THE OXFORD HANDBOOK OF

PERCY BYSSHE SHELLEY

PERCY BYSSHE SHELLEY

Edited by

MICHAEL O'NEILL

and

ANTHONY HOWE

With the Assistance of

MADELEINE CALLAGHAN

OXFORD
UNIVERSITY PRESS

OXFORD
UNIVERSITY PRESS

Great Clarendon Street, Oxford, OX2 6DP,
United Kingdom

Oxford University Press is a department of the University of Oxford.
It furthers the University's objective of excellence in research, scholarship,
and education by publishing worldwide. Oxford is a registered trade mark of
Oxford University Press in the UK and in certain other countries

British Library Cataloguing in Publication Data
Data available

Library of Congress Cataloging in Publication Data
Data available

ISBN 978–0–19–955836–0

Printed in Great Britain by
MPG Books Group, Bodmin and King's Lynn

ACKNOWLEDGEMENTS

Anthony Howe and Michael O'Neill would like to thank all the contributors for their fine essays, and for all their hard work, good humour, patience, and responsiveness to editorial suggestions.

Anthony Howe and Michael O'Neill have worked closely on all aspects of the book. As noted on the title page, Madeleine Callaghan's contribution has been highly significant, especially in helping with the final stages of preparation of the typescript and with editorial input. Others who have helped greatly while working as research assistants on the book include Dr Paige Tovey, Stephanie Dumke, and Oliver Clarkson at Durham University. The book was completed while Michael O'Neill was Acting Executive Director of the Institute of Advanced Study at Durham University, and the editors are grateful to Audrey Bowron at the Institute for her superb secretarial support. Paige Tovey took principal responsibility for preparing the Index.

The editors would also like to thank all those at Oxford University Press who have overseen the book, especially Andrew McNeillie who commissioned it and Jacqueline Baker who has been a helpful guiding presence at a later stage. Michael O'Neill would like to thank the Department of English Studies at Durham University for funding help.

The editors are grateful to the Bodleian Libraries, University of Oxford, for permission to cite from Bodleian manuscripts, and to Dr Robin Darwall-Smith, and The Master and Fellows of University College, Oxford, for permission to reproduce the image of the Shelley Memorial on page xxii.

CONTENTS

PART III POETRY

PART IV CULTURES, TRADITIONS, INFLUENCES

PART V AFTERLIVES

NOTE ON TEXTS AND ABBREVIATIONS

Each chapter indicates which edition of Shelley is being used. Prose works are normally set in italics as are longer poems; shorter poems are set in roman. Titles of the same work may vary: e.g. *The Sensitive-Plant* is thus if quoted from *Longman* or *Norton*, but *The Sensitive Plant* if quoted from *Major Works*.

Bieri James Bieri: 2 vols.; vol. I; *Shelley: A Biography: Youth's Unextinguished Fire, 1792–1816*. Newark, Del.: University of Delaware Press, 2004; vol. II; *Percy Bysshe Shelley: A Biography: Exile of Unfulfilled Renown, 1816–1822*. Newark, Del.: University of Delaware Press, 2005. Also cited from the one-volume version *Percy Bysshe Shelley*. Baltimore: Johns Hopkins University Press, 2008. Where a volume is indicated, the work is cited from the 2004–5 version; where not, from the 2008 version.

BSM Bodleian Shelley Manuscripts, gen. ed. Donald H. Reiman. 22 vols., New York: Garland, 1986–97: vol. I: '*Peter Bell the Third*' [...] *Bodleian MS. Shelley adds. c. 5* [...] *and* '*The Triumph of Life*' [...] *Bodleian MS. Shelley adds. c. 4, folios 18–58*, ed. Donald H. Reiman (1986); vol. II: *Bodleian MS. Shelley adds. d. 7*, ed. Irving Massey (1987); vol. III: *Bodleian MS. Shelley e. 4*, ed. P. M. S. Dawson (1988); vol. IV: *Bodleian MS. Shelley d. 1*, ed. E. B. Murray, 2 parts (1988); vol. V: *The 'Witch of Atlas' Notebook* [...] *Bodleian MS. Shelley adds. e. 6*, ed. Carlene Adamson (1997); vol. 6: *Shelley's Last Notebook* [...] *Bodleian MS. Shelley adds. e. 20* [...] *with Bodleian MS. Shelley adds. e. 15* [...] *and Bodleian MS. Shelley adds. c. 4, folios 212–246*, ed. Donald H. Reiman and Hélène Dworzan Reiman (1990); vol. VIII: *Bodleian MS. Shelley d. 3*, ed. Tatsuo Tokoo (1988); vol. IX: *The 'Prometheus Unbound' Fair Copies* [...] *Bodleian MSS. Shelley e. 1, e. 2, and e. 3*, ed. Neil Fraistat (1991); vol. X: *Mythological Dramas* [...] *Bodleian MS. Shelley d. 2* [...] *with 'Relation of the Death of the Family of the Cenci'* [...] *Bodleian MS. Shelley adds. e. 13*, ed. Betty T. Bennett and Charles E. Robinson (1992); vol. XI: *The Geneva Notebook of* [...] *Shelley* [...] *Bodleian MSS. Shelley adds. e. 16 and adds. c. 4, folios 63, 65, 71, and 72*, ed. Michael Erkelenz (1992); vol. XII: *Shelley's 'Charles the First' Draft Notebook* [...] *Bodleian MS. Shelley adds. e. 17*, ed. Nora Crook (1991); vol. XIII: *Drafts for 'Laon and Cythna'* [...] *Bodleian MSS. Shelley adds. e. 14 and adds. e. 19*, ed. Tatsuo Tokoo (1992); vol. XIV: *Shelley's 'Devils' Notebook* [...] *Bodleian MS. Shelley adds. e. 9*, ed. P. M. S. Dawson and Timothy Webb (1993); vol. XV: *The 'Julian and Maddalo' Draft Notebook* [...] *Bodleian MS. Shelley adds. e. 11*, ed. Steven E. Jones (1990); vol. XVI: *The 'Hellas' Notebook* [...] *Bodleian MS. Shelley adds. e. 7*, ed. Donald H. Reiman and Michael C. Neth (1994); vol. XVII: *Drafts for 'Laon and Cythna'* [...] *Bodleian MS.*

Shelley adds. e. 10, ed. Steven E. Jones (1994); vol. XVIII: *The Homeric Hymns and 'Prometheus' Draft Notebook [...] Bodleian MS. Shelley adds. e. 12*, ed. Nancy Moore Goslee (1996); vol. XIX: *The Faust Draft Notebook [...] Bodleian MS Shelley adds. e. 18*, ed. Nora Crook and Timothy Webb (1997); vol. XX: *The 'Defence of Poetry' Fair Copies [...] Bodleian MSS. Shelley e. 6 and adds. e. 8*, ed. Michael O'Neill (1994); vol. XXI: *Miscellaneous Poetry, Prose and Translations [...] Bodleian MS. Shelley adds. c. 4, etc*, ed. E. B. Murray (1995); vol. XXII, Part One: *Bodleian MS Shelley adds. d. 6 [...]*; vol. XXII, Part Two: *Bodelian MS. Shelley adds. c. 5 [...]*, ed. Alan M. Weinberg (1997), See also vol. XXIII; *A Catalogue and Index of the Shelley Manuscripts in the Bodleian Library [...]*, ed. B. C. Barker-Benfield and Tatsuo Tokoo (London: Routledge, 2002)

CC The Journals of Claire Clairmont, ed. Marion Kingston Stocking. Cambridge, MA: Harvard University Press, 1968

CPPBS The Complete Poetry of Percy Bysshe Shelley, ed. Donald Reiman, Neil Fraistat, and Nora Crook. Baltimore: Johns Hopkins UP. 3 vols. to date. 2000, 2004, 2012

H The Complete Poetical Works of Percy Bysshe Shelley, ed. Thomas Hutchinson. Oxford: Clarendon, 1904. Issued 1905 and 1934 as Oxford Standard Authors edition; corrected by G. M. Matthews, 1970

Journals: MWS The Journals of Mary Shelley, ed. Paula R. Feldman and Diana Scott-Kilvert. Oxford: Oxford UP, 1987. 2 vols. Reprinted pbk as one volume by Johns Hopkins UP, 1995

Julian The Complete Works of Percy Bysshe Shelley, ed. Roger Ingpen and Walter E. Peck. London: Benn; New York; Scribner's. 10 vols. 1926–30

Letters: MWS The Letters of Mary Wollstonecraft Shelley, ed. Betty T. Bennett. Baltimore: Johns Hopkins UP, 1980–8. 3 vols.

Letters: PBS The Letters of Percy Bysshe Shelley, ed. Frederick L. Jones. Oxford: Clarendon, 1964. 2 vols.

Longman The Poems of Shelley, ed. Kelvin Everest and G. M. Matthews. London: Longman. 3 vols. to date. 1989, 2000, 2011

Major Works Percy Bysshe Shelley: The Major Works, ed. Zachary Leader and Michael O'Neill. Oxford: Oxford UP, 2003, 2009 (corr.)

Murray: Prose The Prose Works of Percy Bysshe Shelley, ed. E. B. Murary. Oxford: Clarendon, 1993. 1 vol. published

MYR Manuscripts of the Younger Romantics: Shelley, gen. ed. Donald H. Reiman. New York: Garland, 1985–97. 9 vols: vol. I: *The Esdaile Notebook*, ed. Donald H. Reiman (1985); vol. II: *The Mask of Anarchy* (1985), ed. Donald H. Reiman; vol. III: *Hellas: A Lyrical Drama* (1985), ed. Donald H. Reiman; vol. IV: *The Mask of Anarchy Draft*

Notebook [...] Huntingdon MS. HM 2177, ed. Mary A. Quinn (1990); vol. V: *The Harvard Shelley Poetic Manuscripts*, ed. Donald H. Reiman (1991); vol. VI: *Shelley's 1819–1821 Huntington Notebook [...] Huntington MS. HM 2176*, ed. Mary A. Quinn (1994); vol. VII: *Shelley's 1821–1822 Huntington Notebook [...] MS. HM 2111*, ed. Mary A. Quinn (1996); vol. VIII: *Fair-Copy Manuscripts of Shelley's Poems in European and American Libraries*, ed. Donald H. Reiman and Michael O'Neill (1997); vol. IX: *The 'Frankenstein' Notebooks [...]*, ed. Charles E. Robinson (1996)

Norton 1 Shelley's Poetry and Prose, ed. Donald H. Reiman and Sharon B. Powers. New York: Norton, 1977 (3rd printing, corrected, 1982)

Norton 2 Shelley's Poetry and Prose, ed. Donald H. Reiman and Neil Fraistat. New York: Norton, 2002

SC Shelley and his Circle: 1773–1822. 10 vols. to date. 1961–. Cambridge, MA: Harvard UP. Ed. Kenneth Cameron, Donald H. Reiman, and Doucet Devin Fischer

Webb Percy Bysshe Shelley: Poems and Prose, ed. Timothy Webb, with critical selection by George Donaldson. London: Dent, 1995

Notes on Contributors

Ian Balfour is Professor of English at York University. He is the author of several books, including *The Rhetoric of Romantic Prophecy*, which won the MLA's Scaglione Prize for Comparative Literature and the Barricelli Prize from the International Conference on Romanticism. He co-edited *Subtitles: On the Foreignness of Film* (MIT) as well as *And Justice for All? The Claims of Human Rights*, a special issue of *South Atlantic Quarterly*. He was also the sole editor of an *SAQ* volume on *Late Derrida*. He has taught as a visiting professor at the Johann Wolfgang Goethe University in Frankfurt, UC Santa Barbara, SUNY at Buffalo, Stanford, Williams College, and at Cornell as the M. H. Abrams Distinguished Visiting Professor of English. He has twice been a Fellow at the Getty Research Institute in Los Angeles. He is currently finishing an interminable book on the sublime.

Shahidha Bari is Lecturer in Romanticism at Queen Mary, University of London, and works in the fields of literature, philosophy, and politics, with special interests in the Romantic period and the ideas of ethical subjectivity that emerge from it. Her current research examines the Romantic engagement with Islam and the East, through an exploration of early English translations of the *Arabian Nights* and nineteenth-century Islamic art. She has also written about the philosophers Martin Heidegger and Jacques Derrida.

Bernard Beatty is Senior Fellow in the School of English at Liverpool University and Associate Fellow in the School of Divinity at St Andrews. He is the author of many works on Byron and other authors and topics, and was, 1988–2005, the Editor of the *Byron Journal*.

Stephen C. Behrendt is University Professor and George Holmes Distinguished Professor of English at the University of Nebraska. His most recent book is *British Women Poets and the Romantic Writing Community* (2009). In addition to his scholarly work, he is also a widely published poet whose most recent book is *History* (2005).

James Bieri began his research on Shelley's life while teaching his favourite course at the University of Texas (Austin), 'Psychology and Literature'. His biography, *Percy Bysshe Shelley*, was published in two volumes by University of Delaware Press (2004–5) and in a one-volume second edition by Johns Hopkins UP (2008).

Arthur Bradley is Senior Lecturer in the Department of English & Creative Writing at Lancaster University. He is the author of *Negative Theology and Modern French*

Philosophy (2004); *Derrida's Of Grammatology: A Philosophical Guide* (2008) and (with Andrew Tate) *The New Atheist Novel: Fiction, Philosophy and Polemic after 9/11* (2010). His most recent book is entitled *Originary Technicity: The Theory of Technology from Marx to Derrida* (2011).

Frederick Burwick, Professor Emeritus at UCLA, has taught courses on Romantic drama and directed student performances of a dozen plays. Author and editor of twenty-eight books and 130 articles, his research is dedicated to problems of perception, illusion, and delusion in literary representation and theatrical performance. His *Illusion and the Drama* (1991) analyses affective theories of the drama from the Enlightenment through the Romantic period. His *Poetic Madness and the Romantic Imagination* (1996) won the Barricelli Book of the Year Award of the International Conference on Romanticism. He has been named Distinguished Scholar by both the British Academy (1992) and the Keats–Shelley Association (1998). Recent monographs include *Romantic Drama: Acting and Reacting* (2009) and *Playing to the Crowd: London Popular Theatre, 1780–1830* (2011).

Madeleine Callaghan received her BA and PhD from the University of Durham and is a Lecturer in Romantic Literature at the University of Sheffield. She is currently preparing a monograph on Byron, Shelley, and Yeats for publication and has published various articles and chapters on Romantic poetry. She has also co-edited, with Professor Michael O'Neill, a Blackwell Guide to Criticism entitled *Twentieth-Century British and Irish Poetry: Hardy to Mahon* (2011).

Teddi Lynn Chichester is the author of *Shelley's Mirrors of Love: Narcissism, Sacrifice, and Sorority* (1999); she teaches in UCLA Writing Programs.

Benjamin Colbert is Reader in English and Co-Director of the Centre for Transnational and Transcultural Research at the University of Wolverhampton. His publications include (ed.) *British Satire 1785–1840*, vol. III (2003), *Shelley's Eye: Travel Writing and Aesthetic Vision* (2005), (ed.) *Travel Writing and Tourism in Britain and Ireland* (2012), and (ed.) *Women's Travel Writings in Post-Napoleonic France*, vols. V–VII (2012), part of Pickering & Chatto's Chawton House Library Series. He has served on the Steering Committee of the International Society for Travel Writing (2006–11) and is Book Review Editor for *European Romantic Review*.

Richard Cronin teaches at the University of Glasgow. His most recent books are *Paper Pellets: British Literary Culture after Waterloo* (2010) and *Reading Victorian Poetry* (2012).

Nora Crook, Jamaican by birth and education, received her degree from Cambridge University and is Emerita Professor of English Literature at Anglia Ruskin University, Cambridge. Most of her publications are on the Shelleys. She is the General Editor of twelve volumes of Mary Shelley's works and has edited two of Shelley's notebooks. She is currently a General Co-Editor, with D. H. Reiman and Neil Fraistat, of *The Complete Poetry of Percy Bysshe Shelley* (in progress).

Stuart Curran, Vartan Gregorian Emeritus Professor of English at the University of Pennsylvania, is the author of *Shelley's* Cenci: *Scorpions Ringed with Fire* (1970), *Shelley's Annus Mirabilis: The Maturing of an Epic Vision* (1975), *Poetic Form and British Romanticism* (1986), and numerous essays centred on the Shelley circle. He is President of the Keats–Shelley Association of America.

Jack Donovan was formerly Reader in English at the University of York. He was one of the editors who prepared the second and third volumes of the Longman edition of *The Poems of Shelley* and is currently part of the team preparing the fourth volume.

David Duff is Professor of English at the University of Aberdeen, and Chair of the Council for College and University English. His books include *Romance and Revolution: Shelley and the Politics of a Genre* (1994), *Scotland, Ireland, and the Romantic Aesthetic*, co-edited with Catherine Jones (2007), and *Romanticism and the Uses of Genre* (2009), which won the 2010 Book Prize awarded by the European Society for the Study of English. He is editor of the forthcoming *Oxford Anthology of Romanticism* and *Oxford Handbook of British Romanticism*.

Kelvin Everest is Bradley Professor of Modern Literature at the University of Liverpool, and Pro-Vice-Chancellor of the University. He has published widely on English Romantic Poetry, and is co-editor of the Longman Annotated English Poets edition of Shelley's complete poetry.

Marilyn Gaull moved from New York University to the Editorial Institute at Boston University in 2007. Her publications include *English Romanticism: The Human Context* (Norton), *Northanger Abbey* (Longman), articles, introductions, and reviews in literature and the sciences. She is founder and editor of *The Wordsworth Circle*, and several book series including *Nineteenth-Century Major Lives and Letters* (Palgrave). She founded the Wordsworth Summer Conference with Richard Wordsworth in 1970, serving as American Director until 2005, and is a member of the Council of Editors of Learned Journals, and the Wordsworth–Coleridge Association of which she serves as Executive Director. She currently lectures on climate history, mathematics, publishing history, literature, and the environmental sciences.

Nancy Moore Goslee, Professor of English and Distinguished Professor of Humanities Emerita, University of Tennessee, has published essays and monographs in two broad areas: visual and verbal relationships in Romantic poetry, including aspects of material textuality, and Scottish Romanticism. In addition to *Uriel's Eye: Miltonic Stationing and Statuary in Blake, Keats, and Shelley,* she has edited one of Shelley's notebooks in the Bodleian Shelley Manuscripts series and has just published *Shelley's Visual Imagination.* She is now returning to interests begun with *Scott the Rhymer.*

Paul Hamilton is Professor of English at Queen Mary University of London. He published a short book on Percy Shelley in 1999. His more recent books include *Coleridge and German Philosophy: The Poet in the Land of Logic* (2007) and *Metaromanticism* (2003). He is currently working on a comparative study of European Romanticism.

Anthony John Harding is Professor Emeritus, University of Saskatchewan. With the late Kathleen Coburn, he co-edited volume V of *The Notebooks of Samuel Taylor Coleridge* (2002). In 2008 and 2010, he taught as guest professor in Kiel, Germany. His recent publications include 'Radical Bible: Coleridge's 1790s West-Country Politics', *English Romantic Writers and the West Country*, ed. Nicholas Roe (2010), 129–51; 'The Fate of Reading in the Regency', *Grasmere 2010: Selected Papers from the Wordsworth Summer Conference*, ed. Richard Gravil (2010), 149–72; and 'An Ethics of Reading: A Conflicted Romantic Heritage', *Keats–Shelley Journal* 57 (2008), 27–47. He lives in Nova Scotia, Canada.

Daisy Hay is the author of *Young Romantics: The Shelleys, Byron and Other Tangled Lives*, for which she was awarded the Rose Mary Crawshay Prize by the British Academy. She has held a Bye-Fellowship at New Hall, Cambridge, and the Alistair Horne Fellowship at St Antony's College, Oxford. She is currently a Visiting Scholar at Wolfson College, Oxford.

Diane Long Hoeveler is Professor of English at Marquette University, Milwaukee, Wisconsin. She is author of *Gothic Riffs: Secularizing the Uncanny in the European Imaginary, 1780–1820* (2010), which won the Allan Lloyd Smith memorial award from the International Gothic Association, *Gothic Feminism* (1998), and *Romantic Androgyny* (1990). In addition to publishing some sixty-five articles on a variety of literary topics, she co-authored a critical study of *Charlotte Brontë*, and edited the Houghton Mifflin volume of *Wuthering Heights*. Her ten co-edited volumes of essays include *Approaches to Teaching Jane Eyre*; *Approaches to Teaching the Gothic* (both for the MLA); *Interrogating Orientalism*; *Comparative Romanticisms*; *Romanticism and its Other Discourses*; *Romantic Drama*; *Romanticism and the Law*; *Women of Color*; *Women's Literary Creativity and the Female Body*; and the *Historical Dictionary of Feminism*. More recently, she co-edited the *Blackwell Encyclopedia of Romanticism* (2011) and a Broadview edition of Edgar Allan Poe's *Narrative of Arthur Gordon Pym* (2010). She served as President of the International Conference of Romanticism 2001–3, and is now co-editor of the *European Romantic Review*.

Jerrold E. Hogle, whose PhD is from Harvard University, is University Distinguished Professor and Director of Undergraduate Studies and Honors in the Department of English at the University of Arizona. His books include *Shelley's Process* (Oxford UP), *Evaluating Shelley* (co-edited with Timothy Clark, Edinburgh UP), *The Undergrounds of 'The Phantom of the Opera'* (Palgrave), *Frankenstein's Dream* (Romantic Circles Praxis online), *The Cambridge Companion to Gothic Fiction* (Cambridge UP), and *The Cambridge Companion to the Modern Gothic* (forthcoming), and he has published numerous essays on the Shelley circle, Romanticism, literary theory, and the Gothic in journals and essay collections.

Gavin Hopps has been a Lecturer in English at the universities of Aachen, Oxford, and Canterbury Christ Church, and is currently a Lecturer in Literature and Theology at the University of St Andrews. He has published numerous articles on Romantic writing, a co-edited collection of essays on Romanticism and religion, and a monograph on the singer-songwriter Morrissey. He is co-editing Byron (with Jane Stabler) for Longman.

Anthony Howe studied at the University of Liverpool before gaining a PhD at Cambridge. He has published articles on Byron and Shelley, and is the editor (with Bernard Beatty and Charles E. Robinson) of *Liberty and Poetic Licence: New Essays on Byron* (2008). A monograph on Byron is forthcoming. He has taught at Cambridge and Oxford and is currently Senior Lecturer in English Literature at Birmingham City University.

Steven E. Jones is Professor of English and Co-Director of the Center for Textual Studies and Digital Humanities at Loyola University Chicago. He is co-creator, with Neil Fraistat, of the *Romantic Circles* website. His publications include editions of Shelley's notebooks as well as *Shelley's Satire* (1994), *Satire and Romanticism* (2000), *Against Technology: From the Luddites to Neo-Luddism* (2006), and *The Meaning of Video Games* (2008). *Codename Revolution: The Nintendo Wii Platform*, which he co-authored with George K. Thiruvathukal, is forthcoming from MIT Press, 2012.

Michael O'Neill is a Professor of English at Durham University. He is the author of books, chapters, and essays on Shelley, including *The Human Mind's Imaginings: Conflict and Achievement in Shelley's Poetry* (1989) and the entry on Shelley for the *New Dictionary of National Biography* (2004). He is the editor of *The 'Defence of Poetry' Fair Copies* (1994) and the co-editor (with Donald H. Reiman) of *Fair-Copy Manuscripts of Shelley's Poems in European and American Libraries* (1997). With Zachary Leader, he is the co-editor of *Percy Bysshe Shelley: The Major Works* (2003). He is also the author of *Romanticism and the Self-Conscious Poem* (1997) and *The All-Sustaining Air: Romantic Legacies and Renewals in British, Irish, and American Poetry since 1900* (2007). With Timothy Webb, he is co-editing *The Prose of Percy Bysshe Shelley 1818–1822* for Oxford University Press.

Ralph Pite is Professor at the University of Bristol. He has published widely on Romantic period poetry, on ecocriticism, and on the work of Thomas Hardy. He is co-editor of *Romans and Romantics* (Oxford UP, forthcoming) and is currently writing a study of Robert Frost and Edward Thomas (Harvard UP).

Jessica K. Quillin is a researcher, writer, and entrepreneur. She received her PhD in English from the University of Cambridge and has published widely, including a book, *Shelley and the Musico-Poetics of Romanticism* (2012).

Donald H. Reiman is co-editor of *Shelley and his Circle* at the Carl H. Pforzheimer Collection, New York Public Library. He is general editor, with Neil Fraistat and Nora Crook, of *The Complete Poetry of Percy Bysshe Shelley* (three volumes published to date). His publications also include, as co-editor with Neil Fraistat, *Shelley's Poetry and Prose* (2002) and, as general editor, *The Bodleian Shelley Manuscripts* (23 vols., 1996–2002) and *The Manuscripts of the Younger Romantics* (1985–97). A founder of the Romantic Circles website, he has written, edited, or co-edited some 200 volumes of literary and textual criticism.

Jeffrey C. Robinson has recently published a collection of poems based upon Romantic idiom and theme, *Untam'd Wing: Riffs on Romantic Poetry* (2010), (co-edited with Jerome Rothenberg) *Poems for the Millennium, 3: The University of California Book of Romantic and Postromantic Poetry* (2009, American Book Award, 2010), *Unfettering Poetry: The Fancy in British Romanticism* (2006), a paperback edition of *The Walk: Notes on a Romantic Image* (2005), and *Wordsworth Day by Day: Reading his Work into Poetry Now* (2005). He is Honorary Senior Research Fellow at the University of Glasgow.

Michael Rossington is Senior Lecturer in Romantic Literature in the School of English Literature, Language, and Linguistics, Newcastle University. He has contributed to volumes II and III of the Longman Annotated English Poets edition of *The Poems of Shelley,* eds. Kelvin Everest and Geoffrey Matthews, 3 vols. to date (1989, 2000, 2011). He is editing the fourth and fifth volumes of this edition with Kelvin Everest, Jack Donovan, and Cian Duffy.

Mark Sandy is a Senior Lecturer in English Studies at Durham University and is author of *Poetics of Self and Form in Keats and Shelley* (2005) and co-editor with Michael O'Neill of *Romanticism: Critical Concepts in Cultural and Literary Studies* (4 vols., 2006). He co-edited a volume of essays on *Romantic Echoes in the Victorian Era* (2008) and more recently edited a collection of critical essays on *Romantic Presences in the Twentieth Century* (2012). He is currently completing a book on *Romanticism, Memory, and Mourning.*

Michael Scrivener, Professor of English at Wayne State University, has published books on Percy Shelley (*Radical Shelley*, 1982), John Thelwall (*Seditious Allegories*, 2001; *Two Plays by John Thelwall*, 2006), Romantic verse in political periodicals (*Poetry and Reform*, 1992), and cosmopolitanism (*Cosmopolitan Ideal in the Age of Revolution and Reaction, 1776–1832*, 2007). His new monograph, *Jewish Representation in British Literature, 1780–1840: After Shylock*, was published in 2011 by Palgrave.

Jane Stabler is Reader in Romantic Literature at the School of English, University of St Andrews. She is working on the Longman Annotated English Poets edition of Lord Byron's works and a monograph on exile in Italy.

Paige Tovey is the holder of a MHRA Research Associateship (2010–12) awarded to the Durham University English Department. She is working on *The Prose of Percy Bysshe*

Shelley 1818–1822, eds. Michael O'Neill and Timothy Webb, which is contracted to Oxford University Press. Her primary research interests are British Romanticism, twentieth-century American poetry, and manuscript editing, and she has published essays on Gary Snyder and Shelley's prose.

Alan Weinberg is an Emeritus Professor of English at the University of South Africa and is contracted to the University Research Directorate. He has a record of many articles and essays on Shelley. He is the author of *Shelley's Italian Experience* (1991), and has edited vol. XXII (2 parts) of the *Bodleian Shelley Manuscripts* (1997). More recently he has collaborated with Timothy Webb on a collection of essays entitled *The Unfamiliar Shelley* (2009). At present a second volume is in progress which further draws attention to the marginalization of many significant works in Shelley's oeuvre.

Susan J. Wolfson is Professor of English at Princeton University; Past President of the Association of Literary Scholars, Critics, and Writers; and General Editor of the Longman Cultural Editions. Her most recent critical books are *Romantic Interactions: Social Being & the Turns of Literary Action* (2010) and *Borderlines: The Shiftings of Gender in British Romanticism* (2006). Her editorial work includes, most recently, *John Keats: A Longman Cultural Edition* (2007), and she has gathered and contributed to the critical anthology *'Soundings of Things Done': The Poetry and Poetics of Sound in the Romantic Ear and Era* (2008). Her essay on Shelley here reflects on and revisits questions first explored in *Formal Charges: The Shaping of Poetry in British Romanticism* (1997).

Sarah Wootton is a Senior Lecturer in English Studies at Durham University. She is the author of *Consuming Keats: Nineteenth-Century Representations in Art and Literature* (2006) and co-editor, with Mark Sandy, of a special issue of *Romanticism and Victorianism on the Net* (August 2008). Her second book, *The Rise of the Byronic Hero in Fiction and on Film*, is under contract with Palgrave-Macmillan, and she has co-edited (with Michael O'Neill and Mark Sandy) a collection of essays, entitled *Venice and the Cultural Imagination* (2012). She is also a co-director of the Romantic Dialogues and Legacies Research Group at Durham University.

Ann Wroe is the Obituaries and Briefings editor of *The Economist* and the author of *Being Shelley: The Poet's Search for Himself* (2007). She is the author of five other books, including *Pilate: The Biography of an Invented Man* (1999) which was shortlisted for the Samuel Johnson prize, and *Orpheus: The Song of Life* (2011), which won the 2011 Criticos prize. She holds a doctorate in medieval history from Oxford University, and is a fellow of the Royal Historical Society and the Royal Society of Literature.

The Shelley Memorial By permission of The Master and Fellows of University College, Oxford

INTRODUCTION

MICHAEL O'NEILL

> All high poetry is infinite; it is as the first acorn which contained all oaks potentially.
>
> (Shelley, *A Defence of Poetry, Major Works*, 693)

I

If Percy Bysshe Shelley (1792–1822) seemed 'more arrestingly contemporary than ever' to Kelvin Everest in 1983, his poetry has, to adapt Ezra Pound, continued to stay news in the decades that followed.[1] This *Oxford Handbook* seeks both to reflect and to shape current Shelleyan scholarship and criticism. The present is a stimulating time to take stock of and advance beyond recent developments in the study of a significant Romantic poet, one whose influence on later poetry and culture has been remarkable.

Shelley has occupied a strangely unsettled position in English poetry. He enjoys an almost mythological status, on one influential line of interpretation, as a poet who embodies the quintessence of poetry. Harold Bloom writes that 'Shelley is a unique poet, [...] and he is in many ways *the* poet proper, as much so as any in the language'. He is so, Bloom continues, because 'His poetry is autonomous, finely wrought, in the highest degree imaginative'.[2] This is hyperbole that captures a vital truth. Yet Shelley is also a writer whose canonical status has never been entirely secure. *Adonais* effectively constructs the idea of the canon as an 'abode where the Eternal are' (495; quoted from *Major Works*). But Shelley

---

[1] Kelvin Everest, 'Introduction', in Kelvin Everest (ed.), *Shelley Revalued: Essays from the Gregynog Conference* (Leicester: Leicester UP, 1983), p. xiv. For the maxim that 'Literature is news that STAYS news', see Ezra Pound, *ABC of Reading* (London: Faber, 1951), 29.

[2] See Harold Bloom, 'The Unpastured Sea: An Introduction to Shelley', in *The Ringers in the Tower: Studies in Romantic Tradition* (Chicago: University of Chicago Press, 1971), 87.

depicts himself as 'borne darkly, fearfully, afar' (492), on his own, caught between such an 'abode' and 'the trembling throng' who are dismissed with aristocratic hauteur as those 'Whose sails were never to the tempest given' (489–90). Aware of his condition as a liminal, exilic figure, poised between past and future, Shelley's self-description looks ahead to the view expressed by Timothy Clark and Jerrold E. Hogle that 'His value as poet or thinker' was fated to remain 'as problematic as the nature of culture'.[3]

Shelley is a poet who imagines change, transformation, potentiality, both in his larger political and cultural visions, and through details of his poetic craft.[4] The metaphorical shifts characteristic of his writing's 'grammar of vision' (265), to employ Jack Donovan's phrase in his contribution to the present volume, provide a suggestive analogy with his hopes for 'some unimagined change in our social condition or the opinions which cement it' (*Major Works*, 231). The word 'unimagined' enacts the wish to find a language that 'indicates', in Timothy Webb's words, 'not only a negative negated but an energy unquenched or a potential not realized, perhaps not even recognized'.[5] The poet who asks, with Asia, 'Shall we pursue the sound?' (*Prometheus Unbound*, II. i. 188) is forever searching to recognize and realize such potential, often redefining and questioning normal modes of perception, as in the 'Life of Life' lyric in II. 5 of *Prometheus Unbound*. Shelley presents his ideal here as dazzlingly indefinable and elusive, quickening the imagination to embrace 'the beautiful which exists in thought, action or person, not our own' (*Major Works*, 682).

Poets have always recognized Shelley's importance. Thomas Lovell Beddoes paid early and majestic tribute in his 'Lines Written in a Blank Leaf of the "Prometheus Unbound"' (published 1822) in which a conceit is sustained that makes Shelley both source and substance of a world of 'bright creations' (8); the sixteen lines of blank verse behave as though they had initial designs to be a sonnet and shrugged them off, impelled beyond formal limits by their subject, 'An Intellect ablaze with heavenly thoughts' (2).[6] The line encapsulates Shelley's capacity to make a new body of poetic thought from the intellectual endeavours of thinkers such as Godwin, whose intricately twisting arguments in *Enquiry Concerning Political Justice* maintain both the mind's passivity in perception (and therefore its freedom from censure about its contents) and its agency (through freeing itself from others' regulating opinions).[7] Yeats's late reference to the Witch of Atlas in

---

[3] Timothy Clark and Jerrold E. Hogle (eds.), *Evaluating Shelley* (Edinburgh: Edinburgh UP, 1996), 1. For work on the figure of the poet in Shelley, see Judith Chernaik, *The Lyrics of Shelley* (Cleveland: The Press of Case Western Reserve University, 1972) and Timothy Clark, *Embodying Revolution: The Figure of the Poet in Shelley* (Oxford: Clarendon, 1989).

[4] For the idea of potentiality in Shelley, see D. J. Hughes, 'Potentiality in *Prometheus Unbound*', *Studies in Romanticism* 2 (1963), 107–26.

[5] Timothy Webb, 'The Unascended Heaven: Negatives in *Prometheus Unbound*', in Everest (ed.), *Shelley Revalued*, 57.

[6] *The Works of Thomas Lovell Beddoes*, ed. H. W. Donner (London: Oxford UP, 1935).

[7] See William Godwin, *Enquiry Concerning Political Justice* (1798), ed. Isaac Kramnick (Harmondsworth: Penguin, 1976), 373, 568 (where in a striking anticipation of the end of the third section of 'Mont Blanc' Godwin speaks of scepticism about 'government' as inciting us to 'look for the moral improvement of the species, not in the multiplying of regulations, but in their repeal').

'Under Ben Bulben' turns Shelleyan motifs into stores of esoteric lore: 'Swear by what the sages spoke | Round the Mareotic Lake | That the Witch of Atlas knew' (1–3).[8]

For readers such as Beddoes and Yeats, tropes, tones, and themes pour forth from the burning fountain of Shelley's work; they scatter themselves among and live on in the verses of his poetic legatees. The process of literary influence can involve resistance and contestation as much as imitation and admiration. Robert Browning's fervent enthusiasm for Shelley in *Pauline* (1833) passes into a complex negotiation with his Romantic precursor in poems such as 'Two in the Campagna'; there, the ending's discovery of 'Infinite passion, and the pain | Of finite hearts that yearn' (59–60) shows the continued presence in Browning's work of a concern with Shelleyan scenarios of desire and disappointment, such as that embodied in the knowingly artful and self-undermining rhapsody of *Epipsychidion*: self-undermining because the poet and poem recognize that longing and failure are fated to coexist.[9]

Again, Shelley's autumnal leaves may end up in Hardy's 'During Wind and Rain' as diminished, beyond resurrection, 'sick leaves' that 'reel down in throngs' (7).[10] But they bear witness to the intensity and resourcefulness with which Hardy read his Romantic forebear. In their criticism Matthew Arnold and T. S. Eliot may have deplored aspects of Shelley's life and style, yet their poetry shows a strong if divided response to his work.[11] In his essay 'The Figure of the Youth as Virile Poet' Wallace Stevens turns to *A Defence of Poetry* for aid when seeking to articulate the role of poetry and the poet in the twentieth century, quoting with watchful and feline approval a number of his forebear's 'impressions' and 'approximations' in support of his view that 'In spite of the absence of a definition and in spite of the impressions and approximations we are never at a loss to recognize poetry.'[12] More generally, Shelley is a presence actively at work in Stevens's attempt to produce a modern poetry that has its 'own meaning for reality'.[13]

Academic criticism has followed its own trajectory. In recent decades, the dislike for Shelley expressed by New Critics and Leavisites has been abandoned, as it has become evident that the hostile press Shelley received in those quarters resulted from shamefully

---

Shelley read *Political Justice* in the 1793 first edition, which contains this passage. For more on Shelley and Godwin, see P. M. S. Dawson, *The Unacknowledged Legislator: Shelley and Politics* (Oxford: Clarendon, 1980) and Pamela Clemit, 'Shelley's Godwin, 1812–1817', *Durham University Journal* NS 54 (1993), 189–201.

[8] *W. B. Yeats*, Oxford Authors, ed. Edward Larrissy (Oxford: Oxford UP, 1997).

[9] *Robert Browning*, Oxford Authors, ed. Adam Roberts, introd. Daniel Karlin (Oxford: Oxford UP, 1997). For the view that '*Pauline* undoubtedly owes a great deal to Shelley's *Epipsychidion*, especially to its "improvisatory" form', see Catherine Maxwell, *The Female Sublime from Milton to Swinburne: Bearing Blindness* (Manchester: Manchester UP, 2001), 133.

[10] Thomas Hardy, *Selected Poems*, ed. Tim Armstrong (London: Longman, 1993).

[11] For discussion of Shelley, Arnold, and Eliot, see Michael O'Neill, 'The Burden of Ourselves: Arnold as a Post-Romantic Poet', *Yearbook of English Studies* 36 (2006), 109–24, and ch. 3 of Michael O'Neill, *The All-Sustaining Air: Romantic Legacies and Renewals in British, American, and Irish Poetry since 1900* (Oxford: Oxford UP, 2007).

[12] *Wallace Stevens: Collected Poetry and Prose*, ed. Frank Kermode and Joan Richardson (New York: Library of America, 1997), 669, 670.

[13] 'The Noble Rider and the Sound of Words'. Ibid. 658.

sloppy and polemically simplified reading, of a kind rarely inflicted on any other poet comparable in stature. Part cause and part consequence of this change in the default view of Shelley has been the veritable editorial industry that has sprung up round his work since the mid-1980s. All critics and readers of Shelley need to take note of the fact that, until recently, many texts of Shelley's poetry and prose have been fraught with error. Shelley died young, leaving many works unpublished, even unfinished. He also lived in Italy for the last four years of his life; major works such as *Prometheus Unbound* appeared in print, full of mistakes, often the result of Shelley not having been sent proofs. Editions of the poetry in print were, until selections by Geoffrey Matthews, Donald H. Reiman and Sharon B. Powers, and Timothy Webb, unreliable and full of error. The prose fared even worse; only the few works edited by Reiman and Webb could by the mid-1980s lay claim to reliability. Shelley was for many years served ill by the academy, especially in the UK: a poet caricatured and read badly, in deficient texts.

The revival in Shelley's critical fortunes in the 1960s and afterwards can be traced to the interpretative and critical acumen of critics who, in the main, came from North America, especially Carl Grabo, Carlos Baker, C. E. Pulos, Kenneth Neill Cameron, Earl R. Wasserman, and Harold Bloom, and the bibliographical and editorial work of Charles H. Taylor, Jr. and Donald Reiman.[14] A number of these authors published significant work way before the full-scale restoration of Shelley's reputation, providing the basis for that restoration. So, Grabo made clear Shelley's fascination with science and Baker his deep involvement with a mythmaking poetic inherited from Spenser and Milton, while Pulos provided a brilliant sketch of how sceptic and idealist lodged in the same poetic sensibility, making possible a probabilism that licensed 'the human mind's imaginings' ('Mont Blanc', 143). Building on Pulos's work, Wasserman gave an account of an intellectually coherent Shelley who reconciled materialism and idealism by means of a system of ideas which in *On Life* he calls 'the intellectual philosophy' (*Major Works*, 635). This coherence has proved a suggestive yet perplexing bequest to later commentators, some of whom wish to admire Shelley more for his ability to stage conflict and provoke questions than to supply final answers.[15] Bloom threw the gauntlet down to the attackers of Shelley, showing how his work seeks to establish imaginative relationships and transform the real. Cameron grounded Shelley's work in his commitment to social and political improvement. For their part, other critics began to offer nuanced and

[14] See Carl Grabo, *The Magic Plant: The Growth of Shelley's Thought* (Chapel Hill, NC: University of North Carolina Press, 1935); Carlos Baker, *Shelley's Major Poetry: The Fabric of a Vision* (Princeton: Princeton UP, 1948); C. E. Pulos, *The Deep Truth: A Study of Shelley's Scepticism* (Lincoln, NE: University of Nebraska Press, 1954); Kenneth Neill Cameron, *Shelley: The Golden Years* (Cambridge, MA: Harvard UP, 1974); Earl R. Wasserman, *Shelley: A Critical Reading* (Baltimore: Johns Hopkins UP, 1971); Harold Bloom, *Shelley's Mythmaking* (New Haven: Yale UP, 1959); Charles H. Taylor, Jr., *The Early Collected Editions of Shelley's Poems: A Study in the History and Transmission of the Printed Text* (New Haven: Yale UP, 1958); Donald H. Reiman, *Shelley's 'The Triumph of Life': A Critical Study* (Urbana, IL: University of Illinois Press, 1965).

[15] See Michael O'Neill, *The Human Mind's Imaginings: Conflict and Achievement in Shelley's Poetry* (Oxford: Clarendon, 1989).

thoughtful defences of Shelley, to explain and explore his abilities as a translator, to examine his engagement with contemporary politics and political ideas, and, above all, to analyse the poetry's generic sophistication and artistic merit.[16]

In the meantime, Donald Reiman, along with G. M. Matthews, Timothy Webb, Kelvin Everest, and others, saw and acted on the all-important need to establish accurate texts. As noted above, a crucial spur to the enhanced understanding of Shelley's work has been recognition of the significance of his manuscripts. Thanks to two series from Garland, both under the general editorship of Reiman, *The Bodleian Shelley Manuscripts*, 23 vols. (1986–2002) and *The Manuscripts of the Younger Romantics*, nine volumes (1985–97), most of these manuscripts have been made available in carefully annotated and edited form. To this valuable toil must be added the editorial and scholarly labours of the *Shelley and his Circle* series.

Running in parallel with this work and building upon it have been a number of important editorial ventures. In particular, there are two ongoing editions of the poetry, the Longman edition, edited by Kelvin Everest and others, three volumes published to date, due to consist of five volumes by completion, and the Johns Hopkins edition, edited by Donald H. Reiman, Neil Fraistat, Nora Crook, and others, two volumes completed to date, a third just out, the series to consist of eight volume by completion. Edited on rather different principles (Longman modernizes, Johns Hopkins does not; Longman follows the chronological order of composition, Johns Hopkins the chronological order of publication), these editions are revolutionizing the study of Shelley's poetry, even as they are themselves the beneficiaries of new insights generated by recent criticism and scholarship. There has also been a major edition of Shelley's prose work up to 1818 by E. B. Murray; this edition is currently being completed by Michael O'Neill and Timothy Webb. Significant comment on the critical implications of these editorial discoveries appears in a recent collection of essays.[17]

The determination to establish what Shelley wrote is part of a concerted effort to see his work in a new, fairer light. Viewed broadly, modern criticism has dispelled one-sided accounts of the poet that make him into the embodiment of an essence: whether of self-delighting radical paradoxicality (Hazlitt), pure lyricism (Arnold's beautiful but ineffectual angel), commitment to sloganizing revolutionary abstractions (Eliot), or sentimentalizing and egotistical evaporation of a solid world of objects (the burden of Leavis's infamous onslaught). In its place is a poet whose 'workmanship of style', in Wordsworth's phrase, has been recognized, and whose learning, allusiveness, and

---

[16] See Timothy Webb, *Shelley: A Voice Not Understood* (Manchester: Manchester UP, 1977); Timothy Webb, *The Violet in the Crucible: Shelley and Translation* (Oxford: Clarendon, 1976); Dawson, *The Unacknowledged Legislator*; Michael H. Scrivener, *The Philosophical Anarchism and Utopian Thought of Percy Bysshe Shelley* (Princeton: Princeton UP, 1982); Stuart Curran, *Shelley's Annus Mirabilis: The Maturing of an Epic Vision* (San Marino, CA: Huntington Library, 1975); Richard Cronin, *Shelley's Poetic Thoughts* (London: Macmillan, 1981); William Keach, *Shelley's Style* (London: Methuen, 1984); Angela Leighton, *Shelley and the Sublime: An Interpretation of the Major Poems* (Cambridge: Cambridge UP, 1984).

[17] Alan M. Weinberg and Timothy Webb (eds.), *The Unfamiliar Shelley* (Farnham: Ashgate, 2009).

command of different generic possibilities have been praised.[18] A major impetus for this volume is the wish to explore and affirm Shelley's many-sidedness and the many dimensions of his achievement, as well as his receptivity to different approaches and possibilities. The volume represents a celebration of Shelley's ability to persuade his readers to 'Fancy another situation | From which to dart [their] contemplation, | Than that wherein [they] stood' (*Peter Bell the Third*, 300–2). This Shelley is a poet peculiarly open to different critical approaches and questions, whether framed from a neo-formalist, post-structuralist, psychoanalytic, gender-based, or Marxist perspective.[19] He is a poet who frequently calls into question the validity of any single approach to his work; if Lucretius offers a model and an inspiration, the Shelleyan *clinamen* or swerve from precursors and contemporaries establishes his poetic voice as one that is most itself when most differentiating itself from the belief-systems adopted by others.[20] The multiple critical avenues that can lead profitably into the metropolis of his work are showcased in the present *Handbook*. Shelley's legacy as a thinker, which takes in poetics, philosophy, politics, psychology, linguistics, translation, science, the arts, history, and religion, is immensely varied. Shelley criticism, as a response, has needed to be able to think in many places at once. But individual studies cannot always follow all of the different paths that Shelley suggests, meaning that a volume such as this, which brings together an unprecedented range of expertise, is the perfect medium for understanding such an intellectually and artistically multifaceted figure.

Various Shelleys can be discerned at present, bearing witness to the way in which his work generates 'new relations' and is continually 'the source of an unforeseen and an unconceived delight' (*A Defence of Poetry, Major Works*, 693). They range from a red, revolutionary poet to a distinctly green one, from an anarchistic firebrand to a gradualist reformer, from a deconstructive sceptic to a celebrant of decentred process, from an Oedipally challenged figure ready for Lacanian analysis to a healer of psychoanalytical wounds.[21] Nor is controversy absent. The old battles are always ready to reassume a novel

---

[18] See William Hazlitt, unsigned review of Shelley's *Posthumous Poems* (1824) in *The Edinburgh Review* July 1824, in Theodore Redpath, *The Young Romantics and Critical Opinion 1807–1824* (London: Harrap, 1973); Matthew Arnold, 'Shelley', in *The Last Word: The Complete Prose Works of Matthew Arnold*, vol. XI, ed. R. H. Super (Ann Arbor: University of Michigan Press, 1977), 306; T. S. Eliot, 'Shelley and Keats', in *The Use of Poetry and the Use of Criticism* (London: Faber, 1964); F. R. Leavis, 'Shelley', in *Revaluation* (London: Chatto & Windus, 1936); Wordsworth's comment is quoted in James E. Barcus (ed.), *Shelley: The Critical Heritage* (London: Routledge, 1975), 2.

[19] For accounts of critical approaches to Shelley, see George E. Donaldson's 'Shelley and his Critics' at the end of Timothy Webb (ed.), *Percy Bysshe Shelley: Poems and Prose* (London: Dent, 1995), 479–529, Michael O'Neill's introduction to *Shelley*, Longman Critical Readers, ed. Michael O'Neill (London: Longman, 1993), 1–26, and Jerrold E. Hogle's chapter in *Literature of the Romantic Period: A Bibliographical Guide*, ed. Michael O'Neill (Oxford: Oxford UP, 1998), 118–42.

[20] See Jerrold E. Hogle, 'Shelley as Revisionist: Power and Belief in *Mont Blanc*', in G. Kim Blank (ed.), *The New Shelley: Later Twentieth-Century Views* (Basingstoke: Macmillan, 1991), 115–16 for relevant commentary.

[21] Representative examples include Paul Foot, *Red Shelley* (London: Sidgwick and Jackson, 1980); Timothy Morton, *Shelley and the Revolution in Taste* (Cambridge: Cambridge UP, 1994); Paul de Man, 'Shelley Disfigured', in Harold Bloom et al., *Deconstruction and Criticism* (New York: Continuum,

mask. The author of exquisite love lyrics anthologized in Palgrave's *Golden Treasury* is also the figure whose treatment of women, especially his first wife Harriet, continues to disturb many readers and who turns out, on at least one account, to be the ruthless exploiter of vulnerable young women.[22] By contrast, the infamous atheist expelled from Oxford emerges as having more than a smack of the negative theology fellow traveller about him.[23] For others, the challenge posed by Thomas McFarland when he remarks that 'modern Shelley scholars […] simply ignore the fact that Hazlitt, Arnold, and Leavis […] all call into severest question Shelley's poetic quality and importance' has still adequately to be confronted.[24] But the unthinking condescension that often characterized treatment of Shelley in the Anglo-American academy for many years in the twentieth century has been effectively banished.

Again, a life which once attracted extreme views, some writers bestowing a halo, others diabolic horns, has been placed more carefully in the contexts supplied by biographical research. What has emerged from the biographical work of Holmes, Cameron, Reiman, and others is the picture of a brilliant young man at the heart of his restless times, simultaneously conditioned by his age and seeking to model it anew. In Shelley criss-cross strains come together.[25] An aristocrat by birth, he rebelled against the political orthodoxies of his time, looking ahead to the values enshrined in modern political democracies, describing himself to Leigh Hunt as 'one of those whom nothing will fully satisfy, but who am ready to be partially satisfied by all that is practicable' (*Letters: PBS* II, 153), 'We shall see', he continues, and the tide of progressive political and cultural opinion has flowed with Shelley; the figure who seemed shockingly heterodox in his own day now seems to formulate ideas at the heart of our best hopes. And yet Shelley is an ethical thinker in politics and religion who has a strong sense of the limits of 'Ethical science'; 'nor is it', he writes with that command of sardonic polemic that shows him to be the heir of Burke and Paine, 'for want of admirable doctrines that men hate, and despise, and censure, and deceive, and subjugate one another' (*A Defence of Poetry*, *Major Works*, 681), the drum-roll of verbs ushering human hypocrisy into the glare of

1979); Jerrold E. Hogle, *Shelley's Process: Radical Transference and the Development of his Major Works* (New York: Oxford UP, 1988); Barbara Gelpi, *Shelley's Goddess: Maternity, Language, Subjectivity* (New York: Oxford UP, 1992); Stuart M. Sperry, *Shelley's Major Verse: The Narrative and Dramatic Poetry* (Cambridge, MA: Harvard UP, 1988).

[22] See Janet Todd, *Death and the Maidens: Fanny Wollstonecraft and the Shelley Circle* (London: Profile, 2007). Reviewing Todd's book for *The Observer* on 1 July 2007, Hilary Spurling notes that it 'confronts more frankly than anyone has done before the fact that Shelley spent virtually his entire adult life trying to lure young girls away from the protection of their families' (online access).

[23] See Arthur Bradley, '"Until Death Tramples it to Fragments": Percy Bysshe Shelley after Postmodern Theology', in Gavin Hopps and Jane Stabler (eds.), *Romanticism and Religion from William Cowper to Wallace Stevens* (Aldershot: Ashgate, 2006), 191–206.

[24] Thomas McFarland, 'Recent Studies in the Nineteenth Century', *Studies in English Literature: 1500–1900* 16 (1976), 694. Critics who have taken up this challenge, though in different ways (the former to defend Shelley, the latter to attack him), include Michael O'Neill, *The Human Mind's Imaginings* and Simon Haines, *Shelley's Poetry: The Divided Self* (London: Macmillan, 1997).

[25] See Richard Holmes, *Shelley: The Pursuit* (London: Weidenfeld and Nicholson, 1974); Cameron, *Shelley: The Golden Years*; Donald H. Reiman, *Percy Bysshe Shelley* (updated edn. Boston: Twayne, 1990).

shamed self-contemplation. In many respects, Shelley's importance has to do with his twin sense that poetry is profoundly imaginative and that, as it 'awakens and enlarges the mind itself by rendering it the receptacle of a thousand unapprehended combinations of thought' (*A Defence of Poetry*, *Major Works*, 681), it spurs us on to 'act that which we imagine' and regain 'the poetry of life' (*A Defence of Poetry*, *Major Works*, 695).

II

The Oxford Handbook of Percy Bysshe Shelley contains forty-two essays by forty contributors. It is divided into five parts. The first part, 'Biography and Relationships', provides information about and reflections on the poet's biography. Shelley himself argued that 'The poet & the man are two different natures' (*Letters: PBS* II, 310). Yet the remark is itself of biographical interest, foreshadowing tensions at the heart of Yeatsian and Eliotic ideas about the antithetical relationship between the self and anti-self, and the impersonality of poetry. Shelley's turbulent life and times have attracted much comment, sometimes exculpatory, often censorious. In a sense, our entire book is fascinated by biography, construing that word as having a wide range of implications: along with his life-experiences in Britain and Italy, for example, there is discussion of his poetry's quasi-filial textual relations with Spenser and Milton, and its afterlife in the poetry of later poets.

The first part builds, as does the book as a whole, on research undertaken over the last half-century and beyond. Richard Holmes's and Kenneth Cameron's contrasting but seminal works in the 1970s have been reinforced more recently by biographies (equally different in mode) from James Bieri and Ann Wroe.[26] The time is propitious for biographical studies that will reconcile the poetry and prose, allowing for a negotiation between the accumulated details which distinguish Bieri's account and the sympathetic inwardness that is a marked feature of Wroe's book. Throughout this part, contributors distil, examine, and nuance the biographical record. Chapters consider Shelley's life and travels in Britain and Italy; they look at his extraordinary final year in which he saw visions, wrote masterpieces, sailed, fell in love with Jane Williams, and planned *The Liberal*, an anti-establishment periodical to be edited with Leigh Hunt and Byron; they give particular attention to relationships with women, creative as well as amorous, and look too at his fraught dealings with publishers, through whom he sought to mediate his often thwarted attempts to reach an audience.

In the second part, 'Prose', the *Handbook* ensures that comparatively under-investigated prose works are given the detailed attention that more restricted studies cannot provide, complementing in this respect significant new work appearing in *The Unfamiliar Shelley*. Contributors explore Shelley's philosophical positions, which

---

[26] James Bieri, *Percy Bysshe Shelley: A Biography*, first published with different titles in two volumes in 2004 and 2005 (Baltimore: Johns Hopkins UP, 2008); Ann Wroe, *Being Shelley: The Poet's Search for Himself* (London: Cape, 2007).

involve a very particular blend of materialism, scepticism, and idealism, and which benefit, therefore, from multiple perspectives and expertise. One concern that emerges is whether it is possible to see Shelley as consistent in his philosophical thinking: does he, or does he not, for instance, succeed in creating a coherent fusion of Hume and Plato? Other essays in this part explore Shelley's moral and religious views; his political ideas about social reform set out most carefully in his unfinished *A Philosophical View of Reform*; his ideas about love, involving detailed consideration of his engagement, among other things, with Plato's *Symposium*, which he translated in 1818; his use of satire in support of political progressivism; his theories of poetry, especially as articulated in his prefaces to poems and in *A Defence of Poetry*. They look, too, at Shelley's early Gothic novels and the later (and fragmentary) *The Assassins* and *The Coliseum* and his letters (often too hastily dismissed as less interesting than Keats's, and thus too little read).

The third part devotes itself to the poetry. These chapters seek to draw in and appeal to first-time readers of the work, and reinvigorate and extend the understanding of seasoned readers. Shelley is and should be at the forefront of debates about the priority of the aesthetic and the imaginative in Romantic literature, and chapters in this part bring out the creativity apparent in his drafts, before looking across the range of his career, one in which he showed his capacity to excel in many different genres. One essay discusses his lyric practice from the early *Esdaile Notebook* up to and including the 'Hymn to Intellectual Beauty' and 'Mont Blanc'; another analyses his lyrics to women. Others examine his handling of the long poem in *Queen Mab* and *Laon and Cythna*, his deployment of a more conversational style in poems such as *Julian and Maddalo*, his command of tragic form, his experiments with lyrical drama, his writing of odes and sonnets, his achievement in *Alastor* and *Epipsychidion* of a quest poetry of near-tragic intensity, his sophisticated use of the revolutionary ballad form and popular song in *The Mask of Anarchy* and associated poems, his creation of a narrative visionary poetry in *The Sensitive-Plant* and *The Witch of Atlas*, and his manipulation of pronouns and modes of address in his lyrics, *Hellas*, *Adonais*, and *The Triumph of Life*. The part is organized so as to bring out Shelley's variety of voices and achievements across a range of genres, and to help readers find different ways through what is a wealth of pre-existing critical material.

The fourth part seeks to understand Shelley's response to past and present literary cultures, within both an English and a comparative context. The scope of the current volume will, for the first time, allow for a simultaneous investigation of the various strands of Shelley's complex literary heritage, especially his immersion in historical and contemporary European literature (involving responses to figures such as Dante, Ariosto, Tasso, Calderón, Goethe, and Rousseau). Shelley's creative flair as a translator underpins and pervades these chapters, and is recognized elsewhere in the volume. Placing Shelley in an identifiably English tradition is also an important aim of this part. Essays explore Shelley's dealings with the Bible; with mythology and classical tradition; with Italian culture; with French, Spanish, and German cultures; with Milton; with Spenser and Pope; and with his contemporaries.

The second aim of this part is to draw on and expand recent scholarly work in the broader cultural field of Romanticism. Shelley's immersion in the culture of his day, not just in the arts, but also in terms of his well-known interest in science and technology, was diverse; and the ways in which his work is energized by such immersion still require extensive investigation. Essays explore his response to music; to Shakespeare and theatre; to the visual arts (and their attitude to Shelley); to science; and to tourism and travel.

In the fifth part, essays explore Shelley's literary and cultural afterlife. George Eliot's Ladislaw provokes comparisons with Shelley in *Middlemarch*, as does Hardy's Angel Clare in *Tess of the D'Urbervilles*. Shelley is also a vital influence in the poetry of the nineteenth century: Arnold, Browning, Tennyson, Emily Brontë, Swinburne, and Wilde, to give some of the most prominent examples. As already noted, his influence in the twentieth century on writers such as Yeats and T. S. Eliot is strong, and his presence continues to be felt up to the present day. The section also analyses the ways in which Shelley's writings have been edited, from his own lifetime, through pirated editions in the 1820s and the 1830s, Mary Shelley's highly influential but flawed editions, the significant editions produced by Forman and Rossetti, to the Hutchinson edition, and up to the present.

This fifth part also reflects on Shelley's critical reception. These reflections take in the friendly and hostile reactions of contemporaries such as Hunt and Hazlitt, the complex responses of Arnold and other Victorians, and the seminal role that Shelley's writings played in the rise of post-structuralism, notably in the criticism of de Man and Derrida. In this part, then, essays look, in turn, at Shelley's influence in the nineteenth century and in twentieth- and twenty-first-century poetry (especially, changing the usual angle of focus in we think a profitably surprising way, in the sphere of American open-field poetics); at the editing of his work; and at criticism of him from the Romantics to the Modernists, and from Deconstructionist and other more recent perspectives. In exploring the afterlife of the work of a great poet, *The Oxford Handbook of Percy Bysshe Shelley* wishes also to extend it, to establish a basis for its exciting future.

Select Bibliography

Allott, Miriam. 'Attitudes to Shelley: The Vagaries of a Critical Reputation'. *Essays on Shelley*. Ed. Miriam Allott. Totowa, NJ: Barnes & Noble, 1982. 1–38.
Blank, G. Kim. Ed. *The New Shelley: Later Twentieth-Century Views*. Basingstoke: Macmillan, 1991.
Cameron, Kenneth Neill. *Shelley: The Golden Years*. Cambridge, MA: Harvard UP, 1974.
Clark, Timothy and Jerrold E. Hogle. Eds. *Evaluating Shelley*. Edinburgh: Edinburgh UP, 1996.
Curran, Stuart. 'Percy Bysshe Shelley'. *The English Romantic Poets: A Review of Research and Criticism*. Ed. Frank Jordan. 4th edn. New York: Modern Language Association of America, 1985.
Everest, Kelvin. Ed. *Shelley Revalued: Essays from the Gregynog Conference*. Leicester: Leicester UP, 1983.

Hogle, Jerrold E. 'Percy Bysshe Shelley'. *Literature of the Romantic Period: A Bibliographical Guide*. Ed. Michael O'Neill. Oxford: Clarendon Press, 1998. 118–42.

Morton, Timothy. Ed. *The Cambridge Companion to Shelley*. Cambridge: Cambridge UP, 2006.

O'Neill, Michael. *Percy Bysshe Shelley: A Literary Life*. London: Macmillan, 1989.

—— Ed. *Shelley*. London: Longman. 1993.

Weinberg, Alan M. and Timothy Webb. Eds. *The Unfamiliar Shelley*. Farnham: Ashgate, 2009.

White, Newman Ivey. *Shelley*. 2 vols. New York: Alfred A. Knopf, 1940.

PART I

BIOGRAPHY AND
RELATIONSHIPS

CHAPTER 1

....

SHELLEY AND THE
BRITISH ISLES

....

DONALD H. REIMAN AND JAMES BIERI

CHILDHOOD AND EARLY REBELLIONS

PERCY Bysshe Shelley was born on 4 August 1792 at Field Place, in the West Sussex parish of Warnham, near the market town of Horsham. The Shelley ancestral manor house of Field Place, with its many acres of farmland, woods, and ponds, dated from medieval times. Shelley, called Bysshe by his family, delighted in the natural beauty of Field Place but would become aware of the sharp contrast between his family's wealth and privilege and the poor living conditions of his father's farm workers. In this Arcadian setting, Shelley's primary companions were his younger sisters and the fantasy creatures inhabiting his precocious, fertile imagination, fed by his omnivorous reading and wanderings through nearby St Leonard's Forest. Shelley may have known his father's illegitimate son, older than Shelley, who possibly lived briefly at Field Place.[1] Shelley's second cousin, Tom Medwin, lived in Horsham where his father was a solicitor. The Gothic novels young Shelley read helped foster his own adolescent novels (*Zastrozzi* and *St. Irvyne*) and the aerial boat travels of Paltack's *Peter Wilkins* would resonate in his poem *Alastor*.[2] The teenaged Shelley, finding the social and intellectual milieu of his home increasingly stultifying, wrote on vacation from Eton in 1809 to a classmate calling Field Place 'this temple of Solitude' and complaining that 'Dissipation & Pleasure are stagnant at Horsham—and after a few Balls ill attended every thing is now silent' (*Letters: PBS*, I, 2).

His elders, including his parents Timothy and Elizabeth Pilfold Shelley and his grandfather (Piercey) Bysshe Shelley, helped make Field Place and Horsham displeasing to young Shelley. Old Bysshe, American born in New Jersey in 1731, inherited most of his grandparents'

---

[1] James Bieri, 'Shelley's Older Brother', *Keats–Shelley Journal* 39 (1990), 29–33.
[2] Bieri, 49–50.

modest estate and became a large landowner by eloping with an heiress. After she died in childbirth, he married a wealthier heiress, who suffered the same fate. Taking a mistress, old Bysshe fathered more children, including a son named Bysshe, born in London a few weeks after Shelley's birth.[3] In politics old Bysshe supported Charles Howard, eleventh Duke of Norfolk, who controlled a large bloc of Whigs in the House of Commons by buying up election votes in 'rotten boroughs'. Timothy Shelley, old Bysshe's eldest son, supported Norfolk while serving as an MP in Sussex boroughs. For his political services, Bysshe Shelley was created a baronet in 1806, during the brief Whig-led administration. By that year the newly minted, avaricious Sir Bysshe Shelley had built Castle Goring, his large, gaudy mansion near Norfolk's Arundel Castle. In January 1812, Shelley wrote to Elizabeth Hitchener about his grandfather: 'He is a complete Atheist and builds all his hopes on annihilation. He has acted very ill to three wives. He is a bad man. [...] I always regarded him as a curse on society' (*Letters: PBS* I, 239). Three years later when Sir Bysshe Shelley died, his eldest son became Sir Timothy Shelley and Shelley was next in line to inherit the title and the family estate. However, Sir Bysshe designed his will to prevent his heirs—especially Shelley—from dissipating his fortune. Timothy and each of his heirs could spend only the income from the estate without 'wasting' the principal. This hindered Shelley from giving large sums of money to his friends without putting his own family's finances at risk.[4]

Sir Timothy, who now owned Field Place and property in five English counties and in Wales, had been submissive to his father's power and was unprepared when Shelley challenged him during their generational disputes. Shelley despised the sexual hypocrisy of both his grandfather and his father, who told Shelley that he could have as many children out of wedlock as he liked but should not make a misalliance. An eyewitness wrote that Shelley's 'ardent mind, and somewhat natural haughtiness of disposition, rendered him very impatient of control. [...] His father did not appear [...] to be particularly bright, though [...] inclined to exercise his parental authority, with most injudicious despotism.'[5] These paternal conflicts throughout Shelley's childhood helped foster in him a rejection of all forms of political, religious, and social authoritarian control, and his espousal of social justice, equality, and political freedom.

Alongside these patriarchal conflicts, Shelley's relationship with his mother was intensely ambivalent. His was a special place as his mother's firstborn child and her only son until 1806. The pervasive maternal imagery in Shelley's poetry includes powerful mother and sister figures who supersede their male counterparts. Shelley's maternal great-grandmother and maternal grandmother had rebellious streaks and only his mother's expressiveness in her letters provides any hint of parental influence on his literary genius.[6]

As a boy Shelley won the hearts of the Field Place servants and he always considered his first tutor, the Revd Evan 'Taffy' Edwards, Welsh curate of Warnham Church, his only effective teacher. Shelley enlisted his four sisters in his childhood games and pranks and encouraged them to write. He was especially close to his eldest sister Elizabeth who

---

[3] Bieri, 9–11.   [4] Bieri, 301–2.

[5] John Joseph Stockdale, in *Stockdale's Budget*, 20 December 1826.

[6] Bieri, ch. 2; Thomas Frosch, *Shelley and the Romantic Imagination* (Newark, DE: University of Delaware Press, 2007); Barbara Gelpi, *Shelley's Goddess* (New York: Oxford UP, 1992).

collaborated in his early writings. Shelley left this feminine family nest to spend two unhappy years (1802–4) at the all-male Syon House Academy, a boarding school west of London. There and subsequently at Eton (1804–10), Shelley was tormented by older schoolfellows but he resisted fagging. By the time he made his mark as a precocious scholar, he had identified these schoolyard persecutions with the injustices of England's political, social, and religious establishments. Shelley's lifelong interest in science was first fostered by lectures at Syon House. At Eton he came under the protective wing of the liberal polymath Dr James Lind, a physician at Windsor. Lind shielded Shelley from his father's intrusiveness, and his ministrations would be represented in Shelley's later poetry. Lind had scientific interests and exposed Shelley to classical and contemporary literature that provided models for reform, especially William Godwin's *Enquiry Concerning Political Justice* and *The Enquirer*.[7]

After one memorable encounter with injustice at Eton in 1809 or 1810, Shelley experienced an epiphany that inspired his commitment to the ideals of truth, justice, and love that he had encountered in his reading. Multiple portrayals of this event appear in Shelley's poems, including 'Hymn to Intellectual Beauty' and the dedication 'To Mary' that opens *Laon and Cythna*. The earliest version (1809), appearing in *The Esdaile Notebook*, begins 'I will kneel at thine altar', specifies the evils that he hoped to overthrow—'Prejudice, Priestcraft, Opinion, and Gold' (30)—while he vows to help the poor and to support love, non-violence, and social reform.[8]

This commitment to improve the world made Shelley feel more isolated and he turned outside his immediate family for someone to share his deepest feelings (1818 draft 'On Love'; *Norton 2*, 503–4). He initially chose in 1808 his cousin Harriet Grove, a year older than he. Her mother and Shelley's mother were sisters. Harriet's diaries (1809–10) contain details of this Shelley–Grove courtship.[9] Harriet and her family in Wiltshire were more pious Anglicans than Shelley's family. Yet in early 1810, Harriet Grove received and read a manuscript copy of Shelley's long subversive poem *The Wandering Jew* and defended it against the opinion of her parents and siblings. That March Harriet received Shelley's first published book, the Gothic 'Romance' *Zastrozzi*. The conservative Groves, already leery of Shelley's liberal views, agreed to stop only overnight at Field Place in April. Shelley and Harriet took long walks near Field Place and for ten days in late April and early May, the two families spent time together in London, where Shelley asked Harriet to call him 'Percy' rather than 'Bysshe', signalling his intended break from his family's controls.[10]

Although Shelley and Harriet felt that they would eventually marry, her father's misgivings dated from 1804, when Shelley, visiting the Groves, persuaded the younger

---

[7] Shelley probably first read *Political Justice* from Dr Lind's library during 1809–10 while at Eton. He ordered a copy from Stockdale in November 1810 and told Godwin in early 1812 that it had been 'more than two years' since he first read it. Bieri, 66; *Letters: PBS* I, 21, 227.

[8] *CPPBS* (all quotations from the poetry cited from this edition unless otherwise stated) II, 105–6; *SC* IX, 67–90; 146–68.

[9] *SC* II (1961); Desmond Hawkins, *Shelley's First Love* (London: Kyle Cathie, 1992) and *The Grove Diaries: The Rise and Fall of an English Family, 1809–1925* (Wimborne: Dovecote Press, 1995).

[10] Hawkins, *The Grove Diaries*, 71–8; *Shelley's First Love*, 38–9.

Grove brothers to join him in chopping down newly planted trees.[11] Harriet and her older sister Charlotte began to question their good opinion of him when, in mid-September 1810, Harriet received from Shelley a copy of *Original Poetry; by Victor and Cazire* (i.e. Shelley and his sister Elizabeth). Harriet and Charlotte were offended by the second poem, which implied that Charlotte's visit to their uncle Captain John Pilfold was a husband-hunting foray.[12] The finale came when the Groves wrote to the Shelleys breaking off Harriet's implied engagement with the young poet, who began complaining of being persecuted by Christian bigots. Shelley probably received the bad news just before his residence began at University College in October 1810. A short poem that he wrote at Oxford began 'Oh wretched mortal, hard thy fate!' and ended, ' "The lover is the vilest slave" ' (16).

At Oxford, Shelley soon met John Munday, bookseller and printer, and, at dining hall, Thomas Jefferson Hogg, who recalled that the two students became virtually inseparable until after their expulsion. Hogg, who had entered University College one term before Shelley arrived, was considered bright, but was unpopular with his fellow students. Shelley found in Hogg someone to fill the void of his loss of Harriet Grove, a partner in his quest to reform the world.[13]

ENGLAND REJECTED

Upon entering Oxford Shelley was becoming an *anti*-Englishman, despite writing in early March 1811 to Leigh Hunt of probably assuming his father's seat in parliament.[14] Seeking to publish *The Wandering Jew*, his first book-length poem, he submitted his manuscript to John Ballantyne in Edinburgh who replied in September 1810 that the poem was too liberal for 'the bigoted narrow spirit' of the Scots.[15] From *The Wandering Jew* to *Hellas* (1822), Shelley identified himself with the legendary Jew who, after rejecting Jesus on the way to his crucifixion, was doomed to be a homeless solitary wanderer, experiencing every form of pain and denied the power to die. Shelley's rejection of England is reflected in his major poems, most of which are located outside England. His poems and prose that deal primarily with England and English politics either attack English injustice or satirize English folly.

The work of apprenticeship that transformed Shelley's juvenile versifying into artistic mythmaking poetry appears in *The Esdaile Notebook*, poems he wrote over several years (some as early as 1806) but collected and revised by him in 1812–13, when he completed

[11] Hawkins, *Shelley's First Love*, 4.
[12] See *CPPBS* I, 9–10, 164–5 and Hawkins, *The Grove Diaries*, 86.
[13] Thomas Jefferson Hogg, *Shelley at Oxford*, introd. R. A. Streatfeild (London: Methuen, 1904); reprinted from Hogg's papers in *New Monthly Magazine* (1832–3); Bieri, 93–126.
[14] *Letters: PBS* I, 55; Bieri, 118–19.
[15] *Letters: PBS* I, 17–18 (note). For the Wandering Jew legend and Shelley's poem, see *CPPBS* I, 189–204.

Queen Mab. Attacks on the state religion and unjust monarchs were staples of English literature; *Piers Plowman* and Shelley's *Esdaile* poems are vividly subversive, condemning the actions of the English people, their rulers, and their heroes alike in satires and diatribes that end, not imagining an idealized England, but by exposing the injustice, corruption, and hypocrisy at the basis of English society.

Shelley's first attempt to write a long narrative poem was 'Henry and Louisa', drafted in 1809. The first part relates how Henry, a soldier thirsting for glory, leaves his faithful Louisa to fight the French army that Napoleon had left in Egypt after the 1798 Battle of the Nile. In the first two stanzas, the omniscient narrator vilifies Henry for following 'legal murderers' instead of honouring his vows of love to Louisa. Henry argues that he must fight for God against Napoleon, 'the Tyrant of the World' (72), but when the lovers part, the poet addresses Louisa as a 'Sweet flower! in dereliction's solitude' (135) and attributes human misery to 'Religion! Hated cause of all the woe | That makes the world this wilderness' (144–5).

The poem's second part is set in Egypt during a night battle, after which the poet considers the plight of 'the Genius of the south' (166), who 'Looked over Afric's desolated clime, | Deep wept at slavery's everlasting moan' (168–9). Amid 'waste and ruin' (175) the English lovers play out their personal tragedy. Louisa, disguised as a man, crossed the sea that bore 'Britannia's hired assassins on | To victory's shame or an unhonored grave' (II, 186–7). Rushing to the battlefront, Louisa finds Henry 'death-convulsed and ghastly' (224), and after he dies from his wounds, Louisa commits suicide to rejoin her lover: 'Sacred to Love a deed is done!' (291). The poem ends with a hope for a non-supernatural yet somehow spiritual triumph of the lovers: 'Despising self, their souls can know | All the delight love can bestow' (298–9). In this poem, Shelley not only castigated the officers who won the first British land campaign against revolutionary France, but also rebuked the English poets who praised the war.

Other poems in *The Esdaile Notebook* also twist the British lion's tail. Following 'Henry and Louisa' is Shelley's poetic translation of *La Marseillaise*, entitled 'A Translation of The Marsellois Hymn,' partially drafted in June 1811 at Field Place. In 'Zeinab and Kathema' Shelley's anti-English feelings reached a new extreme. A shipload of British freebooters reached India and 'over-ran the plain, | Ravaging, burning, and polluting all' (33–4). After slaughtering Zeinab's Muslim family, the 'Christian murderers' (33) carry her off to England. Her Hindu lover Kathema persuades another British ship to follow her and upon reaching 'Albion's changeful skies and chilling wind' amid a people whose 'hearts are more uncongenial than the zone— | Gross, spiritless, alive to no pangs but their own' (91, 95–6), Kathema finally finds Zeinab's corpse hanging from a gibbet, executed for crimes committed after she was 'dragged to live in love's untimely tomb' (165) as a prostitute. Shelley's final couplet sums up his view of his nation: 'A universe of horror and decay, | Gibbets, disease, and wars and hearts as hard as they' (179–80).

The wars that Shelley condemned included not only England's conquests abroad, but also English suppression of the Irish and Welsh (Shelley agreed with Norfolk and other Whigs who advocated civil rights for Roman Catholics). In short, Shelley's poems defend the oppressed against the oppressor, and his moral position on 'good wars' asserts that subject peoples may fight to defend their liberty. *Esdaile* poems pursuing this issue include 'On leaving London for Wales', 'To Liberty', 'On Robert Emmet's tomb', and 'a Tale of Society as it is', 'To the Republicans of North America', and 'The Tombs'. In 'A retrospect of Times of Old', Shelley cites as additions to history's 'list of legal murderers. [...] Frederic of Prussia, Buonaparte, Suwarroff, Wellington and Nelson [as] the most skilful and notorious scourges of their species of the present day' (*CPPBS* II, 73). Finally, Shelley, summarizing his relationship with British society in 'The Retrospect', described his social circle thus: 'My darksome spirit sought. It found | A friendless solitude around.—' (84–5). Those classmates 'might shine in courtly glare, | Attract the rabble's cheapest stare, | [...] They might be learned, witty, gay, | Foremost in fashion's gilt array, | On Fame's emblazoned pages shine, | Be princes' friends, but never mine!' (104–5, 108–11).

Exiled from Oxford and Field Place

Much of *The Esdaile Notebook* remained unpublished until 1964, but Shelley's other early writings were sufficiently provocative. While at Eton, he published his first Gothic romance *Zastrozzi* and wrote most of *The Wandering Jew* (first published in 1829). Shelley and his sister Elizabeth published *Original Poetry by Victor and Cazire*, though it was immediately suppressed because Shelley included a plagiarized poem.[16] At Oxford, Shelley published pamphlets in poetry and prose, including *Posthumous Fragments of Margaret Nicholson*, attributed to the mad washerwoman who in 1786 had tried to stab King George III.[17] Its six poems feature political radicalism (including praise for tyrannicide), erotic cries of 'Suck on, suck on [...]', and sexual innuendo creating a vulgar word posing as a typographical error.[18] In November 1810 John Stockdale, who published and suppressed *Original Poetry*, prepared proofs for *St. Irvyne*, Shelley's second Gothic romance containing poems harking back to his infatuation with Harriet Grove the previous April. Its inchoate plot perhaps was an intentional parody of Shelley's broken engagement.

During the 1810 Christmas holidays at Field Place Shelley's letters reveal his mounting anger and depression about his loss of Harriet Grove.[19] On 22 January 1811 Shelley left for London to meet 15-year-old Harriet Westbrook, a school friend of his younger sisters. Within days he directed Stockdale to send his new Harriet a copy of *St. Irvyne*. As a daughter of a retired London coffee house owner, Harriet would not be considered a suitable match for the entailed heir to large landed estates. However, Shelley's parents, by keeping him away from his sisters, helped drive him into Harriet's arms, ably assisted by Harriet's elder sister Eliza, who manoeuvred to bring the young couple together.[20]

---

[16] See *CPPBS* I, 154–9; 178–9 and Bieri, 88; 696 (n. 12).   [17] See *CPPBS* I, 91–104; 235–59.
[18] See *CPPBS* I, 98; 239–41; 254–5.   [19] See *Letters: PBS* I, 26–48 and *SC* II, 668–717.
[20] See Louise Schutz Boas, *Harriet Shelley: Five Long Years* (London: Oxford UP, 1962).

The Westbrook sisters soon won Shelley's gratitude and affection, and he dedicated his poem *Poetical Essay on the Existing State of Things* to 'Harriet W[est]b[roo]k'. *Poetical Essay* (rediscovered in 2006), intended to raise money for the imprisoned radical Irish journalist Peter Finnerty, featured Shelley's well-developed anti-war and anti-monarchical sentiments.[21]

Shelley's radical writings were about to sever both his ties to his father's Whig politics and his tenure at Oxford. Long aware of his father's hypocrisy about religion, Shelley at Field Place over Christmas had argued with his sire about Christianity. Back at University College in late January, he brought copies of *The Necessity of Atheism*, his philosophical tract based on arguments in the long letters that he and Hogg exchanged during the vacation.

Although Shelley slipped an advertisement for *Necessity* into Munday's weekly *Oxford University and City Herald* on 9 February, Munday refused to sell the pamphlet. Shelley defiantly placed copies in the bookshop's windows, where a college don saw it and ordered Munday's employees to burn the copies. About the same time, Shelley apparently mailed or delivered additional copies to college and church officials at Oxford and elsewhere. Only five copies of *Necessity* are known to survive.

On 15 March, William Kirkpatrick Sharpe, Shelley's acquaintance at Oxford, wrote in a letter about four Shelley publications that were circulating at the university—*Margaret Nicholson, Poetical Essay, St. Irvyne*, and *Necessity*.[22] On 25 March 1811, the Master of University College summoned Shelley, demanding to know if he had written *Necessity*. When Shelley refused to affirm or deny authorship, he was expelled. Hogg then implicated himself to the authorities and was also expelled. The next morning the two were on the coach to London and found lodgings on Poland Street. Each proceeded to make demands to their fathers. Shelley's plan to share his inheritance with his sisters and mother was especially galling to his father. The £20 that Shelley had borrowed from Munday's junior partner's brother, Henry Slatter, was soon spent and by mid-April Hogg capitulated to his father's wishes, agreeing to spend a year in the office of a York convey-ancer.[23] The senior Hogg had taken a more moderate stance towards his son than had Timothy Shelley. Hogg departed London, leaving Shelley alone and refusing to submit to his father's proposals about his future. Timothy, at a loss about his recalcitrant son, now gave his London solicitor Whitton sole responsibility for dealing with Shelley.[24] Whitton proved as unbending as Timothy.

On 18 April, a lonely Shelley was visited by his 'little friend' Harriet Westbrook, accompanied by Eliza, aged 28, upon whom Harriet depended. The Westbrook sisters remained Shelley's only female friends as he plied London's streets in his isolation. His strong dislike for London was portrayed some years later in *Peter Bell the Third* (1819),

[21] See H. R. Woudhuysen, 'Shelley's Fantastic Prank', *TLS*, 12 July 2009.
[22] Alexander Allardyce (ed.), *Letters from and to Charles Kirkpatrick Sharpe, Esq.* (Edinburgh: Blackwood, 1888), I, 442–3.
[23] See Winifred Scott, *Jefferson Hogg* (London: Jonathan Cape, 1951), 33.
[24] Roger Ingpen, *Shelley in England* (Boston: Houghton Mifflin, 1917), 235–7; *Letters: PBS* I, 60–1; *SC* II, 721–53.

where he depicted its citizens as both corrupt and pitiable and predicts its sinking into 'ruins in the midst of an unpeopled marsh' (*Norton* 2, 341).

Shelley now reached out to Leigh Hunt, who invited him to breakfast on 5 May. Hunt was impressed by 'this youth, not come to his full growth; very gentlemanly [...] quoting the Greek dramatists'.[25] Shelley also sought out his maternal uncle Captain John Pilfold, soon his ally in Shelley's paternal war. Shelley returned to Sussex, the guest of his uncle Pilfold in Cuckfield, ten miles from Field Place. Pilfold soon persuaded Timothy Shelley to relent. On 12 May, the day before Shelley was readmitted to Field Place, he wrote to Hogg comparing the two Westbrook sisters: Eliza 'improves upon acquaintance' but Harriet was 'more noble' (*Letters: PBS* I, 83). At Field Place, Shelley wrote to Hogg that 'My Mother is quite rational—she says "I think *prayer* & thanksgiving of no use. If a man is a good man, atheist or Xtian he will do very well in whatever future state awaits us"' (*Letters: PBS* I, 85). More importantly, Timothy agreed to give his son £200 per annum.

Edward Fergus Graham, the Shelley family's music master, was seven years older than Shelley and lived in London. Graham had been Shelley's confidant and helper.[26] During Shelley's struggle with Timothy, Graham's neutrality possibly led Shelley to punish Graham's disloyalty by writing a letter accusing Graham of an affair with Shelley's mother (*Letters: PBS* I, 85). It is not known whether Timothy did receive this accusatory letter and, if so, whether it was written by Shelley. More important than this note are two salacious verse letters that Shelley certainly sent to Graham. In the first Shelley warns Graham that 'Killjoy' (Timothy) is 'eaten up with Jealousy' and is 'hot with envy' of both Graham and Shelley. Although he doubts that Graham could be tempted by 'ancient dames' like his mother (twenty-two years older than Graham), Shelley suggests that Graham might as well cuckold 'Killjoy'. Some three weeks later, Shelley sent Graham a longer verse letter warning him that not even sackcloth and ashes will appease Timothy. A note by Shelley's mother on this letter suggests she was possibly in collusion with Shelley by using a secret Horsham address to receive letters from Graham.[27]

In late May Shelley, visiting his uncle at Cuckfield, met Elizabeth Hitchener, an intellectual woman in her late twenties who ran the school that Pilfold's daughter attended. Finding Hitchener a challenging conversationalist, Shelley extended his visit to early June. Upon receiving a letter from her, Shelley replied promptly in the first of forty-seven long letters that he wrote to Hitchener up to June 1812.[28] Although Shelley had shifted his affection from Harriet Grove to pretty, malleable Harriet Westbrook, his most intense letters were to Elizabeth Hitchener, whom he idealized as his 'soul sister'.

After receiving his first quarterly stipend of £50, Shelley went from Field Place to London on 1 July with Hogg, who had unsuccessfully tried to meet Shelley's sister

[25] James Henry Leigh Hunt, *The Autobiography of Leigh Hunt* (New York: Harpers, 1850), II, 221; Bieri, 142.
[26] *SC* IX, 116–26; 140–68.
[27] *SC* IX, 146–68; *CPPBS* I, 140–4, 313–22; Bieri, 146–7.
[28] For Hitchener's letters to Shelley, see footnotes of *Letters: PBS* I. On the strange provenance of the original MSS. of Shelley's letters to her, see *MYR* VIII, 38; *SC* IX, 146–68; *CPPBS* I, 140–4; 313–22.

Elizabeth.[29] Hogg went to York while Shelley saw the Westbrooks but not Hitchener, who expected to meet him in London. Soon Shelley was off for Wales to visit his cousin Thomas Grove at his estate, Cwm Elan. For a month, a lonely, depressed, and introspective Shelley wandered around the estate, composed nature poems, read Erasmus Darwin, and began a vegetarian diet. His letters to Hitchener omitted mentioning his relationship with Harriet, which he wrote about at length to Hogg. Shelley initially told Hogg that he was 'assuredly yours' and then wrote that he would bring Harriet to York, as 'she has thrown herself upon my protection'. Shelley was 'almost convinced' by Hogg's 'arguments' against Godwin's anti-matrimonialism (*Letters: PBS* I, 117–31).

Shelley returned to London on 5 August, having just turned 19 and after receiving Harriet's urgent letter, probably written on 1 August, her sixteenth birthday. Staying at Graham's Piccadilly lodgings, Shelley became stalled in negotiations with the Westbrooks but confided in his cousin Charles Grove about his elopement plans. Shelley made several trips to Field Place and his suspicious father began tracking his son's activities. At Cuckfield, Shelley's uncle was supportive and a letter arrived there from Harriet clinching the plans to elope to Edinburgh and be married. Shelley, stopping in Horsham, elicited £25 from Thomas Medwin senior, who was unaware of Shelley's plans.

In London on the morning of 25 August Shelley and Charles Grove waited at an inn for Harriet, who was late. The couple caught an afternoon coach and at a midnight stop in York Shelley penned a note to Hogg announcing the elopement and asking Hogg to mail him a ten-pound note to Edinburgh. Instead, Hogg made plans to join the honeymoon. The couple arrived on 28 August and may have received advice about marriage from Gilbert Hutchinson, a lawyer they befriended in their coach. That same day, with their new landlord as witness, they were married by a minister who years later was defrocked for performing irregular marriages. The marriage certificate listed Shelley as 'Farmer, Sussex'. Shelley, concerned about his marriage's legality, made plans to be remarried when he returned to England.

During September Shelley wrote numerous letters from Edinburgh to his father defending his marriage and asking in vain for his allowance. Timothy Shelley, soon having heard of his son's elopement, stopped his stipend and refused to respond to his letters. Captain Pilfold was more forthcoming with money. Shelley, Harriet, and Hogg were back in York early in October lodging together. Shelley wrote to Hitchener about his marriage: 'My dear friend Hogg that noble being is with me, & will be always, but my wife will abstract from our intercourse the shadow of impropriety' (*Letters: PBS* I, 145). Perhaps the fathers' interest in keeping the two youths apart was to dispel any thought they were homosexuals. Hogg pursued only women with whom Shelley was infatuated—Shelley's sister Elizabeth, Harriet Westbrook, Mary Godwin, and Jane Williams.

Shelley then left Harriet and Hogg together and returned to Cuckfield on 19 October to do financial battle with his father with the aid of his uncle. Shelley's brief visit to Field Place produced only his violent outburst, causing Timothy Shelley to order his household to shun him. Before scurrying to London with his uncle, Shelley angrily wrote to

---

[29] *SC* II, 820–9; Bieri, 152.

his mother, charging her with promoting a marriage between his beloved sister Elizabeth and Graham in order to hide her (alleged) affair with the music master. This letter and others were sent unopened by Timothy to his solicitor Whitton.[30]

Returning to York, Shelley soon learned why Harriet's sister Eliza was there in command of their household. Hogg had tried unsuccessfully to seduce Harriet, with whom he had secretly fallen in love in Edinburgh. Harriet wrote immediately to her sister, who came promptly to York. Shelley, after confronting an unrepentant Hogg, slipped away with the two sisters for Keswick in the Lake District, home of Robert Southey, then one of Shelley's favourite poets. After Shelley's ten-day visit to the Duke of Norfolk at nearby Greystoke, tactful letters from Norfolk and Shelley (plus John Westbrook's offer of an annual allowance of £200 for Harriet) induced Timothy Shelley to provide an equal sum to Shelley. At Keswick, Shelley's letters to Hogg contained effusive expressions of love while those to Hitchener said she was his 'second self' whose 'letters are like angels sent from heaven on missions of peace' (Letters: PBS I, 140, 193). He was imploring her to come and live with him and Harriet. These Keswick letters to Hitchener contain poems that evolved into The Esdaile Notebook and stanzas, including those influenced by Southey and Coleridge, that became The Devil's Walk. Early in December he mentioned to Hitchener his intention to visit Ireland and that he was 'in contemplation of a Poem' (Queen Mab). His letters to her expressed thoughts germane to Queen Mab, but he put the poem aside to write political essays for Ireland—An Address to the Irish People and Proposals for an Association of Philanthropists.[31]

Shelley appreciated the hospitality of Southey, who recognized the young poet's genius. However, he became disillusioned with Southey's conservatism when they discussed Irish politics and Catholic Emancipation. Seeking a mentor more congenial to his beliefs, Shelley wrote to William Godwin on 3 January 1812. A week later he wrote again with words that caught Godwin's eye: 'I am the Son of a man of fortune in Sussex' (Letters: PBS I, 219–22, 227).

In late January 1812 Shelley had the first of several 'attacks' of panic and flight that he would experience intermittently to the end of his life. Feeling persecuted and anxious about possible political attacks in Ireland, Shelley was at odds with his Keswick landlord and neighbours because of his outdoor pistol practice, flaming balloons, and chemical experiments. On 16 January Shelley wrote to Hitchener that he had started taking laudanum for his 'nervous attack', noting his 'reputation for madness' (Letters: PBS I, 232, 235). On the evening of 19 January, after reports circulated about robbers in town, Shelley said he was knocked senseless by 'ruffians' when he answered his door. He recovered quickly and his landlord came on the scene after the attackers had fled. Some townsfolk questioned whether the attack occurred and Shelley told Hitchener that 'assassination' is one of 'the phantoms of a mind'.[32]

---

[30] Letters: PBS I, 155; Ingpen, Shelley in England, 341–9; Bieri, ch. 10.

[31] Murray: Prose, 41–55, 338–48; Letters: PBS I, 189, 190, 199, 217, 224–6, 235–7; for the texts and commentaries of Queen Mab and poems in The Esdaile Notebook, see CPPBS II.

[32] Letters: PBS I, 248; Bieri, 191–3.

Irish and Devon Politics

The three travellers left Keswick in early February and arrived in Dublin nine days later after delays on the Isle of Man and a gale that blew them off course. Shelley's seven weeks in Dublin were his most energetic period of political activism. The *Address* was soon printed, advertised, and distributed with the help of an Irish servant, Daniel Healey. The high point in Dublin was Shelley's 28 February hour-long speech to the meeting of Daniel O'Connell's Catholic Committee in the Fishamble Theatre. Six local papers reported his speech, citing loud applause, noting his publications, and giving his brief biography. Government agents in attendance reported his speech to the English Home Secretary, and Shelley's London subversive activity file began. Shelley kept a disapproving Godwin informed of his (stillborn) plan to form political associations but did not mention his broadside publication, *Declaration of Rights*. Godwin urged him to come to London, commenting that his 'three daughters' were interested in him. In mid-March Harriet wrote to Hitchener to distribute the *Declaration*, shipping them to her in a box with the other pamphlets that was intercepted by authorities in Holyhead. These writings were added to his government file and Hitchener came under surveillance.

Shelley became disillusioned with the local political figures and the Dublin poor he tried to help. His entourage, including Daniel Healey, left Dublin in early April. They settled on a farm in Wales, Nantgwillt, near Cwm Elan. Harriet became depressed, money was short, and rumours circulated in Sussex that Hitchener was to become Shelley's mistress. Shelley, unable to lease Nantgwillt, in June moved the family briefly to Cwm Elan; he thought of residing in Italy. They travelled south, settling in Lynmouth on the Devon coast where Hitchener joined them. Shelley, maturing his prose style, composed *A Letter to Lord Ellenborough*, which became a classic statement in defence of freedom of the press.[33] He had 1,000 copies printed in Barnstaple, sending many to the London bookseller Thomas Hookham to distribute to 'any friends *who are not informers*' (*Letters: PBS* I, 319). Also printed was his revised *The Devil's Walk*. Shelley, collecting his *Esdaile* lyrics and composing *Queen Mab*, began broadcasting his seditious works airborne in fire balloons or enclosed in corked bottles set afloat in the Bristol Channel. Local agents observed these launchings and Home Secretary Sidmouth took notice. Shelley's plans to flee were clinched with Daniel Healey's arrest and imprisonment in Barnstaple for circulating Shelley's broadsides.

Tanyrallt

Shelley's party, without Healy, hurriedly left for Wales as August ended, unbeknownst to Godwin who arrived too late in Lynmouth to visit his disciple. Attracted by William Madocks's reclamation project in Merioneth, Shelley rented Tanyrallt, Madocks's

---

[33] *Murray: Prose*, 327–57.

isolated house above Tremadoc. John Williams, who oversaw the project, introduced Shelley to local officials in the poet's efforts to raise funds for the bankrupt project. In early October the Shelleys, Eliza, and Hitchener returned to London where Shelley learned that Harriet was pregnant. Shelley had long talks with Godwin but Hitchener, now Shelley's 'Brown Demon', was ejected from the family. At Hookham's bookstore Thomas Love Peacock first met Shelley.

Returning to Tanyrallt, Shelley, who earlier had been arrested for debt in Caernarvon, now became sceptical of the Tremadoc project. His radical writings elicited a Tory neighbour's enmity and Shelley grew suspicious of his friend Williams. On the night of 26 February 1813, after Shelley transcribed the poetry of *Queen Mab*, he experienced two successive 'attacks', exchanging pistol shots with an intruder who escaped before Daniel Healey, just back from jail, entered the room. This may have been another delusional episode or a ruse allowing the Shelleys to leave Wales without paying their debts.[34] A week later Shelley and his family took the ferry to Dublin, proceeding on to stormy Lake Killarney.

Shelley was in London in early April, avoiding Godwin but visiting John Newton and his family, vegetarian devotees of nude air-bathing. Especially pleasing to Shelley was the company of Harriet Boinville and her lovely married daughter, Cornelia Turner. After Harriet had a baby girl, Eliza Ianthe Shelley, on 23 June 1813, Shelley moved his family to Bracknell, close to Mrs Boinville and Cornelia. Often in London, Shelley was evading his creditors while trying to raise money for Godwin. His marriage beginning to unravel, Shelley in early October crowded his family and Peacock into his new carriage for Edinburgh.

Peacock and Harriet were together in Edinburgh while Shelley socialized with his lawyer friend Gilbert Hutchinson. William Kirkpatrick Sharpe, who lived near Shelley, brought him and Hutchinson to a dance at Mrs Balfour's home, having assured her that the two 'danced quadrilles eternally'.[35] Shelley wrote to Hogg that he was returning 'by himself' to London, but they all returned together at the end of November. Shelley found a house in Windsor but was often absent, disengaging from Harriet and her now-despised sister Eliza. At this time, Shelley feared he had elephantiasis. He overcame his hypochondriacal concern and by late 1813 had completed *A Refutation of Deism*. This philosophical dialogue, in the manner of Hume and Cicero, reflected Shelley's development as an Academic sceptic.[36]

THE SECOND ELOPEMENT

In March 1814 Shelley was living sporadically with Harriet in Bracknell, preferring his room at Mrs Boinville's, where Cornelia helped him learn Italian. His infatuation with Cornelia and his erotic lyrics about her resulted in his banishment by Mrs Boinville.[37]

[34] Bieri, 238–52; *SC* IX, 196–204.   [35] Bieri, 166.

[36] C. E. Pulos, *The Deep Truth: A Study of Shelley's Scepticism* (Lincoln, NE: University of Nebraska Press, 1954); Donald H. Reiman, 'Intervals of Inspiration': The Skeptical Tradition and the Psychology of Romanticism (Greenwood, FL: Penkevill Publishing, 1988).

[37] *CPPBS* I, 145; *Norton* 2, 91; Bieri, 272.

Harriet Shelley became pregnant about the time that she and Shelley remarried on 24 March to assure their union's legality. Shelley in early May met Mary Wollstonecraft Godwin, recently returned from Scotland. They had briefly met in November 1812 and Mary, now 16, rejoined her half-sister Fanny Imlay Godwin, aged 20, her 16-year-old stepsister Claire Clairmont, her younger half-brother William Godwin, her loathsome stepmother, and her adored father. Godwin and his wife Mary Jane, unaware of the attraction between Mary and Shelley but fearing Fanny's attraction to Shelley, sent Fanny to visit relatives in Wales. Mary Wollstonecraft's grave at Old St Pancras Church was a June rendezvous spot for the couple. Godwin was furious when late that month Shelley told him he loved his daughter. Although the lovers were apart, they communicated, and after Shelley almost overdosed on laudanum, Mrs Boinville looked after him. Shelley told Mary he believed that Harriet had been unfaithful to him and the couple planned their elopement. They fled London on 28 July for Calais, joined by Claire.

The three, rambling through war-torn France, reached Brunnen, Switzerland, in late August. Shelley began dictating his story *The Assassins* to Mary, who was pregnant. Destitute, they started home down the Rhine, arriving in mid-September in London. The ensuing months of 1814 they struggled financially, dodged bailiffs, and tried to restore relationships with the Godwins and their friends. Shelley and Claire often went out together and Hogg frequently visited Mary, who returned his flirtations. Harriet's son and new Shelley heir Charles Bysshe was born on 30 November. Harriet, sure of Shelley's paternity, thought the babe looked just like 'his unfortunate father'.[38]

Early in January 1815 Shelley's grandfather Bysshe died. Sir Timothy, forced to deal with his son, gave him a £1,000 annual income. From this, Shelley gave Harriet £200 annually. Hogg professed his love for Mary, who sent him a lock of her hair as she awaited her child, a seven-months baby girl born on 22 February. Gloom settled over the household when the unnamed infant died two weeks later. Shelley, again unwell, was consulting physicians about his spasms.

Trying to distance themselves from Hogg, Shelley and Mary spent several days at Salt Hill, near Eton, where she again became pregnant at the end of April. Mary, jealous of the time Claire and Shelley spent together, succeeded in May in arranging Claire's departure for Lynmouth. After Mary and Shelley toured the west, in August they rented a Bishopsgate cottage next to Windsor Great Park, their home until the following May. Peacock and Claire's brother Charles soon planned a boat trip up the Thames with Shelley and Mary. They visited Oxford and at Lechlade Shelley composed 'A Summer Evening Churchyard'.

The river trip perhaps influenced the imagery of *Alastor; or, The Spirit of Solitude*, the poem Shelley wrote that autumn. In *Alastor*, Shelley shifted from the Godwinian ideology of *Queen Mab*, examining his fundamental ideals from newer, darker perspectives, narrating a lonely poet's quest for love ending in death. The poem's autobiographical elements were not unnoticed by his associates, Timothy noting that his son 'wanted to find out one person on earth the Prototype of himself'.[39]

---

[38] *Letters: PBS* I, 422 (n. 2).   [39] See Ingpen, *Shelley in England*, 463.

Godwin resumed corresponding with Shelley after a year's lapse, but was silent on 24 January 1816 when Mary gave birth to a son, William. Shelley soon wrote to Godwin that he was considering living in Italy. Claire, back in London, used money Shelley provided and found lodgings in Marylebone to advance her scheme to meet Lord Byron. Claire proceeded quickly, carrying on her affair with Byron from mid-March into April, and even brought Mary to meet him. Byron left for the Continent on 23 April, leaving Claire pregnant with his child. Determined to follow Byron, Claire convinced Shelley that they should go to Geneva, Byron's destination. Meanwhile, a Chancery decision limited Shelley's access to his estate but his father continued his allowance and covered some of his debts.

The Shelley ménage set off on 2 May for Geneva, where they waited almost two weeks for Byron to arrive with his young physician, Polidori. The two poets soon bonded, finding adjacent houses and jointly buying a sailboat to circumnavigate Lake Geneva. The summer's literary fallout was positive for everyone except Claire, who was rebuffed by Byron before and after learning of his unborn child. Mary's *Frankenstein* proved the most notable creative monument from that summer, but Shelley was inspired to compose 'Hymn to Intellectual Beauty' and 'Mont Blanc', the former a deeply personal expression of his creativity, the latter his most philosophically probing verse to date.

Shelley's group, with their Swiss nursemaid Elise, arrived in Portsmouth in early September, Shelley going to London, the others to Bath to await the birth of Claire's child. Shelley saw Fanny in London but was with Mary in Bath in early October when Fanny passed through that city for Bristol. There she wrote Mary an alarming note. Before Shelley could locate her, Fanny committed suicide in Swansea. Shelley, shaken and depressed, expressed his guilt in lines beginning 'Her voice did quiver as we parted' (*Longman*, 1, 550–3).

On 1 December the first favourable notice of Shelley as a poet appeared in Hunt's *Examiner*, where 'Hymn to Intellectual Beauty' was printed (in January). Shelley visited Hunt in early December, where he met John Keats and Horace Smith. Returning to Bath, Shelley received Hookham's letter informing him that Harriet had drowned herself in the Serpentine several days before her body was found (10 December). Harriet probably had been living with an army officer who was sent abroad, leaving her alone and pregnant. Both Peacock and Hunt later observed that Shelley was severely shaken, his guilt turning into 'a deep and abiding sorrow'.[40]

Shelley was determined to retrieve his two children by Harriet, but her father petitioned Chancery to retain Ianthe and Charles. In late March 1817 Shelley and Hunt listened as Lord Eldon decided in the Westbrooks' favour and guardians were appointed. Sir Timothy later grew fond of Charles, who died aged 11 at Field Place. His father was unmentioned on his headstone. Ianthe married, the only child to provide descendants of the poet.

[40] Bieri, 363–5.

FAREWELL TO ENGLAND

After Harriet's death, Mary (more than Shelley) was eager to be married. The ceremony at St Mildred's on 30 December 1816 was attended by Godwin, now effusively accepting of the couple whom he had ostracized. Claire's daughter Allegra (initially, Alba) was born in Bath on 12 January 1817 and in late March they all moved into Albion House in Marlow, Shelley's final English home. Earlier in March Shelley's new publisher, Charles Ollier, began selling *A Proposal for Putting the Reform to the Vote Throughout the Kingdom*, Shelley's political treatise urging reform moderation but reaching out to radicals. Perhaps the press publicity of the *Shelley* v. *Westbrook* Chancery trial led Shelley to use the pseudonym 'The Hermit of Marlow'.[41] Mary was completing *Frankenstein* despite the many visitors to Albion House, including Godwin, Peacock, Hogg, and Hunt's family, who stayed many weeks. Keats, never intimate with Shelley, resisted his invitation to visit. With his close friends, Hunt and Horace Smith, Shelley engaged in poetry writing contests; one between Smith and Shelley yielded 'Ozymandias'.

By April Shelley had begun *Laon and Cythna*, finding solitude composing in his boat on the Thames and in nearby Bisham Wood. Solicitous of Marlow's poverty-stricken workers, he visited them regularly with gifts of money and blankets. Shelley translated Aeschylus' *Prometheus Bound* and read Homer, Plutarch, and Spenser. He congratulated Hogg for reading Lucretius, saying, 'I am well acquainted with Lucretius' (*Letters: PBS* I, 545). When Mary completed *Frankenstein* in May, Shelley wrote the Preface for it (having contributed 4,000–7,000 words to the text).[42] Mary next edited the journals and letters from their 1814 trip, published anonymously as *History of a Six Weeks' Tour* and containing 'Mont Blanc'. Shelley began composing *Rosalind and Helen*, later completed in Italy. More to Shelley's liking than this poem were his erotic verses expressing his feelings for Claire, whose 'snowy fingers' played the piano that he obtained for her. The longest poem, 'To Constantia', transcribed by Claire, was published in Munday's Oxford newspaper.

After Mary's baby Clara Everina was born (2 September), Shelley's health declined and he saw his physician William Lawrence, who advised he stop writing poetry. Shelley was often in London seeking money to help support Hunt, Godwin, and Peacock. *Laon and Cythna*, completed in September, was accepted by Ollier based on several sheets Shelley had submitted. Although advertised in October, when the printer read its blasphemous contents, no further copies came off the press. Besides being anti-religious, the title reflected its incestuous brother–sister relationship. Ollier came to Marlow and Shelley accepted changes, deleting passages which threatened legal action. Cythna became an 'orphan', and the new title was *The Revolt of Islam*.

Shelley traded barbs with Godwin, who disliked *Laon and Cythna* and was upset about his going to Italy. However, Shelley favourably reviewed Godwin's novel

---

[41] *Murray: Prose*, 419; Bieri, 376–7

[42] Mary Wollstonecraft Shelley (with Percy Bysshe Shelley), *The Original Frankenstein*, ed. Charles Robinson (Oxford: Bodleian, 2008), 25.

Mandeville. Mary and Shelley, briefly in London in November, were visited by Keats. The nation mourned the death of Princess Charlotte but not the three leaders of the Derbyshire uprising who were brutally executed for insurrection. Outraged, Shelley wrote *Address to the People on the Death of Princess Charlotte*. Its bitter epigraph from Paine's *Rights of Man*, 'We Pity the Plumage, but forget the Dying Bird', perhaps preventing the pamphlet's circulation until years later.[43]

Shelley's sonnet 'Ozymandias', signed 'Glirastes', appeared in Hunt's *Examiner* as 1818 began. Copies of *Frankenstein* arrived and Shelley, asserting he was not the author, sent one to Walter Scott (*Letters: PBS* I, 590). Perhaps aggravated by Godwin's visit, Shelley's ophthalmia and lung complaints recurred and he ceased translating Homer's *Hymns*. In early February Shelley met Keats at Hunt's house; another sonnet competition apparently was won by Hunt. Shelley departed Albion House finally on 7 February and soon the entire household was lodged on Great Russell Street. Peacock was a constant companion for Claire, who resisted his marriage proposal. She dreaded the idea of leaving her adored Allegra with Byron in Italy and recorded in her journal the operas and plays the family attended before their departure.[44] Shelley's last visit to Keats was at Hunt's house on 11 February. Horace Smith invited Keats to dinner with Shelley, but the younger poet declined, saying 'Remember me to Shelley'.[45] Godwin avoided the christening of Mary's two children, probably still believing that Shelley had fathered Claire's child.

On 11 March the group left for Dover and the next day crossed a stormy channel for Italy, the final resting place for Shelley and the three children.

SELECT BIBLIOGRAPHY

Bieri, James. *Percy Bysshe Shelley: A Biography*. Baltimore: Johns Hopkins UP, 2008.

Boas, Louise. *Harriet Shelley: Five Long Years*. London: Oxford UP, 1961.

Cameron, Kenneth Neill. *The Young Shelley: Genesis of a Radical*. New York: Macmillan, 1950.

Dowden, Edward. *The Life of Percy Bysshe Shelley*. 2 vols. London: Kegan Paul, Trench, 1886.

Feldman, Paula R. and Diana Scott-Kilvert. Eds. *The Journals of Mary Shelley: 1814–1844*. 2 vols. Oxford: Clarendon Press, 1987.

Hawkins, Desmond. *Shelley's First Love: The Love Story of Percy Bysshe Shelley and Harriet Grove*. London: Kyle Cathie, 1992.

Medwin, Thomas. *The Life of Percy Bysshe Shelley: A New Edition*. Ed. H. Buxton Forman. London: Oxford UP, 1913.

Murray, E. B. Ed. *The Prose Works of Percy Bysshe Shelley*. Vol. I. Oxford: Clarendon Press, 1993.

O'Neill, Michael. *Percy Bysshe Shelley: A Literary Life*. New York: St Martin's, 1990.

Reiman, Donald H. *Percy Bysshe Shelley*. Updated edn. Boston: Twayne, 1990.

Scott, Winfred. *Jefferson Hogg*. London: Jonathan Cape, 1951.

Stocking, Marion Kingston. Ed. *The Journals of Claire Clairmont*. Cambridge, MA: Harvard UP, 1968.

[43] *Murray: Prose*, 400; 451.

[44] *The Journals of Claire Clairmont*, ed. Marion Kingston Stocking (Cambridge, MA: Harvard UP, 1968), 79–87.

[45] Bieri, 397, 740.

CHAPTER 2

....

SHELLEY AND ITALY

....

RALPH PITE

I

....

THE first letter Shelley wrote from Italy was addressed to his friend the poet and satirical novelist Thomas Love Peacock. 'Behold us arrived at length at the end of our journey', Shelley announced on 8 April 1818, two days after reaching Milan (*Letters: PBS* II, 3). He, Mary, their two infant children, William and Clara, Mary's half-sister Claire Clairmont, and her daughter Allegra (fathered by Lord Byron) had travelled together through France and crossed the Alps via the Cenis; they reached Milan, after passing through Susa and Turin and, initially at least, they planned to go no further. Shelley and Mary looked into renting somewhere to live on the shores of Lake Como nearby—a place which, Shelley told Peacock (writing on 20 April 1818), 'exceeds anything I ever beheld in beauty' and whose surrounding 'range of lower hills' (lower than the mountains beyond) has 'glens & rifts opening to the other such as I should fancy the *abysses* of Ida or Parnassus'. Shelley continues:

> Here are plantations of olives & orange & lemon trees which are now so loaded with fruit that there is more fruit than leaves, & vineyards. [...] The union of culture & the untameable profusion & loveliness of nature is here so close that the line where they are divided can hardly be discovered. But the finest scenery is that of the Villa Pliniana, so called from a fountain which ebbs & flows every three hours described by the younger Pliny which is in the courtyard. This house which was once a magnificent palace, & is now half in ruins, we are endeavouring to procure. (*Letters: PBS* II, 6–7)

Shelley's delight and excitement in this letter reflects the sense of physical and personal renewal he reported two weeks earlier: 'no sooner had we arrived in Italy', he wrote in his first letter to Peacock, 'than the loveliness of the earth & the serenity of the sky made the greatest difference in my sensations' (*Letters: PBS* II, 3).

The sense of relief is no doubt connected to the fact that their journey was over. Transporting three young children, their mothers, and servants across France and

Switzerland must have imposed considerable strain on Shelley. He makes no mention of those circumstances, choosing instead a more impersonal narrative in which (following a long-standing convention) he describes arriving in Italy as an entry into Eden.[1] In Shelley's description, the shores of Lake Como appear superlatively fruitful and display an ideal harmony between man and the natural world—a harmony so perfect that human activity and organic process can barely be distinguished.

Moreover, in Italy the classical past visibly survives; parts of it may even be 'procured' by the visitor. He or she might linger here and settle into a pastoral scene: one filled with scattered, fragmentary traces of the classical past and yet in itself still whole and undiminished. The profusion of natural growth, conjoined with and enhanced by human activity, implies that what appears to lie in ruins continues, in truth, still full of vitality. By inhabiting the ruined palace, the visitor can become part of a living tradition, aligned with it while able also to claim that he or she is reviving only the best of the old. Ruins may declare, in other words, not only the decline and fall of the classical past, its corruption and degeneracy, but also the opposite of that: the virtues lost through decline and overthrow. Ruins survive as traces of the ancient ideal which the modern traveller can retrieve and revive. There is, furthermore, an effortlessness and naturalness to that process of recovery: as nature and culture blend into one another, so may ancient and modern, and so even may alien and native.[2]

Similarly, the hills around the lake contain glens and rifts which, for Shelley, are such as he should 'fancy the *abysses* of Ida or Parnassus'. Peacock was a devoted classicist (whose own correspondence frequently switches between English, Latin, and Greek and whose fictional prose is dotted with classical tags).[3] Shelley speaks to Peacock's enthusiasm for the widely assumed and admired 'serenity' of the classical world, finding in Italy likenesses of Mount Ida, from where the gods observed the tragic conflict of the Trojan War, and Mount Parnassus, sacred to Apollo and home of the Muses. Modesty compels him to place himself on only the lower slopes of these mountains of inspiration, and his modesty becomes hyperbolic when he describes these lower slopes as the very lowest possible, the 'abysses' of magnificent elevations.

Such exaggeration of feeling becomes, when addressed to Peacock, a moment of banter and self-parody. Peacock was at the time writing a portrayal of Shelley as Mr Scythrop in his novel *Nightmare Abbey* (1818), and making fun there of Shelley's fondness for morbid extremes of hope and despair. Shelley, though he did not read the novel until 1819, evidently knew of the project: 'See, I have sent you a study for Night Mare Abbey' he says in his letter of 20 April. In the novel, Scythrop condemns Mr Cypress (a Lord Byron figure) for travelling abroad and claims that he 'should [himself] have no pleasure in

---

[1] Thinking of Italy as a paradise, reached by crossing the desolate wastes of the Alps, is a Grand Tour commonplace, dating back to Petrarch. See my 'Shelley in Italy', *Yearbook of English Studies* 34, guest editor David Seed (Leeds: Modern Humanities Research Association, 2004), 46–60 (49–51).

[2] On this subject, see Anne Janowitz, *England's Ruins: Poetic Purpose and the National Landscape* (Oxford: Blackwell, 1990) and Anne Janowitz and Carolyn Springer, *The Marble Wilderness: Ruins and Representation in Italian Romanticism, 1775–1850* (Cambridge: Cambridge UP, 1987).

[3] See *The Letters of Thomas Love Peacock*, ed. Nicholas A. Joukovsky, 2 vols. (Oxford: Clarendon Press, 2001), I, 105–12 (a letter to Thomas Forster, in typical polylingual style, and one to William Roscoe, in Latin).

visiting countries that are past all hope of regeneration' or in wandering 'among a few mouldy ruins, that are only imperfect indexes to lost volumes of glory'.[4] Here, while doing precisely what, according to Peacock, he would condemn in other people, Shelley pre-empts his friend's amusement. These 'abysses of Ida or Parnassus' are, he acknowledges, what his friend would expect him (the gloomy, Gothic Scythrop-Shelley) to find in Italy. By finding them, and registering his self-awareness about the figure he cuts, Shelley gives the impression that he has escaped Scythrop's melodrama; the improvement in his physical well-being ('the greatest difference in [his] sensations' engendered by Italy) has had, it seems, a comparable, beneficial effect on his mental well-being.

Peacock was, naturally, just as amused by Shelley's expressions of eager optimism as he would have been by his conforming to Gothic type. He told their mutual friend Thomas Jefferson Hogg that Shelley 'seems in excellent health and spirits and is full of sanguine expectations of finding paradise on the banks of the Lake of Como'.[5] Such high hopes are vividly displayed in Shelley's first letter—the one that Peacock is talking of here; Italy possesses 'loveliness' and 'serenity', the sound of the language is delightful after 'that nasal & abbreviated cacophony of the French', Milan is 'very agreeable' and most strikingly:

> A ruined arch of magnificent proportions in the Greek taste standing in a kind of road of green lawn overgrown with violets & primroses & in the midst of stupendous mountains, & a *blonde* woman of light & graceful manners, something in the style of Fuseli's Eve were the first things we met in Italy. (*Letters: PBS* II, 3–4)

Consistent with his later, longer description of the landscape around Lake Como, Shelley sees Italy as a classical Eden, where Eve may be found among ruins of Greek architecture and monuments of human greatness blend into the green lawn of an ideal natural world.

Between these two descriptions, however, Shelley voices more difficult feelings. His second letter to Peacock begins with a sense of surprised regret that letters between Italy and England take so long to arrive, and disappointment too that Peacock will not be able to travel out to join them but is, instead, 'obliged to remain at Marlow'. Shelley adds:

> I often revisit Marlow in thought. The curse of this life is that whatever is once known can never be unknown. You inhabit a spot which before you inhabit it is as indifferent to you as any other spot upon the earth, & when, persuaded by some necessity you think to leave it, you leave it not,—it clings to you & with memories of things which in your experience of them gave no such promise, revenges your desertion. (*Letters: PBS* II, 6)

Such labile shifts in mood between euphoria and despondency were, as Peacock knew (and as Shelley knew he knew), characteristic of him. They also characterize his conflicted state as a traveller into—and, later on, as a resident in—Italy. Although he remained abroad for the rest of his life (until his death by drowning in 1822), Shelley continually revisited England in thought. He continued to be preoccupied by British politics and the great majority of his poetry written in Italy comments directly or

---

[4] Thomas Love Peacock, *Nightmare Abbey* (London: T. Hookham, 1818), 152, 153.
[5] Peacock to T. J. Hogg, [?1–27 April 1818] (*Letters*, ed. Joukovsky, I, 122).

indirectly on events taking place in his home country. Similarly, although he learnt Italian and sought acquaintance with Italians, Shelley encouraged (sometimes entreated) his English friends to join him abroad. The Edenic paradise of Italy was also, for Shelley, a place of personal and political exile so that he experienced Italy as, at once, an idyll, a slope of Ida or Parnassus, and as an abyss.

The ability to see himself caught between those two extremes becomes, furthermore, both an attraction and a pitfall; the ironic self-perception he conveys to Peacock can appear an escape from feverish extremes (a paradise) and as a loss of access to true feelings and commitments (an exile). Consequently, the serenity that Italy offers seems increasingly to Shelley to be enmeshed with self-distance and passivity because haunted by loss: if he can mimic Italy's perfect calm only by ironizing himself, the calm he attains is always exposed to irony too; it may be no more than a self-deception (vulnerable to the fear that he is not essentially serene at all) and may, equally, become—or come to appear—a compromise: an acceptance of the world and its manifold injustices that he has made in order to maintain personal equanimity.

Similarly, by allowing paradise to appear, manifest within nature, Italy seems to realize an ideal; at the same time it reveals that this must remain an impossibility because the real inevitably impedes and falsifies ('stains') the ideal. The presence of an ideal brings with it an awareness of our distance from it (as visitors and exiles); accompanying this sense of personal exclusion is the more profound sense that the realized ideal reveals its falling away from that ideal simply by virtue of being realized, in time and history. The presence of the Edenic comes to appear innately illusory and deceptive because it offers perfection within an imperfect world.

In other words, the 'Paradise of exiles' (57), as Italy is described in *Julian and Maddalo*, has in truth the effect of exiling paradise. It becomes a pressing question for Shelley the political idealist, how far his idealism is a delusion and self-deluding, and for Shelley the poet, how far and in what way the ideal may be perceived and then conveyed without being captured and/or diminished.[6] He addresses such questions most directly and fully in his final, unfinished poem, *The Triumph of Life*. Similar questions and concerns are present, however, from the beginning of his time in Italy, as these early letters to Peacock suggest.

II

One reason for staying on Lake Como was the hope that Lord Byron, then living in Venice, would come to visit Shelley's party there.[7] Shelley had had a number of motives for travelling to Italy: his doubtful health; the fear that he would be denied custody of his

---

[6] Shelley's concerns parallel Keats's and Coleridge's preoccupation with the ambiguities of 'indolence'. See Willard Spiegelman, *Majestic Indolence: English Romantic Poetry and the Work of Art* (New York: Oxford UP, 1995).

[7] Lady Morgan remarks that the 'union of classic interest with picturesque beauty, has rendered Como the sojourn of the elegant, and the haunt of the learned', terms that mirror Shelley's praise and

children by Mary (as he had lost custody of Ianthe and Charles, his children by Harriet Westbrook); and, thirdly, the scandal which had greeted his publication of *Laon and Cythna*. He was also involved in mediating between Byron and Claire Clairmont over the future of their child. It had been agreed that 'Byron would send for the child when it was old enough to leave its mother and that Claire would have the right to see it when she desired'.[8] How exactly this vague understanding would work out in practice remained to be seen, but Como seemed somewhere that offered Claire the best hope of remaining in contact with a child she was devoted to.

Byron, however, at this point and subsequently, proved stubbornly uncooperative, combining possessiveness about his daughter with contempt for her mother. He refused to leave Venice and sent a messenger to fetch Allegra. Though Shelley offered to look after Claire and Allegra whatever happened, Claire ultimately gave in to Byron and handed Allegra over; soon afterwards, the Shelleys left Como for Tuscany. They spent the remainder of the spring at Livorno, retreating from the heat of summer to Bagni di Lucca, in the hills nearby. That autumn, once more attempting a reconciliation with Byron, Shelley took Claire with him to Venice. Mary followed a little later, bringing the children, but, tragically, Clara Shelley died on 24 September, a few days after arriving in the Veneto.

The following winter and spring were nomadic: the party lingered at Este, in the Euganean Hills, until November (in a villa leased by Byron); then they travelled south, visiting first Rome and then Naples where they spent the winter. At the end of February 1819 they moved back to Rome, where they lived until June. In Rome, however, they lost the second of the children, William, who died (probably of malaria) aged three and a half; soon afterwards they retreated north to Tuscany, moving first to Livorno once again, then to Florence, and, in January 1820, to Pisa, where they settled for the next two years.

Outwardly, then, the Shelleys' movements in Italy correspond quite closely to those of their fellow tourists. When the Continent reopened after Waterloo, English travellers journeyed across Europe in the footsteps of the eighteenth-century Grand Tour. Visitors to Italy would cross the Alps (rather than making the sea passage from, for example, Marseille to Genoa), take in Turin and Milan, before travelling south, usually via Florence to Rome and Naples, often for the winter. They would visit Venice on their return journey, if they had not done so on the way south, so that this unique, notorious, and spectacular city was established as the first or final Italian destination.[9]

Though the Shelleys undertook much of this itinerary, at each stage they had personal and frequently painful reasons for following it. Moreover, unlike Lord Byron, Shelley

---

suggest his obedience to conventional taste at this stage (*Italy*, 2 vols. as 1 (London: Henry Colburn, 1821), I, 172).

[8] Daisy Hay, *Young Romantics: The Tangled Lives of English Poetry's Greatest Generation* (New York: Farrar, Strauss, Giroux, 2010), 91; see 146–7. See also Richard Holmes, *Shelley: The Pursuit* (London: Weidenfeld & Nicolson, 1974), 342–3, 418–19.

[9] See James Buzard, *The Beaten Track: European Tourism, Literature, and the Ways to Culture, 1800–1918* (Oxford: Clarendon Press, 1993), 97–107 and his 'The Grand Tour and After (1660–1840)', in Peter Hulme and Tim Youngs (eds.), *The Cambridge Companion to Travel Writing* (Cambridge: Cambridge UP, 2002), 37–52.

travelled as a family man, with all the associated responsibilities and constraints. The opportunity for self-cultivation and self-realization which the Grand Tour was customarily understood to afford (to young people on the brink of adulthood) was denied him by the presence of several dependants and the depth of his attachment to them. Shelley's unusual circumstances placed him, therefore, on the margins: among Italians, his circumstances meant he could assimilate only to a limited extent (unlike the solitary Lord Byron who could 'go native' in Venice); meanwhile, among tourists Shelley stood out as a quasi-resident, unable to participate in the licence of the traveller.

Shelley's remedy for his double exclusion was to align himself with other expatriate 'Anglo-Italians'. His decision to leave Como was prompted by Byron's recalcitrance over Allegra, but the choice of Livorno (Leghorn) as their destination was decided by the fact that Maria Gisborne was living there. Maria was an old friend (and old flame) of Mary Shelley's father William Godwin, who had looked after Mary and her sister Fanny when their mother Mary Wollstonecraft died. The Shelleys sought out similar family connections, including Amelia Curran, in Rome in 1819 and when they returned to Tuscany in 1820.[10] Jeffrey N. Cox argues that Shelley's behaviour shows his desire to create abroad an equivalent to the liberal, progressive Hampstead set Leigh Hunt had formed in London.[11] Pisa, Livorno, and Florence all possessed long-standing communities of expatriates, from England and (of particular interest to Shelley) from Ireland too; many in these circles were in sympathy with Shelley's politics, loathing Britain's Castlereagh administration and supporting the cause of Italian unification and independence.[12] Had Clara not died in autumn 1818, the family might well have settled in Tuscany from the beginning, since the Anglo-Italian identity suited their situation and their allegiances so well. As it was, their year journeying around Italy (from autumn 1818 to autumn 1819) looks (and may have felt to them) like a period of internal exile.

Personal factors, then, ensured that Shelley was neither a tourist visitor nor an assimilated resident nor, until 1820, a settled member of an expatriate community. That dislocated condition placed him in between the various perspectives on Italy implied by these other ways of being there. Each perspective became an option which Shelley could adopt and investigate, with the detachment of the uncommitted. He gained a dubious freedom, a disinterestedness which was potentially advantageous and even, in a sense, ideal, but whose flipside was a sense of emptiness and deracination. Specifically, in Shelley's case, separation from both traveller and resident made him look sceptically at and into the privileges of the tourist.

Italy, after 1815, became a highly contested space, in which the proliferating guidebooks became politically controversial. Two of the most prominent—John Chetwood Eustace's *A Classical Tour of Italy*, first published in 1813 and in its sixth edition by 1821,

---

[10] See Maria Schoina's admirable study of these groups, their dynamics, and Shelley's place in them: *Romantic 'Anglo-Italians': Configurations of Identity in Byron, the Shelleys, and the Pisan Circle* (Farnham: Ashgate, 2009).

[11] Jeffrey N. Cox, *Poetry and Politics in the Cockney School: Keats, Shelley, Hunt, and their Circle* (Cambridge: Cambridge UP, 1998), 187–8.

[12] See Paul O'Brien, *Shelley and Revolutionary Ireland* (London: Redwords, 2002), 143–6.

and Lady Sydney Morgan's *Italy*, an immediate bestseller when it appeared in 1821—reveal the nature and the intensity of the differences.

Both writers attracted as much hostility as enthusiasm; the *Historical Notes* to Byron's *Childe Harold*, canto IV, written by John Cam Hobhouse, Byron's friend and travelling companion, assault Eustace.

> The extreme disappointment experienced by choosing the *Classical Tourist* as a guide in Italy must be allowed to find vent in a few observations [...]. This author is in fact one of the most inaccurate, unsatisfactory writers that have in our times attained a temporary reputation, and is very seldom to be trusted even when he speaks of objects which he must be presumed to have seen.[13]

Shelley joined in this chorus of disapproval: 'Consult Eustace if you want to know nothing about Italy', he exploded to Peacock in a letter written in November 1818 (*Letters: PBS* II, 54). Morgan, though, was placed by the *Edinburgh Magazine* of 1821, with Hobhouse, among Eustace's natural enemies. Eustace is 'the amiable and diligent author of the Classical Tour' whose 'literary merits' can be ignored only by the partisan and the corrupted. Hence:

> there is a very natural reason why he [Eustace] should have been exceedingly disagreeable both to Hobhouse and this woman [Lady Morgan]. His 'Antigallican Phillipics' necessarily rendered him obnoxious to the former, and his habitual respect for taste, decency, religion, and regular government, to the latter.[14]

As E. R. Vincent has revealed, Hobhouse relied on the Italian émigré poet Ugo Foscolo when writing the historical notes to *Childe Harold*; contemporaries (without knowing Foscolo's involvement) registered nonetheless the liberal bias of the work.[15] Moreover, as Maurizio Isabella notes, they were right to align Lady Morgan with Hobhouse and Foscolo:

> Proposing a positive image of northern Italy, [Lady Morgan's] book also reflected the views of the Italian Romantic elites, and advanced a brand of liberalism which tallied with that of the Italian Romantics and with their political aspirations.[16]

For Lady Morgan, then, Italy was, as Donatella Badin says, 'an ideal community in which a sense of nation was just beginning to prevail'; as a scene of opportunity for progressive politics it became a vantage point for Byron. According to Jerome McGann, both Byron and Stendhal delight in Italy because they can 'transform' it, creating from the country 'a geopolitical myth through which they can criticize the deficiencies of contemporary

[13] Lord Byron, *The Complete Works* (Paris: Galignani, 1837), 170.
[14] Quoted from *The Literary and Scientific Repository, and Critical Review* 4 (1822), 203.
[15] E. R. Vincent, *Byron, Hobhouse and Foscolo: New Documents in the History of a Collaboration* (Cambridge: Cambridge UP, 1949).
[16] Maurizio Isabella, *Risorgimento in Exile: Italian Emigrés and the Liberal International in the Post-Napoleonic Era* (Oxford: Oxford UP, 2009), 196.

Europe, on the one hand, and intimate more generous and vital forms of human civilization on the other'.[17]

Morgan and Hobhouse both draw attention, therefore, to the presence of nineteenth-century Italians, inhabiting their venerable antiquities and under the yoke of the Austrian occupation; hence their travel writing violates the classical sanctity of the landscape. This policy disturbs the dignity and repose of the classical tourist, whose focus on the everlasting truths of art and religion (visible in the ruins situated amidst picturesque rurality and in the ecclesiastical grandeur of the eternal city) allowed native concerns and their politics to be forgotten. Creating such an aesthetic posture in relation to Italy was, however, evidently an escape neither from history nor from contemporary concerns.

As Benjamin Colbert has pointed out, Eustace's apparent indifference to present-day Italian concerns masks an agenda as fully contemporary as Lady Morgan's or Lord Byron's. The *Classical Tour* invokes William Wilkins's recent architectural survey of southern Italy, *The Antiquities of Magna Graecia* (1807), in which, according to Colbert:

> scientific data and picturesque views combined to promote Italy as a palimpsest beneath which Greek lineaments could be clearly discerned. Eustace refers to Wilkins in order to ally the *Classical Tour* with the Greek Revival's programme of reimagining the classical world in Grecian terms and applying these to contemporary tastes in literature, architecture, and fashion.[18]

On a larger scale, Eustace was defending via his classicism the ascendancy of the cultural, religious, and political status quo, while Morgan's and Hobhouse's liberal position highlighted contemporary Italian virtues in order to argue for political change. This polarity was consolidated by the reviewers at the time, who placed Eustace in one camp, Hobhouse and Morgan in the opposing one, shadowed by their *éminence grise*, the disreputable Lord Byron.[19]

Colbert rightly perceives that this polarization oversimplifies Eustace, whose praise for Mme de Staël's *Corinne ou l'Italie* (1807) sits oddly with his anti-Risorgimento reputation. Colbert also registers how these differences of view and their positioning within the politicized culture wars of the day affected Shelley. 'Lines Written among the Euganean Hills', for example, Colbert sees as:

> synthesising through a Byron-Eustace dialectic, [Shelley's] own cross-cultural understanding of the relation between the modern British sightseer and sights seen, the alienated subject and the outward signs of social, political and intellectual mutability.

[17] Donatella Badin, *Lady Morgan's Italy: Anglo-Irish Sensibilities and Italian Realities* (Bethesda: Academic Press, 2007), 159; Jerome McGann, 'Rome and its Romantic Significance', in *The Beauty of Inflections: Literary Investigations in Historical Method and Theory* (Oxford: Clarendon Press, 1985), 96.

[18] Benjamin Colbert, *Shelley's Eye: Travel Writing and Aesthetic Vision* (Farnham: Ashgate, 2005), 134.

[19] Lady Morgan saw the differing views of Italy in these terms: 'To trace the result of this European revolution in Italy [...] is the object of the following pages [...] For while the classical annals of Italy [...] make a part of the established education in England, the far nobler history of the Italian republics [...] remains but little known' (Lady [Sydney] Morgan, *Italy*, 2 vols. in 1 (London: Henry Colburn & Son, 1821), I, 17).

These interests and the poetry that follows from them parallel, moreover, a wider concern of the post-Waterloo moment:

> By 1818, travellers increasingly turned their attention to the Italian sites of the Grand Tour, once again interrogating how classicism might be incorporated into a modern British cultural consciousness.[20]

'Interrogating' and 'synthesising', though apparently at opposite extremes, imply a more settled stance than the one Shelley was able to adopt. *Lines Written among the Euganean Hills* and Shelley's following work, *Julian and Maddalo: A Conversation*, probe the landscapes of northern Italy and Venice, the restlessness of the poet's eye corresponding to the poems' unease with the received depictions of these places and the self-constructions they imply.

Padua—seat of one of the great medieval universities, now in decline—is presented within the contradictory perspectives of classical and liberal tourist:

> By the skirts of that grey cloud
> Many-domed Padua proud
> Stands, a peopled solitude,
> 'Mid the harvest-shining plain,
> Where the peasant heaps his grain
> In the garner of his foe,
> And the milk-white oxen slow
> With the purple vintage strain,
> Heaped upon the creaking wain,
> That the brutal Celt may swill
> Drunken sleep with savage will; [...][21]

The pastoral elements ('the peasant [who] heaps his grain', the 'milk-white oxen', and 'purple vintage') evoke a classical world in moments of vividness. Shelley sets up this familiar image of the Italian landscape, however, only to knock it down via references to present-day injustices: the peasant's harvest stored 'in the garner of his foe', the wine gathered and transported only in order that 'the brutal Celt', the Austrian rulers of this part of Italy, 'may swill | Drunken sleep'. A classicizing view appears to be being debunked by this strategy; there is though an unexpectedly rehearsed quality to the contrasts Shelley constructs, such that Morgan's or Hobhouse's perspective does not win out over Eustace's. Rather, the two points of view coexist, mingled and, by implication, interdependent. The contemporary scene both clashes with the pastoral idea and is absorbed in it, because as the peasants labour in the 'harvest-shining plain' (and lead their 'milk-white oxen' and 'creaking wain'), they are taken up into the poeticism of Shelley's descriptions, his use of standard epithets from eighteenth-century poetic diction ('milk-white', 'purple', 'creaking') and of its characteristic means to novelty, double epithets like 'harvest-shining'. The energy with which pastoral illusions are broken down (when the

---

[20] Colbert, *Shelley's Eye*, 3, 142.
[21] *Lines Written among the Euganean Hills*, 214–24; *Norton 2*, 108 (all quotations from Shelley's poetry taken from this edition, unless otherwise stated).

turn of a line-break reveals the lie, as in 'the peasant heaps his grain | In the garner of his foe' or 'upon the creaking wain, | That the brutal Celt')—is dissipated when the mode of description continues unaltered, flowing onward unchallenged. An almost gleeful and certainly ill-founded triumphalism then infects the supposed revelations of the liberal, Risorgimento sensibility. They seem to be (perhaps unconsciously) participating in a merely theatrical subversion of the status quo, and emerge as dependent upon the moral clarities produced by a pastoral convention for their opportunity to show its inappropriateness to (and its distortions of) the 'reality'.

More prominent in the poem than the attack on the classical tourist (which these lines superficially imply and Shelley's letters might lead one to expect) is a seeming disdain for the places that the liberal conscience hopes to rescue. Venice, for all its magnificence, deserves to 'perish' if it cannot break free of foreign oppression. 'Earth can spare ye' is Shelley's brusque dismissal of La Serenissima. Padua, likewise, is a lost cause: the spark of its ancient university 'lies dead [...] Trampled out by tyranny'. Worse, its lamp of learning is like a meteor 'lost over the grave of day, | Its gleams betrayed and to betray'.[22] Since it is bound now to mislead further, to betray more men, we should not lament its demise.

These are surprisingly harsh sentiments, motivated by Shelley's radical loyalties and in part by his wish to distinguish his own perspective from those of others—liberal or conservative. An apocalyptic radicalism comes through in the poem as Shelley suggests that tyranny's destruction of Padua is all to the good because it will act as a distraction for those same forces of tyranny, blinding them to the greater danger they face: the Europe-wide conflagration of popular uprising that has been set in train by the original spark of Enlightenment learning, extinguished in its place of origin but vigorously burning still elsewhere (see 269–84). In the same vein, Venice may be spared, 'while' (i.e. so long as) 'like flowers, | In the waste of years and hours, | From your dust new nations spring | With more kindly blossoming' (163–6). This qualification also has the effect of making the preceding gesture of contempt ('Earth can spare ye') appear excessive and, again, theatrical.

English travellers were fond of condemning Venice; Eustace declared that the city:

> for so many ages the seat of independence, of commerce, of wisdom, and of enterprise, gradually sunk from her eminence, and at length became the foul abode of effeminacy, of wantonness, and of debauchery.

Its history was, for him:

> A tremendous lesson [...] to prove, if such proof were wanting, that independence must be preserved, as it can only be obtained, by the sword [...]; that submission excites contempt; and that determined heroic resistance, even should it fail, challenges and obtains consideration and honour.[23]

---

[22] *Lines Written among the Euganean Hills*, 160, 163, 258–60, 267–8.
[23] John Chetwode Eustace, *A Classical Tour through Italy*, 2nd edn., 2 vols. (London: Mawman, 1813), I, 76, 78.

Lady Morgan is less moralizing because more disheartened:

> such images of desolation and ruin are encountered, in every detail of the moral and
> exterior aspect of the city, as dissipate all visionary anticipations, and sadden down
> the spirit to that pitch, which best harmonizes with the misery of the once superb
> mistress of the waves.[24]

Shelley's dismissal of Venice resists both these readings. The city is neither to be condemned nor its subjection to the Austrians bemoaned. Its art, its palaces, its romantic
grandeur do not make it a special case. Rather, Shelley says, the city is valuable insofar as
its history and example may inspire democracy and independence movements
elsewhere.[25]

Via these moves, Shelley takes issue with Eustace's judgemental rejection of the city.
Both might say 'Earth can spare ye' but for quite different reasons. This implies a critique
of Eustace's patriotism and cultural self-confidence while Shelley's willingness to part
with Venice brings out the self-indulgence present in Lady Morgan's fond misery.
Shelley, therefore, is resisting both Eustace's self-separation from the foul abode of
Venice and Lady Morgan's alignment of her feelings with the place, to the extent that her
sad spirit 'harmonizes' with the city's condition. Instead, he places himself at one remove
both from the city itself and from the usual interpretations travellers bring to it. By taking the city to be (from some points of view) comparatively insignificant and *un*exceptional, Shelley reveals the true unwillingness (despite appearances) of other visitors to
see it either as exceptional or as itself, in their attempts to align its fate with their own
historical narratives, political agendas, moral precepts, or habitual sentimentality.
Likewise, the tensions present within Shelley's descriptions of Italian scenes expose the
attempt by other travellers to avoid or deny their perplexity in the face of the country's
radical ambiguity—their reaching for some (usually rather desperate) means of establishing coherence, however partial, partisan, or self-reflexive that might be.

In a more direct attack on contemporary views of Venice, he claims that the city
should be remembered for offering refuge to Lord Byron. '[L]et there only be [...] one
remembrance, more sublime | Than the tattered pall of time':

> That a tempest-cleaving Swan
> Of the songs of Albion,
> Driven from his ancestral streams
> By the might of evil dreams,

---

[24] Morgan, *Italy*, II, 451. See also Louis Simond, *A Tour through Italy and Sicily* (London: Longman,
Rees, Orme, Brown, and Green, 1828), 35, where Venice appears as 'A confused heap of very old
buildings, shabbily fine, with pointed windows half-Gothic, half-Grecian, out of which dirty beds were
thrust, for the benefit of air, and once or twice dirtier utensils emptied of their contents. Half-rotten
piles supported blocks of marble richly carved, serving as landing-places to these miserable hovels.'

[25] Similarly, Maddalo interrupts Julian's touristic rapture over Venice's 'fabrics of enchantment',
promising to show him 'A better station'. The gloomy madhouse ('A windowless, deformed and dreary
pile') shows Venice as a place of contemporary oppression and not only romantic decay and this sets in
train the two characters' discussion of perfectibility and political idealism (ll. 87, 92, 101).

> Found a nest in thee; and Ocean
> Welcomed him with such emotion
> That its joy grew his.
>
> (167, 171–2, 174–80)

Even visitors, such as Lady Morgan, who did not set out to inveigh against Venice's corruption and luxury tended to be coy about Lord Byron's presence there, since his notoriously and flagrantly debauched behaviour conformed precisely to the belief that Venice was a den of iniquity.[26] Shelley boldly reverses this: Byron is the glory of Venice; the city's welcome of the exiled poet is proof of its still uncorrupted condition.

This, the most fervent moment in the poem, occurs when Shelley finds in Venice a 'nest' for Byron and thus a realization of the hope with which he began, that 'Many a green isle needs must be | In the deep wide sea of Misery' (1–2). He returns to this idea at the end, urging that somewhere there must be 'some calm and blooming cove, | Where for me, and those I love, | May a windless bower be built'. There:

> the Spirits of the Air,
> Envying us, may even entice
> To our healing Paradise
> The polluting multitude;
> But their rage would be subdued
> By that clime divine and calm.
>
> (342–4, 353–8)

Though the poem attacks the pastoral impulse of Eustace and, to a similar extent, the liberal optimism of Lady Morgan, it still articulates a utopian ideal, placing that beyond the actual world of Italy yet also glimpsing something equivalent in the real—in Venice's reception of Byron.

The impulse to find some hint of Eden in Italy, despite seeing this as a mistake and a temptation, is probed in *Julian and Maddalo*, particularly near the end. Having seen the Maniac's suffering, Julian remarks:

> If I had been an unconnected man
> I, from this moment, should have formed some plan
> Never to leave sweet Venice,—for to me
> It was delight to ride by the lone sea
> [...] I imagined that if day by day
> I watched him, and but seldom went away [...]
> I might reclaim him from his dark estate.
>
> (547–50, 568–9, 574)

---

[26] See Lady Morgan's telling silence in *Italy*, II, 454: '"Palazzo di Lord Byron," said the capo of our gondolieri, as we rowed by it. The next object he announced was the Rialto.' Similarly, Anna Jameson in her *The Diary of an Ennuyée*, new edn. (London: Henry Colburn, 1826), reports meeting a lady who knew Byron while he was living in Venice, but then gets coy: 'Several little anecdotes which she related I need not write down; I can scarcely forget them, and it would not be quite fair as they were told *en confiance*' (77).

Venice becomes for Julian another green isle or windless bower: 'one may write | Or read […] Unseen, uninterrupted', he says, and enjoy the company of friends. Maddalo's 'wit | And subtle talk would cheer the winter night' (551–2, 554, 559–60), just as Julian's company will subdue the Maniac's grieving rage. Julian imagines, in other words, another 'healing Paradise'. That conventional hope produces the clichés of travel writing: the place becomes 'sweet Venice' and a few lines later 'bright Venice' (583), by striking and disappointing contrast with the detailed descriptions of the opening. It also leads to no actual help: Julian leaves Venice, 'urged by his affairs' (582), and abandons the Maniac to his fate.[27]

The poem remains secretive about its view of Julian's wish to be of help followed by his rapid departure. Blitheness and self-deception are suggested without Julian's actions being condemned exactly. He acknowledges readily that nothing came of his plans but claims that this incident was nonetheless exceptional: whereas usually such 'dreams of baseless good' vanish and are forgotten, 'what I now designed', he says, 'Made for long years impression on my mind' (578, 580–1). This claim, although it is not fully supported by the poem, is not exposed to withering irony either. As Shelley directs towards his own idealizing perspective the same scepticism that he brought to both conservative pastoral and liberal naivety, he attains a curiously dispassionate acceptance of the pitfalls of his own position, recognizing its vulnerability to the criticism that someone like Maddalo might make. Yet the logic of disillusionment is not followed through in this poem and, in the remainder of Shelley's output, he does not renounce or abandon idealism; he will still, sometimes obstinately, 'talk Utopia' (*Julian and Maddalo*, 179).

III

When he first arrived in Italy, Shelley found a quiet corner in Milan Cathedral where he could read Dante (see *Letters: PBS* II, 8) and Dante's influence on Shelley's Italian poetry is evident, especially in *The Triumph of Life*. Dante's *Purgatorio* in particular assisted Shelley in reflecting on the marginality of his own position, exiled in Italy, and on the role that idealism could play in the task of addressing sad realities, the actualities of historical conditions and personal limitations.

Evidence of *Purgatorio*'s importance comes from Shelley's drafting a translation of the first fifty lines of *Purgatorio* 28, at some point between summer 1818 and spring 1820;[28] Dante's renewed significance to him is apparent also from 'The Woodman and the Nightingale', written in *terza rima*, and from 'Marenghi' (or 'Mazenghi'), a Dantean poem in its preoccupation with Florentine politics and exile. Both poems were written and left unfinished during Shelley's winter in Naples (1818–19), a period which Mary Shelley describes as one of misery: 'many hours were passed when [Shelley's] thoughts,

---

[27] See my 'Shelley in Italy', 52–5.
[28] See *BSM* V, *The Witch of Atlas Notebook*, ed. Carlene A. Adamson, p. xlv.

shadowed by illness, became gloomy,—and then he escaped to solitude, and in verses, which he hid for fear of wounding me, poured forth morbid but too natural bursts of discontent and sadness.'[29] 'Stanzas, Written in Dejection Near Naples' bear witness to this state of mind, as do fragments from the same period such as 'Apostrophe to Silence' and 'My Head is Wild with Weeping' or the sonnet, 'Lift not the painted veil'.

In 'The Woodman and the Nightingale', in a passage reminiscent of *Purgatorio* 28, Shelley imagines an idyllic woodland, tended by wood-nymphs who:

> kept ever green
> The pavement and the roof of the wild copse,
> Chequering the sunlight of the blue serene
>
> With jaggèd leaves,—and from the forest tops
> Singing the winds to sleep.
>
> (43–7; *H* 563)

'Wild' stands out here amidst the orderliness of the space and its unchangingness. The word's dissonance in the lines is accentuated, perhaps, by the root-meaning of 'copse', which derives from 'coppice'; a copse is by definition cultivated woodland, and so precisely not 'wild'. Similarly, 'jaggèd' is unexpected, clashing with 'the blue serene' from a moment before and, through the closeness in sound and rhythm, bringing out a harsher quality from 'Chequering'. You sense the dappling of the shade as light is being 'checked', held back, interrupted by foliage that is tough and spiny, more needle than leaf. By these means, Shelley brings 'the thorns of life' into a place of serenity; he also allows, however, that 'Nature's gentle law' dictates that the nymphs chequer the light, keep the wild copse green without entirely taming it and water it with 'Nature's pure tears which have no bitterness' (42, 50; *H* 563). Wildness and jaggedness seem innate and, curiously, to be tied in to the kindliness and generosity of nature. The dictional tension and intricacy of the writing reflects Shelley's grief at the seemingly inherent cruelty of events (which had robbed him of his daughter Clara) and, secondly, his aspiration to find in these sad realities signs of a 'gentle law' in operation. That aspiration, as the use of *terza rima* perhaps reveals, was mediated by Dante.

Purgatorio begins with an escape from Hell. Dante, who has climbed out from the centre of the earth and reached the surface at the Antipodes, is gladdened by the dawn: 'Dolce color d'oriental zaffiro [...] alli occhi miei ricominciò diletto [...] tosto ch'io usci' fuor dell'aura morta.'[30] The 'Sweet hue of eastern sapphire [...] to mine eyes | Unwonted joy renew'd [...] soon as I scap'd | Forth from the atmosphere of deadly gloom' (in the version by Henry Cary, the pre-eminent English translator of Dante in the period, which Shelley read).[31] As Shelley wrote in *Peter Bell the Third*, 'Hell is a

---

[29] See *Poetical Works*, ed. Hutchinson, 570. Shelley had used *terza rima* earlier in his career, in 'Prince Athanase' (written in 1817).

[30] *Purgatorio* 1, ll. 13, 17; *La Divina Commedia*, ed. Natalino Sapegno, 3 vols. (Florence: La Nuova Italia Editrice, 1984), II, 4.

[31] Henry Cary, *The Vision of Dante*, ed. Ralph Pite (London: J. M. Dent, 1994), 123. Shelley began a translation of *Purgatorio* 1, 1–6 (see *BSM* V, 71, 374).

city much like London—| A populous and smoky city' (147–8) and, as he remarked to Peacock (noted above): 'no sooner had we arrived in Italy, than the loveliness of the earth & the serenity of the sky made the greatest difference in my sensations' (*PBS: Letters* II, 3). Dante's narrative exactly paralleled his own, lending new resonances to the familiar, Edenic associations of Italy. Specifically, Dante's example allowed the paradisal to be coloured by suspense and anxiety as well as hope.

Shelley enthused more than any of his contemporaries about Dante's *Paradiso* and he composed a translation of the opening of *Purgatorio* canto 28, in which Dante enters the Earthly Paradise. Nonetheless, the settings of Dante's Purgatory and his Ante-Purgatory, from the earlier cantos of *Purgatorio*, figure with greater intensity in Shelley's poetry than do echoes of the *Paradiso*. The opening lines of *The Triumph of Life* adopt many elements from *Purgatorio* 1 and 2; the 'waking dream' that follows parallels Dante's 'Valley of the Princes' (*Purgatorio* 7 and 8). The narrator sees a pageant of legislators: 'Voltaire, | Frederic, and Kant, Catherine, and Leopold' (42, 235–6). Writers and philosophers are coupled with the rulers of the world so that the bearing of thought on events, of theory and practice, becomes the focus of the poem. 'And so my words were seeds of misery', Rousseau cries, 'Even as the deeds of others.' The narrator comforts him by challenging that fear, '"Not as theirs," | I said'. Rousseau, though, disputes this, pointing to a company of 'Anarchs old whose force and murderous snares | Had founded many a sceptre bearing line' and declares:

> 'Their power was given
> But to destroy […] I
> Am one of those who have created, even
>
> If it be but a world of agony.'
>
> (280–1, 285–6, 292–5)

The narrator's absolute distinction between the tyrant and the thinker is not collapsed but the relation between the two sides looked at more closely.

Similarly, the narrator's disdain for historical actors is rebuked:

> 'Let them pass'—
> I cried—'the world and its mysterious doom
>
> 'Is not so much more glorious than it was
> That I desire to worship those who drew
> New figures on its false and fragile glass […]'

Rousseau replies first that all are equally insignificant ('Figures ever new | Rise on the bubble, paint them how you may'). Secondly, after the narrator's aloofness shifts towards misery ('Mine eyes are sick,' he says, 'of this perpetual flow | Of people, and my heart of one sad thought'), Rousseau urges him to commit to the involvement he recoils from: 'But follow thou, and from spectator turn | Actor or victim in this wretchedness.' No longer 'forbear[ing] | To join the dance' makes one risk being destroyed by it, but also means one may do the world some good. By turning actor or victim, Rousseau continues, 'what thou wouldst be taught I then may learn | From thee'. Disciple will be teacher, follower, leader, and the chain of history broken by this reversal of temporal sequence; isolated despair at the perpetual flow of people will be relieved by exposure to it.[32]

Shelley presented himself as lying 'asleep in Italy' when he wrote 'The Mask of Anarchy'. His poems in response to the Peterloo massacre are paralleled by writings on the uprisings in Spain, Naples, and Greece. He recognized his proneness to over-investment in these causes: 'With no strong personal reasons to interest me, my disappointment on public grounds has been excessive' (*Letters: PBS* II, 291), he told Byron when the Neapolitan rebellion was put down. Yet the alternative seemed to be oblivion. *The Mask of Anarchy* and *The Triumph of Life* both rebuke the sleepy self-marginalization of the expatriate and, at the same time, vindicate it, since the dreams that come during the 'wondrous trance of thought' may inspire passive resistance (as in *The Mask*) and its intellectual equivalent: the stance searched after in *The Triumph of Life* in which the visionary hope continues even as it fades into the light of common day:

> 'So knew I in that light's severe excess
> The presence of that shape which on the stream
> Moved, as I moved along the wilderness [...]
>
> A light from Heaven whose half extinguished beam
>
> 'Through the sick day in which we wake to weep
> Glimmers, forever sought, forever lost. [...]'
>
> (424–6, 429–31)

The 'Valley of the Princes' in Dante's *Purgatorio*, cantos 7–8 provides the template for Shelley's concerns over commitment, negligence, hesitation, and necessary patience.

The valley is another 'windless bower' (or abyss of Ida) in which pastoral beauty offers a foretaste of paradise; Dante discovers there an assembly of the great and the good, comparable to the gathering of poets in *Inferno* 4 and to the pageant of rulers in Shelley's *Triumph*. Dante's princes are, however, required to wait for their salvation to begin because, while alive, they did too little or acted too late. Dante's rage over the fragmentation of Italy (which resonated so deeply with Foscolo and his compatriots) is voiced in *Purgatorio* 6, just before he encounters the princes. Their neglect of their duty colours, therefore, the reader's experience of their enforced idleness and observation of their religious devotion. The princes sing the Catholic liturgy as evening falls, the leader 'ficcando li occhi verso l'oriente, | come disse a Dio: "D'altro non calme"' (fixing his gaze on the east, as if he were saying to God, 'Nothing else concerns me'), and then the whole group singing, 'avendo li occhi alle superne rote' (their eyes directed towards the heavenly spheres) (*Purgatorio* 8, 11–12, 18; Sapegno, *Divina Commedia* II, 83). Under constraint, amidst disappointment and self-rebuke, the princes look still towards what is rising out of the eastern sky and also towards the eternal and the ideal, visible in the

---

[32] *Triumph of Life*, 188–9, 243–7, 248–9, 298–9, 305–7.

unchanging stars. Shelley's stance in Italy, in the face of political setbacks, artistic rejection, and personal tragedy, is revealed by Dante's princes, involved in their waiting.

Select Bibliography

Bandiera, Laura and Diego Saglia. Eds. *British Romanticism and Italian Literature: Translating, Reviewing, Rewriting*. Amsterdam: Editions Rodopi, 2005.

Brand, C. P. *Italy and the English Romantics: The Italianate Fashion in Early Nineteenth-Century England*. Cambridge: Cambridge UP, 1957.

Colbert, Benjamin. *Shelley's Eye: Travel Writing and Aesthetic Vision*. Farnham: Ashgate, 2005.

Crisafulli, Lilla Maria. Ed. *Immaginando l'Italia: itinerari litterari del romanticismo inglese*. Bologna: CLUEB, 2002.

Curreli, Mario and Anthony L. Johnson. Eds. *Paradiso degli esuli: Shelley e Byron a Pisa*. Salzburg Studies in English Literature: Romantic Reassessment. Salzburg: Universität Salzburg, 1988.

Eustace, John Chetwode. *A Classical Tour through Italy*. 2nd edn. 2 vols. London: Mawman, 1813.

Folliot, Katharine. *Shelley's Italian Sunset*. Richmond: H&B Publications, 1979.

Isabella, Maurizio. *Risorgimento in Exile: Italian Emigrés and the Liberal International in the Post-Napoleonic Era*. Oxford: Oxford UP, 2009.

Marshall, Roderick. *Italy in English Literature 1755–1815: Origins of the Romantic Interest in Italy*. New York: Columbia UP, 1934.

Morgan, Lady [Sydney]. *Italy*. 2 vols. in one. London: Henry Colburn & Son, 1821.

Pfister, Manfred. *The Fatal Gift of Beauty: The Italies of British Travellers. An Annotated Anthology*. Amsterdam: Editions Rodopi, 1996.

Pite, Ralph. *The Circle of our Vision: Dante's Presence in English Romantic Poetry*. Oxford: Clarendon Press, 1994.

Rogers, Samuel. *Italy: A Poem*. London: John Murray, 1823.

Rossington, Michael. 'Shelley's Neapolitan-Tuscan Poetics: "Sonnet: Political Greatness" and the "Republic" of Benevento'. *The Unfamiliar Shelley*. Ed. Alan M. Weinberg and Timothy Webb. Farnham: Ashgate, 2009. 137–56.

Schoina, Maria. *Romantic 'Anglo-Italians': Configurations of Identity in Byron, the Shelleys, and the Pisan Circle*. Farnham: Ashgate, 2009.

Webb, Timothy. *The Violet in the Crucible: Shelley and Translation*. Oxford: Clarendon Press, 1976.

Weinberg, Alan M. *Shelley's Italian Experience*. Basingstoke: Macmillan, 1991.

Woolf, Stuart. *A History of Italy 1700–1860: The Social Constraints of Political Change*. London: Methuen, 1979.

CHAPTER 3

....

RESOLUTIONS, DESTINATIONS

Shelley's Last Year

....

ANN WROE

ONE night in June 1822, at Villa Magni near Lerici on the north-west Italian coast—the sky moonless, the sea rough, rain falling—Shelley saw himself standing beside his bed. His own shadow drew him to the hall and asked him 'Are you satisfied?' He did not record an answer. His wife Mary thought he screamed wildly in his dreams; he knew he was awake, calm, rational. He had met himself before, a day-appearing dream walking on the narrow terrace that almost overhung the sea, and knew what he would say. 'How long do you mean to be content?' he had asked himself, and vanished.[1]

Some months earlier, Faust-like, he had plucked the petals from 'various flowers', real or imagined, to ask whether he was loved:

> and every one still said
> 'She loves me, loves me not.'
> And if this meant a Vision long since fled—
> If it meant Fortune, Fame, or Peace of thought
> If it meant—(but I dread
> To speak what you may know too well)—
> Still there was truth in the sad oracle.[2]

The day before, he had asked 'her'—probably Mary, but perhaps Jane Williams, with whom he was falling hopelessly in love—'if she believed | That I had resolution' (49–50). He recorded no answer, as he gave no answer to his double, and as he had received no answer from the flower. He did not know.

---

[1] Edward J. Trelawny, *Records of Shelley, Byron and the Author* (London: Pickering, 1878), II, 163–4; *Letters: MWS* I, 180–1.

[2] 'To—("The serpent is shut out from Paradise")', 34–40. Quotations from poetry and major prose works are from *Major Works* unless otherwise stated

To his friends, the last year of Shelley's life was full of portents of his death. They saw fate in everything: the white arcaded house he had taken for the summer at San Terenzo, so isolated and austere, too near the sea; his new yacht the *Don Juan*, so foolishly rigged and engineered for speed; his wistfulness for the past; his bad dreams. Hindsight coloured every corner of the scene. Yet Shelley—for all his careless remarks about dying in his thirtieth year, for all the presentiments of death by drowning from *Queen Mab* onwards—was still taken by surprise. Until the blue-green waters of the Bay of Spezia closed over him at around 7 o'clock in the evening on 8 July 1822, his mind contained ambition as well as resignation.

He had plans, and meant to achieve them. He would assist the birth of a radical new quarterly, the *Liberal*, with Byron and Leigh Hunt; urge on the Greek revolution with what writings and efforts he could; see Hunt and Claire Clairmont, to both of whom he sent money and intimate, confiding letters, set up somehow. He would perhaps visit Greece, once it was free, or even seek some 'entirely new sphere of action' as far away as India. He was anticipating, too, what he would do with his father's estate when he succeeded to it, down to the sale of timber *in absentia* (*Letters: PBS* II, 278, 361, 408). In the winter of 1821–2 he was tackling a grand historical subject in his drama of *Charles the First*; by late May he was writing, in *The Triumph of Life*, the most ambitious and technically assured poem he had yet undertaken. Yet every act of resolution was dogged by its opposite, and every confident statement tinged with despair. 'I am full of thoughts and plans,' he told Hunt in his last August, 'and should do something, if the feeble and irritable frame which incloses it was willing to obey the spirit' (*Letters: PBS* II, 345). Nine months later came a quieter, paradoxical thought, freighted with a deeper sadness: 'I hope to forget what I might have been in my content with what I am' (*Letters: PBS* II, 439).

To this conflict, death increasingly offered an answer. Dissolution or liberation, in one touch. Death did not need to step forward, though at times it did so, as stark embodied fears and premonitions. It merely had to sit at the corner of Shelley's mind, the inevitability he would not forget. Several of his letters had the feel of tying things up, stocktaking, making lists, so that death could enter unregretted. He feared it, being mortal; and he strode towards it, holding out both his hands.

Time, he knew, was playing tricks on him. The 'false' hours flew, yet they dragged. Teetering between the unfaceable future and the unendurable past, as if he stood at the brink of a precipice to which he had slowly, arduously climbed, he was glad if the heaven above him was calm for the passing moment. Perhaps, like Faust, he could stop time then, crying, 'Remain thou, thou art so beautiful' (*Letters: PBS* II, 436). Yet the present, too, was often unbearable, the new day he fled from as soon as it appeared. To pause in such a place was to be becalmed among terrors. And it was far too dangerous to go back.

The past he had always hated, memory's ashes and the cicatrices of pain: lost children, dead children, a dead wife, passion gone. But now he found himself haunted by it, nostalgic for the clouds of long-gone summers:

> Something is not there which was.
>
> (Stanza, 'If I walk in Autumn's
> even', 4, *H* 659)

Would the hours, he wondered in his last letter—hours passing so soon, returning so slowly—ever bring such happiness again as he and Edward and Jane had known in the summer of 1822? Or would they never return? Jane in reply, in a letter he never saw, asked why he was thinking that way. 'Are you going to join your friend Plato or do you expect I shall do so soon?' (*Letters: PBS* II, 445 and n.). But Shelley, again, was trying simultaneously to shake himself free from stasis and to cling to it, dreading the alternative. A very late pencilled poem, dated June 4/July 4 as if dates no longer mattered, seemed to catch the mood he was submerged in:

> Time is flying
> [Joy] is dying
> Hope is sighing
>   For there is
>
> Far more to fear
> In the coming year
> Than desire can bear
>   In this[3]

His divided state showed itself physically. A watercolour by his friend Edward Williams, undated but plainly from the last months in Pisa, showed Shelley hunched over a chair-back, eyes exhausted, mouth slack, his curling sideburns white as an old man's. At 28 or 29, he was worn out. It was time to leave 'my winter life' (*MYR* VII, 28–9). Yet it seemed to his friends that he was healthier than he had been for years: his chest fuller, his muscles firmer, his skin tanned and freckled with the Italian sun. Edward Trelawny, bathing with him often in the early summer of 1822, found him 'strong as a young Indian', vigorous and lithe (*Records*, I, x). Shelley himself, in *Adonais*, noted the paradox:

> On the withering flower
> The killing sun smiles brightly: on a cheek
> The life can burn in blood, even while the heart may break.

> (286–8)

He confessed to Claire that body and soul, mind and frame, 'me and my rebel faculties' were in a state of permanent struggle. The 'unnatural connexion' of soul and body was prolonged partly for her sake (*Letters: PBS* II, 292, 403, 404). Too many people depended on him: Hunt, for lodgings and furniture in Italy, as well as the *Liberal*; Claire herself, for money and emotional support over the custody of Allegra, her daughter by Byron; William Godwin, Mary's father, for funds to stave off bankruptcy. It seemed that no one came into his circle without needing and draining him; and that, increasingly, he could not replenish what he instinctively wanted to give.

Mary, too, depended too much on him. She had made him a part of her, binding him into her depression and despair. Love was still there somehow, a ghost at the hearth, though devoid of sympathy or understanding; duty remained, as well as a listless determination to confine the pain somehow. Their house in Pisa had brought rooted

---

[3] Donald H. Reiman, *Shelley's 'Triumph of Life': A Critical Study* (New York: Octagon, 1979), 247.

domesticity, with pot plants in the windows and their first bought Italian furniture arranged on the marble floors. But home was cold again.

> As the heart when joy is [fled]
>   dead
> As the night when sleep is fled
> I [am] now [left] alone—
>   alone,
>   left lone, alone—
>   (*MYR* VII, ed. Quinn, 24–5)

When Godwin continued to pester them for money, Shelley hid his letters from Mary to prevent the hurt to her. When Mary was ill—and she was often ill, languid with pregnancy and hating the San Terenzo house—he endeavoured to protect her. Lerici was a paradise where he would live always, he told Horace Smith, were it not that 'Mary has not the same predilection' (*Letters: PBS* II, 443). He would carry out her commissions if he remembered them, change his jacket to look 'proper' if she insisted, sign his letters 'Yours affectionately S', as usual. He would subdue his own wishes for her sake. But it was Jane to whom he wrote 'only […] for the pleasure of tracing what will meet your eyes' (*Letters: PBS* II, 445).

Ghosts also haunted the marriage. The summer of 1821 brought the scandal stirred up by Byron's friends the Hoppners, in which Shelley stood accused of fathering a child by Claire and abandoning it to the Naples foundling hospital. That child, Elena Adelaide Shelley, had died in 1820 of teething and fever, her true identity and history ruthlessly kept secret. Shelley had last shown such efficiency to shield Claire and Allegra from scandal in 1816; but in April 1822 Allegra too, a blue-eyed beauty with whom he had recently skipped and run like a child himself, had died of typhus fever. He saw her ghost a month later in the waves at Villa Magni, a naked child in the moonlit foam, clapping her hands for him to play again (Williams, *Journal*, 57–8). Death, he supposed, infected all those connected with him. And phantoms—including his own—had taken to returning.

Memory and thought, close-linked, now caused him disabling pain. He struggled actively to suppress them by sailing, frenetic exercise, or wild behaviour. Trelawny in the last months remembered him full of 'high glee' and shrieking laughter, spirits and fun. They hid the other side: feelings scratched so violently in dull pen over pencil that the whole page seemed to quake and hurt.

> Vultures who build yr. bowers
> High in the Futures towers
> Wake, for the spirits blast
> Over my peace has past
>   -------------
>
> Wrecked hopes on hopes are spread
> Dying joys choked by dead
> Will serve your beaks for prey
>   Many a day.
>   (*MYR* VII, 290–1; *H* 637)

That same notebook was full of the random scribbles of a child to whom the notebook had probably been handed: as if it did not matter, and as if he did not care.

Laudanum helped him. The small brown bottle was stuffed in a pocket, the dosing furtive and ashamed. In August 1821, though, after a fleeting and secret visit to Claire (that old addiction, too, bitter-sweet and unbreakable), he told her that he had slept as well 'as one might naturally sleep after taking a double dose of opium', as if he had done so (*Letters: PBS* II, 314). Laudanum stilled not only pain and breathing, but time itself, smoothing the moments out into eternity; it dissolved the body into the wider scene, a boundless immensity of being. At the dawning of that day he had rowed out with Claire in the harbour at Livorno to float among the white sails and the mist (*CC*, 245). This strange scene was his last birthday morning.

He was young, yet he was old. He was also pure; yet he was damaged and stained. 'How am I fallen', he told the wondering Hunt in April 1822, 'from the boasted purity in which you knew me once exulting!' (*Letters: PBS* II, 405). The Hoppner accusations were part of it; but when these had surfaced Shelley had been defiant in his conviction of his own 'exalted nature' and his pure soul's disdain. He longed only to withdraw to some lonely island from 'this hellish society of men' (*Letters: PBS* II, 319, 339). Yet he knew there was no escape that way. There was no denying the false masks, the layers of lies and pestering, evil thoughts, that flaked and fluttered from the faces of the hapless human processants in *The Triumph of Life*—his own masks too, concealing his own face. The outward Shelley was no better than those he mixed with, or obsessively avoided. And social isolation could not protect him from the hell that lay inside him.

His vegetarianism, once a sign of his purity, had now become random. He ate cold meat for lunch, and fished with Williams from the rocks on the shore at San Terenzo. He was still one of the *Sunetoi*, the elect, for whom he had written *Epipsychidion*; a man so confident in his pureness of mind and body that he could pause, perfectly naked and dripping with water from the sea, to argue with a female dinner guest who objected to him (Trelawny, *Records*, I, 166–9). Yet his indomitable sense of righteousness, that self-esteem he clung to as fiercely as love and hope, had been knocked aside by something. Self-doubt had entered in.

Some of it stemmed from his 'intolerable' closeness to Byron, a bond vexed by 'the demon of mistrust & of pride' (*Letters: PBS* II, 393, 324). He longed to break away, but was unable to. In Pisa from November 1821 they were neighbours across the river, shooting, playing billiards, riding, arguing, with Shelley's nerves 'shaken to pieces' at Byron's claret-fuelled dinner parties (*Letters: PBS* II, 379). He had long been disgusted by Byron's mode of life, his immorality and laziness with his talent; but when, in the autumn of 1821, Byron seemed at last to produce a great work in *Don Juan*, Shelley found its beauty and transcendence irrevocably mixed up with 'what is worst in human nature' (*Letters: PBS* II, 357). With disgust, he felt his censure slide into envious worship and even sycophancy; in his 'Sonnet to Byron' he became a 'worm', Byron his God (4, 14). Almost his last vicarious contact with him was the name *Don Juan* blazoned in black on the mainsail of his yacht. He retained the name, though he had wanted to call his new boat *Ariel*; but he had the sail scrubbed with every known cleanser, and then patched, to remove the pollution Byron had painted there.

Perhaps, too, he had been reading too much *Faust*, devouring Goethe's play 'over & over again' in the spring of 1822. That too was a paradox, his pleasure deriving directly from 'despair & a scorn of the narrow good we can attain in our present state'. Perhaps his 'discontent with the *less*' did indeed imply 'a just claim to the *greater*'; perhaps, with a small, select company, he was really 'in the right road to Paradise' (*Letters: PBS* II, 406). Or, his hesitancy implied, the path to destruction. Translating *Faust* involved brushing with obscenity, 'which is ever blasphemy against the divine beauty in life':[4] naked witches straddling broomsticks, apple trees yawning into dark vulva-clefts, the 'agonizing pleasure' of frantic sex he was to find again among the maddened firefly dancers of *The Triumph of Life*. Maurice Retzsche's sparely erotic engravings also caught those scenes: the Harz revellers half-dancing, half-coupling in their tangled hair, or the full, soft, devouring kiss of Faust and Margaret in the summer house. It made all the pulses of his head beat, Shelley told John Gisborne, merely to touch the back of the page on which that picture lay (*Letters: PBS* II, 407). The pulses of his heart, he could not help adding, 'have been quiet long ago'. But they were not so quiet that he, too, had not felt delight turn to poisonous desire that caught him, moth to flame, and consumed him. One instant in particular, with Claire or with Jane, perhaps a kiss ('Sweet lips'), was almost too searing to record:

> [Delusion madness & ruin]
>   [And memory]
>   [...]
>   [too sweet]
>   (*MYR* VII, 276–7)

Among the concepts he now struggled to express, finding the mundane word 'too often profaned' to catch its depth, force, and gentleness, was love.[5]

Translation itself was a sign of his frustration. He used it as a distraction from limping projects, a way past blocks. He was translating a good deal in those last months, from Calderón's *El mágico prodigioso* as well as *Faust*, perhaps because *Charles the First* would not take wing. With Spanish he was fluent and assured; Goethe was harder. He spent unmoving hours balancing *Faust* and the German dictionary on the marble mantelpiece of his study, running his long fingers distractedly through his hair. He once told Trelawny that he had 'lost a day' doing this (*Records*, I, 94): days of whose passing he was now painfully aware.

The matter he translated, from both authors, shared a theme of bargains with the devil: an immortal soul for magic powers, worldly pleasures, a woman's love. Both Calderón's Cypriano and Faust imagined themselves striding the air and marshalling the stars, as Shelley in *Prometheus Unbound* had seen man himself (IV, 418–23). Those dreams turned to ashes. Faust's Margaret cut her throat; Cypriano's Justina, on the point of ravishment, became a cloaked skeleton who filled his arms with death.

---

[4] *A Defence of Poetry: Major Works*, 685.
[5] 'To— ("One word is too often profaned")', *passim*. See also *Fragments of an Unfinished Drama*, 40–4 (*H* 484)

Both Faust and Cypriano were alchemists. In this dangerous, synthesizing science they believed their magic lay, as Shelley did. His magisterial essay of 1821 on his own powers and duties, *A Defence of Poetry*, had described poetry as 'secret alchemy', which 'turns to potable gold the poisonous waters which flow from death through life' (*Major Works*, 698). It was 'indeed something divine [...] at once the centre and circumference of knowledge' (696), and he controlled it, sunlike and godlike in the play of his imagination, directly in line from Homer, Dante, Bacon, Shakespeare, Milton. He too heard 'the echo of the eternal music', and beheld in the present the shape of what was to come (677).

Three instalments had been envisaged for the *Defence*. He had managed one, and offered Charles Ollier, his publisher, the second for nothing in September 1821 (*Letters: PBS*, II, 275, 355); but he did not write it. His surpassing statement of his own duties and his own divinity had dwindled into silence. Those 'happiest and best moments of the happiest and best minds', out of which his magic flared (*Major Works*, 697), seemed consigned to the unvisitable past. He remembered them acutely, even from childhood: the slow dropping of the noonday pine cones, the hum of gnats, while he closed his eyes to find the 'fire-trailed stars' of the universe inside (*MYR* VII, 308–9, 300–1). Now the lamp was destroyed, the lute broken, and the landscape one of naked branches and cold, roaring gales that no longer carried his spirit to the heights.

> No song—but sad dirges,
> Like the wind through a ruined cell
> Or the mournful surges
> That ring the dead seaman's knell.
>
> ('When the lamp is shattered', 13–16)

His high prophetic voice could sometimes be recovered. In the epigram to his lyrical drama *Hellas*, written in the autumn of 1821 under the sharp spur of the Greek rebellion against the Turks, he was the dove above the battlefield anticipating 'glorious struggles'; in the Prologue he soared among 'splendour-winged' and golden worlds, the green and azure sphere of earth turning below him, at the dawn of created time (20, 53–64). Prince Alexander Mavrocordato, who had become a friend in Pisa, would organize insurrection on the ground; Shelley, Freedom's voice on Freedom's wing, would radiantly shadow forth the Greece to come, once more the world's source of liberty and light. He too was Greek ('I try to be what I might have been'), writing in conscious imitation of Aeschylus' *The Persians* (*Letters: PBS*, II, 364); he too, therefore, according to his Preface, was that divine mirror, a being 'stript of all but that ideal energy, which is all we would be or would become':[6]

> Another Athens shall arise,
> And to remoter time
> Bequeath, like sunset to the skies,
>   The splendour of its prime,
> And leave, if nought so bright may live,
> All earth can take or Heaven can give.
>
> (1084–9)

---

[6] *A Defence of Poetry*: *Major Works*, 684.

But such enthusiasm had become rare. Even *Hellas*, his Preface admitted, was 'a mere improvise', produced with such emotion that much of the draft was barely legible. And even its most exhortatory passages were touched with the valediction he felt towards his own life.

> Could aught that is, ever again
> Be what it once has ceased to be:
> Greece might again be free.
>
> (*BSM* XVI, 244–5)

The scheme to set up the *Liberal* was also part of the cause of civilization, inspiration, and social improvement. But Shelley hung back, consenting to be 'only a sort of link' between Hunt and Byron in the enterprise, and then even less: 'I am, and I desire to be, nothing' (*Letters: PBS* II, 344).

His drama *Charles the First*, too, was no revolutionary appeal. Whatever his initial hopes for the play ('King Lear is my model,' he told Trelawny (*Records*, I, 117)), it had none of the cold steel of *The Cenci*, and proved in the end, in his uncharacteristically strong phrase, 'a devil of a nut […] to crack' (*Letters: PBS* II, 373). His characters spoke tamely, in competent but laboured verse; his notebooks were filled with careful historical points cribbed from Hume, though he hated history. Either of his rebel heroes, Sir Harry Vane or Hampden, might have been Shelley's fond projection of himself, but they barely entered the action before he abandoned it. Instead Shelley's favourite was Archy, the court fool, a mad singer babbling of blindness and rat-traps, corpses and rainbows. Archy saw truth, but his nonsense obscured it again; his words had wings, but rather than the soaring bird of prophecy he was the other, shyer poet of the *Defence*, 'a nightingale who sits in darkness, and sings to cheer its own solitude with sweet sounds'; sad sounds.

> There was no leaf upon the forest bare,
>   No flower upon the ground,
> And little motion in the air
>   Except the mill-wheel's sound.
>
> (V, 13–16; *H* 507)

A fundamental strangeness lay in this English subject. Shelley had been away from England now for more than three years. His exile, self-imposed and intended as temporary, had become his life. He still sought out the *Indicator*, and expatriate English friends made up most of his narrow society. But friends in England wrote rarely, and his letters back to them asked no political questions. He confided to Thomas Love Peacock that he knew his 'cause' was lost in England; he told Gisborne that he would not return, even when his father died (*Letters: PBS*, II, 331, 409). He had written no reformist works since *A Philosophical View of Reform*, his best and most ambitious, had petered out in mid-sentence in 1820; his good genius, he said, had urged him not to (442). Since then he had felt closer to revolts in Naples and Spain than to any stirrings north of the Channel. He still clung to moral and political hope, he told Byron, 'like a drowner to a plank' (291); but whatever revolutionary hopes he had nourished for England had faded like the land itself. The chatter in his house was of Italian domestics; his roof (the roof of his prison and charnel house, as he continued to regard the world) was the blue Italian sky; his 2-year-old son Percy, though fair and fat as any English child, babbled in Italian in his arms.

His books, besides, did not sell in England, and had never sold. *Prometheus Unbound* had had some fair reviews; but increasingly, the hassle of unseen proofs and public indifference weighed on Shelley. His publisher Charles Ollier was so dilatory and uncommunicative that he dreamed of 'ex-Ollierization' (*Letters: PBS* II, 388), but could not effect it. He turned in July 1821 to an Italian printer for *Adonais*, now his favourite among his poems; the types of Didot were beautiful, but the reviews remained scathing. If *Adonais* excited no interest, he told Hunt, he had no incentive to go on. 'I write nothing,' he confided to his friend the next March. 'What motive have I to write.' Without the certainty of finding sympathy, he told friends, there was no point (*Letters: PBS* II, 382, 394, 368, 436). Hunt, swept into his violent embrace at last in Italy, found him the same as ever, 'with the exception of less hope'.[7] But hope was crucial. Shelley's sense of lost purity was also bound up with the loss of his ideals.

Nonetheless his solitary days were still devoted to the chance of visions appearing and lines coming: in the pools and pine glades of the Pisan forest or in the caves and shallows round Lerici, his boat rocking under him in the light-play of the sea. Both Trelawny and Williams were told that he wrote better in the open air, seeking that 'secret correspondence of the heart' between flowing water, the wind in the leaves, and the motion of spirit in his body.[8] The source of inspiration had not changed. But the sense of divine beauty hidden, of music fled, tended to become a more prosaic list of obvious enthusiasms: flowers, grass springing, dawns, women's smiles.[9] Even in *Adonais*, what he loved became a bitter jingle.

> As long as skies are blue, and fields are green,
> Evening must usher night, night urge the morrow,
> Month follow month with woe, and year wake year to sorrow.
>
> (187–9)

Trelawny, surprising him one day in the Pisan forest, found scrawled, smudged sheets scattered in the grass and received from Shelley an almost crude, dismissive account of how his poems appeared: boiled off from his seething brain like scum on liquor, breeched like 'bantlings', or bastards (*Records*, I, 107–8). The high poet's voice of the *Defence* was mocked by the man's, as though they were strangers to each other. 'The poet & the man', he told the Gisbornes in July 1821, 'are two different natures: though they exist together they may be unconscious of each other, & incapable of deciding upon each other's powers & effects by any reflex act' (*Letters: PBS* II, 310). The poet sat alone, waiting, dreaming; the man gathered up those 'alms for oblivion' and hastened back to Mary, 'the quick coupled with the dead' (*Records*, I, 105).

He was perhaps less dead than indifferent: to society, parties, 'polite human faces', inert at Mary's side (*Letters: PBS* II, 292). In his mind he was 'the Snake' as Byron now

---

[7] Leigh Hunt, *Lord Byron and Some of his Contemporaries*, 2 vols. (London: Colburn, 1828), I, 22.

[8] *On Love, Major Works*, 632; Trelawny, *Records*, I, 170; Williams, *Journal*, 20.

[9] 'The Zucca', 33–40 (*H* 665); Song, 'Rarely, rarely comest thou', 31–6.

called him, sly, subversive, outcast, and reviled. His detachment from the world was increasing. His body he described as a cage, a shell or skin soon empty and left without regret. To Gisborne he explained that 'my error—and it is difficult for spirits cased in flesh and blood to avoid it—consists in seeking in a mortal image the likeness of what is perhaps eternal' (*Letters: PBS* II, 434). Thus, with apparent lightness, he now dismissed *Epipsychidion*, the beauty and terror of mystical love and the rapturous transfiguration of the united soul. Perhaps what he had felt and seen was true. Perhaps, on the other hand, it was only 'a production of a portion of me already dead' (*Letters: PBS* II, 262–3). He could no longer look at it, evidently, because his passion for Emilia Viviani was over. Or because it was unbearable to recall where for an instant he had been, and what he had been: transfigured, bodiless, complete.

He sought love desperately, as always; but first he sought calm. The chief attractions of Jane Williams, gradually brought into focus, were her amiability, her lack of words, her gentleness. The Williams household, on the floor below his in Pisa, offered a respite from thought and pressing time. Again and again he visited, slipping 'too melancholy' verses to them that were not by him but by 'my friend', or were 'the torn leaf of a book out of date' (*Letters: PBS* II, 437, 384). With Jane, too, he left the house for the forest. In her company he gazed into the unmoving pools, more beautiful in their green and purple shades than the world above; with her the wide landscape of Apennine mountain, sea, and shore found a focus in smiling, silent love. He was agitated as fleeting, surface water; she was still. He would 'take what this sweet hour yields', the illusory ecstasy of the present moment, tacitly acknowledging that with her he had no past and no future. His poet-self made it otherwise, sure that in some previous life or state he had been her Ariel, her soul-guide, 'flitting on, your prow before | Like a living meteor'. But now Ariel was silent, unlit, imprisoned 'in a body like a grave', or in the wood of the guitar he gave her. Her music alone would release him as it touched the nervestrings of his heart.[10]

Under her attempts at Mesmerism in the saloon at Pisa, or sitting, trembling, with her on the moonlit beach at San Terenzo, he let her hand caress his brow with infinite tenderness. But he was not healed. He could not be, because she was Edward's and he, despite himself, Mary's. In this too he was divided. The Poet knew that 'Memory gave me all of her' and that to his depths he was possessed by Jane, to love, to sleep, and to forget. The man, polite and grateful, knew that pity was all she could offer him. When she left him alone on the beach he was 'disturbed and weak', aroused but unrelieved; once again, the pain-daemon 'reassumed his throne | In my faint heart.' Still in trance at Pisa he had lied, in answer to her question of how he did, that he was 'Better, quite well'. But only breaking 'my chain' could cure him: the chain of his marriage, of time, or of his life.[11]

---

[10] 'The Pine Forest of the Cascine near Pisa', 65–104 *passim*; 'To Jane: The Recollection', 87–8; 'To Jane: The Invitation', 32; 'With a Guitar, To Jane', *passim*.

[11] 'Lines Written in the Bay of Lerici', 21–41; 'The Magnetic Lady to her Patient', 1–4, 28–45; *Adonais*, 234.

The background question was whether he had resolution: in the case of Jane, and in the general case of himself. In 'The serpent is shut out from Paradise', he answered it:

> One who *had*
> Would ne'er have thus relieved
> His heart with words, but what his judgement bade
> Would do, and leave the scorner unrelieved.

(50–3)

He was still capable, despite his disclaimer, of steely and sometimes frightening resolve. At Byron's shooting parties outside Pisa he could often fire straightest and fastest at the target, his eye unblinking, his hand rock-steady. When Mary in June 1822 almost died of a miscarriage, it was he who had ice brought, overbearing all resistance and pre-empting all medical advice, to fill a bath with it and by 'unsparing application' (Mary's still shivering, terrified words) stanch the bleeding (*Letters: MWS*, 1, 244). And when in March 1822 an Italian dragoon insulted a party of them at the Pisa city gate, Shelley plunged so keenly into the mêlée that followed that a sabre-blow knocked him from his horse and made him sick.

These headstrong episodes, however, did not prove that there was resolution in his life. Between the spring of 1821 and the summer of 1822 there was a sense of drift interspersed with sudden dramas, shocks that might even release him into another state. He once rowed Jane and her infants out to sea at Lerici in his tiny coracle of woven reeds and, oblivious to them, rested in dejection on the oar over deep water (Trelawny, *Records*, I, 156–61). Suddenly, brightening, he cried, 'Now let us together solve the great mystery!' With difficulty, she dissuaded him.

How actively he desired death was hard to say. His old imaginings of his own grave, strewn with rue and pansies and unwatered by tears, now had an exact geography in the meadows of the Protestant Cemetery in Rome where his small son William lay buried, 'so sweet a place' (*Adonais*, Preface). He wrote of sleep, 'soft as love, and calm as death' (*Hellas*, 12) with a new intensity, and sighed for night as the dawn came. In *Adonais* Death, the lover, pulled him down, embracing him:

> —oh, dream not that the amorous Deep
> Will yet restore him to the vital air.

(25–6)

At some stage too he wrote neatly, carefully, on the corner of a notebook page, 'Killing Self' (*BSM* XII, 10–11). Boldly under it stood a tree, one of 'my' trees as he thought of them, leafy and deep-layered, still growing. The words were in faint pencil; so faint, that he might have rubbed a hand across to blur the intention. He told Claire that, despite 'the strong motives which should impel me to desire to exist under another form', he also longed to live (*Letters: PBS* II, 288, 296). On balance, too, he rowed Jane and her children back to the beach at Villa Magni.

Yet he gave the impression that if a chance came to answer the question that had 'teazed' him all his life, he would take it. He would not struggle. Instead he would lie at the bottom of the pool, stretched like an eel, until something or someone plucked him out; or he would let himself go limp, as in the thrashing spume at Lerici, until he was carried to the shore. 'My curiosity on this point', he told his cousin Tom Medwin, 'never amounts to solicitude' (*Letters: PBS* II, 341). To find what he sought, as he noted in *Adonais* (464–5), he knew he must die first.

Most practically, he wrote to Trelawny in June 1822 requesting, at 'any price', prussic acid, or essential oil of bitter almonds, 'that golden key to the chamber of perpetual rest' (*Letters: PBS* II, 433). He did not mean to use it then, just to have it by him: 'A single drop, even less, is a dose & it acts by paralysis.' He was good at vanishing; on Trelawny's first visit in January 1822, after holding the rough-cut sailor spellbound for a while with Calderón, he suddenly disappeared 'like a spirit', as Jane said (*Records*, I, 22). Out of the obstructed life and the impossible loves, out of the stiffening, dying body, he would slip away.

Lerici was a step towards the edge. It was only a temporary reprieve; at summer's end the trunks and furniture would go back to Pisa. But that escape was sought with all Shelley's famous urgency, up and down the coast, by foot and boat. The villa itself, little more than a whitewashed boathouse, commended itself to him for one overriding reason: it stood, as his Poet-selves had so often stood, with its back to the enclosing mountains and its face to the wide, blue, beckoning bay, time stretching out into infinity.

> Who shall put forth on thee,
>   Unfathomable Sea?
>
> ('Time', 9–10; *H* 637)

The waves might almost come to fetch him: roaring in the lower storey like artillery, flooding in his dreams.

No particular destination drew him. His sea, like Homer's, was pathless and trackless; he committed himself almost wildly to the waves, and to wind and current. Nothing had changed, now that proper sea-sailing had entered his life. Steering and navigation were both joyously careless. His voyages in both the little green-and-white Arno punt, acquired in April 1821, and the 'beautiful' *Don Juan*, delivered in May 1822, were mostly random. 'In the evening we sail about', he told Claire in June, and in the daytime the vessel was pitted against all comers in impromptu races, usually beating them 'as a comet might pass the dullest planet of the Heavens' (*Letters: PBS* II, 427, 422). The yacht also went out merely to challenge squalls, storms, and winds. The end was unknown; the point was speed, motion, and the heeling of the undecked boat, with its multiple sails sometimes almost grazing the surface of the sea.[12] The point was flying, as nearly as was possible, in a vessel that made almost no barrier between the elements and himself. Ecstatically, Shelley stopped time this way. He probably died this way.

A journey without a destination was also the theme of much of the writing he was doing on shore. In *The Triumph of Life*, begun in May, left unfinished, a procession of dusty souls surged along a highway, ignorant and desperate:

> All hastening onward, yet none seemed to know
>   Whither he went, or whence he came, or why
> He made one of the multitude [...]
>
> (47–9)

---

[12] See Donald B. Prell, 'The Sinking of the *Don Juan* Revisited', *Keats–Shelley Journal* 56 (2007), 136–54.

Behind them rushed a chariot driven by Life, blindfolded, as Destiny had been in *Hellas*. Again Shelley heard the relentless turning of the wheels of existence, bringing-to-be and destroying, never ceasing. Humanity streamed past as bubbles jostling, breaking, and vanishing, leaving only thin foam behind them. Pure, he would not join them; impure, he would have no choice. The Earth itself was a bubble, a 'false and fragile glass' on which men threw their shadows before they faded (243–51). In *Hellas*, too, the whole fabric of human life, past, present, and future, firmaments and worlds, were 'motes of a sick eye, bubbles and dreams'. Thought alone 'and its quick elements, Will, Passion | Reason, Imagination', could not die (776–81, 795–801). The rest—mortal Shelley, his earthly life— was formed out of random atoms and went to nothing, whirled aimlessly as he watched.

He had asked in *Adonais* whether he was an actor or spectator in what seemed to be his life (184–5). He was both, perhaps, a dream observing dreams. In *The Triumph of Life* he once more faced his own phantom in the eyeless, withered root that was the ghost of Rousseau, battering him with his urgent questions: where he was from, where he was going, why. Rousseau could not answer, and radiant daylight offered only a cup of forgetfulness. Then Life's 'cold bright car' crossed the forest again, sweeping up this 'I', this 'me', the Rousseau-who-was-Shelley, carrying him to 'bright destruction' down the stream of life, now a river, now almost the tumultuous sea that was soon to overwhelm him.

> ' [...] I among the multitude
> Was swept, me sweetest flowers delayed not long,
> Me not the shadow nor the solitude,
> [...]
>
> —but among
>
> The thickest billows of the living storm
> I plunged, and bared my bosom to the clime
> Of that cold light, whose airs too soon deform.—'
>
> (460–2, 465–8)

Death caught him before the poem ended. Yet he meant to go on; and, almost certainly, there would have been a destination. His Poet-voyages had always been less a leap into the unknown than a statement of violent desire, though what he desired could not be named until he was there, embraced by it, possessed. Where Shelley arrived was often a place he already knew: one of those green isles, rising from the sapphire sea, in which he had walked in the woods, heard the nightingales, gazed into diamond-glinting wells, and disturbed the sleeping deer. An inward light, the sunset, star-springing light of love or of the heart, illuminated them, the 'sweet evening beams' he had tried to describe in the draft of *The Triumph of Life*.[13] He had been there in *Epipsychidion* and at the end of *Lines Written among the Euganean Hills*; he was there again in *Hellas*, in 'the Evening land' that was partly America and partly no place known on earth (1038–57). Even in *Charles the First* Hampden embarked from Westminster to find them: 'floating Edens' shining to the west, his idealized and perfect world (IV, 19–25; H 505).

[13] Reiman, *The Triumph of Life*, 181.

Shelley's last poem, too, might have ended in such a place: horror replaced by hope, and the apparent by the real. As he left the narrative, no sign of an up-beat was visible. The very rhythm of the *terza rima*, interweaving, to and fro, suggested the eternal ebb and flow of the strong tides at Lerici, ever aspiring and falling back, to the future, to the past, pausing at neither. His own mastery of the form, after years of trying, now allowed him to control it like an ocean; having acquired Dante's music, he too might be able to progress from his Inferno to his Paradise. As he broke off from the *Triumph* a boat was edging its way on to the folded page, his perennial hope of rescue and transfiguration.

What was life? Where was he going? He had asked the same question in *Adonais*, his elegy for Keats, and had answered it in different ways. The dead Keats, who was also himself, would never wake: he would decay, like all material things. On the other hand,

> Nought we know, dies. Shall that alone which knows
> Be as a sword consumed before the sheath
> By sightless lightning?
>
> (177–9)

Implicitly, the answer was no. The Poet would become 'one with Nature' both physically and spiritually, 'a portion of the loveliness | Which once he made more lovely' and of the unknown Power beyond it (370, 379–81). Though the body would vanish, his spirit would move, touch, and illuminate, even press to passion and reaction, as Shelley's would. The unacknowledged Poet, the writer of unsellable books and unnoticed pleas for reform, would become part of 'the one Spirit's plastic stress' that would mould and change the world. He himself would become the wind, the lightning, and the song and, after death, know something of 'Fame's serene abode' (45) among the actor and spectator stars.

One particular metaphor haunted him in his last year. It involved a strange plant, seeded deep in the earth and there creeping, growing, and mutating, like the snake he increasingly joked he was, from the soil to the grass to the water. Frost should have killed it ('The Exotic [...] droops in this frost'[14]), but it survived somehow, nourished by starlight and tears. In both 'The Zucca' and *Fragments of an Unfinished Drama* the snake-plant appeared; both stories broke off ambiguously, the journey unfinished. But in the *Drama* the plant rested, 'some light cloud' on the surface of a garden pool, mirroring all the hues and forms around it, like some chameleon poet; like himself.

> And thus it lay in the Elysian calm
> Of its own beauty, floating on the line
> Which, like a film in purest space, divided
> The heaven beneath the water from the heaven
> Above the clouds [...]
>
> (228–32; H 487–8)

These plants seemed to have cast themselves to earth, with the plant of the *Drama* 'panting forth light among the leaves and flowers | As if it lived, and was outworn with speed; | Or that it loved' (131–3). A similar journey was described, too, among his most chaotic

---

[14] 'The Exotic' being himself. *Letters: PBS* II, 367.

drafts for *Adonais* and *Hellas*: another story of a star or a monad, pure love and liberty, plunging from heaven to beat somehow in the dark, deep earth, 'unextinct in that cold source [...] a ray of the eternal' (*BSM* XVI, 242–3). And jotted in pencil in one 1822 notebook, among scattered, familiar fragments of despair ('[Vision of a fatal year | Tempt me not to hope or fear]'), were repeated attempts to pin down one star's history.

> There was a star [in] when Heaven was young
> That [from the]
>   twin with Hesper sprung—
> The music that without a lyre
> [Wandered oer the sea]
>   [...]
>
> By the music of heaven
>   A star out of
>
>   [...]
>
> [By]   [night]
>   [came out of the deep]
> [A star from [?Shelley's bower]]
> [Heaven[s] music enkind]
> [Soothes [to] its sleep of sounds & light]
> [By Heavens l[o]ve]
> [And love with its ascendant]
> [the world]

(*MYR* VII, 12–13, 31, 35)

In *Hellas* he observed more immortal monads or beings descending to the bubble-world, briefly clothing themselves in matter and reascending, 'according to the degree of perfection which every distinct intelligence may have attained':

> Bright or dim are they as the robes they last
> On Death's bare ribs had cast.

(209–10)

He did not mean to dogmatize, he said. His rational self remained sceptical, insisting to Trelawny that he could not believe in immortality without good evidence (*Records*, I, 92), and concluding in the second note to *Hellas* that, 'in our present state' (a concept that now seemed to nag at him), a solution to the puzzle of life after death, or before it, could never be found. Yet there remained that imagery of the star falling and rising, drawn by eternal music or by love. There remained that 'inextinguishable thirst'.

He knew for certain that love, or rather the lack of what he loved (invoking that truth that he had long ago retrieved from Plato's *Symposium*), was still the motivation of his life. But this was not the lustful earth-love of *The Triumph of Life*, nor the water-love of music and magnetism he was trying to share with Jane Williams. Instead, he desired 'more in this world than any understand'. As he explained in 'The Zucca',

> I loved, I know not what—but this low sphere
> And all that it contains, contains not thee,
> Thou whom seen no where, I feel every where [...]

(20–2; *H* 665)

Some representative of that unseen power, a phantom that glimmered like 'the ghost of a forgotten form of sleep', moved beside Shelley-Rousseau in *The Triumph of Life*, 'forever sought, forever lost' (428, 431). In draft this was his herald and guide, 'a light from Heaven'.[15] This was the morning star, almost extinguished by the false, lurid sun of earthly life; and it was also his inner poet's light that had shone through *Adonais* from the opening epigram, 'Thou wert the morning star among the living'. This ghost, too, was himself.

In *Adonais* Shelley's own phantom, crowned with dying pansies and with his thyrsus in his hand, came last in the line of mourners, a stranger even to his own Muse, a 'frail form' that was clearly on the verge of leaving life. But this form was also 'a Power | Girt round with weakness', 'A Love in desolation masked', a billow already breaking into the infinite, resounding sea (289–303). He was a dream dissolving, but into the shocking, godlike essence of himself: 'A portion of the Eternal', infinite strength and infinite Love.

At the end of *Adonais* this radiance at last shone on him, unmisted and unmediated.

> The Light whose smile kindles the Universe,
> That Beauty in which all things work and move,
> That Benediction which the eclipsing Curse
> Of birth can quench not, that sustaining Love
> Which through the web of being blindly wove
> By man and beast and earth and air and sea,
> Burns bright or dim, as each are mirrors of
> The fire for which all thirst; now beams on me,
> Consuming the last clouds of cold mortality.

(478–85)

He had anticipated this. The experience of it, known as he wrote it, lay across the rest of his life. His scepticism never quite disavowed it, and his spells of despair never buried it. He would die 'the death which lovers love',[16] living in the fire he sought.

Beneath his physical and mental strugglings lay 'the god of my own heart', quietly acknowledged in a late letter for the first time (*Letters: PBS* II, 394). He had also been reading Plato constantly, finding there 'all that could be said' on the immortality of the soul.[17] Behind his temporal, trapped agitation was a curious calm.

The last days of June 1822 brought glassy, unmoving heat. In that stillness it was almost impossible to sail, but he had promised to meet Hunt in Livorno and discuss their plans. As the weather broke on 8 July, whipping into action the oily, languid sea, he was sailing home.

In the ecstasy of the present moment, the scream of wind, sky, and water, he could just cram Keats's *Lamia* volume into his pocket, folded back on itself where he would not

---

[15] Reiman, *The Triumph of Life*, 195.   [16] 'The Boat on the Serchio', 108–9 (*H* 657).
[17] *On the Moral Teaching of Christ BSM* XXI, ed. E. B. Murray.

lose the place. He had time for nothing else. Books, clothes, flesh, face, dissolved into silt and the sea. And what would burn of him burned.

He was borne 'darkly, fearfully, afar'. And he was already there.

SELECT BIBLIOGRAPHY

Jones, Frederick L. Ed. *Maria Gisborne and Edward E. Williams, Shelley's Friends: Their Journals and Letters*. Norman, OK: University of Oklahoma Press, 1951.
Morpurgo, J. E. *The Last Days of Shelley and Byron*. London: Folio Society, 1952.
Reiman, Donald H. *Shelley's 'Triumph of Life': A Critical Study*. New York: Octagon, 1979.

CHAPTER 4

....

SHELLEY AND WOMEN

....

NORA CROOK

WHY not 'Shelley and Men'? Why not, indeed? Shelley's relationships with men were no less important than those with women; several biographers and critics have treated them, as, in effect, much more so.[1] The memoirs left by Shelley's friends Thomas Medwin, Thomas Jefferson Hogg, Thomas Love Peacock, and Edward John Trelawny testify to the indelible impression that he made on them when young, and their association with him has pleaded for oblivion against their names. At one extreme this can manifest itself as total devotion (confessions that Shelley was a personal beau-ideal of all that a man should be); at the other, as a compulsion to record the often risible eccentricities of a dominant personality (Shelley licking turpentine off pine trees, or suddenly declaring his intention of becoming a clergyman, or walking naked into mixed company). But they also demonstrate, taken with Shelley's correspondence, his deep attachment to his male friends, his need for fraternity, for their companionship and stimulus, his reproaches when he felt neglected by them, and the importance of their shared activities (translating Greek, reading and criticizing each other's writings, raising an altar to Pan, vigorous walking, sailing). His youthful conversion to the tenets of William Godwin's *Political Justice* and subsequent 'adoption' of Godwin as surrogate parent, guide, philosopher, and friend was to have the profoundest consequences on his thought and actions. His bitter quarrel with his father was a defining event of his life, intimately bound up with his lifelong fight against the patriarchal authority of Church and State, and one source of the evil tyrant-figures that appear in his work. After he eloped with Godwin's daughter Mary, his adoptive filial relationship was to prove as fraught as that with his

---

The citations match the text and lineation of *H, Longman, Norton*, and *CPPBS*, unless otherwise stated; in a few cases composition dates have been corrected.

[1] The tradition began with Edward Trelawny, who claimed, using Thomas Medwin as authority, that 'women cannot write men's lives and characters—they don't know them: much less his—he was so different from ordinary men' (*Records of Shelley, Byron, and the Author* (London: Pickering, 1878), II, 21). It continued with H. J. Massingham's *The Friend of Shelley: A Memoir of Edward J. Trelawny* (London: Cobden-Sanderson. 1930).

blood-parent. His wary friendship-cum-rivalry with Byron, dating from the summer in 1816 that he and his entourage (Mary Godwin, Claire Clairmont) spent in Geneva in Byron's company, is one of the great poetic pairings, second in importance in the history of British Romanticism only to that of Wordsworth and Coleridge.[2] The radical journalist and poet Leigh Hunt, with whom he became intimate in the same year, became the first to hail him publicly as a rising star in a galaxy of new poetic talent, and the first to publish his lyrics in a periodical; Hunt was a vigorous defender of Shelley's poetry and character and, with Mary Shelley, chief among those who ensured that Shelley was not forgotten after his death. The relationship was symbiotic: Shelley needed a public platform and supportive circle while Hunt needed money, but the friendship of the two was none the less sincere. It was through Hunt that Shelley met Keats, without which there would have been no *Adonais*. Moreover, Shelley in his person and in his writing defined one of the forms of nineteenth-century masculinity, a paradoxical one, in which ill health, a high-pitched voice, and boyish face, the conventional markers of feminization, are counteracted by 'masculine' physical stamina, mental energy, and moral force.

Nevertheless, despite the many temptations to spread its net wider, this chapter sticks to the traditional topic of Shelley and Women. Although the subject merges into the wider discourse on Romanticism and gender, or Shelley and sexuality/androgyny, historically speaking the category 'Women' has been as inseparable from 'Shelley' (and as problematic) as 'Politics' or 'Irreligion' or 'Nature' in a way that is not similarly true of Shelley and 'Men'. He casts women as agents in his works to a greater degree than any of his male contemporaries. His most important literary collaboration was with a woman. His works testify to the influence of remarkable women. And whether he is one of the most pro-feminist of male writers or the subtlest of self-deceiving male dominators is a debate that emerged early and continues to be perpetually reconfigured. During his lifetime, and for some time afterwards, this debate hinged on whether his views on the 'relationship between the sexes' was theoretical only, or had been acted out, for good or ill.

SHELLEY, WOMEN, AND SCANDAL

Hogg, writing reminiscently in 1858, recalled Shelley as 'most conspicuously great in that particular excellence, which [...] has been invariably the characteristic distinction of the greatest of mankind—he was pre-eminently a lady's man. [...] The moment he entered a house, he inspired the most lively interest into every woman in the family'. One of these ladies twittered to Hogg that Shelley was 'so modest, so reserved, so pure, so virtuous [...] what terrible havoc he would make, if he were at all rakish!' Hogg retorted, 'If he were less modest, he would be less attractive, and therefore less dangerous.'[3]

---

[2] The classic study of the Shelley–Byron dialogue is Charles E. Robinson's *Shelley and Byron: The Snake and Eagle Wreathed in Fight* (Baltimore: Johns Hopkins UP, 1976).

[3] Thomas Jefferson Hogg, *Life of Percy Bysshe Shelley*, 2 vols. (London: Moxon, 1858), I, p. xxiii, II, 308–9.

Hogg refers particularly to 1813 (the year in which Shelley had *Queen Mab* printed for private circulation), a good part of which he spent in London with his first wife Harriet. Within twelve months he had left Harriet, and had eloped with Mary Godwin to the Continent, taking also her stepsister Jane (Claire) Clairmont. On his return, rumours began to circulate that William Godwin had sold the young women to Shelley, who was living incestuously with both; these spread after their going abroad again in July 1816 and associating with Byron in Switzerland,[4] and still further in early 1817, when Shelley unsuccessfully tried to obtain custody in the Court of Chancery of his children by Harriet after her suicide. *Queen Mab* had announced Shelley's credentials as torch-bearer of the Godwinian antimatrimonialism and Wollstonecraftian feminism of the 1790s. Although reaching only a small readership before 1821, this poem crucially affected the Chancery ruling. Shelley lost his suit (unprecedentedly; the law almost invariably favoured a father's claims) partly on the grounds that he had not recanted the contempt for marriage expressed in *Queen Mab*, and therefore could not be trusted to provide a stable home for his children.

He responded defiantly in 1817/18 with his epic romance *Laon and Cythna* (censored and reissued as *The Revolt of Islam*). For his heroes he chose 'a youth nourished in dreams of liberty' and 'a woman such as he delighted to imagine—full of enthusiasm for the same objects; and they both, with will unvanquished, and the deepest sense of the justice of their cause, met adversity and death', wrote Mary Shelley, circumspectly omitting that the lovers in the uncensored version are siblings.[5] *Laon and Cythna* drew a famous attack from the *Quarterly Review* in 1819. The reviewer, though conceding that it had 'not much ribaldry or voluptuousness' (there is in fact no ribaldry, but many readers have found voluptuousness), savaged the work, ending stingingly: 'If we might withdraw the veil of private life, and tell what we now know about [Shelley], it would be indeed a disgusting picture'; the universal love extolled in the poem masked 'cold selfishness' and 'unmanly cruelty'.[6] After the pirate republication of *Queen Mab* in 1821 the fiercest *ad hominem* attack of all appeared in the *Literary Gazette*:

> A disciple following his tenets, would not hesitate to debauch, or, after debauching, to abandon any woman [...] to rob a confiding father of his daughters, and incestuously to live with all the branches of a family whose morals were ruined by the damned sophistry of the seducer; to such it would be sport to tell a deserted wife to obtain with her pretty face support by prostitution; and, when the unhappy maniac sought refuge in self-destruction, to laugh at the fool while in the arms of associate strumpets.[7]

Hogg's observation about Shelley being a 'lady's man', potentially dangerous because modest, undermines even as it seemingly endorses the image of Shelley, cultivated by Mary Shelley and by Leigh Hunt, as a man 'of a more spiritual nature than ordinary, partaking of the errors and perturbations of his species, but seeing and working through

---

[4] *Byron's Letters and Journals*, ed. Leslie Marchand, 12 vols. (London: John Murray, 1973–82), VI, 76.
[5] Mary Shelley, *Poetical Works of Percy Bysshe Shelley*, 4 vols. (London: Moxon, 1839), I, 376.
[6] [John Taylor Coleridge], 'Review of *Laon and Cythna*', *Quarterly Review* 21 (April 1819), 462, 471.
[7] [William Jerdan], 'Review of *Queen Mab*', *Literary Gazette and Journal of Belles Lettres* 226 (19 May 1821), 305–8.

them with a seraphical purpose of good'.[8] As Hogg would have known in 1858, the very success of this Shelley, and the stream of Shelley editions issuing from Moxon's publishing house from 1839 onwards, provoked a reaction of anxiety, even hysteria; women were warned that Shelley was an angel with horns. As with Rousseau in the generation of the 1790s, the charge against Shelley was that his poetry dressed up depravity as refined and exalted sentiment; he corrupted the intellect and the heart. A source of alarm was Shelley's being *like* a woman; the *locus classicus* is Charles Kingsley's comparing the increase of Shelley-reading in Britain in the 1850s to another growing female addiction, the secret sipping of eau-de-cologne:

> Shelley's nature is utterly womanish. Not merely his weak points, but his strong ones, are those of a woman. Tender and pitiful as a woman—and yet, when angry, shrieking, railing, hysterical as a woman. The physical distaste for meat and fermented liquors, coupled with the hankering after physical horrors, are especially feminine. The nature of a woman looks out of that wild, beautiful, girlish face.[9]

'And pants in that maternal bosom', Kingsley might have added, had he known the story of how Shelley in 1813, despairing lest the wet-nurse's soul should enter his baby daughter Ianthe, attempted vainly to persuade Harriet to breast-feed the child, and, failing, tried to suckle Ianthe himself.[10] For trashy Victorian novelists indicating danger lurking for maid or matron, Shelley's very name was a sweet, insidious whisper. In *Greatheart* (1866) Dr Bradbrain has but to croon 'There was a little lawny islet' to Mrs Tolpedden as he weaves a violet-chain for her neck, and the reader divines his serpentine intentions, even without the author's nudge: 'Dangerous dalliance with evil! Sporting on the brink of a volcano!'[11] (Dr Bradbrain duly has his comeuppance, and drowns.)

Biographies of the 1880s, John Cordy Jeaffreson's *The Real Shelley* (1885) and Edward Dowden's *Life* (1886), exposed the omissions in the portraits of Shelley by Hunt, Mary Shelley, Medwin, Hogg, and particularly Lady Shelley's *Shelley Memorials* (1859). The hostile Jeaffreson told a story that subsequent biographers have passed over, but which he thought justified the *Literary Gazette*'s charge (which otherwise looks like a total fabrication) that Shelley had urged Harriet to support herself by prostitution. According to Jeaffreson, Harriet told William Jerdan (editor of the *Literary Gazette* in 1821 and inferred author of the review) that in July 1814, when Shelley announced that he was leaving her:

> she said that on hearing her doom, she exclaimed imploringly, 'Good God, Percy! what am I to do?' In answer to this pathetic question Shelley, extending his right hand to her in vehement gesticulation [...] replied in the highest and most discordant

---

⁸ P. B. Shelley, *The Masque of Anarchy*, introd. Leigh Hunt (London: Moxon, 1832), p. xxx.

⁹ Charles Kingsley, 'Thoughts on Shelley and Byron', *Fraser's Magazine* 48 (November 1853), 572.

¹⁰ *Life and Letters of Stopford Brooke*, ed. L. P. Jack (New York: Scribner, 1917), 506–7. The story has a respectable source in Thomas Love Peacock.

¹¹ Walter Thornbury, *Greatheart*, 3 vols. (London: Hurst and Blackett, 1866), III, 60–1.

pitch of his voice, 'Do? Do?—Do what other women do. They know what to do. Do as they do.'[12]

As Jeaffreson later stated that he did not begin to research Shelley's life until 1883, i.e. after Jerdan's death, he would seem to have heard the story at second hand, and some garbling has almost certainly occurred: there is no record of Harriet Shelley meeting Jerdan.[13] Yet an anecdote deriving ultimately from her own words is likely to have informed Jerdan's virulence, even though Jerdan and Jeaffreson no doubt put the worst possible construction on Shelley's alleged utterances. We find in a letter written around the time of the separation, rediscovered in 1930, that Shelley hoped Harriet *would* find someone else, 'a lover as passionate and faithful, as I shall ever be a friend affectionate & sincere!' (*Letters: PBS* I, 390). While this is very far from enjoining her to embark on a harlot's progress, Harriet was soon to spike Shelley's hopes that she would go quietly, and when cornered he was liable to explode in fury, and say outrageous things. Dowden was in some ways more damaging than Jeaffreson. As authorized biographer, he could not be dismissed as a witness for the prosecution. Everyone remembers Matthew Arnold's calling Shelley an 'ineffectual angel' in his review of Dowden; fewer recall his lament that Dowden's revelations had spoiled Mary Shelley's portrait of Shelley for him forever:[14]

> In one important point [Shelley] was like neither a Pythagorean nor an angel: he was extremely inflammable. [...] God forbid that I should go into the scandals about Shelley's 'Neapolitan charge,' about Shelley and Emilia Viviani, about Shelley and Miss Clairmont, and the rest of it! I will say only that [...] when the passion of love was aroused in Shelley (and it was aroused easily) one could not be sure of him; his friends could not trust him.[15]

Attempts to sanitize Shelley and to excuse his treatment of Harriet faded out during the second half of the twentieth century, as Richard Holmes's 'darker and more earthly, crueller and more capable figure' replaced Victorian excesses of worship and demonizing.[16] If, today, the longest-standing Shelley biographical mystery were to be cleared up, and it were to turn out that the baby whom he falsely registered in Naples in February 1819 as the child of himself and Mary Shelley was, after all, the child of a lady, still possibly alive in 1876, with whom he had 'got into' a 'Scrape',[17] he might emerge a degree more earthly than the Shelley of Holmes's portrait, but the fact would be unlikely to shock anyone much.

---

[12] John Cordy Jeaffreson, *The Real Shelley*, 2 vols. (London: Hurst and Blackett, 1885), II, 219.

[13] Jeaffreson, *A Book of Recollections*, 2 vols. (London: Hurst and Blackett, 1894), II, 150–4; Jerdan's most likely source was Thomas Hookham (1787–1867), Shelley's publisher, who sided with Harriet, and was later to shock Robert Browning with revelations about Shelley's conduct towards her. For another surmise see R. S. Garnett (ed.), *Letters about Shelley* (London: Hodder and Stoughton, 1917), 142.

[14] Matthew Arnold, 'Shelley', *Essays in Criticism: Second Series* (1888; London: Macmillan, 1913), 206.

[15] Ibid. 243.

[16] Richard Holmes, *Shelley: The Pursuit* (London: Weidenfeld and Nicolson, 1974), p. ix.

[17] See Bieri, 431–48.

SHELLEY, WOMEN'S FRIEND
AND LIBERATOR, AND LATER DEBATES

During the later nineteenth century, and especially among left-wing intellectuals, Shelley's 'womanishness' operated, on the whole, in his favour, in spite of the *Literary Gazette*, Kingsley, Jeaffreson, Dowden, et al. He was allowed 'that attribute of genius, which is said to partake of the feminine as well as the masculine'.[18] Even though 'Shelley himself, we must confess, fell short of the ideal standard of humanity',[19] he was seen as a male poet whose dual nature gave him a particular rapport with the desires of women for sexual liberation and political equality. Shelley, disciple of Mary Wollstonecraft, who had imagined a future in which women and men were free, equal, fearless friends and lovers, was an immensely attractive and genuinely inspirational figure for the British and American women's movement. Leading feminists who might be called Shelleyans included pioneers like Frances Wright, Margaret Fuller, and Harriet Taylor, and their successors Mathilde Blind, Eleanor Marx, Olive Schreiner, and Charlotte Despard. The works mentioned most often in this context are *Queen Mab* and *Laon and Cythna* (which was republished, unexpurgated, in 1873). Shelley's Cythna is a model for the emergent woman public-speaker and the *fin-de-siècle* New Woman—and the debates concerning them.[20] For example, the eloquence of Lyndall, the Wollstonecraftian figure in Schreiner's *Story of An African Farm* (1883; see especially chapter 4, part II), draws on Cythna's words, particularly her famous 'Can man be free if woman be a slave?' (II. xliii). A late-flowering variant on Shelley as brother-lover is Virginia Woolf's *Orlando* (1928), where Shelley is playfully transformed into the spouse of a cross-gendered free spirit. Shel (Marmaduke Bonthrop Shelmerdine Esquire), explorer and muse of the once-male, now female Orlando, knows the entire works of Shelley by heart, is 'as strange and subtle as a woman', comes and goes with the wind, is usually away at Cape Horn (allowing Orlando to write poetry), but arrives by aeroplane when called.[21] If Orlando must have a husband, this updated skylark is surely the least unsatisfactory one conceivable.

In the 1970s, with the application of feminist literary theory to Gothic and Romantic texts the old lines were redrawn. Nathaniel Brown, following Kenneth Neill Cameron, presented Shelley as a proto-feminist with a high sex-drive, a forerunner of the 1970s consciousness-raiser and 'a champion of women'. Shelley 'incorporated a feminist ideal directly contradicting the period's sexist norms' and an 'erotic psychology necessitating

---

[18] Leigh Hunt, *The Autobiography of Leigh Hunt*, 3 vols. (London: Smith, Elder, 1850), II, 103. Hunt is speaking particularly of Shakespeare.

[19] *Letters from Percy Bysshe Shelley to Elizabeth Hitchener*, ed. Bertram Dobell (London: Bertram Dobell, 1908), p. xxii.

[20] Victor Luftig, *Seeing Together: Friendship between the Sexes in English Writing from Mill to Woolf* (Stanford, CA: Stanford UP, 1993), 93–119.

[21] Virginia Woolf, *Orlando, a Biography*, Oxford World's Classics (Oxford: Oxford UP, 1998), 239–52, 312–13.

equality between the sexes', dissolving the ideology of separate spheres.[22] Brown's thesis was contested, by, notably, Anne Mellor and Barbara Gelpi, while Teddi Chichester Bonca gave it a nuanced qualification. Gelpi emphatically denied that Shelley was a feminist; rather, she argued, he reinscribes traditional sex roles. Bonca maintained that it would be 'more accurate to call Shelley a "detractor of men"' than a 'champion of women'; his poetry evinces his yearning to escape from masculinity, and his idealized women are mirrors of the self that he wanted to be.[23] An uncollected letter to Felicia Browne (later Hemans) signed with the feminized sobriquet 'your affectionate Philippe Sidney', and discovered only in 1991, seems corroborative.[24]

Gelpi particularly noted Shelley's characteristic projecting of personal relationships as mythic archetypes, images of the universal, or, to adapt Mary Shelley's phrase, his idealizing of the real. We now turn to some of these. They are compartments with porous boundaries. Shelley's female familial archetypes are erotic and militant, his female preceptors are maternal soul sisters. These persons are never, of course, purely familial in origin.

SHELLEYAN TYPES: MOTHERS, NURSES, DIOTIMAS

In 1950 Cameron remarked on the 'extraordinary' neglect of Shelley's mother by biographers, and suggested that, as a strong-minded and talented woman of warm affections (qualities attested to by memoirists), she might have 'attempted to execute her own unfulfilled ambitions through her son'.[25] In Shelley's close childhood relationship to his mother, and the (conjectured) trauma of separation when sent to boarding school at the age of 10, Cameron located a major source of not only the numerous redemptive female figures in Shelley's poetry but also of the inconstant divinities and semi-divinities who irradiate the world, or reveal the possibilities of transforming it, and then withdraw, such as Intellectual Beauty and the Witch of Atlas. Notable psychobiographical critical readings that have developed or reinterpreted Cameron's perception include those of Christine Gallant, Gelpi, and Bonca, while James Bieri has discovered and assembled new material concerning Shelley's family and its gender dynamics.[26] Gallant, using a (mainly) Kleinian approach,

---

[22] Nathaniel Brown, *Sexuality and Feminism in Shelley* (Cambridge, MA: Harvard UP, 1979), 3, 198.

[23] Anne K. Mellor, Review of Brown, *Sexuality and Feminism*, *Criticism* 22 (1980), 178–81 and, *passim*, *Mary Shelley: Her Life, her Fiction, her Monsters* (New York: Routledge, 1988); Barbara Charlesworth Gelpi, *Shelley's Goddess: Maternity, Language, Subjectivity* (Oxford: Oxford UP, 1992), p. viii; Teddi Chichester Bonca, *Shelley and the Mirrors of Love: Narcissism, Sacrifice, and Sorority* (New York: Stonybrook University of New York Press, 1999), 227 (n. 48). For a recent, severe view of Shelley, see Janet Todd, *Death and the Maidens: Fanny Wollstonecraft and the Shelley Circle* (London: Profile, 2007).

[24] Letter of ?13 or ?19 March 1811, Bodleian MS. Don.c.180, fos. 13–16; Bruce C. Barker-Benfield, 'Hogg–Shelley Papers of 1810–1812', *Bodleian Library Record* 14.1 (1991), 14–29.

[25] Kenneth Neill Cameron, *The Young Shelley: Genesis of a Radical* (London: Victor Gollancz, 1950), 4.

[26] See Bieri, ch. 2.

read the poetry as repeating a cycle of 'love, then hate, then guilt, then reparation',[27] predicated upon conflicted feelings towards the mother. Gelpi, linking psychoanalytic theory, myths of primal matriarchy, and anthropology, focused on the themes and imagery of maternity, suckling, thirst, and the breast that run throughout Shelley's work. Her analysis of the scanty data on Shelley's mother produced a persuasive picture of a household where she was a Queen Bee, resentful of her husband, with an ally in her son, until Shelley's sudden accusation (1811) that she had taken the music master, his friend, as her lover.[28]

A variant of the mother-figure is the Diotima figure, so called after Socrates' instructress in *The Symposium*, who teaches him the lore of divine love; in Shelley's actual life, she is part of the make-up of the amiable 'lady of 45, very unprejudiced and philosophical' (*Letters: PBS* II, 180), who frequently acted as his foster-mother and mentor. While such friendships were among Shelley's more serene ones, they, too, were liable to sudden rupture. Harriet de Boinville, or 'Maimuna', the cultivated female with the young face and grey hair, who helped his recovery after his breakdown of late 1813, introducing him to the novels of Wieland and the mysteries of making panada (a pabulum for invalids), broke with him when his attentions to Cornelia, her daughter, threatened the latter's marriage. Shelley's friendships in Italy with Maria (Reveley) Gisborne and with Margaret, Lady Mount Cashell ('Mrs Mason'), of Pisa endured, though there was an ugly incident in late 1820 when he suspected the Gisbornes of betrayal. Both had connections with his surrogate parents: the widowed William Godwin had wished to marry the widowed Maria Reveley, and 'Mrs Mason' had been Wollstonecraft's pupil. Shelley's elegant and delightful *Letter to Maria Gisborne* (1820), his testament of friendship, was written when he was being blackmailed by a man-servant threatening to spread rumours concerning the Naples baby affair. There is a subtext of despair kept at bay, and repeated imagery of longed-for green retreats—the silkworm's cocoon amidst the mulberry leaves, grape-vine bowers. Shelley turns to memories of hope—the recent liberal revolution in Spain, the summer of 1819 when he had learned Spanish with this 'wisest lady' and discovered the plays of Calderón with her:

> —thou wert then to me
> As is a nurse—when inarticulately
> A child would talk as its grown parents do.
>
> (184–6)

By the end of the poem there appears a sudden reference to Shelley's own family amidst plans for a winter reunion with Maria Gisborne (which includes comfort food of tea, toast, sweet desserts, and philosophy):

> We will have books, Spanish, Italian, Greek;
> And ask one week to make another week
> As like his father as I'm unlike mine,
> Which is not his fault, as you may divine.
>
> (298–301)

---

[27] Christine Gallant, *Shelley's Ambivalence* (New York: St Martin's Press, 1989), 14.
[28] *Shelley's Goddess*, 105–30.

Mary Shelley omitted the last line from her editions. Ostensibly Shelley is boastfully confessing that he is a disobedient son; but he is also dropping a hint (for Maria Gisborne to 'divine') that the 'fault' might be his *mother's*—the old joke that only the woman knows for sure that she is the biological parent; he may be only nominally his father's son, hence his different nature.

A complex Diotima figure appears in *Rosalind and Helen* (1819), which Shelley finished shortly after translating *The Symposium*. Lionel's mother, 'bright and wise' with 'silver locks and quick brown eyes' (2111–12) has invented a religion and raised a shrine to Fidelity, for which the enfeebled reformer Lionel has carved a veiled, androgynous, suffering, and smiling marble image. As Bonca, in a witty and perceptive examination, says of this 'strange set-piece': '[I]n one of his more outrageous moves, Shelley has Lionel's mother in effect worshipping the image of her martyred son.'[29] Lionel dies in his mother's temple in the arms of his love, Helen, having been over-excited by her sweeping a wild air on his mother's harp. Helen goes mad; Lionel's mother nurses her and dies. The recovered Helen gives birth to Lionel's child (engendered, we are to infer, as he breathes his last). Helen finds happiness with her friend Rosalind, and their children marry. This work is at once Shelley's most explicit treatment of matriarchy and sorority, and the one where the tangle of substitutions, doublings, and disguises is densest. Why, to ask two questions of many that might be asked, is the wise mother's worship of Fidelity in some way implicated in the death of her son, and is her death some kind of expiation?

SISTERS

The prevalence of the 'soul sister' and 'sister spouse' figures in Shelley is ascribed by Brown and others not only to a Romantic challenging of established morality, but also to Shelley's exceptional closeness to his eldest sister, Elizabeth. His visionary women are often figured as sisters; he wishes that he and 'Emily' in *Epipsychidion* (1821) were 'twins of the same mother!' (45). But, as Brown pointed out, the salient point is not any 'putative desire for incestuous connection, conscious or repressed'; incest in *Laon and Cythna* is rather the poem's 'symbolic core, the metaphor of total sexual equality [...] the paradigm of sympathetic communion between the sexes.'[30]

As numerous commentators have noticed, Shelley's family position—the eldest brother with four younger sisters—gave a permanent direction to his character and his poetry. Holmes writes of the 'society of sisters' that made up his Edenic childhood, and his 'disinclination to live entirely in the company of one woman for more than a few hours at a time' (or what Mellor calls his 'self-serving "harem psychology"').[31] This pattern shows itself in both his marriages, where the trio of himself, Harriet Shelley, and

[29] Bonca, *Shelley and the Mirrors*, 102.   [30] Brown, *Sexuality and Feminism*, 215, 216.
[31] Holmes, *Shelley*, 12, 79; Mellor, *Mary Shelley*, 73.

Elizabeth Hitchener, the soul sister schoolmistress who became a 'Brown Demon' and 'Hermaphroditical beast' when they fell out in late 1812 (*Letters: PBS* I, 150, 336), was later replicated in the Mary Shelley and Claire Clairmont ménage (which Mary's half-sister Fanny might have joined, but for her suicide). Shelley offered Hitchener a role upon announcing his marriage in October 1811: '[A]ssist me to mould a really noble soul into all that can make it[s] nobleness useful and lovely' (*Letters: PBS* I, 163)—in short, she was to continue as soul sister, but, additionally, become Harriet's preceptor. With this sentence Shelley summed up a relational situation that was to shape the 'plot' of *Queen Mab*.

Queen Mab's opening is a singular one. Henry regards his sleeping beloved, Ianthe. Sleep reminds him of Death, and immediately he imagines her 'peerless form' putrefying into a state of 'loathsomeness and ruin' (I. 12, 20). Queen Mab in her enchanted car arrives to arrest this disturbing train of thought; she rescues Ianthe's soul from decay by instructing her in Shelley's revolutionary creed, including the transformed relations between men and women in the future renovated world, eventually restoring her soul to the body, which Henry has been brooding over. In this triangle, Ianthe is an idealization of Harriet and Henry of Shelley, while Elizabeth Hitchener is apotheosized as the Fairy Queen, moulding Ianthe into a noble soul. For the real Hitchener, from Fairy Queen to Brown Demon was but a single step. Nevertheless, Shelley found a way of transfiguring the fallen Hitchener also: in his shortened version of *Queen Mab*, the *Dæmon of the World* (1816), the hermaphroditical Demon (fiend) became an androgynous Dæmon (intermediary between the numinous and the earthly).

The circle of sisters clustering around the elder brother has its clearest idealization in *Prometheus Unbound*, where Prometheus, reunited with his consort Asia, acquires two 'sister nymphs', Panthea and Ione, and says to them, 'Henceforth we will not part' (III. iii. 8–10, 27). In *Epipsychidion*, Emily is the Sun, but the Poet's universe is not complete unless the Moon (Mary Shelley) and the 'Comet beautiful and fierce' (Claire Clairmont) are also permitted their orbits (345–84). Bonca, however, acutely remarks on the pathos of Shelley's characterization of sorority as unselfish, pure devotion, 'perfect intimacy', marked by the absence of all reserve.[32] 'Tell me then if you want cash,' he writes to Hogg in April 1811, 'I have nearly drained you, & all delicacy, like sisters stripping before each other is out of the question—' (*Letters: PBS* I, 75). The bevy of sisters was only a stage in Shelley's larger plan for a community of friends, male and female, bound together by ties of mutual consentaneous love.

EARLY LOVES

The figure of the early love or first love is firmly identified with Harriet Grove, Shelley's cousin, who broke her engagement with him in early 1811 because of his rejection of Christianity. But there were others. Among the last glimpses we have of Shelley is one

---

[32] Bonca, *Shelley and the Mirrors*, 96–7.

from Captain Gronow, an Eton school friend, who saw him a few weeks before his death, 'making a true poet's meal of bread and fruit':

> He at once recognized me, jumped up, and appearing greatly delighted, exclaimed, 'Here you see me at my old Eton habits [...] I only wish I had some of the excellent brown bread and butter we used to get at Spiers's: but I was never very fastidious in my diet.' Then he continued, in a wild and eccentric manner: 'Gronow, do you remember the beautiful Martha, the Hebe of Spiers's? She was the loveliest girl I ever saw, and I loved her to distraction.'[33]

Martha may have been one of three sisters who ran Spiers, an Eton shop selling hot rolls and 'sock' (eatables).[34] The *amour fou* that is inseparable from brown bread is the passion of Werter for Charlotte, 'most lovely of women', whom Werter first sees with a 'brown loaf... cutting slices of bread and butter' and feeding the little ones. The path to his suicide has begun.[35] The Werteresque passion was always part of Shelley's erotic landscape: 'she abhors me as a Deist,' he wrote to Hogg in January 1811 of Harriet Grove's disaffection; 'I cannot avoid feeling every instant as if my soul were bursting, but I *will* feel no more. [...] I slept with a loaded pistol & some poison last night but did not die' (*Letters: PBS* I, 36). Ten years later, 'Emily' holds out the promise of lost early love restored: 'Youth's vision thus made perfect' (42). Shelley's view of this 'vision' often involves ambivalence. The traveller in 'The Two Spirits' (1818), in an interval of sleep as he traverses the world's wilderness, envisions the passing shape of his 'early love' with 'her wild and glittering hair' (45–6). Yet the possibility that the vision is an illusion that has arisen from the morass, an *ignis fatuus* of the mind, is not totally dispelled. The imprisoned Tasso sees the silver shape of Leonora, but knows it is only an exhalation from his dungeon damps ('Song for "Tasso"', 1818). The 'Shape all light' in *The Triumph of Life* (1822) awakens Rousseau to sexual passion by offering him her cup of 'bright Nepenthe' (359, 400) and then deserts him. The early love sustains and betrays. Holmes commented on the 'appalling implication'[36] of the climax of Shelley's translation, *Scenes from the Faust of Goethe* (1822). Seeing the simulacrum of Margaret, a 'lifeless idol', Faust cries, 'That is the breast that Margaret yielded to me— | Those are the lovely limbs which I enjoyed!' Mephistopheles answers, 'It is all magic, poor deluded fool! | She looks to everyone like his first love' (II. 386, 392–5). 'First love' is Shelley's twist; Goethe has simply 'sein Liebchen'—'his darling'.

---

[33] Rees Howell Gronow, *The Reminiscences of Captain Gronow* (London: Smith, Elder, 1862), 214–15.

[34] C. Allix Wilkinson, *Reminiscences of Eton (Keate's Time)* (London: Hurst and Blackett, 1888), 25.

[35] [Goethe], *The Sorrows of Werter*, trans. Daniel Malthus (London: J. Dodsley, 1789; facsimile repr. Oxford: Woodstock, 1991), 27, 34, 32.

[36] Holmes, *Shelley*, 694.

THE PASSIONATE WOMAN

For many of Shelley's female idealisms, familial relationships are less relevant than historical and literary archetypes and the tradition of personifying abstractions as female. His women in a state of passionate abandon, or desire, are most often Oriental (rather than Spanish, Italian, or even Greek), following the conventional Western association of the East with the female and the emotional. Examples include the speakers of the dramatic lyrics 'From the Arabic' (1821) and 'The Indian Serenade' (1821–2), the Enchantress and the deserted Lady, both in his 'Unfinished Drama' (1822). In *Alastor* (1816) the Poet is visited in Cashmire by a veiled dream-maiden who speaks to him of 'divine liberty' (159), and whose passion arouses him to frenzy (140–91). The Lady of the Garden in 'The Sensitive Plant' (1820), whose breast heaves with passion at the coming and going of the wind, has an Indian basket and tends Indian plants. Though these women feel unsatisfied desire and bring desolation when they depart, they are associated above all with pleasure, enjoyed or anticipated, and often, too, with song.

Such pleasure contrasts with a persistent association in Shelley's earlier writings of auto-eroticism with violence. The villainess of *Zastrozzi* (1810) repeatedly stabs her rival; the rejected lover of Wolfstein in *St. Irvyne* (1811) snatches his dagger, and 'plunged it into her bosom. Weltering in purple gore, she fell' and 'expired in torments, which her fine, her expressive features declared that she gloried in'.[37] Eroticized violence was shortly to become a site within which Shelley explored unresolved contradictions as to how to effect revolutionary change. In his second collection of poetry, *Posthumous Fragments of Margaret Nicholson* (1810), woman's violence is channelled into political action. Shelley assumes two roles: the madwoman who had attempted to assassinate George III with a kitchen knife, and her 'nephew', editor of his deceased aunt's poetry. Most relevant here is 'Fragment. Supposed to be an Epithalamium of Francis Ravaillac and Charlotte Cordé'. Two more stabbers, one the assassin of a king (Henry IV), the other of a revolutionary tyrant (Marat), exult in their noble work; both have been executed, and, as Liberty's martyrs, their spirits enjoy the reward of a rapturous sexual union.

FROM CHARLOTTE CORDAY TO ANTIGONE; THE TRANSFIGURED WOMAN

With Shelley's mature poetry the Charlotte Corday figure modulates into the woman who actively resists patriarchal state authority to the death. A key work in this transition is *Laon and Cythna*. Cythna rides into battle on a 'black Tartarian' horse, beneath whose

---

[37] *Zastrozzi: a Romance; St. Irvyne, or, The Rosicrucian: a romance*, ed. Stephen C. Behrendt (Peterborough, Ont.: Broadview, 2002), 142, 206.

hoofs 'the living bleed', waving a sword, but to rescue Laon, not to kill (2497–514). In *Prometheus Unbound*, Asia is an agent in the overthrow of Jupiter, not personally, but through her questions, which arouse the power (Demogorgon) that overthrows him. In *The Cenci*, Beatrice Cenci, an 'Angel of Parricide' like Corday,[38] hires murderers to kill her father, but only because she faces inescapable and repeated rape by him. For Shelley the tragedy consists in the tension between the teaching of Christ and Socrates (it is better to suffer wrong than to do wrong) and outrage that anyone should be required to suffer such wrong. In a draft passage written for *Hellas* but eventually dropped, the Chorus of Greek captive women accuse the Sultan's favourite slave, the Indian Fatima, of self-deception: only the free, they say, can love. They invoke the Apocryphal figure of the beautiful Jewish patriot who decapitated the enemy leader by pretending that she would become his concubine: 'Judith loved—not her enslaver.'[39] Fatima, whose royal master, during a brief panic, commands her to show her loyalty by drowning herself so as to be united with him in Paradise, replies that such reasoning assigns false limits to love. The Chorus, however, avoid the polarities of slavishly adoring the enemy and killing him as he sleeps. Instead they disturb his sleep with unsettling songs prophetic of end of empire and the liberation of Greece.

Shelley's model for non-violent resistance was Sophocles' Antigone. 'How sublime a picture of a woman!' he wrote to John Gisborne in October 1821. 'Some of us have in a prior existence been in love with an Antigone & that makes us find no full content in any mortal tie' (*Letters: PBS* II, 363). Like Antigone, Shelley's mortal heroines are raised to the level of the sublime: Cythna in glory at sunset on the mountain's edge, her shadow floating on a river of light (4225–51); Asia, in *Prometheus Unbound*, radiating the light of love from a snowy mountain summit (II. v); Emily, the 'image of some bright Eternity' (*Epipsychidion*, 115). This deification of woman is matched by Shelley's feminization of abstractions—Intellectual Beauty, the maniac maid Hope in *The Mask of Anarchy*, and above all, the glorious phantom of Liberty.

WOMAN LOATHSOME, DEAD, RESURRECTED, AND BEYOND

The obverse of such bright idealizations is the sublime of horror, the attraction of repulsion, of which Shelley's 'On the Medusa of Leonardo da Vinci in the Florentine Gallery' (*c.* October 1819) is the supreme representative. The Medusa's head, a female Laocoön, lies on a mountain top (unlike Cythna, who *stands*), snaky locks writhing, gazing at the heavens (in accusation?), its image reflected in its own dying breath, beautiful and horrible in its death agony. Other types that manifest Kingsley's 'hankering after physical horrors'

---

[38] A connection made by Medwin; see *Longman*, 2, 722.
[39] Bodleian MS. Shelley adds. e. 7, pp. 60, 92–5 (*BSM* XVI, 66–7, 98–101).

are hideous witch-forms: the 'hellish shape' who turns to a 'lady fair' (*Rosalind and Helen*, 150–4); the 'foully disarrayed' women of the *Triumph of Life* (165), kin to Eliza Westbrook, Harriet's detested sister, a ghoul, said Shelley, who would expose her breasts, which had eyes instead of nipples.[40] There are deceivers, like the 'One whose voice was venomed melody' in *Epipsychidion* (256), who leaves the poet ruined and prematurely grey; the furies, infernal sisters with hydra tresses and iron wings, ministers of hate and fear; or simply evil women, 'ugliest of all things evil' (*Prometheus Unbound*, I. 326–7, 463; III. iv. 46). Or the loathly lady is a hideously aged mother-figure. In a suppressed second stanza to the canonical 'Tomorrow' (1820), Shelley brings together both Chaucer's 'Wyf of Bath's Tale', and a ribald verse letter of 1811, 'As you will see I wrote to you', in which he compared his mother unfavourably to Ninon de Lenclos, the octogenarian courtesan (*CPPBS* I, 141–2). The vain pursuit of the infinite possibility of 'To morrow' inevitably ends in disappointment, as when a youth 'steals towards the odorous bed' of his love, only to find 'his old brown grandmother'.[41] Sometimes the lovely/loathsome woman is the mortal form of beauty, like the envisaged dead Ianthe, or the Lady of the Garden, decayed into a 'heap | To make men tremble' ('Sensitive Plant', III. 20–1) or Princess Charlotte, 'a putrid corpse, who but a few days since was [...] a woman young, innocent, and beautiful'.[42] Such decay is often averted, as in *Queen Mab*, or evaded, as when Shelley advances the 'modest creed' that the Lady has been sublimed into the eternal Platonic form of delight and love, or substitutes for the corpse of Charlotte that of British Liberty, hoping that

> [...] if some glorious Phantom should appear, and make its throne of broken swords and sceptres and royal crowns trampled in the dust, let us say that the Spirit of Liberty has arisen from its grave and left all that was gross and mortal there, and kneel down and worship it as our Queen. (*Murray: Prose*, 239)

Between such extremes of idealization and loathing we find a sober truth-telling about Shelley's self-conflictedness; this note is increasingly sounded in the last year of Shelley's life, giving a peculiar poignancy to his late poetry. By 1821–2 there seems little that could have been said to him about his relations with women that he did not already—at least subliminally—know, or could not make superb poetry out of. In 'The Zucca' he admits that he has loved 'I know not what', though recognizing it fleetingly in 'the rare smile of woman' (20, 37); in the *Triumph of Life* the 'Shape all light' is 'forever sought, forever lost' (431). The exquisite lyrics to Jane Williams attempt to hold in precarious balance his yearning and her unattainability: she is a healer ('The Magnetic Lady'), a musician who speaks to him of some world 'far from ours' ('To Jane' ['The Keen Stars were Twinkling'], 22); she brings a brief moment of peace as they wander by the pools in the pine-forest of the Cascine ('To Jane. The Recollection'). In 'Lines Written in the Bay of Lerici', among

---

[40] Henry Reveley, 'Notes and Observations' (*SC* X, 1135).

[41] Timothy Webb, 'Naming "I—t": Incest and Outrage in Shelley', in James Hogg (ed.), *Shelley 1792–1992*, Romantic Reassessment 112; Salzburg Studies in English Literature (Lewiston: Edwin Mellen, 1993), 187–9; *BSM* VI, 118–19.

[42] *An Address to the People on the Death of the Princess Charlotte* (*Murray: Prose*, 231).

the very last verses Shelley wrote, she has retired from the scene of the moonlit bay, whereupon 'The demon reassumed his throne' (28).

SHELLEY AND WOMEN AS WRITERS

Shelley's promotion of women as published writers through patronage, encouragement, and collaboration awaits a contextualized reassessment. He had his sister Hellen's poetry printed when she was a child, praising the line 'an old woman in her bony gown'. According to Medwin, some chapters of *Zastrozzi* were by Harriet Grove,[43] and his first published collection, *Original Poetry by Victor and Cazire* (1810), was jointly written with his sister Elizabeth. He was unsuccessful in finding a publisher for Claire Clairmont's novel, but he encouraged her 'Germanizing' and her (never completed) translation of Goethe's *Dichtung und Wahrheit*.[44] His chief collaboration was, of course, with Mary Shelley, most famously with *Frankenstein* (1818). The discovery in the early 1970s of the greater part of most of the *Frankenstein* intermediate draft and some of the fair copy, with corrections and additions in Shelley's hand, prompted James Rieger to suggest that he should be assigned a measure of authorship.[45] This revived speculations, which date back to 1824,[46] that he, not she, was responsible for everything remarkable about *Frankenstein*. On the other hand, Anne Mellor saw him as an appropriative editor, imposing on the work his own Latinate diction and, to a degree, ideas.[47] In two judicious studies of the manuscripts, *The Frankenstein Notebooks* and *The Original Frankenstein*, the latter of which offers two reading texts of the surviving draft MSS. in a form enabling general readers to review the evidence for themselves, Charles E. Robinson finds, with Mellor, that Shelley sometimes improves, at other times pointlessly inflates, Mary Shelley's colloquial diction ('a great deal of wood' becoming 'a great quantity of wood', for instance); he considers that some of Shelley's alterations substantially 'deepen our understanding of the domestic, scientific and political issues'; his conclusion, however, is that while *Frankenstein* is unquestionably a collaboration, Shelley's contribution remains firmly editorial. One might add, too, that many of Shelley's poetic heightenings of the language are to the good; Mary Shelley's 'he was carried away by the waves, and I soon lost sight of him in the darkness & distance' is already a haunting final sentence, but Shelley's reworking 'he was soon borne away by the waves, & lost in the darkness of distance' hones it into memorability (the sentence has become a hexameter).[48]

---

[43] Hogg, *Life*, I, 15; Thomas Medwin, *The Life of Percy Bysshe Shelley*, 2 vols. (London: Newby, 1847), I, 69.

[44] *Letters: PBS* I, 561; II, 267–8, 401, 403; Marion K. Stocking (ed.), *The Clairmont Correspondence*, 2 vols. (Baltimore: Johns Hopkins UP, 1995), I, 179.

[45] James Rieger (ed.), *Frankenstein or, the Modern Prometheus: The 1818 Text* (1974; corr. ed. Chicago: University of Chicago Press, 1982), p. xliv.

[46] *Knight's Quarterly Magazine* 3 (August–November 1824), 195–9.

[47] Mellor, *Mary Shelley*, 57–68, 219–24.

[48] Robinson, *Original Frankenstein*, 24–8 (see Select Bibliography for full details); *MYR* IX, Pt. ii, 772 [*Frankenstein Notebooks* II].

After *Frankenstein*, Shelley continued to encourage Mary Shelley's authorship; he urged a translation of Alfieri's *Mirra* (unfinished, but it bore fruit in her 1819 novella *Matilda*). He supplied lyrics for her mythological dramas *Proserpine* and *Midas* (1820). She was, at points, contributor to his translation of Spinoza's *Tractatus Theologico-Politicus*, complete at his death; its disappearance is one of the great losses from the Shelley canon.[49] Nor was this a one-way process. He protests in the *Witch of Atlas* against her discouragement of his 'visionary rhyme' (8), but without her predilection for the historically based it is unlikely that we would have *The Cenci* or valuable fragments such as 'Mazenghi', 'Ginevra', and *Charles the First*.

An up-to-date inventory of and comprehensive commentary on the books by female writers that Shelley read, and a sifting of those that he has been inferred to have read, has yet to be compiled, though it would not be a daunting task. The reading lists kept by Mary Shelley during 1814–20 contain few titles by women. Byron owned, and put up for sale in 1813, novels of Jane Austen; Shelley appears to have been completely unaware of her. Caroline Lamb's *Glenarvon* is the only recorded woman-authored novel that he read hot from the press during those years. This is partly an effect of the preponderance in the Shelleys' reading of the classics, history, philosophy, poetry, and drama over novels, correspondence, and memoirs (with Mary Shelley and Claire Clairmont only partly redressing the balance). But as no detailed record of Shelley's reading before 1814 or for 1821–2 was kept there are undoubtedly lost items. His letters, and Medwin's and Hogg's memoirs, show that the tally could be enlarged from pre-1814 reading. Medwin testifies to Shelley's immersion in Gothic novels, specifying those of Ann Radcliffe and Charlotte Dacre's *Zofloya* (a marked influence on *Zastrozzi*), while, according to Hogg, he took lodgings in Poland Street in 1811 because the name reminded him of Jane Porter's *Thaddeus of Warsaw* (1803).[50] Sydney Owenson's 'perfect' Luxima, priestess-heroine of *The Missionary* (1811), influenced the conception of Cythna (*Letters: PBS* I, 107, 112, 130). An enthusiastic subscriber to Janetta Phillipps's *Poems* (Oxford, 1811), he may first have encountered her as the author of *Delaval* (1802), a two-volume Minerva Press novel (Jones, editor of Shelley's *Letters*, thought her a 'young genius' but she appears to have been an older woman).[51] Evidence that Shelley read women poets of the 1790s during the pre-1814 years accumulates as echoes of their work are detected; it is now virtually certain that he knew some of the poetry of Charlotte Smith, for instance.[52] Joanna Baillie's drama *Orra* (1812) left its impress on *The Cenci*.[53] He wrote 'On the Medusa of Leonardo Da Vinci' two months after reading Mary Lamb's poems on paintings by Leonardo and on Salome with the Baptist's head (*Letters: PBS* II, 110, 126). Reading

---

[49] *Letters: PBS* II, 39; *Journals: MWS* I, 306, 312–15; *Letters: MWS* I, 135, 262.

[50] Medwin, *Life*, I, 30; Hogg, *Life*, I, 297.

[51] *Letters: PBS* I, 88–9; *Cardiff Corvey: Reading the Romantic Text*, 12 (Summer 2004); <www.cardiff. ac.uk/encap/journals/corvey/articles/engnov4.pdf>.

[52] See, e.g., *CPPBS* I, 246 and *Longman*, 2, 214.

[53] Stephen Hancock, '"Shelley Himself in Petticoats": Joanna Baillie's *Orra* and Non-violent Masculinity as Remorse in *The Cenci*', *Romanticism on the Net* 31 (August 2003), <www.erudit.org/ revue/ron/2003/v/n31/008699ar.html>.

Catharine Macaulay's republican *History* (1763–83) appears to have been the tipping point that decided him to attempt the stage-drama *Charles the First*. Collation of Macaulay with Shelley's other known sources and his abandoned draft shows that he had her work in mind or to hand during composition.[54]

But if Shelley's reading of women writers was narrow (though less narrow than it has often appeared) the influence of a select few women writers on his work was lasting and deep, and still awaits an overview and a gathering-together of dispersed criticism. Among these are Sappho, whose extant works he ordered in 1812 (*Letters: PBS* I, 344); the effect of her famous Fragment 31 is seen in his representation of passion *in extremis*, most clearly in the 1817 'To Constantia' ('Thy voice, slow rising like a spirit'), where upon hearing Constantia sing, he exclaims, 'My brain is wild, my breath comes quick [...] And thronging shadows fast and thick | Fall on my overflowing eyes' (5–8). Germaine de Staël's works (of which he undoubtedly read more than is on record) widened his knowledge of German culture beyond the Gothic 'shudder-novel', his awareness of the interaction between literature and national character (particularly Italian), and his interest in the female *improvvisatrice*. But the profoundest influence of all was undoubtedly that of Wollstonecraft, for him an avatar of Venus, Antigone, and Intellectual Beauty all in one. Shelley knew parts of her work by heart, as shown, for instance, in his weaving together of phrases from her *Letters Written in [...] Sweden* (1796) and from *The Wrongs of Woman; or, Maria* (1798) into the lines, long thought to be written to William Shelley, but addressed to the dead Fanny Godwin, 'Thy little footsteps on the sands' (1816/1817); he mourns Fanny as the daughter of Wollstonecraft and Wollstonecraft herself (*Longman*, 1, 552–3). If we gloss 'eyes' as comprehending 'minds', Shelley might, indeed, have claimed these words of Shakespeare's Biron for himself:[55] 'From women's eyes this doctrine I derive; | They are the ground, the books, the academes | From whence doth spring the true Promethean fire.'

SELECT BIBLIOGRAPHY

Bennett, Betty T. and Stuart Curran. Eds. *Shelley: Poet and Legislator of the World* Baltimore: Johns Hopkins UP, 1996.

Bonca, Teddi Chichester. *Shelley and the Mirrors of Love: Narcissism, Sacrifice, and Sorority.* New York: Stonybrook University of New York Press, 1999.

Brown, Nathaniel. *Sexuality and Feminism in Shelley*. Cambridge, MA: Harvard UP, 1979.

Cafarelli, Annette Wheeler. 'The Transgressive Double Standard: Shelleyan Utopianism and Feminist Social History'. *Shelley: Poet and Legislator of the World*. Ed. Betty T. Bennett and Stuart Curran. Baltimore: Johns Hopkins UP, 1996.

Gallant, Christine. *Shelley's Ambivalence*. New York: St Martin's Press, 1989.

Gelpi, Barbara Charlesworth. *Shelley's Goddess: Maternity, Language, Subjectivity*. Oxford: Oxford UP, 1992.

---

[54] See commentary on *Charles the First* in *CPPBS* VII (in preparation at time of writing).
[55] *Love's Labour's Lost*, IV. iii. 302–4 (Riverside edition).

Hay, Daisy. *Young Romantics: The Shelleys, Byron, and Other Tangled Lives*. London, Bloomsbury, 2010.

Kelly, Gary, 'From Avant-Garde to Vanguardism: The Shelleys' Romantic Feminism in *Laon and Cythna and Frankenstein*'. *Shelley: Poet and Legislator of the World*. Ed. Betty T. Bennett and Stuart Curran. Baltimore: Johns Hopkins UP, 1996.

Luftig, Victor. *Seeing Together: Friendship between the Sexes in English Writing from Mill to Woolf*. Stanford, CA: Stanford UP, 1993.

Robinson, Charles E. Ed. and introd. *Frankenstein [...] The Original Two-Volume Novel of 1816–1817 from the Bodleian Shelley Manuscripts by Mary Wollstonecraft Shelley (with Percy Shelley)*. Oxford: Bodleian Library, 2008. [Cover title: *The Original Frankenstein*].

CHAPTER 5

··

SHELLEY AND HIS
PUBLISHERS

··

STEPHEN C. BEHRENDT

DURING Shelley's lifetime, an author's relations with his or her publisher were much different from how they are in the contemporary world. Publishers held far greater power, in terms both of financial arrangements and of the actual content of individual works and the ways in which that content was to be put before a readership. Some authors were handsomely paid, especially if they had enjoyed sensational debuts like Scott's in 1802 or Byron's in 1812, or were already reliably profitable authors like Ann Radcliffe, who in 1797 was paid an extraordinary £800 for the copyright to *The Italian*. Most authors, however, received relatively little for their efforts. Even authors of the wildly popular novels published by the Minerva Press usually received little for their work: £25 was fairly typical and as little as £5 was not unusual, even for a multi-volume novel. Authors depended for their livelihood upon their publishers and the booksellers with whom they dealt, and these relationships, which were always complex and which benefited publishers far more than authors, placed individual authors in often humiliating subservience. Moreover, even after the passage of copyright reforms in eighteenth-century England there remained a thriving trade in unauthorized (or 'pirated') editions, for which authors received nothing, while enterprising booksellers like James Lackington began in the 1790s to trade successfully in 'remaindered' editions, unsold books purchased from their original publishers at large discounts and then re-sold for a fraction of their original prices—but still at a profit. Wary of losing profits on account of such schemes, publishers offered prospective authors as little as possible for the rights to their works, and they often required the author to finance publication by securing subscriptions—payments made in advance for copies to be delivered upon publication—or by paying directly for the expenses of publication. It was a precarious environment for any neophyte author, and not for the faint of heart—or of pocketbook.

Today we might imagine that Romantic-era publishers invested considerable time, expense, and effort in publishing both now-familiar authors like Shelley or Byron and other authors whose lives and works have long been ignored or even forgotten. In fact, though, the publishing industry was driven, then as now, by the contemporary market economy, which meant that what made successful publishers succeed was their skill in publishing diverse books that appealed to many different readerships. This skill became increasingly important in the early nineteenth century, when improvements in the mechanical technology of book production facilitated far larger press runs than had been possible earlier, and at less expense. At the same time, the expansion of literacy in Britain during the Romantic era meant not only that the *total* potential reading audience was growing ever larger, but also that this once relatively homogeneous audience was splitting into an array of more specialized audiences whose patterns of consumption varied according to their means, their classes, their occupations, and their individual interests. The London publisher Joseph Johnson, who in the 1790s published radical writers like Thomas Paine, Mary Wollstonecraft, and William Godwin (and who published Wordsworth's first printed poem, *An Evening Walk*, in 1793), is usually regarded as a radical publisher. An unabashed supporter of liberal causes and the authors who promoted them, Johnson was also a savvy businessman, and he appreciated that success meant attracting readers of diverse interests and convictions, and so he published both broadly and even eclectically. Politics mattered to Johnson, of course, just as they did to most publishers during the era, but the economic 'bottom line' mattered more. This point needs bearing in mind when we assess the relationship of any author—in the present case, Percy Bysshe Shelley—to his or her publishers.

We can gain some perspective on Shelley's activities as an author by considering the businesses of two of his publishers, John Joseph Stockdale, who in 1811 published Shelley's second Gothic romance, *St. Irvyne*, and Charles and James Ollier, his primary publishers beginning in 1817. Stockdale's father John had operated in Piccadilly since 1783 and had built a strong trade in children's books (he had begun publishing Thomas Day's immensely successful *Sandford and Merton* in 1783), travel and geography, political tracts, and works relating to America.[1] His son John Joseph had established his own business in 1807, and by the time he brought out *St. Irvyne*, he too was publishing in subjects ranging from travel narratives and the British colonial empire to works on morality (like Thomas Comber's *Adultery Analyzed*, 1810), European history (Comber's *History of the Parisian Massacre*, 1810), economics, and political commentary ranging from speeches to analyses of government ministries and issues of public policy from the local to the national. During this four-year period Stockdale published nearly 300 titles (including the first of what would be a dozen or so novels and romances, *St. Irvyne* among the earliest), a number that places in perspective both the position in his list that

---

[1] Useful and detailed information about the names and addresses of Romantic-era British printers and publishers, their preferences, and their publications in literature can be found in several particularly important sources: William Todd, *A Directory of Printers and Others in Allied Trades: London and Vicinity, 1800–1840* (London: Printing Historical Society, 1972); Peter Garside, James Raven, and Rainer Schöwerling (gen. eds.), *The English Novel 1770–1829: A Bibliographical Survey of Prose Fiction Published in the British Isles*, 2 vols. (Oxford: Oxford UP, 2000); J. R. de J. Jackson, *Annals of English Verse 1770–1835: A Preliminary Survey of the Volumes Published* (New York: Garland, 1985); see also the sources identified in the Select Bibliography.

he apparently expected Shelley's youthful romance to occupy and the surprising extent to which he interested himself in the young author's affairs.

With the Olliers, the matter is significantly different. For one thing, their operation was a much smaller one; between late 1816 or early 1817, when they began publishing, and 1822, when Shelley drowned, volumes bearing the Olliers' imprint number only about fifty. Moreover, most of these were literary texts, among which Shelley's are especially prominent. They published poetry by Leigh Hunt, John Keats, 'Barry Cornwall' (Bryan Waller Procter), and Eaton Stannard Barrett, as well as prose by Charles Lamb, William Hazlitt, and Thomas Love Peacock (including *The Four Ages of Poetry*, 1820). Given both the narrowness of the market they thus defined and their decision to feature writers whom the conservative critic John Gibson Lockhart, writing in *Blackwood's Magazine* in 1817, had derisively dubbed the 'Cockney school', it is little surprise that the Olliers' business, which included both a circulating library and a retail bookselling establishment, never prospered. Indeed, by 1825 they were effectively out of business.

Shelley was an inveterate reader and writer from his earliest years, avidly consuming poetry and fiction (Gothic thrillers like Charlotte Dacre's 1806 *Zofloya; or The Moor* were among his favourites) already by the time he was attending Eton, 1804–10. Shelley's first contact with a potential publisher seems to have come while he was still at Eton, in fact. In May 1809 he wrote to the most prominent Romantic-era publisher, Longman, to offer a still-unfinished 'Romance' that may have been his youthful Gothic tale *Zastrozzi*. Longman, whose principal interests at the time were in religious and educational books, was 'reluctant to accept any text that was not safely mainstream',[2] although someone at Longman wrote on his letter 'We shall be happy to see the MS. when finished' (*Letters: PBS* I, 5). While it is unclear whether Shelley actually sent Longman the completed manuscript, he never gave up on this powerful publisher, later offering them both his *Laon and Cythna* (revised as *The Revolt of Islam*) and Mary Shelley's *Frankenstein*. Both offers were turned down. Meanwhile, *Zastrozzi* was issued in 1810 by the diversified London publishers G. Wilkie and J. Robinson, who had published Fanny Burney's *Geraldine Fauconberg* in 1808 but who were better known for books on constitutional history, animal husbandry, rhetoric and linguistics, and for educational texts. Shelley would not find a steady publisher until 1817, when his relationship with the Olliers began.

In fact, Shelley's earliest experiences as an ambitious author were like those of many of his contemporaries. 'New' authors typically printed their work at their own expense and then attempted to interest booksellers in selling them or adding them to the subscription-based circulating libraries maintained by many publishers. Often these multilateral ventures involved more than one publisher, as indicated by title pages that bear multiple publishers' names (and business addresses). For example, the title page of the early and derivative *Original Poetry by Victor and Cazire* (by Shelley and his sister Elizabeth) informs the reader that the book, printed at Worthing, has been 'Printed by C. & W. Phillips, for the Authors and Sold By J. J. Stockdale'. In the case of radical prose

[2] William St Clair, *The Reading Nation in the Romantic Period* (Cambridge: Cambridge UP, 2004), 159.

works like *The Necessity of Atheism* (1810) and *A Refutation of Deism* (1814), no publisher is identified, although, as required by British law, the copies bear the names of their printers. The title page of the particularly incendiary *Queen Mab*, printed in 1813 and quickly suppressed by its author, indicated that the poem had been 'Printed by P. B. Shelley'. There seem to have been 250 copies produced, some of which Shelley apparently sent to major contemporary poets after carefully cutting out the name of the actual printer; the approximately 180 copies that remained at the time of Shelley's death were purchased by the radical publisher Richard Carlile (St Clair, *Reading Nation*, 649).

Shelley's early letters teem with comments about all his writing projects, and for some years he appears to cast about for publishers willing to risk publishing a relative 'unknown' whose works were undeniably controversial from the very beginning. He got an early start. When his father, Sir Timothy Shelley, installed him at University College, Oxford, in 1809, he told the Oxford publisher and bookseller Henry Slatter that 'My son here has a literary turn; he is already an author; and do pray indulge him in his printing freaks' (Bieri, I, 120). Slatter's partner John Munday published the liberal weekly *Oxford University and City Herald*, and Shelley cultivated both men (and their clienteles) as instruments for publishing and circulating his work in the venerable university community and beyond. In these early years Shelley identified as his chief projects novels and romances; he distinguishes between the two, evidently regarding 'novels' as more intellectually, philosophically, and politically substantial than Gothic-inflected sensational 'romances' like *Zastrozzi* (1810) and *St. Irvyne* (1811). In 1812, for example, Shelley was working on one of these more intellectually substantial works, having apparently completed 'about 200 pages' of a 'novel' called *Hubert Cauvin* which he called 'a tale in which I design to exhibit the cause of the failure of the French Revolution and the state of morals and opinions in France during the latter years of its monarchy' (*Letters: PBS* I, 218). It is a pity that nothing of this ambitious tale seems to have survived, since its composition coincided with the period during which, as he told William Godwin in early 1812, he had been powerfully affected by his future father-in-law's influential *Political Justice*, which was first published in 1793. It is clear from this sketchy account that Shelley recognized that literature could serve as a vehicle for promulgating an ideologically driven programme of social control, whether it took the form of sensational fiction, the 'novel of ideas', or polemical poetry. This appreciation of the power of the printed word remained fundamental to his thinking and to his relations with the publishers whom he hoped to enlist in his liberal antinomian agenda.

During 1812 Shelley also became acquainted with Thomas Hookham, Jr., and his brother Edward, young liberal publishers who printed and sold books to a relatively exclusive and aristocratic clientele at their father's circulating library in the fashionable locale of Old Bond Street, to which Shelley subsequently subscribed and from which he continued to purchase even after he left Britain in 1818. The Hookhams published novels and romances especially, including the work of the satirical novelists Sarah Green and, later, Thomas Love Peacock, whose poetry they were already publishing by 1812. Shelley evidently tried to enlist Thomas Hookham to distribute polemical works like *A Letter to Lord Ellenborough*, written in Ireland in support of the radical publisher Daniel Isaac

Eaton and printed in 1812 at Shelley's own expense by a minor printer and bookseller in Barnstaple. Believing he had found in Hookham a kindred activist spirit, Shelley sent twenty-five copies of the *Letter* to Hookham in London with instructions to 'shew them to any friends who *are not informers*' (*Letters: PBS* I, 319). Although Hookham declined to publish the *Letter* formally himself, Shelley soon informed him about other projects he was contemplating, including 'a vol[ume] of essays moral & *religious*' (*Letters: PBS* I, 324), and he also sent him his own copy of *The Necessity of Atheism* and a preliminary manuscript of *Queen Mab*, along with a collection of 'Biblical Extracts' based on the words of Jesus (*Letters: PBS* I, 332). That this subsequently untraced collection of extracts, which Shelley must have intended to include his own commentary, was neither orthodox nor uncontroversial is suggested by his question to Hookham, 'Would not Daniel I. Eaton publish them?—Could the question be asked him in any manner?' (*Letters: PBS* I, 340). Shelley evidently figured out that Hookham was unwilling to risk his clientele—and indeed himself—with a work of this sort, but he also recognized in Hookham an intermediary who might provide useful contacts with other publishers, like Eaton, who were less cautious. Nevertheless, in January 1813 Shelley still promised Hookham the completed *Queen Mab*, with its 'long & philosophical' notes, which he finally sent him in March with the ominous instructions that 'If you do not dread the arm of the law, or any exasperation of public opinion against yourself, I wish that it should be printed & published immediately' (*Letters: PBS* I, 361). If Hookham demurred on the 'Biblical Extracts', he must have been more alarmed still by *Queen Mab*, although he seems to have had the poem handsomely printed (without mention of his agency in the act), leaving it to Shelley to suppress the poem immediately (Bieri, I, 293; *Journals: MWS* I, 9 n.).

Meanwhile, Shelley's relationship with Stockdale had soured after Shelley and his college friend Thomas Jefferson Hogg were expelled from Oxford in 1810 after publishing and distributing their jointly authored essay, *The Necessity of Atheism*. Stockdale apparently conspired with Shelley's father Sir Timothy against both Shelley and Hogg, who had sent him the manuscript of a novel, *Leonora*, which Stockdale rejected. Over the next several years Shelley published a number of works, all at his own expense, including several overtly political ones dating from his brief stay in Ireland in 1812 with his young wife Harriet. After completing his *Alastor* volume at the beginning of 1816 he paid the Surrey printer Samuel Hamilton for 250 copies, which he then offered to the prestigious London publisher John Murray, Byron's publisher, who was not interested. He eventually ended up placing the *Alastor* volume with Baldwin, Cradock, and Joy, successors after 1816 to Henry Baldwin and his sons, who had been publishing in London since 1772 and who were by now publishing Peacock's novels (including *Headlong Hall*, 1816) along with extensive offerings in history, politics, natural science, travel and geography, children's books, and both poetry and novels. *Alastor*'s co-publishers were Carpenter and Son, a smaller-scale publisher who had operated at 140 Old Bond Street since 1800 and who were now publishing books on the arts (including one by Benjamin Robert Haydon on the Elgin marbles, 1816) as well as Thomas Moore's poetry, with which Shelley had become acquainted (apparently unfavourably at first) as early as 1811 (*Letters: PBS* I, 44).

Shelley's most long-standing relationship with a publisher, however, involved Charles and James Ollier, the former of whom Shelley had met through Leigh Hunt, the liberal journalist with whom Shelley had struck up a correspondence after his and his brother John's imprisonment in 1812 on a charge of libel against the Prince Regent. The Olliers operated a small publishing house in London and published most of Shelley's work beginning in 1817, when they published—at Shelley's own expense—his prose treatise, *A Proposal for Putting Reform to the Vote throughout the Kingdom.* The ambitious print run of 500 copies suggests Shelley's optimism about his prospects as a political activist, an impulse to engage the public sphere that was never out of his view as poet or prose essayist. Like many of their contemporaries, the Olliers operated a retail bookshop, where they sold their own books as well as those of other publishers, whose works they sold on consignment, often as part of a cooperative arrangement for sharing both profits and expenses. These arrangements, which were common, worked to everyone's advantage while reducing each publisher's financial risk, especially when they were publishing an author like Shelley, whose works never sold well, or one who was simply unknown. The Olliers also maintained a circulating library, which had also failed by 1825, after the brothers tried in 1823 to recoup some of their losses by last-ditch schemes like issuing remaindered editions of Shelley's works under the title of *Poetical Pieces by the Late Percy Bysshe Shelley.*

Publishers and booksellers—which were not always one and the same during Shelley's lifetime—often stocked and sold one another's publications on a commission basis, paying each other and the authors (when they did so at all) on a percentage basis agreed upon in advance among the booksellers. That Shelley understood this arrangement is clear from his correspondence with his publishers; his terms with Charles and James Ollier apparently were set at 20 per cent, although Charles Ollier seems to have charged him only half that amount (*Letters: PBS* II, 177, 200). Shelley's 1817 *Proposal*, written during the Shelleys' residence at Marlow and published by the Olliers, illustrates Shelley's understanding of these matters of production and distribution. He instructed Charles Ollier to advertise the pamphlet heavily '& get as many booksellers as you can to take copies on their own account. Sherwood Neely & Co. *Hone* of Newgate St. Ridgeway, & Stockdale are people likely to do so—Send 20 or 30 copies to Messrs. Hookham & Co. Bond St.' (*Letters: PBS* I, 533). While Ridgeway was a minor London publisher, Sherwood, Neely, and Jones were originally engaged as co-publishers of *Laon and Cythna*, which was stopped before its actual publication when Ollier's printer convinced him to abandon the original version out of concern about the poem's controversial contents. When Ollier apparently informed Shelley in December 1817 that he was withdrawing as publisher Shelley angrily objected to Ollier's unilateral decision, writing that 'Sherwood and Neely wished to be the principal publishers' (*Letters: PBS* I, 580). Ollier may have objected less to suggestions in the text about incest (which were easily remedied) than to the poem's spirited attacks on religion, for which—as their publisher—Ollier could have been prosecuted for blasphemous libel (*Journals: MWS* I, 187 n.).

How Shelley had come to be associated with Sherwood, Neely, and Jones in the first place is unclear, although they had been one of the publishers who had been involved, earlier in 1817, in republishing—as a pirated edition—Robert Southey's revolutionary drama *Wat Tyler* (1794), at the instigation of Southey's enemies and to the embarrassment and consternation of the now conservative Poet Laureate. Shelley had visited Southey in Keswick in 1811 and had been disillusioned by his evident conservatism in matters both poetic and political. Given Shelley's enmity by 1817 toward Southey, approaching Sherwood, Neely, and Jones may have struck Shelley as a particularly appropriate touch of irony. Indeed, when the *Quarterly Review* attacked Shelley's poem in April 1819, Shelley mistakenly attributed the attack to Southey; it was in fact written by John Taylor Coleridge.

Shelley's suggestion that Ollier send copies of his *Proposal* to the radical journalist William Hone (whose name he underscored and whose addresses in 1817 included both 67 Old Bailey and 55 Fleet Street—but never Newgate Street) further indicates how anxious he was to gain access to the sort of radical republican audience cultivated by Hone, who also had a hand in republishing *Wat Tyler* in 1817. Another participant in that 1817 republication was the radical publisher Richard Carlile, who would in a few years publish his own pirated editions of Shelley's works, including *Queen Mab*, from 183 and then 62 Fleet Street, while Carlile's wife Mary Ann set up shop in 1819 at Hone's old address of 55 Fleet Street.

Not only did Shelley hope to place copies of his pamphlet with these booksellers, he also furnished a list of prominent individuals to whom copies were to be sent; these included the reformist MP Sir Francis Burdett and radicals like the Whig MP Henry Brougham and the journalist William Cobbett, as well as the activist reform Hampden clubs of Birmingham and London (which received five and ten copies, respectively). The Hampden clubs had been formed in 1812 by Major John Cartwright (to whom Shelley also instructed Ollier to send a copy) to unite working-class radicals and more moderate middle-class citizens in the cause of reform; the Birmingham club was a particularly active one and would be instrumental in a large reform gathering in 1819. Shelley also specified that copies should go to the editors of several London papers, including the *Morning Chronicle*, the *Independent Whig*, and *The Statesman*, which the radical journalist Thomas Wooler edited before founding the era's best-known radical paper, *The Black Dwarf*, which made its appearance in January 1817. Soon after his first letter, Shelley wrote to Ollier: 'Had you not better advertise the day (an early one) of publication[?] Advertise it in *all* the morning papers of note' (*Letters: PBS* I, 534). For Shelley, who was an instinctive propagandist, *visibility* counted as much as venue and vehicle.

Shelley understood that books and pamphlets were not the only vehicles for disseminating ideas, especially socio-political ones. Daily and weekly newspapers and journals had proliferated in the last quarter of the eighteenth century, and by Shelley's time their circulation had reached previously unimagined numbers, owing in part to improvements in printing technology and in physical distribution. Papers and journals were available in coffee houses and other public meeting places, where they were examined by countless readers and read aloud for the benefit of the still unlettered. During this period Cobbett's *Political Register*, the periodical most widely read by the working class, for example, reached a circulation of some 40,000 copies, which translated into many more actual readers and auditors. Moreover, most periodicals were fiercely partisan, many of them receiving subsidies from political parties and from the government itself to promote these groups' ideological agendas and to attack each party's enemies, both in politics and in the arts, including literature. As instruments of social control, therefore, the periodical press represented an increasingly important vehicle, especially for radicals and reformers, and the government's repeated efforts to silence oppositional voices are evident in the series of repressive measures beginning with the Treason Trials of 1794 and continuing through the 'Blasphemous and Seditious Libels Act' and the 'Newspaper and Stamp Duties Act', two of the notorious 'Six Acts' of 1819. Their particular targets were radical organs like Cobbett's 'twopenny trash' (the cheap version of his weekly *Political Register*, produced as a single sheet to evade the newspaper tax) and Wooler's *Black Dwarf*, but they included also more moderate reformist organs like John and Leigh Hunt's *Examiner*.

Like other Romantic-era poets who published, sometimes pseudonymously, in the daily press, Shelley saw the periodical press's potential for spreading his beliefs and promoting his causes. After the notorious 'Peterloo Massacre' of 16 August 1819, for example, Shelley sent Hunt a series of hotly indignant political poems to publish in *The Examiner*. Safely insulated (and isolated) in Italy, Shelley had no need to worry about the consequences of publishing shorter poems like 'England in 1819' and 'Song to the Men of England' or longer ones like *The Mask of Anarchy*. Hunt enjoyed no such security, however, so it is little surprise that in those repressive years he chose not to publish the poems, keeping *The Mask*, for instance, until the passage of the Reform Act in 1832 made him feel safe enough to publish it.

After he left England in 1818 (never to return, as it turned out), Shelley had to rely upon intermediaries to transact business with the Olliers and others on his behalf. Leigh Hunt was foremost among these. In November 1819, for example, Shelley sent Hunt the manuscript of his satire on Wordsworth, *Peter Bell the Third*, which he instructed Hunt to give to Ollier for anonymous publication after Hunt had himself 'be[en] kind enough to take upon yourself the correction of the press' (i.e. correcting the galley proofs; *Letters: PBS* II, 134–5). Other friends served Shelley in comparable fashion, including Thomas Love Peacock, to whom he sent *The Cenci* in September 1819 for submission to Covent Garden for performance (it was turned down) and whom he asked to supervise correction of the proofs of *Julian and Maddalo* (which did not appear during Shelley's lifetime). Shelley's friend John Gisborne was also assigned the task of correcting *Prometheus Unbound* for Ollier, although it was Peacock who finally did the job (*Letters: PBS* II, 196, 244).

Correcting printers' proofs was more critical two centuries ago than it is today, if only because the process opened up so many more opportunities for errors along the way. Typically, after composing any work, an author would prepare a 'fair copy'—a clean copy of all corrected drafts of the volume. This fair copy would go to the printer, who would set the movable type and print one or more proof impressions, which would be sent to the author for his or her inspection. After the author marked up the proof with any and all corrections of printer's errors and with any substantive revisions to the text, the proof would be returned to the printer, who would make the corrections and then produce the finished pages for binding (or, more commonly, for stitching, since books were usually sold stitched in plain paper covers so that individual purchasers could have them custom bound to their own specifications). Many authors, Shelley among them, turned to others to produce the fair copy; after 1814 Percy Shelley's fair copies were usually prepared by Mary Shelley, whose handwriting was neater and generally more legible. Even so, what the printer was receiving was still a handwritten document, so that errors were frequent, especially in matters of punctuation and emphasis. When author and printer were located conveniently near one another, correcting the proofs was fairly efficient and speedy, and the finished product was relatively accurate. But once Shelley left England for Italy, the process became complicated indeed. Fair copy manuscripts had to be sent by post, through intermediaries, and the proof copies were most often checked by Shelley's representatives in England, who frequently were forced to guess about Shelley's intentions when they read the proofs. Nor was there time for exchanging letters and enquiries about these matters, since printers had to get on to the next job and could not wait endlessly for corrections. Many of Shelley's complaints about being ill served by his publishers are a result of his inability directly to supervise the preparation of his works.

These limitations notwithstanding, however, almost from the start of his career Shelley displayed a shrewd sense of how the publishing business operated, and of what today we might call 'marketing strategies'. The young Shelley was sufficiently acquainted with circulating libraries—which he was patronizing even before his move to Oxford in 1810—to suggest to Stockdale that *St. Irvyne* 'is a thing which almost *mechanically* sells to circulating libraries, &c.' (*Letters: PBS* I, 20). But neither the circulating libraries nor the retail booksellers were entirely reliable venues, no matter how 'mechanical' (i.e. automatic) it seemed that one's work would appear there. This is evident from Shelley's admonition to Ollier in January 1818 following the publication of the revised *Laon and Cythna* as *The Revolt of Islam*: 'Can't you *make* the Booksellers subscribe [for] more of the Poem?' (*Letters: PBS* I, 593).

There were other marketing strategies, however. When he published *Zastrozzi* in 1810, for example, he instructed his London contact Edward Fergus Graham to be sure that the reviewers were 'pouched'—bribed—to provide favourable reviews (*Letters: PBS* I, 5–6). He understood, too, that particularly negative reviews could usefully draw attention to works that the reading public might otherwise overlook. Writing to Graham late in 1810 he mentions that 'I shall possibly send you the abuse today, but I am afraid that they will not insert it.' Frederick L. Jones suggests that Shelley is talking about a negative review of the *Posthumous Fragments* that he had himself composed for insertion in some periodical (*Letters: PBS* I, 23). Certainly Shelley understood the capacity of all reviews for publicizing new works. Although he suppressed *Queen Mab* immediately after publishing it in 1813, Shelley undoubtedly authored the poem's only contemporary review, a notice containing long extracts from the poem that was spread across five consecutive issues of *The Theological Inquirer; or Polemical Magazine*, thereby both publicizing the (suppressed) poem and placing its actual contents before the public in a way that evaded legal prosecution. It is surely no coincidence that also during 1815 the same journal published, over six consecutive months, Shelley's 101-page 1814 treatise *A Refutation of Deism*. Shelley also recycled one of *Queen Mab*'s long explanatory notes on vegetarianism by publishing it as a separate pamphlet, *A Vindication of Natural Diet*; its title page announced that it was being published by 'J. Callow, Medical Bookseller', suggesting that the young Shelley appreciated the utility also of 'niche' publishers. This market savvy is further apparent in his instructions in 1813 to Hookham about the format for printing *Queen Mab*: he asked for 'A small neat Quarto, on fine paper & so as to catch the aristocrats: They will not read it, but their sons & daughters may' (*Letters: PBS* I, 361). Sometimes his concern for his publications *as physical artefacts* in fact outweighed more practical considerations that would have occurred to his publishers. When he sent Ollier the finished manuscript of *Prometheus Unbound, and Other Poems* in 1820, he called the great lyrical drama 'my favourite poem' and ordered Ollier 'specially to pet him and feed him with fine ink and good paper'. Even given Shelley's light-hearted tone here, the already financially strapped Ollier must have winced when Shelley continued, 'the "Prometheus" cannot sell beyond twenty copies', unlike *The Cenci*, of which Shelley had also sent him copies that had been printed in Pisa and which he assured Ollier, who was to prepare an English edition, 'is written for the multitude, and ought to sell well' (*Letters: PBS* II, 174).

Shelley also tried to use his connection with the Olliers to assist others. After his cousin Thomas Medwin's return from India in 1821, for example, Shelley encouraged him to send Charles Ollier his *Sketches in Hindoostan, with Other Poems*, which Ollier published in 1821, perhaps at least in part at Shelley's urging: 'May I challenge your kindness to do what you can for it?' (*Letters: PBS* II, 246). He was less successful on his wife's behalf, though. After sounding out Ollier in July 1821 about publishing Mary Shelley's new novel *Valperga*, Shelley followed up with letters in September and November pressing him to do so, but Ollier seems to have responded with complete silence and the novel was published in 1823 by G. and W. B. Whitaker. Shelley also tried unsuccessfully, at about the same time, to interest Ollier in publishing his new friend John Taaffe's *Comment on Dante* and his translation of *The Divine Comedy*; when Ollier remained silent again, John Murray published it, at Byron's particular insistence, in 1822.

The Olliers continued as Shelley's principal publishers—typically at a loss, if Charles Ollier's complaints are to be credited—for the remainder of Shelley's short life. Most often, they published Shelley's works in editions of 250 copies, and by 1821 the dispirited author, who mistakenly believed that his work was simply ignored when it was not pilloried by the reviewers, told Ollier that probably a hundred copies of *Epipsychidion* would be sufficient (*Letters: PBS* II, 263), although Ollier must have printed 250, since in 1823 160 copies remained (St Clair, *Reading Nation*, 650). The comparatively large edition of *The Revolt of Islam* (750 copies) was printed at Shelley's expense and never did sell out, despite Shelley's and the Olliers' best efforts. Shelley asked Ollier twice in 1821 whether there was any chance of a second edition (*Letters: PBS* II, 263, 354), but in 1829 there were still enough copies remaining of the first for the radical pirate John Brooks to publish an unauthorized edition. Brooks also reissued remaindered copies of *The Cenci* and Percy and Mary Shelley's *History of a Six Weeks' Tour*, which had been printed in 1817 (also at Shelley's expense) and sold by Hookham and the Olliers, the only time these two publishers converged in a Shelley project. Although Shelley expressed increasing impatience with Charles Ollier (calling him 'negligent' to Leigh Hunt in 1820; *Letters: PBS* II, 186), after the wrangle over the suppression of *Laon and Cythna* and its revision as *The Revolt of Islam*, Ollier seems to have served Shelley relatively faithfully (at least during the first years of their relationship), considering his own financial straits and the poor profits Shelley generated; indeed, Shelley's works account for nearly a quarter of the total volumes that the Olliers' short-lived operation published.

But Shelley concluded that Ollier was not doing enough to promote either him or his works. Particularly upsetting was Ollier's surprising neglect of *Adonais*. After he learned of Keats's death, Shelley rapidly composed his elegy in early June 1821. Having experienced so many problems over the years with printer's errors in his texts, Shelley had copies of his poem printed in Pisa and then sent some of these to Ollier so that he could publish the poem in England from an already corrected, printed (rather than handwritten) copy. That Shelley intended an imposing volume is evident from his comment to Ollier in July that he was sending him 'a sketch for a frontispiece to the poem "Adonais"' (*Letters: PBS* II, 310) which means that he intended the poem to have at least this one engraved illustration. Ollier never followed through and actually published the intended English edition of *Adonais*, however, although he did sell some of the copies of the Italian edition that Shelley had sent him. More and more, in fact, he neglected new work that Shelley sent him, while growing ever more unresponsive to Shelley's increasingly heated letters to him.

Not surprisingly, then, even before these problems with Ollier became acute Shelley had begun exploring alternatives, asking Hunt in May 1820, for example, whether he might recommend some other publisher for his *Philosophical View of Reform* (unpublished until 1920), which he described as a 'boldly but temperately written' book intended 'for the philosophical reformers politically considered, like Jeremy Bentham's something, but different & perhaps more systematic' (*Letters: PBS* II, 201). In 1822, more discontent than ever with Ollier, Shelley inquired of Hunt about his unfinished drama, *Charles the First*: 'Would no bookseller give me 150 or 200 pounds for the copyright of this play? [...] Write to Allman your bookseller, tell him what I tell you of Charles the Ist and do not delay a post' (*Letters: PBS* II, 380–1). T. and J. Allman, relatively new Hanover Square publishers who had quickly developed a strong list in history, geography, and travel literature, and who also offered classical and contemporary literature, had published Hunt's translation of Tasso's *Amyntas* in 1820. Shelley undoubtedly hoped that Hunt would therefore prove a productive 'contact' with them.

In the event, while Shelley remained with the Olliers, he had seemingly lost all patience with them. In January 1822, at about the same time that Mary Shelley wrote to Maria Gisborne that Ollier 'treats us infamously in every way' (*Letters: MWS* I, 215), Shelley implored her husband John, who was then in London, to act as his agent in extricating him and his works from Ollier's hands: 'I wish now to have done with Ollier as a publisher, & should feel exceedingly grateful to you if you would undertake to extract me from his clutches. I give you hereby, full authority, to settle my accounts with him, & to take from him all the unsold copies of my works, which I wish to be transferred to another publisher, & a fresh title printed to each with his names & advertisements issued in course' (*Letters: PBS* II, 387). This was a serious move: substituting new title pages would have removed all material connection between Shelley and the Olliers, and it is clear that Shelley wanted to settle his account with Ollier, both financially and personally, and be done with him. But Shelley was 725 miles (1,165 km) away, in Pisa, and could do little to help Gisborne secure another outlet for his work. All he could do was rage—and suggest names as best he could: 'I would not, for the sake of a trifle, continue my connexion [*sic*] with Mr Ollier a single day after you have found another bookseller—The same bookseller as publishes for Hunt or Barry Cornwall, or Tailor [*sic*] & Hess[e]y the publishers of Keats's poems[;] would none of them refuse to be mine[?] My idea is that they should publish simply on my account. […] I will have nothing more to do with Ollier on *whatever terms* or for *whatever apology*' (*Letters: PBS* II, 387–8).Yet three months later, he expressed what seems like unfeigned satisfaction with the copy of *Hellas* which the Olliers had just published, writing that it 'is prettily printed & with fewer mistakes than any poem I ever published' (*Letters: PBS* II, 406). Without another publisher upon whom to rely, Shelley apparently decided to be diplomatic and make the best of the Olliers, which was about all he could do in the face of his physical distance from the London publishing scene. Mary concurred; she wrote to Maria Gisborne that doing so 'is the best [option] after all I agree' (*Letters: MWS* I, 222).

Shelley's dealings with his printers and publishers frequently left them the losers—at least financially. The Oxford printers John Munday and Henry Slatter, for example, who had published the *Posthumous Fragments of Margaret Nicholson* at their own (principally Slatter's) expense, were never paid (*Letters: PBS* I, 26), and Stockdale later observed that Shelley had never paid him either (*Letters: PBS* I, 130), while as late as spring 1822 Ollier was claiming that Shelley had a negative balance with him (*Letters: PBS* II, 410). Ironically, it was only after his death that Shelley's works began to be profitable commodities for their publishers. Shelley's isolation in Italy left him only partially—and incorrectly—informed about his growing reputation in England and the seriousness with which his work was now being taken in all quarters. His frequently anguished comments about his ill fortunes and fate are touching reminders of the terrible cost to an activist writer like Shelley of detaching oneself from the cultural milieu in which one instinctively—even compulsively—has invested such energy and emotion. On the heels of the Olliers' posthumous 1823 editions (there were two variants) of Shelley's *Poetical Pieces* came Mary Shelley's 1824 *Posthumous Poems*, subsidized by admirers like Thomas Lovell Beddoes and 'Barry Cornwall', published in an edition of 500 by John and Henry Hunt, and angrily suppressed by Shelley's father Sir Timothy after some 309 copies had been sold. Sir Timothy, who had all remaining copies destroyed, threatened to cut off all support for Mary Shelley and his sole remaining grandchild, Percy Florence, if she published anything further by or about the son he had effectively disowned. Only in 1839 did Sir Timothy relent, leading to the 1839 and 1840 editions of Shelley's poetry and prose that Mary Shelley edited for the London publisher Edward Moxon, who had, ironically, become Wordsworth's publisher beginning in 1835.

In the meantime appeared a succession of 'pirated' (unauthorized) editions of Shelley's works, beginning in 1826 with two different editions (one cheap, the other longer and relatively sumptuous) prepared by the well-known pirate William Benbow. The Paris publishers Galignani followed in 1829 with an edition that bound Shelley's works with those of Coleridge and Keats; their edition, to whose preparation Mary Shelley may have contributed materially, was the most complete and accurate one that had appeared to that point. In 1834 another pirated edition surfaced, a virtually complete edition prepared by John Ascham that reflects reasonably professional editorial standards. Charles Daly published his own editions of Shelley in London in 1836, 1837, and 1839; excepting the dated title pages, these were virtually identical. In 1839 appeared still another pirated edition, this one published by William Dugdale, whose second volume includes *Peter Bell the Third* and *Oedipus Tyrannus*, neither of which had appeared before Mary Shelley included them in her one-volume 1839 edition. Meanwhile, other poems had made their way into print in the intervening years. Hunt had published *The Mask of Anarchy* (spelling it *Masque*) in 1832, the same year in which Medwin published several additional poems in *The Athenæum* and in which Thomas Jefferson Hogg began a series of contributions to *The New Monthly Magazine* that ran over into 1833 and that included excerpts of Shelley's poetry and prose. Finally, it is important—as it surely would have been gratifying to Shelley—to remember that even before his death some of his most radical poems—*Queen Mab* in particular—had been seized upon by radical publishers like Richard Carlile, whom Shelley had defended at length in an unpublished November 1819 letter to Hunt that was intended for *The Examiner* on the occasion of Carlile's trial for blasphemous libel for publishing excerpts from Thomas Paine's *Age of Reason* and the Deist Elihu Palmer's *Principles of Nature*. Carlile's former employee William Clark published a pirated edition of *Queen Mab* in 1821, and Carlile republished it with a new title page in 1822 and again in 1826, while yet another pirate, John Brooks, produced an edition in 1829, as did Carlile's wife and sons in 1832 and then Ascham in 1834 and Daly in 1836. Shelley would have been gratified, had he survived, to observe the prominent role this poem came to play in working-class radical culture in the 1820s. The small-format 1832 edition became a touchstone text for the Chartist movement, and at least fourteen editions had appeared by 1845 (Bieri, I, 293).

Although other editions appeared after Mary Shelley's for Moxon, Henry Buxton Forman was the first to apply sophisticated scholarly editorial methods to Shelley's texts. By comparing first editions (including pirated ones) with later ones and with manuscripts in the poet's and Mary's handwriting, Forman produced the most 'correct' texts of the poetry to that time. These he published in 1876–7 and then followed them in 1880 with four volumes of Shelley's prose. Then, in 1926–30, Roger Ingpen and Walter E. Peck published what is known as the 'Julian Edition', which added significant quantities of both prose and poetry to what Forman had published. Shelley's prose has historically been overlooked or judged inferior to the better-known poetry, but both his prose fiction and his non-fiction has begun to attract new attention and study during the past several decades. Oxford's Clarendon Press began a project to publish a full scholarly edition of Shelley's prose, but only the first volume (1993), edited by E. B. Murray and ending with March 1818, has appeared.

Meanwhile, 'academic' publishers began in the twentieth century to produce a variety of Shelley texts, both in 'complete works' formats like the one that was published in 1905 in the Oxford Standard Authors series, edited by Thomas Hutchinson, and in numerous anthologies of works selected principally from the poems—often with the addition of all or part of *A Defence of Poetry*. Because the contemporary market for texts intended for college and university use is a competitive and often lucrative one, such selected editions continue to proliferate. Of course, Shelley's works appear in broader-ranging anthologies (like those devoted to 'British literature'), where the selections have become increasingly predictable.

Most recently, two publishers have undertaken to produce complete 'scholarly' editions of Shelley's poetry, complete with elaborate bibliographical, historical, and critical apparatus. The first of these is being published by the Longman group, an irony that Shelley would surely have found irresistible, given that it was Longman to whom he offered his first major literary effort in 1809—and was turned down. Three volumes of this projected five-volume edition have appeared (1989, 2000, 2011) and the fourth is reasonably close to publication.[3] This edition's editors aim at an accessible format in which spelling and punctuation are modernized and regularized and editorial notes and commentary appear on the page together with Shelley's words. The other edition, which is being published by the Johns Hopkins University Press,[4] adopts a more technical and 'text-centred' editorial procedure in which Shelley's poems are presented on the page as faithfully as modern publishing permits; the very extensive annotations, editorial commentaries, full collations, and appendices of especially relevant contextual materials all appear at the end of each volume. To date, three volumes (2000, 2004, 2012) of this edition (projected at eight volumes) have appeared.

Once the publication of both these very substantial editions is finished, readers will have two options for a 'complete' poetic Shelley. The Johns Hopkins edition will assess not just the various printed copies and relevant manuscript materials, but also the historical and cultural contexts for those documents. The Longman edition, on the other hand, will serve the reader less concerned about the technical *minutiae* and more eager to 'read' the poems in an accessible format with annotations ready to hand.

Shelley made virtually no money during his lifetime from his poetry or prose; indeed, the evidence suggests that both he and his publishers lost repeatedly in the bargain. Ironically, Shelley is today one of the most widely published Romantic poets and essayists. Nearly 200 years after his premature death, publishers around the world continue to reap profits from Shelley's writing, a trend that shows little sign of abating—and for very good reason.

[3] *The Poems of Shelley*, I: *1804–1817*, ed. Geoffrey Matthews and Kelvin Everest (London: Longman, 1989); *The Poems of Shelley*, II: *1817–1819*, ed. Kelvin Everest and Geoffrey Matthews, contributing editors Jack Donovan, Ralph Pite, and Michael Rossington (Harlow: Longman, 2000); *The Poems of Shelley, III: 1819–20*, eds. Kelvin Everest, Jack Donovan, Michael Rossington, and Cian Duffy.
[4] *The Complete Poetry of Percy Bysshe Shelley*, ed. Donald H. Reiman, Neil Fraistat, and Nora Crook (Baltimore: Johns Hopkins UP, vol. I, 2000; vol. II, 2004; vol. III, 2012).

ADDITIONAL READING

Shelley's relations with his publishers are necessarily connected with his understanding (and occasional misunderstanding) of the readerships toward which he directed his works in various genres. While some of these matters have been examined in cursory fashion in the major biographical studies (especially Holmes and Bieri) and documented in bibliographical resources like *Shelley and his Circle* and *Manuscripts of the Younger Romantics*, several studies are particularly relevant to this topic, chief among them Stephen C. Behrendt, *Shelley and his Audiences* (1989) and Kim Wheatley, *Shelley and his Readers* (1999). Both of these examine in detail the calculated strategies Shelley employed to engage his readers and to manipulate the ways in which they read and processed his works. Two other studies pay particular attention to the political contexts for Shelley's textually mediated relationships with his readers: Michael Henry Scrivener, *Radical Shelley* (1982) and Steven Jones, *Shelley's Satire* (1994). The best study of the broader world of Romantic-era publishing is William St Clair, *The Reading Nation in the Romantic Period* (2004), which provides a rich analysis of the conditions under which publishers and booksellers—and the authors in whose works they dealt—did their work. St Clair also provides invaluable documentary evidence about the pricing and circulation of books, about numbers of copies produced and payments to authors, and about circulating libraries and pirate publishers. More limited, but nevertheless valuable, contextual studies include R. K. Webb, *The British Working Class Reader, 1790–1820* (1955) and Jon Klancher, *The Making of English Reading Audiences, 1790–1832* (1987).

SELECT BIBLIOGRAPHY

Behrendt, Stephen C. *Shelley and his Audiences*. Lincoln, NE: University of Nebraska Press, 1989.
—— 'The History of Shelley Editions in English'. *The Reception of P. B. Shelley in Europe*. Ed. Susanne Schmid and Michael Rossington. London: Continuum, 2008. 9–25.
Jones, Steven. *Shelley's Satire: Violence, Exhortation, and Authority*. DeKalb, IL: Northern Illinois UP, 1994.
Klancher, Jon. *The Making of English Reading Audiences, 1790–1832*. Madison: University of Wisconsin Press, 1987.
St Clair, William. *The Reading Nation in the Romantic Period*. Cambridge: Cambridge UP, 2004.
Scrivener, Michael Henry. *Radical Shelley: The Philosophical Anarchism and Utopian Thought of Percy Bysshe Shelley*. Princeton: Princeton UP, 1982.
Webb, R. K. *The British Working Class Reader, 1790–1820: Literacy and Social Tension*. London: Allen & Unwin, 1955.
Wheatley, Kim. *Shelley and his Readers: Beyond Paranoid Politics*. Columbia, MO: University of Missouri Press, 1999.

PART II

PROSE

CHAPTER 6

....

SHELLEY AND PHILOSOPHY

On a Future State, Speculations
on Metaphysics and Morals, On Life

....

ANTHONY HOWE

I

....

DURING the freezing Welsh winter of 1813 Shelley wrote to his publisher Thomas Hookham that 'I certainly wish to have all Kants [*sic*] works' (*Letters: PBS* I, 350). The great German philosopher did not become one of the key influences to which this essay must restrict itself, but the request is nevertheless typical of Shelley, who was, from an early age, a voracious reader of philosophy from a variety of countries and historical epochs.[1] Perhaps the obvious place to start is with Shelley's much-loved Plato, although how we understand Shelley's 'Platonism' depends in turn upon the knotty issue of how we understand Platonism itself.[2] Shelley was influenced by Plato in his metaphysics, political science, and poetics,[3] and frequently redeploys, in his poems, images and ideas taken from his deep study of the philosopher's writings. His passion for the experience of reading Plato, however, exceeds his agreement with many of the latter's apparent doctrines, both in their own right, and insofar as they have been transformed through the interpretative traditions of Christianity. In the unfinished Preface to his notable translation of *The Symposium*, he describes Platonism as something 'in which a long series and an incalculable variety of popular superstitions have sheltered their absurdities from the slow contempt of mankind'. As for Plato's own 'views into the nature of

---

[1] The range of Shelley's reading is suggested by *Letters: PBS* II, 467–88 (appendix VIII).

[2] James A. Notopoulos specifies three relevant concepts of 'Platonism': 'indirect', as being engaged in the larger historical tradition of Platonic interpretation; 'direct', as adhering to Plato's specific doctrines; and, thirdly, as a sharing of a '*similar* awareness' of thought as a 'living process'. *The Platonism of Shelley: A Study of Platonism and the Poetic Mind* (Durham, NC: Duke UP, 1949), 6, 8.

[3] For insightful comment on Shelley's response to the politics of Plato's Greece see Timothy Webb, *Shelley: A Voice Not Understood* (Manchester: Manchester UP, 1977), esp. 196–8.

mind and existence', Shelley writes that they 'are often obscure', although only 'because they are profound'. Moreover, while Shelley takes the view that Plato's 'theories respecting the government of the world, and the elementary laws of moral action, are not always correct', he adds that 'there is scarcely any of his treatises which do not, however stained by puerile sophisms, contain the most remarkable intuitions'.[4] Shelley's response to Plato, in other words, is itself, like the dialogic form the latter bequeathed, dynamic, often beginning critically with respect to specific doctrines before moving to a celebration of a more general profundity or intuition. This dialogic response is inseparable from Shelley's estimation of Plato as a pre-eminent *literary* writer. Plato was for Shelley—as the latter wrote, in *A Defence of Poetry*—'essentially a poet—the truth and splendour of his imagery and the melody of his language is the most intense that it is possible to conceive' (*Norton 2*, 514). Although he may be found wanting with respect to individual judgements or opinions—partly a symptom of social change and diversity, partly of the warping effect of Platonic tradition—he is, as a poet (in the extended Shelleyan sense), almost unparalleled in his truthfulness. Shelley's 'philosophy' is in this sense double, weaving between theoretical agreements and disagreements, but also puzzled and energized by elusive literary truths that seem to escape theoretical location. Thus he can also find 'poetry in the doctrines of Jesus Christ' (*A Defence of Poetry*; *Norton 2*, 524) while espousing aesthetical views and holding the bulk of Christian dogma, in its contemporary state-implicated form, to be deeply corrupt.

The textures of Shelley's thought are complex, notably in poems such as *The Triumph of Life*, where the conventional quest for knowledge is referred over to a mode of knowing that seems to offer at once the apparent contraries of oblivion and definition. Within a vision that answers to the poet's own 'thirst of knowledge',[5] Rousseau's request of the 'shape all light' (352), a plea for epistemological anchorage ('Shew whence I came, and where I am, and why' (398)), is answered by the 'shape' with prophetic, but proleptic, assurance: 'Arise and quench thy thirst' (400). He is promised not an answer, but a more vital sustenance; this takes the form of a vision (within a vision) that is ushered in through a moment of dissolution ('my brain became as sand' (405)) that is the prelude to a description of exquisite imaginative precision:

> 'Where the first wave had more than half erased
> The track of deer on desert Labrador,
>   Whilst the fierce wolf from which they fled amazed
>
> 'Leaves his stamp visibly upon the shore
>   Until the second bursts—so on my sight
> Burst a new Vision never seen before.—
>
>   (406–11)

Shelley's precarious yet indelible imagery is itself, in constituting an extended simile, anticipative of another vision that continues and demonstrates the poet's magnificently

---

[4] Quoted in Notopoulos, *The Platonism of Shelley*, 402–3.
[5] *The Triumph of Life*, 194. Shelley's poetry is quoted throughout from *Norton 2*.

undulating, dynamic sense of what knowledge—and thus what philosophy—might be; and it was in Plato perhaps more than in any other writer that Shelley discovered a depth of poetry always available not so much to answer questions as to pressurize the inevitable assumptions with which they emerge into the context of a scientific and rational modernity.

A very different, and in many respects an earlier, strand of Shelley's thought comes from the French materialists, of whom he read Laplace, Condorcet, Volney, Cabanis, and Holbach. Holbach, whom he translated in the summer of 1812, seems to have been particularly influential, his radically anti-Christian masterpiece *Système de la nature* (1770) being quoted at length in the notes to *Queen Mab*. There, in *The Necessity of Atheism*, and in a number of letters written in 1811–12 (notably to William Godwin and Elizabeth Hitchener), Shelley often discusses, in approving terms, materialist and necessitarian beliefs.[6] His consistent preference for a universal actuating principle over a conscious deity also appears to derive from this period of his intellectual development.

Although it is difficult to be precise, it seems that at some point from around 1813 Shelley began to drift away from materialist dogma towards the less systematic views we encounter in the later prose, a change he reflects upon in the short, enigmatic essay *On Life*, thought to be written in 1819:

> The shocking absurdities of the popular philosophy of mind and matter, and its fatal consequences in morals, their violent dogmatism concerning the source of all things, had early conducted me to materialism. This materialism is a seducing system to young and superficial minds. It allows its disciples to talk and dispenses them from thinking. But I was discontented with such a view of things as it afforded; man is a being of high aspirations 'looking both before and after', whose 'thoughts wander through eternity', disclaim alliance with transience and decay, incapable of imagining to himself annihilation, existing but in the future and the past, being, not what he is, but what he has been, and shall be. (*Norton* 2, 506)

Throughout his life, Shelley consistently attacked dualism, which he saw, at its worst, as an intellectually fraudulent attempt to rationalize a Christian worldview that in turn leads to a catastrophic diminishment of human potential. It was this, we are told, which led the young Shelley to materialism and its subversive critique of conventional mind or spirit versus matter dichotomies (Shelley's fascination with Spinoza's monism is also key here). But although—unlike Wordsworth—he didn't turn his back on the radicalism implicit in Holbach's materialism, and he does remain true to certain materialist-inflected positions (notably the non-creativity of mind), he nevertheless came to see the limitations of a system that argues for an entirely determined universe. As his dogmatic necessitarianism foundered upon Hume's theory of causality and a reconsideration of Godwin's coldly rational ethics (on grounds, often especially difficult to distinguish in Shelley's case, both philosophical and personal), he came to think of the universe proposed by the materialists as deeply inadequate to human 'aspirations'. Whether such a shift of alignment constitutes

---

[6] See, for instance, Shelley's letter to Godwin of 29 July 1812 (*Letters: PBS* I, 315–18).

a change of philosophical 'position', or whether it represents a change of attitude towards philosophy itself, is a question to which we will return.

Shelley's apparent shift away from materialism also has implications for his development as a poet. The most materialist of his major poems, *Queen Mab*, is also one of his most interesting formal experiments, although one he never repeated. Its subtitle ('A Philosophical Poem with notes') is something of an understatement given that the supplementary prose outweighs the poetry itself, a fact which might be taken to imply some distrust of poetry as a means of—as Shelley put it to his bookseller—'propagating my principles' (*Letters: PBS* I, 350). Shelley's sometimes brilliant, sometimes rather conventionally eighteenth-century verses can at times seem almost apologetic when read alongside their more modern-sounding, substantial, and scientifically and statistically thorough prose annotations. As Shelley moves away from materialist dogma, however, he also moves away from the assumptions that would appear to determine the formal choices of *Queen Mab*. Prose remains important, especially through Shelley's numerous Prefaces, to his work as a poet, but after *Queen Mab* it is not allowed to underwrite poetry to such an extent; nor does it assume such a scientific, explicatory role. Shelley's drift away from materialism, then, is bound up in an increasing trust in poetry as a convictive force, or at least in a reflexive wish for poetry to be trustworthy in this sense.

Perhaps the most important philosopher of all for Shelley was David Hume. Thomas Jefferson Hogg, in describing Shelley's unorthodox studies at Oxford, wrote that the 'soul of Hume passed [...] into the body of that eloquent young man'.[7] It is an insight that, although irrelevant to the ethereal, mystical poet-prophet Shelley favoured by the Victorians, has returned to the centre of Shelley studies, especially since the 1970s, when Kenneth Neill Cameron noted of Shelley criticism that 'in recent years the "Platonist" tide has begun to turn, and the emphasis has been placed on the British empiricists, especially Hume'.[8] The marks of the internalization described by Hogg are widely apparent. Shelley's polemical *Essay on a Future State*, for instance, draws heavily both on Hume's scepticism and his psychological account of belief.[9] In section ten ('Of Miracles') of *An Enquiry Concerning Human Understanding*, Hume famously argues that our evidence for miracles—the various recorded testimonies of miraculous events—is highly questionable, riddled as it is with inconsistency and the ulterior motives of religious dogmatism. As such, it should in no way, if we are to think aright, overbalance our instinctive and amply evidenced belief in the immutability of the laws of nature. It is the duty of rational beings, Hume concludes, to doubt miracles, and, implicitly, the religious accounts of the world they seek to uphold. Hume uses a process of what he calls 'mitigated' (or 'Academical') scepticism, by which he means radical or 'excessive' scepticism that has

[7] Quoted in Bieri, 102.

[8] Kenneth Neill Cameron, *Shelley: The Golden Years* (Cambridge, MA: Harvard UP, 1974), 151.

[9] For the essay's publication history and the difficult question of dating see *Julian*, VI, 361 and *Shelley's Prose or The Trumpet of a Prophecy*, ed. David Lee Clark (Albuquerque, NM: The University of New Mexico Press, 1966), 175. See also P. M. S. Dawson, *The Unacknowledged Legislator: Shelley and Politics* (Oxford: Clarendon Press, 1980), 283 for a proposed date of September–December 1818, and Steven E. Jones, in *BSM* XV, for a date 'from late 1818 to early 1819', 176.

been 'corrected by common sense and reflection'.[10] He makes no definitive or dogmatic claim either way, but does suggest that as it is impossible to live in a state of total sceptical indecision, we should, on the basis of the available evidence, incline our belief to what is most probable, which in this case would be the negative side of the question.

Shelley's case, in his *Essay*, that the 'desire to be for ever as we are' is the 'secret persuasion which has given birth to the opinions of a future state' (*Julian*, VI, 209) takes Hume's argument as its model. The essay seems in transit from materialist dogma to scepticism, approvingly introducing a materialist perspective, but stopping short of wholehearted agreement: 'Some philosophers—and those to whom we are indebted for the most stupendous discoveries in physical science, suppose [...] that intelligence is the mere result of certain combinations among the particles of its objects.' The 'suppose' just about keeps dogma at arm's length: it suggests inclination rather than certainty, and openness rather than decision. Shelley next, and in classical sceptical fashion, brings another dogma into play by introducing those who argue for 'the interposition of a supernatural power, which shall overcome the tendency inherent in all material combinations, to dissipate and be absorbed into other forms' (*Julian*, VI, 205). The tone implies Shelley's opinion of such views, yet his philosophical model remains Hume's 'mitigated' scepticism in that he now proceeds to investigate the contending claims of each side. He plays the arbiter, accusing both positions of a tendency to confuse contingency with necessity: were the existence of an intelligent God to be proven, he claims, this would not in turn prove the existence of life after death. Conversely, if an atheist account of the universe were to be established as fact, it would not necessarily follow that an 'animating power' does not survive the body (*Julian*, VI, 206).

Hume described this form of scepticism as a 'necessary preparative to the study of philosophy, by preserving an impartiality in our judgements, and weaning our minds from all those prejudices, which we may have imbibed from education or rash opinion' (*EHU* 200). Similarly, Shelley writes that in order to examine such a 'subject' as the immortality of the soul, it is necessary that 'it should be stript of all those accessory topics which adhere to it in the common opinion of men' (*Julian*, VI, 205–6). He also follows Hume in drawing what sounds like a 'mitigated' sceptical conclusion, that it 'is enough that such assertions [that there is an afterlife] should be either contradictory to the known laws of nature, or exceed the limits of our experience, that their fallacy or irrelevancy to our consideration should be demonstrated' (*Julian*, VI, 209). Strictly, Hume argues that such assertions are highly improbable rather than demonstrably fallacious (a negative dogmatic claim), although very high probabilities can for Hume amount to 'proofs',[11] which may explain Shelley's phrasing.

While Shelley often deploys sceptical procedures of this kind, there remain a number of considerations to bear in mind in discussing Shelley's scepticism. First, as we will see, there are times where he appears to reach beyond scepticism towards what has appeared

[10] David Hume, *An Enquiry Concerning Human Understanding*, ed. Tom L. Beauchamp (Oxford: Oxford UP, 1999), 207 (hereafter *EHU*).

[11] See section 6 of *EHU* ('Of Probability').

to more than one critic as a form of secularized Berkeleyan idealism. Second, 'mitigated' scepticism, although potentially subversive in the particular Humean manifestation discussed above, has historical and political associations inconsistent with Shelley's anti-establishment stance. A similar model, for instance, underpins the religious conservatism of anti-Reformation thinkers such as Montaigne, who argued (adapting classical Pyrrhonism) that the limitations of human reason should lead us to acquiesce in the face of established theological authority (a form of fideism) rather than create new metaphysical fictions that are necessarily meaningless from a philosophical (sceptical) point of view. It is risky, in other words, to de-contextualize and generalize Shelley's 'scepticism'—or, indeed, scepticism more generally—because it needs to be understood with reference to the specific historical conditions that determine its ideological impetus. Third, to identify the presence of particular philosophical traditions within a writer's oeuvre is not the same as offering an account of that writing in its literary specificity; this is certainly true for Shelley, whose fitting into philosophical tradition can seem at odds with the misfitting energies of his prose. While self-consciously following Hume's model, his tone and diction are typically more decisive. Even taking into account the point made above about Hume's notion of 'proof', he is less skilled, or less interested, in smoothing the tensions that inevitably accompany scepticism into an environment coloured by the passions and convictions of the individual mind. His prose is more immediately responsive to the fluctuations of his thought, composed less in the wake of a pre-decided conclusion that, when it does arrive, forms the least interesting part of the whole. The form of probabilism that Shelley partially inhabits, in other words, although identifiable on the spectrum of intellectual history with reference to Hume, becomes, amidst the shaping forces of a singular rhetoric, less easy to place.

Often, the literary forces he sets in motion break up polemic surfaces, leaving productive conflicts and ironies that enact a form of 'scepticism' no less powerful than the more self-conscious, ordered version proposed by Hume. This might work at the level of form, as it can in the philosophical dialogue, or within particular passages of literary animation. Here, for instance, while pointing to the emotional basis of most beliefs in an afterlife, Shelley suddenly becomes bound up in the thoughts and feelings of a man confronted with the passing of a loved one:

> The body is placed under the earth, and after a certain period there remains no vestige even of its form. This is that contemplation of inexhaustible melancholy, whose shadow eclipses the brightness of the world. The common observer is struck with dejection at the spectacle. He contends in vain against the persuasion of the grave, that the dead indeed cease to be. The corpse at his feet is prophetic of his own destiny. Those who have preceded him, and whose voice was delightful to his ear; whose touch met his like sweet and subtle fire; whose aspect spread a visionary light upon his path—these he cannot meet again. (*Julian*, VI, 20)

Although identifying the distortions inflicted upon philosophy by emotion, Shelley's own tone is far from critical and detached. Where earlier in the essay he patronizes the benighted 'common opinion of men', here, in moving from general to specific, he dignifies his subject, investing him with a refined, humane imagination. He becomes him, finding in the poetry of memory a moment of genuine rather than prejudiced human connection and recognition that overpowers initial purpose. The imperative assumptions of reason are decentred by the stark, unremitting fact that the corpse at our feet is prophetic of all our destinies, whatever philosophical views we may entertain. Through a turn to human immediacy the weak pulse of dogmatic atheism rises to a stronger beat.

What we witness here, amidst finely discriminated frictions, is an abrasive coming together of the generalizing theoretical and emotively immediate casts of mind that are both strong (and often complementary) in Shelley. Thus, while the passage might be cited quite legitimately as evidence of particular Shelleyan philosophical inclinations, this requires a zooming out from the textures of the prose that risks missing the peculiar ways in which the local modifies an always hankered-after Shelleyan universal.

II

While the *Essay* suggests some emphases of Shelley's thought, a fuller, and more complex picture emerges from a reading of *On Life* as well as the fragments that, following Mary's posthumous designation, have become known as *Speculations on Metaphysics* and *Speculations on Morals*.[12] Shelley's very definition of 'metaphysics' in the fragments as the 'science of all that we know, feel, remember and believe' (*Julian*, VII, 62–3) is, in its exclusive emphasis on human interiority, instructive. He accepts, that is, the empiricist position that philosophical discussion must restrict itself to sensory evidence and its combinations, a belief that can be extended to doubt the existence of a material reality external to mind. Although widely discussed in eighteenth-century philosophy, it was in the work of Sir William Drummond, who is quoted by Shelley as early as *Queen Mab*, that the poet found what he considered the most forcible discussion of this issue. Drummond's *Academical Questions*, a crucial source for *On Life*,[13] is a work of thoroughgoing scepticism that rigorously polices what it sees as philosophy's constant extension of itself beyond the verifiable. This, Drummond complains, has rendered us hopelessly confused about the true nature of things:

> We are not satisfied with speaking of the objects of our perception—of what we feel and understand. We seek to attach ideas to mere abstractions, and to give being to pure denominations. The dreams of our imaginations become the standards of our faith. Essences, which cannot be defined; substances, which cannot be conceived; powers, which have never been comprehended; and causes, which operate, we know not how; are sounds familiar to the language of error.[14]

[12] Again, exact dates of composition are difficult to determine. On this and other issues of textual history see *Julian*, VII, 341, *Shelley's Prose*, ed. Clark, 181 and *BSM* XXI, 188–91.

[13] The essay was written the same year that Drummond visited Shelley in Rome. See Bieri, 454.

[14] Sir William Drummond, *Academical Questions* (London, 1805), 166–7.

Misled by words that have come to substantiate delusions, we overlook the fact that we have no direct knowledge of these 'substances' and 'powers' whatsoever, and therefore no basis upon which to make claims about them. In this respect *Academical Questions*, the promised second volume of which did not appear, is largely a work of preparatory scepticism of the kind recommended by Hume. Shelley recognizes this when he writes, in *On Life*, that Drummond 'establishes no new truth', but works as a 'pioneer' to clear away 'the growth of ages'. Scepticism, he adds, leaves us with a 'vacancy', a 'freedom' of mind that allows unbiased clarity of thought (*Norton 2*, 507). According to Hoagwood, it is this recognized emancipation, as offered by the sceptical tradition, rather than a developed dogma or theory, that constitutes the 'philosophical field in which [Shelley's] work belongs'. Scepticism, in this reading, is for Shelley not simply a clearing away of error as preliminary to a systematic pursuit of truth, but represents in itself a valuable, and politically resonant, set of procedures that yield their own 'progressive value'.[15]

It was the possibility of a cautious reassertion of dogma, however, rather a wish to reclaim Pyrrhonian energies that drove—and divided—the British empiricists. Locke's dualism was an attempt to circumvent the radical scepticism suggested by the empiricism to which he also subscribed. This was contested by Berkeley (as it would be by Hume and Drummond), who proposed his idealist theory in its place. Berkeley jumped, that is, from scepticism about an external world of matter to the claim that existence *is* perception, that 'ideas', rather than being different in kind from the reality they apparently represent, are in fact constitutive of that reality. A similar jump appears to be taken for granted by the older Shelley,[16] who has, for that reason, often been associated with Berkeley.[17] In *On Life* he writes that 'I confess that I am one of those who am unable to refuse my assent to the conclusions of those philosophers, who assert that nothing exists but as it is perceived.' This 'intellectual system' (*Norton 2*, 507), as Shelley terms it, is readily acknowledged to be counter-intuitive, a 'decision against which all our persuasions struggle'. That 'the solid universe of external things is "such stuff as dreams are made of"', however, was—at least by 1819, and almost certainly before—something about which he appears to have entertained few doubts (*Norton 2*, 506).

Despite some clear similarities, however, we need to be cautious about Mary's claim that Shelley was a 'disciple' of Berkeley. As scholars have pointed out, any association of the two must be limited with reference to the latter's theology.[18] In Shelley's universe there is no room for a standardizing, overarching entity (for Berkeley, the Christian God)

[15] Terence Allan Hoagwood, *Skepticism and Ideology: Shelley's Political Prose and its Philosophical Context from Bacon to Marx* (Iowa City: University of Iowa Press, 1988), pp. xiv, 55.

[16] Shelley first read Berkeley at the suggestion of Southey, but was far from convinced, writing to Godwin that 'I have read Berkeley, & the perusal of his arguments tended more than anything to convince me that immaterialism & other words of general usage deriving all their force from mere *predicates* in *non* were invented by the pride of philosophers to conceal their ignorance even from themselves' (*Letters: PBS* I, 316).

[17] Mary claimed, after the poet's death, that Shelley 'was a disciple of the Immaterial Philosophy of Berkeley' (*Julian*, V, p. ix).

[18] See C. E. Pulos, *The Deep Truth: A Study of Shelley's Skepticism* (Lincoln, NE: University of Nebraska Press, 1962), 108.

to explain experiential consistency.[19] This absence raises some problems for Shelley, notably solipsism, which, as we will see, is rejected out of hand in *On Life*. A further implication, one Shelley recognizes, is that there can be no difference in kind—only in 'force' or social utility—between 'distinct thoughts' (those that appear to be universally experienced) and those 'obscure and indistinct' mental phenomena such as 'hallucinations, dreams, and the ideas of madness' (*Julian*, VII, 59). Where Berkeley proposes—as it were— a form of dualism within his monism in order clearly to distinguish between apparently objective experience and the freaks of subjective imagination, Shelley, without a clear, external point of reference, is less able to do this, and must conclude that the world really does consist of 'such stuff as dreams are made of'. These beliefs help us to understand the unique reality, one often experienced as unusually 'abstract', encountered in much of Shelley's poetry. Compared to Byron, say, who took a Johnsonian line on Berkeley (see the opening of *Don Juan*, canto XI), and who crams his satires full of vivid tangibles, Shelley is less interested in the feel of hard edges (there are exceptions), less comically and tragically involved in the relation of things to the spaces they occupy. In his universe 'material' objects have no privileged status, whereas visionary experience is largely impervious to the suspicions of common-sense dualism.

But if Shelley doesn't follow Berkeley (or at least follows him only so far), then where does he go instead? Part of the answer begins with the form of the fragments. In Clark's edition they are consolidated under the title *A Treatise on Morals (A Fragment)*, on the assumption that Shelley appears to have intended to write a full, systematic work in that tradition. While this is perhaps an overstatement of the work's coherence, it does appear that Shelley had ambitions in that direction, writing, as late as January 1819, that 'I consider poetry very subordinate to moral and political science, and if I were well, certainly I should aspire to the latter' (*Letters: PBS* II, 71). One of Shelley's models here would again be Hume, who proposes an objective 'science of human nature' (*EHU* 87) that begins with a naturalistic psychology and builds towards a practical ethics. Hume's assumption, one reflected by the progression from the first to the second enquiry (concerning, respectively, 'Understanding' and 'Morals'), is that a comprehensive study of human mental process will yield robust, generalizable principles concerning the moral nature of man, which will in turn enable a more accurate understanding of how that nature is best to be governed. Shelley's progression from 'metaphysics' to 'morals', although inflected by his reading of both Berkeley and Godwin, works along similar lines. If 'nothing exists but as it is perceived', and these perceptions are susceptible to taxonomic oversight (as the incipient form of Shelley's 'Little treatise' (*Julian*, VII, 79) implies), then it will be possible to produce an objective science of the mind: a 'catalogue of all the thoughts of the mind, and of all their possible modifications', as Shelley puts it, 'is a cyclopedic history of the Universe' (*Julian*, VII, 59). If we also accept, as Shelley does, the necessitarian view that we can no more escape the tendencies of our nature than 'the clouds can escape from the stream of the wind' (*Julian*, VII, 83), then through a 'determination of that arrangement of [distinct ideas] which produces the greatest and

[19] See Earl R. Wasserman, *Shelley: A Critical Reading* (Baltimore: Johns Hopkins UP, 1971), 144–5.

most solid happiness', we would be in a position to establish objective, ameliorative rules of government, or what Shelley calls a 'moral science' (*Julian*, VII, 71).

The bulk of the fragments on 'morals' is dedicated to sketching out, as a practical application of the proposed 'moral science', a social vision and attendant ethics that is atheist and broadly perfectibilarian in character. Shelley's utopia centres on the promotion of virtuous actions that are 'fitted to produce the highest pleasure to the greatest number of sensitive beings' (*Julian*, VII, 71). Religion has no place in this society because of its 'tendency to pollute the purity of virtue' (*Julian*, VII, 80) by reducing it, through its promises of heaven and threats of hell, to questions of self-interest and fear. Shelley also takes the anti-essentialist and Godwinian view that evil is not inherent in human nature, as well as accepting that virtue is a social construct, although the latter position is modified by the claim (one evidenced by a dubious and very un-Godwinian account of pre-Christian heroism) that 'benevolent propensities are [...] inherent in the human mind', and that we are naturally predisposed to virtue because we 'experience a satisfaction in being the authors of [others'] happiness' (*Julian*, VII, 77).

The question of where Shelley's 'metaphysics' tend, then, can be answered with reference to the poet's revisionary political agenda. He is not engaged in an abstract pursuit concerned with cosmic solutions, but with providing a philosophical foundation upon which a just society might be built. But while this conclusion fits the fragments in terms of tradition, form, and general intellectual momentum, there are moments where Shelley's rhetoric takes on a visionary colouring that appears to gesture beyond political science. He writes, for instance, that by 'considering all knowledge as bounded by perception [...] we arrive at a conception of Nature inexpressibly more magnificent, simple and true, than accord[s with] the ordinary systems of complicated and partial consideration' (*Julian*, VII, 60). What begins in quite conventional terms—at least in the context of Shelley's intellectual inheritance—moves in the direction of an ineffable 'conception' that while inviting metaphysical interpretation is given no obvious metaphysical value ('God', the Sublime', etc.). We start with a set of identifiable philosophical procedures that are further stabilized with reference to a clear political agenda, yet we arrive at something very different, and seemingly beyond the point where reason and language can claim effective control.

The fragments provide considerable information about Shelley's philosophical interests and how they shaped his thought, yet it is perhaps their failure—their ironic textual status as incomplete system—that tells us most about Shelley as a writer. Shelley couldn't do philosophy like Locke or Hume, not just because of his fragile health, but because his mind was always rushing to a point of ultimate significance (but also resistance) that as both ending and beginning identifies the methodologies of system as secondary. He comes to be most interested in systematic philosophy (as he is with Drummond's) not for its own sake but insofar as it allows him to realize his own distinction between 'thinking' and 'talk'. His own later theoretical prose correspondingly becomes less systematic and more full-blooded in its literariness; it is most engaged and engaging at points of interruption or challenge, such as where form becomes a dominant semantic mode, or where the ashes of systematic ambition become the seedbed of poetry.

Poetry has a way of making its voice heard, of suggesting its possibilities, even in some of the more unpromisingly dry areas of Shelley's philosophical prose. Here, in the third 'metaphysical' fragment (*Difficulty of Analyzing the Human Mind*), Shelley confronts the vanity, or at least the extreme complexity, of attempting to render the chaos of subjectivity as an orderly 'science':

> But thought can with difficulty visit the intricate and winding chambers which it inhabits. It is like a river whose rapid and perpetual stream flows outwards;—like one in dread who speeds through the recesses of some haunted pile, and dares not look behind. The caverns of the mind are obscure, and shadowy; or pervaded with a lustre, beautifully bright indeed, but shining not beyond their portals. (*Julian*, VII, 64)

This galloping of metaphors marks an incipient recognition not only that a scientific 'metaphysics' is beyond (or beneath) Shelley, but that his path as a writer lies elsewhere. The writing suggests the problem at stake by confronting the reader with a gush of similes that in its suggestiveness and compression pressurizes cognitive discrimination (a technique used to great effect in *The Triumph of Life*). But while this literary dynamism participates in a sceptical economy by proposing that thought escapes orderly analysis, it also, in realizing an approximation of mind and word, suggests a more optimistic epistemology, at least in its own terms. The mind is a 'perpetual stream' but so, in prolepsis, is the flow of Shelley's prose. If, in recognizing this, we accept the possibility of formal as well as analytic veracities, we potentially come to transcend the assumptive framework that Shelley lays down in his fragments, just as the poet himself found it insufficient to contain his mind. It is from here that we begin to understand the very different—essayistic and literary—formal and stylistic choices Shelley makes when he writes his best 'philosophical' prose.

III

On Life, an essay with no desire to be a thoroughgoing or systematic work of philosophy, is amongst other things an attempt to pursue the 'conception' that Shelley runs up against in the fragments. Rather than a definition of purpose and terms, the essay opens with a passionate avowal of 'Life, and the world, or whatever we call that which we are and feel' (*Norton 2*, 505). This notion of 'life' is derived by Shelley from Drummond's 'system'. Where the latter's scepticism 'establishes no new truth', it does, Shelley believes, suggest a particular direction for speculation: the 'view of life presented by the most refined deductions of the intellectual philosophy is that of unity' (*Norton 2*, 508). If we replace a 'complicated' dualism grounded in the idea of individual material entities with a monism that considers all existence to be of the same 'intellectual' nature, then we are conducted to a radically different 'view' of things from the one commonly accepted. 'Pursuing the same thread of reasoning', Shelley arrives at a striking claim:

> the existence of distinct individual minds similar to that which is now employed in questioning its own nature is found to be a delusion. The words, *I, you, they*, are not signs of any actual difference subsisting between the assemblage of thoughts thus indicated, but are merely marks employed to denote the different modifications of the one mind. (*Norton 2*, 508)

This stated, Shelley realizes that in questioning the 'existence of distinct individual minds' he might be taken to imply solipsism, and is quick to exclude the possibility that 'I, the person who now write and think, am that one mind' as a 'monstrous presumption'. The writer is 'but a portion of' existence, one of many 'modifications' of an infinitely larger 'assemblage' of perceptions (*Norton 2*, 508). This caveat in place, Shelley proceeds to explain that his 'view' appears so counter-intuitive because it has become lost to us, that our intuitions have become reconfigured by the false but overwhelmingly dominant logic of dualism. Drummond's complaint that we are misled into a philosophically invalid understanding of things by 'the language of error' is taken to indicate a profound failure, or lapse, of perception. 'Life' is the 'great miracle [that] we admire not'. We have become inured to it, unresponsive; it has receded into a 'mist of familiarity [that] obscures from us the wonder of our being' (*Norton 2*, 505). 'Our whole life', with its habitual, repetitive processes and abstracting linguistic systems, is (in a phrase that echoes Drummond) 'an education in error' (*Norton 2*, 507). This perceptual deterioration will become apparent if we reflect upon our childhood when 'we less habitually distinguished all that we saw and felt from ourselves'. As adults, we are reminded of this condition if we enter the 'state called reverie', when we feel as if we were 'dissolved into the surrounding universe' (*Norton 2*, 507).

There is something here of the Shelleyan sublime:

> Dizzy Ravine! and when I gaze on thee
> I seem as in a trance sublime and strange
> To muse on my own separate phantasy,
> My own, my human mind, which passively
> Now renders and receives fast influencings,
> Holding an unremitting interchange
> With the clear universe of things around;
>
> ('Mont Blanc', 34–40)

That sudden slowing as Shelley ponders his 'human mind' is a moment both of alienation and revelation, a recognition that what is 'familiar', however fundamentally it defines our sense of self, is finally inauthentic, a 'separate phantasy'—or fantasy of separation—that must be overcome in order for 'mind' and 'clear universe' to be recognized in their true alignment.

Given the dense and often abrupt intellectual allusiveness—both within and without Shelley's oeuvre—of *On Life*, it is perhaps not surprising that the question of how we are to understand the 'one mind' has provoked considerable debate. Pulos, rejecting Platonic or quasi-Berkeleyan interpretations, sees it not as a metaphysical but a psychological concept, which he likens to a Jungian theory of 'collective unconscious'. The poet, he claims, 'exhibits the sincere idealism of the transcendentalist, but not his dogmatism'.[20] Wasserman agrees with Pulos that the idea develops out of Shelley's 'native scepticism', but goes further to argue for Shelley's proposal of an 'objective idealism dependent upon a non-theistic and nontranscendent Absolute'.[21] Wasserman's upgrading of the 'one mind' to the 'One Mind' (perhaps thinking also of the 'One' of *Adonais*),[22] however, has been widely contested, most severely perhaps by Hoagwood, who, in arguing for Shelley's sceptical rejection of any such dogmatic postulate, dismisses Wasserman's account as 'densely contradictory'.[23] On a different tack, Timothy Clark offers a demystifying and historicist counter-reading, arguing that the 'one mind may be compared to the popular notion, in critical works of the period, of the "public mind" as an atmosphere of public opinion within which all think and act'.[24] It might be asked why such a 'notion' required such an intense engagement with technical philosophy; but, this aside, Clark usefully reminds us not to depoliticize Shelley's vision. Although *On Life* lacks the fragments' incipient formal commitment to political solutions, it is, as with almost all of Shelley's writings, a work with clear political ramifications. Before he describes its philosophical basis in the 'most refined abstractions of logic', Shelley has already established a political value for his subject. In its 'astonishing' magnificence, 'life' has some of the obliterating force of the 'lone and level sands' ('Ozymandias', 14) of 'Ozymandias': 'What are changes of empires, the wreck of dynasties with the opinions that supported them; what is the birth and extinction of religious and of political systems to life?' (*Norton 2*, 505). Shelley's reading of 'life' as a magnificent unity of which we have lost sight is at least as much a revolutionary allegory as it is an act of philosophical positioning. And although the essay's rhetoric has, on the face of it, little to do with the realities of early nineteenth-century political culture, we should not forget the extent to which these realities forged Shelley's literary character. He is clearly writing in a broad 'metaphysical' tradition that takes in, among others, Berkeley and Drummond, but he is also writing in a utopian tradition (including Plato's *The Republic* and his own *Revolt of Islam*) that takes as its destination a just and fair society, something that, from where Shelley was standing, may well have appeared an almost unimaginable other. While critics have tended to emphasize one tradition at the expense of the other, then, it is perhaps a peculiar challenge of Shelley's thought that they are conceived of as occupying the same place.

Where *On Life*, by naming the 'one mind' with reference to a wider metaphysical disquisition, does give grounds for an interpretation of Shelley's thought in terms of a partially developed system of idealist dogma, any such paraphrase is likely to miss its

[20] Pulos, *The Deep Truth*, 53, 8.   [21] Wasserman, *Shelley: A Critical Reading*, 147.
[22] Ibid. 149.   [23] Hoagwood, *Skepticism and Ideology*, 60.
[24] Timothy Clark, *Embodying Revolution: The Figure of the Poet in Shelley* (Oxford: Clarendon Press, 1989), 40.

complexity and fullness as an erratic but powerful living process. The 'one mind' is finally an ironic postulation, a brief, frustrated suspension of the linguistic scepticism that drives the essay: 'How vain is it to think that words can penetrate the mystery of our being' (*Norton 2*, 506). The 'one mind' is in these terms an emanation of Shelley's own vanity, and one that finds itself immediately corrected:

> It is difficult to find terms adequately to express so subtle a conception as that to which the intellectual philosophy has conducted us. We are on the verge where words abandon us, and what wonder if we grow dizzy to look down the dark abyss of—how little we know. (*Norton 2*, 508)

The words 'one mind' do correspond to a particular 'view' suggested by a particular 'metaphysical' direction that Shelley believes to be correct, and should not therefore be ignored or transferred over to the terms of a different debate; they are also, however, acknowledged as being used beyond the 'verge where words abandon us' and thus represent an admission of inadequacy more than a belief that something has been accurately described in any Lockean sense.

This leaves us with a stalemate of sorts, a halting of intellectual (and political) ambition in the face of a scepticism that recognizes the impossibility of any such project, at least insofar as it is carried through in the standard terms of philosophical disquisition. This might be seen, with Hoagwood, as a moment of emancipation, a finding in the energizing dialectics of philosophical doubt what becomes meaningless as philosophical dogma. On the other hand, Shelley's frustrated sense of abandonment hardly suggests sceptical acceptance in the face of mystery; the poet's education in 'how little we know' is written more as a cosmic, Promethean struggle than the calm acquisition of Pyrrhonian or Socratic wisdom. Shelley feels the pain of bewilderment and contradiction—and resists it—more than the philosophical sceptic does. The latter may acknowledge insufficiency, but he also puts it aside in favour of probabilism or (the deeply un-Shelleyan) *ataraxia* or tranquillity. Granted, sceptical and literary casts of mind have much in common, and if we broaden the field of 'scepticism' sufficiently it would be easy enough to find in it a place for Shelley (and many other poets). But if we wish to say that he 'belongs' to the 'philosophical field' of scepticism, that he stands as a *philosopher* in the tradition of philosophical scepticism, then we could do so only by closing ourselves to the particularities of literary experience. We would need to overlook Shelley's rhetorical abrasion of scepticism in the interests of paraphrase, and to read the 'philosophical' prose without reference to its own formal qualities, and, more generally, to assess Shelley-as-philosopher without reference to Shelley the poet. What would be needed, that is, is precisely the kind of enforced separation of the philosophical from the literary upon which Hoagwood's case explicitly rests.[25]

Such an approach is questionable, not only because it excludes the complicating thoughtfulness of form from our consideration of a poet's thought, but because Shelley explicitly argues that it is in poetry—rather than in systematic philosophy of any kind—that we find a solution of sorts to the problem we run up against in *On Life*.

---

[25] See Hoagwood, *Skepticism and Ideology*, pp. xiii–xiv.

In *A Defence of Poetry*, amidst the elevated sentences of which we witness an unprecedented coming into alignment of Shelley's theoretical and aesthetic commitments, it is claimed that a vitally creative and original poetry, in marking the 'before unapprehended relations of things' (*Norton 2*, 512), works to overcome our subjection to an ordinary language that has become moribund and limiting. Poetry dispels the familiar and 'withdraws life's dark veil from before the scene of things' (*Norton 2*, 533); it is a revelatory, prophetic force, a radical, disruptive energy that offers our main chance of actualizing truth. Such beliefs give Shelley's own poetry (including the prose-poetry) a peculiar philosophical interest, and make it an essential source for our assessment of him as a philosopher; where philosophy for Shelley breaks down at the moment where 'words abandon us', poetry works through a different kind of linguistic functionality that for Shelley has profound implications for the human search for truth. If we assume that Shelley's own poetry is informed by such thinking, then it follows that close attention to that poetry's linguistic, intellectual, emotional, and formal singularity must be a primary rather than an incidental mode of enquiry with respect to Shelley-as-philosopher. To privilege the philosophical prose as evidence in establishing 'a philosophical account of Shelley's philosophical work' is thus,[26] while not in itself unreasonable, to risk a decidedly un-Shelleyan distancing of theory from form.

The intense investment in poetry we encounter in *A Defence* relegates 'philosophy', understood as the systematic exposition of ideas and theories, to a supporting role in the thought of Shelley's maturity, except where it is judged (as in the case of Plato) to transcend this and become poetry in its own right. It is in these terms that Shelley places such a high value on the 'intellectual system', to which he responds not primarily as a set of rational procedures—albeit it is derived from such—but as an aesthetic artefact, a thing of wonder, a dizzying vision like a sublime poem or a stunning natural prospect. It is 'philosophical' not because of its systematic intellectual status, but insofar as it manifests remarkable intellectual possibilities that have the capacity to stimulate and reorganize degraded perception. It was thus inevitable that *On Life* must bury its own most striking words ('the one mind') and resurrect its problematics within the great poetry that Shelley wrote around the time of its composition. This enweaving of philosophy and poetry, or the redefinition of the former in the latter's terms, is suggested in the passage (quoted above) in which Shelley makes his crucial distinction between 'thinking' and 'talk'. It is striking that this is elaborated not in terms of a theoretical recognition, or a changing of systems—materialism to idealism or scepticism—but through a change of prose texture and a paired allusion to the pinnacles of English poetic thought, *Hamlet* and *Paradise Lost*: 'man is a being of high aspirations "looking both before and after," whose "thoughts wander through eternity"'. These invocations—both of tradition and of a consciously unsystematic mode of thought—signal a real but never complacent subsuming, for Shelley, of philosophical activity by poetic meaning; they also suggest the extent of the task facing scholars of Shelley's philosophy, something which can be approached, but not finally understood, through traditional methods of intellectual history and paraphrase.

---

[26] Hoagwood, *Skepticism and Ideology*, p. xiv.

SELECT BIBLIOGRAPHY

Cameron, Kenneth Neill. *Shelley: The Golden Years*. Cambridge, MA: Harvard UP, 1974.

Cronin, Richard. *Shelley's Poetic Thoughts*. London: Macmillan, 1981.

Hamilton, Paul. 'Literature and Philosophy'. *The Cambridge Companion to Shelley*. Ed. Timothy Morton. Cambridge: Cambridge UP, 2006. 166–84.

Hoagwood, Terence Allan. *Skepticism and Ideology: Shelley's Political Prose and its Philosophical Context from Bacon to Marx*. Iowa City: University of Iowa Press, 1988.

Hogle, Jerrold E. *Shelley Process: Radical Transference and the Development of his Major Works*. Oxford: Oxford UP, 1988.

Keach, William. *Shelley Style*. New York: Methuen, 1984.

King-Hele, Desmond. *Shelley: His Thought and Work*. London: Macmillan, 1960.

Notopoulos, James A. *The Platonism of Shelley: A Study of Platonism and the Poetic Mind*. Durham, NC: Duke UP, 1949.

Pulos, C. E. *The Deep Truth: A Study of Shelley's Scepticism*. Lincoln, NE: University of Nebraska Press, 1962.

Reiman, Donald H. *Intervals of Inspiration: The Skeptical Tradition and the Psychology of Romanticism*. Greenwood, FL: Penkevill, 1988.

Wasserman, Earl R. *Shelley: A Critical Reading*. Baltimore: Johns Hopkins UP, 1971.

Williams, Merle A. 'Contemplating Facts, Studying Ourselves: Aspects of Shelley's Philosophical and Religious Prose'. *The Unfamiliar Shelley*. Ed. Alan M. Weinberg and Timothy Webb. Farnham: Ashgate, 2009. 199–219.

CHAPTER 7

···

RELIGION AND ETHICS
The Necessity of Atheism, A Refutation
of Deism, On Christianity

···

GAVIN HOPPS

IN 1816, the year without a summer, in a hotel visitors' book in the Vale of Chamonix, Percy Shelley famously added after his name, in Greek, 'Democrat, Philanthropist, and Atheist.'[1] Visiting the same hotel, though not before Southey had seen and been scandalized by Shelley's inscription, Byron discreetly erased the entry, commenting, according to Hobhouse's *Recollections*, 'Do you not think I shall do Shelley a service by scratching this out?'[2] Quite a lot has been made in recent years of the act of erasure or disfiguration, so it is hard not to notice the symbolic resonances of Byron's 'scratching out'. Writing of *The Triumph of Life*, for instance, Paul de Man suggested that the poem's nebulous and fugitive figures, its radically ambiguous syntactic tangles, and its paratactic series of receding questions present us with a self-effacing narrative that allegorizes its own inscrutability.[3] On a historical level, and closer to our immediate concerns, Martin Priestman has helpfully highlighted the ways in which writers, editors, and critics of the Romantic period have sought to erase the vital and varied atheism which he contends was 'central to the age'.[4] The discreet effacement of Shelley's atheism at the hands of Byron may, however, I would like to suggest, present us with an allegory of another kind. For in spite of considerable critical attempts to distance the poet from his own declarations, the label 'atheist' persists with a 'near miraculous suspension' in the public perception of Shelley.[5] In this chapter, I shall examine the legitimacy of this association, based on the evidence of his writing on religion in prose.

---

[1] As Gavin de Beer has shown, there were in fact no fewer than four such inscriptions. See 'An "Atheist" in the Alps', *Keats–Shelley Memorial Bulletin* 9 (1958), 1–15.

[2] Baron John Cam Hobhouse Broughton, *Recollections of a Long Life* (New York: Charles Scribner's Sons, 1909), II, 9.

[3] 'Shelley Disfigured', in *The Rhetoric of Romanticism* (New York: Columbia University Press, 1984).

[4] Martin Priestman, *Romantic Atheism: Poetry and Freethought, 1780–1830* (Cambridge: Cambridge UP, 1999), 2.

[5] The phrase in quotation marks is from 'Shelley Disfigured', *The Rhetoric of Romanticism*, 109.

I

Shelley hated Christianity with a vengeance and raged against it from an early age. Writing to Hogg in 1810, for example, encouraged by disappointment in love with his cousin Harriet Grove, he exclaimed:

> Oh! I burn with impatience for the moment of Xtianity's dissolution, it has injured me; I swear on the altar of perjured love to revenge myself on the hated cause of the effect which *even now* I can scarcely help deploring.[6]

His early Gothic romances *Zastrozzi* and *St. Irvyne* are similarly laced with anti-religious views, and even at Eton, according to Hogg, he was known as 'Shelley the Atheist'.[7] However, it was the publication of a seven-page pamphlet in 1811 that ended Shelley's academic career and commenced his lifelong association with atheism.

Whilst there is a certain amount of recycling in his prose writings on religion (the note to 'There is no God' in *Queen Mab*, *A Refutation of Deism*, and the essay *On Christianity* all rework material from *The Necessity of Atheism*), there are also significant alterations in his views—especially in his attitude towards Christ. It will therefore be helpful to set out the claims of his principal anti-religious prose works separately, before considering more generally in what sense, if at all, they merit the label 'atheistic'.

Although it is difficult to say precisely who did what, and although the witnesses give conflicting statements—and often don't even agree with themselves—it seems safe to say that *The Necessity of Atheism* was jointly authored by Shelley and Hogg.[8] It also seems clear that 'the central atheistic argument' was Hogg's (though it is based on Locke's *Essay Concerning Human Understanding* and Hume's essay *Of Miracles*) and that this had its origin in a letter to Shelley in January 1811.[9] The poet's reply, from Oxford, on 17 January, appears to be more concerned with the fate of Hogg's manuscript of *Leonora*; however, the seed had been sown and Shelley declared: 'Your systematic cudgel for Xtianity is excellent.'[10]

---

[6] 20 December 1810. *Letters: PBS* I, 27.

[7] Thomas Jefferson Hogg, 'The Life of Percy Bysshe Shelley', in Humbert Wolfe (ed.), *The Life of Percy Bysshe Shelley*, vol. I (London: Dent, 1933), 91. There is some dispute as to whether the phrase has any real theological significance; as Kenneth Neill Cameron notes: 'Hogg claims that Shelley informed him that this title referred to a kind of schoolboy office—"youths of the greatest hardihood might be considered as boys commissioned for executing the office of Lord High Atheist"—and hence, had no theological connotation. But Dowden [...] failed to find any trace of such an "office" at Eton, and while Shelley may have received the title partly for his defiance of the masters (the Gods of Eton), it is probable, in view of Hogg's practice of toning down Shelley's views, that [...] the title also indicates anti-religious sentiments.' Cameron, *The Young Shelley: Genesis of a Radical* (New York: Octagon Books, 1973), 326 n. 156.

[8] For a summary discussion of the questions surrounding joint authorship, see *The Prose Works of Percy Bysshe Shelley*, vol. I, ed. E. B. Murray (Oxford: Clarendon Press, 1993), 321–2 (hereafter cited as *Murray: Prose*).

[9] Cameron, *The Young Shelley*, 329 n. 179.   [10] *Letters: PBS* I, 47.

This 'systematic cudgel' was edited, polished, and fitted with introductory and concluding material by Shelley, and arrived back from the printers in Worthing around St Valentine's Day, 1811.[11] According to Hogg, Shelley was especially pleased with the 'potent characters' QED with which it ends, on account of 'their efficacy in rousing antagonists'.[12] As the story of the pamphlet's efficacy in this respect is well known, let us turn to the substance of the argument itself.[13]

The pamphlet begins with an untraced quotation allegedly from Bacon's *De Augmentis Scientiarum*, and is followed by an 'Advertisement', whose perfectly judged modesty is part of its provocation:

> *As a love of truth is the only motive which actuates the Author of this little tract, he earnestly entreats that those of his readers who may discover any deficiency in his reasoning, or may be in possession of proofs which his mind could never obtain, would offer them, together with their objections to the Public, as briefly, as methodically, as plainly as he has taken the liberty of doing.* Thro' deficiency of proof. AN ATHEIST.[14]

The argument proposes, with terse, temperate, textbook neutrality, to 'consider the nature of Belief', which, following Locke, the authors maintain is an involuntary 'passion of the mind', which 'perceives the agreement or disagreement of the ideas of which it is composed'. These ideas or 'degrees of excitement'—upon which 'our knowledge of the existence of a Deity' is based—are held to come from three sources: (i) the evidence of the senses; (ii) reason; and (iii) the testimony of others. The pamphlet considers each in turn and finds none of them sufficient to furnish a conviction. The authors are thus able, on the basis of their syllogistic reasoning, to draw two conclusions: first, that since proof on all three counts is lacking, 'the mind *cannot* believe the existence of a God'; and, second, if what we believe is involuntary, 'no degree of criminality can be attached to disbelief'.[15]

In 1813, between the appearance of *The Necessity of Atheism* and *A Refutation of Deism*, Shelley published his first major poem, *Queen Mab*, which is even more elaborate and vitriolic in its denunciation of Christianity. Indeed, in the effervescence of his anti-religious polemic, Shelley seems to want to have his cake and eat it, by suggesting that God is malicious *and* doesn't exist. The poem's Notes repeat the argument of *The Necessity of Atheism* and anticipate the subject matter of *A Refutation of Deism*, so won't be discussed in any detail here. Although there is one point on which the Notes differ from *The Necessity of Atheism*, which is worth highlighting. In the note to the line 'There is no God!' (VII, 13), Shelley qualifies the Fairy's declaration: 'This negation must be understood solely to affect a creative Deity. The hypothesis of a pervading Spirit co-eternal with the universe remains unshaken.'[16] The addition of the word 'creative', whilst obviously denying an essential attribute of the Judaeo-Christian God, makes explicit what is implicit in *The Necessity of Atheism*—namely, that Shelley has not

---

[11] Richard Holmes, *Shelley: The Pursuit* (London: Weidenfeld and Nicholson, 1974), 49.

[12] Hogg, *The Life of Percy Bysshe Shelley*, I, 165.

[13] See Holmes, *Shelley: The Pursuit*, 50–60, for a detailed description of the antagonists' arousal.

[14] *Murray: Prose* 2.   [15] Ibid. 3, 5.   [16] Ibid. 309.

abandoned the idea of God entirely, and still adheres to a belief in some sort of indwelling Spirit of Nature or Soul of the Universe.

A Refutation of Deism was probably written towards the end of 1813 and published anonymously in 1814. It is considerably longer than *The Necessity of Atheism* and takes the form of a dialogue between a Christian and a Deist (which may have been modelled on Hume's *Dialogues Concerning Natural Religion*). The work is also a good deal more complicated than *The Necessity of Atheism*, though it can be divided into two discrete parts for the convenience of discussion: an attack upon Christianity by the Deist, Theosophus, and an attack upon Deism by the Christian, Eusebes.

The dialogue opens with a pre-emptive defence of Christianity—which in fact provides the ammunition for its own demolition—and skilfully elicits the reader's animosity towards the position it purports to defend. And then the serious sport begins.

The anti-Christian speech of Theosophus commences with a prefatory section reiterating the argument from *The Necessity of Atheism* that belief is involuntary and hence cannot be a 'legitimate object of merit or demerit'.[17] He thereafter sets out to demonstrate that Eusebes' position is 'destitute of rational foundation'.[18] His assault proper begins with a sarcastic summary of the biblical narrative of Fall and Redemption, from which he draws a series of objections to Christianity. These pertain to: the violent, anthropomorphic conception of the Old Testament God and the barbarity of the early Church; the 'scandal of particularity'; the pernicious nature of Christian morality; the degree of evidence afforded by miracles and prophecies; and, by way of sarcastic conclusion, the apparent insufficiency of divine revelation.[19] Somewhat less hubristically than in his opening speech, Eusebes responds by conceding the difficulty of solving such objections 'by the unassisted light of reason'. However, he claims to be able to show how reason alone 'conducts to conclusions destructive of morality, happiness, and the hope of futurity, and [is] inconsistent with the very existence of human society'. Having thus set reason and faith over against each other, Eusebes then asks Theosophus to choose between 'cold and dreary Atheism' and Christianity, and—following a denunciation of the former by Theosophus—invites him to state 'the grounds of [his] belief in the being of God'. In this way, having persuaded Theosophus to reject reason as a 'faithless' guide, since this is alleged to conduct to atheism, Eusebes narrows the options to a debate between Deism and Christianity.[20] All that remains then for him to do is to undermine the credibility of the Deist's position, and Christianity—so Eusebes appears to reason—will be the last one standing.[21]

---

[17] *Murray: Prose* 99.   [18] Ibid. 100.

[19] Many of these complaints of course resurface in Shelley's poetry; in *Queen Mab*, for instance, he speaks of God as the 'almighty fiend', from whom there came a 'special sanction to the trade of blood' and who provoked in his followers an 'unnatural thirst | For murder, rapine, violence, and crime' (VI, 222; II, 157; VI, 128–9).

[20] *Murray: Prose* 122; 110; 111; 110.

[21] The arguments put forward by Theosophus, and duly refuted by Eusebes, follow traditional deistical lines: the argument from design; the universality of belief; and the ultimate causality implied by motion. For a detailed discussion of Shelley's sources and a contextualizing account of anti-religious literature, see Cameron, *The Young Shelley*, 274–9.

There is a dramatic irony to the dialogue though, which is lost on its participants; for Theosophus' speech has already vitiated Eusebes' position to an 'irrational' fideism. Thus, the latter's effective refutation of Deism means that the two arguments appear to cancel each other out, and the most plausible position at the end of their dispute turns out ironically to be atheism—which is slyly presented as a matter of fact, if only we had the courage to own it.[22]

Of Shelley's principal prose writings on religion, the essay *On Christianity* is the hardest to date and was left in the most fragmentary condition. The most likely date of composition, according to E. B. Murray, is late 1817, which may be conjectured from its presence in a notebook that includes drafts of poems written no later than January 1818.[23] The essay can be divided into four parts: a short introductory section on Christ's significance and the provenance of his teachings; a much longer section on Christ's conception of God and various Christian doctrines; a brief reflexive section on Christ's rhetorical strategies and the poet's own interpretative principles; and a final section on the equality of mankind. As, somewhat surprisingly, the essay *On Christianity* is in a sense the most original and 'creative' of Shelley's prose writings on religion, it will be instructive to consider each of these sections in a little more detail.

The introductory fragment asserts the superlative significance of Christ (the 'being who has influenced in the most memorable manner the opinions and the fortunes of the human species') but seeks to separate his humanity from his divinity, which is consistently bracketed throughout the piece: 'I protest against any prejudication of the controversy (if indeed it can be considered a disputable point) as to whether Jesus Christ was something divine or no. I make an abstraction of whatever miraculous or mysterious is connected with his character and his history. Enough remains to afford a theme for amplest elucidation.'[24] Shelley then sketches the socio-political context out of which, he claims, Christ's teachings emerged—which, as Cameron remarks, appear curiously parallel to the poet's own.[25] The second and longest but also fragmentary section is headed 'God' in the manuscript. This begins with some general conjectures concerning Christ's 'Romanticised' notion of God and Shelley's 'Romanticised' notion of Christ—whose heart is attuned by Scripture to the 'still, sad music of humanity'. (If the style of *The Necessity of Atheism* may be characterized by the language of syllogistic reasoning, and that of *A Refutation of Deism* may be described as a spirited academic dispute, the section

---

[22]   As Earl R. Wasserman notes, 'the absence of any atheist to argue his own position is a strategic irony that makes atheism all the more insidiously compelling'. *Shelley: A Critical Reading* (Baltimore: Johns Hopkins UP, 1971), 14.

[23]   *Murray: Prose* 460.

[24]   Ibid. 246–7. Whilst Shelley protests against any 'prejudication' of the matter of Christ's divinity, he is rather less opposed to such pre-emptive judgements in his notes to *Queen Mab*: 'Jesus was sacrificed to the honour of that God with whom he was afterwards confounded. It is of importance, therefore, to distinguish between the pretended character of this being as the Son of God and the Saviour of the world, and his real character as a man, who for a vain attempt to reform the world, paid the forfeit of his life to that overbearing tyranny which has since so long desolated the universe in his name.' *The Complete Poetical Works of Percy Bysshe Shelley*, ed. Neville Rogers, I: *1802–1813* (Oxford: Clarendon Press, 1972), 319.

[25]   Kenneth Neill Cameron, *Shelley: The Golden Years* (Cambridge, MA: Harvard UP, 1974), 163.

on God in the essay *On Christianity* is undoubtedly the most poetic.) Christ's God, according to Shelley, is 'the interfused and overruling Spirit of all the energy and wisdom included within the circle of existing things'; he—or it—is 'something mysteriously and illimitably pervading the frame of things' and 'a power by which we are surrounded, like the atmosphere in which some motionless lyre is suspended, which visits with its breath our silent chords, at will'.[26] The remainder of this section is given over to a consideration of certain Christian doctrines, the traditional interpretation of which Shelley seeks to show is false, as he assumes 'the rhetorical posture of both exegete and higher critic of the New Testament'.[27]

The first of Christ's teachings he considers in detail is the Sermon on the Mount, which Shelley reinterprets—or rewrites—in two ways. 'Blessed are the pure in heart, for they shall see God.' What this means, according to Shelley, is simply 'that virtue is its own reward'; and any metaphysical construals of 'seeing God' are 'the idle dreams of the visionary or the pernicious representations of imposters who have fabricated from the very materials of wisdom a cloak for their own dwarfish and imbecile conceptions'.[28] Having bracketed the first part of Christ's teaching ('Blessed are the pure in heart') whilst reinterpreting the second ('for they shall see God'), he then brackets the second whilst reinterpreting the first, and allows the possibility of 'seeing God', but in a 'Romanticised' context:

> He [Christ] affirms that a being of pure and gentle habits will not fail in every thought, in every object of every thought, to be aware of benignant visitings from the invisible energies by which he is surrounded. Whosoever is free from the contamination of luxury and licence may go forth to the fields and to the woods inhaling joyous renovation from the breath of Spring, or catching from the odours and the sounds of autumn some diviner mood of sweetest sadness which improves the solitary heart. [...] he has already seen God.[29]

The second doctrine that Shelley considers is Christ's teaching on vengeance or retribution. Here, he more polemically contends that 'the doctrine of what some fanatics have termed a peculiar Providence, that is of some power beyond and superior to that which ordinar<il>y guides the operations of the Universe interfering to punish the vicious and reward the virtuous, is explicitly denied by Jesus Christ', and that according to Christ 'it is foreign to [God's] benevolent nature to inflict the slightest pain'.[30] Shelley's reinterpretation of the 'absurd and execrable doctrine of vengeance' is supported by a carefully reasoned argument in which he claims that since Christ 'instructed his disciples to be perfect as their father in Heaven is perfect', and since perfection required 'refraining from revenge or retribution in any of its various shapes', it therefore follows that 'the divine character' is 'incapable of malevolence or revenge'.[31]

---

[26] *Murray: Prose* 250, 251.   [27] Ibid. 461.   [28] Ibid. 251.   [29] Ibid. 251; 252.

[30] Ibid. 259; 252. For a discussion of Shelley's selective and self-serving citation of the Bible, see Bryan Shelley, *Shelley and Scripture: The Interpreting Angel* (Oxford: Clarendon Press, 1994), 56–62.

[31] *PWPBS* 259. For all the apparent orthodoxy of Shelley's reasoning, his arguing from man to God involves an *un*orthodox inversion of the scriptural logic of the *imago Dei*, and exhibits what Timothy Webb has referred to as a 'relocation of the centre of power in man rather than in God' (*Shelley: A Voice Not Understood* (Manchester: Manchester UP, 1977), 171).

In the midst of his consideration of vengeance and retribution, Shelley turns his attention to the subject of heaven and what happens after death. His account of Christ's teaching is worth quoting at length, since it involves an extraordinarily powerful visionary description of communion the other side of death:

> Another and more extensive state of being, rather than the complete extinction of being will follow from that mysterious change which we call death. There shall be no misery, no pain, no fear. The empire of the evil Spirit extends not beyond the boundaries of the grave. The unobscured irradiations from the fountain fire of all goodness shall reveal all that is mysterious and unintelligible until the mutual communications of knowledge and of happiness throughout all thinking natures constitute a harmony of good that ever varies and never ends. This is Heaven, when pain and evil cease, and when the benignant principle untram<mel>led and uncontrolled visits in the fullness of its power the universal frame of things.[32]

Following Shelley's examination of vengeance, there is a short section on Christ's rhetorical style (which is highly praised), the methodology of the Gospel writers (which is roundly condemned), and Shelley's own interpretative principles (which are somewhat problematical).[33] The final section of the essay—headed 'Equality of Mankind' in the manuscript—has in a sense the least to do with Christianity. It begins with a portrait of Christ as a social radical, who continues the work of Plato and Diogenes, and who wanted to establish 'an egalitarian republic'.[34] At this point, however, the essay becomes more of a sermon or a rallying cry than a description of Christ's teachings—exhorting the reader, apostrophizing mankind, and introducing an emotive personal perspective—at the end of which Shelley appends the clause 'Such […] appear to have been the doctrines of Christ'. The focus then shifts to Rousseau, who is described as 'the philosopher among the moderns who in the structure of his feelings and understanding resembles most nearly the mysterious sage of Judea'. In this final unfinished section of the essay, Shelley attempts to clarify what is meant by the injunction—attributed to Christ and Rousseau—to lead 'a pure and simple life', and argues that the Church's attempt to establish a 'system of equality' failed. To conclude, he offers a rousing statement of what is required for 'the annihilation of the unjust inequality of powers and conditions subs<is>ting in the world'.[35]

II

Now that we have before us a summary of his principal writings on religion in prose, we are in a better position to consider the legitimacy of ascribing the epithet 'atheist' to Shelley. In order to assess the matter precisely, it will be necessary to distinguish between

---

[32] *Murray: Prose* 255–6.

[33] Shelley's 'rule of criticism'—that we should form a general impression and then take or leave particular details according to whether or not they agree with this—obviously allows him considerable licence.

[34] Cameron, *The Golden Years*, 168.   [35] Ibid. 265; 266; 267; 270.

Shelley's views on ethics, theology, the Church and Christ, and second, to be cognizant of alterations in his views over time. It will also be helpful to be aware of the peculiarly modern conception of God against which Shelley's atheism defines itself. With these discriminations in mind, let us consider each of the texts in turn.

The first obvious problem we encounter when considering the legitimacy of describing Shelley as an atheist on the basis of his most notorious pamphlet is that he isn't exactly its author. As Cameron notes—and as the poet's letters in December and January 1810–11 reveal—whilst Shelley was 'the moving spirit behind [the pamphlet's] public appearance', the 'argument on the non-existence of a deity is Hogg's'.[36] The second problem, if we address the question to its joint authors, is that it doesn't actually give us what it says on the tin. As Carlos Baker points out, 'The title of his college pamphlet should have been *The Necessity of Agnosticism* rather than *The Necessity of Atheism*, for the general argument developed there is not that God does not exist, but rather that no proofs of his existence thus far adduced will stand up under rational scrutiny.'[37] This point has been reinforced recently by the theologian Alister McGrath:

> The essay actually makes a case for a practical agnosticism—or perhaps a sceptical empiricism—rather than atheism, in that Shelley's argument leads only to the conclusion that an informed mind cannot reach a reliable conclusion on the existence of God on the basis of the available evidence.
>
> Without in any way wishing to call the reliability of Shelley's judgement into question, it is very difficult to avoid the conclusion that his essay [...] does little more than make a point already familiar to generations of Christian theologians— that the existence of God cannot be proved and is ultimately a matter of faith. [...] The title of the treatise simply does not represent its contents; nor do its contents entail what the title proclaims.[38]

These assessments are confirmed by Richard Holmes, who observes that had Shelley chosen to defend the pamphlet on intellectual grounds, instead of refusing to acknowledge his part in its authorship, there's a good chance he wouldn't have been expelled:

> The fact is that Shelley must either have lost his temper or his nerve in choosing to defend himself in this oblique way. The pamphlet stood on the proposition that 'disbelief' could not be criminal; and that the whole object of the argument was to seek rebuttal. The authorship of the pamphlet was clearly known. If, then, Shelley had freely admitted that he (with Hogg) was the author, and that he had never claimed to make an outright statement of atheism, but merely demanded a proper intellectual inquiry into the matter on the logical principles of Hume and Locke (both academically respectable), his position would have been very strong.[39]

[36] *The Young Shelley*, 76.
[37] *Shelley's Major Poetry: The Fabric of a Vision* (New York: Russell & Russell, 1961), 29.
[38] *The Twilight of Modern Atheism: The Rise and Fall of Disbelief in the Modern World* (New York: Doubleday, 2004), 122.
[39] Holmes, *Shelley: The Pursuit*, 54–5.

Such complicating qualifications shouldn't surprise us, since they correspond to Shelley's mixed pronouncements on the subject of religion in the years around writing 'The Necessity of Atheism'. In January 1811, for example, in a letter to Hogg, he distinguishes his religious views from those of his co-author by writing:

> The word 'God' has been [and] will continue to be the source of numberless errors until it is erased from the nomenclature of Philosophy.—it does not imply 'the Soul of the Universe the intelligent & *necessarily* beneficent principle'—This *I* believe in; I may not be able to adduce proofs, but I think that the leaf of a tree, the meanest insect on wh. we trample are in themselves arguments more conclusive than any which can be adduced that some vast intellect animates Infinity [...].[40]

Just over a week later, and whilst inveighing against the moral system of Christianity, he writes again to Hogg: 'Oh! that this Deity were the Soul of the Universe, the spirit of imperishable love.—Indeed I believe it.'[41] And later the same year, he assures Elizabeth Hitchener that he acknowledges a God—defined as 'the *existing power of existence*' or 'the *essence* of the universe'—and would 'as gladly perhaps with greater pleasure admit than doubt his existence'.[42] In light, then, of the foregoing qualifications, which find positive corroboration in his correspondence, it seems reasonable to conclude, with David Lee Clark, that whilst Shelley exhibited an 'anti-clerical deism'[43] and raged against the Christian system of morality, he cannot at this period of his life be described as an atheist in the commonly accepted sense of the term.[44]

Since in the prefatory 'Advertisement' to *The Necessity of Atheism* the authors 'earnestly entreat' the reader to point out 'any deficiencies in [their] reasoning', it may be worth pausing for a moment to note that precisely the kind of rebuttal they invite is provided in the writings of John Henry Newman—whose Christian faith was itself vitally shaped by his reading of the Romantics.[45] Briefly, Newman agrees with the argument of 'The Necessity of Atheism' that our knowledge of the existence of God comes from reason, the evidence of our senses, and the testimony of others. He also agrees that none of these amounts to a conclusive proof. However, against the authors of *The Necessity of Atheism*, he argues that faith is based on an accumulation or convergence of things which *in themselves* are not a sufficient foundation, but which taken together can furnish conviction.[46] It might additionally be noted that such an account of faith—which seems to correspond to Shelley's actual practice[47]—leaves room for the will, for it

---

[40] 3 January 1811, *Letters: PBS* I, 35.   [41] 12 January 1811, ibid. 45.

[42] 11 June 1811, ibid. 101.   [43] Cameron, *The Young Shelley*, 73.

[44] David Lee Clark, *Shelley's Prose: Or, The Trumpet of a Prophecy* (Albuquerque, NM: University of New Mexico Press, 1966), 6.

[45] See John Henry Cardinal Newman, *Apologia Pro Vita Sua* (New Haven: Yale UP, 2008), 212.

[46] John Henry Newman, *An Essay in Aid of a Grammar of Assent* (Oxford: Clarendon Press, 1985). See also his *Essay on the Development of Christian Doctrine*, in which he speaks of a 'collection of weak evidences' which 'makes up a strong evidence' and of how 'one strong argument imparts cogency to collateral arguments which are in themselves weak'. *Conscience, Consensus, and the Development of Doctrine: Revolutionary Texts by John Henry Cardinal Newman* (New York: Doubleday, 1992), 125.

[47] See the letter to Hogg, quoted above, in which the poet defends a belief for which no proof can be adduced.

acknowledges that we are dealing with probabilities rather than certainties.[48] Thus, the act of assent is a commitment which is neither a simple perception of agreement nor a violent or arbitrary coercion of our inclinations.

One might also more radically object that the pamphlet's Advertisement is a loaded challenge, which pre-emptively narrows the range of admissible answers, since its methodological presuppositions—that God is an investigable object of thought, whose univocally conceived being is subject to 'proof', and that 'reasoning' is the ultimate arbiter of 'truth'—reflect a distinctively modern epistemology, which rules out in its very framing of the issue certain alternative conceptions of God.[49] By contrast, a pre-modern or postmodern theologian might want to reject altogether the premises of such an enterprise on the grounds that it involves an idolatrous anthropocentric episte-mology and a 'domestication' of divine transcendence.

Assessing the nature of Shelley's anti-religious views is a much more complicated task with respect to *A Refutation of Deism*. This is because of the ironic dialogical framework he employs as a way of articulating his critique of Christianity and the Deism of which he was previously an enthusiastic advocate.[50] The problem is not merely the ambiguity that attends a position which is negatively constituted and the consequent lack of an 'autho-rial' voice. The dialogue is also hard to assess because it is so obviously a staged fight, in which the speakers' defences seem designed more to allow their opponent to demolish their case than to reflect their ostensible positions. Indeed, it starts to seem a little like an episode of *The Sweeney*, as the antagonists conveniently bump each other off. Moreover, the Christian Eusebes is so clearly in both his rhetorical style and the arguments with which he espouses his cause an example of what Slavoj Žižek identifies as the over-conforming subversive—who sabotages his own cause through an all-too-literal support of it[51]—that it is difficult to assess the significance of Shelley's criticism.[52] Nevertheless, however staged their demolition of each other's perspective, and however imperfectly the speakers repre-sent their professed causes, it is evident that the author has an animus towards them. So what exactly are Shelley's targets, and what, if anything, does he leave undisputed?

---

[48] In spite of his assiduously rationalistic stance in *The Necessity of Atheism*, Shelley was evidently prepared to espouse the sort of fideism he appears to disdain in *A Refutation of Deism* and countenance believing what reason denies. As he writes to Elizabeth Hitchener: 'I have considered it in every possible light & reason tells me that death is the boundary of the life of man. Yet I feel, I believe the direct contrary.' 16 October 1811, *Letters: PBS* I, 150.

[49] As Gavin Hyman notes, 'pre-modern theological epistemology began with divine revelation and used this to extrapolate to and illuminate human realities. Modern epistemology did precisely the opposite. It began with human realities (notions of rationality, logic and so forth), and then extrapolated from these in order to reach transcendent truths.' *A Short History of Atheism* (London: I. B. Tauris, 2010), 142.

[50] May 1811, To Janetta Phillips, *Letters: PBS* I, 89.

[51] *The Plague of Fantasies* (London: Verso, 1997), 22.

[52] We find the poet employing a similar strategy in *Queen Mab*, where God is presented as a kind of stage villain, who brags about the things of which Shelley would accuse him: 'From an eternity of idleness | I, God, awoke; in seven days' toil made earth | From nothing; rested, and created man: | I placed him in a paradise, and there | Planted the tree of evil, so that he | Might eat and perish, and my soul procure | Wherewith to sate its malice, and to turn, | Even like a heartless conqueror of the earth, | All misery to my fame' (VII, 106–14).

If we draw the two sets of objections together, we can see that Shelley's critique of religion pertains on the one hand to ethics and ecclesial history (the wrathful God of the Old Testament, the violence of the early Church, and effects of Christianity's system of morals) and on the other to dogmatic apologetics (the lack of any proof for the existence of God, the fact that belief doesn't rest upon reason, the irrationality of prophecy and miracles, and the apparent insufficiency of revelation). What *A Refutation of Deism* does *not* dispute, however, is the possibility of a belief based on faith—or a combination of faith and reason, after the manner of Newman; and what, according to David Lee Clark, Shelley's polemic leaves a space open for is 'God as the soul of the universe—the animating principle of all life'.[53] Once again, this peculiar Shelleyan holding on to some kind of extra-materialistic belief in the face of an atheistic storm of his own making is corroborated in his correspondence. As he wrote to Elizabeth Hitchener in January 1811:

> I have lately had some conversation with Southey which has elicited my true opinions of God—he says I ought not to call myself an Atheist, since in reality I believe that the Universe is God.—I tell him I believe that God is another signification for the Universe.—I then explain—'I think reason and analogy seem to countenance the opinion that life is infinite—that as the soul which now animates this frame was once the vivifying principle of the *infinitely* lowest Chain of existence, so it is ultimately destined to attain the highest [...]'[54]

On the evidence of *A Refutation of Deism*, then, the description 'atheist' would once again appear not entirely to apply, for whilst Shelley is even more vigorous and extensive in his criticism of the Church, Christian ethics, and apologetics, he is unwilling to renounce a belief in 'something mysteriously and illimitably pervading the frame of things'—even if his scepticism keeps him from any further specification of this 'something'.

In Earl Wasserman's view, 'the real contest [in *A Refutation of Deism*] is implicitly between fideistic religion and rational atheism'[55]—which intriguingly correspond to what Wasserman identifies as the two most profound but opposing aspirations that 'persist unequivocally' in the 'labyrinthine confusion of Shelley's early intellectual probings'.[56] If this is the case, it suggests against the customary reading that the conclusion of *A Refutation of Deism*—whose ostensible openness appears irresistibly to steer us towards atheism—may in fact be a *genuine* openness that leaves undecided and unforeclosed the two opposing possibilities between which the poet himself is torn.

This is obviously not the place for a historical assessment of the effect of Christianity on Western civilization—however contestable Shelley's polemical account of it is (an impressive, corrective reading of this has in any case recently been advanced by David Bentley Hart[57]). Extending the invitation of *The Necessity of Atheism* to comment on the reasoning of

---

[53] *Shelley's Prose*, 118. Cameron similarly argues that the final section of *A Refutation of Deism* supports a belief in a 'coeternal spirit' and contains the roots of Shelley's future 'Berkeleian idealism'. *The Young Shelley*, 286.

[54] 2 January 1811, *Letters: PBS* I, 215.   [55] *Shelley: A Critical Reading*, 13.   [56] Ibid. 3.

[57] *Atheist Delusions: The Christian Revolution and its Fashionable Enemies* (New Haven: Yale UP, 2009).

the authors' critique, however, one might raise a question about the underlying logic of Shelley's rejection of Christianity. The problem with this—if one considers the matter in the strictly rational spirit of *The Necessity of Atheism*—is that Shelley tends to proceed by means of *argumentum ad conseqentiam*; that is to say, by arguing backwards from consequences. This is his self-conscious principle in forming his judgements ('all religions are good which make men good'[58]) and clearly a function of his faith in Godwinian perfectibility. Yet the desirability of a consequence has no logical bearing on the truth claim of the premiss. Thus, leaving aside the legitimacy of the complaint for a moment, if it could be established that Christianity is violent, oppressive, and unconducive to human flourishing, this does not mean that its God does not exist. One might of course conclude—as Shelley does—that such a God is morally repugnant. However, this is a different complaint altogether (and one that would require the kind of omniscience the atheist denies in order to assess its legitimacy). Hence, insofar as Shelley's rejection of Christianity involves a covert crossing over from ethics to ontology, the logic of its procedures may be called into question.

It is furthermore necessary to keep in view the historical specificity of Shelley's rejection and the conception of God upon which it is based; for as Gavin Hyman has shown, the evolution of atheism is inextricably bound up with the advent of modernity, and the God whose existence modern atheism denies is 'a specifically modern conception of God'.[59] To point out that such a God is 'a modern innovation and [...] in no way integral to religion itself'[60] does not of course constitute a decisive argument against atheism as such. However, it does make clear that 'atheists' like Shelley—or Richard Dawkins for that matter—whose denial is a mirror image of Enlightenment theism—reject a God that most postmodern and pre-modern theologians would reject too. What Shelley would make of postmodern conceptions of a God 'without' or 'otherwise than' being is hard to say. Yet it is also hard to say whether someone who rejects the existence of an idolatrous God may appropriately be described as an atheist.

The third of Shelley's major prose texts on religion is undoubtedly the most positive, though perhaps also the most conflicted. This is because it is, on the one hand, as vehement as ever in its censure of the Church and Christian teaching, and yet on the other hand speaks with awe and in superlatives of their founder (even if Shelley first of all remodels him after his own image). Similarly, whilst the essay in one sense consistently brackets metaphysical questions—in passing over Christ's divinity in silence—it is at same time continually drawn towards metaphysical concerns, in its poetic meditations on God and the afterlife. Of course, it's possible to argue that Shelley's imagination is freed and his scepticism suspended by the fact that he's speaking as it were 'second-hand' about Christ's notion of God and the afterlife. Yet as an absolute explanation this is unconvincing for a number of reasons. First, there is an obvious, elaborate, and consistent correspondence between the descriptions of God in the essay *On Christianity*—as a benign Power 'by which we are surrounded [...] which visits with its breath our silent chords'—and Shelley's own

---

[58] *An Address, to the Irish People*, 10. See also Shelley's well-known letter to Southey denouncing Christianity, in which he speaks of 'judg[ing] of the doctrines by their effects'. 17 August 1820, *Letters: PBS* II, 230.

[59] *A Short History of Atheism*, 63.   [60] Ibid. 119.

imaginings of such a Power in his poetry.[61] Second, when Shelley *doesn't* agree with an aspect of Christian teaching—or when he wishes to defer judgement (as in the case of Christ's divinity)—it is hardly his custom to be reserved about saying so. Nevertheless, there is still perhaps an element of truth in the objection, as a closer examination of Shelley's description—and his response to his own description—of the afterlife reveals.

Having presented us with a powerful visionary account of the nature of divine communion, the other side of 'that mysterious change which we call death', Shelley attempts to distance himself from his own imaginings by adding:

> How delightful a picture even if it be not true! How magnificent and illustrious is the conception which this bold theory suggests to the contemplation, even if it be no more than the imagination of some sublimest and most holy poet [...].[62]

What his reflexive scepticism takes away with one hand, however, in retrospectively casting his description as a hypothesis, it surreptitiously returns with the other; as the need he feels to disown the account suggests a defensive recognition—as though he were embarrassed in front of his own scepticism—of how much of himself is invested in it. We should also notice that it is left as an 'if'—so that his sceptical gainsaying is itself half gainsaid. (There is as well an odd kind of double-crossing logic to the apparent put-down 'even if it be *no more than* the imagination of some sublimest and most holy poet', since for Shelley of course there *is* nothing higher.) What we can see here, then, is the poet yearning in spite of himself for something he can't quite allow himself to believe in, which in turn won't allow his disbelief sovereignty either.

It should be apparent from the irruptions of Shelley's self-censuring scepticism, along with his contempt for the Church as well as some of its doctrines, that the author of the essay *On Christianity* is a long way from the conversion that Browning envisaged, if only Shelley had lived long enough.[63] Yet it should be equally clear, in view of the poet's serial infidelity to his own scepticism, his superlative assessment of the character of Christ, and his powerful affirmation of a Romanticized deity, that it would inappropriate to describe its author as an 'atheist'.

In conclusion, then, if we consider the three texts together, whilst there are some variations in Shelley's conception of the Power that 'mysteriously and illimitably pervad[es] the frame of things',[64] and whilst his hostility is fairly evenly divided between a range of religious targets, a consistent pattern seems to emerge, which is perhaps best rendered

---

[61] Interestingly, this correspondence isn't simply apparent in a pantheistic swerve away from orthodoxy; we also find both in his poetry and his prose works on religion a counter-tendency in his depictions of divinity, inchoately carrying them back towards orthodoxy, in their shuttling to and fro across the border of personhood. An obvious poetic example of such wavering personhood is the Dantesque 'One' in *Adonais*, who—or which—is described as 'That Light whose smile kindles the Universe' (54).

[62] *PWPBS* 256.

[63] *An Essay on Shelley*, in *The Oxford Authors: Robert Browning*, ed. Daniel Karlin (Oxford: Oxford UP, 1997), 586.

[64] See Clark, *Shelley's Prose*, for a summary of the poet's evolving conception of the deity in which he was 'unable entirely to disbelieve'. (The phrase in quotation marks is borrowed from Southey, Preface to *A Vision of Judgement*.)

by the paradoxical logic of the formula 'I know very well, but nonetheless.' For Shelley is on the one hand unfailingly contemptuous of institutionalized Christianity, which he believed had 'fenced about all crime with holiness';[65] and he is equally scornful of what he took to be some of its doctrines and its system of morality—whose 'Large codes of fraud and woe' 'blast the human flower | Even in its tender bud'.[66] He is also withering in his criticism of traditional theological apologetics, in particular concerning the role of reason—or lack thereof—in religious belief, and attempts to prove the existence of God. And yet, on the other hand, he was passionately attached to the founder of the system he hated so much—whom he praised as the 'most just, wise, and benevolent of men'[67]—and he was prepared to argue for 'a benevolent agency at work in the universe and, in some essential form, for a future state'.[68] This isn't quite a contradiction, though it was, for Shelley, a constant problem; since orthodox religion was, simultaneously, a witness and an obstacle to what he most wanted to believe in.[69] Even in *Queen Mab*—which has Voltaire's 'ÉCRASEZ L'INFÂME!' as one of its epigraphs—we find the poet ferociously attacking the Church, its doctrines, and the God of wrath, whilst also affirming an 'eternal world' pervaded by an 'active, living spirit', in which 'One aspires to Heaven' and 'Pants for its sempiternal heritage'.[70] As the poet succinctly phrases it himself, 'the eternal world | Contains at once the evil and the cure'.[71] These conflicting attitudes are inextricably conjoined in the personification 'killing Truth', which signifies Christ in *Hellas*:

> A Power from the unknown God
> A Promethean Conqueror came;
> Like a triumphal path he trod
> The thorns of death and shame.
> [...]
> The Powers of earth and air
> Fled from the folding star of Bethlehem;
> Apollo, Pan, and Love—
> And even Olympian Jove—
> Grew weak, for killing Truth had glared on them.
>
> (211–14; 230–4)

---

[65] *Queen Mab*, VII, 27.   [66] Ibid. IV, 104.

[67] Note 8 to *Hellas* (*Percy Bysshe Shelley: The Major Works*, ed. Zachary Leader and Michael O'Neill (Oxford: Oxford UP, 2003), 587).

[68] *Murray: Prose* 367.

[69] The conflict is explained by Walter Peck as follows: 'Not Christianity, but the accompaniments of Christianity—ritualism, that had grown upon the body of the church, or had been superimposed upon it as the faith of Christ fought its way forward through the Holy Land [...]; intellectual death that had followed the subjection of reason to faith in dogma; hypocrisy, in a church which, though it had arisen from a teaching of self-sacrifice, and love, and the forgiveness of sins, had since shut its New Testament, worshipped wealth and ease, countenanced war, and preached endless torment for the wayward sinner—it was upon these things that Shelley declared war' (*Shelley: His Life and Work*, I: *1792–1817* (Boston: Houghton Mifflin Company, 1927), 112–13). Carlos Baker argues similarly: 'Shelley's anti-Christian prejudice entered his thinking early and remained to the end. It was not so much that he disliked the ethical thought of Jesus Christ, which as a youth he had not understood, though he came later to a profound admiration for it. It was rather that in his opinion the whole teaching of Christianity had been utterly perverted and falsified by successive generations of theologians' (*Shelley's Major Poetry*, 29).

[70] IV, 139; I, 148–9.   [71] *Queen Mab*, VI, 31–2.

In Shelley's eyes, Christianity was fatal to truth in a dual sense, as it is responsible for a system of 'sophisms' which 'dim [...] | Bright reason's ray',[72] and yet, at the same time, in the sublime moral character of its founder and in its vision of a paradise of 'perpetual peace', 'across the night of life',[73] it bears witness to 'sacred and eternal truths' which eclipse all others.[74] It therefore seems that there was something prophetic about Byron's erasure of Shelley's atheism in the Vale of Chamonix in 1816, since on that occasion too the association persisted in spite of a lack of material evidence. Attempting to separate the 'evil' from the 'cure' is the underlying, heroic aim of Shelley's major prose writings on religion—a project which, however baffled by his own prejudices, cannot legitimately be described as 'atheistic'.

SELECT BIBLIOGRAPHY

Baker, Carlos. *Shelley's Major Poetry: The Fabric of a Vision*. New York: Russell & Russell, 1961.
Beatty, Bernard. 'P. B. Shelley'. *The Blackwell Companion to the Bible in English Literature*. Ed. Rebecca Lemon, Emma Mason, Jonathan Roberts, and Christopher Rowland. Chichester: Wiley-Blackwell, 2009.
Clark, David Lee. *Shelley's Prose: Or, The Trumpet of a Prophecy*. Albuquerque, NM: University of New Mexico Press, 1966.
Jones, Frederick L. 'Hogg and the Necessity of Atheism'. *PMLA* 52.2 (1937), 423–6.
McGrath, Alister. *The Twilight of Modern Atheism: The Rise and Fall of Disbelief in the Modern World*. New York: Doubleday, 2004.
O'Neill, Michael. ' "A Double Face of False and True": Poetry and Religion in Shelley'. *Literature and Theology* 25.1 (2011), 32–46.
Shelley, Bryan. *Shelley and Scripture: The Interpreting Angel*. Oxford: Clarendon Press, 1994.
Vaughan, Percy. *Early Shelley Pamphlets*. New York: Haskell House Publishers, 1972.
Wasserman, Earl R. *Shelley: A Critical Reading*. Baltimore: Johns Hopkins Press, 1971.
Webb, Timothy. *Shelley: A Voice Not Understood*. Manchester: Manchester University Press, 1977.
—— 'The Unascended Heaven: Negatives in *Prometheus Unbound*'. *Shelley Revalued: Essays from the Gregynog Conference*. Ed. Kelvin Everest. Leicester: Leicester UP, 1983. 37–62.
—— ' "The Avalanche of Ages": Shelley Defence of Atheism and *Prometheus Unbound*'. *Keats-Shelley's Memorial Bulletin* 35 (1984), 1–39.
Williams, Merle A. 'Contemplating Facts, Studying Ourselves: Aspects of Shelley's Philosophical and Religious Prose'. *The Unfamiliar Shelley*. Ed. Alan M. Weinberg and Timothy Webb. Aldershot: Ashgate, 2009. 199–220.

---

[72] Ibid. IV, 114–15.

[73] Ibid. IX, 238; *Prometheus Unbound*, III. iii. 172.

[74] This is how Shelley refers to the teachings of Christ in *A Defence of Poetry* (*Percy Bysshe Shelley: The Major Works*, 690).

CHAPTER 8

··

LOVE, SEXUALITY, GENDER

On Love, Discourse on Love, *and* The Banquet of Plato

··

TEDDI LYNN CHICHESTER

It seems that I must bid the Muse go pack
Choose Plato and Plotinus for a friend
Until imagination, ear and eye,
Can be content with argument and deal
In abstract things: or be derided by
A sort of battered kettle at the heel.

(W. B. Yeats, 'The Tower')

WHILE for Yeats, ascending his ancient tower in his sixty-third year, the battered kettle at the heel that marched him toward the sonorous music of Plato was the clanging 'caricature | Decrepit age', a more complex cacophony propelled Percy Shelley, not yet 26, into 'the splendour and harmony' of Plato's world and words.[1] After an often wretched final two years in England—marked by ill health, the suicide of Shelley's abandoned wife Harriet, and the poet's failed bid to gain custody of his and Harriet's two children— Shelley and his ménage ensconced themselves during the summer of 1818 in the idyllic Italian retreat Bagni di Lucca. While Italy promised some respite from personal scandal

I wish to thank Julie Giese, generous friend and ideal reader, and Jennifer Fordyce, my excellent research assistant.

[1] Shelley, Preface to *The Banquet of Plato*, in James Notopoulos, *The Platonism of Shelley* (Durham, NC: Duke UP, 1949), 402. Shelley translates the *Symposium* as *The Banquet*. Depending on context, I will alternate between these two titles. All quotations from *The Banquet* and *Ion* translated by Shelley, the Preface to *The Banquet*, and *A Discourse on the Manners of the Antient Greeks Relative to the Subject of Love* (hereafter *Discourse on Love*) are from Notopoulos. I cite *Laon and Cythna* and *Athanase* from *Longman*. Unless otherwise indicated, my text for Shelley's other writings is *Norton 2*.

and tragedy, it did not immediately release the poet's creative energies nor restore his artistic confidence, recently eroded by the forced revision—evisceration—of his most ambitious poem to date, *Laon and Cythna*, composed in the summer of 1817. Derided or ignored by the English critics and stalked by the shadow of his great rival and friend Lord Byron, also now residing in Italy, Shelley found his shaping spirit of Imagination, to use Coleridge's words, suspended, his sense of artistic mission blunted. As Michael O'Neill points out, 'the first months in Italy were a time of stocktaking, reading, and making literary plans', and Plato, especially the *Symposium*, his splendid dialogue on love, remained firmly at the centre of these endeavours.[2] If Shelley's Muse had, unbidden, packed up and left, Plato not only invited him to 'deal | In abstract things', but also to partake in the Greek philosopher's 'Pythian enthusiasm of poetry' until imagination, ear and eye rediscovered both the sensual music of love, and its even diviner chords, played most thrillingly by Socrates and Diotima in the *Symposium*'s sublime finale (*Banquet*, Preface, 402).

Not long before departing England—permanently—in March 1818, Shelley had been swept into the 'irresistible stream of musical impressions' of Plato's prose, and into the limpid channels of Platonic thought that he found both revelatory and liberating: artistically, intellectually, and erotically (*Banquet*, Preface, 402). Most recently, Plato had helped interweave various strands of Shelley's character—'the poet, the philosopher, and the lover' (*Alastor*, Preface, 73)—within his intimate circle of fellow writers and philhellenists in bucolic Marlow, where the Shelleys settled from the winter of 1817 until the following February. Along with Leigh Hunt, Thomas Jefferson Hogg, and the supreme classicist of them all, Thomas Love Peacock, Shelley turned his Marlow home, Albion House, into a kind of shrine to the Greek spirit and formed what Marilyn Butler has called the 'Cult of the South', where classicism, mythmaking, artistic innovation, radical politics, and paganism—the latter fully flush with sexual heat—fruitfully interfused.[3]

For both Shelley and Peacock it was the *Symposium* that proved most enchanting as they conjured 'sacred Hellas', both within their impassioned talks and their literary efforts (*Athanase*, 15 [cancelled sequence following l. 129]). While Peacock penned his Platonic verse romance *Rhododaphne*, Shelley composed his semi-autobiographical *terza rima* narrative *Athanase*, in which his hero, 'Philosophy's accepted guest', recalls Shelley's own youthful introduction to 'the story of the feast' (*Athanase*, 15, 193). According to Mary Shelley, the poem would have developed Plato's theme of Uranian (heavenly) and Pandemian (earthly and carnal) love. Both *Athanase* and Shelley's major poem of the summer, *Laon and Cythna*, feature semblances of the poet's beloved Dr Lind, the teacher and father-figure who made Shelley's years at Eton bearable and, most

---

[2] Michael O'Neill, *Percy Bysshe Shelley: A Literary Life* (London: Macmillan, 1989), 64.

[3] See *Romantics, Rebels, and Reactionaries: English Literature and its Background 1760–1830* (Oxford: Oxford UP, 1981), 113–37, and *Peacock Displayed: A Satirist in his Context* (London: Routledge, 1979), 19–25, 37–40, 102–9. Calling English Romantic Hellenism 'a tendency rather than a tangible ideology', Timothy Webb highlights the 'exotic and erotic' nature of Shelley's Greece, which the poet never actually visited ('Romantic Hellenism', in Stuart Curran (ed.), *The Cambridge Companion to British Romanticism* (Cambridge: Cambridge UP, 1993), 155).

crucially, ushered him into what was then the arcane, rather exotic world of Platonic studies. While the kindly, aged Hermit helps Laon rediscover 'love's benignant laws' (*Laon and Cythna*, V. ix. 1800), the white-haired Zonoras invites Athanase to recall the one mystic night when 'Plato's words of light' taught them both 'Of love divine':

> 'Dost thou remember yet
> When the curved moon then lingering in the West

> 'Paused in yon waves her mighty horns to wet,
> How in those beams we walked, half entered on the sea?
> 'Tis just one year ... sure thou dost not forget,

> '[   ]Plato's words of light in thee and me
> Lingered like moonlight in the moonless East,
> For we had just then read—thy memory

> 'Is faithful now—the story of the feast;
> And Agathon and Diotima seemed
> From death, and Dark [   ] released

> 'To talk with us of all they knew or dreamed,
> Of love divine

(Athanase, 185–97)

This passage richly demonstrates how the 'soul-sustaining songs and sweet debates' comprising Plato's *Symposium* served for Shelley as a unifying and mediating power—akin to the Romantic imagination itself—that links the heavens with the earth (the moon dips into the sea) and man with them both (Zonoras and Athanase seem here both to walk in the moon's beams and in/on the sea itself) (*Athanase*, 8 [cancelled sequence following l. 129]). The characters' Platonic reminiscences also link past with present ('thy memory | Is faithful now'), self with other ('thee and me' of l. 190 become 'we' in l. 192), and the dead and the living (Agathon and Diotima seem 'From death [...] released | To talk with us'). Finally, with the quickness of intuition that Shelley so often ascribes to his sympathetically charged fictive lovers, Zonoras spontaneously 'reads' Athanase's dawning remembrance, just as together they had instinctively divined Plato's radiant words. As Shelley declares in one of his earliest compositions, 'Congenial minds will seek their kindred soul, | E'en though the tide of time has rolled between.'[4] In the later poem, the kindred souls who find each other are Plato, his expositors of love, Diotima and Agathon, and their two latter-day disciples.

It was the congenial mind of Plato which helped bridge for Shelley his own past and present as he revisited in 1817–18 the author whom his own Zonoras, Dr Lind, had illuminated so many years before. During Shelley's first Italian summer, Plato also provided a conduit between the poet's former life in England and his new life on the

---

[4] *Longman*, 2, 120: *Fragment. Supposed to be an Epithalamium of Francis Ravaillac and Charlotte Cordé*, ll. 42–3 (1810).

Continent, spiritually transporting the convivial Marlow 'Academy' to the lovely Baths of Lucca, where nature provided the 'the luxury of voluptuous delight' that Shelley received from Peacock's 'Greek and Pagan' *Rhododaphne*.[5] In his dialogue on poetry and rhetoric, the *Ion*, which Shelley would translate in 1821, Plato develops a rich metaphor for the type of influence, inspiration, and often subliminal communication shared among art's divine source, its direct recipient (here, a poet), its performers (rhapsodists), and its audience.

> [...] you are not master of any art for the illustration of Homer [Socrates tells Ion] but it is a divine influence which moves you, like that which resides in the stone called Magnet by Euripides, and Heraclea by the people. For not only does this stone possess the power of attracting iron rings but it can communicate to them the power of attracting other rings; so that you may see sometimes a long chain of rings and other iron substances attached and suspended one to the other by this influence. And as the power of the stone circulates through all the links of this series and attaches each to each, so the Muse communicating through those whom she has first inspired to all others capable of sharing in the inspiration the influence of that first enthusiasm, creates a chain and a succession. For the authors of those great poems which we admire do not attain to excellence through the rules of any art but they utter their beautiful melodies of verse in a state of inspiration and, as it were, *possessed* by a spirit not their own. (Shelley's translation of the *Ion*, 472)

We might see Plato himself here as the lodestone, or 'divine influence', for Shelley in his own creative endeavours, both at Marlow and at Lucca, where Shelley felt deserted by his poetic Muse but impelled by *The Banquet* towards prose composition. In a more fundamental sense, the powerful source of 'universal and reciprocal attraction' that Socrates presents resembles deific Love itself, inspiration of poetry as well as of human sympathy and affection for both Plato and Shelley (*Ion*, 475). This passage suggests the kind of sympathetic energy that flowed within Shelley's Marlow circle, as well as within Shelley's own more private communion with the Greek philosopher at Lucca, a communion that engendered Shelley's three most important prose meditations on love: a soaring translation of the *Symposium* (entitled by Shelley *The Banquet*), a starkly confessional essay *On Love*, and a rather daring *Discourse on the Manners of the Antient Greeks Relative to the Subject of Love*.

In his magisterial study *The Platonism of Shelley*, James Notopoulos suggests how Shelley's deep connection with Plato and his ardent 'participation in the divine influence' of *The Banquet* and the *Ion* helped forge intimate, 'magnetic' bonds within his social and domestic circles (*Ion*, 473): 'Shelley was himself a veritable magnet of Greek and Platonism. Claire Clairmont [Mary's half-sister] is to be included among his converts to Greek and Plato. Like Harriet [Westbrook Shelley] and Mary [Godwin Shelley] she took up the study of Greek to please Shelley' (464). If the Marlow 'Cult of the South' involved a kind of fraternity of classical enthusiasts, Shelley's home life, from childhood until his last

---

[5] Shelley's review of *Rhododaphne*, in *The Prose Works of Percy Shelley*, ed. E. B. Murray, vol. I (Oxford: Clarendon, 1993), 285.

days in Italy, invariably took on a more feminine tone, with various 'sister-spirits' helping him recreate the sororal atmosphere that the young poet had enjoyed with his four adoring female siblings.[6] Shelley's immersion in Plato during the summer of 1818 was inspired in part by his desire 'to give Mary some idea of the manners & feelings of the Athenians', and her complex role as student, audience, transcriber, and lover certainly coloured Shelley's creative conversation with *The Banquet* (*Letters: PBS* II, 20: 10 July 1818).

Expanding on his metaphor of the Heracleotic stone, Socrates explains to Ion the audience's role as both recipient and (magnetic) conductor of eloquent poetry: 'Know then that the spectator represents the last of the rings which derive a mutual and successive power from that [...] stone of which I spoke' (*Ion*, 474). Socrates' subsequent reference to 'the power transmitted' first from the magnet and then from the primary iron ring—the poet—highlights the essential hierarchy of poet and audience, teacher and student; yet his emphasis, in both passages cited above, on mutual influence suggests how Percy's primary audience, Mary, could both receive and bestow the creative, cohesive energy flowing from the divine source: 'the power circulates through all the links in this series', 'the stone communicate[s] [...] the power of attracting other rings', and the chain involves a 'universal and reciprocal attraction' (*Ion*, 474, 472, 475).

Immersed in a culture that saw women as the embodiments of virtue, benevolence, compassion, and sympathy, and shaped by the sisterly companionship of his early years, Shelley fervently embraced the feminine, both as a general social and spiritual 'purifying' force and as a personal ideal—even, in fact, a cherished self-image. As students and muses, Shelley's beloved women entered the world and texts of Periclean Greece and allowed the poet to re-imagine Plato's exclusively male drinking party as transfused with the power of feminine sympathy, a word that signals Shelley's ideal of mutual affection and deep intimacy, and denotes a contemporary theory that posited a '*cognate effluvia*' binding together both individuals and the fields of psychology, ethics, philosophy, and science, as Roy R. Male's still unsurpassed 'Shelley and the Doctrine of Sympathy' has shown.[7] 'Sympathy' also conveys the comprehensive act of imagination that allowed the poet to join Plato's symposiasts as translator, participant (offering his own eloquent 'speech', an essay *On Love*), and cultural liaison, introducing his nineteenth-century audience to the decidedly different erotic 'manners' of the ancient Greeks—as well as introducing into this vividly recreated world a harsh critique and partial corrective of its pervasive misogyny.

Central to the Oxbridge curriculum, as well as those of the elite public schools Eton, Shelley's alma mater, and Harrow, where Byron matriculated, the classics had

---

[6] Nearly all of Shelley's biographers—most recently, James Bieri (*Percy Bysshe Shelley*, 2 vols. (Newark, DE: University of Delaware Press, 2004, 2005))—note what Richard Holmes calls 'the pre-Lapsarian land of Field place [...] constructed from a society of sisters' (*Shelley: The Pursuit* (London: Weidenfeld & Nicholson, 1974), 12). Both Barbara Charlesworth Gelpi and I trace many of Shelley's poetic themes and psychological patterns to his childhood Eden. See Gelpi, *Shelley's Goddess: Maternity, Language, Subjectivity* (Oxford: Oxford UP, 1992) and [Chichester] Bonca, *Shelley's Mirrors of Love: Narcissism, Sacrifice, and Sorority* (Albany, NY: State University of New York Press, 1999).

[7] Roy R. Male, 'Shelley and the Doctrine of Sympathy', *Texas Studies in English* 29 (1950), 183–203.

long been an exclusively male and aristocratic province. Inviting Mary—as well as Harriet and Claire—into this rarefied world, Shelley was performing the kind of liberating act that compels some readers, most notably Nathaniel Brown, author of *Sexuality and Feminism in Shelley*,[8] to view the poet as staunchly feminist in his politics, poetry, and personal relationships. In light of Shelley's sometimes callous treatment of the women in his life, and of his romantic ideal of a mirroring 'second self' without a genuine identity of her own, it is rather difficult to regard, as Brown does, the poet's 'enduring legacy to women' as purely emancipatory (*Laon and Cythna*, II. xxiv. 875; Brown, 195). The question 'Can man be free if woman be a slave?' does ring throughout Shelley's writings, but it is man's bondage to what the poet calls the 'principle of Self' that most troubles him (*Laon and Cythna*, II. xliii. 1045; *Defence*, 531).

Beginning with his earliest writings, Shelley voices grave (self-)suspicions of what he calls in the *Discourse* 'the sexual impulse', especially as experienced and expressed by men (408). As Plato's *Symposium* reveals, Venus Pandemos, purveyor of sexual and cosmic blight, lurks behind the beautiful and benignant love inspired by her gracious sister, the Uranian Venus. Invariably linked to what Shelley identifies as 'the dark idolatry of self' (*Laon and Cythna*, VIII. xxii. 3390), rape, seduction, and libertinage call forth from the poet the most vehement denunciations and thus remind us that his rhetoric of romantic love, as William Ulmer's *Shelleyan Eros* has brilliantly shown,[9] can be harsh and even violent, as well as astonishingly mellifluous.

The lively gathering of Athenian men that Plato commemorates ultimately allows Shelley to investigate, through his translation and the two prose-pieces that accompany it, how masculinity, sexuality, and desire may find release from the kind of destructive and 'malignant selfishness of sensuality' that Shelley consistently condemned (*Murray: Prose*, 142: review of Hogg's *Prince Alexy Haimatoff*). While his recoil from the idea of (penetrative) homosexual lovemaking—called a 'detestable violation' in the *Discourse* (411)—has earned him the label 'homophobe',[10] Shelley's writings often veer from the physical expression of even heterosexual love, displacing it onto passionate flora (*The Sensitive-Plant*) or heavenly bodies (Act IV of *Prometheus Unbound*); relegating it to dreams (*Alastor* and the *Discourse*, in which reverie supplies the satisfaction that the body cannot); or coupling it with death, as in *Epipsychidion*, where the lovers' erotic bliss culminates in 'one annihilation' (587).[11] As he reflected on the various facets of love during the summer of 1818, Shelley (re)discovered in Plato's *Symposium* a fertile site in which to explore how private passions could lead to 'wider sympath[ies]', how emotionally intimate, 'sentimental' and fully sexual love may harmonize within the 'proper Paradise' of sympathetically attuned lovers, and how the male eros might

---

[8] Nathaniel Brown, *Sexuality and Feminism in Shelley* (Cambridge, MA: Harvard UP, 1979).

[9] William Ulmer, *Shelleyan Eros: The Rhetoric of Romantic Love* (Princeton: Princeton UP, 1990).

[10] See, for example, Louis Crompton's *Byron and Greek Love: Homophobia in 19th Century England* (Berkeley and Los Angeles: University of California Press, 1985), 284–311.

[11] Ulmer's *Shelleyan Eros* powerfully plumbs the darker currents of Shelley's love poetry, with its alliance of Eros, Thanatos, and repression of the (sexual) body.

achieve 'the intensity of disinterested love' and glimpse 'the wide ocean of intellectual beauty' that so radiantly inspires it (*Laon and Cythna*, II. xxxvi. 984; *On Love*, 504; *Discourse*, 411; *Banquet*, 449).

Entering *The Banquet*

Shelley's intense communion with Plato during the summer of 1818 brought him face to face with the most contested—both within himself and, later, among his critics—aspect of his own philosophy of love: whether it propels us out of our own world of self or instead pulls us further inward, creating a vortex or 'eddy' of self-involved desire that prevents any real connection with others—or, as he puts it in the Platonically inflected language of the *Defence*, 'with the beautiful which exists in thought, action, or person, not our own' (517). His project of translation and transmission in fact lucently reflects this (self-)debate. The cluster of texts that emerged that summer required Shelley (and his readers) to transport themselves imaginatively, sympathetically into the unfamiliar world of ancient Athens, with its 'widely different' sexual 'manners and opinions' (*Discourse*, 407). At the same time, these writings allowed the poet to explore his own private passages of desire, where Eros may lead to a labyrinthine hall of mirrors rather than an effulgent 'Sea reflecting Love' (*Prometheus Unbound*, IV. 384).

Some scholars, including Donald H. Reiman, who first definitively traced the essay *On Love* to July 1818, distinguish between Shelley's concept of mirroring lovers—the 'prototype' and 'antitype' invoked in *On Love* (504)—and his 'mature doctrine of love'[12] as 'a going out of our nature', in the words of the *Defence* (517). Jerrold E. Hogle and William A. Ulmer,[13] among others, see an essential continuity between these versions of Shelleyan love. 'The differing emphases that Reiman notes are merely complementary aspects of a single self/other model', writes Ulmer—one, I might add, whose dualism, at least for the poet, nonetheless posits an underlying unity that the lover, the social reformer, and the spiritual seeker long to glimpse.[14]

Shelley's passionate engagement with *The Banquet*, and especially with the erotic teachings presented by the prophetess Diotima, allowed him to employ and even channel 'the daemoniacal nature' of Eros as he explored not just the subject and object of desire but, perhaps more importantly, the interstices between them (*Banquet*, 443). Love, Diotima tells Socrates, is 'something intermediate', born of lack, of poverty, yet at the same time filling—or at least travelling, perpetually and fruitfully, within—the space between, for example, self and other and divine and human (441). As Shelley boasts in a note appended to his own *Discourse on Love*, 'I should say in answer [to the dialogue's

---

[12] Reiman (ed.), *Shelley and his Circle 1773–1822*, vol. VI (Cambridge, MA: Harvard UP, 1973), 646.

[13] See Hogle, 'Shelley's Poetics', *Keats–Shelley Journal* 31 (1982), 188 and Ulmer, *Shelleyan Eros*, especially 3–24.

[14] Ulmer, *Shelleyan Eros*, 5 n. 8.

pressing question 'What is Love?'] that Ερως neither loved nor was loved, but is the cause of Love in others—a subtlety to beat Plato' (Notopoulos, *Platonism*, 461). That is, as Richard Isomaki has shown,[15] Eros resides neither in lover nor beloved but instead, like gravitation, like magnetism—the permeative power that Shelley's beloved Lucretius as well as Plato tapped—in and as the 'intervals and interstices whose void for ever craves fresh food' (*Defence*, 488).

Within the dialogue itself, both the poverty and the power of vacancy[16] assert themselves most dramatically in the speeches of Aristophanes and of Diotima (or Diotima-Socrates for those who see the prophetess as Socrates' fictive persona). Aristophanes' tragicomic account of circular, double-faced, multi-limbed primitive human beings, each with 'two organs of generation', in fact emerges from a space made empty first by his inconvenient hiccups and then by the gaps in Eryximachus' discourse, itself an 'attempt to fill up what [Pausanias, the previous speaker] left unfinished' (429, 426). Eryximachus, who elaborates on Pausanias' portrait of a 'double Love' comprised of the beneficent Uranian and the destructive Pandemian Venus, highlights in his opening and concluding remarks the double nature of vacancy—a doubleness that informs both Shelley's epistemology (in the oddly self-cancelling 'vacancy' that crowns Mont Blanc, both the mountain and the poem) and his view of love (as in the companionless, perpetually yearning, Love-identified mimosa whose 'deep heart' nonetheless 'is full' (*The Sensitive-Plant*, 76)). 'Pausanias, beginning his discourse excellently, placed no fit completion and development to it,' announces Eryximachus, whose own contribution to the debate leaves an opening for the next symposiast: 'Probably in thus praising Love, I have unwillingly omitted many things; but it is your business, O Aristophanes, to fill up all that I have left incomplete' (426, 428).

Yet Aristophanes only continues the cycle of fertile lack and false fulfilment, both by breaking away from his predecessors' focus on heavenly vs. vulgar love and by constructing a myth of 'mutual Love' whose very premiss depends on loss and fragmentation. In Aristophanes' tale, Eros, in its strictest sense as romantic and sexual desire, emerges only when circular or 'whole' beings become 'imperfect portions [...] perpetually necessitated to seek the half belonging to him' (431). What were originally males, females, and androgynes separate into homosexual couples, lesbians, and heterosexual lovers, but all share the same desire: to find the (lost) 'second self'—as Shelley would call it—and then to regain wholeness, 'to be melted together' permanently (432). However, in adapting Aristophanes' myth of dissevered and reconnected 'twin' lovers, which infiltrates Shelley's writings on love well before he translated *The Symposium*, the poet remains more absorbed in 'the *pursuit* of integrity and union' than in its realization; it is 'those lost and concealed objects of our love'[17] that magnetically pull both him and his

---

[15] 'Love as Cause in *Prometheus Unbound*', *Studies in English Literature* 29 (1989), 655–73.

[16] In *Shelley and Greece: Rethinking Romantic Hellenism* (London: Macmillan, 1997), Jennifer Wallace examines the permutations of 'vacancy' within Shelley's writings, pointing out that in *Alastor* and elsewhere 'It is uncertain whether negation or plenitude [in the sense of potential] is implied' (50).

[17] Shelley's translation here highlights a sense of bereavement and frustration absent in, for example, the Loeb version, which simply reads 'our proper favorites' (Notopoulos, *Platonism*, 578).

desire-driven speakers and characters toward but never quite *to* discovery and (re)connection (432; emphasis added).

In his groundbreaking *Shelley's Process*, Jerrold Hogle traces the poet's intellectual restlessness and fascination with change, mirrored in his ever-shifting style, to a 'sub-liminal impulse' that Hogle calls 'radical transference': any '"bearing across" between places, moments, thoughts, words, or persons that refuses closure or commitment to an originative—or terminal—"One"'.[18] For Shelley, 'Desire is carried on, generated and revived perpetually, by a moving recollection seeking an image that looks elsewhere to yet another point' (16). This 'transpositional' energy that Hogle discerns (re)charges itself most potently in the space that exists on a cosmic level—'the intense inane' of *Prometheus Unbound*—as well as within individual consciousness: 'we find within our own thoughts the chasm of an insufficient void,' as Shelley declares in his essay *On Love* (*Prometheus Unbound*, III. iv. 204; *On Love*, 503). In Plato's dialogue, particularly in Diotima's climactic discourse, the 'great Daemon' Eros, darting between heaven and earth, lover and beloved, spirit and body, and speaker and speaker, both opens up this gap and temporarily bridges it as it urges us upward 'through [...] transitory objects which are beautiful towards that which is beauty itself' (441, 449).

Yet these 'transitory objects', especially those who most perfectly reflect our own (self-)ideal 'of everything excellent or lovely [...] as belonging to the nature of man' (*On Love*, 504), never completely disappear, but are instead irradiated with what Shelley might call 'an electric life' that 'burns within' their mortal vestments, and within the words uttered by Plato's Love-inspired encomiasts and their nineteenth-century apostle (*Defence*, 535). These earthly beauties also gain a kind of immortality by creating within the beholder the bliss and torment of 'love's sweet want', as Shelley puts it in *The Sensitive-Plant* (12), a passionate, and perpetual—because ultimately unquenchable—desire to possess, preserve, and even coalesce with the 'beautiful forms' we encounter along life's way (*Banquet*, 448).

In Shelleyan terms, we thirst and find no fill; all that we, like Eros himself, acquire ceaselessly 'flows away' from us (*Banquet*, 443). That yearning cradles us into song, pro-pels us toward philosophy, poetry, politics, and spurs us to seek the highest Good, all activities that flow *into* and fructify the social sphere. As Agathon declares in his lyrical tribute to the god whom he calls 'a wise poet', 'Love divests us of all alienation from each other, and fills our vacant hearts with overflowing sympathy' (437). David K. O'Connor and Michael O'Neill both note the extraordinary power of this final section of Agathon's discourse.[19] As O'Connor points out, Agathon's 'splendid peroration' is 'not quite a literal translation of Plato', and it strikes a quintessentially Shelleyan note with its interpolation of 'vacant hearts' and 'overflowing sympathy' (p. xxxii). O'Neill's nuanced reading of Agathon's superb prose-poem and his remark that Shelley 'lavish[es] verbal attention on

---

[18] Jerrold E. Hogle, *Shelley's Process: Radical Transference and the Development of His Major Works* (Oxford: Oxford UP, 1988), 15.

[19] See *The Symposium of Plato: The Shelley Translation*, ed. David K. O'Connor (South Bend, IN: St Augustine Press, 2002) and Michael O'Neill, 'Emulating Plato: Shelley as Translator and Prose Poet', in Alan Weinberg and Timothy Webb (eds.), *The Unfamiliar Shelley* (Farnham: Ashgate, 2009), 239–55.

a passage whose attitudes [he] knows will be superseded in the dialogue' beautifully highlight Shelley's remarkable artistry here (254). Yet I would say that Agathon's encomium is absorbed and enriched rather than superseded by Socrates-Diotima's speech, which gains access—through the power of sympathy, or magnetism, that Agathon conducts—to the fount of 'poetic enthusiasm' itself: Love, the 'author of all the arts of life' (*Banquet*, 436). Just as each of the stages of love—personal sexual desire on through to the worship of transcendental Beauty—remains crucial and present as the lover ascends towards the divine vision, so too does each note in the symphony that together Plato's symposiasts create. Love is the deity, declares Agathon, 'whose footsteps everyone ought to follow, celebrating him excellently in song, and bearing each his part in that divinest harmony which Love sings to all things which live and are, soothing the troubled minds of god and men' (437). As for Shelley himself, his own great love for the Platonic dialogue allowed him to see a space for himself within its symphony and song, not only as translator—linguistic and cultural liaison between ancient Athens and Regency England—but also as composer of his own memorable contributions and counterpoints to 'the irresistible stream of musical impressions' with which Shelley harmonized during his first Italian summer (*Banquet*, Preface, 402).

PRIVATE PASSIONS AND WIDER SYMPATHIES: ON LOVE AND DISCOURSE ON LOVE

In his essay 'The Relations between Poetry and Painting', Wallace Stevens writes, 'The world about us would be desolate except for the world within us. There is the same interchange between these two worlds that there is between one art and another, migratory passings to and fro, quickenings, Promethean liberations and discoveries.'[20] The suite of texts that emerged from those warm, ripe days at Bagni di Lucca invites us to trace such migratory passings as they quicken Shelley's imaginative powers and light up the filaments that connect the world without and the world within, and that link the various art forms—translation, prose-poem, and expository essay—through which Shelley explored love's 'transforming presence', in the words of *Prometheus Unbound* (I. 832). The restless movements of Eros as it inspires and then eludes each of Plato's speakers not only dissolve the barriers between lovers, but also between genders and forms of sexuality. Moreover, the great Daemon whom Diotima extols infuses the very labours of the translator, who must fluidly cross from Greek to English (his 'source' and 'receptor' languages, respectively) as well as from symposiast to symposiast while he (re)constructs the dialogue, the drama[21] that Plato presents. Finally, and most visibly in his *Discourse*

[20] Wallace Stevens, 'The Relations between Poetry and Painting', in *The Necessary Angel: Essays on Reality and the Imagination* (New York: Vintage, 1942), 169.
[21] 'For [so] the lively distinction of characters and the various and well-wrought circumstances of the story almost entitle it to be called,' writes Shelley in his Preface to *The Banquet*, 403.

on Love, Shelley must channel the erotic, or mediating, spirit as he identifies and 'bears across' to his readers—first Mary and then others unfamiliar with Athenian culture—the 'widely different manners and opinions' of this ancient world, especially regarding 'the regulations and the sentiments respecting sexual intercourse' (*Discourse*, 407).

According to Donald Reiman, Shelley began the more personal response to Plato's dialogue, the breathlessly lyrical essay *On Love*, just as he completed his translation, with the *Discourse* following shortly after.[22] While both texts nimbly negotiate the boundaries of identity and difference within the world of erotic desire, the earlier piece is much less certain that love can in fact, in the words of Agathon, 'divest us of all alienation from each other' (Notopoulos, *Platonism*, 437). As presented in *On Love*, difference enkindles a kind of desperate desire for one's ideal mirror, for a perfect sensual, intellectual, and spiritual 'correspondence', doomed, it seems, to failure and frustration (504). Shelley's revision of Aristophanes' myth keeps the dissevered lovers in continual suspension, their 'nerves, like the chords of two exquisite lyres', vibrating in unison but never actually intersecting (*On Love*, 504). The complex interplay of pronouns within the piece underscores the seemingly unbridgeable distance between self and other. As the original manuscript reveals, after abruptly opening with the question 'What is Love?'—a query which he shortly and rather belligerently ascribes to the reader ('*Thou* demandest what is Love'; Shelley's emphasis),—the poet haltingly begins his response with 'The' and then 'We', both of which he cancels in favour of 'I'.[23] This personal pronoun in turn launches a series of complaints involving misunderstanding, isolation, 'repulse and disappointment' (503). Clearly, the writer is feeling 'the chasm of an insufficient void', 'within [his] own thoughts' as well as externally—a gap dividing the lone 'I' from his 'other': lover or reader, or perhaps both in the person of Mary Shelley (503).

The essay is replete with images of separation and obstruction, yet clearly Shelley's own creative powers have been regenerated by their (erotic) encounter with Plato's poetic genius. In spite of the kinds of vacancy that the essay itself invokes—solitude, ever-widening intervals between 'points of sympathy', a sense of desertion within a crowd, and love-abjuring man as a 'living sepulchre' or 'mere husk'—Shelley himself has found ample room within *The Banquet* to give birth to 'the airy children of [his] brain' (*On Love*, 503, 504). These poetic offspring both express crucial aspects of Shelleyan Eros and reveal the poet's fascination with, as well as participation in, Diotima's doctrine of spiritual pregnancy. For a man who once tried to suckle his infant daughter,[24] the plethora of female imagery featured in *The Banquet* must have been extremely appealing. A group of eloquent and emotionally open philosophers presided over by a powerful prophetess, the mother goddess whom Barbara Gelpi has so compellingly situated within Shelley's thought: viewed in tandem with Shelley's *On Love* and *Discourse on Love*, this gathering resembles an idealized, because feminized, version of the Marlow circle, especially when

[22] *SC* VI, 639.
[23] *Bodleian Shelley Manuscripts* (MS. Shelley adds. e. 11), vol. XV, ed. Steven E. Jones (New York: Garland, 1994), 3.
[24] Newman Ivy White, *Shelley*, 2 vols. (New York: Knopf, 1940), 1, 326, chronicles this incident, provoked by Harriet Shelley's desire to hire a wet-nurse rather than suckle the child herself.

we recall that Mary and Claire were the first readers of Shelley's Platonic productions, as well as de facto members of the philhellenic 'Cult of the South', now translated/transported back to warmer climes. Besides illuminating, through his own fluid style, 'the streams of sympathy' that flow among Plato's 'unreserve[d]' and 'delicate' symposiasts (*Discourse*, 221), Shelley imports into ancient Athens the concept of 'sentimental love', associated with the love of and for women and with an aesthetic considered feminine during Shelley's day, as well as our own. This aesthetic, often embraced by the poet since his earliest writings, permeates the essay *On Love*, where Shelley refers to his 'inmost soul', 'trembling and feeble' spirit, and 'tears of mysterious tenderness' (503, 504). As we will see shortly, the poet also turns to sentimental, and heterosexual, love in order to evade the physical realities of homoeroticism, as well to elide the body itself.

Diotima most radically feminizes the practice of philosophy, and thus its male practitioners, with her account of the sensually and spiritually questing lover, 'pregnant, and [...] bursting with the load of his desire', bringing forth wisdom and, of paramount import to Shelley, poetry through intercourse with incarnate and then divine beauty (445). The unlikely figure of Alcibiades, drunk and crashing the party just as Socrates has finished speaking, further contributes to the dialogue's feminine aura. As Angela Hobbs observes, even the virile Alcibiades 'embraces' the feminine: he 'arrives crowned with violets and ribbons, conjuring up an image of the often androgynous Dionysus'.[25] More crucial, though, is the interloper's comparison of Socrates, already identified with a wise woman instructor, to a statue of Silenus, rough-hewn and even ridiculous, yet filled or 'pregnant' with lovely miniature statues of the gods, an image that Shelley found most captivating as he explored within his own meditation *On Love* the 'internal constitution[s]' of other potential readers/lovers and of himself (*Banquet*, 453, 454, 459). Alcibiades' declaration that 'those Silenuses that sit in the sculptors' shops [...] when divided in two, are found to contain withinside the images of the gods' obliquely glances back to Aristophanes' severed lovers—here implicitly rescued from desolation and even deified—as well as suggests with that doubled interiority of 'withinside' just how difficult this treasure may be to find and excavate. Hopeful in its hint that 'to divide is not to take away', yet disquieting in its intimation of a too-deeply buried beauty, this ambiguous image perfectly captures the poet's own uncertainty as he develops his theory of the romantic prototype and antitype (*Epipsychidion*, 161).

When he explores in 1815 the dangers of narcissism in *Alastor*, where the 'insatiate' Poet pursues to his 'untimely grave' an idealized, feminine version of himself, Shelley invokes the term 'prototype', stating in the Preface that the Poet 'seeks in vain for a prototype of his conception' (72, 73). While Shelley claims that 'the picture [of the Poet's baffled quest] is not barren of instruction to actual men', the Poet himself, it seems, *is* indeed barren; to return to the language of *On Love*, the young visionary wastes into the 'sepulchre of himself' in part because he does not recognize the prototype (as) within—that is, as the soul within his soul that Diotima and then Shelley himself sees enwombed inside

[25] 'Female Imagery in Plato', in J. H. Lesher, Debra Nails, and Frisbee C. C. Sheffield (eds.), *Plato's Symposium: Issues in Interpretation and Reception* (Cambridge, MA: Harvard UP, 2006), 267.

the ardent philosopher-poet, male or female (*Alastor*, Preface 73; *On Love*, 504). With its paired prototype and antitype, *On Love*, unlike *Alastor*, does create space for a necessary and liberating self-search that ideally will inspire that 'going out of our own nature', that 'identification of ourselves with the beautiful which exists in thought, action, or person, not our own', called by the poet 'the great secret of morals', Love itself (*Defence*, 517).

Together, the figures of Diotima and Alcibiades helped Shelley envision a paradoxically fertile inner void experienced by all sentimental lovers. This 'insufficient chasm' in fact contains the seed of desire, the yearning to commune with and bring forth the beautiful both 'within our own thoughts' and 'beyond ourselves' (*On Love*, 503). It is only the quest for our 'antitype', the elusive inner ideal of the perfectly sympathetic, thoroughly corresponding beloved, that can create or 'awaken' a 'community' between our inner lives and the beings surrounding us. The *Alastor* Poet searches in vain for his own prototype because he neither peers deeply enough into his inmost soul, where his 'miniature', ideal self dwells *in utero*, nor looks outward, where his antitype may exist, perhaps even in the warmly human form of an amorous Arab girl, ignored in favour of an intangible dream-maiden (*On Love*, 504). As Wallace Stevens declares in the passage cited earlier, 'the world about us would be desolate except for the world within us', yet the opposite is also true; and Shelley's philosophy of love, especially as it is touched by what Walter Pater calls Plato's 'mystical, intimate prose', travels ceaselessly and fruitfully between these two realms.

If the essay *On Love* remains largely cloistered within the private world of personal passion, Shelley's *Discourse on Love* reaches outward to a whole culture, performing an act of transmigration that goes beyond the linguistic and, to cite Goethe's maxims regarding translation, brings a foreign nation across to us and simultaneously urges us to 'go across to what is foreign and adapt ourselves to its conditions, its use of language, its peculiarities'. For Shelley's countrymen and women, the most troubling 'peculiarity' among the ancient Athenians involved male same-sex love, the homoeroticism that kept Plato largely unavailable, even in the British universities, where as Peacock's Dr Folliot dryly observes in *Crotchet Castle*, the philosopher 'is held to be little better than a misleader of youth; and they have shown their contempt for him, not only by never reading him [...] but even by never printing a complete edition of him'.[26] Just as Shelley's rendition of *The Banquet* contains, as Pater says of the imaginative prose that he himself perfected, 'an appeal to the reader to catch the writer's spirit, to think with him', so too does Shelley's *Discourse* ask the reader to 'catch the tone of [Greek] society', to cross over and comprehend, without 'prudery' or 'outrage', its dramatic 'difference in manners' relative to sexuality and sentimental love (*Discourse*, 407).

While the *Discourse* thus enacts and encourages that 'sympathetic going out of our own nature' germane to Shelleyan love, its willingness to embrace difference only goes so far. Rather than delivering on his promise 'to show the Greeks precisely as they were', Shelley instead imports ideals from his own culture, as well as inscribes in the text the 'imperious want[s]' of his own heart (407, 409). According to the *Discourse*, it is because Greek women lacked cultivation, social equality, and 'moral and intellectual loveliness'

[26] '*Nightmare Abbey*' and '*Crotchet Castle*', ed. Raymond Wright (London: Penguin, 1969), 187.

that homoeroticism emerged as a compensatory practice, an erotic mode that Shelley disingenuously claims is now obsolete because of women's improved status (*Discourse*, 408). While seeing the same-sex love of ancient Greece as simply a substitute for the 'natural' heterosexuality prevalent in modern Europe, Shelley also superimposes onto the highly complex, ritualized world of Athenian homoeroticism the contemporary concept of sentimental love, the 'universal thirst for a communion not merely of the senses but of our whole nature, intellectual, imaginative and sensitive' (*Discourse*, 408).

Shelley's own psychosexual imprint, refined and deepened by contact with Plato's multi-voiced 'hymn in honour of Love', is most visible in his remarks on love as 'something within us'—a prototype in *On Love*, an archetype in the *Discourse*—'that thirsts after its likeness', as he writes in the earlier piece (*Banquet*, 419; *On Love*, 504). In the words of the *Discourse*, 'This [...] archetype forever exists in the mind, which selects among those who resemble it, that which most resembles it' (408). Closely connected to Shelley's concept of mirroring lovers is his idealization of the feminine, an impulse consistently yoked with intense distrust of the masculine will, linked with the 'principle of Self', father of violence, oppression, the 'venal interchange' of commerce, and—most dangerously in the context of Shelley's meditations on love—lust and libertinism (*Queen Mab*, 5, 38). As he 'rehabilitates' Greek homosexual 'manners' in his *Discourse*, Shelley creates a three-part strategy that celebrates romantic friendship, feminizes the male participants in same-sex love, and altogether bypasses the sex act itself.

As he confesses in his brief *Essay on Friendship*, which Barbara Gelpi suggests was written during his Platonizing summer of 1818, Shelley himself experienced a 'devoted attachment' to a young school friend, a 'profound and sentimental attachment'[27] that involved long and intimate conversations, goodnight kisses, and, as Gelpi notes, the disapproval of Shelley's mother. We can further witness Shelley's enthusiasm for such friendships in his youthful, volatile relationship with the 'brother of his soul' Thomas Jefferson Hogg, as well as in his rhapsodic description of a statue of Bacchus and Ampelus that he saw in Rome which embodied 'that tender friendship towards each other which has so much of love'.[28] Shelley also praises in the *Discourse* the romantic friendships commemorated by Shakespeare and other Renaissance poets. Yet his depictions of such attachments invariably feminize the men (and boys) involved, suggesting that the same-sex love he held most dear and longed to participate in featured women rather than men, ardent sisters of the soul like Rousseau's Claire and Julie or 'the delicately sculptured [...] likeness of two female figures, whose [...] eager and half-divided lips seemed quivering to meet' that appears in Shelley's fragmentary tale *The Colosseum* (*Shelley's Prose*, 224). Shelley's young schoolmate, for example, is delicate and gentle, 'the tones of his voice [...] soft and winning' (*Shelley's Prose*, 338). But it is the bodies of the male romantic friends that Shelley most thoroughly sculpts into the likeness of women as he contemplates homoerotic desire in the *Discourse*. As Nancy Goslee asserts, 'Shelley attempts [in the *Discourse*] a sympathetic explanation of [the Athenian] difference in

---

[27] *Shelley's Prose; or, The Trumpet of a Prophecy*, ed. David Lee Clark (London: Fourth Estate, 1966), 338.
[28] Shelley, *Notes on Sculptures in Rome and Florence*, in *Shelley's Prose*, 347.

sexual orientation; and he mediates that explanation through an appeal to the beautiful forms of the sculpted human figure.'[29] 'The men of Greece', Shelley writes, 'corresponded in external form to the models which they have left as specimens of what they were'; their forms were 'firm yet flowing', their physiques and faces beautiful, their voices musical (*Discourse*, 409). Shelley would note a similar grace in the sculpted figure of Bacchus, with his gentle and tender expression and 'soft[ly] astonish[ing]' loveliness; the 'flowing fulness and roundness of breast and belly' bring to mind the pregnant philosophers of Diotima's oration.[30]

Along with transforming the male lovers of ancient Greece into ideal, because feminine, (self-)images, Shelley also translates love's 'visible link', sexual intercourse[31] into the ethereal minglings of dreamers, caught up in a reverie that allows a 'state of abandonment' and sexual release without penetration, or even physical contact (*Discourse*, 409, 411). Just as Shelley insists in his *Essay on Friendship* that (his) same-sex romance is 'wholly divested of the smallest alloy of sensual intermixture', so are the homoerotic attachments presented in the *Discourse*, the phrasing nearly identical in both pieces (*Shelley's Prose*, 338; *Discourse*, 413).

While Shelley's tortuous attempt in the latter text to evade the physical realities of homosexual love is understandable in light of his (potential) contemporary readers, his vision of erotic reverie—where, in the language of the essay *On Life*, lovers dissolve into each other, 'conscious of no distinction'—in fact suggests that for Shelley 'the sexual and intellectual claims of love' for same-sex or heterosexual desire may find their highest expression within that 'exalted state of sensibility' that fuses 'all sympathies': 'intellectual, imaginative and sensitive' (*On Life*, 507; *Discourse*, 411, 410, 408). In what is perhaps Shelley's greatest—and sexiest—love scene, Act II, scene i of *Prometheus Unbound*, the radiantly transfigured Titan, with his 'soft and flowing limbs', erotically intermingles with his sister-spirit Panthea inside a (literally) steamy mutual dream, where 'vaporous fire' dissolves the boundaries between them and brings them both the 'intoxication of keen joy' (73, 75, 67). Within this dream, this reverie, we can glimpse Shelley's own Platonic reveries, most powerfully kindled as he imaginatively transported himself during the summer of 1818 to ancient Athens, to the house of Agathon, to the gathering of symposiasts whom he joined in praise of love.

Shelley's immersion in Plato's writings and world that summer helped return him, as he'd hoped, to 'original composition', including *Julian and Maddalo*, 'Lines Written among the Euganean Hills', and the beginnings of his masterpiece, *Prometheus Unbound* (*Letters: PBS* II, 472). It also enabled him to strengthen his skills as a prose writer of real power. It is hard to imagine either the grand historical sweep of *A Defence of Poetry* without the probing cultural analysis achieved in the *Discourse on Love*, or the *Defence*'s soaring lyricism and remarkable insights into the human heart without the intimate,

---

[29] Nancy Moore Goslee, 'Shelley's Cosmopolitan *Discourse*: Ancient Greek Manners and Modern Liberty', *Wordsworth Circle* 36 (2005), 2.

[30] Shelley, *Notes on Sculptures*, in *Shelley's Prose*, 348.

[31] Shelley most forcefully banishes anal sex—which he calls an 'operose and diabolical machination'—from his vision of lovemaking (*Discourse*, 411).

eloquent essay *On Love* hovering in the background. Yet Shelley neither completed nor published his passionate responses to *The Banquet*. Both of his Platonic meditations break off rather abruptly, and thus embody that imperfection, that want so central to Diotima's doctrine of love and so alluring to readers, who must themselves—sympathetically, affectionately, and imaginatively—fill the interstices within and between them.

SELECT BIBLIOGRAPHY

[Chichester] Bonca, Teddi Lynn. *Shelley's Mirrors of Love: Narcissism, Sacrifice, and Sorority.* Albany, NY: State University of New York Press, 1999.

Brown, Nathaniel. *Sexuality and Feminism in Shelley.* Cambridge, MA: Harvard UP, 1979.

Gelpi, Barbara Charlesworth. *Shelley's Goddess: Maternity, Language, Subjectivity.* Oxford: Oxford UP, 1992.

Goslee, Nancy Moore. 'Shelley's Cosmopolitan *Discourse*: Ancient Greek Manners and Modern Liberty', *Wordsworth Circle* 36 (2005), 2–5.

Kinnell, Galway. 'Shelley'. *The New Yorker* (26 July 2004), 68.

O'Neill, Michael. 'Emulating Plato: Shelley as Translator and Prose Poet'. *The Unfamiliar Shelley.* Ed. Alan Weinberg and Timothy Webb. Farnham: Ashgate, 2009. 239–55.

Ulmer, William A. *Shelleyan Eros: The Rhetoric of Romantic Love.* Princeton: Princeton UP, 1990.

CHAPTER 9

....

POLITICS AND SATIRE

....

STEVEN E. JONES

IN March 1817, Shelley began what would turn out to be his final year's residence in England, moving into a house in Great Marlow, Buckinghamshire, in the rural Thames river valley.[1] This was his first stable home in England since eloping with Mary Godwin in 1814, and it remained their home together for one year, at which point they left again for the Continent. Mary Shelley had specifically expressed a desire for a house with a garden, and Albion House included extensive grounds. Shelley took numerous hikes in nearby Bisham Wood, organized group picnics and river trips, and entertained an expanding circle of friends in a household that included a number of children, Shelley and Mary Shelley's son (and, later in the year, their daughter) as well as Claire Clairmont's daughter with Lord Byron (born in January) and several visiting locals. Though it might seem as if he were seeking a retreat in this rural and domestic setting, in fact, Shelley used Marlow as a base from which to engage in public discourse. Soon after establishing himself, he began to write an ambitious twelve-canto epic in Spenserian stanzas on revolution, radical leadership, religious intolerance, and political persecution, *Laon and Cythna* (later revised as *The Revolt of Islam*). During the same period he also wrote a good deal of prose (E. B. Murray's volume includes thirteen separate prose works dated to 1817). Much of this prose was politically engaged and satirical in tone, and it included two important pamphlets—*A Proposal for Putting Reform to the Vote Throughout the Kingdom* and *An Address to the People on the Death of the Princess Charlotte*—written under the pseudonym, 'The Hermit of Marlow'.

Besides offering a legal screen against prosecution, the name is interesting for what it reveals of Shelley's attitude towards his role as a pamphleteer. Writing as a hermit may seem at first another sign of Shelley's desire to retreat from public conflict, which would be an understandable reaction, given the personal and legal troubles Shelley faced upon returning to England. In the early nineteenth century the figure of the hermit was associated with retreat to picturesque simplicity and a refuge close to nature. This kind of

---

[1] The biographical context for the residence at Marlow I take from Bieri, II, 32–54.

romantic hermit, often depicted in a grotto or out in the moonlight, was everywhere a common figure in popular culture at the time. Indeed, Shelley created one such romantic hermit character for *Laon and Cythna*, an old man who nurses the hero back to health in his crumbling tower on a remote shore (*Julian*, I, III, 27 ff.). But this hermit also makes an intellectual contribution to the revolution which Laon leads: over the years he has 'collected language to unfold | Truth to [his] countrymen' (III, 12). He writes about 'human power' and inspires hope and passion. Like his fictional hermit, Shelley as the Hermit of Marlow would be a figure of influence writing from a secure place of retirement. He may invoke a romantic setting, but his writing is topical and politically engaged.

The hermit who writes satirical or critical commentary from a position outside society goes back at least to Horace and forms a context in which Pope, for example, was nicknamed the Hermit of Twickenham. The idea of publishing from a rural retreat would also have invoked Montaigne, who retired to the tower of his estate to write the *Essais*, and whom Shelley was reading at around the time he wrote the pamphlets of 1817. More immediately, Shelley had just spent the previous summer in Geneva and could also have been thinking of Rousseau, who famously wrote as an exile from the republic of his citizenship. Among French Enlightenment figures, another likely inspiration would have been Voltaire, who was known as 'The Hermit of Ferney' late in life, during which period he produced the satirical tale *Candide*, and his *Dictionnaire philosophique*. Though Shelley criticized Voltaire, he also admired his position as a sceptical Deist who resisted religious persecution. *Queen Mab* had as its epigraph Voltaire's personal declaration of war on religion, *Écraser l'infâme!* (which Shelley once translated loosely as 'Crush the Demon'[2]).

Shelley spent a good deal of time during the summer of 1817 with his friend Thomas Love Peacock, who had arranged for the move to Marlow in the first place and who lived nearby. In the year that followed, Peacock would caricature Shelley as Scythrop Glowry in his novel *Nightmare Abbey* (1818), a volatile romantic poet who frequently escapes to his tower. For his part, Shelley seems to have aspired to the kind of subtle but effective satire that he admired in Peacock, whose 'wit | Makes such a wound, the knife is lost in it'.[3] Shelley was always ambivalent about wielding satirical weaponry, but he did so anyway, especially in response to tyranny and its apologists. It is important to remember that during the Regency a 'satire' could refer to any act of ridicule, any effort to expose hypocrisy or denounce corruption. For example, the term was commonly applied to graphical prints that attacked some public person or some customary aspect of society, even those containing very little 'satire' in the formal, literary sense. Shelley's Hermit of Marlow is satiric in just this general sense: he is a writer who denounces the system of existing authority in

---

[2] *Letters: PBS* I, 35.
[3] *Letter to Maria Gisborne*, *Julian*, IV, 3–12; 9. An epigraph to Peacock's *Nightmare Abbey* indicates a source for part of Shelley's phrase in Ben Jonson: 'Your true melancholy breeds your perfect fine wit, sir.'

varying tones, from pragmatic rationality to scoffing ridicule to moral outrage, by way of rapidly published pamphlets.

Shelley's turn to the national arena in his pamphlets of 1817 came at a time of great personal tragedy for him. In August 1816 he returned to England; in October, Mary's sister Fanny Godwin committed suicide. In December Shelley's wife Harriet Westbrook was found dead, having committed suicide by drowning herself in the Serpentine. Within weeks, Shelley and Mary Wollstonecraft Godwin were married in anticipation of taking custody of Shelley and Harriet's two children, Charles and Ianthe. Instead, Chancery proceedings were begun by the Westbrook family that by March 1817—just before he settled at Marlow—would deprive Shelley of custody, on the grounds of his immorality, radicalism, and atheism. Politically, this was the period of the second wave of Luddite riots, the Spa Fields riots, and the Pentridge uprising in Derbyshire, which was instigated by government spies and led to the arrest and trial of radical leaders on charges of treason. In January 1817 the Prince Regent's carriage was attacked by a mob as he was leaving parliament. By 4 March Habeas Corpus was suspended. Shelley was not the only one who believed that a general popular uprising might be imminent. After losing the Chancery battle, Shelley completed the move to Marlow but, as we have seen, he did not retreat. For one thing, he continued to travel back and forth to London on literary and personal business. For another, he immediately acted to publish topical and legally actionable works such as the *Proposal for Putting Reform to the Vote throughout the Kingdom*, the first pamphlet attributed to the Hermit of Marlow, produced in late February. In it Shelley calmly sets forth a plan for altering the system of representation, calling for meetings and a vote (by landowning male citizens), pledging 10 per cent of his own annual income in support of the effort. But it is significant that, even in this most hortative and pragmatic of publications, Shelley sometimes adopts a bitterly satiric tone and exposes the fundamental ideological underpinnings of the system: 'An hospital for lunatics is the only theatre where we can conceive so mournful a comedy to be exhibited as this mighty nation now exhibits,' he writes near the beginning of the pamphlet, and of the people's reluctance to accept reform, he declares: 'perhaps Custom is their only God, and they its fanatic worshippers will shiver in frost and waste in famine rather than deny that Idol.'[4] Addressing a national crisis, Shelley used stirring language meant to awaken and persuade, but sometimes he began with satire. There is a sense in which his personal crises of 1817 inform the intensity of the effort, insofar as he is motivated to turn his energies outward from domestic troubles to the problems facing the nation. Shelley's pamphlets, essays, letters, and reviews from that year (and forward at least to late 1819) represent entangled themes of domestic affections and public reputation, home and inheritance, mourning and legal succession, blasphemy and prosecution, reform and oppression, and the possibility of a popular revolution.

---

[4] *A Proposal for Putting Reform to the Vote Throughout the Kingdom*, in *Murray: Prose*, 169–76 (171). And see Scrivener in the present volume.

An Address to the People on the Death
of the Princess Charlotte

Shelley's material inheritance as the errant son of a Whig MP was directly threatened in 1817, as were his own paternal rights. His first wife had been discovered dead and his new wife (whose mother died in giving birth to her) was struggling to avoid being ostracized by her famous father, William Godwin. Against this personal background, and in a perhaps not unconnected response to momentous public events, Shelley wrote the second Hermit of Marlow pamphlet about a woman who had died from complications of childbirth, *An Address to the People on the Death of the Princess Charlotte*. In a letter to Byron written on 17 January 1817, which goes into the Chancery case and the charges against him as a 'REVOLUTIONIST, and an *Atheist*', Shelley opens with a chilling short sentence: 'My late wife is dead' (*Letters: PBS* I, 529). After alluding to 'circumstances' of 'awful and appalling horror'—perhaps meaning the reports that Harriet had been pregnant when she died—Shelley continues in the rest of the letter with defensive and distancing remarks about her death and the custody case. But, whether consciously or not, the blunt syntax of that simple opening sentence would come back to him ten months later when he composed the pamphlet. It begins by with the declarative: 'The Princess Charlotte is dead.'[5] It then continues with an emotional address that echoes Wordsworth's 'A slumber did my spirit seal:'

> She no longer moves, nor thinks, nor feels. She is [as] inanimate as the clay with which she is about to mingle. It is a dreadful thing to know that she is a putrid corpse, who but a few days since was full of life and hope; a woman young, innocent, and beautiful, snatched from the bosom of domestic peace, and leaving that single vacancy which none can die and leave not. (231)

'Thus much the death of the Princess Charlotte has in common with the death of thousands,' Shelley comments, and then goes on to remind his audience of the countless women who have died in childbirth or 'in penury or shame' and particularly of the suffering among 'the poorest poor'. 'Yet', he points out, 'none weep for them—none mourn for them—none when their coffins are carried to the grave (if indeed the parish furnishes a coffin at all) turn aside and moralize upon the sadness they have left behind' (232). Shelley here reveals the fundamental rhetorical device underlying the pamphlet as a whole: to compare the royal death with all-too-common deaths among 'the people' to whom the pamphlet is addressed, and in particular to compare the death of a princess to the near-simultaneous political executions of the working men convicted for taking part, goaded on by government spies and *agents provocateurs* such as the notorious 'Oliver', in a planned general insurrection in June 1817. This uprising included an armed march from the village of Pentridge towards Nottingham led by a framework knitter

---

[5] *An Address to the People on the Death of the Princess Charlotte*, in *Murray: Prose*, 229–39 (231).

(who may have once been a Luddite), Jeremiah Brandreth.[6] He and his insurrectionaries were arrested on the way. Brandreth, along with Turner and Ludlum, was publicly hanged and then beheaded on 7 November 1817, the day after the Princess died—a day set aside for national mourning of *her* loss, commemorations that the government surely hoped would divert attention from the executions. But radical publishers and journalists turned the juxtaposition around and made it the focus of their outrage. With his pamphlet, Shelley aimed to take his place among them.

'The news of the death of the Princess Charlotte, and of the execution of Brandreth, Ludlam, and Turner, arrived nearly at the same time' (233). The Princess, Shelley allows, 'was the last and the best of her race'. But there were thousands of others equally distinguished as she, 'when it comes to personal virtues'. And, though he says, 'in compassion: let us speak no evil of the dead', he makes in clear that the Princess had accomplished nothing significant during her brief public life.

> Such is the misery, such the impotence of royalty.—Princes are prevented from the cradle from becoming any thing which may deserve that greatest of all rewards next to a good conscience, public admiration and regret. (233)

But the execution of the three radical working-class men was, Shelley says, 'an event of quite a different character', since they were locked up in 'a horrible dungeon, for many months, with the fear of a hideous death and of everlasting hell thrust before their eyes; and at last were brought to the scaffold and hung'. The comparison itself is violently levelling. Shelley aims to humanize the Princess as less than her public persona while humanizing the executed reformers as more than theirs. At Marlow in the first week of November he was inspired by the reactions of the radical press to these events. Thomas Wooler's *The Black Dwarf* put it bluntly: 'That the death of the Princess Charlotte should have been immediately followed by such a scene of blood as that exhibited upon the scaffold at Derby, is as shocking to the understanding, as it is abhorrent to the feelings.'[7]

Shelley leverages that shock and abhorrence for the purposes of enlightening the people. As he will do in the sonnet 'England in 1819', and in *The Mask of Anarchy*, he structures the pamphlet's final emotional appeal around the formal figure of an interrupted procession, in this case the funeral procession for the beloved and lamented daughter of the Regent. Shelley would shift the intense national sympathy for Princess Charlotte in a radical direction. Near its end the essay suddenly changes registers, turning from conventional mourning to a sublime triumph, abruptly substituting one queen for another in a kind of positive usurpation:

> A beautiful princess is dead:—she who should have been the Queen of her beloved nation, and whose posterity should have ruled it for ever. She loved the domestic affections, and cherished arts which adorn, and valour which defends. She was amiable and would have become wise, but she was young, and in the flower of youth the despoiler came. LIBERTY is dead! Slave! I charge thee disturb not the depth and solemnity of our grief by any meaner sorrow. (239)

---

[6] E. P. Thompson, *The Making of the English Working Class* (New York: Vintage, 1966), 667–8.

[7] *The Black Dwarf*, as quoted in Kenneth Neill Cameron, *Shelley: The Golden Years* (Cambridge, MA: Harvard UP, 1974), 126.

The primary rhetorical device here is substitution, and it builds to a surprising climax. The pamphlet leads the reader to transfer his or her loyalties from the lost future Queen to an abstract 'sovereign', LIBERTY, as its syntax prompts the reader to imagine the one standing in the place of the other, living Liberty succeeding dead royalty. Shelley's writing models and would initiate the collective psychological process of substitution that will be necessary if the people are to accept the necessity of radical reform, if they are to allow one system to succeed another, if they are to worship something other than 'Custom'. In this way, Shelley prepares his audience emotionally to accept the peroration's final anti-monarchical image:

> and if some glorious Phantom should appear, and make its throne of broken swords and sceptres and royal crowns trampled in the dust, let us say that the Spirit of Liberty has arisen from its grave and left all that was gross and mortal there, and kneel down and worship it as our Queen. (239)

This most Shelleyan of images—a spirit of light triumphing over the signs of worldly power—is in fact highly conventional among the multiple forms of popular culture in his day. Graphical prints, for example, which made use of a visual language, allusive iconography, and various kinds of special effects in multiple media, were extremely popular with a wide and diverse audience of varying literacy. One well-known example published just a few years later celebrated another Queen, Caroline, during the scandal surrounding her divorce proceedings; it was the climactic transparency from George Cruikshank's *the political showman—at home!* (1820; British Museum #14150). The emblematic image of this print was also exhibited as a transparency—as a show-cloth or backlit curtain—during the general illumination of London in honour of the Queen in 1820. It depicts Liberty (or Britannia in the role of Liberty) lit by the radiance of a free press (represented by the literal image of a printing press). She holds in one hand a lance or pike topped with a liberty cap and in the other a portrait head of Caroline. Light disperses clouds of murk all around, which still partially conceal various caricatured politicians represented as scampering vermin with identifiable human heads— the accusers of the wronged and now transfigured Queen. Just as in Shelley's earlier image ('if some glorious Phantom should [...] make its throne of broken swords and sceptres and royal crowns trampled in the dust'), in the print the illuminated figure of Liberty triumphs over the symbols of corrupt power. Shelley's image of Liberty as Queen shares with this print a whole history of such images, which are based on a readily understood visual vocabulary and often employ spectacular special effects, for example, in the case of prints, the use of sequential images and of literal transparency or translucence (created by varnishing the paper, for example) to signify metaphorical layered meanings, a mood of sublime awe, transformations, and revelations. Shelley's representation of the Spirit of Liberty in the place of Princess Charlotte depends on the audience's familiarity with such images of glorious apotheosis, but it also depends on the audience knowing from diverse experience that these significations were always contested, potentially unstable in terms of who or what precisely the people should 'worship' as their ideal.

The visual vocabulary and structural conventions of satiric prints were matched elsewhere in popular culture during the Regency, especially for example in the theatrical pantomime, which Leigh Hunt called in 1817 'the best medium of dramatic satire' and which Shelley attended in London.[8] Princess Charlotte was already associated in the popular imagination with the heroine, Columbine, who was the daughter of a tyrannical father, Pantaloon. In his attempt to write for a popular audience, Shelley may have meant to tap into the rest of the tradition by putting his Columbine/Charlotte through a conventional pantomime climax—the 'transformation scene'. In the pantomime, the characters of the first part would suddenly be transformed by the actions of a Benevolent Agent (often a fairy godmother or Mother Goose) into their true identities—the stock characters descended from *commedia dell'arte*, Harlequin and Columbine, for example. On the stage, the actors might remove a 'big head' mask as the music swelled and the audience cheered. In his pamphlet, Shelley aims for a similarly stirring transformation scene by using the devices of accelerating syntax, vivid imagery, and linguistic substitution, as one thing replaces another in rapid succession: Liberty replaces the future Queen, a 'spirit' replaces a corpse, a vital ideal replaces a moribund institution, the Crown. In this way the pamphlet makes a *formal* argument for the transfer of popular reverence from the Princess to the more worthy object of veneration, Liberty. If, as the *Proposal for Putting Reform to the Vote* had suggested, the people are the 'fanatic worshippers' of 'Custom', then powerful persuasion will be needed to convince them to transfer their hopes and loyalties to a new political ideal.

For some time before her death Princess Charlotte had been cast in the role of the nation's best hope. Heiress apparent, she was beloved especially by the opposition forces who despised her father the Regent and was thus at the heart of party conflict, made into a symbol of Whig aspirations and the desire for change. With the loss of her stillborn child leading to her own death in 1817, those aspirations and hopes were dramatically destroyed and the line of succession was broken. In British history, threats to an orderly succession have always been moments of deep-seated political anxiety, and this was no exception. An heir was wanted, and the descent was rapidly established with some manoeuvring of a hasty marriage for the Duke of Kent, whose daughter Victoria would be born in 1819. From one point of view, the Regency itself was a structure of vicarious rule for the purpose of ensuring a proper succession, a measure intended to avoid the threat of a dangerously volatile interregnum. The whole Hanoverian line leading to George IV was the result of an earlier succession crisis and settlement. The death of Princess Charlotte represented a new moment of crisis in the national identity, and Shelley's pamphlet from Marlow was intended to intervene in that crisis and redirect the popular energies the crisis had released.

The actual printing and publishing of the pamphlet, however, is somewhat obscured.[9] Mary Shelley's journal records Shelley's beginning (on 11 November 1817) and completing

---

[8] *The Examiner*, 26 January 1817, 57. For the tradition of pantomime in relation to Shelley's satire, see Steven E. Jones, *Shelley's Satire: Violence, Exhortation, and Authority* (DeKalb, IL: Northern Illinois UP, 1994), 113–15.

[9] For the textual history of the *Princess Charlotte* pamphlet see *Murray: Prose*, 447–51.

(12 November 1817) what is very likely the pamphlet (*Journals: MWS* I, 183–4). Shelley wrote to his publisher Ollier on 12 November saying that he wanted an unnamed 'pamphlet' to be sent to press immediately, 'without an hours delay', and that 'the subject tho treated boldly is treated delicately' (*Letters: PBS* I, 566). These certainly sounds like references to the pamphlet on Princess Charlotte. But no manuscript or copy of a printed first edition survives. The text that comes down to us is based on a 'facsimile reprint' of 1843. Thus Shelley's attempt to publish in the moment, to influence a contemporary popular audience at a crucial turning point, seems to have been frustrated in this case.

ON THE DEVIL, AND DEVILS

Shelley had seen publication as a political act since his youth. Part of the evidence used against him during the Chancery hearings was his own radical poem from 1812, *Queen Mab*, even though he had distanced himself from it to a degree by 1817. At the hearings he was accused of having published works such as this that 'blasphemously derided the Truth of the Christian revelation and denied the existence of God'.[10] It seems clear that Shelley was actually in some real danger of being prosecuted for blasphemy, not just deprived of the custody of his children, as a result of the evidence brought out during the hearings. Following the generic division between verse and prose that Shelley had no doubt originally intended when he composed *Queen Mab*, the Chancery action objected not to the poetic stanzas but to the prose footnotes attached to them, in particular the notes to the lines 'There is no God!' and 'I will Beget a Son.' These polemical essay-length notes do indeed reveal that Shelley was an enemy of the received idea of divinity—'the God of Theologians'—which he insists 'is an hypothesis'. They also contain logical arguments against the doctrine of 'a future state of punishment' or damnation. In the note to the line 'I will beget a son', Shelley summarizes it in this way:

> During many ages of misery and darkness this [biblical] story gained implicit belief; but at length men arose who suspected that it was a fable and imposture, and that Jesus Christ, so far from being a God, was only a man like themselves. But a numerous set of men, who derived and still derive immense emoluments from this opinion, in the shape of a popular belief, told the vulgar, that if they did not believe in the Bible, they would be damned to all eternity; and burned, imprisoned, and poisoned all the unbiassed and unconnected enquirers who occasionally arose. They still oppress them, so far as the people, now become more enlightened, will allow. (*CPPBS* II, 263–77; 284–93; 284)

That rejecting this kind of theism, along with the doctrine of eternal damnation, was itself not only damnable but prosecutable, and that many others were being prosecuted in England for publishing such rejections, rendered the issue particularly urgent for Shelley in 1817, when *Queen Mab* was brought into evidence against him. It came down

---

[10] Quoted in Bieri, II, 28.

to the injustice of being prosecuted for what according to Shelley were the most advanced forms of imaginative speculation and expression. That one could suffer severe legal penalties for disavowing not just the divinity of Jesus, for example, but the reality of hell and the devil, was particularly galling to Shelley, since as myths they represented in the first place a deeply perverted idea of justice based on vengeance. He expressed his exasperation with this entanglement of the English political and judicial systems and the popular religion in a number of texts over the course of his career, including satirical fragments drafted in his notebooks (the 'Satire upon Satire' in particular),[11] and his published satire *Peter Bell the Third*, but nowhere more pointedly than in the satirical essay *On the Devil, and Devils*.

Seen in the context of Shelley's personal and political turmoil since returning to England at the end of 1816, this essay, which was most likely written sometime between late 1819 and early 1820, looks less like an academic exercise in theological speculation and more like another strategic political intervention.[12] It targets the English system of justice under which, just as under the authority of the 'popular religion', exposing injustice for what it is could legally be 'answered by the most conducive of syllogisms—persecution'.[13] In the essay, Shelley associates the devil (in his role as the 'Accuser') with the spies and informants of the current government, such as those who had goaded on Brandreth, Ludlum, and Turner, as part of the system that then condemned and executed the men:

> he is at once the Informer, the Attorney General, and the jailor of the Celestial tribunal. It is not good policy, or at least cannot be considered as constitutional practice to unite these characters. The Devil must have some great interest to exert himself to procure a sentence of guilty from the judge; for I suppose there will be no jury at the resurrection—at least if there is it will be so overawed by the bench and the counsel for the Crown, as to ensure whatever verdict the court shall please to recommend. No doubt, that as an incentive to his exertions half goes to the informer. What an army of spies and informers Hell must afford under the direction of that active magistrate, the Devil! (94)

In this way Shelley satirizes with sarcastic understatement both religious and political injustice, and implies that they are structurally related, manifestations of the same underlying ideology.

> The dirty work is done by the devil, in the same manner as some starving wretch will hire himself out to a King or Minister to work with a stipulation that he shall

---

[11] For Shelley's still relatively unknown and often blasphemous satiric fragments, see Jones, *Shelley's Satire*, 32–6, 64–7, 78–93.

[12] The essay was probably written between November 1819 and January 1820; see *BSM* XIV, *Shelley's 'Devils' Notebook, Bodleian MS. Shelley adds. e. 9*, ed. P. M. S. Dawson and Timothy Webb (New York: Garland, 1993), p. xvii. Mary Shelley intended to include it in her volume of 1840. A printer's proof for this volume became the basis for later texts. On internal evidence for dating, based mostly on Shelley's reading, see Stuart Curran and Joseph Wittreich, 'The Dating of Shelley's "On the Devil, and Devils" ', *Keats–Shelley Journal* 21–2 (1972–3), 83–94 (cited in *BSM* XIV, p. xvii).

[13] *On the Devil, and Devils*, in *Julian*, VII, 87–104; 91.

have some portion of the public spoil, as an instrument to betray a certain number
of other starving wretches into circumstances of capital punishment, when they
may think it convenient to edify the rest, by hanging up a few of those whose
murmurs are too loud. (94)

The allusion to the use of spies and informers in the Pentridge uprising is unmistakable.
Both political and theological work of this kind is 'dirty work', Shelley asserts, and in a
deliberately shocking analogy, he compares the cosmic injustice of 'judging, damning,
and tormenting' not only to political double-dealing but to the disposition of 'old maids
eunuchs & priests' and to 'a troop of idle dirty boys baiting [he had first written
'tormenting'] a cat', followed by an escalating list of other acts of wanton cruelty to
animals (95; *BSM* XIV, 69).

In his earlier satirical ballad *The Devil's Walk* (1812), Shelley had represented the devil
as a kind of cartoon gentleman, a dandy with intimate ties to wealth and power. The essay
On the Devil, and Devils takes a slightly different tone. Shelley knew Lucian's satirical
dialogues, and he himself characterized this essay as 'Lucianic',[14] witty and scoffing, sometimes sarcastic, in the spirit of the Greek rhetorician and pagan satirist of early
Christianity. Like Lucian, Shelley writes as an outsider from Christianity, which he repeatedly refers to in the essay as 'the European mythology', 'the popular superstition', 'the
modern mythology', and 'the Christian mythology'. By implication, he compares it with
the now-outmoded systems of Greek mythology, for example, treating it as 'one more
superstition' to be added 'to those which have already arisen and decayed upon the earth'
(92). In this spirit he pretends in his Lucianic voice to consider seriously 'the sphere of the
operations of the Devil'—which is, as he says (again with sarcastic understatement),
'difficult to determine'—in relation to the known cosmos in his day. Some have said,
absurdly enough, that the devil dwells in the sun. According to Shelley, this merely
illustrates the fact that the nature of the stellar and planetary systems was 'not known during the gradual invention of the Christian mythology' (96–7), and, by implication, that
theology is itself a form of mythmaking. We may as well suppose, he suggests,

> that the devil occupies the centre and God the circumference of existence, and that
> one urges inwards with the centripetal, whilst the other is perpetually struggling
> outwards from the narrow focus with the centrifugal force, and that from their per-
> petual conflict results that mixture of good and evil, harmony and discord, beauty
> and deformity, production and decay, which are the general laws of the moral and
> material world. (100)

But, no. Such complex metaphysics lie beyond the bounds of conventional religious faith:

> Alas, the poor theologian never troubled his fancy with nonsense of so philosophi-
> cal a form, and contented himself with supposing that God was somewhere or other;
> that the Devil and all his angels, together with the perpetually increasing multitude

---

[14] In an 1821 letter to his printer, Shelley refers to reading a 'quotation from Schlegel about the way
in which the popular faith is destroyed—first the Devil, then the Holy Ghost, then God the Father'.
He says he was amused by this and that he 'had written a Lucianic essay to prove the same thing'
(*Letters: PBS* II, 258).

of the damned were burning alive to all eternity in that prodigious orb of elemental light, which sustains and animates that multitude of inhabited globes, in whose company this earth revolves. (100–1)

In the escalating language of this passage Shelley overwhelms 'poor' theology with the sublimity of the cosmos and with the power of his own demonstrated philosophical and poetic imagination.

From innumerable stars and the multitude of inhabited planets Shelley shifts the focus to numerous devils, and turns to the 'droll story' from the Gospels of the 'legion' of demons cast out by Jesus into a herd of Gadarene swine, which then ran over a cliff. 'These were a set of hypochondriacal and high-minded swine, very unlike any others of which we have authentic record', he remarks (98), then speculates absurdly about the devils leaving the pigs and entering the fish and thus the food chain. He ends the digression by turning again to syncretic mythology, putting Christianity into a pagan context by wondering what Ulysses might have said to Eumaeus if he were told that 'all pigs had drowned themselves in despair because a wandering prophet had driven a legion of Devils into them'. For his part, Shelley, says, 'If I were a pig herd, I would make any [excuse] rather than that, to a master renowned for subtlity [sic] of penetration, and extent and variety of experience' (99).[15] This is strategic satiric blasphemy with a political end, satire cloaked in the guise of serious Enlightenment study of comparative mythological narratives. The 'droll story' from the Bible is set against Homer, the 'wandering prophet' of the Gospels against the wily hero of the *Odyssey*. Late in the essay Shelley decries the way in which 'Christians contrived to turn the wrecks of the Greek mythology, as well as the little they understood of their philosophy, to purposes of deformity and falsehood' (103). The pagan imagination conceived of Pan and the 'Sylvans and Fauns'; Christianity transformed these imaginary creatures into devils.

Shelley's essay *On the Devil, and Devils* may have been originally inspired by his own reading of the Gospels. Mary Shelley's journal notes that he read the New Testament, Luke in particular, during November or December 1819 (*Journals: MWS* I, 302, 304–6). One of his notes on Luke includes this remark: 'Who the devil is the Devil?' (*BSM* XIV, p. xvi). The ultimate point of the essay, however, is not merely to debunk Scripture or satirize Christianity for the sake of attack, though Shelley admits in both the essay and his letter about it that he is interested in the devil because he understands that the figure is 'the weak place of the popular religion' (87). Instead, Shelley's pro-pagan attack on *l'infâme* of contemporary Christianity was part of his larger political agitation for reform and against the injustices that he believed were based on the ideological foundation of religion. The essay is a satiric performance of the very expressions of unbelief for which a number of radicals were at that very moment being punished by the state. There was a dangerously fine line between blasphemy and sedition during the wartime and post-war years. The libel laws were deployed on multiple fronts in a government and loyalist

---

[15] *Julian* leaves a blank where 'excuse' appears in Shelley's hand in the manuscript (see *BSM* XIV, 85). Shelley added above the line in the manuscript the arguably blasphemous reference to Jesus as 'a wandering prophet'. He had first written 'some one' (see *BSM* XIV, 85).

society-sponsored campaign against radicalism. The question of blasphemy was therefore necessarily at the heart of radical assertions of free speech, and Shelley in this regard merely joined the radical publishers and pamphleteers he admired, such as William Hone and Richard Carlile, in making the crime of blasphemy at once his target and his strategic weapon. Rather than merely debating the issue, he defied the ban himself by flagrantly *performing* blasphemy in print.

LETTER TO *THE EXAMINER* ON RICHARD CARLILE

Late in 1819, perhaps at around the same time that he was writing the essay *On the Devil, and Devils*, Shelley composed a letter to his friend Leigh Hunt, the editor of *The Examiner*, on Richard Carlile's October 1819 conviction for blasphemous and seditious libel. Carlile had published Tom Paine's *Age of Reason* as well as his own radical journal, *The Republican*, and, beginning in January 1819, a journal mostly reprinting earlier material called *The Deist: or Moral Philosopher*. For this he was sentenced to three years' imprisonment in Dorchester Jail and was fined £1,500. From inside, Carlile continued to see that *The Republican* was published. Indeed, a series of surrogate editors, starting with his wife and including his sister, were to be prosecuted for the same crime. His highly visible case became a rallying point for radicals and reformers. Carlile had been one of the scheduled speakers at Peterloo on 16 August 1819, and afterwards he protested the resulting massacre in the pages of *The Republican*. In the event he was caught up in what historian E. P. Thompson has called 'the most sustained campaign for prosecutions in the courts in British history'.[16] The first such wave of government and private-society prosecutions during the post-war era had taken place in 1817, just at the time when Shelley was writing as the 'Hermit of Marlow', and had culminated in the public trials of radical journalists and publishers Thomas Wooler and William Hone. 'Percy B. Shelley, Marlow' had himself contributed £5 to Hone's cause and Shelley had remained engaged in English politics as best he could since leaving for the Continent in March 1818. No longer a rhetorical hermit but an exile in fact, he read *The Examiner* and other journals and newspapers, as well as private correspondence, and usually reacted rapidly to events as he received news of them. He sent *The Mask of Anarchy* back to Leigh Hunt in England for publication within weeks of hearing about Peterloo, for example, though Hunt chose not to publish the poem at the time, just as he apparently chose not to publish Shelley's letter on Carlile.

The charge of blasphemy became the target of Shelley's letter. Carlile was a Deist, and Shelley uses the word in his polemic, but the letter shows little interest in fine theological distinctions between Deism and atheism, for example. Under the libel laws at the time,

---

[16] Thompson, *The Making of the English Working Class*, 700.

even expressions of general scepticism could lead to prosecution if they were politically radical enough and directed to the volatile popular audience. As he does in the essay *On the Devil, and Devils* Shelley here points to the fundamental problem of getting a fair trial by jury in England. Carlile himself had opened his own defence by raising questions about the close connections between the Crown and the jurors.[17] Shelley, however, takes an apparently more theological tack. The letter to *The Examiner* makes a legal argument that Carlile could not have been tried by a jury of his peers: 'Who are the peers of a Deist? Deists, to be sure.'[18] As a practical matter Shelley concedes that an ideal jury could be composed of half Deists and half Christians—but of course he knows that this is a highly unlikely scenario. From the opposition he anticipates the argument that, after all, murderers are not empanelled on juries hearing cases of murder. In response, Shelley points out that 'Deism is no crime by the law of England' (139). He argues that 'mere disbelief is perfectly legal', and at any rate Carlile was accused not of Deism or disbelief per se but of the crime of blasphemy—the act of 'speaking injuriously of a certain religious persuasion' (139). This prohibition against blasphemy Shelley admits is the law of the land, but he sees it as a 'scandal' that should be 'erase[d]' by 'some legislative enactment' as soon as possible (139). In the meantime, strictly as a matter of logic, Carlile could not possibly have received a fair trial under the prevailing system, because it is the same system outside which he is accused of standing, a system built upon the very ideology whose authority he has refused to acknowledge. The blasphemed religion, Christianity, and its members and officials—'the persons who are injured & provoked by the blasphemy' (139)—cannot fairly stand in judgement of the alleged blasphemer.

Shelley's overall aim in the passage is to expose the deeply unjust circularity of such a trial. In the process of making this case, he also relativizes Deism and Christianity, along with other religious persuasions, by treating Christianity as if it were merely one among many possible belief-systems: 'Deism is no crime by the law of England any more than Sandimonianism or Unitarianism is a crime' (139). Indeed, as he observes, the Unitarian

> openly denies the divinity of Christ, or rather, if I understand his tenets, he asserts that every great moral teacher is divinely inspired in exact proportion to the excellence of the morality which he promulgates, & that Jesus Christ was a moral teacher of surpassing excellence. He considers whole passages of the Bible as interpolations & forgeries. (140)

Shelley then lists eminent Deists such as David Hume, William Drummond, William Godwin, and Jeremy Bentham, concluding with a question: 'What men of any rank in society from their talents are *not* Deists whose understandings have been unbiassed by the allurements of worldly interests?' (142). In contrast to these well-known and well-connected Deists Shelley describes Carlile as a 'starving bookseller' who must work to support his family (143). The point is not only to expose the inequalities of social class, but to expose the hypocrisy of the whole campaign against blasphemy. As Shelley

---

[17]   Kevin Gilmartin, *Print Politics: The Press and Radical Opposition in Early Nineteenth-Century England* (Cambridge: Cambridge UP, 1996), 142.

[18]   'To The Editor of *The Examiner*, London', 3 November 1819, in *Letters: PBS* II, 136–48 (139).

declares, in reality 'the prosecutors care little for religion, or care for it only as it is the mask & garment by which they are invested with the symbols of worldly power. In prosecuting Carlile they have used the superstition of the Jury as their instrument for crushing a political enemy, or rather they strike in his person at all their political enemies' (143).

Into this climate of political persecution masquerading as a religious cause, Shelley sent his letter defending Carlile to Leigh Hunt to be published in the liberal *Examiner*. Publication (which however Shelley was unable to achieve in this case) was intended as an act of defiance, a performance of solidarity with Carlile and other radical reformers. Though he calls for a subscription to raise money to support Carlile and vows to contribute to it himself, Shelley's most impassioned act of support in the letter comes near its beginning. There, deploying a rhetorical strategy like that of the essay *On the Devil, and Devils*, Shelley himself commits the same act of blasphemy for which Carlile is being prosecuted—and calls attention to the fact:

> for what was Mr. Carlile prosecuted? For impugning the Divinity of Jesus Christ? I impugn it. For denying that the whole mass of antient Hebrew literature is of divine authority? I deny it. I hope this is no blasphemy, & that I am not to be dragged home by the enmity of our political adversaries to be made a sacrifice to the superstitious fury of the ruling sect. But I am prepared both to do my duty & to abide by whatever consequences may be attached to its fulfilment. (137)

Some readers may be tempted to find in this passage signs of the kind of Shelleyan persecution complex they have come to expect from the author of *Alastor* and *Adonais*. But it is important in assessing Shelley's political and satirical prose to recognize the deliberate strategy at work in his rhetoric. The effect of the passage relies on the fact that it was to be published, since only the act of publishing such opinions would flout as well as criticize the libel laws and judicial system. The performative constructions here—'I impugn it. [...] I deny it'—*do* something by *saying* something; or rather, they *do* something by engaging in the act of *publishing* something. Thus they perform defiance by breaking one of the bad laws that 'tempt and slay' in post-war England ('England in 1819'). At his trial, Carlile himself had read aloud the blasphemous work he was accused of publishing, thus putting into the record Paine's *Age of Reason*, defiantly performing it in public and hoping to get it recorded by printed accounts of the proceedings.[19] From his own position as a once-privileged member of society who was now an exile (if not really a hermit), Shelley attempted in his letter to *The Examiner* to intervene forcefully in the politics of the moment by going on the record, by publishing that which was prosecutable while exposing the ideology that supported such prosecutions. In this instance, however, as in so many others during his short career, he was unable to publish, and the opportunity for timely intervention, if not the textual record of his attempt, was lost.

[19] Gilmartin, *Print Politics*, 139. See also Joel H. Wiener, however, in *Radicalism and Freethought in Nineteenth-Century Britain: The Life of Richard Carlile* (Westport, CT: Greenwood Press, 1983).

SELECT BIBLIOGRAPHY

Cameron, Kenneth Neill. *Shelley: The Golden Years*. Cambridge, MA: Harvard UP, 1974.

Gilmartin, Kevin. *Print Politics: The Press and Radical Opposition in Early Nineteenth-Century England*. Cambridge: Cambridge UP, 1996.

Hoagwood, Terrence Allan. *Skepticism and Ideology: Shelley's Political Prose and its Philosophical Context from Bacon to Marx*. Iowa City: University of Iowa Press, 1988.

Jones, Steven E. *Shelley's Satire: Violence, Exhortation, and Authority*. DeKalb, IL: Northern Illinois UP, 1994.

Marsh, Joss. *Word Crimes: Blasphemy, Culture, and Literature in Nineteenth-Century England*. Chicago: University of Chicago Press, 1998.

Scrivener, Michael Henry. *Radical Shelley: The Philosophical Anarchism and Utopian Thought of Percy Bysshe Shelley*. Princeton: Princeton UP, 1982.

Thompson, E. P. *The Making of the English Working Class*. New York: Vintage, 1966.

Wiener, Joel H. *Radicalism and Freethought in Nineteenth-Century Britain: The Life of Richard Carlile*. Westport, CT: Greenwood Press, 1983.

CHAPTER 10

POLITICS, PROTEST, AND SOCIAL REFORM

Irish Pamphlets, Notes to Queen Mab, Letter to Lord Ellenborough, A Philosophical View of Reform

MICHAEL SCRIVENER

INTRODUCTION

WHEN Thomas Hutchinson, in his 1905 Oxford edition of Shelley's poetry, placed *Queen Mab* and its extensive notes in the 'Juvenilia' section, he was following and reinforcing cultural and literary norms which have been largely abandoned a century later. If *Queen Mab* was a juvenile work, it did not have to be read seriously or at all, and if working-class radicals and socialists persisted in reading such a text—by far Shelley's most popular work in the nineteenth century, the so-called Chartist's Bible—such ill-informed reading habits only proved the vulgar reading taste of the masses. Modern scholars have long rejected the Victorian era's class and political quarrels over Shelley's radicalism, but important questions continue to be asked about his political works of 1812–13, and how his early radical prose relates to later reflections on politics.

Was Shelley's Irish expedition a presumptuous intervention or was it a measured, politically responsible action? Did the activism of 1812–13 lead to disillusionment and retreat, or did Shelley intervene politically in later periods? How are we best to characterize the political philosophy of 1812–13? How does his earliest political writing relate to the later *Philosophical View of Reform* (1819)? In terms of philosophical orientation, did Shelley begin as a materialist and then develop a more sceptical and Platonically idealist position?

TEXTS

Carefully annotated and edited according to the most rigorous textual standards, E. B. Murray's volume I of the *Prose Works of Percy Bysshe Shelley* (*Murray: Prose*) contains prose pieces that used to be regarded as among Shelley's juvenilia: *An Address to the Irish People*, *Proposals for an Association of Philanthropists*, *A Declaration of Rights*, and *A Letter to Lord Ellenborough*. Although manuscript material does not exist for any of these works, Murray was able to use a corrected copy of the *Address* which Shelley sent to his father. The corrected copy, part of the Pforzheimer Collection, has shaped the editing only of the Murray version of the essay, which for now is the definitive version.[1]

The textual history of *Philosophical View of Reform* is more complicated in part because it was never published in Shelley's lifetime. A holograph of the text has been transcribed and expertly edited by Donald H. Reiman (*SC* VI, 945–1065).[2] Mary Shelley, preparing the text for her own 1839 edition of the essay, transcribed the essay from the holograph, but she declined to publish the essay because she was afraid Sir Timothy Shelley would object to its politics. The essay was not published until 1920 when T. W. Rolleston published his edition of the work, upon which the modern editions have been based. Now Mary Shelley's own transcription of the holograph has been reproduced in a volume of the *Bodleian Shelley Manuscripts* edited by Alan M. Weinberg (*BSM* XXII, 58–249). Anyone doing scholarly work on the essay should consult the Reiman edition of Shelley's holograph and Mary Shelley's own transcription in the *Bodleian Manuscripts* series. Reiman has done an extraordinary job collating the variants between the holograph, Mary Shelley's transcription, and the editions of Rolleston and Peck, but there needs to be also a newly edited, reliable reading text of the essay to take the place of the Ingpen and Peck edition (*Julian*, VII, 1–55); the Julian text is flawed by its omissions (restored in the *SC* and *BSM* versions) and its structuring the material into what looks more like a finished essay than the manuscript material can sustain.[3]

IRELAND

William St Clair, reflecting what used to be the received opinion, views Percy's Irish expedition as a disillusioning failure. According to St Clair, the poorly written and poorly conceived pamphlets—rambling, repetitive, earnest exhortations, a 'bad sermon'—provoked

[1] *Murray: Prose* includes valuable editorial commentary (327–59), textual commentary (537–40), and textual collations (500–1) for the three Irish pamphlets and the *Letter to Lord Ellenborough*. The not wholly reliable reprinted texts in David Lee Clark's *Shelley's Prose: Or the Trumpet of a Prophecy* (Albuquerque, NM: University of New Mexico Press, 1954) remain useful, if out of print. Roland A. Duerken's inexpensive *Political Writings by Percy Bysshe Shelley* (New York: Meredith, 1970) has the two longest Irish pamphlets (but not *Declaration of Rights*), *A Letter to Lord Ellenborough*, and *A Philosophical View of Reform*. Donald H. Reiman and Neil Fraistat edited a hypertext of *Declaration of Rights* for the *Romantic Circles* website (<www.rc.umd.edu/editions/shelley/devil/declright.html>). The prose notes of *Queen Mab* are in *H* and volume II of *CPPBS*.
[2] *SC* VI, 945–1066.
[3] For a new reading text of most of the essay, see the version in *Major Works*, 636–74.

his mentor William Godwin to warn harshly that Shelley's political activism was preparing a 'scene of blood', a warning that led Shelley to leave Ireland in the spring of 1812, and never again to try to 'change things by organized political activity'.[4] This view ignores Shelley's extensive post-Dublin efforts to 'change things' politically. A partial list would include distributing pamphlets in Devon later in 1812, collaborating with the Spencean George Cannon and others associated with the *Theological Inquirer* in 1815, publishing the two Hermit of Marlow pamphlets in 1817, working on the Popular Songs of 1819–20, and cooperating on *The Liberal* with Byron and Hunt. One could quarrel over the meaning of 'organized political activity', but these later political interventions suggest a continuity of purpose and direction from his Irish expedition, not something wholly different. To be sure, Shelley did not pursue again plans to form a political association of 'philanthropists', but he found other ways to be active politically.

That the 19-year-old Shelley and his young wife Harriet came to Dublin in early 1812 was not wholly eccentric because the public anticipated that the Prince Regent and the Whigs might be granting the Irish their principal political demand, Catholic Emancipation. Irish political affairs were a pervasive reality in Shelley's world long before he came to Ireland, as his father was connected with the Whig leader, the Duke of Norfolk, one of the most powerful advocates for Catholic interests in parliament. As Paul Dawson illustrates in his study of Shelley's politics, the Whig influence on Shelley's political understanding was fundamental.[5] Ireland, in terms of its population—about half of England, Scotland, and Wales—and economic importance, was also anything but peripheral in British politics in 1812.

The first pamphlet, written in England, *An Address, to the Irish People*, was published by John Stockdale, a radical Dublin printer who had been imprisoned for his association with the United Irishmen in the 1790s. Stockdale probably published all three Irish pamphlets but his name is withheld in each case, presumably to avoid legal difficulties. Although the *Proposals for an Association of Philanthropists* has 'I. Eton' of Winetavern Street on the title page, there is no evidence that such a publisher ever existed.[6] The press was anything but free in 1812, especially in Ireland. At that time Irish journalist Peter Finnerty was serving a two-year sentence, as was William Cobbett, a London journalist, and Leigh Hunt with his brother John would serve two years starting in 1813. Kenneth Neill Cameron depicts the political atmosphere of 1812 as one marked by repression and revolutionary anger—with the Luddite riots—and revolutionary hope—with an insurrection in Mexico. The Shelley who completed his visit to Dublin 'saw his country with new eyes, a country of social conflict and predatory war, of cynical dictatorship and rising protest, of arrogant suppression and courageous resistance'.[7]

The *Address, to the Irish People* starts with an attack on Catholicism in a way almost all critics agree is rhetorically inept. Addressing Irish Catholics who have been victimized

[4] William St Clair, *The Godwins and the Shelleys: The Biography of a Family* (New York: W. W. Norton, 1989), 327.

[5] See the first chapter of P. M. S. Dawson, *The Unacknowledged Legislator: Shelley and Politics* (Oxford: Clarendon Press, 1980).

[6] Paul O'Brien, *Shelley and Revolutionary Ireland* (London: Redwords, 2002), 76.

[7] Kenneth Neill Cameron, *The Young Shelley: Genesis of a Radical* (New York: Collier, 1950), 180.

because of their religion, Shelley's persona, which claims to be neither Protestant nor Catholic, extensively criticizes Catholicism for its intolerance, its persecution of Protestants and heretics, papal authoritarianism, sexual immorality, clerical domination, and economic exploitation of the faithful (*Murray: Prose*, 10–16). Paul O'Brien, one of the strongest defenders of Shelley's Irish expedition, nevertheless points to the obvious flaws of the first pamphlet: that it is too focused on larger political issues, insufficiently focused on immediate Irish concerns, and wholly misreading the Catholic situation. Additionally, it is 'overlong, repetitive' and patronizing. O'Brien excuses Shelley for the frequent exhortations to the Irish to stay sober and peaceful because such appeals to self-control were standard political gestures from the 1790s, when they were frequently made by the United Irishmen themselves. O'Brien thus finds credible and worthy Shelley's general idea of carving out a political position to the left of Daniel O'Connell's Catholic Committee.[8]

After the wrongheaded attack on Catholicism, the essay moves more effectively into a vigorous defence of religious toleration and free speech, transitioning finally to proposals for forming political associations for discussion, education, and advocacy. Obviously outside the orbit of the Catholic Committee, these associations are urged to pursue intellectual independence with reading, discussion, and reflection. These probably illegal associations will constitute a public sphere to criticize political affairs. The essay seems to anticipate repression and hostility, asking: 'Are you slaves, or are you men?' Moreover, when repression comes, the proper response is non-violence: 'When one cheek is struck, turn the other to the insulting coward' (*Murray: Prose*, 30). The pamphlet concludes with a re-emphasis on non-violence and press freedom, highlighting Peter Finnerty's imprisonment (without mentioning, however, that Shelley had earlier directed the profits from *Posthumous Fragments of Margaret Nicholson* to be sent to Finnerty, for whom he also had raised £100).[9]

Whether the Catholic Committee had read Shelley's pamphlet carefully or at all, it invited him to its public meeting at the Fishamble Theatre where he delivered a fifteen-minute speech—not the hour-long speech he thought he had given—which all the Dublin papers reported favourably, never mentioning the hisses at Shelley's anti-religious comments.[10] The politically savvy Catholic gentry was not interested in confronting the young son of a Protestant English MP connected with the pro-Catholic Whig interest.

Shelley's brief sojourn in Dublin attracted the attention of John Lawless, political journalist and activist to the left of O'Connell, and the working-class radical Catherine Nugent. These veterans of earlier political struggles took Shelley and his ideas quite seriously and O'Brien persuasively states that 'given time and hard work, a small but significant movement could have been built to influence the political agenda in a more radical direction'.[11]

---

[8] O'Brien, *Shelley and Revolutionary Ireland*, 103–4.
[9] Ibid. 32–3.
[10] The newspaper accounts are in *Murray: Prose*, 291–302.
[11] O'Brien, *Shelley and Revolutionary Ireland*, 121.

The second Irish pamphlet, written and published in Dublin, proposed an association of 'philanthropists' who would be educated political idealists rather than dispensers of wealth. The essay, much more effectively put together, works better as a piece of rhetoric than the first pamphlet by focusing on the function and rationale for the association. How precisely this association relates to the ones sketched out in the first pamphlet is not entirely clear because the audience for the first was the poor and for the second, the well educated. Presumably the philosophical enlighteners who are addressed in the second pamphlet will teach and lead the people who are addressed in the first. Using the same rhetoric one finds in his correspondence with Elizabeth Hitchener and William Godwin to whom he wrote about his novel *Hubert Cauvin* on the failures of the French Revolution,[12] Shelley constructs a complex analysis of the French Revolution as having not achieved its full potential because of the failures of the Enlightenment. Voltaire, Rousseau, Helvetius, Condorcet, and even Shelley's mentor Godwin are accused of varying degrees of error and ineffectiveness. A better-organized, more philosophically systematic and coherent, and more energetic enlightenment process would have prevented the revolution from its various horrors, but sound philosophical principles 'were little understood in the Revolution' (*Murray: Prose*, 52). The essay concludes by turning back to Ireland's situation, which the proposed philanthropic association is invited to address, to promote Catholic Emancipation and repeal of union.

The third Irish pamphlet, the single-sheet *Declaration of Rights*, designed to be displayed on public doors and walls, fuses an emphasis on rights from Paine with an emphasis on rational deliberation from Godwin. Its thirty-one epigrammatic paragraphs constitute a manifesto of democratic insurgence with some surprising aspects, like a 'right' to 'universal citizenship' (no. 20), the denial of an absolute right to property and wealth, the concomitant implication of a moral rather than a laissez-faire economy (no. 28), and a 'right' to leisure (no. 29). It is not clear that any of these broadsheets were ever distributed in Dublin but some were posted in Devon, where Shelley's servant Dan Healy was arrested, convicted, and imprisoned for six months. Political activism in 1812 was dangerous, as indicated by the Home Office file that was being developed on Percy Shelley's activities and publications.[13]

If one gets beyond Shelley's youthful, English arrogance and the first pamphlet's rhetorical mistakes, *Declaration of Rights* seems to be as remarkable as the rest of his literary career. Contrary to those who find the activism and writing readable as an Orientalist fantasy and adolescent indulgence, it turns out that Shelley was right in terms of winning Catholic Emancipation, for it was secured in 1829 largely along the lines sketched out by Shelley.[14] Shelley underestimated the difficulty of achieving the repeal of the union, which would not be achieved for another century, but he was hardly alone in that particular miscalculation. The achievements and failures of the French Revolution and the Enlightenment would continue to be central points of focus in his political poetry and prose. Although his ideas developed more complexity over time, even his very last poem, the unfinished *The Triumph of Life*, has important continuities with the Irish pamphlets

---

[12] *Letters: PBS*: I, 218, 223, 229, 267.   [13] St Clair, *The Godwins and the Shelleys*, 377–8.
[14] Dawson, *The Unacknowledged Legislator*, 164.

of the 19-year-old Shelley. Viewing all three pamphlets together, however different each one is, one notices points of similarity to which he will keep returning in later writing: a civic republican construction of citizenship and a notion of educating the public through politics and discourse, a cosmopolitan understanding of what it means to be a literary intellectual and responsible member of the world community, and an absolute and unwavering commitment to civil liberties, which ensure the health of a public sphere. It is also impossible to ignore those Shelleyan qualities that are definitely not simply products of youthfulness: his contempt for a traditional Catholic culture that had resisted English dominion for centuries, his blindness about his own exercising of power, and his impatience with the minute particulars of everyday materiality.

NOTES TO QUEEN MAB

The most valuable commentary on *Queen Mab* the poem and its Notes is that found in Kenneth Neill Cameron's incomparable *The Young Shelley* (1950). Unlike so many other literary critics of his day, Cameron actually loved *Queen Mab*, a poem he declared 'the most revolutionary document of the age in England' (301). Note the choice of word, 'document', for the poem with its Notes is not a tidy work with unity, organic or otherwise. The epic poem with numerous, lengthy, and asymmetrical notes was fairly commonplace in the eighteenth and early nineteenth century but its vogue passed with the rise of stringently Romantic aesthetic norms. Within the norms of postmodern textuality, perhaps readers are ready again for something like *Queen Mab*, truly a loose and baggy monster. My favourite moment in terms of form is Note 3, which recontextualizes a passage from Godwin's *The Enquirer* to comment on an anti-war passage in canto IV, then transitions to a poem authored by Shelley: 'Falshood and Vice: A Dialogue', as if the poem were completing the line of thought, poetic and philosophical. Pastiche and quotation are joined with a separate poem, all to comment on the so-called main text, another poem. It is also perfect that the poem deployed as a response to the Godwin extract is a dialogue, two more voices that can hardly achieve semantic closure.

That the Notes owe much to the radical Enlightenment is hardly in dispute. Note 13 announces, 'There is no God!' Rejecting a creative deity but not a 'Spirit coeternal with the universe', Shelley seems to allow for a Spinozan kind of God but one is not entirely sure (*CPPBS* II, 263). The Notes are extreme in both content and rhetorical effect. Note 12, for example, affirms a doctrine of Necessity from Holbach that constructs a nature completely indifferent to humanity (*CPPBS* II, 260). As Paul Hamilton remarks on this Holbachian emphasis, it is 'surprising' but it illustrates Shelley's zeal in attacking religion. A wholly impersonal and mechanistic Necessity gives no quarter to Christianity or Deism.[15] Rationalistic science to undermine religious illusions and delusions, a staple of

---

[15]   Paul Hamilton, 'Literature and Philosophy', in Timothy Morton (ed.), *The Cambridge Companion to Shelley* (Cambridge: Cambridge UP, 2006), 173.

the radical Enlightenment, is deployed in half a dozen Notes. Note 2, for example, on the 'plurality of worlds' insists that the perspective opened up by astronomy destroys utterly any possible attachment to Judaeo-Christianity (*CPPBS* II, 239–40). Although Shelley is attacking what religious modernists would consider a childish notion of monotheistic religion, that was the form of religion most people in his culture at the time understood as the only legitimate kind—otherwise Lyell and Darwin later in the century would not have had such a devastating effect on religious opinion. Another example of rhetorical intensity is Note 9 on the selling of love: 'Prostitution is the legitimate offspring of marriage and its accompanying errors' (*CPPBS* II, 254). If prostitution is the 'legitimate' product of marriage, one wonders what the other 'errors' could be. Note 17 on vegetarianism rewrites the Fall, a central Western myth, in terms of meat-eating and cooking. The Shelleyan Fall from a vegetarian diet to Promethean meat-eating is correctable whereas the Christian Fall requires the whole sacrifice of Christ and the various mechanisms of faith. From cooking and meat-eating comes the necessity of spices, which is to say conquering other lands.[16] These Notes are meant to provoke, to upset, to disturb, and to irritate. Like Blake in *The Marriage of Heaven and Hell*, Shelley wants to give full voice to the antithetical powers that are ordinarily muffled and held in check.

LETTER TO LORD ELLENBOROUGH

The principal reason Lord Ellenborough sentenced the elderly radical Daniel Isaac Eaton to eighteen months in jail and to the pillory in May of 1812 for the 'blasphemous libel' contained in one of Thomas Paine's anti-religious essays was not mysterious. At a time when more British soldiers were trying to thwart the English Luddites than were engaged in doing battle against Napoleon, the government was worried about social unrest (*Murray: Prose*, 355). Religion as part of the state was an important instrument of social control. A veteran publisher for the London Corresponding Society in the 1790s, Eaton (1753?–1814), whose judicial punishment killed him, enjoyed considerable public support but it was not powerful enough to force his release. Shelley's essay, which falsely claims to be the first to protest Eaton's conviction,[17] was published in July of 1812 by a Devon printer by the name of Syle who destroyed many of the thousand copies after he comprehended his possible legal danger. Only one copy survived into the twentieth century to be reprinted (*Murray: Prose*, 353–9).

Identified by Cameron as Shelley's 'first important work of literature' and 'among the classics' of free-speech arguments, the *Letter to Lord Ellenborough* has an intended audience that is, depending on the critic, indefinite (Behrendt), popular (Cameron), or educated

---

[16] Timothy Morton, in *Shelley and the Revolution in Taste: The Body and the Natural World* (Cambridge: Cambridge UP, 2004) and other writings, has developed this dimension of Shelley's work.

[17] Stephen C. Behrendt, *Shelley and his Audiences* (Lincoln, NE: University of Nebraska Press, 1989), 74.

(Scrivener).[18] The uncertainty may derive from the double role played by the persona of the *Letter*, for he acts both as a legal analyst attempting to rebut the constitutionality of the conviction and as a fellow sceptic who casts doubt on the authority of Scripture in the manner of Eaton and Paine. The constitutional debater and the freethinker have more and less polite styles.

The constitutional argument is that the state has no business trying to regulate public opinion on religion or anything else. The legal authority by which Lord Ellenborough condemned Eaton was illegitimate because the judicial precedents were 'antiquated' and had long been obsolete (*Murray: Prose*, 63). The judge failed to maintain a court of impartiality by allowing the prosecution to inflame the jury's prejudice as Christians against the Deist Eaton (64). Accordingly, Eaton was victimized as were Socrates and Jesus. The essay deploys these two examples recurrently, especially the latter one, to illustrate the hypocrisy of a classically educated Christian like Ellenborough violating the spirit of the culture and religion for which he is supposedly an advocate and defender. The pamphlet also points to the specifically Catholic instances of persecuting and burning heretics, trying to remove the basis for an affirmation of Protestant superiority. If the judge claimed that Eaton and Paine were undermining morality, Shelley's persona was ready to develop all the paradoxes and contradictions of doing something immoral in the name of morality. To protect so-called morality 'Socrates was poisoned' and 'Jesus Christ was crucified' (*Murray: Prose*, 69). In fact, it is only for his opinions that Eaton is being prosecuted, opinions that should be protected constitutionally, as print culture should debate the controversial points of theology. 'If the truth of Christianity is not disputable, for what purpose are these books [of philosophy and theology] written? If they are sufficient to prove it, what further need of controversy? *If God has spoken, why is not the universe convinced?*' (*Murray: Prose*, 71–2). Here the two roles are merged, for the persona affirms the constitutionality of rational argument and echoes the scepticism of Eaton and Paine concerning Christianity.

The pamphlet concludes with a call to universal solidarity and toleration—'when the Mahometan, the Jew, the Christian, the Deist, and the Atheist, will live together in our community, equally sharing the benefits which arise from its association, and united in the bonds of charity and brotherly love' (*Murray: Prose*, 73). The constitutionalist not the sceptic is the one who speaks those words and who is the one belonging to 'our community'. Shelley argues for a cosmopolitan, multicultural community appealing to the secularized religious values of charity and love; in later works, most notably *Prometheus Unbound*, he continues to refine and deepen his understanding of how charity and love have communitarian power.

The pamphlet is designed to move someone already sympathetic to Eaton to a more philosophically informed position, to understand the legitimate role of free speech as 'unrestrained philosophy' in its perennial battle with 'superstitious custom'.[19] Shelley's

---

[18] Cameron, *Young Shelley*, 209–10; Behrendt, *Shelley and his Audiences*, 78; Michael Scrivener, *Radical Shelley: The Philosophical Anarchism and Utopian Thought of Percy Bysshe Shelley* (Princeton: Princeton UP, 1982), 65–6.

[19] Scrivener, *Radical Shelley*, 65–6.

investment in working against the restrictions on, and the disabilities attached to, violating the government's conception of what constitutes a legitimate print culture is powerful and lifelong. With some notable exceptions like Cameron, criticism before the 1960s largely ignored Shelley's experience with and thinking about political repression. Recent critics, however, have paid attention to the ways repression affects Shelley's writing.[20]

A PHILOSOPHICAL VIEW OF REFORM

Remaining unpublished for a century, Shelley's *A Philosophical View of Reform* was drafted in a notebook between December 1819 and January 1820. First mentioning it in December 1819 as an 'octavo on reform' and then again in May 1820 as 'a kind of standard book' after Jeremy Bentham 'for the philosophical reformers' (*SC* VI, 953), Shelley for unknown reasons never carried the work to completion. Behrendt correctly describes the draft as a series of false starts with uncorrected errors.[21] Not a unified essay, it should not be treated as one but rather as several rhetorical lines of development centred around some intellectual concerns that are provoked by the issue of political reform. After Peterloo—the massacre of peaceful demonstrators in Manchester on 16 August 1819—it was widely expected that the reform forces had momentum on their side and would force government to alter the system of representation at least to approximate to what was called 'moderate' reform, but Lord Liverpool's government passed instead the repressive Six Acts to silence the reform movement, which revived in 1820 during the raucous Queen Caroline Affair (when the rejected wife of George IV tried to claim her title with great popular support). The moderate reform that was expected by many did not become a reality until 1832, more than a decade later. Writing from Italy and depending on newspaper reports filtered through his own wishful thinking, Shelley—like many others on the left and right—thinks that a political 'crisis' is approaching.

Philosophical Reform has two general areas of interest, the practical dimensions of a possible reform and the theoretical issues such a reform entails. Shelley's approach to the practical issues is consistent with his earlier political writing in its emphasis on moderation to avoid the failures of the French Revolution. For Shelley moderation is the best form of radicalism. As Dawson points out, moderate reform was the end-goal for most of its advocates but for Shelley it was just a beginning.[22] The complexities of moderation should not be dismissed, for the goal is to achieve as much of the political ideal as conditions will bear, but the nature of those conditions is not obvious. Although he looks forward to a fully egalitarian society, the kind of ideal equality sketched out by Christ, Plato, Rousseau, Godwin (the draft also alludes to Moses—*SC* VI, 1044), the task for

---

[20] Terence Allan Hoagwood, *Skepticism and Ideology: Shelley's Political Prose and its Philosophical Context from Bacon to Marx* (Iowa City: University of Iowa Press, 1988), 45–7, deals with repression in *Letter to Lord Ellenborough* and other Shelley texts.

[21] Behrendt, *Shelley and his Audiences*, 213.

[22] Dawson, *The Unacknowledged Legislator*, 188–9.

reformers is 'with the difficult and unbending realities of actual life' and 'accommodating our theories to immediate practice' (*Julian*, VII, 43).[23] Too ambitious movement toward the ideal results in regressive disorder and violence, but too timid an approach results in 'incurable supineness', a passivity he associates with cowardly members of parliament and Oriental despotism (*Julian*, VII, 50).

Shelley's plan of action for the reform movement, which is only one of five threads of thought developed in the fragmentary *Philosophical View of Reform*, coherently sets out a series of bold steps. He proposes moderate reform as an initial move to prod the government to enlarge the franchise (*Julian*, VII, 46; *SC* VI, 1050), but if parliament does not reform itself, then 'my vote is for universal suffrage and equal representation' (*Julian*, VII, 47). Moreover, he unambiguously prefers aggressively resisting an unreformed government to passive inaction. Cameron labelled Shelley's position on reform and revolution as conflicted,[24] but there seems to be no hesitation in the proposed series of actions: large open-air meetings of the united reformers to advocate radical reform; non-violent resistance to military aggression; efforts to win over the soldiers to reform; ceaseless political activity, risking jail, contesting public opinion in 'perpetual contest and opposition' (*Julian*, VII, 49). A proposal with reference to the seventeenth-century revolution is tax resistance, one of the activities that led eventually to the toppling of Charles I (*Julian*, VII, 51). A petition campaign from assemblies would be coordinated with 'memorials' composed by the nation's reformist writers—'poets, philosophers and artists' such as Godwin, Hazlitt, Bentham, Hunt, and Byron (*SC* VI, 1059–60). And if all this activity did not move parliament to reform? 'The last resort of resistance is undoubtedly insurrection' (*SC* VI, 1061). Shelley's view of civil war is anything but sentimental, for he delivers a harsh reminder of how authoritarian and dehumanizing any kind of war is, but even this, war with all its horrors, is much better than abject passivity and perpetual tyranny (*Julian*, VII, 53–54). The plan of action is practicable, reasonable, plausible, and unyielding in trying to move society toward radical reform.

The plan is consistent with the unequivocal defence of executing Charles I as a way of teaching other nations how to bring tyrants to justice (*SC* VI, 967). Although Shelley also pens a proposed note that somewhat moderates the regicidal affirmation— 'criminals' should be 'pitied & reformed'—republican rhetoric is evident throughout *Philosophical Reform*. A dimension of republican thinking governs Shelley's rejection of the secret ballot, an aspect of his reform programme that puzzles Cameron and Hogle.[25] Secret ballots are like secret political associations that conceal motives which should be part of public discourse. A face-to-face interchange between politician and voters at a large public meeting generates 'common sympathy' and 'excitements of a popular assembly'; moreover, 'a mass of generous & enlarged & popular sentiments [would] be awakened,

---

[23] When quoting the essay, I rely on the Julian edition, which is a reading text, except when the draft provides something that the Julian edition lacks.

[24] Kenneth Neill Cameron, *Shelley: The Golden Years* (Cambridge, MA: Harvard UP, 1974), 145.

[25] Cameron, *Golden Years*, 142; Jerrold E. Hogle, *Shelley's Process: Radical Transference and the Development of his Major Works* (Oxford: Oxford UP, 1988), 248.

which would give the vitality of That republican boldness of censuring & judging one another' (*SC* VI, 1047). Public opinion requires the exercise of open debate. As in the civic republican tradition, politics is educative;[26] citizens who must explain their voting preferences become accustomed to debate and non-violent conflict and 'learn to be free by practicing freedom, exercising the will, imagination, intelligence, and capacity to love'.[27] Public voting has the Godwinian emphasis on rational argument,[28] but Godwin preferred reading and small-scale discussions; he mistrusted large political assemblies which he feared would be emotionally rather than logically swayed.

Another intellectual thread in the *Philosophical View of Reform* is the understanding of history, most pointedly the replacement of the Whiggish 1688 by the republican 1641. It will be recalled that Richard Price and Edmund Burke were debating the meaning and implications of 1688 in 1789–90, but both assumed that 1688 was the proper touchstone for mainstream political thinking and national identity. Shelley puts the normative focus on the Long Parliament of 1641–8, which represented 'all classes of people' and initiated massive changes, abolishing feudalism, securing personal liberty, and in short carrying out what amounts to a bourgeois revolution (*SC* VI, 997–8). The role of William III was putting a 'seal' on the revolution and permitting the drift toward the crisis of political representation, for the one to five ratio of represented to unrepresented citizens had in the nineteenth century become a huge one to many thousands. It was the 'unrepresented multitude'—the tens of thousands of urban and rural labourers who had emerged from the new economic conditions of a 'double aristocracy' and an ever expanding national debt—that created a constitutional crisis of political legitimacy. To resolve this crisis the point of historical reference for Shelley was 1641, not the 'compromise' with tyranny that constituted the meaning of 1688 (*SC* VI, 998–1000).

An important focus of this fragmentary essay is economic, as Shelley explores the nature of legitimate and illegitimate property as well as the contentious issue of the national debt. Lacking in the Julian edition of *Philosophical View of Reform* but present in both Mary Shelley's transcription (*BSM* XXII, Part 1, 137) and Shelley's holograph (*SC* VI, 1004) is the clear heading, 'Of the National Debt', followed by a lengthy analysis. The Julian version, which sets up three chapters, gives a distorted sense of what this piece of writing is actually doing. Clearly deriving in part from William Cobbett's essay *Paper against Gold*, to which Shelley makes explicit reference (*SC* VI, 1014), Shelley's analysis of the national debt and the paper money controversy goes beyond Cobbett in several important respects, as pointed out by Cameron: instead of reducing the interest paid on the debt, as recommended by Cobbett, Shelley boldly wants to abolish the debt, forcing the wealthiest people to absorb the financial loss; Shelley, unlike Cobbett, does not see a return to the gold standard as resolving the economic crisis. Although Cameron correctly notes

---

[26] Dawson, *The Unacknowledged Legislator*, 192.   [27] Scrivener, *Radical Shelley*, 214.
[28] Hogle, *Shelley's Process*, 248.

Shelley's 'county' bias against city speculators,[29] and Reiman persuasively describes Shelley's 'agrarian' bias (*Norton 2*, 589–99), the most exciting aspects of the economic analysis are semiotic, its penetrating understanding of money as a sign system, as pieces of paper with writing on them. The constitution of value that Shelley describes anticipates Marx's interpretation of commodity fetishism and Lukacs's conception of reification (*SC* VI, 1009–23). Similarly, in the section on legitimate and illegitimate property, he gives more credibility to the dichotomy than it surely deserves, as Hogle recognizes, when he points to the 'limits of Shelley's proto-Marxism' in the comments especially of the 'discretion' of the legitimate property owner to dispose of his wealth according to individualist rather than moral-political criteria.[30] Shelley tries to align the writer with the labourer, rather than the privileged rich, but sooner than base the affiliation on solidarity alone, he argues that writers and others with skill and wisdom produce legitimate personal property as opposed to the fraudulent wealth produced by the rich (*SC* VI, 1032). Perhaps betraying the uneasy conscience of the eldest son of a baronet, Shelley insists on the production aspect of writing and intellectual activity as a way to link himself with labourers and artisans.

The final intellectual thread upon which I want to comment is the section on history and poetry, which is clearly an early version of some of the key ideas in the *Defence of Poetry*. That *Philosophical View of Reform* is, as Hoagwood phrases it, the 'most sustained exposition of Shelley's philosophical skepticism' seems correct, as Shelley's text pursues a dialectic of enquiry and mental construction contextualized often by references to the history of philosophy.[31] *Philosophical View of Reform*'s critique of ideology, which Hoagwood compares with the thinking in Marx's *German Ideology*, can also be seen in Hogle's terminology of 'transference' or Weinberg's understanding of the text's logic of how social injustice gets reproduced by a 'paradigm of deceit' governing the logic of political institutions. The 'falsity of entrenched ideologies' has its origin in the 'deliberate deception of the governed'.[32] What Shelley calls poetry is that discursive moment of rupture when something new and powerful emerges that is capable of attracting sufficient sympathetic identification to warrant calling the phenomenon unacknowledged legislation (*SC* VI, 992–3). Shelley's understanding is that cultures 'produce' great poets and great poets produce cultures, that the creativity of the most original artists is truly revolutionary but that the most remarkable creativity is also socially and culturally determined. That shrewd sense of both what an individual artist can do and the inevitable dependence of even the greatest artist to the 'spirit of the age' is something Shelley articulated better and more clearly than anyone else.

---

[29] Cameron, *Golden Years*, 139.

[30] Hogle, *Shelley's Process*, 235.

[31] Hoagwood, *Skepticism and Ideology*, 209, 183.

[32] Ibid. 169–70; Alan M. Weinberg, '"These Catchers of Men": Imposture and its Unmasking in "A Philosophical View of Reform"', in Alan M. Weinberg and Timothy Webb (eds.), *The Unfamiliar Shelley* (Farnham: Ashgate, 2009), 258.

CONCLUSION

Although it still makes sense to call Shelley's political project a form of philosophical anarchism, as both Paul Dawson and I have argued, it is now apparent to me that other emphases are equally important. Shelley was indeed a radical, as O'Brien makes all too clear, but he was never reckless and impulsive (at least in politics). That he was not a liberal is illustrated by his opposition to the secret ballot, a typical product of liberal political philosophy. Shelley wanted the rough and tumble world of the noisy political meeting, the give and take of debate and oratory, the stir and excitement of bodies in close connection. The solitary voter in the isolated polling booth—perfectly understandable within Benthamite liberalism—violates the Shelleyan spirit of civic republicanism and revolutionary forms of association. His society of philanthropists never got anywhere but his political thinking always assumed a place for such associations. The London Corresponding Society, the Friends of the People, the Society for Constitutional Information, the Hampden Clubs, the Society of Spencean Philanthropists—Shelley assumed politics meant having structures like these, even if he himself never found an organization to join.

Shelley was a radical, to be sure, but he was not anti-liberal, as is evident in his unwavering defences of civil liberties and his several arguments of a constitutionalist nature. Certain phases of the French Revolution, of which Shelley was well informed, contemptuously turned aside considerations of free expression, free press, and individual liberties for a revolutionary-populist rhetoric. He explicitly argued against such tendencies in the reform movements of his own day. Like John Thelwall, Shelley expected the radical societies and reform movements to conduct their affairs with reason, intelligence, and restraint—as the London Corresponding Society almost always conducted itself, as Laon and Cythna lead the revolutionaries in *The Revolt of Islam*, and as *The Mask of Anarchy* urges the non-violently resisting crowd. Although not really a part of the liberal tradition, non-violent resistance is an essential part of Shelley's political writing.

From the Irish pamphlets to the unpublished manuscript of *Philosophical View of Reform* there is not a movement from naive materialism to philosophical idealism, as at one time was the received wisdom in Shelley scholarship. Rather, there is a kind of materialism to all the writing, which, as Paul Hamilton points out, has the Platonic quality of dialogism.[33] Vegetarianism is a form of materialism, as is the wild textuality of the *Queen Mab* Notes, as is the deconstruction of the national debt and paper money. The Holbachian materialism was only one moment, to be taken seriously but not definitively. Dialogue-like materialism pervades Shelley's political oeuvre, as it does the poetic work. Paine versus Godwin, Catholic versus Protestant, Irish versus English, elite versus working class, religious versus sceptical, moderate versus radical, Shelley's political writing puts into play different voices and logics for both rhetorical and dialectical purposes.

---

[33] Hamilton, 'Literature and Philosophy', 169.

Shelley even debates with himself, as seems evident in parts of *Philosophical View of Reform* where he struggles to define morally and politically legitimate forms of property.

Finally, Shelley, an original and serious political writer, absorbed influences like Godwin, Paine, and Rousseau, made them his own, and moved in new directions. He is a serious writer in that he is not a superficial tourist simply observing exotic ideas to be entertained, but he carries out his thinking with rigour and moral care. Who else could have invented the approach of non-violent resistance, to which he gave rich philosophical and poetic attention? Although he does indeed anticipate Marx in a number of texts, he has a political outlook more nuanced in many respects than Marx's, for Shelley's reading of the French Revolution acknowledges the power of class but is not reductionist. A new synthesis of Shelley's political worldview would integrate the more recent emphases like ecocriticism and postcolonial critique with the long recognized proto-Marxism, philosophical anarchism, civic republicanism, non-violence, and liberalism.

SELECT BIBLIOGRAPHY

Behrendt, Stephen C. *Shelley and his Audiences*. Lincoln, NE: University of Nebraska Press, 1989.

Bradley, Arthur. 'Shelley, Ireland and Romantic Orientalism'. *English Romanticism in the Celtic World*. Ed. Gerald Carruthers and Alan Rawes. Cambridge: Cambridge UP, 2003.

Cameron, Kenneth Neill. *Shelley: The Golden Years*. Cambridge, MA: Harvard UP, 1974.

—— *The Young Shelley: Genesis of a Radical*. New York: Macmillan, 1950.

Clark, David Lee. Ed. *Shelley's Prose or The Trumpet of a Prophecy*. Albuquerque, NM: University of New Mexico Press, 1954.

Dawson, P. M. S. *The Unacknowledged Legislator: Shelley and Politics*. Oxford: Clarendon Press, 1980.

Duerksen, Roland A. Ed. *Shelley: Political Writings*. New York: Meredith, 1970.

Hoagwood, Terence Alan. *Skepticism and Ideology: Shelley's Political Prose and its Philosophical Context from Bacon to Marx*. Iowa City: University of Iowa Press, 1988.

Hogle, Jerrold E. *Shelley's Process: Radical Transference and the Development of his Major Works*. Oxford: Oxford UP, 1988.

Morton, Timothy. Ed. *The Cambridge Companion to Shelley*. Cambridge: Cambridge UP, 2006.

Murray, E. B. Ed. *The Prose Works of Percy Bysshe Shelley*. Vol. I. Oxford: Clarendon Press, 1993.

O'Brien, Paul. *Shelley and Revolutionary Ireland*. London: Redwords, 2002.

Roberts, Hugh. 'Setting Minds Afloat: Shelley and Barruel in Ireland'. *A Brighter Morn: The Shelley Circle Utopian Project*. Ed. Darby Lewes. Lanham, MD: Lexington Books, 2003.

Scrivener, Michael. *Radical Shelley: The Philosophical Anarchism and Utopian Thought of Percy Bysshe Shelley*. Princeton: Princeton UP, 1982.

Webb, Timothy. ' "A Noble Field": Shelley Irish Expedition and the Lessons of the French Revolution'. *Robespierre and Co.: atti della ricera sulla letteratura francese della Revoluzione*. Ed. Nadia Minerva. Vol. II. Bologna: Edizione Analisi, 1990.

Weinberg, Alan M. ' "These Catchers of Men": Imposture and its Unmasking in "A Philosophical View of Reform" '. *The Unfamiliar Shelley*. Ed. Alan M. Weinberg and Timothy Webb. Farnham: Ashgate, 2009. 257–76.

CHAPTER 11

POETICS

PAUL HAMILTON

SHELLEY's 'poetics', or theory of poetry, is given definitive treatment in one explicit manifesto, *A Defence of Poetry*, towards which he builds through a series of Prefaces he wrote to a number of his poems. Other prose fragments contain speculations, thought-experiments, and position papers which contribute to his central views on poetry. But the habit of prefacing, and the diversity of input which his Prefaces make to poems, show that Shelley's habit of theorizing was important to him as a poet, especially to the extent that the self-conscious, reflective dimension created for his poetry by prefacing is frequently relevant to the poetry's interpretation.

Sources for Shelley's ideas about poetry can be found in classical and near-contemporary philosophical precedent. None of these, however, ever provides a satisfactory explanation or comprehensive account of the way he thinks about poetry. It is more helpful, this chapter tries to show, to present Shelley as fluent in the philosophical idioms of his day, a theorist articulating his own thoughts in a generally available speculative language. Shelley can then be seen to be unusually eclectic: from the British empirical tradition he makes sophisticated use of Lockean semiotics and Humean scepticism; he deploys views about the interdependence through desire of the identity of self and other deriving from German idealism; he also capitalizes on ideas of aesthetic education which Friedrich Schiller had put high on the philosophical agenda. He uncannily exploits those moments when Romantic philosophy anticipates rationalizations of a modernity to come—historicist notions of untimeliness, and theories locating meaning in difference, which lead through Nietzsche to Derrida. Just as his poetry is profoundly European in its erudition and setting, arguably if silently bearing comparison with Goethe and Leopardi as much as with Shelley's British contemporaries, so his theory shows its pedigree more in its practice than by explicit reference.

Shelley's first major poetic project, and one of his most influential ones, was the long poem *Queen Mab*, written over almost a year between April 1812 and February 1813. Shelley's bulletins to friends and publisher on its progress at first suggest that he sees poetry as a safe-house for his radical opinions rather than their most effective organ of dissemination. While he claims not 'to have tempered my constitutional enthusiasm in that Poem', he has done so in the belief that a 'Poem is safe' from the attention of 'the iron-souled Attorney general'. Outrageous politics or inordinate ambition ('The Past, the Present, & the Future are the grand & comprehensive topics of this Poem') testify to the traditional 'genus irritabile vatum' of the poet, absolving him from being taken altogether seriously (*Letters: PBS* I, 324). This view of poetry has to be understood in the context of Shelley's other writings of this time which were highly risky—*A Letter to Lord Ellenborough, An Address, to the Irish People, Proposals* [...] *for an Association of Philanthropists*—nevertheless it is striking that at this time poetry is the means of unrealizing his opinions. To be an infidel and republican democrat in poetry apparently excused the author from being held to account for these views. This is an isolated remark, however. Thereafter in letters Shelley insists on the unwaveringness of his opposition to all orthodoxies, although he imagines few will appreciate the poetry of his radicalism. But his initial willingness to capitalize on a traditional view that 'the poet nothing affirms', as Sir Philip Sidney's *Apology for Poesie* (1695) had it, is not simply a strategic disguise.[1] It shows how pointedly his poetics set up poetry as an alternative juridical system opposed to all legal establishments and their Attorney Generals. There is no suggestion in *A Defence of Poetry* that current 'unacknowledged legislators of the World' (*Norton 1*, 508) should never be acknowledged; in some historical cases where Shelley's flexible notion of poetry allows itself to be found in 'institutions' they most clearly were recognized and obeyed.

Ironically, *Queen Mab*, or the 'The Chartist's Bible' as it came to be known, was the most politically influential poem Shelley wrote. It also was a poem which had copious endnotes but no Preface. Its *parerga*, or framing devices, were more explanatory and didactic than the poem's story, in that disconcerting way that some of the later Prefaces were. Shelley's Prefaces are henceforth the ambiguous and subtly implicated manifestos of the idea of poetry he thinks his poems embody. Prefaces never quite take up the objective stances to which they pretend, disinterestedly telling us how the subsequent poem should be read, but often put forward views which the poetry then outmanoeuvres. Put another way, the Prefaces voice their poetics through a character who has his place within the poem's plot rather than outside it. The implication is that these ambiguities are material to the interpretation of the poetry, and that the difficulty of finding transcendental rather than immanent meanings for any statement of what poetry is about is often part of the poem's meaning.

So in *Alastor; or, The Spirit of Solitude*, the speaker of the Preface sounds tendentious in the interpretation offered, even before one has read the poem. His or her *ad hominem* criticism of the 'youth' or hero of the poem, while specific to this character, is also clearly situated within poetic polemics of the day—disagreement between the first and second generation of British Romantics as to how poetry should be written. From the Preface, we receive 'instruction' about the dangers of 'self-centred seclusion' represented by the

[1] Sir Philip Sidney, *An Apology for Poetry (or The Defence of Poesy)*, ed. Geoffrey Shepherd, rev. and expanded R. W. Maslen (Manchester: Manchester UP, 2002), 103.

'youth' or hero of the poem (*Longman*, 1, 462–3s).[2] Many critics have taken this straight-forwardly and joined in the castigation of the hero's pursuit of his own imaginative ide-als at the expense of social interaction or an awareness of the needs of the others around him. Shelley's poem, the speaker of the Preface instructs us, is understood as attacking a Wordsworthian poetry of introspection whose apparent sympathy for the plight of oth-ers is actually a celebration of his own powers of imaginative sympathy. But the Preface also deplores those who are 'deluded by no generous error'. What is this 'error'? It is to cease to be content with the infinite possibilities of nature around one and to desire something more. Since, by definition, such satisfaction is not objectively available, it has to be invented. In fact, it is only in the activity of making up that natural infinity can be surpassed. Hence derives the hero's concentration on his own imaginative powers, and his disastrous immuring in his own solipsism. But hence, also, will derive the Preface's sense of his 'generous error': the *super*-infinity he tries to find through self-consciousness, and the Preface's own delusion, perhaps, that it can both critique the hero and celebrate the imaginative powers revealed by his reflexive turn.

But the Preface's critique of internalization is further complicated when it coincides with Shelley's growing belief that we are largely dependent on the imagined responses of others for our own sense of self. By the time Shelley writes his fragment *On Love* (*Norton 1*, 473–4, probably written in July 1818) things have gone even further: the logic of reflec-tion has become the prime force in epistemology. Far from being straightforwardly con-demned, the 'generous error' of the 'youth' in *Alastor* has become the mechanism by which we advance beyond received orders of knowledge, systems of ethics, or political establishments. Lacking ourselves the sense of what we truly are, conceived in its full potential, we entrust this responsibility to the lover, a figure for an ideal realm of perfect sympathy. The lover sets the pattern for that desired correspondence in which external reality underwrites or reflects back to us confirmation of our infinite capacities. The lan-guage of Shelley's explanation ranges from the scientifically forensic language of 'meet-ing with an understanding capable of clearly estimating the deductions of our own', to the political imaginary of 'the enthusiasm of patriotic success' (474). One might have reasonably suspected that the narrator of the Preface to *Alastor* was nursing his own fan-tasy in the figure of the 'youth' when he re-described 'self-centred seclusion' as 'generous error', himself responding over-generously. But now the logic of reflection explains the continuity here, and only urges, in addition, that we recognize the dialectic involved. Shelley's fragment of a year later, *On Life* (*Norton 1*, 474–8), continues his polemic against a materialism fixed in its ways in contrast to a materialism—the 'Necessity' valorized in *Queen Mab*—which undermines any establishment and so is better described as 'the intellectual system' (476).

How can 'materialism' also furnish an 'intellectual system' or 'science of mind' as Shelley seems to claim? Aren't they opposites? Many influential critics have taken Shelley's scepticism to show that he is not a materialist but an idealist thinker who conceives of the

---

[2] References to Shelley's poetry are taken either from *Longman*, or where not already in its first two volumes, from *Norton 1*, which is also the edition from which Shelley's prose is quoted.

world as mental in character, tailored to our modes of understanding it.[3] Materialism requires us to believe in final, physical determinants of our mental activity. Shelley appears to resist this determinism, but he is immersed in the ambiguities of its dominant empiricist expression—our subjection to fixed patterns of ideas and impressions. Imagination, in the Humean empiricism with which Shelley principally engaged from *The Necessity of Atheism* onwards, consolidates the regularities of this input from the senses rather than freeing us from its authority. We imagine the world in which we can believe.[4] Our reliance on imagination for our belief in a stable world makes Hume himself a sceptic about that world's external existence; it makes Shelley a sceptic not about the world's externality but about its established character. In *On Life*, Shelley effectively turns Hume's scepticism inside out to argue that the world organizes itself as a semiotic system which gives a different lead to our speculations about it, disrupting their conservative psychology to ensure they never become conclusively stabilized. Shelley insists that even 'all familiar *objects* are signs, standing not for themselves but for others, in their capacity of suggesting one thought which shall lead to a train of thoughts,—our whole life is thus an education of error' (477) (emphasis added). The activity by which objects reflect each other becomes the principle of natural organization. Materialism *is* an intellectual system, but one which progresses our mental states rather than being prescribed by them as in idealism. At all levels of sentience, from highly self-conscious subjects to inanimate objects, progressive differentiation keeps our educative 'error'—generous to a fault—on the move.

Where does this leave the poetics of the Preface to *Alastor*, though? The ongoingness of the linguistic organization of things, the constant movement of desire within the activity of knowing, as one word seeks corroboration in another, overcomes aesthetic establishments too. The 'error' is perhaps too generous to be policed conventionally. Poetry can no longer be the hiding place of opinions wanting to de-clutch themselves from other more legally accountable discursive activities. All are signs for each other. The philosophy of Shelley's older contemporary, Hegel, rather than our post-Saussurean semiotics, seems a fitting commentary on this dynamic intertwining of significance with desire in the service of progress.[5] But then how is poetics possible? Aren't we always overpowered by the life-stories on which Prefaces try to pronounce? Aren't would-be objective critics actually interested narrators? *Alastor* speaks a language in which we can tolerate the contradictions that have stretched the credibility of the Preface's response. The Preface can only represent the poem's dilemma in a more limited form.

The 'self-centred seclusion' for which the Preface of *Alastor* indicts its hero does not allow for the formative influence of others; but extreme openness to the world is a

---

[3] See Earl Wasserman, *Shelley: A Critical Reading* (Baltimore: Johns Hopkins UP, 1971), 31–153; and contrast Timothy Clark in *Embodying Revolution: The Figure of the Poet in Shelley* (Oxford: Clarendon Press, 1989), 39–43.

[4] Anthony Flew's *Hume's Philosophy of Belief* (London: Routledge and Kegan Paul, 1961) is still the clearest introduction.

[5] Contrast Jerrold E. Hogle's *Shelley's Process: Radical Transference and the Development of his Major Works* (New York: Oxford UP, 1988).

'generous error' which underpins the educative principle as Shelley (and Hegel) understands it. Eventually Shelley addresses this conflict head-on in his final poem, *The Triumph of Life*, an unfinished project in which life's irresistible progress triumphs over its *Triumph*, or its generic handling within poetry. By that I mean that the poem shows that 'life' makes history out of all those whose reflexive self-understanding—'thought's empire over thought' (211)—has tried to detain it. To object to this, to find it insupportable, is like objecting to history, like wanting it to stop. But the poetics of this precept produces a strikingly open or self-undermining attitude which uses genre in order to show us its limitations. Poetry is there to be disenchanted.

But this power to disenchant itself is its supreme creativity. In other words, poetry for Shelley is the discourse whose purpose is *transparently* educative. It turns 'error' from mistake into exploration. The narrator of *The Triumph of Life*, 'Rousseau', identifies with his own written life of sensibility, and all that is left him as a result is the irredeemable decay and decomposition of that historical expression. The poem in which he appears, on the other hand, already suspects its own character. How can we have a 'Triumph', in the manner of Petrarch's great series of poems, not of the usual subjects of love, fame or death, but a 'Triumph' of life, the very element in which we move and have our being? The unspoken suggestion seems to be that 'life' is poetically unmanageable. Poetry here stands in for any establishment hoping to arrest the progress of things, but does so knowingly. 'Vitally metaphorical', according to *A Defence of Poetry*, poetry itself is never self-identical but always a figure or allegory of a fulfilment still to come, 'the before unapprehended relations of things' (482). A poem capable of getting on terms with life must already be writing itself as history, as a creation which will be outlived in another form, but whose knowledge of this historicity makes it willingly generate its afterlife, ceding the ground to its successors. Even the most flagrant of a poem's concessions to its unmanageable subject matter must look dated. Expanding on the conclusion to the 'Ode to the West Wind', Shelley's 'Triumph' summons the greatest resources of Western thought and chains them to the 'car' of life. Its modern, English fluency in a *terza rima* rhyme scheme marvellously recreates Dante and his outmoded theology, so expressive still for us in terms different from its original religiosity. Poetry here becomes exemplary as its creativity advertises the 'error' of any historical view of things, historicizing it in a manner revelatory of a sense of modernity, of the poet's now, his 'life'. It educates us in the historical difference which will eventually err from its own poetic specifics. But whichever bio-political discourse becomes the next developer of the poem's insights, it too will be historically subjected to radical renovation. To know this is to recover the poetic moment and escape the mouldering redundancy of 'Rousseau'. A language which is not open to such rehabilitation 'will be dead to all the nobler purposes of human intercourse' (482); conversely, we can only image life, according to Shelley, as the vitality of a language continually differing from itself. Poetic figuration is and stands for this vitality, 'at once the representation and the medium, the pencil and the picture, the chisel and the statue, the chord and the harmony' (481). *A Defence* keeps making this crucial transition between poetry in 'a more restricted sense' (483) and poetry which 'unveil[s] the permanent analogy of things' (485).

How does Shelley arrive at the destructive poetics of his last, unfinished poem?[6] He follows a path through his Prefaces towards *A Defence of Poetry*'s definition of poetry as capable of exceeding its 'restricted sense', a discursive self-transcendence which, though, seems nurtured by excellence in 'the more restricted sense' of prosodic felicities (*Norton 1*, 483). In the Advertisement to 'Rosalind and Helen', we find that 'the highest style of poetry' is 'calculated to excite profound meditation' (*Longman*, 2, 268). In the poem itself, it is noted that 'Alas we know not what we do | When we speak words' (1194–5). Again, the particular surrender to music or measure appropriate to the appreciation of poems is unrestricted by the historical meanings of the words. It is thus like the recognition in any creative view of human nature, not only one which is formally poetic, that a prophetic understanding includes its own historical way of putting things in its sense of what is to be surpassed. *A Defence* tells us that the need to arrange in 'rhythm and order', in accordance with appropriate canons of 'the beautiful and the good', is the poetic idiom in which we recognize 'new materials of knowledge, power and pleasure' (503). Poetry in high style, a poem which conspicuously draws attention to its own poetic features, is, the argument goes, more conducive to getting its readers to think about the prophetic ambitions which a poem might encode for discourse in general. Consequently, poetry just by being poetry can, like Milton's *Paradise Lost*, 'contain within itself a philosophical refutation of that system of which, by a strange and natural antithesis, it has been a chief popular support' (498). At the end of *A Defence*, Shelley states baldly that 'poetry, in a restricted sense, has a common source with all other forms of order and beauty according to which the materials of human life are capable of being arranged, and which is poetry in an universal sense' (507). This connection of poetry with a poetic of *all* human understanding can then explain some of Shelley's more outrageous claims for poetry 'in its most extended sense'—that it lets the poet enjoy a 'character' in which he 'participates in the divine nature as regards providence, no less than as regards creation' (492). Hence also his provocative claims that it is 'an error to assert that the finest passages of poetry are produced by labour and study' (504). This makes more sense if it is tied to the belief that poetry is the discourse that advertises the fact that true progressiveness also critiques the terms in which it is currently expressed. Poetry has therefore, following Milton's claim, to be 'unpremeditated' (504), escaping prescription. The footsteps of the quasi-divine nature with which it interpenetrates our own are erased, or are traceable only as signs whose meaning has overtaken them. Footsteps fascinate Shelley in *A Defence*, whether Bacon's, Astraea's, or those of sheer inspiration, and in each case he stresses that the power to signify only comes with the passage of meaning somewhere else. The poetry of this mobility does not simply defamiliarize, it 'creates anew the universe'. It starts from Shelley's basic linguistic principle, his universal semiotic, that 'all familiar things' gain significance by standing not for themselves but for others (493, 504, 505).

---

[6] Helpful here is William Keach's qualification of Paul de Man's 'Shelley Disfigured': 'he recognizes that Shelley's fragment [*The Triumph of Life*] affirms an irreducible power in the arbitrariness of language, without which language would not be able to question its own mode [e.g. Poetic] of meaning.' *Shelley's Style* (New York: Methuen, 1984), 194.

Is poetic untimeliness always a virtue? Couldn't it also describe a kind of historical malfunctioning? In his Preface to *Laon and Cythna*, Shelley discusses the failure of the French Revolution in ways that make it sound like the poetry he is commending to his readers. The poem to follow is an 'experiment on the temper of the public mind', we are told (*Longman*, 2, 32). 'Experiment' recalls both Burke's use of it as a term of opprobrium for those who, like the French revolutionaries, tinker with a country's constitutional inheritance; it also echoes Wordsworth's view of his own *Lyrical Ballads*, now usually thought to mark a rural retreat from a public to a domestic register of discussion. Shelley's 'experiment', though, is 'in contempt of all artificial opinions or institutions', and these include the 'system' (*Longman*, 2, 38) which critics from Jeffrey to Byron abhorred in Wordsworth's poetry, despite his denials of having one. Shelley eschews the didacticism that went with writing to a system because he hopes to 'awaken' a sympathetic reception to the narrative he then proceeds to summarize. His abstract is then followed by a short verdict on the French Revolution which describes how it too exhibited the untimely disparity between enlightened opinion and existing institutions (*Longman*, 2, 35). But now the contempt for conformity, shared by the poetic experiment, appears to be a symptom of political failure. This looks like an embarrassment until one remembers that the poetic 'experiment' Shelley has just proposed was a practical one intended to have results. Rather like William Godwin's progressive anarchism, the poem seeks to have an effect on its readers that will tend to further the 'cause' in which it is written and thus help establish the truth it proclaims. Coleridge told Wordsworth that great poets should create the taste by which they are to be enjoyed, and Shelley here argues that it is the displacing of didacticism by affect that in fact morally and politically empowers his poem. His poem is written to 'kindle' that 'virtuous enthusiasm' whose presence at first it appeared merely to be trying to detect (*Longman*, 2, 32). Shelley is now trying to incite the sympathies for which he seemed earlier only to be testing. He is beginning to contrive an aesthetic education, the preparation which the French revolutionaries disastrously lacked, as a prerequisite for the success of another revolution. In other words the Preface, if somewhat obliquely (or tactfully), is actually endeavouring to create the conditions for establishing that missing conformity between enlightened opinion and a political establishment. He risks the Burkean riposte that he has shown that the French Revolution might have been all very well as a speculative, poetic idea, but then was a catastrophe practically. He plants the idea that the power of poetry is to engage with us in such an effective way that the 'enthusiasm', which thinkers from Shaftesbury onwards saw as a power to be civilized in a progressive cause, could indeed produce political reform.[7]

Such poetic dynamism, he tells us, is 'poetry in its most comprehensive sense' (*Longman*, 2, 40). In a footnote alluding to his mentor Godwin, he further argues that such generosity makes poetry as much as science the possible agent of 'perfectibility'

---

[7] Anthony Ashley Cooper, Third Earl of Shaftesbury, 'A Letter Concerning Enthusiasm', in *Characteristics of Men, Manners, Opinions, Times*, ed. Lawrence E. Klein (Cambridge: Cambridge UP, 1999), 4–29.

(40 n.). Repeatedly Shelley's prose defences of poetry risk dissolving poetry's discursive specificity in the educational range he attributes to its aesthetic power. For Shelley, 'the poetry of life' (*Norton 1*, 502) is sometimes something we have lost, at other times what poetry endeavours to establish, even at the cost of its own *poetic* survival. No tactic could be better calculated to offend the literary establishment of his day which required art to stay in its allotted place, and which fiercely attacked any examples of taking its traditionally emancipatory or universal ambitions as serving particular lobbies for social enfranchisement, whether of class, sex, or nonconformity in general. Poetry for most of Shelley's contemporary reviewers became something else as soon as its idealism became realized in actual social recommendation. Shelley must have seen Anna Barbauld's *Eighteen Hundred and Eleven* prominently vilified in *The Quarterly Review* as incompetent catachresis or wilful oxymoron because of its ambitions to be a political poem.[8] When Keats translated the classical register of educated poetasters into flesh and blood gods and goddesses, he was ridiculed as uneducated, depraved, and as having made a category mistake disqualifying his poetry from aesthetic status. Shelley, as learned in the classics as any of his enemies, similarly historicized the classics as part of a desire he would share with the narrator of Keats's *The Fall of Hyperion* for poetry to disseminate or anticipate practical virtue and material good. Like Keats's narrator, he desired a poetry whose author was not isolated, 'a fever of thyself', but outgoing, 'a sage; | A humanist, physician to all men'.[9] *Adonais*, the elegy he wrote for Keats, culminates, I will argue, in an affirmation of this common practice.

For Shelley, it was just poetry's transformative but non-didactic power which confirmed that the originating poetic moment had been a genuine one. The Preface commends an aesthetic education not locked in the categories of its own 'unmingled good' (*Longman*, 2, 36) as, arguably, was the influential theory of the *Letters on the Aesthetic Education of Mankind* (1795–1801) which Friedrich Schiller wrote in reaction to the French Revolution. The absence of such a transfiguring, educational force explains the historical failure of a revolution in which those breaking out of slavery could not be expected to become 'liberal-minded, forbearing, and independent' (*Longman*, 2, 36) overnight.

Already Shelley's lithe and sinuous prose style is devising a new versatility for poetics, in which the primacy of the literary imagination usually associated with the Romantics is allowed to undermine its seeming centrality by a kind of calculated overreaching. Thus, sympathies awakened in others by poetry are allowed a different kind of expression altogether, one adapted to their needs and their situation. Poetry's subjection to historical circumstance reminds writers that 'each is in a degree the author of the very influence by which his being is thus invaded' (*Longman*, 2, 41): the maker of something no longer bearing an exclusively literary character because of poetry's powers of historical shape-shifting. We get the poetry we deserve. The Preface to *Laon and*

[8] *Quarterly Review* 7 (1812), 309–13.
[9] *The Fall of Hyperion*, 1, 169, 189–90, in *The Poems of John Keats*, ed. Miriam Allott (London: Longman, 1970).

Cythna is strikingly engaged with the central philosophical problem of hooking up aesthetics to the world we know and in which we act. The dispensability of poetry in the process of realizing its virtue is a subject to which Shelley repeatedly returns in both prose discussion and poetic theme. He personalizes the anxieties belonging to this adventurousness in 'Ode to the West Wind' and he universalizes them in *The Triumph of Life*. This willingness to forgo poetic sovereignty in the interests of a discursively more democratic legacy is very different from submitting poetry to a strict critique of its limitations and insisting on the critical proprieties. In one passage, he states baldly that 'Poetry, and the art that professes to regulate and limit its powers, cannot subsist together' (43). Shelley is instead interested (already) in poetry's power to push its own figures towards their own historical transfiguration so that they can re-materialize with fresh authority elsewhere in the discoveries they have anticipated. In a curious follow-up, he has Lucretius as the exemplary poetic transformer, here of poetry into 'the basis of our metaphysical knowledge' (44). The critics of Lucretius are the product of a Roman Republic gone wrong, the Greek and Asian diaspora resulting from Roman imperialism, whose slave mentality militates against the virtue and benevolence which poetry typically dispenses.

In the Preface to Shelley's great revolutionary poem of 1818–19, *Prometheus Unbound*, Shelley's argument continues to work primarily through a series of transitions between restricted and unrestricted senses of poetry. Whenever poetry appears reduced to the one meaning, Shelley's enthusiasm carries it towards the other, and in the process shows poetry's unrivalled power to reveal the spectrum of significance. In contrast to the Preface to *Laon and Cythna*, the later one is happier to acquiesce in the interaction between the current historical state of opinion and poetic innovation. We hear that 'the equilibrium between institutions and opinions is now restoring, or is about to be restored' (*Longman*, 2, 474). The obligation to observe the intellectual forms of the age is a 'subjection the loftiest do not escape' (475). Yet, Shelley's imagery for historical conditioning can now be quite positive. The unpremeditated 'uncommunicated lightning' with which the creative individual irradiates inherited literary forms sounds homogeneous with the 'collected lightning' of the 'cloud of mind' to which she or he can as a result contribute. In this cloud inhere 'the opinions' which 'cement' our social condition. Poets are caught in this circle in which they are 'in one sense the creators and in another the creations of their age' (474–5). The restricted sense in which they are original authorizes their transition to the sense in which they contribute to the *Zeitgeist*. Shelley thus develops his experimental alternative to the 'didactic poetry' which is his 'abhorrence', and again his imagery suggests his abiding ambition of getting his writing on terms with life-process:

> My purpose has hitherto been simply to familiarise the highly refined imagination of the more select classes of poetical readers with beautiful idealisms of moral excellence; aware that until the mind can love, and admire, and trust, and hope, and endure, reasoned principles of moral conduct are seeds cast up on the highway of life which the unconscious passenger tramples into dust, although they would bear the harvest of his happiness. (475)

The rhythm of poetry and the order of ethics harmonize once more when the heightened perceptions of poetry make us conscious of moral possibility as growth-points in our lives without which we fail to flourish as human beings.

Shelley's writing on poetry is never 'Romantic' in a clichéd sense. Writing on 'imitation' in the Preface to *Prometheus Unbound*, he can sound like a neoclassical or Augustan writer. Imitation is of nature, but in nature is included human nature. Just imitations of nature also reflect the proper proportions and ratios of human understanding. What might have been a Romantic theory of expressiveness, in which our renderings of the world are fervid projections of our fantasies, is instead a sober placing of individual aspiration within the boundaries of generally accepted possibility. Shelley appears as distrustful of a pure originality as was Dr Johnson. He concedes that in portraying nature he has imitated the representations he has inherited from others, just as did the poets before him from Homer to Pope: 'one great poet is a masterpiece of nature, which another not only ought to study but must study' (474). On the other hand, when he, Shelley, goes back to the origins of tragedy, the context in which Aeschylus' *Prometheus Bound* was written, one uncovers a pervasive arbitrariness. It is in order to win the prize for the best tragedy at Greek religious festivals that the first tragedians rewrote 'national history or mythology' (472). Employing the same licence, Shelley rewrites Aeschylus' lost play *Prometheus Unbound*, which was reputed to have reconciled Prometheus with his and mankind's tyrannical oppressor, Jupiter. His poetically self-serving bid for originality, however, makes space for us to see again the crucial connection between poetry in a 'restricted' sense and poetry in a 'universal' sense. For, it is in strengthening this connection that Shelley hopes to advance on his predecessor's achievement. So 'moral interest' and 'high language' (472) turn out to be inseparable, the virtuous and the poetical are conjoined, and apparent one-upmanship becomes a furtherance of Shelley's conception of poetry's historical dynamic. Equally, this movement lets Shelley's work claim that it departs from that of his contemporaries, since to stress the poetics of his work, its theoretical dimension, involves representation of 'the operations of the human mind', something 'unusual in modern poetry' (473), and so a redoubled assertion of Shelley's originality.

There must be some humour in this. Shelley's skilfully opportunistic approach to classical imitation, and his occasionally capricious tone, are un-ignorable. In a way, though, this lightness of touch is a tactic in which he pretends to discount his personal ambitions in order to suggest the life-process that his own calculated transparency makes visible. Poetry historically reviewed at length as it is in *A Defence* renders history circumstantial and exposes its attempt to turn what could have been different into an unarguable establishment of some kind. The personal views of Dante and Milton are 'merely the mask and the mantle in which these great poets walk through eternity enveloped and disguised' (*Norton 1*, 498). In other words, it is the extraordinary ability to produce writings coterminous with history at every stage which singles out great poets. To transform one's personality into a mask becomes the counter-intuitive touchstone of poetic sincerity. In the Preface to Shelley's play *The Cenci*, written just after *Prometheus Unbound*, we hear of the heroine Beatrice that

The crimes and miseries in which she was an actor and a sufferer are as the mask and the mantle in which circumstances clothed her for her impersonation on the scene of the world. (*Longman*, 2, 735)

It is impossible to separate artifice from integrity in Beatrice's 'impersonation' here. She wouldn't have a personality were it not for these historical circumstances which nevertheless appear as masks, as disguises of something more genuine. But such authenticity would once again be her untimeliness, something uncommunicated or only communicable through a kind of casuistry which bends or tailors a universal law to the individual instance. Paradoxically it is the universal, ongoing life-process that is represented by turning her into a 'dramatic character' through and through. Within the play her rapist father, by contrast, self-defeatingly claims personal adequacy to infinite process when he uses the language of fixed religious and patriarchal institutional thinking, styling himself as the 'scourge' of God and the narcissistic creator of others in his own likeness through the generations (IV. i. 141–58).

Shelley resumes the attack on critics found in the Preface to *Laon and Cythna* in the Preface to *Adonais*, where in hyperbolic manner he castigates the murderous reviewer of the *Quarterly* whose contemptuous notice of *Endymion* sent his young contemporary, the poet John Keats, into a 'rapid consumption' (*Norton 1*, 391). It is not at all clear that the critical assault by John Wilson Croker, or the genuinely vicious one by John Gibson Lockhart in *Blackwoods Edinburgh Magazine*, had this fatal effect on Keats. Shelley sets up contemporary criticism of Keats as committed to terminal interpretations against which Shelley then pits poetry's own power to translate itself beyond critical limitation, turning extinction into rebirth. He does this by writing an elegy, perhaps the most reflexive of all poetic genres, always keen to make a theme of the theory of what it is. In this case, Shelley exploits to the full the traditional elegiac trope of nature mourning in sympathy with the mourner. Immortality is granted Keats through the survival of his idiom and the currency of his expression: 'He is made one with Nature: there is heard | His voice in all her music' (370–1). The poetics of elegy, which has to balance the sad duty to remember with the joyful afflatus accompanying success in creating a great monument, is managed by Shelley in the Romantic, *sentimentalische*, or self-conscious twist of introducing the poet 'who in another's fate now wept his own' (300). We know that Milton was similarly self-regarding in *Lycidas*, but he could not make a virtue of this transgression of the proprieties of mourning. Shelley, though, appearing as 'a pardlike Spirit' (280), presumably the familiar of Dionysus rather than Apollo, openly celebrates his poem as a place where all economies can be breached and outstripped. His gift of an elegy to Keats and the dead poet's gift to him of a poetic occasion are equally un-returnable, and escape all logics of exchange. The poem's own thought about itself, then, answers in no uncertain terms the restricting critics demonized in the Preface, and so is itself an exercise in the philosophy of poetry. A hugely literary exercise written in the Spenserian stanza which Shelley praised in the Preface to *Laon and Cythna* for 'the brilliancy and magnificence of sound' belonging to its 'measure' (42) progressively exceeds its metrical character. As in a key moment of the development of Cythna's character in *Laon and*

Cythna, it weaves 'a subtler language' (VII. 3112) within its conventional diction. This 'key of truths' (VII. 3113), or of what in *Adonais* is called 'the One', survives ruins and fatalities of all kinds—the end of Keats, the fall of Rome, the passing of seasons, all ephemera. Ultimately, though, poetic scope becomes a call to—death; but, again, I think we must not see this as a perversely literal invitation, but a self-consciously poetic realization that the discourse's own ends can only be realized by subsumption in others, by losing its 'heart', by abandon to a 'breath' initially evoked in song, yes, but whose destiny is to journey out of its sphere, 'borne darkly, fearfully afar', into the self-surpassing realm of great poetry of the past (443–95).

In the Advertisement to *Epipsychidion* (*Norton* 1, 373–4), Shelley quotes from number XXV of Dante's mixture of poetic theory, autobiography, and love poetry, *La vita nuova*, the well-known passage concerning the disgrace (*grande vergogna*) which will be his who, when challenged, does not know how to denude his rhymes of the figure or rhetorical colour in which wise or manner he had meant truth (*in guisa che avessero verace intendimento*).[10] The context of Dante's remarks is different but, to Shelley, apparently relevant. Dante is defending modern, vernacular poetic licence with reference to its classical, Latin past; but, in case uneducated readers misunderstand him, he emphasizes that such translation of ancient rhetoric into modern poetic technique is justified in the same way as poetic translation in general. Shelley's famously sceptical attitude towards translation in *A Defence of Poetry*, probably written straight after *Epipsychidion*, repays close examination:

> Hence the vanity of translation; it were as wise to cast a violet into a crucible that you might discover the formal principle of its colour and odour, as seek to transfuse from one language into another the creations of a poet. The plant must spring again from its seed or it will bear not flower—and this is the burthen of the curse of Babel. (*Norton* 1, 484)

This subtle passage gives back what it takes away. Translation is impossible, but perhaps poetic virtue can be replanted and diversify? The story of Babel is reinterpreted to emphasize the new growth required of poetry in order for it to have meaning for another audience. Shelley can't mean that the vanity of translation means that you shouldn't do it. He himself was a prolific translator, not only literally in his especially fine versions of Goethe, Dante, and Plato, but also in the imitative virtuosity which allows Calderón to power his 'Ode to the West Wind' or, again, Dante to become an engine of *The Triumph of Life*. But poetic transplantation still implies for Shelley a break from its original radical enough for the image of Babel to apply. On the other hand, it is a family of languages within which the disparities of Babel exist. Against this human kinship, though, militates the difference of translation, and so on. But poetry does appear, for Shelley, to stand for a creativity, a moral energy, a virtue whose power lies in its survival of being replanted and in the traceability of its new effect back to a sometime poetic original. The Advertisement to *Epipsychidion* sets up a series of translations, some vain, some belonging to

---

[10] Dante Alighieri, *La vita nuova*, ed. G. A. Ceriello (Milan: Signorelli, 1977), 54.

fundamental modes of human organization and progress, for which the example of poetic translation crystallizes the difficulties and the necessity. The series begins with the very words of the unfortunate Italian lady the narrator is enamoured of, whose loving soul creates for its own satisfaction another world, very different (*diverso assai*, 373) from this one. The ironic tone which the Preface author takes with the narrator evinces scepticism of a too easy trust in translations of this kind. And the entire poem, from its title to its anaphoric imagery of a self infinitely protracted through love's projections, repeatedly poses the problem. Love itself appears not as the creature personified relatively straightforwardly by the Ovid quoted in Dante's defence of his own poetic style, his *dolce stil nuovo*'s updating of classical precedent. This love is a complicated investment, more like the problematic fantasy of the 'poet' of *Alastor*, or the psychology of Shelley's prose fragment 'On Love'. Shelley's title, *Epipsychidion*, suggesting a miniature soul within a soul or simply a treatise on the soul, can signify a tragic diminution through desire or a transcendental empowerment. Its exaggerated reliance on the response of an Other to reflect back the self revealed in that desire for the Other furnishes a self-consciousness that progresses. This unfolding, rolling sense of self, is enhanced by a love-heightened perception of nature that in turn renders a new visibility to the enquiring subject. But the poem ends in an orgasmic expiration that sends us back to the Preface's discussion of poetics.

By 1821, in the Preface to his 'lyrical drama' *Hellas*, Shelley is dealing with a political future desired for modern Greece which strains even his confidence in the poetic evocation of a national change only to be achieved by new growth: 'a new race has arisen throughout Europe, nursed in the abhorrence of the opinions which are its chains, and she will continue to produce fresh generations to accomplish that destiny which tyrants foresee and dread' (*Norton* 1, 410). In the meantime, awaiting this new life, Shelley finds the subject of a modern, liberated Greece 'insusceptible of being treated otherwise than lyrically' (408). To call it a 'drama' as he has done is, he confesses, a misnomer except as it points to its dialogue. This is not only because of the difficulty of accomplishing the revolution which Greece, like so many other European countries, needs to secure its democratic freedom after the post-Napoleonic settlement of the Congress of Vienna. The translation of the ancient Greeks into a modern version raises in a final acute form Shelley's problems in hooking poetic idealism onto reality. The heroes of the Greek republics are 'glorious beings whom the imagination almost refuses to figure as belonging to our Kind' (409). Continuity between them and the Greece that might be established by defeating the Turks is almost inconceivable, not because the modern country could not live up to the ancient example, but because Greece for Shelley is so poetic that, again, the poetic description of it can only work by in substantial part declaring its own failure—the drama or 'impersonation' it itself now suffers rather than confers significance on the incommunicability of people like Beatrice Cenci. The disparity between opinion and institution is intensified by poetry's *own* struggle to connect its 'opinions' of the Greeks to a recognizable human solidarity. The triumph of life in this case will be to produce a new race for whom the poetry of the past can be completed and so enjoy the translation into political discourse which at present it is denied. This is rather different from the anxiety of losing poetry in its reincarnations within the terms of other discourses, like the shift from Aeschylus to Plato Shelley toys with in the Preface to *Prometheus Unbound*. It is more a worry about the adequacy of poetry to move successfully from the restricted to the unrestricted sense as it does elsewhere. One can try to see this dilemma as Shelley's pessimism about the Greek situation—and the poem is pessimistic—but it is more as if poetry here is blocked by its own untimeliness which has become a kind of limbo rather than 'the trumpet of a prophecy'.

Earlier in the same year (1821) that he wrote *Hellas*, though, Shelley had completed his major work on poetics, *A Defence of Poetry*. This text has been interleaving my discussion throughout. The commonplace, found in Kames, Rousseau, Herder, and many others, that 'poetry is connate with the origin of man' (*Norton 1*, 480), is complicated by Shelley's almost immediate addition that poetry, in effect, is also coeval with human progress. Typically, he solders poetry to an Enlightenment anthropological fact which he then transforms in a very modern-sounding theory of a self-differing identity linked to a reflective epistemology. Child and poet grasp themselves in an imagined antitype which evidences our understanding of ourselves through otherness and of otherness through self. This key binary interaction then directs *A Defence*'s entire investigation of poetry in the 'restricted' sense in which it is confined to literary genres and the 'unrestricted' sense in which its creativity can put its own specificity at risk through its uniquely creative power to adapt to historical change. This chapter has isolated a number of the changes Shelley rings on this argument. In each instance, poetry in the 'unrestricted' sense is liberated to contribute to an ongoing human inventiveness.

> [Poets] are not only the authors of language and music, of the dance and architecture and statuary and painting: they are the institutors of laws and the founders of civil society, and the inventors of the arts of life [...] (482)

When poetically established, Shelley insists, these instaurations are all forward looking. To be timely is to be prophetic: to think in a manner adequate to the progressive character of humanity.

But where, one might reasonably ask, does all this lead? How specific is Shelley about the destiny 'unrestricted' poetry proposes for the human project? He has little time for theological or eschatological end-games. Despite sympathy for Godwin's philosophy, neither does he appear to buy into any rational millenarianism. Critics have noted that *Hellas* seems to allude, in its final Chorus, to Virgil's fourth *Eclogue*, but only to refute the messianic overtones detected by Christian readers with a cyclic pessimism, rather than a secular alternative. The answer is that 'Poetry is ever accompanied with pleasure' (486), along with poetry's enforcement of the realization that this pleasure comes from a future conjured but not apprehended. Shelley's poetics are animated by a poetics of hope, in which current satisfactions derive from their orientation towards what is to come. Because poetry has always done this, it gives us an idea of eternity in which we both feel targeted by poetry of the past and are properly sensible of the present when we detect how it is underwritten by its future. Just as poetry links pleasure to hope, it binds, as we saw, error to generosity. Its education, then, is not reducible to specific 'effects' but lies in acquainting us with the 'cause' of its intrinsic generosity. Poetry shows us that progress is not a journey over whose interpretation religious and other ideologies compete, but an experience. At every stage, poetry shows us the opportunity to deploy our 'imagination'—the blanket, Romantic term Shelley eventually uses for this constantly available resource.

A *Defence* lists and illuminates for us spectacular deployments of imagination, but nowhere suggests its effects are cumulatively quantifiable. The exercise of imagination is its own reward. It generates a temporary pleasure in the fullest self-realization of which we are historically capable. Nevertheless, a teleological timbre resonates unavoidably in progressive language. It is so difficult to think of progress as a good in itself without some sort of defining road-map popping up. But not to grant Shelley this intransitive progressive virtue is to regard him as the vague purveyor of an ill-defined futurity—as Matthew Arnold's 'ineffectual angel'—a pale shadow of the bold opponent of 'a substitution of the rigidly-defined and ever-repeated idealisms of a distorted superstition for the living impersonations of the truth of human passion' (490).[11] The new anthropology, which Shelley's poetics does champion, anticipates the materialist visions to come of Marx, Nietzsche, and Freud but is itself unusually enhanced by its power to impersonate, and so insists forthrightly on its connection with poetry in its 'restricted' sense. The poetic communication which Shelley so fundamentally values thus works equally between poet and audience and between poetry and the invention of humanity. And it is in that renewed invention, Shelley argues, that 'Poetry ever communicates all the pleasure which men are capable of receiving' (493).

SELECT BIBLIOGRAPHY

Alighieri, Dante. *La vita nuova*. Ed. G. A. Ceriello. Milan: Signorelli, 1977.

Clark, Timothy. *Embodying Revolution: The Figure of the Poet in Shelley*. Oxford: Clarendon Press, 1989.

Cooper, Anthony Ashley, Third Earl of Shaftesbury. 'A Letter Concerning Enthusiasm'. *Characteristics of Men, Manners, Opinions, Times*. Ed. Lawrence E. Klein. Cambridge: Cambridge UP, 1999.

de Man, Paul. 'Shelley Disfigured'. *The Rhetoric of Romanticism*. New York: Columbia UP, 1984. 93–125.

Duff, David. 'Shelley and the "Great Poem"'. *Romanticism and the Uses of Genre*. Oxford: Oxford UP, 2009. 201–12.

Flew, Anthony. *Hume's Philosophy of Belief*. London: Routledge and Kegan Paul, 1961.

Hogle, Jerrold E. *Shelley's Process: Radical Transference and the Development of his Major Works*. New York: Oxford UP, 1988.

Keach, William. *Shelley's Style*. New York: Methuen, 1984.

Milton, John. *Complete Prose Works of John Milton*. Ed. Don M. Wolfe. 8 vols. New Haven: Yale UP, 1959.

[11] Matthew Arnold, 'Shelley', *Essays in Criticism: Second Series* (1888; London: Macmillan, 1913), 206.

Morton, Timothy. *Shelley and the Revolution in Taste: The Body and the Natural World*. Cambridge: Cambridge UP, 1994.

Ruston, Sharon. *Shelley and Vitality*. Basingstoke: Palgrave Macmillan, 2005.

Sidney, Sir Philip. *An Apology for Poetry (or The Defence of Poesy)*. Ed. Geoffrey Shepherd, rev. and expanded R. W. Maslen. Manchester: Manchester UP, 2002.

Wasserman, Earl R. *Shelley: A Critical Reading*. Baltimore: Johns Hopkins UP, 1971.

CHAPTER 12

PROSE FICTION

Zastrozzi, St. Irvyne, The Assassins, The Coliseum

DIANE LONG HOEVELER

PERCY Shelley was once described by his wife Mary as 'more apt to embody ideas and sentiments in the radiance of beautiful imagery, and […] melodious verse […] than to invent the machinery of a story'.[1] Although not generally thought of as a writer of prose fiction, Percy Shelley did write two short Gothic novels and two pieces of short prose that seem to be introductions to tales or romances he soon decided to abandon. This chapter will focus on the themes and structures, literary sources and devices, and ideological agendas of these works, particularly his two Gothic romances, *Zastrozzi, A Romance* (composed in the spring of 1809; published 1810) and *St. Irvyne; or, The Rosicrucian: A Romance* (composed 1810; published December 1810 but dated 1811), both of them written when he was between the ages of 18 and 19 and in his final year at Eton. Within two years of their composition, however, Shelley was attempting to distance himself from the two Gothic novels, claiming to William Godwin that he wrote them in 'the state of intellectual sickliness and lethargy into which I was plunged two years ago, and of which *St. Irvyne* and *Zastrozzi* are the distempered although unoriginal visions'.[2] It is fair to say at the outset that these works were not particularly well received by contemporary reviewers upon their publication, nor generally have they been viewed with favour by Shelley critics in more recent years (although *Zastrozzi* has rather improbably been adapted twice in recent years, as both a play and a television series).[3] A writer for the *Critical Review* denounced the character of Zastrozzi, for instance, as 'one of the

---

[1] Mary Shelley, Preface to *Frankenstein* (1831 edn.), ed. James Rieger (Chicago: University of Chicago Press, 1982), 225.

[2] *Julian*, VIII, 287. All quotations from *Zastrozzi, St. Irvyne, Assassins*, and *The Coliseum* will be taken from the Broadview text edited by Stephen Behrendt (2002), cited as Behrendt, with page numbers provided.

[3] In 1977 the Toronto Free Theatre produced George F. Walker's *Zastrozzi: The Master of Discipline* and Channel Four Films (Britain) presented its own adaptation in 1986, a four-part mini-series written and directed by David G. Hopkins, with music by Martin Kiszko.

most savage and improbable demons that ever issued from a diseased brain,[4] while the reviewer for *The Anti-Jacobin Review and Magazine* speculated that the author of *St. Irvyne* was most likely 'some "Miss" in her teens', indulging in 'description run mad' with 'uncouth epithet' and 'wild expression'.[5]

Similarly, the majority of literary critics of our own era have not been particularly sympathetic to these two novels, frequently dismissing them as either juvenilia or self-conscious and flat attempts to spoof the outlandish characters and plots of the popular Gothic potboilers and chapbooks that Shelley had read as an adolescent. For instance, Kenneth Neill Cameron has seen Shelley's Gothic interests as no more than a 'dreary spectacle' that causes us to 'heave a sigh of relief that he finally (via Godwin or anyone else) found that he had social "duties to perform"' and therefore no time for such silliness.[6] Dismissed as 'mere juvenilia' by E. B. Murray, these two works were not included in his definitive modern edition of Shelley's prose up to 1818.[7] As Stephen Behrendt, their best modern editor, states, such a decision 'devalues' and 'marginalizes' the texts, while at the same time it reveals how consistently Shelley scholars have been 'embarrassed' by these works, not simply for their awkward style and language, but for their 'derivative' nature.[8] Most recently, Tilottama Rajan has attempted to make a case for their importance as textual practices and spaces where Shelley played with some of the hyperbolic characters, metaphysical issues, and poetic devices (such as anamorphosis) that eventually emerged in full-blown maturity in *Prometheus Unbound* (see Select Bibliography). Whether such claims are justified or not, it seems only fair to examine the works on their own terms, as novelistic practices by a writer who would soon find his more authentic voice as a philosophical poet.

Because the two Gothic romances are so little known or studied today, this chapter will provide a summary of their plots before examining their structures, sources, and techniques. *Zastrozzi* is a Gothic revenge fantasy predicated on a son's consuming need to avenge his mother's sexual honour. The novel presents its eponymous character as a mysterious and ominous embodiment of fate, so consumed with hatred for Verezzi (Il Conte Verezzi) that he plots Verezzi's 'destruction' 'urged by fiercest revenge' (61). Zastrozzi's intention is nothing less than to force Verezzi's suicide so that his eternal soul will be damned. After drugging and kidnapping Verezzi, Zastrozzi has him chained for weeks to the wall of an underground cavern where lizards and 'large earth-worms, which twined themselves in his long and matted hair, almost ceased to excite sensations of horror' (63). When lightning strikes the cavern, shattering it, Verezzi is moved to a deserted cottage where he finally has the opportunity to confront his tormentor, Zastrozzi, and declares: '"I fear nothing [...] from your vain threats and empty

---

[4] S3, V. 21 (November 1810), 329; cited in Behrendt, 279.
[5] 41; (January 1812), 6972; cited in Behrendt, 286.
[6] *The Young Shelley* (1950; repr. New York: Collier, 1962), 51.
[7] *Murray: Prose*, p. xxiii.
[8] Stephen C. Behrendt, 'Introduction' to Percy Shelley, *Zastrozzi, A Romance; St. Irvyne: or The Rosicrucian: A Romance*, ed. Stephen C. Behrendt (Peterborough, Ont.: Broadview Press, 2002), 9–10. All quotations from the two novels are taken from this edition.

denunciations of vengeance: justice, Heaven! is on my side, and I must eventually tri-umph." What can be a greater proof of the superiority of virtue than that the terrible, the dauntless Zastrozzi trembled' (68). One could claim to hear in this overwrought dia-logue early echoes of the Prometheus/Jupiter dispute that is so central in Shelley's later major work *Prometheus Unbound*, and certainly there is, as Rajan has claimed,[9] a hyper-bolic quality to the latter work that may very well have had its origins in the experiments of this early Gothic novel.

After escaping his hapless captors, Verezzi lives incognito in a Bavarian cottage while the focus of the action shifts back to the diabolical schemes of Zastrozzi. It is at this point in the narrative that we are introduced to Zastrozzi's double, the villainous femme fatale Matilda (La Contessa di Laurentini), who demands to know if Zastrozzi has accom-plished her stated command: ' "Are we revenged on Julia? am I happy?" ' (76). The text does not provide the background information to allow the reader to understand what Julia has done to merit Matilda's rage, but at this point the reader of Gothic texts knows enough to fill in the blanks: Julia (La Marchesa de Strobazzo) is Verezzi's true love, and Matilda is a passionate aristocratic nymphomaniac who has fixated her obsessive lust on him. Julia deserves death, according to Matilda, because she has stood in Matilda's way as a competitor for Verezzi's love and sexual favours. Just to show the reader how serious they are, Zastrozzi in collusion with Matilda kidnaps Julia's servant and protector, the loyal Paulo, and after he begs for his life, they poison him so that he will not stand in the way of yet another assassination attempt on the life of Julia (78).

After futilely searching for Verezzi in the grip of a frustrated sexual frenzy, Matilda finally decides on suicide and leaps off a bridge in Bavaria only to be rescued from the water by the passing Verezzi. His initial words to her suggest that she has been stalking him for quite some time: ' "did I not leave you at your Italian castellan? I had hoped you would have ceased to persecute me, when I told you that I was irrevocably another's" ' (82). But Matilda is not one to moderate her declarations: ' "I adore you to madness—I love you to distraction. If you have one spark of compassion, let me not sue in vain—reject not one who feels it impossible to overcome the fatal, resistless passion which consumes her" ' (83). Described twice in the text as 'wily', Matilda is likened to the serpent in Milton's *Paradise Lost* as well as the temptress Circe,[10] and she now begins in earnest her campaign to seduce and then marry Verezzi. Believing that Julia is dead, Verezzi dashes his head against a wall and develops a life-threatening brain fever, eventually recovering only to live in the deepest mourning for Julia. Only after Verezzi is attacked by Zastrozzi in dis-guise and Matilda steps in to take the blow herself (a plot that they arranged together) does Verezzi begin to soften toward Matilda and propose marriage. Warned by Zastrozzi, who claims to have killed Julia, not to move to Venice, Matilda and Verezzi promptly move there, and within days Matilda receives a summons to appear before the 'il consiglio de dieci', the Council of Ten, the Venetian Republic secret service (132–3), perhaps for

[9] Tilottama Rajan, 'Shelley's Promethean Narratives: Gothic Anamorphoses in *Zastrozzi, St. Irvyne*, and *Prometheus Unbound*', in *Romantic Narrative: Shelley, Hays, Godwin, Wollstonecraft* (Baltimore: Johns Hopkins UP, 2011), pp. xix; 49; 52; 66; 72
[10] See Behrendt's edition, 84 n., 113.

the crime of killing Paulo or perhaps, as Matilda herself suggests, for 'heresy' (135), although neither of these charges is ever made clear in the text. Complications multiply quickly when Zastrozzi arranges for Verezzi to see the very much alive Julia with his own eyes and then realizes that he has been duped into marriage by the machinations of his new wife. Confronted by Julia in the palazzo he shares with Matilda, Verezzi kills himself after a passionate denunciation of his evil wife. Matilda, using the same knife, then stabs Julia in a manic fury, only to sink into a spiritual despair: 'her soul had caught a glimpse of the misery which awaits the wicked hereafter, and, spite of her contempt of religion— spite of her, till now, too firm dependence on the doctrines of atheism, she trembled at futurity; and a voice from within, which whispers, "thou shalt never die!" spoke daggers to Matilda's soul' (143).

Arrested along with Zastrozzi by the secret police, Matilda confesses her sins and seeks and receives forgiveness, while Zastrozzi is defiant to the end: '"Am I not convinced of the non-existence of a Deity? Am I not convinced that death will but render this soul more free, more unfettered? Why need I then shudder at death? Why need any one, whose mind has risen above the shackles of prejudice, the errors of a false and injurious superstition"' (153). Zastrozzi admits to the court that he has been motivated to destroy Verezzi because Verezzi's father had seduced and then abandoned Zastrozzi's mother. Zastrozzi killed his own father, the seducer, and then sought to kill his half-brother, Verezzi, because his mother on her deathbed had asked him to revenge her honour. Sent to the rack, Zastrozzi declares his defiance and actually brags that he has accomplished his life's work: '"I know my doom; and instead of horror, [I] experience some degree of satisfaction at the arrival of death, since all I have to do on earth is completed"' (156).

Nicola Trott has described *Zastrozzi* as 'a mock Minerva novel, with stock Gothic names and characters'. For her, 'Shelley's manipulation of the Gothic ranges all the way from pranking and pastiche to the profoundest speculation.'[11] Other critics, in particular Stephen Behrendt, have read it as an early but serious attempt to confront the question of character and destiny, the dangers of pride and revenge, and the follies of sexual passion and infatuation. For Behrendt, it is important to 'take the prose romances seriously and on their own terms, bearing in mind that the elements of playfulness and calculated excess that enter into them with some frequency foreshadow—even if occasionally crudely—many of the transgressive and destabilizing elements we associate with the poetry (especially) that would follow' (32–3, 14). Rajan's recent reading of the work takes it quite seriously, reading the villain Zastrozzi as a 'Symbolic, adolescent mask for the Promethean transgression whose incoherences [he] masks'.[12]

The second and slightly later novel, *St. Irvyne*, is structured so that we seem to be reading two separate and parallel narratives, first the robber/Faust/Wandering Jew/ghost-seer tale of Wolfstein and his doppelgänger Ginotti, and secondly, the sentimental romance of Eloise, a beautiful orphan, seduced and sold in a gambling wager by the libertine Frederic de Nempere. The dual structure of the novel has received the most

---

[11] Nicola Trott, 'Shelley, Percy Bysshe (1792–1822)', in Marie Mulvey-Roberts (ed.), *The Handbook to Gothic Literature* (New York: New York UP, 1998), 216–17.

[12] Rajan, 'Shelley's Promethean Narratives', 54.

critical attention, with critics arguing that the two narratives parallel and illuminate each other or that the use of both genres within the master-text collapses these two discrete discourse forms, the Gothic and the sentimental, and suggests the exhaustion and limitations of both genres.[13] The novel begins with 'the high-souled and noble' (164) Wolfstein fleeing from his native land because of some horrific crime he has committed. Very quickly he is captured by a group of banditti led by the ruthless Cavigni, who forces Wolfstein into full participation with their activities (these early scenes strongly recall Friederich von Schiller's popular drama *Die Räuber* (1781), which had been translated into English by 1792 and later adapted by George Cruikshank as the popular Gothic chapbook *Feudal Days; or, The Noble Outlaw*). So desperate about his capture and forced banditry that he begins to contemplate suicide, Wolfstein decides that he would rather take up his pen and write poetry that is, in fact, the same poem that Shelley used in *Original Poetry by Victor and Cazire*, itself a plagiarism of a ballad from the anonymous *Tales of Terror* (1801), 'The Black Canon of Elmham; or St. Edmond's Eve'.[14]

Almost immediately the beautiful Megalena de Metastasio is captured and also held in the same underground cavern, and the action escalates. Within a day she is told that she will be forced to marry Cavigni, so Wolfstein decides to murder Cavigni and escape with the beautiful Megalena with whom he has fallen instantly in love. Like Wolfstein, Megalena is also prone to writing poetry as an act of cathartic therapy. In her case, however, Megalena plagiarizes her poetic offering from Byron's 1807 edition of *Hours of Idleness* (174), an act that is repeated by Eloise St. Irvyne when she is asked to sing a song of her own composition (211–12). Also inhabiting the banditti cave and seemingly possessed of preternatural powers of foreknowledge, Ginotti ('some superior and preterhuman being', 183) becomes a shadowy force who haunts the footsteps of Wolfstein, always turning up to help him at a crucial moment and then demanding that Wolfstein swear an oath of allegiance to him should he, Ginotti, ever request assistance himself. The Wolfstein/Ginotti doubling recalls the action of Schiller's *Ghost-Seer* (1789), while the pact with the devil is similar to the one that occurs in both Marlowe's *Dr Faustus* (1604), and Goethe's version of the *Faust* tale (Part One; 1808), which we know Shelley read and admired.[15] There are also echoes here of the legend of Ahasuerus, the Wandering Jew, doomed to wander the earth for all eternity because he mocked Christ on his way to the cross, a subject that the young Shelley had also been exploring in his 'The wandering Jew's soliloquoy' (1811?), excerpts from which form the epigraphs to chapters II, VIII, and X of *St. Irvyne*.

---

[13] See Andy P. Antippas, 'The Structure of Shelley's *St. Irvyne*: Parallelism and the Gothic Mode of Evil', *Tulane Studies in English* 18 (1970), 59–71 and Tilottama Rajan, 'Promethean Narrative: Overdetermined Form in Shelley's Gothic Fiction', in Betty T. Bennett and Stuart Curran (eds.), *Shelley: Poet and Legislator of the World* (Baltimore: Johns Hopkins UP, 1996), 240–52.

[14] See Douglass H. Thomson, 'Introduction' to *Tales of Wonder by Matthew Gregory Lewis* (Peterborough, Ont.: Broadview Press, 2009), 35.

[15] Thomas Love Peacock, 'Memoirs of Percy Bysshe Shelley', in Howard Mills (ed.), *Memoirs of Shelley, and Other Essays, and Reviews* (New York: New York UP, 1975), 43.

After moving to Genoa with Megalena, Wolfstein succumbs to a dangerous gambling addiction (a stock vice in anti-aristocratic Gothic texts), and begins to be stalked by Ginotti, who appears only to mutter ominously, '"Attend to these my directions, but try, if possible, to forget me. I am not what I seem. The time may come, *will* most probably arrive, when I shall appear in my real character to you. You, Wolfstein, have I singled out from the whole world to make the depositary—"' (195), and then the sentence abruptly stops. Clearly, Ginotti lures and seduces Wolfstein with tantalizing hints about his knowledge of the secret of immortality, but the reader is as confused as Wolfstein about the nature and identity of Ginotti, who is sometimes depicted as a villain and sometimes as a powerful Promethean avenger. At the climax of the Wolfstein/Megalena tale, her double, the nymphomaniac Olympia della Anzasca, attempts to seduce Wolfstein and is discovered by the jealous Megalena in a compromising position with him. Demanding revenge, Megalena insists that Wolfstein murder Olympia, who then commits suicide when she realizes that she has been irrevocably rejected by Wolfstein. Fleeing to Bohemia, Wolfstein and Megalena are not safe for long because Ginotti suddenly appears and demands fulfilment of his sworn oath. At this same meeting Ginotti also gives Wolfstein the secret of immortality, an elixir that he says he has purchased from the devil at the cost of his everlasting soul. Instructed by Ginotti to go to the abbey of St. Irvyne in France on a certain evening, Wolfstein arrives at midnight to discover the dead Megalena and the emaciated Ginotti, who again seeks in Wolfstein a substitute for his own pact with the devil. When Wolfstein refuses to renounce his belief in God, the devil appears and transforms Ginotti into an enormous skeleton.

Juxtaposed with the robber/Faust/Wandering Jew/ghost-seer story operating fairly crudely in the Wolfstein/Ginotti plot is the sentimental story of the beautiful French orphan Eloise de St. Irvyne (whose ancestral home had been the setting for the ill-fated Wolfstein–Ginotti climax). Seduced by a mysterious dark stranger who goes by the name of Nempere (name of the father?; not a father?), Eloise is pregnant by him when she is sold to an Englishman, the Chevalier Mountfort, in order to settle a gambling debt that Nempere incurred. She is then passed by the Englishman to an Irish idealist named Fitzeustace, who accepts her baby as his own, marries her, and proposes to take her to England to escape the evils of continental life (this plot is similar to any number of sentimental seduction tales, notably Mary Wollstonecraft's *Maria* (1798) or Charlotte Dacre's *Confessions of the Nun of St. Omer* (1805)). In a denouement that quickly and awkwardly attempts to connect the two narratives, the text baldly states: 'Ginotti is Nempere' and 'Eloise is the sister of Wolfstein'. Suffice to say that this conclusion did not satisfy Shelley's publisher, who wrote to complain to him about its abruptness.[16] Contemporary critics have tended to read the two narrative lines more positively, claiming, in fact, that they detect a greater level of narrative sophistication in the second novel. For example, Peter Finch has asserted that *St. Irvyne*, with its overlapping Gothic and sentimental storylines, is the 'much more accomplished and intriguing textual performance', while Rajan sees the novel as 'Shelley's first metadiscursive text, in that it is about the functioning of

---

[16] Behrendt, 'Introduction', 25.

the signifier. In that sense it is also a commentary on the form of *Zastrozzi*, on the problems in signification and emplotment that complicate the writing and reading of the texts we shape out of the political unconscious.'[17]

As far as tracing literary influences on these two novels, we know that Shelley was an enthusiastic reader of Gothic chapbooks as a child and was later a purchaser of the Gothic Minerva Press titles while he was a student at Eton (1804–10). We also know that he read Ann Radcliffe's *The Italian* (1794), but his first attempt at a Gothic novel was very clearly inspired by what, according to Thomas Medwin, was an 'enraptured' reading of Charlotte Dacre's *Zofloya; or the Moor* (1806), a fact that was elaborated on by Peck close to 100 years ago.[18] While it has been customary to cite *Zofloya* as the primary source for the names, plot, and themes of *Zastrozzi* and, in fact, to accuse Shelley of something like a virtual plagiarism of that work, it is also necessary to point out that *Zofloya* itself is close to a plagiarism of a number of other earlier Gothic novels, George Moore's *Theodosius de Zulvin, the Monk of Madrid* (1802) being its primary and overlooked source apart from Matthew Lewis's *The Monk* (1796). The popularity of *Zofloya* in turn led to a number of other imitations of it in chapbook and novel form, ones that Shelley most certainly would have had access to: Lucy Watkins's Gothic romance *Cavigni of Tuscany. A Terrific Romance* (1814?), from which numerous characters, situations, and themes are borrowed (or, in fact, virtually stolen); the anonymous *The Avenger; or The Sicilian vespers* (1810); and Isaac Crookenden's *Horrible Revenge; or The Monster of Italy!!* (1808). And *St. Irvyne* itself, somewhat ironically, was plagiarized as an anonymously published chapbook sometime between 1815 and 1818 entitled *Wolfstein; or The Mysterious Bandit*.[19]

There are echoes of numerous other Gothic novels in *Zastrozzi*, and, as Edith Birkhead has pointed out, names such as 'Julia' and 'Matilda' are most likely borrowed from Radcliffe's *A Sicilian Romance* (1791), and Lewis's *The Monk*, while 'Verezzi' is also a character in Radcliffe's *Mysteries of Udolpho* (1794).[20] Names, however, are the least of the borrowings. The murder and suicide scenes are Gothic staples, as are the Inquisition trials, the revenge theme, and the detailed depictions of sexual dysfunction. *St. Irvyne* is also obviously indebted to the legend of the Wandering Jew, which so intrigued Shelley that he wrote about the figure as challenging God, or, in Shelley's words, the 'Tyrant of Earth', to explain the sufferings that this God has in fact caused: 'Or the Angel's two-edged sword of fire that urged | Our primal parents from their bower of bliss | (Reared by thine hand) for errors not their own, | By thine omniscient mind foredoomed, foreknown?' (150).

David Seed claims that one of the major influences on this novel, as well as Shelley's earliest attempts to write political prose fiction, can be found in his reading of the works

[17] Peter Finch, 'Monstrous Inheritance: The Sexual Politics of Genre in Shelley's *St. Irvyne*', *Keats–Shelley Journal* 48 (1999), 35–68 (36) and Rajan, 'Shelley's Promethean Narratives', 65.

[18] Thomas Medwin, *The Life of Percy Bysshe Shelley*, ed. H. Buxton Forman (London: Oxford UP, 1913), 25 and Walter Edwin Peck, *Shelley: His Life and Work*, 2 vols. (Boston: Houghton Mifflin, 1927), II, 305–13.

[19] Reprinted in Behrendt's edition, 307–20.

[20] Edith Birkhead, *The Tale of Terror: A Study of the Gothic Romance* (London: Constable, 1921), 111.

of William Godwin, particularly *St Leon: A Tale of the Sixteenth Century* (1799), which includes an Inquisition scene and a Wandering Jew character who gives the elixir of life to St Leon. Godwin's *Caleb Williams* and *Mandeville* are also inscribed in the action and themes of *St. Irvyne*, while Behrendt, following Peck, cites Lewis's *The Bravo of Venice* (1805) as a possible source text.[21] As far as Gothic chapbooks with very similar scenes, characters, and plots are concerned, Shelley would have had access to such works as *The Black Forest; or, the Cavern of Horror* (1802); *The Bloody Hand, or The Fatal Cup* (1810); and *The Sorcerer; A Tale from the German of Veit Weber*, translated by Robert Huish and published in 1795.

In tracing Shelley's possible sources it is also important to recognize that, besides his readings in the canonical and pulp British tradition, he was also an admirer of the four Gothic works of the American novelist Charles Brockden Brown; according to Peacock, 'nothing so blended itself with the structure of his interior mind as the creations of Brown'. But he was also an avid reader of, as Mary Shelley tells us, 'such German works as were current in those days'.[22] By setting both of his novels partially in Germany, Shelley was tapping into the vogue for all things Germanic in this particular strain of British Gothic sensibility. In fact, in *St. Irvyne* Shelley introduces a character named Steindolph who is described as 'famed for his knowledge of metrical spectre tales, and the [banditti] gang were frequently wont to hang delighted on the ghostly wonders which he related' (177). Steindolph tells a gruesome Gothic ballad that he learned in Germany about a monk and his dead nun-lover Rosa, but the reader of Anne Bannerman's 'The Penitent's Confession' (1802) will find the ballad extremely familiar in tone and content.

Huish's *The Sorcerer* is itself an adaptation of the German Gothic classic Friedrich von Schiller's *Der Geisterseher* (1789), translated into English as *The Ghost-Seer or the Apparitionist* (1795), immensely popular in England, and, I think, an obvious and over-looked source for Shelley's early Gothic works. The dialogue between Enemonde and Francesco about the nature of God and the devil in Huish's *The Sorcerer* is very similar to the conversations that occur later in Lewis's *The Monk* and then in Shelley's *St. Irvyne* when Ginotti traces his education in 'Natural Philosophy' to Wolfstein (234–5). In short, disputing about the existence and nature of God and the possibility or impossibility of an afterlife were two of the most prominent themes in Germanic Gothic novels, and Shelley it would appear is simply repeating in *St. Irvyne* what would have been an extremely familiar dialogue in any number of earlier Gothic texts, and which he himself adapted and expanded on again only a few months later in his pamphlet *The Necessity of Atheism* (1811).

Both of Shelley's novels employ a series of veritable Gothic clichés and conventions: the motivating and mysterious vendetta, banditti roaming around dark forests, the besieged and orphaned heroine, the demonic seducer, the Venetian Inquisition, and

[21] David Seed, 'Shelley's "Gothick" in *St. Irvyne* and after', in Miriam Allott (ed.), *Essays on Shelley* (Liverpool: Liverpool UP, 1982), 39–70 (53–4) and Behrendt, 'Introduction', 22–3.
[22] Peacock, 'Memoirs of Percy Bysshe Shelley', 43; Mary Shelley, Notes to *Queen Mab*, 1839; repr. in *The Complete Poetical Works of Percy Bysshe Shelley*, ed. George E. Woodberry (Boston: Houghton Mifflin, 1892), I, 404.

chance encounters of the most fantastical sort. Characters are frequently doubled (virgin/whore; redeemer/seducer) and the convention of supposedly missing chapters is used in both works, while the themes of 'apprehension, danger, resistance, struggle, sexual tension, and intense awareness of surroundings are stock in trade of the Gothic fiction'.[23] Shelley does employ a device that, while not original, takes on an increased poetic and psychological depth in *St. Irvyne*: namely, the dream-vision. We can see the first of these attempts to portray a dream-like state when Matilda foresees the attack on Verrezi that she has planned with Zastrozzi in the first novel (121–2). But in *St. Irvyne* we see an extended dream-vision, very similar in descriptive details to the one that the *Alastor* poet would undergo in Shelley's later poem (1815). In this version, Wolfstein dreams that he is standing 'on the brink of a frightful precipice, at whose base, with deafening and terrific roar, the waves of the ocean dashed'. In great danger from a 'figure, more frightful than the imagination of man is capable of portraying', Wolfstein is suddenly rescued from 'the grasp of the monster' by Ginotti (191). Uncertain as to how to interpret the dream, Wolfstein decides that Megalena is his enemy and Ginotti is his hero. Eloise has a similar dream-vision in which she meets a 'fascinating, yet awful stranger' who embraces her, only to find herself suddenly standing with him over a yawning pit and an ominous landscape (213). Finally, Ginotti himself recounts to Wolfstein the most elaborate of all these dream-visions: of Satan coming amidst 'rays of brilliancy' and a 'blood-red moon' to drag him to a precipice (236–7).

Shelley's two Gothic romances present yet another interesting problem for the literary critic: what are we to make of what appear to be intensely conservative domestic, religious, and ideological agendas when we know that the author, in fact, held diametrically opposite opinions and beliefs at the time of composition? Behrendt refers to the conservative tone taken by these and other Gothic works as 'the rhetoric of moral stewardship',[24] and such is, indeed, an apt characterization of a sort of double-voiced quality to so much of these works. On one hand, they deal in shocking and aberrant behaviours, such as nymphomania, libertinism, and murder, all the while condemning in the name of social decency and moral middle-class standards the very acts they have so lovingly detailed. For instance, one of the dominant discourses in *Zastrozzi* is Promethean hedonism and self-aggrandizement, heard very clearly when Zastrozzi says to Matilda: '"No—any purpose undertaken with ardour, and prosecuted with perseverance, must eventually be crowned with success. Love is worthy of any risque. [...] for whatever procures pleasure is right, and consonant to the dignity of man, who was created for no other purpose but to obtain happiness, else, why were passions given us?"' (102). This discourse on the justification of the passions is extremely similar to the debates that occur throughout Charlotte Dacre's novels, in particular *The Passions* (1811), as well as her earlier novel *The Libertine* (1807), both of which Shelley may have read. Debating about the control of the emotions was part and parcel of an emerging bourgeois agenda,

[23] Jack Donovan, 'The Storyteller', in Timothy Morton (ed.), *The Cambridge Companion to Shelley* (Cambridge: Cambridge UP, 2006), 85–103 (89).
[24] Behrendt, 'Introduction', 26.

and associating extreme emotions with the aristocracy was part of the 'Whiggish' Gothic ideology that characterizes the novels of Dacre in particular.[25]

Gothic novels frequently focused their ideological agendas on the questions that surround the climate of growing secularization and religious angst, and certainly we can hear a number of these concerns in both of Shelley's novels. Zastrozzi plays the role of existential transgressor in the first novel, while Ginotti/Nempere is the embodiment of the demonic in St. Irvyne. Being a devil in human form, however, means that one can seduce, tempt, and trick the protagonist into forfeiting his eternal soul, and that attempted seduction is sketched in fairly crude terms in both novels. In Zastrozzi the title character frequently puts forward views that the narrator characterizes as 'sophistically argued' (102), as when Zastrozzi says to Matilda, '"As for the confused hope of a future state, why should we debar ourselves of the delights of this [world], even though purchased by what the misguided multitude calls immorality?"' (102). Meant to shock the orthodox, Zastrozzi's sentiments echo those of Matilda in Lewis's The Monk, a demon in the guise of a woman who tempts the doomed monk Ambrosio to fall into sexual licentiousness and damnation. But for every blasphemous statement made by Zastrozzi, the narrative voice is there to denounce and chide: 'His soul, deadened by crime, could only entertain confused ideas of immortal happiness; for in proportion as human nature departs from virtue, so far are they also from being able clearly to contemplate the wonderful operations, the mysterious ways of Providence' (102–3). So while the villain Zastrozzi quizzes Matilda about theological issues ('"do you believe that the soul decays with the body, or if you do not, when this perishable form mingles with its parent earth, where goes the soul which now actuates its movements? Perhaps, it wastes its fervent energies in tasteless apathy, or lingering torments"'), the narrator condemns the 'sophistical' discourse altogether and traces its influence to the destruction of Matilda's decency: 'by an artful appeal to her passions, did Zastrozzi extinguish the faint spark of religion which yet gleamed in Matilda's bosom. In proportion as her belief in an Omnipotent Power, and consequently her hopes of eternal salvation declined, her ardent and unquenchable passion for Verezzi increased, and a delirium of guilty love filled her soul' (103–4).

A similar conservative narrative voice emerges in St. Irvyne, particularly during the Eloise section of the novel. Here the narrator condemns Eloise's seducer, warning: 'Reflect on this, ye libertines, and, in the full career of the lasciviousness which has unfitted your souls for enjoying the slightest real happiness here or hereafter, tremble!' (229). The censorious sexual ethic implied throughout these texts is not far from some of the positions that Shelley would take later, particularly as they are spelled out in his Discourse on the Manners of the Antient Greeks Relative to the Subject of Love (1818), one of two Prefaces he wrote to his translation of Plato's Symposium. Here Shelley argues that the homosexual acts as well as pederasty that were practised by Greek men could be explained by the inferior status and intellectual inadequacies of the women during that

---

[25] See my Gothic Feminism: The Professionalization of Gender from Charlotte Smith to the Brontës (University Park, PA: Penn State Press, 1998), 143–58.

period. For Shelley, 'the practices and customs of modern Europe are essentially different from and comparably less pernicious than either [the Greeks and Romans]'. He continues, 'in modern Europe the sexual and intellectual claims of love, by the more equal cultivation of the two sexes, so far converge towards one point so as to produce, in attempt to unite them, no gross violation in the established nature of man'.[26]

The Assassins consists of only four chapters of what appears to have been intended as a 'romance' on the scale of the two earlier Gothic works. Begun during the late summer of 1814, abandoned by September of that same year, and then briefly revived about a year later, the tale focuses on the Assassins, a group of Christian Gnostics that Shelley had read about in Edward Gibbon's Decline and Fall of the Roman Empire and the Abbé Augustin Barruel's Mémoires pour server a l'histoire du Jacobinisme.[27] The fact that Shelley presents these Gnostics in a sympathetic light suggests that perhaps his attitudes toward Christianity and what he considered to be the institutionalized corruptions of the religion were more complex than has generally been recognized. The fragment also serves as something of a transition between Shelley's early Gothic novels and a political prose-poem like Queen Mab (1813), itself written partly as a poem and partly as prose, and his later more mature poetic work. As Richard Holmes has noted, 'with its grim and fantastic gothic imagery, and its fiery, energetic, hate-filled language, [The Assassins] brings Shelley one step further towards his best political poetry'.[28]

Shelley begins his idealistic portrait of the Assassins by presenting them as having nothing but 'contempt for human institutions' because they are people who, like him and his circle, were able to reject 'pagan customs and the gross delusions of antiquated superstition' (254). By linking paganism and 'superstition' (a coded term for Catholicism at the time), Shelley participates in the Gothic's well-established anti-Catholic discourse, something he also does in Epipsychidion, with its denunciation of the treatment of a young and beautiful woman forced against her will into a convent, and Queen Mab, with its condemnation of 'priests [who] dare babble of a God of peace | Even whilst their hands are red with guiltless blood'.[29] Valorizing the 'human understanding' and 'the energies of mind', the Assassins are true Christians (unlike, Shelley implies, the masses of ignorant Catholics) who are committed to 'an intrepid spirit of enquiry as to the correctest mode of acting in particular instances of conduct that occur among men' (254). Peaceful, committed to 'benevolence and justice', and 'unostentatious', the Assassins are the saving remnant who flee Jerusalem and Rome in order to settle in Lebanon in a utopian valley called 'Bethzatanai' (256). The physical landscape of Bethzatanai sounds very much like the idealized psychic/natural inscape of Shelley's Alastor, full of 'dark chasms like a thousand radiant rainbows', a 'grove of cypress', 'precipitous mountains', 'starry pyramids of snow', and 'overhanging rocks' (257). And the inhabitants of Bethzatanai are

---

[26] Shelley's Prose: or, The Trumpet of a Prophecy, ed. David Lee Clark (London: Fourth Estate, 1988), 221.
[27] See Murray: Prose, 385. The Assassins is quoted from Behrendt's edition.
[28] Holmes, Shelley: The Pursuit (New York: New York Review of Books, 2003), 246.
[29] The Complete Poetical Works of Percy Bysshe Shelley, ed. George E. Woodberry (Boston: Houghton Mifflin, 1892), I, 58.

'men who idolized nature and the God of nature, to whom love and lofty thoughts and the apprehensions of an uncorrupted spirit were sustenance and life' (258). In other words, the Assassins share the same values and beliefs as Shelley.

While Rome falls and the rest of the civilized world falls into 'perverseness and calamities', the Assassins continue to live in their benevolent 'Republic', shielded from the sinfulness and destruction that mars the outside world (261). But the evil of the outside world threatens the sanctuary that is Bethzatanai, and at the end of the sixth century the valley is suddenly visited by a mysterious young man who is found 'impaled on a broken branch' with a serpent and worms eating away at his chest (264). This strange descent of a Promethean Christ-figure, with a 'bitter smile of mingled abhorrence and scorn' on his lips, suggests something like a composite figure or a doubled Gothic hero/villain whose message is oddly ambivalent (264–5). On one hand the man talks of suicide and death and on the other hand of human love and delight. In short, the figure demands that one of the Assassins take him home, where he states that he needs to be accepted and loved as a member of the family. The text abruptly ends as the stranger is introduced to the Assassin's two children who are sitting on the side of a pool of water and talking to a small snake that is peacefully coiled at their sides. Shelley uses the serpent in canto I of *Laon and Cyntha* (1817) as a positive force of good drawn into combat with the eagle, the power of evil according to Zoroastrianism, but at this date he could have simply been reversing the meaning of the serpent of Genesis. *The Assassins* is too brief and truncated to present a coherent theme or ideology; however, it is obvious that Shelley is even at this date attracted to the possibilities of political and religious prose, although the 'vehement style' of the text itself would appear to indicate that his ideas would be more effectively expressed in the sort of epic poetry he would ultimately pen in *Prometheus Unbound*.[30]

The Coliseum was written in Rome during November 1818, in a lull between the composition of Acts I and II of *Prometheus Unbound*. Organized as a conversation between an elderly blind man, his daughter Helen, and a young, mysterious outsider figure named 'Il Diavolo di Bruto', or Brutus' Devil, the work attempts to explore a persistent Shelleyan theme: the need to renounce self-interest and ego in favour of empathy with others and the greater good of the community. Binfield has suggested that the work may have begun as a response to Byron's *Childe Harold's Pilgrimage*, canto IV (January 1818), the historical cynicism of which Shelley found offensive. In Shelley's alternative meditation on Hellenism, aesthetics, the 'psychology of violence', and the 'anti-elegiac attitude to historical monuments',[31] Shelley advocates 'the interconnectedness and therefore the mutual interdependence of all things and beings',[32] as well as 'an awareness of the life beyond the narrow circle of self'.[33] Using an ambiguously named and effeminately featured young man as his mouthpiece, Shelley introduces yet another fallen angel, this

---

[30] *BSM* XXII, Part 2, 128.

[31] Timothy Clark, 'Shelley's "The Coliseum" and the Sublime', *Durham University Journal* 54 (1993), 225–35 (233, 231).

[32] Behrendt, 'Introduction', 46.

[33] Kevin Binfield, '"May they be divided never": Ethics, History, and the Rhetorical Imagination in Shelley's "The Coliseum"', *Keats–Shelley Journal* 46 (1997), 125–47 (129).

time associated in name with both the assassin of Julius Caesar and Lucifer, as well as the earlier idealized Brutus, founder of the original Roman Republic. Set during the 'feast of the Passover' which is also 'the great feast of the Resurrection', the text immediately situates itself between two competing religious traditions: the Jewish and the Christian. Suggesting that the two religions are actually the same and that therefore religious wars and persecutions are pointless, the text next collapses gender differences in the introduction of the 'emaciated' young man of 'exquisite grace' whose face resembled the 'impassioned tenderness of the statues of Antinous' as well as the 'timid expression of womanish tenderness and hesitation' (Behrendt, 270–1). The androgynous ideal appears throughout Shelley's poetry, and the introduction here of yet another androgynous figure is certainly consistent with Shelley's larger ideological agenda: the denial of a narrow selfhood in favour of merging and denying oppositions and all socially constructed dichotomies.[34] In addition to its truncated religious theme, *The Coliseum* can perhaps best be understood as yet another manifestation of the enthusiasm for ruins that dominates the writings of René Chateaubriand, Germaine de Staël, and Byron. The set-piece here is the visit to the Colosseum by moonlight which was inspired by Chateaubriand's 1804 letter from Italy and printed in the *Mercure*: 'Rome sleeps amidst its ruins. This star of the night, this globe one imagines as finite and deserted wanders in its pale solitude over the solitude of Rome.' After reading this, Staël wrote to a friend: 'To stay in Rome, as Chateaubriand says, calms the soul. It is the dead who live in it, and each step one takes here is as eloquent as Bossuet on the vanity of life. I will write a sort of novel that will serve as framework for a trip to Italy and I think many thoughts and feelings will find their proper place in it.'[35] This scene in *Corinne, or Italy* (1807), made the Colosseum by moonlight a *locus romanticus* for poets like Byron in *Childe Harold* and *Manfred*, and, it would appear, Shelley. When Brutus' Devil confronts the old man and his daughter in the Colosseum, he states: '"Strangers, you are two; behold the third in this great city, to whom alone the spectacle of these mighty ruins is more delightful than the mockeries of a superstition which destroyed them"' (272). Blaming the rise of Catholicism for the destruction of Rome, the young man minutely describes the ruined Colosseum to the blind man, who enunciates the great Shelleyan theme: 'The internal nature of each being is surrounded by a circle, not to be surmounted by his fellows; and it is this repulsion which constitutes the misfortune of the condition of life' (275). The ruined columns of the Colosseum represent the 'circles' that close us off from each other so that we can never fully experience what the old man calls 'Love. This is the religion of eternity, whose votaries have been exiled from among the multitude of mankind' (275).

Invoking the very masculine force of 'Power' and praying to 'Love, Author of Good, God, King, Father!', the blind man requests that the forces of 'justice', 'liberty', 'loveliness', and 'truth, which are thy footsteps' will never divide father and daughter (276). But recognizing that he will die before his beloved Helen, the old man asks that his 'hopes,

---

[34] See Hoeveler, *Romantic Androgyny*, 249–60.

[35] Quoted in Madelyn Gutwirth, *Madame de Staël, Novelist: The Emergence of the Artist as Woman* (Urbana, IL: University of Illinois Press, 1978), 164. Shelley read *Corinne* in 1818, while in Naples (See Bieri, 100).

and the desires, and the delights' that he now has will 'never be extinguished in my child' (276). This conversation—very similar to the *improvvisatori* performance of Tommaso Sgricci that Shelley witnessed in Italy—cannot ultimately resolve the question of 'that mystery, death' (277), and the old man concludes by warning the two others only that all he can say is that death is 'something common to us all' (277). But in the face of the certainty of death, Shelley proposes one answer: 'communion'. The youth, who has been silent while the old man has spoken, announces that he has lived a life in which he has not been understood by his peers, all of whom have consistently rejected his values. He concludes: 'Not but that it is painful to me to live without communion with intelligent and affectionate beings. You are such, I feel' (278). The fragment ends on these words, unable to present a specific vision of a positive 'communion' that would enable individuals to resist and overcome the pessimism inherent in the ruins discourse.

Although he loved to read fiction and was married to a successful novelist, Percy Shelley's literary talents clearly did not lie in the realm of fiction. He himself disparaged the 'story' as a mere 'catalogue of detached facts' in contrast to the superior synthesis of form and meaning that could be achieved in a poem.[36] In fact, Shelley was far less interested in character development, convincing plot, and actions than he was in the play of language, imagery, and symbolism in itself. That he continued to try to compose in prose as late as 1818 suggests that the lure of fiction continued to fascinate him, or perhaps it is fairer to say that it continued to elude him. In the final analysis, Shelley was a poet whose ideas found their clearest and most powerful expression, not in his prose exercises, but in the poetic works that grew out of these early and abortive experiments.

SELECT BIBLIOGRAPHY

Antippas, Andy P. 'The Structure of Shelley's *St. Irvyne*: Parallelism and the Gothic Mode of Evil', *Tulane Studies in English* 18 (1970), 59–71.

Behrendt, Stephen C. 'Shelley's Narrative Fiction Fragments'. *The Unfamiliar Shelley*. Vol. II. Ed. Alan M. Weinberg and Timothy Webb. Aldershot: Ashgate, forthcoming.

Bieri, James. *Percy Bysshe Shelley: A Biography*. Cranbury, NJ: Associated University Presses, 2006.

Binfield, Kevin. ' "May they be divided never": Ethics, History, and the Rhetorical Imagination in Shelley's "The Coliseum"'. *Keats–Shelley Journal* 46 (1997), 125–47.

Birkhead, Edith. *The Tale of Terror: A Study of the Gothic Romance*. London: Constable, 1921.

Cameron, Kenneth Neill. *The Young Shelley: Genesis of a Radical*. 1950; repr. New York: Collier, 1962.

Clark, Timothy, 'Shelley's "The Coliseum" and the Sublime'. *Durham University Journal* 54 (1993), 225–35.

Donovan, Jack. 'The Storyteller'. *The Cambridge Companion to Shelley*. Ed. Timothy Morton. Cambridge: Cambridge UP, 2006. 85–103.

Finch, Peter. 'Monstrous Inheritance: The Sexual Politics of Genre in Shelley's *St. Irvyne*'. *Keats–Shelley Journal* 48 (1999), 35–68.

---

[36] *A Defence of Poetry*, in *Shelley's Poetry and Prose*, ed. Donald H. Reiman and Sharon B. Powers (New York: Norton, 1977), 485.

Hoeveler, Diane Long. *Romantic Androgyny: Then Women Within*. University Park, PA: Penn State Press, 1990.

—— *Gothic Feminism: The Professionalization of Gender from Charlotte Smith to the Brontës*. University Park, PA: Penn State Press, 1998.

Hogle, Jerrold E. 'Shelley's Fiction: "The Stream of Fate"'. *Keats–Shelley Journal* 30 (1981), 78–99.

Holmes, Richard. *Shelley: The Pursuit*. New York: New York Review of Books, 2003.

Rajan, Tilottama. 'Promethean Narrative: Overdetermined Form in Shelley's Gothic Fiction'. *Shelley: Poet and Legislator of the World*. Ed. Betty T. Bennett and Stuart Curran. Baltimore: Johns Hopkins UP, 1996. 240–52.

—— 'Shelley's Promethean Narratives: Gothic Anamorphoses in *Zastrozzi, St. Irvyne,* and *Prometheus Unbound*'. *Romantic Narrative: Shelley, Hays, Godwin, Wollstonecraft*. Baltimore: Johns Hopkins UP, 2010.

Seed, David. 'Shelley's "Gothick" in *St. Irvyne* and after'. *Essays on Shelley*. Ed. Miriam Allott. Liverpool: Liverpool UP, 1982. 39–70.

Shelley, Percy Bysshe. *Zastrozzi, A Romance*; *St. Irvyne: or The Rosicrucian: A Romance*. Ed. Stephen C. Behrendt. Peterborough, Ont.: Broadview Press, 2002.

CHAPTER 13

SHELLEY'S LETTERS

DAISY HAY

THE PURSUIT OF SHADOWS

On 24 March 1822, Shelley wrote a letter to his stepsister-in-law, Claire Clairmont. Claire had become increasingly frantic about the fate of her daughter Allegra, who had been placed by her father Lord Byron in the care of the nuns at the Capuchin Convent at Bagnacavallo. She was convinced that Byron would never allow her to be reunited with Allegra, and wrote to Shelley to demand his assistance in kidnapping the child from the convent. He was horrified by this proposal, and by what he perceived to be her obsessive fixation with her daughter. 'If you would take my advice,' he wrote with some finality, 'you would give up this idle pursuit after shadows' (*Letters: PBS* II, 400).

Anyone who searches for Shelley in his correspondence might do well to heed his advice. His letters are shot through with the shadows of his life, and for over a century have been used by biographers and literary critics eager to pursue the poet through his own words. This is hardly surprising, since the letters appear to offer the illusion of privileged insight into their writer's mind, and to present an unmediated image of Shelley's self.

In this chapter I will argue that Shelley is particularly engaged with the illusory nature of the epistolary self, and that, as a result, he is both obscured and revealed by his correspondence. As we pursue him through that correspondence, we have to remember that we are in pursuit of a shadow, of an idealized, constructed identity. We also have to remember that the letters stand apart from Shelley's other prose works, that they are texts in constant dialogue with their biographical context, genre, and material history. They are, first and foremost, a sequence of communicative gestures, which are shaped in complicated ways by their recipients. Alongside the shadow of Shelley himself, the shadows of these idealized recipients people his correspondence, and breathe life into every letter he wrote.

READING SCRAWLS

Writing to Thomas Jefferson Hogg in October 1821, Shelley noted wryly that Thomas Love Peacock—newly married, and much occupied with his position at the East India Company—had 'something better to do than read scrawls' (*Letters: PBS* II, 362). Shelley was always doubtful about the value of his own letters, and frequently inscribed this doubt into his correspondence. The troubled textual history of this correspondence, however, points to the value of his 'scrawls', the physical and intellectual ownership of which has been contested ever since his death.

Mary Shelley understood better than most the importance of letters in the creation of a legacy. From childhood she had watched Godwin copy and curate his correspondence and, as Betty T. Bennett has argued, his example taught her how to 'value the personal letter as a component of public history'.[1] She had acted on this example when she included letters by both her and Shelley in *History of a Six Weeks' Tour* (1817), and in the months following her husband's death she began the slow process of collecting his correspondence, writing to Peacock and others to request both copies and originals of the letters in their possession. It took her until 1840 to publish the results, in large part because her father-in-law prohibited her from bringing his son's name before the public, and in the intervening years a small number of Shelley's letters appeared in print in volumes such as Leigh Hunt's *Lord Byron and Some of his Contemporaries* (1828). But Sir Timothy Shelley's strictures did not stop Mary from collecting Shelley's letters, which she bought whenever they appeared on the open market. In this she was assisted, after 1848, by her daughter-in-law Jane Shelley, who was passionately interested in her husband's literary ancestry. The efforts of the two women to preserve Shelley's correspondence had one unfortunate side effect, as William St Clair has noted, since they inadvertently encouraged the activities of forgers, and at various points Mary felt compelled to purchase letters of dubious authenticity in order to remove them from circulation.[2]

After Mary's death in 1851, Jane Shelley enthusiastically assumed the mantle of defender of the Shelleyan faith. She was a less scrupulous and more partisan editor than her mother-in-law, and she exerted tight control over the documents in her possession. This brought her into conflict with Hogg, whose 1858 biography of the poet shamelessly cut and manipulated his friend's letters for his own ends. Jane punished Hogg for his editorial transgressions by withdrawing access to the family archive, and by publicly castigating his uncompleted biography as a 'fantastic caricature' in the Preface to her *Shelley Memorials* (1859).[3] The repercussions of this dispute were felt for decades, as Jane reacted

---

[1] Betty T. Bennett, 'Mary Shelley's Letters: The Public/Private Self', in Esther Schor (ed.), *The Cambridge Companion to Mary Shelley* (Cambridge: Cambridge UP, 2003), 221–5 (214).

[2] William St Clair, *The Godwins and the Shelleys* (London: Faber, 1989), 494.

[3] Jane Shelley, *Shelley Memorials: From Authentic Sources*, 3rd edn. (1859; London: Henry S. King and Co., 1875), pp. vii–viii.

by preventing further scrutiny of Shelley's papers. Instead of allowing those interested in Shelley to work from original documents, she produced a privately printed source book, *Shelley and Mary*, which presented silently edited texts of the letters, and with which nineteenth-century biographers of both Shelleys had to be content.

Jane died in 1899, and with her passing, restrictions on the publication of Shelley's letters eased. This did not mean, however, that battles over the ownership of the correspondence faded into historical oblivion. In 1909 Roger Ingpen published the first comprehensive edition of the correspondence, and his *Letters of Percy Bysshe Shelley* remained the standard text until 1964, when it was superseded by Frederick Jones's two-volume edition of the same title. Jones's volumes provoked a quarrel with the editors of *Shelley and his Circle* (1961–), who objected to his decision to include in the edition letters owned by the Pforzheimer Collection, which were destined for first publication in the *Shelley and his Circle* volumes. A war of words ensued in the front matter of the rival editions, over a century after Jane Shelley had condemned Hogg from a similar platform. The outline of this episode can still be traced in Jones's *Letters* (which implied that the Pforzheimer Collection's policy was unjustifiable) and in volume III of *Shelley and his Circle*, in which Jones was accused of 'misrepresentation', 'unauthorized use of material', and of 'apparent violations of usual professional ethics' (*SC* III, p. xxii).

Today, the chief result of this dispute is that, uniquely among the canonical Romantic poets, Shelley's letters are not available in a single authoritative edition. Jones's texts of the Pforzheimer letters are taken predominantly from Ingpen's 1909 edition and differ from the manuscripts in subtle but important ways. Shelley's grammar and punctuation is polished, as in Ingpen's edition, resulting in texts which lack the impetuous, idiosyncratic immediacy of the originals. The *Shelley and his Circle* texts, in contrast, are meticulously transcribed and annotated, but are deprived of the context of the bulk of Shelley's correspondence. In addition, at the time of writing *Shelley and his Circle* does not include those letters written after 1820, although two further volumes of the title are projected which should ultimately fill this gap.[4]

One of the consequences of this state of affairs is that Shelley's letters have not received the literary critical attention they deserve.[5] Textual instability exacerbates a more general critical reluctance to engage with letters as artefacts, as documents which are more

---

[4] In this essay, I use texts from *Shelley and his Circle* where possible, and Jones's edition for letters not published in those volumes.

[5] There are exceptions to this: John Freeman has written on Shelley's early letters, Enno Ruge on the correspondence with Elizabeth Hitchener, and Benjamin Colbert on the travel letters to Peacock. In addition, at a conference on Shelley at University College, Oxford, in September 2007, Michael O'Neill gave a plenary lecture which looked in some detail at Shelley's late epistolary style. See Freeman, 'Shelley's Early Letters', in Kelvin Everest (ed.), *Shelley Revalued: Essays from the Gregynog Conference* (Leicester: Leicester UP, 1983), 109–28 and 'Shelley's Letters to his Father', *Keats–Shelley Memorial Bulletin* 34 (1983), 1–15; Ruge, '"Is the Entire Correspondence a Fiction?" Shelley's Letters and the Eighteenth-Century Epistolary Novel', in Werner Huber and Marie-Luise Egbert (eds.), *Alternative Romanticisms* (Essen: Studien zur Englischen Romantik 15, 2003), 111–21; and Colbert, *Shelley's Eye: Travel Writing and Aesthetic Vision* (Aldershot: Ashgate Publishing, 2005).

than deposits of biographical information.[6] However, the existence of rival texts of the same letter is by no means wholly negative, since it emphasizes that printed letters are always editorially constructed, and that the published epistle has a separate existence to the autograph 'scrawl'. This is particularly evident in the differences between Jones's volumes and *Shelley and his Circle*, since in many respects the former reads like an epistolary novel, in which editorial commentary and replies from recipients jostle for space with the letters themselves. In *Shelley and his Circle*, by contrast, the reader is given a much clearer sense of the letter as physical object, blotted by sealing wax, ink stains, and postmarks. Such differences have a profound effect on the ways in which the reader experiences the letters, and serve as a salutary reminder of Betty T. Bennett's words of warning to the naive letter-reader. 'There are no neutral facts or neutral editors,' she writes. 'There are only theoretical and interpretative editorial processes that, like "the awful shadow of some unseen Power," should not float unrecognised among us'.[7]

Adieu to Egotism, Part One

Shelley's letters bear witness to the truth of Clara Brant's observation that 'identity [...] is manifested in relationships'.[8] He placed great importance on what Godwin, in the *Enquiry Concerning Political Justice*, termed 'the collision of mind with mind',[9] and, like Keats, was innately aware of the ways in which, within its own limitations, letter-writing could mimic that collision. But while Keats conceded that 'Writing has this disadvan[ta]ge of speaking. one cannot write a wink, or a nod, or a grin, or a purse of the Lips, or a *smile*',[10] Shelley sought to challenge the limitations of the written word by throwing the focus of his letters from the self to his relationship with his correspondent. As a result, while his letters are intrinsically self-conscious, they are also intensely focused on the particular characteristics of their recipient. This is especially true of the letters of Shelley's maturity, in which the shadows of self and interlocutor are frozen in a delicate balance. 'Adieu to egotism I am sick to Death at the name of *self*,' Shelley tells Hogg on 1 January

---

[6] Timothy Webb has drawn attention to this, writing of 'our slowness in evolving a poetics of the letter', and his engagement with Keats's letters as literary texts in their own right demonstrates the potential of the epistolary poetic he describes. See Timothy Webb, '"Cutting Figures": Rhetorical Strategies in Keats's *Letters*', in Michael O'Neill (ed.), *Keats: Bicentenary Readings* (Edinburgh: Edinburgh UP, 1997), 144–69.

[7] Betty T. Bennett, 'The Editor of Letters as Critic: A Denial of Blameless Neutrality', *Text: Transactions of the Society for Textual Scholarship* 6 (1994), 222.

[8] Clara Brant, *Eighteenth-Century Letters and British Culture* (Basingstoke: Palgrave Macmillan, 2006), 334.

[9] William Godwin, *Enquiry Concerning Political Justice*, in *Philosophical Writings of William Godwin*, ed. Mark Philp (London: Pickering and Chatto, 1993), III, 15. This phrase, and Godwin's own correspondence, is discussed by Pamela Clemit in 'Holding Proteus: William Godwin in his Letters', in Heather Glen and Paul Hamilton (eds.), *Repossessing the Romantic Past* (Cambridge: Cambridge UP, 2006), 100.

[10] John Keats, *Letters*, ed. Hyder Rollins, 2 vols. (Cambridge, MA: Harvard UP, 1958), 2, 205.

1811 (*SC* II, 679). The letters he writes over the course of the ensuing decade do not bear out the truth of this assertion, but they do show him complicating the idea of self until it is transformed into a source of epistolary possibility.

In order to demonstrate this, I am going to focus on the letters Shelley wrote, from 1816 onwards, to two of his closest friends, Leigh Hunt and Thomas Love Peacock. The letters to Hunt and Peacock reveal Shelley at his most alert to the problems and possibilities of epistolary communication, and they show the ambitiousness with which he attempted to reshape his sense of self through his correspondence. In the case of Leigh Hunt, the letters formed part of a relationship which was central to Shelley's intellectual and emotional existence. This was also a relationship originally conjured into being by letters, as the two men built their friendship through the pages of their correspondence.

Shelley's letters from the winter of 1816 demonstrate how their epistolary exchange, which began in earnest after the publication of Hunt's 'Young Poets' article, transformed the older man into his chief confidant. On 8 December he wrote to acknowledge two letters from Hunt, and attempted to convey how much those letters had moved him. 'Your letters [...] give me unmingled pleasure', he reported. 'I have not in all my intercourse with mankind experienced sympathy & kindness with which I have been so affected, or which my whole being has so sprung forward to meet and to return.' The remainder of the letter testifies to the accuracy of this statement, as it articulates polite conventions in order to ignore them. 'Let me lay aside preliminaries,' Shelley implores. 'Let me talk with you as an old friend' (*Letters: PBS* I, 516).

This is a letter which gives no indication of the slim ties binding writer and recipient. Instead, it reads as if written to an intimate acquaintance, as Shelley confesses his feelings of alienation to Hunt:

> With you, & perhaps some others (tho in a less degree, I fear) my gentleness & sincerity finds favour, because they are themselves gentle and sincere; they believe in self-devotion & generosity because they are themselves generous & self devoted. Perhaps I should have shrunk from persisting in the task which I had undertaken in early life, of opposing myself, in these evil times & among these evil tongues, to what I esteem misery & vice; if I must have lived in the solitude of the heart. Fortunately my domestic circle incloses that within it which compensates for the loss.—But these are subjects for conversation, & I find that in using the priviledges which you have permitted me of friendship, I have indulged that garrulity of self-love which only friendship can excuse or endure. (*Letters: PBS* I, 517–18)

Shelley portrays himself as an exile deserving of Hunt's sympathy, as he aligns himself with him by endowing them both with 'gentleness & sincerity', and by positioning them both as opponents of 'evil tongues'. He demonstrates how crucial sympathy is to him, as he describes his 'domestic circle' to a man famous for his celebrations of domesticity. In sharing the pain of loneliness and the consolations of domestic affection Shelley emphasizes his suitability to be Hunt's companion, in a gesture which offers as well as celebrates friendship. And as he acknowledges that his letter deals with topics better suited to conversation than to correspondence, he once again proclaims the strength of his connection to Hunt, as he excuses the 'garrulity' of his 'self-love'. By highlighting his disregard for epistolary convention, Shelley solidifies a friendship created entirely through the exchange of sympathetic letters.

If Shelley and Hunt's friendship was made by letters such as this, it was also sustained by them, when, after Shelley's departure for Italy in 1818, they were forced to rely on letters to keep their friendship alive. Both understood the importance of expressing their concern and affection for the other, but it was Hunt who established a model of epistolary theatricality which allowed them to bridge the distance between them imaginatively. 'Whenever I write to you', he told both Shelleys in a letter dated 23 August 1819, 'I seem to be transported to your presence. I dart out of the windows like a bird, dash into a southwestern current of air, skim over the cool waters, hurry over the basking lands, rise like a lark over the mountains, fling like a swallow into the vallies, skim again, pant for breath' (SC VI, 879–80). Images such as this allowed Shelley and Hunt to write proximity into their letters, and represented one of the techniques they developed to prevent their dialogue from subsiding into rehearsed paragraphs. Shelley responded to Hunt's example by relating conversations held with Hunt's portrait, which he positioned as a signifier of his absent friend, and by treating the *Examiner* and *Indicator* as an extension of their correspondence.

Such epistolary techniques created an illusion of immediacy, but brought with them their own problems. Shelley could write of his pleasure at receiving Hunt's portrait, but its presence in his Italian home ultimately served to emphasize Hunt's absence. And his decision to treat Hunt's periodical writing as part of their private correspondence put his conception of his interlocutor under strain. The Hunt of Shelley's letters is not just a sympathetic friend: he is also a public figure on whom specific demands can be made. 'What a state England is in!', Shelley writes, in the aftermath of Peterloo, 'but you will never write politics':

> I dont wonder; but I wish then that you would write a paper in the Examiner on the actual state of the country; & what, under all the circumstances of the conflicting passions & interests of men, we are to expect [...] Every word a man has to say is valuable to the public now, & thus you will at once gratify your friend, nay instruct & either exhilarate him or force him to be resigned & awaken the minds of the people. (SC VI, 1107)

Through rapid transitions in person and perspective Shelley reminds Hunt of his responsibility to his readers, using the privileges of private correspondence to recall him to a public duty. He makes both himself and his recipient impersonal in the process: Hunt is abstracted into 'a man' with something valuable to say; Shelley becomes representative of his public; an auditor waiting to be guided. This reconfiguration of their relationship stems from that most private of things: a desire, or a 'wish'. As Shelley requires Hunt to be both the ideal friend and the champion of the people, he makes himself into a dual figure as well, an individual whose capacity for wonder allows him to understand Hunt's rhetorical withdrawal, but who is nevertheless part of an expectant 'we'.

In the aftermath of Peterloo, this doubling of both Shelley and Hunt's epistolary personas introduced a note of restraint into the correspondence, as Hunt declined to explain his retreat from politics to Shelley, and subsequently implicated Shelley in that retreat by refusing to publish his *Mask of Anarchy*. Yet despite this and other moments of tension, Shelley's creation of an idealized public and private Hunt comes in the letters to exemplify a crucial relationship between private form and public concern. As private interlocutor Hunt receives Shelley's frankest explorations of friendship (an ideal which he valorizes in *Foliage*), but as editor of the *Examiner* he becomes a mediator through whom Shelley is able, in the words of Clara Brant, to write as a citizen: to participate 'in a culture of letter-writing that had a widely recognised power to represent, misrepresent and contest political processes'.[11] When the public and private Hunts are brought together in a single letter, it results in a bold experimentation with the boundaries of the epistolary form.

This is most evident in the dedicatory letter to *The Cenci*, directed to Hunt but in fact written for a much wider audience. In the Dedication Shelley takes the personal, sympathetic communicative style he and Hunt had developed and uses it to make a public, political point about his dedicatee. 'My dear Friend,' he begins, 'I inscribe with your name, from a distant country, and after an absence whose months have seemed years, this latest of my literary efforts.' From this modest opening, the Dedication broadens out into a celebration of all that Shelley admires in Hunt:

> Had I known a person more highly endowed than yourself with all that it becomes a man to possess, I had solicited for this work the ornament of his name. One more gentle, honourable, innocent and brave; one of more exalted toleration for all who do and think evil, and yet himself more free from evil; one who knows better how to receive, and how to confer a benefit, though he must ever confer far more than he can receive; one of simpler, and, in the highest sense of the word, of purer life and manners I never knew: and I had already been fortunate in friendships when your name was added to the list. (*Norton* 2, 140)

Here the gestures and compliments of personal exchange are put to public use: to announce allegiance with Hunt, and to defend him against the slander of critics, levelled in the *Blackwood's* 'Cockney School' articles and elsewhere. Yet while the expressions of admiration for Hunt are shadowed in the private correspondence, here they are reformulated and distanced, so that Hunt becomes emblematic of his own good qualities. Through an extended comparison with an unrealized superior being, Hunt is made into an abstract embodiment of simplicity and purity. Friendship itself is abstracted in the process, until Shelley's formal characterization of himself as one 'fortunate in friendship' is as objectively distanced as his depiction of Hunt.

The result, however, is a dedication which merges Shelley's public and private conceptions of Hunt, making the private virtues a matter of public record. Hunt's heroic qualities are held up as an example to all those who fight stigma and isolation, and they emphasize the disjunction between the critical opprobrium directed towards him and the benefit his actions have already conferred on his fellow men. The letter thus reveals the possibilities of an abstracted version of a private form made public, as Shelley

---

[11] Brant, *Eighteenth-Century Letters and British Culture*, 211.

employs the epistolary genre to situate *The Cenci* in a politically and culturally oppositional context, and as he redeploys in public the rhetorical techniques of private exchange.

Ultimately the double nature of Shelley's conception of Hunt allowed the two men to maintain a frank epistolary relationship, and it enabled that relationship to survive periods of silence as they disagreed about the direction of Hunt's writing. The mutual sympathy established in their letters sustained their friendship in spite of their differences, and allowed their correspondence to develop and flourish. Their epistolary dialogue ceased only with a letter written by Hunt after Shelley and Edward Williams had set sail from Livorno on 7 July 1822. 'Shelley Mio,' Hunt wrote, 'pray let us know how you got home the other day with Williams, for I fear you must have been out in the bad weather, and we are anxious.'[12]

ADIEU TO EGOTISM, PART TWO

The intersection of public and private in Shelley's correspondence takes on a further degree of complexity in the letters he wrote to Peacock from Italy in 1818–19. These letters are epistolary travelogues, and are quite distinct from those he wrote to the rest of his friends. They form one of the most striking portions of his correspondence, and include some of his most ambitious and experimental communications. Peacock was the ideal recipient of such epistles: scholarly and sympathetic, he was able to respond intuitively and articulately to the detail of Shelley's descriptions. He and Shelley had discussed their shared love of classical writers in Bishopsgate and Marlow in 1815 and 1817, and these conversations formed an intellectual backdrop for Shelley's mediations on scenes of Italianate classical grandeur.

Colouring this backdrop further were the letters Shelley wrote to Peacock from Switzerland in 1816, which were subsequently published in *History of a Six Weeks' Tour*. The 1816 letters, partly written while Shelley was reading Rousseau's epistolary novel *Julie*, served as a paradigm for the Italian correspondence, both in their presentation of a self-consciously subjective travel narrative and in their complicated conception of their audience. Although initially written for Peacock the Swiss letters were, in *History of a Six Weeks' Tour*, made available to a much wider readership, memories of which pervade the 1818–19 correspondence, Shelley's protestations to the contrary notwithstanding. Even while he assured Peacock that 'I am more pleased to interest you than the many' (*Letters: PBS* II, 70) he emphasized the importance of his letters, which stood in place of a travel journal. It seems more than likely that he wrote them with publication in mind, a supposition confirmed by Mary Shelley, who instructed Peacock to keep the letters safe so that she could copy them on her return to England.

---

[12] David Cheney, 'The Letters of Leigh Hunt' (unpublished typescript). David Cheney Collection, University of Toledo, Ohio. Box 16, file 10.

Nor, even in the first instance, were the travel letters written for Peacock's eyes alone. Instead they were designed to be shared with Hunt, Hogg, and others in Shelley's abandoned London circle. Peacock duly circulated them among his friends, acting on Shelley's instructions as he did so. 'I consider the letters I address to Peacock as nearly the same things as a letter addressed to you,' Shelley told Hogg. 'They contain nothing but long accounts of my peregrinations which it would be wearisome to transcribe' (*Letters: PBS* II, 68).

The Italian letters to Peacock were thus written for a triple audience: Peacock himself, a circle of sympathetic friends, and the anonymous body of the travelogue-reading public. As a result, there is a contradiction at the heart of the letters. On the one hand they are among Shelley's more private communications, in that they focus almost exclusively on his own experience of the sights he sees, rather than on the more communal concerns—about friends and relationships—discussed in his correspondence with Hunt. Yet they are also among his most impersonal epistles, in that they are written with publication in mind, for audiences other than their primary interlocutor. As Benjamin Colbert has shown in his study of Shelley's travel writing, Shelley is quick to capitalize on this contradiction. 'The private letter', Colbert writes, is 'a mode of expression less inhibited by the genre and gender expectations imposed on published travel accounts— [Shelley] crosses at will from "masculine" discourses of classical and antiquarian inquiry to "feminine" discourses of emotional response'.[13] The inbuilt audiences of the travel letters allow Shelley to rationalize his reaction to Italy through a focus on his own aesthetic experience: a focus which is both intimate and distanced.

In order to illustrate this, I will explore the complexities of a single letter, written from Rome on 23 March 1819 (*Letters: PBS* II, 83–90). This was one of the last letters Shelley wrote to Peacock before the travel correspondence ceased with William Shelley's death at the beginning of June, and it is particularly rich in both detail and scope. It suggests that Rome tested Shelley's powers of expression to their full extent, but it also highlights the limits of language in order to encapsulate the city's grandeur. 'What shall I say to you of Rome?' Shelley asks towards the beginning of the letter, pointing to the impossibility of conveying the city's totality. 'If I speak first of the inanimate ruins [...] will you not believe me insensible to the vital, the almost breathing creations of genius yet subsisting in their perfection?' He extends the conceit by ventriloquizing Peacock, as he acknowledges his own descriptive inadequacy:

> What has become you will ask of the Apoll{o} the Gladiator the Venus of the Capital? What of Apollo of Belvedere, the Laocoon? What of Raphael and Guido? These things are best spoken of when the mind has drunk in the spirit of their forms, and little indeed can I who must devote no more than a few months to the contemplation of them hope to know or feel their profound beauty.

By articulating Peacock's response and his own inability to express the beauty he sees, Shelley gestures towards Rome's magnitude, and towards his own aesthetic experience

---

[13] Colbert, *Shelley's Eye*, 123.

of that magnitude. He thus establishes a conversation between spectator, scene, and interlocutor, in which the spectator becomes the medium through which the witness to his reactions views the city.

This conversation continues throughout the letter. 'What shall I say of the modern city?' Shelley asks, as he shifts the focus of his description. Elsewhere he breaks off his account to ponder its worth. 'The tourists tell you all about these things, & I am afraid of stumbling upon their language when I enumerate what is so well known.' And, in a crucial passage, which is worth quoting at some length, he shows how an acknowledgement of the limits of expression can express more than page upon page of guidebook prose. His subject is the Baths of Caracalla:

> In one place you wind along a narrow strip of weed-grown ruin; on one side is the immensity of earth & sky, on the other, a narrow chasm, which is bounded by an arch of enormous size, fringed by the many coloured foliage & blossoms, & supporting a lofty & irregular pyramid, overgrown like itself by the all-prevailing vegetation. Around rise other crags & other peaks all arrayed & the deformity of their vast desolation softened down by the undecaying investiture of nature. Come to Rome. It is a scene by which expression is overpowered: which words cannot convey. Still further, winding half up one of these shattered pyramids by the path through the blooming copse wood you come to a little mossy lawn, surrounded by the wild shrubs; it is overgrown with anemones, wall flowers & violets whose stalks pierce the starry moss, & with radiant blue flowers whose names I know not, & which scatter thro the air the divinest odour which as you recline under the shade of the ruin produces a sensation of voluptuous faintness like the combinations of sweet music. The paths still wind on, threading the perplexed windings;—other labyrinths, other lawns, & deep dells of wood & lofty rocks & terrific chasms. When I tell you that these ruins cover several acres, & that the paths above penetrate at least half their extent your imagination will fill up all that I am unable to express, of this astonishing scene. I speak of these things not in the order in which I visited them, but in that of the impressions which they made on me, or perhaps as chance directs.

Alongside Peacock and his circle of readers, we are shown the Baths of Caracalla through Shelley's eye as he moves his narrative through the Baths' overgrown pathways. His gaze shifts promiscuously, taking in crumbling masonry, the colours of wild flowers, the height and depth of the unfolding scene, as well as views in which buildings are transformed into mountains, with peaks and crags as sublime as anything nature can boast. As the buildings are reclaimed by weeds they become elemental, part of the natural landscape. Through a direct address to the reader, encompassed via the informal second person plural—'you wind along a narrow strip', 'you come to a little mossy lawn'—Shelley unveils his scene through a personal, subjective perspective which, in the multiplicity of its detail, manages to appear all-encompassing. Colour and scent are thrust before the reader's notice, and sentences linked by conjunction after conjunction perform the perplexed windings of the paths along which Shelley and his readers tread. Interrupting this rhetorical passage through the Baths are moments of frustration, acknowledgements that language is stifled by that which it tries to describe. 'Come to Rome', Shelley pleads. Or, failing that, imagine the gap between expression and reality. 'Your imagina-tion', he tells Peacock, 'will fill up all that I am unable to express, of this astonishing scene.' Peacock's aesthetic sensitivity is co-opted by Shelley, transformed from something autonomous into a weapon in his own descriptive armoury. If 'expression is overpow-ered' and the scene one which 'words cannot convey' then all Shelley can do is to depend on Peacock—figured in the letters as his ideal reader—to become a participant in his rhetorical drama, so that two minds may together reach towards an understanding of the enormity of that which he describes. As the eye through which the scene is visual-ized, Shelley can only speak of what he sees in the order of 'the impressions which they made on me'—a haphazard approach belied by the passage's meticulous construction.

The epistolary form enables Shelley to capture his response to Rome through a rhetorical appropriation of his interlocutor's imagination. His notebooks suggest that he drafted his descriptions before synthesizing them into letters,[14] but it was only in the letters that these descriptions were brought to life through Shelley's insistent acknowl-edgement of his recipient's perspective. Betty T. Bennett has argued that a letter's addressee is its writer's 'unacknowledged collaborator',[15] an idea supported by Shelley's correspondence with Peacock. The collaborative nature of this correspondence allows Shelley to write of himself even as he focuses on statuary and landscape. And as he becomes merely the eye through which that landscape is viewed, he writes a new degree of subjectivity into his travelogue, where everything he describes is mediated through his experience. The letters to Peacock therefore allow him to know himself better as, in testing the limits of his powers of expression, he interrogates his response to that which he tries to portray. The result is both self-aware and self-effacing, and produces letters which simultaneously celebrate and transcend the essential subjectivity of their form.

THE CURSE OF TANTALUS

On 18 June 1822, Shelley wrote his last long letter. His correspondent was John Gisborne, an expatriate resident of Livorno who had recently returned to London. 'Italy is more and more delightful to me,' Shelley reported. 'I only feel the want of those who can feel, and understand me. Whether from proximity and the continuity of domestic intercourse, Mary does not [...] It is the curse of Tantalus, that a person possessing such excellent powers and so pure a mind as hers, should not excite the sympathy indispensable to their application to domestic life' (*Letters: PBS* II, 435).

This letter was written two days after Mary Shelley suffered a miscarriage which nearly killed her. Given this, at one level it is strikingly lacking in empathy in the way in which it ignores her suffering as it apportions blame for a mutual failure of communication.

[14] The Arch of Titus, for example, is described both in the letter of 23 March and elsewhere in draft. See *Julian*, VI, 309.
[15] Bennett, 'The Editor of Letters as Critic', 221.

However, it also contains an acknowledgement that sympathy and understanding are crucial to Shelley's conception of himself, and that without true friends around him, his creativity is stifled. In this context Mary's withdrawal, regardless of its cause, has a profoundly negative impact on Shelley. 'I write little now,' he tells Gisborne. 'It is impossible to compose except under the strong excitement of an assurance of finding sympathy in what you write' (*Letters: PBS* II, 436). Faced with critical disdain and an uninterested public, Shelley turns inwards to his domestic circle in search of the understanding he desires. But he cannot find it at the Villa Magni, the isolated house on the Bay of Lerici where he lived out the end of his life with Mary Shelley, Claire Clairmont, and Jane and Edward Williams. Like his wife he suffers the curse of Tantalus, which in his case means he is not able to find among his friends the community of his dreams. So he retreats into correspondence, producing, through June 1822, letters which are intensely focused on the idealized images of others. These letters demonstrate the impact of his exchanges with Hunt and Peacock on his epistolary style, as they combine the complicated self-consciousness of the Italian travel letters with the idealized conception of sympathy developed in collaboration with Hunt.

The letters of this period are full of ghosts: of Shelley's former self, of the poet he once hoped to become, and of his friends. The recipients of individual letters continue to loom large, yet Shelley seems distanced from them, as if he no longer needs more than the idea of friendship to shape his correspondence. He asks Edward Trelawny, the Byronic caricature who had arrived in Pisa the previous winter, to procure him a small quantity of '*Prussic Acid*, or *essential oil of bitter almonds*', so that he has the relief of knowing death to be a possibility. 'I need not tell you I have no intention of suicide at present,' he tells Trelawny, in an assurance deliberately undermined by its qualifications and negative formulations. 'But I confess it would be a comfort to me to hold in my possession that golden key to the chamber of perpetual rest' (*Letters: PBS* II, 433). Shelley's image valorizes and idealizes death, presenting it as a blissful retreat, available only to those in possession of its 'golden key'. It does so in the context of an illicit admission ('I confess') in which Trelawny is imagined as a pagan confessor, and which gives the illusion of intimacy. Shelley, however, reveals nothing of the circumstances which lead him to make his request, preferring to leave it as an enigmatic indicator of hidden dramas. He becomes a stoic distanced from the petty concerns of his fellow men, who nevertheless plays off the drama of Trelawny's theatrical, plagarized identity.

A similarly distanced self-representation is visible too in a letter to Horace Smith, written two days before Shelley left the Villa Magni for Pisa. Writing of the proposed journal collaboration between Byron and Hunt, Shelley confesses to Smith that 'I greatly fear that this alliance will not succeed, for I, who could never have been regarded as more than the link of the two thunderbolts, cannot consent to be even that,—& how long the alliance between the wren and the eagle may continue I will not prophesy' (*Letters: PBS* II, 442). Hunt and Byron are anthropomorphized into birds, an idea derived from Hunt's earlier depiction of himself in flight to the Shelleys at Livorno. Shelley, in contrast, will not play a part in their relationship, and denies himself a place in his friends' interaction even as he dramatizes them as 'two thunderbolts'. He claims that he 'cannot consent' to link them, but enigmatically declines to provide a context for his refusal. Instead, in his pointed silence, he merely hints at circumstances which inform his actions, but which he will not confide to his interlocutor. To Hunt himself, whose presence in Italy Shelley had originally orchestrated and which he had eagerly anticipated, he writes of their proposed reunion in curiously detached tones, which suggest new distance between him and Hunt. 'All will go well,' he insists, but as he addresses Hunt's lack of funds and Byron's lack of interest in the journal project, he acknowledges the disjunction between the fantasy of community which has sustained him and Hunt during the long years of their separation and the difficulties of reality (*Letters: PBS* II, 441).

Shelley's analysis of self, friends, and community is at its most sustained and complex in the long letter to Gisborne with which this section opened (*Letters: PBS* II, 434–7). Gisborne was unusual among Shelley's correspondents in that he received some of the poet's most personal letters even though he was not one of his closest friends (indeed, their relationship had been badly disrupted by a period of estrangement in 1820). Shelley came to view Gisborne as one of his most trustworthy correspondents, to whom he could write without fear of complicating a delicate personal relationship. Gisborne made few demands on Shelley, who was therefore able in his letters to focus on himself, rather than on his interlocutor. Moreover, Gisborne's residence in Italy made him a particularly valuable correspondent, since he knew at first hand the difficulties Shelley had been compelled to confront there. He and his wife Maria were among the few people who knew of the existence of Elena Adelaide Shelley, the baby for whom Shelley assumed responsibility at Naples in the winter of 1819–20, and, uniquely among Shelley's acquaintance, they saw Mary Shelley at her most depressed and withdrawn following the death of her son. After he returned to England Gisborne acted for Shelley in negotiations with his publisher and, as a result, came to understand the frustrations Shelley faced as he tried to get his work printed.

Gisborne's knowledge of Shelley's Italian life and his English circle made him an ideal correspondent, with whom Shelley was able to contemplate his situation with absolute freedom. No explanation is needed to foreground discussion of Mary, Claire, Byron, Trelawny, Hunt, Hogg, and Jane and Edward Williams, all of whom make an appearance in the letter of 18 June. Again, however, Shelley is distanced from them all. He has become the sole proprietor of his boat to 'escape' Trelawny; the society of Byron and his friends is 'hateful and tiresome'. Hunt 'can neither see nor feel any ill qualities from which there is a chance of his personally suffering' but Claire is at least 'restored [...] to tranquillity' and somehow easier to 'like' since the death of her child; and the Williamses are charming company. But still Shelley remains separate, as he contemplates his own past, present, and future. He begins his meditation on his former self by considering his infatuation with the abstracted women of *Epipsychidion*, which he summarizes as an 'idealized history of my life and feelings'. 'I think', he acknowledges, 'one is always in love with something or other; the error, and I confess it is not always easy for spirits cased in flesh and blood to avoid it, consists in seeking in a mortal image the likeness of what is perhaps eternal.' Of his future, he writes in a manner which is both self-reflexive and objective:

I feel too little certainty of the future, and too little satisfaction with regard to the past, to undertake any subject seriously and deeply. I stand, as it were, upon a precipice, which I have ascended with great, and cannot descend without *greater*, peril, and I am content if the heaven above me is calm for the passing moment.

As Shelley places his own position under scrutiny he turns to metaphor to visualize his predicament. Analytical discussion and subjective commentary combine to allow him to write of his own life and work with the same distance with which he considers the activities of his friends. It is as if he has become once more the all-seeing eye of the letters to Peacock: the subjective yet separate witness via whom the shadows of self and of friends can be seen.

There is, however, one moment in the letter of 18 June when its distanced perspective briefly vanishes. That moment comes as Shelley describes his boat:

> It is swift and beautiful, and appears quite a vessel. Williams is captain, and we drive along this delightful bay in the evening wind, under the summer moon, until earth appears another world. Jane brings her guitar, and if the past and the future could be obliterated, the present would content me so well that I could say with Faust to the passing moment, 'Remain, thou, thou art so beautiful.'

In this evocative account description is extended and elongated through context and intertext, until the poet is glimpsed in his own words, as a vital being in the boat which brings him happiness. As the passage's grammar shifts from third to second to first person he becomes part of the boat's movement, his epistolary persona brought to life through the portrayal of wind and sea. The painful past and the problematic future cease to exist, and the present remains frozen in Shelley's prose. Richard Holmes has written that Shelley's biography is caught 'in the glamorous headlights of [his] death',[16] but here Shelley is caught in his own words, not as an idealized shadow of himself, but as an animate, joyous being, revelling in the delights of the boat which will kill him. The resultant image is perhaps the single most moving testament to his epistolary powers.

TRACING THE VEILED COUNTENANCE

In conclusion, I would like to turn to what was almost certainly the final letter Shelley wrote. Its recipient was Jane Williams, and it was dated 4 July 1822:

> I fear you are solitary & melancholy at Villa Magni—& in the intervals of the greater & more serious distress in which I am compelled to sympathize here, I figure to myself the countenance which has been the source of such consolation to me, shadowed by a veil of sorrow— (*Letters: PBS* II, 445)

Jane's countenance is 'figured' in Shelley's imagination, just as all his letters figure their recipients. This letter, though, becomes an act of homage to its idealized interlocutor, who

---

[16] Richard Holmes, 'Death and Destiny', *The Guardian*, 24 January 2004.

is shadowy, veiled, apparent only in outline. 'How soon those hours past,' he continues, recalling the time spent living with the Williamses at the Villa Magni. 'Adieu, my dearest friend—I only write these lines for the pleasure of tracing what will meet your eyes'.

As Shelley traces the lines he writes for Jane, he leaves us a richly suggestive image with which to comprehend the complex variety of his correspondence. His letters are like the silhouettes cut by Marianne Hunt: partial portraits, in which the writer's outline is captured in words on the page. But his countenance, like those of his recipients, remains veiled behind an idealized image of the self. This essay opened with Shelley advising Claire Clairmont to give up her 'idle pursuit after shadows'. He recommended instead that she should 'seek in the daily & affectionate intercourse of friends a respite from these perpetual & irritating projects'. Shelley himself adopted this advice as he shaped his correspondence, and as he sought in his interlocutors both respite and inspiration. He and his friends remain in his letters as silhouettes traced in words, shadows cast against the wall of Plato's cave. Perhaps we too should take his advice and cease our pursuit of those shadows, remaining instead content to witness their enigmatic forms.

SELECT BIBLIOGRAPHY

Bennett, Betty T. 'The Editor of Letters as Critic: A Denial of Blameless Neutrality'. *Text: Transactions of the Society for Textual Scholarship* 6 (1994), 213–23.
—— 'Mary Shelley's Letters: The Public/Private Self'. *The Cambridge Companion to Mary Shelley*. Ed. Esther Schor. Cambridge: Cambridge UP, 2003. 211–25.
Brant, Clara. *Eighteenth-Century Letters and British Culture*. Basingstoke: Palgrave Macmillan, 2006.
Clemit, Pamela. 'Holding Proteus: William Godwin in his Letters'. *Repossessing the Romantic Past*. Ed. Heather Glen and Paul Hamilton. Cambridge: Cambridge UP, 2006. 98–115.
Colbert, Benjamin, *Shelley's Eye: Travel Writing and Aesthetic Vision*. Aldershot: Ashgate Publishing, 2005.
De Ricci, Seymour. *A Bibliography of Shelley's Letters, Published and Unpublished*. 1927. New York: Burt Franklin, 1969.
Favret, Mary A. *Romantic Correspondence: Women, Politics and the Fiction of Letters*. Cambridge: Cambridge UP, 1993.
Freeman, John. 'Shelley's Early Letters'. *Shelley Revalued: Essays from the Gregynog Conference*. Ed. Kelvin Everest. Leicester: Leicester UP, 1983. 109–28.
—— 'Shelley's Letters to his Father'. *Keats–Shelley Memorial Bulletin* 34 (1983), 1–15.
Ruge, Enno. '"Is the Entire Correspondence a Fiction?" Shelley's Letters and the Eighteenth-Century Epistolary Novel'. *Alternative Romanticisms*. Ed. Werner Huber and Marie-Luise Egbert. Essen: Studien zur Englischen Romantik 15, 2003. 111–21.
St Clair, William. *The Godwins and the Shelleys*. London: Faber, 1989.
Webb, Timothy. '"Cutting Figures": Rhetorical Strategies in Keats's *Letters*. *Keats: Bicentenary Readings*. Ed. Michael O'Neill. Edinburgh: Edinburgh UP, 1997. 144–69.

PART III

POETRY

CHAPTER 14

....

SHELLEY'S DRAFT
NOTEBOOKS

....

NANCY MOORE GOSLEE

Toward the front of a cheaply bound pocket-sized notebook, Percy Shelley finds a blank page and begins a poem that he will later title 'The Two Spirits: An Allegory'. With a blunt pen full of chestnut-coloured ink, he first writes a line in iambic pentameter: 'Two genii stood before me in a dream'. Whether prompted by literary convention, an actual dream, or both, the line gestures toward a mysterious origin for its own creation. On the notebook page, however, creativity struggles to describe itself. Shelley cancels the line and only on his third try does his lyric take off. Abandoning both the distancing dream-vision and the spatial immediacy of placing those 'genii' before the narrator, he instead lets one of those spirits begin by urgently addressing the other: 'O Thou who plumed with strong desire […] A shadow tracks thy flight of fire | Night is coming.' Then, with more difficulty, he introduces the opposing voice of the second spirit.[1] In the notebook drafting of this brief poem, we as critical readers can track the compositional struggles that led from Shelley's cancelled attempts to represent dream or reverie into the intricately balanced music and argument of his completed lyric, a lyric almost ready for publication. In the completed lyric, moreover, we can see an analogous movement from dramatic yet still visionary encounter to a more narrative contextualizing of that vision in a public, social human world. These two movements, one textual and the other thematic, will structure my larger argument in this chapter, an argument that interprets manuscript evidence from Shelley's draft notebooks. Out of this rich archive, I focus upon two pairs of examples. First, I examine his drafting of 'The Two Spirits' and trace its relationship to adjacent lyric passages of *Prometheus Unbound*, Act I. Second, I look briefly at a lyric duet that develops through several

---

[1] Bodleian MS. Shelley adds. e. 12, 13; *Bodleian Shelley Manuscripts XVIII: The Homeric Hymns and 'Prometheus' Drafts Notebook*, ed. Nancy Moore Goslee (New York: Garland, 1996). Although I have worked extensively with these manuscripts, work that has led me to the development of this essay, I have used the facsimiles as well; all quotations are taken from the facsimiles.

draft notebooks from isolated song into the cosmic dance of a new fourth act for *Prometheus.*

First, the material processes of revision shown in the drafting of this lyric illustrate Shelley's compositional practices more generally. Moving from preliminary images, sound patterns, and line fragments, though often beginning with a clearer sense of verse form than here, his drafts move through stanzaic and thematic development traceable on the still-private notebook pages, through neater copies, then Mary Shelley's fair copying, to print. In the case of this lyric, the copying and publication occur posthumously, so that Shelley's manuscript revisions become all the more important for us to consider.[2] Further, its notebook context exemplifies Shelley's habit of accompanying his verbal drafts with visual sketches. Ranging from near-graffiti to finished drawings, they reflect alternating moments of graphic inscription, first writing a verbal text and then pausing to sketch. As he draws, he may listen to the rhythms or the logic of what he has written and is about to write. Moreover, this liminal interplay between verbal and visual expression leads toward the completed poem's oscillations between heard voices and seen—often barely seen—figures, shapes, spirits, genii, or human characters.

The second strand of my argument pursues this oscillation of voice and glimpsed shape in terms of what I will call 'lyric performativity', a generic turn from private, subjective emotion to scenes of more public, communal conflict and agency. This turn in 'The Two Spirits', I argue, points toward—and helps Shelley to define—the crucial turn of his Prometheus at the end of Act I. Listening to a relay of lyric spirit-voices, the Titan recommits himself to a love both private and public. Although both this oscillation of voice and vision and the development from an originating lyric impulse to a more dramatic, more public structure might seem limited to 'The Two Spirits' and to the mixed, ambiguous genre of 'lyrical drama', I argue that this model functions, if less explicitly, in most of Shelley's poetry.

I

Opening the notebook in which Shelley drafts 'The Two Spirits' and substantial sections of *Prometheus Unbound*, a notebook now known as Bodleian MS. Shelley adds. e. 12, we find an apparently chaotic mix of poetic lines or stanzas often from different works, visual sketches, and financial calculations. This mix characterizes most of Shelley's notebooks. Often a sequence of lines from one work is interrupted by passages from another work, either because Shelley turns his attention to the second work or because that 'interrupting' passage from the second work was already on the page, so that he must skip over it. Moreover, tracing the progress of a given work often leads from one notebook to another, each with a repertoire of visual sketches and with a new context of

---

[2] Judith Chernaik, *The Lyrics of Shelley* (Cleveland: Case Western UP, 1972), 280.

verbal drafts from other poems or essays. Thus each germ or node of a work finds its material existence in a welter of overlapping visual and textual constellations and develops its coherent order in spite of and—I would argue—because of this complex creative matrix.

Looking at these draft notebooks yields, of course, the narcissistic pleasure of identifying with the poet: as we read, we imagine ourselves sharing his creative agency. Yet following the cancellations and revisions also develops the critic's power to interpret, to recognize what William Godwin called a 'tendency' as the writer decides 'not that, but this'.[3] Following Godwin, genetic textual scholars now argue that even cancelled drafts are not lost but exert a shadowy formative influence on the completed work.[4] And, given the interlocking sequences of Shelley's notebooks, spatial puzzles of drafts from one work jostling against drafts from another within a single notebook or across multiple manuscripts, the reader becomes better attuned to themes or motifs that may be drawn in from neighbouring drafts.

To study the visual sketches in these notebooks along with the verbal drafts is to enrich the sense of entering into that creative process. Many of Shelley's more finished drawings show thematic links to Shelley's verbal texts (for example, sketches of imagined devils in a realistic landscape fill the front endpapers in a notebook containing his essay *On the Devil and Devils*). A notebook that the Shelleys took to Geneva in 1816 contains finished drawings of Alpine lakes as well as prose journal entries intended to describe the scenes for armchair travellers; in it Percy Shelley also drafted 'Mont Blanc' and 'Hymn to Intellectual Beauty', lyrics which evoke the visual world yet question what knowledge or values that world offers us. Visual sketches may reflect verbal texts or may even generate them. Even accidental marks such as ink blots may be incorporated into verbal figures, as in the manuscripts of the 'Ode to Liberty' and *The Triumph of Life*.[5] Further, both finished representational sketches and other less developed but recurrent ones such as boats, trees, or profiles have another function, less mimetic than gestural. For the moment of visual sketching seems to be one in which the poet's flow of verbal inscription has paused but the graphic impulse continues. These sketches occur most often as he writes, cancels, and revises verse. Not only do his drafts of poetry, particularly lyric poetry, offer more white space between stanzas or in the margins, but Shelley seems to listen more

---

[3] Tilottama Rajan, *The Supplement of Reading: Figures of Understanding in Romantic Theory and Practice* (Ithaca, NY: Cornell UP, 1990), 168–9.

[4] Daniel Ferrer, 'The Open Space of the Draft Page: James Joyce and Modern Manuscripts', in George Bornstein and Theresa Tinkle (eds.), *The Iconic Page in Manuscript, Print, and Digital Culture* (Ann Arbor: University of Michigan Press), 249–67; Neil Fraistat and Elizabeth Loiseaux (eds.), *Reimagining Textuality: Textual Studies in the Late Age of Print* (Madison: University of Wisconsin Press, 2002); Hans Walter Gabler, 'On Textual Criticism and Editing: The Case of Joyce's Ulysses', in George Bornstein and Ralph G. Williams (eds.), *Palimpsest: Editorial Theory in the Humanities* (Ann Arbor: University of Michigan Press), 195–224.

[5] Bod. MS. Shelley adds. e. 9; Bod. MS. Shelley adds. e. 16; Bod. MS. Shelley adds. e. 6, 119–11 rev.; Bod. MS. Shelley adds. c.4, fos. 42^r–43^v.

closely to its sounds and rhythms than to those of prose. Both the verbal and the visual habits of composition I've described complicate Shelley's eloquent claims for inspiration formulated in his 1821 *Defence of Poetry*. There he famously describes 'the mind in creation'

> as a fading coal which some invisible influence, like an inconstant wind, awakens to transitory brightness [...] [W]hen composition begins, inspiration is already on the decline. [...] I appeal to the greatest Poets of the present day, whether it be not an error to assert that the finest passages of poetry are produced by labour and study.[6]

The very poetry of his prose convinces us that his creative work is instantaneous, inscrutable, and innocent of rational revision. Yet Shelley introduces key qualifications to this powerful claim for a mysterious and powerful force fanning the passive mind into energy. The 'influence' may be transcendent and external, like Milton's Holy Spirit, or subjective and only semi-rational or semi-conscious. The 'most glorious poetry [...] is *probably* [my italics]', he conjectures about the experience of other writers, 'a feeble show of the original conception of the poet'; and only 'the finest passages of poetry' are the ones not 'produced by labour and study'.

Second, although earlier in the *Defence* he argues that language is more faithful to the motions of the imagining mind than are all other arts (513), the passage above goes on to suggest that the intuitive, irrational, and passively organic process of inspiration also informs the visual and plastic arts. And clearly the graphic, material processes of his own inscription and revision, even in the drafts of this prose essay but even more in successive drafts of his poetry, show laborious revisions that then leap into ongoing acts of imagination. Further, even if the poet's final aim is to create a verbal text, not a composite art like Blake's, the visual sketches within and around his verbal drafts have some part both in the intuitive leaps that precede writing and in the graphic process of inscribing the verbal text. We might conjecture that their early presence in the drafting process raises precisely the kind of questions Shelley explores in his 1816 lyrics, in Demogorgon's cryptic speech about the unrepresentability of 'deep truth' in *Prometheus*, II. iv, and in his *Defence*, questions about how or which different arts best express the mind's insights, on the one hand, and how or whether those insights and their expression may correspond to any external reality or power. In other words, the differences between the capacities of the two arts, visual and verbal, help to define the scepticism that challenges both firm claims to a transcendent inspiration and to an underlying, knowable order of the universe and its visible world. *Prometheus Unbound* enacts this instability of representation as Asia's sisters Panthea and Ione repeatedly hear lyric voices and try to see the speakers, thus prompting us as readers of this closet drama to imagine its staging, a staging always in the process of emergence toward a public audience.

---

[6] *Norton 2*, 531.

II

Even strong undergraduate students reading *Prometheus* tend to ignore its lyrics, reading the blank verse as a transparent medium for conveying action and significance in the struggle for liberation. A strikingly similar focus, though one working at a much more sophisticated level, appears in several excellent critical essays that address timely questions of punishment and justice in this play. Melynda Nuss and Theresa Kelley both argue, if in somewhat different ways, that Shelley's play cannot fully resolve the problems raised by Prometheus' complicity with Jupiter's violence, and that, as a result, the lyric celebrations of political and cosmic harmony, particularly those in Act IV, are suspect.[7] On the other hand, Jessica Quillin argues that contemporary opera provides Shelley, as it did Byron in *Manfred*, with a genre that integrates song and text.[8] In her key example, however, this integration of music and text dramatizes a challenge to conventional social harmonies and pieties. For Mozart's *Don Giovanni* anticipates both in its composite mode and in its thematic action the pattern of the Promethean rebel against established authority, a rebellion that finds no clear resolution in the opera or in Byron's drama as it does at least prophetically in Shelley's *Prometheus Unbound*.

While the analogy with opera implies performance, or at least the mental performance of unheard melodies, those generated by the skill of Shelley's shifting lyric rhythms and his dramatic blank verse, the ethical analyses of plot I noted above imply a different sort of performativity. Nuss draws evidence from Aeschylus' involvement in a civic theatre linked to a civic commitment to public justice and punishment,[9] and Theresa Kelley analyses (through late Derrida) the speech-act performativity of Prometheus' curse— both its original utterance and its repetition by the phantasm of Jupiter—as central to what she views as his complicity in the violent tyranny of Jupiter.[10] To bring together these formal analyses of lyrical and dramatic harmony and thematic analyses of the ethics of Promethean action—or at least to raise some preliminary possibilities for doing so—I will suggest a model of 'lyric performativity': the performance through lyric of the self's and the community's idealizing visions entering into the troubled external social and political world and their testing as they materialize. As Karen Weisman writes about all of Shelley's lyrics, though not specifically about those in *Prometheus Unbound*, 'the space that Shelley occupies in his lyric poetry in particular is essentially a space between contraries. More important, perhaps, it is also a space between self-reflexion and the

[7] Melynda Nuss, 'Prometheus in a Bind: Law, Narrative, and Movement in *Prometheus Unbound*', *European Romantic Review* 18.3 (2007), 417–34; Theresa Kelley, 'Reading Justice: From Derrida to Shelley and Back', *Studies in Romanticism* 46.3 (2007), 267–87.

[8] Jessica Quillin, '"An Assiduous Frequenter of Italian Opera": Shelley's *Prometheus Unbound*', 9, 12, in Gillen D'Arcy (ed. and introd.), *Romanticism and Opera*, *Romantic Circles* <www.rc.umd.edu/praxis/opera.quillin>; Peter Conrad, *Romantic Opera and Literary Form* (Berkeley and Los Angeles: University of California Press, 1977), 72–3; Stuart Curran, *Poetic Form and British Romanticism* (New York: Oxford UP, 1986), 198–203.

[9] Nuss, 'Prometheus in a Bind', 427–9.   [10] Kelley, 'Reading Justice', 277.

outward gaze. [...] His self-reflexiveness is constantly questioning, constantly checking, the efficacy of his utterances.'[11] Writing about Shelley's dramas, Jeffrey Cox builds on Walter Benjamin's analysis of the *Trauerspiel* or 'sorrow-play' to suggest that Shelley in *Prometheus* and in *Hellas* 'returns to Greek tragedy as a model to open up the sorrow-play's formal limits', and 'to break out of [its] vision of entrapment in history [...] to shape a kind of secular apocalypse in which we neither transcend human material life nor confront an absolute gap between immanent historical fact and eternal ideals, as in the *Trauerspiel*, but instead discover the ideal in history, find the order we long for not in a realm after or beyond human life but in its historical fulfilment.'[12] That discovery is created through performance or an implied performance prophetic of the realization of its vision first on stage and then in the political arena, as Michael Simpson suggests.[13] It is also enabled, I suggest, through the specific expressiveness of a lyric performativity.

While each of the examples of lyric development I analyse in this chapter is witnessed by the visuality of the material texts—manuscript or print—and each moves toward an imagined if still closeted visual and auditory performance on a stage, the dramatic context and even the internal gestures of the lyrics themselves repeatedly emphasize the evanescent, temporary visuality of the singers. Their visuality is as passing as spoken or sung words, songs, or curses. Both sets of my examples play with contraries and the possibility of a space between them, to adapt Weisman's model for characterizing Shelley's lyrics. The first leads to an intensified dissonance, an absence of such space, and the second to harmony—yet a harmony with undertones of danger for its stability.

No early drafts exist for most of *Prometheus Unbound* Act I, possibly because Shelley was using large, loose sheets to accommodate its many sections of blank verse. On 22 September he writes from Padua to Mary at Este, arranging for her to bring their very ill 1-year-old daughter Clara to Venice for treatment; he also reminds her to bring 'the sheets of "Prometheus Unbound" which you will find numbered from 1 to 26 on the table of the pavilion' (*Letters: PBS* II, 39–40). In a letter to Peacock on 8 October, he relays the sad news that Clara had died as soon as they arrived at Venice, on the 24th, and that they 'have all had bad spirits enough'. In the same letter he also tells Peacock, amazingly, that he has finished the first act of *Prometheus Unbound* (*Letters: PBS* II, 42–3). In late January, however, he writes to Peacock from Naples both to describe classical ruins and to say again that he has finished the first act (23–4 January 1819; *Letters: PBS* II, 70–1). In Shelley adds. e. 12 are the only extant early passages for Act I. On page 23 he drafts a version of lines 217–18, at the end of Earth's speech explaining that mysterious second realm containing 'the shadows of all things that think and live', from which Prometheus might summon up a form to repeat his curse. Thus any response from Jupiter would attack only shades, 'As rainy winds thro the abandoned gate | Of a fallen palace'—these are the lines in adds. e. 12. The other drafts from Act I all come from the passage

[11] Karen Weisman, 'The Lyricist', in Timothy Morton (ed.), *The Cambridge Companion to Shelley* (Cambridge: Cambridge UP, 2007), 50.
  [12] Jeffrey Cox, 'The Dramatist', in *The Cambridge Companion to Shelley*, 73.
  [13] Michael Simpson, *Closet Performances: Political Exhibition and Prohibition in the Dramas of Byron and Shelley* (Stanford, CA: Stanford UP, 1998), 112, 156–72.

I mentioned earlier, a passage that leads late in the act to the very gradual, uncertain steps Prometheus takes from the recanting of his curse to the need for love and the recognition of its vulnerability.

Shelley's and Mary's understandably 'bad spirits' at Clara's death are closely related, I suggest, both to these passages and to Shelley's composition of 'The Two Spirits', drafted on pages 13–17 of adds. e. 12. The debate between the two spirits in the independent lyric, Charles Robinson argues, grows out of Shelley's debates with Byron, begun in Geneva in the summer of 1816 and resumed as they met in Venice from late August through October of 1818.[14] In contrast to the conversational, urbane couplets of *Julian and Maddalo*, conceived if not actually yet written during that autumn, 'The Two Spirits' is formally and tonally influenced by Byron's lyrical drama *Manfred*, yet challenges its thematic arguments as Julian challenges Maddalo's philosophy.

The title he gives his lyrical dialogue, 'The Two Spirits: An Allegory', reflects the complex doublings of its structure. First, these two 'spirit' voices debate over what humans might aspire to: whether, as the more Byronic first spirit argues, we should brace ourselves in stoic, even tragic acceptance that 'Night is coming', or whether, as the second spirit counters, we carry our own light within and can 'make night day'. Second, it reflects the final paired stanzas of the poem, which offer two alternative histories or legends, as Earl Wasserman describes them,[15] legends that narrate the outcome or fate of each belief. 'Some say' that around a tree clinging to an Alpine precipice, a winged form circles endlessly yet continually renews its energy to do so, a resistance like that shown in Byron's 1816 lyric 'Prometheus'. On the other hand, 'Some say' that a form materializes in the shape of a traveller's early love, so that he awakes and like Shelley's 1818 Prometheus at the end of Act I 'finds night day'.[16] Thus this delicate, eerie, and yet sublime 'allegory' already includes its own mysterious commentary, one that in turn both provokes and challenges interpretation.

Shelley himself never published the poem, nor did he edit it beyond this rough draft in adds. e.12. When Mary Shelley copied it out and then published it in her 1824 edition of Shelley's posthumous poems, she left it undated; in her 1839 edition she included it in the poems of 1820 (*BSM* XVIII, 280). Most recent critics and editors focus on a period from the Shelleys' journey through the Alps in March 1818 to winter 1819.[17] Here I will follow Robinson's dating of late summer to early autumn but broaden his biographical focus upon Byron to include Mary Shelley. For the notebook context and cancelled phrases from Shelley's draft point toward what we might call a feminine trace, a ghostly presence that links the poem to a child's death, to a mother's grief, and to the reaffirmation of love late in Act I of *Prometheus*.

[14] Charles Robinson, *Shelley and Byron: The Snake and Eagle Wreathed in Fight* (Baltimore: Johns Hopkins UP, 1976), 111–12.

[15] Earl R. Wasserman, *Shelley: A Critical Reading* (Baltimore: Johns Hopkins UP, 1971), 43.

[16] Bod. MS. Shelley adds. e. 12, p. 17, line 12. In citing line numbers for these drafts, I refer to those I assigned in my facsimile edition, *BSM XVIII*.

[17] Robinson, *Shelley and Byron*, late summer or early autumn of 1818; Goslee, *BSM XVIII*, second half of 1818; Reiman and Fraistat, October 1818–February 1819 (*Norton 2*, 137 n. 1).

Although Shelley may have made a few entries in this small notebook as early as 1814 and had used it in late 1817–early 1818 to translate the 'Homeric' hymns from Greek, he apparently began to use it more consistently on the trip north from Bagni di Lucca to Venice, a trip prompted by Mary's stepsister Claire Clairmont's anxiety to see how Allegra, her 2-year-old daughter with Byron, was faring in her father's reportedly licentious household.[18] Shelley then sent for Mary and their two children to stay with Claire at Este. One reason to suggest a date earlier than the second week of November 1818 for 'The Two Spirits' is that at least two verse drafts that follow it in the notebook correspond to letters written as the Shelleys begin to travel south toward Naples. Leaving Venice on 5 November, they spent the sixth and seventh in Ferrara. On page 27 Shelley writes a verse fragment describing autumn vines—a fragment corresponding to his letter of November 6 describing the scenery between Venice and Ferrara (*Letters: PBS* II, 45). Then on pages 39–40 are drafts for a 'Song for Tasso'. Though he had been considering a play about Tasso since the summer (Robinson, *Shelley and Byron*, 83–7), it seems reasonable to think that visiting Ferrara and seeing the Renaissance poet's prison (*Letters: PBS* II, 48) might have prompted this song.

On pages 2 and 4–6 are lines related to *Prometheus Unbound* I and II. On page 2, Shelley wrote in a large pencil hand the lines 'Twin nurslings of this all sustaining air | Whom one nest sheltered'.[19] Although these lines, scrawled above a pencil tree-sketch running in reverse direction, might well have been inserted after Shelley drafted 'The Two Spirits', they are again closely linked to that lyric—for the 'twin nurslings' in the completed text are the two spirits who appear to Panthea and Ione, reporting that they have witnessed the winged shapes of Love and Despair, the latter following and haunting the former. On page 4 is a Greek phrase, in English 'Asia wife of Prometheus'. Neil Fraistat identifies the source as Herodotus, whom Shelley had been reading from 16 July to 2 August.[20] This phrase, then, possibly written just before he and Claire set off for Venice on August 17 (*Journals: MWS*, 224), may mark the beginning of this small notebook's involvement in the large project of drafting the verse drama. It also points toward the transition from angry resistance to love at the end of Act I. On pages 4–6, beginning below the Greek phrase, is a rhymed lyric fragment that describes 'the utmost wildernesses | Of Indian Scy thia', as if testing the mountainous landscapes through which Asia travels in Act II.

On pages 7 to 11 are two lyrics drafted in pencil; and on page 18, immediately following 'The Two Spirits', two and a half lines of another pencil lyric. All three of these describe moments of alienation from a beloved and—in the first and second—pleas for reconciliation. The third describes only alienation: 'How pale & cold thou art in thy despair | One who from many mourners might be chosen | To imitate the very peak of grief'. Beginning 'When passions ~~storm~~ trance is overpast', the first lyric consists of three stanzas on page 7, the last one left incomplete. On pages 8–11 follows another pencil draft, 'Mine eyes were dim with tears unshed'. The first lyric speaks of alienation and hope for

---

[18] *Journals: MWS*, 223 n. 2; 14 July.   [19] These become I. 753–4 in *1820* text, *Norton 2*, 232.
[20] *Journals: MWS*, 219; *BSM* IX, p. lxv.

the sustaining of a calmer love figured as a renewal of spring. Its third stanza falters, however, ending with 'Alas we know not what we do [...] & I to thee | I [?have] That have been false'. This revision of Jesus' speech from the cross also appears, correctly quoted, in the final Fury's taunting speech to Prometheus: 'Many [...] would be just,— | But live among their suffering fellow men | As if none felt—they know not what they do' (I. 630–41; *Norton 2*, 229). In the pencil lyric, the 'we' acknowledges the speaker's identification with those who 'would be just'—those who crucify Christ. The second describes an earlier time when the addressee had recognized his agony of unshed tears and had taken pity on him: 'your accents sweet | Of [...] peace and pity feel like dew | On flowers half dead [...] thy lips did meet | Mine tremblingly'—but it goes on to say, at the top of page 11, 'We are not happy, ~~love~~/sweet', as some estrangement separates them and he pleads for reinstatement.

Mary Shelley changed her mind repeatedly about dating these lyrics.[21] While one factor in this confusion is undoubtedly Shelley's habit of repeating emotional patterns in the sequence of his relationships, here he deliberately chronicles these patterns from a retrospective viewpoint. In this reading, Shelley may speak first to Harriet in 1814, then to Mary in the present recalling how she listened in 1814 to his unhappiness as his relationship with Harriet waned. The 'present' for the second narrative—and in effect for both—then may be the early autumn of 1818, as Mary grieves over the death of their daughter Clara on 25 September and blames him for asking her to bring the children north on such a long journey in the summer heat. On page 8 an ink note about Plato appears to be written over the pencil of 'Mine eyes were dim', since no graphite sparkle shows above the ink—and Shelley was reading Plato on 20 October (*Journals: MWS* 230). This would not, of course, preclude a much earlier date for the pencil drafts—say, for example, 1814—but the tense sequence 'Were', 'are', suggests a reference back to an earlier time within the present of the poem. Further, Shelley's use of Jesus' words in the Fury's speech and in 'passions trance' reinforces the possibility that they were written at the same time, late summer to early autumn 1818.

On page 12, a fragment experiments with two of the same poetic devices used in 'The Two Spirits', which begins on the facing recto: images of light and shadow and a *terza rima* verse pattern.[22] Resembling the 'Hymn to Intellectual Beauty', this fragment shifts from prayerful invocation to speak in the voice of the descending mysterious spirit itself, whose 'shadow' descends 'upon mankind', upon the earthbound, who cannot see the 'flight of fire' (ll. 2–2a, 7d) beyond or above the shadowy tempest.

While the verse form of 'The Two Spirits' is not technically *terza rima*, because its metrical pattern is iambic tetrameter like that of Byron's 'Prometheus', its rhyme scheme surely develops out of Dante's. What looks like a simple alternating rhyme in each speech—ababab—is divided into mirroring tercets by the intervening refrains: aba [refrain], bab [refrain]. Further, these triple rhymes do not carry over from the paired

---

[21] She published 'When passions trance' in 1824 with no date, and in 1839 dates it in 1821; she copied 'Mine eyes were dim' into her fair-copy notebook (Bod. MS. Shelley adds. d. 9), dating it in 1814, published it in 1824 with no date but near poems dated 1818–19, and in 1839 dated it too in 1821.
[22] Wasserman, *Shelley*, 42 n. 84.

stanzas of one voice to the opposing paired stanzas of the other. In contrast to the evenly oppositional arguments of *Julian and Maddalo*, the confrontation here is asymmetrical: Spirit 1, a more critical version of the narrator of *Alastor*,[23] focuses upon and is even obsessed by Spirit 2, as he utters concerned warnings about the dangers of its 'flight of fire'.

In its graphic cancellations and revisions, the manuscript shows two stages of Shelley's struggle to give these spirits a vocal performative agency. First is a cluster of cancelled and revised lines at the bottom of page 13, as Shelley completes Spirit 1's opening speech and prepares to begin Spirit 2's answer. These are written in the same wet chestnut ink used for the whole of his primary drafting stage. The second consists of the additions Shelley made in a brown ink with a finer, drier point; we might describe these as editing. Spirit 1 has already hesitated in Shelley's faltering lines 13–13b, as he tries to warn Spirit 2 of an approaching storm: '[?Beware] [...] when winds'; and his refrain 'Night is coming' intensifies the danger. Given the intensely figurative nature of the lyric thus far—'O Thou who plumed with strong desire | Would float [...] above the Earth'—it is not surprising that critics interpret the warning of this spirit-voice as they do the similar figuration of approaching storm and darkness in the 'Ode to the West Wind', which Shelley would work on a year later in the same notebook: storm and night signify personal, political, even apocalyptic times of crisis.[24] Peterfreund reinforces his reading by pointing out a significant echo from the Gospel of John, when Jesus prepares to give the blind man sight and reveals at the same time his own glory: 'I must work the works of Him that sent me while it is day. The night cometh, when no man can work. As long as I am in the world, I am the light of the world' (KJV 9: 3–6). Once his physical sight is restored, the man asserts to the spiritually blind Pharisees and then to Jesus his faith—his sharing of spiritual light. Peterfreund extends the Johannine influence to include the prologue to the Gospel and thus to read Spirit 2 as 'Logos-made Light', but I would argue that the very splitting of the Gospel perspective between the two opposing spirits points toward a more sceptical, less ontological reading—a reading supported, I'll suggest below, by the poem's title.

As Shelley struggles to start the second spirit's response at the bottom of page 1, he alludes to an earlier miracle in the same Gospel. Line 16 reads, 'O what What I have to do with', echoing Jesus' admonition to his mother at the wedding in Cana. When Mary tells him that the wine has run out, he answers, 'Woman, what have I to do with thee? mine hour is not yet come' (KJV John 2: 4). As one biblical scholar comments, 'Jesus is placing himself beyond family relationships even as he demanded of his disciples.'[25] Even though he seems to reject involvement, however, he goes on—in the first miracle John describes, and a miracle described only in this Gospel—to turn water into wine so that he

---

[23] Ibid. 42.

[24] Chernaik, *The Lyrics of Shelley*, 141; Angela Leighton, *Shelley and the Sublime: An Interpretation of the Major Poems* (Cambridge: Cambridge UP, 1984), 157; Thomas Frosch, *Shelley and the Romantic Imagination: A Psychological Study* (Newark, DE: University of Delaware Press, 2007), 31–2; Stuart Peterfreund, *Shelley among Others: The Play of the Intertext and the Idea of Language* (Baltimore: Johns Hopkins UP, 2002), 218.

[25] Raymond E. Brown (trans., introd.), *The Anchor Bible* (New York: Doubleday, 1966), 112.

'manifested forth his glory' (KJV John 2: 11). While this allusion reinforces Peterfreund's reading of Spirit 2 as a figure for Christ, it places Spirit 1 in the position of Mary, his mother, here concerned with earthbound things and earthbound relationships. It may thus also link Spirit 1 to Mary Shelley, pleading for emotional support and family responsibility—or at least link Spirit 1 to Percy Shelley's own internalized yet dramatized sense of guilt for the cost of pursuing his imaginative vision. Although he cancels the allusion, its traces mark Spirit 2's response. For if that fiery flight discovers light beyond all storms in 'the deathless stars above' or in attendant meteors, it also carries 'Within my heart [...] the ~~light~~ lamp of love'. Further, his turn on pages 16 and 17 focuses also on more earthly and concrete, if still starkly sublime, settings and thus lessens the opposition between the two opposing views. The first set of human observers reports a bleak struggle that might confirm Spirit 1's view of Spirit 2's fate. 'Some say' that the 'winged shape' circles forever around a blasted Alpine tree. Yet is it trapped in that circle by its optimistic persistence or is its continued high flight sufficient reward, 'aye renewing | Its aery fountains' (ll. 13–14)? Shelley's pen is so blunt at this point that its excess ink runs down the page from 'fountains', making the word's meaning visual. 'Some' others then report that a traveller, even perhaps repeated travellers, are caught at night where 'the death dews sleep on the morass', and where 'Sweet whispers' may only be treacherous will-o'-the wisps to tempt him astray even if they 'makes night day'. And here, with one more sub-stanza to go (the end of the second 'Some say' speech), Shelley's chestnut ink runs out, for he changes to a finer point and to a lighter, browner ink.

Writing in a much smaller hand to fit into the limited space above his pencil sketches of stylized vine-covered trees (or perhaps a vine-covered initial B) and his ink financial calculations, he alleviates the sense of danger: a '~~winged~~ | a ~~silver~~ Shape like his early love doth pass | ~~But Before his eyes~~ is borne by her wild & glittering hair | [...] [I omit several cancelled lines] And when he awakes on the fragrant grass | He finds night day'. Danger turns to recalled, if momentarily recalled, fulfilment, dream finds some reality in wakening.

With the same light brown ink and finer point, Shelley returns to the beginning of his draft and edits—or, perhaps, still not quite sure how to finish, he begins this editing and waits for inspiration about his conclusion. A new phrase on page 13 that he then cancels recalls both the cancelled line 'O what What have I to do with' and the redemptive haunting of the traveller by the radiant 'Shape' of his early love. Above his originating line, 'Two genii stood before me in a dream', he writes in the top margin, 'The good die first—'. This phrase misquotes a passage from Book I of Wordsworth's *Excursion* (I. 500–2), which reads 'young' for 'first'. Shelley had used the same misquoted phrase as an epigraph to his 1816 narrative *Alastor* (Norton 2, 73), where it sets up that poem's examination of the appealing but destructive power of hope. In *The Excursion*, Margaret's hope for the return of her missing-in-action husband leads to a suspension of living in an incomplete grieving. If the irrational intensity of hope links the second of the two spirits in this lyric to the visionary of *Alastor*, it continues the qualification of that hope by the joyous and yet elegiac recalling of the traveller's 'early love'. Moreover, the phrase seems more ambiguous here than in *Alastor*. For if the 'good' who die first include in *The Excursion* both

Margaret's dead baby and Margaret herself, strangely admirable in the intensity of her grief, here it also may include the Shelleys' dead daughter and point toward both grieving parents, Mary despairing and Percy imagining hope in the face of despair. Shelley leaves the phrase uncancelled, but Mary Shelley omits it from her published version of the poem. Perhaps she recognized both an undesirable repetition of its earlier use and the painful if ambiguous appropriateness of its allusions to grief and hope. She may also have recognized a connection with the three pencil lyrics that frame this draft of 'The Two Spirits'.

Below this trial epigraph and between two early cancelled attempts at first lines, Shelley writes a title: 'The Two Spirits: An Allegory'. Marking the entry of the spirits' lyric debate into a still more public space than that of the commenting observers—those 'Some [who] say'—it also wryly anticipates the various ways critics have since read it: as a model for Shelley's own internal dialogues manifested both in his poetry and his prose through much of his career. Harold Bloom suggests, seconded by Michael O'Neill, that 'A Shadow tracks thy flight of fire' reflects the shape of Shelley's poetry after 1819. Robinson suggests the line as a model for his debates with Byron; Frosch, Chernaik, and Leighton as a model for possible responses to the failure of the French Revolution; Peterfreund as a messianic confirmation of the poetic imagination.[26] All of these readings except the last also point toward more sceptical, even post-structuralist readings of allegory in which a slippage remains between sign and some elusive signifier—so that neither spirit's view of the world's significance can claim ultimate certainty and our decision to follow one or the other must rest on pragmatic ethical grounds. The lingering effects of Shelley's allusions to the Gospel of John, then, point toward hope but not certainties, not a confirmed Logos.

Although Shelley's 'allegorical' commentary brings the creeds of his two spirit-voices closer together, the lyrics that form the sub-scene at the end of *Prometheus Unbound* Act I prove threatening because the poles tend to collapse into one another. As we learn from the completed 1820 text, though not from these drafts in adds. e. 12, Earth has called up spirits 'from the caves of human thought' to console Prometheus, countering the Furies' taunts over how his gifts to humans have gone awry. The first four spirits indeed present benevolent human acts that counter hostile acts.[27] The fifth and sixth spirits, however, the speakers in these adds. e. 12 drafts, thematize—or better, allegorize—these oppositions and undermine their optimism—an effect intensified in the published version. These spirits are the 'Twin nurslings' described on page 2 of the notebook. On page 25, Shelley drafts what will become part of the vision reported by the Fifth Spirit:

The music
Of | It is delight when

---

[26] Harold Bloom, '"The Unpastured Sea": An Introduction to Shelley', in *The Ringers in the Tower: Studies in Romantic Tradition* (Chicago: University of Chicago Press, 1971), 89; Michael O'Neill, *Percy Bysshe Shelley: A Literary Life* (Basingstoke: Macmillan, 1989), 130; see n. 24 above.

[27] Robinson, *Shelley and Byron*, 129–30.

. . . .

on

from   wings

~~OLove the God & King~~ [?] | descend ~~with~~ world embracing ?limbs…

Scattering the liquid joy of life ~~& these dream [?people]~~

slumbers

From thine immortal

the world   [?tresses]

~~[?Let /Were /thy/Thy] footsteps pave with light~~ [?hair] (ll. 3–4, 6b–8)

Only the first long line reveals the eventual heptameter (I. 766 in *1820*; *Norton 2*, 233). Leaving a white space which he fills in with oscillating rows of dots, Shelley drafts what will become the Sixth Spirit's portrayal of 'desolation': it is 'a delicate thing' that 'walks not on the Earth, it floats not on the air | But ~~seeks~~ […] treads with lulling footsteps, & fans with silent wings | T | The ~~tender s~~hearts | soft hopes […] ~~lulled to false~~ repose by [?] | the fanning plume above […] | Dream-visions of aerial joy, & call the monster Love' (ll. 15–9). At the bottom of page 26, on the verso, Shelley squeezes in below a lyric fragment unconnected to the drama a second draft of the fifth spirit's speech, beginning: 'Hast thou beheld the ~~shape of Love~~?' In the fair copy Shelley attributes this question to the fifth spirit but then changes it to the chorus (*BSM IX*, 239; e. 2, fo. 16ᵛ). In the fifth spirit's report its own energy-filled motion reappears in the spirit it describes: 'I sped, ~~upon the~~ sightless ~~winds which~~ […] like some swift cloud | that wings the wide | air's wilderness' (ll. 14–16). What he sees, though not in this draft, is a 'planet-crested Shape' that 'swept by on lightning-braided pinions' (*Norton 2*, 233; I. 765).

Page 35 has a draft in the same metrical pattern which may be an addition, more cynical in tone, to the sixth spirit's account of desolation. In the published text the fifth spirit's speech more clearly represents Love and Ruin as separate if sequential, and 'hollow Ruin' as more closely connected to the tableaux of idealism gone awry staged by the Furies earlier—'Great sages bound in madness | And headless patriots and pale youths who perished unupbraiding' (I. 768–9). Then the Sixth Spirit links the two even more closely. In other words, Shelley's revisions of this consolatory lyric exchange tie the two opposing spirits of the 'Allegory' lyric more closely together and make the task of untwining them even for a short revolutionary moment that much harder. This reframes the difficulties of agency and of the delegation of responsibility that Prometheus must come to terms with. Admiring the beauty of 'these airborne shapes' as they speak or sing to him on stage, he also seems to admire the ambiguous beauty of the compounded forms they describe and interpret as Love and Desolation. Because Love and Death are so closely linked, he is poised to give up his struggle against the ruin Jupiter, his delegated agent, has made. Yet he does opt, in Shelley's final version of the act, for the risky hope of love, as if sustained by the memory of a 'Shape like his early love'.

My second example of lyric performativity, moving from expression to dramatic public commitment, comes from Act IV of *Prometheus Unbound*, from the lyric duet between the Spirits of Earth and Moon. As Fraistat has proposed, this duet generates the composition of the new act in late summer 1819 (*BSM* IX, p. lxxi). It begins in HM 2176 on fo. *17ᵛ with an address by an unnamed speaker (though probably named Earth on a missing leaf) to a 'Green & azure moon [with 'orb' written over 'moon' in pencil]'.[28] A stanza below attributed to 'The Moon' then describes either herself or the first speaker as 'G̶r̶e̶e̶n̶ ̶&̶ ̶a̶z̶u̶r̶e̶'. Shelley then cancels this phrase, so that the moon, not yet blossoming, defines herself as 'thy <u>chrystal</u> paramour' and an 'enamoured maiden'. With the exception of one stanza on fo. *23ʳ later assigned to the Moon, for the next seven pages he composes a long, sustained lyric to be sung by Earth—though he later rearranges the order of the stanzas. Neither the maternal Earth of Act I, given a voice but no human shape, nor the flirtatious young male spirit of Act III, this articulate voice gives itself the shape of a material, geological globe. As life now pours into its caverns, the voice emerges, uncloseted and performative, from those abysses as did the earlier spirits from the caves of human thought. The voice of this Earth also resembles the one that speaks so mysteriously 'As if from Earth' to sustain Hope's agency through the 'Men of England' in *The Mask of Anarchy* which he was drafting almost at the same time (Fraistat, *BSM* IX, p. lxx; Goslee, *BSM* XVIII, pp. xxi–xxx). Retaining maternal qualities in spite of the moon's casting him as male, its song is both individually expressive and collective. We can then return to Michael Simpson's idea of a closeted drama—not in this case a closeted lyric—moving into the public sphere. Yet here the public realm includes not only the social but the material universe, as Earth initiates their cooperative, disciplined dance.

The next stage of this turn of Earth's and Moon's duet toward the public moves through Shelley's development of a dramatic architecture not at all clear in HM 2176 and only partially clear in adds. e. 12. In this second stage he writes first another set of lyrics, the barely glimpsed procession of hours and still more spirits from the human mind. Shelley then drafts—or copies in from elsewhere—Panthea and Ione's detailed visual descriptions of the chariots of Earth and Moon Spirits, recalling his visual sketches of moon-boats in HM 2177 and Bod. MS. Shelley adds. e. 11, notebooks which contain drafts from the earlier three acts of *Prometheus Unbound*. Thus the singers of the duet acquire quasi-human forms. In the published version, all of these chariots and charioteers enact a doubly dramatic function, an epithalamial Triumph staged in front of the cave to which Prometheus and Asia have withdrawn. Like them, we readers form an audience for this celebration—and Earth's lyrics map out millennial hopes. Yet once Shelley places his duet between Earth and Moon spirits in this fully dramatic context, he then makes it vanish visually, unbuilding it again as the cloud does in the lyric also included in Shelley's 1820 volume containing *Prometheus Unbound*. Panthea says, 'I rise as from a bath of sparkling water [...] Out of the stream of sound', and then—in a reversal of their usual roles—Ione responds, teasingly and sceptically, 'Ah me, sweet sister, | The stream of sound has ebbed away from us | And you pretend to rise out of its wave | Because your words fall like the clear soft dew | Shaken from a bathing wood-nymph's limbs and hair'

---

[28] Huntington Manuscript 2176; *Percy Bysshe Shelley*, VI: *Shelley's 1819–1821 Huntington Notebook*, ed. Mary A. Quinn (New York: Garland, 1994).

(*Norton 2*, *Prometheus Unbound*, IV. 500, 502–9). It is as if Panthea has created them, through an imagination that employs both sound and sight, as if this lyric performativity retreats from the actualized drama to an earlier lyric stage, yet one that is framed in its own reflexivity—and in its sense of ongoing temporality. This very experience of the idealizing lyrics then gives way to Demogorgon's ode-like final lyric, in which he both celebrates and warns. Yet this time, Demogorgon suggests, Ruin might be severed from Love, or Love might re-emerge from Ruin, if a liberated humanity can 'Defy Power, which seems omnipotent', can foresee a non-violent resistance to that power. Earth's lyric has generated both a celebration of the possibility of choice and an acceptance of the responsibilities and dangers of such choice—and of delegating power to others given such choices.

SELECT BIBLIOGRAPHY

Chernaik, Judith. *The Lyrics of Shelley*. Cleveland: Case Western Reserve UP, 1972.

Ferrer, Daniel. 'The Open Space of the Draft Page: James Joyce and Modern Manuscripts'. *The Iconic Page in Manuscript, Print, and Digital Culture*. Ed. George Bornstein and Theresa Tinkle. Ann Arbor: University of Michigan Press, 1998. 249–67.

Fraistat, Neil and Elizabeth Loiseaux. Eds. *Reimagining Textuality: Textual Studies in the Late Age of Print*. Madison: University of Wisconsin Press, 2002.

Gabler, Hans Walter. 'On Textual Criticism and Editing: The Case of Joyce's *Ulysses*'. *Palimpsest: Editorial Theory in the Humanities*. Ed. George Bornstein and Ralph G. Williams. Ann Arbor: University of Michigan Press, 1993. 195–224.

Goslee, Nancy Moore. 'Shelleyan Inspiration and the Sister Arts'. *The Unfamiliar Shelley*. Ed. Alan Weinberg and Timothy Webb. Burlington, VT: Ashgate, 2009. 159–79.

——*Shelley's Visual Art*. Cambridge: Cambridge University Press, 2011.

Peterfreund, Stuart. *Shelley among Others: The Play of the Intertext and the Idea of Language*. Baltimore: Johns Hopkins UP, 2002.

Robinson, Charles. *Shelley and Byron: The Snake and Eagle Wreathed in Fight*. Baltimore: Johns Hopkins UP, 1976.

Wasserman, Earl R. *Shelley: A Critical Reading*. Baltimore: Johns Hopkins UP, 1971.

....

CHAPTER 15

LYRIC DEVELOPMENT

Esdaile Notebook *to Hymns of 1816*

....

DAVID DUFF

BY 1816 Shelley had made himself into a great lyric poet. The process by which he did so is not well understood, and studies of his lyrical output rarely reach back before 1815. Until the publication of the Esdaile Notebook in 1964, there were good reasons for this, since this vital collection of poems which holds many of the clues to his early poetic development was known to the public only in fragmentary and dispersed form. Even when made available in its entirety, however, the Esdaile collection—a substantial volume of mostly lyrical poems which Shelley prepared for press in 1812–13 but left unpublished—attracted limited critical attention and failed to dispel the long-standing assumption that Shelley's early poetry was of poor quality and unconnected with his later achievements. The impression of discontinuity is reinforced by the fact that in the following two years Shelley wrote little verse that has survived, and when he resumed writing poetry in late 1815 it was to compose the allegorical narrative *Alastor, or, The Spirit of Solitude*, which appears to mark a radical departure from his previous work in both theme and style (though the shorter poems published alongside it in the volume of 1816 have more obvious links with the past, one being carried over from the Esdaile collection and two others being reworkings of parts of *Queen Mab*). The Swiss hymns of summer 1816, 'Hymn to Intellectual Beauty' and 'Mont Blanc', represent a further departure, introducing a new style of philosophical lyricism different from anything that preceded it—but richly indicative of the future direction of his talents. Shelley's progress from the shrill emotionalism and Gothic extravagance of his first two poetry collections, *Original Poetry by Victor and Cazire* (1810) and *Posthumous Fragments of Margaret Nicholson* (1810), to the dazzling lyric artistry of 'Mont Blanc' remains an enigma, notwithstanding the wealth of contextual information provided by recent critical editions and the impressive body of commentary on the post-1815 poems.

Attempting to isolate Shelley's development as a lyricist from other aspects of his literary development is of course a somewhat artificial exercise, and 'lyric' itself is a term with many meanings, then as now. A full inventory of Shelley's efforts at lyrical poetry in the years up to 1816 would need to include his compositions in traditional forms like the sonnet, ode, and hymn; the fifteen poems in the *Victor and Cazire* volume and interspersed through his Gothic novel *St. Irvyne; or, The Rosicrucian* (1811) and long poem *The Wandering Jew* (1811) labelled 'songs' (at least two of which were set to music by his friend Edward Fergus Graham, though the scores have not survived); an 'epithalamion' or 'supposed fragment' thereof (in reality, a dream-vision celebrating the politics of assassination); another early poem with a quasi-musical designation, 'Melody to a Scene of Former Times'; several self-styled 'ballads', including his satirical broadside *The Devil's Walk* (1812); and many other poems which, though not labelled as such, can be identified as lyrics by virtue of their subject matter, style, or verse form. The normal (non-musical) definition of lyric as a short poem expressive of intense personal feeling needs adjustment in Shelley's case because alongside confessional lyrics there are political and philo-sophical lyrics which are equally intense and personal; lyrics in which the speaking voice is not his own; and other types of lyrical writing which are primarily descrip-tive rather than expressive. His sonnet 'Feelings of a Republican on the Fall of Bonaparte' (from the *Alastor* collection), with its foregrounding of a private emo-tional response to a major public event, is an example of a personalized political lyric, while 'Hymn to Intellectual Beauty' is illustrative of a type of lyric, also char-acteristic of Shelley, which combines philosophic exposition with autobiographical revelation. Of first-person lyrics in which the speaking voice is not his own, the *Posthumous Fragments* volume provides obvious examples, Shelley's adoption of the Margaret Nicholson persona (and of other voices, male and female) enabling him to explore extreme states of mind to political or sometimes comic effect. 'The Wandering Jew's Soliloquy' (from the Esdaile collection) is another example, its tor-mented lyricism combining with aggressive anti-religious polemic in a way that is again typical of the young Shelley. His early endeavours at lyric include, too, parts of his philosophical poem *Queen Mab*, the descriptive passages of which are set in what he calls 'blank lyrical measure' (unrhymed irregular metre), while the didactic passages are in 'blank heroic verse' (unrhymed iambic pentameter).[1] Like his mixing of genres, Shelley's blending of lyric metres with other verse forms is a recurrent fea-ture of his work, as his later experiments with 'lyrical drama' demonstrate; and his mastery of the technical demands and expressive possibilities of lyric develops in conjunction with other aspects of his verse craft.

In this sense, the idea of tracing in Shelley's early work the origins of some quintessen-tial lyric voice is misleading. From the start, Shelley speaks in different voices, and his lyric utterances, though acutely personal at times, span various registers and take many differ-ent forms. This is something critics have increasingly recognized in relation to his later work. Geoffrey Matthews, in an influential essay, took issue with Victorian and Modernist accounts of Shelley as a poet of self-expression—of the 'lyrical heart-cry'—by pointing

---

[1] *Letters: PBS* I, 352.

out that, from the *Alastor* volume onwards, Shelley published in book form only four lyrics (excluding dedications) which were strictly personal or semi-personal, and that he went to considerable lengths to prevent publication of most of the later personal lyrics for which he is best known, these appearing only posthumously in Mary Shelley's editions.[2] Emphasizing Shelley's reticence rather than his emotional exhibitionism, Matthews also noted that many seemingly personal poems are actually dramatic lyrics voicing the imagined feelings of another person (real or fictitious), or, alternatively, lyrics shaped by the conventions of a particular genre rather than simple acts of self-expression. The mis-titling of poems in the posthumous editions—leading in some cases to poems intended as draft speeches for plays being presented as autobiographical lyrics—fuelled the tradition of misreading, a situation which Matthews and other modern editors have sought painstakingly to correct. Though some dispute remains about exactly which poems were originally dramatic in conception, Matthews's claim that the 'dramatic impulse was at least as strong in Shelley as the lyrical, and that the two were often inseparable' (691) is now widely accepted, as is his related argument that most if not all of Shelley's lyrical poetry is shaped to some degree by generic convention, even where he subverts traditional codes. One of my aims in the present chapter is to show that the generic awareness characteristic of many post-1816 poems can also be found in the earlier lyrics.

Another factor that has deepened our understanding of Shelley's lyrics is recognition of their allusive or, in Tilottama Rajan's term, 'interdiscursive' quality.[3] Earlier characterizations of Romantic lyric as a type of monologue or soliloquy (the poet speaking to himself, 'overheard' by the reader) have been superseded by a virtually opposite model which sees the poetry of the period as strongly dialogical and context-sensitive.[4] One indication of this, Rajan notes, is the way lyrical discourse is frequently interwoven with, or framed by, narrative discourse, or exteriorized into drama, a mixing of modes which is part of a broader Romantic trend towards composite forms of art. Even the most 'pure' kinds of lyric prove, in Shelley's case, to be dialogical rather than self-enclosed, rhetorically targeted rather than merely expressive (the paradigm is the 'Ode to the West Wind', a lyrical speech-act which demands to be heard, not overheard, and in which the speaking voice is an oratorical construct as much as a vocalization of the author's self). Recent work on Shelley's audiences,[5] actual and imagined, has underlined the pragmatic orientation of his writing, which is dialogical in the full Bakhtinian sense in that it not only presupposes previous utterances but also anticipates

---

[2] G. M. Matthews, 'Shelley's Lyrics', in D. W. Jefferson (ed.), *The Morality of Art: Essays Presented to G. Wilson Knight* (London: Routledge and Kegan Paul, 1969), reprinted in *Norton 1*, 682.

[3] Tilottama Rajan, 'Romanticism and the Death of Lyric Consciousness', in Chaviva Hošek and Patricia Parker (eds.), *Lyric Poetry: Beyond New Criticism* (Ithaca, NY: Cornell UP, 1985), 206.

[4] John Stuart Mill's definition (1833), cited by M. H. Abrams, *The Mirror and the Lamp: Romantic Theory and the Critical Tradition* (New York: Oxford UP, 1953), 23–5.

[5] Stephen C. Behrendt, *Shelley and his Audiences* (Lincoln, NE: University of Nebraska Press, 1989); Kim Wheatley, *Shelley and his Readers: Beyond Paranoid Politics* (Columbia, MO: University of Missouri Press, 1999).

further ones,[6] shaping itself proleptically around an expected response or making the juxtaposition of voices and viewpoints its main organizing principle, as in antiphonal lyrics such as 'The Two Spirits: An Allegory' or realistic dialogue poems like *Julian and Maddalo: A Conversation*. Though generally associated with his later poetry, this pattern is already visible in his early lyrics, many of which address named auditors, incorporate direct or reported dialogue, or solicit active reader-response—often through tactics of provocation.

A second form of dialogue, equally indispensable to Shelley, is the conversation with other writers. No Romantic poet's work has been altered more profoundly by the revolution in critical method which replaced traditional source study with influence analysis, and recognized creative dialogue with precursors and contemporaries as a decisive factor in the formation of the poetic self. Shelley's work has, indeed, been a testing ground for modern theories of poetic influence, the subject of a book-length study by the foremost influence-theorist Harold Bloom[7] and of at least six other monographs devoted to questions of intertextuality and influence.[8] Bloom's claim that Shelley came into being as a poet through the influence of Wordsworth is now axiomatic, though evidence of that influence has been found much earlier than the *Alastor* volume, which Bloom took as his starting point, and scholars have traced other formative influences. These include Southey and Coleridge, the other members of the Lake School triumvirate; fashionable lyric and narrative poets like Scott, Moore, Campbell, and Byron; the Gothic poet-novelist M. G. Lewis; and—a line of influence still needing further investigation—female poets such as Charlotte Dacre, Sydney Owenson, and Felicia Browne (later Hemans). The impact of poets from earlier periods is also evident but the key influences on the young Shelley are living writers, theirs being the current literary idioms through and against which he defined his own voice. His allusive techniques range from citation and imitation to various forms of revisionism, or corrective rewriting, and also include several instances of outright plagiarism, the motives for which remain obscure. What is clear is that Shelley is an intertextual writer through and through, the extreme derivativeness of some of his earliest poems and the boldly revisionary quality of his later ones being part of a continuum—different manifestations of the same dialogic impulse. Moreover, the dialectic of influence is central to his *theory* of poetry: as he states in the Preface to *Prometheus Unbound* (1821), it is through the influence of contemporaries that a writer becomes part of, and in turn helps to shape, the 'spirit of the age'; and 'one great poet is a masterpiece of nature, which another not only ought to study but must

---

[6] Mikhail Bakhtin, *The Dialogic Imagination: Four Essays*, ed. Michael Holquist, trans. Caryl Emerson and Michael Holquist (Austin, TX: University of Texas Press, 1981). Bakhtin himself denies the dialogic possibilities of lyric poetry, calling it a 'monologic' genre (297).

[7] Harold Bloom, *Shelley's Mythmaking* (New Haven: Yale UP, 1959).

[8] In addition to works by Blank, West, Robinson, and Brewer cited below, see Stuart Peterfreund, *Shelley among Others: The Play of the Intertext and the Idea of Language* (Baltimore: Johns Hopkins UP, 2002); and Jerrold E. Hogle, *Shelley's Process: Radical Transference and the Development of His Major Works* (New York: Oxford UP, 1988).

study' (*Longman*, 2, 474). The successive phases of such 'study' define the course of Shelley's poetic development.

With these considerations in mind, this chapter will focus on three pivotal moments in Shelley's early career: the Esdaile collection (to which I will refer by the title which Shelley used in his correspondence, the 'Volume of Minor Poems'),[9] the *Alastor [...] and Other Poems* volume, and the hymns of summer 1816. Although the 'Minor Poems' remained unpublished, despite Shelley's efforts, the fact that almost half of its fifty-one poems draw directly on personal experience, referring by name to people he knew or places he visited, or recalling events in his life, necessitates some rethinking of Matthews's conclusions about Shelley's 'reticence'. The 1813 volume was in fact a daring exercise in autobiography, founded on a belief, stated explicitly in Shelley's letters and elsewhere, that candid self-portraiture could be philosophically and politically beneficial.[10] This conviction of Shelley's occasioned some dispute with his newly adopted mentor William Godwin, who, after once holding similar views, had by 1812 arrived at precisely the opposite conclusion, namely that autobiographical disclosure was self-defeating and politically counter-productive (the disastrous reception of Mary Wollstonecraft's posthumous writings, publication of which Godwin arranged, was probably one of the reasons for his change of mind). In defending his plan to publish autobiographical verse, and insisting that it appear under his own name rather than pseudonymously as in his previous collections, Shelley was aligning himself with the confessional poetics of Wordsworth and Coleridge, who had created a new form of lyric poetry predicated on the link between introspection and political radicalism. Shelley's discovery of this poetics in late 1811 and early 1812, during a visit to the Lake District which was almost certainly motivated in part by a desire to make personal acquaintance with the Lake poets, was a decisive moment in his literary development. He succeeded in meeting only Southey, but the fresh insight he gained at this time, through reading and conversation, into the work of all three Lake poets had a dramatic effect on his writing, leading to compositions different in kind and quality from what had gone before.

The stylistic transformation can be seen very clearly in the blank verse lyric that begins 'It is not blasphemy', one of five poems entitled 'To Harriet' which punctuate the 1813 collection. The Harriet in question is Harriet Westbrook, his wife as of August 1811, rather than his former girlfriend Harriet Grove, to whom he had also written love poems, one of which had appeared in *Victor and Cazire* and two of which ('How eloquent are eyes' and 'Hopes that bud in youthful breasts', both labelled '1810') were included in the 'Minor Poems'. The earlier love lyrics were written in a conventional sentimental idiom that had been fashionable since the 1770s, a style replete with personifications, inversions, and other forms of poetical diction. By contrast, 'It is not blasphemy', written in 1812, is couched in a language that is unmistakably and overwhelmingly Wordsworthian, its vocabulary, syntax, and verse form, as well as many of its ideas,

[9] *Letters: PBS* I, 340.
[10] For the autobiographical significance of the collection, see David Duff, '"The Casket of my Unknown Mind": The 1813 Volume of Minor Poems', in Alan Weinberg and Timothy Webb (eds.), *The Unfamiliar Shelley* (Aldershot: Ashgate, 2009), 41–67.

deriving from 'Lines Written a Few Miles above Tintern Abbey'. Wordsworth's great lyric is only secondarily a love poem—the affectionate tribute to his 'dear, dear sister' Dorothy in the final paragraph follows a much longer autobiographical section devoted to his shifting relationship to Nature—but Shelley reassembles the ingredients of 'Tintern Abbey' to produce an impassioned love lyric with its own blend of erotic affirmation, personal reminiscence, and metaphysical speculation. Recalling his previous loneliness and misery, Shelley credits Harriet with the restorative powers ascribed in Wordsworth's poem to Nature and to Dorothy, and reworks the pantheism of 'Tintern Abbey' into a new expression of one of his favourite themes, the relationship between earthly and heavenly bliss.[11] There are certainly traces in the poem of his earlier styles: the opening phrase, with its blunt challenge to religious orthodoxy, recalls the polemical manner of his Oxford pamphlet *The Necessity of Atheism* (1811), and the reference to Harriet's 'spirit-beaming eyes' (11) echoes the 'eloquent eyes' theme of his lyric to the *other* Harriet (another phrase from which, 'When Time shall be no more', is carried over verbatim—part of a pattern of recycling that is an important compositional feature of the 1813 collection). But the Wordsworthian influence soon makes itself felt as Shelley describes, in the part-physical, part-spiritual language of 'Tintern Abbey', 'those nameless joys | Which throb within the pulses of the blood' (2–3) and the 'soft suffusion' that breathes 'magnetic sweetness through the frame | Of my corporeal nature' (11–16).[12]

Later in the poem, the echoes of Wordsworth become even more pronounced as Shelley, re-enacting the time shift in the last paragraph of 'Tintern Abbey', turns from the past and present to an imagined future. Wordsworth, after reflecting on the intense experiences of his youth, looks forward to 'after years, | When these wild ecstasies shall be matured | Into a sober pleasure' (138–9), describing Dorothy's mind as 'a mansion for all lovely forms' and her memory 'a dwelling-place | For all sweet sounds and harmonies' (139–42).[13] Shelley elaborates these hints into an extended declaration of faith in the durability of his 'holy friendship' with Harriet:

> Nor when age
> Has tempered these wild extacies, and given
> A soberer tinge to the luxurious glow
> Which blazing on devotion's pinnacle
> Makes virtuous passion supercede the power
> Of reason, nor when life's æstival sun
> To deeper manhood shall have ripened me,
> Nor when some years have added judgement's store
> To all thy woman sweetness, all the fire
> Which throbs in thine enthusiast heart, not then

---

[11] For other examples, see David Duff, 'Shelley's "Foretaste of Heaven": Romantic Poetics and the Esdaile Notebook', *Wordsworth Circle* 3.3 (2000), 149–58.

[12] All quotations from the 'Minor Poems' are from vol. II of *CPPBS*, which prints the collection alongside *Queen Mab*, as Shelley at one point intended it to be published. I have capitalized titles. All other Shelley poems are quoted from *Longman*.

[13] All Wordsworth quotations are from his *Poetical Works*, ed. Thomas Hutchinson, rev. Ernest de Selincourt (Oxford: Oxford UP, 1936).

> Shall holy friendship (for what other name
> May love like ours assume?) not even then
> Shall custom so corrupt, or the cold forms
> Of desolate world so harden us
> As when we think of the dear love that binds
> Our souls in soft communion, while we know
> Each other's thoughts and feelings, can we say
> Unblushingly a heartless compliment,
> Praise, hate or love with the unthinking world
> Or dare to cut the unrelaxing nerve
> That knits our love to Virtue—can those eyes,
> Beaming with mildest radiance on my heart
> To purify its purity e'er bend
> To soothe its vice or consecrate its fears?
>
> (32–55)

To say that these lines merely 'allude' to Wordsworth is to understate the debt, and to mis-conceive the appropriative strategy involved; Shelley's poetic language is saturated in the terminology and cadences of 'Tintern Abbey'. Whole phrases such as 'wild extasies' are carried over intact, and numerous nouns, verbs, and adjectives—*judgement, power, passion, feeling, heart, nerve, form, store, custom, dare, dear, sweet, holy*—are reused with exactly equivalent emphasis. Light imagery, central to Wordsworth's metaphoric encoding of the maturation process, reappears with minor variations: the 'light of setting suns' and 'sober pleasure' of Wordsworth's poem become the 'soberer tinge' and 'æstival sun' of Shelley's. The syntactic influence is equally palpable: Wordsworth's distinctive 'nor' construction, used no fewer than six times in the last paragraph of 'Tintern Abbey', is redeployed by Shelley with comparable frequency and to similar rhetorical effect, namely to reinforce, through a cumulative logic of pseudo-negation and double negation, the defiant affirmations with which the poem concludes (in Shelley's case, the laddering effect of the multiple 'nors' and 'not thens' stretches almost to breaking point the grammatical coherence of his twenty-four-line sentence). Shelley's first attempt at a blank verse lyric lacks the grace of Wordsworth's poem, but it opens up a new poetic register that allows him to articulate, however clumsily, a new kind of lyric consciousness.

   In Bloomian terms, Shelley's poem is a 'scene of instruction',[14] marking a rapturous initiation into a new influence-relationship. Artistically, the lyric is as much a love poem to Wordsworth as to Harriet, and the cognitive transformation it describes owes as much as to his literary precursor as it does to his female companion. Yet, while enthusiastically adopting the Wordsworthian mode, Shelley introduces a crucial modification. 'Tintern Abbey' is a loco-descriptive poem which transcends its setting; the internalization is so powerful and the imaginative transcendence so complete that not only salient details of the external scene but also vital biographical and historical facts which explain Wordsworth's altered state of mind are displaced or concealed. Shelley counteracts this

---

[14] Harold Bloom, *A Map of Misreading* (New York: Oxford UP, 1975), ch. 3.

abstracting, eliding tendency of the lyric mode he employs by insisting on the political ramifications of his heightened consciousness:

> Dark Flood of Time!
> Roll as it listeth thee. I measure not
> By months or moments thy ambiguous course.
> Another may stand by me on the brink
> And watch the bubble whirled beyond the ken
> Which pauses at my feet—The sense of love,
> The thirst for action, and the impassioned thought
> Prolong my being. If I wake no more
> My life more actual living will contain
> Than some grey veteran's of the world's cold school
> Whose listless hours unprofitably roll,
> By one enthusiast feeling unredeemed.
>
> (58–69)

The language of this apostrophe is again Wordsworthian: the 'Flood of Time' metaphor echoes the literal and figurative waters of 'Tintern Abbey', the address to the river Wye and the famous lines about 'A motion and a spirit, that impels | All thinking things, all objects of all thought, | And rolls through all things' (101–3; note Shelley's repetition of *roll*, a key word for both poets, and the metaphoric intensification that turns river into flood). However, the philosophical content—regarding the relativity of our perception of time—derives primarily from Godwin, as is confirmed by a note to *Queen Mab* where Shelley quotes these lines and glosses them with a cross-reference to Godwin's *Enquiry Concerning Political Justice* (1793) (*CPPBS* II, 295). Once again, though, Shelley modifies his source: first, by personalizing Godwin's hypothetical comparison between the 'indolent man', oblivious of the passage of time, and the man in 'acute pain, or uneasy expectation', for whom time passes uncomfortably slowly, into a much more pointed opposition between an aged reactionary, 'grey veteran of the world's cold school', and himself, the hot-blooded young radical whose life, even if cut short, 'more actual living will contain' by virtue of sheer intensity of experience; and, secondly, by insisting that, alongside 'the sense of love' and 'the impassioned thought', what creates that intensity and 'prolong[s] my being' is 'the thirst for action'—something conspicuously absent from the speculative utopia of *Political Justice* and the internalized, tranquillized world of 'Tintern Abbey'.

The interweaving of personal and political themes is found throughout the 'Minor Poems', a pattern that becomes a hallmark of Shelley's work. Some of the poems refer directly to the political activities of his youth. Two sonnets, for example, record his attempts to circulate radical propaganda (his *Declaration of Rights* and *Devil's Walk* broadside) via bottles launched into the sea and by hot-air balloon, unorthodox methods of dissemination which the young poet clearly found imaginatively appealing. In 'Sonnet: To a Balloon, Laden with *Knowledge*', the metaphor of his airborne writings as an 'unquenchable' fire, a 'spark [...] gleaming on the hovel's hearth' which will one day roar 'thro' the tyrants' gilded domes' (10–11), resurfaces seven years later in the 'Ode to the West Wind' as one of his most famous images of poetry's inspirational power: the poet's words as 'ashes and sparks' from an 'unextinguished hearth', scattered among mankind by the 'incantation' of verse (65–7). As so often with Shelley, the germ of later, greater lyrics—themes, images, verbal motifs—is found in the early poems, a form of self-inspiration and creative recycling which is part of the transmission process he describes.

More complex autobiographical poems like 'On Leaving London for Wales' connect politics and personal experience in subtler ways. Here, Shelley allegorizes a journey he made in November 1812 from London, where he had gone to raise funds for the Tremadoc embankment project, via Snowdon to his home at Tanyrallt in North Wales as an exodus of almost biblical significance from a place of confinement to a land of freedom. Like the balloon sonnet, the poem contains the seeds of later works: its lurid picture of the political corruption and social decay of the metropolis ('Thou miserable city! where the gloom | Of penury mingles with the tyrant's pride' (1–2)) anticipates the vision of London as 'Hell' in *Peter Bell the Third* (1819), and the descriptions of Snowdon and its surroundings introduce motifs and vocabulary that recur in other mountain poems like 'Mont Blanc' and *Prometheus Unbound*. What is striking, though, about this earlier lyric is the rawness of the psychological content, and the directness with which it is linked to the equally raw political content. Private and public frames of reference are made to intersect in almost disconcertingly abrupt ways. Thus, while evoking the long tradition of political-allegorical mountain poetry that began with Milton's *L'Allegro* (whose reference to 'The mountain nymph, sweet Liberty'[15] provides Shelley's central conceit), and mapping this onto the political situation of early nineteenth-century Britain, Shelley also probes his innermost thoughts and feelings at a moment of personal crisis. Written in Spenserian stanzas, one of Shelley's favourite forms, but relying for its lyrical dynamic on the conventions of the sublime ode, the poem is built round a sequence of apostrophes in which Shelley addresses 'Cambria', the personified spirit of Wales, asking urgent rhetorical questions to which he supplies his own equally forthright answers. In the course of this imaginary dialogue, he reveals the horror he felt at the deprivation he encountered in London, his frustration at his powerlessness to alleviate it, and his potential guilt at removing himself from a scene of public suffering to enjoy the private pleasures of the Welsh countryside.

It is this guilt—the temptation of 'selfish peace' (28) and inertia—that the poem above all struggles with, as Shelley galvanizes himself with a series of emphatic denials, promising to redouble his efforts to serve the cause of freedom. In true 'enthusiast' fashion, the poem builds to a frenzy as Shelley fantasizes about taking direct political action, imagining himself clasping a dagger to execute revenge upon 'the pert slaves whose wanton power had grasped | All hope that springs beneath the eye of day' (48–9), but then checking that impulse by reminding himself that what is needed is not a massacre but a 'bloodless victory' over despotism. The rugged landscape that inspired Shelley's violent fantasy becomes in turn the means for exorcizing it, as Shelley calls upon 'wild Cambria' to 'calm each struggling thought' and 'Cast thy sweet veil of rocks and woods between' (55–6). As the 'visions fade', the poem moves to its conclusion, like many of Shelley's lyrics, with a self-addressed prayer:

---

[15] Line 36, in *Poems of John Milton*, ed. John Carey and Alastair Fowler (London: Longman, 1968).

> Let me forever be what I have been,
>> But not forever at my needy door
> Let Misery linger, speechless, pale and lean.
>> I am the friend of the unfriended poor;
> Let me not madly stain their righteous cause in gore.

(59–63)

In purely political terms, the poem can be seen as an early dramatization of one of the unresolved issues of Shelley's political thought: the problem of revolutionary violence, Shelley's ambivalent attitude to which is revealed here in a peculiarly stark form. In aesthetic terms, the poem is a potent demonstration of how, by 1812, lyrical poetry—notably the technique of apostrophe and the conventions of the sublime—has become a vehicle not for mere rhetorical display, as in his earliest poems, but for the working through of difficult psychological and intellectual issues.

To turn from the 'Minor Poems' to the *Alastor* volume is to see not the radical stylistic break posited by previous generations of critics who wrote without full knowledge of the earlier collection, but rather a systematic complication of the premises of the earlier poetry brought about by changes in Shelley's personal circumstances and in his relation to his literary precursors. The tangled quest narrative of the title poem is examined elsewhere in this volume. The accompanying poems include one, 'The pale, the cold, and the moony smile', which had formed part of the 1813 collection, plus eight others (including two translations) composed in the intervening years, along with two revised extracts from *Queen Mab* retitled as 'Superstition' and 'The Daemon of the World'. Two of the new poems are of particular interest in that they show Shelley confronting precursors who had long been formative influences on his work, but with whom he now saw reason to quarrel. Our main evidence that the lyric 'O! there are spirits of the air', which opens the 'Other Poems' section, 'was addressed in idea to Coleridge' is a note by Mary Shelley in her 1839 edition, a suggestion that has triggered modern interpretations of the lyric as a diagnostic, revisionary text which turns Coleridge's psychoanalytic method back upon himself.[16] Read in this way, the poem is an attempt to explain how Coleridge's visionary imagination—his capacity to summon 'spirits of the air' and commune with the forces of nature—has become instead an instrument of self-torment, because, rather than trusting his inner lights, he built his hopes on 'the false earth's inconstancy' (20) and fell prey to the 'wiles' of the 'faithless' (24–5): 'Thine own soul still is true to thee, | But changed to a foul fiend through misery' (29–30). This theme links the poem both to 'Alastor', another psychological allegory about a poet's visionary idealism metamorphosed into self-destructive despair ('alastor' is a Greek word for an evil spirit), and to Shelley himself, whose personal demons the *Alastor* collection as a whole seems to be an attempt to exorcize.

More explicitly confrontational is the sonnet actually entitled 'To Wordsworth', a textbook case of the 'revisionary strife' postulated in Bloom's theory of influence,[17] except that

---

[16] See e.g. Sally West, *Coleridge and Shelley: Textual Engagement* (Aldershot: Ashgate, 2007), 43–50.
[17] Bloom, *Map of Misreading*, 10.

here ideological disagreement rather than imaginative competitiveness is the cause of the strife, and the governing emotion is not repressed anxiety but angry disappointment. Addressing Wordsworth as the 'Poet of Nature', Shelley perceptively identifies the psychological core of his poetry as the experience of loss, and begins by acknowledging that he shares Wordsworth's sorrow that 'things depart which never may return: | Childhood and youth, friendship and love's first glow' (2–3). His empathy comes across all the more strongly because he expresses it in Wordsworth's own elegiac language, filling the sonnet with verbal echoes of 'Tintern Abbey' and the Immortality Ode. The form of the poem, too, is an implicit tribute to Wordsworth, who had helped to revive and popularize the sonnet, and whose 'Sonnets Dedicated to Liberty' from *Poems in Two Volumes* (1807) were an important model for Shelley's many experiments with the genre. Shelley alludes to one of the most famous of these, 'London, 1802', where Wordsworth addresses *his* precursor Milton with the resonant statement 'MILTON! thou shouldst be living at this hour' (the connection is underlined by Shelley's reuse of the metaphor of the 'lone star', an emblem of both literary influence and political independence). But, having established common cause with Wordsworth, Shelley then turns the tables on him. Still using Wordsworthian phrasing but exploiting the capacity of the sonnet form to 'turn', or alter direction (the *volta*), Shelley accuses Wordsworth of giving him another 'loss' to grieve, one 'Which thou too feel'st, yet I alone deplore' (6), by having deserted his youthful radicalism and ceased to be the radical poet whose 'voice did weave | Songs consecrate to truth and liberty' (11–12). A poem that began as a tribute ends as a critique and, more damning still, a lament, Shelley's imputation being that the Wordsworth whom he once honoured, though actually alive, is now politically dead. Quite when he first learned about Wordsworth's altered political views is not clear, but the fact is that by 1813 the one-time republican and semi-atheist was now a tax official on the government payroll, actively supporting the local Tory candidate and the established Church. The scale of his apostasy had been brought home to Shelley by his reading of *The Excursion* in 1814, his reaction to which Mary recorded in her diary: 'he is a slave' (*Journals: MWS* I, 25). The sonnet gives further expression to that same disillusion, confirming Shelley's problematized relationship with his still indispensable but now fatally compromised precursor.

The corrective dialogue with Wordsworth continues in Shelley's unpublished lyric 'Verses Written on Receiving a Celandine in a Letter from England', written soon after his arrival in Switzerland in May 1816. Here, the dialogue is conducted emblematically, using a revisionary technique Shelley had experimented with several years earlier in his poem 'Passion' (from the Esdaile collection), a highly charged lyric about emotional and sexual betrayal modelled on Wordsworth's 'A Poet's Epitaph' and centred on the symbol of deadly nightshade. The 'Verses', whose theme is also betrayal but whose target is now Wordsworth himself, prosecutes its case by ironically recycling one of Wordsworth's favourite emblems (he had published three poems about celandines) to show how the seemingly 'deathless Poet' had 'changed and withered' (27–9), just like the flower he had once described. Severed from its stem, the celandine now betokens not liberty but 'Love sold, hope dead, and honour broken' (72).

The fact that Wordsworth remained, nonetheless, a source of inspiration to Shelley is confirmed by the two interconnected lyrics that are the most important fruits of his summer in Switzerland and the French Alps, 'Hymn to Intellectual Beauty' and 'Mont Blanc'. The former is a metaphysical hymn in the tradition of Spenser's 'Hymn of Heavenly Beauty', one of a pair of poems written, as Spenser's dedication of 1596 informs us, 'to amend, and, by way of retraction to reform' his two earlier 'Hymns of earthly or natural love and beauty',[18] which had been deemed too philosophically heterodox. Whether or not Shelley was aware of it, this textual history is significant because his poem too centres on the question of natural versus supernatural explanations of the world, and offers its own revisionary assessment of the claims for transcendence made by Christianity and other philosophical systems. Like Spenser's hymn, Shelley's includes an *ekstasis* in which the essence of beauty is beheld, but whereas in Spenser's it is achieved by contemplation, through a carefully gradated process of meditation, in Shelley's the revelation occurs suddenly and unexpectedly, leading some critics to interpret it as an actual biographical event. The Neoplatonism of Spenser's hymns (more apparent in the earlier than the later, amended pair) is retained in Shelley's poem, but modified by the latter's reading of more recent philosophical expositions of 'intellectual beauty', notably in Sir William Drummond's *Academical Questions* (1805), a long-time favourite of Shelley's.

Artistically, Shelley's main achievement is to weld the form of the philosophical hymn to a more modern form of lyric, the autobiographical ode, since the poem's other main structural model—particularly evident from the fifth stanza onwards, where Shelley switches from the third to the first person—is Wordsworth's Immortality Ode. This too is a poem about intellectual beauty which dabbles in Neoplatonism, but it is Wordsworth's exploration of the experiential sources of his perception of beauty and his beauty-making power ('the visionary gleam'), his analysis of the shifting relationship between mind and Nature, and his dialectic of imaginative loss and gain in the transition from childhood to adulthood, that captivate Shelley, who offers his own version of the predicament set out and worked through in the Immortality Ode. Employing, like Wordsworth, the form of the neo-Pindaric 'progress' ode, but regularizing its stanzaic structure, Shelley's bold rewriting of Wordsworth's crisis-lyric involves, among other things, a massive foregrounding of the problem of 'mutability', already the title of a poem in the *Alastor* volume and implicitly the subject of much of Shelley's other poetry. Unlike Wordsworth's Ode, though, the 'Hymn' offers no resolution, either metaphysical or psychological, of the predicament it describes, but instead ends in the way we have seen before, with a prayer for personal 'calm' and an undertaking that Shelley will use his visionary powers for the public good, 'to free | This world from its dark slavery' (69–70).

The philosophical subtleties of the 'Hymn to Intellectual Beauty', and the ingenious stylistic strategies Shelley deploys in his attempt to convey the ineffable, have fascinated critics, and it remains one of his most frequently analysed poems. Critical interest intensified when a new version of the 'Hymn', differing significantly from the text published in *The Examiner* in 1816, came to light in 1976 in the Scrope Davies Notebook.

---

[18] Edmund Spenser, *The Shepherd's Calendar and Other Poems*, ed. Philip Henderson (London: Dent, 1932), 328.

The Notebook also contained a variant text of 'Mont Blanc', known previously in the version published (with the subtitle 'Lines Written in the Vale of Chamouni') in the Shelleys' jointly authored *History of a Six Weeks' Tour* (1817), and a manuscript draft. Though it has much in common with the 'Hymn', 'Mont Blanc' is a different kind of poem and its artistic achievement—whichever version we consider—is arguably even greater.[19] It is here that Shelley unleashes the full force of his poetic imagination, and starts to write lyric verse that is both technically brilliant and intellectually compelling. The stimulus of Wordsworth is, once again, one of the enabling factors. 'Mont Blanc' extends the revisionary work of the 'Hymn', probing further the Immortality Ode's claims for transcendence (the Wordsworthian code-word for which is 'gleam', reused here by Shelley both as noun and verb), while developing further the sceptical metaphysic which puts all such claims in question. An even stronger influence is 'Tintern Abbey', whose innovative method of combining literal descriptions of nature with a metaphorical landscape of the mind provides Shelley's basic technique. Especially seminal are the lines already quoted about a 'motion and a spirit' that 'rolls through all things', echoes of which begin in the opening lines of 'Mont Blanc' ('The everlasting universe of things | Flows through the mind, and rolls its rapid waves' (1–2)), and recur throughout the poem. The crude borrowings from 'Tintern Abbey' in 'To Harriet' are replaced by a much subtler mode of creative transformation in which ideas, images, rhythms, and syntactic features from Wordsworth's poem are subjected to skilful elaboration, recombination, and semantic re-coding, showing the process of poetic influence in its strongest and most paradoxically original form.

Moreover, 'Mont Blanc' is a poem *about* poetic influence: its grand philosophical themes—the relation between the individual and the universal mind, the nature and sources of power, the problem of self-knowledge, mirrored in the symbolic geography of the poem in the relation between the river Arve, its tributary the Arveiron, the creeping glaciers that feed them, and the mighty river Rhone into which the waters eventually flow—are focused, in part at least, on the more specific and personal question of the relation between a writer and his precursors, and the mechanisms by which a new poetic voice makes itself heard, 'with a sound but half its own' (6). As G. Kim Blank notes, 'the "universe of things" holds the same power relationship to the mind as the "spirit of the age" holds to the individual poet', and the mountain becomes 'a symbol for the enigmatic source and power of influence'.[20] The self-reflexive quality of the poem is particularly evident in the second section, where Shelley turns from the external scene to meditate, with an equal sense of wonder, on the psychological origins of poetry:

> Dizzy Ravine! and when I gaze on thee
> I seem as in a trance sublime and strange

---

[19] Quotations below are from the text in *History of a Six Weeks' Tour*, as given in *Longman*. For a comparison with other versions, see Michael O'Neill, 'Shelley's Lyric Art' (1997), reprinted in *Norton 2*, 616–26; and Robert Brinkley, 'Spaces Between Words: Writing *Mont Blanc*', in Robert Brinkley and Keith Hanley (eds.), *Romantic Revisions* (Cambridge: Cambridge UP, 1992), 243–67.

[20] G. Kim Blank, *Wordsworth's Influence on Shelley: A Study of Poetic Authority* (Basingstoke: Macmillan, 1988), 175, 177.

To muse on my own separate fantasy,
My own, my human mind, which passively
Now renders and receives fast influencings,
Holding an unremitting interchange
With the clear universe of things around;
One legion of wild thoughts, whose wandering wings
Now float above thy darkness, and now rest
Where that or thou art no unbidden guest,
In the still cave of the witch Poesy,
Seeking among the shadows that pass by,
Ghosts of all things that are, some shade of thee,
Some phantom, some faint image; till the breast
From which they fled recalls them, thou art there!

(34–48)

The dialectic of rendering and receiving described here closely foreshadows the theorization of poetic influence in the Preface to *Prometheus Unbound*, but the poem's phrasing adds further resonance: 'fast influencings' conveys Shelley's sense of the exhilarating speed of creative transfer, and 'unremitting interchange' of its tireless demands. Yet there is nothing deterministic about this process: 'legion of wild thoughts' is a reminder of the unpredictable nature of imaginative activity—the fecund chaos from which art springs— while the essential mystery of artistic creation is captured by the image of the 'cave of the witch Poesy', which fuses Plato's myth of the Cave, signifying the simulacrum of the Real to which human perception is confined, with traditional iconography of the artistic *daemon* or muse; Shelley cleverly maps this symbolism onto the actual caves (more precisely, cave-like indentations in the glaciers) of Mont Blanc. The multiplicity of literary echoes in the passage, which, besides Wordsworth, include Coleridge's 'The Eolian Harp', canto III of *Childe Harold's Pilgrimage*, and other Byron poems from 1816 (Shelley and Byron being in daily proximity at this time, reading Wordsworth together and imaginatively feeding off one another),[21] make it, like the poem as a whole, a powerful demonstration of the 'influencing' process it describes.

   Another key model, or counter-model, for 'Mont Blanc' is Coleridge's 'Hymn before Sun-rise in the Vale of Chamouni', whose title Shelley echoes in his subtitle but whose theological interpretation of the Alpine landscape he systematically challenges. The note Coleridge appended to his 'Hymn' when it first appeared in the *Morning Post* in 1802, though probably not seen by Shelley (who knew the poem from a later reprinting in *The Friend*), encapsulates its fervent rhetoric: 'the whole vale, its every light, its every sound, must needs impress every mind not utterly callous with the thought—Who *would* be, who *could* be an Atheist in this valley of Wonders!'[22] Such a response to Europe's highest mountain was, by the turn of the century, wholly conventional; similar sentiments had

---

[21] Charles E. Robinson, *Shelley and Byron: The Snake and Eagle Wreathed in Fight* (Baltimore: Johns Hopkins UP, 1976), 31–9; William D. Brewer, *The Shelley–Byron Conversation* (Gainesville, FL: University of Florida Press, 1994), 22–7.
[22] Quoted in *Longman*, 1, 535 (headnote).

been uttered in similar language by numerous writers including the clergyman-poet Thomas Sedgwick Whalley in his *Mont Blanc: An Irregular Lyric Poem* (1788), which, alongside the expected theology, deploys a royalist symbolism which would have been equally inimical to Shelley, picturing Mont Blanc as a 'monarch Mountain' around which other 'vassal ALPS' crowd and cower.[23] Shelley confronts this tendentious literary legacy with a resolutely secular and politically radical interpretation of the scene, mobilizing his sceptical intelligence to probe 'the secret strength of things | Which governs thought' (139–40). Where, in answer to the question of the Ultimate Cause, the anthropomorphized landscape of Coleridge's poem thunders the word 'GOD!', Shelley's by contrast 'teaches awful doubt' (77); and his 'great Mountain', rather than exerting tyrannical dominion as in Whalley, uses its voice 'to repeal | Large codes of fraud and woe' (80–1).

Unlike Coleridge, whose 'Hymn' is a free translation of a poem by the Danish-German poet Friederike Brun (a fact he did not initially acknowledge), Shelley actually visited the valley of Chamonix, and no account of the poem's literary provenance should forget that Shelley's primary inspiration was first-hand experience of this spectacular landscape.[24] When introducing 'Mont Blanc' in the *History of a Six Weeks' Tour*, which sets the poem alongside letters and journal entries describing the same scene, Shelley emphasizes that the poem was composed on location and was, above all, an effort of mimesis: 'an attempt to imitate the untameable wildness and inaccessible solemnity from which those feelings sprang' (*Murray: Prose*, 181). Comparison of the poem with his prose descriptions, eloquent and imaginative in themselves, shows Shelley utilizing the full resources of the poetic medium, condensing and intensifying his descriptive language, substituting metaphorical for literal statement, and carrying further the daring speculations in the prose. As critics have noted,[25] stylistic features such as the extensive use of enjambment and irregular rhyme, the pluralization of voices (multiple apostrophes to different addressees), the rapid turnover of metaphors, and the succession of mythological analogues, all help to convey the awesome wildness of the scene and what Shelley calls the 'undisciplined overflowing of the soul' (*Murray: Prose*, 180–1) it occasioned. The 'oscillating utterance'[26] that results is both a classic rendition of the aesthetic of the sublime (the 'rapidly alternating attraction and repulsion' Kant posits as the mind's response to the sublime object's 'outrage on the imagination')[27] and an

[23] Page 8 (no line numbers). For this and other precedents, including Friederike Brun, see Morton D. Paley, '"This Valley of Wonders": Coleridge's *Hymn before Sun-rise in the Vale of Chamouni*', *European Romantic Review* 12.3 (2001), 351–80; and Angela Esterhammer, 'Coleridge's "Hymn before Sun-rise" and the Voice Not Heard', in Nicholas Roe (ed.), *Samuel Taylor Coleridge and the Sciences of Life* (Oxford: Oxford UP, 2001), 224–45.

[24] For details, see Benjamin Colbert, *Shelley's Eye: Travel Writing and Aesthetic Vision* (Aldershot: Ashgate, 2005), 81–115.

[25] Judith Chernaik, *The Lyrics of Shelley* (Cleveland: Press of Case Western Reserve University, 1972), 40–52; William Keach, *Shelley's Style* (New York: Methuen, 1984), 194–200; Hogle, *Shelley's Process*, 79–85.

[26] Hogle's phrase: *Shelley's Process*, 80.

[27] Immanuel Kant, *The Critique of Judgement*, trans. James Creed Meredith (Oxford: Clarendon Press, 1952), 107, 91. For a reading of 'Mont Blanc' against the British tradition of the sublime, see Angela Leighton, *Shelley and the Sublime: An Interpretation of the Major Poems* (Cambridge: Cambridge UP, 1984), 58–72.

example of the linguistic slippage that is a distinctive mark of Shelley's poetic style, mirroring the epistemological predicament it describes. The abrupt formal transitions between the five verse paragraphs are another aspect of the mimesis, a structural feature of the irregular ode perfectly suited to Shelley's philosophical musings, which are 'undisciplined' only in the sense that the ode form is alleged to be; what actually defines the genre, as its best theorists and practitioners understood, is apparent lawlessness together with underlying artistic control.[28] Shelley's mastery of this poetic logic, already evident in the odes of illustrious contemporaries like Coleridge and Wordsworth, marks another important breakthrough in his lyric development, pointing forward to the equal and greater accomplishments of his later years.

SELECT BIBLIOGRAPHY

Blank, G. Kim. *Wordsworth's Influence on Shelley: A Study of Poetic Authority*. Basingstoke: Macmillan, 1988.

Bloom, Harold. *A Map of Misreading*. New York: Oxford UP, 1975.

Chernaik, Judith. *The Lyrics of Shelley*. Cleveland: Press of Case Western Reserve University, 1972.

Cronin, Richard. *Shelley's Poetic Thoughts*. London: Macmillan, 1981.

Duff, David. '"The Casket of my Unknown Mind": The 1813 Volume of Minor Poems'. *The Unfamiliar Shelley*. Ed. Alan Weinberg and Timothy Webb. Aldershot: Ashgate, 2009. 41–67.

—— *Romanticism and the Uses of Genre*. Oxford: Oxford UP, 2009.

Hogle, Jerrold E. *Shelley's Process: Radical Transference and the Development of his Major Works*. New York: Oxford UP, 1988.

Keach, William. *Shelley's Style*. New York: Methuen, 1984.

Matthews, G. M. 'Shelley's Lyrics'. *The Morality of Art: Essays Presented to G. Wilson Knight*. Ed. D. W. Jefferson. London: Routledge and Kegan Paul, 1969. Reprinted in *Norton 1*, 681–94.

O'Neill, Michael. '"And All Things Seem Only One": The Shelleyan Lyric'. *Percy Bysshe Shelley: Bicentenary Essays*. Ed. Kelvin Everest. *Essays and Studies 1992*. Cambridge: D. S. Brewer, 1992. 115–31.

Peterfreund, Stuart. *Shelley among Others: The Play of the Intertext and the Idea of Language*. Baltimore: Johns Hopkins UP, 2002.

Rajan, Tilottama. 'Romanticism and the Death of Lyric Consciousness'. *Lyric Poetry: Beyond New Criticism*. Ed. Chaviva Hošek and Patricia Parker. Ithaca, NY: Cornell UP, 1985. 194–207.

Weisman, Karen. 'The Lyricist'. *The Cambridge Companion to Shelley*. Ed. Timothy Morton. Cambridge: Cambridge UP, 2006. 45–64.

West, Sally. *Coleridge and Shelley: Textual Engagement*. Aldershot: Ashgate, 2007.

---

[28] David Duff, *Romanticism and the Uses of Genre* (Oxford: Oxford UP, 2009), 86–8.

CHAPTER 16

....

EPIC EXPERIMENTS

Queen Mab *and* Laon and Cythna

....

JACK DONOVAN

I

....

THE critical reputation of Shelley's two narrative poems of epic scope and design, *Queen Mab* (1813) and *Laon and Cythna* (1817), is marked by peculiarities that make it difficult to approach them without pre-formed expectations.[1] This is because over time each has acquired the aspect of a 'case' whose constituent features are implicated with an eventful reception-history, dramatically contentious in its time, which has affected understanding ever since. In consequence, any consideration of these substantial and ambitious early works proceeds unavoidably on two fronts. While polemical accretions make it indispensable to try to look at each poem distinctly and in itself, due weight must none-theless be given to important cultural bearings which would be lost by abstracting what are intentionally controversial works from the controversies they provoked. These controversies have also had a broader influence on the formation of Shelley's reputation as man and writer. The most virulent attacks on his ideas, morals, and character—which in his lifetime painted him as demonic blasphemer and monster of depravity, a distorted likeness that persisted for decades after his death—were occasioned by the two long poems that form the subject of this chapter. The response to *Queen Mab* is the more con-sistently overwrought and injurious; contemporary reaction to *Laon and Cythna*, some of which is hardly less so, will be considered together with that poem in section III.[2]

---

[1] Recent critical editions of *Queen Mab* are in *Longman*, 1 and *CPPBS* II, of *Laon and Cythna* in *Longman*, 2. Quotations from both poems are from the *Longman* edition; references are given in the text.

[2] Contemporary reviews may be found in Newman Ivey White, *The Unextinguished Hearth: Shelley and his Contemporary Critics* (1938; New York: Octagon Books, 1966), and in Donald H. Reiman (ed.), *The Romantics Reviewed: Contemporary Reviews of British Romantic Writers*, 3 parts (New York: Garland, 1972), Part C, vols. I and II.

Shelley did not arrange for the commercial publication of *Queen Mab* but had it printed and distributed privately in a well-produced and relatively expensive edition of 250 copies. His purpose in this was (so he put it, with casual bravura) to appeal not to those 'aristocrats' who could afford to buy the volume but to their children (*Letters: PBS* I, 361)—an early instance of that strategic targeting of a modest but select band of influential readers which he would continue to claim as his appropriate and preferred audience. Contrary to his calculation, the poem achieved far wider circulation than he could have hoped, though not until cheaper pirated editions started to appear in 1821. Yet even before then *Queen Mab* had begun to attract the articulate partisans of radical and progressive persuasion who would guarantee its influence right through the nineteenth century, notably among Chartists, followers of the early socialist Robert Owen, and free-thinkers. The advocacy of this dedicated and active readership from the labouring classes was a factor in the hostile reviews *Queen Mab* attracted for its frank and comprehensive assault on established political institutions, sanctioned social customs, and orthodox religious belief.[3]

It is possible to track in some detail the evolution and fortunes of *Queen Mab* from its conception in December 1811 to Shelley's public repudiation of the piracy by the bookseller William Clark in June 1821. The first idea for the poem was prophetic and utopian: 'by anticipation a picture of the manners, simplicity and delights of a perfect state of society', he wrote to the Sussex schoolmistress Elizabeth Hitchener in December 1811 (*Letters: PBS* I, 201). (Shelley's letters to her, to T. J. Hogg, to William Godwin, and to the bookseller Thomas Hookham in the years 1811–13 constitute a primary and illuminating commentary on *Queen Mab*.) Composition seems to have begun in April 1812 or soon after; in August he wrote to Hookham of his plan to imagine a total conspectus of universal history—'the Past, the Present, & the Future are the grand & comprehensive topics of this Poem'—taking care to mollify the bookseller's entirely justified fear of prosecution on account of its forthright anti-monarchical and anti-Christian sentiments. Poetry of obvious literary sophistication and addressed to educated readers, he claimed, is *ipso facto* unassailable: 'a Poem is safe, the iron-souled Attorney general would scarcely dare to attack "genus irritabile vatum"' (the excitable race of poets). The decision to attach discursive prose notes (some of which were already written, some even in print) after the example of modern poems such as Robert Southey's *Thalaba the Destroyer* (1801) or Walter Scott's *The Lady of the Lake* (1810) appears to have been taken in the course of composing the verse. The following spring he changes tack to reassure Hookham (who eventually declined to publish) that the polemical broadside against Christianity 'will be unnoticed in a Note' (*Letters: PBS* I, 324, 361, 368). In the event copies of the poem were not offered regularly for sale but distributed by the author because neither he nor any bookseller was prepared to stand the risk of prosecution.

Two sorts of legal intervention laid down what might be called the institutional basis of the poem's infamy. In January 1817 John and Elizabeth Westbrook, the father and sister

---

[3] H. Buxton Forman, *Vicissitudes of Shelley's* Queen Mab: *A Chapter in the History of Reform* (London: privately printed, 1887); Bouthaina Shaban, 'Shelley and the Chartists', in Betty T. Bennett and Stuart Curran (eds.), *Shelley: Poet and Legislator of the World* (Baltimore: Johns Hopkins UP, 1996), 114–25.

of Shelley's late wife Harriet, petitioned the Court of Chancery to allow them to become guardians of Charles and Ianthe, the children of the marriage. The petitioners submitted that Shelley was morally unfit to rear the children, and that in *Queen Mab* and other writings he had 'blasphemously derided the truth of the Christian Revelation and denied the existence of God as the Creator of the Universe'.[4] In March 1817 the Lord Chancellor Eldon himself delivered the judgement that Shelley should be denied custody of Charles and Ianthe because of his avowed principles and the conduct to which these had led him in abandoning Harriet and cohabiting with Mary. This decision effectively asserted that where a relation of cause and effect could be determined between a parent's professed convictions and his immoral and vicious conduct (as the court deemed it), he could be declared unsuited to educate his own children lest he inculcate the same principles in them.[5] Lurid rumours of sexual promiscuity, even a 'league of incest' (for which see section III), involving Byron, Shelley, Mary Shelley, and Claire Clairmont had been in circulation for some time and were later turned to account by scandalized reviewers of the 1821 piracies of *Queen Mab*. These claimed to discover in Shelley's life and work the same malign combination of outrageous opinions, personal depravity and subversive writing that Eldon had identified, though in quite another key. Deploring the promulgation of doctrines that 'drive their odious professors' to 'abominations', *The Literary Gazette* for March 1821, to take an egregious example, specifies the iniquities of the diabolical author in question:

> We declare against receiving our social impulses from a destroyer of every social virtue; our moral creed, from an incestuous wretch; or our religion, from an atheist, who denied God, and reviled the purest institutes of human philosophy and divine ordination.[6]

Over against such vilification should be set two kinds of defence. The radical publisher and bookseller Richard Carlile—an interested party since he himself pirated *Queen Mab* in four editions—frankly praised the poem's beauty in 1822 in his journal *The Republican*, as well as its 'merit' in the 'exposure and denunciation of Kingcraft and Priestcraft', while insisting that its publication must be defended on 'the principle of free discussion'. A more circumspect and tolerant stand is taken by *The London Magazine and Theatrical Inquisitor*, which in the same year focused its exclusive attention on the poem's 'poetical merits', which it regarded as the fruits of 'original genius', pointedly declaring both extreme opinions and 'private scandal' to be irrelevant to criticism.[7]

Although often fined and imprisoned for his publishing activities, Carlile escaped the attentions of the authorities in the case of *Queen Mab*.[8] Not so the bookseller William

---

[4] *The Life of Percy Bysshe Shelley by Thomas Medwin*, ed. H. Buxton Forman (Oxford: Oxford UP, 1913), 464.

[5] Edward Dowden, *The Life of Percy Bysshe Shelley*, 2 vols. (London: Kegan Paul, Trench, 1886), II, 90.

[6] White, *Unextinguished Hearth*, 56.

[7] Ibid. 95–7, 53–4.

[8] In autumn 1819 Shelley wrote a brilliant defence of Carlile after his conviction for blasphemous libel, which he sent to Leigh Hunt's *Examiner* but which Hunt never published (*Letters: PBS* II, 136–48).

Clark, who was responsible for the first of the piratical editions in 1821, and who was prosecuted on the instigation of the Society for the Suppression of Vice, a self-appointed warden of public morals; convicted of publishing an 'Atheistical libel', he was sentenced to four months' imprisonment. The many unauthorized editions that followed Clark's managed to elude prosecution, only for Edward Moxon, the publisher of Mary Shelley's one-volume edition of Shelley's *Poetical Works* (1840), to fall foul of the law after restoring at Mary's behest the (largely anti-religious) passages that she had previously removed at his insistence from her four-volume edition of 1839.[9]

Shelley's own later evaluations of *Queen Mab* are complicated by both the continuing danger of prosecution and the disadvantages of opprobrium to a writer wishing to attract sympathetic readers, if only in modest numbers. Hence the revised version of Parts I and II—the notes removed and all contentious matter prudently tempered—which he included under the title of *The Daemon of the World* as the final poem in the *Alastor* volume of 1816, together with a similarly pruned excerpt (VI, 72–102) entitled *Superstition*. He also drafted a toned-down recasting of Parts VIII and IX but did not publish it.[10] The following year he candidly admitted that *Queen Mab*

> is full of those errors which belong to youth, as far as arrangement of imagery & language & a connected plan, is concerned.—But it was a sincere overflowing of the heart & mind, & that at a period when they are most uncorrupted & pure (*Letters: PBS* I, 566)

—before going on to declare his continuing and increased attachment to the principles which had originally inspired the poem. But he vigorously disowned the Clark piracy of 1821 in order, he said, to distance himself from the enterprise of 'one of the low booksellers in the Strand' and 'for the sake of a dignified appearance' (*Letters: PBS* II, 300–1). His public disavowal in the *Examiner* on 15 July claims that *Queen Mab* was written two years earlier than it actually was and that it had not been intended for publication, while branding it 'crude and immature' from a literary point of view and in 'all that concerns moral and political speculation as well as in the subtler discriminations of metaphysical and religious doctrine'—without, however, renouncing the 'principles' he had reaffirmed in 1817 (*Letters: PBS* II, 304). There was method in this careful positioning. By summer 1821 the great *Prometheus Unbound* volume had appeared, *The Cenci* had gone into a second edition, and *Adonais* had been completed and sent to be printed. Shelley was anxious to forestall any further notoriety that would damage his chances of finding the readers he had long been seeking by diverting attention to a poem which was sure to offend many and which was out of keeping with the styles and modes from which he now hoped for success.

Mary Shelley appended the disclaimer in the *Examiner* to her 'Note on Queen Mab' in the *Poetical Works* of 1840.[11] Shelley's estimate of the poem ten years after writing it, and clearly influenced by the specific set of circumstances outlined above, thus became part of the standard paratext of *Queen Mab*. So did the idealized biography of the schoolboy and student Shelley—as he had done, Mary gave his age as 18 and not 20/21 when he

---

[9] *CPPBS* II, 509–18.   [10] *Longman*, 1, 489–91, 500–8.   [11] *H* 838.

wrote it—which she inserted as an obvious antidote to the aggressively *ad hominem* denunciations the poem had attracted. Her character-sketch exhibits a youthful Shelley who is ardent, independent, unworldly, and generous; a fervent lover of truth, a heroic rebel against all forms of tyranny; already at school a victim and martyr to these unshakable convictions, steadfast in his dedication to the brotherhood of man, tragically persuaded that only a year or two more of life remained to him, and determined to devote his allotted span to lofty ends of general benefit. She assures her readers that Shelley desired to accomplish 'the noblest work that life and time permitted him. In this spirit he composed *Queen Mab*.'[12] Such instances of out and out attack or defence, glimpses of the cloven foot or rustle of the angel's wing, combined to create a *succès de scandale* such that in 1887 the doyen of nineteenth-century Shelley editors, H. Buxton Forman, lamented that 'there are ten who know Shelley as the author of *Queen Mab* for one who knows that he wrote *Prometheus Unbound*'.[13]

Academic criticism has continued to assign *Queen Mab* a notably modest place in the Shelley canon. The informed and thoughtful book that can claim to have initiated modern critical attempts to view his verse as a whole, Carlos Baker's *Shelley's Major Poetry: The Fabric of a Vision*, to take a signal example, frankly declared of all the poems of 1812–17: 'None of them has intrinsic importance as a work of art.'[14] Few would now subscribe to such an assessment. Yet vestiges of the prepossessions which underlie it, and which are rooted in the history of the poem's reception, can still be encountered in apologetic or downright dismissive evaluations of *Queen Mab*. The works by Cameron, Curran, and Duff listed in the Select Bibliography have done much to establish a more informed and discerning view of the poem from which the present chapter has benefited and which it takes as point of departure.

II

Queen Mab is an eclectic mix of literary forms and features, a notable instance of the generic hybrid frequent in the poetry of the Romantic period. Numerous sources and analogues have been pointed out, some of them indicated in the text itself and its notes, such as Lucretius' *De Rerum Natura* and Milton's *Paradise Lost*. Commentators have located a large number of antecedents—discovering, for example, broad resemblances to eighteenth-century neo-Spenserian 'moral allegories' that deliver counsel for right living, such as James Thomson's *The Castle of Indolence* (1748). Shelley's visionary frame and setting show close resemblances to Sir William Jones's *The Palace of Fortune* (1772), in which the Tibetan maiden Maia is conducted in a golden chariot drawn by peacocks to the celestial palace of the goddess Fortune from which she surveys the far-off globe of the earth. Here are staged for her moral education a series of allegorical visions which

---

[12] *H* 837.   [13] Buxton Forman, *Vicissitudes of* Queen Mab, 27.
[14] Carlos Baker, *Shelley's Major Poetry: The Fabric of a Vision* (Princeton: Princeton UP, 1948), 5.

the goddess interprets for her. In the languorous couplets of Erasmus Darwin's *The Botanic Garden* (1791), which Shelley admired, a vegetation goddess instructs a young woman in the wonders of vegetable nature with copious scientific notes appended in support.[15] For some of *Queen Mab*'s central political ideas and its conception of mental and cultural history Shelley drew substantially on *Les Ruines; ou méditations sur les révolutions des empires* (1791) by the French theorist of revolution Constantin Volney (1757–1820).[16] This unequivocally radical tract displays a conspectus of human history as sinister alliance between religious imposture and usurped authority enforced by military power. So much is revealed from a cosmic vantage point by a local deity, a spirit that haunts tombs and ruins, to the soul of a traveller through the ancient kingdoms of the Near East.[17]

The imparting of visionary instruction by a supernatural being to an individual marked out for a historical destiny is a commonplace of epic tradition. Familiar instances include the enlightenment of Aeneas in the underworld by the shade of his father Anchises in Book VI of the *Aeneid* and of Adam by the Archangel Michael in Books XI and XII of *Paradise Lost*. The succession of visions revealed to Shelley's Ianthe by Queen Mab represents the poem's chief structural debt to classical and neoclassical epic as well as to scenes of instruction in works such as those mentioned in the previous paragraph. To consider *Queen Mab* as an example of Romantic epic is therefore to apply the term not in a strictly formal sense but with the licence authorized by the breadth and flexibility of its usage in the Romantic period itself. This new range of meaning, which accompanied the extraordinary number and variety of epic poems published in the late eighteenth and early nineteenth century, is illustrated in William Hayley's influential *An Essay on Epic Poetry* (1782). In order to create poems of encyclopedic compass which incorporated major themes of public significance and imagined exceptional individuals engaged in actions that addressed the pressing concerns of their time, Hayley urged poets to free themselves from the restrictive prescriptions of neoclassical theory. Instead, the epic for a new age should be approached in a generous and innovative spirit without dogmatic attachment either to critical codes or arbitrary preferences, which together had hardened into doctrine. The natural field for British writers undertaking to create a national epic was British history. Hayley commended as privileged subject the progress of British liberty as furthered by the heroic figures of the past towards its current state of advanced development. National poems on this decidedly Whiggish theme were indeed written in considerable numbers in the period, as were biblical epics inspired by Milton's example.[18]

Both these types of poem emerged from mainstream British historical and religious culture. For *Queen Mab* Shelley drew upon currents of thought which stood squarely in

[15] Carl Grabo, *A Newton among Poets: Shelley's Use of Science in* Prometheus Unbound (Chapel Hill, NC: University of North Carolina Press, 1930), 30–79.

[16] Kenneth Neill Cameron, *The Young Shelley: Genesis of a Radical* (London: Victor Gollancz, 1951), 239–74; *Longman*, 1, 265–423; *CPPBS* II, 491–670.

[17] Baker, *Shelley's Major Poetry*, 23–8; *Longman*, 1, 268–9; *CPPBS* II, 501–7.

[18] Stuart Curran, *Poetic Form and British Romanticism* (Oxford: Oxford UP, 1986), 158–79.

opposition to both. His own notes and the efforts of commentators have identified his sources in detail. There is general agreement that the most important are the Roman poet Lucretius (98–*c*.55 BCE), Thomas Paine (1737–1809), William Godwin (1756–1836), the French *philosophe* Baron d'Holbach (1723–89), and Constantin Volney, who was both sceptical mythographer and member of the revolutionary national assembly. From these radical writers and an impressive library of other progressive thinkers Shelley derived the critical perspectives and the chief intellectual and political positions that he develops in *Queen Mab*. The poem's exposition of scientific materialism, of rational atheism, of the principles of necessity, and of perfectibility can be traced to them, as can its uncompromising critique of monarchical despotism, of biblical and institutional religion, of the restricting of the freedom to love by rigid marriage laws, and of the blighting sway of commerce. In all of these areas Shelley adopts what he calls a 'cosmopolitical' view (*Letters: PBS* I, 340), a supranationalism that excludes any celebration of that national destiny which tradition deriving from the *Aeneid* had consecrated as the first ambition of the epic.

Further generic orientations throw light on other aspects of *Queen Mab*. Both general and particular resemblances have been noticed to, for example, Edward Young's discursive and didactic poem *Night Thoughts* (1742–5) as well as to Southey's *The Vision of the Maid of Orleans*, which originally formed part of his epic *Joan of Arc* (1795) and in which Joan is granted a view of future human happiness and equality.[19] Duff makes an interesting case for the underlying force of the romance tradition in shaping *Queen Mab*'s narrative structure and ends.[20] To these may be added the fairy tale. The name of Mab, queen of the fairies, provides the title for two collections of such tales that were current in England at the end of the eighteenth century and beginning of the nineteenth. The long title of one is revealing: *Queen Mab; or Fairy Adventures, Being a Series of Incidents Wonderful and Surprizing, In which are Painted the Happiness attendant on Virtue; and the Punishment that necessarily follows Vice, Illustrated by Example.*[21] An engraving showing the fairy Amazona in a chariot of diamonds drawn through the sky by six swans introduces the text. *Queen Mab: Containing A Select Collection of only the Best, most Instructive, and Entertaining Tales of the Fairies* is largely made up of *contes* translated from the French of the Comtesse d'Aulnoy (*c*.1650–1705) which appends to each a short verse to point its moral, without exception a variant of 'But Heav'n by Miracle doth soon or late | The Virtuous favour, and their Deeds reward'.[22] Annexed to the main series of stories is 'Queen Mab's Song' in which her fairy band describe their nocturnal activities—

> When Mortals are at Rest,
> And snoring in their Nest,
> Unheard and unespy'd,
> Thro' key-holes we do glide—

[19] Stuart Curran, *Shelley's Annus Mirabilis* (San Marino, CA: Huntington Library, 1975), 13–14; *Longman*, 1, 268.

[20] David Duff, *Romance and Revolution: Shelley and the Politics of a Genre* (Cambridge: Cambridge UP, 1994), 79–93, 111–14.

[21] London: W. Lane, 1796.   [22] 5th edn. (London: Verner and Hood and J. Barker, 1799), 62.

which consist in dispensing small rewards and punishments according as a household is well kept or slovenly (366–7). The master-narrative of the tales as a group involves princes and princesses whose fitness to succeed to their elders is confirmed through ordeals that test their generosity, courage, and perseverance. As they undergo such trials, which typically pit them against wicked and treacherous relations, they regularly benefit from the assistance of beneficent fairies. A marriage to the object of desire ultimately rewards their sufferings and consecrates their prerogatives of beauty, riches, and power. These brief romances, conventional illustrations of the myth of the intrinsic worth of royal lineage, elevate the sons and daughters of monarchs to pre-eminence as actors in a drama in which innate virtue receives its due and recommends them as patterns of behaviour to young readers.

The allusion to tales of this kind in the title of Shelley's poem both varies and sharpens the irony that is its dominant rhetorical mode. An awareness of the moralized form of the fairy tale described above and the social values that underwrite it repeatedly invites mordant contrasts with (to consider only these examples) *Queen Mab*'s portrait of the cold-hearted king enslaved within his own palace, its insistence on the tyranny of marriage laws and customs, and on the injustice of accumulated riches. The series of religious, social, and political counter-narratives that make up the bulk of the poem are enclosed within the developing scene of Ianthe's education which provides them with a grand ironic frame. In this the Queen of the Fairies imparts not edifying moral parables that endorse the natural aptness of royalty to rule but the critical knowledge required to see through the pernicious fictions that mask the arbitrary character of established power and sustain its structural inequalities.

That contemporary fairy fictions adapted to the instruction of the young should be one reference point for *Queen Mab*'s broad polemical dimension is appropriate to the character of Ianthe, poised as she is between child and woman. Resemblances between her and Harriet Shelley, who was 15 years old when Shelley met her, and 16 when he began to write the poem, have a particular relevance to the education theme outlined above inasmuch as within the couple Shelley had adopted the role of mentor and tutor. Two months after their marriage, in a letter of October 1811 to Elizabeth Hitchener, he spoke of the deeply unhappy relations with family and school that had prompted him to elope with Harriet: 'Suicide was with her a favorite them[e and] her total uselessness was urged as its defence.' He goes on to invite Miss Hitchener to join him in a project to complete the formation of a mind:

> If Harriet be not at sixteen all that you are at a more advanced age, assist me to mould a really noble soul into all that can make it[s] nobleness useful and lovely.
> —Lovely it is now, or I am the weakest slave of error. (*Letters: PBS* I, 162–3)

Such a pedagogical model of his relations with Harriet finds its equivalent in the major elements of *Queen Mab*'s narrative frame: the death/sleep ambiguity with which the poem opens, the dramatic intervention of the Fairy, Ianthe's education for usefulness. This quality is to be understood in the sense it had acquired in utilitarian social philosophy, as the power to promote general benefit: 'Learn to make others happy' (II, 64) is

Mab's cardinal injunction to Ianthe's spirit. The poem represents the fashioning of an individual possessing exceptional moral qualities for the practical life such qualities demand: it directs personal goodness to the threshold of committed social action for the advantage of all.[23] In view of this explicit object, an additional narrative irony may be intended in relation to the pious practice of commending one's soul to divine protection at bedtime, as in the traditional prayer taught to children:

> Now I lay me down to sleep,
> I pray the Lord my soul to keep;
> If I should die before I wake,
> I pray the Lord my soul to take.

Mab visits the sleeping Ianthe, who at first appears to be dead, and conducts her soul to a palace in the heavens. So far the poem mimics the movement of the prayer. But Mab informs her pupil that this cannot be the goal of her being:

> were it virtue's only meed, to dwell
> In a celestial palace, all resigned
> To pleasurable impulses, immured
> Within the prison of itself, the will
> Of changeless nature would be unfulfilled.
>
> (II, 59–63)

Self-realization is not a matter of completing one's individual salvation in a transcendent realm but can only be achieved in the world of human beings, and in relation to all of them.

Ianthe is brought to mental maturity through Mab's systematic revision of the myths that established political regimes routinely impose on children through a subservient culture. Her aptness to develop under such instruction can be appreciated by taking as co-ordinates three words repeatedly used in relation to her—*virtue, purity,* and *wonder,* together with their cognates and synonyms. Shelley is very precise in characterizing the pre-eminent virtue that qualifies Ianthe for her enlightenment by supernatural intervention; innately gifted with goodness and sincerity, she has

> struggled, and with resolute will
> Vanquished earth's pride and meanness, burst the chains,
> The icy chains of custom
>
> (I, 125–7)

that is, shown herself superior to the arbitrary dictates and petty hierarchies of social convention and so become fit to understand and confront the deeper mental structures that sustain unjust systems of power. The sense of purity as it is applied to her ranges from clear suggestions of virginity—her 'tresses shade' her 'bosom's stainless pride' (I, 41–2) and she sleeps a 'maiden's sleep' (I, 78)—to an innocence of all worldly motive.

---

[23] Further autobiographical elements in the poem are noticed in, for example: Stuart Sperry, *Shelley's Major Verse: The Narrative and Dramatic Poetry* (Cambridge, MA: Harvard UP, 1988), 1–20 and Bieri, I, 160–290.

Wonder bears a central significance for her as representative consciousness. She is repeatedly told that Mab's office is 'the wonders of the human world to keep' (I, 167–8; VII, 50–1; VIII, 48–9); while her full awakening is achieved when Mab can assure her that 'Earth's wonders are thine own' (IX, 144). The enigmatic opening to the poem, 'How wonderful is Death, | Death and his brother Sleep!', is resolved by redefining wonder in relation to her fresh perception of both human love and natural marvel when she awakes at the end of the poem to look about her 'in wonder' (IX, 236). The capacity for wonder that Mab's revelations bring to perfection was regarded in eighteenth-century aesthetic theory as lying at the origin of the human creative impulse:

> To Admiration, source of joy refin'd!
> Chaste, lovely mover of the simple mind!
> [...]
> To her, sweet Poesy! we owe thy birth,
> Thou first encomiast of the fruitful Earth!

—as Hayley's *Essay on Epic Poetry* (VIII, 107–12) puts it. That the *Essay* goes on to imagine the birth of poetry at the dawn of time as arising from spontaneous praise of God the creator of the earth, so providing religion with its earliest form of prayer, suggests an additional ironic dimension to the secular wonder that Mab fosters. Shelley quite specifically defines the critical faculty of wonder that Ianthe acquires in opposition to such impulses to natural theology in the note to a passage describing the interminable extent and dazzling beauty of the celestial bodies in motion—'a sight of wonder'(I, 242–63)—conventional stimulus to the religious sublime. He cites the words of Psalm 8 which summons 'the heavens, the work of his fingers' to bear witness to the glory of God, altering the biblical text to 'The works of his fingers have borne witness against him'.[24]

The capacity for genuinely spontaneous wonder has another function than divesting nature's extraordinary manifestations of false theological accretions; it can transform a set of natural surroundings of dramatic beauty into a scene of imaginative vision, as it does in the thirty-nine lines that open canto II. The language and architecture of images in these lines, which can claim to be one of the foundation-passages of Shelley's verse, lay down what might be called a grammar of vision, elements of which reappear at pivotal moments in later visionary poems such as *Laon and Cythna* and the *Triumph of Life*. Shelley emphasizes the weight he attaches to the passage, situated so as to serve as prelude to the entry to Mab's celestial palace, by shifting the rhetorical mode from narration to direct address to the individual reader. The scene he constructs is liminal both physically (seashore) and temporally (sunset). But also perceptually: the boundaries of ocean, earth, and sky become fluid before the viewer's gaze, finally running into one another at the moment before the sun disappears. The reader is apprised that although the Fairy's dwelling, built up from this dazzling spectacle, is more 'wonderful' than the sum of its natural components, her visionary palace yet remains rooted in natural phenomena:

[24] *Longman*, 1, 278–9, 360–1, and see Cian Duffy, *Shelley and the Revolutionary Sublime* (Cambridge: Cambridge UP, 2005), 13–48.

'Yet likest evening's vault, that faery Hall'. An intimate and dynamic relation is thus defined between the natural and the visionary planes of reality; minds capable of wonder are invited to negotiate creatively between them.

III

If *Queen Mab* was for decades after Shelley's death the most influential of his major poems, *Laon and Cythna* was surely the least read—and no doubt remains so. If *Queen Mab* has passed through a variety of afterlives, *Laon and Cythna* has struggled to find even one. Shelley began to compose what would become the 4,818 lines of his epic romance around the middle of March 1817, some five years after he began *Queen Mab*. In the earlier poem a figure from popular fairy lore reveals the true state of the contemporary world to an exceptional individual by situating the present aright in relation to time past and future. In *Laon and Cythna* a barely developed narrator receives a similar revelation from a female character who is clearly supernatural but who has lived as a human being through the revolutionary age that has just ended. Shelley condenses the exposition of universal history that she delivers to symbolic and mythical form near the beginning rather than unfolding it piecemeal through the poem, the bulk of which is given over to a narrative which he described as exhibiting the '*beau ideal* as it were of the French Revolution' (*Letters: PBS* I, 564). To create this purified image he re-imagines what he regarded as the pivotal event of the age as an elemental conflict between humane and progressive principles and a regime both oppressive and treacherous. By 23 September he had completed a draft of the whole; between then and the beginning of December when the poem was offered for sale, he had added a prose Preface of over 3,000 words and a long verse Dedication to Mary Shelley.

The principal narrative introduces its anonymous narrator, who is in despair at the failure of the French Revolution, at the moment when he encounters a beautiful woman sorrowing for the same defeat. She discloses to him that from the beginning the world has been governed by twin deities of opposed and equal power, one good, the other evil—the latter having been in the ascendant from the beginning of human memory. An enchanted boat transports narrator and guide to the temple of the Spirit of Good. Here he witnesses the arrival of a heroic couple who have contended on earth in the service of the Spirit; an account of their struggle against evil occupies the remaining eleven cantos of the poem. They are Laon (who recounts their story as an autobiography) and Cythna, brother and sister, modern Greek patriots dedicated to the liberation of their country from Ottoman rule. Captured by the soldiers of the tyrant Othman, Laon is exposed to die, Cythna sent as a slave to the tyrant's harem. After seven years, following Laon's rescue and Cythna's expulsion and imprisonment, they meet in the Golden City, a version of the Ottoman capital Constantinople, where a peaceful revolution inspired and led by Cythna is under way. Viciously attacked by the tyrant's soldiers, Laon and a band of patriots resist until they are nearly annihilated. Laon is rescued from certain death by

Cythna. During a brief interlude they consummate their love before recalling to one another the course of their lives since their separation. Foreign monarchs league together to send armies in support of the Ottoman tyrant. Plague and famine follow the battle, which the tyrant's priests persuade him are a sign of divine wrath, insisting that Laon and Cythna, who have surrendered themselves, should be burnt at the stake to propitiate the offended deity. After their death a child in the form of a winged spirit (their own imaginative offspring) conducts their eternal selves to the temple of the Good Deity, bringing the narrative round to the point at which the first canto ended.

Within a few days of *Laon and Cythna* going on sale the publisher Charles Ollier, intimidated by objections and threats on the part of some customers at his bookshop, withdrew the volume from sale and removed his name from the title page. He feared, with good reason, that the poem's forthright attack on the Christian religion as complicit with oppressive political power rendered him liable to prosecution for blasphemous libel and the stringent fines and imprisonment that could be—and were—imposed for the offence. In addition, the poem's representation of incestuous love, explicitly prohibited in the Bible and the Book of Common Prayer, at the least constituted an affront to most readers' sensibilities; in combination with the anti-religious strain it could make *Laon and Cythna* appear outrageously provocative and purposely offensive. Without realistic hope of finding another publisher willing to accept such a risk, Shelley compromised with Ollier. All lines identifying Laon and Cythna as brother and sister were rewritten; passages disparaging to Christianity and to biblical theism were toned down. The title was changed from *Laon and Cythna; or, the Revolution of the Golden City: A Vision of the Nineteenth Century* to *The Revolt of Islam*. What had been a frankly prophetic title announcing a generalized revolutionary future, in its altered form obscurely suggests an insurrection on the fringe of Europe. The covert significance of the new title is dependent on readers recognizing the sense of Islam as 'submission, resignation'. The revised poem was reissued in January 1818.[25]

To these extraordinary circumstances Shelley's grand fiction of 'such a Revolution as might be supposed to take place in an European nation' owes its peculiar textual condition of existing virtually since publication in alternative versions which differ significantly (*Letters: PBS* I, 563). Shortly thereafter it became the subject of a polemical dispute in two journals of opposed political tendency, Leigh Hunt's liberal weekly *The Examiner* and the conservative *Quarterly Review*. Hunt's paper advertised the appearance of *The Revolt of Islam* as well as devoting three articles to a sympathetic exposition of the poem and its inherent social and ethical doctrines, as Hunt construed them. The *Quarterly's* reviewer, John Taylor Coleridge, sets the titles of both versions at the head of his review and uses them to convict the author of equivocation: 'he has reproduced the same poison, a little, and but a little, more cautiously disguised.' His first sentence identifies Shelley as 'one of that industrious knot of authors' loyal to and supported by Hunt's progressive newspaper. There follows an unsparing assault on *Laon and Cythna*'s system of ideas, as the reviewer interprets them, accompanied by an equally unsparing personal

---

[25] *Longman*, 2, 15–19; *SC* V, 141–69.

attack on the author as cowardly, vain, cruel, immoral, and dissolute.[26] Hunt replied with a defence of poet and poem in a further series of three articles in *The Examiner* in autumn 1819. The controversy represents a signal instance of frankly partisan reviewing not of a political tract but of an original narrative poem developing a critical view of established authority and institutions in the tense and polarized atmosphere of public debate post-Waterloo. From the middle of October 1819, when a copy of the *Quarterly*'s review reached Shelley in Florence, its aggressive condemnation of himself and his work had a material effect on his conception of his role as poet and on the poetry he wrote, influencing notably such masterpieces as *Prometheus Unbound*, 'Ode to the West Wind', and *Adonais*.

The double aspect of *Laon and Cythna/The Revolt of Islam* has continued to shape the poem's presentation and critical reception. Mary Shelley's editions of Shelley's *Poetical Works* from 1839 onwards print the *Revolt of Islam* text without reference to its original form. Nor in her accompanying Note does she mention the polemical debate the poem had aroused. Nonetheless, the charges laid against Shelley's character and behaviour are clearly in her mind when she alludes to 'the saddest events' of autumn 1816; that is, to the suicides of Fanny Godwin and Harriet Shelley, for both of which he had been held responsible. She goes on to construct a narrative of poetic creation which incorporates a portrait of Shelley drawn after his own visionary paradigms in which a compensatory and sublimating process turns the painful trials he had endured to the brilliant idealisms of a poem that he intended only to benefit his countrymen. As in Mary's Note on *Queen Mab*, the Shelley that appears here is both victim and alchemist, selflessly transmuting his own sufferings in the cauldron of his art to an enduring image designed to promote high and general good. The first of the nineteenth-century collected editions to prefer the text of *Laon and Cythna*, H. Buxton Forman's (1876–7), relegates the changes made for the *Revolt of Islam* to footnotes. Thereafter editors have typically chosen one of the two as the received text, displaying the other's readings as variants. The consensus nowadays is that *Laon and Cythna* demands primacy of attention as conforming to Shelley's unconstrained aims, *The Revolt of Islam* issuing from a set of circumstances so exceptionally coercive as to deny it both integrity and authority.

The day after he finished drafting *Laon and Cythna* Shelley wrote to Byron of the new poem: 'It is in the style and for the same object as "Queen Mab", but interwoven with a story of human passion, and composed with more attention to the refinement and accuracy of language, and the connexion of its parts' (*Letters: PBS* I, 557). So far as it goes, this is a fair estimate of the relation between the earlier and the later poem. Instead of the sustained scene of education that is *Queen Mab*, in *Laon and Cythna* Shelley constructs an intricate narrative drawing largely on the European romance tradition that runs from the late medieval Italian poems of Ariosto and Tasso through Spenser's *Faerie Queene* to Southey's *Thalaba the Destroyer* (1801) and *The Curse of Kehama* (1810). Strategically interspersed through the episodes are briefer scenes of instruction delivered in different

---

[26] For contemporary reviews see White, *Unextinguished Hearth*, 117–50; the two quotations in this paragraph are on pp. 134, 133.

voices. The intention is to mitigate what in the Dedication to *The Cenci* Shelley qualifies as 'the presumptuous attitude of an instructor', in a clear reference to both *Queen Mab* and *Laon and Cythna* (*Longman*, 2, 726). Freedom and equality remain central concerns as do the chief obstacles to their realization, those political and religious institutions so vehemently castigated in *Queen Mab*; so does Shelley's enduring conviction that an enlightened understanding of both must inform the will to a liberating revolution.

There are important additions and shifts of emphasis, however, which arise from Shelley's altered conception of the scope and function of poetry on grand public themes in the five years since 1812. In the first place religion is treated with a circumspection absent from *Queen Mab*. Not that *Laon and Cythna* is without exhibitions of hostility in this regard—witness the judicial execution of the two title characters, at the behest of a zealous Christian priest, which develops with increase of lurid detail the episode of the atheist's burning in *Queen Mab* (VII, 1–13). But a comparison of the attack on institutional religion in cantos VI and VII of *Queen Mab* with Cythna's long speech in canto VIII (3244–396) of *Laon and Cythna* on the implicated interests of religion, money, and power reveals a decided muting of the aggressive and accusatory in favour of a broader critique appealing to human reason and sympathy. Beyond this general toning-down, Shelley strategically places scenes of mythic scope and power which aim to supply the religious dimension traditional in epic by conspicuously revising received biblical originals. His aim is both to focus the poem's ironic and critical dimension and to quicken its imaginative appeal. The two most important of these scenes, although they appear in the introductory first canto, were composed after cantos II–XII were completed, with the evident purpose of furnishing the narrative of revolution with both a cosmic and an affective rationale.

In the first scene the narrator's supernatural instructor reveals that at the formation of the universe the first human being was confronted with a spectacular manifestation of the divided empire of the world:

> Lo! afar
> O'er the wide wild abyss two meteors shone,
> Sprung from the depth of its tempestuous jar:
> A blood-red Comet and the Morning Star
> Mingling their beams in combat—as he stood,
> All thoughts within his mind waged mutual war,
> In dreadful sympathy—when to the flood
> That fair Star fell, he turned and shed his brother's blood.
>
> (353–60)

The cosmogony and theogony here recalled, in which conflict emerges simultaneously with the primeval natural order, Shelley means to be set over against the creation of the world as uniformly good in the first chapter of *Genesis*. In the Bible discord is introduced (and human guilt perpetuated) only when the serpent successfully tempts Adam and Eve; in *Laon and Cythna* the original sin, evidently a version of the murder of Abel by Cain, is re-imagined as violence towards another rather than disobedience to the divine creator's command. Its continuing effect in human affairs corresponds within the human sphere to the elemental opposition of benign and malign forces present in nature since its foundation. Such an account of origins reduces the poem's theological design to a minimum and anchors it in the thought of French Enlightenment mythographers like Holbach and Volney who traced the birth of the religious impulse to the primal human experience of nature's creative and destructive powers. Shelley returns to this primordial confrontation of man and nature in order to define a radically purified religious idea which is prior to theological obfuscation, sectarian strife, and the fraudulent alliance between institutional religion and political power.[27]

The second strategic revision of biblical narrative in canto I recalls both a familiar incident from the New Testament and its earlier use in *Queen Mab*. Ianthe was singled out to receive her revelation because of pre-eminent virtue, inviting an analogy with the Virgin Mary who was 'highly favoured' and 'blessed among women' in the account of the Annunciation in Luke 1: 26–38. For her part, the woman who educates the narrator in *Laon and Cythna* recounts how her own simultaneous awakening to sexual desire and elation at the commencement of the French Revolution had left her in a state of high excitement. She is laid asleep and dreams of a supernatural lover who delivers a message contrasting radically with both the biblical prototype and Mab's address to Ianthe: 'a Spirit loves thee, mortal maiden, | How wilt thou prove thy worth?' (505–6). The dream enters her psyche as a directing awareness which leads her to a city, manifestly revolutionary Paris, from which she returns, disappointed but not despairing, endowed with those prophetic powers which she now exercises for the narrator's benefit. The trinity composed of her supernatural lover, Venus as the morning star, and the Spirit of Good emerges in the course of the unfolding narrative as so many manifestations of a single divine being. Such a nexus affirms the essential connection between an animating erotic force, the human impulse to freedom, and the defining event of recent history—the French Revolution, which in this mythic context is exhibited as the latest expression of a force for good which has been inherent in the world since its emergence from chaos.

By frankly linking cosmic, sexual, and revolutionary energy and grounding the alliance in such revisionary parables Shelley invests *Laon and Cythna* with its peculiar originality. This bold and very risky procedure allows him to engage pertinently with two areas of experience that are notably underrepresented in *Queen Mab*. For one, the earlier poem seems deliberately to restrain its potential for erotic development. The Dedication to Harriet Shelley evokes love essentially as incitement to virtue and philanthropy, while the devoted watch over Ianthe by her lover Henry at the poem's close is a solicitude that shades into veneration of a saint. A conventional evocation of the lover's delight in his beloved (VIII, 31–40) is followed by one of the poem's central assertions, the absolute independence of erotic love from the 'fetters of tyrannic law' (IX, 79)—but this is concluded in no more than sixteen lines (IX, 76–92). *Laon and Cythna* can be regarded as both elaboration and testing of that assertion through an intricate narrative that encompasses a range of erotic situations and circumstances including the transgressive, the disruptive, the obsessive, and the tragic. Shelley's Preface declares that in his poem 'love

---

[27] *Longman*, 2, 22–6.

is celebrated everywhere as the sole law which should govern the moral world' (*Longman*, 2, 47), intending this first principle to find its definitive instance in the love, which extends to sexual intimacy, of the brother and sister of the title. Principle and illustration were on his part equally acts of defiance in view of the rumours then circulating of a 'league of incest' which imputed promiscuous sexual exchanges to the group formed by Byron, Shelley, Mary Godwin, and her stepsister Claire Clairmont.[28] But the seminal importance of the erotic narrative of *Laon and Cythna* lies elsewhere, in its implication with the narrative of revolution. Although the actions of the poem, set in modern Greece, are clearly offered as fictional, Shelley's Preface as well as numerous details in the poem unequivocally recommend as example to the future an idealized version of the French Revolution, an event on which his silence in *Queen Mab* is conspicuous. That ambition in part explains its hostile reception, appearing as it did not three years after the Battle of Waterloo. Moreover, its complex and sometimes abstruse narrative makes serious demands on its readers' attention, and like all long poems it is not without its *longueurs*. But it also marks the decisive entry into Shelley's poetry of one of its leading themes, which he critically re-examines in various forms to the end of his career: to be fully realized, the mental and material liberation promised by the revolutionary age that had begun must incorporate an understanding of sexuality in all its amplitude and variety.

Select Bibliography

Baker, Carlos. *Shelley's Major Poetry: The Fabric of a Vision*. London: Oxford UP, 1948.

Butler, Marilyn. 'Shelley and the Empire in the East'. *Shelley: Poet and Legislator of the World*. Ed. Betty T. Bennett and Stuart Curran. Baltimore: Johns Hopkins UP, 1996. 158–68.

Cameron, Kenneth Neill. *The Young Shelley: Genesis of a Radical*. London: Victor Gollanz, 1951; repr. 1962.

Curran, Stuart. *Shelley's Annus Mirabilis: The Maturing of an Epic Vision*. San Marino, CA: Huntington Library, 1975.

—— *Poetic Form and British Romanticism*. Oxford: Oxford UP, 1986.

Donovan, Jack. 'Incest in *Laon and Cythna*: Nature, Custom, Desire', *Keats–Shelley Review* 2 (1987), 49–90.

—— 'The Storyteller'. *The Cambridge Companion to Shelley*. Ed. Timothy Morton. Cambridge: Cambridge UP, 2006.

Duff, David. *Romance and Revolution: Shelley and the Politics of a Genre*. Cambridge, Cambridge UP, 1994.

—— *Romanticism and the Uses of Genre*. Oxford: Oxford UP, 2009.

Kucich, Greg. *Keats, Shelley, and Romantic Spenserianism*. University Park, PA: Pennsylvania State UP, 1991.

Sperry, Stuart M. *Shelley's Major Verse: The Narrative and Dramatic Poetry*. Cambridge, MA: Harvard UP, 1988.

Wilkie, Brian. *Romantic Poets and Epic Tradition*. Madison: University of Wisconsin Press, 1965.

[28] *Longman*, 2, 47.

CHAPTER 17

....

QUEST POETRY

Alastor *and* Epipsychidion

....

MARK SANDY

SHELLEY'S quest poetry has been praised for its literary and mythical resonance, psychological depth, philosophical sophistication, formal complexity, historical significance, sexual politics, and deconstructive potential.[1] This chapter explores Shelley's poetics of desire at the heart of his re-imagining of romance. With its visionary interiority, *Epipsychidion* brings into sharp focus Shelley's transformation of the romance genre with its central motif, the quest.[2] Shaped by a narrating consciousness that no longer feigns a connection with the world outside, the poem illustrates the degree to which the earlier complexities addressed in *Alastor*—described by Shelley as 'allegorical of one of the most interesting situations of the human mind'[3]—exerted a constant pressure on his imagination. Both *Alastor* and *Epipsychidion* explore the quest of the human mind and heart for a mysterious power manifest in the physical world, the inherent dangers of pursuing such ideals, and the inadequacies of poetic language. Inextricably bound to Shelley's poetics of desire is an internalization of the romance quest that opens up this literary form into an endless series of creative possibilities that are, according to Harold

---

[1] For representative studies of these approaches see Harold Bloom, *Shelley's Mythmaking* (1959; Ithaca, NY: Cornell UP, 1969); Earl R. Wasserman, *Shelley: A Critical Reading* (Baltimore: Johns Hopkins UP, 1971); William Keach, *Shelley's Style* (London: Methuen, 1984); Michael O'Neill, *The Human Mind's Imaginings: Conflict and Achievement in Shelley's Poetry* (Oxford: Clarendon, 1989); William A. Ulmer, *Shelleyan Eros: The Rhetoric of Romantic Love* (Princeton: Princeton UP, 1990); Barbara Charlesworth Gelpi, *Shelley's Goddess: Maternity, Language, Subjectivity* (Oxford: Oxford UP, 1992); and Tilottama Rajan, *Dark Interpreter: The Discourse of Romanticism* (Ithaca, NY: Cornell UP, 1980).

[2] *Epipsychidion* and *Adonais* mark a re-engagement with the earlier interiority of *Alastor*. See David Duff, *Romance and Revolution: Shelley and the Politics of a Genre* (Cambridge: Cambridge UP, 1994), 2.

[3] Preface to *Alastor* in Donald H. Reiman and Neil Fraistat (eds.), *Shelley's Poetry and Prose: Authoritative Texts*, 2nd edn. (New York: Norton, 2002), 72. All quotations from this edition. Hereafter *Norton 2*.

Bloom, as difficult to define as the nature of love. Like love itself, romance, resisting the immediate claims of the present, exists forever in potential and gestures towards what it yet might become.[4]

In the summer of 1818, Shelley's own response to the question 'what is Love?' in the fragmentary essay *On Love* defines love as a sympathetic yearning which reaches out of, and beyond, ourselves, commingling the material with the immaterial, so that 'another's nerves should vibrate to our own, that the beams of their eyes should kindle at once and mix and melt into our own' (*Norton 2*, 503) Anticipating W. B. Yeats,[5] Shelley elaborates his conception of love into a continual quest for an 'antitype' and anticipated discovery of:

> [...] an imagination which should enter into and seize upon the subtle and delicate peculiarities, which we have delighted to cherish and unfold in secret, with a frame whose nerves, like the chords of two exquisite lyres strung to the accompaniment of one delightful voice, vibrate with the vibrations of our own; and of a combination of all these in such proportion as the type within demands: this is the invisible and unattainable point to which Love tends; and to attain which it urges forth the powers of man to arrest the faintest shadow of that without the possession of which there is no rest or respite to the heart over which it rules. (*Norton 2*, 504)

Adapting Coleridge's harmonious image of the mysterious, barely discernible, organic operations of the Æolian harp, Shelley finds an analogy for how love unfurls itself and 'tends' towards its own 'invisible and unattainable point'. Writing several years later, in *A Defence of Poetry*, Shelley reaffirms this comparison between 'a corresponding antit-ype'—with its modulating echo of an initial 'impression'—and the Æolian 'lyre [which] trembles and sounds after the wind has died away' (*Norton 2*, 511). *On Love* looks back to the autumn and winter of 1815, when Shelley wrote, in *Alastor*, about a poet-figure who 'images to himself the Being whom he loves' and hastens his demise through questing 'in vain for a prototype of his conception' (Preface, *Norton 2*, 73).

Beyond these thematic and verbal echoes of *Alastor*'s preface, Shelley's definition of love and its 'corresponding antitype' is a reminder both of the promised soothing power in *Epipsychidion* of 'A lute, which those whom love has taught to play' (65) and of the less positive imagery of the lyre framing the events of *Alastor*.[6] By the conclusion of the latter poem's proem (ll. 1–49), the narrator's account of his quest to discover nature's 'deep mysteries' (23) leaves only a sense of abandonment and desolation:

> [...] As a long-forgotten lyre
> Suspended in the solitary dome [...]
> I wait thy breath, Great Parent, that my strain
> May modulate with murmurs of the air,

[4] Harold Bloom, *The Ringers in the Tower: Studies in Romantic Tradition* (Chicago: University of Chicago Press, 1971), 34–5.

[5] See Michael O'Neill, *The All-Sustaining Air: Romantic Legacies and Renewals in British, American and Irish Poetry since 1900* (Oxford: Oxford UP, 2007), 42–3.

[6] On the lyre imagery as transgressive see Timothy Morton, 'Nature and Culture', in Timothy Morton (ed.), *Cambridge Companion to Shelley* (Cambridge: Cambridge UP, 2006), 190, 185–207.

And motions of the forests and the sea,
And voice of living beings, and woven hymns
Of night and day, and the deep heart of man.

(42–9)

Spoken by a narrator in Wordsworthian vein, *Alastor*'s proem outlines the narrator's love of nature and sceptical search, founded on a 'dark hope' (32), for a power within the natural world that will 'render up the tale | Of what we are' (27–8). Infused with the language of Wordsworth's commitment to nature, the appeal of Shelley's narrator to the 'Earth, ocean, air, beloved brotherhood!' (1) revises and qualifies Wordsworth's belief in the elemental trinity 'Of something far more deeply interfused | Whose dwelling is the light of setting suns | And the round ocean and the living air'.[7] Hopeful faith in the revelatory power of nature, enabling us, as Wordsworth assures, 'to see into the life of things' ('Tintern Abbey', 49), gives way in the hands of Shelley's narrator to a darker realization that such revelation is merely an 'incommunicable dream' (*Alastor*, 39). The narrator's sense of failed vision and abandonment by the force of nature finds a subsequent reiteration in the description of the broken body of the poet-figure, a description which recalls the narrator's image of himself as a 'long-forgotten lyre':[8]

A fragile lute, on whose harmonious strings
The breath of heaven did wander—a bright stream
Once fed with many-voiced waves—a dream
Of youth, which night and time have quenched for ever,
Still, dark, and dry, and unremembered now.

(667–71)

This deliberate echoing of the bereft Æolian harp, as an earlier image of failed quest and lost inspiration, suggests that Shelley's narrator and poet-figure are mutually implicated. Raised by Shelley's imagistic doubling in *Alastor*, questions over the precise nature of the relationship between the narrator and poet-figure have been much debated by critics. Focusing on the Greek meaning of *alastor* as 'evil genius' and the poem's subtitle, 'The Spirit of Solitude', early critics read Shelley as unequivocally condemning Wordsworth's emphasis on the solitary and argued that the poet-figure's actions were morally culpable, as his self-seclusion becomes his own curse in the form of an avenging spirit.[9] More intricate accounts of Shelley's anti-Wordsworthian stance, advocated by Earl R. Wasserman and Karen A. Weisman, have stressed the dichotomy between *Alastor*'s narrator and the questing poet-figure to advance a dialectical understanding of the interplay between scepticism and idealism in the poem.[10] Other recent critics, including

[7] William Wordsworth, in *William Wordsworth: The Major Works*, ed. Stephen Gill (1984; Oxford: Oxford UP, 2000), 'Lines Written a Few Miles above Tintern Abbey', 97–9.
[8] See Rajan, *Dark Interpreter*, 82.
[9] For these earlier readings see Carlos Baker, *Shelley's Major Poetry: The Fabric of a Vision* (London: Oxford UP, 1948), 41–60.
[10] See Wasserman, *Shelley: A Critical Reading*, 18–34, 41 and Karen A. Weisman, *Imageless Truths: Shelley's Poetic Fictions* (Philadelphia: University of Pennsylvania Press, 1994), 27, 38.

Tilottama Rajan and Timothy Clark, have questioned these dialectical readings of the relationship between Shelley's narrator and poet-figure, arguing that they act as mutual analogues of one another. For me, these mirrored sympathies between the narrator's opening dedication and the poem's main narrative enable and underscore *Alastor's* self-reflexive interrogation of a Wordsworthian mode of recollection.[11]

Shelley's portrayal of the narrator, as a sceptical or even failed Wordsworthian poet, shares an affinity with the final fate of the questing poet-figure, whose 'blood | [...] ever beat in mystic sympathy | With nature's ebb and flow' (651–3). The quests of both poet-figure and narrator end up resembling an incommunicable 'dream | Of youth' (38–9). Reminiscent of the narrator's solipsistic watching of nature's 'shadow, and the darkness of thy steps' (21), Shelley's poet-figure pursues 'the bright shadow of that lovely dream' (233) to the perilous exclusion of all else. Both the narrator and the poet-figure exemplify the ardent inward drive for an 'antitype' which, as Shelley identifies in *On Love*, 'urges forth the powers of man to arrest the faintest shadow' (*Norton 2*, 504) or trace of this elusive other wherever its presence is manifest.

This personal, emotional, and poetic quest for the manifestation of love in the world is recorded by the autobiographical narrative of *Epipsychidion*, recognized by Shelley, in a letter to John Gisborne, as 'an idealized history of my life and feelings'.[12] As is the case for *Alastor*, Shelley's chosen title for his poeticized autobiography is the cause of much critical speculation and *Epipsychidion* has been taken by a variety of commentators to mean 'On the Subject of the Soul', 'soul within the soul', 'upon a little soul', and, in conjunction with *epithalamion*, as 'a song about a wedding'.[13] Supposedly written between December 1820 and 16 February 1821, *Epipsychidion* has been understood as occasioned by Shelley's introduction to the 19-year-old Countessa Teresa Viviani, daughter of Count Niccolò Viviani. Teresa, now eligible for marriage, had been placed by her father in customary confinement at the Covent of St Anna, in Pisa, whilst he sought to make her a suitable marital match. Undoubtedly, such impulsive feelings governed the poem's finalized published form but, as recent critics, most notably Nancy Moore Goslee and Tatsuo Tokoo, have shown, some of the fragments, commonly associated with *Epipsychidion*, pre-date Shelley's meeting with Teresa by as much as a year.[14] That Shelley's infatuation with Teresa's beauty and unfortunate circumstances was fleeting is evident by the spring of 1821, when he commented to his publisher, Charles Ollier, that *Epipsychidion's*

---

[11] Tilottama Rajan, *Dark Interpreter*, 76–8. Timothy Clark, *Embodying Revolution: The Figure of the Poet in Shelley* (Oxford: Clarendon, 1989), 137–42. See Vincent Newey, 'Shelley's "Dream of Youth": *Alastor*, "Selving" and the Psychic Realm', in Kelvin Everest (ed.), *Percy Bysshe Shelley: Bicentenary Readings*, Essays and Studies 45 (Cambridge: Brewer, 1992), 1–23. O'Neill, *The Human Mind's Imaginings*, 11–29. See also my *Poetics of Self and Form in Keats and Shelley: Nietzschean Subjectivity and Genre* (Aldershot: Ashgate, 2005), 34.

[12] *The Letters of Percy Bysshe Shelley*, ed. Frederick L. Jones (Oxford: Clarendon, 1964), II, 434. Subsequent quotations from this edition. Hereafter *Letters: PBS*.

[13] See Wasserman, *Shelley: A Critical Reading*, 418–20.

[14] See Nancy Moore Goslee, 'Dispersoning Emily: Draft as Plot in *Epipsychidion*', Norton 2, and Tatsuo Tokoo, 'The Composition of "Epipsychidion": Some Manuscript Evidence', *Keats–Shelley Journal* 42 (1993), Special Issue Bicentenary Tribute to the Achievement of Percy Bysshe Shelley, 97–103.

'advertisement is no fiction' because it is 'a production of a portion of me already dead' (*Letters: PBS* II, 262–3). No matter how short-lived, the intensity of personal feelings and emotions behind the poem's cosmological tropes and figures can be estimated from Shelley's request to Ollier to publish the poem anonymously in London, 1821.

In the cosmic poetics of *Epipsychidion*, Teresa Viviani is transformed into the ideal-ized figure of Emilia or 'Emily', a name indebted to Boccaccio's *Teseida*[15] and adopted for her by the Shelleys, symbolized as the sun. Shelley, represented in the poem as the earth, reflects on his complex emotional life and love for Mary Shelley, depicted as the moon, and Claire Clairmont, signified as a comet. In part these complex, and complicating, patterns of cosmic imagery in *Epipsychidion* play out Shelley's triangulated desire and divided affections for these three women.[16] Imaginatively drawing on the Old Testament's Song of Solomon and Dante's celebration of love's eternal constancy in *Vita nuova* and *Convivio*,[17] as the advertisement published with the poem makes clear, Shelley's allego-rizing mode and poetic enquiry within *Epipsychidion* extend beyond speculating about the spiritual alone to an intermingling of the spiritual and material. At the outset, Shelley's invocation outlines the poet's relationship with Emily and melds eternal spirit with physical decay, immaterial soul with material body, and mind with matter:

> [...] the brightness
> Of her divinest presence trembles through
> Her limbs, as underneath a cloud of dew
> Embodied in the windless Heaven of June
> Amid the splendour-winged stars, the Moon
> Burns, inextinguishably beautiful [...]
> In her mild lights the starry spirits dance,
> The sun-beams of those wells which ever leap
> Under the lightnings of the soul—too deep
> For the brief fathom-line of thought or sense.
>
> (77–81; 87–90)

Here Shelley's allegorical depiction of Emilia as Emily, whose 'divinest presence trem-bles through | Her limbs', achieves a coalescence of incorporeal spirit and physical embodiment. According to Shelley's retrospective and allegorized account of their first historical meeting, Emily's mercurial form exists as a 'shade | Of unentangled intermix-ture, made | By Love, of light and motion' (92–3) on the very edge of 'thought or sense' (90). This paradoxical account of Emily's presence as a 'motion which may change but cannot die' (114) echoes Shelley's description of the poet-figure's inspirational 'bright

[15] See *Norton 2*, 390.

[16] See Newman Ivey White, *Shelley*, vol. II (London: Secker, 1947), 259–69 and Kenneth Neill Cameron, *Shelley: The Golden Years* (Cambridge, MA: Harvard UP, 1974), 275–88; Richard Holmes, *Shelley: The Pursuit* (1974; Harmondsworth: Penguin, 1987), 633–5; and Ann Wroe, *Being Shelley: The Poet's Search for Himself* (London: Cape, 2007), 82–3; 367–8. See also Stuart M. Sperry, *Shelley's Major Verse: Narrative and Dramatic Poetry* (Cambridge, MA: Harvard UP, 1988), n. 1, 220–1.

[17] For Dante's influence on Shelley see Alan M. Weinberg, *Shelley's Italian Experience* (London: Macmillan, 1991), 135–72.

silver dream' (67) and his unsettling faded vision of the 'veiled maid' (151) in *Alastor*. The next line of *Epipsychidion* evokes again the poetic diction of *Alastor* as it compares Shelley's primary encounter with the trembling, changing, eternal, diffuse, and all-pervasive presence of 'Emily' to an enticing and elusive 'shadow of some golden dream' (116). Emily's form, for all her immediacy, erotic presence, and contradictory power, threatens to evade—as does the visionary 'fleeting shade' (206) of *Alastor* with 'her glowing limbs beneath the sinuous veil' (176)—the present and resist an adequate definition in language.[18] Shelley guards against this appeal of past vision with a present-tense testimony to Emily's commingled presence: 'See where she stands! a mortal shape indued | With love and life and light and deity' (112–13).[19]

When Shelley's invocation of Emily as a physical manifestation of divine light melts into a meditation on the nature of true love, *Epipsychidion* is marked by an increasing self-consciousness about the creative pressure under which the poetry operates to generate these serial images and this anxiety shows in the poet's own questioning of his imaginative quest and purpose: 'What have I dared? where am I lifted? how | Shall I descend, and perish not?' (124–5). This self-conscious creative crisis prefigures Shelley's presentation of Emily as 'A Metaphor of Spring and Youth and Morning; | A Vision like incarnate April' (120–1), an image which discloses the poetry's mounting self-awareness of its own poetic workings. *Epipsychidion* responds to this potential representational crisis through a succession of images in a bid to recapture and re-inscribe Emily's 'divinest presence' (78) by amassing evanescent imagery of a 'windless Heaven of June' (80), 'the splendour-winged stars' (81), and even 'the sun-beams of those wells which ever leap | Under the lightnings of the soul' (88–9). Growing out of these numerous images, Shelley's meditation on the nature of love culminates in a simile, binding pure emotion to a revelatory light:

> Love is like understanding, that grows bright,
> Gazing on many truths; 'tis like thy light,
> Imagination! Which from earth and sky,
> And from the depths of human phantasy,
> As from a thousand prisms and mirrors, fills
> The Universe with glorious beams, and kills
> Error, the worm, with many a sun-like arrow
> Of its reverberated lightning.
>
> (162–9)

Derived from the physicality of the 'earth', intangibility of the 'sky', and partaking of the illuminating light of poetic consciousness, 'True love' is an elemental presence in the universe which in kind 'differs from gold and clay' (160). Love's light acts as both a benign gaze turned towards those interior and exterior 'many truths' and a belligerent assailant (armed with an incandescent arsenal of 'reverberated lightning') of serpentine 'Error'. These powerful 'glorious beams' of love irradiate outwards into the world

---

[18] See Sperry, *Shelley's Major Verse*, 164–9 and Bloom, *The Ringers in the Tower*, 50, 50–2.
[19] See O'Neill, *The Human Mind's Imaginings*, 164–6.

(refracted by 'a thousand prisms') and inwards to the very 'depths' of our being (multiply reflected by 'a thousand [...] mirrors').[20] These myriad refractions, reflections, and intensifications of these 'beams' of love, operating externally and internally, find a compelling counterpart in Shelley's account of how love functions as 'a mirror whose surface reflects only the forms of purity and brightness: a soul within a soul that describes a circle around its proper Paradise which pain and sorrow or evil dare not overleap' (*On Love, Norton* 2, 504).[21]

Shelley's description of this sympathetic, arguably self-projected mirroring of vibrations finds poetic expression in the central passage of *Alastor* concerned with the poet-figure's instance of vision when:

> He dreamed a veiled maid
> Sate near him, talking in low solemn tones.
> Her voice was like the voice of his own soul
> Heard in the calm of thought [...]
>
> (151–4)[22]

Subsequent loss of vision leaves the poet-figure bereft and determined, like the speaker of *Epipsychidion*, to recapture the absent-presence of 'That beautiful shape' (*Alastor, Norton* 2, 211). Shelley's poet-figure embarks upon a dizzying quest transgressing, as indicated by a further allusion to *Paradise Lost* (IV. 179–83), the limits of the earth, mind, time, space, and life, when 'He eagerly pursues | Beyond the realms of dream that fleeting shade; | He overleaps the bounds' (205–7). The 'visioned wanderings' (191) later recounted in *Epipsychidion* occupy a similar transgressive space of sexual desire central to the tragic tale of the poet-figure in *Alastor*. Shelley's reworking of failed transgression in *Alastor* into a poetic, emotional, and sexual triumph within *Epipsychidion* is evident in his description of 'true love never yet | Was thus constrained: it overleaps all fence' (397–8). Shelley's words again unmistakably echo Milton's account of Satan's treacherous breach of the boundaries of Paradise and hint at the possibility of the poem's own imaginative self-deception.[23]

In *Epipsychidion*, Shelley's invocation of, and address to, the figure of the one true Emily provides a prelude to an 'idealized history' of the poet's life and sensibilities unfolding, according to a biographical sequence, as Sperry, Wasserman, and other critics have noted,[24] already rehearsed in *Alastor* (67–106) and 'Hymn to Intellectual

---

[20] See O'Neill, *The Human Mind's Imaginings*, 167.

[21] See Barbara Charlesworth Gelpi, 'Keeping Faith with Desire: A Reading of *Epipsychidion*', in Timothy Clark and Jerrold E. Hogle (eds.), *Evaluating Shelley* (Edinburgh: Edinburgh UP, 1996), 188, 180–95. See Jerrold E. Hogle, *Shelley's Process: Radical Transference and the Development of his Work* (Oxford: Oxford UP, 1988), 281–2.

[22] See Keach, *Shelley's Style*, 61. For an alternative view, see O'Neill, *The Human Mind's Imaginings*, 18–19. See also Sally West, *Coleridge and Shelley: Textual Engagement* (Aldershot: Ashgate, 2007), 68.

[23] Stuart Peterfreund, *Shelley among Others: The Play of the Intertext and the Idea of Language* (Baltimore: Johns Hopkins UP, 2002), 277–8.

[24] See Sperry, *Shelley's Major Verse*, 168–9; Wasserman, *Shelley: A Critical Reading*, 432; Keach, *Shelley's Style*, 205; and Peterfreund, *Shelley among Others*, 275–6.

Beauty' (49–73). A familiar pattern is discernible in Shelley's symbolic record of his youthful encounter, in *Epipsychidion*, with a female 'Spirit [that] was the harmony of truth' (216):

> There was a Being whom my spirit oft
> Met on its visioned wanderings, far aloft,
> In the clear golden prime of my youth's dawn,
> Upon the fairy isles of sunny lawn,
> Amid the enchanted mountains, and the caves
> Of divine sleep, and the air-like waves
> Of wonder-level dream, whose tremulous floor
> Paved her light steps [...]
>
> (190–7)

Typically, this idealized biography of the poet begins in the revelatory mode of visionary dream ('divine sleep') and with a sense of connection between the self and all that is spiritually and intellectually beautiful and good in the universe. Such vision, inevitably, ends with a waking, troubled, consciousness that embarks upon a potentially fatal quest to recapture the ideal figure of lost vision in 'one form resembling hers, | In which she might have masked herself from me' (254–5). Playing out a similar predicament, the poet-figure's unquenchable desire for knowledge of the 'sacred past' (73), in *Alastor*, is a product of his highly individuated consciousness that separates him from both his fellow beings and the material universe. His quest for self-knowledge becomes a search for meaning across time and space amongst the ruins of civilization (109–15) which, finally, through the contemplation of 'mute thoughts on the mute walls around' (120) and 'speechless shapes' (123), reveals 'The thrilling secrets of the birth of time' (128). Through uncovering the origins of time itself and translating the hieroglyphs, the poet-figure emerges as a consciousness more far-seeing than the poem's narrator, who is incapable of deciphering those hieroglyphics or the 'thrilling secrets of time'.[25] At the same time, the narrator may confer upon the poet-figure a displaced and compensating capacity for vision. Restoring significance to these 'speechless shapes' causes the poet-figure to acknowledge an incongruity between meaning and language and increases his own anxiety that reality will never match those idealized visions of his adolescence.

Recollecting Wordsworth's 'fled visionary gleam' ('Ode: Intimations of Immortality', 56), *Epipsychidion*'s account of the passage from childhood to adulthood reveals an equally painful process of individuation which irrevocably separates the poet-speaker from the once all-pervasive presence of the Spirit of his dream-vision. Growing up only teaches the idealized and idealizing poet his limitations. A mortal 'man with mighty loss dismayed' (229), he is unable to track the flight of his visionary Spirit, as she departs 'like a God throned on a winged planet [...] | Into the dreary cone of our life's shade' (226, 228). As the poet-speaker attests:

---

[25] See Ronald Tetreault, *The Poetry of Life: Shelley and Literary Form* (Toronto: University of Toronto Press, 1987), 51.

> I would have followed, though the grave between
> Yawned like a gulph whose spectres are unseen:
> When a voice said:—'O Thou of hearts the weakest,
> The phantom is beside thee whom thou seekest.'
> Then I—'where?'—the world's echo answered 'where!'
>
> (229–33)

Shelley's final line draws to itself resonances from the ill-fated mythological relationship of Echo and Narcissus in order to capture the mutual self-reflections, absorptions, projections, and identifications that it suggests are inseparable from love itself and from the emotional quest, in *On Love*, for the self-identical 'one delightful voice' that can 'vibrate with the vibrations of our own' and is a 'soul within our soul' (*Norton* 2, 504), or, as in *Epipsychidion*, for the absent 'fled [...] soul out of my soul' (238). That the natural world only echoes the poet-speaker's questioning 'where?' tragically indicates that the Spirit, whose 'voice had come to [him] through the whispering woods' (201), has withdrawn from the physical world and abandoned him amidst a Dantean 'wintry forest of our life' (249).[26] These desperate circumstances of the forlorn visionary recall Shelley's portrayal of the poet-figure's predicament, in *Alastor*, as 'he started from his trance' (192) to discover that:

> The cold white light of morning, the blue moon
> Low in the west, the clear and garish hills,
> The distinct valley and the vacant woods,
> Spread round him where he stood. Whither have fled
> The hues of heaven that canopied his bower
> Of yesternight? The sounds that soothed his sleep,
> The mystery and the majesty of Earth,
> The joy, the exultation? His wan eyes
> Gaze on the empty scene as vacantly
> As ocean's moon looks on the moon in heaven.
>
> (192–202)

Whereas in 'his infancy' the poet-figure had delighted in 'Every sight | And sound from the vast earth and ambient air' (68–9), his present situation leaves him with a series of questions unanswered by the natural world comprised entirely of 'the vacant woods' and 'empty scene'. Later the poet-figure's sighting of a swan 'Scaling the upward sky' (278) reminds him of the airy transcendental heights to which he aspires as well as his own alienated state and human limitations. Disturbed by the presence of this 'Beautiful bird', the poet-figure questions why he 'should linger here' (281, 285) amidst the 'deaf air' and 'blind earth, and heaven | That echoes not my thoughts?' (289–90).[27] Unlike the poet-speaker in *Epipsychidion*, the poet-figure does not receive the faintest echo in response to his heartfelt questionings. Shelley's comparison in *Alastor* of the poet-figure's 'wan eyes' with the 'vacantly' watery reflection of the 'ocean's moon' looking 'on the moon in heaven' conflates observing subject with perceived object, confusing a sense of whether

---

[26] The 'gloomy wood' (*selva oscura*) is in Dante, *Inferno*, 1. 2.

[27] See Richard Cronin, *Shelley's Poetic Thoughts* (London: Macmillan, 1981), 84–94.

the moon mirrored in the sea is either a projection of, or distinct entity from, the moon in the night sky. Pointing to the dangers of self-absorption behind the myth of Echo and Narcissus, the 'ocean's moon' is a mirrored version of the moon's own reflection of light from the sun and neither the moon itself nor its reflected image is a source of light.[28]

By implication the reflected image of the moon and the actual moon gaze 'vacantly' back at one another as the vacant poet looks upon the vacancy of nature. Such vacancy may either originate in a self-projection of the poet-figure's own 'vacant' gazing or register a real change in the material world. Whether this irrevocable change has occurred internally or externally, the poet-figure's subsequent desire (*eros*) to revive his vision of the 'beautiful shape' (211) is bound up with a self-destructive death-drive (*thanatos*).[29] Deprived of his visionary maiden, the natural world no longer speaks to the poet-figure of the idealized joys of youth and becomes a constant reminder of the fragility of human existence and the inevitability of death. The poet-figure's dejected state causes him to represent the surrounding ordinary world through a negative poetic language that points directly back to his acute sense of loss and unfulfilled vision.[30] Even the iridescent reflection of a rainbow amidst cloudy skies is imaged by the poet-figure as its own negation and transformed into a symbol of desperation and death:

> Does the bright arch of rainbow clouds,
> And pendent mountains seen in the calm lake,
> Lead only to a black and watery depth […]
>
> (213–15)

Desire and death are also identified by *Epipsychidion* as fused together after the feminine 'Spirit' (216) of the poet-speaker's vision has abandoned the world to leave him only with the trace of 'The shadow of that idol of my thought' (268). Whether the poet-speaker's action of springing 'from the caverns of my dreamy youth' (217) is the cause of, or response to, his visionary abandonment is ambiguous; what is more definite is that his 'flight' (220) 'towards the loadstar of [his] one desire' (219) is, at worst, as futile as 'a dead leaf's in the owlet light' (221) and, at best, a destructive ascent to 'a radiant death' (223).

As in *Alastor*, the poet-speaker of *Epipsychidion* embarks on a desperate quest for a sign that his absent vision is incarnate amongst 'the many mortal forms' (267); he searches in vain to discover that 'some were fair—but beauty dies away: | Others were wise—but honeyed words betray: | And One was true—oh! why not true to me?' (269–71). What emerges from the poet-speaker's quest is a common Shelleyan division between the 'One' and the 'many'—formulated later in *Adonais* as 'The One remains, the many change and pass' (460)—and a distinction woven into Shelley's scathing attack on monogamy as 'that great sect, | Whose doctrine is, that each one should select | Out of

---

[28] Sperry notes this allusion in *Shelley's Major Verse*, 31.
[29] See Hogle, *Shelley's Process*, 53–7 and Peterfreund, *Shelley among Others*, 284–5.
[30] See my *Poetics of Self and Form*, 39, 36–44 and Rajan, *Dark Interpreter*, 78, 76–8.

the crowd a mistress or a friend' (149–51),[31] as well as into the fabric of the poet-speaker's visionary quest in *Epipsychidion*:

> If I could find one form resembling hers,
> In which she might have masked herself from me.
> There,—One, whose voice was venomed melody
> Sate by a well, under blue night-shade bowers;
> The breath of her false mouth was like faint flowers,
> Her touch was as electric poison,—flame
> Out of her looks into my vitals came,
> And from her living cheeks and bosom flew
> A killing air, which pierced like honey-dew,
> Into the core of my green heart […]
>
> (254–63)

Shelley's description of this false 'One' conveys an energy of sexual awakening, corruption, and erotic desire concomitant with death, an energy that contaminates with a 'venomed melody' and 'electric poison' the youthful 'green heart' within these deadly 'blue night-shade bowers'. Anticipating Shelley's claim in *Adonais*, Emily's one true 'Heaven's light forever shines' whilst 'Earth's shadows fly' (461), shadows whose falsity, 'like a dome of many-coloured glass, | Stains the white radiance of Eternity' (462–3). Mistakenly identified by the poet-speaker as a concrete manifestation of the true 'One', only ever met 'robed in such exceeding glory | That I beheld her not' (199–200), this figure is one of the 'many mortal forms' (267) that comprise a thinly disguised biographical catalogue of the women Shelley encountered before meeting Emily. Some biographers speculate that behind this episode is Shelley's sexual experience with a prostitute and contraction of a venereal illness during his brief time as an Oxford undergraduate. By blurring the boundaries between art and life, artist and poetic persona, Shelley's poem invites, and frustrates, such biographical speculations. On one hand, *Epipsychidion* attests to its autobiographical and factual origins and, on the other, distances authorial presence from the poetry through its own phantasmagoric vision.[32]

At the level of symbol, the poet-speaker's idealized vision of a 'shadow of some golden dream' (116) gives rise to its darker malevolent antitype as a result of his misplaced identification of concealment ('she might have masked herself') within the many as the transcendent presence of the 'One'. This process of idealization coupled with a mistaking of materiality for spiritual transcendence produce a malignant female figure, whose killing words of 'honey-dew' are both similar and dissimilar to Emily's life-engendering powers which are 'like fiery dews that melt | Into the bosom of a frozen bud' (109–10).[33]

---

[31] See Peterfreund, *Shelley among Others*, 279–80.

[32] For biographical speculations see Sperry, *Shelley's Major Verse*, 170–1; n. 19, p. 222. On the difficulties of biographical readings see Madeleine Callaghan, ' "This Soul out of my Soul": The Trial of the Hero in Shelley's *Epipsychidion*', Richard Gravil (comp.), *Grasmere 2008: Selected Papers from the Summer Wordsworth Conference* (Penrith: Humanities-Ebooks, 2010), 146–54.

[33] Verbal echoes noted in Wasserman, *Shelley: A Critical Reading*, 433–4. For interpretations of this figure see Sperry, *Shelley's Major Verse*, 169–71, and Peterfreund, *Shelley among Others*, 280–1. See also Hogle, *Shelley's Process*, 281.

In *Epipsychidion*, the poet-speaker's imaginative capacity for vision originates in a self-destructive erotic and imaginative desire which, simultaneously, generates the idealized creation of an epipsyche and its attendant apocalyptic opposite. This collapse of idealized prototype into terrifying antitype occupies territory mapped out by Shelley's *Alastor*, where the poet-figure's experience of transcendent vision discovers its counterpart in a tragic realization of earthly limitations.

Subtle differences between how *Alastor* and *Epipsychidion* mediate these interpenetrating visionary modes of idealized creativity and destructive despair are evident in Shelley's contrasting use of the figure of the antelope within the poems. Early in *Alastor* we witness the poet-figure's affinity with the natural world, as he observes 'the wild antelope, that starts whene'er | The dry leaf rustles in the brake, suspend | Her timid steps to gaze upon a form | More graceful than her own' (103–6). Shelley's description frames the visionary youth as the subject of another's creaturely 'gaze' to imply affinity and difference between the antelope and the poet-figure who is both looked upon and onlooker, as he possesses a 'form' that exceeds in 'grace' the delicately poised presence of the watchful antelope. Shelley's figural representation of the antelope in *Alastor* is open to the dissolution of the boundaries between subject and object, but remains grounded in an external referent and world. In *Epipsychidion* Shelley re-imagines this figure when he writes: 'An antelope, | In the suspended impulse of its lightness, | Were less ethereally light' (75–7). This image dissolves the antelope's elegant physical 'lightness' into Emily's celestial light and suspends, at least within the interiority of the poet-speaker's vision, any recourse to an external ground, referent, or frame of observing consciousness. Shelley's treatment of these figures of the antelope points to a fundamental difference in the poetic constitution of *Alastor* and *Epipsychidion*. Resisting those self-secluded, potentially narcissistic visions of the poet-figure, Shelley entrusts the episodes of *Alastor* to a third-person narrator who (taking the form of a separate consciousness) provides an outside point of reference to authenticate or deny the poet-figure's life and vision. Even then the narrator's positive or negative experiences of nature remain ultimately unverifiable to the reader of *Alastor*.[34] No such appeal to an external vantage point exists to validate or refute the self-enclosed, and enclosing, visions of *Epipsychidion* which are narrated entirely in the first person by Shelley's poet-speaker.

This inwardly turned visionary perspective of the poet-speaker's quest in *Epipsychidion*, starting from those 'caverns of [...] dreamy youth' (217) to the final revelatory 'living light' (342), culminates in an encounter with Emily the 'glorious One' (336)—who had been 'sought through grief and shame' (322)—as 'an Incarnation of the Sun' (335). As a prelude to this instance of fulfilled vision, the poet-speaker is redeemed from the 'venomed melody' (256) of those untrue Emilys by 'One' (277) who, as the poet-speaker admits, is 'like the glorious shape which [he] had dreamed' (278) and associated with a light 'like the noon-day dawn' (276) that 'warms not but illumines' (285). Her light is of 'the Moon, whose changes ever run | Into themselves' (279–80), combining the transient with the transcendental, as the poet-speaker had aspired and failed to do in his

---

[34] On narrative frames see Rajan, *Dark Interpreter*, 81–3 and on the 'antelope' trope see O'Neill, *The Human Mind's Imaginings*, 163–4.

earlier succession of images in the poem. Under the Moon's influence, the poet-speaker falls into a death-in-life sleep in which his 'being became bright or dim | As the Moon's image in a summer sea' (296–7). Through the explicit allusion of these lines to the lunar imagery of *Alastor*, Shelley's peaceful 'image' of reciprocity also ushers in the prospect of the unsettling, unrequited love of Echo for Narcissus.

Biographically, the brightness of Emily's celestial beauty eclipses the once desired, now 'chaste cold bed' (299) of Mary Shelley. Through Shelley's interplay of cosmological imagery, Mary Shelley is unflatteringly represented as a 'cold chaste' (281) and overshadowed female figure of the Moon, who provides a momentary haven and the repose of a 'calm mind' (289). Fittingly when her 'Illumining' (293) lunar presence wanes, the poet-speaker is set adrift on the tempestuous inner turmoil of his own confused and conflicting emotions, leaving his soul bereft as 'a lampless sea' (311). From this chaotic voyage of self-struggle and misdirected wanderings amongst the Dantean 'obscure Forest' (321) comes calm enlightenment and recognition of 'the Vision veiled from me | So many years—that it was Emily' (343–4). This harmonious reunion between poet-speaker and sought-for vision is reflected in Shelley's imaginative effort to cohere the disjointed planetary imagery of the earlier sections of *Epipsychidion* into a more orderly and regulated cosmos.[35] With an entreaty to Emily, Mary Shelley, and Claire Clairmont, Shelley closes this second movement of *Epipsychidion* by uniting the emblems of sun, moon, comet, and earth in a powerful vision of emotional and universal harmony born of 'their many-mingled influence' (358), integrating mind and matter, soul and body, transience and permanence, life and death:

> Thou too, O Comet beautiful and fierce,
> Who drew the heart of this frail Universe
> Towards thine own; till, wreckt in that convulsion,
> Alternating attraction and repulsion,
> Thine went astray and that was rent in twain;
> Oh, float into our azure heaven again!
> Be there love's folding star at thy return;
> The living Sun will feed thee from its urn
> Of golden fire; the Moon will veil her horn
> In thy last smiles; adoring Even and Morn
> Will worship thee with incense of calm breath
> And lights and shadows; as the star of Death
> And Birth [...]
>
> (368–80)

In spite of Shelley's hoped-for cosmic reconciliation, these lines acknowledge turbulent past times that witnessed the cataclysmic upheavals, caused by the 'fierce' Comet's 'convulsions', which tore asunder the poet-speaker's 'world of love' (346). This cosmos can only be reconstructed if the Comet returns to the 'azure Heaven' transformed from its prior force of sudden destruction into a steadying and mediating power of 'alternating

---

[35] See Sperry, *Shelley's Major Verse*, 434–5.

attraction and repulsion'—mirroring the motions of the Sun and Moon—in the form of Venus, the morning and evening star ('adoring Even and Morn') and the planet whose namesake is the goddess of love. As a symbol of equilibrium between night and day, light and shadow, creation and destruction, birth and death, the Comet's presence will restore cosmic balance to the universe and enable the Sun and the Moon to become again, as the poet-speaker envisages, 'Twin Spheres of light who rule this passive Earth, | This world of love, this *me*' (345–6).

No such cosmic or natural equilibrium exists in *Alastor*'s final tragic scene of the poet-figure's death, dominated by the sinking crescent moon whose 'two lessening points of light alone | Gleamed through the darkness' (654–5). These fading 'points of light' are a reminder of the poet-figure's tendency to perceive the universe as a perpetual stream of self-projected and ever-changing fictions and recall his 'intense pensiveness' (489) required to find 'Two starry eyes, hung in the gloom of thought' (490), even amidst the 'evening gloom | Now deepening the dark shades' (485–6), as he 'images to himself the Being whom he loves' (Preface, *Norton 2*, 73). The physical deterioration of the poet-fig-ure, whose body is reduced to a 'shadowy frame' (416), is unconsolingly bemoaned by the narrator. Instead he acknowledges that the universe is irrefutably changed by the poet-figure's absence for 'Nature's vast frame, the web of human things, | Birth and the grave, that are not as they were' (719–20). In response to the poet-figure's death, Shelley's narrator produces his own fiction of negation, forbidding tears through their evocation and prohibiting the authoring of elegiac 'high verse' (707) in the act of initiating his own elegy. Closely echoing the poet-figure, the narrator's elegy rehearses a negatively charged poetics shaped in answer to his earlier failed expectations of transcendence:

> Art and eloquence,
> And all the shews o' the world are frail and vain
> To weep a loss that turns their lights to shade.
>
> (710–12)

'Art and eloquence' can no longer sustain those abandoned in a world made darker by the poet-figure's demise because, for all their grace and beauty, they only point up how much darker existence has become. On two levels, the narrator's elegy is a complex nega-tion of itself. First, the grief originating from the poet-figure's death is voiced through the trope of absent tears, albeit at the level of 'thought' (703), and, secondly, this figure triggers a series of negative tropes that form precisely the kind of 'high verse' (707) that it warns against.

Failed imaginative transcendence leads back only into the past and an alleged recount-ing by the narrator of the origins and spent life of the poet-figure who can 'no longer know or love the shapes | Of this phantasmal scene' (696–7). As much as *Epipsychidion* reaches backwards into an irrecoverably Edenic past, the narrative also extends towards an imagined future absconding with Emily to 'an isle under Ionian skies | Beautiful as a wreck of Paradise' (422–3).[36] The closing sequence of *Epipsychidion* comprises this invitation

---

[36] See Ulmer, *Shelleyan Eros*, 143–53.

and one further entreaty to Emily to 'Scorn not these flowers of thought, the fading birth | Which from its heart of hearts that plant puts forth | Whose fruit, made perfect by thy sunny eyes' (384–6), recalling the hoped for restoration of cosmic harmony that will 'into birth | Awaken all [Earth's] fruits and flowers' (346–7) and reminds us of the poem's earlier self-consciousness about the fragile power of poetic language. Eventually, this recognition of imaginative limitation terminates the desired union of Emily and the poet-speaker in a past or future state of indivisible prelapsarian delight, as 'one | Spirit within two frames' (573–4). At the limits of poetic vision, Shelley's diction in *Epipsychidion* prefigures the uncertain visionary voyage embarked upon at the end of *Adonais*. With its visionary flight dramatically curtailed, *Epipsychidion* acknowledges that poetic language may not sustain the aspiration of the poet's soul to a transfigured union with Emily's celestial presence and that its own verse risks ironically exhausting the imagination and incarcerating his spirit:[37]

> Woe is me!
> The winged words on which my soul would pierce
> Into the height of love's rare Universe,
> Are chains of lead around its flight of fire.—
> I pant, I sink, I tremble, I expire!
>
> (587–91)

Such imaginative shortcomings and limitations of poetic desire tether the poet-speaker's 'flight of fire' to the earth, restricted as much by his mortality as by any poetic shortcomings. Any utopian dream of an earthly paradisal island as a permanent retreat for the lovers recedes from Shelley's *envoi* to the poem, affirming that 'Love's very pain is sweet | But its reward is in the world divine | Which, if not here, it builds upon the grave' (596–8) and reiterating Emilia Viviani's prefatory words to *Epipsychidion* that 'the loving soul launches beyond creation, and creates for itself an infinite world all of its own' (Preface, *Norton* 2, 392).[38]

It is appropriate that the quest of *Epipsychidion* terminates with the ambiguous use of the pivotal word 'here' which both projects itself into the infinite beyond the limits of mortality and recognizes that the constraints of human existence culminate in the confines of the grave.[39] There is scope for qualified faith in the transcendent, but also an encroaching awareness of the limitations of imaginative vision, love, life, and poetic meaning. By the close of *Epipsychidion*, the poet-speaker has fallen silent and a chorus commands Shelley's failed 'Weak Verses, go, kneel at your Sovereign's [Emily's] feet' (592). There is genuine concern expressed about whether poetic words can successfully envisage a future utopia or embody Emily's celestial brilliance. A comparable failure to capture vision in words and in the world haunts *Alastor* and precipitates the poet-figure's doomed search 'for intercourse with an intelligence similar to itself' (Preface, *Norton* 2, 73) and

---

[37] See Timothy Webb, *Shelley: A Voice Not Understood* (Manchester: Manchester UP, 1977), 40–1.

[38] 'L'anima amante si slancia fuori del creato, e si crea nel infinito un Mondo tutto per essa' (translation Reiman and Fraistat).

[39] See Wasserman, *Shelley: A Critical Reading*, 461.

subsequent tragic demise. The narrator's recounting of the visionary poet-figure's life instructs us that existence, without the possibility of imaginative transcendence, constitutes merely a dark 'web of human things' (719). Confirming Shelley's lyrically bittersweet sense of how 'Our sweetest songs are those that tell of saddest thought' ('To a Skylark', 90), these romance quests are motivated by a virtuous love for an idealized antitype but, invariably, such love transmutes into a tainted self-destructive desire born of the disappointment of failed vision, lost meaning, and demonic self-absorption.

SELECT BIBLIOGRAPHY

Allott, Miriam. Ed. *Essays on Shelley*. Totowa, NJ: Barnes, 1982.

Bloom, Harold. 'The Internalisation of Quest-Romance', *Romanticism and Consciousness: Essays in Criticism*. Ed. Harold Bloom. New York: Norton, 1970.

—— *The Ringers in the Tower: Studies in Romantic Tradition*. Chicago: University of Chicago Press, 1971.

Cameron, Kenneth Neill. *Shelley: The Golden Years*. Cambridge, MA: Harvard UP, 1974.

Clark, Timothy. *Embodying Revolution: The Figure of the Poet in Shelley*. Oxford: Clarendon, 1989.

Cronin, Richard. *Shelley's Poetic Thoughts*. London: Macmillan, 1981.

Duff, David. *Romance and Revolution: Shelley and the Politics of a Genre*. Cambridge: Cambridge UP, 1994.

Gelpi, Barbara Charlesworth. *Shelley's Goddess: Maternity, Language, Subjectivity*. Oxford: Oxford UP, 1992.

—— 'Keeping Faith with Desire: A Reading of *Epipsychidion*'. *Evaluating Shelley*. Ed. Timothy Clark and Jerrold E. Hogle. Edinburgh: Edinburgh UP, 1996.

Goslee, Nancy Moore. 'Dispersoning Emily: Drafting as Plot in *Epipsychidion*'. *Shelley's Poetry and Prose: Authoritative Texts*. 2nd edn. Ed. Donald H. Reiman and Neil Fraistat. New York: Norton, 2002.

Hall, Spencer. '"Beyond the Realms of Dream": Gothic, Romantic and Poetic Identity in Shelley's *Alastor*'. *Gothic Studies* 3 (2001), 8–14.

Hogle, Jerrold E. *Shelley's Process: Radical Transference and the Development of his Work*. Oxford: Oxford UP, 1988.

Jones, Frederick L. Ed. *The Letters of Percy Bysshe Shelley*. 2 vols. Oxford: Clarendon, 1964.

Keach, William. 'Obstinate Questionings: The *Immortality Ode and Alastor*'. *Wordsworth Circle* 12 (1981), 36–44.

—— *Shelley's Style*. London: Methuen, 1984.

Lokash, Jennifer. 'Shelley's Organic Sympathy: Natural Communitarianism and the Example of *Alastor*'. *Wordsworth Circle* 28 (1997), 177–83.

McDayter, Ghislaine. '"O'er Leaping the Bounds": The Sexing of the Creative Soul in Shelley's *Epipsychidion*'. *Keats–Shelley Journal* 52 (2003), 21–49.

Makdisi, Saree Samir. 'Shelley's *Alastor*: Travel beyond the Limit'. *Romantic Geographies: Discourses of Travel 1775–1844*. Ed. Amanda Gilroy. Manchester: Manchester UP, 2000.

Morton, Timothy. Ed. *Cambridge Companion to Shelley*. Cambridge: Cambridge UP, 2006.

Newey, Vincent. 'Shelley's "Dream of Youth": *Alastor*, "Selving" and the Psychic Realm'. *Percy Bysshe Shelley: Bicentenary Readings*. Ed. Kelvin Everest. Essays and Studies 45. Cambridge: Brewer, 1992.

O'Neill, Michael. *The Human Mind's Imaginings: Conflict and Achievement in Shelley's Poetry.* Oxford: Clarendon, 1989.

Peterfreund, Stuart. *Shelley among Others: The Play of the Intertext and the Idea of Language.* Baltimore: Johns Hopkins UP, 2002.

Rajan, Tilottama. *Dark Interpreter: The Discourse of Romanticism.* Ithaca, NY: Cornell UP, 1980.

Reiman, Donald H. and Neil Fraistat. Eds. *Shelley's Poetry and Prose: Authoritative Texts.* 2nd edn. New York: Norton, 2002.

Sandy, Mark. *Poetics of Self and Form in Keats and Shelley: Nietzschean Subjectivity and Genre.* Aldershot: Ashgate, 2005.

Schulze, Earl. 'The Dantean Quest of *Epipsychidion'. Studies in Romanticism* 21 (1982), 191–216.

Sperry, Stuart M. *Shelley's Major Verse: Narrative and Dramatic Poetry.* Cambridge, MA: Harvard UP, 1988.

Steinman, Lisa M. 'Shelley's Scepticism: Allegory in *Alastor'. ELH* 45 (1978), 255–69.

Tetreault, Ronald A. *The Poetry of Life: Shelley and Literary Form.* Toronto: University of Toronto Press, 1987.

Ulmer, William A. *Shelleyan Eros: The Rhetoric of Romantic Love.* Princeton: Princeton UP, 1990.

Wasserman, Earl R. *Shelley: A Critical Reading.* 1971. Baltimore: Johns Hopkins UP, 1975.

Webb, Timothy. *Shelley: A Voice Not Understood.* Manchester: Manchester UP, 1972.

Weinberg, Alan M. *Shelley's Italian Experience.* London: Macmillan, 1991.

Weisman, Karen A. *Imageless Truths: Shelley's Poetic Fictions.* Philadelphia: University of Pennsylvania Press, 1994.

White, Newman Ivey. *Shelley.* 2 vols. London: Secker, 1947.

Wroe, Ann. *Being Shelley: The Poet's Search for Himself.* London: Cape, 2007.

....

CHAPTER 18

LYRICAL DRAMA

Prometheus Unbound *and* Hellas

....

STUART CURRAN

WORDSWORTH's famous remark that 'Shelley is one of the best *artists* of us all: I mean in workmanship of style'[1] is an assessment by a writer who, despite his aversion to Shelley's politics and personal values, admitted on several occasions his great admiration for the younger poet's craftsmanship. Although the main thrust of this remark is directed at Shelley's stylistic abilities, its general thrust could be extended as well to his formal experimentation, an area of expertise in which Wordsworth, in his famous preface to the second edition of *Lyrical Ballads* (1800), had pointedly prided himself as a serious literary innovator. From sonnets to odes to pastoral, wherever Shelley adopts a genre, he also adapts it, with a rare scrutiny of its history and formal characteristics evident in the result. Needless to say, since 'lyrical drama' is an innovative form that, above all others, we associate with Shelley's experimental genius, we should anticipate the same kind of attention to the attributes of the particular forms of which it is a hybrid.

And yet, in his own public representation of those terms, this is hardly the case at all. The second paragraph of the 'Preface' to *Hellas, a Lyrical Drama* does immediately focus on the question of genre, as if the work's mode rather than its propagandistic thrust were the more pressing issue confronting a reader. But the definition there is uncharacteristically naive: 'The subject in its present state, is insusceptible of being treated otherwise than lyrically, and [...] I have called this poem a drama from the circumstance of its being composed in dialogue [...]' (*Norton* 2, 430). Instead of settling the matter, then, this bland statement is rather like the poet's ensuing apology for falling back on 'newspaper erudition' (*Norton* 2, 431), when he had at first the counsel of his dedicatee, the future secretary of state and premier of liberated Greece Prince Alexander Mavrocordato, and, after that imposing figure left to help lead the revolution against the Turkish occupation, reports from the cadre of eager Greek exiles he left behind in Pisa. It is, in other words, almost deliberately misleading, of a piece with Shelley's concerted attempt throughout

[1] Christopher Wordsworth, *Memoirs of William Wordsworth* (London: Moxon, 1851), II, 474.

the prefatory matter to reconfigure his recondite neo-Greek drama to the concerns of a general audience.

'Lyrical drama', like the similar designation of the previous generation, 'lyrical ballad', is, instead, a deliberate assault on the integrity of the tripartite generic division—epic, drama, lyric—inherited from Aristotle and Horace and reinforced throughout the eighteenth century by major arbiters of neoclassical criticism. Unlike Wordsworth and Coleridge's 'lyrical ballad', however, Shelley did not actually invent the combinative term 'lyrical drama' as a generic designation, and his employing it as a generic designator for both *Prometheus Unbound* and *Hellas* surely suggests that he had a more refined sense of its characteristics than as mere dialogue surrounding lyrical effusions. The term has two different, if loosely linked, applications in eighteenth-century literary nomenclature, both of which seem pertinent to what Shelley formally realizes in these works. Although there is no direct evidence tying Shelley's reading or his generalized cultural background to either of them, still, the fact that the term is itself already in the air suggests that a writer as self-aware and conscious of the traditions he inherits as Shelley should not be considered as blindly operating in the literary vacuum he implicitly posits in the 'Preface' to *Hellas*.

The first of the generic categories associated with the term 'lyrical drama' is, indeed, that of a neo-Greek drama. Richard Jodrell, in his *Illustrations of Euripides, on the Alcestis* (1789), writing on imitations of Euripides first among Latin authors and then in the Italian Renaissance, notes, apropos versions of the Alcestis legend in the seventeenth century, that 'there were three lyrical dramas of this title; one by Prospero Bonarelli in 1647, another by an anonymous Author in 1665, and the last by Donato Cupeda in 1699' (361). Closer to home for a poet in the English tradition, the term is associated with two dramas on early British themes by William Mason, *Elfrida* (1755) and *Caractatus* (1759), which were much heralded in their day and were both originally styled by subtitle, *a Dramatic Poem written on the model of the ancient Greek tragedy*. Both were theatrically produced with music at Covent Garden, and subsequently a separate publication was made for each with the common lead-in, *The lyrical part of the drama of* [...], with *Caractatus* so truncated in 1776 and *Elfrida* in 1779. This generic designation was then refined for a final neoclassical dramatic work, *Sappho, a Lyrical Drama*, published posthumously in a third volume of Mason's *Works* in 1796.[2] The evolution of Mason's generic thinking in this succession may be indicated by a note he introduced in his *Essays, historical and critical, on English Church Music* (London: J. Robson; York: J. Todd, 1795), 102:

> How great a dramatic writer would Metastasio have been, had he not been compelled, in subserviency to his musical Composers, to furnish them only with *Libretti!*

---

[2] *Sappho* was reprinted in London by Thomas Bulmer (1809), then translated into Italian the same year—*sul modello toscano*, according to a Tuscan model—by Thomas James Mathias, whose translation was once again printed, after his removal to Italy, in Naples in 1818. Mathias prefaces this translation with a brief exposition on the work and its mode, citing the celebrated early eighteenth-century opera librettist Pietro Metastasio as its prime influence. This is in accord with the note appended to the *dramatis personae* in the original printing of *Sappho*: 'N. B. The types in the following pages are arranged in the manner of METASTATIO's Operas, Paris Edit. *1755* in order to distinguish the Airs, Duetts, etc. from the Recitative' (*Poems*, 1797), III, 144.

It must however be allowed, that his Lyrical Dramas, as originally written, in respect to theatrical contrivance and judicious developement of the story, infinitely excel the generality of our modern Tragedies.[3]

The citation of Pietro Metastasio here, in turn, establishes the linkage between neoclassical drama interspersed with choruses and eighteenth-century opera, for which Metastasio, based in Vienna, had emerged as the recognized premier librettist in the 1730s. His operatic subjects, in keeping with the mode of *opera seria*, were drawn from classical myth and history, and his arias, written in an elevated poetic diction, constituted for the late Enlightenment a pan-European repertory of song for translators. Whether or not the proliferation of the term 'lyrical drama' was owing principally to Metastasio, with him it certainly became a synonym for an operatic libretto. Well before Metastasio's appearance on the scene, however, there was a modest attempt at theorizing around these two contrary components as the special province of opera, as can be gleaned from the preface John Hughes penned for his opera *Calypso and Telemachus* (1712): 'An Opera, I think, is to be consider'd as a Species of Poetry, compounded out of the Lyric and Dramatick Kinds, admitting of all the Beauty of the first, united with Part of the latter' ('Preface', vii). By later in the century opera and lyrical drama are interchangeable terms, as they overlap in the excursus on Parisian opera to which Rousseau devotes a letter in *Julie; ou la nouvelle Héloïse* (1761), where he refers to the form by the term 'drame lyrique' (2nd Part, letter 23 [1925], 398).[4] In nineteenth-century Italy, as 'dramma lirico', the term firms into a generic category: the librettos of most Verdi operas and all of Puccini's feature this phrase as a subtitle.[5] With Massenet, in his divergence from the sprawling historical panoramas of Meyerbeer, the fusion likewise becomes common in the French musical world. In Britain, as late as 1907 the libretto to Frederick Delius' *A Village Romeo and Juliet* is subtitled 'a lyrical drama'.

Before turning to *Prometheus Unbound* and *Hellas* as the focus of this chapter, it might be useful for contextual purposes to recapitulate Shelley's interests in and practices with dramatic form. As was noted some years ago, once the poet arrived in Italy, he became almost obsessed with dialogic works, beginning with his translation of Plato's *Symposium* and Euripides' *Cyclops*, and continuing through his modern eclogues *Rosalind and Helen* and *Julian and Maddalo*, at which point Shelley also began translating from

---

[3] This statement is produced with minor alterations in a much more accessible volume, Charles Burney, *Memoirs of the life and writings of the abate Pietro Metastasio*, 3 vols. (London: G. G. and J. Robinson, 1796), III, 385.

[4] The anonymous translator of the standard late eighteenth-century English version of *Julie*, in picking up on the term, multiplies it, inscribing it twice in this letter (letter 88 [London, 1795], II, 37, 38).

[5] The exception is *Aida*, referred to as 'opera' or as 'melodramma' or, as it occurred with the printed libretto accompanying the first London performance, a 'grand romantic opera' (London: Royal Italian Opera, 1876). The distinction is between a work centred on human interaction and a 'grand opera' focused on historical spectacle. By the later nineteenth century the notions of opera and of lyrical drama are fused, as can be discerned from the sculpture by Jean-Joseph Perraud, *Le Drame lyrique* (1869) on the façade of the Palais Garnier, seat of the Paris Opera. In English, compare, for example, H. Sutherland Edwards, *The Lyrical Drama: Essays on Subjects, Composers, & Executants of Modern Opera*, 2 vols. (London: W. H. Allen & Co, 1881).

Calderón's dramatic oeuvre and simultaneously culminated this tutelage by writing two exemplary though wholly different dramatic works, *Prometheus Unbound* and *The Cenci*.[6] It should be noted that all of these productions explicitly in dramatic form contain lyric elements—songs and conspicuously rhymed passages—and this characteristic is to be found as well in Shelley's later original dramatic fragments such as *Charles the First* and translations like those he completed from Goethe's *Faust*. It is clear, then, that Shelley conceived of lyric as an essential aspect of drama, and it has been argued, indeed, that this concerted embedment of lyric at the heart of drama signals his concern with the multiplicity of illusionary frameworks in which we all find ourselves as well as his recognition that all action is subordinate to the preliminary mental conceptions that spur it.[7]

The two works Shelley characterized as lyrical dramas are thus not to be seen as merely formal investments derived from neoclassical or operatic prototypes, however one may discern discreet elements from these forms within them. Rather, they constitute, in a concentrated mode to which the author wished to call specific attention, embodiments of a carefully realized notion of what the dramatic form could be stretched to accommodate beyond the objectification of reality to which Aristotle had confined it. However formally these dramas appear to cast an eye to the past, then, they may be understood as conceived to be radical experiments concerned with the very nature of the dramatic, or, to employ the figurative vocabulary of Shelley's *A Defence of Poetry*, 'mirrors of the gigantic shadows which futurity casts upon the present' (*Norton* 2, 535).

Still, the prototypes for lyrical drama exist, and in keeping with his skilful employment of genre throughout his mature writings, Shelley seems intent on exploiting their associations. Of his two lyrical dramas *Hellas* is the most obviously conceived according to a Greek tragic model. Roughly a third of its 1,101 lines are choral in nature, and four different messengers are employed to report the external dramatic action. Yet, even with so obvious a neoclassical cast to the work there is a distinct paradox to be observed. The Greek drama descending to the modern world is with a single exception itself, so to speak, neoclassical in its import, recycling myths from a dim cultural memory, with occasional resonances, like the choral ode to the greatness of Athens in Sophocles' *Oedipus at Colonus*, to the living moment of its original enactment. Otherwise, the events of the entire corpus exist within an irretrievable past, oddly like those dramatic originals from the fifth century BCE inspiring neoclassical drama across Europe throughout the eighteenth century. The exception is the play to which Shelley turns as a model for *Hellas*, *The Persians* (472 BCE) of Aeschylus, whose focal point is the defeat of Xerxes' forces at the Battle of Salamis eight years before this play was performed. And yet, even as Shelley adopts many of Aeschylus' structural elements, preserving a strict unity of time and place and relying heavily on those successive messengers to relate ongoing events, he forecasts an uncertain future rather than, as with his model, recreating a historical past. It is exactly because of his need to project history as possibility, indeed, that

---

[6] See Stuart Curran, 'Shelleyan Drama', in Richard Allen Cave (ed.), *The Romantic Theatre: An International Symposium* (Garrards Cross: Colin Smythe, 1986), 63–4.

[7] Ibid. 68–77.

in his 'Preface', as already noted, he claims that he must substitute a lyrical potentiality for dramatic assurance. 'The subject in its present state, is insusceptible of being treated otherwise than lyrically': which is to say, that the actual must be suspended upon the thought processes that will eventually force it into being.

This, of course, is exactly the focus of the more elaborated lyrical drama, *Prometheus Unbound*, that preceded *Hellas* by three years. In the preface to that work, Shelley is even more explicit in stressing the priority of lyric, as the province of psychological states, to drama, the action that ensues from them: 'The imagery which I have employed will be found in many instances to have been drawn from the operations of the human mind, or from those external actions by which they are expressed' (*Norton 2*, 207). The ensuing first act exemplifies the process articulated in this formulation. There, Prometheus, having failed to elicit from the Earth or her component attributes (Mountains, Springs, Air, Whirlwinds) a repetition of the curse he had bestowed upon Jupiter, and then having called Jupiter's Phantasm forth as a second self to objectify the utterance, turns inward to condemn the adversarial mental state that had relied on cursing another to affirm its own righteousness. But rather than discovering release through this return of the repressed, the later aim of such a psychoanalytical procedure, Prometheus must instead confront the Furies of his own mind, a flood of uncertainties about the implications of altering that mental state and doubts over the results that will ensue from eschewing a reactionary defiance. Although Prometheus initially identifies these Furies as objective embodiments of 'the all-miscreative brain of Jove' (I. 448), he immediately registers a psychological affinity with them: 'While I behold such execrable shapes, | Methinks I grow like what I contemplate | And laugh and stare in loathsome sympathy' (I. 449–51). The First Fury immediately dispels the Titan's illusion that these 'shapes' are objective at all: 'We are the ministers of pain and fear | And disappointment and mistrust and hate | And clinging crime' (I. 451–4). When Prometheus recognizes their inner character— 'Yet am I king over myself and rule | The torturing and conflicting throngs within' (I. 492–3)—the Furies redouble the torture by presenting visions of an externalized conflict, an objective failure of human liberation represented by the crucifixion of Jesus and the bloodbath of the French Revolution. It is telling, however, that they do so by exchanging the blank verse with which they have been haranguing Prometheus (I. 442–91) for the most elaborate choral passagework yet encountered in the drama, involving intricate rhyming, separate solo exchanges, and internal divisions into semichoruses. In other words, the dramatic exposition that has represented an introspective psychological analysis by Prometheus has given way to a process that is ostensibly external but in its visionary nature is far from constituting a dramatic realism. It is, rather, an allegorical pageant that stresses its own representational character and to which Panthea responds (I. 584–93) as if it were a *tableau vivant*. The formal source for this unanticipated shift in dramaturgy will be investigated later. At this point what is essential to understand about the visions concocted by the Furies and the Chorus of Spirits that follows them is that in the final third of Act I allegory has replaced enactment, the symbolic idea has affirmed its priority over the action that is impelled by it. By the end of the act Prometheus finds himself at a standstill, his internal debates having brought him to a point where no action seems possible: 'There is no agony and no solace left; | Earth can console, Heaven can torment no more' (I. 819–20).

In a less radical reconception of the nature of dramatic agon the ensuing act would supply the action that the first forestalls. And with Panthea's arrival in the vale where Asia has been sequestered some event seems promised. But when Panthea instead brings her memories of Act I reconfigured as dreams and Asia reads them through her eyes, 'dark, far, measureless, | Orb within orb, and line through line inwoven' (II. i. 116–17), we are confronted with a complexity of representation that makes the rich allegorical pageantry of the first act seem simplistic in comparison. And the lyrical element increases exponentially, as Echoes and Spirits who are unseen constitute the choral element within the multiple ensuing scenes of Act II. Here even the notion of pageantry is internalized, so that the reader actually witnesses only the descent of Asia and Panthea to Demogorgon's realm but overhears what gives this journey both its meaning and momentum and must interpret its significance accordingly at a step removed from the actuality of representation. This inversion of the notion of action and the actual is clearly deliberate on Shelley's part, ensuring that the reader will come to understand Asia to be Prometheus' consort in like-mindedness as well as in function. When at last she is in Demogorgon's presence and can attempt to unveil the secrets of a universe gone so wholly wrong, the terms of her enquiry should not surprise us. 'Who made the living world?' (II. iv. 9) is her first question; but then she goes on to stipulate what it is that this 'living world' entails: 'Who made all | That it contains—thought, passion, reason, will, | Imagination?' (II. iv. 9–11). Without any action intermediate that readers might identify as concrete events, we have come a very long way from Prometheus' opening invocation in Act I of the elements of his world: Mountains, Springs, Air, Whirlwinds. Asia's world is informed by thought processes alone. In this conception things change because thoughts change: drama is impossible without the lyric; indeed, it is solely enabled by the lyric.

It should be no surprise, therefore, that we will re-encounter Asia's sense of the world's content as thought processes when, in *Hellas*, the frightened Sultan Mahmud calls upon the seer Ahasuerus to give him hope that his forces will triumph over the growing revolt in Ottoman territories and the threat of a Russian intervention. Against the exigencies of preserving the Ottoman empire within the vagaries of history, Ahasuerus posits another reality and does so pointedly echoing Asia's formulation of its five constituents, but taking its implications to an extreme assault on a conventional sense of reality:

> Thought
> Alone, and its quick elements, Will, Passion,
> Reason, Imagination, cannot die;
> They are, what that which they regard, appears,
> The stuff whence mutability can weave
> All that it hath dominion o'er, worlds, worms,
> Empires and superstitions—what has thought
> To do with time or place or circumstance?
>
> (795–802)

Although at the very end *Hellas* represents the Turkish empire surviving the multiple threats to its integrity, Shelley's intended contribution to a growing British disgust with such a predicated outcome, Mahmud is so unnerved by the counter-vision of Ahasuerus as to leave the stage thinking his unexpected victory a profound defeat.

To return to the dynamics of *Prometheus Unbound*, it will be seen that only in Act III lies what conventionally we would consider a truly articulated dramatic action: Jupiter's fall and the various consequences of that event on the actual face of the earth. And Act III—quite consciously it would appear on Shelley's part—is conspicuously devoid of choral intervention, even of rhymes: for the present moment of exhausted liberation blank verse reigns from one end to the other of the regenerated earth. In contrast, the first and second acts, in which initially the agon of Prometheus is enacted and then the emotional depths of Asia are plumbed, however different they are in their dramatic structure, are curiously alike in representing 36–7 per cent of their contents chorally. After the comparatively prosaic blank verse of Act III, the fourth act, where we witness the enormous potentiality unleashed by the simple shift of consciousness that has impelled the drama, relies on chorus and song for 89 per cent of its 578 lines. This includes exuberant metrical patterning and intricate rhyming devices: its first appearances, 'A Train of dark Forms and Shadows' (IV. 9 s.d.), sing in a succession of seven triplets, and the act ends with Demogorgon's final pronouncement of 'Victory' (IV. 578) in a concluding, emphatic triplet. The regenerate universe cannot have too much rhyme as its reason.

Given the proliferation and variety of choral and song elements within its structure, it is true that no drama from classical antiquity is as invested in the lyric as *Prometheus Unbound*, and this fact might alert us to the ways in which, grounded as it formally is in the practices of Greek drama, in the end its form transcends its model. Yet, also in *Prometheus Unbound* the actual form of lyrical drama, unlike that of Greek drama or of the formulaic eighteenth-century *opera seria*, under Shelley's command attains something of an ideological cast, as Shelley not only employs lyrical elements for the metadramatic purposes outlined above, but in the process also appears to conceptualize the inner nature of choral harmonies and the spontaneities of song. Here, his formulation bears the imprint of his friend Leigh Hunt and the recent attempt by that poet to resurrect a third form of lyrical drama in *The Descent of Liberty, a Mask* (1815). The allegorical pageantry of *Prometheus Unbound*, Act I, the supernal voices that intrude upon Act II, and the complex representational configuration of Act IV, all have their counterparts in the development of the seventeenth-century masque in Britain, as Hunt, with some disdain for the examples he cites, distinguishes its history in 'Some Account of the Origin & Nature of Masks', a treatise introductory to the work itself. There, too, Hunt defines the masque in such terms as we have already observed used for eighteenth-century opera: 'a mixed Drama, allowing of natural incidents as of every thing else that is dramatic, but more essentially given up to the fancy, and abounding in machinery and personification'.[8] Moreover, Hunt directly ties the characteristics of the seventeenth-century masque

---

[8] *The Descent of Liberty, a Mask* (London: Gale, Curtis, and Fenner, 1815), p. xxiv.

to the practices of Dryden and his contemporaries in creating operatic librettos (xlviii). So Shelley would have had before him, as he read Hunt's treatise, an exemplary binding of the masque with the development of opera, as he already had through eighteenth-century *opera seria*'s fixation on classical thematics, an established link between opera and classical drama.

Yet, it is not that Shelley needed either Hunt's critical dissertation or the historical examples it embodied for his own conception of lyrical drama. What is of most direct significance to the underlying ethos he mapped out for *Prometheus Unbound* and, with a greater sense of historical contingency, *Hellas* is the surprisingly apocalyptic cast of Hunt's work, a radical departure from the masque's purpose in the Stuart courts to reify the status quo through symbolic representation of their divinely sanctioned empower-ment. Hunt begins from an opposite extreme, carefully positioning himself as a celebra-tor of the overthrow of autocratic and imperial power. Pointedly signing his dedication, 'Surrey Jail, 10th July 1814' (p. iv), reminding his readers of his having recently been jailed for daring to satirize the Prince Regent, Hunt likewise appends to his title page an epi-graph of remarkable tonality by the sixteenth-century poet Celio Magno, himself renowned as a celebrator of the republican Venice of the Renaissance: 'Aprite, O Muse, i chiusi fonti, aprite. | Cominci omai da questo dì giocondo | Più che mai bello a rinovarsi il mondo.—Open, O Muses, your sealed fountains, open them; begin now from this happy day, more than ever beautiful, to renovate the earth.'[9]

The day in question in *The Descent of Liberty* is that of Napoleon's initial surrender on 11 April 1814. His abdication is accompanied by a universal amelioration of the atmos-phere that is unaccountable to the simple shepherds who open the first scene, and it is heralded, like the development of *Prometheus Unbound*, Act II, by faint music that grows increasingly strong and varied as the scene develops. The music represents the as-yet unseen presence of liberty restoring to freedom both individuals and their collective societies: music will be the constant and constantly varying background to the allegori-cal pageant unfolding across the drama proper. The first scene closes with the shepherds joining the maiden Myrtilla (representing innocent, peaceful love) and her almost deaf father Eunomus (whose name is an allegorical cipher for good government). When the latter, so long enfeebled by chaotic war, is unable to command the unseen singer's atten-tion, Myrtilla, in the tradition of the Lady in Milton's *Comus*, sings to it. The Spirit responds by recasting her own words, and in turn her final word, 'rejoice' (15) is echoed by two other, unseen voices, whom the Spirit identifies: ''Tis my brethren of the sky, | Couriers we of Liberty' (16).

There is no need to follow Hunt's dramatic allegory into its all-but-ludicrous account of the monarchical systems opposing Napoleon becoming reformed agents themselves of liberty. Rather, the development of the opening scene sets the model for the far more complex allegorical positioning of Shelley in *Prometheus Unbound* where the second act, especially, adopts a similar patterning of voice and echo to draw Asia down to

---

[9] 'On the naval victory over the Turkish host at the Cursolari Islands', ll. 1, 19–20, a celebration of the Venetian victory in the Battle of Lepanto (7 October 1571).

Demogorgon's realm. There, too, music is the harbinger of a liberty celebrated by the ever-varied song that constitutes the fourth act. Hunt's example, however, seems to have been conceptualized even more thoughtfully by Shelley than this account demonstrates. For, though in both the first and second acts of *Prometheus Unbound* there are innumerable antiphonal choral passages, perhaps suggestive of an as-yet unrealized collectivity, it is not until Asia's transformation in Act II, scene v, that genuine song is empowered. As with the beginning of *The Descent of Liberty*, we overhear an unseen 'VOICE (*in the air, singing*)' (II. v. 48) to which Asia will respond with 'My soul is an enchanted boat' (II. v. 72), the passage that concludes the act wherein, 'by the instinct of sweet Music driven' (II. v. 90), the lovers are regenerated and with them the earth. The larger implications of this renovation (to recall Celio Magno's specific verb) are suspended until Act IV. There, after the breathtaking array of metrical and rhythmic choral exposition, at last the drama again reverts to song, in the love duet of the Earth and Moon (IV. 319–502), which seems meant as a symmetrical parallel to that of Prometheus and Asia in Act II.

In Shelley's conception of a lyrical drama, then, song is at core the expression of spontaneous human desire for the perfection of love; choral song is its collective embodiment. When Demogorgon summons the various components of his universe to the culminating epode of *Prometheus Unbound*, his grand final conclave, the various stars and planets respond, 'Our great Republic hears' (IV. 533), intimating the political composition of that choral collective. This understanding is implicitly transposed into the nature of *Hellas* as well. There, like Hunt writing from Surrey Jail, the collective voices that open the drama and intermittently comment on its development are composed of a 'CHORUS OF GREEK CAPTIVE WOMEN', doubly enslaved by gender and nationality. It is they who, at the end, against the reactionary thrust of the dramatic events, utter the paradoxical, tendentious aspiration that has driven both these lyrical dramas, 'The world's great age begins anew, | The golden years return' (1060–1). To a remarkable extent, this apocalyptic renewal is the ideological thrust that Shelley conceives as the heart of his hybrid 'lyrical drama', the counterpart in action of its revolutionary fusion of metaphysical opposites.

SELECT BIBLIOGRAPHY

Cheeke, Stephen. 'Wrong-Footed by Genre: Shelley's *Hellas*'. *Romanticism* 2.2 (1996), 204–19.

Cox, Jeffrey N. 'Staging Hope: Genre, Myth, and Ideology in the *Dramas* of the Hunt Circle'. *Texas Studies in Literature and Language* 38.3–4 (Fall–Winter 1996), 245–64.

Curran, Stuart. *Poetic Form and British Romanticism*. New York: Oxford UP, 1986.

—— 'Shelleyan Drama'. *The Romantic Theatre: An International Symposium*. Ed. Richard Allen Cave. Gerrards Cross: Colin Smythe, 1986.

—— *Shelley's Annus Mirabilis: The Maturing of an Epic Vision*. San Marino, CA: Huntington Library, 1975.

Erkelenz, Michael. 'Inspecting the Tragedy of Empire: Shelley's *Hellas* and Aeschylus' *Persians*'. *Philological Quarterly* 76.3 (1997), 313–37.

Everest, Kelvin. '"Mechanism of a Kind Yet Unattempted": The Dramatic Action of *Prometheus Unbound*'. *Coleridge, Keats and Shelley*. Ed. Peter J. Kitson. New York: St Martin's, 1996. 186–201.

Kipperman, Mark. 'History and Ideality: The Politics of Shelley's *Hellas*'. *Studies in Romanticism*
    30.2 (1991), 147–68.
Quillin, Jessica K. '"An Assiduous Frequenter of the Italian Opera": Shelley's *Prometheus
    Unbound* and the *Opera Buffa*'. *Romanticism and Opera*. Ed. Gillen D'Arcy Wood. Romantic
    Circles Praxis, <www.rc.umd.edu/praxis/opera/index.html>. College Park, MD: University
    of Maryland, 2005.
Tetreault, Ronald. 'Shelley at the Opera'. *ELH* 48.1 (Spring 1981), 144–71.

CHAPTER 19

....

TRAGEDY

The Cenci *and* Swellfoot the Tyrant

....

MICHAEL ROSSINGTON

In *A Defence of Poetry*, Shelley posits 'the Drama [to be] that form under which a greater number of modes of expression of poetry are susceptible of being combined than any other' (*Major Works*, 686). According such an elevated position to dramatic poetry is characteristic of Romantic aesthetics. It resonates with Hegel's assertion that 'drama [...] must be regarded as the highest stage of poetry and of art generally'.[1] Moreover, Shelley would have concurred with Schopenhauer that 'Tragedy is to be regarded [...] as the summit of poetic art'.[2] In the mature phase of his poetic career Shelley was increasingly occupied with tragic drama. He extemporized translations of *Prometheus Bound* to Byron in Switzerland in 1816, and to Mary Shelley in Marlow in 1817.[3] Soon after arriving in Italy in April 1818, he planned a tragedy of his own, on the madness of Tasso.[4] He approached the task self-deprecatingly, telling Thomas Love Peacock: 'I have taken the resolution to see what kind of a tragedy a person without dramatic talent could write' (*Letters: PBS* II, 8). In the spring and summer of 1819 he wrote *The Cenci*, 'rather to try my powers than to unburthen my full heart' (*BSM* VII, 178–9), as he put it later in the draft Preface to *Adonais*. The currency of the Cenci story in contemporary Rome confirmed it as 'a subject [...] fitted for a tragedy',[5] because, as the Preface to *The Cenci* argues, it 'has already received from its capacity of awakening and sustaining the sympathy of men, approbation and success' (*Major Works*, 316). It was printed in Livorno in late

---

[1] G. W. F. Hegel, *Aesthetics: Lectures on Fine Art*, trans. T. M. Knox, 2 vols. (Oxford: Clarendon Press, 1975), II, 1158.

[2] Arthur Schopenhauer, *The World as Will and Representation*, trans. E. F. J. Payne, 2 vols. (Indian Hills, CO: Falcon's Wing Press, 1958), I, 252.

[3] Ernest J. Lovell (ed.), *Medwin's Conversations of Lord Byron* (Princeton: Princeton UP, 1966), 156; *BSM* XXII, Part 2, 190–235; *Journals: MWS* I, 177.

[4] Some drafts of this abandoned project survive; see 'Scene for *Tasso*' and 'Song for *Tasso*', Longman, 2, 365–9, 445–7.

[5] *The Poetical Works of Percy Bysshe Shelley*, ed. Mary Shelley, 4 vols. (London: Edward Moxon, 1839), II, 274.

summer 1819 and published in London early the following year. Written for 'popular effect', Shelley asked Peacock to 'procure' this revenge drama's performance on the London stage, the character of Beatrice being 'precisely fitted for' Eliza O'Neill (*Letters: PBS* II, 102). But the theatre manager to whom it was sent 'pronounced the subject to be so objectionable, that he could not even submit the part to [her] for perusal'.[6] Its blasphemous and incestuous content made it 'unperformable' in public until a century after it appeared in print.[7] Over a much briefer period, in the summer of 1820, he composed the two-act tragedy cum satire *Swellfoot the Tyrant*, which appeared anonymously in pamphlet form before the end of the year. It was immediately suppressed as a 'seditious and disloyal libel'.[8] In the Preface to *Hellas*, in wry allusion to the etymology of the word 'tragedy', he described *The Cenci* as '[t]he only *goat-song* which I have yet attempted' (*Major Works*, 549), confirmation that *Swellfoot the Tyrant* resists classification as tragedy *tout court*. Earlier in 1820 he had begun to meditate in earnest the 'Historical Tragedy' of *Charles the First* (*Letters: PBS* II, 219–20, 372). The extant drafts and notes show this play to have been projected on a larger scale than the two that are the subject of this chapter, and it remained unfinished at his death in 1822. Translations of scenes from Goethe's *Faust. Eine Tragödie* (1808) and Calderón's *El mágico prodigioso* (1637) appeared posthumously. Creations of tragedies of his own, and of translations of its finest classical and modern exemplars, were thus central to his later poetic ambitions. The focus of what follows is Shelley's view of drama's purpose, and *The Cenci* and *Swellfoot the Tyrant* as national tragedies. First, though, their Greek characteristics are outlined.

I

Hazlitt argued that 'the highest efforts of the Tragic Muse are in general the earliest'.[9] That Shelley's conception of tragedy to a great extent derived from ancient Greece is to be expected given his claim in the Preface to *Hellas* (1822) that 'Our laws, our literature, our religion, our arts, have their root in Greece' (*Major Works*, 549). The depth of his linguistic and critical engagement with Athenian tragedies may be gleaned from the several manuscript notebooks that contain transcriptions, quotations, notes, and translations from them. The 'wonderful poetry' of *Agamemnon* and its 'almost unfathomable depth' in *Oedipus Tyrannus* compelled him in scholarly as well as aesthetic terms (*MYR* IV, 320–1, 396–7). In the last three years of his life he consumed these plays ever more avidly, enjoying *Agamemnon* with Maria Gisborne in April 1820, and informing her husband

    [6] Ibid. 279.
    [7] Susan Staves, 'Tragedy', in Jane Moody and Daniel O'Quinn (eds.), *The Cambridge Companion to British Theatre, 1730–1830* (Cambridge: Cambridge UP, 2007), 88.
    [8] Horace Smith, 'A Graybeard's Gossip about his Literary Acquaintance, No. IX', *New Monthly Magazine and Humorist* 81.323 (November 1847), 293.
    [9] William Hazlitt, 'On Modern Comedy', *The Round Table*, 2 vols. (London: Longman, Hurst, Rees, Orme and Brown, 1817), I, 54.

John in October 1821 that, 'I read the Greek dramatists [...] forever.' (*Letters: PBS* II, 186, 364) His cousin Thomas Medwin's claim that the verse translations of *Prometheus Bound* and *Agamemnon* he published in the 1830s bear Shelleyan hallmarks is credible since they studied the former play together and the latter with Prince Alexander Mavrocordato in the winter of 1820–1.[10] Aeschylean drama exercised a particular hold after Shelley's arrival in Italy when, Mary Shelley noted, 'the sublime majesty of Æschylus filled him with wonder and delight.'[11]

Geoffrey Matthews once observed that 'Except in the most trivial ways [*The Cenci*] is quite un-Shakespearian, in versification as in content.'[12] Its Greekness, however, is pronounced. If indebtedness to *Prometheus Bound* and *Persae* is overt in *Prometheus Unbound* (1820) and *Hellas* respectively, the plays of Aeschylus, as well as of those of Sophocles and Euripides, inform *The Cenci*. The wording of a cancelled draft title, the 'Family of the Cenci' (*MYR* IV, 446–7), invokes the spirit of the *Oresteia*, epitomized by R. P. Winnington-Ingram as 'the story of a doomed house.'[13] In Beatrice's lengthy speeches in Act V there are echoes of Cassandra's in *Agamemnon*, especially her final scene, a favourite of the most erudite of Shelley's Greek scholar-companions, Peacock.[14] Equally, her violent challenge to the patriarchal order recalls Clytemnestra, 'the man-woman who threatens the principle of male domination' in that play.[15] Behind Beatrice also lies Antigone, whose wish to bury her brother Polyneices in Aeschylus' *Seven against Thebes* is expressed as an openly defiant act: 'I will not be ashamed to display such disobedient insubordination to the city.'[16] Of her stance, expressed most fully in Sophocles' *Antigone*, Shelley had asked his fellow undergraduate Thomas Jefferson Hogg in 1811, 'Did she wrong when she acted in direct in noble violation of the laws of a prejudiced society' (*Letters: PBS* I, 81) Another Sophoclean heroine, Electra, popular in eighteenth-century stagings of Greek tragedy in Britain has recently been proposed as a prototype.[17] If in *Electra* and *Antigone* 'the family curse has its importance', the same is true of *The Cenci*.[18] Francesco Cenci's excoriation of his daughter (IV. i. 114–36, 140–59), Gothic in its excess, only reinforces the sense in which her fate is as much familial as

[10] Medwin's translations of these plays were first published as pamphlets in 1832; they appeared in modified form, along with his translations of four further tragedies by Aeschylus, in *Fraser's Magazine* between 1832 and 1838. For his acknowledgement of Shelley's scholarly influence, see Aeschylus, *Prometheus Bound*, trans. Thomas Medwin (London: William Pickering, 1832), p. iv; H. Buxton Forman (ed.), *The Life of Percy Bysshe Shelley by Thomas Medwin* (London: Oxford UP, 1913), 242–3, 263; *BSM* XII, p. xl. That *Prometheus Bound* was authored by Aeschylus was not put in doubt until later in the nineteenth century.

[11] *Poetical Works of Shelley*, ed. Shelley, II, 131.

[12] G. M. Matthews, *Shelley* (Harlow: Longman, 1970), 22.

[13] R. P. Winnington-Ingram, 'Aeschylus', in P. E. Easterling and B. M. W. Knox (eds.), *The Cambridge History of Classical Literature*, I: *Greek Literature* (Cambridge: Cambridge UP, 1985), 284.

[14] Letter to Thomas Forster, 13 February 1812, in *The Letters of Thomas Love Peacock*, ed. Nicholas A. Joukovsky, 2 vols. (Oxford: Clarendon Press, 2001), I, 81–2.

[15] Winnington-Ingram, 'Aeschylus', 286.

[16] Alan H. Sommerstein (ed.), *Aeschylus*, 3 vols. (London: Harvard UP, 2008), I, 269.

[17] Edith Hall and Fiona Macintosh, *Greek Tragedy and the British Theatre 1660–1914* (Oxford: Oxford UP, 2005), 180.

[18] Hugh Lloyd-Jones (ed.), *Sophocles*, 3 vols. (London: Harvard UP, 1994–6), I, 4.

individual. A further model is the young Alcestis, whose nobility in the face of death is the subject of a tragedy by Euripides that Shelley described as 'exceedingly beautiful' on a first reading in 1817. He returned to the play in June 1818 within a few weeks of Claire Clairmont recording in her journal for 25 May, 'We are much with the Gisbornes. Read the manuscrit [*sic*] History of the *Cenci* family' (*Letters: PBS* I, 542; *Journals: MWS* I, 166, 213; *SC* V, 455). Given that the books Mary Shelley read after Shelley's death evidence his tastes, it is notable that she transcribed the first hundred lines or so of *Alcestis*, adding some word-for-word translations into English and Latin, a decade later (*BSM* XXII, Part Two, 328–39; *BSM* XXIII, 21). The legacy of these heroines allows the definitive article in the play's title to be understood as a translation of the name '*La Cenci*', given to Beatrice, according to the play's Preface, by Shelley's Italian servant on recognizing his copy of her portrait (*Major Works*, 316). It may therefore be read as a reference to her alone, in Greek tragic style, rather than to the family as a whole.

Shelley's familiarity with Greek tragedy is expressed exuberantly, and to satiric ends, in *Swellfoot the Tyrant*, not least in the lese-majesty of its full title. *Oedipus Tyrannus; or, Swellfoot the Tyrant* translates the sombre hero of the first play in the Theban trilogy into the gouty incumbent of the British throne, latterly the Prince Regent, now King George IV. Debates from Plato's dialogues to Leigh Hunt's *Examiner* about the legitimacy of monarchical government are invoked through the English rendition of the Greek τύραννος, 'Tyrant', that recalls the language of Milton's defence of liberty in the mid-seventeenth century. The laboured 'Advertisement' by the 'Translator' presents the play as the first and only surviving tragedy of a trilogy about a mythical royal house:

> This Tragedy is one of a triad, or system of three Plays (an arrangement according to which the Greeks were accustomed to connect their Dramatic representations), elucidating the wonderful and appalling fortunes of the SWELLFOOT dynasty. [...]
> Should the remaining portions of this Tragedy be found, entitled, *Swellfoot in Angaria*, and *Charité*, the Translator might be tempted to give them to the reading Public. (*Longman*, 3, 655, 657)

The allusion to England's post-Peterloo political crisis in the imperative on the title page, 'Choose Reform or civil-war' (quoted from I. 113 and II. i. 153), implies that recent events are only the first instalment of the tragic cycle of the Hanoverian dynasty whose further playings-out will inflict yet more suffering on the people. However, in its burlesque qualities, *Swellfoot the Tyrant* also displays some of the excess and ribald humour associated with the satyr play that in the ancient Greek tradition 'was the normal fourth play of a tragic tetralogy'.[19] The only complete, extant example is Euripides' *The Cyclops*, translated by Shelley between May 1818 and November 1819.[20] Adrian Poole's observation that his translation 'anticipates a ruder and more carnal aspect to Greek drama [...] with which the nineteenth century negotiated nervously, when it did not simply ignore or deplore it' points to Shelley's striking awareness of the ways in which Greek drama allows for the proximity of

---

[19] David Kovacs et al. (eds.), *Euripides*, 8 vols. (London: Harvard UP, 1994–2008), I, 53.
[20] See *Longman*, 2, 371–3 where a composition period in the summer of 1818 is proposed.

the comic and the tragic.[21] In *Swellfoot the Tyrant*, this juxtaposition is palpable in the absurd song of the Gadfly who tells of having driven Iona Taurina ('Joan Bull') from Italy to London (I. 220–60). The allusion to the return from exile of Queen Caroline is thereby juxtaposed with the fate of the nymph Io in *Prometheus Bound* to which the reader is referred in a cursory note to I. 153. In the Aeschylean tragedy, Io, an innocent victim of Zeus's lust who has been transformed into a heifer by Juno and driven by a gadfly from Greece to Egypt, is treated by the Chorus with pitying tenderness. Aristotle's *Poetics* roots tragedy in the dithyramb or choral song in honour of Dionysus, and comedy in phallic songs.[22] *Swellfoot the Tyrant*, which abounds in elaborate choruses and sexual innuendo, accommodates the tragic and comical aspects of Caroline's situation in equal measure.

II

Notwithstanding his compulsive absorption in Athenian drama, Shelley claimed that '*King Lear* [...] may be judged to be the most perfect specimen of the dramatic art existing in the world' on account of its 'modern practice of blending comedy with tragedy' for ends 'universal, ideal and sublime' (*Major Works*, 684, 683). This shows his willingness to see tragedy as assuming an equal or perhaps even more exalted form in a later age. The admission of Shakespeare and Sophocles to one another's company—he calls Sophocles 'the Greek Shakespeare' (*MYR* IV, 396–7)—is, however, distinct from the promotion of 'modern' over 'classical' tragedy systematized by contemporaries including Madame de Staël. Whereas Staël had argued that 'la tragédie a dû suivre les progrès de l'esprit humain' ('improvement in tragedy arises from the increased progress of the human intellect'),[23] for Shelley, Shakespeare's parity with Sophocles instead demonstrates that, 'A Poet participates in the eternal, the infinite and the one; as far as relates to his conceptions, time and place and number are not' (*Major Works*, 677). Indeed it is Shelley's resistance to any innovation in tragedy that would divert it from models bequeathed by the Greek tragedians and their comparators, Shakespeare and Calderón, that sets him apart from Byron. He summarized their significant disagreement thus in a letter to Horace Smith of September 1821:

> He is occupied in forming a new drama, and, with views which I doubt not will expand as he proceeds, is determined to write a series of plays, in which he will follow the French tragedians and Alfieri, rather than those of England and Spain, and produce something new, at least, to England. This seems to me the wrong road; but genius like his is destined to lead and not to follow. (*Letters: PBS* II, 349)

[21] Adrian Poole, 'Greek Drama', in Peter France and Kenneth Haynes (eds.), *The Oxford History of Literary Translation in English*, IV: *1790–1900* (Oxford: Oxford UP, 2006), 184.

[22] Aristotle, *Poetics*, ed. Stephen Halliwell (London: Harvard UP, 1995), 41, 43.

[23] Madame de Staël, *De la littérature considérée dans ses rapports avec les institutions sociales*, ed. Gérard Gengembre and Jean Goldzink (Paris: Flammarion, 1991), 110; *The Influence of Literature upon Society*, 2nd edn., 2 vols. (London: Henry Colburn, 1812), I, 113.

Shelley's antipathy to neoclassical tragedy had been excited through *Über dramatische Kunst und Literatur. Vorlesungen* (1809–11) by August Wilhelm Schlegel, 'the learned critic' (*BSM* V, 140–1), as he styled him, who admonished French writers for their largely contemptuous attitude towards Greek dramatic literature.[24] He read Schlegel's lectures aloud in Black's English translation en route to Italy in March 1818 (*Journals: MWS* I, 198–9), and, as Jacqueline Mulhallen points out, *A Defence of Poetry* 'suggest[s] that his opinion of theatre was influenced by [them].'[25] Shelley's appreciation of 'the intense power of the choral poetry' in Greek drama and of masks to mould a 'dramatic character [...] into one permanent and unchanging expression' (*Major Works*, 683–4), for example, resonates with Schlegel's view that the chorus is 'the incorporation into the representation itself of the sentiments of the poet', and the mask 'absolutely essential' to 'the expression of the passion' in ancient Greek theatre.[26] Schlegel, then, offered Shelley a model of how to engage critically with Greek tragedy from a self-consciously modern but nonetheless sympathetic perspective.

Further suggestions that Greek tragedy shadows *The Cenci* may be found in the play's metatheatrical qualities. These include the dramatic irony registered in Lucretia's reaction to the arrival at the Castle of the Pope's Legate after the murder of Francesco Cenci: 'All was prepared by unforbidden means | Which we must pay so dearly, having done' (IV. iv. 29–30; quoted from *Major Works*). Such self-reflexivity haunts the play. Orsino's belief that he might exploit the 'self-anatomy' of the Cenci ("tis a trick of this same family | To analyse their own and other minds' (II. ii. 110, 108–9)) for his own ends is, by his own admission, foiled by a higher power:

> I thought to act a solemn comedy
> Upon the painted scene of this new world,
> And to attain my own peculiar ends
> By some such plot of mingled good and ill
> As others weave; but there arose a Power
> Which grasped and snapped the threads of my device
> And turned it to a net of ruin [...]
>
> (V. i. 77–83)

This 'Power' also conditions Beatrice's existence. According to the Preface, 'The crimes and miseries in which she was an actor and a sufferer are as the mask and the mantle in which circumstances clothed her for her impersonation on the scene of the world' (*Major Works*, 319). She is to be pitied because what the play's Dedication to Hunt describes as the 'sad reality' (*Major Works*, 314) of her situation is more suited to a classical performance of mythical proportions than a life endured just over two centuries previously. In short, her story has the same claim as the tales of Oedipus and King Lear to tragic treatment. But more salient than her life-story meeting the credentials of tragedy is the way that the Preface carries self-awareness, so notable a feature of this play's

[24] A. W. Schlegel, *A Course of Lectures on Dramatic Art and Literature*, trans. John Black, 2 vols. (London: Baldwin, Cradock, and Joy, 1815), I, 48.
[25] Jacqueline Mulhallen, *The Theatre of Shelley* (Cambridge: Open Book Publishers, 2010), 72.
[26] Schlegel, *A Course of Lectures*, I, 78, 63.

characters, over to the audience. In reminding us that had Beatrice reacted to her circumstances morally, 'she would never have been a tragic character', Shelley deploys Orsino's terminology to point up the reader's dilemma: 'It is in the restless and anatomizing casuistry with which men seek the justification of Beatrice, yet feel that she has done what needs justification [...] that the dramatic character of what she did and suffered, consists' (*Major Works*, 316–17). Of greater importance to Shelley than the fulfilment of Aristotelian conventions of tragedy (the key terms of *Poetics*—plot, action, *hamartia*, *catharsis*—are largely absent from his writing), is an understanding of its effect. Here, again, the Greek dimension of Shelley's thought, particularly his, in certain respects, Platonic understanding of tragedy, is illuminating.

On the final page of the text of *Agamemnon* in Shelley's pocket copy of Aeschylus, possibly salvaged from the wreck of the *Don Juan* after his death, is a barely legible pencilled note: 'This, & the two following plays may be considered as the distant [?acts] of our great drama—The two first end with an expectation. In the first the wicked triumph & the [?reader] is [?revealed] to a desire of moral & poetical justice.'[27] Both *The Cenci* and *Swellfoot the Tyrant* permit the suggestion that Shelley's purpose in his tragedies is no less than to educate his audience to 'a desire of moral & poetical justice'. That Plato's dialogues are instrumental to this end but opposed to the means demands elaboration given Shelley's reverence towards them. In his comment to Peacock of November 1820 that 'Plato and Calderon have been my gods' (*Letters: PBS* II, 245) lies an ostensible contradiction. How, in the same sentence, could he worship a philosopher whose *Republic* vows 'not to admit [the imitative poet] into a city which is going to be well governed',[28] and a dramatist, one of whose plays he had 'intentionally' plagiarized in *The Cenci* (*Major Works*, 755)? Martha Nussbaum's conception of Plato's dialogues as 'anti-tragic theater' is helpful here: 'If the dialogues are a kind of theater, owing a debt to tragic models, they are also a theater constructed to supplant tragedy as the paradigm of ethical teaching.'[29] However, Shelley strives for a bolder, more strategic accommodation by claiming in *A Defence of Poetry* that 'Plato was essentially a poet', who 'rejected the measure of the epic, dramatic and lyrical forms, because he sought to kindle a harmony in thoughts divested of shape and action' (*Major Works*, 679). Furthermore, his praise of the best drama—which 'teaches [...] self-knowledge and self-respect'—is expressed in notably Platonic terms:

> The drama, so long as it continues to express poetry, is as a prismatic and many-sided mirror, which collects the brightest rays of human nature and divides and reproduces them from the simplicity of these elementary forms; and touches them with majesty and beauty, and multiplies all that it reflects, and endows it with the power of propagating its like wherever it may fall. (*Major Works*, 685)

However, that great dramatic poetry mirrors to an audience 'the brightest rays of human nature' negates Plato's claim in *Republic* that it is civically corrosive in encouraging all

[27] *Æschyli Tragœdiæ ex editione Chr. Godofr. Schütz* (Oxford: N. Bliss, 1809), Bodleian [pr.] Shelley adds. g.1, p. 276. Quoted by kind permission of the Bodleian Libraries, University of Oxford.

[28] Plato, *The Republic*, ed. G. R. F. Ferrari, trans. Tom Griffith (Cambridge: Cambridge UP, 2000), 326.

[29] Martha C. Nussbaum, *The Fragility of Goodness: Luck and Ethics in Greek Tragedy and Philosophy*, rev. edn. (Cambridge: Cambridge UP, 2001), 129.

but the best citizens to succumb to their weakest, least rational impulses. Instead, with fifth-century BCE Athens in mind, Shelley asserts a correlation between the most advanced societies and the most aesthetically satisfying plays: 'the highest perfection of human society has ever corresponded with the highest dramatic excellence' (*Major Works*, 686). In times of degeneration (unlike those in which *A Defence of Poetry* was composed in early 1821, when, Shelley believed, political events heralded social change in Europe), the symptoms displayed by tragedy include 'a weak attempt to teach certain doctrines, which the writer considers as moral truths' (*Major Works*, 685). The Preface to *The Cenci* had laid the ground for this theory of tragedy. It professes an aversion to vulgar didacticism and promotes drama as a form uniquely placed to achieve elevated ethical ends:

> There must [...] be nothing attempted to make the exhibition [on the stage] subservient to what is vulgarly termed a moral purpose. The highest moral purpose aimed at in the highest species of the drama, is the teaching the human heart, through its sympathies and antipathies, the knowledge of itself; in proportion to the possession of which knowledge, every human being is wise, just, sincere, tolerant and kind. (*Major Works*, 316)

For Shelley, then, the eminence of tragedy rests on a Socratic paradigm. It should elicit the most worthwhile kind of knowledge, that which is grounded in sympathy ('the teaching the human heart [...] the knowledge of itself'), for goals such as the 'moral & poetical justice' noted in his pocket Aeschylus. Not only does he therefore undo Plato's objections to drama, he argues that more than any other literary form it has the potential to be transformative in social terms.

III

Shelley's response to hearing news of Peterloo in early September 1819 was to cite to Charles Ollier, his publisher, Beatrice's reaction to her rape: 'something must be done; | What, yet I know not' (III. i. 86–7) (*Letters: PBS* II, 117). This suggests his confidence that, notwithstanding its geographically and historically remote setting, *The Cenci* would have spoken directly to the national crisis in Britain had it been staged. Moreover, the word 'ITALY' on the title page of the first edition points to contemporary struggles to achieve nationhood abroad. In these terms, Beatrice, like the heroine of Staël's *Corinne* (1807), symbolizes the anguish of a frustrated people. That tragedy was a particularly potent means of mobilizing a national spirit is expressed by Oswald in Staël's novel: '"De tous les chefs-d'œuvres de la littérature, il n'en est point qui tienne autant qu'une tragédie à tout l'ensemble d'un peuple"' ('"Of all literary masterpieces there are none so intimately linked to a whole people as a tragedy"').[30] The dramatizations of generational

---

[30] Madame de Staël, *Corinne ou l'Italie*, ed. Simone Balayé (Paris: Gallimard, 1985), 190; Madame de Staël, *Corinne, or Italy*, trans. and ed. Sylvia Raphael, introd. John Isbell (Oxford: Oxford UP, 1998), 121.

conflict in *The Cenci* and of class division in *Swellfoot the Tyrant* may in this way be seen as attempts to forge in the audience a consensus about the grounds of justice. Their focus is on the fate of two women who take on the state, are tried, and then embraced power-fully in the popular imagination. Beatrice is ultimately destroyed where Iona Taurina, with Shelleyan flourish, is imagined as triumphing in the end, her final chorus with the Swine described by Timothy Morton as 'a muddier version of the psychedelics of *Prometheus Unbound* IV, with its exhilarating dance of reforming desire'.[31] However, Michael Simpson's sober perception of continuities between the treatment of Shelley's Beatrice and that of the historical Caroline is pertinent: '*The Cenci* seems proleptically to cite the Queen's [i.e. Caroline's] trial in the proceedings against Beatrice'.[32]

Within both plays lies an interrogation of Burke's *Reflections on the Revolution in France* (1790), the founding text in the revolutionary debate thirty years earlier. They call into question Burke's view that the national interest depends upon a social hierarchy, the patriarchal family, and the Church. The 'Chorus of the Swinish Multitude' in *Swellfoot the Tyrant* (Longman, 3, 659; play quoted from this edition), which sings that 'the Pigs are an unhappy nation!' (I. 60), builds on the numerous satirical responses since the 1790s to Burke's fearful portrayal of the masses. In telling Orsino that he and his father 'Are now no more, as once, parent and child, | But man to man; the oppressor to the oppressed' (III. i. 283–4), Giacomo appeals to an external agency to arbitrate his situa-tion. The result for him, his siblings, and their stepmother is an awareness that there is no escape from any one of the numerous manifestations of the patriarchal order because they all reinforce one another. The Pope's bitter irony, '"Authority, and power, and hoary hair | Are grown crimes capital"' (V. iv. 23–4), reported by Camillo in the final scene, is itself ironical in another sense for it invites us to see institutionalized authority in the play as equatable with capital crime. From the very first lines in which we learn of Count Cenci paying the Pope to buy silence for another murder, religion is seen as a licence for anarchy and a source of immorality. As the Preface puts it, 'Religion pervades intensely the whole frame of society, and is according to the temper of the mind which it inhabits, a passion, a persuasion, an excuse, a refuge; never a check' (*Major Works*, 317). Thus Beatrice's reply to the Judge's 'Art thou not guilty of thy father's death?' captures the essence of George Steiner's remark that, '[*The*] *Cenci*, in particular, come[s] closest in our literature to being what Tourneur had entitled *An Atheist's Tragedy*':

> Or wilt thou rather tax high-judging God
> That he permitted such an act as that
> Which I have suffered, and which he beheld;
> Made it unutterable, and took from it
> All refuge, all revenge, all consequence,
> But that which thou hast called my father's death?
>
> (V. iii. 78–83)

[31] Timothy Morton, 'Porcine Poetics: Shelley's *Swellfoot the Tyrant*', in Alan M. Weinberg and Timothy Webb (eds.), *The Unfamiliar Shelley* (Farnham: Ashgate, 2009), 291.

[32] Michael Simpson, *Closet Performances: Political Exhibition and Prohibition in the Dramas of Byron and Shelley* (Stanford, CA: Stanford UP, 1998), 394.

For Steiner, *Prometheus Unbound* and *The Cenci* 'press claims of human justice, of compassion, of reason against the arbitrary tyranny of the gods and the hypocritical despotism of religious institutions'.[33] Manuscript accounts of the narrative on which *The Cenci* is based came to light in the eighteenth century on the back of antiquarian research that challenged the power of the Church. Shelley's play offers an Enlightenment perspective on early modern Europe even as it reminds its audience of the proximity of aspects of a rebarbative age.

SELECT BIBLIOGRAPHY

Carlson, Julie A. 'A Theatre of Remorse'. *In the Theatre of Romanticism: Coleridge, Nationalism, Women*. Cambridge: Cambridge UP, 1994. 176–212.

Cox, Jeffrey N. 'The Dramatist'. *The Cambridge Companion to Shelley*. Ed. Timothy Morton. Cambridge: Cambridge UP, 2006. 65–84.

Curran, Stuart. *Shelley's* Cenci: *Scorpions Ringed with Fire*. Princeton: Princeton UP, 1970.

Erkelenz, Michael. 'The Genre and Politics of Shelley's *Swellfoot the Tyrant*'. *Review of English Studies* NS 47.188 (November 1996), 500–20.

Hall, Edith and Fiona Macintosh. *Greek Tragedy and the British Theatre 1660–1914*. Oxford: Oxford UP, 2005.

Jones, Steven E. '"Rough Festivals" and Charisma in *Oedipus Tyrannus; or, Swellfoot the Tyrant*'. *Shelley's Satire: Violence, Exhortation, and Authority*. DeKalb, IL: Northern Illinois UP, 1994. 124–48.

Morton, Timothy. 'Porcine Poetics: Shelley's *Swellfoot the Tyrant*'. *The Unfamiliar Shelley*. Ed. Alan M. Weinberg and Timothy Webb. Farnham: Ashgate, 2009. 279–95.

Mulhallen, Jacqueline. 'Practical Technique—*The Cenci*', and 'Satirical Comedy—*Swellfoot the Tyrant*'. *The Theatre of Shelley*. Cambridge: Open Book Publishers, 2010. 85–113, 209–34.

Parker, Reeve. 'Reading Shelley's Delicacy'. *Romantic Tragedies: The Dark Employments of Wordsworth, Coleridge, and Shelley*. Cambridge: Cambridge UP, 2011. 180–221.

Reiman, Donald H. 'Shelley's *Swellfoot*: Critics' Stepchild'. *SC* X, 772–812.

Richardson, Alan. '"Self-Anatomy" and Self-Consciousness in *The Cenci*'. *A Mental Theater: Poetic Drama and Consciousness in the Romantic Age*. University Park, PA: Pennsylvania State UP, 1988. 100–23.

Schlegel, A. W. *A Course of Lectures on Dramatic Art and Literature*. Trans. John Black. 2 vols. London: Baldwin, Cradock, and Joy, 1815.

Shelley, Mary. Trans. 'Relation of the Death of the Family of the Cenci'. Ed. Betty T. Bennett. *BSM* X, 157–272.

Simpson, Michael. 'Role Playing in *The Cenci*'. *Closet Performances: Political Exhibition and Prohibition in the Dramas of Byron and Shelley*. Stanford, CA: Stanford UP, 1998. 375–99.

Staves, Susan. 'Tragedy'. *The Cambridge Companion to British Theatre, 1730–1830*. Ed. Jane Moody and Daniel O'Quinn. Cambridge: Cambridge UP, 2007. 87–102.

Steiner, George. '"Tragedy," Reconsidered'. *New Literary History* 35.1 (Winter 2004), 1–15.

---

[33] George Steiner, '"Tragedy," Reconsidered', *New Literary History* 35.1 (Winter 2004), 7.

CHAPTER 20

SHELLEY'S 'FAMILIAR STYLE'

Rosalind and Helen, Julian and Maddalo, and Letter to Maria Gisborne

ANTHONY HOWE

I

IN *A Defence of Poetry* Shelley writes that

> poetry defeats the curse which binds us to be subjected to the accident of surrounding
> impressions. […] It makes us the inhabitants of a world to which the familiar world
> is a chaos. It reproduces the common universe of which we are portions and percipi-
> ents, and it purges from our inward sight the film of familiarity which obscures from
> us the wonder of our being. (*Norton 2*, 533)

For Shelley here 'familiarity' is a 'curse', a cataract-like 'film' upon the 'inward sight'; it is
the glass through which we see the 'universe' darkly. Poetry, however, has the capacity to
remove this obstruction; it 'purges' our vision, allowing us to behold the true 'wonder of
our being'. It 'lifts the veil from the hidden beauty of the world, and makes familiar
objects be as if they were not familiar' (*Norton 2*, 517), a process of visionary enlightenment that for Shelley finds a parallel in political emancipation: through the 'abolition of
personal slavery', he writes, the 'familiar appearance and proceedings of life' become
'wonderful and heavenly' (*Norton 2*, 525).

This pejorative take on 'familiarity' has significant implications for Shelley as both
poet and political writer. Given his account of poetry as a positive force for *de*familiariz-
ing the world, any attempt to write a 'familiar' poetry would, according to Shelley's own
logic, risk compromising the writer's capacity to effect change. However, as a poet with
political aspirations—one who had been involved in disseminating polemical literature
for a general audience (including the literate working class)—Shelley also knew that his
potential success was linked to his ability to find a publicly appealing voice. The most
successful radical writers of the day, notably Thomas Paine, typically used a clear and

direct prose style, accessible to readers with limited literary education. Shelley, however, although frustrated by the limited extent of his audience (a situation made all the worse by the proximity of the hugely popular Byron), remained, on the whole, true to his poetics of defamiliarization and to a hope that the future would understand what the present chose largely to ignore. He tended to prefer those of his works which most fully embodied the aesthetic and political ideals of *A Defence*, notably the demandingly abstract *Prometheus Unbound*, which, in the poet's own short lifetime at least, was little read.

Despite his apparent preferences, however, Shelley, an experimental writer and one always conscious of audience, was by no means a purely abstruse writer. *The Mask of Anarchy*, as well as its own ironies and insecurities, possesses some of the full-tilt, earnest radicalism of *Queen Mab*, whereas *The Witch of Atlas* is a fruitful experiment in a plausible serio-comic style. Then there are the poems it is the task of this chapter to describe, which are not like *Prometheus Unbound* or *Queen Mab*, but which are not satires or comedies either (although *Letter to Maria Gisborne* has strong comic elements). They are, rather, poems grounded in forms of idealized biography that emerge from the flow and exchange of intimate social experience. Their interest derives in part from the provisional resistance of such experience to the authoritative stances typical of visionary and didactic writing. Their fascination lies in their unofficial status, in their rising to poetry despite their author's hierarchical sense of poetic style.

Of *Julian and Maddalo*, Shelley wrote to Hunt that

> I send you a little Poem to give to Ollier for publication but *without my Name*. [...] I wrote it out with the idea of offering it to the Examiner, but I find that it is too long. It was composed last year at Este; two of the characters you will recognize; the third is also in some degree a painting from nature, but, with respect to time and place, ideal. You will find the little piece, I think, in some degree consistent with your own ideas of the manner in which Poetry ought to be written. I have employed a certain familiar style of language to express the actual way in which people talk with each other whom education and a refinement of sentiment have placed above the use of vulgar idioms. I use the word *vulgar* in its most extensive sense; the vulgarity of rank and fashion is as gross in its way as that of Poverty, and its cant terms equally expressive of bare conceptions, and therefore equally unfit for Poetry. Not that the familiar style is to be admitted in the treatment of a subject wholly ideal, or in that part of any subject which related to common life, where the passion exceeding a certain limit touches the boundaries of that which is ideal. [...] But what am I about. If my grandmother sucks eggs, was it I who taught her? (*Letters: PBS* II, 508)

Although prepared to work in a 'familiar style of language', Shelley insists, as did Hazlitt, that such a style must be free from 'vulgarity', regardless of its social origin.[1] But even with this caveat in place, Shelley still seems uncertain about his 'familiar' work, referring

---

[1] 'It is not easy to write a familiar style. Many people mistake a familiar for a vulgar style, and suppose that to write without affectation is to write at random. On the contrary there is nothing that requires more precision, and, if I may so say, purity of expression, than the style I am speaking of. It utterly rejects not only all unmeaning pomp, but all low, cant phrases, and loose, unconnected, *slipshod allusions*.' William Hazlitt, 'On Familiar Style', in *The Selected Writings of William Hazlitt*, ed. Duncan Wu, vol. VI (London: Pickering and Chatto, 1998), 217–22 (217).

to it condescendingly as a 'little Poem' and a 'little piece' (despite its acknowledged length). Compared to *Prometheus Unbound*—'the most perfect of my productions' and 'in my best style' (*Letters: PBS* II, 519)—*Julian and Maddalo* was clearly thought of by its author as a second-class citizen in the world of poetry.[2] While proposing a similar literary mode, Shelley was less comfortable than Hazlitt in championing the apparent spirit of literary democracy that also informs Wordsworth's theorization of the *Lyrical Ballads*. This does not mean that Shelley treats of less momentous subjects with his 'familiar style'—on the contrary *Julian and Maddalo* and *Prometheus Unbound*, both structurally and thematically, have much in common[3]—but that Shelley's disrespect for authority rarely extended to literary form and tradition. Indeed, Shelley's attenuated investment in the familiar could be seen as motivated as much by his immersion in (from a modern egalitarian perspective) elitist cultures as democratic enthusiasm. As Donald Davie noted, 'urbanity', that tone of 'unflurried ease between poet and reader', which, despite the 'whole pressure of Shelley's age [being] against anything of the kind', is a distinctive presence in the poet's oeuvre.[4] Shelley may have quotably said that 'I had rather err with Plato than be right with Horace' (*Letters: PBS* II, 75), but he was, nevertheless, much less concerned than some of his contemporaries to throw off Augustan poetic practice.

The 'familiar' Shelley persists in the face of his unlikeliness; he is—as Davie recognized in a way that historicism's revision of Arnold's ineffectual angel has on the whole not—a source of energy and fruitful complication, a fact nowhere more apparent than at the end of the passage above. Perhaps conscious of his patrician air, Shelley suddenly assumes a more familiar, even 'vulgar' ('If my grandmother sucks eggs, was it I who taught her?') idiom. As William Keach points out, he strikingly modulates his style even in discussing it.[5] It is a liberty licensed by friendly correspondence, but one that speaks, nonetheless, to an intriguing tension that humanizes a political and aesthetic vision too often subjected to dry paraphrase.

II

Shelley began writing *Rosalind and Helen, a Modern Eclogue* in Switzerland in the summer of 1816 and finished it, after a number of interruptions, in Italy in August 1818.[6] The poem thus bridges a personal and creative gap between a worried, but semi-nostalgically remembered home life in England and a life of exile in Italy that offered the possibility of finding a home. It was published under Shelley's name by Ollier in 1819

[2] Shelley wrote to Ollier: 'if you print *Julian and Maddalo* I wish it to be printed in some unostentatious form' (*Letters: PBS* II, 196). With *Prometheus Unbound*, however, Ollier was instructed 'specially to pet him and feed him with fine ink and good paper' (*Letters: PBS* II, 551).

[3] See G. M. Matthews, ' "Julian and Maddalo": The Draft and the Meaning', *Studia Neophilologica* 35.1 (1963), 57–84 (73).

[4] Donald Davie, *Purity of Diction in English Verse* (1952; Manchester: Carcanet, 2006), 118.

[5] William Keach, *Arbitrary Power: Romanticism, Language, Politics* (Princeton: Princeton UP, 2004), 57.

[6] See *Longman*, 2, 266–8 for full composition details.

as the title poem of a volume that also included 'Lines Written among the Euganean Hills', 'Hymn to Intellectual Beauty', and 'Ozymandias' (entitled 'sonnet' in the original volume). The poem received a relatively large amount of contemporary critical attention, including some praise (primarily from Hunt in *The Examiner*), although it was mainly used by critics to attack Shelley's heterodox views and unconventional lifestyle.[7]

Hunt's review immediately recognizes Shelley's attempt to write a 'more popular style of poetry' by describing an impacted domestic experience very different from the refined introspection of *Alastor* or the epic political idealism of *Laon and Cythna*.[8] *Rosalind and Helen* is a 'human interest' poem of the kind that Mary, who laid claim to it as 'my pretty eclogue' (*Letters: MWS* I, 43), and who provides the model for Helen, seems often to have urged Shelley to write.[9] The poem's interest is also decidedly female and, through its critique of male domestic tyranny, arguably feminist, a fact which pays tribute to Mary's familial heritage, but which may also signal an attempt to engage a growing female readership. For the generous Hunt these developments are unequivocally positive: the 'humanity', he avers, 'is brought nearer to us, while the abstractions remain as lofty and noble' (442). Shelley, however, was typically reticent about his more 'familiar' poetry. Anticipating his uncertainty about *Julian and Maddalo*, he writes, in the Advertisement to the collection, that the poem is 'not an attempt in the highest style of poetry' (*Longman*, 2, 268) and, in letters to both Peacock and Ollier (*Letters: PBS* II, 29, 31), refers to it a 'little poem' (it is over 1,000 lines). Shelley's sense of his poem as 'light and unstudied' (*Letters: PBS* II, 31) has been generally accepted by critics, of whom Reiman is representative in claiming that '*Rosalind and Helen* [is] the weakest of Shelley's longer poems'.[10]

As *Longman* notes, *Rosalind and Helen* has often been read primarily in terms of its political content (2, 269), Kenneth Neill Cameron, for instance, seeing the poem as 'a passionate exposition of [Shelley's] social beliefs'.[11] The observation is accurate, but its expression has infrequently coincided with an attempt to understand the poem's complex generic and formal thoughtfulness. This is especially problematic because the poem is arguably at its weakest precisely when it is at its most polemical. Quick to exploit this was John Gibson Lockhart, who, although less fashionable in his politics, demonstrates a surer sense of the poem's style than many of his critical descendants. Lockhart praises the poem's frequent touches of beauty and acknowledges Shelley's huge potential as a poet, before turning, with a destructive intent fortified by his stylistic engagement, to Shelley's anti-establishment politics. The 'cold, bald, clumsy, and lifeless parts of this poem', Lockhart complains, 'are those in which [Shelley] obtrudes upon us his

---

[7] John Taylor Coleridge dismissed the poem in a single line of the *Quarterly Review* before launching into an extensive, highly personal demolition of Shelley's work and character. *Quarterly Review* 21 (April 1819), 460–71; reprinted in Donald H. Reiman (ed.), *The Romantics Reviewed: Contemporary Reviews of British Romantic Writers* (New York: Garland, 1972), Part C, II, 770–6.

[8] *The Examiner*, 9 May 1819, 302–3; reprinted in *The Romantics Reviewed*, C, I, 442–4 (442).

[9] See Shelley's note to Mary at the head of *The Witch of Atlas*.

[10] *The Romantics Reviewed*, C, I, 442. A notable exception is John Donovan, '*Rosalind and Helen*: Pastoral, Exile, Memory', *Romanticism* 4.2 (1998), 241–73.

[11] Kenneth Neill Cameron, *Shelley: The Golden Years* (Cambridge, MA: Harvard UP, 1974), 253.

contemptible and long-exploded dogmas. Then his inspiration deserts him.'[12] He is in part right: *Rosalind and Helen* more often stumbles than glides into its politics, as with Helen's stilted couplet: 'But the youth, for God's most holy grace, | A priest saved to burn in the market-place' (165–6).[13]

Lockhart's mistake was not a failure of literary sensitivity, but lies in his de-radicalizing of the majority of a poem blemished by a politics too insecure to encounter the literary on its own terms. Lionel, Helen's dead lover and the poem's anti-authoritarian authority figure, may be the Shelleyan self-portrait 'that renders most of the essential spirit of Shelley',[14] but it is also perhaps the most intrusive with respect to its own poetic environment. Lionel is an idealized martyr to British tyranny who bravely confronts the severe legal sanctions that Shelley's self-exile may well have evaded, yet his heroic death also leaves him lifeless with respect to the poem's stylistic achievement. The only point at which we hear his voice directly, through Helen's incorporation into her narrative of a tear-blotted poem of his discovered 'on the ground' (762), is also a rare moment of formal orthodoxy. Lionel's poem is formed of two rather forced *ottava rima* stanzas (764–79), which, when compared to the emotional close attention of Helen's surrounding speech, seem lacking in nuance, both formally and politically.

Shelley was clearly diffident about what he saw as the lower style of *Rosalind and Helen*, but he was also (as he would be with *Julian and Maddalo*) exercised in his discussions of the poem as a stylistic experiment. In the Advertisement he writes that 'I resigned myself, as I wrote, to the impulse of the feelings which moulded the conception of the story; and this impulse determined the pauses of a measure, which only pretends to be regular inasmuch as its corresponds with, and expresses, the irregularity of the imaginations which inspired it' (*Longman*, 2, 268–9). Similarly, he wrote to Peacock that the poem's 'metre corresponds with the spirit of the poem, and varies with the flow of the feeling' (*Letters: PBS* II, 29). Both to the public and even to his more politically sympathetic friends Shelley stresses not his poem's political vision, but its stylistic innovation. Indeed, as Donovan notes, it was—or was at least perceived to be by the establishment literary press—an 'outrage to a sensibility schooled to value a classical appropriateness of style'.[15]

Rosalind and Helen, however, is far from being a calculated affront to aesthetic orthodoxy; it is a poem caught between a generalizing or 'idealizing' impulse and a tense proximity to home, biographically and generically as well as formally. Rosalind's brutal husband is based on David Booth, the controlling husband of Rosalind's original Isabel Baxter (Shelley used 'Isabel' instead of 'Rosalind' throughout his notebook draft), whose broken friendship with Mary provides the biographical basis of the poem.[16] Booth is negatively 'idealized' as a malicious domestic tyrant, but even in departing from life

---

[12] *Blackwood's Edinburgh Magazine* 5 (June 1819), 268–74; reprinted in *The Romantics Reviewed*, C, I, 104–10 (110).

[13] Shelley's poetry is quoted from *Longman* unless otherwise stated.

[14] H. Buxton Forman, *Rosalind and Helen, A Lecture* [to the Shelley Society] (London: printed for private circulation, 1888; not paginated).

[15] Donovan, '*Rosalind and Helen*: Pastoral, Exile, Memory', 253.   [16] See Bieri, 278.

(Booth may have been severe but he was no monster) Shelley re-echoes it through the husband's cruel will (which deprives Rosalind of her children), a reference to the poet's own failed custody battle by which he was deprived of the children of his marriage to Harriet Westbrook. Generically, the poem is also fraught in its holding to, yet scrambling of, allusion. Shelley explicitly evokes Virgil in his subtitle, but complicates this positioning via a series of generic references, including Shakespearian comic pastoral (Rosalind's name is probably borrowed from *As You Like It*), *Lyrical Ballads*, and Southey's 'Botany-Bay Eclogues', the clustered ironies of which are reconstituted by Shelley to interesting effect.[17]

Formally, the poem repeatedly 'pretends' to a regularity that although never sustained to the point of habituation (familiarity), is nevertheless grounded in, without any ironic show of pretence, standard forms of English metrical composition. The majority of the poem is written in tetrameter rhyming couplets and tetrameter alternating rhymes (together creating some of the feel of the version of *terza rima* used in 'Ode to the West Wind'), although we also encounter triplets, unrhymed lines (which often cut short developing patterns), envelope rhymes, half rhymes, eye rhymes, sudden injections of anapaest, nine- and ten-syllable lines, and inserted, stand-alone lyrics. It is a poem of hectic propriety, composed in the face of an approached but finally resisted dissolution. Its feel is more *déjà vu* than *coup d'état*.

The result, while uneven, is distinguished by a remarkable sensitivity to emotional transition. Helen's insecure nostalgia, which no doubt reflects Shelley's own complex feelings about the England he had recently left behind, is introduced in the tension between an over-musical triplet and a lonely mono-rhyme:

> Those heathy paths, that inland stream,
> And the blue mountains, shapes which seem
> Like wrecks of childhood's sunny dream:
> Which that we have abandoned now,
> Weighs on the heart like that remorse
> Which altered friendship leaves. I seek
> No more our youthful intercourse.
>
> (24–30)

The quick chimes of nostalgia terminate in 'abandoned now', a present state which finds no echo in what comes before or after. This leads to a bitter, bolted down sentence— 'I seek | No more our youthful intercourse'—that in turn gives way to an outpouring of increasingly desperate, imperative neediness:

> That cannot be! Rosalind, speak,
> Speak to me. Leave me not.—When morn did come,
> When evening fell upon our common home,
> When for one hour we parted,—do not frown:
> I would not chide thee, though thy faith is broken:
> But turn to me.
>
> (31–6)

[17] See Donovan, '*Rosalind and Helen*: Pastoral, Exile, Memory', 251.

Helen's release into longer, de-regularized pentameter lines both liberates her and wrings her out. Caught somewhere between the sharp speech patterns of Jacobean Tragedy and the peculiar realism of the Romantic Ballad, her vocal oscillations represent well a poem that is repeatedly, and thus never quite entirely, familiar.

III

Shelley wrote *Letter to Maria Gisborne* in June 1820 in Leghorn (Livorno), Italy, where he and Mary were staying in the house of their friends John and Maria Gisborne, who were in London, trying to settle the future of Henry Reveley, Maria's son by a previous marriage. The Shelleys first met the Gisbornes two years earlier when they made the first of three visits to Livorno. Although they found the place dull, Maria, a friend of William Godwin (he had proposed marriage to her), was, according to Mary, a 'saving grace', 'a lady of great accomplishments', with a 'frank and affectionate nature', an 'intense love of knowledge', and 'a delicate and trembling sensibility'.[18] Her husband, although an edu-cated man (this is clear from Shelley's letters to him), made less of an impression, Shelley calling him a 'great bore' (*Letters: PBS* II, 119) in one letter to Peacock. Henry Reveley, from whose workshop the poem imaginatively emerges, was an aspiring nautical engi-neer who was attempting to build, with Shelley's financial help, a commercial steamboat to run from Marseille to Livorno.

Shelley's *Letter* was sent to London with a more conventional prose letter to the Gisbornes in early July 1820.[19] The poet's wishes regarding publication are difficult to determine because he said very little on the subject. Mary insisted to Maria, in a letter of 7 July, that it must 'on no account be published' (*Letters: MWS* I, 153), although she did include it in her posthumous edition of 1824, where she gave it the title by which it has come to be known. It is also clear that the poem was not intended exclusively for Maria's eyes, although she is the primary addressee. Shelley clearly expected that the manuscript would be shown to John and especially Henry, who is remembered warmly through Shelley's descriptions of his workshop. The poem also encourages its own wider dissem-ination among mutual London acquaintances, several of whom, including Godwin, Hogg, Hunt, Peacock, and Horace Smith, are referred to directly in the poem through a mixture of courteous flattery and familiar repartee. Coterie correspondence of this kind was not unusual for the Shelleys, whose letters often specify a multiple audience—a practical as well as sociable tactic when disseminating news from abroad (letters were expensive and might be lost in transit). Shelley's letters to Hunt and Peacock from Milan in 1818, for instance, are described as 'common property' (*Letters: PBS* II, 14) to Hogg;

---

[18] *The Poetical Works of Percy Bysshe Shelley*, ed. Mary Wollstonecraft Shelley (London, 1839), IV, 50.
[19] On this issue see N. I. White, 'Probable Dates of Composition of Shelley's "Letter to Maria Gisborne" and "Ode to a Skylark"', *Studies in Philology* 36 (1939), 524–8. There is an excellent account of the poem's history in the notes to the forthcoming (at the time of writing) Longman edition. I would like to thank Dr Rossington for showing me a draft of his work.

they were not written just for the eyes of the addressee, but were meant for other mutual friends as well.

But despite being an occasional piece of writing apparently limited in terms of its potential audience, Shelley's *Letter* seems always to be straining against its familial tethering. Partly this is the effect of a complex invocation of poetic tradition. It is striking that what seems one of Shelley's most temporary works is also one of his most intricate acts of positioning in relation to literary precedent. *Letter* alludes formally, generically, and thematically to a range of poetic-epistolary precursors, including Donne, Dryden, Pope, Prior, Cowper, and Cotton.[20] There are flavours, also, of Jonson's 'Inviting a Friend to Supper' (with vegetarian options) and of a more comedic version of the Coleridgian conversation poem—through Shelley's eager imagining from remote isolation: 'But what see you beside?—a shabby stand | Of Hackney coaches—a brick house or wall [...]' (265–6).[21] We are reminded also of Shelley's admiration for Byron's *Don Juan*. *Letter* is a poem, as Timothy Webb notes, crammed full of 'unyielding material' that 'insists on its own intransigence',[22] even at the expense of formal decorum. As with *Rosalind and Helen*, this accumulation of generic allusion establishes its own kind of frenetic familiarity, as well as raising the question of the poem's apparent impermanence by linking it to other occasional, but in some cases canonical, poems.

Letter begins in defiance of expectation, with an introspective account of the poet's literary isolation rather than the second person address we might anticipate:

> The spider spreads her webs, whether she be
> In poet's tower, cellar, or barn, or tree;
> The silk-worm in the dark green mulberry leaves
> His winding sheet and cradle ever weaves;
> So I, a thing whom moralists call worm,
> Sit spinning still round this decaying form,
> From the fine threads of verse and subtle thought—
> No net of words in garish colours wrought
> To catch the idle buzzers of the day—
> But a soft cell, where when that fades away,
> Memory may clothe in wings my living name
> And feed it with the asphodels of fame
> Which in those hearts which must remember me
> Grow, making love an immortality.
>
> (1–14)

There is at once here a strongly critical sense of the contemporary literary scene (with its 'idle buzzers', 'garish colours', and sham 'moralists') and an involving, evasive combination of reflexive metaphors less inviting of paraphrase. As Michael O'Neill

---

[20] See Ann Thompson, 'Shelley's "Letter to Maria Gisborne": Tact and Clutter', in Miriam Allott (ed.), *Essays on Shelley* (Liverpool: Liverpool UP, 1982), 144–59 (144–7).

[21] The poem is quoted from *Norton 2* unless otherwise stated.

[22] Timothy Webb, 'Scratching at the Door of Absence: Writing and Reading "Letter to Maria Gisborne"', in Alan M. Weinberg and Timothy Webb (eds.), *The Unfamiliar Shelley* (Aldershot: Ashgate, 2009), 119–36 (131).

points out, Shelley projects a 'fascinating indecision' about his status as writer by playing between the figures of the spider and the silkworm.[23] The former is curiously ironic in demonstrating Shelley's knowledge of the literary past (he has in mind, among other sources, Swift's *The Battle of the Books*) while at the same time apparently identifying with those—for Swift risible—writers who treat, roughly speaking, of the present and self over the accumulated universal wisdom of tradition. Through the silkworm, however, Shelley enters a very different possibility, that of his being taken up into 'immortality'. His present death—or exile from the poet's true sphere—anticipates a more glorious future life, just as the insect, in creating its cocoon or 'soft cell', is at once spinning his 'winding sheet and cradle'. This future, however, seems highly uncertain, depending as it does on the poem's immediate—and politically precocious—readers, those who, Shelley seems hopefully to insist, 'must remember me'.[24] Shelley seems caught between possibilities and audiences, drawn between the local and the universal, the transitory and the permanent, the familiar and the ideal.

Amidst the paraphernalia of the workshop, Shelley pictures himself—perhaps recalling some humorous banter with Henry—as a 'mighty mechanist' (16), using 'figured spells' (20) to bring a 'machine portentous' (19) to life. The jovial parallel between engineer and poet brings to mind the creative role of the latter as one who works on his disparate materials through a historically extensive and politically charged imagination. Following in a way the logic of *A Defence*, his own mental clutter of familiar images is reorganized into a new and surprising whole:

> For round the walls are hung dread engines, such
> As Vulcan never wrought for Jove to clutch
> Ixion or the Titans:—or the quick
> Wit of that man of God, St. Dominic,
> To convince Atheist, Turk or Heretic;
> Or those in philanthropic council met,
> Who thought to pay some interest for the debt
> They owed to Jesus Christ for their salvation,
> By giving a faint fortaste of damnation
> To Shakespeare, Sidney, Spenser and the rest
> Who made our land an island of the blest,
> When lamp-like Spain, who now relumes her fire
> On Freedom's hearth, grew dim with Empire—

(23–34)

Henry's 'dread engines' bring to mind Zeus's torture of Ixion, which rapidly turns to anti-Christian sentiment as Shelley alludes to the Catholic Church's apparent use of torture to 'convince' non-believers to change their faith. St Dominic was active in the Spanish Inquisition, which leads to Spain's sixteenth-century crusade against Protestant

[23] Michael O'Neill, 'The Mind which Feeds this Verse: Self- and Other-Awareness in Shelley's Poetry', in Michael O'Neill and Mark Sandy (eds.), *Romanticism: Critical Concepts in Literary and Cultural Studies*, vol. I (Abingdon: Routledge, 2006), 244–74 (260).
[24] Shelley sounds even less certain in an important transcript of the poem by John Gisborne (followed to different degrees by *Longman* and *Major Works*) where 'must' reads as 'most'.

England (as well as politicizing his poem here, Shelley is also personalizing it: Maria taught Shelley Spanish primarily so that he could read the great dramatist Calderón in the original).[25] This also brings to mind the great English poets of that age, who, Shelley implies, prospered under the relatively tolerant rule of Elizabeth. Spain's oppressive past is also contrasted with its liberated present as Shelley celebrates the country's recent military uprising and constitutional revolution (in 1820), which, as *Longman* notes, led to the abolition of the Inquisition.[26] The missing element from this historical patterning is the England of Shelley's birth, which, from the poet's perspective at least, nicely completes the reversal of national fortunes in being rather closer to old Spain than to new. Certainly its poets, who are castigated by the establishment press and variously exiled, are far from flourishing.

This flitting between past and present (one thinks again of the poet of *A Defence*, for whom 'time and place and number are not' (*Norton 2*, 513)) as well as private and public is a characteristic of the poem again evident when, later in his monologue, Shelley returns to his Spanish lessons:

> Or how I, wisest lady! Then indued
> The language of a land which now is free
> And winged with thoughts of truth and majesty
> Flits round the tyrant's sceptre like a cloud,
> And bursts the peopled prisons, and cries aloud,
> 'My name is Legion!'—that majestic tongue
> Which Calderón over the desert flung
> Of ages of nations; and which found
> An echo in our hearts, and with the sound
> Startled oblivion—thou wert then to me
> As is a nurse when inarticulately
> A child would talk as its grown parents do.
>
> (175–86)

Spain's 'majestic tongue' has banished the conditions ('the familiar appearance and proceedings of life') that enabled its downtrodden past, a linguistically driven reawakening which for Shelley is crucially aligned with the country's literary tradition. The seamless emergence of this polemical thread from Shelley's own progress as Hispanist also suggests a place for the poet himself in this process of literary-political development, and thus hints at his own potential emancipative role. The true poet is for Shelley one who re-appropriates linguistic energy and refigures establishment rhetoric, as he does here by turning 'majesty' and 'majestic' against the 'tyrant's sceptre' and by using biblical allusion to figure the overthrow of a Church-sponsored state.

The poem's mode of political and psychological projection is especially complex. We encounter a plausible, mutually grounding mixture of self-preoccupation, ironic

---

[25] In a letter to Peacock Shelley wrote that Calderón 'exceeds all modern dramatists with the exception of Shakespeare; whom he resembles however in the depth of thought & subtlety of imagination of his writings, & in the rare power of interweaving delicate and powerful comic traits with the most tragical situations without diminishing their interest' (*Letters: PBS* II, 515).

[26] Compare Shelley's letter to Peacock of 23–4 January 1819 (*Letters: PBS* II, 75).

potential, and dauntless universal interest. Shelley's 'familiar style' is in this respect an attempt to naturalize such simultaneity. Yet this intriguing persona finds its strength in a process that also points to the likelihood of its final defeat. The poet's immediate surroundings may be transmuted, through a quicksilver imagination, into a partial vision of human emancipation, but his status as exile—both emotional and political—always acts as a reminder of the marginalized status of the visionary.

In the tradition of Calderón (as Shelley read him at least), the poem interweaves comic and 'tragic' traits without losing the force of either; it observes, as in this powerfully vulnerable address to Maria, dramatic mood swings:

> How I ran home through last year's thunder-storm,
> And felt the transverse lightning linger warm
> Upon my cheek—and how we often made
> Feasts for each other, where good will outweighed
> The frugal luxury of our country cheer,
> As well it might, were it less firm and clear
> Than ours must ever be;—and how we spun
> A shroud of talk to hide us from the sun
> Of this familiar life, which seems to be
> But is not:—or is but quaint mockery
> Of all we would believe, and sadly blame
> The jarring and inexplicable frame
> Of this wrong world: [...]

(148–60)

Shelley is here both child and adult. The first line, with its breathless, fast-slow rhythms, sees him returning to a recollected, fantasy 'home' now emptied of its maternal presence by the needs of a real son. As if conscious of the slip, Shelley is quick to assert the equality of the friendship in their subsequent provision 'for each other', a return to adult reality accompanied by a shift from touchingly comic familiarity to existential angst. This both looks back to the poem's opening and anticipates the powerful account of the 'familiar world' in *A Defence*. Recalling the silkworm spinning his 'winding-sheet' that is also a 'cradle', Shelley describes how together the friends spun a 'shroud of talk' to escape the unreal reality of 'this familiar life'. The metaphor suggests that the poet's existence in such a world is a form of living death, animated by nothing more (although also nothing less) than the sympathy and conversation of fellow exiles and a faith in poetry as a form of immortality. There seems no easy way to the optimism of *A Defence* here: the 'familiar' is not a veil to be torn aside by the visionary, but a 'sun' under which the dissident must find shade as best he might. To know that the world 'seems to be | but is not' is all very well, but such knowledge makes that world no less 'inexplicable' or 'wrong'. The 'wondrous' life beyond, for all Shelley's belief therein, seems impossibly distant, a confirmation of the political and philosophical exile of the poet. The 'familiar style' cannot be fully endorsed because of its immersion in self and present and its consequent tendency to obscure the ideals Shelley held most dear. On the other hand, this most touchingly familiar poetry reveals a mode of life that for all its huddled seeming is no less profound than Shelley's highest idealizations.

IV

In August 1818 Shelley travelled to Venice to speak to Byron on the tricky subject of the latter's illegitimate daughter. Soon after Shelley's arrival, the two poets, who had not met since 1816, rode together along the Lido. The event is immortalized by the opening lines of *Julian and Maddalo: A Conversation*.[27]

A short prose preface introduces the poem's main characters: Julian, another, and perhaps the most self-critical, of Shelley's self portraits, is a political idealist of 'good family', 'a scoffer at all things reputed holy' and 'passionately attached to those philosophical notions which assert the power of man over his own mind'. He is also 'rather serious' (*Longman*, 2, 661–2). Count Maddalo is a broodingly Byronic nobleman of 'ancient family and great fortune', a 'consummate genius' but 'proud' and consumed by his own 'impatient feelings'. He derives, 'from a comparison of his own extraordinary mind with the dwarfish intellects that surround him, an intense apprehension of the nothingness of human life' (*Longman*, 2, 660–1). The third main character, the Maniac, is less easy to pin down in biographical terms, although the enigmatic revelation that he is 'in some degree a painting from nature' has prompted much speculation.[28]

The narrative is composed almost entirely of loose pentameter rhyming couplets. It opens with Julian—now as narrator—revelling in an intense, mutual solitude:

> I love all waste
> And solitary places; where we taste
> The pleasure of believing what we see
> Is boundless, as we wish our souls to be.
>
> (16–19)

The pair converse in an atmosphere of 'merriment' (27), their talk rapid, witty, instinctive, something Shelley captures perfectly with the savouring progression through 'waste'—'places'—'taste'. This is precisely what Shelley intended for his 'familiar style'—a musically heightened, educated voice grounded in ordinary diction and the tones of conversation:

> So, as we rode, we talked; and the swift thought,
> Winging itself with laughter, lingered not,
> But flew from brain to brain,—such glee was ours— [...]
>
> (28–30)

Rather than the threatening isolation of Shelley and Maria, this solitary scene is accompanied by an expansive sense of optimism—yet the 'glee' is as fleeting as the

---

[27] See *Letters: PBS* II, 36–7 for Shelley's account of the meeting. For the biographical and compositional background see *Longman*, 2, 656–7.

[28] Cameron asserts that 'there can be little doubt that the madman is Shelley' (*Shelley: The Golden Years*, 262) and Bieri, more cautiously, that the Maniac's agonized feelings and thoughts are those of Shelley' (Bieri, 478). The Maniac has also been identified with both Byron and with Tasso (Matthews, '"Julian and Maddalo": The Draft and the Meaning', 82).

thought by which it is animated. As soon as the fragile 'I' gives way to the collective 'we taste',[29] that vast unknown of audience that haunts even Shelley's most private moments, Julian is on borrowed time. Pleasure must give way to disagreement, to the dark pedagogy of the Maniac, and to a struggle to rescue hope from despair.

The poem is structured by, and conventionally read in terms of, the debate between Shelleyan optimism and Byronic pessimism set out in the Preface. Shelley's arrogation of narrative authority has prompted some critics to see the poem as playing out a victory of the former over the latter.[30] But this is to underestimate the pressure applied to Julian's seriousness. On more than one occasion his argumentative flow is interrupted by events that resist the more immediately assimilative tendencies of Shelleyan polemic. The stunning prospect of the Lido sunset, for instance, suspends debate in poetic animation:

> Those famous Euganean hills, which bear
> As seen from Lido through the harbour piles
> The likeness of a clump of peaked isles—
> And then—as if the Earth and Sea had been
> Dissolved into one lake of fire, were seen
> Those mountains towering as from waves of flame
> Around the vaporous sun, from which there came
> The inmost purple spirit of light, and made
> Their very peaks transparent.
>
> (70–8)

Via an initial touch of tourist vulgarity, Julian's voice is called from its opposition to Maddalo's 'darker side' (49) to the creative undoing of this Turneresque magnificence. Argument—a testing of subjectivity—is subsumed in a process of defamiliarization that recalls *A Defence* and its implication that style and form can only gain revolutionary potential at the expense of direct address.

It is a complex sense of this predicament that distances Shelley from Julian and which allows Maddalo to transcend the apparent containment of the Preface. The poem's philosophical argument, that is to say, is grounded in and finally referred over to a literariness that holds adjudication at bay. Symbol both pre-exists and survives the conflicting conclusions it generates, as it does when Maddalo manoeuvres Julian into his first glimpse of the Maniac's forlorn abode:

> I looked, and saw between us and the Sun
> A building on an island; such a one
> As age to age might add, for uses vile;
> A windowless, deformed and dreary pile.
>
> (98–101)

---

[29] Shelley heavily revised this section of his poem in his draft notebook, where he initially used the second person ('you taste', 'you see') before changing it to 'we' (*BSM* XV, 66).

[30] Charles E. Robinson, *Shelley and Byron: The Snake and Eagle Wreathed in Fight* (Baltimore: Johns Hopkins UP, 1976), 101.

This slow-vowelled accretion of 'uses' immediately becomes the centre of debate, each observer reading it from his peculiar philosophical perspective. For Julian, the monkish 'madhouse' offers an opportunity to scoff at religion and its deleterious effects, as he understands them, through history. As the building stands 'between us and the Sun', so superstition intervenes, rather like the 'film' of *A Defence*, between Man and existential self-realization. Maddalo, however, takes a more generous attitude towards religion (as Byron tended to do, especially in his Italian years), blaming man's debasement not on tyranny and superstition but on his own irredeemably fallen nature. Julian 'should' be right, Maddalo concedes, but the hard enervations of Byronic experience have taught him otherwise. This argument-through-interpretation continues the next morning when Julian, on visiting Maddalo and his young daughter, takes the child, with her eyes that 'seem | Twin mirrors of Italian heaven' (147–8), as a sign of human perfectibility. Maddalo, however, refuses to admit such optimism and counters with a cautionary tale about an acquaintance of his—the Maniac—who held similar opinions to Julian and who is now 'gone mad' (198). We are brought not to a conclusion but to a deferral, to a choice of readings that will be offered once more, immediately prior to the silence of ending. Julian may, in Maddalo's characteristically Byronic phrase, make his radical-idealist 'system refutation-tight', but only as 'far as words go' (194–5). His victory, in a poem that witnesses the confrontation of Enlightenment faith by a reluctant mustering of the forces of irrationalism is far from certain.

Any claim for a philosophical outcome to the poem, moreover, needs to account for the presence of the Maniac, whose defining psychological abnormality, and its compelling expression, again works to displace the poem's organizing 'conversation' (Julian confesses that in the latter's presence 'our argument was quite forgot' (520)). Attendant upon this is the abolition of the 'familiar style', the Maniac's fractured logic and jagged lines (which come to dominate the poem) having little in common with the earlier descriptions of urbane exchange. This silencing also calls into question—at least provisionally—Shelley's suggestion (in the letter to Hunt) that the poem's achievement be judged with final reference to its familiarity. The Maniac is, as Shelley told Hunt, 'with respect to time and place, ideal'; he thus transcends the 'familiar', which, we also recall, is not 'to be admitted in the treatment of a subject wholly ideal'. The poem's initial environment of fragile emancipation, this overwriting of styles seems to suggest, must be broken apart and remade if we are to achieve the true freedom Shelley invokes in *A Defence*.

It is the Maniac, therefore, and not the fictional Byron or Shelley, who is the poem's true poet. Cursed in his moment yet potent in the poet's timeless element, his madness and his poetry are inextricably one:

> The colours of his mind seemed yet unworn;
> For the wild language of his grief was high,
> Such as in measure were called poetry.

> (540–2)

This 'wild language' is a tragically located ideal Shelleyan poetry, an uneasy alignment that helps us to understand the claim, made in the poem's Preface, that the 'unconnected exclamations of [the Maniac's] agony will perhaps be found a sufficient comment for the text of every heart' (*Longman*, 2, 663). The Maniac's rewriting of the poem's familiarity, that is, opens onto the possibility of a universal—and specifically textual—process of self-realization. The familiar is cast aside to reveal truth in its beyondness. But just as the present moment cannot be securely transcended in *Letter*, so the Maniac's unhinged poetry cannot escape the cell of its author's dislocation. Weighed down by self and the maddening impositions of a 'cold world' (617), it remains 'wild', unmeasured, and fails to actualize the transformative potential of the ideal artist. The Maniac's lines are thus doomed to permit the possibility of being read—and quite legitimately—as 'tiresome and unpoetic'.[31]

The madman's cell stages and represents Shelley's darkest reflection on poetry. It is a space in which the fundamental sanities of poetic communication come under impossible stress:

> How vain
> Are words! I thought never to speak again,
> Not even in secret,—not to my own heart—
> But from my lips the unwilling accents start
> And from my pen the words flow as I write,
> Dazzling my eyes with scalding tears [...] my sight
> Is dim to see that charactered in vain
> On this unfeeling leaf which burns the brain
> And eats into it [...] blotting all things fair
> And wise and good which time had written there.
>
> (472–81)

If writing and talking simultaneously seems appropriate to a man of dislodged reason, it also speaks of the distressed sense of audience that lies behind Shelley's predicament as a poet. Those delicately musical parallel lines beginning 'But from' and 'And from' run together the optimistic charge and pessimistic reflux of Shelleyan poetics: the vanity of words, their unwillingness to escape subjective entrapment with respect to their ideal potentiality, is succeeded by their flowing into ink, and its potential, to borrow Byron's rhyme, to make millions think. The possibility of reaching an audience—which relies in turn upon a capacity for the familiar—is troublingly mixed up in the poet's stymied reaching out to truth. Beyond the death-life of the insect's softer cell in *Letter*, the Maniac becomes a powerful symbol of the tensions caused by Shelley's apparently incompatible theories of poetry and public vocation.

But the poem does not end here; there are enough pieces to pick up in the final thirty lines or so to offset maniacal finality and to anticipate the directions in which Shelley's words will flow. There is the undimmed 'bright Venice' that Julian leaves the following morning and there is also Maddalo's daughter, 'of transcendent worth | Like one of Shakespeare's women' (591–2), a reminder both of human potential and the ineradicable benevolence of tradition. Then there is the return, through the re-uptake of Julian's narration, of the 'familiar style', which persists as a mode of poetry and life even in the face

---

[31] Davie, *Purity of Diction in English Verse*, 122.

of its apparent secondariness. This is no glorious victory over the questions posed by deep truth, nor does it take us very far—only to the poem's final, inscrutable act of withholding ('the cold world shall not know' (617))—but it does register something of life's irrepressibility and its value even in its triteness. It hints to us that if *Julian and Maddalo* is a poem of depression, then it is one that incorporates the logic of its own cure.

SELECT BIBLIOGRAPHY

Buxton, John. *Byron and Shelley: The History of a Friendship*. London: Macmillan, 1968.

Bradley, Arthur. '"Winging itself with laughter": Byron and Shelley after Deconstruction'. *Romantic Biography*. Ed. Arthur Bradley and Alan Rawes. Farnham: Ashgate, 2003. 152–68.

Cronin, Richard. *Shelley's Poetic Thoughts*. London: Macmillan, 1981.

Davie, Donald. *Purity of Diction in English Verse* [first published 1952]. Manchester: Carcanet, 2006.

Donovan, John. '*Rosalind and Helen*: Pastoral, Exile, Memory'. *Romanticism* 4.2 (1998), 241–73.

Everest, Kelvin. 'Shelley's Doubles: An Approach to *Julian and Maddalo*'. *Shelley Revalued: Essays from the Gregynog Conference*. Leicester: Leicester UP, 1983. 63–88.

Hall, James M. 'The Spider and the Silkworm: Shelley's "Letter to Maria Gisborne"'. *Keats-Shelley Memorial Bulletin* 20 (1969), 1–10.

Hill, James L. 'Dramatic Structure in Shelley's *Julian and Maddalo*'. *ELH* 35 (1968), 84–93.

Matthews, G. M. '"Julian and Maddalo": The Draft and the Meaning'. *Studia Neophilologica* 35.1 (1963), 57–84.

O'Neill, Michael. *Romanticism and the Self-Conscious Poem*. Oxford: Clarendon Press, 1997.

Robinson, Charles E. *Shelley and Byron: The Snake and Eagle Wreathed in Fight*. Baltimore: Johns Hopkins UP, 1976.

Thompson, Ann. 'Shelley's "Letter to Maria Gisborne": Tact and Clutter'. *Essays on Shelley*. Ed. Miriam Allott. Liverpool: Liverpool UP, 1982. 144–59.

Webb, Timothy. 'Scratching at the Door of Absence: Writing and Reading "Letter to Maria Gisborne"'. *The Unfamiliar Shelley*. Ed. Alan M. Weinberg and Timothy Webb. Aldershot: Ashgate, 2009.

CHAPTER 21

··

SONNETS AND ODES

··

MICHAEL O'NEILL

SHELLEY may be, as Harold Bloom put it eloquently, the author of a poetry that 'is autonomous, finely wrought, in the highest degree imaginative'; he is at the same time responsive and recreative in his dealings with other poets.[1] Hugh Roberts notes the 'circulatory vision of cultural (re-)creation' evident in Shelley's work generally and in his Prefaces, in particular. For Roberts, these Prefaces urge 'the reader to see [Shelley's] texts as existing within a noisy pre-existing universe'.[2] Simultaneously sympathetic to Bloom's and Roberts's emphases, this chapter explores how in his sonnets and odes Shelley sustains a vision that is at once solitary and collective, heroic and democratic, lyrical and dramatizing.

I

··

Especially as catalysed by the 1807 'Sonnets Dedicated to Liberty', Wordsworthian influence on Shelley's sonnets is undeniable. In the sestet of 'Milton! thou should'st be living at this hour', Wordsworth praises his mentor in terms that Shelley picks up with ironic resonance, both in his early sonnet 'To Wordsworth', deploring the senior poet's falling-off, as the younger poet saw it, from his early political radicalism, and in *Adonais* which co-opts for its own purposes Wordsworth's central symbol of praise, expressed in the following lines in the older poet's lines:

> Thy soul was like a Star and dwelt apart:
> Thou hadst a voice whose sound was like the sea;
> Pure as the naked heavens, majestic, free,
> So didst thou travel on life's common way,

[1] Harold Bloom, 'The Unpastured Sea: An Introduction to Shelley', in *The Ringers in the Tower: Studies in Romantic Tradition* (Chicago: University of Chicago Press, 1971), 87.
[2] Hugh Roberts, 'Noises On: The Communicative Strategies of Shelley's Prefaces', in Alan M. Weinberg and Timothy Webb (eds.), *The Unfamiliar Shelley* (Farnham: Ashgate, 2009), 197, 196.

In chearful godliness; and yet thy heart
The lowliest duties on itself did lay.

(9–14)[3]

After the indignation of the octave, in which 'England' is said to be 'a fen | Of stagnant waters' (2–3), these lines, the evident point of departure for Shelley's 'To Wordsworth' (published in *Alastor and Other Poems* (1816)), themselves imply loss as well as celebration. 'Thou hadst a voice' is a formulation that suggests that 'we' do not possess it. 'To Wordsworth' pushes further at the implications of the phrase to suggest that Wordsworth had a voice, one able to 'weave | Songs consecrate to truth and liberty' (11–12), but has now forsaken it.[4] Shelley's poem contains a complex set of intertextual references to Wordsworth's poetry, 'Ode: Intimations of Immortality' featuring in particular alongside the sonnet to Milton. Its construction disputes the 'legitimate' or Petrarchan form used by Wordsworth. Shelley's rhyme schemes in his sonnets vary from poem to poem in concord with their redefining moods and themes. In 'To Wordsworth' he rhymes the octave as two quatrains, follows this with a couplet, then finishes with another quatrain in alternating rhyme:

> Poet of Nature, thou hast wept to know
> That things depart which never may return:
> Childhood and youth, friendship and love's first glow,
> Have fled like sweet dreams, leaving thee to mourn.
> These common woes I feel. One loss is mine
> Which thou too feel'st, yet I alone deplore.
> Thou wert as a lone star, whose light did shine
> On some frail bark in winter's midnight roar:
> Thou hast like to a rock-built refuge stood
> Above the blind and battling multitude:
> In honoured poverty thy voice did weave
> Songs consecrate to truth and liberty,—
> Deserting these, thou leavest me to grieve,
> Thus having been, that thou shouldst cease to be.

Shelley does not use the poem's one couplet at the end for summary, for a reproving axiom, but places it at the head of his sestet to re-evoke Wordsworth's former greatness, the couplet reinforcing a sense of him as 'a rock-built refuge' who 'stood | Above the blind and battling multitude'.[5] The formulation suggests how one side of Shelley's imagination, so far as a poet's politics is concerned, warms to the heroic and shows a wariness of the 'multitude'.[6] Yet the last two lines' syntactical and semantic separateness, along

---

[3] Quoted from *21st-Century Oxford Authors: William Wordsworth*, ed. Stephen Gill (Oxford: Oxford University, 2010).

[4] In this chapter poems are quoted from *Longman*.

[5] See Karen Weisman for the suggestion that 'the oddly placed couplet' hints at lurking 'fault lines' in 'Wordsworth's commitment', 'The Lyricist', in Timothy Morton (ed.), *The Cambridge Companion to Shelley* (Cambridge: Cambridge UP, 2006), 45–64 (54).

[6] *Longman* 1 glosses as ' "thoughtless followers of the doctrine of self-interest" rather than the common people as such' (455 n.), but this distinction is not entirely clear from Shelley's words.

with the closeness in sound of the words in the rhyme position ('grieve' and 'be'), retains something of the effect of a couplet without any tendency to jingling triteness. Indeed, the last line, in particular, underscores how the sonnet thrives on evoking the dynamics of influence.[7] In its preference for monosyllables and its plangent use of the verb 'to be', 'Thus having been, that thou shouldst cease to be' could almost be mistaken for a line from Wordsworth at his barest and most elegiacally stark.

The cunning of Shelley's sonnet is to direct such Wordsworthian effects against Wordsworth himself. 'To Wordsworth' addresses a mentor who has made poetry possible for younger writers, then let them down. It twists and turns, using Wordsworthian phrases, now to celebrate, now to qualify. 'These common woes I feel' is a salute to the poet who is alive, in 'Ode: Intimations of Immortality', to the baleful impact on 'the vision splendid' (73) of 'the light of common day' (76). It is also faintly disdainful, suggesting that Wordsworth's elegiac radar has detected relatively easy targets, 'Childhood and youth, friendship and love's first glow', 'common' just hinting, on Shelley's part, at the establishment of distance. Where mentor and disciple cleave asunder begins in the same line: 'One loss is mine | Which thou too feel'st, yet I alone deplore'. That 'alone' has a for-lornness, a sense of being 'deserted' (to use a form of the word that Shelley employs at the start of the poem's penultimate line), which carries on into and yet plays against the next line's reference to the 'lone star' that Wordsworth once was. And yet, competing with this forlornness is a sense that Shelley's 'aloneness' has a newly significant status; the poem is an assertion of his capacity to 'deplore'. His capacity for critique of Wordsworth indicates his power over the older poet. Shelley writes an elegiac farewell which declares that Wordsworth has, like his Lucy in 'She dwelt among th'untrodden ways', 'ceased to be' (see l. 10 of Wordsworth's poem). Bringing out 'The difference to me' ('She dwelt among th' untrodden ways', 12), Shelley weaves a song 'consecrate to truth and liberty' by plaiting his own inflections with and setting them against those of Wordsworth.

In a sonnet, finally entitled 'Political Greatness', fair-copied in 1820 and copied for the press in 1821,[8] Shelley sought to clarify what political 'truth and liberty' might be. The sonnet was written in the wake of the failed rising in the Neapolitan town of Benevento against King Ferdinand (an earlier fair copy was entitled 'To the Republic of Benevento'). Michael Rossington writes persuasively in the light of the poem's context in February 1821 (when it received its title 'Political Greatness') that it 'chides the Tuscans generally [...] for their unwillingness to assist the Neapolitan cause'.[9] Characteristically of Shelley, it aims to locate an underlying ethical principle beneath the historical specifics:

---

[7] See, among other essays, Graham Allen, 'Transumption and/in History: Bloom, Shelley, and the Figure of the Poet', *Durham University Journal* NS 54 (1993), *Percy Bysshe Shelley: Special Issue*, guest ed. Michael O'Neill, 247–56.

[8] See *Longman*, 3, 618–19, for details.

[9] See *Longman*, 3, 621; Rossington quotes from Shelley's letter to Claire Clairmont of 18 February 1821, in which Shelley deplores those who mock the Neapolitan rebels, describing such mockers as 'a set of slaves who dare not to imitate the high example of clasping even the shadow of freedom' (quoted *Longman*, 3, 621).

> Nor happiness, nor majesty nor fame,
> Nor peace nor strength, nor skill in arms or arts
> Shepherd those herds whom Tyranny makes tame:
> Verse echoes not one beating of their hearts;
> History is but the shadow of their shame;
> Art veils her glass, or from the pageant starts
> As to oblivion their blind millions fleet
> Staining that Heaven with obscene imagery
> Of their own likeness. What are numbers, knit
> By force or custom? Man, who man would be,
> Must rule the empire of himself; in it
> Must be supreme, establishing his throne
> On vanquished will; quelling the anarchy
> Of hopes and fears; being himself alone.

The poem directs its rapid, tight-lipped hostility towards 'those herds whom Tyranny makes tame'. It derives its tone of forensic clarity from its Godwinian emphasis on an ethic of self-rule.[10] In a manner familiar from *Prometheus Unbound*, with its subversion of regal and imperial language, it contends that the only 'empire' over which the truly free man should rule is that 'of himself'; the only 'throne' he should occupy or respect is that 'established' over 'vanquished will'; the only victory is that which has 'will' and 'anarchy' as its foes. But the poem is more than doctrine in verse as Shelley uses his control of pace, of speeding and slowing, with great expressiveness. A variation on a reversed Petrarchan sonnet, the poem's opening six lines (the inverted sestet) flow beyond any division, capturing the way in which the 'blind millions fleet' towards 'oblivion'. If every 'modern sonnet becomes partly a sonnet about sonnets', Shelley's sonnet has a particular interest in the function of the 'Verse' that 'echoes not one beating of their hearts', where 'beating' anticipates the self-reflexive suggestions of 'numbers, knit | By force or custom'.[11]

In *Longman* 3 'numbers' is glossed as possibly having the 'sense of "metrical periods or feet; lines, verses"', a suggestion seen as implying that art has the power to criticize tyranny.[12] Yet Shelley depicts 'art' as being potentially complicit with tyranny, failing to speak to or of the 'blind millions', or as parodied by the 'blind millions', said sardonically to be 'Staining that Heaven with obscene imagery | Of their own likeness'. The antecedent of 'that Heaven' is the heaven of Art, but 'oblivion' flickers for a second as a possibility. It is almost as if, in the process of taking a sideswipe at the crowd for their obscene staining, Shelley attacks Heaven itself as merely a form of oblivion towards which everything hurtles, including Art. The phrasing in 'obscene imagery | Of their own likeness' arrests: the poem is itself in danger of succumbing to just such an 'obscene imagery', and, as though aware of the danger, the sonnet stops short, letting the fleeting

---

[10] See *Longman*, 3, 622.

[11] A. D. Cousins and Peter Howarth, 'Introduction', in A. D. Cousins and Peter Howarth (eds.), *The Cambridge Companion to the Sonnet* (Cambridge: Cambridge UP, 2011), 3.

[12] *Longman*, 3, 624 n.

imagery whirl by, and settles for restrained statement, rather like a man taking deep, deliberate breaths in an effort to articulate precisely after an outburst. The effect is to prevent statement from just being statement: the language of the close visibly exercises self-control, establishing its 'throne | On vanquished will' in a series of curt syntactical gestures that seek to affirm some stay against 'the shadow of […] shame' that 'History' can all too easily seem to be.

The syntactical structure of the last few lines recalls the close of Wordsworth's 'I grieved for Buonaparte', a sonnet which most clearly influenced Shelley's sonnet in the *Alastor* volume, 'Feelings of a Republican on the Fall of Bonaparte', where initial hate passes into something more subtly qualified: 'I know | Too late, since thou and France are in the dust, | That virtue owns a more eternal foe | Than force or fraud' (10–13). There, the restlessly enjambed lines imply a political consciousness disturbed out of simplistic dualisms, while the dance of abstractions bears witness to an intensity of redefinition. At the end of 'I grieved for Buonaparte', Wordsworth describes the influences that should shape 'The Governor who must be wise and good' (6). 'Books, leisure, perfect freedom, and the talk | Man holds with week-day man in the hourly walk | Of the mind's business: these are the degrees | By which true Sway doth mount; this the stalk | True Power doth grow on; and her rights are these' (10–14). Wordsworth's concept of heroism involves emphasis on the ordinary and the mind, and his notions of 'true Sway' and 'True Power' are antithetical to any vainglorious idea of greatness. The appositional phrases themselves give us a sense of 'degrees'. In 'Political Greatness', Shelley appears to have adopted or adapted Wordsworth's concluding cadences, with their clipped run of phrases. But in doing so he departs from the sense of domestic virtue at the heart of Wordsworth's vision, replacing it with a turbulent overcoming of turbulence, and ending with the enigmatically virtuous condition of 'being himself alone'. The lack of absolute calm is a clue to the poem's power; it halts, but the rhythmic wheels still spin. That the final word is 'alone' supports the sonnet's metapoetic dimension; in keeping with the poem's theme, its very form revitalizes convention by insisting on the significance of individuality, an impression sharpened by the rhyme scheme that disturbs as it reverses the division into octave and sestet. 'Political Greatness' opposes the knitting performed by 'force or custom', while allowing its emergent ideals to stay in vibrant relationship with their opposites. Creative rule wards off, yet cannot quite banish, the memory of misdirected energy as the sound held in 'fleet' carries over (in a half-rhyming way) to 'knit' and 'it'. The fact that the key phrase 'Man, who man would be' rhymes with the 'anarchy' which he must 'quell' keeps open such 'anarchy' as an ever-present possibility.

'Political Greatness' takes the shopworn word 'great' and invites us to look at it differently. In the earlier 'Ozymandias' Shelley deals with a fallen, parodic form of political greatness, allowing imperial pretension and regal arrogance their boastful, hollow sonority:

> I met a traveller from an antique land,
> Who said—'Two vast and trunkless legs of stone
> Stand in the desert... near them, on the sand,
> Half sunk a shattered visage lies, whose frown,

And wrinkled lip, and sneer of cold command,
Tell that its sculptor well those passions read
Which yet survive, stamped on these lifeless things,
The hand that mocked them, and the heart that fed;
And on the pedestal these words appear:
My name is Ozymandias, King of Kings,
Look on my Works ye Mighty, and despair!
Nothing beside remains. Round the decay
Of that colossal Wreck, boundless and bare
The lone and level sands stretch far away'.—

Unlike Horace Smith's sonnet 'Upon a Stupendous Leg of Granite [...]', probably written in friendly competition with Shelley, the poem does not allow itself an easy passage from ruin to reflection. Smith's sonnet is a virtually regular Petrarchan sonnet, with a clear break between octave and sestet; it turns the 'gigantic Leg' (2), 'The only shadow that the Desert knows' (3), into a remnant of a 'forgotten Babylon' (8) that induces a 'Wonder' (10) which may be felt, too, by some future 'Hunter' (9) who comes across similar fragments when he moves 'thro' the wilderness | Where London stood' (10–11).[13] The poem is stylish but facile. Shelley's sonnet stages a more disturbed and disturbing encounter between art and history. A mediated traveller's tale, it depends for its effectiveness on concise implication: the reported legend on the pedestal—'My name is Ozymandias, King of Kings, | Look on my Works ye Mighty, and despair!'—gets its come-uppance in the brief three-word sentence which follows, 'Nothing beside remains'. The final vista of 'lone and level sands' stretches alliteratively beyond the sway and grasp of 'that colossal Wreck' in a mesmerizing figuration of time's 'levelling' erosions, a levelling which has a politically democratic flavour.

The report comes from 'an antique land', both ancient Egypt and 'an antic' place that is a mirror of contemporary imperialist projects.[14] The poem's 'I' is the reverse of the egotistical self at the heart of the sonnet from Petrarch onwards; he drops out, having passed on to the 'traveller'. In turn, the traveller repeats the self-imploding words which Ozymandias presumably decreed should be incised on his 'pedestal'. The traveller also makes us aware of a further crucial figure, the 'sculptor' who, in seeming to praise an all-powerful ruler, reveals his alertness to his master's 'passions [...] | Which yet survive, stamped on these lifeless things'. Empires crumble; artistic indirections 'survive', shaping a truth about history through a dissembling show of complicity. The sculptor's work shows that he 'well those passions read | [...], | The hand that mocked them, and the heart that fed'. The sonnet is about 'reading', interpretation, activities fundamental to any historical perspective. Yet the syntax immediately points up difficulties in any process of reading, since we have to wait until line 8 to realize that 'survive', which has appeared to be used in an intransitive sense, does, in fact, function transitively. The traveller's interpretation of the sculptor's interpretation brings out the

---

[13] Quoted from *Longman* 2.
[14] For a possible pun on 'antic', see Derek Guiton and Nora Crook, *Shelley's Venomed Melody* (Cambridge: Cambridge UP, 1986), 99.

latter's power. Without 'The hand that mocked them', that is, the hand of the sculptor working in imitative and subliminally scornful mode, there would be no evidence of the ruler's 'passions' or of 'the heart that fed' them. A poem about that Enlightenment topos, the inevitable subjection of empire to temporal ruination, speaks too of art's capacity to ensure 'survival'.[15] Yet there is little sense of triumph in art's powers of insight; rather, the sonnet suggests the challenge posed by history to art. Its form reinforces impressions of a near-inevitable progression towards 'decay' and all that stretches beyond it (including the potentiality for change and hope), and of the tenacity needed by the artist in tracking such a progression. Here, the poem's 'I', understood as an organizing principle, re-enters, presiding over the avoidance of easy symmetry, for example. This avoidance shows in the heterodox handling of the sonnet; the rhyme scheme disrupts any neat division into octave and sestet while connecting the poem's vestigial sections through the rhyme in lines 7 and 10.[16] At the same time, a driving pattern of aligned sounds (an instance is the linkage set going across the poem by 'met' culminating in the last line's 'level' and 'stretch') bears witness to a concentrated intensity of vision.

Comparable intensity and tension between sonneteering self and an alter ego appear in Shelley's more metaphysical sonnets. 'Lift not the painted veil' is a reversed Petrarchan sonnet that starts with admonition and ends with evocation of the quest against which we are warned. 'Lift not the painted veil which those who live | Call Life; though unreal shapes be pictured there, | And it but mimic all we would believe | With colours idly spread' (1–4): the sonnet's opening makes strange 'Life', suggesting a compulsion heralded by the second line's 'though' to get beyond the 'unreal shapes' that are 'pictured there' (2), even as it critiques the compulsion on the grounds that behind the veil there are only further unrealities, 'shadows' (6) woven by 'Fear | And Hope' (4–5). At the back of these veils, pictures, and shadows, none of them taking on more than momentarily adumbrated reality, is a 'chasm, sightless and drear' (6). Shelley suggests that the deep absence of truth is imageless, and yet the poem derives pathos from its account of a quester who sounds like a version of the self, one unable to heed the poem's opening injunction, driven by a longing for 'things to love' (8). This figure is the subject of that fine balance of empathy and detachment evident in many of Shelley's portraits of alter egos. What told in the first person would be insufferable egotism seems more like fated idealism when reported in the third person. Again, Shelley sets the individual against the 'many' in a sonnet: 'Through the unheeding many he did move, | A splendour among shadows, a bright blot | Upon this gloomy scene, a Spirit that strove | For truth, and like the Preacher found it not' (11–14). Originally, in an anticipation of 'Political Greatness', the poem concluded, 'I should be happier had I never known | This mournful man—he was himself alone'.[17] But that 'aloneness' is less principled ideal, as it is in the later poem, than existential predicament. Shelley's revision supplies a wryly

---

[15] For subtle reflections on the way the poem's textual fortunes participate in the temporality which is its subject, see Kelvin Everest, '"Ozymandias": The Text in Time', in Kelvin Everest (ed.), *Percy Bysshe Shelley: Bicentenary Essays* (Cambridge: Brewer, 1992), 24–42.

[16] See *Longman*, 2, 309n.   [17] Quoted from *Longman*, 2, 415n.

ironic affinity between dissatisfied quester and disillusioned author of Ecclesiastes, concluding the poem with the phrase 'found it not', in turn rhyming with the oxymoronic 'bright blot' which the quester cannot but be in a world that is, were it not for his longing desire, merely a 'gloomy scene'. The sonnet's love of oppositions allows Shelley to produce a distilled x-ray in the poem of the invidious choice between meaningless endurance and idealistic self-destruction which he explores in *Alastor*. Yet the poem's flicker of humour in 'like the Preacher' permits it not wholly to endorse either of the possible attitudes it sketches at the close. The sonneteer's own control and ironies hold open the door for future explorations, should the need to find 'splendour' amidst 'shadows' reassert itself.

II

'Ah! that once more I were a careless child!' (14): Coleridge's line at the close of his 'Sonnet to the River Otter' uses its artful patterning of sound to hold sentimentality at arm's length; the line is less an immersion in self-pity than an expert miming of an unrealizable wish.[18] It is an influence at work in the crucial fourth section of 'Ode to the West Wind', Shelley's virtuosic conversion of *terza rima* sonnets into an ode. A further Coleridgean influence, on this as on other Shelleyan odes, is the older poet's 'France: An Ode', which, according to Medwin, Shelley thought 'the most perfect of compositions,—the most faultless in spirit and truth in our language'.[19] 'France: An Ode' shapes an intricate stanza form out of the sonnet-form, its twenty-one lines adding half a sonnet to itself; Shelley's *terza rima* breaks the sonnet-form into small units which are then overwhelmed by ongoing enjambment. Coleridge's poem identifies 'Freedom' (88), in an accelerating alexandrine, as 'The guide of homeless winds, and playmate of the waves' (98). Shelley's 'Ode to the West Wind' both aspires to and struggles with such homelessness, housed within its formal confines.[20]

In the fourth section of 'Ode to the West Wind', the poetic 'I' enters the poem explicitly for the first time after three sections evoking the tumultuous operation of the wind on land, in the air, and in the sea. Shelley takes the Coleridgean wish for simplified consciousness and makes it the pivot of a poem that wrestles with the question of the poet's role, which at this point is found to be overwhelming, Shelley bringing the section's series of conditional clauses to an anguished focus:

[18] Quoted from Samuel Taylor Coleridge, *The Complete Poems*, ed. William Keach (London: Penguin, 1997).

[19] Thomas Medwin, *The Life of Percy Bysshe Shelley*, ed. H. Buxton Forman (London: Oxford UP, 1913), 344.

[20] For a comparison between these poems, see my essay 'The Romantic Sonnet', in *The Cambridge Companion to the Sonnet*, 199.

> If even
> I were as in my boyhood, and could be
>
> The comrade of thy wanderings over Heaven,
> As then, when to outstrip thy skiey speed
> Scarce seemed a vision, I would ne'er have striven
>
> As thus with thee in prayer in my sore need.

(47–52)

Like Coleridge, Shelley yearns for 'boyhood', seeing it, however, less as time free from care than as a period when capability seemed to match desire. Now, in adult life, the poem records the onset of 'vision' (in the sense of an imagining known to be illusory) and conflict, a conflict caught in the way in which 'Heaven' enters into a tensely rhymed relationship with 'striven'. Shelley, as commentators have noted, assumes biblical accents as he depicts himself striving 'As thus with thee in prayer in my sore need'.[21] The word 'thus' gives self-aware immediacy to the entire poem; it is such striving 'in prayer', the reader recognizes, that has characterized the poem's pattern of invocations and entreaties, especially the repeated cry that the wind should 'hear' (14, 28, 42).[22] Shelley's ode adapts the quasi-religious quality of the ode form, a form that often involves meditation on and supplication of a higher power, to his own conception of his role, function, and career as a poet. That career seems at the close of section IV, where he cries, 'I fall upon the thorns of life! I bleed!' (54), to have brought him to a point where the appropriate analogues are with the poetic outcries of his contemporaries. Near-blasphemous as it suggests comparison with Christ's suffering, the entire passage conveys a mood of sinking and abasement, of exhausted energies, a mood enhanced by the stressed monosyllables. In the section the poet comes to terms with, and is evidently weighed down by, his own subjectivity and the 'heavy weight of hours' (55) which he has had to endure. Just hinting at an escape from abasement is the proud line which concludes the section, 'One too like thee: tameless, and swift, and proud' (56).

Momentarily Shelley has anticipated the great post-Romantic American poet Wallace Stevens, who writes in 'Men Made out of Words' of being 'torn by dreams, | By the terrible incantations of defeats | And by the fear that defeats and dreams are one'.[23] The Romantic poet asserts in the fifth section a powerful, affecting will to rise above such a 'fear'. Building on the glimpse of identity postulated in 'One too like thee', Shelley's strategy, as he seeks to lift himself out of a vision of 'defeats', is to fuse his creative destiny with the wind's force: 'Make me thy lyre, even as the forest is' (57) is how the final section begins. Yet 'even as' has a calculated over-assertiveness; it shows and betrays the poet's knowledge that, as the possessor of a consciousness capable of 'striving' (see 51), he can never quite be 'as the forest is'. In some moods, Shelley may have been persuaded 'that inspiration originates in a power independent of the mind'.[24] Yet in the fifth section of

---

[21] Bloom speaks of the section as 'Jobean in quality', *Shelley's Mythmaking* (New Haven: Yale UP, 1959), 84.

[22] Again there is a biblical echo. Compare Psalm 102: 1, 'Hear my prayer, O Lord, and let my cry come unto thee.'

[23] Quoted from *The Collected Poems of Wallace Stevens* (London: Faber, 1955).

[24] *Longman*, 3, 211n.

the ode, a contrary or complementary persuasion, that inspiration is generated by the self, is also evident. Shelley scrawled in Greek below a draft of the final lines the words 'In virtue I, a mortal, surpass you, a great god', a quotation from Euripides' *Hercules Furens* line 342,[25] and the gradual movement from beseeching prayer to commanding imperative in the final section marks an equivalent assertion by the poet.

'Thy', 'thou', 'my', and 'me' are the markers of attempted union and a final settling for relationship, one in which the wind and poet employ one another. 'Be thou me, impetuous one!' (62) is at once request and command; it is, we sense, aware in its very insistence that it is doomed not to be fulfilled, almost as though it were anticipating Stevens's wry commentary in 'Notes Toward a Supreme Fiction', 'Bethou him, you | And you, bethou him and bethou. It is | A sound like any other. It will end' ('It Must Change', VI). Stevens's text suggests that 'bethou' is nothing more than a rhetorical gesture; Shelley's poem shapes the capacity to articulate 'A sound' into a sign of imaginative energies that rival those of the wind, as he cries exultingly, in an 'incantation' that may leave its mark on Stevens's 'Men Made out of Words', 'And, by the incantation of this verse, | Scatter, as from an unextinguished hearth | Ashes and sparks, my words among mankind!' (65–7). Shelley here discovers the positive aspect of being a figure not at one with the natural elements; he can shape 'this verse', the poem we are reading, and in doing so, turn the wind into an instrument of his will that his words reach 'mankind'. Assertiveness coexists with qualification; two stress shifts at the start of successive lines bring home the fact that Shelley expects the wind to 'Scatter' his words, both to disseminate them widely and to let them fall in an almost random way; there are, too, suggestions of something sacrificial in the scattering, as though Shelley were an Orphic poet whose words were to be dismembered by a wind which destroys as well as preserves (see 14) and has already been associated, in its effects on the cloudy tumult of 'the approaching storm' (23), with 'some fierce Maenad' (21). Greek and Christian mythologies, drawn on by the poem, coalesce in a vision of the inevitable symbiosis of extinguishing and rekindling. The poet's words are 'Ashes and sparks', simultaneously that which has burned itself out and that which can give rise to new fires. The poem may long to assist in the bringing on of some political change if we wish so to allegorize 'the approaching storm', yet it allows, too, for the poet's words to fall where they will, to compose, above all, a 'prophecy' (69) of a 'new birth' (64). 'Be through my lips' (68) is Shelley at his most commanding, the preposition 'through' meaning 'by means of' but also 'as a result of the agency of', yet hope is self-chastening in this poem that, having seen despair at close quarters, recognizes that the poet's imagination is, at best, 'an unextinguished hearth' (66) and that the 'earth' he wishes to reach is 'unawakened' (68). Shelley concludes with a question, 'O wind, | If Winter comes, can Spring be far behind?' (69–70), which already, for all its rhetorical form, retreats from the certainty of the draft reading, 'When Winter comes Spring lags not far behind' (see *BSM* V, 137 rev.). The poem invites us to consider the aptness of analogues between the natural worlds and the worlds of politics and creativity. The assurance that spring will follow winter is only a frail guarantee that freedom will follow

[25] See *Longman*, 3, 210–11n.

tyranny, or that creativity will follow a loss of imaginative power. Yet that frail guarantee has its own tenacity in this ode that glimpses the deconstruction of its best hopes, without allowing self-critique the final word.[26]

Shelley's other major uses of the ode also exhibit a high degree of poetic self-awareness. Ghosting 'Ode to the West Wind' and its forerunner, 'Hymn to Intellectual Beauty' is Wordsworth's 'Ode: Intimations of Immortality', a poem full of plangent loss and maturation. In both cases, even as Shelley rewrites aspects of the representation in Wordsworth's Ode of the poet's predicament, he arrives at his own variation on the sober colouring of the older poet's final, complex synthesis. Wordsworth asserts that 'We will grieve not, rather find | Strength in what remains behind' (182–3), where 'Strength' takes a confidence-inspiring emphasis, even if the exorcism of grief deliberately fails to convince after the affecting expression of loss which has preceded it: 'Though nothing can bring back the hour | Of splendour in the grass, of glory in the flower' (180–1). Shelley's 'Hymn to Intellectual Beauty' acknowledges that 'there is a harmony | In autumn' (74–5), but qualifies Wordsworthian sadness with accelerating delight in the limits of sensory knowledge: such a 'harmony' and 'lustre' 'through the summer is not heard or seen, | As if it could not be, as though it had not been!' (76–7). There, the 'as' clauses make clear that to settle for limited perspectives is to do less justice to what may 'be', Shelley imbuing Wordsworth's signature verb with a different, revisionist intuition of being's possibilities. Yet his new creation recognizes that these possibilities inhere, too, in Wordsworth's endlessly rebalancing Ode, for that poem, as Bloom puts it, 'suffers a great defeat, even as it retains its greater dream'.[27]

'Hymn to Intellectual Beauty' exploits the ode's fascination with different perspectives, implicit in the pattern of strophe and antistrophe typical of the form and embodied in the varying rhyme scheme and line-lengths of the twelve-line stanzas. As Stuart Curran writes, 'The major hymn of British Romanticism is, in fact, an ode.'[28] Stanza 3, for example, switches from nominalist deconstruction, depicting Christian invocations of 'God, and ghosts, and Heaven' (27) as 'Frail spells' (29), to construction of its own 'Frail spell' as it addresses with sceptical fervour 'Thy light alone' (32). This light emerges in subsequent figures as highly insubstantial, 'like mist o'er mountains driven' (32), yet the figure is consciously wispy and elusive; it sets itself in calculated tension with the poetry's claim that Intellectual Beauty possesses a Logos-like capacity to supply 'grace and truth to life's unquiet dream' (36).[29] Moving between awareness of precariousness and affirmation of belief in something close to a fiction, the poem creates a new and dynamic structure of spiritual feeling out of self-conflict. The poem's finest writing occurs when

---

[26] See Ronald Tetreault's reading of the poem as inviting the reader to engage with the poem's latent uncertainties, *The Poetry of Life: Shelley and Literary Form* (Toronto: University of Toronto Press, 1987), esp. 219–20.

[27] Harold Bloom, *The Anxiety of Influence: A Theory of Poetry*, 2nd edn. (1973; New York: Oxford UP, 1997), 10.

[28] Stuart Curran, *Poetic Form and British Romanticism* (New York: Oxford UP, 1986), 63. See also Richard Cronin, *Shelley's Poetic Thoughts* (London: Macmillan, 1981), where he says the poem 'is not a hymn, but an ode', 224.

[29] Compare John 1: 17: 'but grace and truth came by Jesus Christ'.

this self-conflict sends a powerful charge through its rhythms and images. At the end of stanza 4, for example, just after asserting that Intellectual Beauty, were it to be steady and not inconstant, would make 'Man [...] immortal, and omnipotent' (39), Shelley uses a simile and a mode of address (close to an imploring cry) that reveal anxiety: 'Thou—that to human thought art nourishment, | Like darkness to a dying flame! | Depart not as thy shadow came' (44–6). In such odic poetry shadows and substance commingle; so, too, do darkness and flame, departure and arrival, what is with what is not.

'The Cloud' and 'To a Sky-lark' also have covert commerce with the tradition of the ode. 'To a Sky-lark' may have as a precedent the Anacreontic ode, a poem celebrating drink and pleasure, though the drink in which Shelley takes pleasure is not wine but a song that surpasses description and evokes a stream of comparisons.[30] Claiming originality for his praise of the bird's song, a song that symbolizes an inspiration desperately longed for by the poet, Shelley asserts: 'I have never heard | Praise of love or wine | That panted forth a flood of rapture so divine' (63–5). The final alexandrine captures the panting forth of the 'flood of rapture' in such a way that Shelley seems to possess the inspiration he desires; at the same time, the recognition of some 'hidden want' (70) latent in even the best human poetry both impels Shelley's drive to imitate the skylark and explains his poem's sense of exclusion from the 'clear keen joyance' (76) that it admires. Building into the poem an interplay between celebration and desire, want and inspired emulation, Shelley endows 'To a Sky-lark' with a mercurial version of the dialectical structure evident in his odes.

Taking its point of departure from Aristophanic chorus and Hunt's practice in *The Nymphs*, 'conceived', as Shelley put it, 'with the clearest sense of ideal beauty and executed with the fullest and most flowing lyrical power' (*Letters: PBS* II, 152), 'The Cloud' finds a voice for the presence in nature of ceaseless change.[31] Its speaker is at once ethereal and robust, airily basking 'in heaven's blue smile' (29), yet vigorously wielding 'the flail of the lashing hail' (9). A lyric flight yet meteorologically grounded, 'The Cloud' transforms the choral ode into a *sui generis* poetic work in which the same persona plays many parts.[32] 'I change, but I cannot die' (76) describes the persistence of identity through change in relation not only to the cloud but also the form of the ode, deceptively hidden amidst the lilting anapaestic rhythms and internal rhymes. Strophe and antistrophe coexist in the same lyric moment, composed from a dialectic of 'remaining' (28) and 'dissolving' (30) that empowers and drives the rapid shifts of perspective in Shelley's 'Ode to Heaven', in which a trochaically light metre conveys and revises different ideas of an endlessly shifting word in the poet's vocabulary.

In Shelley's major political odes, 'Ode to Liberty' and 'Ode to Naples', he updates classical tradition, while, most evidently in the former poem, re-energizing more recent poetic modes. 'Ode to Liberty' draws on the example of the 'progress' poem by writers such as Thomas Gray in his 'The Progress of Poetry: A Pindaric Ode' (1757). Gray's poem

---

[30] For the comparison with Anacreon, see Parks C. Hunter, Jr., 'Undercurrents of Anacreontics in Shelley's "To a Skylark" and "The Cloud"', *Studies in Philology* 65 (1968), 677–92.

[31] See *Longman*, 3, 356–7 for comments on Aristophanes and Hunt.

[32] For the poem's meteorological accuracy, see *Longman*, 3, 357.

focuses on poetical rather than political progress, but, in doing so, has unexpected affinities with Shelley's ode. Pindar's daring example is important to both poets, Gray concluding with an evocation of the 'Theban Eagle' (Pindar) 'Sailing with supreme dominion | Thro' the azure deep of air' (115, 116–17), Shelley beginning with an allusion in his account of how 'Liberty [...] | Gleamed' (2, 5) to Pindar's Pythian ode, 8. 95–7, in lines transcribed in a notebook around which is a draft of the opening to 'Ode to Liberty' (BSM V, 143 rev.).[33] Gray's lines have a musicality at odds with the conviction that such sublimity is 'heard no more' (111), and yet, for him, poetic power is located in the achievements of the past. For Shelley, poetic power is the unstable herald and follower of the equally complex abstraction 'Liberty' which, imitating Coleridge's practice in 'France: An Ode', he at once exalts and complicates. By the end of his turbulent recantation Coleridge locates 'The spirit of divinest Liberty' (21) in the 'mind' and 'God in Nature', outside the domain of 'any form of human government'.[34] Shelley's initial outburst of enthusiasm at the resurgence of the spirit of liberty in Spain, where Ferdinand VII had been obliged to restore the Spanish Constitution of 1812, passes into a chronicle of the manifestations of liberty in Athens, republican Rome, the England of Alfred, the Italian city-states of the twelfth and thirteenth centuries, the Lutheran Reformation, the glorious Revolution, the War of American Independence, and the French Revolution. Liberty is both transhistorical and located in specific social and historical structures, much as Shelley's fifteen-line stanzas contain triple rhymes at strategic places as though to arrest Liberty's quicksilver career, yet give the impression, too, of hurling themselves headlong past breathing pauses and line-endings.

This is the significance of the double-edged word 'again' in the opening lines: 'A glorious people vibrated again | The lightning of the nations' (1–2). If the unusual transitive form of 'vibrated' grants 'A glorious people' political agency, the fact that they are acting 'again' makes them the medium through which liberty sweeps. 'Herodias' daughters have returned again' (118), from the final section of Yeats's 'Nineteen Hundred and Nineteen', involves a grimmer use of the temporal adverb by one of Shelley's major heirs, and underscores the cyclical vision encoded in the word's application to historical process.[35] The poem and poet rise to the occasion with a conscious determination to quell despair: 'My soul spurned the chains of its dismay, | And, in the rapid plumes of song, | Clothed itself, sublime and strong' (5–7). Yet this active clothing of the soul in the rapid plumes of song takes the form of submitting the poetic self to a visionary power both within and beyond itself, depicted as 'The Spirit's whirlwind' (11) which leaves Shelley to 'record' 'A voice out of the deep' (15). It is this voice, which, on the poem's fiction, communicates liberty's course across the centuries and between cultures, a voice depicted as though beyond the historical and yet continually at the mercy, in its inflections of delight and anxiety, of political settlements.

---

[33] Gray is quoted from *Eighteenth-Century Poetry: An Annotated Anthology*, ed. David Fairer and Christine Gerrard (Oxford: Blackwell, 1999); for the notebook reference to Pindar, see *Longman*, 3, 386.

[34] Quoted from the argument added to the poem in its 1802 *Morning Post* printing; see *The Complete Poems*, ed. Keach, 518.

[35] Quoted from *The Variorum Edition of the Poems of W. B. Yeats*, ed. Peter Allt and Russell K. Alspach (New York: Macmillan, 1957).

The poem's highly conscious patterning of rhyme, sound, and image bears a relationship to its themes that is analogous to liberty's visitations throughout history. A poet's visions may seek to shape understanding of liberty, but they are themselves shaped by extra-poetic forces. An emphatic triple-rhyme in stanza II asserts that, without liberty, 'this divinest universe | Was yet a chaos and a curse, | For thou wert not'; all that happens, rather, is the spectacle which haunts the poem of 'power from worst producing worse' (21–3). If nature without liberty is a 'chaos and a curse', the Miltonic fiat of 'For thou wert' (72), the act of bringing into being which it is poetry's privilege to enact, has a countervailing power.[36] Yet 'Art's deathless dreams' (57) and the murmurings of 'Verse' (59) exercise, at times, a marginal resistance to the human propensity to 'unlearn' liberty's 'sublimest lore' (113). Indeed, in this eighth stanza, Liberty is thought of, after its flight from the Roman Empire, as an elegiac poet without audience save 'the woods and waves, and desert rocks' (110), an Ovid in exile murmuring the tristia of its neglect and rejection.

Shelley's tone in the poem is one of sustained and exalted praise of liberty. But the poem's structure foregrounds conflicts, the potential at any historical moment for destruction as well as creation. The stanzas forego the closure of the sonnet, their extra line propelling the poem forwards to some new turn in the historical road. When libertarian victories come, they never wholly dispatch their foes. So the achievement of Dante and his successors was one in which 'from the human spirit's deepest deep | Strange melody with love and awe struck dumb | Dissonant arms' (131–3). Yet those 'Dissonant arms' have been only too evident, the poem recognizes, in recent history, while art, liberty's 'ardent intercessor' (249), is an ineffectual angel if it cannot prevent exploitation and economic suffering (253–5). The poet's own language is enmeshed in contradiction. Longing to rid the world of such ideological markers of oppression as 'king' (212) and 'PRIEST' (228), Shelley expresses the desire that words might be 'stripped of their thin masks and various hue' (237). The poem's close, though, with its richly figured and ambivalent account of inspiration's withdrawal, gives the lie to that wish; a series of similes precedes and follows the evocation of how 'My song, its pinions disarrayed of might, | Drooped' (281–2), and that 'might' consists of flinging forth images of hope and its endless shadowy counterpart, despair. The poem concludes with an image of its own sounds drowning under the weight of their 'tempestuous play': 'o'er it [the poets' song] closed the echoes far away | Of the great voice which did its flight sustain, | As waves which lately paved his watery way | Hiss round a drowner's head in their tempestuous play' (282–5). Previous stanzas have asked for liberty to lead forth 'Wisdom' (259) as its necessary companion, but philosophical and ethical wisdom surrender themselves at the end to the element of a self-reflexive creativity, which knows its own powers as it imagines its final destruction. The triple rhyme of 'dismay' (5), 'prey' (9), and 'ray' (11) in the first stanza records the emergence from 'dismay' into an inspired state; the same rhyme, used four times at the end, announces the subsidence of creativity, a creativity whose very guarantee is its own provisional instability.[37]

[36] Judith Chernaik compares *Paradise Lost*, III. 8–9; *The Lyrics of Shelley* (Cleveland: The Press of Case Western Reserve University, 1972), 119n.

[37] For discussion of 'the ambivalence with which poetry is implicitly treated throughout the poem', see Weisman, 'The Lyricist', 52; for a sympathetic reading of the poem's dealings with ideology, see

'Ode to Liberty' thus participates in the preoccupation with the poet's role and the concerns with wide-ranging, culture-crossing renovation that are marked features of the *Prometheus Unbound* volume in which it first appeared. In his 'Ode to Naples', first published in the *Morning Chonicle* on 26 September 1820, Shelley attempts to speak urgently to contemporary events, in this case, the initially peaceful 'proclamation of a constitutional government at Naples', as Mary Shelley put it.[38] He does so in a poem that the editors of *Longman* 3 consider exists in two forms, accentuating its impression of experimenting with a strict Pindaric form: Shelley's Text A (quoted from here and submitted for publication) preserves the Greek headings of Strophe, Antistrophe, and Epode but departs from tradition by surrounding Strophes and Antistrophes with Epodes at the start and finish; Text B (a manuscript fair copy) dispenses with the headings and the initial two Epodes. In Text A, the poetic self is to the fore from the beginning, evoking a state of being visited by 'the Power divine' (21) familiar in poems such as 'Hymn to Intellectual Beauty', but doing so with a new care for place and affect. 'I stood within the City disinterred' (1), which Shelley's note identifies as Pompeii, is more akin to Byron's self-stationing in *Childe Harold's Pilgrimage* than to the soul's shaking off of chains of 'dismay' in 'Ode to Liberty', and the poem suggests the speaker's role as shaper as well as receiver of impressions through a series of active verbs. Even the line 'Around me gleamed many a bright sepulchre' (12) locates the poet at the centre of the entranced vision in which 'the crystal silence of the air' (20) prompts the answering speech of the ode. The second Epode sees the poet as borne (probably) by the 'Power divine', yet the very vagueness of the antecedent of 'It' in 'It bore me, like an Angel o'er the waves | Of sunlight' (32–3) shows a quality of assurance on the poet's part; as he connects his celebration of Neapolitan liberty with the work of 'the dead Kings of Melody' (39), identified in a note as 'Homer and Virgil', it is as though the fierce 'strife' with an originating Power evident in 'Ode to the West Wind' and 'Ode to Liberty' has yielded to a less overwhelmed sense of being the conduit for 'Prophesyings which grew articulate' (50).

This is not to say the poem is undemanding. But Michael Erkelenz is right to note its rhetorical shrewdness, even opportunism; addressed to the well-educated readers of the *Morning Chronicle*, the poem shows Shelley 'using a high-art form to influence an urgent political crisis'.[39] As Judith Chernaik comments, 'The past informs the poet's vision of present Italy' and this 'vision' was well suited to 'the kind of reader likely to be enamored of the classical past'.[40] The ode's Pindaric gesture is suited more to public discourse than the enactment of inner conflict. The dynamizing strength of Shelley's finest work in the form of the ode is to set poet and public sphere, word and world, in relationships of energizing tension. Yet even in the less turbulent 'Ode to Naples' the poet's concern with

---

Mark Kipperman, 'Shelley and the Ideology of the Nation: The Authority of the Poet', in Betty T. Bennett and Stuart Curran (eds.), *Shelley: Poet and Legislator of the World* (Baltimore: Johns Hopkins UP, 1996), 56–8.

[38] See *Longman*, 3, 626, 629.

[39] Michael Erkelenz, 'Unacknowledged Legislation: The Genre and Function of Shelley's "Ode to Naples"', in Bennett and Curran (eds.), *Shelley: Poet and Legislator of the World*, 72.

[40] Chernaik, *The Lyrics of Shelley*, 112; Erkelenz, 'Unacknowledged Legislation', 69.

creativity, with the poet as self-aware utterer of a redeeming Logos, is apparent, both in the form of negation, when he depicts the Austrians, 'The Anarchs of the North', as leading forth 'their legions | Like Chaos o'er Creation, uncreating' (137–8), and, more positively, when he assumes biblical inflections and intercedes on behalf of peaceful freedom with that 'Great Spirit! deepest Love! | Who rulest, and dost move | All things which live and are, within the Italian shore' (149–51). In the way that the final phrase restrains the poem's universalism to impressive effect, one glimpses the particular achievement of 'Ode to Naples'.[41] Prophecy is sustained; no collapse of inspiration is mimicked. For once, the Shelleyan relationship with genre is suavely transformative rather than brilliantly conflicted.

Select Bibliography

Allen, Graham. 'Transumption and/in History: Bloom, Shelley, and the Figure of the Poet'. *Durham University Journal* NS 54 (1993), *Percy Bysshe Shelley: Special Issue*, guest ed. Michael O'Neill. 247–56.

Chernaik, Judith. *The Lyrics of Shelley*. Cleveland: Press of Case Western Reserve University, 1972.

Cronin, Richard. *Shelley's Poetic Thoughts*. London: Macmillan, 1981.

Curran, Stuart. *Poetic Form and British Romanticism*. New York: Oxford UP, 1986.

Erkelenz, Michael. 'Unacknowledged Legislation: The Genre and Function of Shelley's "Ode to Naples"'. *Shelley: Poet and Legislator of the World*. Ed. Betty T. Bennett and Stuart Curran. Baltimore: Johns Hopkins UP, 1996. 63–72.

Everest, Kelvin. '"Ozymandias": The Text in Time'. *Percy Bysshe Shelley: Bicentenary Essays*. Ed. Kelvin Everest. Cambridge: Brewer, 1992. 24–42.

Hunter, Parks C., Jr. 'Undercurrents of Anacreontics in Shelley's "To a Skylark" and "The Cloud"'. *Studies in Philology* 65 (1968), 677–93.

Kipperman, Mark. 'Shelley and the Ideology of the Nation: The Authority of the Poet'. *Shelley: Poet and Legislator of the World*. Ed. Betty T. Bennett and Stuart Curran. Baltimore: Johns Hopkins UP, 1996. 49–59.

O'Neill, Michael. 'The Romantic Sonnet'. *The Cambridge Companion to the Sonnet*. Ed. A. D. Cousins and Peter Howarth. Cambridge: Cambridge UP, 2011. 185–203.

Wagner-Lawlor, Jennifer A. *A Moment's Monument: Revisionary Poetics in the Nineteenth-Century English Sonnet*. Cranbury: Fairleigh Dickinson UP, 1996.

Weisman, Karen. 'The Lyricist'. *The Cambridge Companion to Shelley*. Ed. Timothy Morton Cambridge: Cambridge UP, 2006. 45–64.

---

[41] See Acts 17: 28: 'in him we live, and move, and have our being'; *Longman*, 3 (644n) cites the close of Dante's *Paradiso*.

CHAPTER 22

POPULAR SONGS AND BALLADS

Writing the 'Unwritten Story' in 1819

SUSAN J. WOLFSON

UNACKNOWLEDGED LEGISLATORS, UNWRITTEN STORY

'PAINFUL to read'. That's how the close of Shelley's *Defence of Poetry* (drafted 1821) struck Raymond Williams:

> The bearers of a high imaginative skill become suddenly the 'legislators', at the very moment when they were being forced into practical exile; their description as 'unacknowledged', which, on the theory, ought only to be a fact to be accepted, carries with it also the felt helplessness of a generation.[1]

'Poets are the unacknowledged legislators of the World' is the now famous last sentence, chiming with the close of chapter I of *A Philosophical View of Reform* (drafted late 1819), there, with commendable company: 'Poets and philosophers are the unacknowledged legislators of the world.'[2] But the world saw neither tract in Shelley's lifetime. It is not just this immateriality that bothers Williams but also the tendency of Shelley's defence to 'dismiss [...] considerations which might involve an inquiry into the principles of society itself, and restrict our view to the manner in which the imagination is expressed upon its forms.'[3]

---

[1] Raymond Williams, 'The Romantic Artist', in *Culture and Society, 1780–1850* (New York: Columbia UP, 1958), 47.

[2] *Shelley's Prose, Or the Trumpet of Prophecy*, ed. David Lee Clark (Albuquerque, NM: University of New Mexico Press, 1954), 241. For *A Defence* I use the first publication (most proximate to the first publications of most of Shelley's popular poems), *Essays & c*, ed. [Mary] Shelley, 2 vols. (London: Edward Moxon, 1840); here, I, 57.

[3] Shelley, *Defence* 4.

Yet if Shelley seems to be offering poetic science in place of political science, his view of expressive forms, poetic and political, reckoned with social principles. 'The system of society as it exists at present must be overthrown from the foundations with all its super-structure of maxims & of forms,' he wrote to Leigh Hunt in May 1820, warming up to asking if he knew of 'any bookseller who would like to publish a little volume of *popular songs* wholly political, & destined to awaken & direct the imagination of the reformers' (*Letters: PBS* II, 191). He had in mind 'Lines Written during the Castlereagh Administration', 'Song to the Men of England', 'Similes for Two Poetical Characters', 'What Men Gain Fairly', 'A New National Anthem', 'England in 1819', 'Ballad of the Starving Mother', and perhaps a fresh plea for the blazing centrepiece, *The Mask of Anarchy: Written on the Occasion of the Massacre at Manchester* (cooling on Hunt's shelf for over half a year).[4]

A few weeks on, Shelley was prodding Hunt about *A Philosophical View of Reform*.[5] Yet he was not without ironic self-regard. 'I see you smile', he assures Hunt, 'but answer my question' (*Letters: PBS* II, 191). This relay of practical realism and philosophical resolve reverberates in the difficulty many have had with Shelley's auditions in political voice and political poetics. The iconic case is that *Mask*, a dream-vision spun in far-away Italy. Cast as 'a public poem with revolutionary intentions', its 'generating consciousness, the poet's mind', comments Thomas Edwards, 'is in no position to do more than write a poem'.[6] Roger Sales attempts a game spin: by 1819 Shelley was favouring the dormant activist, poetic agency detached from the 'political arena', in a dream ultimately 'more important than the politician's programme'.[7] Or, argues Anne Janowitz with another spin, poetry is the programme: its force is not the expression of any individual consciousness but a vision of class aspiration (92)—one fulfilled in the 'Red Shelley' (Paul Foot's hero) that gave a voice to the labour class in the Reformist 1830s, to the Chartists in the 1840s, to Victorian labour halls, to progressive movements across the globe ever since.[8]

[4] Titles in quotation are editorial tradition from first publications—most in the post-Reform 1830s, by Shelley's cousin Thomas Medwin, in the *Athenæum*, and in Mary Shelley's *The Poetical Works of Percy Bysshe Shelley*, 4 vols. (London: Edward Moxon, 1839), hereafter *1839*. Not until 1990 did a 'marvellous, cheap' 'little volume' appear: *Shelley's Revolutionary Year* (£3.95), developed by Paul Foot to meet 'the enthusiasm' in the Socialist Workers Party 'for Shelley's revolutionary writings' (9) and a resource for teaching their children 'the poetry which carries revolutionary ideas through the centuries' (26). Foot includes two 'high-flown' lyrics (18) from *Prometheus Unbound &c* (1820): 'Ode to the West Wind' (written October 1819) and 'Ode on Liberty' (spring 1820).

[5] 'Do you know any bookseller who w^d publish for me [this] octavo volume [...]? It is boldly but temperately written—& I think readable—It is intended for a kind of standard book for the philosophical reformers politically considered' (26 May; *Letters: PBS* II, 201). It wasn't published until 1920, in a limited edition for the Shelley Society. Foot includes it to 'reinforce' the poetic pedagogy.

[6] Thomas R. Edwards, *Imagination and Power: A Study of Poetry on Public Themes* (Oxford: Oxford UP, 1971), 160.

[7] Roger Sales, *English Literature in History 1780–1830: Pastoral and Politics* (New York: St Martin's Press, 1983), 196.

[8] Anne Janowitz, '"A Voice from across the Sea": Communitarianism at the Limits of Romanticism', in Mary A. Favret and Nicola J. Watson (eds.), *The Limits of Romanticism: Essays in Cultural, Feminist, and Materialist Criticism* (Bloomington, IN: Indiana UP, 1994), 92. For the reverberations of 'Rise like lions', see Timothy Morton, 'Receptions', in *Cambridge Companion to Shelley* (Cambridge: Cambridge UP, 2006), 40–1. Writing in the 1840s, Frederick Engels notes Shelley's prophetic genius.

Whatever the argument, this poetry was unpublishable in 1819 (or soon after). In *Formal Charges*, I described it as a medium for Shelley to vent, or to address a 'few select spirits' in a fantasy of political agency (*Letters: PBS* II, 191). For all its proto-Marxist acumen, it seemed to me less 'wholly political' than a romance of politics, beautifully figured but in sum a fantasy of public agency. While it is hard to prevent that murmur, I want to consider more deliberately Shelley's politics of 'unwritten story'. This is the horizon of history he projects in *The Mask of Anarchy* (148).[9] Its agents in the present are 'companions and forerunners of some unimagined change in our social condition or the opinions which cement it' (so the narrative is cast in the Preface to *Prometheus Unbound*).[10] On the arc of 'un-' (with 'unimagined' and 'unbound') the potential of 'unwritten' gathers: a prevailing story that could be unbound, unwritten, rescinded;[11] a story not yet written, or waiting to be written. For this prefix, Shelley had good forerunners. In the revolutionary 1640s, Milton referred to 'unwritten lawes and Ideas which nature hath ingraven in us', this alternative authority nicely sounded in the links of 'ingraven' and 'in us'. Blackstone began *Commentaries on the Laws of England* (1765) observing that 'municipal law' abides both in 'the *lex scripta*, the written, or statute law' and in 'the *lex non scripta*, the unwritten, or common law'.[12] Shelley's *Defence*, drafted in the wake of his popular songs, deploys 'un-' for poetic power: it 'awakens and enlarges the mind' with 'a thousand unapprehended combinations of thought' (16), 'marks the before unapprehended relations of things' (5). 'Marks' is a nice supplement: takes notice of, identifies, makes legible. Across his *Defence* Shelley drives the negative prefixes into positive claims, clinched in those closing sentences, where poets, agents of 'unapprehended inspiration', are hailed as 'unacknowledged legislators' (57).

The flashpoint in 1819 for this legislative theory—and, no less, its knotty complications—was that 'Massacre at Manchester'. On 16 August some 100,000 labourers and their families gathered at St Peter's Field for peaceful parading and to hear Henry 'Orator' Hunt declare their right of assembly, voice their grievances, and urge parliamentary reform. Intent on suppression and to make an example, a sabre-wielding yeomanry—shopkeepers, mill-owners, merchants, packed with British Hussars (regular cavalry, many veterans of Waterloo)—rode into the crowd, wreaking fifteen deaths and 400–700 injuries. The attack may have been prompted by Home Secretary Lord Sidmouth, or just cheered after the fact, with the Prince Regent's endorsement, for 'preservation of public peace'. Shelley read about the atrocity in Hunt's *Examiner*. The news

---

[9] For *The Mask* I follow *Norton 2*'s text, based on the press transcript reviewed by P. B. Shelley, with Norton's corrections from an intermediate stage.

[10] *Prometheus Unbound: A Lyrical Drama in Four Acts* (London: C. and J. Ollier, 1820), p. xii.

[11] See, for example, Keats writing to Shelley in 1820 about some poems which he wishes he could 'unwrite' (see *John Keats: A Longman Cultural Edition*, ed. Susan J. Wolfson (New York: Pearson, 2007), 426).

[12] See John Milton, *The Reason of Church-Government*; 2 books (London: E.G. for John Rothwell, 1641), 1. III, 11. William Blackstone, *Commentaries on the Laws of England;* 4 books (Oxford: Clarendon Press, 1765), I, 63; Blackstone hastens to add that, from long custom, *leges non scriptae* have the force of written law (I, 64).

blazed on the front page of the 22 August issue, fuelled within by reports from *The Times* and seven 'Letters from Manchester'. Ensuing issues kept up the front-page accounts, with angry letters and trenchant verses on 'Peterloo'—the *Manchester Observer's* sardonic riff, quickly minted, on Waterloo triumphalism.[13]

Shelley was 'writing the Cenci, when the news of the Manchester Massacre reached us; it roused in him violent emotions of indignation and compassion', recalled Mary Shelley in *1839* (III, 205). It was no stretch for him to summon Beatrice Cenci (just after her father raped her). 'The torrent of my indignation has not yet done boiling in my veins', he fumed to his publisher Ollier on 6 September; 'I wait anxiously hear how the Country will express its sense of this bloody murderous oppression of its destroyers. "Something must be done [...] What yet I know not"' (*Cenci* III. i; *Letters: PBS* II, 117). Shelley knew what Beatrice had done. Published in England in early 1820, *The Cenci's* desperate parricide registered as post-Peterloo discourse.[14]

By 21 September 1819 Shelley's boiling had cooled to a caution. Writing back to Peacock, he sounds Beatrice's murmur not only without quotations (muting the allusion to *The Cenci*) but also counters it with admiration for Henry Hunt's composure amid the 'infernal business': 'What is to be done? Something assuredly. H. Hunt has behaved I think with great spirit & coolness in the whole affair' (*Letters: PBS* II, 120). Though suppressed, arrested, and forced to run a violent gauntlet on the steps of the magistrate's house (Thompson, *English Working Class*, 688), then sent to London for trial, Hunt did not rage for revolution. This was some salve to Shelley's disturbance (even before he learned of Peterloo) about England's 'very disturbed state'. 'I wonder & tremble', he wrote to Peacock, 24 August 1819; 'change should commence among the higher orders, or anarchy will only be the last flash before despotism' (*Letters: PBS* II, 115). Yet the referent of 'anarchy' is syntactically ambiguous: does it refer to a despotic higher order? or to civil war rising from the lower orders, and a new (*vide*: France) revolutionary despotism? Shelley's popular songs vibrate with the question. In 1819 there wasn't yet a forceful reform movement in the middle orders, and no leadership in the higher orders. The agitation was from below.

---

[13] *Examiner* 608 (22 August 1819), 529–31: 'Disturbances at Manchester' [Leigh Hunt]. For the events, see E. P. Thompson, *The Making of the English Working Class* (1963; New York: Vintage, 1966), 681–9; Richard Holmes, *Shelley: The Pursuit* (1974; New York: E. P. Dutton, 1975), 529–31; and Stephen Behrendt's edition, 74–115.

[14] Parricide is the scandal of Edmund Burke's *Reflections on the Revolution in France* (London: J. Dodsley, 1790): one 'should approach to the faults of the state as to the wounds of a father, with pious awe and trembling sollicitude', and 'look with horror on those children of their country who are prompt rashly to hack that aged parent in pieces' as the way to 'regenerate' the social order (143). For Shelley's conflicted perspective on Beatrice's parricide, see my '"Something must be done": Shelley, Hemans, and the Flash of Revolutionary Female Violence', in Beth Lau (ed.), *Fellow Romantics: Male and Female British Writers, 1790–1835* (Aldershot: Ashgate, 2009), 101–23.

RISING WORDS: 'AS IF' IN
THE MASK OF ANARCHY

Shelley wavered. He was convinced (Mary Shelley recalls) 'that a clash between the two classes of society was inevitable, and he eagerly ranged himself on the people's side'; but he didn't book the next boat home. He 'had an idea of publishing a series of poems adapted expressly to commemorate their circumstances and wrongs'; but he knew 'in those days of prosecution for libel they could not be printed' (1839 III, 207). Then there's the character of the poetry itself. William Keach, a social activist and subtle literary critic, argues for the importance, 'politically as well as critically', to query the 'things that do not fit, or that fit only uneasily, with the "enthusiasms" that Foot so engagingly transmits'.[15] Even Foot is vexed by Shelley's tacking between 'direct and deliberate appeals to the masses to rise up and trample their oppressors' and 'vaporous appeals' that 'duck real issues'—especially *The Mask of Anarchy*, now 'counselling the people to behave constitutionally, and to protest within the system', then, resonantly at the end, openly advocating revolution.[16]

Nor can he decide about Hunt, who had *The Mask* in time for the 23 September *Examiner*, but held it back for a dozen years, and didn't help out with the other political projects either. Lacking the mischievous moxie of a Carlile, Cobbett, or Wooler, Hunt 'became, uncomfortably but firmly, the censor of some of the most powerful political writing in the English language'.[17] Yet Foot concedes that Shelley, recreating in Italy, 'risked nothing'. It would be Hunt, veteran of two years of jail-time (1813–14) for 'libelling' the Prince Regent, who would take the heat for publishing Shelley's sustained mockery of the monarchy, in prelude to almost 200 lines of rousing address to 'Men of England, heirs of Glory' (147).[18] More than nod to the Glorious Revolution of 1688, these words are urgently activist:

> 'Rise like Lions after slumber
> In unvanquishable number
> Shake your chains to Earth like dew
> Which in sleep had fallen on you—
> Ye are many—they are few.'

> (151–5)

This voice is no '*un*acknowledged' legislator; it is populism for '*un*vanquishable number' (and potent poetic numbers). At stake is a politics not only of words, but *as* words,

---

[15] William Keach, 'Rise Like Lions? Shelley and the Revolutionary Left', *International Socialism* 75 (Summer 1997): <http://www.marxists.de/culture/shelley/keach>.

[16] Paul Foot, *Red Shelley* (London: Sidgwick & Jackson, 1980), 169; Paul Foot, *Shelley's Revolutionary Year* (London: Redwords, 1990), 16.

[17] Foot, *Red Shelley*, 219.

[18] Shelley was following the prosecution of Carlile for publishing Paine's *Age of Reason*. For Hunt to publish poetry denouncing 'KING' to the labouring classes and urging their rights could expose him to fines, even imprisonment (Donald Reiman, *'The Mask of Anarchy': A Facsimile Edition* (New York: Garland Press, 1985), p. xiv; Holmes, *Shelley: The Pursuit*, 539–41; Foot, *Red Shelley*, 34–6, 220–1).

unwriting things as they are: the present is sleep not fixity; chains are dewy ephemera; power abides in many, not few.

The opening sally of *The Mask* is a brash rewriting of Lord Chancellor Eldon's arraignment of Manchester as a 'shocking choice between military government and anarchy'. Shelley writes magistrate Eldon as a child-murdering Hypocrite Fraud, and unwrites government into its antonym Anarchy in 'a kingly crown' (34), avatar of Milton's Death, wearing 'the likeness of a kingly crown'.[19] The master-trope takes a cue from Hunt's excoriation in the 22 August *Examiner* of 'Men in the Brazen Masks of power' acting 'against an assemblage of Englishmen irritated by every species of wrong and insult'.[20] The master-allusion is the seventeenth-century court masque, those elaborate pageants of divine grace upon the grand, social harmony of the monarchy.[21] Shelley's *Mask* (ringing with the subtitle word *Massacre*) issues a caustic parody of masque as the artifice of tyranny, no less specious, no less factitious in 1819 than during 'the reign of Charles II, when all forms in which poetry had been accustomed to be expressed became hymns to the triumph of kingly power over liberty and virtue' (*Defence*, 24).

Mocking the fulsome hymns, Shelley produces popular-culture ballad stanzas and scurrilous political cartoons. In another parody of *masque*, Anarchy's 'ghastly masquerade' is a triumphal parade of allied 'Destructions'—Murder, Fraud, Hypocrisy—the parts played by the stars of 1819: Castlereagh, Eldon, Sidmouth (5–34).[22] Their hymns, Regency-styled, chorus the tautologies of tyranny. Anarchy's brow proclaims, 'I AM GOD, AND KING, AND LAW!' (37), echoed by 'hired Murderers who did sing | Thou art God, and Law, and King' (60–1). The *King-sing* rhyme cues the chiming monopoly of accord:

> Lawyers and priests, a motley crowd.
> To the earth their pale brows bowed;
> Like a bad prayer not over loud,
> Whispering—'Thou art Law and God.'—
>
> Then all cried with one accord;
> 'Thou art King, and God, and Lord;

[19] For Eldon, see Thompson, *English Working Class*, 684. For a sharp genealogy of 'anarchy' from Milton to Shelley, see William Keach, 'Radical Shelley?', *Raritan* 5.2 (1985), 120–9. Shelley is conspicuous for using *Anarch* to denote the ruling orders; see 'Ode to Liberty', 43. John Milton, *Paradise Lost*, II. 673, *John Milton: The Complete Poems*, ed. John Leonard (London: Penguin, 1998), 159.

[20] *Examiner* 608 (22 August 1819), 530.

[21] Shelley considered for his title a patent genre-satire, 'Masque of Anarchy' (Letter to Hunt, November 1819, *Letters: PBS* II, 152). The poem Hunt eventually helped publish would be titled *The Masque of Anarchy* (London: Edward Moxon, 1832).

[22] Robert Stewart (Viscount Castlereagh), Foreign Secretary and Tory leader of Commons, was reviled for the violent suppression of Ireland and alliance with reactionary European monarchies. Shelley despised Lord Chancellor John Scott (Baron Eldon) for depriving him of his children by his first wife. Home Secretary Henry Addington (Viscount Sidmouth) fostered programmes of religious instruction to mollify workers, and on the intractable set *agents provocateurs*, to lure them into actions prosecuted into death sentences. For Shelley's shrewd genre-play with the seventeenth-century masque, see Stuart Curran, *Shelley's Annus Mirabilis: The Maturing of an Epic Vision* (San Marino, CA: Huntington Library, 1975), 186–8.

> Anarchy, to Thee we bow,
> Be thy name made holy now!'
>
> (66–73)

Shelley exposes, to mordant parody, the political arts of anarchy.

Yet for all this, its poet-artist exposes the complication that bothers Foot (*RS* 221):

> As I lay asleep in Italy
> There came a voice from over the Sea,
> And with great power it forth led me
> To walk in the visions of Poesy.
>
> (1–4)

If the plan is to lionize this slumber, the poetry is not exactly auspicious. A sleepy phonotext slides from 'As I lay asleep' to the dream-site 'Italy', lapping over the 'Sea', a passive 'me', and the medium, 'Poesy'. 'Poesy', moreover, occupies uncertain syntax. In a genitive 'visions of', Poesy is a visionary agency; as prepositional object, Poesy is a visionary dreamscape. It's a foundational conceptual dilemma.

Shelley's design is to propel the dreaming 'I' onto the scene of crisis. 'I' next appears as an eyewitness reporter—'I met Murder on the way' (5); 'this mark I saw' (36)—then as a Peterloo orator ('whilst I speak'; 171). The emergence of this last 'I' (Shelley's intimate epipsyche) is heralded by a transformation of poetic syntax that takes the circumstance '*As I* lay asleep' into a potently visionary, dreamscaped '*As if*':

> These words of joy and fear arose
>
> As if their own indignant Earth
> Which gave the sons of England birth
> Had felt their blood upon her brow,
> And shuddering with a mother's throe
>
> Had turned every drop of blood
> By which her face had been bedewed
> To an accent unwithstood,—
> As if her heart had cried aloud:
>
> 'Men of England, heirs of Glory,
> Heroes of unwritten story [...]'
>
> (138–47)

At this crux, with words 'unwithstood' hailing 'unwritten' story, 'As if' launches into political force. Philosopher Hans Vaihinger helps deliver the syntactic thrust: the simile-signifier 'as' gains an 'if' that, while conceding 'something unreal or impossible', produces an 'apperceptive construct'; an 'impossible case' can be 'posited for the moment as possible or real'.[23]

---

[23] *The Philosophy of 'As if': A System of the Theoretical, Practical and Religious Fictions of Mankind*, trans. C. K. Ogden (1911; 1924; London: Routledge and Kegan Paul, 1949), 91–3, 258–9. For Keach, such syntax serves collective consciousness (see 'Rise Like Lions?')—an effect he also discerns in *Prometheus*

Shelley mobilizes 'As if' to summon political vision as uncontingent natural force: England's Earth, a ground of authority that recalls Milton's ascription of 'unwritten lawes' as nature's agency.[24] He will launch 'Ode to Liberty' (1820) on the same natural authority: 'there came | A voice from out the deep: I will record the same' (14–15).

In *The Mask* 'unwritten story' rises as a reflex of a story too deeply engraved. The forerunner is a punned 'maniac maid' (a maniac made by Anarchy): 'her name was Hope, she said: | But she looked more like Despair' (86–9). The contradiction contrasts Shelley's similes for the rule of anarchy, in which tenor and vehicle, policy and agent, are so complicit as to be synonymous:

> I met Murder on the way—
> He had a mask like Castlereagh—
>
> (5–6)
>
> Next came Fraud, and he had on,
> Like Eldon, an ermined gown;
>
> (14–15)
>
> Like Sidmouth, next, Hypocrisy
>
> (24)

The name of Hope against the look of Despair is a disturbance of language that holds potential for 'unwritten story', in antithesis to names too well written:

> 'What is Freedom?—ye can tell
> That which slavery is, too well—
> For its very name has grown
> To an echo of your own.'
>
> (156–9)

The phonics of this last rhyme spell out the slavery. Its name has literally 'grown' (sounding a pun on 'groan') into the oppressed, 'your own'.

Across this relay from a story that seems all there is to 'tell' to 'unwritten story', Shelley presses the syntax of 'as' from condition to mordant analogy:

> "Tis to work and have such pay
> As just keeps life from day to day
> In your limbs, as in a cell
> For the tyrants' use to dwell
>
> So that, ye for them are made
> Loom, and plough, and sword, and spade.'
>
> (160–5)

Unbound (see William Keach, 'The Political Poet', in *Cambridge Companion to Shelley* (Cambridge: Cambridge UP, 2006), 140–1).

[24] Janowitz's reading of 'communitarian' mode, 'plural and social' (89), even elides *As if* to take 'female Earth' (94–5) as direct authority.

Simile compresses into synonym in the severe double-grammar of this pedagogy: tools are made for workers and workers are made tools for tyrants. 'What is slavery—' asks Shelley in *A Philosophical View of Reform*, with a philosophical review: 'It is a system of insecurity of property, and of person' (43). To name 'system' is to allow its unwriting into the antonym *Freedom*, refusing the false report: it is 'not, as impostors say, | A shadow soon to pass away, | A superstition, and a name' (210–15).

Yet for all this sharp philosophy, *The Mask* will soon entertain a story so peculiar as to seem Sidmouth's ghost-writing for sedating class unrest:

> 'Science, Poetry, and Thought
> Are thy lamps; they make the lot
> Of the dwellers in a cot
> So serene, they curse it not.'

> (254–7)

This 'delicious stanza', Hunt coos in his 1832 Preface to *The Masque of Anarchy*, is 'a most happy and comforting picture in the midst of visions of blood and tumult' (p. x). No surprise that in this Reform Act year he's also happy to stress Shelley's 'political anticipation' in recommending against 'active resistance, come what might […] a piece of fortitude, however effective, which we believe was not contemplated by the Political Unions: yet, in point of the spirit of the thing, the success he anticipates has actually occurred, and after his very fashion […] The battle was won without a blow' (pp. x–xi). Hunt fashioned *The Masque* as a polite parlour book, graced with roman-numeral stanza headings. Three stanzas appealing to 'the old laws of England' (331) as antidote to the 'laws […] sold' in modern England (231–2) were featured in italics.[25] Gone was Shelley's Massacre-blaring subtitle (now, *A Poem*). Gone, too, the naming of Eldon and Sidmouth and a stanza that called the Bible the cloak of Hypocrisy.[26]

In a front-page review, a Shelley-friendly *Athenæum* took the genre-cue. If *The Masque* is 'political', Shelley was 'too much of a poet to be a good politician', 'too lofty in his conceptions'. For all the instruction in 'strong and simple words', the 'account of the Peterloo affair […] is not in the customary style of reports'.[27] Even so, as this review also made clear, by 1832 the notoriety of 'Peterloo' was not in question.[28] *Athenæum* could even feel able to publish (in December) 'LINES Written during the Castlereagh Administration', which Shelley opens with a terse tercet of indictments:

---

[25] LXXXI–LXXXIII (42–3; cf. ll. 327–9), along with a singular footnote praising 'the sober, lawful, and charitable mode of proceeding advocated and anticipated by this supposed reckless innovator […] a picture and a recommendation of "*non-resistance*," in all its glory' (41).

[26] ll. 22–5. Hunt blanked out Sidmouth (still alive) with three asterisks but left Eldon (also alive) decodable in 'Lord E—'. With no risk of libel, suicide Castlereagh (d. 1822) could be (and was) named. Mary Shelley used Hunt's text in *1839*.

[27] *Athenæum* 262 (3 November 1832), 705.

[28] The 'moral consensus of the nation outlawed the riding down and sabreing of an unarmed crowd' and endorsed 'the right of public meeting' (Thompson, *English Working Class*, 710).

> CORPSES are cold in the tomb;
> Stones on the pavement are dumb;
> Abortions are dead in the womb.

While a headnote did concede 'something fearful in the solemn grandeur' of this report, this could be taken as an aesthetic effect, with no 'chance of exciting either personal or party feeling'.[29]

Yet a chance, apparently, had to be managed. It was Shelley's cousin Medwin who devised the back-then title. In Shelley's manuscript it was categorically 'England'—an epitaph for Liberty vanquished by a Tyrant, and 'Albion, free no more' (5), a vast national graveyard:

> Her sons are as stones in the way;
> They are masses of senseless clay;
> They are trodden and move not away,
> The abortion with which *she* travaileth
> Is Liberty, smitten to death.

The oratory is urgent and urging. 'Masses of senseless clay': if the sense of 'the populace' or 'lower orders' was yet to emerge, Keach discerns an anticipation here, building on the tyrannical reduction of human subjects to brutal matter.[30] No small risk is Shelley's gambit in turning the report to a sarcastic ode to power and its victims' fatal complicity:

> Then trample and dance, thou Oppressor!
> For thy victim is no redresser;
> Thou are sole lord and possessor
> Of her corpses, and clods, and abortions,—they pave
> Thy path to the grave.
>
> (6–15)

The reformer's gambit to indict and incite also sounds like a voice of exasperation.

In *The Mask of Anarchy*, Shelley's counsel is redress in symbolic form. For 'Ye who suffer woes untold' (291)—'untold' in story as well as in the numerical mass—the orator envisions speech-activism in a grand figurative performance of a reformed parliament, many voices unanimous on one theme:

> 'Let a vast assembly be,
> And with great solemnity
> Declare with measured words that ye
> Are, as God has made ye, free—
>
> Be your strong and simple words
> Keen to wound as sharpened swords,
> And wide as targes let them be
> With their shade to cover ye.'
>
> (295–302)

---

[29] 'Original Papers'; *Athenæum* 267 (8 December 1832), 794.
[30] Keach, 'Rise Like Lions?'

In the poetry of politics, words are agents. Shelley imagines a war in words, shaping a simile that incorporates vehicle into tenor: 'words' are lettered into, projected into 'swords' (with an edge from 'sword!'—an old oath for 'by God's word!'). The rhyme is there for the reading.[31]

Is this a poet's mere dreaming? Some still hear 'the sing-song of instructive nursery-rhymes or routine political oration' or feel that the 'superstructure of maxims' (notwithstanding Shelley's agenda) is being reproduced rather than reformed,[32] or tremble that a school of passive resistance could turn slaughterhouse for those armed only with words. Yet it is worth remembering that the oppressors were already hearing words 'as sharpened swords', and seeing in the parades at St Peter's Field a well-honed, proto-revolutionary formation.[33]

SIMILE TO SIMULTANEITY

In *The Mask of Anarchy*, Shelley's syntaxes of 'as' work into political rhetoric by a deft grammatical transformation. Such is the taut dramatic arc of another political song:

> *Similes.*
>
> As from an ancestral oak
>   Two empty ravens sound their clarion,
> Yell by yell, and croak by croak,
> When they scent the noonday smoke
>   Of fresh human carrion:—
>
> As two gibbering night-birds flit
>   From their bowers of deadly yew,
> Through the night to frighten it,
> When the moon is in a fit,
>   And the stars are none, or few:—
>
> As a shark and dog-fish wait
>   Under an Atlantic isle,
> For the negro-ship, whose freight
> Is the theme of their debate,
>   Wrinkling their red gills the while—
>
> Are ye, two vultures sick for battle,
>   Two scorpions under one wet stone,

---

[31] At least two-thirds of the factory proletariat were literate (Sidney Pollard, *The Genesis of Modern Management: A Study of the Industrial Revolution in Great Britain* (Cambridge: Harvard UP, 1965), 180; cited by Michael Henry Scrivener, *Radical Shelley: The Philosophical Anarchism and Utopian Thought of Percy Bysshe Shelley* (Princeton: Princeton UP, 1982), 7).

[32] Edwards, *Imagination and Power*, 165.

[33] The '*discipline* of the sixty or a hundred thousand who assembled' itself aroused alarm (Thompson, *English Working Class*, 682).

> Two bloodless wolves whose dry throats rattle,
> Two crows perched on the murrained cattle,
> Two vipers tangled into one.[34]

The last stanza unveils the sequence of scenes marked by 'As' to have been an extended simile, with the force of temporal report: all the events are happening under a tyrannous reign, enabled by it, imaging its policies. The catalogue of predatory pairs, across which two act with one intent, writes a feral form of simile logic, culminating in a Gothic antithesis of the caduceus, the Roman herald's peace sign.

With reciprocal grammatical punning, Shelley launches the visionary syntax of 'As' in *The Mask* by joining conceptual similes to temporal conjunctions. Hope is about to surrender,

> When between her and her foes
> A mist, a light, an image rose,
> Small at first, and weak, and frail
> Like the vapour of a vale:
>
> Till as clouds grow on the blast,
> Like tower-crowned giants striding fast
> And glare with lightnings as they fly,
> And speak in thunder to the sky,
>
> It grew—a Shape arrayed in mail
> Brighter than the Viper's scale,
> And upborne on wings whose grain
> Was as the light of sunny rain.
>
> On its helm, seen far away,
> A planet, like the Morning's, lay,
> And those plumes its light rained through
> Like a shower of crimson dew.
>
> With step as soft as wind it past
> O'er the heads of men—so fast
> That they knew the presence there,
> And looked,—but all was empty air.
>
> As flowers beneath May's footstep waken
> As stars from Night's loose hair are shaken
> As waves arise when loud winds call
> Thoughts sprung where'er that step did fall.
>
> (102–25)

In this vision of poesy (with a poet's pun at the cadenced 'step'), comparison vibrates with simultaneity, climaxing in the triple anaphora of 'As' to produce, in one syntax, similes for the rising of new thoughts and temporal accompaniments in nature. The ensuing oratory carries a logic of generated effect: 'These words of joy and fear arose' (138).

---

[34] 'Memoir of Shelley', *Athenæum* 252 (25 August 1832), 554. Medwin's headnote hewed to Hunt's tact, naming Castlereagh only. For *1839* Mary Shelley used Medwin's title (III, 188) and, with minor variants, his text (deleting the first two dashes; *hue* instead of *yew* at 7). Not specifying the referents, she better interpreted Shelley's general indictment.

The high stakes on which Shelley plays these words send them along multiple chan-nels.[35] Impostors of power may hear indictment and warning; *Examiner*-readers may hear the argument for reform; and workers, an exhortation to act.[36] Shelley's reprise of the inaugural 'Rise like Lions' stanza as a closing refrain displaces the dream-frame (which, by convention, should return at the close), to propose a new national anthem for the oppressed:

> 'And these words shall then become
> Like oppression's thundered doom
> Ringing through each heart and brain,
> Heard again—again—again—'

The repetition of *again* performs itself, in prelude to the reprise:

> 'Rise like lions after slumber
> In unvanquishable number—
> Shake your chains to earth like dew
> Which in sleep had fallen on you—
> Ye are many—they are few.'
>
> (364–72)

'Lions' transposes royal iconography to popular force. The plural 'many' is the activated assembly of 1819 and after, its horizon in unwritten story. One draft even lacks a last clos-ing quotation mark (just a prospective dash).[37]

From 'As if' to 'may'

Shelley himself rang the words again in 'Song to the Men of England', a pithy abstract on labour oppression. The first four stanzas issue a barrage of couplet-memorable challenges:

> MEN of England, wherefore plough
> For the lords who lay ye low?

---

[35] Noting that agency is left to 'somehow', Michael Scrivener decides that in 'England in 1819', the argument is necessarily symbolic rather than practical (*Radical Shelley*, 207). Stephen Goldsmith is sceptical, reversing the force of Shelley's *as if* with his own: 'the transformation from silence to speech, from death to life [...] ends oppression automatically, as if the dismantling of power on the terrain of political discourse were somehow a *generic* dismantling of domination itself', which 'appears to be insubstantial, a mere language effect that evaporates the moment one brings to an end its monopoly over representation' (*Unbinding Jerusalem: Apocalypse and Romantic Imagination* (Ithaca, NY: Cornell UP, 1993), 256).

[36] For historically alert soundings of the rhetorical strata, see Stephen C. Behrendt, *Shelley and his Audiences* (Lincoln, NE: University of Nebraska Press, 1989), 199–202. Keach proposes that Shelley's compound 'joy and fear' registers 'all the complications and contradictions and fears' that attend 'powerful political protest' ('Rise Like Lions?'); hence his question mark.

[37] Reiman (ed.), *Facsimile* (32); while this draft was 'not intended as press copy' (1), Mary Shelley's press-copy (which Shelley reviewed) also lacks a closing quotation mark. It has a terminal point and 'The End' (50), as does Hunt's text (47). Hunt blazons the last stanza with capitals at 'unvanquishable NUMBER!' and the last line: 'YE ARE MANY—THEY ARE FEW'.

> Wherefore weave with toil and care,
> The rich robes your tyrants wear?
>
> (1–4)

And so forth, into blunt recapitulations:

> The seed ye sow, another reaps;
> The wealth ye find, another keeps;
> The robes ye weave, another wears;
> The arms ye forge, another bears.
>
> (17–20)

Poetically potent in themselves, the repetitions also evoke the horrific repetitions of labour-history and its dehumanizing mechanizations. Shelley's unwriting issues in reverse-imperatives:

> Sow seed,—but let no tyrant reap;
> Find wealth,—let no imposter heap;
> Weave robes,—let not the idle wear;
> Forge arms,—in your defence to bear.
>
> (21–4)

Yet a tonal shift in the final two stanzas once again raises a potential insult:

> Shrink to your cellars, holes, and cells;
> In halls ye deck another dwells.
> Why shake the chains ye wrought? Ye see
> The steel ye tempered glance on ye.
>
> With plough and spade, and hoe and loom,
> Trace your grave, and build your tomb,
> And weave your winding-sheet, till fair
> England be your sepulchre.
>
> (25–32)

Shelley's poetry lets the Men of England hear themselves written as unwitting anti-poets, tracing, building, weaving the life out of the nation. When the President of the National Secular Society read this *Song* on the centenary of Shelley's birth in 1892 to a large audience of 'working men who took Shelley quite seriously', it met 'thunders of applause'. Taking no insult, these men of England cheered the unveiling of oppressor-ideology, the cynicism of power (hear the voice of the lords!).[38] Shelley's couplets speak in acid rhymes: 'loom' linked to the workers' 'tomb'; the cant of 'fair England' linked to 'sepulchre'. The steel that glances on them deftly wounds them and, in punning, surveys their labour.

---

[38] The anecdote is from George Bernard Shaw, 'Shaming the Devil about Shelley', *Albemarle Review* (September 1892). Shelley's tone troubles Keach, who also notes K. N. Cameron 'puzzling' over it ('sardonic' in mood, 'shaming' in intent (343)); Behrendt proposes 'a calculated challenge' in the 'bitter irony' (*Shelley and his Audiences*, 195–6).

This 'Song to' is cast without a speaking 'I'. Another report, also issued without an 'I', and with a climax for a national 'our', is the sonnet Shelley sent to Hunt on 23 December (*Letters: PBS* II, 167), 'England in 1819'—the categorical crisis-title given by Mary Shelley to Shelley's now most famous political poem.[39] Undeluded about publishability, Shelley indulged his most radical revolutionary imagination and found his most compelling political voice:

> An old, mad, blind, despised, and dying King;
> Princes, the dregs of their dull race, who flow
> Through public scorn,—mud from a muddy spring;
> Rulers who neither see nor feel nor know,
> But leechlike to their fainting country cling
> Till they drop, blind in blood, without a blow.
> A people starved and stabbed in th'untilled field;
> An army, whom liberticide and prey
> Makes as a two-edged sword to all who wield;
> Golden and sanguine laws which tempt and slay;
> Religion Christless, Godless—a book sealed;
> A senate, Time's worst statute, unrepealed—
> Are graves from which a glorious Phantom may
> Burst, to illumine our tempestuous day.

'Liberticide' was a word coined in 1790s France for the agents and policies of anti-republican factions and conspiracies, thence imported by English reformers (Francis Burdett in the 1790s and Jeremy Bentham in 1817) to censure its repressive ministry and monarchy.[40] Making good on the argument of *A Mask* (295–6), Shelley wields a sword of words for a massive political indictment, each wrong end-punctuated, and the whole arrayed in rhymes that repeal old patterns.[41] The syntax is the very action, accreting, in parody both of Burke's famous swelling periods and an epic catalogue, an argument for revolution, converging on the blunt unifying predicate, 'Are graves'. This, moreover, is no conclusion, but a dynamic pivot into a pregnant infinitive, 'to illumine'.

It's a breathtaking tour de force. Yet it is at this very climax that the shifts of Shelley's political poetics emerge in their most extreme measure. One crux is that 'glorious Phantom'. It seems conjured to answer the 'unformed spectre' that is the Revolution-apocalypse in Burke's story of regicide France:

> out of the tomb of the murdered Monarchy in France, has arisen a vast, tremendous, unformed spectre, in a far more terrific guise than any which ever yet have over-powered the imagination and subdued the fortitude of man. Going straight forward

---

[39] *1839* III, 193; I use *N2*, based on Percy Shelley's fair copy.
[40] Francis Burdett, 3 January 1798, *Parliamentary Register*, 12 vols. (London: J. Debrett, 1797–1802), IV, 543; Jeremy Bentham, *Plan of Parliamentary Reform* (London: R. Hunter, 1817), p. cccxxix.
[41] Hunt echoed Shelley's 'without a blow' (6) when he noted in his Preface to *The Masque* that the 1832 Reform Act was achieved 'without a blow' (p. xi).

to it's end, unappalled by peril, unchecked by remorse, despising all common maxims and all common means, that hideous phantom overpowered those who could not believe it was possible she could at all exist.[42]

Shelley not only refuses Burke's scandal-spectre; he also revises the familiar sense of 'phantom'—nonentity, delusion, ghost, illusion—into an exposure of the 'phantasm' (the etymological ancestor) pretending to fact. 'Phantasm' would be the word used by a writer in 1850 to channel Wordsworth's French Revolution mind: 'Men had already asked themselves the question, shall we continue to obey phantasms, or shall we search for realities [...]?'[43] Shelley's version of this 'or' conjures Phantom to unwrite the grave story of England in 1819.

Or, with a relay from Burke's outrage, England in 1817: Shelley's sonnet reprises, with a difference, the iconic figure in the closing sentence of a pamphlet in which he set the national grief over the death of Princess Charlotte against the brutally cheered execution of the leaders of the Pentridge rebellion (the hatching of an *agent provocateur*):

> Let us follow the corpse of British Liberty slowly and reverentially to its tomb: and if some glorious Phantom should appear, and make its throne of broken swords and sceptres and royal crowns trampled in the dust, let us say that the Spirit of Liberty has arisen from its grave and left all that was gross and mortal there, and kneel down and worship it as our Queen.[44]

In the hypothetical future, a Phantom redeems the corpse of Liberty with precise political logic: a glorious revolution erecting its authority on the debris of the old order. This is also the logic of Shelley's *New National Anthem*, where the refrain 'God save the Queen' refers to Liberty, in rebuke to the present King, her ruiner. The plea to 'save' is blatantly not the old-anthem sense, 'preserve', but is politically rebranded to 'rescue, redeem' Queen Liberty from what *save* has to rhyme with in 1819, 'England's grave'.[45]

For 'England in 1819', Shelley takes the speculative proposition of his 1817 pamphlet and puts its 'grave' in a plot of historical contingency. James Chandler goes so far as to argue Shelley's 'commitment to the notion of changing history *by* interpreting it', the 'act

---

[42] *Two Letters [on] Proposals for Peace with the Regicide Directory of France* (London: F. and C. Rivington, 1796), I, 6–7.

[43] 'Wordsworth's Autobiographical Poem', *Gentleman's Magazine and Historical Review* 34 (November 1850), 466. This reviewer registers the force of form in both political and literary revolutions: if Wordsworth's poetry amounts to 'one of the greatest literary revolutions the world has ever seen', the 'nerve and purpose to work it were braced and formed under the influence of a corresponding convulsion in politics' (466).

[44] P. B. Shelley, *An Address to the People on the Death of the Princess Charlotte*, Murray: *Prose*, 239. The full title (troping Paine's sneer at Burke in *The Rights of Man*) is 'We Pity the Plumage, but Forget the Dying Bird': *An Address to the People on the Death of the Princess Charlotte*. Shelley printed twenty copies. Although Thomas Rodd (likely proxy for Shelley's usual publisher, Ollier) issued a limited facsimile 'reprint' in 1843, it did not gain wide audience until 1888 (just after the foundation of the Shelley Society), in R. H. Shepherd's edition of *Prose Works*.

[45] Text from Foot, *Shelley's Revolutionary Year*, 105–6.

of reading' itself performing a revolutionary 'resurrection'.[46] I am touched by this teach-erly hope, but it's telling (and winningly honest) that Chandler concedes his students' scepticism. The problem is not just the romance of reading as action, but also the hing-ing of the action, at Shelley's climax, on an unexpected auxiliary, 'may', written into com-plications of syntax and grammar, with philosophy at stake. Where a Shakespeare-pattern sonnet would clinch its case, Shelley mutes the rhyme with syntax that drives 'may' over the line into a percussive 'Burst'. In the visionary aftershock, the closing rhyme is scarcely heard, scarcely (even) read.

One of Shelley's most sensitive readers, Stuart Curran, finds this event poetically and politically resonant, risking all:

> Shelley pivots his poem on a syntactic potentiality—'may'—that yields to the burst-ing of its formal bonds in a movement parallel to the revolutionary explosion that will invert the anti-forms repressing contemporary society. The form symbolically consumes itself, as surely as does the society it catalogs.[47]

This is the strong allegory; but is the form so sure? The modality of 'may' (and the idea-tional consequence) is evasive: perhaps? is enabled? is empowered to? maybe a tact of not overplaying the phantom-hand? A 'glimpse of some far goal in time', remarks Jerome McGann, is Shelley's signature 'ideology of hope', and it is 'deeply allied [...] to his sense of hopelessness'.[48] To F. R. Leavis (in line with Arnold's iconic 'ineffectual angel') it all seems 'pathetic weakness': the 'oddly ironical stress' that 'results from the rime position' sustains no more than a Phantom of miraculous agency.[49] Reading the same couplet, Timothy Webb admits the ghost of 'improbability' but also admires a brave 'intellectual honesty' in the 'ironical and limiting' mode.[50] The letter to Hunt in which Shelley sent the sonnet plays its own cagey 'may'. 'I do not expect you to publish it, but you may show it to whom you please' (*Letters: PBS* II, 167). Yet if giving the 'may' to Hunt makes him the agent for a collective 'our', it is Shelley who has written the show. And so 'may' rhymes and unrhymes, sustaining hope and desire, but hesitating about the force of poetry, and its forms, in releasing an unwritten story from the graves of 1819. The debate is the epit-ome, and epiphenomenon, of Shelley's political poetics—an imagination of popular agency amid present oppression in an historicism of possibility.

Utterly familiar with *The Tempest*, Shelley surely knew the phrasing of outrage as 'our tempestuous day' activates the etymology of 'time' in 'tempestuous': for this time, a day, not for ever. Shelley's persistence in writing poems tempered with a sense of a future day (if the French Revolution is any reminder) often, quite often, resides in the compromise

---

[46] James Chandler, *England in 1819: The Politics of Literary Culture and the Case of Romantic Historicism* (Chicago: University of Chicago Press, 1998), 31.

[47] Stuart Curran, *Poetic Form and British Romanticism* (New York: Oxford UP, 1986), 55.

[48] Jerome J. McGann, *The Romantic Ideology: A Critical Analysis* (Chicago: University of Chicago Press, 1983), 112–13.

[49] F. R. Leavis, 'Shelley', *Revaluation: Tradition and Development in English Poetry* (London: Chatto & Windus, 1936), 213.

[50] Timothy Webb, *Shelley: A Voice Not Understood* (Atlantic Highlands, NJ: Humanities Press International, 1977), 107–8.

of what poetry can 'illumine' at the moment. It's an unusual verb, 'illumine' ('illuminate' is far more common). I think Shelley is tuning it against its two singular events in *Paradise Lost*. The first, resonantly, is Milton's plea to his Spirit: 'What in me is dark | Illumine' (I. 22–3). The second is an ironizing sequel, from the rebels' defiant swords: 'The sudden blaze | Far round illumin'd hell' (I. 665–6). If Milton gives 'illumine' to authority, and gives God the gloat on the outlaws, Shelley illumines the hell on earth in the mask of Law and God. Even as the strong grammar of 'to' in 'burst, to illumine' is 'so as to', or 'with power to', Shelley's poetic forming of his final line allows 'to illumine our tempestuous day' to shimmer as infinitive. In this phantom syntax is a transition from hell ringing with 'the tempestuous cry | Of the triumph of Anarchy' (*Mask*, 56–7) to historical potential.

This is the poetry, not a proven argument, Shelley was writing out in that final paragraph of his *Defence of Poetry*. The poets who 'measure the circumference and sound the depths' of human potential are also working through poetry, its measure and sound. Not just writers of words, poets become their words: 'Poets are […] the words which express what they understand not.' This is potential for other agents as 'legislators of the World'— *World* itself holding 'word'.

The immediate days were not heartening. 'Every thing seems to conspire against Reform', Shelley conceded to Peacock in March 1820 (*Letters: PBS* II, 176). Across the next months he wrote that 'Ode to Liberty', which closes in a poet's despair, 'As waves which lately paved his watery way | Hiss round a drowner's head in their tempestuous play'—rhyming with a difference the last words of 'England in 1819'.[51] By May 1820 the 'vast assembly' imagined in *The Mask* had devolved into 'little unanimity in the mass of the people' and 'a civil war impend[ing] from the success of ministers and the exasperation of the poor' (to Peacock, *Letters: PBS* II, 193). Yet if this seemed the proximate story, Shelley would still hope for poetry to preview an unwritten story in the illumining of a tempestuous day, its darkness visible, and a phantom of possibility.

Select Bibliography

Behrendt, Stephen C. *Shelley and his Audiences*. Lincoln, NE: University of Nebraska Press, 1989.
——Ed. *Percy Bysshe Shelley: A Longman Cultural Edition*. New York: Pearson, 2010.
Chandler, James. *England in 1819: The Politics of Literary Culture and the Case of Romantic Historicism*. Chicago: University of Chicago Press, 1998.
Curran, Stuart. *Poetic Form and British Romanticism*. Oxford: Oxford UP, 1986.
Edwards, Thomas R. *Imagination and Power: A Study of Poetry on Public Themes*. Oxford: Oxford UP, 1971.

---

[51] Keach, with characteristic nuance, proposes 'a trajectory of commitment to "Liberty's" unfinished cause', recognizing its coursing, even in Shelley's optimistic vision, with questions of 'its historicity, its actuality, as well as its very representational status' (William Keach, *Arbitrary Power: Romanticism, Language, Politics* (Princeton: Princeton UP, 2004), 158, 157).

Foot, Paul. *Red Shelley*. London: Sidgwick & Jackson, 1980.

—— *Shelley's Revolutionary Year*. London: Redwords, 1990.

Goldsmith, Stephen. *Unbinding Jerusalem: Apocalypse and Romantic Imagination*. Ithaca, NY: Cornell UP, 1993.

Janowitz, Anne. '"A Voice from across the Sea": Communitarianism at the Limits of Romanticism'. *The Limits of Romanticism: Essays in Cultural, Feminist, and Materialist Criticism*. Ed. Mary A. Favret and Nicola J. Watson. Bloomington, IN: Indiana UP, 1994. 83–100.

Keach, William. *Arbitrary Power: Romanticism, Language, Politics*. Princeton: Princeton UP, 2004.

—— 'Radical Shelley?' *Raritan* 5.2 (1985), 120–9.

—— 'Rise Like Lions? Shelley and the Revolutionary Left', *International Socialism* 75 (Summer 1997): <http://www.marxists.de/culture/shelley/keach>.

—— *Shelley's Style*. London: Methuen, 1984.

Morton, Timothy. Ed. *The Cambridge Companion to Shelley*. Cambridge: Cambridge UP, 2006.

Redfield, Marc. *The Politics of Aesthetics: Nationalism, Gender, Romanticism*. Stanford, CA: Stanford UP, 2003.

Reiman, Donald. *'The Mask of Anarchy': A Facsimile Edition*. New York: Garland Press, 1985.

Sales, Roger. *English Literature in History 1780–1830: Pastoral and Politics*. New York: St Martin's Press, 1983.

Scrivener, Michael Henry. *Radical Shelley: The Philosophical Anarchism and Utopian Thought of Percy Bysshe Shelley*. Princeton: Princeton UP, 1982.

Thompson, E. P. *The Making of the English Working Class*. 1963; New York: Vintage, 1966.

Williams, Raymond. *Culture and Society, 1780–1850*. New York: Columbia UP, 1958.

Wolfson, Susan J. *Formal Charges: The Shaping of Poetry in British Romanticism*. Stanford, CA: Stanford UP, 1997.

CHAPTER 23

VISIONARY RHYME

The Sensitive-Plant *and* The Witch of Atlas

JERROLD E. HOGLE

IN his verse-dedication 'To Mary' introducing *The Witch of Atlas*, stanzas left out of its initial publication in 1824, Shelley, deflecting his wife's fear that such a work lacks 'human interest' (*Norton 2*, 367), applies the phrase 'visionary rhyme' to this highly fanciful and explicitly mythological poem (8).[1] That label may point partly to what his dedication calls this piece's 'Light [...] vest of flowing meter' (37). *The Witch* does use the *ottava rima* form of eight-line iambic stanzas with a distinctive rhyme scheme associated at the time with serio-comic Italian epic-romance, as in the *Il Ricciardetto* (1738) of Niccolo Fortiguerri, and with the 1819 early cantos of Lord Byron's *Don Juan*, including their ironic and satiric distance from the realities they depict.[2] But the 'visionary' reach of *The Witch* also exceeds these flights from everyday realism to celebrate the mythic nature of the poet's own pre-texts that most helped him generate this epyllion in San Giuliano, Italy, largely over three days in August, 1820.[3] Shelley is here extending his own brief fancy about a personified 'witch Poesy' in her 'cave' in his 1816 lyric 'Mont Blanc' (44) and his own rendering of the demigoddess 'Asia', the 'transforming presence' who is the distant love-object of his hero and the 'Child of Light' whose 'soul' becomes 'an enchanted boat', once it is lifted onto the 'waves' of her lover's 'sweet singing', in the ultra-mythological *Prometheus Unbound* as it was published that very August (see I. 832 and II. v. 56, 72–4). It is surely this classical idealization of a feminized force that led the poet's friend Leigh Hunt to describe *The Witch* later as 'a personification of the imaginative faculty in its most airy abstractions', though Hunt admits that this poem in its 'fairy region' is occasionally '*dreaming* of mortal strife'.[4]

---

[1] All my citations from Shelley's works come from *Norton 2*.

[2] See *Norton 2*, 365, and Richard Cronin, *Shelley's Poetic Thoughts* (London: Macmillan, 1981), 55–7. All further citations of 'Cronin' in my text are drawn from this book.

[3] See Bieri, II, 203. All my other references to Bieri will appear in my text.

[4] From 'Hunt's Critique of Shelley's *Posthumous Poems*' (published 1828) in Theodore Redpath, *The Young Romantics and Critical Opinion, 1807–1824* (New York: St Martin's Press, 1973), 409.

As it happens, too, both Shelley's 'visionary' label and this suggestion of an abstracting 'personification' can be applied as readily to his earlier poem of the spring of 1820, *The Sensitive-Plant*, which appeared in his *Prometheus* volume. This variation on Erasmus Darwin's *Loves of the Plants* (1789) somewhat echoes the latter's emphasis on the erotic outreach of every living 'vegetable' that seeks its own reproduction in the 'garden' that is the world.[5] Yet Shelley's garden, visualized in quatrains of tetrameter couplets reminiscent of Southey's 'God's Judgment on a Bishop',[6] is at first an 'undefiled Paradise' (Part First, 38) filled with 'Naiad-like lily of the vale' and the 'hyacinth purple' that recalls the bloodied Hyacinthus turned to a flower by Apollo (21–5), both allusions to the transformations of people into plants in the Graeco-Roman myths that compose Ovid's *Metamorphoses* (8–10 CE). Moreover, the 'Lady' who is the life-sustaining 'Power' in the world of *The Sensitive-Plant* (Part Second, l. 1) is another goddess-like reworking of Asia as the 'Life of Life' (*Prometheus Unbound*, II. v. 48), and all that is mythologized in her garden turns out to be the merest 'shadows of the dream', of a timeless beyond where 'For love, and beauty, and delight | There is no death nor change' (Conclusion, 3–14, 21–2). As much as Shelley soars to the 'airy' and insubstantial in other poems, there are no writings of his more qualified than these two to be the 'winged Vision' to which he confesses aspiring often (17) in the *Witch of Atlas* dedication.

These 'abstracting' drives in both poems, to be sure, have tempted some interpreters to see their deeper meanings in very Platonic terms, particularly in the face of the poet's fascination with Plato's *Symposium*, which Shelley translated as *The Banquet* starting in 1818. As Earl Wasserman writes, *The Sensitive-Plant* appears to argue that 'the perceptible mutable world is an illusion and the ideal world is real and eternal', an echo both of Plato and of the play *Life is a Dream* (1635–6) by the Spanish dramatist Calderón de la Barca, whom Shelley also translated.[7] Numerous scholars have also concurred with Carl Grabo that *The Witch of Atlas* is Shelley's vision of the transcendently self-sufficient 'goddess of love and intellectual beauty animating the deeps of life'.[8] Even the exactitude of the older verse forms that Shelley employs in these poems, ones previously associated with absolutist visions such as Boccaccio's late medieval poems in *ottava rima*, have been evidence for many that Shelley's *Plant* and *Witch* point to transcendent Essences as absolute and supersensible as the Ideas in Plato's dialogues. Nevertheless, I now want to argue, building on the most important scholarship about these two poems over the last few decades, that a strictly Platonic reading of his 'visionary rhymes' fails to grasp

---

[5] I refer, when 'Darwin' is noted in my text, to *The Loves of the Plants* in the Woodstock reprint edition, introd. Jonathan Wordsworth (Oxford: Woodstock, 1991), which describes the 'Sensitive Plant' in canto I, ll. 247–62.

[6] Nora Crook and Derek Guiton, *Shelley's Venomed Melody* (Cambridge: Cambridge UP, 1986), 203. Other citations of 'Crook/Guiton' will come from this source.

[7] See Wasserman, *Shelley: A Critical Reading* (Baltimore: Johns Hopkins UP, 1971), 154–69. Further citations from 'Wasserman' are from this book. Note also Pedro Calderón de la Barca, *Life is a Dream*, trans. and ed. Edwin Honig (New York: Hill and Wang, 1970), from which I draw my later references to 'Calderón'.

[8] Grabo, *The Meaning of 'The Witch of Atlas'* (Chapel Hill, NC: University of North Carolina Press, 1935), 87. Further references to 'Grabo' are all to this work.

Shelley's radically liberal challenges to all hierarchical systems subordinated to primary Absolutes. These poems offer profoundly sceptical alternatives to such philosophical and political schemes that for Shelley tyrannize over human beings by positing a level of emanating Centres and Truths at which 'Power' lies and from which human absolute powers fictively claim to draw their authority.

Just as he resists such claims as they appear in orthodox and institutionalized Christianity and in the government rhetoric of imperial Britain and more ancient empires, Shelley also asserts in his 'Preface' to *The Banquet* that its author's 'theories respecting the government of the world, and the elementary laws of moral action, are not always correct', despite Plato's 'remarkable intuitions' of how the 'human mind' moves between levels of thought.[9] *The Sensitive-Plant* and *The Witch of Atlas*, consequently, are really disruptions of many of the sources, the belief-systems, and verse-patterns with which they seem to begin. Just at those points where they might intimate absolute fixities beyond their many and rapid transfers among thoughts and words, they suggest that this very movement across different figures (un-centred, un-fixed, perpetually self-transformative) can be—and should be—radically reclaimed as the key underpinning of thought and language that can best ensure the dissolution of tyrannical constructs. Once those aims are exposed in these poems' most basic assumptions, as I hope to show in what follows, we can even see how further interpretations of great value have emerged from this revised understanding and helped it stunningly redefine what being 'visionary' really is in the poetry of Shelley's final years.

The Sensitive-Plant, as some scholars have realized, starts with the transfers between different figures that are already endemic to its primary 'vehicle', the *mimosa pudica* or 'sensitive-plant' itself. Since the fifth century BCE, ancient Greek botanical philosophy and poetry have asserted analogies between the 'organic order' in plants and the life 'force' that 'runs through all' entities; human beings have thus had rationales over several centuries for defining themselves by analogies to plants.[10] Starting in the seventeenth century CE in Europe, the *mimosa pudica*, though small, native to Brazil, and able to reproduce without a counterpart of its own kind (*Norton* 2, 286), has thus become a focal point for many such analogies. It is unusually responsive to sensory contact (curling into a tighter shape when touched), opens out rapidly to light (even changing colour) but closes inward with the coming of darkness, and so reveals humanistic sensitivity to all stimuli, making it a most apt correlative for the 'sensibility' increasingly celebrated as a central human attribute by the end of the eighteenth century (Maniquis, 140–4). The sensitive-plant analogy makes it seem so biologically human, in fact, that it can be likened to the male phallus—'it rears its *head* | Flushes, as 'twere, a kindly red, | And courts thy lovely hand' (10–12)—throughout James Perry's salacious *Mimosa: or, the Sensitive Plant* (1779), which certainly prepares the way for Darwin's eroticizing of the whole

---

[9] 'Preface to the Banquet of Plato', in James A. Notopoulos, *The Platonism of Shelley: A Study of Platonism and the Poetic Mind* (Durham, NC: Duke UP, 1949), 402. Further references to Shelley's renderings of Plato, cited with 'Notopoulos', come from this volume.

[10] Robert M. Maniquis, 'The Puzzling *Mimosa*: Sensitivity and Plant Symbols in Romanticism', *Studies in Romanticism* 8 (1969), 130, hereafter cited in my text as 'Maniquis'.

botanic kingdom in *The Loves of the Plants*.[11] But even Darwin, as Shelley knew, expands well beyond Perry and makes the very self-contained *mimosa* 'chaste' and feminine rather than masculine, the ultimate locus of transfers between subjects and objects *or* subjects and subjects as she 'feels, alive through all her tender form, | The whisper'd murmurs of the gathering storm' (Darwin, 25, I. 251–2). At no point in its history as any kind of symbol, it turns out, has the *mimosa pudica* in literature been anything other than the analogical transformation of what has always been a metaphor.

Shelley thus makes his 'sensitive-plant' the quintessential passage point for the 'Spirit of love felt every where' in a garden that could be a private preserve, a nation, or the whole world (Part First, 1–6). Such a Spirit is manifestly a process of transference very like the basis of metaphor itself, especially when it is embodied in such forms as 'plumed insects' that dart from plant to plant 'Like golden boats on a sunny sea' (82–3). The *mimosa*, as the metaphoric vehicle of this Spirit's tenor, 'Received more than all—it loved more than ever' (72), being primarily a receptor and emitter of love's ongoing transferences. It is a hermaphroditic 'it' rather than a 'he' or 'she' and thus not driven to turn the great interplay into one act of intercourse with just one other. Shelley's 'it' 'loves' so generally that it is 'even like Love' itself in its subtle movements (76). In that way only, it 'desires what it has not—the beautiful' (77), enacting the sheer human longing for what is always out of longing's reach. Yet it spawns a partial signifier, which differs from yet defers to that objective,[12] in the 'small fruit' (70) that is a synecdoche for the fundamental process of giving and receiving that Love most fully is. Shelley's poem of spring 1820 has gone back to the primal interplay of analogies, rather than a single Essence, that made the metaphoric interplay of human-as-plant arise in ancient Greece and has brought it forward through its later transformations to become the very give-and-take-and-give of love in the world that his sensitive-plant channels in being both unique among its species and what that species can be at its most sensitized.

Such a vivid expansion of an already metaphoric figure consequently generates several more acts of transference. In the first place, the sensitive-plant's metaphoric 'roots' make it, as vehicle, able to incarnate a wide continuum of tenors. It can suggest Shelley himself at a 'companionless time' in Pisa cut off from an estranged Mary and feeling 'frustration' at his ineffectual isolation from England while simultaneously producing some 'fruit' in a *Prometheus* volume that few will read (Bieri, II, 186–90). Yet this same plant also points to the general condition of any real poet as a conduit for a larger energy of give-and-take surging across the whole history of poetry, even as poets, often subject to painful rejection, can only feebly intimate the 'beautiful' yet to be realized (*Defence*, 535). On top of all this, Shelley's *mimosa* hints at the elemental condition of any good human being: nakedly vulnerable, selflessly disinterested, vibrating in all its senses, and desirous of the transformative Love it keeps striving to channel—yet still left quite incomplete and fearful of being rejected at every turn, forced to always wait for more lasting fulfilments even as he or she strives to open the self not to one linkage but to the many ways through which the

---

[11] See Perry, *Mimosa: or, the Sensitive Plant* (London: W. Sandwich, 1779), esp. 1–2.

[12] This is one indication of my ongoing debt throughout this chapter to the late Jacques Derrida, especially in *Of Grammatology*, trans. Gayatri Chakravorty Spivak (Baltimore: Johns Hopkins UP, 1976), 30–65.

plant/person might help instigate the improvement of humanity's 'garden'. This multiplicity of levels is not a hierarchy of lesser to more divine, as in the medieval allegories of plants that call us Platonically from the literal to the moral to the anagogic planes. It is the metaphoric interfacing of all these levels on the *same* plane, the sensitive-plant's as Shelley renders it, as it is washed over, like all sentient beings, by an 'ocean of dreams', the spectres of earlier perceptions, that 'impress | The light sand which paves [the surface of fluid thought]—Consciousness' (*Sensitive-Plant*, Part First, 103–5).

That centreless mobility, in point of fact, helps to create as much as it seems to pour out from the 'Lady' of Shelley's garden. Like Asia in *Prometheus Unbound* and the 'veiled maid' of the Poet's 'dreams' in Shelley's *Alastor* (1816, 51–91), the 'Eve in this Eden' is a 'ruling grace' to the garden (Part Second, l. 2), yet only to the degree that she is a 'wonder [...] | Whose form was upborne by a lovely mind, | Which, dilating, had molded her mien and motion | Like a sea-flower unfolding beneath the ocean' (5–8). Even as the Lady therefore resembles a goddess emerging from the sea, as in Sandro Botticelli's painting *The Birth of Venus* (c.1482), she is the product for Shelley, not of any Divinity, but of a 'mind' with a small 'm' that enables her very 'motion' as an emanation of thought. This Lady, then, is very like Asia: the kind of projection that thought can fashion in Shelley's essay *On Love* (1818) when that 'powerful attraction' of the sensitive subject towards 'all that we conceive or fear or hope beyond ourselves'—the primal transference-impulse of love within us all that is also a force beyond any one individual—projects metaphorically into an 'antitype' or 'mirror' of the projector 'the ideal prototype of everything excellent or lovely that we are capable of conceiving', thereby seeming to build, as the Lady does in *The Sensitive-Plant*, 'a circle around its proper Paradise which pain and sorrow or evil dare not overleap' (*Norton 2*, 503–4).

True, even in *On Love*, Shelley insists on the genuine alterity of this 'other' lest she be but the onanistic vision of the *Alastor* Poet (Shelley's earlier critique of his own solipsism). This whole process in *The Sensitive-Plant* thus surges back towards the projecting subject from an external counterpart. All the garden's 'music' cannot be perceived to be there, in fact, without her projected and mobile 'Power' appearing to infuse it (*Sensitive-Plant*, Part Second, l. 1), however much that transferential movement actually comes from the 'sensitive' subject, who feels that some such 'soul of his soul' must be 'out there' so that the life of the garden can be sustained by a love beyond any single mind. Consequently, the 'Lady' of the garden, being the product of a metaphoric projection, can, like the plant, be analogous to number of particular figures on her own: perhaps the Mary who once returned Shelley's love but had now frequently withdrawn from him; the maternal Mrs Mason who sustained him greatly till it came time to think of leaving the Casa Frassi in Pisa, where he wrote this poem (Bieri, II, 188); or even the lady 'Liberty' of Shelley's *The Mask of Anarchy* (written in 1819) who can arouse the oppressed of England 'As flowers beneath May's footsteps' (*Mask*, 122) but can also be killed by 'tyranny's denial of nurture' so often visible in the 'garden' that is the Britain Shelley perceived.[13]

---

[13] Michael Henry Scrivener, *Radical Shelley: The Philosophical Anarchism and Utopian Thought of Percy Bysshe Shelley* (Princeton: Princeton UP, 1982), 235.

Yet the Lady of this poet's garden is still the primary externalization of the inward and outward movement of transfer and transformation, which is a challenge to all absolutist regimes even in Ovid's anti-Augustan dance across myths so often reinvoked in this 'visionary rhyme'.[14] 'So soon as this want or power is dead' or perceived to be so, 'man becomes the living sepulcher of himself, and what yet survives is the mere husk of what he once was' (*On Love*, 504). Such is the state to which the sensitive-plant and all its neighbours are reduced in Shelley's 'Part Third' once the Lady and all she channels suddenly appear to die, and 'The garden once fair became cold and foul | Like the corpse of her who had been its soul' (Part Third, 17–18)—no longer a state of perfect rhyme, with the 'soul' now linked only to the 'foul'-ing of it.

Granted, the 'Conclusion' of *The Sensitive-Plant* strives to counter this loss by suggesting that perception's level of mere seeming can be overcome by the 'creed' that 'love, and beauty, and delight' have a 'might' that 'exceeds our organs' and so can be seen as transcending 'death' and undergoing no 'change' in their fundamental natures. As much as this resurgence of hope alludes to the *Symposium*, however, it radically alters Plato's locations of love, beauty, and delight. In *The Banquet* as Shelley translates it, the priestess Diotima tells Socrates that 'beauty' alone is 'eternally uniform' to the point of being 'monoeidic with itself', while 'love' is but a 'desire' in pursuit of beauty's union of 'immortality' with ultimate 'good', and 'delight' is an emotion that arises when 'the lover touches the consummation of his labor', that moment when desire verges on attainment but has not achieved full knowledge (Notopoulos, 445–9). What Plato places on three different levels Shelley places on the same plane of 'truth' beyond immediate awareness in *The Sensitive-Plant* (Conclusion, 19–21). He thereby draws the process of love and the nature of delight, both transitional and transformational for Plato, up to 'beauty's' level, making it coequal with them. There is thus as much of a process of becoming and seeking in 'beauty' as in there is in 'love' and 'delight', so much so that the 'Garden sweet, that lady fair, | And all sweet shapes and odors there | In truth have never passed away', being examples of an eternal process forever projecting an Eden that is the larger energy in the 'ocean of dreams' sweeping into and across 'Consciousness' if we will but attend to it (Part First, 103–5). Since therefore 'all things exist as they are perceived: at least in relation to the percipient', a key tenet of Shelley's scepticism by 1820 (*Defence*, 533), we can choose, individually and collectively, to perceive the garden-life we long for as decaying and our ego-ideals (such as the Lady) dying as experience destroys Edenic innocence. Yet we can also choose to harness the movement of transference in and beyond us so that any earthly pattern of growth and death, including momentary failures of progress towards a better world, can seem only one level of perception which a fuller consciousness can overcome by finding ways (such as this poem) by which the 'garden' can keep living on in further transfigurations.

In suggesting all this, of course, Shelley is quite aware that his final 'creed' must declare itself as 'modest' and thus not fully certain (Conclusion, 13) so that it will not seem the

---

[14] See Horace Gregory, 'Introduction', *Ovid: The Metamorphoses*, trans. Gregory (New York: New American Library, 1958), pp. ix–xxviii. My citations of 'Ovid' are all from this translation.

dogma of Absolute Essences. This modesty must therefore be emphasized in *The Sensitive-Plant*'s Conclusion, partly in its being driven by the earthly mobility of thought visible in all the earlier segments. Shelley's allusion to Calderón in 'the shadows of *the dream*' (emphasis added), we must realize, invokes the original *Life is a Dream* right at the point where its hero, Segismundo, sees the life of the immediate senses as a 'passing shadow' mainly because a man's 'dreams' prevent our higher awareness, not of God directly, but the fact that human dreams themselves are only part of the greater 'dreaming', only part of the process for the fulfilment of our hopes that is broader and more lasting—and possibly as illusory—as humankind's 'passing shadows' (Calderón, 76–7). Hence *The Sensitive-Plant* must admit, with 'saddened irony', that even its final 'affirmation expresses [nothing] more [conclusive] than subjective longing' in a 'consciously unsettled and unsettling fiction'.[15] However much the poem's verse form seems to contradict this process by aping Southey's conservative attempt at couplet-and-quatrain closure, even this scheme is finally diverted from an absolutist containment. First there is the way Shelley often uses enjambment to make his lines and stanzas pour over into each other, as when 'each [plant in the garden] was interpenetrated | With the light and the odour its neighbor shed | Like young lovers' (Part First, 66–8). Then, too, there is the manner in which many of his rhymes refuse to be clearly unifying echoes, as in the 'foul'/'soul' succession noted earlier and in the poem's inconclusive ending, where the 'might' of 'love, and beauty, and delight', already redefined, 'Exceeds our organs—Which endure | No light—being themselves obscure' (Conclusion, 21–4). All at once the refusal of closure in another enjambment is echoed by a line that first juxtaposes permanence ('endure') with its negation ('No light') and then links the persistence of deeper movements with how our senses 'obscure' them even while we still sense the 'endurance' of Love's larger process. Shelley has served notice by employing the most ordered of stanza-patterns as well as some final abstractions the most likely to recall the absolutes of Plato. He has shown us conclusively that both of these can be undermined within themselves to reveal a non-hierarchical process of redemptive transfiguration, the ultimate resistance to all the older hierarchies that still try to suppress or destroy it.

This basic view of *The Sensitive-Plant*, however, is not exclusive to me but is the mobile underpinning of several interpretations that have emerged over the last few decades. One such perspective embraces revisionist psychoanalysis to argue that Shelley's sensitive-plant works through the primal human 'longing for symbiotic union with [some being like] the mother [here the Lady, only to see that quest] replaced by a fearful [...] image of abandonment' (O'Neill, 171). Salvation from such Oedipal desire and its denial can be remedied psychologically, in this view, only by an awareness that the primordial 'combination of symbiotic and erotic' longing does 'remain in the hidden reality of unconscious desire', the transferences eternally occurring in the human unconscious itself.[16] A quite different, but equally decentred, approach has developed the 'new

    [15] Michael O'Neill, *Romanticism and the Self-Conscious Poem* (Oxford: Clarendon, 1997), 177–9, to be cited hereafter as 'O'Neill'.
    [16] Here I quote (from 227 and 251) the epitome of this reading: Richard S. Caldwell, '"The Sensitive Plant" as Original Fantasy', *Studies in Romanticism* 15 (1976), 221–52.

historicist' penchant for placing poems in the context of the many discourses that warred with each other around it. This reading reveals *The Sensitive-Plant* as immersed in the scientific debates of the day also crucial to Mary Shelley's *Frankenstein* (1818), particularly the quarrels over whether the essential 'vitality' of life, the cause of the plant's sensitivity, stems from an electrical 'fluid' that enters matter from outside it or arises in the very structural interplay of material particles as they combine.[17] Shelley in this view resolves that conflict in his poem by making 'the ideological and the physical' metaphorical of each other, thereby suggesting that 'the transient and mutable character of matter' is an eternal mobility inherent in the principle of life (Ruston, 152).

Most recent new-historicist interpretations, though, recover the calls for political reform even in the most mythic of Shelley's works. Such approaches place *The Sensitive-Plant* within the frame of Shelley's anti-imperialism and his and his fellow liberals' sense of Europe as beset by the disease of reactionary tyranny that causes whole peoples and especially sensitive minds to wither just as the plant and the entire garden do in Part Third of this poem. All 'declines produced by social inequity' in this reading 'result [...] in the collapse of the habitable environments produced by rational, social labor' while the principles of greater equality and interactive freedom ('love, and beauty, and delight') remain eternal verities and drives obscured behind political repressions that remain to be overthrown.[18] At the same time, in another political reading, the loving sexuality pervading *The Sensitive-Plant*'s garden decays with the death of enlightened Lady Liberty into a 'blight' of 'obnoxious weeds' that 'evoke syphilis' (Crook/Guiton, 205) once 'social corruption' eats away 'all sensibility to pleasure' of the best kind and 'distributes itself thence as a paralyzing venom' (*A Defence, Norton 2*, 522). Beneath and beyond this disease-inducing level, only the transference-based, imaginative drives of Poetry in the broadest sense—and only if we choose to perceive and re-enact them—can survive as the 'invisible effluence' which eternally 'contains within itself the seeds at once of its own and of social renovation' (*Defence*, 522).

A dynamic range of readings, we find, has been opened up for *The Sensitive Plant* by a recovery from repression of the metaphoric movement that more strictly Platonic readings have failed to grasp in that poem. The same is true for *The Witch of Atlas*, I now want to show, though in some ways a revisionist understanding of this mini-epic or serio-comic romance has been more difficult to achieve. After all, perhaps more than *Prometheus Unbound*, this poem seems the supreme example in Shelley's writing of what Wasserman and others have called his 'syncretic mythology', his drawing together of myriad classical and Christian myth-figures into such a total, Ovidian coalescence— here in one pantheistic figure—that the reader supposedly gains intimations of 'the mind's extraordinary apprehensions of perfect unity' (Wasserman, 271–2). Just as Carlos Baker has written, Shelley's Witch or demi-goddess is 'a female counterpart of the prank-ish Hermes of the [ancient] Homeric Hymn', hence another 'messenger' between the

---

[17] See Sharon Ruston (henceforth 'Ruston'), *Shelley and Vitality* (New York: Palgrave Macmillan, 2005), esp. 132–56.

[18] Alan Bewell, *Romanticism and Colonial Disease* (Baltimore: Johns Hopkins UP, 1999), 209–19.

godly and human planes; she is 'Una' and 'Alma' from Edmund Spenser's epic-romance *The Faerie Queene* (1595), 'the joyous nymph of [John Milton's] *L'allegro* [1632] bidding loathly melancholy an impolite adieu', even a bit of 'Eve before the Fall' like the life-and-love-giving 'Lady' of *The Sensitive-Plant*—and thus for Baker a 'composite portrait of all the womanly grace, wisdom, beauty, and sympathy' towards which the human imagination strives to transfigure our immediate perceptions.[19]

There is certainly something to be said for this argument. Shelley's 'lady-witch' proliferates her allusions with great profusion, as when her birth from a kind of *aura seminalis* ('insemination by the sun') resembles that of 'Belphoebe' and 'Amoret' in *Faerie Queene* III; her ministering to all things in the Atlas mountains of Africa—where 'the magic circle of her voice and eyes | All savage natures did imparadise' (*Witch*, 3–4)—recalls the beast-taming radiance of 'Una' in Spenser's 'Booke I'; and her journey down the course of the Nile from her and its mythic origins in the Atlas range reminds Spenserians of 'Phaedria' in *Faerie Queene* II, who is ensconced in a 'little Gondelay', turns 'all her pleasance to a scoffing game', and keeps trying 'merry tales to faine' for observers who are at first more mystified than enlightened as she voyages by.[20] In addition, this allusiveness crosses belief-systems, as well as national and continental boundaries. While taking on aspects of the Graeco-Roman Astraea, Diana, Aurora, Minerva, Venus, Orpheus, and even Apollo (her supposed father), all intermixed with Byron's 'Witch of the Alps' from *Manfred* (1817), Shelley's Witch in Africa appropriately plays out fabled aspects of Isis and Osiris from ancient Egyptian mythology, as when 'Under the Nile, through chambers high and deep | She past, observing [and sometimes inspiring] mortals in their sleep' as those old deities were said to do (*Witch*, 527–8). As these once-African figures are brought into the Witch, moreover, the surroundings of her birth-forest and her movement down the Nile come to be populated by Graeco-Roman renditions of Egyptian (as well as classical and biblical) mythography as if she were wandering across the now-falsified geography and spectres of African myth as imagined for thousands of years.[21]

Ultimately, though, this 'syncretism' is not in the service of some supreme Absolute Beauty. As I read this 'Witch', Shelley is even more boundary-breaking and iconoclastic here than he is in *The Sensitive-Plant*. He wrote this poem down in August 1820 just after he returned to San Giuliano from climbing Monte San Peligrino towards 'a rocky shine to the Virgin Mary' near the top, already a known 'pilgrimage spot for Catholics' (Bieri, II, 203). Such shrines contained a statue of the Virgin surrounded by glass containers of candles or oil that were lit, and left lit, in her honour. All of this is parodically echoed in *The Witch of Atlas* by the virginal title character residing in her birth-cave filled with 'chrystal vials' holding 'substances unknown' in 'phials which' indeed, like candles, 'shone | In their own golden beams' (182, 201–6).

[19] Carlos Baker, *Shelley's Major Poetry: The Fabric of a Vision* (Princeton: Princeton UP, 1948), 213–14.

[20] See *The Faerie Queene*, III. vi. 5–10, I. iii. 3–14, II. vi. 2–9, in *Spenser: Poetical Works*, ed. J. C. Smith and E. de Selincourt (Oxford: Oxford UP, 1966).

[21] For more details, see Grabo, 3–20, and Frederick S. Colwell, 'Shelley's "Witch of Atlas" and the Mythic Geography of the Nile', *ELH* 45 (1978), 69–92.

Strongly opposed to the restrictiveness of Catholic iconography in Italy as much as to what he viewed as the tyranny of Church-and-state in England, Shelley is taking the shrine on San Peligrino, enlarging and satirizing it simultaneously, and then shattering its supposed Catholic unity by filling his Witch-cave with an array of pagan, Christianized, and non-religious artefacts all intermixed. This cave is chock-a-block with 'magic treasures' containing samples of the ancient Greek elements of Air, Earth, Fire, and Water *and* more modern remnants of the perceptions that enter the mind from the senses of smell, sight, hearing, taste, and touch in the more recent empirical philosophies of John Locke and David Hume (see 153–84).[22] This pre- and post-Christian panoply is augmented in the same cave, too, by 'scrolls of strange device' that mix pagan, empirical, and Christian schemes with the 'works of some Saturnian Archimage' prior to Jupiter's deposing of Saturn and the Titans in Graeco-Roman mythology (185–6). As much as this allusion recalls Spenser once more in alluding to the wizard Archimago, again from *The Faerie Queene* (I. i. 36), the Witch's scrolls reverse the power-plays of so evil a figure to teach instead the 'expiations' (*Witch*, 186) by which the lost golden age before the Truth/Error split can be restored to its less oppositional mingling of many 'bright natures' (52). The boundary-crossing figures interplaying with each other around and in Shelley's Witch, it turns out, emphasize, rather than suppressing, the differences in time, origin, and belief-systems between them all. They do not merge into any subsuming Oneness but rather continue as figures being moved between and linked before being moved beyond and decoupled in the endless play of the Witch and her poem across various textual contexts. Lest we miss such a metaphoric drive among once-separate allusions at the base of the Witch's birthplace and actions, Shelley has her become, from the moment she is born from a transference of the sun's light into a daughter of the demigods Atlas and Hesperus, a series of fast metamorphic, but also metaphoric, shifts: 'changed into a vapour | And then into a cloud [...] then into a meteor [...] | Then, into one of those mysterious stars | [...] between the Earth and Mars' (65–72). She momentarily settles into 'a dewy Splendour' in the 'cave' (78), but even that amorphous fluidity continues the primal acts of transference as the Witch goes on to weave a 'subtle veil' for her multivalent beauty out of 'threads of fleecy mist' and 'lines of light' (146–51). If the Witch is textually disruptive and metaphoric, she is so as a new incarnation of the metamorphic process that the anti-Augustan Ovid, like the anti-Catholic Shelley, sees as the animating principle of the entire universe and its history of transfigurations in the climactic Book XV of *The Metamorphoses* (Ovid, 413–41).

All of this is why the best scholarly explanation of what Shelley's Witch 'is' to date may well be Jean Watson Rosenbaum's description of her as 'a metaphor for the state of mind [...] a moment of total possibility [...] in which all irreconcilable things are not yet unified', are 'one step back from form'.[23] This reading does match what the Witch is in her

---

[22] The great importance for this poet of both Locke and Hume and their senses of basic perceptions is best confirmed by Shelley's own *On Life, Norton 2*, esp. 506–8.

[23] Rosenbaum, 'Shelley's Witch: The Naked Conception', *Concerning Poetry* 10 (1977), 37–8.

birth from many transfigurations and later in her emergence from her recess, veiled but still changing, as she fashions a boat for a voyage down the Nile that has no one clear object or destination except a transference out from an origin that is already a series of transferences on its own. Such an interpretation provides greater precision to, without denying, Hunt's view of the Witch as the Shelleyan play of 'imagination' personified at its 'most airy'. Yet it also satisfies Shelley's claim in his dedication that his 'winged Vision' cannot and should not be allegorized, that no reader should try to 'unveil my Witch' in a way that would satisfy a 'Priest or Primate' searching for a fixed reference to a single Truth (46–8). *The Witch's* vision of numerous metaphoric possibilities avoiding the 'form' of any one analogy opens up delightful hopes of many new interconnections freeing human thought from its most established constructs, a mobile standard against which more hierarchical and centred ideologies should now be satirized. At the same time, however, it points to the bathos of disappointment that can occur—and does on occasion in *The Witch of Atlas*—when such playful re-imaginings have to take forms that contain and restrict the liberating transference of imagination and poetry. Here lies the principal irony within this work: that nearly all settled products of primal transference, from the Witch's veil to the Hermaphrodite she fashions, are 'fallen' coverings and suppressions of the greater imaginative mobility by which this Lady, true poetry, and potential readers can break apart the older myths that confine their possibilities of thought and action.

Faced with the Witch's supremely metamorphic beauty, after all, the animals and nymphs and 'herdsmen' of the Atlas forest (129) find 'every thing' they perceive to be 'like the fleeting image of a shade' (138–9), an insufficient 'object' that cannot match the range of her shape-shifting 'splendour' (152). That very discrepancy becomes satirically humorous when her preconscious influence on the thoughts of tyrants along the Nile, like that of Isis and Osiris, leads a 'King' to 'dress up an Ape in his crown' and thereby reveal how monarchy's past repressions of transferential love can reduce the potential of a man to the official 'chatterings of [a] monkey' (633–7). Then, too, the Witch's sculpting of '"Hermaphroditus"' (388) out of 'fire and snow', while it does produce a 'fair Shape' blurring once-fixed oppositions (521–5), nevertheless creates a 'sexless thing' of 'such perfect purity' (329–36) that the transferential interplay of 'busy dreams' across its 'countenance' (363–4) is ultimately restricted to what Ovid's 'Pygmalion' first saw in his female statue (328): a cold and narcissistic 'Image' of 'folded wings and unawakened eyes' (361–2). Diane Long Hoeveler, it turns out, has been right to see *The Witch of Atlas* as projecting an Asia-like 'feminine muse' that aims at mobile, liberating 'androgeny', yet to find it also acting out 'the contradictions found in poetic creativity', and hence satirizing itself, when the cross-sexual 'merger of psychic characteristics within the imagination' (the Witch at her most mobile) symbolizes its multiplicity in 'a parody of the androgynous ideal',[24] a mainly static hermaphrodite that only mirrors her internal multiplicity back in an arrested state.

---

[24] Hoeveler, *Romantic Androgyny: The Women Within* (University Park, PA: Pennsylvania State UP, 1990), 249–51, the book I henceforth cite in my text as 'Hoeveler'.

In fact, this combination in *The Witch* of a wild metaphoricity dancing across different myths and ideologies and a need to wrench that dance into sequences of concrete 'form' (including *ottava rima* stanza-frames) has caused several critics to highlight its 'incongruity between different verbal registers and the areas of experience with which they are associated' (Cronin, 63). As such readings rightly show, *The Witch's* 'beauty-making fictions distort [their] distortions of the real', the words and references with which those fictions began; they both distance reused words affirmatively from the older 'realities' (actually ideologies) for which they once stood and expose how such revisionist fictions can devolve negatively into distortions of them, all of which keeps poets and their readers in a 'dialectic of skepticism and belief' (O'Neill, 127, 178). It is within these extensions of Rosenbaum's reading that Stuart Sperry is correct to say that 'the Witch is Shelley's metaphor for art's power to arouse and attract' through its sublime transfigurative energy but also for 'the sense [that art] leaves us of the limits of our powers and experience' during any finite stretch of time, making this work its author's greatest piece of 'Romantic Irony'.[25]

Even so, as we acknowledge this poem's double stance and its shifting tonality throughout its playful mixture of mini-epic, romance, satire, and myth, we should also embrace its suggestions for how its readers may avoid the despair of helpless indecision to which a strictly ironic reading might lead. Most of the Witch's plays among differences, we find, are positively re-creative and thus, unlike the hermaphrodite, so transformative of older mythic structures that they reinvigorate most observers in the Atlas mountains or along the mythic Nile caught in the traps of their fixed belief-systems. When, above the 'Austral waters' of Timbuktu (423), the Witch 'ascend[s]' the 'streams of upper air' to 'win the spirits' already projected there by human perception (488–92), the 'Mortals' who observe this remaking of existing mythology find 'That on those days the skies were calm and fair', whatever the apparent weather—since 'all things exist as they are perceived'—and that the 'upper air' seems underwritten by 'mystic snatches of harmonious sound' unnoticed by older myths about the heavens (492–6). The cure for the ephemeral nature of all mythic reconstructions, after all, is the shift towards new metamorphic activity that the Witch initiates when any state or act of hers seems to be settling into a fixed condition. Just when she seems most prone, lying 'in trance [...] within the fountain' inside her cave, she sees in those waters the universe's 'constellations reel and dance | Like fire-flies' in transformative motion (265–71). She must therefore enact that mobility, first by moving herself to yet another 'well [...] Amid a wood of pines and cedars' where she can 'dream' a sped-up forecast of the seasonal changes across the world (277–88) and then by entering a 'boat' of 'woven tracery' (313, 308) composed from several different myths (289–312), into which she infuses a 'living spirit' (314) to carry her visionary process down the sources and course of the Nile. If the hermaphrodite that she places at the prow of that boat threatens to freeze her and its mobile foundations into an un-reproductive coldness, she counters that tendency by commanding

[25] Sperry, *Shelley's Major Verse: The Narrative and Dramatic Poetry* (Cambridge, MA: Harvard UP, 1988), 147.

'It' to be the agent of her vessel's changes of direction into 'The labyrinths of some many winding vale' (386–92). After that point, the sexless 'Image' is never mentioned again, and so the Witch drives on, as the dreamy 'soft step [that] deepens slumber' (522), 'Scattering sweet visions from her [mobile] presence sweet | Through fane and palace-court and labyrinth' (524–5). The only way of truly fulfilling the Witch's energy and her possibilities for the humanity that often refuses to sense her power (the basis of poetry, as in *The Sensitive-Plant*) is thus for her not to stop nor rest but for her to continue 'the pranks she played among the cities | Of mortal men' beyond even Africa (665). The poem therefore has to break off with the promise of 'another time' in which the poet may describe what her 'sweet ditties' could do to 'sprites | And gods' as well as 'mortal men' as yet untold (666–9). To end this poem as though it were some epic or romance fulfilling the main character's destiny with some form of closure would be for Shelley to deny this Witch's, as well as *ottava rima*'s now-Byronic, resistance to closure and her status for him as the spirit of transference that makes all such mythologies and all revisions of them possible.

It should be no surprise, then, that, as with the recent history of *The Sensitive-Plant*, this liberated view of Shelley's iconoclastic *Witch* has led to exfoliations of its many suggestions that have opened this poem to several important contexts not linked to it before. Hoeveler's reading of 1990, for example, has enabled us to grasp the way this poem both anticipates and questions modern feminism and gender theory. To get beyond the tyrannies rooted in male dominance, Shelley in Hoeveler's account turns his own previous 'idealized beloveds' into a masculine-feminine 'merger of psychic characteristics within the imagination' and so redefines the classic nature of a Muse as a figure of 'androgynous reintegration' combining traditionally 'female' sympathy and nurturance with 'masculine' authority and cross-cultural education (Hoeveler, 249–52). At the same time for Hoeveler, though, Shelley fears the resistance of his culture to such an androgynous multiplicity, and so he has to present its process in *The Witch* as continually impeded in fulfilling its potential by the 'flawed ideals' it produces (Hoeveler, 249). Alice Jardine, however, has rescued what the Witch acts out, her manifesting of 'the *process* which moves beyond/behind/through [all human] fantasies',[26] and shown it to be an intensification of a long-standing construct: '*a space coded as feminine*' by Western culture within and underlying male discourse that should now be re-exposed as the 'alterity' within language prior to the conventional discourse that often represses what really it depends upon. By mythologically reconfiguring this alterity, Shelley's *Witch* has intimated the primacy of what Jardine calls '*gynesis*—the putting into discourse of "woman" as that process beyond' and underlying 'Man's Truth' that is 'never stable' and yet is the source of any movement across figures by which male logic is fundamentally constituted.

Such an emphasis on the central character's femininity, moreover, has also drawn history-of-ideas, new historicist, and cultural-studies readings of Shelley's *Witch* towards connecting its intertextual mobility with both the science and imperialism of Shelley's

---

[26] I cite Alice Jardine from 'Gynesis', *Diacritics* 12 (1982), as repr. in Hazard Adams and Leroy Searle (eds.), *Critical Theory since 1965* (Tallahassee, FL: University Presses of Florida, 1986), 560–70.

time and place. The much-discussed scientific idea of a 'living fluid that Romantic natural philosophers thought might run through the nerves of all creatures', as Denise Gigante has recently shown,[27] was frequently described before 1820 through variations on the figure of Mother Nature (the way we have seen in *The Sensitive-Plant*). Gigante therefore argues that *The Witch of Atlas*, as poem and figure, 'is Shelley's poetic equivalent of living form' (158). It is precisely because Shelley's Witch is a metaphor of 'self-generating and self-renewing life, not constricted to preformed structures of the past', as we have established above, that she can symbolize a fluid generative 'power' that springs from its own inherent process instead of the creation of a masculine God who has transmitted his life-force into existing forms (Gigante, 159, 186). This part of Gigante's reading, to be sure, raises the question of whether this 'epigenesis' in the Witch is more a deep force of nature outside, as well as inside, the psyche for Shelley or a projection of the imagination's and language's transformative metaphoricity into the 'nature' apparent to perception. Gigante suggests that Shelley avoids this conundrum by wilfully accepting 'a cultural moment' of intertextual confluence in which 'vital power was being biologically confused with soul' (Gigante, 175); hence the fluidity in the soul's process of perception can be, as Shelley suggests in *The Witch*, both a product of the 'life' in nature and a projection of the psyche's own life-force into the world outside it. Whatever the case, this reading is now available for debate because we have come to see how dynamically vital Shelley's *Witch* is in being an iconoclastic critique of older and more hierarchical visions of earthly existence.

At the same time, though, we have to admit that too little has been said in all this about Shelley's choice of *Africa* as a location for *The Witch*. Is the use of Africa by such an iconoclastic poet actually a *dis*-location that places the certainty of European norms, including their senses of the 'dark continent', under genuine (and again satirical) scrutiny? Fortunately, we know that the answer is 'yes' because we now have a reading that places the newly fluid sense of Shelley's *Witch*, including its feminization, squarely in the context of England's imperialist mappings and investigation of Africa from the 1790s into the 1820s. Debbie Lee has truly broken open *The Witch of Atlas* by showing how this poem echoes treatises of the day in which Africa is interpreted for Europeans through the ways all *her* 'feminine beauty and fertility' help the explorer see himself reconstituted 'in the midst of a vast wilderness' (Lee, 176–8).[28] Shelley, by this account, recalls his solipsistic Poet in *Alastor* projecting what 'dark Aethiopia in her desert hills conceals' (115) and critiques both that figure and the recent accounts of explorers by having the speaker of his *Witch* offer a series of Western mythological projections as a means of placing the poet's imagination in the 'interior' of Africa as Europe has already mythologized it. So that the imperialism of Britain's explorers is exposed for what it is, the Witch in Shelley's poem is indeed made feminine—but as a 'playful' *gynesis*-figure of self-transformation

---

[27] Starting with the foregoing quotation from 189, I cite Gigante throughout this paragraph from *Life: Organic Form and Romanticism* (New Haven: Yale UP, 2009), 155–207.
[28] I quote Lee from 'Mapping the Interior: African Cartography and Shelley's *The Witch of Atlas*', *European Romantic Review* 8 (1997), 169–84.

'that resists colonization'—even as she also manifests 'an enactment of imperialistic mapping and naming', the very force of colonization that has feminized Africa in the first place (Lee, 182).

The Witch of Atlas thus joins with *The Sensitive-Plant*, we must conclude, in showing us the capacity of this extraordinary writer to explode restrictive patterns in the many forms of hierarchical writing he knew so as to produce 'visionary' correctives of transference and transformation that decentre his readers away from such older confines, an iconoclasm that is the greatest poetic achievement in Shelley's eyes by time he wrote these works in 1820. Yet these same two poems, as we can see in the recent history of interpreting them both, can also remind us of what we need to keep working to escape: our temptations towards the excessive domination of the world empowered by centred systems of myth, belief, and poetic form that can still entrap us and control us, and make us try to control others, if we choose to let such visions be the lenses through which we keep viewing human, and even cosmic, existence.

SELECT BIBLIOGRAPHY

Caldwell, Richard S. '"The Sensitive Plant" as Original Fantasy'. *Studies in Romanticism* 15 (1976), 221–52.

Colwell, Frederick S. 'Shelley's "Witch of Atlas" and the Mythic Geography of the Nile'. *ELH* 45 (1978), 69–92.

Cronin, Richard. *Shelley's Poetic Thoughts*. London: Macmillan, 1981. 55–76.

Crook, Nora and Derek Guiton. *Shelley's Venomed Melody*, Cambridge: Cambridge UP, 1986. 203–7.

Gigante, Denise. *Life: Organic Form and Romanticism*, New Haven: Yale UP, 2009. 155–207.

Grabo, Carl. *The Meaning of 'The Witch of Atlas'*. Chapel Hill, NC: University of North Carolina Press, 1935.

Hoeveler, Diane Long. *Romantic Androgyny: The Women Within*. University Park, PA: Pennsylvania State UP, 1990. 249–60.

Hogle, Jerrold E. *Shelley's Process: Radical Transference and the Development of his Major Works*. New York: Oxford UP, 1988. 211–19 and 286–94.

Lee, Debbie. 'Mapping the Interior: African Cartography and Shelley's *The Witch of Atlas*'. *European Romantic Review* 8 (1977), 169–84.

Maniquis, Robert M. 'The Puzzling *Mimosa*: Sensitivity and Plant Symbols in Romanticism'. *Studies in Romanticism* 8 (1969), 129–55.

O'Neill, Michael. *Romanticism and the Self-Conscious Poem*. Oxford: Clarendon Press, 1997. 119–79.

Rosenbaum, Jean Watson. 'Shelley's Witch: The Naked Conception'. *Concerning Poetry* 10 (1977), 33–43.

Ruston, Sharon. *Shelley and Vitality*. New York: Palgrave Macmillan, 2005. 132–56.

Sperry, Stuart. *Shelley's Major Verse: The Narrative and Dramatic Poetry*. Cambridge, MA: Harvard UP, 1988. 143–57.

Wasserman, Earl R. *Shelley: A Critical Reading*, Baltimore: Johns Hopkins UP, 1971. 154–79.

CHAPTER 24

LYRICS AND LOVE POEMS

Poems to Sophia Stacey, Jane Williams, and Mary Shelley

SHAHIDHA BARI

THE various lyrics and love poems dedicated to Sophia Stacey, Jane Williams, and Mary Shelley illustrate the intricate entanglement of Shelley's personal life and poetic ambition. The image of Shelley that emerges through these texts is that of a lover who is as ardent and idealist as the early poet-protagonists of *Alastor* and *Epipsychidion*, but whose professions of devotion are also adumbrated by more serious reflections. The poems disclose Shelley's understanding of the real and complex sexual politics that subtend the idealisms of courtly poetics, dispelling his reputation for reckless radicalism and moral laxity that could extend to the casual advocacy of experimental polyamory. The poems attest, instead, to the importance of the women in his life and indicate an intellectual engagement with questions of intimacy, attachment, and desire. While the etherealized women of *Alastor* and *Epipsychidion* present 'a human shape of his ideal', the poems addressed to the very real Sophia Stacey, Jane Williams, and Mary Shelley allow Shelley's romantic idealizations to intersect with the erotic realizations of his domestic life.[1]

It is unclear whether the relationships with Sophia and Jane extended beyond flirtation but, independently of any biographical verification, the poems warrant attention for their startlingly earnest accounts of experiences of attachment and alienation. Although G. M. Matthews cautions against biographical hermeneutics, and counsels an investigation into 'the *nature* and *function*' of the poems as a corrective to speculative readings, Nora Crook makes an equally persuasive case for recognizing in Shelley's more enigmatic work the 'turning loose of personal emotion'.[2] This chapter does not enquire how far these poems are biographical but instead examines how the different poems attached to Sophia,

---

[1] Judith Chernaik, *The Lyrics of Shelley* (Cleveland: Case Western Reserve UP, 1972), 13.
[2] G. M. Matthews in *Norton 2*, 688. Nora Crook, 'The Enigma of "A Vision of the Sea", or "Who Sees the Waterspouts?"', in Timothy Clark and Jerrold E. Hogle (eds.), *Evaluating Shelley* (Edinburgh: Edinburgh UP, 1996), 152–63 (152).

Jane, and Mary seem to produce from Shelley different emotional and psychological insights that might refer back to the particularity of those relationships without being bound to them. Private life does not master poetic fiction in such a reading, nor vice versa, rather each surpasses and supplements the other in Shelley's varied lyric forms. While the poems to Sophia, Jane, and Mary might prompt biographical reading, they also illuminate the ways in which feelings, whether real or imagined, readily fasten onto thought and take poetic form in compelling ways. The poems relay a personal sense of Shelley's emotional and erotic life, but they indicate too his acute understanding of the inequalities of romance, the imbalance of a desirous one to a resistant other, and the dynamics of submission and domination implicit in the experiences of desire and denial. In these poems, Shelley movingly recognizes the precarious happiness that romantic union promises and from which he is debarred.

Although each series of poems narrates the vicissitudes of a particular relationship, pieced together they form the arc of a broader narrative from which one might draw a fuller conception of Shelley's romantic life. They are not easily generalized into a systematic poetics of love, but they do indicate a development, where each relationship yields a different kind of self-understanding, expressed in the varying tones, modes, and registers of each series. If the experimental stanzas to Sophia sustain a confident courtly levity, the extended lyrics to Jane depict a more complex psychological drama. By contrast, the terse, tense verses to Mary impart the intensity of a relationship whose psychological intricacy and emotional insecurity remains for Shelley bitterly unresolved to the very end. None of these relationships, as we might understand them from the poems, suggests the self-serving erotics of free love; rather, they indicate a seriousness that belies Shelley's reputation for casual cruelty. Indeed, as Nathaniel Brown argues, Shelley's advocacy of free love itself might be best understood as the culmination of his considered Godwinian and proto-feminist sympathy for sexual equality.[3] Shelley delineates this vision with an unabashed boldness in *Epipsychidion* when he denounces monogamous hetero-normativity as a 'great sect', reasoning instead 'That to divide is not to take away. | Love is like understanding, that grows bright, | Gazing on many truths [...]' (*Epipsychidion*, 161–3).[4]

The passage romantically euphemizes the argument for polyamory by casting monogamy as an impediment to understanding and creativity. Brown reads Shelley's conception of free love as a feminist alternative to the restricted identity of wifehood, and he recognizes the sophisticated feminism of Shelley's presentation of women who are both attributed more than a reductive erotic function and urged to claim their equal rights to erotic fulfilment. What might have been named promiscuity is, for Brown, redeemed as a political championship of sexual identity. Yet, for Shelley, liberated sexual congress signifies more than a political ideal. In his essay *On Love*, the fleshiness of 'Love' is

---

[3] Nathaniel Brown, *Sexuality and Feminism in Shelley* (Cambridge, MA: Harvard UP, 1979), see, for example, 98, 187.

[4] All poetic citations are taken from *Major Works*, except the poems to Sophia and Mary which are taken from *MYR* VIII, *H*, and *Longman*.

sublated into more ethereal elements, symbolizing the intellectual union and cosmic communion of all things in romantic congress:

> We would that another's nerves should vibrate to our own, that the beams of their eyes should kindle at once and mix and melt into our own, that lips of motionless ice should not reply to lips quivering and burning with the heart's best blood. This is Love. This is the bind and the sanction which connects not only man with man, but with every thing which exists. (*Norton 2*, 503–4)

Shelley's account of vibrating nerves, kindling eyes, and burning blood elevates the materiality of bodily relations into a metaphorical heat whose sensuous coalescence mixes and melts into 'Love', binding and connecting with 'every thing'. The idea of a transformative 'Love', that moves fluently between the singular, the relational, and the communal, its register shifting from the bodily to the elemental and the cosmic, emerges as a recurrent motif of the poems to Sophia, Jane, and Mary.

SOPHIA STACEY

Born in 1791, the daughter of Flint Stacey, mayor of Maidstone, Sophia was entrusted to the care of Shelley's paternal aunt following her father's death in 1802. This familial connection allowed her entrance into Shelley's circle when she visited Florence in 1819, where she occupied rooms at the same *pensione* on the Via Valfonda. In his headnote to the poems to Sophia in *MYR* (277–8), Reiman observes that their relationship was likely to have remained platonic, noting the absence of any documentary evidence of romance and Sophia's relative age to Shelley. Edmund Blunden speculates that relations between the parties at the *pensione* were close enough for Sophia to select for the newborn Shelley boy the middle name of 'Florence'. Blunden concludes that 'Sophia was a wide-eyed listener to Shelley's talk on the established church, love, liberty, death, music and books; played the harp, and sang very sweetly; could join in all his family and Sussex recollections. He was enchanted and said so in melodious verse.'[5]

'Melodious verse' refers here particularly to the poem beginning 'Thou art fair, and few are fairer', sometimes titled 'To Sophia' which is characterized by its musicality (four sestets of largely trochaic tetrameter), and the fluency of Shelley's ready, romantic gallantry.[6]

> Thou art fair, and few are fairer
>   Of the Nymphs of earth or ocean;
> They are robes that fit the wearer—
>   Those soft limbs of thine, whose motion

---

[5] Edmund Blunden, *Shelley: A Life Story* (Glasgow: Collins, 1948), 213.

[6] Blunden might also have been referring to 'The Indian Girl's Song', sometimes titled 'The Indian Serenade'. Although the note to the text of 'The Indian Girl's Song' in *Major Works* (511) observes that a copy of the poem was given to Sophia, *MYR* suggests that a text was transcribed for Sophia but that a later version may have been intended for Jane Williams (see 331, 336).

Ever falls and shifts and glances
As the life within them dances.

Thy deep eyes, a double Planet,
    Gaze the wisest into madness
With soft clear fire,—the winds that fan it
    Are those thoughts of tender gladness
Which, like zephyrs on the billow,
Make thy gentle soul their pillow.

If, whatever face thou paintest
    In those eyes, grows pale with pleasure,
If the fainting soul is faintest
    When it hears thy harp's wild measure,
Wonder not that when thou speakest
Of the weak my heart is weakest.

As dew beneath the wind of morning,
    As the sea which whirlwinds waken,
As the birds at thunder's warning,
    As aught mute yet deeply shaken,
As one who feels an unseen spirit
Is my heart when thine is near it.
(quoted from *H*, without stanza nos)

In the poem, Shelley obediently adopts the romantically unrequited pose of the courtly poet-lover who desires but is denied a chaste, unobtainable beloved. The hyperbolic likenesses and passionate declarations follow familiarly in the vein both of an urbane English tradition of Sidney, Marvell, and Donne, and an exalting Italian tradition of Dante and Petrarch. Yet if Sophia's limbs, eyes, and shapely form are accordingly emblazoned, the poem is also infused with a peculiarly Shelleyan regard for the immanent and un-bodied, privileging 'the life within' that animates exterior beauty. The musical metaphor serves Shelley here insofar as Sophia's immanent 'life within' is, like music, 'unseen' and only felt. The poem makes much of its own musicality; anaphoric beginnings ('As the dew', 'As the sea', etc.) close with feminine rhymes, conveying the auditory serenity of a natural landscape. The winds, seas, even thunder are only quietly stirred, as Shelley is by Sophia's nearness: 'mute yet deeply shaken'. Although Shelley is silenced by Sophia's music, professing to be 'weakest', subject to the power she wields, the poem betrays another logic at work in Sophia's form that is reduced to metaphorical insubstantiality even as it is praised as 'spirit'; her eyes are 'soft clear fire', her thoughts 'like zephyrs on the billow'. The likenesses achieve for Shelley a romantic elementality, but they also diminish Sophia's seeing and thinking corporeality. Indeed, the 'double Planet' of Sophia's eyes only passively reflect back that upon which they gaze. In the mode of Narcissus, Shelley recovers from Sophia's eyes his own image, which the poem ultimately conjures in place of Sophia. The poem's focus repeatedly returns from the beloved to the reflective poet, betraying more self-concern than romance, and perhaps suggesting a relationship of Platonic dependence rather than sexual entanglement.

This pattern emerges again in 'The Fountains mingle', another lyric addressed to Sophia, in which the beloved's image is only an aside to a more subtle set of meditations on love. Sophia functions to facilitate Shelley's extension of the fluent conception of love described in 'On Love', where Shelley analogizes the union of two bodies in a kiss with the elemental communion of a natural landscape. The tone is playful, persuasive, and smart:

> The Fountains mingle with the River
>   And the Rivers with the Ocean,
> The winds of Heaven mix for ever
>   With a sweet emotion;
> Nothing in the world is single;
>   All things by a law divine
> In one spirit meet & mingle.
>   Why not I with thine?—
>
> See the mountains kiss high Heaven
>   And the waves clasp one another;
> No sister-flower would be forgiven
>   If it disdained its brother;
> And the sunlight clasps the earth
>   And the moonbeams kiss the sea:
> What is all this sweet work worth
>   If thou kiss not me?

Published by Hunt in the December 1819 *Indicator*, Mary Shelley interestingly subtitled the poem 'An Anacreontic', referencing the Greek lyric form that traditionally deals lightly with love and wine. Her subtitle connects the poem's mode of romantic propositioning and its opening image of easily mingled fluids with the literal fluency of wine and the kind of intoxicated sexual forwardness that might be as encouraged by alcoholic consumption as it is by desire. In this regard, the poem achieves the mock-seriousness of a courtly appeal that knows the vanity of the supplication it makes and the absurdity of the likenesses it draws; that the mingling of fountain, river, and ocean could resemble the mingling of saliva in a kiss, is persuasive only to those intoxicated by love or wine. A winning gallantry is combined with a knowing reflexivity—the conclusion, 'What is all this sweet work worth?', seems to refer both to the cosmic mingling of sea and sky, but also the sophisticated rhetorical efforts of the poem itself, otherwise wasted without the prize of a kiss. The lover's suit is propelled by the temerity of his invention; the scale of the metaphors ('mountains' and 'moonbeams') deployed in quest of a kiss might themselves be said to wobble, intoxicatedly, between romantic entreaty and teasing bathos. The poem though is steadied by the balance of its equal stanzas and alternating rhymes; the two octaves, although united in the appeal they make, figure the resolute separateness of lover and silent addressee. Shelley might invoke a 'law divine' that they should 'In one spirit meet & mingle', but the poem also depends upon the separateness of mine from 'thine'. If the metaphorical fluency of river and ocean suggests the romantic mingling Shelley angles for in this poem, the even octaves gracefully insist on separation.

Shelley's figuration of heaven-kissing mountains and sea-kissing moonbeams renders kissing an airy, un-bodied act, effortlessly executed, and so unlike the solid contact of real kisses that require mutual consent. Indeed kissing a real body might even require a degree of force, which Shelley acknowledges implicitly in the word 'clasp', jarringly repeated in the second stanza. Clasping requires hands that grasp, grip tenaciously even, and the repetition of 'clasp' subvocally invokes the sense of being held too close for too long. Force is intimated in the unsettling double 'clasp', but it is also audible in the hypometric contractions of the last line of each octave ('Why not I with thine?' and 'If thou kiss not me?'), forming questions that are issued with the slightest abruptness. Those direct questions, no longer couched in romantic metaphor, suggest perhaps how the mode of courtly address disguises what is, ultimately, a proposition of the very direct sort, and with which the object of desire is confronted. If the poem's romantic appeal has succeeded, the contracted close of each octave might be taken to signal the collapsed proximity of 'I' and 'thine', 'thou' and 'me' now on the verge of a kiss and joined in a metrical unity. Yet the hypometricality might also impart the impression of an appropriative compression in which the union of lover and beloved entails something more than effortless mingling and mixing. Shelley only suggests this in his double 'clasp' and subvocally in the compression of rhythm and the force of rhyme. If his elegant evocation of an elemental coalescence supplies an analogy for the romantic commingling of lovers, the poem betrays in more measured ways the inadequacies of that analogy and the implicit dynamics of force and resistance in a relationship.

The poems to Sophia provide for Shelley a space to explore these ideas and they are extended in the quieter lyric to Sophia titled 'Goodnight', written in 1819. In the poem, Shelley retains the tone of urbane reasoning, toying with the leave-taking sense of 'goodnight' that would part him from his lover, and the night made 'good' by their 'remain[ing] together still'. The reluctantly parted 'goodnight' and the sexually gratified 'good' night are playfully differentiated. The 'night' that 'severs those it should unite' is patiently woven through each verse, repeated in homophones and rhyme, so that what severs the lovers in actuality ironically binds a poem together in textuality. This cross-stanzaic binding of the poem formally figures the mingling romantic intimacy for which the poet makes an ardent case. Yet his assessment that the *good* night is that in which 'goodnight' is 'not said, thought or understood', seeks to silence only his lover's speech, since he himself does not abstain from that utterance in making his case—indeed, he repeats 'night' to excess whilst hushing a beloved who is poised on the cusp of taking leave. The silenced 'goodnight' of the female subject presents an ironic inversion of Juliet's fevered 'A thousand times good night!', that most famous of romantic partings. Juliet, though, avows, in her excessive articulations, to lure her lover back until she is 'hoarse, and may not speak aloud', like her mythic predecessor, Echo.[7] At first, Shelley's inversion implicitly seems to figure the inequality of the articulating poet and the silent addressee, but, as for Juliet and Echo, the silencing that comes from the hyper-articulation of love is itself a powerful metaphor for

---

[7] William Shakespeare, *Romeo and Juliet*, ed. Brian Gibbons, The Arden Shakespeare (London: Methuen, 1980), II. ii. 154.

female passion that remedies that seeming inequality. Shelley's closing vision of 'hearts that on each other beat', posits its own image of mutuality, each heart equally resting and dependent upon the beating of the other, rectifying the poem's initial imbalance. The lovers' deferral of the 'goodnight' which extends their unity from 'evening close to morning light' recalls and inverts again Romeo and Juliet's aubade, in which both conspire to prolong the night of their sexual union and defer the day of their parting. Just as Shelley's poem is implicitly presented as a dawn-deferring aubade, the night-time attentions of the voluble poet might also be understood as a lullaby for the muted other, whose silence is not forced but willingly complicit, rendering them not equal nor less, but privileged. The intimacy of 'hearts that on each other beat' intimates both a sexual proximity, chest to chest, but also the more tender responsibility of a relationship in which one rests upon the other's care. More lullaby than aubade, Shelley's poem ends with the surprising innocence of 'nights as good as they are sweet', one dependent figure in the watchful care of another from 'evening close to morning light'. 'Goodnight' then ultimately deletes the sexuality of Shelley's relationship with Sophia, and substitutes for it a friendship of mutual dependence. Indeed, this friendship vitally enables Shelley's writing and allows him to entrust to Sophia the most significant confidences that inform his work.

Of the poems to Sophia, the lyric 'Time Long Past' attests to this intimacy most powerfully. Darker than 'Goodnight', the poem melancholically reflects upon an unspecified 'Time long past'. Interlocked, cross-stanzaic rhymes impart an idea of motion that is halted each time by emphatic closing triplets. The lingering vowels of the repeated rhymes, 'cast', 'last', and 'past', extend that sense of a stalled continuity. The solicitous night-time responsibility of 'Goodnight' is left behind and replaced with the subtle 'regret, almost remorse' of retrospection, replacing a lullaby with a lament. The opening image of the unnamed 'ghost of a dear friend dead' is accented by the hauntingly repeated rhymes of each stanza. The modulated refrain 'Time long past' further marks this ghostly emptiness in its catalectic metricality, where the repetition of silence acts as a kind of aural haunting; there is something not fully articulated in this poem that lingers and makes its presence felt by absence. Superficially, the poem presents romantic retrospection, but something unspoken also passes through it, distinguishing its tone from that of the other poems addressed to Sophia. Shelley reflects that in this mysterious 'Time long past', memories whether of 'sadness or delight' are indistinguishable from those who once shared the intimacy of each other's confidence, but this affective elision is itself symptomatic of traumatic experience, an unspoken but still present event to which the poet can barely allude. This unnamed presence obscures the poem but also renders it profoundly intimate in the exclusivity of its closed address. Its secret is perhaps betrayed by its most striking figuration, that of 'A father who watches' a 'child's beloved corse'. Shelley notes that this is only a likeness, a metaphorical father whose watchful guardianship only models that of the poet's care for a mysterious 'Time lost past', but the image is so unexpected that it overwhelms the poem and betrays Shelley with its image of paternal grief at infant mortality. That this poem was given to Sophia indicates the intimacy of the confidence they shared, and articulates perhaps the watchful solicitude with which each regarded the other in a relationship that extended beyond romantic proposition into the care of friendship.

JANE WILLIAMS

Jane Williams is also a source of solicitude for Shelley, but 'The Indian Girl's Song', written around 1820–1, reveals a new urgency and drama in his verse. Apostrophic and exclamatory ('O beloved as thou art!'), what was previously romantic compliment is now fired with a heated corporeality: 'I die, I faint, I fail!'[8] Where the lover of 'Goodnight' envisages the companionable contingency of 'hearts that on each other beat', here only 'My heart beats loud and fast', prompting a desperate entreaty for reciprocation. Although a version of the poem seems to have been given to Sophia Stacey in 1819, O'Neill makes a strong case against it being included amongst those poems intended for her.[9] Its almost onanistic urgency indicates a relationship of a different order from that which Shelley had established with Sophia, and more readily resembles that of other poems dedicated to Jane, including 'With a Guitar. To Jane', 'To Jane ("The keen stars were twinkling")', 'To Jane. The Invitation', 'To Jane—The Recollection', 'The serpent is shut out from Paradise', 'The Magnetic Lady to her Patient', and 'Lines Written in the Bay of Lerici'. Yet if these poems form a series, they are themselves varied, presenting the different tonalities of an uncertain relationship that was deeply to affect Shelley's emotional and psychological well-being, and whose exact nature remains contested. As O'Neill observes, the poems to Jane are 'at once serene and frustrated, saddened and accepting, pastoral but with more than a hint of tragedy [...] lamenting the gap between the human lot and "some world far from ours | Where music and moonlight and feeling | Are one"'.[10]

Jane, with her musical accomplishments, exotic Anglo-Indian background, and interests in therapeutic mesmerism, did indeed seem to promise to Shelley the glimpse of a 'world far from ours' when she arrived in Pisa in early 1821 with her common law husband, Edward Elleker Williams. Born Jane Cleveland in 1798, she, like Shelley, had already behind her a failed marriage when she met Edward Williams, a naval officer on a commission in India. Edward's friendship with Thomas Medwin, Shelley's cousin, provided the fateful connection that ultimately ended with the death of both men in the fateful waters of the Gulf of Spezia in July 1822. But in January 1821, the Williamses had entered easily into Shelley's circle, occupying rooms beneath his own in the Tre Palazzi di Chiesa. Shelley, increasingly unhappy in his own marriage, was charmed, writing to John Gisborne:

> I like Jane more and more, and I find Williams the most amiable of companions. She has a taste for music, and an elegance of form and motions that compensate in some degree for the lack of literary refinement [...] I have a boat here [...] Williams is the captain, and we drive along this delightful bay in the evening wing under the summer moon, until earth appears another world. Jane brings her guitar, and if the past

---

[8] The text of 'The Indian Girl's Song' is taken from *Major Works*, as are the texts of all the poems to Jane discussed here.

[9] See the note to the text in *Major Works*, 795 and *MYR* 336 for fuller discussion.

[10] *MYR* 352.

and the future could be obliterated, the present would content me so well that I could say with Faust to the passing moment, 'Remain, thou, thou art so beautiful'.[11]

The letter, striking for its foreshadowing of fatal events to come, also presents a record of contented companionship. Acknowledged as a co-recipient of the letters to Jane, Edward emerges as a benign presence, a co-actor in a curious domestic drama. Shelley notes of 'The Magnetic Lady to her Patient' that the lyric is 'For Jane & Williams alone to see' and specifies further on the wrapping, 'To Jane. Not to be opened unless you are alone, or with Williams', indicating perhaps the exclusivity of a relationship from which only Mary Shelley was debarred.[12] That the attachment to Jane entailed a dual attachment to Edward further obscures the exact nature of the relationship between Jane and Shelley. These poems pose once more the broader question of how a poetic corpus relates to biographical fact. The emotional and psychological acuity of the Jane poems rearticulates the circuit formed by art and life, and sets against each other the competing truths of fantasy and fact. If these poems draw from and lead back to 'real' events, the question of biographical truth remains quite separate from the veracity of a poetic form; if the former is difficult to verify retrospectively, then the latter, at least, is attested to in the persuasiveness of a reading.

Tilar Mazzeo's reading of the Jane poems in the context of Shelley's musical interests, for example, makes an especially persuasive case.[13] Music that produces harmony as well as melody presents an idealized figuration of love for Shelley, and 'To Jane ("The keen stars were twinkling")' accordingly binds feeling to song in an ideal ethereality. Each stanza recycles the same terms, 'keen stars', 'fair moon', and 'sweet tones', until they cohere in 'some world far from ours, | Where music and moonlight and feeling | Are one' (22–4). This state of romantic coalescence is indeed a world far from the grim truths of Shelley's actual life in which his wife had recently miscarried. Unsurprising, perhaps, then that Shelley should prefer music of the sort that promises the extraterrestrial transport of its listeners. The poem's strictly syncopated tercets (sequential lines of tetrameter, pentameter, and bimeter) build into the poem regular rests that might be filled by instrumental parts. Indeed, Shelley's note to Jane describes the poem as 'some words for an ariette'.[14] Paul Vatalaro notes the poem's striking auditory features, including the lengthened vowels and nasal consonants ('Jane', 'moon', 'again', 'own', 'thrown') that suggest the lingering vibrations of plucked strings.[15]

Indeed, the lyric 'With a Guitar. To Jane' records Shelley's gift of a guitar to Jane, and recalls the courtly tradition of lyrics appended to tokens of affection. Here, Jane is cast as *The Tempest's* Miranda, with Edward her Ferdinand, and Shelley as Ariel, the spirit charged with their safe return to Naples. The poem extends the Shakespearian scene,

---

[11] *Letters: PBS* II, 435–6.   [12] See note to text in *Major Works*, 814.
[13] Tilar Mazzeo, 'The Strains of Empire: Shelley and the Music of India', in Michael Franklin (ed.), *Romantic Representations of British India* (London: Routledge, 2006), 180–96.
[14] See note to text in *Major Works*, 815.
[15] Paul Vatalaro, 'The Semiotic Echoes in Percy Shelley's Poems to Jane Williams', *Keats–Shelley Journal* 48 (1999), 69–89.

boldly dramatizing the dynamics of their real relationship in which Shelley/Ariel vacillates between the part of a protective guardian and an excluded third. Although Ariel's role is precisely to disenchant the lovers, undoing the fantasy in which they have been mired so as to return them to a non-magical realm, Shelley's rendering of the scene clings to the possibility of a fantasy in which he could continue to exert his influence, infiltrating the reality he is not permitted to enter. The guitar given to Jane has its own magic, yielding to her solicitation and articulating 'more than ever can be spoken'. Like the 'silent guitar' to Jane's touch, Shelley promises to overturn the unspeaking part to which he is relegated in her relationship with Edward. The poem poses the possibility of an articulation capable of that circumvention. The effortlessly harmonized couplets conceal the jostling for real-life positions that the poem figures. It is, at once, a whimsical fiction that dramatizes the companionable friendship of the three, and a more subtle articulation of Shelley's frustration.

In 'The Magnetic Lady to her Patient', Shelley attempts to refigure again the dynamics of his relationship with Jane in the context of a real attempt at hypnotic therapy. Tim Fulford records the interest in therapeutic mesmerism in the period, noting that Shelley himself had undertaken treatment in 1820 for kidney stones.[16] For Shelley, Jane's professed proficiency in mesmerism would have held the additional attraction of an intimate consultation and the implicit erotics of submission and domination the process might entail. In the poem though, Jane offers a gentle reproof. Its incantatory rhythms and fluid images of transference ('from my fingers flow') cede to a strictly separate allocation of the 'powers of life' which 'brood on thee, but may not blend | With thine' (5, 6, 8–9); the diagnosis is tantamount to a sexual rejection. Jane's implacable assertion 'I love thee not' (10) is fortified by her reference to Edward, whose invocation acts as a deterrent against any improper intimacy. Even Jane's sympathy for Shelley is mediated through Edward who 'Might have been lost like thee' (14). Jane's happiness is as contingent on Edward's as Shelley's is on Jane's; the poem efficiently delineates the problematic of this triangulation.

As Nigel Leask notes, the Romantic interest in mesmerism focused on the exercise of 'the magnetizer's will in the therapeutic operation', and the poem duly details the restaging of a process in which Jane's active part subjects Shelley to passivity.[17] Yet Shelley's alert sense of this encounter heightens the very desires that Jane prohibits. Her determined rejection cannot curb his passion; he draws from her domination his own pleasure of submission, responding to her question 'What would cure your head and side?' with a playful puzzle: 'What would cure that will kill me, Jane' (41, 42). Jane is both cure and cause, and therefore a remedy not to be sought, not only insofar as Shelley draws pleasure from his pain but also since Jane's submission to Shelley's will would ultimately 'break | My chain' (44–5). Just as Jane invokes Edward, Shelley implicitly acknowledges the restraints of his own marriage. The poem presents through the erotics of

[16] Tim Fulford, 'Conducting the Vital Fluid: The Politics and Poetics of Mesmerism in the 1790s', *Studies in Romanticism* 43.1 (Spring 2004), 57–78.

[17] Nigel Leask, 'Shelley's "Magnetic Ladies": Romantic Mesmerism and the Politics of the Body', in Stephen Copley and John Whale (eds.), *Beyond Romanticism* (London: Routledge, 1992), 53–78.

surrender and submission, domination and denial, the complex dynamics of a relationship in which Shelley must acknowledge both Jane's independent will and the constraint of his own will by his commitment to Mary.

More pastoral in style, the lyric, 'To Jane. The Invitation' and its companion, 'To Jane—The Recollection' present differing accounts of an excursion taken by Jane, Mary, and Shelley through a Pisan forest in 1822. That Mary was present at this trip and subsequently elided from the poem is itself a striking feature.[18] Shelley's attention is exclusively Jane's in the fragile moment that is anticipated in 'The Invitation' and recalled in 'The Recollection'. Where 'The Invitation' is buoyant with rhyming couplets, 'The Recollection' strays into alternate rhymes, as though the seeking of aural consonance might imitate the harder, restorative work of reflection after the event. In 'The Invitation', Shelley defers long-term consequences for the joy of the immediate in which 'Today is for itself enough' (40). The poem enthusiastically culminates in the coherent figure of 'the universal Sun' (69), but is betrayed by the coming prospect of darker things that 'may come tomorrow' (33). The illusion that 'all things seem one' (68) is revealed as only a semblance of unity in 'The Recollection', but 'The Invitation' too acknowledges the fragility of this seeming unity. It carries tragedy latently, opening with the inchoate figuration of a 'cradle' and an 'unborn spring', the intimation of a beginning barely begun. Later the emergent daylight that, parent-like, 'kissed the forehead of the earth' (12) subtly underscores the images of infancy implicit in the poem. Jane comes, Shelley notes, 'to those in sorrow' (3); the significance of that passing reference to himself (and perhaps Mary) as sorrowful is easily missed, except for that recurring intimation of an incipient infancy so inchoate it is barely articulated. The pleasure of Jane's company momentarily subsumes the sorrow of infant death and the poem appeals to her for the temporary relief only she can inspire.

The arboreal canopy that temporarily shelters Shelley and Jane in 'The Invitation' is in 'The Recollection' ominously remembered as 'Tortured by storms to shapes as rude | As serpents interlaced' (23–4). The entire scene, in sober recollection, is muted, like the 'silent deep' (31), in an 'inviolable quietness' (37) that is peaceful but also 'lifeless' (52) apart from the restorative figure of Jane. The 'magic circle' (50) she casts is an enchantment of 'momentary peace' (47). Shelley insists that 'the silence' is bound as though by a 'chain' (33, 34), but the robustness of the image belies the poem's tentativeness. The repeated pausing ('We paused amid the pines […]', 'We paused beside the pools […]') imparts the sense of a fragile stillness, easily disturbed and all the more frail by dint of its recollected nature. The stillness and pausing amplifies the intense psychological drama of Shelley's own self-understanding. The pool of winter rain, which in 'The Invitation' reflects back an idyllic 'roof of leaves' (51), is played back now as a dangerous self-romance 'in the water's love | Of that fair-forest green' (71–2). A reworking of the Narcissus myth, Shelley professes to perceive in the pool not his own image but the forest's natural 'leaf and lineament | With more than truth expressed' (79–80). This more than truthful image is disturbed by an 'envious wind' (81), just as the recollection of Jane's 'dear image' is disturbed by Shelley's own unpeaceful mind, but the likeness between the rippled pool and an agitated mind reinstates Shelley where he had

---

[18] See note to text in *Major Works*, 813.

professed to efface himself: Narcissus contemplating his own image in the pool. The idea of a representation that could exceed the verities of what it presents, the pool that 'more than truth expressed', indicates more acutely Shelley's own delusive desire for an imaginative recollection capable of blotting out bleaker realities. The image impressed upon the pool's fragile surface promises 'more than truth', but the 'softer day below' in its 'dark water's breast' (76, 78) is ominously deep and alluring. In the poem's obscured last stanza, Shelley's Narcissus is lured by the promise of those depths; the poem sustains this sublated contemplation of suicide as the means of obtaining a permanently inviolable quietness.

The darker edge of Shelley's poetics emerges again in 'The Serpent is Shut Out from Paradise', where Shelley is figured as an interloper in the Williamses' paradisal scene. Again, the scene allegorizes a real relationship from which he is excluded though he celebrates it, and which he tests even as he admires it. Mazzeo, among other critics, notes that the serpent image plays on Byron's nicknaming of Shelley as 'Snake', after the music-charmed snakes of Kashmirian myth.[19] Everest notes that the connection to Byron is affirmed in the poem's *ottava rima* form, observing that the varied metre presents a snaking form on the *mise-en-page*, but this modulation intimates too the ambiguous effect of Jane's charms, which both delight and distress in the ebb and flow of 'a mitigated pain' (8). Shelley is tormented by the Williamses' happiness, even as he seeks refuge from his own unhappiness with them. The comfort Jane ministers both assuages and exacerbates the loneliness of his 'cold home' (25). The last phrase posits Mary, again, as the absent centre of a poem which forms around her. Absorbed in his unhappiness, Shelley reads the 'sad oracle' of torn flowers as indicative of 'Fortune, Fame, or Peace of Thought', but he cannot quite bring himself to articulate another possibility, signalling only his 'dread | To speak what you may know too well' (37–9). 'Dread' displaces 'dead' as an unspoken rhyme, but its possibility lingers subvocally nonetheless; suicide, an implicit presence in the poem, intimated by Shelley and perhaps intuited by Jane.[20] It emerges in the metaphorized 'bursting heart' of a billowing ocean whose waves break 'and die in foam | And thus, at length, find rest' (45–6). 'These verses', Shelley acknowledges with a reflexive clarity, 'were too sad | To send to you' (54–5). The poem attests to a friendship he valued deeply enough to disclose the bleakest confidence, but it is also one which he can neither sustain nor sever. The recognition of that dilemma and the sadness it effects further illuminates his hesitant instructions to Edward Williams regarding the poems: 'You may read them to Jane, but to no one else—and yet on second thought I had rather that you would not.'[21] The poem suggests both the seriousness of his alienation from Mary and the frustration of his predicament with the Williamses. In the 'Lines Written in the Bay of Lerici', moonlight, music, and feeling can no longer effect a cosmic consonance, but leave him alone and pensive. The poem's irresolution reflects Shelley's uncertain sense of his future. He leaves the final lines in disrepair with a dangerous textual crux: 'Seeking life alone, not peace' or 'Destroying life alone, not peace' (58).

---

[19]   Mazzeo, 'Strains of Empire', 181.
[20]   See Bieri for a detailed discussion of Shelley's suicide fantasies.
[21]   *Letters: PBS* II, 384.

MARY SHELLEY

The varied lyrics and love poems to Sophia and Jane indicate the passionate attachments that Shelley was capable of forming and the significant ways in which they shaped his work. If the poems to Sophia are at times arch, absorbed in the guile of their own gallantries, they are also playful and persuasive, their artistry itself an expression of affection. The poems to Jane are tender even when they are tenacious, curious combinations of candid self-examination and veiled intimations. Yet the coherency of the fictional worlds they conjure is tested by the reality of Shelley's marriage and Mary's suppressed presence. Apart from the dedication of *Laon and Cythna*, Shelley's poetic addresses to Mary are characterized by brevity and brokenness. The lyrics are terse, tense expressions of an almost overwhelming intensity, suggesting Shelley's difficulties in writing about a relationship that seemed more complex than any available form could bear. Although lyric form invites expressions of personal feeling, the relationship with Mary is, perhaps, too intensely felt, but after 1819, Shelley's difficulties might also be understood as symptoms of profound emotional and psychological trauma. The lyrics to Mary might be divided into two phases, dating before and after the infant William Shelley's death in Livorno, June 1819. Those that precede the event are brief but ebullient, while the poems that follow are devastatingly bleak and broken. Mary is imaged both as the figure and the failure of the idealized romantic relationship Shelley envisages.

The fragment beginning 'What Mary is', dated 1815 and remarkably footnoted as lines 'scratched by Shelley on a window-pane at a house wherein he lodged' (*Longman*, 1, 447), indicates an intimacy that inspires Shelley to praise even as it reduces him to incoherence:

> What Mary is when she a little smiles
> I cannot even tell or call to mind,
> It is a miracle so new, so rare.[22]

Similarly, the brief,

> arise sweet Mary rise
> For the time is passing now

easily discarded as ephemera, might also attest to the difficulty of writing about Mary. The more substantial 'Listen, listen, Mary mine' that presents as a sonnet, unusually split into septets of varying line length, begins by simulating the image of the oceanic 'ebb and flow' it invokes, but then struggles to maintain this formal confidence and falteringly tails off. The compact lyric 'O Mary dear, that you were here' is also not fully complete, although its lack of finish accentuates the poem's simple sincerity. Drafted between August and September 1818 during a period of separation, the poem's unaffected charm impresses the sense of a powerful intimacy in which the well-being of each is entrusted

---

[22] Texts of lyrics to Mary taken from *Longman*.

to the care of the other. Shelley issues to the absent Mary a direct warning to encourage her return, the truth of which becomes starkly clear in later poems; 'I am not well whilst thou art far'. Whilst the sentiment is simple, it also portends a dangerous contingency, painfully explored in the lyrics following William Shelley's death and the extended period of Mary's depression.

What is only a romantic appeal in 'O Mary dear, that you were here' is more keenly felt in the later 'My dearest Mary, wherefore hast thou gone':

> My dearest Mary, wherefore hast thou gone
> And left me in this dreary world alone?
> Thy form is here indeed, a lovely [?]
> But thou art fled,—gone down the dreary road
> Which leads to Sorrow's most obscure abo[de]
> Thou sittest on the hearth of pale despair
> If [   ] where
> For thine own sake I cannot follow the[e]
> Do thou return for mine—

The various lacunae make visible again Shelley's difficulty in writing of and to Mary, but the breaks and spaces are as elegantly expressive of her absence as the final, forsaken entreaty, 'For thine own sake I cannot follow the[e] | Do thou return for mine'. The relationship of loving entrustment articulated here amplifies the devastation effected by Mary's self-secluding grief that leaves Shelley 'in this dreary world alone'. The word 'dreary' emerges recurrently in the lyrics written in the post-1819 period to Mary, as, for example, in the lyric beginning, 'The world is dreary | And I am weary | Of wandering on without thee Mary'. A useful half-rhyme with 'Mary', its repetition also has a deflationary effect, seemingly exhausting the word and emphasizing the repeated failure of Shelley's repeated entreaties; its semantic emptiness matches Mary's own absence, and Shelley's unvarying loneliness. In the poem he struggles with Mary's detachment, which seems to him beyond any appeal he could issue.

Shelley's grief is not without its own subtle articulation; 'The world is dreary', for instance, closes 'With the lullaby | Of birds that die | On the bosom of their own harmony', a muddled image in which the 'bird' that dies on the bosom seems to figure William and Mary but curiously entwines and blurs their living and dead forms in a 'harmony'. That the dead child takes with him the mother's song seems to relegate Mary even further from the living. The lyrics to Mary are frequently interleaved with images of infancy, often understated and strangely awry. In the lyric beginning 'Wilt thou forget the happy hours', Shelley reminds Mary of the happiness 'we buried' in 'Love's sweet bowers', the last image intimating something like a cradle. The grimly decaying 'blossoms' heaped over that Love's 'corpses cold' invert the romance of a spring flowering, intimating William's early death and unrealized maturation. Shelley's tangled imaging of infancy seems itself to speak of his own unresolved grief, and the doubled sense of loss he feels with Mary's estrangement. This is articulated in the lyric titled and addressed to a personified 'Misery' that is evidently synonymous with (as well as sounding like) Mary. The poem is characterized by the peculiar buoyancy of its successive rhyming couplets and triplets which only signals further the false cheer of Shelley's words of encouragement and the forced resolve with which he challenges Mary's unwavering grief:

> Come, be happy, sit near me
> Shadow-vested Misery,
> Coy, unwilling, silent bride,
> Mourning in thy robe of pride,
> Desolation deified.

The identification of 'Misery' as 'Desolation deified', is not without judgement; the poem wavers between gentle chastisement and harsher reproof, and so carries too the subtle guilt of that criticism. Later the poem issues an imploringly heartfelt but sharply sensible reproach:

> Misery!—we have known each other
> Like a sister and a brother
> Living in the same lone home
> Many years: we must live some
> Hours or ages yet to come.—
>
> 'Tis an evil lot, and yet
> Let us make the best of it—
> If love can live when pleasure dies
> We two will love; till in our eyes
> This heart's Hell seem Paradise.

The simplicity of the line 'Let us make the best of it' is more pragmatic than poetic, but it asserts again a Shelley who is frank in the analysis of his broken marital life, and it is enjoined to the still romantic possibility of a loving gaze in which each retrieves in the other's eyes their own reflection in a kind of 'Paradise'.

This loving absorption in each other Shelley posits as a possible remedy, but it is one which betrays the loneliness of their current estrangement. The likeness of misery to the non-sexual fraternity of 'a sister and a brother' presents an intimate confession concealed in a simile. The invitation to 'lie thee down | On the fresh grass' and the offering of his arm as 'thy pillow' on which peaceful natural sounds 'shall lull | Us to slumber', promises a restored intimacy, but one which remains non-sexual and whose paternalistic mode of care (particularly the lullaby intimated by 'lull') also reserves the latent image of the lost child. The imagined scene yields to another of a bitterly cold domestic life: Shelley imagines himself and Mary as silent bedfellows, he vigilant with anxiously 'burning heart', and she grievously cold with 'frozen pulse' and 'icy bosom'. The needy, perhaps sexual, embrace Shelley yearns for from his wife, and which would restore them to a relationship of entrustment, is revealed as 'soft, but chill and dead', with Mary appropriating the corpse-like cold of her dead child. The image of the 'bridal bed' spread 'Underneath the grave', is not only overshadowed by grief, but also profoundly claustrophobic; the implicit reference to the buried child transfers to the deathly embrace of a marriage in which one might feel as though they are buried alive.

The desperate loneliness of these last poems to Mary informs the longing expressed in the poems to Jane. Yet they also delineate with an arresting simplicity Shelley's conception of a marriage in which the happiness of one is entrusted to the care of the other and contingent on their well-being. That this mode of caring entrustment is imaged in the 'lullaby' of a night-time vigilance, both here and in the poems to Sophia, lends to it an additional plangency and indicates the ways in which the experience of infant mortality tests Shelley's marriage in the most profound way and finds it wanting. In 'Misery', Shelley imagines the stoic resolve of a love that outlives death and bears out the hardships of grief, but he also indicates the devastating reality of a relationship in which that is simply not possible. If all of the poems to Sophia, Jane, and Mary disclose the ways in which Shelley allows his life to inform his work and his work, in turn, to be infused by the truth of sentiment, in all its complexities and uncertainties, it is perhaps the broken verses to Mary that present the surest sense of desire and devastation.

SELECT BIBLIOGRAPHY

Blunden, Edmund. *Shelley: A Life Story*. Glasgow: Collins, 1948.

Brown, Nathaniel. *Sexuality and Feminism in Shelley*. Cambridge, MA: Harvard UP, 1979.

Cœuroy, Andre. 'The Musical Inspiration of Shelley'. *Musical Quarterly* 9.1 (1923), 83–95.

Frosch, Thomas. '"More than Ever Can Be Spoken": Unconscious Fantasy in Shelley's Jane Williams Poems'. *Studies in Philology* 102.3 (2005), 378–413.

Fulford, Tim. 'Conducting the Vital Fluid: The Politics and Poetics of Mesmerism in the 1790s'. *Studies in Romanticism* 43.1 (2004), 57–78.

Keach, William. *Shelley's Style*. London: Methuen, 1984.

Leask, Nigel. 'Shelley's "Magnetic Ladies": Romantic Mesmerism and the Politics of the Body'. *Beyond Romanticism: New Approaches to Texts and Contexts 1780–1832*. Ed. Stephen Copley and John Whale. London: Routledge, 1992. 53–78.

Matthews, G. M. 'Shelley and Jane Williams'. *Review of English Studies* 12.45 (1961), 40–8.

Mazzeo, Tilar. 'The Strains of Empire: Shelley and the Music of India'. *Romantic Representations of British India*. Ed. Michael Franklin. London: Routledge, 2006. 180–96.

Vatalaro, Paul. 'The Semiotic Echoes in Percy Shelley's Poems to Jane Williams'. *Keats–Shelley Journal* 48 (1999), 69–89.

CHAPTER 25

....

SHELLEY'S PRONOUNS

Lyrics, Hellas, Adonais, *and* The Triumph of Life

....

MICHAEL O'NEILL

I

....

JOHN Fuller's spoof memoirs of Laetitia Horsepole, supposedly addressed to Shelley, contain towards their end a meditation on the self as composed of so many donned and now doffed 'Attitudes': 'At my Age, there is nothing left to be done. I have run through all my Possibilities, like a Chest of Cloaths, each of which I have put on & acted out its Part, as though a Bequest of theatrical Costume. These are now the meer Ghosts of me, left in the Darkness like Attitudes without an Audience.'[1] The word 'I' turns out to contain multitudes that are at the same time 'meer Ghosts'. Offering a wryly comic evocation of Romantic agonizing over selfhood, Fuller's well-managed pastiche may at first sight bring to mind here less Shelley than Byron at his most performative: a poet for whom the 'Possibilities' of self can seem to fold into 'a Bequest of theatrical Costume'. 'What am I? Nothing; but not so art thou, | Soul of my thought!' (*Childe Harold's Pilgrimage*, III. 50–1), Byron retorts with self-abnegating self-display to his stanza's earlier, more collective assertion: ''Tis to create, and in creating live | A being more intense, that we endow | With form our fancy, gaining as we give | The life we image, even as I do now' (III. 46–9).[2]

The stanza derives its unpredictable force from the interplay between 'we', 'I', and 'thou', as is also the case in much of Shelley's work. Typical of Byron is the way in which the self-emptying 'Nothing' follows hard on the heels of the self-assertive, 'even as I do now'. The emphasis on the scene of composition allows the poet to parade his virtuosity and discover his nothingness and, indeed, his vulnerability to the ravages of 'thought'. 'Yet must I think less wildly' (55), the next stanza begins. At the same time, 'thou, | Soul

[1] John Fuller, *The Memoirs of Laetitia Horsepole, by Herself* (London: Chatto, 2001), 196.
[2] Quoted from *Lord Byron: The Major Works*, ed. Jerome J. McGann (Oxford: Oxford UP, 2003), with 'image' preferred to 'imagine'.

of my thought' exists in a hazardous realm of serenity, hazardous because clearly a projection, a self-conceived ideal, and here, as this chapter will argue, Byron foreshadows, for all his tonal differences, a central and productive artistic conundrum in Shelley's later work.

Byron knows the self is a theatrical performance, even as he longs (here, at any rate) for an authenticity guaranteed by an ascent to the sublime. Shelley at once fears and hopes that the self may be a fiction: 'hopes' since all finiteness poses a bar to the illimitable; 'fears' since the illimitable can only be broached through the finite and, if the finite self is a fiction, the desires for which it serves as conduit may be illusory. In constant dialogue with Byron, a dialogue that is rarely straightforwardly oppositional, Shelley, too, gives the sense in some of his later work that he has, in Fuller's words, 'run through all [his] possibilities'. In 'To—("The serpent is shut out from Paradise")', he writes a confessional lyric that thrives on doubt about what is being confessed and to whom. Addressing or seeming to address Edward Williams, Jane Williams's common-law husband, Shelley observes: 'When I return to my cold home, you ask | Why I am not as I have lately been? | *You* spoil me for the task | Of acting a forced part in life's dull scene' (25–8). The modified *ottava rima* calculates to a nicety the emphasized pronominal crux of '*You* spoil me', where '*You*' might be Edward, Jane, or Edward and Jane, an effect that takes us back to and intensifies the complexity of address involved in the previous stanza: 'if now I see you seldomer, | Dear friends, dear *friend*, know that I only fly | Your looks, because they stir | Griefs that should sleep, and hopes that cannot die' (17–20).[3] The question mark in line 26, evident in the manuscript fair copy, requires us to hear the 'you ask' clause as a direct question rather than as indirectly reported speech. The pressure of another person, changing the self, can be felt. If the cadencing of Shelley's lament is Wordsworthian— 'Why I am not as I have lately been' recalls the phrasing and rhythms of the 'Ode: Intimations of Immortality'—the self seems vulnerable to others in ways that are foreign to the older poet. Who I am depends on who you are, and on whom I take you to be, or on whom I take you to suppose that I am.

These knots are quotidian realities rather than visionary mysteries. But the late lyrics delicately and powerfully foreground 'I' and 'you'. Nothing, Shelley's later writing indicates, is so tricky or so eloquent of the tensions involved in both personal intimacies and wider perspectives as a pronoun. When his figures sound most assured of their identity, we sense a counter-intuition. In the 'Song of Apollo' the speaker announces with triumphant near-solipsism, 'I am the eye with which the Universe | Beholds itself, and knows it is divine' (31–2). This moment of pure cognition, a circling self-reflexivity in which the 'I' and the 'Universe' reinforce one another's self-knowing interpenetrating identities, might take us to the loftier reaches of *Biographia Literaria*, the opening 'I am' challenging comparison with Coleridge's definition of 'The primary IMAGINATION' as 'a repetition in the

---

[3] See William Keach, 'Shelley's Last Lyrics', for an analysis of how the poem 'dramatizes its own uncertainty', in Michael O'Neill (ed.), *Shelley* (London: Longman, 1993), 201. Shelley is quoted from *Major Works*, unless indicated otherwise.

finite mind of the eternal act of creation in the infinite I AM'.[4] But Apollo's voice, with its moments of what Wasserman rightly identifies as 'too-insistent boastfulness',[5] must contend with something less certain throughout Shelley's oeuvre, and its immediate counter-voice sounds in the 'Song of Pan', which suggests a different notion of self, a different poetry: 'And then I changed my pipings' (29), Pan says in the final stanza, subjecting his metre to an expressively fractured 'change': 'Gods and men, we are all deluded thus!— | It breaks on our bosom and then we bleed' (32–3). The use of 'we', there, lacks the sense of joyous community evident at the poem's start ('From the forests and highlands | We come, we come', 1–2) and pinpoints a shared participation in delusion, a near-inevitable fall into pain and suffering.[6]

Apollo's affirming 'I' becomes Pan's fracturing 'we'. Elsewhere, Shelley breaks away from the manacles of self, as at the end of 'Stanzas Written in Dejection', a lyric that accepts but tests the nature of subjective isolation. The poem opens in an other-centred way: 'The Sun is warm, the sky is clear, | The waves are dancing fast and bright' (1–2). But the focus on externals tacitly communicates the suppressed self's alienation, indicated explicitly for the first time in the poem by the exclamatory line at the close of the second stanza: 'How sweet! did any heart now share in my emotion' (18). 'Sharing' is made subtly strange by Shelley; readers find themselves assuming the position of a secret sharer. If the solitary self asserts 'I sit upon the sands alone' (14), the poem's close sashays away from the 'I' who is named three times within five lines (37, 38, 41), as Shelley presents himself as 'one | Whom men love not, and yet regret; | Unlike this Day, which, when the Sun | Shall on its stainless glory set, | Will linger though enjoyed, like joy in Memory yet' (41–5). The poem finishes with 'joy in Memory yet', and with a glimpse of what life might be like stripped of self-concern, though only self-concern makes possible its imagined opposite.

This is Shelley, improbably enough, as a forerunner of the Philip Larkin of 'Sad Steps', dependent on the very self by whom he is dissatisfied for epiphanic glimpses of how youth is 'for others undiminished somewhere' (18). This 'diminished' self enters the poem, 'Groping back to bed after a piss' (1), Larkin's crude diction registering a refusal to romanticize. Yet it is this self which responds to the moon in a vein of Symbolist rapture, that, for all its parodic air of sending up an outmoded style and despite the subsequent negation of 'No' (12), opens itself to a vision, triggered by the moon, of 'Immensements' and 'wolves of memory' (12). Tellingly, Larkin's final if liminal state involves an altered pronoun, 'One shivers slightly' (13).[7]

---

[4] *Coleridge's Poetry and Prose*, selected and ed. Nicholas Halmi, Paul Magnuson, and Raimonda Modiano (New York: Norton, 2004), 488.

[5] *Shelley: A Critical Reading* (Baltimore: Johns Hopkins UP, 1971), 48.

[6] For commentary on the dialectic between the two Songs, see Wasserman, *Shelley: A Critical Reading*, 46–56; for discussion of the poem's metrical skill, see the section of Milton Wilson, *Shelley's Later Poetry: A Study of his Prophetic Imagination* (New York: Columbia UP, 1959), repr. in George M. Ridenour (ed.), *Shelley: A Collection of Critical Views* (Englewood Cliffs, NJ: Prentice-Hall, 1965), 157.

[7] Quoted from the *Norton Anthology of Poetry*, 5th edn., ed. Margaret Ferguson, Mary Jo Salter, and Jon Stallworthy (New York: Norton, 2005).

For his part, Shelley is able to make pronouns dance to the tune of pipings that wish to celebrate states of excited unknowingness, scenes of potential discovery. A *locus classicus* is the close of the second section of 'Mont Blanc', where the poet exclaims 'thou art there!' (48), a brief instantiation of hoped-for presence that occurs in the very moment of 'Seeking among the shadows that pass by, | Ghosts of all things that are, some shade of thee, | Some phantom, some faint image' (45–7). What catalyses this section's rendering of 'an unremitting interchange' (39) between self and other is the self's glimpse of its mental processes: 'and when I gaze on thee', writes Shelley, 'I seem as in a trance sublime and strange | To muse on my own separate fantasy, | My own, my human mind' (34–7). The syntax of those lines includes 'sublime and strange' qualifications and modifications that imply a 'mind' other than the 'human mind'. Shelley clings to selfhood as to a newly discovered reality amidst the flux of perception. Without endorsing Wasserman's reading of the poem as investing belief in some Universal Mind, one might note how Shelley both privileges and questions the status of 'My own, my human mind'.[8]

Again, pronouns in 'Written on Hearing the News of the Death of Napoleon' play a prominent part in what feels like a lyric anticipation of themes explored more meditatively in *The Triumph of Life*. 'I feed on whom I fed' (32) exults the Earth over the death of Napoleon, rhyming yet again with manic verve on the repeated sound that closes each of the poem's five stanzas. Indeed, the poem's obsessive mono-rhyming (or duo-rhyming) suggests that History does indeed have but one story, and that such a story is one of exhausted possibilities stimulating a train of new and themselves inevitably exhausted possibilities. Such possibilities are embodied here in Earth's voice, which may have the last word, but never wholly refutes the speaker's apparent dismay at its continued vitality. The poem brings together human speaker and the non-human figure of 'Earth', depicted as an irrepressibly assertive voice, and its perspectives lurch between the poles of the speaker's opening question, at once awed and slightly contemptuous, 'What! alive and so bold, oh Earth? | Art thou not overbold?' (1–2), and Earth's final '"Aye, alive and still bold," muttered Earth' (33), an utterance both mocking and latently beleaguered. Modes of address and the uncanny interplay of voices result in Shelley's startling vision of history as a vital, terrible dynamic.

Fluidity in the use of pronouns gives imaginative life to metaphysical disquisition. *On Life*, a prose essay that anticipates the concerns of *Adonais* and *The Triumph of Life*, switches from a universally questioning 'We' to a tentatively convinced idealist 'I' in the blink of a paragraph or two:

> What is life? Thoughts and feelings arise, with or without our will, and we employ words to express them. We are born, and our birth is unremembered and our infancy remembered only in fragments. We live on, and in living we lose the apprehension of life. How vain it is to think that words can penetrate the mystery of our being. Rightly used they may make evident our ignorance to ourselves, and this is much. (*Major Works*, 633)

---

[8] Wasserman, *Shelley: A Critical Reading*, 221–38 (223).

Then comes a volley of existential interrogations: 'For what are we? Whence do we come, and whither do we go? Is birth the commencement, is death the conclusion of our being? What is birth and death?' (*Major Works*, 634).[9] The effect of this virtual prose-poem is severe and beautiful. Assumptions are thrown into question, stripped of stable or of assured significance. This is not a question of Shelley forcing language to perform a dance of semantic self-erasure. Rather, words mime a process of enquiry and frustration. Birth, for example, features in a poem written slightly earlier by Shelley, 'Ode to the West Wind', in which he heralds and desires 'a new birth' (64) at the close. But though 'birth' may be an event, being born rouses the questions activated by our contemplation of the universe. It exists, it must have come about, but what is its meaning for the person who was born? 'We are born, and our birth is unremembered'; we remember nothing. The foundational event of our experience is beyond mnemonic access. Shelley asks whether 'birth' is the 'commencement' of our being, possibly wondering with Wordsworth whether we come into this world trailing clouds of glory. If we do not know, how can we know that we did not? How do we know what 'birth' is?

One might reject the foregoing Shelleyan reflections as those of a plate-spinning sceptic, were it not for the skill with which the word 'birth' has been re-articulated in the paragraph and the sinuous empathy by which 'we' have been involved. In the next paragraph Shelley departs from this collective state: 'I confess that I am one of those who am unable to refuse my assent to the conclusions of those philosophers, who assert that nothing exists but as it is perceived' (634). This seeming genuflection towards Berkeley (discussed by Anthony Howe in Chapter 6 on Shelley and Philosophy) is hedged in by guarded wording.[10] Shelley is 'one of those who am unable to refuse my assent', where 'am' rather than 'are' serves, almost awkwardly, to insist on his individuality, in the act of articulating a belief that individuality may be an illusion. The existence of the 'I' making a show of his inability to refuse belief is about to be called into question in the essay. Indeed, in a piece preoccupied by 'the misuse of words and signs, the instruments of [the mind's] own creation' (635), it is fascinating that the word 'I', along with other pronominal markers, turns out to be a signal example of such misuse. If some findings of memory can be trusted, there was a state called 'reverie' when 'We less habitually distinguished all that saw and felt from ourselves' (635). It is as if reality were something from which we are alienated the moment we seek to individuate ourselves: 'The words *I*, and *you* and *they* are grammatical devices invented simply for arrangement and totally devoid of the intense and exclusive sense usually attributed to them' (636).

Comparable tensions run through the dialogue between Mahmoud and Ahasuerus in *Hellas*, where the former sees the latter as a means of imagining a momentary escape from the tyranny of self: 'I honour thee, and would be what thou art | Were I not what I am' (751–2). In reply, Ahasuerus speaks with majestic disdain of the futility of separate

[9] The passage is discussed in Angela Leighton, *Shelley and the Sublime* (Cambridge: Cambridge UP, 1984), 152.
[10] Mary Shelley claims that 'Shelley was a disciple of the Immaterial Philosophy of Berkeley', *Essays, Letters from Abroad, Translations and Fragments by Percy Bysshe Shelley*, 2 vols. (London: Moxon, 1840), I, p. xii.

selves: 'talk no more | Of thee and me [...] | But look on that which cannot change—the One' (766–8). Yet this 'One' beyond selfhood turns out later in the speech to be a virtual synonym for consciousness: 'Nought is but that which feels itself to be' (785). If the 'One' lies beyond 'change', seemingly immutable, occupying a dimension of pure being, it is also the case that 'that which feels itself to be' is identical with absolute reality.[11] Affectingly, a seeming absolute ('the One') turns out to exist only in terms of the very idea of consciousness which is half-discredited in the passage. It is through dramatizing such disjunctions of desire, such splintering connections between desiring self and an object of desire that subsumes the self, that Shelley's later poetry attains its characteristic pitch of questing intensity.

II

In *On Life* Shelley delineates the pronominal pit into which all speakers must fall, using words that imply divisions at odds with a deep intuition of, or longing for, a state of 'unity', the 'view of life presented by the most refined deductions of the intellectual philosophy' (635). But his later poems turn this fall into one that is fortunate, weaving their verbal webs out of the complexities associated with '*I*, and *you* and *they*'. Above all, they sense that 'unity' is a longed-for state, and must compete with the more common-place but heartfelt realization that much human experience is, indeed, 'common', the adjective at which Hamlet sneers but whose implications of a shared mortality he must learn to accept in the Gravediggers' scene; which Wordsworth uses in the Immortality Ode as a token of life's disappointments and, implicitly, the ground for such consolation as can be provided for and by 'the human heart by which we live' (203); and which under-lies Dante's understanding of existence as a pilgrimage, at once individuated and 'com-mon': so Virgil says, *ma noi siam peregrine come voi siete* ('but we, like you, do on a journey go').[12] 'I weep for Adonais—he is dead' (1), so *Adonais*, Shelley's elegy for Keats, begins, its 'I—he' positioning the reverse of that Buberesque 'I-thou' paradigm which a young Harold Bloom sought to find in or impose on Shelley's poetry.[13] Bloom did not devote a chapter to *Adonais* in *Shelley's Mythmaking*,[14] but his model is illuminating for the elegy. It is significant that Shelley for the most part avoids directly addressing the

---

[11] See Jerrold E. Hogle, *Shelley's Process* (New York: Oxford UP, 1988) for suggestive thinking about Shelley's redefinition of 'the One' in his later work, 263–342.

[12] For *Hamlet*, see the exchange between the hero and Gertrude at I. ii. 68–75; for Wordsworth, see 'the light of common day' ('Ode: Intimations of Immortality', l. 76); and for Dante, see *Purgatorio*, 2. 63, quoted from Dante Alighieri, *The Divine Comedy: Text with Translation* by Geoffrey L. Bickersteth (Oxford: Blackwell, 1972).

[13] The basis of Bloom's book is the tension between a 'world of experience' and a 'world of relation', the former confronting the self with a series of 'Its', the latter converting otherness into a 'Thou'; see Harold Bloom, *Shelley's Mythmaking* (New Haven: Yale UP, 1959), 1.

[14] Bloom asserts that the elegy has no connection with 'the dialectic of Shelley's mythopoeia', *Shelley's Mythmaking*, 9.

dead Keats as 'you' or 'thou'. In the Preface we are aware of his own involvement: 'I consider the fragment of *Hyperion*, as second to nothing that was ever produced by a writer of the same years', for example, or 'The genius of the lamented person to whose memory I have dedicated these unworthy verses, was not less delicate and fragile than it was beautiful' (529). The first statement sets up Shelley as an appropriate judge; the second, for all its modesty trope, asserts his status as a fitting elegist. Keats appears in the third person, a 'genius' set apart from the turmoil of a culture antagonistic to poetry. It is Shelley who addresses a representative of this culture directly, singling out the reviewer held responsible for Keats's death: 'Miserable man! you, one of the meanest, have wantonly defaced one of the noblest specimens of the workmanship of God' (530). Shelley is prepared to silence his self-doubt about the existence of a deity to achieve his polemical point.

The elegy pivots on the word 'I', and Shelley's presence is crucial to the poem's effect. This elegy for Keats is less a self-elegy than an opportunity for the elegist to display his poetic power as he presides over and takes an increasingly central role in a 'highly wrought *piece of art*'.[15] Shelley orchestrates, commands, interpolates. He hints at personal sorrow, even as he veils it (in stanza 51, with its allusion to his son's death), and makes his own quest to follow Adonais, now no longer the slain vegetable god, Adonis, but analogous kin to the Hebraic lord, Adonai, the centre of the poem's complexly powerful final stanzas.[16] These complexities show in the poem's different modes of address to the poetic self. In stanza 47, the poem's Spenserian measure, always able to accommodate strains far from the merely melodious, adapts itself in its quickly enjambed movement across the natural stopping points of the fourth and fifth lines to the simultaneous longing for and advised withdrawal from 'the brink' (423). Exhorting a 'Fond wretch' (416) in the second person to 'keep thy heart light' (422), Shelley appears to be speaking to a version of his own self. His way of doing so implies a self at cross-purposes, as it does clearly and affectingly in a later use of the second person when he questions his 'Heart': 'Why linger, why turn back, why shrink, my Heart? | Thy hopes are gone before' (469–70). The triple interrogation takes its syntactical shape from a Dantescan original, Beatrice's remonstrating questions to Virgil (see *Inferno* 2. 121–2), yet it is tense with self-conflict, Shelley implying, to the great benefit of his poem, that he is only too aware, as he seeks to identify death and the goal of his poetic quest in the elegy, of why he lingers, turns back, and shrinks.

The move to address himself as 'thou' reinforces the poem's gradual confrontation with its true subject: Shelley's shaping of ardent but provisional consolations for Keats's death. These consolations pivot on the value of poetry, a value first invested in the figure of Adonais, who emerges in the final section of the poem as a guarantee of permanent poetic lustre. Shelley's declarative rhetoric results in lines that intensify their momentum

[15] *Letters: PBS* II, 294.
[16] See Wasserman, *Shelley: A Critical Reading*, 464–5. For a revisionist view challenging Wasserman's position, see H. J. Jackson, 'The "AI" in "Adonais"', *Review of English Studies* advance access February 2011. Jackson's argument lays emphasis on the fact that 'ai' is Greek for 'woe'; the strength of Wasserman's case is that it sees embedded in the name of 'Adonais' the poem's transformative shift from slain vegetable-god to heroic Lord.

as they endow the pronoun 'He' with worth, building on the earlier reference to Miltonic courage, 'He died, | Who was the Sire of an immortal strain' (29–30). A series of assertions such as 'He has outsoared the shadow of our night' (352) and 'He is a portion of the loveliness | Which once he made more lovely' (379–80) sees Adonais as either transcending the limitations of the mortal condition or as being immanent in all that is best in that condition. Shelley is able to redeem Adonais from the emphatic status of being merely dead which governed the first section—'He will awake no more, oh, never more!' (190)— by virtue of a transvaluation of the elegy's key opposition, death and life, or its related terms, awakening and sleep. And it is in his own resolution of this division through a kind of poetic fiat ('he is not dead, he doth not sleep— | He hath awakened from the dream of life', 343–4) that Shelley anticipates his own central role as poet of unstable affirmation. These affirmations involve Shelley in a review of life's value (or lack of it); so, here, he attaches a definite article to 'dream of life', as though brooking no argument about the phrase's accuracy, and he goes on to emphasize 'We', in calculated opposition to the earlier 'He', only to lament our decayed lot since death's imagery applies more to us than to Adonais: 'We decay | Like corpses in a charnel; fear and grief | Convulse us and consume us day by day' (348–50). Though this is not the elegy's last word on the human condition, it is among its most memorable. Such an inevitability of 'decay' is our unavoidable lot, says the repetition of 'us', a repetition that puts 'us' on the receiving end of two strongly alliterative verbs that fall like blows.

Earlier the poet has sought to establish relationships between elegist and significant others through the use of 'you' or 'thou'. Peter Sacks suggests a major reason for the elegist's reaching out to various 'thous' as well as his use of 'we' in lines 181–5 (and elsewhere) when he writes: 'Shelley [...] cannot bear this burden [of grief] alone'. Sacks's account of how the poet's 'work of mourning' involves an attempt, via the recasting of the figure of Adonais to 'represent the poetic genius [...] as Shelley defines it', does much to explain the poem's motivating dynamic.[17] Yet the poem's awareness of its complicating motives is also evident. Appealing to Urania, Shelley initially employs the forlorn and seemingly upbraiding terms used by Milton in *Lycidas* (see 50–1 in that poem): 'Where wert thou mighty Mother, when he lay, | When thy Son lay, pierced by the shaft which flies | In darkness?'(10–12). Urania, muse of poetry, has failed to defend her 'Son'; the natural order of things whereby a 'Mother' defends her 'Son' has been set aside, and it will be the elegist himself who will finally come up with words that will vanquish the forces that thrive on 'darkness'. This state is soon accepted, apparently (the final third of the poem will overturn any such acceptance): 'But now, thy youngest, dearest one, has perished' (46). In turn, Urania herself is pictured addressing Adonais as 'thou' in stanzas 26–8: 'I would give | All that I am to be as thou now art' (232–3), she asserts, seeking vainly and yearningly to be at one with Keats, conceding that he has outsoared the shadow of her temporal dimension and implicitly preparing us for the idea that Keats, unlike Urania, is not 'chained to Time' (234). He will take his place both in and beyond history as one among 'The splendours of the firmament of time' (388).

---

[17] See 'Last Clouds: A Reading of "Adonais"', in O'Neill (ed.), *Shelley*, 184, 190, 191.

However, the elegist speaks directly to Adonais only twice. The first time occurs in the context of a mythological conceit. 'To Phoebus was not Hyacinth so dear | Nor to himself Narcissus, as to both | Thou Adonais' (140–2). That final phrase 'Thou Adonais' is powerful in its syntactical torsion, but the result is to escort Adonais into a stylized mythological world. Screened off by, as well as linked to, 'the drooping comrades' (143), Phoebus and Hyacinth, Adonais seems a figure, at this stage, protected from the very rawness of elegiac grief which direct address would seem to express. The second occasion occurs in stanza 17 where Shelley uses 'thee' and 'thy' as he acknowledges Keats's achievement through graceful allusion ('Thy spirit's sister, the lorn nightingale', 145) to his 'Ode to the Nightingale', but concludes the stanza by dividing his attention between Keats's 'angel soul' (153) and 'his head who pierced thy innocent breast' (152).

The effects of this restraint in the use of direct address to Keats are threefold: to focus, as the poem's plot requires, on what seems, initially, irrefutable, the fact that Adonais is dead; to indicate how the 'highly wrought' nature of the poem associates itself with Shelley's way of speaking to and about the dead Keats, as though it were a form of high courtesy; and to prepare the reader for the transformation of the dead 'he' into the majestically alive 'he' who sounds throughout the final third of the poem. Shelley employs tact in his reluctance to address Keats/Adonais in the second person; to over-employ the word 'thou' would violate the awful apartness of the sacred dead. He turns away from Milton's direct intensity of address in *Lycidas*, which anticipates, both in likeness and unlikeness, Shelley's ways of speaking to Keats in his elegy. Milton says of Lycidas, 'But O the heavy change, now thou art gone, | Now thou art gone and never must return' (37–8), a tone of plangent loss that Shelley expresses in the third person: 'He will awake no more, oh, never more!' (64). Milton risks an intensity of loss that Shelley reformulates as a severe acceptance of fact. Both authors use the third person to imagine a transcendence of loss and death. So Milton writes: 'For Lycidas, your sorrow, is not dead' (166).

It is as though the use of 'thou' would imply a personal intimacy of a kind the poem does not claim, even as Shelley's intertextual references to Keats's work indicate a wish to imply the living, energy-giving quality of Keats's poetic legacy.[18] Both Greek epigraphs, one from Plato, the other from Moschus, do address their dead poet in the second person, and it is a sign of Shelley's careful plotting of affective response in the poem that he consigns such immediacies of lament to the safety of the epigraphic paratext and the veils of a classical language.[19] Shelley's pronominal complexities serve, too, as a sign that

[18] See Kevin Everest, 'Shelley's *Adonais* and John Keats', *Essays in Criticism* 57 (2007), 237–64. For insightful commentary, see Madeleine Callaghan, '"His Mute Voice": The Two Heroes of *Adonais*', *Keats-Shelley Review* 24 (2010): 'The two poets and their poetry entwine, simultaneously inhabiting and creating alternative spheres of reference', 53. For Shelley's awareness of Keats's writing, see the suggestion that he cancelled the draft line 'The spirit of the great is never dead' because it too obviously echoes the famous first line of [Keats's] sonnet "The Grasshopper and the Cricket"', *Shelley's Last Notebook*, ed. with introd. and notes Donald H. Reiman (New York: Garland, 1990), 369.

[19] Shelley translated the epigraph from Plato thus: 'Thou wert the morning star among the living, | Ere thy fair light had fled;— | Now, having died, thou art as Hesperus, giving | New splendour to the dead' (see *Major Works*, 798), his longer and shorter lines enacting the interplay between the surviving 'Thou' and the 'dead'.

he is conceding the fact that the centre of the elegy is not Keats alone, but the elegist himself, 'Who', in a displacement involving his appearance in the poem under the guise of 'a pardlike Spirit beautiful and swift' (280), 'in another's fate now wept his own' (300). This troubled self-portrait displays division and doubleness, as though Shelley had to undergo the same process of full realization of his potential power as does the figure of Adonais.[20] At this stage, Shelley depicts himself, or a version of himself, as highly conflicted: weak yet strong; close to defeat but driven by an energy which could be creative as well as self-destroying; an outcast, a Cowperesque 'deer struck by the hunter's dart' (297), who is possessed of Dionysiac potency, holding a thyrsus-like 'light spear topped with a cypress cone' (291).

This sense of being a 'Power | Girt round with weakness' (281-2) unites elegist and dead poet. 'Where there is leisure for fiction there is little grief' was Dr Johnson's acute if partial judgement in his 'Life of Milton' about *Lycidas*, the great forerunner of *Adonais*.[21] Milton faces down the criticism by conceding openly that elegy does involve fiction, suggesting the importance of fiction (in the sense of imaginative surmise) for our discovery of meaning, hope, and consolation. Shelley out-manoeuvres the criticism by recognizing the degree to which all human knowledge is metaphorical, rather than metaphysical, and will involve dependence on fiction-making.[22] Shelley is not so much engaged in consuming Keats as in seeking to acknowledge the tricky issue of self-concern (weeping his own fate in another's) and wishing to celebrate the dead.[23] Yet that celebration has about it a quality that seems deliberately willed. Shelley's 'He' is a superman who contrasts vividly both with the Orphically sacrificial self-portrait and with the cur-like reviewer, sent packing by the elegist's contemptuous 'thou', where the second-person expresses the reverse of admiration: 'Live thou', writes Shelley, 'whose infamy is not thy fame!' (325). But 'thou' also serves as a marker of elegiac questioning. Urania asks the stranger-mourner, 'who art thou?' (303), and the murmured interrogation comes close, along with the crucial questions raised in stanzas 21, to the heart of the poem. Those questions in stanza 21 are phrased in a collective form: 'Whence are we, and why are we? Of what scene | The actors or spectators?' (184-5). 'We' do not know, so the questions say, at this stage in the poem, what 'our' purpose is; Urania does not know who the stranger is, even as he is close kin to the poet whose redemptive activity in the poem seeks to answer the elegy's most anguished questions. He can only reply through a gesture and a sign, one of the most riddlingly vexed in Shelley's poetry, as he 'Made bare his branded

---

[20] See Jonathan Wordsworth's suggestive remark that '*Adonais* builds gradually to the full realization of its poetic power', introd. *Adonais* (Oxford: Woodstock, 1992). See also Michael O'Neill, '*Adonais* and Poetic Power', *Wordsworth Circle* 35 (2004), 50-7.

[21] Angela Leighton quotes this comment in arguing that 'The leisured grief of the elegy is not simply a lie', 'Deconstruction Criticism and Shelley's "Adonais"', in Kelvin Everest (ed.), *Shelley Revalued: Essays from the Gregynog Conference* (Leicester: Leicester UP, 1983), 156.

[22] For further discussion, see the central argument of Mark Sandy, *Poetics of Self and Form in Keats and Shelley: Nietzschean Subjectivity and Genre* (Aldershot: Ashgate, 2005).

[23] For a different view, but one significant in any exploration of the elegy's use of pronouns, see James A. W. Heffernan, '"Adonais": Shelley's Consumption of Keats', *Studies in Romanticism* 23 (1984), 295-315.

and ensanguined brow, | Which was like Cain's or Christ's—Oh! that it should be so!'
(305–6). There the exclamation adds to the sense that the 'thou' (303) with which it forms
at least an eye-rhyme, along with 'brow' and 'so', cannot be unperplexed. It is only
through the final section's use of willed assertion, always vibrant with inner conflict, that
the poem can find solutions to its questions and enigmas.

The word 'He', by contrast, calms the poetry's pulse. There is a clarity in its use in a line
and a half such as 'From the contagion of the world's slow stain | He is secure' (356–7)
that is inseparable from a near-despairing commitment to assertion. Definite articles
take on an insistent definiteness, at the very moment that key words—'life', 'dead',
'sleep'—undergo redefinition. It is an insistent definiteness that compensates for a sense
of being in a mist, since another pronoun 'We' emerges as tumultuously central at this
point in the poem: ''Tis we, who lost in stormy visions, keep | With phantoms an unprof-
itable strife' (345–6), Shelley writes, his sense of discovery pointed up by the rhetorical
comma introduced after 'we'. 'Lost in stormy visions' ruffles the unnatural calm that the
poem, through its elegiac tableaux and sculpturesque phrasing, has sought to maintain,
and comes close to supplying a comment on the poem we are reading. 'He' now, the
poem is able to say, 'has outsoared the shadow of our night' (352). It is 'our night'; he is
beyond us. But the Donne-like reversal in 'He lives, he wakes—'tis Death is dead, not he'
(361), where 'He' is chiastically encased in the line, makes it possible for Shelley to turn
with a new mixture of authority and compassion to his personifications: 'Thou young
Dawn' (362), he urges, 'Turn all thy dew to splendour' (363). The personifying mode
shifts in its impact. What was formerly a highly artificial vehicle of grief is now the
co-opted figurative ally in a transformative journey. Keats/Adonais becomes, gracefully,
the recipient of second-person address from all 'whose transmitted effluence cannot die
| So long as fire outlives the parent spark' (407–8), the visionary company of poets.
'"Thou art become as one of us," they cry' (410), where 'Thou' glides into 'us', as though a
barrier had fallen.

As the climax and close of the poem approach, Shelley rings the changes on 'thou'
and 'we'. There is, for example, the gesture of communal sorrow in the phrase,
'Welcoming him we lose with scarce extinguished breath' (450). There is, as noted
above, the suppression of personal grief as Shelley alludes to, and draws attention to the
fact that he is not going to express his emotions about, the presence in the Protestant
Cemetery not only of Keats's body but also that of the elegist's own son, William: 'if the
seal is set, | Here, on one fountain of a mourning mind, | Break it not thou!' (453–5). The
reader may feel rebuked, as though he or she were the potential violators of the seal,
before realizing that Shelley speaks of himself; and yet the emotional mobility here and
in surrounding stanzas makes us realize that he does speak of us, too. Stanzas 52 and 53
bring the drama of the self-addressed 'thou' to the finest pitch and reveal how Shelley
thrives on never finding a way out of the poem's 'stormy visions'; 'thou' is the marker,
the spotlight, the torch, the clue through the labyrinth; but 'thou' is also the unlocatable
place, the unilluminable darkness, the labyrinth itself. Stanza 52 aims to outsoar the
realm of 'I, and *you* and *they*' in its immaculately Platonic figurations of the relationship between 'The One' and 'the many' (460), the stanza's opening opposition recast as

a gradually more complicating matter: 'Life, like a dome of many-coloured glass, | Stains the white radiance of Eternity, | Until Death tramples it to fragments.—Die, | If thou wouldst be with that which thou dost seek!' (462–5). The mighty abstractions of 'Life', 'Eternity', and 'Death' end up entangled in one another; Life's staining is enrichment as well as disfigurement; Death's resolving of the tension between colour and 'white radiance' is also a form of wanton, fragmentary destructiveness. An elegant piece of Platonism fires into vivid and agonized life, as the noun 'Death' turns into the imperative 'Die', placed with perilous urgency at the close of the line. Again, address to the reader is inextricable from self-address; we are part of this journey, realizing a gauntlet has been thrown at our feet, one that recalls Urania's earlier wish to 'be as thou now art'. 'Die, | If thou wouldst be with that which thou dost seek!': the phrasing speaks of *being* (emphasis added) 'with that which thou dost seek', the self and its object each sharing in the other's being, even as the double 'thou' insists on sustaining the self's own individual mode of being in the act of an imagined fusion with its object. The phrase, 'that which thou dost seek', has a yearning, impersonal openness that makes it impossible to gloss it as meaning simply 'Adonais'.

Further modulations include the affectingly severe return to the quotidian suffering self, the elegist addressing his 'Heart' (469) and confessing unhappiness: 'and what still is dear | Attracts to crush, repels to make thee wither' (473–4), a formulation that suggests the flight beyond 'life' is prompted by self-conflicting drives. In the penultimate stanza, Shelley sustains surprises, making amends to the world which has previously been the subject of near-Gnostic contempt:

> That Light whose smile kindles the Universe,
> That Beauty in which all things work and move,
> That Benediction which the eclipsing Curse
> Of birth can quench not, that sustaining Love
> Which through the web of being blindly wove
> By man and beast and earth and air and sea,
> Burns bright or dim, as each are mirrors of
> The fire for which all thirst, now beams on me,
> Consuming the last clouds of cold mortality.
>
> (478–86)

This stanza is itself a complex act of 'Benediction', a secularized litany, a tribute to the transformative forces, the quasi-Dantean sustainers that allow conquest of the 'eclipsing Curse | Of birth' as, configured as a collective network, such forces become a single agency. Shelley rings the changes on alliances between different groupings here, incorporating 'each' into 'all', linking the 'web of being' to 'The fire for which all thirst'. Crucially his rhetoric seems to turn from self-concern to cosmic awareness, before he returns to centre stage in the final couplet, the last word 'mortality' swallowing in its rhyme the word 'me'.

The self may imagine its own mortality being consumed, but such an imagining brings a paradoxically vital energy to its declaration of questing intent in the last stanzas. Rather as a Shakespearian tragic hero may seek to collect all his energies in one final articulation of identity, the elegist seeks to evoke, through his use of 'I', his sense of the value and function of the poetic self: 'I weep for Adonais', the poem begins; it ends with an allusion to his poetic triumph in 'Ode to the West Wind': 'The breath whose might I have invoked in song | Descends on me' (487–8).[24] The descent implies imaginative mastery, but one that displays itself through surrender: 'my spirit's bark is driven | Far from the shore, far from the trembling throng | Whose sails were never to the tempest given' (488–90). It is as though the self is both a medium through which the 'breath' of inspiration pours and an agent whose suspended, questing status offers an exemplary, unfollowable model: 'I am borne darkly, fearfully, afar' (492), he writes, 'borne' towards, we assume, 'the abode where the Eternal are' (495). Adonais takes his place as a star among the 'Eternal', a plural grouping that seems close to an image of canonical poetry, but the poem derives much of its pathos as well as power from the fact that the elegist can only gesture, on his own behalf, towards 'Fame's serene abode' (45).

III

The poet at the end of Adonais wishes to be borne 'darkly, fearfully, afar', to be carried across from one realm into another, 'translated'. Shelley's preoccupation with translation is a form of challenging any fixed subject-position; it permits 'a going out of our own nature, and an identification of ourselves with the beautiful which exists in thought, action or person, not our own' (Major Works, 682). Jeffrey C. Robinson makes the excellent point that Shelley's translation of Dante's sonnet to Cavalcanti, published in the Alastor volume, 'might signify the process of translation in its fantasy of a travelling-across to an ideal community'.[25] Yet in that sonnet, Shelley underscores the fact that such a 'travelling-across' is a fantasy; the poem circles back at the close to the desiring self as he imagines how 'each were as content and free | As I believe that thou and I should be' (13–14; H).[26] Shelley's translating practice demonstrates that 'identification' with the other does not involve straightforwardly what in Epipisychidion he calls the self's 'annihilation' (587). He turns Goethe's Faust into a poem that is, in Timothy Webb's words, 'swifter in motion and less firmly ordered'. If in the same critic's view 'Epipsychidion is [...] an extraordinary example of the way in which translation can interlock with original composition', it brings out, too, the gap between Shelley and Dante whose Vita nuova and first Canzone of the Convito spur and are reworked by the Romantic poem.[27] That it spins to earth and crashes, sending out like smoke-trails a series of first-person pronouns, 'I pant, I sink,

[24] See Stuart Curran, '"Adonais" in Context', in Everest (ed.), Shelley Revalued. 'This is the only occasion in all of Shelley's poetry', writes Curran, 'where in the body of a poem he directly cites his own canon for reference and meaning', 176.

[25] Jeffrey C. Robinson, 'The Translator', in Timothy Morton (ed.), The Cambridge Companion to Shelley (Cambridge: Cambridge UP, 2006), 117.

[26] Quoted from H.

[27] Timothy Webb, The Violet in the Crucible: Shelley and Translation (Oxford: Clarendon Press, 1976), 193, 303.

I tremble, I expire!' (591), bears witness to the way in which translation-influenced creativity enacts the self's longing for what is not its own and discovery of its existential uniqueness and cultural aloneness. Even Plato's *Symposium* assumes Shelleyan inflections as it lives again in cadences and turns of phrase that do justice to desire's varied and restless manifestations.[28]

In *The Triumph of Life*, Shelley's career-long practice of doubling and twinning, a twinning and doubling that is never merely restatement or repetition, takes on a new and disturbing form.[29] What is especially striking about the doubling relations charted in this fragmentary poem, one marked by the accents of a last testament even as it commits itself again to quest and process, is the difficulty of assigning them dialectical meanings. Rousseau's encounter with a 'shape all light' (352) and the narrator's (hereafter Poet's) vision of the 'Shape' (87) within the destructive car of Life may bear the relation of predecessor to successor, young to old. The latter, who sits 'as one whom years deform' (88), may be the corrupted and ominously disfigured 'form' of the former, its 'spent and diminished replica.'[30] If so, the resemblance is lost on the one figure to see them both, namely Rousseau. The Poet and Rousseau seem to haunt one another; as A. C. Bradley noted, they are 'in closer contact than that of two waking men.'[31] It is as though the experience half-remembered by the star-enamoured, dawn-defying Poet, with his sense of having already experienced what he is experiencing ('I knew | That I had felt the freshness of that dawn', 33–4), is that of Rousseau. Yet, as many commentators have observed, such parallels glimmer and are lost in the poem's dissolving uncertainties, an emblem of which might be Rousseau's comment on the Poet's questions. Fending off, yet conceding the interrogative force of the Poet's words, Rousseau replies: 'Whence I came, partly I seem to know' (300). 'Partly I seem to know': the poem suspends us between the ruthless erasures beloved of deconstructionist commentators and the unsatisfied desire for causal coherence.[32]

Terza rima is a perfect form for such imperfect knowledge, especially as practised by Shelley, with its use of elongating, fluidly enjambed sentences.[33] Dante quests, but finds

---

[28] For further discussion, see Michael O'Neill, 'Emulating Plato: Shelley as Translator and Prose Poet', in Alan M. Weinberg and Timothy Webb (eds.), *The Unfamiliar Shelley* (Farnham: Ashgate, 2009), 239–55.

[29] For Shelley and doubling, see Kelvin Everest, 'Shelley's Doubles: An Approach to *Julian and Maddalo*', in O'Neill (ed.), *Shelley*, 56–69.

[30] See Stuart M. Sperry, *Shelley's Major Verse: The Narrative and Dramatic Poetry* (Cambridge, MA: Harvard UP, 1988), 189.

[31] 'Notes on Shelley's "Triumph of Life"', *MLR* 9 (1914), 453.

[32] Major deconstructionist commentaries include Paul de Man's essay, 'Shelley Disfigured', in Harold Bloom et al., *Deconstruction and Criticism* (London: Routledge, 1979), 39–73, and J. Hillis Miller's essay, repr. in O'Neill (ed.), *Shelley* 218–40. Donald H. Reiman's edition and commentary (*Shelley's 'The Triumph of Life': A Critical Study* (Urbana, IL: University of Illinois Press, 1965)) belongs to a less theory-driven age, but contains much that is thoughtful and still of value. For a judicious account of 'the poem's ambiguity', see Tilottama Rajan, 'Idealism and Skepticism in Shelley's Poetry [*The Triumph of Life* and *Alastor*]', repr. in O'Neill (ed.), *Shelley*, 241–63 (245).

[33] See Vidyan Ravinthiran, 'Dante and Shelley's *Terza Rima*', *Essays in Criticism* 61 (2011), 155–72. For Dante and Shelley, see Ralph Pite, *The Circle of our Vision: Dante's Presence in English Romantic Poetry* (Oxford: Clarendon Press, 1994).

answers; his tercets round themselves out; his images are daring and thought-provoking. Shelley quests, but finds only questions; his tercets trail from one to the next; his images haunt, refusing to explain themselves. A shape who expunges thoughts the way that the sun erases starlight is, once lost, depicted as a star erased by the sun (see 387–93, 412–15). Rousseau's response to the shape all light is compared to 'a shut lily, *stricken* by the wand | Of dewy morning's vital alchemy' (401–2; emphasis added), where 'stricken' brings into play ideas of 'deleterious enchantment', in Sperry's words, even as 'the magic practiced' may be only that of 'the natural alchemy of the spring and of the morning'.[34] Whereas a Dantean simile clarifies, a Shelleyan simile weaves together contrapuntal possibilities. Even the opening lines cannot quite identify the sun that springs forth with 'a spirit hastening to his task | Of glory and of good' (1–2). It could be that all that sun and spirit share is swiftness.

Personal identity is the elusive vehicle through which Shelley develops his post-Enlightenment story of quest and sceptical uncertainty. Hume's critique of causality and his interrogation of the self had always fascinated Shelley, whose poems simultaneously operate with, yet call into question, the idea of the self as a means of registering the impact of historical process. In *The Triumph of Life* identity is always on the point of losing its surer contours. Rousseau, prototype of Romantic confessionalism and proof that words might have agency, catalyses in a crucial exchange the Poet's rejection of 'the world and its mysterious doom' (244). In doing so, Rousseau emerges as imperiously non-quietist, but his own best judge and worst enemy, coming close to asserting his own status as Romantic exemplum: 'I was overcome | By my own heart alone, which neither age | Nor tears nor infamy nor now the tomb | Could temper to its object' (240–3). This is the quasi-Byronic, heroic self in a nutshell, one in which the writer might be bounded by limits but count himself as a king of infinite suffering; it seems to glance, with the subtle allusiveness typical of the poem, at Byron's trailing of his bleeding heart in *Childe Harold's Pilgrimage*.[35]

It is not that the poem annuls Rousseau's cry; it is more that it allows us to hear it as a cry. As if on the rebound from his own assertions, his rebuke to the Poet puts matters from another perspective. Rousseau speaks now, not as a Titanic sufferer, but with the voice of one who knows himself merely to be one of many: 'Figures ever new | Rise on the bubble, paint them how you may; | We have but thrown, as those before us threw, | Our shadows on it as it passed away' (248–51). That 'paint them how you may' suggests that figures will 'Rise' whether one paints well or ill; and the use of 'you' might mean 'one' or it might mean 'you', the Poet, who thinks he can be immune from figure-drawing. All of us cast shadows, on this model of human endeavour. The reference to 'the bubble' implies that this world is merely a 'bubble', while providing no assurance of a realm beyond. The final phrase, 'as it passed away' takes on retrospective pathos and irony when one rereads, and knows that Rousseau will tell us that he has already said to the 'shape all light', the ultimate 'Thou': 'Show whence I came, and where I am, and why— | Pass not away upon the passing stream' (398–9).

---

[34] Sperry, *Shelley's Major Verse*, 192.
[35] See Neville Rogers, *Shelley at Work: A Critical Inquiry*, 2nd edn. (Oxford: Clarendon Press, 1967) for relevant comment on Byron and Rousseau, 303–4.

Lines 248–51 do not constitute Rousseau's last word on the subject of last words, and he will reassume a would-be heroic stance. Contrasting himself with imperial and religious tyrants, the former Savoyard Vicar and author of the *Confessions* remarks, the first person dangling proudly at the precipice-edge of a line: 'I | Am one of those who have created, even | If it be but a world of agony' (293–5). The line's comportment wishes to salvage dignity for the creative 'I', the figure emerging from 'the wreckage of Europe', as Ezra Pound will put the matter, as an 'ego scriptor', both the self and the self reconstituted, through its awareness of 'wreckage', as a writer.[36] Such a 'world of agony', the world, that is, created in and by the writer's representations, is no more untrustworthy or less valuable than the 'bubble'. Rousseau's assertion re-balances the self-blame of a previous passage, 'And so my words were seeds of misery— | Even as the deeds of others' (280–1), a view itself modified by the Poet in his quickly checking 'Not as theirs' (281).

Pronominal interchange mirrors the way in which, in *The Triumph of Life*, self passes into self, a passage or interplay that suggests the larger cultural import of dilemmas that are experienced subjectively. Rousseau explains his purpose in telling his story in terms that imply shuttling between states and identities: 'But follow thou, and from spectator turn | Actor or victim in this wretchedness, | And what thou wouldst be taught I then may learn | From thee' (305–8). This passage suggests the possibility of learning and teaching, even if one senses that Rousseau's accents are suffused with irony. Rousseau tells the Poet, in effect, that he has nothing to teach him, except the unavoidable necessity of existential immersion. At the nadir of elegiac doubt and questioning, Shelley asks in *Adonais*, 'Whence are we, and why are we? of what scene | The actors or spectators' (184–5). But at least the elegiac self was able to position itself, by the close, in a central role in the poem's drama, even if Shelley ends up 'borne darkly, fearfully, afar' (492). In *The Triumph of Life* the alternatives oscillate in an unresolved way. Advised by a postmortal shade, the Poet is told that he may have to leave behind the stance of 'spectator', a stance which may be as good as it gets, and gives *The Triumph of Life* some of its unsettled and unsettling poise, as though the poem were able to cling to a spectatorial detachment, as though its reworking of Dante gave it a screen on which to view 'the world and its mysterious doom'. In its very wording the changed condition of 'Actor or victim' has about it a sardonic flick that hardly suggests it is a straightforward advance, and yet it also sketches what the poem indicates to be a necessary fall.

As an 'Actor or victim', the Poet would be able, in turn, to pass on his experiences to Rousseau, a narrative that one anticipates would be as powerful and finally enigmatic as Rousseau's narrative to the Poet. But there is no certainty that such a symmetry of (non) information transfer would have been observed. Maybe the Poet, had the poem been continued, would have learned from Rousseau—in ways that will avoid his being brought to a comparably 'dread pass' (302). The initial signs, it must be said, before the poem was brought to its untimely halt by the accident of Shelley's death, are not that encouraging that anything will be learned or taught: the half line '"Then what is Life?" I said' (544) implies that questions are turning into a driven and compulsive process of repetition.

---

[36] Ezra Pound, *The Cantos* (London: Faber, 1975), canto LXXVI.

Yet if any lessons are to be learned, even if the lesson is that no lessons can be, they will involve transfers between I and thou. Or possibly they will involve momentary abolitions of these markers of identity. At the centre of the 'shape all light' story, an inset narrative into which Shelley seems to pour a career's obsessions with inspiration, trance, and poetry, at the very centre of this narrative occurs a remarkable moment. Rousseau asserts:

> And still her feet, no less than the sweet tune
> To which they moved, seemed as they moved, to blot
> The thoughts of him who gazed on them, and soon
>
> All that was seemed as if it had been not [...]
>
> (382–5)

The sentence unfurls further, into an exquisitely menacing development of figurative affinity between the shape all light and the vision-annihilating light of the sun, a development that is modified (as noted above) when the shape vanishes, as though she, in turn, were the morning star obliterated by 'the coming light' (412). In the lines just quoted, it is fascinating how Rousseau, the great 'I'-sayer, speaks of 'The thoughts of him who gazed on them'. Glimmering through this moment of apparent certainty about the shape's malevolence is an intuition of self-annihilation, though whether annihilation of self has anything positive about it is another of the poem's endlessly open questions. In *A Defence of Poetry*, Shelley asserts that 'The grammatical forms which express the moods of time, and the difference of persons and the distinction of place are convertible with respect to the highest poetry without injuring it as poetry' (677); but in much of his later work it is the pressure brought to bear on 'grammatical forms which express [...] the difference of persons' that lies close to the heart of its imaginative achievement.

SELECT BIBLIOGRAPHY

Bloom, Harold. *Shelley's Mythmaking*. New Haven: Yale UP, 1959.

de Man, Paul. 'Shelley Disfigured'. *Deconstruction and Criticism*. Ed. Harold Bloom et al. London: Routledge, 1979. 39–73.

Everest, Kelvin. 'Shelley's *Adonais* and John Keats'. *Essays in Criticism* 57 (2007), 237–64.

Heffernan, James A. W. '"Adonais": Shelley's Consumption of Keats'. *Studies in Romanticism* 23 (1984), 295–315.

Hogle, Jerrold E. *Shelley's Process*. New York: Oxford UP, 1988.

Keach, William. *Shelley's Style*. London: Methuen, 1984.

Leighton, Angela. *Shelley and the Sublime*. Cambridge: Cambridge UP, 1984.

O'Neill, Michael. '*Adonais* and Poetic Power'. *Wordsworth Circle* 35 (2004), 50–7.

Pite, Ralph. *The Circle of our Vision: Dante's Presence in English Romantic Poetry*. Oxford: Clarendon Press, 1994.

Ravinthiran, Vidyan. 'Dante and Shelley's *Terza Rima*'. *Essays in Criticism* 61 (2011), 155–72.

Sperry, Stuart M. *Shelley's Major Verse: The Narrative and Dramatic Poetry*. Cambridge, MA: Harvard UP, 1988.

Wasserman, Earl R. *Shelley: A Critical Reading*. Baltimore: Johns Hopkins UP, 1971.

PART IV

....

CULTURES, TRADITIONS, INFLUENCES

....

CHAPTER 26

....

SHELLEY AND THE BIBLE

....

IAN BALFOUR

It is a great temptation to want to make the spirit explicit.

(Wittgenstein)

ON the face of it, the topic is hardly auspicious: Shelley and the Bible. One of the first things one tends to learn about Percy Shelley is that he was expelled from Oxford for his part in publishing the pamphlet with the inflammatory, if misleading, title *On the Necessity of Atheism*. Any number of his prose texts rail against Christianity and what are posited as its naive beliefs, many of which amount to sheer superstitions. And if Christianity is, in some respects, a bad thing, because misguided doctrinally and often nefarious institutionally, then, from Shelley's point of view, Judaism, whose scriptures account for the lion's share of the Christian Bible, is even worse. In the schematic histories on display in *Queen Mab* and other poems, the God of the ancient Hebrews is mainly a figure that traffics in blood. 'He is', Walter Bagehot once proclaimed of Shelley, 'the least biblical of poets.'[1] The topic, then, might seem to solicit almost only negatives. Some probing, however, beyond Shelley's obvious repulsion from certain religious doctrines and beyond his counterbalancing, massive debt to ancient Greek literature necessitates a more complicated picture of the poet's stance toward the Bible and how it informs his poetry and prose.

A book order of Shelley's dated 8 December 1815 offers a suggestive emblem, providing a glimpse into the diverse strands of his interests that include, typically, the Bible among other things:

> Gentlemen,
> I would be obliged to you to send the following books, before you complete the list of those which I ordered before, in case you cannot forward them immediately.
>> Locke on the Human Understanding 8vo
>> Lowths Praelectiones Poeseos Hebraeorum

---

[1] Walter Bagehot, 'Percy Bysshe Shelley', in *Literary Studies*, vol. I (London: Longmans, Green & Co., 1897), 115.

> Quintus Curtius Cellari Lipsia 12mo 1688—91.—96
> Lempriere's Classical Dictionary. 4to
> Your obliged Ser.
> P.B. Shelley (*Letters: PBS* I, 437)

The wish list corresponds well to the varying impulses of this open-minded but hardly wishy-washy poet. It includes: one of the masterpieces of British empirical philosophy by a thinker of whom Blake maintained that he 'laught at the Bible in his slieve',[2] the great classical dictionary of the day, so important as a source for Keats, and, perhaps most surprisingly, Lowth's *Lectures on the Sacred Poetry of the Hebrews*, which had for decades been available in English but which Shelley prefers to read in the Latin original. We know from various sources that Shelley was an avid reader of the Bible. When Claire Clairmont records in her journal for 8 January 1820: 'Work in the Evening while Shelley reads the Gospel of Matthew aloud' it seems like business as usual (*CC* 116). The famous list of books he gave to Medwin outlining a core library ended, after the likes of Plato, Shakespeare, Dante, and Calderón, with noting: 'last, yet first, the Bible'.[3] Is it 'last, yet first' because he is somewhat grudgingly admitting the Bible—last—into his canon together with all sorts of non-scriptural texts, the greats of secular and quasi-secular literature? Or 'last, yet first' because it is the most encompassing book, ranging from the beginning to the end of time, a book one drinks in or is force fed as a child in predominantly Protestant England, and to which one might turn to in the end, Alpha and Omega?[4] In any event, the crucial importance of the Bible for Shelley, despite or because of its lofty canonical status, cannot be doubted. Several testimonies, as well as the texture of biblical reception in Shelley's poetry and thought, suggest that he was taken especially with certain *parts* of the Bible. In her 'Note on The Revolt of Islam', Mary Shelley glosses Percy's decision to dedicate himself to poetry rather than to metaphysics thus:

> he educated himself for it [...] and engaged himself in the study of the poets of Greece, Italy, and England. To these may be added a constant perusal of portions of the Old Testament—the Psalms, the Book of Job, the Prophet Isaiah, and others, the sublime poetry of which filled him with delight. (*H* 156)

The 'portions' of the Bible Mary Shelley lists on Percy's behalf are among those that tend to have most impressed a great many poets and literary critics, whether believers or not. This short list is not unlike those singled out by, say, Sir Philip Sidney in his 'Defense of Poesy', though it is closer still to the books foregrounded in Lowth's lectures. It is not clear how literally we are to understand the term 'constant' when applied to Shelley's reading of books of the Bible. It is most likely more accurate to say that the Bible was often either at the forefront or periphery of his thoughts. Bryan Shelley goes too far in

---

[2] William Blake, *The Complete Poetry and Prose of William Blake*, ed. David V. Erdman (Berkeley and Los Angeles: University of California Press, 1982), 613.

[3] Thomas Medwin, *The Life of Percy Bysshe Shelley*, ed. H. Buxton Forman (London: Oxford UP, 1919), 55.

[4] Shelley records in a note to *Queen Mab* how the Bible is 'put into our hands when children'; *H* 819–20.

referring to the poet's 'addiction' to reading the Bible but there's no doubt that some parts struck his imagination and his moral sensibility with great, abiding force.[5]

One should not, however, succumb to the lure of paradox to argue that the Bible is somehow the secret key to Shelley's poetic practice or his thinking. It is not. It is entirely possible for scholars to write extended monographs on Shelley's work, including synthesizing, global studies of the poet, with little or no attention to the Bible, as in extended works by, say, Wasserman or Hogle.[6] Even Northrop Frye, a critic as attuned to biblical resonances and paradigms as can be, finds little need to educe biblical connections in his substantial chapter on Shelley in his *A Study of English Romanticism* specifically devoted to imagery and mythical patterns in the poetry. Indeed, Frye can say: 'For Shelley, the canon of imaginative revelation was Greek rather than Hebrew.'[7] If 'rather than' here entails an either/or scenario, that would be saying too much. If 'rather than' means that Shelley more often than not tended to the Greek over but not to the exclusions of the Hebrew, then that can hardly be gainsaid.[8] The importance of the Bible for Shelley has been obscured by his pointed, sometimes vehement ideological differences with this or that doctrine or passage as well as what counts for Shelley as the disturbing role it often plays in institutionalized Christianity. Yet the Bible figures, nonetheless, in many and sundry forms in Shelley and I shall try to characterize the types and texture of biblical presences in the poetry and prose.

As an impassioned reader of the Hebrew scriptures or what he sometimes called 'the Jewish books', Shelley is following the example of no less than Jesus, at least as Shelley understands the situation. As he notes in his essay 'On Christianity':

> Jesus Christ probably studied the historians of his country with the ardour of a spirit seeking after truth. They were undoubtedly the companions of his childish years, the food and nutriment and materials of his youthful meditations. The sublime dramatic poem entitled *Job*, had familiarized his imagination with the boldest imagery afforded by the human mind and the material world.
> (*Murray: Prose*, 249)

Shelley is akin to the Jesus he comments on insofar as it is clearly the *imagery* of the Bible that most impressed him and its poetry, broadly understood, lives and moves in the

[5] Bryan Shelley, *Shelley and Scripture* (Oxford: Clarendon Press, 1994), 22. This book, however, is an excellent source for understanding Shelley's relation(s) to the Bible, not least for its detailed register of biblical allusions in the poet's work. For a generous, perspicacious review of this study, see Leslie Brisman, 'Review of Bryan Shelley, *The Interpreting Angel*', *Keats–Shelley Journal* 44 (1995), 240–2.

[6] The interesting exception in Wasserman's huge study is a section on *Prometheus Unbound* detailing the importance of Christological imagery and patterns. See *Shelley: A Critical Reading*, 295–305. His key claim for our topic would be this: 'The primary function of the scriptural stratum of the play is to redefine and universalize Aeschylus' Prometheus by assimilating him to a character both a modification of Milton's Satan and a strictly Shelleyan interpretation of Christ.' Earl R. Wasserman, *Shelley: A Critical Reading* (Baltimore: Johns Hopkins UP, 1971), 292.

[7] Northrop Frye, *A Study of English Romanticism* (New York: Columbia UP, 1982), 100.

[8] Frye does, however, point to Shelley's awkward non- or post-biblical homemade trinities of phrases, what he calls 'uneasy triads', such as 'Love, Hope, and Self-esteem', or 'Love, Hope, and Power', syntagma that point to the influence of the Bible and to Shelley's felt need to swerve from them. Ibid. 104.

realm of the imaginative. Shelley was so taken with 'the sublime dramatic poem entitled *Job*' that it was to be the model for a drama he contemplated writing. The Book of Job's extravagant, cosmic, all-or-nothing rhetoric, posing the most essential questions of self and spirit and justice, made a particular mark on Shelley.[9] One notices that these most poetic parts of the Bible feature the 'boldest imagery afforded by the human mind'. The texts that some consider of divine inspiration are thought by Shelley, following the rationalist and philological critiques of the Bible from Spinoza to Eichhorn, to be thoroughly human productions, making it all the more possible for the prophets and the psalmist to be models for all-too-human poets such as Shelley.

A passage in *A Defence of Poetry* similar to the one from the 'Essay on Christianity' makes it clear that these books of the Bible not only impressed Jesus, they seem to have helped make him a *poet*:

> It is probable that the astonishing poetry of Moses, Job, David, Solomon and Isaiah had produced a great effect upon the mind of Jesus and his disciples. The scattered fragments preserved to us by the biographers of this extraordinary person, are all instinct with the most vivid poetry. But his doctrines seem to have been quickly distorted [...] (*Major Works*, 688–9)

As Shelley goes on to say, there is 'poetry in the doctrines of Jesus Christ' (689) but the poetry and the doctrine are soon put asunder by history and the institutionalization(s) of what Shelley sometimes calls 'Xtianity'. It is as if—though Shelley does not say exactly this—the doctrines of Jesus are distorted by virtue of the erasure of their 'poetry'. Shelley envisioned writing a book based on the moral teachings of Jesus Christ, but one in which morality was not simply divorced from the poetry with which it was originally bound up. In various essays Shelley posed the ethical teachings of Jesus against their later institutional incrustations but in a number of private letters, including several to Hogg, he expressed a far dimmer view of Jesus, though even in these unguarded letters Shelley often critiques the use to which Jesus has been put rather than what he said or preached.

Mary Shelley's testimony, noted above, confirmed that it was primarily some *parts* of the Bible that made their sublime mark on Shelley: the prophets, the psalms, and numerous of the more mythical parts of the Bible. One could be forgiven for not finding the Book of Leviticus a goldmine for poetry. More atypically, the early chapters of Genesis are not much drawn on by Shelley, passages on the creation and the Fall that seem so resonant and reusable for other poets, such as Byron in *Cain*, and for Blake and the first generation of Romantics.[10] Yet Shelley's canon within the biblical canon is

---

[9] On the rich tradition of commentary on and reworkings of this text in the period just prior to Shelley, see the excellent study by Jonathan Lamb, *The Rhetoric of Suffering: The Book of Job in the Eighteenth Century* (Oxford: Clarendon Press, 1995).

[10] One of Shelley's mouthpieces in 'A Refutation of Deism' provides a caustic assessment of the biblical story of Fall and Redemption. He also displays relatively little interest in the stories surrounding Noah, Abraham, Isaac, Jacob, and Esau, etc. Shelley does, however, display an interest in the figure of the serpent, as in *Laon and Cynthia* and elsewhere. Bernard Beatty, in a fine analysis of our topic, notes as a gloss on Mary Shelley's note that 'There are a few references to *Exodus* and *Genesis* as we might expect but he makes virtually no use of the historical books.' See 'P. B. Shelley', in Rebecca Lemon et al. (eds.),

largely a familiar one: the same portions tend to appeal to poets, almost regardless of their doctrinal orientations.

That Shelley would take an interest in Lowth's *Lectures on the Sacred Poetry of the Hebrews* probably indicates a concern for the technical (but not merely technical) workings of the biblical poets. Though there was a long-standing intuition as to the poetical character of numerous parts of the Bible, it was really not until Robert Lowth's pathbreaking lectures, delivered at Oxford in the mid-eighteenth century, that the case for much of the Bible being poetry in a strict sense was nailed down.[11] Lowth is usually remembered for his discovery of 'parallelism' as the unacknowledged informing principle of Hebrew verse. Greek and Roman prosody had proved useless when graphed onto the poetry of the Hebrew scriptures. Lowth discerned various sorts of parallelisms, mainly of clauses: phrases that matched one another in structure and length. Coleridge describes the phenomenon in a note to a fragment of a translation of the Song of Deborah: 'each Line or member of a sentence is counter-balanced by the following, either by difference or similitude, or by the repetition of the same thought in different words or with a different Image.'[12] It's not as if parallelism is peculiar to biblical poetry: a good many poems feature caesuras in the middle of lines, balancing one phrase with another on either side of the divide. Shelley's poetry contains its fair share of such phrasing and some of it may well derive especially from the 'wisdom' literature from the Bible whose poetry Shelley prized. Lowth's lectures, however, so famous for the 'discovery' of parallelism, in fact devote far more attention to the sublimity and high passion of biblical poetry, especially in the prophets and the psalms. No less than four of the thirty-one lectures are preoccupied with the sublime. It is the heightened, extreme rhetoric of the biblical poets that makes its mark: forceful, arresting imagery, with stakes often cast in terms of all or nothing, as in Shelley's favoured Book of Job.[13] Numerous verses from Shelley's odes especially—think of the 'Ode to the West Wind' with its impassioned entreaties, prayers even, and the anguished questions—derive from and inscribe themselves in this biblical lineage. Even the simple word 'Hear', to be scrutinized later, owes some of its power to its biblical, prophetic traces.

Probably the most distinctively biblical posture Shelley at times adopts is that of the biblical prophet, variously visionary, even apocalyptic. He does this in far less resolute,

---

The Blackwell Companion to the Bible in English Literature (Chichester: Wiley-Blackwell), 451–62. There are several invocations of the Tower of Babel episode, which is not surprising given Shelley's intense interest in translation.

[11] For the prehistory to Lowth's 'discovery' and for an authoritative understanding of Lowth, see James Kugel, *The Idea of Biblical Poetry: Parallelism and its History* (New Haven: Yale UP, 1981). I take up the importance of Lowth in a slightly different vein in my *Rhetoric of Romantic Prophecy* (Stanford, CA: Stanford UP, 2002). See also James Sheehan, *The Enlightenment Bible* (Princeton: Princeton UP, 2005), especially ch. 6, 'Poetry, National Literature, History, and the Hebrew Bible'.

[12] Samuel Taylor Coleridge, *The Complete Poems*, ed. William Keach (Harmondsworth: Penguin, 1997), 254.

[13] Bernard Beatty argues that *Peter Bell the Third* is a comic version of the Book of Job, legible not least in the comforters who provide no comfort. He also sees *The Triumph of Life* informed by the bleak vision of Job. See Beatty, 'P. B. Shelley'.

less absolute fashion than Blake, but the prophetic strain is unmistakable. Though one might be tempted to align the prophetic in Shelley with the oracular tradition of ancient Greek literature temperamentally more congenial to Shelley, he does seem closer to the biblical prophets primarily for their heterodox spirit. Moreover, one could show how he derives more of his phrasing and imagery from biblical prophecy and apocalyptic than from Graeco-Roman oracles or sibyls. We shall see an extended example of this mode in Shelley in a moment but first let us rehearse how and where the Bible, beginning in the most literal fashion, surfaces in Shelley's poetry.

The Bible figures most directly in Shelley's political poetry, and not always in the best light, when the whole book makes an appearance. Toward the start of the pageant of unsavoury figures in *The Mask of Anarchy*, written in the wake of the Peterloo massacre, we read:

> Clothed with the Bible, as with light,
> And the shadows of the night,
> Like Sidmouth, next, Hypocrisy
> On a crocodile rode by.
>
> (*Major Works*, 400; ll. 22–5)

The Bible doesn't come off well here, aligned with the allegorical figure of Hypocrisy and one of its earthly correlatives, Lord Sidmouth, the Home Secretary for England before, during, and after the massacre. But is it the Bible as such that is the problem? In *Peter Bell the Third*, Shelley's pointed satire aimed at the increasingly conservative and officially Christian Wordsworth, we are throughout in a world of biblical coordinates, including the devil, hell, and its hell-fire, as well as theological terms of art such as 'antitypes'. Even if the hell of the poem is 'a city much like London', the overarching framework is decidedly biblical. That the poem begins with 'Death' as 'Part the First' is not a good sign and, after learning of Peter Bell's demise, we find that all that remains of him and his possessions is this:

> The gaping neighbours came next day—
> They found all vanished from the shore:
> The Bible, whence he used to pray,
> Half scorched under a hen-coop lay;
> Smashed glass—and nothing more!
>
> (420; ll. 71–5)

The book that might have been the key to his salvation seems not to have helped at all: we soon learn Peter Bell has gone not to heaven but to 'the wrong place' (420). So much for the Bible as a book *tout court*.

If it was *parts* of the Bible that impressed Shelley, as noted above, it was even smaller units from the Scriptures that found their greatest resonance in the poet's poetry and prose. The Bible surfaces in Shelley principally in images and phrases, cadences and figures, more than in grand mythopoetic patterns, such as the linked paradigms of paradise, fall, and redemption and the stories they entail. The most common sort of appearance of the Bible comes via quoted phrases or short allusive passages. In *The Mask of Anarchy*, shortly after the passage on Hypocrisy quoted above, we read:

> Last came Anarchy: he rode
> On a white horse, splashed with blood,
> He was pale even to the lips,
> Like Death in the Apocalypse.

(401; ll. 30–3)

It's likely that most readers of Shelley would have caught the allusion to one of the more memorable figures or configurations from the Book of Revelation before the poet spells out his source. The short, clipped lines and the explicitness of the reference to 'Death in the Apocalypse' seem to lampoon the very gesture of seeing things in terms of the Bible, even though they also do just that.

Common too are not just the myriad allusions to the Bible but exact or near-exact quotations. If the devil can quote Scripture, surely Percy Shelley can too. We are told in 'Part the Second' of *Peter Bell the Third* (devoted to 'The Devil') that the archfiend is 'A thief, who cometh in the night'. (421). Here Shelley reverses, by its application to the devil, what was originally a gloss on the Lord or 'the day of the lord'. Already in the letters of Paul (1 Thessalonians 5: 2 and 2 Peter 3: 10) it was rather a paradoxical way to describe the day of the Lord: it's shocking to hear the son of God's coming compared to that of a thief in the night, even if the 'rationale' for the phasing seems to rest on the motif of suddenness, of unexpected entry. The still jarring thing about Shelley's (albeit satirical) passage is that he can so cavalierly apply to the devil the very phrasing associated with the day of the Lord.

Some of these passages sound rife with the angriest sort of atheism or anti-Christian sentiment but they seem to indicate that there are good and bad uses of the Bible, good and bad readings. In the celebrated 'Sonnet: England in 1819', Shelley invokes 'Religion Christless Godless, a book sealed […]' and his political target is a state administration that only appears to be Christian, with the phrase 'a book sealed' perhaps suggesting the hieratic priestcraft Shelley despised. Had it been truly 'Christian', truly in keeping with the teachings of Jesus, there would have been no need for such a political critique to be levelled against the current English regime. The lords responsible had in effect taken the Lord's name in vain. Carlos Baker notes how in these political poems the tone and texture is what he calls 'semi-Biblical' (158). If in *A Defence of Poetry* Shelley made plain his conviction that poetry should avoid direct moral advocacy, lest poetry risk losing what makes it poetry—Milton's 'bold neglect of a moral purpose', for example, is 'the most decisive proof of the supremacy of [his] genius' (*Major Works*, 692)—he has no such scruples when it comes directly to the songs he described to Hunt as 'wholly political', many written, but not published, in the aftermath of Peterloo.[14] In the half-dozen poems

---

[14] Shelley also claims in the *Defence* that 'A Poet, therefore, would do ill to embody his own conceptions of right and wrong' (*Major Works* 682) and goes on to note: 'Those in whom the poetical faculty, though great, is less intense, as Euripides, Lucan, Tasso, Spenser, have frequently affected a moral aim, and the effect of their poetry is diminished in exact proportion to the degree in which they compel us to advert to this purpose' (*Major Works*, 682). See also his dismissal of 'what is vulgarly

written along these lines, only one was published, it being bundled with *Prometheus Unbound* and printed the following year. The poem in question was originally entitled 'Ode to the Assertors of Liberty' (thus with a wide, even cosmopolitical frame of reference), but was subsequently renamed, circumscribing the referent, 'An Ode written October, 1819, before the Spaniards had recovered their Liberty'.[15] It is perhaps the poem of Shelley's most steeped in the language of the Bible, this time not for purposes of sarcasm but for rousing the nation, much as biblical prophets did. This ode is no one's idea of a great Shelley poem (it rarely makes it into even copious selections of his verse) but it is worth citing as an example of his biblically infused verse:

> Arise, arise, arise!
> There is blood on the earth that denies ye bread;
> Be your wounds like eyes
> To weep for the dead, the dead, the dead.
> What other grief were it just to pay?
> Your sons, your wives, your brethren, were they;
> Who said they were slain on the battle day?
>
> Awaken, awaken, awaken!
> The slave and the tyrant are twin-born foes;
> Be the cold chains shaken
> To the dust where your kindred repose, repose:
> Their bones in the grave will start and move,
> When they hear the voices of those they love,
> Most loud in the holy combat above.
>
> Wave, wave high the banner!
> When Freedom is riding to conquest by:
> Though the slaves that fan her
> Be Famine and Toil, giving sigh for sigh.
> And ye who attend her imperial car,
> Lift not your hands in the banded war,
> But in her defence whose children ye are.
>
> Glory, glory, glory,
> To those who have greatly suffered and done!
> Never name in story
> Was greater than that which ye shall have won.
> Conquerors have conquered their foes alone,
> Whose revenge, pride, and power they have overthrown
> Ride ye, more victorious, over your own.

termed a moral purpose' in the Preface to *The Cenci* (316). On the status of the 'wholly' and the implicitly political in Shelley's poetics see the superb analysis in ch. 1 of Forest Pyle, *A Radical Aestheticism in 'Our Romantic Movement'* ('From Which One Turns Away'), forthcoming from Fordham UP (2012).

[15] See James Bieri, *Percy Bysshe Shelley: Exile of Unfulfilled Renown, 1816–1822* (Baltimore: Johns Hopkins UP, 2005), 156.

> Bind, bind every brow
> With crownals of violet, ivy, and pine:
> Hide the blood-stains now
> With hues which sweet Nature has made divine:
> Green strength, azure hope, and eternity:
> But let not the pansy among them be;
> Ye were injured, and that means memory.

$$(H\ 575–6)$$

We encounter here many simple words and images from the lexicon of the Bible, though they are also often so common as not to be identifiable as simply or primarily biblical: 'blood', 'earth', 'bread', 'kindred', 'wounds', 'dead', 'brethren', 'slain', 'chains', 'dust', 'bones', 'grave', 'holy', 'famine', 'toil', 'glory', 'bind', and more, to say nothing of the conjunction of the 'crownals' of flowers in one line followed by 'blood-stains' in the next: it's all but impossible not to have an image of a crown of thorns flash up. Some terms, such as these last, call to mind specific verses but a good many do not: it often does not make much sense to trace or limit its sense to a specific biblical passage (as here with, say, 'dust', or 'blood'). It is not even clear that these biblically charged words are 'allusions' or citations. The terms, taken together, cast a kind of biblical aura over the whole poem, terms whose resonances are made the more emphatic by their proximity to the more direct biblical motifs and quasi-quotations in the poem. These most direct relations to the biblical text have to do mainly with the vatic stance. The simple, prophetic motif that resonates powerfully in Shelley's poem is the repeated call at the outset of some of the verse paragraphs: 'Arise! Arise! Arise!' and even more so 'Awaken! Awaken! Awaken!' These calls have numerous sources throughout the Hebrew scriptures, such as the call to Deborah in Judges 5: 12: 'Awake, awake, Deborah: awake, awake, utter a song' or Isaiah's in 26: 9: 'Awake and sing, ye that dwell in dust'. Poetry's task as well as prophecy's is equally to awake and to sing, and the activities seem linked. The exhortations in Shelley's poem might find their closest parallels in (Second) Isaiah 51 and 52, where three times in rapid succession we encounter the phrase 'Awake, Awake […]'. The overarching section encompassing the three occurrences of this wake-up call is more pivotal than most, outlining the immense change from wilderness to Eden, from desert to garden, with the Lord comforting his people through the mouth of his prophet in exile (thought to be toward the end of the Babylonian captivity), at least a dim analogue to Shelley's being in Italy, far removed from his native land. In the first iteration Isaiah's nation is, through the 'arm of the lord' (51: 9), exhorted to 'put on strength' and Steven Goldsmith, in one of the few good readings of the poem, shows how Shelley revises this passage to be about the oppressed putting on their own strength (though Shelley is perhaps at the same time invoking Isaiah 52: 1 in which Zion is directly urged to 'put on thy strength', which transfers the need for action to the humans).[16] At the same time Shelley's persona or speaker

---

[16] Steven Goldsmith, *Unbuilding Jerusalem: Apocalypse and Romantic Imagination* (Ithaca, NY: Cornell UP, 1993).

wonders about bones in the grave starting and moving, apparently answering in the affirmative the famous question posed in Ezekiel 37: 3: 'can these bones live?' Goldsmith glosses the results of Shelley's invocations and reworkings of so many biblical pre-texts in this way: 'By making the human voice the agent of apocalyptic liberation, Shelley sought to fit his "Popular Songs" into the agenda of the parliamentary reform movement, lending support to one of its primary objectives: the convening of a national assembly in which those deprived of representation would assert their right to speak outside the jurisdiction of the Parliament.'[17] Not all of this can be gleaned immediately from even the whole clutch of political songs but it is true that Shelley saw this group of poems being directly political and that for such poems a prophetic stance, with elementary diction rich in biblical allusion, was an apposite posture. The biblical verses most directly invoked in the 'Ode' have to do with the liberation of Israel and thus are an appropriate source for Shelley's poem so concerned to plead for liberty in his own time. Some of the biblical resonances in Shelley might strike readers as learned or erudite, yet Carlos Baker makes a case for the ready intelligibility of the political songs of 1819 as follows:

> As recently as the preceding summer he had agreed with the proposition that 'in order to move men to true sympathy,' one must use 'the familiar language of man,' although he had immediately specified that 'it must be the real language of men in general, and not that of any particular' class. In such a nominally Christian country as England, the vocabulary and syntax of the English Bible, suitably purged of the less familiar archaisms, will come very close to representing the *lingua communis* which Shelley sought to use as an instrument of communication. This may account for the 'semi-Biblical' tone of these half-dozen political poems.[18]

These political poems are indeed more direct and, in principle, more 'popular' because more simple. One tends not to get lost in these directly political poems the way one can in the vertiginous shifts of figure and ground informing *The Triumph of Life* or 'Mont Blanc'. Shelley suits the idiom to the purpose, calling on the commonly known language of the King James Bible, even when his political designs have nothing to do with religion per se. Often the most resonant allusions are the simplest. Northrop Frye comments as follows in the preface to *The Great Code*: 'Blake's line "O Earth, O Earth return," [...] though it contains only five words and only three different words, contains about seven direct allusions to the Bible. And in many nineteenth-century writers the cadences of the 1611 translation are constantly echoed, giving the effect rather like that of the echoes of popular proverbs in writings of other cultures.'[19]

In a good many of the directly or obliquely or even momentarily political poems, Shelley often draws on prophetic rhetoric, and indeed calls on a voice, as it were, as in the opening of the 'Ode to Liberty' presented as if overwhelming or taking

[17] Ibid. 240.
[18] Carlos Baker, *Shelley's Major Poetry* (New York: Russell & Russell, 1961), 158.
[19] Northrop Frye, *The Great Code* (New York: Harcourt, Brace, and Jovanovich, 1982), p. xii.

precedence over his own.[20] In *A Defence of Poetry*, poetry in general is famously aligned with the prophetic:

> Poets, according to the circumstances of the age and nation in which they appeared, were called, in the earlier epochs of the world, legislators, or prophets: a poet essentially comprises and unites both these characters. For he not only beholds intensely the present as it is, and discovers those laws according to which present things ought to be ordered, but he beholds the future in the present, and his thoughts are the germs of the flower and the fruit of latest time. Not that I assert poets to be prophets in the gross sense of the word, or that they can foretell the form as surely as they foreknow the spirit of events: such is the pretence of superstition, which would make poetry an attribute of prophecy, rather than prophecy an attribute of poetry. A poet participates in the eternal, the infinite, and the one; as far as relates to his conceptions, time and place and number are not. (*Major Works*, 677)

It is clear here and throughout *A Defence of Poetry* that we dealing with poetry in an 'expanded field'. Lord Bacon, Plato, and Livy are all, in Shelley's understanding, poets. The emphasis is on imagination and creativity, on founding and setting up things: hence the perhaps unexpected equation between poets and legislators. The attributes of poetry do not belong to this or that genre, this or that kind of discourse. Shelley's account of prophecy sensibly keeps its distance from a reductive notion of the biblical prophet as a predictor of events. Shelley was well aware of the demystifying rational(ist) criticism of the Bible, especially Spinoza's *Theological-Political Tractatus* (the whole of which Shelley is thought to have translated). The passages of Shelley's translation that do survive have to do mainly with the imagination of prophets, already a rather heterodox notion, since the prophets are understood, in a more orthodox vein, not to have 'imagined' anything but to have quoted and recorded. In the *Defence* Shelley does seem to want to have his visionary cake and eat it too: the poet/prophet has a privileged, authoritative access to the future but can't be pinned down to, much less held responsible for, an accurate, literal vision of the future. The poet/prophet is said to know the *spirit* of the future, even if elsewhere in the passage the same figure is conceived of as vaulting above all history and temporality into the ethereal empyrean of 'the eternal, the infinite and the one'. This accords rather well with the mythopoetic reworking of the Bible ushered in by Lowth's lectures and various allied attempts on the parts of critics to pry loose the mythical, poetic, highly figurative texture of the Scriptures from the narrow referentiality of what formerly counted as sacred historiography.[21] Shelley, moreover, is free to draw on the allegorical character of religious discourse, simultaneously true and false, to recast what might be false, at the level of doctrine or truth claim, into the domain of poetry proper, in which it is only ever

---

[20] Timothy Webb shows the pertinence of a note that seems to sketch out the various stages of the 'Ode to Liberty' and the plan begins with 'Isaiah 13 and 14'. See *Shelley: A Voice Not Understood* (Manchester: Manchester UP, 1977), 158.

[21] On the decline of the hegemony of the historical-referential sense of the Bible in the eighteenth century, see Hans Frei, *The Eclipse of Biblical Narrative* (New Haven: Yale UP, 1974).

true.[22] That Shelley is more interested in the spirit than in the matter of prophecy is in keeping with his poetic borrowings from the Bible which tend to emphasize form, especially the form of vision, over content, and image over idea.

That Shelley lays claim only to the spirit of prophecy fits well with the often rather abstract politics that accompany his prophetic calls. Who could be against, as the mountain is urged in 'Mont Blanc', repealing 'Large codes of fraud and woe' (*Major Works*, 122; l. 81)? Or when the trumpet of a prophecy sounds at the end of 'Ode to the West Wind', is anyone, much less 'unawakened earth', not going to welcome spring not being far behind winter (*Major Works*, 412)? The reader might well fill in these sketchy visions with a desirable politics of his or her own. In many of the prophetic poems, the precise politics are left up in the air. If they tend to come across as progressive or radical ('liberty' is not just any word or principle to invoke in Shelley's time) it is partly because we know from elsewhere Shelley's political views or because the biblical prophets were generally anti-monarchical and relentlessly calling on their people to 'reform'.

A key aspect of Shelley's poetic practice in the light of his theory of poetry as prophecy can be glimpsed in an instance of what might be called, in Hegelian parlance, a 'concrete universal': the chariot or what sometimes used to be called a 'car'. From *Queen Mab* through *Prometheus Unbound* to *The Triumph of Life*, this 'vehicle' is enlisted to allow the poet or his surrogate to transverse and survey broad swathes of history. Shelley's vehicle and his sometime vehicular narrator are on the move, poetry in motion. One source for the omniscient perspective, allowing the poet and us to see all of what is essential in human history, past, present, and future, is the chariot in Ezekiel, sometimes explicitly invoked by Shelley. The dazzling chariot from the opening chapters of Ezekiel, just as he has received his call to be a prophet, features four living figures built into the vehicle, each looking in different directions, which is in effect to say: everywhere. If translated from space to time, this would entail something like the omni-temporal views accorded Shelley's visionaries, from the fairies in *Queen Mab* to the only slightly less transcendent but still human Rousseau in *The Triumph of Life*. When Shelley most explicitly refers to the vision of and by the chariot, he does so with undercutting irony, but the biblical passage casts a shadow over many of his works. Some discontinuous verses from Ezekiel can convey a sense of the complexity and power of this vehicle of vehicles:

[4]   And I looked, and, behold, a whirlwind came out of the north, a great cloud, and a fire infolding itself, and a brightness was about it, and out of the midst thereof as the colour of amber, out of the midst of the fire.

[5]   Also out of the midst thereof came the likeness of four living creatures. And this was their appearance; they had the likeness of a man.

[6]   And every one had four faces, and every one had four wings.

[8]   And they had the hands of a man under their wings on their four sides; and they four had their faces and their wings.

---

[22] On the Janus-like character of Shelley's poetry and thought, see the incisive essay by Michael O'Neill, '"A Double Face of False and True": Poetry and Religion in Shelley', *Literature and Theology* 25.1 (March 2011), 32–46.

[9] Their wings were joined one to another; they turned not when they went; they went every one straight forward.

[12] And they went every one straight forward: whither the spirit was to go, they went; and they turned not when they went.

[13] As for the likeness of the living creatures, their appearance was like burning coals of fire, and like the appearance of lamps: it went up and down among the living creatures; and the fire was bright, and out of the fire went forth lightning.

[16] The appearance of the wheels and their work was like unto the colour of a beryl: and they four had one likeness: and their appearance and their work was as it were a wheel in the middle of a wheel.

[19] And when the living creatures went, the wheels went by them: and when the living creatures were lifted up from the earth, the wheels were lifted up.

[20] Whithersoever the spirit was to go, they went, thither was their spirit to go; and the wheels were lifted up over against them: for the spirit of the living creature was in the wheels.[23]

So many of the Shelleyan motifs are here and in the surrounding verses: cloud, whirlwind, fire, the poet's calling, but especially the chariot or *merkebah*. It is a dazzling passage, inviting yet all but defeating the reader's attempt to visualize the scenario. The chariot is a vehicle that negates any distinction between 'vehicle' and 'tenor', between material and spirit, since we are told as explicitly as can be that the spirit inheres in the very material. Allegory and symbol at one and the same time, the chariot, if one can accept Ezekiel's implicit claims, is the perfect poetic non-arbitrary signifier. One also sees here something that may leave its mark on Shelley more than most poets or at least constitute an affinity: the predominance of simile, the stress on likeness. Romantic poets are generally thought to tend to metaphor over simile.[24] Similes spell out comparisons though in some sense leave things more indeterminate than metaphor, which, on the face of it, entails total identification. Similes, by contrast, tend to be more 'rational', registering only similarities, without necessarily and not more or less absurdly pretending that two distinct entities are identical. Similes are, in a sense, more 'Enlightenment' than 'Romantic', more Humean than Blakean. In texts that have to do with the spiritual and the carnal, the heavenly and the earthly, similes preserve the tension or relation rather than collapse it. All of this fits neatly with Shelley's view of and relation to the Bible, a great source of similes, as we see in spectacular fashion in the opening of the Book of Ezekiel.

Harold Bloom was perhaps the first to draw attention to the stark effects of Shelley's summoning, in *The Triumph of Life*, the grand vision of Ezekiel's chariot only to conscript

---

[23] All passages from the Bible are cited from the King James Version.

[24] Susan Wolfson analyses a related dynamic in Coleridge, arguing that received ideas about organicism and metaphor have obscured the pervasive role of simile in his work. See *Formal Charges: The Shaping of Poetry in British Romanticism* (Stanford, CA: Stanford UP, 1999), ch. 3, 'The Formings of Simile: Coleridge's "Comparing Power"'.

it in a scene that runs counter to its biblical source, for in Shelley's last great, grim poem the charioteer and his chariot team up to have the blind leading the blind:

> So came a chariot on the silent storm
> Of its own rushing splendor, and a Shape
> So sate within, as one whom years deform,
>
> Beneath a dusky hood and double cape,
> Crouching within the shadow of a tomb;
> And o'er what seemed the head of a cloud-like crape
>
> Was bent, a dun and faint ethereal gloom
> Tempering the light. Upon the chariot-beam
> A Janus-visaged Shadow did assume
>
> The guidance of that wonder-wingéd team;
> The shapes which drew it in thick lightenings
> Were lost:—I heard alone on the air's soft stream
>
> The music of their ever-moving wings.
> All the four faces of that Charioteer
> Had their eyes banded; little profit brings
>
> Speed in the van and blindness in the rear,
> Nor then avail the beams that quench the sun—
> Or that with banded eyes could pierce the sphere
>
> Of all that is, has been, or will be done;
> So ill was the car guided—but it passed
> With solemn speed majestically on.
>
>   (86–106)

So many of the motifs fit exactly Ezekiel's vision that the likeness could hardly be more explicit were the name of the prophet invoked. Yet the precedent of Ezekiel's chariot is summoned to heighten the absolute contrast between the vision afforded to Shelley's 'shape' and that accorded to the enthroned charioteer of the Bible. The blindness on display in Shelley's poem is a visual correlative to the recurrent erasing of knowledge so distinctively outlined in the rest of the poem and charted notably by Paul de Man.[25] First the banded eyes of the charioteers imply total lack of vision but then the passage lurches to the diametrical opposite, a vision as total and absolute as can be, in a formula that recalls that associated with the veil of Isis: 'of all that is, has been, or will be done'. No sooner has this vision been summoned, the text returns the mode of error, with the chariot 'ill guided', back on track in the grim procession that Hazlitt glossed as a 'Dance of Death'.[26] How can the passage entertain such diametrically opposed possibilities?

---

[25] Paul de Man, 'Shelley Disfigured', in *The Rhetoric of Romanticism* (New York: Columbia UP, 1984), 93–123.

[26] William Hazlitt, 'Shelley's Posthumous Poems', *The Complete Works of William Hazlitt*, ed. P. P. Howe (London: Dent, 1933), XVI, 273. Hazlitt's review originally appeared in the *Edinburgh Review* 40 (July 1824).

Donald Reiman, after his painstaking work with the manuscript of the poem, thinks that '[t]he muddled syntax of these lines is but another evidence of the unfinished state of the poem'.[27] In any event, the passage as we have it alternates from negative to positive to negative, with the chariot providing the obverse of what Ezekiel's does. It's a key moment in a poem of almost relentless negativity, an apocalyptic poem, but an apocalypse without end, and not just because the poem does not quite end. If it does end, it is not with a bang or a whimper but with a question that suspends the central term or concern of the whole poem: life. The history in *The Triumph of Life*, unlike, say, the Enlightenment narrative of *Queen Mab*, is a history of error, forgetting, and erasure. But is this turning of the Bible against vision and against knowledge part of Shelley's being 'the least biblical' of poets? Not really, not simply. In turning the biblical motifs against their source, Shelley is accepting their imaginative power, which is a huge part of what matters to him.

In closing let us consider a less spectacular but more typical invocation of the Bible, this briefest of sequences, hardly a sequence, namely: the repeated injunction in the 'Ode to the West Wind' of the single word: 'Hear'. This single word cannot profitably be assigned to one and only one passage in the Bible (nor just to the Bible!). The repeated call to 'hear' is addressed to the west wind in a poem hardly pervaded by biblical imagery or ideas. And yet this poem, with its dizzying back and forth between poet and wind as the alternate givers and receivers of breath, of inspiration, ends by invoking the trumpet of a prophecy.

The word 'Hear' recalls many invocations from the prophets, such as this almost paradigmatic one from the opening of Isaiah (1: 2), which happens also to be the first instance of the word in the prophetic books: 'Hear, O heavens, and give ear, O earth: for the LORD hath spoken, I have nourished and brought up children, and they have rebelled against me.' Notice that here, as in Shelley's poem, no human being is addressed. The prophet speaks past, above, or beyond any possible listener or reader to a natural/supernatural entity and yet it is the reader or listener who hears these words. The fictional address adds, paradoxically, and by its very indirection, to the urgency and to the absolute claim of its content, as if of import to the world as such, to all of heaven and earth. Shelley's wind is only slightly less powerful and encompassing an entity than Isaiah's heaven. It is a creative (i.e. poetic) and destructive force that shapes natural and unnatural history. The emphasis on spirit in the ode is typical of Shelley's passionate engagement with a world beyond the immediately material, a world partly learned from Plato but in any event a spirit-realm distinct from but intermittently overlapping with Christian or Hebraic spirituality, in its tonality or imagery, if not its doctrine. For all of Shelley's similes and the odd metaphor, this realm remains 'hauntingly non-figurative', as Geoffrey Hartman remarks incisively.[28] There are, to be sure, some figures offered for the quasi-gods,

---

[27] See Donald H. Reiman, *Shelley's* The Triumph of Life: *A Critical Study, Based on a Text Newly Edited from the Bodleian Manuscript* (Urbana, IL: University of Illinois Press, 1965), 149.

[28] Geoffrey Hartman, 'Gods, Ghosts, and Shelley's "Atheos"', *Literature and Theology* 24.1 (March 2010), 13.

the 'unseen presence' of the 'Hymn to Intellectual Beauty' or the 'Power' of 'Mont Blanc', but they are accompanied by a clear sense of their inadequacy, emphasized by the multiplication of similes that only partly coincide with the posited spirit toward which they gesture. Much of this Shelley learned, despite the counter-example of Ezekiel's chariot whose vision he borrowed but undercut, from the book whose singular position in his canon was 'last, yet first [...]'.

SELECT BIBLIOGRAPHY

Baker, Carlos. *Shelley's Major Poetry*. New York: Russell & Russell, 1961.

Balfour, Ian. *The Rhetoric of Romantic Prophecy*. Stanford, CA: Stanford UP, 2002.

Barnard, Ellsworth. *Shelley's Religion*. Minneapolis: University of Minneapolis Press, 1937.

Beatty, Bernard. 'P. B. Shelley'. *The Blackwell Companion to the Bible in English Literature*. Ed. Rebecca Lemon et al. Chichester: Wiley-Blackwell, 2009. 451–62.

Bieri, James. *Percy Bysshe Shelley: Exile of Unfulfilled Renown, 1816–1822*. Baltimore: Johns Hopkins UP, 2005.

Bloom, Harold. *Shelley's Mythmaking*. Ithaca, NY: Cornell UP, 1959.

Brisman, Leslie. 'Review of Bryan Shelley, *The Interpreting Angel*'. *Keats–Shelley Journal* 44 (1995), 240–2.

—— 'Mysterious Tongue: Shelley and the Language of Christianity'. *Texas Studies in Language and Literature* 23 (1981), 389–411.

Brisman, Susan Hawk. '"Unsaying his High Language": The Problem of Voice in *Prometheus Unbound*'. *Studies in Romanticism* 16 (Winter 1977), 53–86.

Frye, Northrop. *A Study of English Romanticism*. New York: Columbia UP, 1968.

Hartman, Geoffrey. 'Gods, Ghosts, and Shelley's "Atheos"'. *Literature and Theology* 24.1 (March 2010), 4–18.

Jager, Colin. 'Shelley after Atheism'. *Studies in Romanticism* 49.4 (Winter 2010), 611–31.

Kugel, James. *The Idea of Biblical Poetry: Parallelism and its History*. New Haven: Yale UP, 1981.

Medwin, Thomas. *The Life of Percy Bysshe Shelley*. Ed. H. Buxton Forman. London: Oxford UP, 1913.

O'Neill, Michael. '"A Double Face of False and True": Poetry and Religion in Shelley'. *Literature and Theology* 25.1 (March 2011), 32–46.

Shelley, Bryan. *Shelley and Scripture*. Oxford: Clarendon Press, 1994.

Webb, Timothy. *Shelley: A Voice Not Understood*. Manchester: Manchester UP, 1977.

Wasserman, Earl R. *Shelley: A Critical Reading*. Baltimore: Johns Hopkins UP, 1971.

....

CHAPTER 27

SHELLEY, MYTHOLOGY, AND THE CLASSICAL TRADITION

....

ANTHONY JOHN HARDING

SHELLEY saw himself as working in an evolving but unbroken poetic tradition that descended from Homer, Hesiod, Aeschylus, Pindar, Virgil, Horace, and Lucretius, to Dante and Petrarch, Spenser, Shakespeare, and Milton. Indeed, whatever aspect of Shelley the reader turns to—his poetics, his political radicalism, his 'green romanticism', his hostility to religious dogma, or his ideas on sexuality—an understanding of the relevant works will sooner or later need to include how they extend and develop the classical tradition.

This is not to claim that Shelley was a neoclassical writer in the sense that he privileged, on principle, classical modes of thought or classical forms; still less, that he deferred uncritically to classical authorities, as a poet or as a thinker. Though he immersed himself in the literature of ancient Greece and Rome, re-engaging with Greek literature in particular after 1812, his response to the classical tradition was always creative and individual.[1] As Cythna, in *The Revolt of Islam*, expresses the poet's relationship to the past, speaking of the 'good and mighty of departed ages' with an astonishing boldness that immediately claims them as fellow-spirits: 'we | Are like to them—such perish, but they leave | All hope, or love, or truth, or liberty, | Whose forms their mighty spirits could conceive, | To be a rule and law to ages that survive' (*H* 126; 9: 28, ll. 3712, 3716–20). The Shelleyan values—hope, love, truth, liberty—are to be rediscovered through an existing tradition, pre-eminently the classical tradition. But, by a characteristic elision of historical time that avoids any disabling anxiety about the past as a burden, the poet affirms that *we are like to them*. Like them, of course, in being mortal; like them, too, in desiring to create 'forms' of hope, love, truth, liberty. Cythna is speaking to her lover and

---

[1] See the biographical testimony of T. J. Hogg: e.g. 'Shelley's delight was to read Homer, and it grew and strengthened with his years'— *Life of Percy Bysshe Shelley*, introd. Edward Dowden (London: Routledge, 1906), 479.

fellow revolutionary Laon, but the pronoun 'we' in these lines seems inclusive, embracing all readers, or at least all those who desire to be free.

Shelley rejects the notion that a poet's admiration for classical works would automatically lead him to imitate them, or simply repeat the story-lines of classical myths. The Greek tragic poets, he argues in the 'Preface' to *Prometheus Unbound*, 'by no means conceived themselves bound to adhere to the common interpretation, or to imitate in story as in […] title their rivals & predecessors […] The Agamemnonian story was exhibited on the Athenian theatre with as many variations as dramas' (MS. Shelley e.1 f 14^r, *BSM* IX, 58–9). In taking up the story of the Titan Prometheus, Shelley is clearly not engaged in anything we could call 'classicizing'—neither recreating the Athenian worldview, nor decorating a moral allegory with classical allusions—but rather creating his own, contemporary Prometheus. Such mythological language was an integral part of the power of imaging 'the operations of the human mind', as he put it in the Preface: 'the Greek poets, as writers to whom no resource of awakening the sympathy of their contemporaries was unknown, were in the habitual use of this power' (MS. Shelley e.1. f 16^r; *BSM* IX, 66–7).

It is evident, then, that Shelley conceived of classical culture, especially the Greek poets' ways of handling myth, as creatively liberating and as a force for good. 'What the Greeks were was a reality not a promise', he wrote in *A Discourse on the Manners of the Antient Greeks*: and yet, as he adds in a new thought that seems to contradict Cythna's assertion of our similarity to them, 'When we discover […] how far the most admirable community […] ever [formed] was removed from […] that perfection […] to which human society is impelled by some active power within each bosom, to aspire, how great ought to be our hopes, how resolute our struggles. For the Greeks of the Periclean age were widely different from us […]' (Shelley adds.e.11 'pages 28–30'; *BSM* XV, 30–2).

John Lehmann has suggested it was the impact of Italy that infused vitality into Shelley's poetry,[2] but it could be argued that, long before visiting Italy, Shelley had a fully awakened sense of the possibilities for intellectual and political renewal that were latent in the classical tradition. In this respect, Shelley participated in a contemporary, Europe-wide movement, which began some decades before his birth, and which aimed at finding in Greek literature and history the seeds of a new intellectual order that might liberate Europe from its oppressive superstructure of monarchy, aristocracy, and religious dogma.

SHELLEY, REPUBLICANISM, AND HELLENISM

Eighteenth-century revolutionary republicanism found precedents in classical antiquity, particularly in Roman history, for the models of civic virtue, free thought, and republican heroism that it needed. At the height of the 'age of absolutism', the French

[2] John Lehmann, *Shelley in Italy: An Anthology* (London: John Lehmann Ltd, 1947), 8.

monarchist author Perrault had equated the era of Louis XIV with the imperial Rome of Augustus; but revolutionary authors and political leaders, from Rousseau to Robespierre, turned to the history of the Roman republic, and to Athens and Sparta, considering themselves the heirs of Marcus Junius Brutus, Cato, and Lycurgus (legislator of Sparta). With Robespierre, such idealizations became the means of inspiring greater devotion to *la patrie*.[3]

An alternative vision of the ancient world, one that appealed more to most poets and artists, privileged Greek art and literature and the freedom of philosophical enquiry considered characteristic of Athens between the birth of Pericles and the end of the Peloponnesian War. While republican Rome might have evoked ideals of military heroism in the service of the state, it was not admired for artistic or literary achievements: it had no Sophocles, no Phidias, no Plato. As Shelley expressed it in *A Defence of Poetry*, 'the actions and forms of its social life never seem to have been perfectly saturated with the poetical element' (MS. Shelley adds.d.8 'page 26'; *BSM XX*, 202–3). The enthusiasm for all things Greek that gripped much of Europe in the age of Winckelmann, Goethe, Schiller, and Byron was aesthetically a turn away from excessive ornament towards what was perceived as simplicity; but it was also seen as a choice in favour of liberty, meaning both democratic politics and freedom for artists.

Winckelmann made the connection explicit in a pamphlet that was translated into English by Henry Fuseli as *Reflections on the Painting and Sculpture of the Greeks* (London, 1765): 'Art claims liberty'.[4] A later work set out the claim in more historically specific terms: 'In Athens, where, after the expulsion of the tyrants, a democratic form of government was adopted, in which the entire people had a share, the spirit of each citizen became loftier than that of the other Greeks [...] Here the arts and sciences established themselves [...]' (*Geschichte der Kunst des Alterthums* [1764], in Winckelmann, *Writings on Art*, 108).

Winckelmann helped to inspire the passionate Hellenism of Romantic-period writers in both Germany and the British Isles, but his work, rhapsodic rather than discriminating in style, fell out of favour in the 1800s. Nevertheless, one of his key themes did persist almost unchallenged: the argument that Greece, particularly Athens, owed its democratic spirit, its greatness in the arts and letters, and its presumed freedom of intellectual enquiry to the Mediterranean climate. This idea continued in circulation well into the nineteenth century: Schlegel's lectures on drama, delivered in Vienna in 1808, argued that open-air performance was integral to the very nature of Greek drama.

In the British Isles, the Greek Revival also owed much to the activities of the Dilettanti Society, which published a series of lavishly illustrated descriptive volumes on Greek art and architecture. Wealthy Englishmen journeyed to Greece in increasing numbers to see these incomparable works of art for themselves. Many of them, like John Cam

---

[3] See R. A. Leigh, 'Jean-Jacques Rousseau and the Myth of Antiquity in the Eighteenth Century', in R. R. Bolgar (ed.), *Classical Influences on Western Thought* A.D. *1650–1870* (Cambridge: Cambridge UP, 1979), 156.

[4] Johann Joachim Winckelmann, *Writings on Art*, sel. and ed. David Irwin (London: Phaidon, 1972), 64. On Winckelmann, see Timothy Webb, *English Romantic Hellenism 1700–1824* (Manchester: Manchester UP, 1982), 113–15.

Hobhouse, remarked on the painful contrast between the grandeur of the statues, friezes, and other relics, and the squalid conditions in which most modern Greeks had to live. The attractive picture of ancient Athens promulgated by Winckelmann in Germany, and by the Dilettanti Society in England, eventually led to a Europe-wide movement in support of Greek resistance to Ottoman rule.[5]

For Shelley, however, the Greece that mattered most was the Greece of Homer, Aeschylus, Euripides, Socrates, and Plato—that is, of poets and philosophers who raised questions about men's subjection to tyranny, their slavish obedience to the decrees of earthly tyrants and the arbitrary will of the gods. The Greek language, Shelley felt, pre-served the very spirit of the discourse in which these and other writers reflected on—and argued about—the human condition. Classical Greek was therefore a distillation of their minds, 'a type of the understandings of which it was the creation & the image' (*A Discourse*, MS. Shelley adds. e.11, 'page 18', *BSM* XV, 20–1). When unable to work on his own compositions because of personal distress or anxiety, Shelley would habitually turn to translating Greek texts: the elegies of Bion and Moschus in 1817 to 1818, Homeric Hymns from 1818 to 1820, Plato's *Symposium* in July 1818, Euripides' *Cyclops* in (proba-bly) 1819. In some sense, Shelley must have felt that this activity of translation was a way of bringing his burdened mind back to its best source of renewal, the Greek language.[6]

The fearless questioning of language *through* language, which for Shelley was the pre-dominant Athenian virtue, is exemplified in Cythna's story of how she appealed to Othman's sailors, who are taking her back to the Golden City, to free themselves from superstition; and how she then brought the same message to the city's inhabitants: 'with strong speech I tore the veil that hid | Nature, and Truth, and Liberty, and Love' (*H* 122; 9: 7, ll. 3523–4). The privileging of 'Nature' in this series is significant. Where a modern writer might well hesitate before suggesting an affinity between nature and the other concepts in the series, Shelley shared the view of his contemporaries that it was the close-ness of the ancient Greeks to the influences of nature, expressed in the very design of their temples and amphitheatres—which were open to the sky—that enabled them to come closer than any subsequent society has done to a perfect reconciliation of social harmony with individual freedom and accomplishment. As he wrote in a letter of January 1819 to Peacock, 'the Greeks [...] lived in a perpetual commerce with external nature and nourished themselves upon the spirit of its forms. Their theatres were all open to the mountains & the sky [...] Their temples were mostly upaithric; & the flying

[5] On the Dilettanti Society, see R. M. Ogilvie, *Latin and Greek: A History of the Influence of the Classics on English Life from 1600 to 1918* (London: Routledge and Kegan Paul, 1964), 78–9, and William St Clair, *Lord Elgin and the Marbles* (London: Oxford UP, 1967), 176. On European involvement in the Greek uprising, see William St Clair, *That Greece Might Still Be Free: The Philhellenes in the War of Independence* (London: Oxford UP, 1972), 13–65.

[6] For these dates (and analysis of Shelley's reasons for translating these and other works), see Timothy Webb, *The Violet in the Crucible: Shelley and Translation* (Oxford: Clarendon Press, 1976), 35–6, 63–4, 79. The reader interested in more detailed consideration of Shelley's translations from Latin and Greek should refer to chapters I–III of Webb's book, and to Michael O'Neill, 'Emulating Plato: Shelley as Translator and Prose Poet', in Alan M. Weinberg and Timothy Webb (eds.), *The Unfamiliar Shelley* (Farnham: Ashgate, 2009), 239–55.

clouds the stars or the deep sky were seen above' (*Letters: PBS* II, 74–5). The image of the roofless or 'upaithric' temple, which functions as a synecdoche for these notions of Greek imaginative responsiveness to external nature, became a central one in many of Shelley's mature poems.

The Mediterranean colouring of parts of *The Revolt of Islam*, and comparable passages in other works, have misled some readers into thinking that Shelley shared in the purely nostalgic, 'Arcadian' vision of Greece cultivated by some of his contemporaries. In the lines from *Adonais* beginning: 'Nor let us weep that our delight is fled' (l. 334), Shelley does revisit the regretful tone of Peacock's *Rhododaphne*—a poem full of nostalgia for the 'old mythologies'—while giving it a more passionate and protesting edge. But as Reiman argues in noting this debt, Shelley, unlike his friend, 'could not sit apart as a spectator and enjoy the human comedy'.[7] In the strong attraction he felt for the culture of ancient Greece and its Italian colonies, there was little nostalgia. He valued the classical past for what the present might learn from it; and Greek mythology as a poetic expression of the ancient Greeks' responsiveness to the powers of nature and of the human passions.

As Jonathan Sachs has shown, while Shelley invariably refers to both Athens and Rome when he writes about the spread of liberty through the world, Athens is nearer to being his constant ideal and model.[8] Rome occupies a more ambiguous position, its relatively brief existence as a republic being overshadowed by its subsequent history of imperial conquest. However, in the 'Ode to Liberty', written in response to the Spanish liberal revolution of 1820, there is evidence that Shelley had begun to rethink the relationship between Greece and Rome. This poem is the first to present 'a more nuanced vision in which antiquity continues to be relevant for the present, but only as mediated through an understanding of the complex historical process by which the legacy of the past is transmitted to the present'.[9]

The real importance of the distinction between Peacock's dilettantish view of classical literature and Shelley's more engaged and polemical one is apparent in the passage already cited above, from *A Discourse*: 'What the Greeks were was a reality not a promise.' The claim that the history of the Greeks was a 'reality, not a promise' would have been for Shelley's contemporaries a direct blow against the Christian religion.[10] The declaration in Shelley's essay not only holds up the achievements of the Greeks as a 'real' history that—however mediated by later reinterpretation—can still be an inspiration to those

---

[7] Donald H. Reiman, *Intervals of Inspiration: The Skeptical Tradition and the Psychology of Romanticism* (Greenwood, FL: Penkevill Publishing Co., 1988), 226.

[8] Jonathan Sachs, *Romantic Antiquity: Rome in the British Imagination, 1789–1832* (Oxford: Oxford UP, 2010), 148, 155. Ann Wroe's remark is also apt: 'Shelley did not hanker for that Golden Age [...] Instead, he mourned above all the disappearance of the Athenian democracy'; *Being Shelley* (London: Vintage, 2008), 59.

[9] Sachs, *Romantic Antiquity*, 159–60.

[10] In *The Excursion* Book I, the Wanderer, alone among the mountains and immersed in a 'still communion', reflects on 'how beautiful, how bright, appeared | The written promise!'—William Wordsworth, *The Excursion*, I. 215, 222–3, *Poetical Works*, ed. E. de Selincourt and Helen Darbishire, 5 vols. (Oxford: Clarendon Press, 1943–9), V, 15.

who hope for a better future for the human race; it simultaneously undercuts the Christian notion of a covenant between God and humankind by diminishing it to a mere 'promise', based on a superseded metaphysic.

EARLY POETRY TO *THE REVOLT OF ISLAM*

Most of Shelley's biographers mention that, as a pupil at Eton and subsequently at Oxford, Shelley excelled at composing Latin verses.[11] In an era when every boy attending a public school was expected to show competence at such exercises, this talent would be of little interest were it not for the fact that Mary Shelley and T. J. Hogg both connect it to his continued study of poetic form and poetic language. As Hogg puts it, 'he had [...] diligently studied the mechanism of his art before he came to Oxford'.[12] Mary Shelley, in her note on *Queen Mab*, refers to Shelley's 'severe classical taste, refined by the constant study of the Greek poets' (*H* 826). The crucial point here is that both Hogg's account and Mary Shelley's emphasize not only how intensively Shelley studied the classical poets, but how seriously he strove to rise to their level. This remains true despite his reaction against the academic study of Greek and Latin, expressed in a July 1812 letter to Godwin: 'the evils of acquiring Greek & Latin considerably overbalance the benefits' (*Letters: PBS* I, 316).

It is well known that in 1816, when Byron and Shelley were together in Switzerland, Shelley read Aeschylus' *Prometheus Bound* to Byron, translating as he went. Timothy Webb notes that whereas Byron 'did little more translating from the classics after school', for Shelley such work 'became increasingly important'.[13] Since Shelley was a writer for whom language was much more than a passive medium—a writer who knew that to transform language is to transform the world—Shelley's immersion in the classics, and particularly his rededication to the study of the Greek poets, need to be borne in mind by anyone interested in Shelley's poetics or in his ideas about language.

Shelley's career as poet and thinker is marked by the early renewal of his interest in Greek literature, and a corresponding diminishment in his reading of Latin authors, except for Virgil, Horace, Lucretius, and Lucan. In Webb's view, 'his education in Greek really began' in the autumn of 1812, when he met Peacock.[14] Nevertheless, it would be a mistake to assume that classical literature had a negligible influence on his work prior to 1812. The poetry Shelley wrote or co-authored before going up to Oxford is rich in classical quotations and allusions, as one would expect for a young man of his class and educational background. However, some of the allusions go beyond the stock repertoire. The reference to the prophetic powers of the Wandering Jew, in the poem on that popular Gothic subject which he may have co-written with Thomas Medwin—'The past, the present, and to come, | Float in review before my sight' (III. 238–9, *CPPBS* I, 68)—is a common formulation,

---

[11] Hogg's testimony was that 'He composed Latin verses with singular facility'. Thomas Jefferson Hogg, *The Life of Percy Bysshe Shelley*, introd. Edward Dowden (London: G. Routledge & Sons, 1906), 133.

[12] Ibid.   [13] Webb, *The Violet in the Crucible*, 29.   [14] Ibid. 53–4.

usually traced to Virgil's *Georgics* IV. 393: 'quae sint, quae fuerint, quae mox ventura trahantur'.[15] Similarly, the epigraph to canto IV of the poem, five lines from Aeschylus' *Eumenides* spoken by Orestes to the Furies, is a standard classical topos. Other examples, however, show a more inventive deployment of Shelley's already extensive knowledge of the classics. One dramatic instance occurs in a speech Paulo, the Jew, makes to Rosa, in canto I: '"ah!" cried he, "be this the band | Shall join us, till this earthly frame, | Sinks convulsed in bickering flame [...]"' ('The Wandering Jew', I. 261–3, *CPPBS* I, 51). The lines allude to a well-known saying, sometimes attributed to Aeschylus: 'When I die the earth is mingled with fire.' Cicero, who quoted it in *De Finibus*, without attributing it to Aeschylus, commented that it was a 'wicked and inhuman' utterance, since the speaker is implying that he does not care if after his death there should be a universal conflagration (*CPPBS* I, 213). By placing a similar utterance in the mouth of Paulo, the Wandering Jew, Shelley gives Paulo's apocalyptic prediction a still more sinister relevance.

Beyond these individual instances of allusions to classical sources, there is considerable evidence in the early poetry that Shelley was already capable of skilfully adopting poetic forms and rhetorical structures. One of the lyrics in the 'Victor and Cazire' poems, 'Song. To ——', has a rhetorical structure based on a passage in Lucretius, the opening of Book II of *De Rerum Natura*: 'Sweet it is [...] to gaze from the land on another's great struggles [...] But nothing is more gladdening than to dwell in the calm regions [...]'.[16] And in the Esdaile Notebook, poems that adapt or imitate classical forms include 'The Crisis', which imitates the Latin Sapphic used by Horace and Catullus; 'To Death', an irregular Pindaric; and 'A Dialogue—1809', modelled on the classical philosophical dialogue (*CPPBS* II, 338, 411).

In several important ways, Lucretius was a crucial influence on *Queen Mab*. If the materialist philosophy, anti-religious polemic, and progressivist politics of the poem were indebted to the work of the Baron d'Holbach, Thomas Paine, and William Godwin, and the idea of a dream-vision that incorporated a 'cosmic perspective on human history' was derived from Volney's *Les Ruines*, it was in Lucretius that Shelley found a model for the poetic treatment of his themes.

Shelley read *De Rerum Natura* in 1810, and again in 1816, 1819, and 1820.[17] That Shelley should have seen the poem as admirable in itself, and as one model for his own poetry, is perhaps not surprising. At the beginning of the first century BCE, when Titus Lucretius Carus was born, most educated Romans had given up the old religious traditions. Lucretius was a follower of the Greek thinker Epicurus, and in Book I of *De Rerum Natura* he sets out Epicurus' theory that the bodies or masses that form our universe originate from chance collisions of atoms falling through space. Everything that exists can ultimately be explained by the laws of physics. In a universe so constituted, there is no need to hypostatize gods and goddesses, though Lucretius' poem does open with an

---

[15] *P. Vergili Maronis Opera*, ed. F. A. Hirtzel (Oxford: Clarendon Press, 1900), unpaginated.

[16] *Titi Lucreti Cari de Rerum Natura Libri Sex*, ed. and trans. Cyril Bailey, 3 vols. (Oxford: Clarendon Press, 1966), I, p. 237; *De Rerum Natura*, I. 1–2, 7–8.

[17] Paul Turner, 'Shelley and Lucretius', *Review of English Studies* NS 10 (1959), 269.

invocation to Venus, now identified with the creative power of Nature itself. Lucretius clearly saw religion as a harmful institution, and, in lines that Shelley quoted in one of the epigraphs to *Queen Mab*, he states his purpose as being to free his readers from the anxiety and false hopes that still exercise such power: 'because I teach about great things, and hasten to free the mind from the close bondage of religion' ('primum quod magnis doceo de rebus et artis | religionum animum nodis exsolvere pergo'—*De Rerum Natura*, I, pp. 362–3; IV. 6–7). The idea that human beings have a soul that is distinct from the body but not immortal comes from Lucretius (*De Rerum Natura*, III. 136–46). As a moralist, Lucretius also follows Epicurus' reasoning: that one should strive to be moderate in one's desires, taking pleasure in the natural world and viewing human existence from the perspective of a contemplative non-believer.

In addition to these more general ideas, scholars have identified some passages in *Queen Mab* that are direct paraphrases of passages in *De Rerum Natura*. The opening of Book II of Lucretius' poem, with its judgement that 'nothing is more gladdening than to dwell in the calm regions, firmly embattled on the heights by the teaching of the wise [...]' (II. 7–8; I, pp. 236–7), is imitated at the climactic end of *Queen Mab* II: 'The Spirit seemed to stand | High on an isolated pinnacle; | The flood of ages combating below [...]' (*Norton 1*, 27; II. 252–4). In some key passages, the image of the axe of radical reform cutting down the tree of an oppressive monarchy is merged with Lucretius' description of the poisonous tree: 'There is, too, a tree on the great mountains of Helicon, which is wont to kill a man with the noisome scent of its flower' (*De Rerum Natura*, VI. 786–7; I, pp. 554–5). This idea is taken up in *Queen Mab* IV. 82–9; V. 44–5, and VI. 207–8.[18]

Lucretius offered Shelley a strong classical precedent for an anti-religious didactic poem that celebrates in descriptive verse the wonders of the natural world. It seems likely, too, that Shelley felt some empathy with this Roman writer who was a devoted admirer of a Greek philosopher, and whose personal life was troubled. In *A Discourse*, Shelley praised Lucretius along with Virgil and Horace as Roman poets whose dedication to Greek models saved them from the gross lapses of taste, and debased morals, that marred the works of Catullus, Martial, Juvenal, and Suetonius.[19] Later, when he no longer embraced the uncompromising materialism of *Queen Mab*, Shelley expressed regret that Lucretius 'limed the wings of his swift spirit in the dregs of the sensible world', but still ranked him as a poet above even Virgil (*A Defence of Poetry*, *Norton 1*, 494, 499). Shelley continued to draw on what clearly were for him powerful Lucretian images. For instance, the desire to bring light to the darkness of human error, evoked many times in *De Rerum Natura* (I. 146–8, II. 59–61, III. 1–2, 91–3), is claimed by Cythna in *The Revolt of Islam*: 'When I go forth alone, bearing the lamp | Aloft which thou hast kindled in my heart, | Millions of slaves from many a dungeon damp | Shall leap in joy [...]' (*H* 63; I. 44, ll. 1055–8), an allusion to Lucretius' lines addressed to Epicurus at the opening of Book III. The phrase 'daedal earth', which occurs in 'Mont Blanc', 'Hymn of Pan', and 'Ode to

---

[18] The indebtedness of these lines to Lucretius is pointed out ibid. 270, 276.

[19] *A Discourse*, in *Shelley's Prose, or, The Trumpet of a Prophecy*, ed. David Lee Clark (Albuquerque, NM: University of New Mexico Press, 1954), 223.

Liberty', is adapted from Lucretius' 'daedala tellus' (*De Rerum Natura*, I. 7).[20] It could be argued, too, that the 'faith so mild, | So solemn, so serene' of 'Mont Blanc' (*Norton 1*, 91; ll. 77–8) is a version of the Lucretian philosophy.

Yet from about 1814 onwards, as critics since Newman Ivey White have mostly agreed, what took the foremost place in Shelley's intellectual agenda was not Holbachian, Lucretian, or Epicurean materialism, but scepticism—though it should immediately be noted that Shelley's was a scepticism that looked on all attempts to make sense of the universe as creative, and rich in poetic value. Whatever else can be said about Shelley's scepticism, it allowed him the freedom to reinvigorate the imaginative resources of Greek mythology, without which there would have been no *Prometheus Unbound*.

C. E. Pulos, following White, dates Shelley's rejection of materialism between 1814 and 1816, and suggests that *Alastor* was his first poetic attempt to 'adjust his concept of Beauty to a sceptical theory of knowledge'.[21] The image with which the Poet falls in love is not a manifestation of some transcendental power, but a pure creation of his own mind. If this is correct as a gloss on *Alastor*, it also pinpoints the productive tension that existed between Shelley's mature scepticism, which would deny the objective existence of beauty and other values, and the poet's self-dedication to 'intellectual' (that is, non-material) beauty, almost as if such beauty *did* have unchanging though not objective existence, in some other realm. The closing stanzas of *The Revolt of Islam* hint at such a hope.

The parallels between Laon and the poet-figure in *Alastor* become clearer when placed in relation to the lines from Pindar's Tenth Pythian Ode that form the epigraph to *The Revolt of Islam*. These lines recalled for Pindar's audience the unequalled achievement of the father of Hippokleas, victor in the boys' *diaulos* in the Pythian Games of 498 BCE:

> '[The bronze heaven is never his to scale,]
> but as for all the glories which our mortal race
>   attains, he completes the furthest voyage.
> And traveling neither by ship nor on foot could you find
>   the marvelous way to the assembly of the Hyperboreans.[22]

The metaphor of the 'furthest voyage' that a mortal man can take, and the reference to the mythical Hyperboreans, a peaceful, contented nation said to worship Apollo, both suggest the unattainability of the ideal, and yet the heroism of the one who strives to reach it. This theme recurs in later works with a more 'Platonic' colouring, adopting Plato's story (from the *Phaedrus*) of the soul that begins its journey towards the Ideal, borne upward by the chariot of earthly existence, but is increasingly weighed down by mortality, a *mythos* present in both *Adonais* and *The Triumph of Life*.[23]

---

[20] These allusions are also noted by Turner, 'Shelley and Lucretius', 271, 275.

[21] C. E. Pulos, *The Deep Truth: A Study of Shelley's Scepticism* (Lincoln, NE: University of Nebraska Press, 1954), 42, 81.

[22] Pythian Odes X. 27–30, in *Pindar: Olympian Odes, Pythian Odes*, ed. and trans. William H. Race, Loeb Classical Library (Cambridge, MA: Harvard UP, 1997), 361. Shelley omitted the first of these lines. The 'diaulos' is a double-course race: the competitors run up to a mark and then back again.

[23] See James A. Notopoulos, *The Platonism of Shelley: A Study of Platonism and the Poetic Mind* (1949; repr. New York: Octagon, 1969), 312.

The sceptic's way of questioning religious faith appears in Cythna's speech to the sailors, when she undermines their credulous form of religion by explaining to them that the Power they superstitiously worship is merely the narcissistic reflection of an ancient sophist's dark soul: 'The Form he saw and worshipped was his own, | His likeness in the world's vast mirror shown [...]' (*H* 115; VIII. 6, ll. 3246–8). Shelley is paraphrasing a theory advanced by Euripides (who, according to a classical source, put it in the mouth of a character named Sisyphus, in a satyr play): that the invention of the gods can be ascribed to one shrewd man. It is a version of Democritus' theory that the worship of the gods results from the human desire for explanations.[24] In *The Revolt of Islam*, then, Shelley took the sceptical classical account of the invention of the gods, an account found in a fragment by Euripides; and by placing it in the mouth of the prophetess and liberator Cythna, and adding a psychological dimension—the reference to the human tendency to metaphysical narcissism—gave it a distinctly modern, anti-religious twist.

Prometheus Unbound

Though Shelley had been familiar with the works of Aeschylus since his years at Eton, *Prometheus Unbound* marks a new level of complexity in his response to this most mythologically complex of Greek dramatists.[25] Shelley's sense of the poetic power inherent in the Prometheus story is already apparent in one of the Esdaile Notebook poems, 'To Death': 'And on some rock whose dark form glooms the sky | To stretch these pale limbs when the soul is fled, | To baffle the lean passions of their prey, | To sleep within the chambers of the dead!—' (ll. 31–4, *CPPBS* II, 52). Here, however, the attempt to turn the notion of a lonely death into something more heroic is made at the cost of the myth's richer significance. For his own era, as Shelley came to realize, the most potent aspect of the Prometheus story was the recollection that it was Prometheus himself who first gave power to Jupiter; and the related circumstance that the Titan cannot die, but continues to endure, until the hour when his tormentor is overthrown. And yet the attraction of death, offering release from ages of mental anguish, is still a powerful undercurrent in Act I of *Prometheus Unbound*, an ever-present human temptation. Prometheus ('forethinker') can foresee the suffering to come. His compassion for humanity, the 'beloved race', is what makes his refusal to submit truly heroic.

The major dramatic premise of Act I, the seemingly unending trial of wills between Prometheus and Jupiter, is Shelley's point of departure from Aeschylus' *Prometheus Bound*. Aeschylus also provides Shelley with other crucial points in the dramatic situation:

---

[24] The source referred to is a second-century compendium of philosophical opinions, once thought to be by Plutarch, now ascribed to the otherwise unknown author Aëtius. See David T. Runia, 'Atheists in Aëtius: Text, Translation and Comments on *De Placitis* 1.7.1–10', *Mnemosyne* 49.5 (1996), 543–5, 548. See also Martin Ostwald, 'Atheism and the Religiosity of Euripides', in Todd Breyfogle (ed.), *Literary Imagination, Ancient and Modern* (Chicago: University of Chicago Press, 1999), 41.

[25] Mary Quinn summarizes evidence for Shelley's rereading of Aeschylus in 1819–20 in *MYR* IV, p. xxxi.

Prometheus' knowledge of the tyrant-deity's eventual downfall ('the day will come when Zeus, howbeit stubborn of soul, shall be humbled');[26] Hermes' role as both interrogator of Prometheus and reluctant messenger bringing news of Jupiter's decrees; and the agony of Prometheus as he foresees the sufferings of humanity, which in Aeschylus' play are reported by Io, and in Shelley's are evoked by the chorus of Furies. Mercury, in *Prometheus Unbound*, is particularly close to the Hermes figure in Aeschylus' drama. When Mercury asks Prometheus 'Thou knowest not the period of Joves power?', he speaks as does Aeschylus' Hermes, a figure that could be glossed as intelligence in the service of the divinely ordained feudal order. Yet Shelley gives him the strikingly modern characteristic of rather puzzled compassion for Prometheus: 'Alas I wonder at, yet pity thee' (MS. Shelley e.1 f 42^r, 42^v; *BSM* IX, 170–1, 172–3)—reinterpreting Hermes as a servant of the old order, who is aware of his own subjugation, but lacks courage to free himself.

The role played by the Furies—figures derived from Aeschylus' *Oresteia* trilogy—also exemplifies the close intermeshing of 'psychological' with 'political' themes. Their interaction with Prometheus raises the frightening possibility that, if the mind can become good by contemplating a form of virtue, it may equally become evil by looking upon evil. In a sinister version of the Narcissus myth, Prometheus is afraid of becoming what he looks on: 'Methinks I grow like what I contemplate | And laugh & stare in loathsome sympathy' (MS. Shelley e.1 f 43^v; *BSM* IX, 176–7). That the Champion of mankind is here made to glimpse his own 'sympathy' with the agents of despotism is a mark of the maturity and complexity with which Shelley is now handling his classical sources.

Also reconceived in mythological terms is the key moment prepared for in Act II and enacted in Act III when Demogorgon, the 'fatal child' of Jupiter's union with Thetis, commands Jupiter to abandon his throne, and follow him down to the abyss, the place of non-existence. There is powerful dramatic irony in Jupiter's claiming triumph—'Rejoice{\}! henceforth I am omnipotent' (MS. Shelley e.3 f 11^v; *BSM* IX, 376–7)—at the very moment when, as the reader already knows, his reign is about to end. When Jupiter asks the identity of the shape that confronts him, Demogorgon's answer, 'Eternity—demand no direr name', recalls Jupiter's description of Thetis as 'Image of Eternity' (MS. Shelley e.3 ff 13^v, 14^v; *BSM* IX, 384–5, 388–9). The god's very lust for the 'Image of Eternity' has engendered the child that will end his reign.

As the hour of Jupiter's downfall arrives, the refusal of humankind to accept its subjugation is also crucial, as even Jupiter recognizes:

alone

> The soul of man, like unextinguished fire
> Yet burns towards Heaven [...]

---

[26] *Aeschylus*, with translation by Herbert Weir Smyth, Loeb Classical Library, 2 vols. (London: William Heinemann, 1930), I, 297 (*Prometheus Bound*, ll. 908–9). George Thomson's translation is more vigorous: 'And yet one day, for all his arrogance, | This Zeus shall grovel'—*Aeschylus: The Oresteia Trilogy; Prometheus Unbound*, trans. George Thomson, introd. Robert W. Corrigan (New York: Dell, 1965), 154.

In tameless insurrection, which might make
Our antique empire insecure, though built
On eldest faith, & Hell's coeval, fear [...].

(MS. Shelley e.3 f 11ᵛ; *BSM* IX, 376–7)

The passage exposes Jupiter's presumptuous belief that the child he has begotten on Thetis will bring him final victory over the continuing 'tameless insurrection' of the human race against him. In fact, the arrival of Demogorgon signals the emergence of the human race from their long period of subjection to a theology of 'fear'. The Blakean pairing of 'faith' with 'fear', and the reference to Jove's reign as an 'antique empire', make the contemporary relevance of the passage sufficiently pointed; but these terms are also strictly Aeschylean in origin, demonstrating again how successful Shelley was at imaginatively radicalizing his classical sources.

In Act IV, the chorus of Hours becomes a way of registering the complete revolution the world has undergone. Now 'This true fair world of things' (MS. Shelley e.1 f 12ᵛ; *BSM* IX, 52–3) is ruled over by Love, a goddess owing something to Lucretius' Venus in the opening lines of *De Rerum Natura*, who transforms the earth itself as well as the human beings who inhabit and imagine it.

The Witch of Atlas, 'Song of Apollo', 'Song of Pan'

Shelley himself alludes indirectly to the youthful and mercurial characteristics of *The Witch of Atlas* in the dedicatory poem 'To Mary', in which he compares the poem to a 'young kitten' (MS. Shelley d.1 f15ʳ; *BSM* IV, Part 1, 84–5). For Shelley *The Witch of Atlas* was in part an experiment in a new poetic voice and a more playful mode of mythological invention. Its close relationship to the Homeric Hymn which Shelley translated in July 1820 as 'Hymn to Mercury' has long been recognized. As Webb notes, 'the activities of the witch herself seem to be an extension of the playfulness of the child-god, only now the practical jokes have been redirected to the redemption of society [...]'.[27]

For the mythological argument of the poem, however, the account of the Witch's parentage is equally important. Shelley makes her a daughter of Apollo, and thereby (as it were) writes her into the significant relationship that the Homeric Hymn established between the sun-god and his younger brother, Hermes/Mercury. There are clear parallels between the union of Zeus with Maia, which engenders the young god Hermes—'child of Maia & of Jove | Who rules Cyllene & Pastoral Arcady | Heavens messenger!' (MS. Shelley adds.e.9 'page 119'; *BSM* XIV, 126–7)—and the union of Apollo with one of the Atlantides that engenders Shelley's Witch. The 'cavern' in which

---

[27] Webb, *The Violet in the Crucible*, 78.

she is begotten and born recalls the cavern where Jove and Maia lay together, 'unseen by Gods or men' (ibid.):

> with the living form
> Of this embodied Power, the cave grew warm
>   5
> A lovely lady garmented in light
> From her own beauty [...].
>
> (MS. Shelley d.1 f17ᵛ; *BSM* IV, Part 1, 94–5)

The garment of light signifies the Witch's descent from Apollo, while the sea-imagery reflects her mother's role as a sea-nymph. The moon-imagery borrows in a general way from the Homeric Hymn to the Moon (see MS. Shelley adds.e.12, 'pages 226–225 rev', *BSM* XVIII, 266–7). The Witch also resembles Orpheus, in her ability to attract and tame the wild beasts: 'her low voice was heard like love, & drew | All living things towards this wonder new' (MS. Shelley d.1 f18ʳ; *BSM* IV, Part 1, 96–7). She has a mysteriously erotic relationship with Pan (stanza 9), and attracts to her rocky cavern a variety of outlandish mythological creatures and monsters—centaurs, satyrs, 'Polyphemes', and others without names—all of whom her love subdues (stanzas 10–11).

Perhaps the most productive group of images and ideas associated with Shelley's renewed interest in mythology is the cluster of ideas about the 'Orphic' power of language to arouse the feelings of the hearer, and thereby to change his or her perceptions.[28] The notion of music and its sister art, poetry, as a way of subduing destructive passions, and ultimately redeeming a contentious world, informs *Prometheus Unbound* Act IV, *The Witch of Atlas*, the two songs contributed to Mary Shelley's play *Midas*, and stanzas 27–9 of *Adonais* (though *Adonais* is more closely indebted to classical elegies, especially those of Bion and Moschus).

The 'Hymn to Mercury' contains one dramatic example, the story of how Mercury fashions the first lyre out of a tortoise-shell, then, when Apollo is angry with him for stealing his cattle, charms away his older brother's anger by playing to him on the new instrument: 'he changed his plan, & with ~~sweet~~ <strange> skill | ~~Soothed Vanquished~~ Subdued the strong Latonian by the might | Of winning ~~harmony~~ music' (MS. Shelley adds.e.9 'page 161', *BSM* XIV, 168–9). (Shelley's rejection of 'Soothed' then 'Vanquished' in favour of 'Subdued' is worth noting. There is something of this Mercury in the Pan of 'Song of Pan', for Pan also 'changed [his] pipings' to move his hearer's feelings.) Mercury then offers the lyre to Apollo, cleverly flattering him by predicting that Apollo's skill will 'interrogate it well' (MS. Shelley adds.e.9 'page 168'; *BSM* XIV, 176–7).[29]

---

[28] See Rousseau on the power of speech. A simple gesture can demonstrate a fact, but when it's a question of moving the heart, discourse becomes necessary: 'lorsqu'il est question d'émouvoir le cœur et d'enflammer les passions, c'est toute autre chose [...] Le discours sans geste vous arrachera des pleurs'—Jean-Jacques Rousseau, *Essai sur l'origine des langues*, ed. Charles Porset (Bordeaux: Guy Ducros, 1970), 35.

[29] This presumed link between poetic/musical invention and trickery, particularly evident in the Homeric 'Hymn to Hermes', is illuminatingly discussed in chapter 7 of Cora Angier Sowa's *Traditional Themes and the Homeric Hymns* (Chicago: Bolchazy-Carducci Publishers, 1984), 198–211.

The two songs from *Midas* encapsulate in playful, parodic mythological form one aspect of the revaluation of poetic language that was clearly at the forefront of Shelley's thoughts during the writing of *Prometheus Unbound* and afterwards.[30] Poetic language as a form of benign trickery, transforming one thing into another—the 'mercurial' heritage of language—is acknowledged in 'Song of Pan'; and the truth-telling, prophetic, legislative role of language is reflected in 'Song of Apollo'. In the classical account of the contest (Ovid, *Metamorphoses*, Book XI), the presumption is that Apollo, as a member of the Olympian pantheon and the patron of music and poetry, is predestined to be the victor. Mary Shelley's play changes both the order of the songs—Apollo being the first to perform in her version—and the balance of sympathy among the characters, destabilizing the hierarchy implicit in the classical text.

For 'Song of Apollo', Shelley draws on two classical sources in addition to Ovid: the Homeric 'Hymn to the Sun', which he had translated earlier in 1820, and Lucretius' *De Rerum Natura*. The 'Hymn to the Sun' pictures Apollo as a warrior-deity, with 'awe inspiring eyes' from which 'are shot forth afar, clear beams of light' (MS. Shelley adds.e.12 'page 221 rev'; *BSM* XVIII, 260–1). The metaphorical connection between beams of light and weapons—javelins or arrows—is strengthened by association with a passage in *De Rerum Natura* referring to 'bright shafts of day' ('lucida tela diei').[31] Both passages are alluded to in the lines 'The sunbeams are my shafts with which I kill | Deceit, that loves the night & fears the day' (MS. Shelley d.2 f 22ʳ; *BSM* X, 96–7). Pan's song is more attuned to another reality, the human one of change and loss, 'disappointment and suffering'.[32]

Hellas

Shelley's dramatic poem on the War of Greek Independence was written, as Shelley noted in the Preface, 'at the suggestion of the events of the moment'. In one sense, *Hellas* resulted from his lifelong pursuit of the goal of universal human freedom, which was based on the historical 'reality' of what the Greeks had once been. Like other European philhellenes, then, Shelley was immediately fired by sympathy for the 1821 uprising of Greeks against Ottoman rule. His friendship with Prince Alexander Mavrocordato, whom he met in Pisa in December 1820, may have drawn him to identify more closely with the cause, but it was one he was strongly predisposed to support when news of the uprising reached Pisa in April 1821. He began *Hellas* in October of that year.

In taking Aeschylus' *The Persians* as his model, Shelley was basing his own drama on a text already fraught with historical significance: not only the fact that it celebrates the historic victory of the Greek fleet over the Persians at Salamis in 480 BCE, but also that its

[30] See Anthony John Harding, *The Reception of Myth in English Romanticism* (Columbia, MO: University of Missouri Press, 1995), 192.
[31] *De Rerum Natura*, I. 146–8; II. 59–61; III. 91–3. See Turner, 'Shelley and Lucretius', 274.
[32] Milton Wilson, *Shelley's Later Poetry: A Study of his Prophetic Imagination* (New York: Columbia UP, 1959), 34.

long performance history, starting with revivals in the fifth century BCE, perpetuated its reputation as literary testimony to Greek, especially Athenian, military success.[33] To the modern reader it comes as a surprise that Shelley, the prophet of non-violent resistance, would invoke a play that rejoices in the slaughter of many thousands. But, as Carl Woodring has pointed out, *Hellas* ignores the realities of the armed struggle, and is meant rather 'to celebrate the rising of the Greeks in such a way as to arouse English interest, English funds, and patriotic shame at the roles of [English] diplomats [...]'.[34] It champions what Woodring calls 'the Hellenic spirit',[35] which in the opening chorus, spoken by Greek women who are enslaved captives of the Sultan Mahmud, is linked to the universal spirit of freedom. This spirit is envisioned as having emerged first with the victories of the ancient Greeks over the Persian empire at Thermopylae and Marathon, and now, after many long ages, as returning to its ancestral home.

The identification of freedom with the very soil of 'Hellas' is taken directly from Aeschylus. In *The Persians*, the Persian Queen, Atossa, widow of Darius and mother of Xerxes, learns first from the chorus of Persian elders and later from the ghost of Darius himself about the fiercely independent and egalitarian spirit of the Greeks. At the climax of the play, after messengers have brought news of the catastrophic Persian defeat, Darius' ghost tells Atossa that no future ruler should ever lead another army into Greek territory: 'Mark that such are the penalties for deeds like these and hold Athens and Hellas in your memory'.[36] In the earlier scene, in some lines that Shelley copied into one of his notebooks, Atossa asks the chorus of elders about Athens: first, where it is; then about Athenian wealth and military power; and lastly, 'who is set over them [...] ?', to which the Chorus answers, 'Of no man are they called the slaves or vassals'.[37] In other words, the Athenians govern themselves: a notion that astonishes the Persian queen. Aeschylus is obviously reinforcing his audience's sense of their superiority as a proud people who refuse to submit to tyrants; but to Shelley, the value of this passage must have been its claim that even non-Greeks (the Persian elders) recognize the 'democratic' spirit of Athenians. The Persian leader, Darius' son Xerxes, is portrayed as an impulsive, casually cruel despot, and the imperial court as corrupted and feminized by its great wealth.[38] Though Shelley represents Mahmud as a man of some intelligence, sensitivity, and foresight, not as a brutal tyrant, Shelley does repeat the 'Orientalizing' emphasis on the vast wealth and casual cruelty of the foreign power.

Since, at the time Shelley wrote his play, the war was not going well for the Greek side, and the chances of victory over the Ottomans seemed slight, it would have been inappropriate

---

[33] Edith Hall, 'Introduction', *Aeschylus: Persians*, ed. Edith Hall (Warminster: Aris and Phillips Ltd, 1996), 2.

[34] Carl Woodring, *Politics in English Romantic Poetry* (Cambridge, MA: Harvard UP, 1970), 315.

[35] Ibid. 317.

[36] *Aeschylus*, trans. Smyth, I. 181 (*Persians* ll. 823–4).

[37] *Aeschylus*, trans. Smyth, I. 129 (*Persians* l. 242). For Shelley's transcription see *BSM* XIV, 268–9; MS. Shelley.adds.e.9 'page 375'. As noted by Sachs, the invocation of a 'Hellenic' but also world-historical 'spirit of freedom' in *Hellas* reflects the same rethinking of history that lay behind the more nuanced treatment of the Roman republic in *A Defence of Poetry* (Sachs, 'Shelley and Lucretius', 170).

[38] See Hall, 'Introduction', 13.

to end the play with a prediction of the eventual liberation of Greece. Rather, the closing Chorus invokes a cyclic vision of human history—'The world's great age begins anew, | The golden years return'—which seems to foretell the return of the Saturnian time of peace and innocence. And yet, this cyclic vision becomes a background for the expression of a despairing plea that, some day, there will be an end to violence altogether: 'O cease! must hate and death return? | Cease! must men kill and die?' (ll. 1060–1, 1096–7; *Norton 1*, 438, 440).

CONCLUSION

This overview of Shelley's engagements with the classical tradition should be taken as no more than a sketch of future possibilities for research. While excellent work has been done on Shelley's translations from Greek and Latin sources,[39] and several critics have dealt with various aspects of his interpretations of classical myth, there is still a need for detailed and sustained research into how Shelley worked with and developed the classical tradition, as both poet and critic. His creative energies were awakened by and infused with the imagery, rhetoric, and poetic forms of the classical writers. The production of new critical editions of his work, and the availability of manuscript facsimiles, open up unprecedented opportunities for the better understanding of the poet who uniquely in his era combined profound knowledge of classical literature with a passionate belief in the power of language to transform the world.

SELECT BIBLIOGRAPHY

Brisman, Susan Hawk. '"Unsaying his High Language": The Problem of Voice in *Prometheus Unbound*'. *Studies in Romanticism* 16 (1977), 51–86.

Curran, Stuart. *Shelley's Annus Mirabilis: The Maturing of an Epic Vision*. San Marino, CA: Huntington Library, 1975.

Harding, Anthony John. *The Reception of Myth in English Romanticism*. Columbia, MO: University of Missouri Press, 1995.

Kelley, Theresa M. 'Reading Justice: From Derrida to Shelley and Back'. *Studies in Romanticism* 46 (2007), 267–87.

Ogilvie, R. M. Ed. *Latin and Greek: A History of the Influence of the Classics on English Life from 1600 to 1918*. London: Routledge and Kegan Paul, 1964.

O'Neill, Michael. 'Emulating Plato: Shelley as Translator and Prose Poet'. *The Unfamiliar Shelley*. Ed. Alan M. Weinberg and Timothy Webb. Aldershot: Ashgate, 2009. 239–55.

Roberts, Hugh. *Shelley and the Chaos of History: A New Politics of Poetry*. University Park, PA: Pennsylvania State UP, 1997.

Sachs, Jonathan. *Romantic Antiquity: Rome in the British Imagination, 1789–1832*. Oxford: Oxford UP, 2010.

Turner, Paul. 'Shelley and Lucretius'. *Review of English Studies* NS 10 (1959), 269–82.

---

[39] See Notopoulos, *Platonism*, Webb, *The Violet in the Crucible*, and O'Neill, 'Emulating Plato'.

Walker, Constance. 'The Urn of Bitter Prophecy: Antithetical Patterns in *Hellas*'. *Keats–Shelley Memorial Bulletin* 33 (1982), 36–48.

Webb, Timothy. *The Violet in the Crucible: Shelley and Translation*. Oxford: Clarendon Press, 1976.

—— Ed. *English Romantic Hellenism*. Literature in Context Series. Manchester: Manchester UP, 1982.

Wilson, Milton. *Shelley's Later Poetry: A Study of his Prophetic Imagination*. New York: Columbia UP, 1959.

CHAPTER 28

....

SHELLEY AND THE ITALIAN TRADITION

....

ALAN WEINBERG

SHELLEY's interest in the Italian tradition is of singular importance in his development as a writer and thinker. Throughout his literary career, roughly from 1808 to 1822, Shelley encountered, read, studied, conceptualized, and assimilated the work of individual practitioners who, in his estimation, best represented or reflected Italian literary culture.[1] Until March 1818, when Shelley left for Italy, his interaction with the Italians was intermittent, inevitably lacking the immediacy of lived experience in Italy itself. Influenced by his early passion for Enlightenment texts and by Godwin's classically oriented prospectus, Shelley came to the Italians in a less direct manner and allowed his growing acquaintance to embed itself in a general education which encompassed an extensive range of classical literary texts. This pattern was significantly reconfigured once, in self-exile, Shelley adopted Italy as a provisional home, and his response to Italian culture had become vibrant and all-present. At the same time his obsession with ancient Greece and Rome gained in intensity with experience of the remains of the ancient world so visible throughout his travels in Italy. As his direct knowledge increased, so Shelley was able to construct a working model of what Italian authors and artists meant to him and the world, and how they related to each other. That model was increasingly influential and was frequently revised and refined.

While Shelley's direct acquaintance with Italian literature was minimal in his early years at Eton and Oxford (1804–11),[2] his penchant for Gothic adventure exposed him to fictional representations of Italy which were typically exaggerated and stereotyped, but which probably created an imaginary conception that laid the grounds for later refinements. While his own prose romances, *Zastrozzi* and *St. Irvyne* (1809–10), relied almost entirely on standard literary convention for the portrayal of Italian excesses, the Gothic novel could reflect genuine aspects of Italian culture, as in

---

[1] The seminal study of Shelley and Italian literature is Timothy Webb, *The Violet in the Crucible* (Oxford: Clarendon Press, 1976), 276–336.

[2] Thomas Jefferson Hogg, *The Life of Percy Bysshe Shelley*, 2 vols. (London: Edward Moxon, 1858), I, 53.

the case of *The Mysteries of Udolpho* and *The Italian*, the latter a favourite with Shelley.[3] These primitive intimations of an Italian cultural context were tacitly (if unconsciously) reinforced by the Italian models that apparently lay behind the Gothic venture in the first place, since Dante's *Inferno* and several of Boccaccio's tales were themselves considered inherently Gothic.[4]

Italian poetry may well have caught Shelley's attention on his reading, in 1812, of Peacock's *The Genius of the Thames* (1810, rev. 1812) (*Letters: PBS* I, 325).[5] Among allusions to *Orlando furioso*, *Gerusalemme liberata*, the *Inferno*, and some verses of Alfieri is an epigraph drawn from the canzone 'Italia mia', Petrarch's lament for the forsaken patria, which, according to Medwin, Shelley later often recited.[6] In the months ahead, Ariosto and Tasso provided the material for Hogg's and Shelley's early studies in Italian (sometime in 1813–14), prompted by a congenial Italianate circle at Bracknell.[7] Since previously Shelley had by his own admission neglected chivalric romance (*Letters: PBS* I, 303, 307), these poetic encounters with Ariosto and Tasso clearly opened up new worlds, bridging the Romantic present with its Italian antecedents. This opening was clearly enhanced by the discovery of Petrarch's oeuvre. Possibly it was Cornelia Turner who gave an intimation of the exquisite bitter-sweet duality of comfort and sorrow that distinguishes Petrarch's unceasing love for Laura, and which, in Italy, Shelley represents in diverse ways.

That Shelley was by these means drawn to Dante is both implied by Hogg[8] and given further credence in his translation of Dante's sonnet 'Guido, vorrei, che tu, e Lappo, ed io' (*Longman*, 1, 451) probably undertaken in late summer 1815, to memorialize a boat trip via Oxford to the source of the Thames at Lechlade. A key feature of this poem is its embrace of a community of like-minded souls, the three poet-friends and their close female companions. The courtly 'gentilezza' of Dante's style and its 'dolce stil novo' articulations ('[…] would grace | With passionate talk […] | Our time'), is marked by a series of polite subjunctives and conditionals ('would', 'might', 'should', 'might', 'were', etc.) that propose a magic world of 'might-be' and 'would-be'—of poetry itself as of friendship. The decorous fluency of translation, which effortlessly contains the thought in one fourteen-line sentence, seems to result from the elegant influence of mood—that of desire and possibility—over the whole composition, faithfully reproducing the tone and indicating the noble spirit of the original. Notably Shelley avoids Italianisms and is meticulous in sustaining an entirely English form (namely Shakespearian), syntax, and rhythm. The absence of any formal division between octave and sestet gives greater prominence to enchantment ('the bounteous wizard') already adumbrated in Shelley's *magic* ship' and '*charmèd* sails' which are absent in the original. This adaptation keeps pastiche or subordination securely at bay, and establishes a firmer meeting ground between Italian Trecento and English Romantic.

---

[3] Thomas Medwin, *The Life of Percy Bysshe Shelley*, 2 vols. (London: Thomas Cautley Newby, 1847), I, 30.

[4] Diego Saglia, 'From Gothic Italy to Italy as Gothic Archive: Italian Narratives and the Late Romantic Metrical Tale', *Gothic Studies* 8.1 (2006), 75 ff.

[5] Peacock's later friendship must certainly have advanced Shelley's Italian and classical studies.

[6] Medwin, *Life*, II, 39.   [7] Hogg, *Life*, II, 376–80.   [8] Hogg, *Life*, II, 380.

Cavalcanti's address to Dante in the sonnet 'Io vengo il giorno a te infinite volte' (*Longman*, 1, 453–4) was probably also translated at this time. It is notable for its combined praise and blame of Dante and offers both a confirmation of the values of the Florentine school and 'dolce stil' and a forewarning of their easy decline. Shelley could take note of the difficulty of sustaining good fellowship among poets and recognize his own vulnerability, given that Dante himself could so fall from grace in the eyes of his close friend and role model. Dante's 'mild and gentle mind', his disdain for the 'multitude | Of blind and madding men' (an extravagant paraphrase of 'la noiosa gente'='the tedious rabble'), and his 'sweet mood' portray his 'gentilezza'. The breakdown in friendship, however seriously meant, is underscored by Shelley's insistent sentence-breaks within the line, which disrupt the formalities of the Italian; and by changes to the meaning that draw on barely perceptible suggestions. Thus Cavalcanti's claim, 'I then loved thee', substitutes for 'Di me parlavi si coralemente' (lit. 'You spoke of me with such affection').[9] That Cavalcanti's sonnet might dispel the 'false Spirit' in Dante dramatizes the urgency of the complaint, and the efficacy of verse in possibly restoring 'thy [Dante's] true integrity' and a communion of 'Spirits' insisted upon more in Shelley's reading than in Cavalcanti's verse. So, in Shelleyan vein, the sonnet credits poetry itself with ameliorative powers and foreshadows Shelley's deeper reflections on the virtues of the Italian tradition in *A Defence of Poetry*.

The translations of the two sonnets may represent a watershed in Shelley's poetic career, preparatory exercises for the venture south, the creative engagement with the Italians on their own soil, and the prospect of realizing true fellowship among lovers, friends, and poets (later, a recurring Shelleyan motif). Repeatedly Shelley planned residence or exile in Italy.[10] In 1815–16 he reread Ariosto and Tasso (*Journals*: MWS I, 92, 98), as if to reestablish his sense of Italian romance, influenced by the ascendancy of vernacular poetry in medieval Florence by way of Provence. The liberation of the Golden City in Shelley's long epic romance *Laon and Cythna* (1817) clearly owes something to the example of *Gerusalemme liberata*, as the cities in question, Constantinople and Jerusalem, are both strongholds of Islam and tyranny. Specific parallels have been noticed between the two poems, especially the ultimately victorious sacrifice of Shelley's eponymous protagonists, modelled on that of Sophronia and Olindo (*Longman*, 2, 246). Yet Shelley radically displaces Tasso's epic design. His heroes are freethinking Hellenic revolutionaries-in-love, not Christian crusaders, and Islam is temporarily liberated from its own oppression, and not, as in Tasso's epic, conflated with paganism and conquered by Christianity.

Earlier, in 1814–15, readings of Marino's *Adone* and of Alfieri's recent *Life* and neoclassical tragedies (*Letters*: MWS I, 86, 92, *Letters*: PBS I, 435) would have updated the tradition,[11] redefined it, and extended ties between Italian authors and classical antiquity. It would also have brought to acute awareness the continued Italian subjugation to foreign powers and the nascent quest for liberty in Alfieri's bold resistance to tyranny—both

---

[9] *Rime di Guido Cavalcanti*, ed. Antonio Cicciaporci (Florence: Presso Niccolò Carli, 1813), 12.
[10] See *Letters*: PBS I, 305 n. 1, 450, 453, 470, 547, 556, 560, 583.
[11] See also review of Hogg's *Memoirs of Prince Alexy Haimatoff* (1814) in *Murray: Prose*, I, 142.

personally and figuratively in his dramas—modelled on the republican virtues of ancient Rome and medieval Florence.

Familiarity with the broader tradition of Italian writers ensured that, on crossing the border into Italy on 30 March 1818, Shelley was well prepared for the enrichment that lay ahead. In the course of his four-and-a-quarter-year sojourn, only terminated by his tragic drowning off the coast of Viareggio on 8 July 1822, his writings provide ample evidence of the wealth upon which Shelley was able to draw. Nevertheless there were at first notable shortcomings in the poet's knowledge. His repeated request for Cary's rendering of the *Purgatorio* and *Paradiso* in December 1817 (*Letters: PBS* I, 575, 586) points to Shelley's limited acquaintance with the *Commedia* at this time.[12] Enthusiastic reading of the *Purgatorio* in the Cathedral of Milan, shortly after arrival in Italy (*Letters: PBS* II, 8; *Journals: MWS* I, 205), shows a readiness to imbibe new influences, unusually for Shelley in the context of Catholic worship, but also his need to further his Italian education.

Not surprisingly then, Shelley held to certain bold but imprecise conceptions, even as his horizons expanded. This is evident in two prose pieces in which he began, tentatively, to map out a broader historiography of European enlightenment, and to trace its source in Florence. The fragment 'On the Revival of Literature' published posthumously by Medwin in *The Athenæum* has been variously assigned by editors to 1815 or later (there is no surviving manuscript).[13] That the piece belongs to the period of early exile is suggested by the strong positioning of Dante and Petrarch in the sketch of a revival in Europe. Increasing knowledge of these poets and their great reputation in Italy would have signalled their historical importance.[14] In the fragment, Shelley's writing is assured but he oversimplifies his account of the spread of learning by Greek monks in exile, and of superstition in the monasteries and cloisters of Europe, following the fall of Constantinople. His leading comment on Dante and Petrarch is, however, significant, since he rightly gives them pride of place as precursors of a literary re-awakening:

> The writings of Dante in the thirteenth, and of Petrarch in the fourteenth [centuries], were the bright luminaries which had afforded glimmerings of literary knowledge to the almost benighted traveller toiling up the hill of Fame. (*Athenæum*, 761)

The indication of a dearth of inspiring literature at the time is inaccurate and ignores Dante's debt to his literary predecessors and contemporaries in Provence and Italy. Nevertheless, the impression of a dark age succeeded by light, first in the writings of Italian 'luminaries', and then subsequently in the 'new and sudden light' ('quantity of learned [Greek] manuscripts') following 'the taking of Constantinople', is foreshadowed by Petrarch, since he applied the term 'darkness' to the Christian era in general, and the resulting

---

[12] Unlike the *Inferno*, these later volumes (pub. 1814) did not include the Italian text.

[13] No. 265, 24 November 1832, 761–2. Also published in *The Shelley Papers* (London: Whittaker, Treacher, & Co. 1833), 170–4.

[14] A source was possibly Gibbon's *Decline and Fall of the Roman Empire*, vol. VI (1788), requested in August 1817, *Letters: PBS* I, 552.

denigration of ancient knowledge.[15] Officially regarded as the 'father of humanism', Petrarch's efforts were to preserve the inheritance of antiquity at all costs, to the point of recovering many ancient manuscripts. Shelley's readiness to look past Dante's Christian vision is a notable humanist emphasis since, like Bacon, he is unable to come to terms with scholasticism, which he derides in the rest of the fragment. At this stage, Shelley seems unconcerned with the Aristotelian substructure of the *Commedia*, or the way Dante refines and refigures the scholastic reasoning of Aquinas.

That the heralds of a renaissance were themselves illustrious poets would serve as inspiration to Shelley, who was soon to announce his 'passion for reforming the world' in his preface to *Prometheus Unbound* (1819) (*Major Works*, 232).[16] The leading sentence on the Italians in the fragment is isolated and undeveloped, and offset by the main thrust of the piece, which concerns the restoration of Greek literature, 'the finest the world has ever produced' (762). A more subtle variant of this argument is taken up in *On the Manners of the Antient Greeks*, written at Bagni di Lucca in July 1818 as preface to Shelley's translation of the *Symposium*. The essay contextualizes the notion of civilization by exalting the Athenians and their influence, yet conceding limitations in their social practice, most notably in the exclusion of women from the refinements of love (as portrayed in Plato's dialogue). This dual aspect preserves the primacy of Greek culture in Shelley's thought over that of the Italian, while asserting that later advancements were founded on Greek conceptions.

Notwithstanding what was achieved in Athens, Shelley's progressive model allows space for comparative excellence in poetry over the centuries. Assessing the merits of Shakespeare, Dante, Petrarch, and Homer, Shelley finds qualities in the first three that excel even the Greeks. The inclusion of the Italians among the select few here occasions comment on specific talents: that perhaps Dante 'created imaginations of greater loveliness and energy' than his predecessors; and that, in what remains of Greek lyric poetry, there is perhaps no 'equivalent to the sublime and chivalric sensibility of Petrarch'.[17] These brief but carefully chosen distinctions point to uniquely elevating and ennobling attributes. Yet succeeding remarks confine Dante's excellence to a limited area of his work, and intimate what is meant by the plural 'imaginations':

> Nor could Dante, deficient in conduct, plan, nature, variety, and temperance, have been brought into comparison with these men, but for those fortunate isles, laden with golden fruit, which alone could tempt any one to embark in the misty ocean of his dark and extravagant fiction. (Notopoulos, 'Discourse', 405)

Notably at odds with Dante's artistry and temperament, Shelley overlays his comments with Gothic preconceptions of disorderliness, excess, and gloom. He repeats the

---

[15] Petrarch restored 'light' to antiquity at the Church's expense. See Theodore E. Mommsen, 'Petrarch's Conception of the "Dark Ages"', *Speculum* 17.2 (1942), 226–42.

[16] All Shelley's poetry and prose will be quoted from *Major Works* unless indicated otherwise.

[17] James A. Notopoulos, *A Discourse on the Manners of the Antient Greeks Relative to the Subject of Love*, in *The Platonism of Shelley* (Durham, NC: Duke UP, 1949), 405; hereafter cited in text.

contemporary prejudice against Dante's *Inferno*,[18] giving undue weight to it in comparison to the succeeding canticles, and misconstruing the rich classical foundation of Dante's style and conception of the underworld. It would be hard to say which were all the 'fortunate isles' in question, but undoubtedly the Earthly Paradise at the summit of mount Purgatory corresponds to the Islands of the Blest,[19] to which Shelley playfully alludes, thereby Hellenizing Dante's solemn Christian allegory. The idea of Christianity reverting to its pagan origins is always compelling for Shelley, especially given his classical leanings. As 'alone' might suggest, the 'imaginations' do not seem plentiful as yet. While Dante is already a dominant figure in Shelley's thought, his vision has not yet been grasped, assimilated, or reconstituted in terms fully agreeable to Shelley.

The succeeding year and a half of itinerant residence in Italy—from August 1818 to early January 1820—which embraces Shelley's 'Annus Mirabilis', brought to immediate contemplation the great burgeoning of the arts, the surviving ruins of classical antiquity, and continuities between them. The 'Paradise of exiles' reflected exceptional creativity in a cycle of rise and fall,[20] promising rebirth in spite of inevitable decline. Raphael, Guido Reni, or Salvator Rosa provided imagery of transcendence that Shelley would reconstitute for his non-theistic imaginings in *Prometheus Unbound*, or for tragic character portrayal in *The Cenci*.[21] The Italian poets who dominated the literary landscape in Shelley's mind at this time provided analogues for works that Shelley conceived on his travels—as if he were silently acknowledging his predecessors on home territory, whilst drawing on their example to advance his own vision.

Once settled in Italy, Shelley's interest shifted away from Tasso's *Gerusalemme liberata* to the poet's character and trials, in the wake of Byron's *Lament of Tasso* published in 1817.[22] Tasso's pitiable disappointment in love and suffering at the hands of the tyrannic duke (much of this more legendary than true) provided material at first for an abandoned tragedy,[23] and thereafter for the fictional portrayal of the Maniac in 'Julian and Maddalo'. This tormented character exemplifies the poet-figure whose acute sensitivity to injustice and misfortune brings him to the brink of insanity, but not complete despair or hardened defiance. His wild unmediated soliloquy recalls an encounter in Dante's *Inferno*, signalled by allusions to the lustful in canto 5 and the lament of Francesca da Rimini, though 'hell' in this case is a psychological trauma that has no theological justification. It disturbs the urbane dialectic of infinite potential and cynical determinism represented by Julian and

[18] Hunt reflects contemporary disquietudes regarding Dante in *Stories from the Italian Poets* (London: Chapman and Hall, 1846), I, 1–77.

[19] Hesiod, Pindar, Euripides, Herodotus, Plato, and Plutarch, amongst others, refer to these Islands (also associated with the Garden of the Hesperides and Elysian Fields). The reference in *Symposium* (180b) was probably fresh in Shelley's mind. Purgatory is itself a mountain-island.

[20] See *Julian and Maddalo*, 57 and *Letters: PBS* II, 170.

[21] The rare union of 'energy and gentleness' in the portrait of Beatrice Cenci echoes Shelley's praise of Dante (Preface to *The Cenci*, 319).

[22] At Ferrara (November 1818), Shelley observed Tasso's handwriting and the dungeon where he was imprisoned. See *Letters: PBS* II, 46–8.

[23] See 'Scene for *Tasso*', 'Silence; oh well are Death and Sleep and thou', and 'Song for *Tasso*', *Longman*, 2, 365–70, 445–7.

Maddalo (fictional versions of Shelley himself and Byron) and suggests a 'raw' middle position that encompasses both theories, without negating either.

In *Lines Written among the Euganean Hills*, the Petrarchan rhythmic modulation back and forth, from sorrow to joy, in pursuit of the ideal, provides the leitmotif of the paradisal 'green isle' in a 'sea of misery' which besets the solitary mariner in his 'frail bark' (331) (cf. 'frale barca [...] in alto mar senza governo', *Canzoniere* 132, 10–11). Further it provides the model (as drawn from the canzone 'Italia mia') for the lament of an Italian decline, seen by each poet from very different perspectives. In Petrarch's case it is antiquity that represents the lost ideal, but (not without irony) in Shelley's it is Padua and resplendent Venice, seen from afar in the Hills near Arquà, where Petrarch himself found sanctuary and a final resting place. One of the 'flowering isles' (335) that completes the poem is an 'imagination' of community, refuge, and remedial influence that re-proposes Dantean imaginings, anticipating the *invitation au voyage* to Emily in *Epipsychidion*.

In *Prometheus Unbound*, Dante provides the paradigm that, in a subversive form, could take Shelley confidently beyond the constraints of Aeschylean necessity. Dante's epic progression from Hell to Paradise could be stripped of its Catholic trappings, and assume a mythic structure that allowed for Promethean liberation and transcendence of the human predicament within the limits of mortality, and without any recourse to an all-powerful creator. In fact it was the supreme deity who (in the form of the archetypal tyrant, Jupiter) had, in Shelley's epic, to be removed—an effect that, in Dante's case, would have destroyed his vision. The ensuing demise of the tyrant is mocked by the erasure of the curse of Hell: '"All hope abandon, ye who enter here"', III. iv. 136, citing *Inferno* 3. 9. The Tuscan pilgrim's ascent through purgatory to earthly paradise is, in Asia's passage to Demogorgon, inverted as a descent from her Indian vale to the very source of unbounded potential for change: a 'god' who is not creative but makes provision for the occluded 'Life of Life' to be restored. In the celebratory last act, which re-imagines Dante's elevated conception, 'Paradise' reconfigures earthly delight as a timeless cosmic event, a consequence of liberation from theism and its equally oppressive ideological correlatives.[24]

The 'summum bonum' of 'delight' prompted a further inclusion in Shelley's pantheon. In a letter to Hunt of 27 September 1819, Shelley calls Boccaccio 'in the high sense of the word a poet' and 'this most divine writer' (*Letters: PBS* II, 121–2), appropriating an appellation which Boccaccio himself conferred upon Dante's *Commedia*.[25] Divinity in this case is translated back into terms appropriate for Shelley. Each introduction to a new day in the *Decameron* is 'the morning of life stript of that mist of familiarity which makes it obscure to us' (122). That sense of life free from the encrustations of time is not far from the primordial delight that is unmasked and restored to the earth and humanity in *Prometheus Unbound*, and later marks the exordium of *The Triumph of Life*: 'and the mask | Of darkness fell from the awakened Earth' (3–4). The phantasmagoric

---

[24] For extended intertextual commentaries, see Alan Weinberg, *Shelley's Italian Experience* (London: Macmillan, 1991).

[25] See Richard Lansing (ed.), *The Dante Encyclopedia* (New York, Garland, 2000), 113.

vision of relentless obscuring triumph is superimposed upon this primal renewal, as though it did not belong to it. The frame-story's 'lieta brigata' ('happy band') in the *Decameron* inspires Shelley's dream of pleasurable companionship, earlier foreshadowed in Dante's sonnet. Boccaccio's light touch is attractive because it produces 'serious meanings of a very beautiful kind' (*Letters: PBS* II, 122). This style is an advance on Ariosto who, together with Tasso, Shelley now considers as 'children of a later and of a colder day', when 'the corrupting blight of tyranny was already hanging on every bud of genius'. Nevertheless, the light spirit of Boccaccio and Ariosto (and its transmutation in Byron's *Don Juan* or Forteguerri's *Il Ricciardetto*) is present in Shelley's translation of 'Hymn to Mercury' and in *The Witch of Atlas* (July–August 1820), which adopt *ottava rima*, the rhyme scheme most commonly identified with Ariosto but which Boccaccio himself invented.[26] Boccaccio's 'deep sense of the fair ideal of human life' had great appeal for Shelley. Its 'moral casuistry' was 'the opposite of the Christian, Stoical, ready made and worldly system of morals' that Shelley always deplored (122).

If Boccaccio is not 'equal […] to Dante or Petrarch', he now stands with them as 'the productions of the vigour of the infancy of a new nation' (122). Abandoning his view of these poets as rarefied, isolated figures, Shelley now identifies them with the political freedom that prevailed in the commune of medieval Florence (to which all three poets are linked by birth and language).[27] Thus the poets are 'rivulets from the same spring as that which fed the greatness of the republics of Florence and Pisa' (122). An image-complex ('vigour', 'infancy', 'rivulets', 'spring') is central to Shelley's conception here and in subsequent analysis. Autonomy emanates from the first beginnings of nationhood, naturally free from archaic hegemonies. A vitalizing force, like a river at its source, streams without impediment into governance and literary creation, allowing each to realize its potential 'greatness'. Later achievements in the arts result from 'obscure channels'. This paradigm implicitly underplays the later revival of learning, which now seems a foreign tributary that fed into the river, rather than the other way round.

These ideas form the kernel of the argument in *A Philosophical View of Reform* (Florence, late 1819–January 1820). Change is a necessity as the creative will and vitality of the people are stifled in a system of ingrained oppression and privilege. The example of Florence and Pisa gives indication of the promise that suitably awaits England if it were to reform on republican principles. More precise in matters of historical detail, following Sismondi's *Histoire des républiques italiennes*,[28] Shelley is careful to indicate how the predations of 'the all-surrounding tyranny' of Popedom or Empire were resisted and neutralized by Florence in particular. Thus 'Freedom had one citadel wherein it could find refuge from a world which was its enemy' (637). A solitary Promethean sanctuary, holding out against all odds, reveals what is at stake if exceptional creativity is to occur. The sense of tragic beleaguerment (echoing Jupiter's stranglehold in *Prometheus*

---

[26] See e.g. *Teseide* (c.1340) and *Filostrato* (1335/40). For the burlesque influence of Forteguerri, see Alan Weinberg, '*Il Ricciardetto* and Shelley's *The Witch of Atlas*', *Studi d'Italianistica nell'Africa australe* 3.4/4.1 (1990–1), 32–42.

[27] In 'Della tirannide', Alfieri likewise insists that creativity thrives on free governance.

[28] See *Letters: PBS* II, 485, *Journals: MWS* I, 247–8.

Unbound) is nevertheless countered by an extraordinary result, namely, 'the undisputed superiority of Italy in literature and the arts over all its contemporary nations'. Now, for the first time, Dante stands out as the exemplary author, his writings 'distinguish[ed] from all other poets' in their capacity to unite 'energy and beauty' (637). In this reading, the great scope and intensity of Dante's vision is at one with its artistry. From this point on, Dante becomes the key figure in Shelley's thinking about his own poetry and literature in general.

A slightly earlier letter to Hunt (24 August 1819) anticipates this new concentration on Dante. Here, there are just a 'few distasteful passages of the Inferno' while 'exquisite tenderness & sensibility & ideal beauty' elevate Dante above all other poets except Shakespeare (*Letters: PBS* II, 112). The 'flowering isles' which previously seemed dispersed are now exempla of what Dante achieves more generally in the succeeding canticles. It is probably on this account that Shelley attempted translations of two of the episodes he mentions: 'the Spirit coming over the sea in a boat' from *Purgatorio* 1, and 'Matilda gathering flowers' from *Purgatorio* 28. The dating of these attempts is uncertain but the evidence points to the following spring of 1820 (*BSM* V, p. xlv). The first is just three lines, but the second covers the first fifty-one lines of canto 28 and is a rough incomplete draft.[29] This latter literally portrays a 'flowering isle': the scene is one of perpetual spring in the calm and protective seclusion of the *divina foresta* in contrast to the *selva oscura* ('dark wood') of *Inferno* 1, in which Dante loses his way. Along the river bank appears a *genius loci*, Matilda, 'singing' and 'gathering flower after flower' as she moves (*Webb*, p. 314), to whom Dante is led without fear by some benign influence.

In context, the passage is an immediate prelude to the restoration of Beatrice's love for the pilgrim, his cleansing from sin, and his vision of the gryphon and Church triumphant. On their own, however, the lines are free of any obvious links with pilgrimage or the broader scope of the *Commedia*. This works to Shelley's advantage. It allows him to focus on the extract as if it had less to do with Christian or prelapsarian emblems than with the earthly ideal itself and its elusiveness. At the end of canto 28, Matilda concedes that the poets of old foreshadowed the Christian paradise in the myth of the golden age. This was perhaps Shelley's lead. He could attempt to emulate Dante, as a lesson in the art of poetry, by using *terza rima*, and finding an English analogue for Dante's visual lucidity, stylistic elegance, architectural symmetry, and magisterial poise of narration. In Shelley's translation, there are strikingly few Miltonisms, unlike Cary, and the style, receptive to measured rhythm and cumulative syntax, allows the scenic description to unfold clearly and naturally, *terzina* by *terzina*, until the sudden appearance of Matilda. Accord, such as Shelley achieves, is the necessary ground for difference, since he also displaces Dante's emphasis: updating him in terms of Romantic predilections, or backdating him to the pre-Christian roots which Dante had assimilated and transformed. Shelley intensifies the impact of the scene with emotive modifiers ('bare', 'blithe', 'perfect', 'bleak', 'turbid', 'charmed', 'blank', 'besprent', '[b]right') and enjambments that, at times, hurry the pace. Complementing this process, the link between Matilda and Proserpine

---

[29] Text in *Webb*, 313–14.

in the concluding *terzina* submerges the implicit theme of the Fall, bringing out rather the inevitable loss of spring and the grief of mother earth, for whom her daughter is 'more dear', a phrase absent in Dante. Shelley bridges past and present by interweaving Milton's famous reference to Proserpine 'gathering flours',[30] implicitly reversing Milton's Christian parable as well as Dante's. Overall, Shelley continues to assimilate Dante's voice to his own, thus anticipating the narrative style in *The Triumph of Life*.

Translation of the canzone 'Voi che 'ntendendo il terzo ciel movete',[31] in the summer or autumn of 1820, brought Shelley closer to Dante's intensely personal autobiography of love, rendered in the form of an 'idealized history'. In the canzone, the poet's love of an angelic figure (Beatrice) is supplanted by a new, powerfully attractive 'donna gentile'. Sensing betrayal, Dante submits to a seemingly irresistible influence, that of the intelligence that 'moves' the third Heaven (Venus). Submission is not achieved without an intense struggle. The dynamics of love and their metaphysical machinery, reinforced by Shelley's later reading of the *Vita nuova* (January 1821, *Journals: MWS* I, 351), provided a model for his own 'idealized history', soon to find renewed expression in *Epipsychidion* (February 1821).[32]

Dante's commentary on the canzone in Book 2 of the *Convivio* would have further guided Shelley in finding a suitable poetic mode and rationale for his own 'platonics'.[33] Significantly, Dante's distinction between literal and allegorical meanings disallows the crude assumption that a personified beloved must necessarily be a person. Thus the 'donna gentile' turns out to be an abstraction, Lady Philosophy, and not a flesh and blood rival of Beatrice. It is on these grounds that the relationship with 'Emily' in *Epipsychidion* should not be reduced to an ordinary affair of passion, but rather be regarded as imbued with 'platonic' significance. The union of the Lady with Beatrice in the *Commedia* eventually resolves Dante's dilemma, prefiguring Emily, both 'Seraph' and oracle of the wisdom of 'True Love' that, like Charity in *Purgatorio* 15. 55–7, is infinitely expansive, increasing the more it is shared.

Shelley's translation of 'Voi che' ntendendo' attempts to trace and undergo Dante's poetic thought-process: it is complete (but for a single line in the third stanza) and the form, structure, and diction adhere to the original, except where Shelley's understanding seems inexact. His risk of the word 'intelligent' (for the participle *intendendo*) in the first line underlines Dante's reference to the Angelic Intelligences, and is not a personal emphasis. Likewise the 'third Heaven' belongs strictly to Dante's Ptolomeic cosmology (founded in Aristotelian physics), as does the 'glorious lady throned aloft' (Beatrice at the feet of God (*nostro Sire*; lit. 'our Lord')) which Shelley, without any sign of dissent, translates 'our Father'. Care for such detail continues in the reference to 'her | Who came on the refulgence of your sphere [=*stella*, Venus]',[34] displacing the 'bright seraph [=*angela*] sitting crowned on high'.[35] Dante presents love as a primal stellar force which entirely captivates and illuminates the soul, and finds its true expression in poetry

---

[30] *Paradise Lost*, IV. 269.   [31] Text in *Webb*, 292–3.
[32] See also the Italian prose-poem 'Una favola' (dated 1821, *MYR* VI, xl–liii).
[33] Shelley annotated the *Convivio* in 1820.   [34] See *Epipsychidion*, 116–17.   [35] *Webb*, 292.

(since the planet Venus is the sphere of Love and Rhetoric). In *Epipsychidion*, Shelley's 'platonics' are re-imagined in the language and philosophy of Dante which, in contrast to the Socratic dialogues, wholly affirm poetry and the feminine embodiment of the beloved, whether human or intellectual or both.

In the advertisement to *Epipsychidion*, Shelley quotes the entire last stanza or *congedo* of his translation of 'Voi che 'ntendendo'. The *congedo* speaks for Dante as for Shelley, establishing their accord. Acknowledging the difficulty of understanding love's metaphysics, the Dantean frame device requires that art should be a stimulus for further insight: it enjoins the mystified reader to 'own that thou [the poem] art beautiful'. Shelley's fluent and elegant rendering of Dante's lines departs finally from the original by insisting that those who miss the poet's meaning are 'dull' or 'base' (p. 293).[36] In this way he exalts his work above the common reader with a disdain that is Petrarchan rather than Dantean.

Written in the aftermath of *Epipsychidion*, *A Defence of Poetry* (February to March 1821) recapitulates Shelley's estimation of the Italian tradition and advances it significantly. The five major Italian poets—Dante, Petrarch, Boccaccio, Ariosto, and Tasso—are again considered in their varying contexts: chivalry, the revival of learning, republicanism, love, imagination, idealized vision, etc. However the contexts are now themselves occasions for a celebration of poetry.

Within an historical overview anchored in the exceptional achievements of Homer and the Greek tragedians, Dante yet takes centre stage and is of all writers the key exemplar of Shelley's theoretical argument: that poetry is in the forefront of knowledge and human advance. Remarks on the Italian poets occur in the light of Dante's eminence. An exception seems made for Petrarch who, in the introductory discussion of the 'religion of love', receives glowing tribute. Reiteration of Petrarch's excellence in conveying 'the delight which is in the grief of Love' (690) is emphatic and eloquent. It indicates that, in *Epipsychidion*, the exuberance yet sense of inadequacy or imperfection of the Shelleyan persona, caught up in overwhelming admiration for Emily's divine presence and the quest to exalt and to unite with it, is a Petrarchan as much as Dantean derivative. So too is the constant juxtaposition of transcendence and mortality. In fact, Emily has much in common with Laura as a figuration of intellectual beauty or of poetry itself.[37]

Yet Dante is said to have 'understood the secret things of love even more than Petrarch'. While in the *Vita nuova* his 'idealized history' is an 'inexhaustible fountain of purity of sentiment and language', its further treatment in the *Commedia* is more elevated. In this work, Dante's 'apotheosis of Beatrice in Paradise and the gradations of his own love and her loveliness, by which as by steps he feigns himself to have ascended to the throne of the Supreme Cause, is the most glorious imagination of modern poetry' (690–1). Shelley dissolves the superstructure of Dante's vision to reveal the anagogical progression of the full narrative. In so doing he unsuspectingly points forward to the apotheosis

---

[36] Citing the *Vita nuova* in the 'Advertisement', Shelley implies that the esoteric meaning of his poem is plainly intelligible and that he could explain it without difficulty.

[37] See e.g. 'Thou Harmony of Nature's art' (30), or 'A Metaphor of Spring and Youth and Morning' (120).

of Keats in *Adonais* (April to June 1821), depicted as arising out of the elegist's gradual ascent from mortal sorrow to affirmation of the immortality of poets (the third Heaven). In the *Defence*, the ladder of ascent portrays, in finely imagined sequence, the exalted divinity of Beatrice, the pilgrim's measured advance from Hell to Paradise, the bond of love that marks the journey's progress, and fulfilment in the loftiest realm of being. The association of Beatrice with the Supreme Cause registers Dante's originality and daring, laying bare his refined conception of the divine will, and underlining the motive force of 'loveliness' as imaged in the figure of sublime feminine beauty. Stylistically, Shelley imaginatively relives his assertion, thus eliding the centuries that separate the two poets. In one small detail—the unobtrusive phrase 'he feigns himself'—Shelley adopts the very advanced view that Dante's journey is a fictional, and not a true, mystic experience. 'Feigning', for Shelley, throws the emphasis on 'glorious imagination' as an integral body of thought (now encompassing the whole poem and not specific scenes) in accordance with his defence more broadly, and eschews literal-mindedness, even on the most elevated plane of signification. The glorification of Beatrice is a destabilizing construct, however much Dante may have personally subscribed to it or allowed his vision to be conditioned by it.

Shelley's greater regard for the *Purgatorio* and *Paradiso* matches his conviction that triumphant love and chivalry have liberated women from ancient constraints, by sensitizing human consciousness. In this context, Shelley re-envisions Ariosto and Tasso more positively, regarding them jointly with Dante and Petrarch, and their great successors of more recent times, as having 'celebrated the dominion of love; planting as it were trophies in the human mind of that sublimest victory over sensuality and force' (691). The fusion of romance and epic results in the subjection of superheroes to the elixir, love, in both *Orlando* and *Gerusalemme*. Recognition of the powerful civilizing influence of love poets culminates in a germinal idea: that 'The poetry of Dante may be considered as the bridge thrown over the stream of time which unites the modern and the ancient world' (691). At a decisive point of transmission, continuity is ensured, and the past freshly absorbed into modern consciousness. Ancient thought (providing the framework and scaffolding for Dante's conceptions) is preserved and integrated into a personalized and feminized imaginary that is foreign to the classical world, but characterizes our own. The image of 'time' recalls Shelley's earlier analogy of source and flow in the letter to Hunt, the stream now extending beyond Florence into the distant past and forward to the immediate present, where Dante's influence holds sway.

Aware that cultural transmission could not be free of ostensible barriers, Shelley adds a significant rider:

> The distorted notions of invisible things which Dante and his rival Milton have idealized are merely the mask and the mantle in which these great poets walk through eternity enveloped and disguised. (691)

A similar use of 'mask and mantle' describes Beatrice Cenci's 'crimes and miseries' (Preface to *The Cenci*, 319) which circumstances did not permit her to avoid, but which also did not break her spirit. Shelley understands that the theology espoused by Dante and Milton was an expedient, masking an epic truth that remains viable for all time. Dante's adherence to the Catholic system of the afterlife, predicated on divine judgement with its eternally direful as well as benign consequences, provides the theological and moral framework for his poem. Its rigorous application in the *Commedia*, structurally and thematically, as an idealized construct, does not preclude exceptions, deviations, or adaptations that test out the framework to the limit. Shelley gives the prime instance of Riphaeus who, though a pagan, earns his place in Paradise among the just Christian saints for single-handedly defending Troy at the cost of his life. Virgil, on the other hand, is excluded from salvation, let alone Paradise, yet, for Dante, he is his guide and leader: the exemplary poet, the figure of reason, the advocate of Rome and Empire, and the legendary prophet of Christianity. Aptly, Dante's source for Riphaeus is the *Aeneid* (a work of fiction), where Virgil himself calls him 'justissimus unus', as Shelley points out, lamenting the injustice of the gods. The extraordinary disparity between these two figures, Riphaeus and Virgil, creates a dramatic tension in the *Commedia* that seems unresolvable, but may surreptitiously open the door to all possibilities. Remarking mischievously, but acutely, that Dante 'observ[es] a most heretical caprice in his distribution of rewards and punishments' (691), Shelley once more underlines the challenge to orthodoxy that Dante, like Milton, has written into his poem whilst maintaining the semblance of outward conformity. Calling Christianity the 'modern mythology', Shelley deflates its claim to historic truth and permanence but, with reversed logic, acknowledges its poetic potential. This eventually extinct 'superstition' will only remain interesting for future historians because 'it will have been stamped with the eternity of genius' (692).

In fellowship with Milton and Homer (as second 'among the sons of light' (*Adonais*, 36)) Dante is an epic poet whose works 'bore a defined and intelligible relation to the knowledge, and sentiment, and religion, and political condition of the age in which he lived, and of the ages which followed it: developing itself in correspondence with their development' (692). The great compass of the epic imagination points to the lesser scope of most other authors, and makes clear the demands of speaking in the present, and prophetically. Shelley registers Dante's European consciousness, his awareness of the fluctuations and dynamics of the broader culture he inhabited, and his incorporation of dramatically changing times into his broader vision. Shelley was no less ambitious than Dante and, in mapping out the latter's task, he was identifying the road that lay ahead for him, and establishing his poetic lineage. In *Prometheus Unbound* Shelley had adopted the epic mode for lyric drama, and an archetypal design that reflected, as well as revised, the fatalistic compromise of the Aeschylean model and the redemptive schema of the *Commedia*; in *The Triumph of Life*, which followed a year after the *Defence*, in April to June 1822, he would embrace the task of epic poet in narrative, largely by following in Dante's footsteps.

As progenitor of reform par excellence, Dante preceded Milton in assimilating and preserving 'the ancient religion of the civilized world' (692) (Shelley's inversion for 'classical myth'), while as first religious reformer, in advance of Luther, he fiercely condemned church abuses. In this context, Dante's prominence in Shelley's pantheon is firmly reinforced: he was 'the first awakener of entranced Europe', removing the spell of centuries of dormancy, superstition, and subjection. His instrument was the creation of Tuscan, musical and persuasive, 'out of a chaos of inharmonious barbarisms'. Refining his suggestion that the Renaissance was a replenished tributary of its source in Florence, Shelley adds that Dante congregated other 'great spirits' like himself to preside 'over the resurrection of learning' (693). The instance of a single mind drawing others to it as overseers of the revival, ensuring its success, broadens Shelley's earlier conception, indicating that the Renaissance might never have taken place were it not for the humanist poets Petrarch and Boccaccio who, inspired by Dante's example, paved the way forward. The inference is that the advancement of knowledge in society is precarious, the contribution of poets towards its attainment vital.

By calling Dante 'the Lucifer of the starry flock which in the thirteenth century shone forth from republican Italy, as from a heaven, into the darkness of the benighted world' (693), Shelley reinvents the *Paradiso* as a heretical manifesto of the sanctity of love and far-reaching thought (Venus/Lucifer), shared by a confraternity of like minds ('starry flock'), whose poetic insight and refinement put to shame the barbarity of Europe. The extravagantly brilliant final salute to Dante, that his every word 'is as a spark, a burning atom of inextinguishable thought' (693), draws on the stellar imagery, identifying an innate power and self-sustaining quality of light that can ignite other minds for all time; just as Dante, in *Paradiso* 1. 34, writes of his poetry that 'Poca favilla gran fiamma seconda' ('a small spark creates a large flame'). So, too, in *Adonais*, the 'transmitted effluence' of the immortals will continue 'So long as fire outlives the parent spark' (407–8). Fittingly Shelley now turns his mind to the precision and vitality of a single word (for which Dante is renowned) and not the overall vision, inasmuch as the former inheres in the latter, and is yet itself unbounded in significance.

The Triumph of Life is a draft fragment that for many marks the tragic incompletion of Shelley's life and works. But there is also a sense in which 'fragmentariness' was an abiding truth for Shelley, whose ideals were well beyond ordinary reach—as may be inferred from his apotheosis of Dante in the heaven of poets. While death itself intervened in the case of *The Triumph of Life*, the poem did, in some sense, fulfil the poet's career, bringing to fruition, in some 548 lines of masterly, yet scarcely revised verse, Shelley's everincreasing affinity with the Italians, and especially Dante. The *Triumph* is saturated with the presence of Dante, to an extent that must be unique in world literature. Not only is it interwoven with the *Commedia*, but its formidable use of *terza rima* and stylistic imitation are constant signals of Dante's example. The degree of this immersion has been charted in detail and its conflation with the iconography of Roman conquest as well as Petrarch's *Trionfi* made clear.[38] Naturally, one cannot underestimate the importance of Petrarch whose successive ultimately liberating 'triumphs' provide the principal model for Shelley's single, condensed, enslaving 'conquest', twice envisioned as in a waking dream, within which Dantean elements, both thematic and formal, are, at every point, inlaid. But it is Dante who seems to be the presiding genius of the poem and this is

---

[38] See Weinberg, *Shelley's Italian Experience*, 202–42.

indicated in repeated, mainly purgatorial motifs, and in the passing homage to Dante which appears close to the end of the fragment:

'[…] Behold a wonder worthy of the rhyme

'Of him who from the lowest depths of Hell
Through every Paradise and through all glory
Love led serene, and who returned to tell

'In words of hate and awe the wondrous story
How all things are transfigured, except Love […]'

(471–6)

In their precise condensation of the whole of the poet's journey, these lines, spoken by Rousseau, seem to echo the several terse reminders to Dante by Virgil of the groundplan of his journey and Beatrice's guidance, so that the map of the whole is always in his and the reader's mind, and neither can lose their way. The steadiness of the writing, the exceptional abstract clarity of the diction (unusual in English poetry), and the unfolding syntax are also Dantean trademarks. The distinct English idiom is infused with Tuscan directness and flair. Yet Shelley reinforces his own independence, allowing the sense to cross over the *terzine*, in order to release Dante's composed and certain progress into the flow and texture of Shelley's own troubled vision—at this point in the narrative disturbingly redolent of Dante's Hell—within which the similitude (itself Dantean) is framed. The *Commedia* seems to stand outside Shelley's text as exemplary—to function on a different plane of signification wherein Dante's vision is both lived and retold—and yet not to be allowed that freedom, least of all because the entire poem is so filled with Dantean echoes (the disillusioned and defeated Rousseau replacing Virgil as Shelley's guide to what lies ahead). The strategic positioning and verbal emphasis of 'Love led serene' (ironically recalling the triple 'Amor' tercets in *Inferno* 5. 100–8) and the play on 'serene' as attribute of Love, mode of its operation, and sign of the pilgrim's well-being, leave unanswered questions as to whether this is the beacon for which Shelley has been searching. Certainly, love's unique surpassing of transfiguration endows it with exceptional 'virtue'. One is left with the poignant impression that, to the very end of Shelley's life, Dante still pointed the way forward or beyond.

Select Bibliography

Eliot, T. S. 'What Dante Means to Me'. *To Criticize the Critic and Other Writings*. London, Faber, 1965. 125–35.

Keach, William. *Shelley's Style*. New York: Methuen, 1984.

O'Neill, Michael. ' "Fashioned from his Opposite": Yeats, Dante and Shelley'. *Journal of Anglo-Italian Studies* 8 (2006), 149–71.

Pite, Ralph, '"The Lucifer of that Starry Flock": Shelley in *Purgatorio*'. *The Circle of Our Vision: Dante's Presence in English Romantic Poetry*. Oxford: Clarendon Press, 1994. 161–98.

Rossington, Michael. 'Theorizing a Republican Poetics: P. B. Shelley and Alfieri'. *European Romantic Review* 20.5 (2009), 619–28.

Saglia, Diego. 'From Gothic Italy to Italy as Gothic Archive: Italian Narratives and the Late Romantic Metrical Tale'. *Gothic Studies* 8.1 (2006), 73–90.

Webb, Timothy. *The Violet in the Crucible: Shelley and Translation*. Oxford: Clarendon Press, 1976.

Weinberg, Alan. *Shelley's Italian Experience*. London, Macmillan, 1991.

CHAPTER 29

ORIGINS OF EVIL

Shelley, Goethe, Calderón, and Rousseau

FREDERICK BURWICK

While yet a boy I sought for ghosts, and sped
Through many a listening chamber, cave and ruin,
And starlight wood, with fearful steps pursuing
Hopes of high talk with the departed dead.
I called on poisonous names with which our youth is fed.

('Hymn to Intellectual Beauty', ll. 49–53, *H* 531)[1]

Although Shelley acknowledged the 'vain endeavour' of 'Frail spells' to conjure ghosts or demons, he remained fascinated throughout his life with the power of evil. On the one hand, he dismissed supernaturalism with his affirmation of atheism; on the other, he persistently conjured both God and Satan as absolute personifications of good and evil. He repeatedly addressed the struggle against the evil of tyranny and corrupt authority, as variously represented in the Sultan of Turkey against whom Laon and Cythna wage their revolution, or in Jupiter opposed by the unremitting Prometheus, or in Cenci whose daughter defies his malignant cruelty. In his exploration of continental literature, too, Shelley focused his attention on prominent expositions of the character of evil, as in Johann Wolfgang von Goethe's *Faust* and Pedro Calderón de la Barca's *El mágico prodigioso*, or in Jean-Jacques Rousseau's account of the social propagation of evil.

In turning to Goethe, Calderón, and Rousseau, however, Shelley found the problematic nature of evil exacerbated rather than resolved. Whence does evil derive its power? How does it propagate its influence? Shelley observed as well the human fallibility in attempting to distinguish between good and evil. At the opening of *The Revolt of Islam* (*H* 42–7) the narrator himself errs in judging a mighty contest, 'An Eagle and a Serpent wreathed in fight'. Reacting in terms of prejudice rather than of knowledge, the narrator

---

[1] Quotations from Shelley's poetry in this chapter are from *H*, unless specified otherwise.

is frightened when a woman cradles the injured serpent, certain that she will become its victim as soon as the serpent revives (320–1). She corrects his misperception. The eagle, not the snake, is the spirit of evil. With the very advent of creation the 'Two Powers' together 'burst the womb of inessential Nought'. In the shape of a 'blood-red Comet', the evil spirit battled the 'Morning Star'. Evil triumphed and cast his rival into the shape abhorred by mankind, the snake:

> 'Evil triumphed, and the Spirit of evil,
> One Power of many shapes which none may know,
> One Shape of many names; the Fiend did revel
> In victory, reigning o'er a world of woe,
> For the new race of man went to and fro,
> Famished and homeless, loathed and loathing, wild,
> And hating good—for his immortal foe,
> He changed from starry shape, beauteous and mild,
> To a dire Snake, with man and beast unreconciled.'
>
> (361–9; *H* 46)

The strategy of evil is not simply to appear more attractive than good, but also to render good repulsive and deformed. Worse than having lost the ability to distinguish good from evil, mankind confounded the two, scorning the former and admiring the latter. The task besetting the narrator of *The Revolt of Islam* is thus to defend the outcast 'Spirit of Good' left to 'creep among | The nations of mankind' (370–6), and to arouse the opposition against 'the conquering Fiend' who reigns in 'Fear, Hatred, Faith, and Tyranny', ever attracting new converts to his dominion: 'His spirit is their power, and they his slaves' (378–96).

In his Preface to *Prometheus Unbound* Shelley declared that 'the only imaginary being resembling Prometheus in any degree, is Satan' (*H* 205). In Act I, however, Shelley presented another comparison. In addition to Satan, Prometheus in his suffering resembles the crucified Christ. The Furies conjure the comparison in taunting their victim for his blighted endeavour to benefit mankind: 'Dost thou boast the clear knowledge thou waken'dst for man?' That knowledge became a curse, just as the words of Christ were adopted as a rationale for persecution and war (I, 542–63; *H* 220). Mercury urged obsequious servitude; the Furies denied that good could possibly prevail against evil. Prometheus cannot refute the Furies' argument that the name of Christ had become a curse (I, 604) and that 'all best things are thus confused to ill' (I, 628); he insists nevertheless that evil prevails only because the sense of the beautiful and good has been repressed. As rebel against Jupiter, Prometheus may resemble Satan, yet Shelley insists that the essential difference lies in presenting his character 'as exempt from the taints of ambition, envy, revenge and a desire for personal aggrandisement'. We may nevertheless sympathize with, and even admire, Satan, because in weighing these faults against a punishment of eternal damnation, we 'excuse the former because the latter exceed all measure' (*H* 205).

In *A Defence of Poetry*, Shelley presented an even stronger case for admiring Milton's Satan, a 'character of energy and magnificence' who cannot be mistaken for the 'popular personification of evil'. For Shelley, it is crucial to distinguish between the motives and actions of the oppressor and the oppressed. 'Milton's Devil as a moral being is as far superior to his God, as one who perseveres in some purpose which he has conceived to be excellent in spite of adversity and torture, is to one who in the cold security of undoubted triumph inflicts the most horrible torment upon his enemy, not from any mistaken notion of inducing him to repent of a perseverance in enmity, but with an alleged design of exasperating him to deserve new punishments' (*Norton 1*, 498–9). The reader of *Paradise Lost* is thus apt to err in the same manner as the narrator of *The Revolt of Islam* upon witnessing the battle of the serpent and the eagle. 'Implacable hate, patient cunning, and a sleepless refinement of device to inflict the extremest anguish on an enemy, these things are evil; and, although venial in a slave, are not to be forgiven in a tyrant' (*Norton 1*, 499). The true source of evil is not the rebellious slave, but the tyrant god. William Blake shared a similar conviction when he declared that Milton 'was a true Poet and of the Devil's party without knowing it'.[2]

Neither Calderón nor Goethe provided Shelley with a model of the absolute corruption of absolute power that had enabled him to redeem the Rebel Archangel and to cast his Prometheus as a character 'of the highest perfection of moral and intellectual nature' (*H* 205). In translating the 'Prologue in Heaven' from Goethe's *Faust*, Shelley encountered a very different interpretation of the relationship between good and evil, God and devil. Goethe's Mephistopheles is granted a divine dispensation to agitate humanity. To be sure, Shelley's Cenci claims a divine authority to act as God's chastising rod, believing that Providence favours him and that 'Heaven has special care of me' (I. iii. 55–65). But Shelley leaves no doubt that Cenci's belief is self-delusion. Although Goethe, too, defined the character of Mephistopheles in terms of a particular set of delusions about his power, he also depicted God sanctioning the intrusion into the life of Faust.

For Goethe, as for Rousseau, the power of evil wells up from no other hell than that which dwells in human desires. In *Peter Bell the Third* Shelley had already adopted this Rousseauistic mode of defining the social origins of evil:

> The Devil, I safely can aver,
>   Has neither hoof, nor tail, nor sting;
> Nor is he, as some sages swear,
> A spirit, neither here nor there,
>   In nothing—yet in every thing.
>
> He is—what we are; for sometimes
>   The Devil is a gentleman;
> At others a bard bartering rhymes
> For sack; a statesman spinning crimes;
>   A swindler, living as he can.
>
>   (*Peter Bell the Third*, 76–85; *H* 349)

---

[2] William Blake, *Marriage of Heaven and Hell*, plate 5, *The Complete Poetry and Prose of William Blake*, ed. David V. Erdman (Berkeley and Los Angeles: University of California Press, 1982), 34–5.

This Devil is an attribute of human character, now a gentleman, now a thief. He resides in the very dwellings occupied by every other inhabitant of the metropolis:

> Hell is a city much like London—
>   A populous and a smoky city;
> There are all sorts of people undone,
> And there is little or no fun done;
>   Small justice shown, and still less pity.

(*Peter Bell the Third*, 147–51; *H* 349)

Shelley's interest in Calderón, Goethe, and Rousseau is directed by their dominant thematic concerns: Rousseau's sense of a paradise lost in the movement from simple rustic nature to the corrupt and corrupting influences of crowded cities; Calderón's interrogation of conflicting systems of social and religious morality; Goethe's insistence that negation and inaction are the source of human failure and downfall.

Mephistopheles no sooner emerges from his dog disguise than the shrewd doctor demands that he declare his true identity. In the first of his three attempts, he states that he is 'A part of that power, | That always wants evil but always creates good' ('Ein Teil von jener Kraft, | Die stets das Böse will und stets das Gute schafft', 1335–6).[3] By itself, this definition seems the opposite of the paradox posed by the Furies, who contended that efforts to do good inevitably ended in evil. Mephistopheles follows with a second definition of self: 'I am the spirit that always negates' ('Ich bin der Geist, der stets verneint'). Here he identifies himself with the decay and corruption, the doom of all material being, the source of the despair that it would be better not to be born. As negation of life and vitality, his natural element is everything known as sin, destruction, and evil (1338–44).

When Faust challenges him to explain what he means about being a part of a more extensive power, Mephistopheles offers his third self-definition: 'I'm part of the Part which at the first was all, | Part of the Darkness that gave birth to Light' ('Ich bin ein Teil des Teils, der anfangs alles war, | Ein Teil der Finsternis, die sich das Licht gebar', 1349–50). Similar to Goethe's appeal to the primal opposition of darkness and light, Shelley, too, gave a cosmic dimension to the battle between the 'blood-red Comet' and the 'Morning Star'. Driven back but not dispelled by the *Fiat Lux*, Darkness remains for Goethe a persistent and necessary 'part' of the divine creation.

Unlike Goethe's Faust, Calderón's Cyprian fails to recognize the Daemon as instigator of evil. In their first encounter they debate on the identity of God. In their second meeting, even though the Daemon narrates a mortal version of the satanic rebellion and fall, Cyprian continues to find him a congenial acquaintance. Because Cyprian's friends Floro and Lelio are at the point of duelling over their love of Justina, Cyprian promises to intervene by visiting Justina in order to determine whether either of them has a place in the lady's affections. The Daemon's plot is to arouse in Justina an irresistible love for

---

[3] *Goethes Faust. Der Tragödie erster und zweiter Teil. Urfaust*, ed. Erich Trunz (Hamburg: Christian Wegner Verlag, 1963).

Cyprian and in Cyprian a passion for Justina that overwhelms his reason. Justina is immediately suspicious and challenges the Daemon to declare his identity:

> JUSTINA.   And who art thou, who hast found entrance hither,
> Into my chamber through the doors and locks?
> Art thou a monstrous shadow which my madness
> Has formed in the idle air?
> DAEMON.   No. I am one
> Called by the Thought which tyrannizes thee
> From his eternal dwelling.
>
> (Scene iii. 101–7)[4]

Although the Daemon denies that he is merely a shadow of her madness, his declaration that he is called by her thought identifies him as conjured by her own mind. Calderón at this point has given evidence that Cyprian, too, mentally summoned the Daemon in his quandary about God's identity, good and evil. In his conviction that he can live a life of reason free from the sway of passion, he renders himself all the more vulnerable. Justina is similarly confident that will and moral rectitude protect her against the Daemon's torment. As the Daemon reminds her, her stronghold has already been penetrated. Her imagination has already sanctioned the seduction. Calderón's Daemon affirms the theological dictum that a sin in thought foreshadows a sin in deed:

> JUSTINA.   So shall thy promise fail. This agony
> Of passion which afflicts my heart and soul
> May sweep imagination in its storm;
> The will is firm.
> DAEMON.   Already half is done
> In the imagination of an act.
> The sin incurred, the pleasure then remains;
> Let not the will stop half-way on the road.
>
> (Scene iii. 109–16)[5]

---

[4] Calderón de la Barca, *El mágico prodigioso*, in *Obras (Teatro doctrinal y religioso)*, ed. Angel Valbuena Prat (Barcelona: Vergara, 1965), 301–403. This text is based on the first edition in *Parte veinte de comedias varias* (Madrid, 1663).

> JUSTINA.   ¿Quién eres tú, que has entrado
> hasta este retrete mío,
> estando todo cerrado?
> ¿Eres monstruo, que ha formado
> mi confuso desvarío?
> DEMONIO.   No soy sino quien, movido
> dese afecto que tirano
> te ha postrado y te ha vencido

[5] Calderón, *El mágico prodigioso*.

> JUSTINA.   Pues no lograrán tu intento;
> que esta pena, esta pasión
> que afligió mi pensamiento,

Similar to Calderón, Rousseau locates the source of evil in the human mind. He differs, however, in assigning the motivation not to emotion in conflict with reason, but to social rivalry, ambition, and greed.

> Man, seek the author of evil no longer. It is yourself. No evil exists other than that which you do or suffer, and both come to you from yourself. General evil can exist only in disorder; and I see in the system of the world an unfailing order. Particular evil exists only in the sentiment of the suffering being, and man did not receive this sentiment from nature: he gave it to himself. Take away our fatal progress, take away our errors and our vices, take away the work of man, and everything is good.[6]

Shelley would have found in Rousseau's works a concern as strong as his own with human fallibility in distinguishing good and evil. Rousseau argued that each person possessed a natural intuition to tell good from evil. This intuition, however, may be altered by society and civil education, so that moral conscience, as 'nature's voice', is drowned out by social prejudices. This argument, in Book 4 of *Émile*, is followed by the 'Profession of a Savoyard Priest', in which Rousseau concludes that institutional religion is as fallible as other social institutions, and therefore equally disruptive of the natural voice of moral conscience.[7] A predominate issue in the *Social Contract*, Rousseau's preoccupation with the corruptive forces of urban conditions and authoritative rule pervades as well the *Confessions*, *Julie*, and *Émile*.[8]

From his earlier casual reading of Goethe,[9] Shelley was prompted by the interest of John Gisborne and Claire Clairmont to undertake a serious study of *Faust* just a year before his death. The first mention of this interest is in a letter to Gisborne (16 June 1821). He subsequently lamented Coleridge's apparent failure to complete his promised translation, and by spring 1822 he was encouraging Claire in her translation of Goethe's autobiography and had sent Gisborne his own translation of passages which had been omitted from the selections accompanying the English edition of Moritz Retzsch's illustrations to *Faust, I*.[10]

> llevó la imaginación,
> pero no el consentimiento.
> Demonio. En haberlo imaginado
> hecho tienes la mitad:
> pues ya el pecado es pecado,
> no pares la voluntad,
> el medio camino andado.

---

[6] Rousseau, *Émile: or, On Education*, trans. Allan Bloom (New York: Basic Books, 1979), Book 4, 282.

[7] Ibid., Book 4, 313.

[8] 'Shelley's Reading', *Letters: PBS* II, 483; Reiman, *Shelley's The Triumph of Life: A Critical Study* (Urbana, IL: University of Illinois Press, 1965), 19–20, 56, 58–9, 74–6. (This edition is used for quotations from *The Triumph of Life*.)

[9] Much of the ensuing commentary on Goethe is adapted from 'Shelley: The "Traces" of *Faust*', in Burwick, *The Damnation of Newton: Goethe's Color Theory and Romantic Perception* (Berlin: De Gruyter, 1986), 257–74. Shelley's first reference to Goethe, in a letter to Jefferson Hogg (2 June 1811), concerns *Die Leiden des jungen Werthers*, which Shelley probably knew from the popular translation of 1802; see: J. M. Carré, *Goethe en Angleterre* (Paris: Plon-Nourrit, 1921), ch. 5.

[10] To Gisborne (12 January 1822 and 10 April 1822), *Letters: PBS* II, 376, 407.

A German edition of Retzsch's line engravings appeared in 1816, and in January 1820 J. H. Bohte published an edition with excerpts translated into English to accompany each of the twenty-six plates illustrated by Retzsch. Independent of Bohte's enterprise, Boosey and Sons issued a similar edition the following month. Although neither offered more than poor piecemeal translations from Goethe's text, both editions sold out quickly. Hoping for even greater success, Thomas Boosey wrote to Coleridge soliciting his 'friendly advice'.[11] Several years had passed since Coleridge had responded to a similar enquiry from John Murray, 'that you wish to have the justly celebrated Faust of Goethe translated; & that some one or other of my partial friends have induced you to consider me as the man most likely to execute the work adequately'.[12] He proposed, in addition to the poetic translation, a separate acting version, in which he would 'compose the whole anew', promising he would 'not repeat or retain one fifth of the original': 'I should re-model the whole, give it a Finale, and be able to bring it thus re-written & re-cast, on the Stage'.[13] As he explained to Byron, he was soon convinced 'that the fantastic characters of its Witcheries and the general tone of its morals and religious opinions would be highly obnoxious to the taste and Principles of the present righteous English Public'.[14] Murray's commission of 1814 may have resulted in no more than a few pages. When Boosey approached him six years later, Coleridge responded with a proposal very similar to the one he had sent Murray. Anonymity would be the indispensable condition: 'Without my name I should feel the objections & the difficulty greatly diminished'.[15] Two days later, he forwarded 'My Advice & Scheme', outlining 'A preliminary Essay', on the same plan proposed to Murray, but also calling for a scene-by-scene analysis with representative passages 'translated in the manner & metre of the original', to be followed by 'Each of the scenes entire [...] on which Ret[z]ch's Plates are founded—translated poetically as for the stage'.[16]

In September 1821, Boosey and Sons published the expanded edition, now entitled *Faustus: from the German of Goethe*.[17] Among the scenes that Coleridge omitted, however, were the 'Prologue in Heaven' and the 'Walpurgis Night', the very scenes in which Goethe had elaborated, respectively, his notion on the necessary coexistence and

[11] Carl F. Schreiber, 'Coleridge to Boosey—Boosey to Coleridge', *Yale University Library Gazette* 20 (July 1947), 9–10; Coleridge to Boosey (10 May 1820), *Collected Letters of Samuel Taylor Coleridge*, ed. Earl Leslie Griggs (Oxford: Clarendon Press, 1959–71), V, 42–3.

[12] Coleridge to Murray (23 August 1814), *Coleridge Letters*, III, 521–3. Samuel Smiles, *A Publisher and his Friends*, 2 vols. (London: Murray, 1891), I, 118, 299.

[13] Coleridge to Murray (31 August 1814), *Coleridge Letters*, 3, 523–5.

[14] Coleridge to Byron (Easter Week, 1815); see also Coleridge to Murray (10 September 1814). *Coleridge Letters*, III, 528; IV, 559–63.

[15] Coleridge to Boosey (10 May 1820), *Coleridge Letters*, V, 42–4.

[16] MS. in the Huntington Library, accession number 131334; transcribed by Griggs in *Coleridge Letters*, V, 43.

[17] See *Faustus, translated by Samuel Taylor Coleridge from the German of Goethe*, ed. Frederick Burwick and James McKusick (Oxford: Oxford UP, 2007). Goethe comments on Coleridge's translation in his correspondence: Goethe to J. C. Hüttner (30 July 1820), *Goethes Werke*, 143 vols. (Weimar: Hermann Böhlau, 1887–1919) = WA, 4, Bd. 33, 137. Boosey to Goethe, in Schreiber, 'Coleridge to Boosey', 9–10. Goethe to August von Goethe (4 September 1820), WA, 4, Bd. 33, 200–1.

reciprocity of good and evil and on the compelling sexual energy of evil. When Shelley announced, 'We have just got the etchings of "Faust"' (*Letters: PBS* II, 376; 12 January 1822), time enough had elapsed for the improved 1821 edition to have reached him.[18] His designation of the work as 'the etchings of "Faust"', however, makes it more likely that he formulated his objections upon looking into the prose passages of the 1820 edition: 'It is not bad, & faithful enough—but how weak! how incompetent to represent Faust!' (*Letters: PBS* II, 407; 10 April 1822). Shelley also had a copy of the excerpts recently published in *Blackwood's* (June 1820).[19] Shelley compared the text accompanying Retzsch's plates with Anster's translation and judged them both 'miserable'. He prized Retzsch's illustrations, for they stimulated his visual access to Goethe's language. Of Retzsch's rendition of the meeting of Faust and Gretchen, Shelley exclaimed: 'It makes all the pulses of my head beat' (*Letters: PBS* II, 376; 12 January 1822). As he began his own translation of *Faust*, he returned again and again to Retzsch for guidance:

> What etchings those are! I am never satiated with looking at them, & I fear it is the only sort of translation of which Faust is susceptible—I never perfectly understood the Har[t]z Mountain scene until I saw the etching.—And then, Margaret in the summer House with Faust!—The artist makes one envy his happiness that he can sketch such things with calmness, which I dared only to look upon once, & which made my brain swim round only to touch the leaf on the opposite side of which I knew that it was figured. (*Letters: PBS* II, 407; 10 April 1822)

Perhaps 'the pencil surpasses language in some subjects', or perhaps 'I am more affected by a visible image', Shelley speculated in trying to explain the extreme sensitivity of his response; in either case, he was sure that in this scene, the etching had excited him 'more than the poem it illustrated' (*Letters: PBS* II, 407; 10 April 1822). In his own poetic effort, Shelley deliberately chose scenes that had not been translated in Boosey's first edition. In lamenting 'how imperfect a representation [...] my words convey', he added his regret, along with Lockhart, that Coleridge had not held to his intention: 'No one but Coleridge is capable of this work.'[20] From Byron, Shelley would have known of Coleridge's earlier negotiations with Murray. From the Gisbornes, he probably had also learned of the recent arrangements with Boosey. The Gisbornes visited Coleridge at Highgate on 25 June 1820, just six weeks after he had submitted his 'Advice & Scheme'. Coleridge's talk reflected his concern with the undertaking, for Maria Gisborne wrote in her journal: 'He should like to translate the Faust [of Goethe], but he thinks that there are parts which

---

[18] Timothy Webb, *The Violet in the Crucible: Shelley and Translation* (Oxford: Clarendon Press, 1976), 148, presumed that Shelley had the 1821 edition; Richard Holmes, *Shelley, the Pursuit* (New York: E. P. Dutton, 1975), 692, claimed that it was the 1820 edition. Byron was unaware of the two editions when he wrote to Douglas Kinnaird (4 December 1821): 'Are there not designs of Faust? send me some—and a translation of it—if such there is—also of Goethe's life if such there be—if not—the original German', *Byron's Letters and Journals*, ed. Leslie Marchand (Cambridge, MA: Harvard UP, 1973–82), IX, 75.

[19] *Blackwood's Magazine* 7 (June 1820), 235–58.

[20] To Gisborne (12 January and 10 April 1822), *Letters: PBS* II, 376, 406–7.

could not be endured in english and by the English, and he does not like to attempt it with the necessity of the smallest mutilation.'[21]

Leigh Hunt had sought the support of Shelley and Byron in launching *The Liberal*, a literary magazine whose 'object [...] is not political, except in as much as all writing now-a-days must involve something to that effect.'[22] If Hunt had thought that a translation of *Faust* might assault the political as well as moral sensibilities of the English, he would have been doubly pleased with Shelley's proposed contribution. Shelley had discovered similarities between Calderón's *Mágico prodigioso* and Goethe's *Faust* and had translated 'several scenes from both', which he intended to present in an essay for this new periodical.[23] As Hunt wrote in the preface to the first issue, 'Italian Literature in particular will be a favourite subject with us; and so was German and Spanish to have been, till we lost the accomplished Scholar and Friend who was to share our task.'[24] Shelley and Williams had sailed in the *Don Juan* to meet Hunt at Livorno; on the return trip, 8 July, the boat was caught in a squall and Williams and Shelley were drowned. The first number of *The Liberal* included Shelley's translation of the Walpurgis Night. The promised essay was never written.

What he wanted to accomplish in his essay on Calderón and Goethe, Shelley had explained to Gisborne. Recalling 'Coleridge's distinction' of the poet and philosopher in the *Biographia Literaria*,[25] Shelley appraised the differences between *Mágico prodigioso* and *Faust*: 'if I were to acknowledge Coleridge's distinction, I should say, Göthe [sic] *was* the greatest philosopher & Calderón the greatest poet.'[26] Shelley went on to declare that Calderón's Cyprian 'evidently furnished the germ of Faust, as Faust may furnish the germ of other poems; although it is different from it in structure & plan, as the acorn from the oak' (*Letters: PBS* II, 407; 10 April 1822). The germination or Germanizing of Cyprian into Faust was a thesis that Shelley had shared with Thomas Medwin. Medwin, in turn, reported how Byron summarized the evidence that Goethe's 'plot is almost entirely Calderon's':

> The fête, the scholar, the argument about the *Logos*, the selling himself to the fiend, and afterwards denying his power; his disguise of the plumed cavalier; the enchanted mirror,—are all from Cyprian. That *magico prodigioso* must be worth reading, and nobody seems to know any thing about it but you and Shelley.[27]

[21] Maria Gisborne and Edward E. Williams, *Shelley's Friends: Their Journals and Letters*, ed. Frederick L. Jones (Norman, OK: University of Oklahoma Press, 1951), 37.

[22] Preface to *The Liberal* (1822), *Prefaces by Leigh Hunt*, ed. R. Brimley Johnson (1927; repr. Port Washington, NY: Kennikat Press, 1967), 59.

[23] To Gisborne (10 April 1822), *Letters: PBS* II, 407. See: W. H. Marshall, *Byron, Shelley, Hunt and 'The Liberal'* (Philadelphia: University of Pennsylvania Press, 1960).

[24] *Prefaces by Leigh Hunt*, 59.

[25] *Biographia Literaria*, ed. James Engell and W. Jackson Bate, *The Collected Works of Samuel Taylor Coleridge*, 7 vols. (Princeton: Princeton UP, 1983), II, 130.

[26] Shelley may have known, through Byron, of Coleridge's proposal to Murray for translations from the Spanish (10 September 1814 and 10 April 1816), *Coleridge Letters*, III, 528; IV, 633. In his notebooks, Coleridge considered an explanation of the pact and struggle with the devil in 'Calderon's Robbers or the Cross' (*La Devoción de la Cruz*), to 'shew that this is no mere frenzy of a Poet' (June–July 1810); *Notebooks of Samuel Taylor Coleridge*, ed. Kathleen Coburn (London: Routledge & Kegan Paul, 1957–73), III, 3924.

[27] *Medwin's Conversations of Lord Byron*, ed. E. L. Lovell, Jr. (Princeton: Princeton UP, 1966), 142.

Especially in the struggle of Prometheus with Jupiter, his rejection of Mercury's debased sycophancy, and the evil casuistry of the Furies, Shelley revealed a thorough comprehension of the same moral issues which provided the dialogue of Calderón's Cyprian and the Daemon, of Goethe's Faust and Mephistopheles.

But what did Shelley mean by his conditional 'if' in acknowledging 'Coleridge's distinction'? Philosophy is distinguished from poetry, Coleridge wrote, because it 'proposes truth for its immediate object, instead of pleasure'. After years of urging Wordsworth to write *The Recluse*, Coleridge could scarcely dismiss a philosophical poem as an abominable self-contradiction. He did argue that, 'till the blessed time shall come, when truth itself shall be pleasure', any attempt to reconcile Horace's *prodesse* and *delectare* shall remain 'unfortunately a small Hysteron-Proteron'. Coleridge, for the purpose of his argument on the 'defects of Wordsworth's poetry', had put aside the reciprocity of the 'philosophical imagination'; he then separated the poet's apprehension of truth from his formal obligation, in poetry, of leading others to truth. In poetry, feeling must guide the reason.[28] Shelley, of course, had offered his own explanation of the relation between reason and imagination, the analytic and synthetic functions of the mind, at the beginning of *A Defence of Poetry* (1821). For Shelley, very much concerned with hysteron-proteron as the confounding of time and space in perception, it was important to define the causal connection: 'Reason is to imagination as the instrument to the agent, as the body to the spirit, as the shadow to the substance.'[29] In designating Calderón as more the poet, Goethe more the philosopher, Shelley entertained a relative sense of their concerns with emotion and reason. Cyprian claimed that he had been wrestling with a passage from Pliny: 'God is one supreme goodness, one pure essence, | One substance, and one sense, all sight, all hands.' But it is the Daemon, not Cyprian, who quotes Pliny's words. When Cyprian cited the faulty deity of Jupiter, the example of his evil is not corrupt power but sexual lust:

> aun a Júpiter le falta
> suma bondad, pues le vemos
> que es pecaminoso en tantas
> ocasíones: Dánae hable
> rendida, Europa robada.[30]

Shelley excised the merely sexual definition of his faults to give him the tyrannic will of Jupiter in *Prometheus Unbound*:

> even Jupiter
> Is not supremely good; because we see
> His deeds are evil, and his attributes
> Tainted with mortal weakness.
>
> (*H* 734)[31]

---

[28] *Biographia Literaria*, I, 241; II, 16–17, 130–1.   [29] *Norton 1*, 480.

[30] Calderón, *Obras*, 308.

[31] *MYR* VII, and *BSM*, XIX. On Shelley and Calderón: Salvador de Madariaga, *Shelley and Calderon* (London: Constable, 1920); Eunice Gates, 'Shelley and Calderon', *Philological Quarterly* 16 (1937), 49–58; Webb, *Violet in the Crucible*, 204–75.

The Daemon answered Cyprian that the stories of the 'gods' were merely a grand disguise for moral lessons on human frailties:

> Ésas son falsas historias
> en que las letras profanes,
> con los nombres de los dioses
> entendieron disfrazada
> la moral filosofía.[32]

> The wisdom
> Of the old world masked with the names of Gods
> The attributes of Nature and of Man;
> A sort of popular philosophy.

> (*H* 735)

Shelley revealed a peculiar relevance of his conditional 'if' when he had Cyprian, in pursuing the argument of good and evil as the conflict of opposing wills, deny that his thinking on divinity had been formed by classical myth. His denial refers back to the Daemon's account of myth. Shelley wanted Cyprian's denial to include both poetic 'wisdom' and 'popular' (not simply 'moral') philosophy: 'That you may not say that I allege | Poetical or philosophic learning' (*H* 735). Cyprian reasons about God but acts according to his emotions. After conducting his logical excursions on God as 'All sight [...] | One cause of all cause', he engages his sight only in his passion for Justina, and, in giving his soul to the Daemon, he surrenders to the dictates of that passion. Calderón's irony is that the Daemon acknowledges Cyprian's ingenuity of reason, but suspends his reason in passion, enthrals his study in a fascination with Justina's beauty, and redirects his ingenuity to the fulfilment of his desire:

> Pues tanto su estudio alcanza,
> yo haré que el estudio olvides,
> suspendido en una rara
> beldad.

> Since thus it profits him
> To study, I will wrap his senses up
> In sweet oblivion of all thought but of
> A piece of excellent beauty.

> (*H* 736–7)

Shelley was clearly aware of the difference in Goethe's dilemma of 'Law and Impulse' ('Pflicht und Neigung') in dramatizing Faust's struggle with reason and passion: 'Two souls dwell, alas! within my breast' ('Zwei Seelen wohnen, ach! in meiner Brust', 1112). In *El mágico prodigioso*, the rational Cyprian is overwhelmed with desire. After the opening scene, he becomes too much involved in his own passion to try the rivalry of reason or test his capacity of vision against the Daemon's. Even in the opening scene, the Daemon mockingly insinuates that Cyprian is not seeing clearly. Faust, although

---

[32] Calderón, *Obras*, 308.

acquiescing to illusion, soon learns to rely on his own perception in opposition to Mephistopheles' way of seeing.

The two scenes from *Faust* which Shelley had completed by April were those omitted by Coleridge: 'Prologue in Heaven' and 'Walpurgis Night'. The 'Prologue in Heaven' begins with a choral hymn to light sung by the Archangels Raphael, Gabriel, and Michael, parallel to the opening of Part II in which Faust proclaims in *terza rima* a reveille upon the rising sun whose light not only revives the permanent form of the ephemeral rainbow, 'des bunten Bogens Wechseldauer', but also provides a symbol for all human striving.[33] Not in the source of light but in its refraction man has life. Goethe's concern in the Prologue is similar, but opposition and conflict rather than reconciliation, in spite of the divine presence, receive the poetic emphasis. Goethe's tripart division is at work: Raphael sings of the source of light, Gabriel of its material refraction, Michael of its dissipation in chaotic darkness. Shelley translated this sequence twice, once for poetic effect and again for literal representation, and in both he reveals a control of the subtle word-play on the negative and positive attributes of light. Goethe's phrase, 'Da flammt ein blitzendes Verheeren' (263), is meant to implicate a 'verherrlichen' as well as the literal devastation, and he has it rhyme with 'verehren'. Shelley cannot hold to the rhyme as he renders the phrase 'There flames a flashing destruction' (literal) and 'A flashing desolation there, | Flames before the thunder's way' (poetic), but in both versions he repeats 'revere' as affective response.[34] The schematic array adapts a traditional division: God is light, Mephistopheles is darkness, and man exists in the refractive middle-ground of colour. Man's perception is influenced by the tension of this middle-ground: the colours closest to white (yellow and red) are positive and the colours closest to black (blue and violet) are negative; the former evoke movement and activity and the latter rest and passivity.[35] The contraries find a ground for reverence in mediation. Shelley translated well Goethe's justification of the ways of God to man:

> The active spirit of man soon sleeps, and soon
> He seeks unbroken quiet; therefore I
> Have given him the Devil for a companion,
> Who may provoke him to some sort of work,
> And must create forever.
>
> (100–4; *Faust*, 340–3)[36]

Because he kept in his translation the dialectics of *Tun* and *Leiden*, action and passion, creation and destruction, life and death, Shelley prepared for Goethe's version of the wager with Mephistopheles. Damnation is to occur when Faust says to any moment, 'Verweile doch, du bist so schön!' (*Faust*, I, 1700). Shelley adapted this very line in

---

[33] *Goethes Faust*, ed. Erich Trunz (Hamburg: Christian Wegner Verlag, 1963); *Faust*, I, 4725–7.

[34] *BSM*, XIX.

[35] 'Sinnlich-sittliche Wirkung der Farbe', *Zur Farbenlehre*, WA, II, Bd. 1, 307–59.

[36] Shelley missed the relevance of 'unbedingte Ruh' to Goethe's idea of 'bedingte und unbedingte Tätigkeit', and he rendered l. 343 in two lines without capturing the predicative emphasis: 'reizt und wirkt und muß als Teufel schaffen'.

'To Jane. The Invitation': 'At length I find one moment's good' (44).[37] To give up the persisting tensions of change in permanence ('Wechseldauer'), is to surrender the vitality of life. Shelley, who never saw Goethe's final dramatization of those fatal words:[38] 'Verweile doch! du bist so schön!' (*Faust*, II, 11582), knew perfectly how they might be turned to address dynamic perpetuity, the permanence in change.

The Walpurgis scene begins with Mephistopheles calling for magic, a broomstick or rutting ram,[39] to aid in the ascent, while Faust praises the regenerative powers at work in nature and the strength he feels in his own limbs. This scene starkly contrasts the way Faust perceives and the way Mephisto perceives. In the earlier demonic scene in the Witch's Kitchen, Faust was caught up in the spell of delusion. Here he asserts confidence in his perception. Complaining of the bad light of the late moon, Mephisto conjures an 'Irrlicht' as a guide. Shelley fully exploited the paradoxical irony of Mephisto's desire to follow an errant gleam:

> But see how melancholy rises now,
> Dimly uplifting her belated beam,
> The blank unwelcome round of the red moon,
> And gives so bad a light, that every step
> One stumbles 'gainst some crag.
> With your permission,
> I'll call on Ignis-fatuus to our aid.
>
> (17–22; 3851–5)[40]

As Shelley realized in his translation, Mephisto seeks to define red in terms of the self-consuming and extinguishing glow of vain mortal greed while Faust celebrates red as the kindling and creative power of dawn light:

> MEPHISTOPHELES.   One may observe from this point
> How Mammon glows among the mountains.
> FAUST.   Ay—

---

[37] Shelley explained this sense of stasis in process in the companion poem, 'To Jane. The Recollection':

> It seemed as if the hour were one
> Sent forth from beyond the skies,
> Which scattered from above the sun
> A light of Paradise.
>
> (17–20)

In his rendition of saying to the 'Augenblick': 'Verweile doch, du bist so schön', Shelley kept the visual purport of the German word for moment, and he added ambiguity (possessive, contractive) in 'one moment's good'.

[38] *Faust, II* was completed in 1831 and published posthumously in 1832. In a letter to the Gisbornes (13 July 1821), Shelley expressed his 'impatience for the conclusion', *Letters: PBS* II, 308.

[39] Shelley translated 'allerderbsten Bock' as 'a good stout ram', he omitted Mephisto's obscene exchange with the old witch (4136–43) and left out such lines as 'es furzt die Hexe, es stinkt der Bock'. As he wrote to Jefferson Hogg, Faust 'has passages of surpassing excellence, though there are some scenes—which the fastidiousness of our taste would wish erased' (22 October 1821), *Letters: PBS* II, 361.

[40] Shelley mistranslates the crescent moon's 'unvollkommne Scheibe' as an 'unwelcome round'.

And strangely through the solid depth below
A melancholy light, like the red dawn,
Shoots from the lowest gorge of the abyss
Of mountains, lightning hitherward: there rise
Pillars of smoke, here clouds float gently by;
Here the light burns soft as the enkindled air,
Or the illumined dust of golden flowers;
And now it glides like tender colours spreading;
And now bursts forth in fountains from the earth;
And now it winds, one torrent of broad light,
Through the far valley with a hundred veins;
And now once more within that narrow corner
Masses itself into intensest splendour.
And near us, see, sparks spring out of the ground,
Like golden sand scattered upon the darkness;
The pinnacles of that black wall of mountains
That hems us in are kindled.

(95–113; 3913–31)[41]

The colour play of kindling red and gold points the way to freedom: not human avarice toiling amidst dearth and death, as Mephistopheles sees, but a release from black physical constraint. Mephisto ushers Faust through frenzy and orgy, urging constantly his way of seeing. Shelley retained Goethe's thematic repetition of verbs of seeing and looking:

I see young witches naked there [...]
Come, I'll lead you
Among them; and what you do and see,
As a fresh compact 'twixt us two shall be.
How say you now? this space is wide enough—
Look forth, you cannot see the end of it—
An hundred bonfires burn in a row.

(224–54; 4056–7)

Even though he missed part of the idiom, he must have delighted in Mephisto's synaesthetic account of the snail's 'tastendens Gesicht':

See you that snail there?—she comes creeping up,
And with her feeling eyes hath smelt out something.

(226–67; 4066–8)

Shelley obviously understood Mephisto's attempt to command the eyes of Faust, and he was alert to that symbolic turn that startles Faust back to the dominion of his own seeing. Faust tells Mephisto what he has seen while dancing with a fair young girl: 'A red mouse in the middle of her singing | Sprung from her mouth' (373–4; 4178–9). Mephisto ironically appeals to the active–passive contrast, 'Be it enough that the mouse was not gray'

---

[41] Shelley's translation retains the contrasts of light and darkness; Goethe's concluding lines to this passage are: 'Doch schau! in ihrer ganzen Höhe | Entzündet sich die Felsenwand', 3930–1.

(375; 4182), but fails to appease the distraught Faust. Then, in the midst of telling more of what he saw, Faust is distracted by what he sees: an image of his beloved Margaret that Mephisto insists is an 'enchanted phantom' ('Zauberbild'). With sight still very much the theme, Mephisto and Faust speak at cross-purposes as they engage their differing perceptions and exchange their conflicting interpretations:

> FAUST.   Seest thou not a pale
> Fair girl [...]
> I cannot overcome the thought that she
> Is like poor Margaret.
> MEPH   [...] it is an enchanted phantom,
> A lifeless idol; with its numbing look
> It freezes up the blood of man; and they
> Who meet its ghastly stare are turned to stone,
> Like those who saw Medusa.
> FAUST.   Oh, too true!
> Her eyes are like the eyes of a fresh corpse
> Which no beloved hand has closed, alas!
>
>   (379–90; 4183–96)

Faust persists in seeing his beloved who has been beheaded; Mephisto, just as relentlessly, insists that he is seeing a dangerous delusion. Shelley's translation closes as the debate dissolves into the theatrical masque of Oberon and Titania. When the 'Walpurgisnachtstraum' passes, Faust awakens to find the prophetic image of Margaret had been all too true: his beloved awaits execution for the murder of her mother and her babe.

In the poems of 1822, Shelley further developed the theme of temporal perception. In 'To Jane. The Invitation', Shelley described a movement of light entering the world. The invitation, 'Best and brightest, come away', and 'Radiant Sister of the day, | Awake, arise and come away' (47–8) not only repeats from *Epipsychidion* the mystic identity of the woman in light, but describes, with the insistent refrain, 'away, away', light moving into the world: 'this halcyon morn | [...] Bending from Heaven in azure mirth' to kiss 'the forehead of the earth' (9–12). From 'azure mirth' of morn to 'blue noon', the only colour references Shelley gave to this poem are the refractions of light into blue and green, the dioptric penetration of light moving away from a beholder who would seek to arrest its flight in 'one moment's good'. 'To Jane. The Recollection' is a Wordsworthian exercise in memory's recreative powers. The colours, of course, are still green and blue, but the movement is no longer a linear 'Away, away'; appropriate to the reflexive process, movement is seen as a 'magic circle' closing upon its centre, much like the 'Feuerstrudel' Faust beholds in the circling dog in the meadow. The conjuring 'magic circle' moves 'from the remotest seat | Of the white mountain-waste, | To the soft flower beneath our feet' (41–4). Within its centre Shelley identifies Jane, now not as the 'Radiant Sister of the day', but still as a 'fair form' reflecting love into the atmosphere.

The Triumph of Life is a poem wrought for comparative analysis. As Donald Reiman has shown in his detailed study, Shelley employs the *terza rima* used by Dante in the *Divine Comedy* and by Petrarch in his seven *Triumphs*. From the latter Shelley adapts the genre of 'triumph', and from the former he repeats a visionary pilgrimage. Dante's guide was Virgil; Shelley takes Rousseau as his guide and interpreter. Much of the description of the visionary car and 'the birth | Of light' can be explained in terms of the Dantesque model,[42] but the influence of Goethe's *Faust* is at work here, too. The poet explains the 'triumphal pageant' in terms akin to Goethe's *Wechseldauer*: the chariot rolls with a procession of the damned, of fallen might, of 'fame or infamy', and is accompanied by dancers as manic and frenzied as those of the 'Walpurgis Night'. 'Swift, first, and obscene | The wild dance maddens in the van' as the dancers 'Mix with each other in tempestuous measure | To savage music' (137–42). Just as Goethe added the farting witch and stinking goat and old Baubo astride a sow, Shelley follows with 'Old men and women foully disarrayed' shaking 'their grey hairs in the insulting wind' (165–6). From the 'Witch's Kitchen' and *El mágico prodigioso* he has also taken the 'Zauberspiegel', a 'false and fragile glass' reflecting the vanity of desires (244–51). From Mephistopheles' perspective of negation, the primary colours are seen in the perversion of history by tyranny and anarchy, 'the plague of blood and gold' (287), and the 'true Sun' is 'quenched' (292). Shelley has Rousseau begin his narrative with perception wearied in the temporal flux: 'Mine eyes are sick with this perpetual flow' (298). But Rousseau goes on to recount his optimism born of the light of 'April prime' burning the forests 'With kindling green, touched by the azure clime | Of the young year' (308–26). Rousseau's vision of 'A shape all light' (343–57) joins company with Shelley's Asia, Emily, and Jane as a bewitchingly ambiguous version of the radiant angel. Shelley elaborates the image of the rainbow Iris, 'A moving arch of victory the vermillion | And green and azure plumes of Iris had | Built high over the wind-winged pavillion' (439–41).

It is easy enough to point to Shelley's translation of the 'Prologue in Heaven' for thematic parallels to 'the birth | Of light' and the stimulation of the vision within the 'transparent [...] scene' and through the 'veil of light' (1–40). The 'obscene' and 'wild dance' of the frenzied 'ribald crowd' within the dim and altered light of their own kindling (137–75) obviously echoes the grotesque pageantry of the rite of witches in the 'Walpurgis Night'. The intertextual dynamic in *The Triumph of Life* of Goethe alongside Dante and Rousseau brings into confluence disparate perspectives on origins of evil. Shelley's visionary narrator must witness the 'captive multitude | [...] subdued, | By action or by suffering' (119, 121–2) before he can raise the question, 'what is Life?' (544). He opened the 'Triumph' with the cosmic image of 'the stars that gem | The cone of night', an image that required the narrator to stand far off in space to behold his planet orbiting through the light of the sun.

With the arrival of the chariot driven by the four-faced Janus, the light is stirred and agitated, so that the day is darkened: 'a cold glare, intenser than the noon | But icy cold, obscured with light | The Sun as he the stars' (77–9). The moon in the twilight sky, 'When on the sunlit limits of the night | Her white shell trembled amid crimson air' (80–1) provided Shelley his visual metaphor for the 'rushing splendour' of the light-eclipsing

[42] Joseph Mazzeo, *Structure and Thought in the Paradiso* (Ithaca, NY: Cornell UP, 1958); see also 'Luce' in the *Enciclopedia Dantesca* (Rome: Instituto della Enciclopedia Italiana, 1978).

chariot. Below huddled the figure of time past, 'a dun and faint etherial gloom | Tempering the light'. Drawing the chariot, 'the wonder-winged team' also baffled sight with their own light, mere 'Shapes' lost 'in thick lightnings'. Above sat the splendid charioteer, but he is blinded, for 'All the four faces of that charioteer | Had their eyes banded'. Eyes that have not learned to see have no notion of their own deficiency. The awful consequence is that the charioteer remains 'blind to its own blindness'. In spite of his 'beams that quench the Sun', potentially able to 'pierce the sphere | Of all that is, has been, or will be done', Janus has utterly acquiesced to the bands before his eyes (77–106). The self-blinded, all-seeing chari-oteer careens through the throng and the mad 'Walpurgis' dance follows.

The Rousseau of *The Triumph of Life* is introduced as a withered root to assume a role like that of Virgil guiding Dante through Purgatory. His first caution is to 'forbear | To join the dance which I had well forbourne' (188–9). But he lapsed in his forbearance: 'if the spark, with which Heaven lit my spirit | Had with purer nutriment supplied | Corruption would not now thus much inherit | Of what was once Rousseau' (201–4). Those who surrender to the dance cannot escape their bondage to the wild careening course of the chariot. Witnessing the plight of the fallen Napoleon, by 'every pigmy kicked' (227), the narrator ponders 'how power & will | In opposition rule our mortal day', and 'why God made irreconcilable | Good & the means of good' (228–30). With the appearance of the 'shape all light' (352), Rousseau is seduced to join the fatal dance.

As Reiman has pointed out, 'the account of Rousseau's life is enriched by its numerous echoes of Saint-Preux's pursuit of Julie' in *La Nouvelle Héloïse*,[43] Saint-Preux and Julie may find their way to a higher plane of love, but the opposite happens to Rousseau whose pursuit of his vision is his downfall. When he drank from the cup offered by the 'shape all light', his 'brain became as sand'. Having acquiesced in the lure of the feminine light, he succumbs to yet another vision. 'Between desire and shame | Suspended' (394–5), he moves through a ghostly dream that becomes increasingly grotesque, crowded with 'vampire-bats', 'Phantoms', and 'Shadows of shadows', which 'like elves | Danced in a thousand unimagined shapes', while 'others sate chattering like restless apes' (480–541). Whether from 'The Witch's Kitchen' and the 'Walpurgis Night', or directly from Goethe's source in Dante's *Inferno*, Shelley crowds these lines with the imagery of evil.

Together with the other captives of the careening carriage, Rousseau is caught in the 'ghastly dance'. His tale is interrupted when the narrator again interrogates his guide. As the vision gains grandeur and profundity, *The Triumph of Life* is broken off abruptly with the high and impatient question: 'Then, what is Life?' (544). Through more than 500 lines the poet has been looking, questioning what he sees, and calling his guide to visual account. This tutelage continues to the very end: 'the cripple cast | His eye upon the car which now had rolled | Onward, as if that look must be the last' (544–5). Here, presuma-bly, would begin a discourse on the consequences—which, of course, was never written.

When Shelley turned to Calderón's *El mágico prodigioso* as an informing antecedent to *Faust*, he unravelled yet another investigation of evil infiltrating the mind. Neither

---

[43] *Julie; ou la nouvelle Héloïse, lettres de deux amants, recueillies et publiées par J. J. Rousseau* (Paris: Garnier frer`es, 1880). See Reiman, *Shelley's The Triumph of Life*, 73–4.

reason nor moral conviction is proof against the impulses of desire and passion. Like Goethe, Shelley became increasingly fascinated with the discovery of sight, how the eyes see, and how much more they see as the mind grows attentive to the process of seeing. Wary of the capacity of evil to disguise itself as good, Shelley was especially attentive to Goethe's use of light and sight in the contrast between Mephisto and God in the 'Prologue' and between Mephisto and Faust in the 'Walpurgis Night'. In both scenes, Mephisto betrays his limitations in seeing and interpreting perception. Not since Milton had an English poet explored the conditions of evil as extensively as Shelley. The authors who devoted similar literary attention to the causality of evil—Calderón, Rousseau, Goethe—each contributed ideas and images to Shelley's vast repository.[44]

Select Bibliography

Brewer, William D. 'The Diabolical Discourse of Byron and Shelley'. *Philological Quarterly* 70.1 (Winter 1991), 47–65.

Cooper, Laurence D. *Eros in Plato, Rousseau, and Nietzsche: The Politics of Infinity*. University Park, PA: Pennsylvania State UP, 2008.

Cox, Jeffrey N. 'Melodrama, Monodrama and the Forms of Romantic Tragic Drama'. *Within the Dramatic Spectrum*. Ed. Karelisa V. Hartigan. Lanham, MD: University Presses of America, 1986. 20–34.

Donovan, Jack. 'Laon and the Hermit: Connection and Succession'. *The Unfamiliar Shelley*. Ed. Alan M. Weinberg and Timothy Webb. Aldershot: Ashgate, 2009. 85–100.

Gross, Kenneth. 'Satan and the Romantic Satan: A Notebook'. *Re-Membering Milton: Essays on the Texts and Traditions*. Ed. Mary Nyquist and Margaret W. Ferguson. New York: Methuen, 1987. 318–41.

Hernández-Araico, Susana. 'The Schlegels, Shelley and Calderón'. *Neophilologus* 71.4 (October 1987), 481–8,

Lokke, Kari. 'Weimar Classicism and Romantic Madness: Tasso in Goethe, Byron and Shelley'. *European Romantic Review* 2.2 (Winter 1992), 195–214.

Reiman, Donald. *Shelley's The Triumph of Life: A Critical Study*. Urbana, IL: University of Illinois Press, 1965.

Roberts, Hugh. 'Mere Poetry and Strange Flesh: Shelley's *The Cenci* and Calderon's *El Purgatorio de San Patricio*'. *European Romantic Review* 20.3 (Summer 2009), 345–66.

Schulze, Earl. 'Allegory against Allegory: "The Triumph of Life"'. *Studies in Romanticism* 27.1 (Spring 1988), 31–62.

Webb, Timothy. *The Violet in the Crucible: Shelley and Translation*. Oxford: Clarendon Press, 1976.

---

[44] Dante must be named here too. See Chapter 28, 'Shelley and the Italian Tradition' by Alan Weinberg.

CHAPTER 30

....

SHELLEY AND MILTON

....

MADELEINE CALLAGHAN

SHELLEY's poetry draws on both the local details and larger designs that he encountered in Milton's work, producing a new creation in the process.[1] Shelley's prose refers to Milton as an exemplar of what the poet ought to be. Thus the preface to *Prometheus Unbound* makes clear the debt that contemporary writers and readers owe to Milton's personal and poetic sublimity: 'the sacred Milton was, let it ever be remembered, a republican, and a bold inquirer into morals and religion' (Preface to *Prometheus Unbound*, 231).[2] Yet Shelley's admiration for Milton never tips into an uncomplicated or narrow form of worship. Shelley responds to Milton in complex, fertile, and multi-layered ways as he explores, nuances, and refigures Milton's authoritative poetry. As Lucy Newlyn suggests, the Romantic response to Milton often prompted an increasing awareness of their predecessor's subtlety and ambiguities, thereby preventing a simplistic response to an authoritarian poetic ancestor.[3] This awareness is at work in Shelley's continuous use of allusions, manifold verbal echoes, and explicit thematic reconceptualizations to illustrate his re-visioning of Milton's already multifaceted poetry.

Milton, for Shelley, is the single most influential poet in the English tradition, one who features for the younger poet as model, mentor, and muse. Shelley names him, after Homer and Dante, as 'third among the sons of light' (*Adonais*, 36), and he lists Milton alongside Shakespeare and Dante as a philosopher of 'the very loftiest powers' (*A Defence of Poetry*, 679). Shelley's *Defence*, a work of prose poetry that meditates musically on the role of the poet, affirms the significance of poetry partly through allusions to Milton. Shelley links his theory to the poetry of 'the sacred Milton', drawing on 'the spirit of his Miltonic muse' to lay claim to an authority endowed on him as the elder poet's inheritor and also as a poetic counter-voice that plays through the prose.[4] While Shelley discusses

---

[1] For a demonstration of Shelley's career-long engagement with Milton's poetic work, see Frederick L. Jones, 'Shelley and Milton', *Studies in Philology* 49 (1952), 488–519.

[2] All references to Shelley's poetry and prose will be from *Major Works* unless indicated otherwise.

[3] Lucy Newlyn, *'Paradise Lost' and the Romantic Reader* (Oxford: Clarendon Press, 1993).

[4] Leslie Brisman, *Milton's Poetry of Choice and its Romantic Heirs* (Ithaca, NY: Cornell UP, 1973), 135.

Paradise Lost at length, and seems to prize Milton's virtues as an epic poet at the centre of his *Defence*, allusions to Milton's lyrical poetry abound throughout the text. When discussing the role of the poet, allusions to 'Il Penseroso' offer Shelley a significant point of reference that strengthens and nuances Shelley's ideas.[5] Shelley's description of the poet is a complex literary performance that recalls Milton even as it possesses its own singular voice:

> Even in modern times, no living poet ever arrived at the fullness of his fame; the jury which sits in judgement upon a poet, belonging as he does to all time, must be composed of his peers: it must be impanelled by Time from the selectest of the wise of many generations. A Poet is a nightingale who sits in darkness, and sings to cheer its own solitude with sweet sounds; his auditors are as men entranced by the melody of an unseen musician, who feel that they are moved and softened, yet know not whence or why. (*A Defence*, 680)

There is a strong impulse toward solitude in this section that seems to counter, and even deny, the importance of the society in which Shelley claims the poet is at the heart. Yet Shelley accepts the presence of unseen auditors; poets are a part of society, but the chosen nature of the company that he keeps is an important caveat. 'The jury' here referred to is to be made up of the poet's peers, and Shelley, by using the image of the nightingale, subtly alludes to Milton's 'Il Penseroso', suggesting the grandeur of his chosen arbiters. As Thomas H. Luxon writes,[6] 'Milton refers to the nightingale more often than any other bird, and Shelley's metaphor of the poet as a nightingale draws on this wealth of potential allusions that stretches from *Paradise Lost* to the Sonnets.' It also provides a possible analogue to the 'unpremeditated art' ('To a Skylark', 5) of Shelley's skylark. 'Il Penseroso' offers one of the most sustained musings on the poet's role, and Shelley takes figurative flight from the Miltonic example:

> 'Less Philomel will deign a song,
> In her sweetest, saddest plight,
> Smoothing the rugged brow of Night,
> While Cynthia checks her dragon yoke,
> Gently o'er th' accustomed oak;
> Sweet bird that shunn'st the noise of folly,
> Most musical, most melancholy!
> Thee chantress oft the woods among,
> I woo to hear thy even-song;
> And missing thee, I walk unseen
> On the dry smooth-shaven green,
> To behold the wand'ring moon,

---

[5] Agnes Péter offers an account of the influence of 'Il Penseroso' on *Epipsychidion* slightly at odds with what is offered above, emphasizing Shelley's corrective urge to Milton's poetic vision. See 'A Hermeneutical Reading of *Epipsychidion*', *Keats–Shelley Journal* 42 (1993), 123.

[6] Thomas H. Luxon (ed.), *The Milton Reading Room*, <http://www.dartmouth.edu/~milton> (accessed October 2010). See notes to *Paradise Lost*, VII. 435.

> Riding near her highest noon,
> Like one that had been led astray
> Through the heav'n's wide pathless way.
>
> ('Il Penseroso', 56–70)[7]

'Il Penseroso', frequently considered to be the more personal poem in comparison to 'L'Allegro', shows Milton meditating on the sober and melancholic calling of the poet. The severe ethical and imaginative discipline required of the poet offers an austere contentment and 'something like prophetic strain' (174): 'These pleasures Melancholy give, | And I with thee will choose to live' (175–6). Though Milton refuses to claim that melancholy can deliver anything more conclusive than *something like* prophetic strain' (emphasis added), the hope for this level of poetic accomplishment is bound up in the virtues of solitary melancholia. The nightingale serves as a type of cloistered existence: the 'Sweet bird' (Philomel) shuns 'the noise of folly', confining itself to hymning the woodland where it lives. An intensity of longing pervades the section, as Milton builds towards an ecstatic exclamation of the bird's beauty. Like the nightingale, Milton remains aloof from the temptations of the town, preferring to move, like the 'wand'ring moon [...] | Through the heav'n's wide pathless way'. Where Milton imagines the nightingale as a separate, though similar creature to the poet himself, Shelley takes the suggestive parallel still further, pushing Milton's lines from suggestive to figurative truth in his metaphoric identification with the bird. Shelley's quotation on the solitude of the poet mirrors the nightingale's solitary song, and the reference to the sweet melody recalls Milton's 'Most musical, most melancholy!' exclamation. In the quotation from *A Defence*, Shelley performs the role of nightingale, along with other poets, and, Milton is, as in 'Il Penseroso', both poet/nightingale and auditor, both ideal poet and ideal jury. This Shelleyan lightness of touch suggests the ways in which he reads Milton with an eye to his unique meditations. Seeing in Milton less an authoritative Bloomian father, and more a powerful ally, Shelley refigures and imaginatively rewrites Milton. The younger poet's 'unpremeditated song' (*A Defence of Poetry*, 696) finds its justification in Milton's exampled 'unpremeditated verse' (*Paradise Lost*, IX. 24).

Shelley's *Prometheus Unbound* forms the centrepiece for any discussion of Milton's influence on Shelley's poetry. *Prometheus Unbound* draws on *Paradise Lost*, *Samson Agonistes*, and *Comus* in support of its multi-generic reinterpretation of Milton's work.[8] Teddi Chichester indicates Shelley's debt to Milton's democratic use of the traditionally courtly masque in *Prometheus Unbound*;[9] Shelley had previously used the masque for

---

[7] John Milton, 'Il Penseroso', *John Milton: The Complete Poems*, ed. John Leonard (London: Penguin, 1998), 27. All subsequent quotations from Milton's poetry will be from this edition unless otherwise indicated.

[8] In *Prometheus Unbound* IV. 135–7 Shelley's Chorus of Spirits use verbal echo of the Spirit who concludes *Comus* (1011–16). *Comus* influences 'pastoral' elements in Act II; see also Jones, 'Shelley and Milton', 503.

[9] 'Milton's *Comus* provided Shelley with a precedent for transporting the masque out of the courtly realm', Teddi Lynn Chichester, 'Entering the Stream of Sound: The Reader and the Masque in Shelley's Prometheus Unbound', *Colby Quarterly* 30.2 (1994), 86 n. 5.

democratic purposes in *The Mask of Anarchy*, which, as Stuart Curran argues, 'is his most considerable achievement in the low style, shrewdly coupling its radical politics to a balladlike meter and framing its exhortations within the iconography of chapbooks, penny pamphlets, and folk pageants'.[10] As with *Comus*' expression of a 'nascent Miltonic libertarianism',[11] the democratic urge is writ large in *The Mask of Anarchy*. Shelley's claim to write for an elect group in *Prometheus Unbound*[12] seems at odds with this earlier pre-occupation, but, as Stephen Behrendt suggests, this alteration seems partially 'a means of psychological self-preservation'.[13] More importantly, Shelley delivers his 'beautiful idealisms' (Preface to *Prometheus Unbound*, 232) to a pantheon of ideal readers distinguished by sensitivity, not social stature. Milton, whose 'soul was like a Star and dwelt apart' (Wordsworth, 'London 1802', 9),[14] becomes part of Shelley's elect group of ideal readers and inspirational figures; to that end, *Comus*, *Samson Agonistes*, and *Paradise Lost* supply more than verbal echoes in Shelley's work. Rather, they represent the kind of poetry Shelley hopes to write—poetry distinguished by its power to soften, to alter, and to liberate hearts and minds.

In Shelley's hands, Milton's theme of tragedy and tragic resistance takes on a different emphasis, Shelley writing for an age in which 'The cloud of mind is discharging its collected lightning' (Preface to *Prometheus Unbound*, 231). In the opening speech of *Prometheus Unbound*, Shelley takes from *Samson Agonistes* one of his most explicit verbal echoes to Milton's poetry, as the younger poet subtly draws suggestive parallels between the two heroes:

> Monarch of Gods and Daemons, and all Spirits
> But One, who throng those bright and rolling worlds
> Which Thou and I alone of living things
> Behold with sleepless eyes, regard this Earth
> Made multitudinous with thy slaves, whom thou
> Requitest for knee-worship, prayer, and praise,
> And toil, and hecatombs of broken hearts,
> With fear and self-contempt and barren hope.
> Whilst me, who am thy foe, eyeless in hate,
> Hast thou made reign and triumph, to thy scorn,
> O'er mine own misery and thy vain revenge.
>
> (*Prometheus Unbound*, I. 1–11)

'Eyeless in hate' alludes directly to Milton's phrase 'Eyeless in Gaza' (*Samson Agonistes*, 40) which Samson uses to convey his outrage at the slavery visited on him. Samson refers

[10]   Stuart Curran, *Shelley's Annus Mirabilis: The Maturing of an Epic Vision* (San Marino, CA: Huntington Library, 1975), 186.

[11]   Angus Fletcher, *The Transcendental Masque: An Essay on Milton's 'Comus'* (Ithaca, NY: Cornell UP, 1971), 18, quoted in Chichester, 'Entering the Stream of Sound', 86 n. 5.

[12]   '[*Prometheus Unbound*] will not sell—it is written only for the elect'; *Letters: PBS* II, 200.

[13]   Stephen C. Behrendt, *Shelley and his Audiences* (Lincoln, NE: University of Nebraska Press, 1989), 162.

[14]   William Wordsworth, 'London 1802', *William Wordsworth: The Major Works*, ed. Stephen Gill (Oxford: Oxford UP, 2000), 286.

less to a specific persecutor than to the horrors of his present condition as he refers to his degraded present in contrast to his predicted glories.

> Ask for this great deliverer now, and find him
> Eyeless in Gaza at the mill with slaves,
> Himself in bonds under Philistian yoke.
>
> (*Samson Agonistes*, 40–2)

The tone of 'great deliverer' contains both an ironic detachment from self, and a genuine hope that the prophecy proclaiming his status comes true. Samson looks into himself to lead his people out of bondage. Prometheus, like Samson, opens the play with a soliloquy about his suffering. Yet, unlike Samson, whose speech seems an expression of his inner suffering overheard by the audience, Prometheus delivers his speech to Jupiter. The reader encroaches into a power struggle; Jupiter, even without being physically present, dominates the lines as Prometheus' Other. As Susan Hawk Brisman shows, at the opening of the play, Shelley characterizes the Promethean voice as the voice of defiance, reacting negatively against Jupiter rather than acting positively through love and sympathy.[15] In contrast, Shelley problematizes Prometheus' heroism as, despite their enmity, Jupiter, the oppressor, and Prometheus, the oppressed, are mirror images. The first mention of 'I' is placed immediately in conjunction with a capitalized 'Thou', gesturing to the immense power of Jupiter in Prometheus' perception, and the imaginative bond forged by their mutual hatred.[16] Like Shelley's perception of *Paradise Lost* in *A Defence of Poetry*, where both God and Satan display 'Implacable hate, patient cunning, and a sleepless refinement of device to inflict the extremest anguish on an enemy' (*A Defence*, 691), Prometheus is imprisoned by his implicit identification with Jupiter. In a parodic parallel to Jupiter's worldly dominion, Prometheus reigns over 'mine own misery and thy vain revenge'; aware of his need for self-autonomy, Prometheus constructs his own kingdom of pain over which to triumph. Shelley, with his typical refusal to assign a single meaning, suggests that Prometheus' attempted self-rule could be a vicious illusion, serving only to underscore Prometheus' dependence on Jupiter as he apes his loathed mirror image. The trials of the two heroes, Samson against his environment, and Prometheus' struggle to become 'king | Over himself' (*Prometheus Unbound*, III. iv. 196–7) seem similar, yet Shelley draws a clear distinction between Milton's and his own hero.

Shelley also makes imaginative use of *Paradise Lost* in the opening act; Prometheus' reference to Jupiter's demand for 'knee-worship' recalls Satan's sneering imaginative projection of the other angels' response to Christ: 'Knee-tribute yet unpaid, prostration vile' (*Paradise Lost*, V. 782). As Jonathon Shears shows, the words of Prometheus' curse 'indicate a Satanic lexis',[17] as Prometheus shares in the Satanic condition of pride, defiance, and hatred (see *Prometheus Unbound*, I. 258–60). By mingling *Samson Agonistes* and

---

[15] Susan Hawk Brisman, '"Unsaying his High Language": The Problem of Voice in "Prometheus Unbound"', *SIR* 16.1 (1977), 52.

[16] As shown by Richard Cronin in *Shelley's Poetic Thoughts* (Basingstoke: Macmillan, 1981), 137–42.

[17] Jonathon Shears, *The Romantic Legacy of 'Paradise Lost': Reading against the Grain* (Aldershot: Ashgate, 2009), 147.

Paradise Lost, Shelley weaves Milton's poetry into a web of allusions which bolster, not detract from, his own lyrical drama.

Paradise Lost remains the master work for Shelley; as Frederick L. Jones shows, Shelley considered it 'both inexhaustible and beyond praise'.[18] While Shelley had, from the first, entertained epic ambitions,[19] *Prometheus Unbound*, his lyrical drama, contains his fullest response to *Paradise Lost*, and, in particular, to Satan. *The Cenci*, written at approximately the same time in Shelley's career, provides an intriguing counter-reading of Satan in its lyrical dramatization of the history of Beatrice Cenci. Lucy Newlyn refers to her as one of 'the most obvious' Romantic character studies of Satanic motivation and, read against Prometheus, the reader can trace another potential Shelleyan response to Milton's Satan.[20] For Shelley, the character of Satan represents an inspiring and troubling creation that drew both his praise and his censure. In his *On the Devil and Devils*, Shelley praises Milton's rendering of Satan, emphasizing Satan's sublimity in contrast to the popular conception of the devil (*On the Devil and Devils, Julian*, VII, 90).[21] He even, in *agent provocateur* mode, suggests an atheist Milton (*On the Devil and Devils, Julian*, VII, 91):

> It is difficult to determine, in a country where the most enormous sanctions of opin-ion and law are attached to a direct avowal of certain speculative notions, whether Milton was a Christian or not, at the period of the composition of Paradise Lost.

Drawing the reader's attention to the restrictive nature of contemporary British society (in both his own and Milton's time), Shelley suggests that Milton's professed position on Christianity could be less straightforward than assumed. Writing in a deliberately neutral tone, Shelley seems to be merely stating an uncertainty. But this studiedly non-committal statement suggests the extent to which Shelley felt he could extricate Milton from his public image and read him on Shelley's own terms.

In this vein, Shelley's presentations of Prometheus and Beatrice Cenci both draw on and refine Milton's presentation of Satan into uniquely Shelleyan creations.[22] Though taking his departure point from Aeschylus' *Prometheus Bound*, Shelley claims that his hero is in the Miltonic mode: 'The only imaginary being resembling in any degree Prometheus is Satan' (Preface to *Prometheus Unbound*, 229). While drawing attention to the near-incomparability of his hero to any other poet's creation, he insinuates the close-ness of his creation to Milton's epic character. Several critics have drawn attention to the complex relationship between Satan and Prometheus, and their different views are

---

[18] Jones, 'Shelley and Milton', 516.
[19] 'It is easy to cavil at *Queen Mab* and *The Revolt of Islam*, but that a poet of Shelley's years should have produced two poems of epic pretension is indicative both of his culture and of his conception of the poet's place in it.' Curran, *Shelley's Annus Mirabilis*, 6.
[20] Newlyn, *'Paradise Lost' and the Romantic Reader*, 97.
[21] As noted by Shears, *Romantic Legacy*, 140.
[22] Many studies focus on this facet of Romanticism; for further reading, see Mario Praz, *The Romantic Agony*, trans. Angus Davidson, 2nd edn. with foreword by Frank Kermode, (1970; Oxford: Oxford UP, 1978); Peter A. Schlock, *Romantic Satanism: Myth and the Historical Moment in Blake, Byron, and Shelley* (London: Palgrave Macmillan, 2003).

suggestive of *Prometheus Unbound*'s allusive intelligence. By suggesting simultaneously his poem's independence from and debt to *Paradise Lost*, Shelley, as Hugh Roberts shows more generally, creates an 'instability' in his preface that moves between attempts to take and then relinquish control over the reader's interpretation of his debt to Milton.[23] As Jonathon Shears writes, Shelley 'strives' for 'irresolution' in his refiguring of Satan,[24] refusing to sketch in full the Satanic character in either Prometheus or Beatrice. Earl Wasserman argues, in turn, that 'they represent, taken together, the antinomies of the skeptical contest as it was waged in Shelley's own mind',[25] yet, though this remark sheds light on the Shelleyan creative process, it understates the ambiguities that pulse through Shelley's refiguring of Satan in the presentations of both the figures. *The Cenci* and *Prometheus Unbound* grow from similar poetic roots. Both *The Cenci* and *Prometheus Unbound* show their protagonists as oppressed by a tyrannical Father-God, and bound into a revenge paradigm. The reader must empathize with Shelley's subtle ethical portrait of Beatrice, which presents her suffering without excusing her revenge, and relate to the play of potential and doubt embodied in Prometheus as he attempts to overcome Jupiter's hold over the self.

The sophistication expected of the reader, who is forbidden to resort to orthodox religious oversimplifications of either character, reveals itself through Shelley's prefaces to both dramas. Wasserman draws attention to the word 'casuistry' that Shelley uses in both the preface to *Prometheus Unbound* and *The Cenci*, demonstrating the preoccupation in both works that the reader should be prevented from mentally diminishing each figure into clean moral absolutes.[26] In the preface to *Prometheus Unbound* there is a moral sternness to Shelley's admonishment: 'The character of Satan engenders in the mind a pernicious casuistry which leads us to weigh his faults with his wrongs, and to excuse the former because the latter exceed all measure' (Preface to *Prometheus Unbound*, 230). Beatrice, like Prometheus, must, for the sensitive reader, evade the binaries of orthodox good and evil. Suffering violation by her father, this 'most gentle and amiable being' (Preface to *The Cenci*, 315) murdered her tormentor. Beatrice attracted Shelley by her potential to avoid moral absolutes, defying 'the restless and anatomizing casuistry with which men seek the justification of Beatrice, yet feel that she has done what needs justification' (Preface to *The Cenci*, 316–17). Shelley insists on the complex response her character and actions provoke. The characterization of Beatrice and Prometheus recalls Shelley's own praise of Milton: his 'bold neglect of a direct moral purpose is the most decisive proof of the supremacy of Milton's genius' (*A Defence*, 692). The ambiguities that abound through *Prometheus Unbound* and *The Cenci* aim to complicate and subtilize the reader's ethical imagination.

---

[23] Hugh Roberts, 'Noises On: The Communicative Strategies of Shelley's Prefaces', in Alan M. Weinberg and Timothy Webb (eds.), *The Unfamiliar Shelley*, The Nineteenth Century Series (Farnham: Ashgate, 2009), 192.

[24] Shears, *Romantic Legacy*, 144.

[25] Earl R. Wasserman, *Shelley: A Critical Reading* (Baltimore: Johns Hopkins UP, 1971), 128.

[26] See ibid. 117–26.

The preface to *Prometheus Unbound* is a complex performance that challenges and admires Milton and his predecessors, seeming, as Michael O'Neill suggests, 'manifestly intent on rivalling and outpacing Aeschylean drama and Miltonic and Dantean epic'.[27] Spelling out the most immediately striking transformation of the hero that he effects in his epic, Shelley makes some of his strongest though admiring criticisms of Milton in his preface to *Prometheus Unbound*, distinguishing the characteristics of his hero in such a way as to argue for the moral superiority of Prometheus in comparison with Satan. Prometheus, according to Shelley, is almost a corrected Satan, a hero that transforms Satanic pride and embittered ambition into 'beautiful idealisms of moral excellence' (Preface to *Prometheus Unbound*, 232). 'Rewriting the epic rule-book',[28] Shelley shows Prometheus' struggle with himself as the centre of the lyrical drama's action: Prometheus must not recount to the reader the circumstances which consigned him to his punishment. Rather, by forgiveness, Prometheus can, in the first act, spark off a series of events that move the reader far beyond conflict, and take him or her to the brink of the 'unascended Heaven' (*Prometheus Unbound*, II. iii. 203) that Shelley suggests is tantalizingly close, even as it remains always out of reach.[29]

This fleetness of poetic foot allows Shelley to come close to identifying Prometheus with Milton's Satan, Christ, and God, without committing to any final interpretative position. His adaptations of *Paradise Lost* demonstrate the different direction that Shelley takes in his presentation of Prometheus. The triumph of rhetoric in Satan's speech from the first book of *Paradise Lost* strongly influenced the Romantic poets:

> A mind not to be changed by place or time.
> The mind is its own place, and in itself
> Can make a Heav'n of Hell, a Hell of Heav'n.
> What matter where, if I be still the same.
>
> (*Paradise Lost*, I. 253–6)

Celebrating the power of the individual mind, Milton's Satan asserts his mental power as he transforms, through language, a hell into a heaven. This speech seals for the damned their defiant stance; the heroic self-mastery promoted by Satan defines itself by its implacable opposition to an omnipotent foe. Prometheus begins in a similar vein of imaginative defiance:

> [...] torture and solitude
> Scorn and despair,—these are mine empire:
> More glorious far than that which thou surveyest
> From thine unenvied throne, O Mighty God!
>
> (*Prometheus Unbound*, I. 14–17)

---

[27] Michael O'Neill, 'Romantic Re-approprations of the Epic', in Catherine Bates (ed.), *The Cambridge Companion to Epic* (Cambridge: Cambridge UP, 2010), 199.

[28] O'Neill, 'Romantic Re-appropriations of the Epic', 200.

[29] See Timothy Webb's essay on Shelley's use of negatives in his poetry, 'The Unascended Heaven: Negatives in *Prometheus Unbound*', Norton 2, 694–711.

Echoing the 'torture without end' (*Paradise Lost*, I. 67) suffered by Satan and his infernal pride, Shelley seems initially to deliver a Satanic double, not an independent character. Yet Shelley more explicitly disrupts Prometheus' speech to display the psychic pain he undergoes as the speech falls into an agonized *cri du cœur* 'Ah me! alas, pain, pain ever, forever! | No change, no pause, no hope! Yet I endure' (*Prometheus Unbound*, I. 23–4). Though an expression of despair, the lyricism of the language carries the lines forward, transforming them from Satanic rhetoric into Promethean poetry. 'No change, no pause, no hope! Yet I endure' contains the musical internal rhyme of 'pause' and 'endure', and renders Prometheus' agony in language; Prometheus is a poet with no audience.[30] As Daniel Hughes suggests, the centre of the drama of *Prometheus Unbound* is 'the unfolding of capabilities within Prometheus himself'.[31] Shelley shows Satanic pride as a form of negative self-mastery which Prometheus must transcend. Shelley seeks to unite the power of Satan's utterance with a high moral end, and the identification of Prometheus with Satan is left deliberately incomplete as the younger poet strives to create a 'type of the highest perfection of moral and intellectual nature, impelled by the purest and the truest motives to the best and noblest ends' (Preface to *Prometheus Unbound*, 230).

Yet even as Shelley creates a suggestive doubling between Satan and Prometheus, he complicates and troubles this identification as he begins to identify Prometheus with Christ.[32] These opposite figures in *Paradise Lost* become central parts of the composite hero in Shelley's analysis. This double identification of Prometheus with Christ and Satan anticipates Shelley's audacious self-presentation as a mixture of Cain and Christ (*Adonais*, 301–6). Yet, rather than stretching the imaginative limits of representation, Shelley uses both figures to fashion a hero capable of sustaining 'the highest perfection of moral and intellectual nature': Shelley draws on the imaginative independence of Milton's Satan whilst retaining the 'unexampled love' (*Paradise Lost*, III. 410) and pity of Christ. As Merle A. Williams notes, 'As intensely as he [Shelley] loathes the perceived perversions of Christianity by the churches, he admires and respects the integrity of Jesus':[33] while admiring Satanic defiance, Shelley requires the ethically superior 'solemn and serene' figure of Christ.[34] Shelley had previously suggested a parallel between himself and Christ in 'The Moral Teaching of Jesus Christ' to suggest, as Stephen Behrendt argues, 'The idea is to make the radical author's opinions palatable, even stimulating, to the reader by making them appear to resemble Christ's. The corollary is clear: to reject Shelley is to reject Christ, while to embrace Christ is to embrace Shelley as well.'[35] Here, to reject Prometheus is also to reject his Christlike quality, which shimmers through

[30] See Daniel Hughes, 'Prometheus Made Capable Poet in Act One of *Prometheus Unbound*', SIR 17.1 (1978), 3–11.

[31] Ibid. 3.

[32] A vital figure for Shelley, Christ stands, as Timothy Webb writes, as both revolutionary hero and virtuous hero of thought. See Timothy Webb, *Shelley: A Voice Not Understood* (Manchester: Manchester UP, 1977), 170.

[33] Merle A. Williams, 'Contemplating Facts, Studying Ourselves: Aspects of Shelley's Philosophical and Religious Prose', in Weinberg and Webb (eds.), *The Unfamiliar Shelley*, 213.

[34] *On Christianity*, Murray: *Prose*, 260.

[35] Behrendt, *Shelley and his Audiences*, 119.

Shelley's presentation of his Romantic hero. While the verbal echoes of Satan's words in Prometheus' speeches, and the emphasis on Milton's Satan in the *Preface*, direct the reader to compare Prometheus to Satan, the idea of Prometheus as a warrior against the Jupiter-enslaved world echoes Shelley's repeated references to Christ as a 'great Reformer' (*A Philosophical View of Reform*, 637). Other characters in the play seem to regard Prometheus in a similar light; the Furies summon an image of Christ as a warning and a torment to the Titan as Promethean passivity and pity begin to parallel Christ as 'a youth | With patient looks nailed to a crucifix' (*Prometheus Unbound*, I. 585–6).[36] Shelley reinforces Prometheus' reforming zeal through his speeches that insist on the impossibility of submission to tyrannical power even as he possesses the Christlike 'meek and majestic demeanour' (*On Christianity, Murray: Prose*, 260):

> Or could I yield? Which yet I will not yield.
> Let others flatter Crime where it sits throned
> In brief Omnipotence [...]
>   [...] I wait,
> Enduring thus, the retributive hour.
>
> (*Prometheus Unbound*, I. 400–6)

As Stuart Curran argues, 'to scan Shelley's career is to realize that one of his major contributions, not only to English literature but to Romantic psychology, is his continuing analysis of passivity'.[37] Yet here the language becomes almost active as Prometheus insists on his 'high language' (Preface to *Prometheus Unbound*, 229) as possessing a dignity and power that deny tyrannical dominion over the mind. Satan, a character whose 'language is sublimely intensified in hell',[38] and Christ, compared repeatedly to a poet-philosopher in *On Christianity*, are both, for Shelley, representative of poets. This poetic bond links Prometheus to his doubles, as Shelley's protagonist is or becomes, as Daniel Hughes has argued, a figure of the 'capable poet'.[39] These poet-figures unite under the umbrella of Shelley's view that 'Poets are the unacknowledged legislators of the World' (*A Defence*, 701). Like 'the sacred Milton' (Preface to *Prometheus Unbound*, 231), Shelley intends to perform as a campaigner against tyranny, imbuing his characters and poems with liberating potential. Yet, like his Milton, his 'Great Original',[40] Shelley retains the creeping doubt and energizing tensions that characterize his finest poetry.

The tension that Shelley injects into *Prometheus Unbound* through his revisionary use of *Paradise Lost* deeply influences his presentation of Demogorgon; as an almost indefinable figure in the poem, his or its cryptic presence disturbs *Prometheus Unbound* and sends ripples of doubt throughout the entire poem. Demogorgon seems representative

---

[36] Newlyn, '*Paradise Lost*' and the Romantic Reader, 148.

[37] Curran, *Shelley's Annus Mirabilis*, 37.

[38] William Flesch, 'The Majesty of Darkness', in Harold Bloom (ed.), *John Milton*, Bloom's Modern Critical Views (Broomall, PA: Chelsea House Publishers, 2004), 166.

[39] This phrase is taken from the title of Daniel Hughes's study of *Prometheus Unbound*. See Hughes, 'Prometheus Made Capable Poet', 3–11.

[40] Harold Bloom, *The Anxiety of Influence: A Theory of Poetry*, 2nd edn. (New York: Oxford UP, 1997), 64.

of a larger artistic mission in the poem, as Shelley uses this complex and indefinable figure to stand for the mysterious and determinedly open structure of *Prometheus Unbound*. Demogorgon is equally revealing of the ways in which Shelley could suggest, re-state, and amplify subterranean issues in *Paradise Lost*. Shelley uses verbal echoes to suggest the connection between Death and Demogorgon while drawing attention to their differences. As Newlyn shows, 'The Miltonic allusion not only gives Demogorgon his deathliness; it also connects him with ideas of uncertainty and of the inexpressible.'[41] These 'ideas of uncertainty' cut to the heart of Shelley's Demogorgon, where Shelley's figure seems neither positive nor negative, and continually evasive of definition. Harold Bloom helpfully lists the volume of critical ideas about Demogorgon, from Carlos Baker's definition of him as 'Necessity' to G. Wilson Knight's definition of him as representing the 'Human Imagination'.[42] This continual avoidance of the single interpretative view is, as we have seen, Shelley's characteristic gesture to retain a sense of ever-refreshing possibilities in poetry. By linking Demogorgon to Milton's Death, Shelley shapes for the figure a new resonance, a resonance that goes beyond any simple identification; the allusions render him a more complicated and complicating force in *Prometheus Unbound*.

In *Paradise Lost*, Milton presents a figure of unmitigated evil, whose shifting description offers a terrifying indeterminacy:

> [...] The other shape,
> If shape it might be called that shape had none
> Distinguishable in member, joint, or limb,
> Or substance might be called that shadow seemed,
> For each seemed either; black it stood as Night,
> Fierce as ten Furies, terrible as Hell,
> And shook a dreadful dart; what seemed his head
> The likeness of a kingly crown had on.
>
> (*Paradise Lost*, II. 666–73)

Burke quotes this passage as an example of the sublime, demonstrating the dizzying abyss on which Milton places the reader by his use of 'judicious obscurity' of the description.[43] The vastness and awfulness of Death, alongside his incomprehensibility, reinforce the terrifying power of the elemental force. Milton presents Death as resisting artistic definition; his shape and substance '*might* be called' (emphasis added) as Death can only 'seem'; Milton amplifies its horror by imprecision. Shelley's portrait of Demogorgon, offered by Panthea, has obvious Miltonic inflections:

> I see a mighty Darkness
> Filling the seat of power; and rays of gloom
> Dart round, as light from the meridian sun,
> Ungazed upon and shapeless; neither limb,

---

[41] Newlyn, '*Paradise Lost*' *and the Romantic Reader*, 201.

[42] Bloom, *Shelley's Mythmaking*, Yale Studies in English 141 (New Haven: Yale UP, 1959), 99.

[43] Edmund Burke, *A Philosophical Enquiry into the Origin of our Ideas of the Sublime and Beautiful*, ed. Adam Phillips, Oxford World's Classics (1990; Oxford: Oxford UP, 2008), 55.

> Nor form, nor outline; yet we feel it is
> A living Spirit.
>
> (*Prometheus Unbound*, II. iv. 2–7)

While offering a similar indeterminacy, complete with references to darkness, shape-lessness, and even retaining the word 'dart' (though as a verb instead of a noun), Shelley's presentation of Demogorgon seems more hypnotic than terrifying. Instead of outright terror, Shelley creates a sense of dread and curiosity. Timothy Webb also suggests that Shelley alludes to 'Dark with excessive bright' (*Paradise Lost*, III. 380) in Milton's presen-tation of God.[44] Shot through with Miltonic influence, this mixed allusive portrait cre-ates a wholly independent portrayal of Demogorgon, who at once embodies Death and yet departs completely from Milton's description. Panthea's tone is calm; the mighty darkness, as 'A living Spirit', invites the gaze, though he is 'Ungazed upon and shapeless'. Yet the reader, aware of Shelley's Miltonic allusions, proceeds with caution. Shelley's ubiquitous negatives reassert themselves. Shelley often uses negatives to introduce darker notes, or disrupt any certain thrust of a line, or, more positively, to gesture towards what, 'though unimagined', is 'yet to be' (*Prometheus Unbound*, III. iii. 56), and here is no exception. Despite becoming Asia's mentor, or more accurately, her mirror,[45] and affect-ing the overthrow of Jupiter, Demogorgon becomes no more knowable. Indeed, the vio-lent action suggests a certain discrepancy from Prometheus' mental revolution.[46] Shelley's presentation of Demogorgon, though drawing heavily on Milton's Death, dis-rupts the dialectic of good and evil. Yeats reacted fiercely against Shelley's refusal to present Demogorgon a straightforwardly evil figure, writing: 'Why is Shelley terrified of the Last Day like a Victorian child [...] Demogorgon made his plot incoherent, its inter-pretation impossible; it was thrust there by that something which again and again forced him to balance the object of desire conceived as miraculous and superhuman, with nightmare.'[47] Yet Yeats, perhaps deliberately, misreads Shelley's artistic achievement here. Demogorgon is not meant to function as an 'evil' or 'good'; he represents the only con-stancy available in Shelley's poetic universe, that of mutability, movement, and change. As Bloom argues in relation to Yeats's reaction against *Prometheus Unbound*, 'Yeats expected what Shelley *on mythmaking principle* refused to give [...] Shelley is fiercely tentative—he gives us not a myth but only a fully conscious exemplification of the experi-ment of mythmaking.'[48] This emphasis on 'the experiment of mythmaking' shows where Shelley differs from Milton, and his predecessors. Shelley exponentially increases the troubled doubt under the surface of *Paradise Lost*, making *Prometheus Unbound* a text that teems with the uncertainty endemic to the Romantic mythmaking project.

Milton continues to feature prominently as an influence in Shelley's poetry after *Prometheus Unbound*. Discussing *The Witch of Atlas*, Hogle depicts Shelley's process of

---

[44] *Webb*, 378.
[45] Richard Cronin, *Shelley's Poetic Thoughts* (London: Macmillan, 1981), 152.
[46] Ibid. 49.
[47] W. B. Yeats, 'Prometheus Unbound', *Essays and Introductions* (London: Macmillan, 1961), 420.
[48] Bloom, *Shelley's Mythmaking*, 123.

creating the poem as a 'stitching of different texts together and a crossing of the spaces within and between them', with Milton as a seminal figure for the poem.[49] Here Shelley revises Milton in the interests of serio-comic play, obliquely calling Milton to his aid when he amusingly chides Mary Shelley in his introductory stanzas for objecting to the poem for 'CONTAINING NO HUMAN INTEREST' (484), repeating and, in the course of the poem, overturning Samuel Johnson's remark that in *Paradise Lost* 'The want of human interest is always felt.'[50] Shelley's deftly inventive poem enlists and adapts Miltonic echoes to suggest that its 'Visions swift' (161) do bear, albeit indirectly, on the human condition. It highlights the value of challenges to orthodoxy through connections between the Witch's 'imperial tent' (465) composed of 'woven exhalations' (466) and the Devils' Pandaemonium that 'Rose like an exhalation' (*Paradise Lost*, I. 711). Rebellious, heterodox, the Witch and the Devils momentarily share in one another's lives, and as the tone of Shelley's poem is largely sympathetic to the Witch he invites a rereading of Milton's epic.

More solemnly, *Adonais* represents a challenge to, even as it celebrates, Milton's *Lycidas*. Shelley both praises Milton as a poetic sire and shows his filial difference from his poetic father in the poem, balancing confrontation with admiration. *Lycidas* offers Shelley an elegiac model for grieving the loss of another poet peer. Yet the younger poet subverts and pushes against the Miltonic example, showing reverence for Milton's artistry even as he suggests that what may have provided consolation and transcendence for the older poet may no longer suffice. Whereas Milton perfects and individualizes the elegiac form, Shelley seems to exhaust it; *Adonais* alludes to *Lycidas* to create a kind of poetic extremity.[51] A contrast between the openings of the two elegies indicates the extent to which Shelley self-consciously refashions *Lycidas* to open the traditional form to Shelley's relentless questioning and exploration of the consolatory possibilities available to the elegy. At the start of *Lycidas*, following the elegy's conventional pattern, Milton demands of the nymphs their whereabouts, before circling back to blame himself for Lycidas' death. 'Where were ye nymphs when the remorseless deep | Closed o'er the head of your loved Lycidas?' (*Lycidas*, 50–1). The 'o' sounds of 'closed o'er […] your' and the elongated 'l's of 'loved Lycidas' slow the line as sound and sense reflect solemnity rather than frantic blame. The manner in which Milton uses ceremony to frame his poem offers a soothing sense suggested by the sombre syntax. Yet Shelley's questioning of Urania, Milton's muse (*Paradise Lost*, VII. 1–12), seems less to follow convention than to demand satisfaction, as he remorselessly repeats himself:

> Where wert thou mighty Mother, when he lay,
> When thy Son lay, pierced by the shaft which flies
> In darkness?
>
> (*Adonais*, 10–12)

[49] Jerrold E. Hogle, 'Metaphor and Metamorphosis in Shelley's *The Witch of Atlas*', *SIR* 19.3 (1980), 345.

[50] Quoted from *The Lives of the Poets* in *Major Works*, 788n.

[51] Peter M. Sacks, *The English Elegy: Studies in the Genre from Spenser to Yeats* (Baltimore: Johns Hopkins UP, 1985), 165.

This foregrounds not Adonais, but Shelley himself; the poet requires a satisfactory answer to his demand, demonstrating what Cronin describes as the 'conflict between conventionality and personality' in *Adonais*, a conflict Shelley catches from Milton and magnifies into Romantic intensity.[52]

Shelley invariably shifts Milton's meaning to nuance and layer the elegy, yet he also heightens the ambiguity of Milton's poetry, or, by his startling use of allusion, returns the reader to Milton's poetry with an eye to his status as the younger poet's great original.[53] Stanza 7 alludes to the 'high capital' (*Paradise Lost*, I. 756) of Pandemonium in *Paradise Lost*, which Milton shows as a city of swarming demons, thronging, building, and marching. Shelley completely removes the sense of industry central to Milton's description; in his own, Death's 'high Capital' and 'his pale court in beauty and decay' (*Adonais*, 56) suggests a faded aristocracy. This allusion uses its departure from Milton to centre Shelley's independent vision, which Milton may bolster, not dominate. Shelley's portrayal of Milton in the fourth stanza situates him as a political poet, emphasizing Milton's disillusionment following the Restoration.

> [...] He died,
> Who was the Sire of an immortal strain,
> Blind, old, and lonely, when his country's pride
> The priest, the slave, and the liberticide
> Trampled and mocked with many a loathèd rite
> Of lust and blood; he went, unterrified,
> Into the gulf of death; but his clear Sprite
> Yet reigns o'er earth; the third among the sons of light.
>
> (*Adonais*, 29–36)

As Webb writes, Shelley highlights Milton's bravery in going 'unterrified, | Into the gulf of death'; yet Shelley's choice of adjective, as he transforms 'terrified' into its antonym by a prefix, also stresses the fearsome nature of death.[54] One senses that, for Shelley, a strange kinship exists with Milton. As Thomas Medwin reports, '[Shelley], like the great object of his admiration, Milton, had a foreboding of his coming greatness, and would quote prophetic words of our English Mæonides: "This I know, that whether in prosing or in versing, there is something in my writings that shall live for ever." '[55] Milton, as 'Sire of an immortal strain', could be said to become the poetic father of the younger poet in these lines as Shelley shapes himself subtly in Milton's image. Emphasizing Milton's last days of disillusionment, Shelley contrasts the older poet's canonical status as a 'clear Sprite' who 'reigns o'er earth' with Milton's crushing disappointment at the hands of society. This serves both to lionize and humanize Milton; his human pain and distress, mitigated by his poetic strength, creates him as a reigning spirit, and Shelley's poetic mission

---

[52] Cronin, *Shelley's Poetic Thoughts*, 191.

[53] See Thomas Medwin, *The Life of Percy Bysshe Shelley*, introd. with commentary H. Buxton Forman (Oxford: Oxford UP, 1913), 421.

[54] Webb, *Shelley: A Voice Not Understood*, 169–70.

[55] Medwin, *The Life of Percy Bysshe Shelley*, 347.

in *Adonais* is to affect the same transformation upon Keats, whom Shelley alters into Adonais. Milton is, at once, the great exemplar and a singular spirit.

Shelley's final poem, *The Triumph of Life*, continues to make use of Miltonic echoes, allusions, and characterizations to nuance and disturb both his poetry and Milton's epic. Shelley uses Dante, Petrarch, along with many others,[56] but Milton remains a major influence. *The Triumph of Life* alludes to *Comus* and *Paradise Lost* at vital junctures during the poem. Death of *Paradise Lost* appears in the guise of Rousseau's altered state as Shelley transports the 'grim feature' (*Paradise Lost*, X. 279) into his presentation of Rousseau, highlighting Rousseau's change from a living being into a fearful figure.[57] Shelley parallels Rousseau with Adam, Eve, and Death in the poem, moving between different possibilities to suggest not only the irreducible nature of identity, but also the inefficacy of such parallels. Each potential parallel leads only to other possible interpretations as Shelley uses allusion to create a 'mighty Darkness' (*Prometheus Unbound*, II. iv. 2), not an interpretative light. *Comus* offers Shelley an opportunity to parallel Circe's transformation of Odysseus' men with Rousseau's change at the hands of the shape all light.[58]

> (For most do taste through fond intemperate thirst)
> Soon as the potion works, their humane count'nance
> Th' express resemblance of the gods, is changed
> Into some brutish form of wolf, or bear,
> Or ounce, or tiger, hog, or bearded goat,
> All other parts remaining as they were.
>
> (*Comus*, 67–72)

As John A. Hodgson suggests in his discussion of these lines, what Milton emphasizes is the likeness of the brutes to the men that they were—Circe's victims become, in some sense, that which they always were. Rousseau's changed appearance, then, ought to reveal him as he is. Yet Rousseau does not seem a possessor of a 'fond intemperate thirst'; he does not gulp greedily down the Shape all Light's potion, nor does he fail to recognize the change which has been wrought upon him. In *Comus*, Circe's victims do not register their disfigurement, and see themselves as more handsome than before ('[…] boast themselves more comely than before, | And all their friends, and native home forget' (75–6)). This alteration from Milton's original does not seek to challenge *Comus* or replace its didactic system with another. As Paul de Man writes, in contrast to *Hyperion* or *Paradise Lost*, 'The text has no room for the tragedy of defeat or of victory among next-of-kin, or among gods and men.'[59] Rather, Shelley blurs the potential parallel between *The Triumph of Life* and *Comus*, closing down the connection as quickly as it is suggested in the poem.

---

[56] *Webb*, 449–50.

[57] See Donald H. Reiman, *Shelley's 'The Triumph of Life': A Critical Study*, Illinois Studies in Language and Literature (Urbana, IL: University of Illinois Press, 1965), 40–1.

[58] John A. Hodgson shows the parallel between Circe and the Shape all light. See 'The World's Mysterious Doom: Shelley's *The Triumph of Life*', *ELH* 42.4 (1975), 608–9.

[59] Paul de Man, *The Rhetoric of Romanticism* (New York: Columbia UP, 1984), 117.

Shelley also alludes to *Paradise Lost*, suggesting a resemblance between Eve's coming to consciousness (*Paradise Lost*, IV. 449–65) and Rousseau's encounter with the Shape (*The Triumph of Life*, 398). As Hugh Roberts argues, 'the parallels are too close to be ignored',[60] yet they are also too faint to be definitive. Shelley creates slippage between the characters; the narrator and Rousseau have shared experiences (like the narrator's 'I knew | That I had felt' (33–4)) and Rousseau's identification with Adam, Eve, and Death mirrors the Shape all light's parallel with Eve and Satan.[61] Eve had been used in a positive context by Shelley in *The Sensitive Plant*, as his Lady is 'An Eve in this Eden' (*Sensitive Plant* 2, 2) and her tending of the plants (*Sensitive Plant* 2, 37–8) echoes Milton's depiction of Eve's similar task (*Paradise Lost*, IX. 427–31). In *The Triumph of Life*, Shelley profoundly alters this nurturing characteristic in the Shape all light, making it a sinister, yet ambiguous portrait of a mysterious figure. The Shape all light also resembles Satan as she tempts the Eve-like Rousseau, and then disappears from the scene, leaving him as 'suddenly my brain became as sand' (*The Triumph of Life*, 405). As Harold Bloom writes, 'The world of the *Triumph* is a world deliberately emptied of myth, a world of *things*. In this world the myth is neither retracted (palinode) nor reversed (reaffirmation). The myth is simply absent, and the poem deals with the consequences of precisely that absence.'[62] Shelley's allusive practice here thrives on the ominous potential that it can draw from Milton's poetry, yet it is independent of Milton's poetic vision. The reader notes the allusive potential, but Shelley prevents us from gaining any stable ground on which to critically pivot. It is not that *The Triumph of Life* is 'deliberately emptied of myth'; rather, Shelley places no mythical handholds for the reader to cling to in the poem.

Like *Prometheus Unbound*'s earlier composite characters, *The Triumph of Life*'s mingling of characters, and the final refusal to commit to any definitive doubling, reveals Shelley's characteristic poetic practice. But in his final poem, Shelley has refined this imaginative principle, replicating in the mind of the reader the shifting sands of consciousness undergone by Rousseau in the poem. Milton is one of many voices in the poem, alongside Petrarch, Dante, Goethe, Calderón, Wordsworth, Southey, and Spenser, 'all like bubbles on an eddying flood' (*The Triumph of Life*, 458) of Shelley's poetic endeavour.[63] Each of Shelley's allusions represents a cumulative poetic effect; he draws strength from his predecessors while retaining control over the direction of his poem. Here in his final and most poetically independent poem,[64] as throughout his finest work, Shelley reveals a sureness of touch and imaginative insight in negotiating Milton's influence.

---

[60] See Hugh Roberts, *Shelley and the Chaos of History: A New Politics of Poetry* (University Park, PA: Pennsylvania State UP, 1997), 212–13.

[61] Reiman makes the connection between Adam and Rousseau, *Shelley's 'The Triumph of Life'*, 60 n. 99.

[62] Bloom, *Shelley's Mythmaking*, 220 n. 1.

[63] As listed by Cian Duffy, in *Shelley and the Revolutionary Sublime*, Cambridge Studies in Romanticism 63 (Cambridge: Cambridge UP, 2005), 190.

[64] 'But so far as the essence of life on earth is in question [in *The Triumph of Life*], the vision's answer is quite explicit, and thoroughly pessimistic.' See Hodgson, 'The World's Mysterious Doom', 595.

SELECT BIBLIOGRAPHY

Brisman, Leslie. *Milton's Poetry of Choice and its Romantic Heirs*. Ithaca, NY: Cornell UP, 1973.

Brisman, Susan Hawk. '"Unsaying his High Language": The Problem of Voice in "Prometheus Unbound"'. *SIR* 16.1 (1977), 51–86.

Curran, Stuart. *Shelley's Annus Mirabilis: The Maturing of an Epic Vision*. San Marino, CA: Huntington Library, 1975.

Goslee, Nancy Moore. *Uriel's Eye: Miltonic Stationing and Statuary in Blake, Keats, and Shelley*. University, AL: University of Alabama Press, 1985.

Hughes, Daniel. 'Prometheus Made Capable Poet in Act One of *Prometheus Unbound*'. *SIR* 17.1 (1978), 3–11.

Jones, Frederick L. 'Shelley and Milton'. *Studies in Philology* 49 (1952), 488–519.

Newlyn, Lucy. *'Paradise Lost' and the Romantic Reader*. Oxford: Clarendon Press, 1993.

O'Neill, Michael. 'Romantic Re-approprations of the Epic'. *The Cambridge Companion to Epic*. Ed. Catherine Bates. Cambridge: Cambridge UP, 2010.

Schlock, Peter A. *Romantic Satanism: Myth and the Historical Moment in Blake, Byron, and Shelley*. London: Palgrave Macmillan, 2003.

Shears, Jonathon. *The Romantic Legacy of 'Paradise Lost': Reading against the Grain*. Aldershot: Ashgate, 2009.

CHAPTER 31

··

SHELLEY AND THE
ENGLISH TRADITION
Spenser and Pope

··

MICHAEL O'NEILL AND PAIGE TOVEY

I

··

THIS chapter seeks to demonstrate the generously responsive yet rigorously revisionary nature of Shelley's relationship with two major figures in the English poetic tradition: one a poet of the English Reformation, Edmund Spenser, the other a poet of the Catholic minority in England in the post-Civil War and post-Restoration settlement, Alexander Pope. There are many other poets from whom Shelley learned; they include Dryden, Gray, and Thomson. But, along with Milton, Spenser and Pope play a special role in Shelley's poetic development, as they do in different ways for Byron. If Spenser licenses Byron's complex reuse of the romance genre in *Childe Harold's Pilgrimage* and Pope prompts his highly individual form of satire in *Don Juan*, both Spenser and Pope are among those poetic predecessors who assist Shelley in fashioning a sophisticated vision of art and experience. Spenser appeals to Shelley partly because of what Harold Bloom calls his 'power to project both the object of desire and the shape of nightmare with equal imaginative freedom'.[1] The older poet with his true and false Duessas, his archetypes of excellence and emblems of horror, often sponsors Shelley's visionary explorations. Pope, for his part, sharpens Shelley's satirical and critical insights and strategies. Both precursor poets feed Shelley's work with forms and images which he adapts to his own purposes.

[1] *The Best Poems of the English Language: From Chaucer through Robert Frost*, selected and with commentary by Harold Bloom (London: Harper, 2004), 61.

II

Edmund Spenser often delighted Shelley's ear and imagination, but occasionally vexed his ideological intelligence. *A Defence of Poetry* manages to forgive the poet of *The Faerie Queene* for being 'a poet laureate' (*Major Works*, 699) since, along with other great poets on Shelley's circular argument, his 'errors have been weighed and found to have been dust in the balance' (*Major Works*, 699). For Shelley in *A Defence* 'Posterity', like 'Time' in Auden's pre-self-censored elegy to Yeats, 'Pardons' Spenser 'for writing well'.[2] Moreover, Spenser was able, like many of Shelley's precursors (Aeschylus, Milton, and Wordsworth are notable examples), to inspire by engaging the younger poet in that imaginative struggle in which he often engages, as a result of which poets, living and dead, even as 'they deny and abjure, [...] are yet compelled to serve, the Power which is seated on the throne of their own soul' (*Major Works*, 701).

Thomas Love Peacock glosses Shelley's allusion in a letter to the 'scale of that balance which the Giant (of Arthegall) holds' in the following way:

> Shelley once pointed out this passage to me, observing: 'Artegall argues with the Giant; the Giant has the best of the argument; Artegall's iron man knocks him over into the sea and drowns him. This is the usual way in which power deals with opinion.' I said: 'That was not the lesson which Spenser intended to convey.' 'Perhaps not,' he said; 'it is the lesson which he conveys to me. I am of the Giant's faction.'[3]

Spenser is clearly opposed to 'the Giant's faction', the Giant's speeches in favour of equality being treated as forms of rabble-rousing demagoguery: the assertion by the Giant that 'Tyrants that make men subiect to their law, | I will suppresse, that they no more may raine' (V. ii. 38) prompts Arthegall's defence of kingship as divinely ordained: 'He maketh Kings to sit in souerainty' (V. ii. 41).[4] From *Queen Mab* to *Prometheus Unbound*, from 'Ozymandias' to 'Ode to Liberty', Shelley's opposition to kings for their usurpation of position and power, and their imposition upon their fellow citizens, remains constant. But Spenser's dramatizing of a contest between an upholder of the status quo and a rebel against it appealed to Shelley since it furnished further grounds for his transformative critique of reactionary politics. Moreover, the subsequent exploration of matters to do with justice and equity in Spenser's fifth book involves the encounter between Radigund the Amazon and Artegall, in which Artegall obeys Radigund, having been overcome by her, until she falls in love with him, as does her handmaiden, Clarinda, sent by Radigund to plead her mistress's suit. The resulting 'subtill nets' (V. v. 52) humanize Artegall to the point where Spenser has to plead his hero's case against readers who may find in him 'Great weaknesse' (V. vi. 1).

---

[2] 'In Memory of W. B. Yeats', in *The English Auden: Poems, Essays and Dramatic Writings, 1927–1939*, ed. Edward Mendelson (London: Faber, 1977), 243.

[3] *Letters: PBS* II, 71n.

[4] Spenser is quoted from *The Poetical Works of Edmund Spenser*, ed. J. C. Smith and E. De Selincourt (London: Oxford UP, 1912).

That a hero should be flawed and find gender relations a difficult area seems calculated to appeal to Shelley, whose own post-Spenserian epic *Laon and Cythna* (1817) has, as Greg Kucich notes, affinities with *The Faerie Queene* in its fascination with 'the drama of psychological collapse and renewal'.[5] Already in his 'Hymn to Intellectual Beauty' Shelley displays his productive compulsion to revise earlier canonical texts by Spenser, here his 'Fowre Hymns', along with responsiveness to the Platonic erotics of the Renaissance poet's vision. Spenser's 'An Hymne of Heavenly Beavtie' uses its stately seven-line stanzas of *rime royal* to establish a Christianized Platonic hierarchy at the top of which is God whose perfection induces the trope of inexpressibility to which Shelley also has recourse.[6] Yet by contrast with Spenser Shelley is all glimpses and hurried fugitive intuitions; his Platonism is no settled scheme of understanding, but a dim background against which his own longings and yearnings flare into speech. There is poise, too, amidst Shelley's uncertainties, as is evident in his opening lines. Spenser appeals directly to God in the form of the Holy Spirit: 'O thou most almightie Spright' (8) 'To shed into my breast some sparkling light | Of thine eternall Truth' (10–11). Shelley states, enigmatically, authoritatively: 'The awful shadow of some unseen Power | Floats though unseen amongst us' (1–2). The idiom suggests a complex transaction with Christian and Platonic traditions. The poet is able to affirm the existence of something close to an absolute, while refusing to locate his intuition within a pre-existing framework of understanding. Shelley writes in the margins almost of Spenser's great Renaissance hymn, yet he does so in a way that finally seeks to reverse the places of text and commentary. The Shelleyan gloss establishes its own secular scripture, according to which revelation comes not from God but from the sceptical, questioning imagination present in 'Each human heart and countenance' (7) and embodied in the very workings of the poem we are reading, with its shifts, transitions, slumps, and rallying.

Spenser argues that 'we fraile wights' (120) are unable to discern 'The glory of that Maiestie diuine' (124) belonging to God; Shelley attacks as 'Frail spells' (29) orthodox Christian attempts to answer questions about the nature of reality, especially its changeableness: questions that provoke from the religious believers answers that involve 'the name of God, and ghosts, and Heaven' (27). The same word points in different directions: humility for Spenser, an awareness of the limits that confront enquiry for Shelley, yet an awareness compatible with trust in the imagination. Addressing and blaming his 'hungry soule' (288) for feeding 'On idle fancies of thy foolish thought' (289), Spenser rejects 'vain deceiptfull shadowes' (291). Shelley finds in similes and comparisons possible analogues for an experience that has much in common with religious fervour save the belief in what Spenser calls 'that great *Deity*' (145) whose 'throne is built vpon Eternity' (152). Value, for Shelley, is conferred upon 'human thought or form' (15) by a 'Spirit of BEAUTY' (13) that agnostically refuses to declare its origins. As Kucich suggests, the difference between the Renaissance and the Romantic poets shows in the adjectives attached to 'beauty' in their titles: 'Heavenlie' in Spenser's poem, 'Intellectual' in

---

[5] Greg Kucich, *Keats, Shelley, and Romantic Spenserianism* (University Park, PA: Pennsylvania State UP, 1991), 274.

[6] This is noted ibid. 263.

Shelley's.[7] Spenser looks to a transcendently 'soueraine light' (295) to give meaning to existence; Shelley to poetic intimations of 'Thy light alone' (32), conveyed through similes that confess and affirm in the same breath that meaning is inseparable from 'fancies'.

With Harold Bloom as a forebear, Kucich uses the word 'revisionism' to explain Shelley's relationship with Spenser, and the word is helpful in its suggestion of purposeful re-orchestration by the later poet of the earlier writer's commitment to a vision of cosmic harmony founded 'Vpon the pillours of Eternity, | That is contrayr to *Mutabilitie*' (VIII. 2). With their opposition between movement and stillness, change and rest, the Mutability cantos appear to have left a deep impression on Shelley's imagination.[8] In *Laon and Cythna*, Shelley explores his sardonically tragic view in 'Mutability', a short poem in the *Alastor* volume, that 'Nought may endure but Mutability' (16).[9] The effect, there, of 'endure' suggests a bitter relish of paradox: all that lasts is the fact of change, with a sidelong glance at the human need to 'endure', in the sense of 'suffer'. Yet that poem suggests a latent exhilaration beneath its mask of sorrow in the fact that, whatever the feeling, 'The path of its departure still is free' (14). The surprising stress on 'its' may bring with it the implication that 'we' are not 'free' from the constraints of change, yet Shelley's embracing of revolution in *Laon and Cythna* brings with it an awareness of a fundamental commitment to change. These meanings are compacted in the poem's subtitle: 'The Revolution of the Golden City, A Vision of the Nineteenth Century, in the Stanza of Spenser'. Shelley seeks to imagine a 'revolution' in accord with his commitment to 'recommending [...] a great and important change in the spirit which animates the social institutions of mankind' (136–7). This commitment involves acceptance of, even a delight in, 'change'.

At the same time the poem wishes to recommend permanent ideals, to believe 'That virtue, though obscured on Earth, not less | Survives all mortal change in lasting loveliness' (XII. xxxvii. 4781–2), locating this survival of 'virtue' in a post-mortal 'Temple of the Spirit' (XII. xli. 4815), to which we have been introduced in the first canto, where the narrator is taken to 'a Temple, such as mortal hand | Has never built' (I. xlix. 559–60). Laon and Cythna instigate a revolution in an imagined human city and Laon's is 'A tale of human power' (I. lviii. 648). But, as Spenser's knights lose their way, or are embroiled in severe trials (Redcrosse's encounter with Despair, for example), so Shelley's hero and heroine must undergo challenges to their revolutionary virtue. The revolution is defeated; Laon burnt at the stake; the voyage to the post-mortal Temple of the Spirit is at once a means of keeping alive dreams and hopes that, for Shelley's generation, had undergone historical defeat, and a confession that the poem's revolution is scarred by traumatic memories of the real-life events in France which Shelley sought to re-imagine and transform.

    [7] Ibid. 262.
    [8] See ibid. 270 for an account of how Shelley was concerned 'with transferring Spenser's drama of mutability and transcendence to a modern, secular context' and *passim* for references to Bloom, especially 7 n., where Bloom is praised for urging 'Spenser scholars to deepen their understanding of *The Faerie Queene* by reading it through the Romantics' revisionary criticism'.
    [9] Unless indicated otherwise, Shelley's poetry in this chapter is quoted from *Major Works*.

'Methinks, those who now live have survived an age of despair', writes Shelley in his Preface to the poem, in which he deplores the liberal defeatism of recent times, as a result of which 'gloom and misanthropy have become the characteristics of the age in which we live' (*Major Works*, 132). That Shelley can make two such contrary pronouncements in rapid succession, one optimistically proclaiming the political health of 'those who now live', the other accepting, even as it fights against, a less buoyant view of 'the age in which we live', prepares us for the swings between confidence and anxiety discernible in *Laon and Cythna*, as they are in *The Faerie Queene*. Indeed, Spenser, it might be argued, gave Shelley the confidence to depict, through 'a succession of pictures' (as Kucich notes, a distinctly Spenserian procedure), the lineaments of 'a liberal and comprehensive morality' (*Major Works*, 131, 130).[10] Part of the 'comprehensiveness' of this 'morality' is that it is conveyed in a work that 'is narrative not didactic' (*Major Works*, 131), allowing for narrative's ramifications to work on the reader's imagination. In Spenser's case this means that though, as a result of Una's upbraidings and heartenings, the Redcrosse Knight does not succumb to Despair's temptations, we still respond to those temptations in all their force, with their sophistical evocations of the desirability of death: 'Sleepe after toyle, port after stormie seas, | Ease after warre, death after life does greatly please' (I. ix. 40). The lines lull and seduce, despite the presence in the poem of a moral scheme urging the rejection of such lulling seductions. In Shelley's case, it means that Cythna's exhortations to welcome the coming political 'Spring' (IX. xxv. 3688) are allowed to pass into a deeply affecting confession of final existential uncertainty: 'All that we are or know, is darkly driven | Towards one gulf' (IX. xxxv. 3779–80). The glimpses of 'Paradise' (IX. xxxvi. 3792) proffered by *Laon and Cythna* avoid the hackneyed by virtue of the poem's ability to gaze into such a 'gulf' and still retain a sense of the revolutionary virtue embodied in a person such as Cythna, Laon's 'Fair star of life and love' and 'soul's delight' (IX. xxxvi. 3788), and Shelley's updated and remodelled version of Una, whose 'celestiall sight' (*The Faerie Queene*, I. xii. 23) fills Redcrosse with wonder at their wedding.[11] Cythna is a post-Wollstonecraftian feminist, full-blooded theological sceptic, and dauntless political agitator; Una is an allegorical type of the true Catholic Church supposedly recovered by the Reformed English religion. But Spenser's idealism (meaning his belief in ideals and his embodiment in words of an idea) is at work as a creative influence in Shelley's *Laon and Cythna*, and means that the relations between the two heroines are not merely those of orthodox thesis and heretical antithesis.

Spenser lies behind *Laon and Cythna*'s 'conjunction of the theme of revolution with the language and form of romance', its highly original use of chivalric romance as the vehicle for Utopian quest.[12] Shelley points out in his subtitle that he is writing 'in the Stanza of Spenser', Spenser being one of the few English poets to have a form named after him. In the Preface Shelley writes that he has 'adopted the stanza of Spenser (a measure inexpressibly beautiful)', because, unlike the 'blank verse of Shakespeare and Milton', it

[10] Kucich, *Keats, Shelley, and Romantic Spenserianism*, 274.
[11] For such remodellings, see ibid. 274.
[12] David Duff, *Romance and Revolution: Shelley and the Politics of a Genre* (Cambridge: Cambridge UP, 1994), 1.

provides some shelter for the 'aspiring spirit'. But he is also 'enticed [...] by the brilliancy and magnificence of sound which a mind that has been nourished upon musical thoughts can produce by a just and harmonious arrangement of the pauses of this measure' (*Major Works*, 135). That is an eloquent tribute to what Spenser's example and bequeathed 'measure' makes possible. Yeats quoted a stanza (VI. xxxiv) from *Laon and Cythna* to show how, in it, 'The rhythm is varied and troubled, and the lines, which are in Spenser like bars of gold thrown ringing upon one another, are broken capriciously'. By contrast with the melodious self-sufficiency of *The Faerie Queene*, in which 'Spenser's verse is always rushing on to some preordained thought', Shelley's meaning 'is bound together by the vaguest suggestion'.[13] Yeats's ear is alert to real differences, and yet the antithesis is cut too cleanly. Shelley's 'thought' may not be 'preordained', but it is consistently fascinated by the possibility of 'confounding' individuals 'into one | Unutterable power' (VI. xxxv. 2641, 2642–3). David Duff is persuasive when he finds in 'the very sound of the poetry the idea of a developing harmony between the individual and the "universal life"'.[14] Spenser, for his part, is no means averse to the 'inspiration of indolent Muses' which Yeats associates with Shelley.[15] P. C. Bayley comes closer than Yeats does to suggesting what Shelley derives from Spenser's poetic form when he writes of the Spenserian stanza as handled by the Renaissance poet that 'it is infinitely varied and intricate'.[16]

Similarly, Kucich is right to argue that Shelley and Byron seek 'to roughen a turbulence already there in Spenser'.[17] 'Turbulence' may not exactly fit the following stanza, one in Keats's mind when urging Shelley to '"load every rift" of your subject with ore'.[18] But the stanza shows how Spenser's style empathizes with his subject, here an account of Mammon's Cave that demands an intuition of weight and covetous, massive strength, qualities that transmit themselves to and through the writing's patterns of stress:

> That houses form within was rude and strong,
>   Like an huge caue, hewne out of rocky clift,
>   From whose rough vaut the ragged breaches hong,
>   Embost with massy gold of glorious gift,
>   And with rich metal loaded euery rift,
>   That heauy ruine they did seeme to threat;
>   And ouer them *Arachne* high did lift
>   Her cunning web, and spred her subtile net,
> Enwrapped in fowle smoke and clouds more blacke then Iet.
>
> (*The Faerie Queene*, II. vii. 28)

[13] W. B. Yeats, 'Edmund Spenser', in *Selected Criticism and Prose*, ed. A. Norman Jeffares (London: Pan in association with Macmillan, 1980), 119.

[14] Duff, *Romance and Revolution*, 192, quoting *Laon and Cythna*, VI. xxix. 2595.

[15] Yeats, 'Edmund Spenser', 119.

[16] Spenser, *The Faerie Queene: Book 1*, ed. P. C. Bayley (1966; London: Oxford UP, 1970 with corrections), 20.

[17] Kucich, *Keats, Shelley, and Romantic Spenserianism*, 279. See also the same critic's observation that Leigh Hunt 'frequently adjured readers to hear the rhythm of passion in Spenser's modulations', 96.

[18] *The Letters of John Keats 1814–1821*, ed. Hyder E. Rollins, 2 vols. (Cambridge, MA: Harvard UP, 1958), II, 323.

'Bars of gold thrown ringing upon one another': in wording thus his sense of Spenser's measure, Yeats may indeed have had this stanza in mind. Yet the sound-patterns intimate danger as much as wealth, and muffle and roughen their music, threading a short 'a' sound through 'ragged', 'massy', 'That', 'Arachne', and 'black' in a way that is less aureate than mimetic of a laboured, 'rude' strength. The caesurae here may seem well behaved and inconspicuous (only two strong medial pauses are present—in the second and eighth lines, and both in a predictable position). But the stanza is 'Embost' with heavy stresses, halting its flow, not permitting any easy way through to a 'preordained' conclusion, and pointing up the surprising appearance of Arachne, her 'subtile net' conspiring with Mammon yet suggestive, too, of self-entrapment, and serving in metapoetic fashion as an image of the very stanza we are reading.

A stanza in Shelley's poem that also describes a cave shows how Shelley can be more harmoniously fluent, when he chooses, than Spenser himself. It occurs in canto VII, when Cythna, imprisoned by the tyrant in a 'cave | Above the waters' (VII. xii. 2929–30; quoted from *H*), effectively turns Plato's myth of the cave (for Plato an image of benighted human consciousness) on its head. Long before Keats's advice, Shelley realized the significance of mining for poetic and political knowledge, as he has Cythna tell Laon:

> My mind became the book through which I grew
> Wise in all human wisdom, and its cave,
> Which like a mine I rifled through and through,
> To me the keeping of its secrets gave—
> One mind, the type of all, the moveless wave
> Whose calm reflects all moving things that are,
> Necessity, and love, and life, the grave,
> And sympathy, fountains of hope and fear;
> Justice, and truth, and time, and the world's natural sphere.
>
> (VII. xxxi. 3100–8)

Cythna, imprisoned in a cave, proves that a prison is not a prison when a metaphor can liberate it by using 'cave' as a metaphor for the stores of 'human wisdom' which she excavates; this 'mine' passes into her discovery of 'One mind, the type of all': an intuited Platonic absolute firmly rooted in rather than transcending the human condition, whose constituents are catalogued in the following list. Spenser's Platonism is more explicitly in accord with traditional exposition; Shelley's more individually inflected so as to take from Plato the idea of enduring value while implicitly calling into question, through the very display of metaphorical association in the stanza, any straightforward conceptual assent to 'the existence of a separate realm of abstract objects called "Forms"'.[19] Shelley's rhythms elsewhere can be termed 'troubled'; here, they are in sympathy with a growth in wisdom and a world-reflecting 'calm', even as the stress shift at the start of the alexandrine hints at a subliminal tension between 'things that are' and things as they ought to be. But as with Spenser's epic, *Laon and Cythna* deploys the space given by the roomy

---

[19] Richard Kraut, 'Introduction to the Study of Plato', in Richard Kraut (ed.), *The Cambridge Companion to Plato* (Cambridge: Cambridge UP, 1992), 8.

nine-line stanza to accommodate stillness and movement, being and becoming, desire and glimpses of fulfilment.

As suggested above, one of the older poet's greatest bequests to Shelley lies in what John Hughes, an early eighteenth-century editor of Spenser, described as his epic poem's 'surprizing Vein of fabulous Invention which runs thro it, and enriches it every where with Imagery and Descriptions more than we meet with in any other modern Poem'.[20] It is in *Prometheus Unbound* that such a 'surprizing Vein' is most evident. A poem written 'in the merest spirit of ideal poetry' (*Letters: PBS* II, 219), the lyric drama abounds in scenes, where, drawing on but also adapting to his own purposes classical and mythological stories, Shelley surprises and delights us through his 'Vein of fabulous Invention', a vein that holds at bay the threat of arid instruction or 'Didactic poetry', his 'abhorrence', as he tells us in his Preface (*Major Works*, 232).

A figure illustrating this vein is Demogorgon, who serves to complicate in enhancing ways the poem's reflections on history. Demogorgon may derive from the first canto of *The Faerie Queene*, where he appears as 'Great *Gorgon*, Prince of darknesse and dead night' (I. i. 37). Shelley recasts him as a less straightforwardly Stygian figure, one who is 'A living Spirit' (II. iv. 7) even as he has 'neither limb, | Nor form, nor outline' (II. iv. 5–6). As 'a mighty Darkness' (II. iv. 2) Demogorgon represents the realm of potentiality rather than evil (or nightmare) and functions as the figure without whom tyranny cannot be deposed. It is he, not Prometheus, who drags Jupiter from his throne, possibly allowing Shelley to displace the problem of violent revolution from his newly forgiving hero to another character, but also allowing him to embody within the lyrical drama the suggestion that a desired change cannot happen simply because the forces of defiance (Prometheus) and love (Asia) combine, though it could not happen without this combination. In the way allegorical thought entangles itself with concrete fabling and invention, Shelley shows himself to have learned much from Spenser's mythmaking, as Harold Bloom and Carlos Baker have argued, among others.[21] In his *Letter to Maria Gisborne*, he depicts himself as a benign version of Spenser's wicked mage, Archimago, whose evil schemes are central to the first book of *The Faerie Queene*: 'And here like some weird Archimage sit I, | Plotting dark spells and devilish enginery' (106–7), where the second line ventriloquizes the paranoid suspicions of what Shelley calls sardonically 'our meek reviews' (110). In this poem, Shelley gestures towards an engagement with Spenser's inventiveness that flowers into individual being in *The Sensitive Plant* and *The Witch of Atlas*. In both poems, Spenser serves as spur and foil. In the former, a fable of seeming mutability and decay that is challenged by a 'modest creed' (Conclusion, 13) of idealist denial of such things, the Lady who tends the garden and dies at the close of Part Second is 'An Eve in this Eden' (II, 2), but also brings to mind, as Jerrold Hogle suggests,

---

[20] Quoted in Kucich, *Keats, Shelley, and Romantic Spenserianism*, 21.

[21] See Harold Bloom, *Shelley's Mythmaking* (1959; Ithaca, NY: Cornell UP, 1969), where Spenser is said to be an exemplar of the 'visionary' school of poetry, and vital for the 'romantic mythmaking of Collins, Blake, Shelley, and Keats', 149; Carlos Baker, *Shelley's Major Poetry: The Fabric of a Vision* (1948; New York: Russell, 1961).

'Spenser's Una'.[22] The delicate interplay between loss and hope in the poem is distinctively Shelleyan in its ability to snatch a provisional affirmation from the jaws of steady-eyed scepticism. Yet the final lines seem to evoke, even as they distinguish themselves from, the movement from melancholy to dignified assurance with which Spenser closes his epic.

The Witch of Atlas, Shelley's most exuberant tribute to 'the poetical faculty' (Major Works, 696), compares the poem being offered to a sceptical Mary to a 'silken-wingèd fly' (9), possibly alluding to Spenser's Clarion, chief of 'the race of siluer-winged Flies' (17), in Spenser's Muiopotmos: or The Fate of the Butterflie.[23] Writing, like Spenser, in ottava rima stanzas, Shelley mourns the ephemerality of his previous and present poems with deeply felt yet nonchalant good humour; now a lonely artist, expecting to be misunderstood, it would seem, he quietly bids farewell to his earlier self-image in the dedicatory stanzas to Laon and Cythna as a Spenserian 'victor Knight of Faery | Earning bright spoils' for his Queen's 'enchanted dome' (3–4). And yet the 'bright spoils' won by The Witch of Atlas include the recognition that a 'liberal and comprehensive morality' may be served best by an art that is bent on proclaiming its autonomy. The creation of the False Florimell in The Faerie Queene (III. viii. 6) mimics, in its blending of 'purest snow', 'wax', and 'fine Mercury', a false art; Shelley's Witch creates Hermaphroditus from 'fire and snow', (321), but does so by 'tempering the repugnant mass | With liquid love' (322–3). Shelley's commitment to art and its condition of free and necessary play does not preclude—indeed, it entails—a wittily sharp-eyed view of art's limits, if we allegorize Hermaphroditus as a product and agent of artistic creativity.

By this stage of Shelley's career Spenser has emerged as an abiding presence in Shelley's imagination. He need not declare ideological war on the Renaissance poet because his swerving from his Christian Platonism is almost second nature. The more individual Shelley's voice as he explores his sense of art's value and limits in a series of poems (The Witch of Atlas and Adonais, in particular), the more strongly he persuades that he has absorbed Spenser deeply into his imagination's bloodstream. In Adonais he produces his most sustained and impressive poem in Spenserian stanzas and, arguably, in any measure. His recurrent concern with Spenser's twin themes of mutability and lasting significance finds memorable expression in an elegy that is indebted to Spenser's elegy for Sidney, Astrophel, and its incorporated lament, The Lay of Clorinda.[24] Clorinda's assertion of 'so diuine a thing' (66) as Astrophel's 'immortall spirit' (61), 'Ah no: it is not dead, ne can it die, | But liues for aie, in blissful Paradise' (67–8), underpins Shelley's pivotal movement from grief to affirmation in stanza xxxix: 'he is not dead, he doth not sleep— |

---

[22] Jerrold E. Hogle, Shelley's Process: Radical Transference and the Development of his Major Works (New York: Oxford UP, 1988), 288. The Bower of Bliss and the Garden of Adonis also feature among the Spenserian archetypes stirred into remembered complementary and contrasting life by the poem's representation of the garden and its destruction. See Bloom, Shelley's Mythmaking, 178–80 for the poem's relationship to the Garden of Adonis in The Faerie Queene III. vi.

[23] See Bloom, Shelley's Mythmaking, 148–55 for an account of this poem's influence on The Sensitive Plant and 170–1 for commentary on the possible allusion in The Witch of Atlas.

[24] Spenser's influence on Adonais is discussed in Hogle, Shelley's Process, esp. 299–301, and Kucich, Keats, Shelley, and Romantic Spenserianism, 326–45.

He hath awakened from the dream of life' (343–4). Shelley's version of 'blissful Paradise' is 'the abode where the Eternal are' (495), an abode that is Platonic, knowingly fictive and secular, and a brave gesture towards transcendence: an abode that is the home of 'eternal' poets such as Keats and Spenser. It exists, in part, as a post-Christian response to Spenser's declarations of belief in eternity and represents Shelley's most significant revision of the older poet's work.

III

In a letter to Lord Byron dated 4 May 1821, Shelley refers to Alexander Pope as 'the pivot of a dispute in taste, on which, until I understand it, I must profess myself neuter'. Knowing that Byron credited Pope as a chief influence on his poetry, and perhaps lightly goading his friend, Shelley continues:

> I certainly do not think Pope, or *any* writer, a fit model for any succeeding writer; if he, or they should be determined to be so, it would all come to a question as to under *what forms* mediocrity should perpetually reproduce itself; for true genius vindicates to itself an exemption from all regard to whatever has gone before—and in this question I feel no interest. (*Letters: PBS* II, 290)

Although Shelley claims to 'feel no interest' in the debate concerning Pope's status as a great writer of the eighteenth century and influence upon the Romantic age, his own works belie such feelings of disinterest. P. M. S. Dawson comments on this passage by noting that Shelley 'did have anxieties on the score of possible influences detectable in his poetry' and that the poet 'took pains in his prefaces to insist that any similarities between his own work and that of eminent contemporaries was to be attributed to the spirit of the age, and not to direct imitation on his part'.[25] Although Shelley's work certainly represents an originality reflective of the 'spirit of the age', Pope's forerunning example is nevertheless felt in the Romantic poet's work. This is not to say that Shelley is a mere imitator of Pope but rather that Shelley's works expound upon and even converse with that of his predecessors in an innovation of new ideas and forms.

From the beginning of Shelley's poetic career, one can trace evidences of Pope. Shelley's early poem, *Queen Mab*, although more obviously containing Spenserian elements, also engages with Pope through allusions and thematic and formal borrowings. Carlos Baker, for example, notes that the verse of *Queen Mab* 'is based on pieces like Pope's *Messiah* and *Essay on Man*' and that 'Pope appears in the poem under a thin disguise'.[26] For instance, Baker points out that Shelley invokes (in canto VIII of *Queen Mab*) the Old Testament utopian image of children playing with asps and cockatrices through

---

[25] P. M. S. Dawson, 'Byron, Shelley, and the "New School"', in Kelvin Everest (ed.), *Shelley Revalued: Essays from the Gregynog Conference* (Leicester: Leicester UP, 1983), 106.

[26] Carlos Baker, 'Spenser, the Eighteenth Century, and Shelley's *Queen Mab*', *Modern Language Quarterly* (March 1941), 81–2, 90.

imitating Pope's version of the same image in his *Messiah*. Both Pope's and Shelley's passages share straightforward similarities: each refers to a green-scaled basilisk rather than using Isaiah's synonym, cockatrice; and both poets invoke the image of the serpent harmlessly licking the feet of either the babe (in Shelley's case) or the pilgrims (in Pope's case).[27] But what is more interesting than occasional borrowings is the way in which Shelley builds upon, reacts, and responds to eighteenth-century influences, and, in particular, Pope's poetic style.

In a letter to Thomas Jefferson Hogg, dated 3 January 1811, Shelley exhibits traces of eighteenth-century influence in the wording and allusion he uses to discuss his ideas concerning atheism, the subject of their controversial pamphlet *The Necessity of Atheism* (for the publication of which Shelley and Hogg were expelled from Oxford less than three months later). Shelley writes: 'I may not be able to adduce proofs, but I think that the leaf of a tree, the meanest insect on which we trample are in themselves arguments more conclusive than any which can be adduced that some vast intellect animates Infinity [...]' (*Letters: PBS* I, 35). The phrase 'meanest insect' recalls the closing lines of Wordsworth's Immortality Ode, and his reflection that 'To me the meanest flower that blows can give | Thoughts that do often lie too deep for tears' (205–6).[28] That Shelley chose the adjective from a poem whose subject is 'Intimations of Immortality', the very subject which Shelley expounds as well as challenges, is no coincidence. Throughout the younger Romantic's career he can be found interacting with, responding to, and even correcting his predecessor. But there are possible sources for 'meanest' which derive from eighteenth-century poetry. Wordsworth in particular (especially given the reference to 'The common sun', a forerunner of the 'light of common day' (77) in the Immortality Ode) and Shelley too appear to draw from Thomas Gray's unfinished '[Ode on the Pleasure Arising from Vicissitude]', probably written in 1754 or 1755, but not published until 1775:

> The meanest flowret of the vale,
> The simplest note that swells the gale,
> The common sun, the air and skies,
> To him are opening Paradise.
>
> (45–8)[29]

For Gray the 'meanest flowret' suggests 'Paradise'; for Wordsworth the 'meanest flower' (which lies under a sky whose clouds 'Do take a sober colouring from an eye | That hath kept watch o'er man's mortality' [200–1]) brings 'Thoughts [...] too deep for tears'; and for Shelley the 'meanest insect' also provokes speculation about what 'vast intellect animates Infinity'. The shift in the use of 'meanest' from Gray to Wordsworth to Shelley is

---

[27] Ibid. 91.

[28] Unless otherwise noted, all Wordsworth quotations are taken from *William Wordsworth: The Major Works*, ed. Stephen Gill (1984; Oxford: Oxford UP, 2008).

[29] Quoted in *The Poems of Thomas Gray, William Collins, Oliver Goldsmith*, ed. Roger Lonsdale (London: Longman, 1969). Lonsdale notes (206n.) the appearance of 'meanest flowret' in Edward Young's *Night Thoughts* (1742), VI, 197, and that work is also a possible influence on both Wordsworth's and Shelley's phrasing.

subtle but noteworthy. For Gray, 'meanest flowret' acknowledges the order of the 'Great Chain of Being', particularly as meanest implies a hierarchy, which the *OED* (def. 3b) defines as 'petty, insignificant, unimportant; inconsiderable'. And yet in insisting that the 'meanest flowret' has the ability to intimate 'Paradise', Gray challenges hierarchical order. For Wordsworth, boundaries undergo major revision as, in a poem obsessed by the nature and limits of seeing, he presents himself as an 'eye | That hath kept watch o'er man's mortality' and suggests that, rather than 'Paradise', the 'meanest flower' can give 'Thoughts that do often lie too deep for tears'. Thoughts become a comparable substitute for paradise; perhaps such thoughts *are* paradise. Going one step further, Shelley replaces the flower with an 'insect on which we trample', and tells Hogg, 'I confess that I think Pope's "all are but parts of one tremendous whole" something more than Poetry, it has ever been my favourite theory' (*Letters: PBS* I, 35). The possibility that, as 'parts of one tremendous whole', the insect and the human being are equals further defies the hierarchical element of the 'Great Chain of Being'. Pope and Gray reappraise as well as reinforce received eighteenth-century beliefs and ideas; Shelley challenges rigidifying notions.

Shelley's *Julian and Maddalo* presents a retrospective conversation with eighteenth-century poetics, especially with such works as Pope's *Essay on Man*. The *Essay on Man* and *Julian and Maddalo* are linked by similarities in both form and subject matter: both poets employ the heroic couplet to present and explore philosophical dualisms. As a central and recognizable form in English poetry since its establishment in the days of Chaucer, the heroic couplet became a commonplace form by the late seventeenth and eighteenth centuries; so much so that Hayden Carruth suggests that 'Dryden chose the couplet because he thought it the plainest mode available'.[30] Pope links his practice to Milton's epic ambitions in *Paradise Lost* when pronouncing his intention, in the opening lines of the *Essay on Man*, to 'vindicate the ways of God to Man' (16).[31] Yet Pope's poem also has commerce with a conversational idiom, a legacy bequeathed to Shelley, who referred to *Julian and Maddalo* as 'a *sermo pedestris* way of treating human nature', asking his publisher, Charles Ollier, that the poem should appear in 'some unostentatious form' (*Letters: PBS* II, 196): in the event it was not published until two years after Shelley's death. Familiar both with Pope's heroic couplet verse and the attack on it by poets such as Hunt who sought to loosen and 'free' the form, Shelley in *Julian and Maddalo* revisits and refashions the Popean heroic couplet. Shelley uses enjambed couplets that differ greatly in their movement from the perfectly balanced couplets of Pope. Richard Cronin observes that 'for Pope [...] the poet's task was only to express gracefully pre-established and generally accepted thoughts', whereas for Shelley 'a poet's speech, not by a loose metaphor but as matter of fact, was an act of divine creation' in

---

[30] Carruth is quoted in John Sitter, 'Pope's Versification and Voice', in Pat Rogers (ed.), *The Cambridge Companion to Pope* (Cambridge: Cambridge UP, 2007), 37–8. Sitter quotes Carruth from 'The Question of Poetic Form', which is reprinted in *Claims for Poetry*, ed. Donald Hall (Ann Arbor: University of Michigan Press, 1982), 59.

[31] All quotations from Pope are taken from *Alexander Pope: The Major Works*, ed. Pat Rogers (1993; Oxford: Oxford UP, 2006).

the same way that the Book of Genesis portrays God's 'primal act of creation' in the 'utterance of a sentence: "And God said, Let there be light: and there was light".[32] This contrast is illustrated in the following passage from Pope and Shelley. In *Essay on Man*, Pope reaffirms man's place in the great chain of being and emphasizes that man's aspirations are a result of his pride:

> The bliss of Man (could pride that blessing find)
> Is not to act or think beyond mankind;
> No powers of body or of soul to share,
> But what his nature and his state can bear.
> Why has not Man a microscopic eye?
> For this plain reason, Man is not a fly.
>
> (189–94)

Each couplet presents a complete statement, functioning as a complete thought, or, grammatically, as a complete sentence. Typically, the second line echoes the first; a pattern of invitation and response emerges. The metre is exact, the rhyme masculine. This is not to say that Pope's heroic couplets are boring or without charm. He does incorporate a fleeting consonance in 'bliss' and '*bless*ing', and one can detect a ghost of assonance in 'nature' and 'state' or '*m*icroscopic' and 'eye'. Nevertheless, Shelley's heroic couplets in *Julian and Maddalo* deliberately defy Pope in both form and subject:

> This ride was my delight.—I love all waste
> And solitary places; where we taste
> The pleasure of believing what we see
> Is boundless, as we wish our souls to be:
> And such was this wide ocean, and this shore
> More barren than its billows;—and yet more [...]
>
> (14–19)

Shelley demonstrates, in this passage, a deliberate subversion of the traditional heroic couplet. Nearly every line is enjambed with caesurae that form a strong contrast with Pope's tidily end-stopped lines. Shelley's lines are replete with additional poetic device; through assonance he pairs 'ride' with 'delight' and 'waste', 'places' and 'taste'; he repeatedly incorporates the word 'we' in several alliterative combinations through successive lines ('where we', 'what we', 'we wish', and 'wide'); he repeats the central '*ie*' vowel sound of 'bel*ie*ving' in 'we see' and again with 'we' and 'be' in the following line; and draws the reader's attention to important words through deliberate, and yet subtle and enjambed, alliteration with 'believing', 'boundless', and 'be'; and he adorns the last line of the quoted passage with a palindromic structure through the repeated 'more' at the beginning and the end of the line. Considered singularly and as the second line of the couplet, the line suggests that the 'shore' is less than 'its billows' by being 'more barren' 'and yet' somehow it is still 'more' in a sense that suggests the barren waste has greater value. But Shelley adds varying possibility to the line, and particularly to the word 'more' with the lines that follow:

---

[32] Richard Cronin, *Shelley's Poetic Thoughts* (London: Macmillan Press, 1981), 4.

> More barren than its billows;—and yet more
> Than all, with a remembered friend I love
> To ride as then I rode; [...]
>
> (14–16)

The grammatical structure, particularly the punctuation, of the lines suggests that 'and yet more' belongs to the assertion that 'more | Than all, with a remembered friend I love | To ride as then I rode'. But the ambiguous placement of 'and yet more' illustrates Shelley's use of enjambment and his ability to create a poem that is 'alive to uncertainties'.[33]

Shelley's poem enacts an interplay between the boundedness of the traditional Popean heroic couplet and the desire for boundlessness expressed by Julian. Byron, too, disciple and defender of Pope, created heroic couplet lines, as in *The Corsair*, that closely follow the couplet of the eighteenth century; and yet Byron makes the poem a place to stage a rebellion between formality and insurrection.[34] In Shelley's case, ambivalence informs his reaction against Pope. He may seem to defy Pope's mandate against overreaching in expressing Julian's wish to 'taste | The pleasure of believing what we see | Is boundless, as we wish our souls to be'. Yet the statement carries with it a suggestion of doubt. Shelley does not insist that 'our souls' are 'boundless', but that 'we wish' them to be. The phrase is a quintessentially Shelleyan expression of hope tempered by doubt; it may, in addition, imply a critique of his speaker's idealizing.

Where Pope's (and Milton's) oppositional poles are man and God, and by extension good and evil, Shelley's binary poetic formation is arranged as a conversation between humanistic optimism and misanthropic cynicism. Pope states in 'The Design', the preface to his *Essay on Man*, that he has aimed at 'steering betwixt the extremes of doctrines seemingly opposite [...] and in forming a *temperate* yet not *inconsistent* [...] system of ethics'.[35] For Shelley, a key feature is the presentation of different perspectives. Where Shelley puts forward a visual image, such as Julian's view of the sky 'roofed with clouds' (71) and the 'wondrous hue | Brighter than burning gold' (73–4) of the sun behind them, he presents a view emblematic of optimism. But just as Julian's musings on the landscape gain momentum, Shelley interrupts them in the second half of a couplet with Maddalo's intervention:

> The inmost purple spirit of light, and made
> Their very peaks transparent. 'Ere it fade,'
> Said my companion, 'I will show you soon
> A better station' [...]
>
> (84–7)

Again, Shelley capitalizes on his use of enjambment. Not only does Maddalo interrupt Julian's cheerful musings, but he also provides a contrasting perspective. Where Julian sees the illuminated aspects of the landscape, Maddalo sees that they will quickly fade.

---

[33] Michael O'Neill, *The Human Mind's Imaginings: Conflict and Achievement in Shelley's Poetry* (Oxford: Clarendon Press, 1989), 54.

[34] For a seminal discussion, see Susan J. Wolfson, 'Heroic Form: Couplets, "Self," and Byron's *Corsair*', in *Formal Charges: The Shaping of Poetry in British Romanticism* (Stanford, CA: Stanford UP, 1997), 133–63.

[35] Pope, *Major Works*, 270.

And, building upon this juxtaposition of views, Maddalo takes Julian to a prospect whereby they are able to see the city rather than, and in stark contrast to, the natural landscape.

This movement from landscape to city governs a movement towards the individually human as Maddalo draws Julian's attention to the 'windowless, deformed and dreary pile' (101), the madhouse in which the Maniac dwells. This switching to and fro of perspectives demonstrates an ambivalence that is similar, in some respects, to the ambivalence in Pope. Laura Brown points out that in Pope's *The Dunciad*, 'the geography of England' has a 'potential for a reversal of place, between ocean and land' and that it has a 'tendency toward movement'. Brown draws our attention to lines 211–18 of Pope's work where he describes the country as a 'watry Landskip', 'pendant Woods', and 'floating Forests'.[36] One finds a great deal of similarity in Shelley's choice of Venice as the setting for *Julian and Maddalo*; for Venice is a 'watry Landskip', a 'floating' city that hangs 'pendant' in the ocean.

Julian and Maddalo caps its changing perspectives with a calculatedly frustrating conclusion, in which Julian learns of the return and subsequent second departure of the Maniac's Lady, but refuses to impart the details to the reader, saying in the final line of the poem that 'the cold world shall not know' (617). It bears comparison in these respects to Pope's *Eloisa to Abelard* (1717), another tale of 'unfortunate passion', as Pope calls it in his opening 'Argument'. Eloisa's letter is a long dramatic monologue that is, in some ways, a model for the Maniac's soliloquy in *Julian and Maddalo*. Both Eloisa and the Maniac's soliloquies express passionate torment, but there is a stark contrast between Pope's articulation of Eloisa's sorrows and Shelley's presentation of the Maniac's pain. Eloisa's plight is particularly representative of what Pope calls 'the struggles of grace and nature, virtue and passion'.[37] In his 'Argument' Pope sets out a strict dichotomy between two poles represented by grace and virtue on the one hand and nature and passion on the other, and he explores Eloisa's vacillations between the two:

> I view my crime, but kindle at the view,
> Repent old pleasures, and solicit new;
> Now turned to heaven, I weep my past offence,
> Now think of thee, and curse my innocence.
>
> (185–8)

These two couplets present a pattern that Pope explores throughout the poem. He gives voice first to grace and virtue, 'I view my crime'; and then answers with nature and passion, 'but kindle at the view'. The second line of the first couplet follows a parallel structure: first articulating grace and virtue, 'Repent old pleasures', and then nature and passion, 'and then solicit new'. And although the second couplet varies its format slightly, dedicating the first line to grace and virtue, followed by a line of nature and passion, the dichotomy is revisited in multiple forms throughout the poem, never straying from a carefully wrought conversation between opposites. Even as Pope articulates Eloisa's passionate torment, he preserves an appearance of artistic and ethical control.

---

[36] Laura Brown, 'Pope and the Other', in Rogers (ed.), *Cambridge Companion to Pope*, 231.
[37] 'Argument' of 'Eloisa to Abelard', Pope, *Major Works*, 137, 138.

By contrast, Shelley's Maniac's soliloquy is a poetic articulation that invites the reader to experience madness from the inside, to glimpse how it must feel to be muddled mentally and emotionally. The Maniac's speech is disjointed and rambling, and Shelley uses asterisks to indicate the separation of the 'unconnected exclamations of his agony', which, he nevertheless suggests, 'will perhaps be found a sufficient comment for the text of every heart'.[38] This idea that 'unconnected exclamations' may be considered 'comment for the text of every heart' intimates the difference between Shelley's soliloquy and its Popean predecessor: from a Romantic perspective, Pope's complete control, his admirable precision, is too perfect to represent passionate sorrow, whereas Shelley's endeavour to create an 'unconnected' monologue more closely represents 'the text of every heart'. The same can be seen in the conclusion of both poems. Pope gives us a robustly clipped ending wherein the parted lovers are finally joined in death ('May one kind grave unite each hapless name, | And graft my love immortal on thy fame!' (343–4)) and live on in memory ('Let him our sad, our tender story tell' (364)). Shelley's poem has a more musing, meditative, and tragic ending where the possibility of representation of such woes is occluded. For Julian, as well as Shelley, it seems as though to articulate 'how | All happened' (616–17) is simply not achievable and the 'cold world' (617) is left to wonder at the poem's state of unresolve.

But Pope's capacity for metaphorical concentration and irony bequeaths a positive legacy to the Romantic poets which they develop in their individual ways. While Pope's satirical and ironic tradition is most evident in the works of Byron, Shelley too was capable of subtle and yet keen irony. One of the most evident instances of Shelleyan irony, which responds to Pope and the eighteenth century, is identified by Patrick Story,[39] who traces connections from the classical triumphs (processional entries of victors into Rome as depicted by poets such as Petrarch and Milton) from Pope to Shelley.[40] Story makes the discerning observation that although Shelley's only reference to Pope's triumphs is in a cancelled line of the October 1819 draft of the preface to *Prometheus Unbound*,[41] there is nevertheless a strong correlation between his and Pope's triumphs, both in the *Dunciad* and what Story calls the 'triumph of Vice' (from the *Epilogue to the Satires*, 131–72).[42]

Shelley's *The Triumph of Life* brings both poetic forebears discussed in this chapter into propinquity. Spenser and Pope shape the account of the chariot of life. The line, 'So ill was the car guided' (105), recalls the account in *The Faerie Queene* of Lucifera's

---

[38]   Shelley, *Major Works*, 213.

[39]   Patrick Story, 'Pope, Pageantry, and Shelley's *Triumph of Life*', *Keats–Shelley Journal* 21–2 (1972–3), 145–59 Harold Bloom, upon whom Story draws, must also be acknowledged for his commentary on Shelley's *Triumph*, and the connections he draws to the triumphal chariots of Ezekiel, Milton, Dante, and even Blake (whom Shelley would not have been aware of) in *Shelley's Mythmaking*, 231–55.

[40]   See in particular Petrarch's *Trionfi*, whose verse form is *terza rima*, which sets the example for, and is widely accepted as a contributing influence upon, Shelley's chosen form.

[41]   Shelley mentions the 'heroes of the Dunciad' in an unused draft passage of the preface to *Prometheus Unbound*. See *Manuscripts of the Younger Romantics: The Mask of Anarchy Draft Notebook: A Facsimile of Huntington MS. HM 2177*, ed. Mary A. Quinn (New York: Garland, 1990), fo. 28ʳ, 127.

[42]   Story, 'Pope, Pageantry, and Shelley's *Triumph of Life*', 146.

procession, where we are told 'the wayne was very euill ledd' (I. iv. 19).[43] So far as Pope is concerned, Story supports his assertion by noting that the 'triumph of Vice' was 'probably the most renowned passage in Pope during Shelley's lifetime'; and because it was featured in Edward Gibbon's *Decline and Fall of the Roman Empire*, a history with which Shelley was familiar, Pope's triumph 'merits consideration as a separate source' for Shelley's *Triumph*. As Story points out, the 'nexus of historical degradation and allegorical convention' between the two poetic triumphs are 'thematically and verbally [parallel]'.[44] The image of Vice, 'In golden chains the willing world she draws | [...] | Lo! at the wheels of her triumphal car' (147–51), anticipates Shelley's presentation of the captivating power of the corrupt and devastating entity, Life.

As Story and many other critics have observed, the title of Shelley's poem is expressly ironic: '"Life" triumphs because it devastates those who live.'[45] Bloom emphasized the fact that 'Shelley's whole vision subsists in this terrifying irony of contrasts, with its wealth of awful meanings'.[46] Just as Pope's Dulness of the *Dunciad* diminishes virtues to vices as she shines in 'clouded majesty' (I. 45), so Shelley's Life in her chariot emits a 'creative ray' which has 'Wrought' from 'Obscure clouds' 'phantoms fluttering' (532–4). Compare the two passages describing Pope's Dulness and Shelley's Life:

> In clouded majesty here Dulness shone;
> Four guardian virtues, round, support her throne:
> Fierce champion Fortitude, that knows no fears
> Of hisses, blows, or want, or loss of ears:
> Calm Temperance, whose blessings those partake
> Who hunger, and who thirst for scribbling sake:
> Prudence, whose glass presents th' approaching gaol.
> Poetic justice, with her lifted scale,
> Where, in nice balance, truth with gold she weights,
> And solid pudding against empty praise.

> (I. 45–54)

Story comments on this passage by saying that 'Pope proposed that the virtues grow out of what seem to be their kindred vices (ii. 183 ff.); in attendance here, Fortitude, Temperance, Prudence, and Justice are appropriately reduced once more to vices by Dulness'.[47] This degenerative 'virtue' is evident in Shelley's Life, as argued by Leader and O'Neill in a note on the text where they observe that 'the car's ray is miscreative and distorting':[48]

> From every form the beauty slowly waned,
>
> 'From every firmest limb and fairest face
> The strength and freshness fell like dust, and left
> The action and the shape without the grace

[43] Baker, *Shelley's Major Poetry*, 261n.
[44] Story, 'Pope, Pageantry, and Shelley's *Triumph of Life*', 146, 148.
[45] *Major Works*, 604n., 815.   [46] Bloom, *Shelley's Mythmaking*, 242.
[47] Story, 'Pope, Pageantry, and Shelley's *Triumph of Life*', 154.   [48] *Major Works*, 818.

'Of life;
....
. Each, like himself and like each other were,
At first, but soon distorted, seemed to be

'Obscure clouds moulded by the casual air;
And of this stuff the car's creative ray
    Wrought all the busy phantoms fluttering there

'As the sun shapes the clouds—thus, on the way,
    Mask after mask fell from the countenance
And form of all [...]

(519–37)

The ghastly image of 'Life' consuming and/or diminishing the 'life' (523) and 'beauty' (519) and 'hope' (524) from the forms along the track draws from and is strengthened by its allusion to Pope, and, behind him, the traditions and legacies, both biblical and classical, of the literary triumph.

In Pope's concluding lines of the *Epilogue to the Satires: Dialogue I*, which immediately follow the 'triumph of Vice', he sets himself apart as one who refuses to join the throng at the feet of triumphal 'Vice'. Although Shelley's poem is unfinished, one can see that the poem's narrator stands separate from the crowd of Life's victims. Perhaps, building upon Pope's example, and recalling his career-long engagement with the Spenserian riddle of mutability, Shelley intended to assert one last expression of defiance in the face of Life's devastation.

SELECT BIBLIOGRAPHY

Baker, Carlos. *Shelley's Major Poetry: The Fabric of a Vision*. 1948. New York: Russell, 1961.
Bloom, Harold. *Shelley's Mythmaking*. 1959. Ithaca, NY: Cornell UP, 1969.
Cronin, Richard. *Shelley's Poetic Thoughts*. London: Macmillan Press, 1981.
Curran, Stuart. *Poetic Form and British Romanticism*. New York: Oxford UP, 1986.
Dawson, P. M. S. 'Byron, Shelley, and the "New School"'. *Shelley Revalued: Essays from the Gregynog Conference*. Ed. Kelvin Everest. Leicester: Leicester UP, 1983.
Duff, David. *Romance and Revolution: Shelley and the Politics of a Genre*. Cambridge: Cambridge UP, 1994.
Hogle, Jerrold E. *Shelley's Process: Radical Transference and the Development of his Major Works*. New York: Oxford UP, 1988.
Kucich, Greg. *Keats, Shelley, and Romantic Spenserianism*. University Park, PA: Pennsylvania State UP, 1991.
Story, Patrick. 'Pope, Pageantry, and Shelley's *Triumph of Life*'. *Keats–Shelley Journal* 21–2 (1972–3), 145–59.
Wolfson, Susan J. *Formal Charges: The Shaping of Poetry in British Romanticism*. Stanford, CA: Stanford UP, 1997.
Yeats, W. B. 'Edmund Spenser'. *Selected Criticism and Prose*. Ed. A. Norman Jeffares. London: Pan in association with Macmillan, 1980.

CHAPTER 32

···

SHELLEY AND HIS
CONTEMPORARIES

···

KELVIN EVEREST

SHELLEY was not a major figure for his contemporaries. His nomadic life was lived in very closed company, and he avoided polite society whenever he could. He spent much of his time in solitude, writing or reading. There is nothing in his career to compare with Byron's lionization in the period of his overnight fame as the author of *Childe Harold's Pilgrimage*, or the celebrity of Wordsworth in his later years. Shelley's financial situation freed him from any need to make a living in the new literary culture of mass print and extended literacy. On the other hand he met with no conspicuous literary success before leaving England for good in March 1818 at the age of 25, and so hardly inhabited the sphere of metropolitan literary culture and its recognized characters. There were no appearances at Holland House *soirées*; no invitations to the legendary literary breakfasts given by the banker and poet Samuel Rogers, such as were regularly enjoyed by Thomas Moore and Byron and the other acknowledged stars of the day. His only direct contact with Rogers seems to have been an interview about a possible loan.[1] He did attract attention from the reviews and magazines of the day, but this was largely because he exemplified so well all that was deplored by the Tory establishment in the few years of his career as a published poet.

Up to the publication of the *Alastor* volume early in 1816, the first of his books to appear under his own name, Shelley's life and contacts were limited almost entirely to his family circle and related acquaintance, and indeed throughout his life most of his dealings outside that immediate circle involved people who wanted money from him. There were however isolated encounters and correspondence with others who were themselves in touch with a much wider world. He introduced himself to Robert Southey, and to William Godwin, though in neither case with any initial extensive personal contact. Through Godwin he met J. P. Curran in Ireland, and also came into contact with the circle of the Newtons, who, while certainly not celebrities, offered a significant widening

---

[1] Bieri, 381.

of the young Shelley's social experience. Shelley came to know Thomas Love Peacock through his bookseller Thomas Hookham, Jr.; and he came into contact with Byron through the liaison initiated in 1816 by Claire Clairmont.

Active and regular interaction with a wider range of living writers came only with Shelley's friendship with Leigh Hunt. Hunt promoted Shelley together with Keats and John Hamilton Reynolds as the next promising generation of 'Young Poets' in an article in the *Examiner* published on 1 December 1816.[2] This recognition marked out both Shelley and Keats as fair game for hostile Tory reviewers. But for Shelley his friendship with Hunt also ushered in a period of some fifteen months in which he did become part of a more inclusive network of writers and intellectuals, many of them at least relatively like-minded in politics. In addition to Godwin and Peacock he met and dined with Keats, William Hazlitt, Horace Smith, Benjamin Robert Haydon, and other lesser but at the time familiar personalities at the more radical end of metropolitan literary society. Shelley's involvements in this circle of literary friends and acquaintances meant that the last month he spent in England, February of 1818, was by far the most sociable of his life.

Shelley's cultural and social experiences throughout the remaining years of exile in Italy were in the main far from sociable. He moved house continually with rootless instability, enduring terrible personal tragedy against a background of striking social isolation. Until the formation of the 'Pisan Circle' from October 1820, Shelley's only significant personal relations, outside his immediate family circle, were with Byron. There was a series of relationships with women in Italy, but they were ephemeral and fundamentally connected with the deep undercurrents of his relationship with his wife, and with Claire Clairmont. The biographical record includes a series of chance encounters with a usually solitary and introspective Shelley by English travellers. Their accounts of these meetings have a dreamlike quality in which Shelley appears oddly disconnected from any social context or human relation.[3] There were friendships during the Italian years, with the Gisbornes and with Lady Mount Cashell, and they brought some connection to wider groups. But only in the short months of the Pisan Circle, with its mix of English émigrés and Italian professional and literary men, did Shelley personally relate with a contemporary social world in any sustained manner. In Pisa, however, this was always a contradictory experience, with many expatriates avoiding Shelley's company because of his reputation (for example Walter Savage Landor),[4] and Shelley himself avoiding such company when he could.

Shelley's one period of immersion in an English literary culture, in the year or so before he left for Italy, itself however calls for careful qualification. He was not much liked by Keats's friends; as Leigh Hunt remarked, 'Keats did not take to Shelley as kindly as Shelley did to him.'[5] The social awkwardness hinted here no doubt owed much to

---

[2] Reprinted in Newman Ivey White (ed.), *The Unextinguished Hearth: Shelley and his Contemporary Critics* (Durham, NC: Duke UP, 1938), 108–9.

[3] See, for example, the account of a chance meeting in James MacFarlane, *Reminiscences of a Literary Life* (1917), quoted in Bieri, 447.

[4] Bieri, 516.

[5] Leigh Hunt, *Autobiography*, 2 vols. (New York: Harpers, 1850), II, 36.

perceived distinctions of social class, of which Shelley made light, but with a personal manner that evidently made his privileged background obvious. But the unqualified extremity of his opinions on politics and religion also attracted hostility. His atheism was regarded by some as offensive and dangerous, and indeed disturbing. More particularly, those of a politically radical persuasion considered his outspoken and uncompromising views, and his heedlessness of local political realities, actually to hinder the radical cause. Hazlitt made no secret of this in his published attacks on Shelley,[6] and the judgement also appeared in inverted form in conservative reviews of Shelley's work which found his opinions basically harmless because so extreme and overt as to read like parodies of themselves, or exercises in *reductio ad absurdum*.[7]

Shelley's life as a poet in England was then characterized by isolation and perceived extremity and eccentricity. And yet, in keeping with other paradoxes in his unusual life, Shelley's alertness to the decisive currents of his own literary culture made their mark on his work, and made his own poetry at once the agent and embodiment of that culture. He had an extraordinary sensitivity to those poetic voices amongst his contemporaries that were distinctive, original, important, and shaping for the future of English poetry. His earliest productions as a serious poet offer differing styles which characterize a contrast that runs right through his oeuvre: on the one hand the politically engaged and outward-facing, radical-visionary *Queen Mab*, hopeful of an audience and a power to change; and on the other the introspective and quasi-autobiographical collection of early, mainly lyric pieces now known as the 'Esdaile Poems'.[8] This contrast is attractive but misleading, because early and throughout his poetry, the public and private modes, the visionary and the plain-speaking demotic, or the intensely lyrical and personal, constantly invade and complicate each other. But the contrast is nevertheless a telling indicator of the most powerful early English poetic influences on Shelley: Robert Southey and William Wordsworth.

Southey was the more dominant early influence, not least through the surviving energies of his youthful radicalism, but more enduringly for Shelley through certain traits of style: epic, Eastern-inflected narratives, whose metrical variety—an underlying short line pattern, with frequent breaks into self-contained complex lyric with elaborate rhyme and long-lined metrical patterns—Shelley seems to have known virtually by heart. But Wordsworth is a much weightier and more constant presence in Shelley, and one whose influence is an essential component of Shelley's own stylistic range. There is an attempt at Wordsworthian self-reflection in the Esdaile poems, but by the time that Shelley came to

---

[6] See William Hazlitt, 'On Paradox and Commonplace', in *Table Talk* (1821–2), *Collected Works of William Hazlitt*, ed. A. R. Waller and A. Glover, 13 vols. (London: Dent, 1902–6), VI, 146–56; and his review of Shelley's *Posthumous Poems* (1824) in the *Edinburgh Review*, July 1824 (40: 494–514), *Collected Works*, X, 256–75.

[7] See, for example, the review of *Prometheus Unbound* in *Blackwood's Edinburgh Magazine*, September 1820 (7: 679–87), *Unextinguished Hearth*, 225–31; and the review of *Prometheus Unbound* in the *Monthly Magazine*, February 1821 (94: 168–73), *Unextinguished Hearth*, 238–40.

[8] See David Duff, '"The Casket of my Unknown Mind": The 1813 Volume of Minor Poems', in Alan M. Weinberg and Timothy Webb (eds.), *The Unfamiliar Shelley* (Farnham: Ashgate, 2008), 21–40.

write *Alastor*, his first serious long poem, the direct Wordsworthian element in that poem's distinctive blank verse is striking and unmistakable. Shelley's manner in *Alastor* is original, certainly, but its effect combines the exotic detail and fantasy elements of Southey's long poems with the kind of deliberated blank verse reflexive narrative that characterizes both *The Excursion*—read by Shelley with dismayed attentiveness in the months before his composition of *Alastor*—and shorter pieces such as 'Lines left upon a Seat in a Yew-tree', a poem which is clearly a direct influence on *Alastor*:

> This lonely yew-tree stands
> Far from all human dwelling: what if here
> No sparkling rivulet spread the verdant herb;
> What if these barren boughs the bee not loves;
> Yet, if the wind breathe soft, the curling waves,
> That break against the shore, shall lull thy mind
> By one soft impulse saved from vacancy.
>
> ('Lines Left upon a Seat', 1–7)

The meditative movement here, with its careful attention to nature, and its undemonstrative voice carried through varied pauses at the line ends, with run-ons and shifting caesural pauses, is cleverly adapted in Shelley's poem:

> Where the embowering trees recede, and leave
> A little space of green expanse, the cove
> Is closed by meeting banks, whose yellow flowers
> For ever gaze on their own drooping eyes,
> Reflected in the crystal calm.
>
> (*Alastor*, 404–8)

Alastor has other affinities with this particular poem, both thematically and in some particulars of diction and phrasing, and there is a broader and pervasive presence of Wordsworthian cadence, and indeed direct allusion.[9] There are of course significant differences. The narrative voice in *Alastor* is less measured, and embraces emotional extremes and Gothic elements that are not Wordsworthian; and Shelley's whole handling of story is more suggestively allegorical and symbolic. It is nevertheless obvious that Shelley's blank verse style is made possible by Wordsworth, and demonstrates the scale of his debt to the older poet. That debt accounts for Shelley's abiding preoccupation with Wordsworth's political apostasy, just as Shelley's outrage in *Adonais* with Southey's supposed part in the death of Keats, and the then Poet Laureate's role in the literary culture as a mouthpiece of reaction in the *Quarterly Review*, was all the more virulent from its contrast with Southey's youthful politics. The sonnet 'To Wordsworth' in the *Alastor* volume ironically invokes Wordsworth's own famous poems of lost passion and intensity (the *Immortality Ode*, the 'Elegiac Stanzas', and 'Surprised by Joy', for example) to lament the older Wordsworth's turning away from the commitments and vision of his early period. That sense of betrayal stayed powerfully in Shelley's view of

---

[9] See *Longman*, 1, 459.

Wordsworth, even while he continued greatly to value the earlier Wordsworth's democratic championing of 'the language really used by men' and his representation of the moral and nurturing power of nature.[10] He was 'dosing' Byron with 'Wordsworth physic' sufficiently insistently in Geneva in 1816 to make a marked impact on the third canto of *Childe Harold's Pilgrimage*.[11] Shelley's recoil from Wordsworth's drift towards reactionary politics and the establishment is all the more emphatic for this continuing sense of indebtedness. The intensified sense of betrayal produced one of Shelley's most remarkable mature poems in *Peter Bell the Third*, a satirical attack on Wordsworth, and on the cultural milieu with which Wordsworth had come to identify himself.

Coleridge too was an enduringly important poetic precursor for Shelley. His work of the 1790s—*The Ancient Mariner, Christabel, Kubla Khan*, but also 'France: An Ode', the Conversation poems, and particularly 'Fire, Famine and Slaughter'—is repeatedly recalled in Shelley. Coleridge's metrical innovations and distinctive workings of ballad verse forms lie behind the vicious choric chanting of the Furies in Act I of *Prometheus Unbound*. The short line of 'Lines Written among the Euganean Hills' strongly suggests the subtle slight variations of stress in *Christabel*. And like Keats (in *Hyperion* for example) Shelley's blank verse displays not just the obvious influence of Milton and Wordsworth, but also of Coleridge's different manner, with its ability to register the shifting of reflective moods, the process of a changing consciousness:

> The point of one white star is quivering still
> Deep in the orange light of widening morn
> Beyond the purple mountains; through a chasm
> Of wind-divided mist the darker lake
> Reflects it—now it wanes—it gleams again
> As the waves fade, and as the burning threads
> Of woven cloud unravel in pale air [...]
>
> (*Prometheus Unbound*, II. i. 17–23)

This delicate evocation of quickening new consciousness, and of a rising sense of joy in the sensory apprehension of nature, derives in part from the blank verse of 'This Lime-Tree Bower my Prison', 'Frost at Midnight', and most especially 'The Eolian Harp', a poem that Shelley echoes often. Shelley's poetic debt to Coleridge was less fundamental than his sense of Wordsworth's presence in his inherited literary tradition, and the intellectual relationship with the still-living older Coleridge was consequently less conflicted and more temperate. The Coleridge who is invoked in the *Letter to Maria Gisborne* is a tortured soul driven to intellectual darkness and difficulty by the pressures of the age:

> You will see Coleridge—he who sits obscure
> In the exceeding lustre and the pure
> Intense irradiation of a mind

[10] Preface to *Lyrical Ballads* (1802), in *William Wordsworth*, ed. Stephen Gill (Oxford: Oxford UP, 1984), 597.

[11] Thomas Medwin, *Conversations of Lord Byron*, ed. Ernest J. Lovell, Jr. (Princeton: Princeton UP, 1966), 194.

> Which, with its own internal lightning blind,
> Flags wearily through darkness and despair—
> A cloud-encircled meteor of the air,
> A hooded eagle among blinking owls.—
>
> (*Letter to Maria Gisborne*, 202–8)

This has nothing of Byron's comical jeering in *Don Juan*—'I wish he would explain his explanation'[12]—and is indeed sympathetic, with a hint of self-identification, and a graceful nod here and throughout the *Letter* to the relaxed discursive pentameter verse made possible by the personal voice of both poets' meditative blank verse, and the break made by the *Lyrical Ballads* with eighteenth-century norms.

Wordsworth and Coleridge are the two English poets amongst Shelley's living contemporaries who exert the most shaping influence on Shelley's own style, but that style of course has many components and sources. Shelley's close familiarity with the choric and lyrical canon of classical Greek drama is fundamental to his taste for fluency within challenging metrical and rhyme constraints. One is also constantly aware in Shelley's style of the cadences and tones of Shakespeare's songs, and of other Elizabethan and Jacobean dramatists, and Milton. Like all literate readers in the early nineteenth century Shelley is saturated in eighteenth-century verse, especially Gray and Collins, but also Blair, Beattie, Young, Cowper, Darwin, Macpherson, Chatterton, Bowles, Landor, and Kirke White. Of his more immediate senior contemporaries apart from Southey, Wordsworth, and Coleridge, Shelley knew Scott's poems very well, and from the start of his efforts in verse he was also attracted by Byron's early volumes.

But one other of Shelley's successful poetic contemporaries stands out as a critical influence. The Irishman Thomas Moore had been important for Shelley from the beginning of his literary life. Moore's readiness to use erotic situations, deliberately skirting the limits of propriety and decorum in the representation of sexual attraction and almost-illicit dalliance, was entirely suited to Shelley's own youthful combination of social revolution and sexual freedom. It would have been especially attractive because joined in Moore with Irish nationalism and its recent heroes and martyrs. As a very young man Shelley was strongly committed to the nationalist cause in Ireland. He travelled to Ireland, was sufficiently active in politics to get noticed, and the British oppression of Ireland fitted more generally with his virulent anti-establishment outlook. Moore's *Irish Melodies* in particular had a powerful appeal in this context, and indeed are almost the defining instance, in the young Shelley's reading of contemporary poetry, of the possibility of association between formally elegant and fluent lyricism with political commitment in the liberal cause. This association becomes central in Shelley's major poetry. It produces some of his most powerful lyric writing, for example in the Choruses of the Furies in the first act of *Prometheus Unbound*, and in the astonishing formal adventure and fluency of the fourth act.

---

[12] Byron, *Don Juan*, 'Dedication', 16, in *Byron*, ed. Jerome J. McGann (Oxford: Oxford UP, 1986), 373.

Moore was also exceptional amongst Shelley's successful poetic contemporaries in that although they never met, Moore was supportive and generous when Shelley contacted him by letter seeking his opinion of *Laon and Cythna*, mindful of Moore's famously huge publisher's advance on his Oriental epic *Lalla Rookh* (1817). Moore responded with appreciative constructive criticism, particularly valuable at that time to Shelley as he was becoming a target for attack in the conservative literary journals.[13] It is striking in fact that this friendliness of Moore's, and his recognition of Shelley's gifts, is virtually unparalleled amongst established figures of London literary high life during the Regency.

It was not only *Irish Melodies* that Shelley admired. If we consider all of the poetry Shelley is known to have written up to the publication of the *Alastor* volume in early 1816, then we can detect a pervasive general influence from Moore, and numerous more specific instances, demonstrating that Shelley was closely familiar with the *Odes of Anacreon*, *Thomas Little*, and the *Odes and Epistles*. Sometimes there is straightforward imitation of Moore's manner in the *Irish Melodies*, and with an Irish theme. Shelley's 'The Irishman's Song' is a good example, from the youthful collection *Victor and Cazire*, though Shelley strikes a note of vigorous resistance which is stronger and more emphatic than Moore. Other poems seem modelled directly on particular Moore lyrics. The 'Supposed to Be Epithalamium of Francis Ravaillac and Charlotte Cordé' is partly modelled on 'The Grecian Girl's Dream of the Blessed Islands' in Moore's *Odes and Epistles*. And Shelley's 'Stanzas.—April, 1814', published in the *Alastor* volume in 1816, is in a very unusual and not quite regular metre which derives from Moore's 'The Irish Peasant to his Mistress' from the third series of the *Irish Melodies*.

The kind of Moore lyric that offers clear affinity with Shelley's style is easy to exemplify. Consider for instance 'Eveleen's Bower' from the second series of *Irish Melodies*:

> Oh! Weep for the hour
> When to Eveleen's bower
> The Lord of the Valley with false vows came;
> The moon hid her light
> From the heavens that night,
> And wept behind the clouds o'er the maiden's shame.[14]

The underlying anapaestic tendency gives an effect of musical and relatively rapid lightness that is very characteristic of Moore. But it is not too emphatic, and the metrical texture is complicated by clusterings of adjacent strong stresses, the graceful variation of end-stopped and run-on lines, and the alternation of short with much longer lines. The unstrained meeting of the rhymes—here recalling a Petrarchan sestet—augments the feeling of fluency; one's impression is of ease within constraint rather than struggle and complicating compression. In thematic terms, and in its evocation of mood, this poem is also characteristic; tinged with sadness and regret, lightly sub-Gothic, a subdued melodrama of love, betrayal, the changes wrought by time, the tribulations of fate. All of these qualities had a strong and enduring appeal for the youthful Shelley. The lyric is

[13] See *Letters: PBS* I, 563–4, 578–83.
[14] Thomas Moore, *Poetical Works of Thomas Moore*, ed. A. D. Godley (London: Oxford UP, 1910), 187.

direct, and its musicality is at one with an accessible clarity of expression, and a precise specification of emotion and the emotional context. There is a lightness of final effect which does not, as one critic has aptly said of Shelley's lyrics, 'occupy the space of its own suggestiveness'.[15] But Shelley's own highly distinctive lyric manner is manifestly related. There is a sophisticated technical facility in Moore that characterizes Shelley's greatest lyrics: extended and involved syntactical structures thrown across a demanding pattern of metre and rhyme, issuing in a fast-moving fluency, a sense of affective expression inside the imposed rigour, which is also the vehicle of a strong emotional charge, again the more powerful for its concentrated lyrical intensity. Think of 'To a Skylark':

> We look before and after,
>   And pine for what is not—
> Our sincerest laughter
>   With some pain is fraught—
> Our sweetest songs are those that tell of saddest thought.
>
> Yet if we could scorn
>   Hate and pride and fear;
> If we were things born
>   Not to shed a tear,
> I know not how thy joy we ever should come near.
>
> ('To a Skylark', 86–95)

Neither stanza here conforms exactly to the implied underlying pattern of the poem as a whole, which is alternating lines of six and five syllables with a fifth final line of twelve syllables, and a rhyme scheme *ababb*. There is a most beautiful effect of apparently careless slight deviation from this pattern right through the poem. The alternation of shortened with noticeably longer lines is particularly characteristic, here gracefully giving the physical conjunction of the Skylark's protracted singing with the apex of its ascending flight and drop. Shelley's style here suggests an intensified and more brilliantly adept development of Moore's technique.

Mary Shelley confirmed the strong direct influence in correspondence with Moore long after Shelley's death:

> Shelley was too true a poet not to feel your unrivalled merits—especially in the department of poetry peculiarly your own, songs and short poems instinct with the intense principle of life and love.[16]

Moore's direct influence is by no means confined to lyric. *Peter Bell the Third* has a lengthy dedication to 'Thomas Brown the Younger', which was Moore's pen-name for his *Twopenny Post-Bag* of 1813. The brilliance of Shelley's virtuoso movement between styles in *Peter Bell the Third* most obviously suggests Byron's *Don Juan*, which Shelley had heard read aloud in October 1818.[17] But Moore's *Fudge Family in Paris* is a further

---

[15] Michael O'Neill, 'Splendour among Shadows: Shelley's Artistry', *MYR* VIII, pp. xi–xxvi, p. xi.
[16] To Thomas Moore, *c.*18 January 1839; *Letters: MWS* II, 308.   [17] *Letters: PBS* II, 42.

clear influence. Peacock sent the Shelleys a copy of *The Fudge Family* in June 1818, and both Shelley and Mary enjoyed it immensely.[18] It is comparable with *Don Juan* in its inclusive attention to the cultural materials, high and low, of Regency London, and in its range of styles. There is also a sharp contemporary political edge to Moore's satire, and a gleeful inventiveness and agility of voice across the several characters, which are picked up brilliantly in Shelley's poem.

Shelley's self-conscious debt to Moore is articulated in the stanzas in *Adonais* where the dead Keats is mourned by grieving contemporary poets. He includes himself, Leigh Hunt (though Hunt is a silent mourner, perhaps to mark Shelley's sense of his unlucky influence on Keats's earlier work), Byron, and Moore. Both of these latter two poets are present as symbolic carriers of the torch of English poetry, and certainly not from any enthusiasm for Keats. Wordsworth and Coleridge are omitted altogether, perhaps from a wish not to lay the poem open to ridicule because of what might easily have been deemed by the reviews a ludicrously inappropriate implied equivalence. *Adonais* brings in Moore with a poised complexity of stylistic allusion:

> the mountain shepherds came,
> Their garlands sere, their magic mantles rent;
> The Pilgrim of Eternity, whose fame
> Over his living head like Heaven is bent,
> An early but enduring monument,
> Came, veiling all the lightnings of his song
> In sorrow; from her wilds Ierne sent
> The sweetest lyrist of her saddest wrong,
> And love taught grief to fall like music from his tongue.

(Adonais, 30, 262–70)

Adonais seeks at every turn to embody an ornate classicism and formal density in rebuke of the reviewers who had derided Keats as an ignorant Cockney guttersnipe, and these lines are no exception in their complex and deliberated allusiveness. The 'mountain shepherds' recall *Endymion*; 'Their garlands sere, their magic mantles rent' compounds several lines from *Lycidas*; the Byron reference is obvious enough; and Moore's own mourning contribution honours his distinctive mix of sweetly lyrical movement with nationalist sentiment. Ireland is given its ancient Greek name Ierne, in keeping with the erudite classicism of the poem's rhetoric. And Shelley gracefully evokes Moore's lyrical style by falling into a metrically extended lilt, musical in its subject's manner, and coinciding with the final alexandrine of the Spenserian stanza.

Shelley never met Wordsworth, Coleridge, or Moore, which given the relatively small absolute scale of metropolitan literary culture is remarkable in itself, and testimony to the extent of Shelley's social isolation, even while his development as a poet drew extensively on the most interesting work of his own immediate milieu. And set against this

---

[18] *Letters: PBS* II, 24; *Letters of Thomas Love Peacock*, ed. Nicholas Joukovsky, 2 vols. (Oxford: Clarendon Press, 1999), II, 130; *Journals: MWS* (1995), 230; Ronan Kelly, *Bard of Erin: The Life of Thomas Moore* (Dublin: Penguin Ireland, 2008), 312–13.

context of his very limited and brief period of social presence, the shocks and challenges of Shelley's personal life were at the same time creating him as a figure of public notoriety in polite English society, which served to underline the sense of exclusion from the main currents and society of his contemporary world. There is an apposite metaphor of Shelley's dual isolation in his English social experience, public and private, in the smugly self-serving account by Thomas Jefferson Hogg of his first meeting with Shelley in Oxford in 1810, which famously recalls Shelley's voice as 'excruciating [...] intolerably shrill, harsh, and discordant [...] it excoriated the ears'.[19] This verdict on Shelley's speaking voice seems to have had some basis in reality and is repeated in the accounts of others who knew him,[20] though his voice was said to modulate beautifully when reading aloud, particularly his own verse. Its quality in Hogg's account is strikingly emblematic of Shelley's general relation to his contemporary society, as perceived by that society. It is hardly surprising to find him considered 'discordant', when he was explicitly opposed in thought and deed to all of the defining norms and assumptions of the age. At Eton and Oxford he experienced the standard induction to the imperial ruling class, and forthrightly rejected its beliefs and customs without concealment or accommodation. His bitter hatred of institutional religion was intensified by successive persecutions because of his atheism and blasphemy. His views on marriage, sex, and free love were not only eloquently articulated in his published poetry and other writings, but acted upon in his relationships, and with publicly known consequences appearing grotesquely to confirm their pernicious effects. In politics, he could easily have taken the option of a career in parliament, like his father; but his views on the franchise, equality, public ownership and finance, his feminism, his vegetarianism, and his pacifism took him far beyond the boundaries of any political party. Shelley had a completely unique ability—unique at least amongst creative writers of his own epoch—to locate the nerve-centres of his contemporary milieu, and to combine fearless critique with prophetic insight into possible better alternatives. And for all his perceived eccentricity at the time, Shelley's bold oppositional critique has proved acute, for most of his intellectual convictions about the right and necessary direction of his own society have been taken up and developed by succeeding like-minded thinkers, and have come to exercise powerful influence.

Shelley seems well to have understood that this unique character of prophetic opposition meant that personal fulfilment and public recognition in his own lifetime were all but impossible. This is the context for the well-known formulations of his major mature prose works, with their defiant and visionary affirmation of the true role and influence of the poetic intellect, and his conception of 'Poets' as creative agents of the human capacity to imagine a better world. The best known of these formulations is the climactic closing passage of *A Defence of Poetry*:

> The most unfailing herald, companion, and follower of the awakening of a great people to work a beneficial change in opinion or institution, is Poetry. (*Norton 2*, 535)

[19] Thomas Jefferson Hogg, *Life of Percy Bysshe Shelley*, 2 vols. (London: Moxon, 1858), I, 56.
[20] Hazlitt refers to Shelley as 'shrill-voiced', in 'On Paradox and Commonplace' (see n. 6).

The essay goes on to close with a triumphant celebration of the poets' calling both to embody the spirit of their age, and to bring into being its future by imagining it; whether or not they recognize or are recognized for this power:

> Even whilst they deny and abjure, they are yet compelled to serve, the Power which is seated upon the throne of their own soul [...] Poets are the hierophants of an unapprehended inspiration, the mirrors of the gigantic shadows which futurity casts upon the present, the words which express what they understand not, the trumpets which sing to battle and feel not what they inspire: the influence which is moved not, but moves. Poets are the unacknowledged legislators of the World. (*Norton* 2, 535)

This conviction in Shelley of the power of poets, to effect through their productions a change anticipated in the imagination, is a motif he returns to often, as in the Preface to *Prometheus Unbound*: the 'great writers of our own age are [...] the companions and forerunners of some unimagined change in our social condition or the opinions which cement it. The cloud of mind is discharging its collected lightning.'[21] It is however a necessarily paradoxical celebration of the power of art and mind, because the scale and significance of the changes made possible by this power in the human condition are chiefly visible and measurable only retrospectively, and can be in painful contrast with the constraining realities of the physical body and its social contingencies. So it proved for Shelley. His aloneness among his contemporaries intensified his conviction in the power of the poetic voice to outlast its material conditions.

The 'Ode to the West Wind' memorably closes with an affirmation of the poem's potential to drive change for future generations. It projects forward the transformational agency of its language: 'by the incantation of this verse | Scatter, as from an unextinguished hearth | Ashes and sparks, my words among mankind!' (65–7). The Ode will render the poet's 'dead thoughts' (63) as sparks which start a fire but themselves go out before the fire spreads beyond control. This image was potent for Shelley.[22] His sense of a power in poets to change mankind, which transformation is deferred to some future realization, goes with the 'unacknowledged' character of the poet as legislator. The possibilities for humanity are imagined into being by creative intellects—'poets' in the most inclusive sense—and most people do not understand that these possibilities originate in that way. But the conception of poets as 'unacknowledged legislators' also carries the personal resonance of Shelley's growing conviction of his own obscurity and want of a public audience amongst his contemporaries. The aspiration to a posthumous affective power is linked with this pessimism, and the close connection in Shelley between a failed life and career, and the promise of great influence in futurity, suggests also the paradoxes of his class position and intellectual outlook. Shelley's radical critique of his social world implies the demise of an educated aristocratic elite of which he was himself a product and an embodiment. This circumstance intensifies the general condition of the prophetic artist as the physically and socially ephemeral agent of great transformation. It is as if

---

[21] *Longman*, 2, 474.

[22] See, for instance, 'Lines Written among the Euganean Hills', 269–84.

Shelley accepts that the sooner his social and physical being is removed, the sooner his true influence can be felt.[23]

Shelley was born in circumstances which gave him access to power. His family was rich and privileged, and although its history had some dark corners, there was serious money, land, and influence. The Duke of Norfolk, one of the most powerful peers in the land, took a direct personal interest in Shelley's difficulties with his father.[24] Byron famously remarked after Shelley's death that his much-misunderstood friend had been 'as perfect a Gentleman as ever crossed a drawing room.'[25] Shelley's upbringing and education was a preparation for the establishment. The privileged elite in which he grew up was a small world. At Eton he was a familiar figure amongst his peers, a great many of them destined for public office, and his brief career at Oxford was nevertheless long enough to reinforce his eccentric identity amongst the tight-knit ruling class to which he belonged. He was from the outset known to this powerful peer group, in strong contrast, for example, with a contemporary such as Keats. He was, indeed, known as an eccentric. But his eccentricity had something unusual and noticeable about it. Shelley's attitudes were shaped in opposition to the dominating conventions and deep assumptions of society, and particularly of the establishment society of which he was a product. He grew up into a kind of antitype of his originally destined social identity.

The most intense and widely noticed episode in Shelley's public career as a writer was the review of The *Revolt of Islam* in the *Quarterly Review* for April 1819. This 'malignant effusion' (Peacock's description) stood out even in a period when offensive party-political hostility in literary reviewing was normal,[26] and particularly associated with the Tory *Quarterly*. Shelley was identified as a special target, as signalled by the *Quarterly*'s decision to review not just the revised *Revolt of Islam*, but also the withdrawn original version *Laon and Cythna*, with its more overt irreligion and incest. He was well known as a highly educated young man of aristocratic birth, whose views were explicit, in print, and could be shown to have led directly to dreadful consequences in his private life. Furthermore he was clearly a serious poet of great talent, and therefore much more of a potential danger to the health of the public mind than a supposed pretentious upstart such as Keats, or an obviously mannered and limited poet such as Leigh Hunt.

The *Quarterly*'s review of *Laon and Cythna* and *The Revolt of Islam* was by John Taylor Coleridge. He had been at Eton with Shelley, and it was probably he who had, in an earlier review in the *Quarterly* of Leigh Hunt's *Foliage*, made thinly veiled and strongly disparaging references to Shelley's personal life. He recalled in the review his own memory of Shelley at Eton 'setting fire to old trees with burning glasses', a perfectly apt image for the kind of threat that Shelley's views, and his capacity powerfully to articulate them, was understood to pose for his class. This review also recounts, alongside dark hints of

---

[23] See Kelvin Everest, 'Shelley's Doubles', in Kelvin Everest (ed.), *Shelley Revalued* (Leicester: Leicester UP, 1983).

[24] Bieri, 174, 256–7.

[25] To John Murray, 25 December 1822; *Byron's Letters and Journals*, ed. Leslie Marchand, 13 vols. (London: John Murray, 1973–94), X, 69.

[26] Cited in *Unextinguished Hearth*, 133.

sexual profligacy leading to 'cruelty and infidelity', the story of Shelley writing 'atheos' after his name in the visiting-book of a Swiss mountain hotel.[27] This was a further damaging aspect of Shelley's public contemporary image: a politically extreme radical, avowedly atheistic, and with attitudes to sex, marriage, and free love that had demon-strably not only broken hearts, but cost lives.

Shelley became increasingly convinced that his poetry had no contemporary readership, a conviction the more bitter and intense for the contrast it formed with Byron's success. *Adonais* assumes with brave self-belief that the court of time—'the selectest of the wise of many generations' (*Norton* 2, 516)—would come to a just verdict, not just on Keats's greatness, but on Shelley's too, looking far beyond the malignant local temporalities of public hostility and critical neglect. Shelley's work, like Keats's, will find a mode of immortality in its influence on future intellects:

> When lofty thought
> Lifts a young heart above its mortal lair
> And love and life contend in it, for what
> Shall be its earthly doom, the dead live there [...]
>
> (*Adonais*, 44, 392–5)

The Preface to *Adonais* betrays a frustrated incredulity on Shelley's part in the face of current reviewing practices in British literary culture. That culture not only lauded Byron, and attacked Shelley. It also sought to promote evidently less gifted writers, on the basis of literary judgements manifestly distorted by political bias. Shelley's Preface to *Adonais* projects his own sense of this injustice onto the context of Keats's critical neglect:

> As to *Endymion*, was it a poem, whatever might be its defects, to be treated con-temptuously by those who had celebrated, with various degrees of complacency and panegyric, *Paris*, and *Woman*, and a *Syrian Tale*, and Mrs Lefanu, and Mr. Barrett, and Mr. Howard Payne, and a long list of the illustrious obscure? Are these the men, who in their venal good nature, presumed to draw a parallel between the Rev. Mr. Milman and Lord Byron? What gnat did they strain at here, after having swallowed all those camels? (*Norton* 2, 410)

Byron's publisher John Murray—who came to a strong dislike of Shelley—had declined to publish *Alastor* in 1816. The titles and authors Shelley mentions in the Preface are mostly linked with Murray: George Croly's *Paris in 1815*, Henry Gally Knight's *Syrian Tale*, *Brutus* by John Howard Payne, and *The Fall of Jerusalem* by Henry Hart Milman had all been published by Murray. These works also share an association with recent numbers of the *Quarterly Review*, which was published by Murray. All of them had been reviewed in the *Quarterly* at least supportively, and some in startlingly glowing terms, with an approving emphasis on their Tory politics. Shelley would certainly have been

---

[27] Review of *Revolt of Islam* and *Laon and Cythna*, *Quarterly Review*, April 1819 (21: 460–71), *Unextinguished Hearth*, 133–42; review of Leigh Hunt, *Foliage*, *Quarterly Review*, May 1818 (18: 324, 328–9), *Unextinguished Hearth*, 124.

closely familiar with all of this, having suffered a series of pointed personal attacks often in the very same issues of the *Quarterly*. Shelley's complaint in the Preface about the injustice of the critical attacks on Keats, from a literary review so cravenly and savagely biased, clearly is expressive also of his own experience. He considered himself not only neglected as a writer, with no readership, no success in publication, nothing remotely approaching Byron's celebrity; he was also repeatedly noticed as an extreme example of immorality, and his private life with its multiple misfortunes was publicly decried as an exemplar of the inevitable real-life consequences of his beliefs. And the history of his personal life also played a more direct part in the outrage of his Preface to *Adonais*. Several of those mentioned by name or as author in the Preface were personally known to Shelley. He had been at Eton with Knight, and Milman had been a contemporary at both Eton and Oxford. In contrast with Shelley's Oxford career, terminating in expulsion after less than two terms, Milman had won a Fellowship at Brasenose College, and was to become Professor of Poetry in 1821. It will have seemed to Shelley that no pitch of poetic achievement would ever enable him to escape from the image of eccentric extremism he presented to his contemporaries.

The circumstances in which Shelley came to write *Adonais* bring to intriguing focus the question of Shelley's literary relations with both Keats and Byron. During the years of his Italian exile these are the only two living English poets who make any significant new impact on Shelley's stylistic development as a poet. In neither case however is it useful to speak of direct influence. Shelley was throughout and after the period of his actual acquaintance with Keats unpersuaded about his true stature as a poet, and considered him limited—as did Byron and Peacock—by a mannered indebtedness to Leigh Hunt's 'Cockney' style with its tripping rhythms, provokingly strained rhymes, frequent feminine endings, and quirky diction and coinages. Shelley did not find *Endymion* easy to read, although he returned to it in Italy and came to a more generous appreciation. But his estimate of Keats was decisively altered once he read the 1820 *Poems*,[28] and the impression made by that volume was greatly intensified when he learned of Keats's death apparently in reaction to the scurrilous politically motivated attacks on him in the Tory reviews. Shelley assumed that the principal critical aggressor was an anonymous Robert Southey in the *Quarterly*, thus bringing into play his sense of betrayal by the older and now apostate generation of major living poets. And there was also a powerful undercurrent of identification by Shelley with Keats's cruelly underestimated and vilified genius, aggravated by the continuing acclaim enjoyed by Byron. Shelley consequently conceived of *Adonais* as an elegy which would in every respect honour Keats as a classic, drawing on classical Greek models of genre and style, steeped in learned allusion to a wide range of classical writers and philosophers, moving with a stately slowness otherwise uncharacteristic, and even sustaining in its printing and paratextual features the manner and elevation of a classical text. Shelley carries this off with astonishing sustained and concentrated assurance. A primary intention of *Adonais* is to essay a programmatic density

---

[28] See Shelley's draft letter to William Gifford, *Letters: PBS* II, 251–3, where however it is misdated '[Pisa,? November 1820]'. The likely date is *c*.18 October 1820; see *Journals: MWS* (1995), 335.

of allusion to Keats's own work and career, thus placing him on a level with the other established writers of the European tradition from classical times. The poem simultaneously offers Shelley the occasion to demonstrate his own powers, as the necessary condition for the success of his elegy in establishing Keats's claims to greatness. Keats's name will last with the lasting presence of *Adonais* itself in the canon.[29]

Adonais is not so much influenced by Keats as indebted to him, brought into being as a brilliantly original conception and extraordinary technical accomplishment by Shelley's complex reaction to the news of his death and the burst of creative evaluation and memorializing that it initiated. Byron offered an almost exactly opposite case, fêted by his contemporary readers to unparalleled extent, apparently impervious to criticism, effortlessly successful in a series of styles and genres. But like Keats, Byron discernibly affects Shelley's stylistic development only obliquely, in ways which accommodate the presence to his own manner and purposes. Shelley's most significant poetic response to Byron's work is in the impression made by the sophisticated colloquial satire of *Beppo* and *Don Juan*. Byron's stanza in these poems is *ottava rima*, with its comical exploration of the possibilities of the sustained double rhyme through six lines, closing on a couplet. Byron made the stanza entirely his own, with a tirelessly inventive comic *brio* which seemingly never fails to seize triumphantly on a rhyme, often all the funnier for being forced. Shelley's own first effort to work in *ottava rima* is his translation of the Homeric 'Hymn to Mercury', written in the summer of 1820. There is clearly a Byronic impulse in Shelley's approach to the translation, but the actual effect is quite different, moderated both by a broader awareness of contemporary and older European models for the verse form, and also by a different comic voice, at once less aristocratically superior and less mocking of human frailty:

> 'I swear a great oath by my father's head-
>   That I stole not your cows, and that I know
> Of no one else, who might or could or did—
>   Whatever things cows are, I do not know
> For I have only heard the name'—this said,
>   He winked as fast as could be and his brow
> Was wrinkled, and a whistle loud gave he
> Like one who hears some strange absurdity.
>   ('Hymn to Mercury', 366–73)

The poise and charm of this tone, wearing with such lightness the enormous intellectual challenge of the difficult Greek, and touching with light humour on the cheeky know-ingness of Hermes, has a welcoming fresh directness that is literally without parallel in translations of Greek into English (only excepting Shelley's own translation of *The Cyclops*). After the exercise of the *Hymn*, Shelley went on immediately to extend the possibilities of his own way of handling *ottava rima* in *The Witch of Atlas*, which retains this combination of un-Byronic joyous light-heartedness with spectacular technical facility and tonal subtlety.

[29] For fuller discussion see Kelvin Everest, 'Shelley's *Adonais* and John Keats', *Essays in Criticism* 57 (2007), 237–64.

It is easy to understand the despondency Shelley came increasingly to feel in his last two years. He lived constantly with the shadows of critical neglect, scandal, and personal unhappiness. His poetry grew in originality and manifest stature, and in subtle and creative relationship with his major living contemporaries. But his personal and social experience rendered these achievements all but invisible. Shelley's literary reputation, like his notoriety, never approached a Byronic scale in his lifetime. He had no significant success as a published poet, and his efforts in print came increasingly to underpin a strong sense of gathering failure. His poetic influence on his own contemporaries was as a consequence quite understandably not marked or noticed. His opinions and ideas were similarly not during his lifetime a powerful stimulus to general opinion or political and social change. He did publish various prose works on political affairs and principles, and there were newspaper accounts of political speeches delivered in his activist days in Ireland and Wales. But these appearances in print were all early in his career, all short, and without public effect. His major prose writings and translations were all published posthumously, and some more than a century after his death.

Shelley's convictions in politics and morality, and the brilliant rich diversity of his poetry, invite for succeeding generations a normalizing perspective. They anticipate and powerfully influence directions that actually were taken in the development of English poetry through the nineteenth century, and in the growth of a radical tradition in politics and society which transmitted Shelleyan ideas to many millions across the world. This Shelleyan cultural afterlife can seem to bring him closer to us. In reality his social experience remained essentially lonely, at the margins of normality and the mainstream; it was in effect defined by his deliberate refusal of the cultural identity into which he was born. The means of his political agency as a force for change were poetic, and, as he rightly understood, posthumous. It is important in that context to bear in mind how wild, dangerous, or simply ridiculous Shelley's convictions appeared to almost all of his contemporaries; and consequently how defiantly courageous was his personal conduct, in the face of almost universal public censure and dreadful personal suffering and misfortune. The absolute singularity of his personal history needs to be held steadily in mind. *The Necessity of Atheism* was the very first openly atheistic publication in England. His proposal, just after his expulsion, to relinquish the entail on a portion of his inheritance was in a way still more extraordinarily exceptional, and certainly seemed to his father a more terrible extremity of conviction. This would have been the first example in English legal history of such an act, let alone with its associated condition that the inheritance should revert to the female line. The decision by Lord Eldon to refuse Shelley the guardianship of his own children by his first wife Harriet set a legal precedent which is still cited. It is hard to think of any other English poet of Shelley's stature for whom moral conviction and personal conduct brought such hostile conflict with his own social world. And yet against these extremities of exclusion from the mainstream, we must acknowledge in Shelley an acute sensitivity and responsiveness to contemporary literary culture, and a remarkable proleptic intelligence which, for all its apparent abstraction from the accepted realities of his age, saw with unmatched insight the future directions that could and would be taken by humanity.

Select Bibliography

Blank, G. Kim. *Wordsworth's Influence on Shelley: A Study of Poetic Authority*. New York: St Martin's Press, 1988.

Butler, Marilyn. *Romantics, Rebels and Reactionaries: English Literature and its Background 1760–1830*. Oxford: Oxford UP, 1981.

Cox, Jeffrey. *Poetry and Politics in the Cockney School: Keats, Shelley, Hunt and their Circle*. Cambridge: Cambridge UP, 1998.

Cronin, Richard. *Shelley's Poetic Thoughts*. London: Macmillan, 1981.

Everest, Kelvin. 'Shelley's Doubles'. *Shelley Revalued: Essays from the Gregynog Conference*. Ed. Kelvin Everest. Leicester: Leicester UP, 1983. 63–88.

—— 'Shelley's *Adonais* and John Keats'. *Essays in Criticism* 57 (2007), 237–64.

Keach, William. *Shelley's Style*. New York: Methuen, 1984.

Kelly, Ronan. *Bard of Erin: The Life of Thomas Moore*. Dublin: Penguin Ireland, 2008.

Robinson, Charles. *Shelley and Byron: The Snake and Eagle Wreathed in Fight*. Baltimore: Johns Hopkins UP, 1976.

Roe, Nicholas. *Fiery Heart: The First Life of Leigh Hunt*. London: Pimlico, 2005.

West, Sally. *Coleridge and Shelley: Textual Engagement*. Aldershot: Ashgate, 2007.

White, Newman Ivey. *The Unextinguished Hearth: Shelley and his Contemporary Critics*. Durham, NC: Duke UP, 1938.

Wheatley, Kim. *Shelley and his Readers: Beyond Paranoid Politics*. Columbia, MI: University of Missouri Press, 1999.

CHAPTER 33

··

SHELLEY AND MUSIC

··

JESSICA K. QUILLIN

IN 1822, Percy Bysshe Shelley made a gift of an Italian guitar to Jane Williams, who, along with her husband Edward Williams, formed part of the Shelleys' intimate circle of friends in Pisa. This famous guitar, which now resides at the Bodleian Library along with a large collection of Shelley's manuscripts, survives as a symbol of the poet's association of music with love of music. In the accompanying poem, Shelley writes:

> The artist wrought this loved guitar,
> And taught it justly to reply
> To all who question skillfully
> In language gentle as thine own;
> [...] and it knew
> That seldom heard mysterious sound,
> Which, driven on its diurnal round
> As it floats through boundless day
> Our world enkindles on its way—
> All this it knows, but will not tell
> To those who cannot question well
> The spirit that inhabits it [...]
>
> ('With a Guitar. To Jane', 58–61; 74–81)[1]

These lines reveal Shelley's conviction in his later poetry that music has a unique connection to the underlying harmony and beauty of the universe and that the poet able to connect his language to instrumental music can comprehend and thus communicate untold universal truths.

By the end of his life, Shelley possessed a great appreciation for the art of music and a significant understanding of the main precepts of contemporary musical aesthetics, particularly more holistic notions in which music and poetry are seen as fundamentally interrelated. Yet, while his early poetry reveals a consistent, though generic, interest in music as a sister art to poetry, music only became a core element of his continually

---

[1] All line references are from *Norton 2*.

evolving conception of poetry after his encounters with the Hunt Circle and other musical acquaintances in late 1816.

MUSIC IN SHELLEY'S LIFE

Shelley was born into one of the most active eras in European musical history. Although discussions of British music from 1780 to 1830 generally note a significant decline in native music-making with the passing of the age of Purcell and Handel, the British musical scene during this period was far from dead, particularly in the arenas of the theatre and the drawing room. Indeed, the age of Beethoven and the first performances of Mozart's operas in London saw such a rapid acceleration in the number of musical performances in the city that several critics have noted that, from the 1790s into the new century, the 'rage' in London was for music.[2] The onset of war on the Continent and other political upheavals, combined with a surge in public access to printed material, made music and literary ideas of music accessible to a wider range of the literate public. These developments contributed to making music and literature popular outlets for current philosophical issues, particularly major ideas on social and political reform. While native British music composition may have been in a decline, the dialect poetry of Robert Burns, the ballads of Sir Walter Scott, and collections like Percy's *Reliques of Ancient English Poetry* and Wordsworth and Coleridge's *Lyrical Ballads* established a uniquely British style of poetry that was purposefully linked to music. The popularization of music-related forms of poetry like the ballad and lyric and the predominance of the image of the poet as minstrel reveal the extent to which writers of the period conceived of poetry and music as conceptually, if not materially, connected. Although this relationship was in part based on the pseudo-historical concept of the common origin of speech and song, as I have argued elsewhere,[3] songs like the French *Marseillaise* and Burns's Scottish airs affirmed the potential of a unified music and poetry to represent, if not inspire, revolutionary feeling. Even though critics have noted that the musical consumerism of the British bourgeoisie did not accelerate until the 1840s with the rise of the music publishing houses and the increased popularity of instruments like the piano in the home,[4] Shelley, like many poets of his time, nonetheless recognized actual and theoretical music as both a platform and a rich tradition of ideas to spread and deepen his radical political agenda.

---

[2] The British press labelled the dominant role of music in the London season the 'rage for music' as early as the 1790s, when the social calendar was dominated by a wide variety of public concerts, operas, and events by amateur music societies. For further reading, see *The Athlone History of Music in Britain*, V: *The Romantic Age, 1800–1914*, ed. Nicholas Temperley (London: The Athlone Press, 1981).

[3] See Jessica Quillin, 'Shelleyan Lyricism and the Romantic Historicization of Musical Aesthetics', *Keats–Shelley Journal* 54 (2005), 133–47.

[4] Nicholas Temperley, 'Music', *Music in Britain: The Romantic Age 1800–1914* (London: The Athlone Press, 1981).

Throughout his life, Shelley took part in music as an active listener and occasional participant, though probably not a very skilled one. Although some accounts of Shelley's childhood mention his early lack of interest or lack of exposure to music,[5] Shelley attended operas and theatrical events with his family as a child, sometimes played the flute and piano, and was known to sing, though rather dissonantly.[6] Nevertheless, Shelley preferred to be an auditor rather than a performer, a role that his use of musical imagery in his poetry supports. While he discouraged both his sister Hellen and later Claire Clairmont from practising music,[7] his early works and personal letters reveal an interest in music as a close sister to his favourite art of poetry. As early as 1810, Shelley wrote letters to his friend, the music master Edward Fergus Graham, full of references to music, including several verse letters and requests for Graham's mentor, the composer Wölfl, to set some of his poems to music.[8] While no settings of Shelley's works by Wölfl survive, there is evidence that some of his poems, such as the 'antiphonal songs' of 'Fragment. Supposed to Be an Epithalamium of Francis Ravaillac and Charlotte Corde' in *Posthumous Fragments of Margaret Nicholson* (1810), 'may have grown out of [Shelley's] knowledge of—or experimentation with—the writing of operatic lyrics' with Graham.[9]

Other important musical figures before 1816 include his cousin Harriet Grove, who is strongly associated with music in many of the 'songs' he wrote for her.[10] This link between music, women, and erotic love was one that would strengthen over the course of his life. Yet, this theme was limited to his erotic relationships with women like Claire Clairmont, Emilia Viviani, Sophia Stacey, and Jane Williams rather than his wives, because neither Harriet Westbrook nor Mary Godwin is depicted as musical in his poetry, despite each having had some training in music. While Mary may not have had the musical talent of her half-sister Claire, she possessed a strong love for music, particularly after she, along with Shelley, became immersed in a world of musical events when they returned from the Continent in the autumn of 1816.

Shelley's interest in music further deepens with the advent of with the inception of his friendship with Leigh Hunt and introduction to his circle of friends and acquaintances.

---

[5]   Newman Ivey White quotes the memoirs of Mme Gataye, the daughter of the Newtons, who recalls how Shelley told ghost stories to the children during one of Mrs Newton's musical evenings (Newman Ivey White, *Shelley* (London: Secker & Warburg, 1947), I, 304). However, there is no evidence to suggest that he did not take interest on other occasions. For example, White also comments how Mrs Newton introduced Shelley and Harriet to the 'lively music' of Vauxhall Gardens (White, *Shelley*, I, 304). For other accounts of Shelley's relative lack of interest in music before 1817, see Jean de Palacio, 'Music and Musical Themes in Shelley's Poetry', *Modern Language Review* 59 (1964), 345.

[6]   Thomas Love Peacock recalls Shelley singing 'a monotonous melody of his own making. His song was "Yáhmani, Yáhmani, Yáhmani, Yáhmani."' Peacock, *Memoirs of Shelley and Other Essays and Reviews*, ed. Howard Mills (London: Rupert Hart-Davis, 1970), 37.

[7]   Shelley, letter to Hellen Shelley, 13 December 1811, *Letters: PBS* I, 206; White, *Shelley*, I, 407.

[8]   See *Letters: PBS* I, 14.

[9]   Donald Reiman, *CPPBS* I, 252.

[10]   One Captain Kennedy, who met Shelley in 1812, writes: 'In music he [Shelley] seemed to delight, as a medium of association [...] There was one [...] an exceedingly simple air, which, I understand, his earliest love was wont to play for him.' Quoted in T. J. Hogg, *The Life of Percy Bysshe Shelley* (London: George Routledge and Sons, 1906). For examples of the poems Shelley penned for Harriet see *CPPBS* I, 20–2.

This group, which included important musical and intellectual figures such as Vincent Novello, John Keats, Robert Benjamin Haydon, William Hazlitt, and Charles Lamb, would often gather at the houses of Novello or Hunt to enjoy 'exquisite evenings of Mozartian operatic and chamber music [...] [which] are things never to be forgotten.'[11] Through his experiences with the Hunt Circle beginning in late 1816, Shelley encountered many different types of domestic, theatrical, and sacred music. In the months leading up to their departure for Italy, Shelley, Mary, and Claire attended a multitude of operas, ballets, and plays in London. Peacock recalls that: '[f]rom this time till [Shelley] finally left England, he was an assiduous frequenter of the Italian opera. He delighted in the music of Mozart, and especially in the *Nozze di Figaro*.'[12] From April 1817 into the beginning of 1818, the Shelleys saw works such as Paisiello's *La molinara*, Paer's *Griselda*, and the latest Mozart and Rossini operas, including *Figaro* three times, *Don Giovanni* six times,[13] and the London première of Rossini's *Il barbiere di Siviglia*. The Shelleys were also impressed with the musical ballets that often followed the operas, particularly the artistry of Mlle Milanie, a ballerina who starred in several pieces produced in the style of the choreographed French *ballet d'action*.[14] These musical months spent in London greatly affected Shelley, giving him a new appreciation and deeper knowledge of music that would substantially affect his writing as well as his conception of poetry for the rest of his life.

Once they reached the Continent in February, 1818, the Shelleys continued to attend many musical events and to meet musical people, including Rossini (who did not take to the young poet) and the *improvvisatore* Sgricci.[15] Yet, like Byron, who kept a box at La Fenice in Venice, the Shelleys were impressed with neither the singers nor the operas they attended while in Italy, though they found the Italians to be naturally musical.[16] Shelley wrote to Hogg from Italy of the 'vine-dressers [...] singing all day *mi rivedrai, ti revedrò* [from Rossini's *Tancredi*] but by no means in an operatic style'.[17] This image of Italian peasants singing 'I'll see you again, you'll see me again' from the nationalistic aria 'Di tanti palpiti' further revealed to Shelley both a strong connection between music and memory, which is a common thread of musical imagery in his poetry, as well as the capacity of music, unlike poetry, which is limited by the written word, to arouse a wide audience, even among people who were very likely illiterate.

[11] Charles and Mary Cowden Clarke, *Recollections of Writers* (London: Gilbert & Rivington, Printers, Sampson Low, Marston, Searle & Rivington, 1878), 19.

[12] Peacock, *Memoirs*, 46.

[13] See Claire Clairmont, *The Journals of Claire Clairmont*, ed. Marion Kingston Stocking (Cambridge, MA: Harvard UP, 1968), 81–6; Mary Shelley, *Letters: MWS* I, 76, 77, 92; White, *Shelley*, I, 520; and Peacock, *Memoirs*, 2, 349–50.

[14] They saw Mlle Milanie in a performance of *Zephyr; or the Return of Spring* after a performance of *Don Giovanni* on 21 February 1818.

[15] See Herbert Lindenberger, *Opera in History: From Monteverdi to Cage* (Stanford, CA: Stanford UP, 1998), 81.

[16] See [Mary Shelley, letter to the Hunts, 6 April 1818], *Letters: MWS* I, 63–4 and [Shelley, letter to Peacock on 4 April 1818], *Letters: PBS* II, 3–4.

[17] Shelley, letter to T. J. Hogg, Livorno, 25 July 1819, in *Letters: PBS* II, 105.

However, for Shelley, the impact of his experiences with the Hunt Circle was not limited to an increased fascination with the public sphere of the opera and theatre, but also extended into the private sphere of his domestic relationships in the form of drawing room music. In the summer of 1817, Shelley wrote to Hunt,[18] asking him to help procure a grand piano for Claire Clairmont for the house at Marlow in order to 'duplicate the musical evenings [they] had enjoyed when visiting the Hunts'.[19] Although the fate of the piano is unknown, these intimate summer evenings with Claire, whose voice her instructor compared to 'a string of pearls', inspired Shelley to write 'no less than four unfinished poems, all begun at Marlow under the influence of music'.[20] Similarly, once in Italy, Shelley continued to form intimate friendships with musically talented women, including Maria Gisborne, who was the sister-in-law of composer Muzio Clementi, Emilia Viviani, Sophia Stacey, and Jane Williams, to whom he respectively wrote many lyrics and longer poems. His consistent use of musical imagery and the intimate nature of these 'private' poems reveal not only his strained relationship with Mary but also his perception after 1817 of a strong connection between music and love. In his 1818 essay *On Love*, Shelley writes that to find love is to discover one's 'antitype [...], with a frame, whose nerves, like the chords of two exquisite lyres strung to the accompaniment of one delightful voice, vibrate with the vibrations of our own [...]'.[21] This musical conception of love stirs Shelley's interest in the idea of music as a vehicle for change after 1817. In this way, while it is important to understand the biographical and cultural context of Shelley's musical experiences, particularly as they inform his knowledge of music at different points in his life, the best way to see the manifest presence of music in Shelley's poetry and in his overall conception of how poetry relates to the imagination is through analysis of his use of musical metaphors and ideas of music as well as a glance at how music affects his poetry.

Musical Aesthetics

Shelley, like all well-educated poets of the early nineteenth century, had access to a vast array of ideas on music from his predecessors as well as his contemporaries. As a voracious reader, he indubitably understood the musical ideas not only of literary sources from Shakespeare to Coleridge as well as those of classical philosophy from Plato to Aristotle; but was also greatly influenced by a range of other sources, including the British sceptical tradition of Smith and Hume, the French materialists and Rousseau, eighteenth-century British writings on aesthetics and the sublime from Shaftesbury to Alison, the German Romanticism of Kant, Goethe, and Schlegel, and the Gothic novels of Matthew 'Monk' Lewis and Mrs Radcliffe. Shelley's remarkable ability to absorb and synthesize concepts from theoretical and poetic ideas of music as well as his experiences

---

[18] Cowden Clarke, *Recollections of Writers*, 196.   [19] White, *Shelley*, I, 507.
[20] White, *Shelley*, I, 507.   [21] Shelley, *On Love, Norton 2*, 504.

with actual performed music caused his views on music to shift constantly throughout his life, which can be seen in both his discussion of music in his prose as well as his use of musical metaphors in his poetry.

In his early poetry and prose, Shelley initially perceives music as flawed because it lacks the intellectual content and physical presence of poetry as language. Although, as Keach and others have shown,[22] his reading of philosophers like Drummond taught him to be constantly sceptical of the representational capacities of language, Shelley nonetheless elevates language over music because it is the material of poetry, which is the highest art for him. The transience of musical experiences forms a major theme throughout his poetry, and Shelley's earlier works portray the impermanent nature of music as a frustrating, even misleading quality, rather than a potentially empowering one, because it reminds him of the inescapably mutable nature of all human experiences and consciousness. Indeed, in poems like *Alastor* and *Queen Mab*, music, though it imparts brief moments of ecstasy and is associated with the more beneficent world of nature, is also a negative force because it creates or heightens the poet's sense of loss or longing to return to that moment of internal ecstasy, thus moving him away from himself and his sense of purpose. The most familiar example of this is the figuration of music in *Alastor*, in which the main character has a vision of a 'veilèd maid' whose musical voice 'like the voice of his own soul | Heard in the calm of thought' (153–4) is at once intoxicating yet toxic to the poet, who embarks on a solipsistic quest to be reunited with the maid from his dream and ultimately dies in the process. Due to the poet's sceptical views about music's expressiveness and his general lack of sustained exposure to performed music, music is at best an undercurrent, rather than a core element, in Shelley's early metaphysics.

Undecided over the representational capacity of art, Shelley vacillates between two perspectives on music throughout his works, particular those written before 1817. Like many eighteenth- and nineteenth-century writers, he was greatly attracted to a mimetic notion of music as a subservient sister of poetry that reflects the natural order of the universe, a conception that was predominant in eighteenth-century aesthetics. On the other hand, building on his understanding of early German Romanticism and the musical ideas of Wordsworth and Coleridge, Shelley was also drawn to a more organic notion of music as the highest form of the arts because of its affective capacity as sound to impact directly the mind and soul of its auditor without the encumbrance of the material—i.e. written language. Twentieth-century criticism, especially postmodernism and then post-structuralism, brought renewed attention to this debate over artistic representation as a central concern of Romanticism.[23] While Shelley wavers between these two perspectives, after 1817 his conception of music is more determined towards an organic point of view, though it is never fixed, as music becomes the locus for revolutionary

---

[22] See William Keach, *Shelley's Style* (London: Methuen, 1984), 32.

[23] For example, see M. H. Abrams, *The Mirror and the Lamp: Romantic Theory and the Critical Tradition* (Oxford: Oxford UP, 1953, Paul de Man, 'The Rhetoric of Blindness: Jacques Derrida's Reading of Rousseau', *Blindness and Insight: Essays in the Rhetoric of Contemporary Criticism*, 2nd edn. (London: Methuen & Co., Ltd, 1983), 102–41, and Kevin Barry, *Language, Music and the Sign* (Cambridge: Cambridge UP, 1987).

change within his overall poetic paradigm precisely because of its ability to bypass reason and directly affect the heart.

Shelley's partial resolution of these two perspectives on music can best be seen in *A Defence of Poetry*, a work that partially expresses his post-1817 attitude towards music. In the *Defence*, he classifies the actual art of music as mimetic yet ultimately relies upon an organic view of music as a 'formless' model of artistic expression in order to define and support his ultimate vision of poetry. Since it 'is arbitrarily produced by the Imagination and has relation to thoughts alone', Shelley argues that poetry 'in a restricted sense' (*Norton 2*, 513) is the highest of the arts because of its basis in language, which is singular in comparison to other modes of expression, such as music. Nevertheless, he describes music as a fundamental characteristic of poetry 'in a general sense' (*Norton 2*, 511) due to his recognition of the representational limits of language as the written word. Utilizing the idea of the common origin of speech and song that was popularized in part by Rousseau's *Essai sur l'origine des langues*, Shelley defines language as inescapably musical, noting that 'the language of poets has ever affected a certain uniform and harmonious recurrence of sound, without which it were not poetry'.[24] This expanded conception of language lends support to his vision of the poet as 'a nightingale, who sits in darkness and sings to cheer its own solitude with sweet sounds' yet whose 'auditors are as men entranced by the melody of an unseen musician, who feel that they are moved and softened, yet know not whence or why' (*Norton 2*, 516). In this vision, poet-musicians, empowered by a musico-poetic conception of language as 'a perpetual Orphic song' (*Prometheus Unbound*, IV, 415), can inspire and effect change simply as 'the hierophants of an unapprehended inspiration [...] the trumpets which sing to battle and feel not what they inspire [...] the unacknowledged legislators of the World'.[25] Despite his self-effacing attitude towards poetry's ultimate effectiveness by itself as a vehicle for his radical political vision, Shelley, in his later works, embraces a conception in which poetry, when modelled after or intertwined with music, can help the poet and, in turn, humanity, come closer to achieving a true liberty of ideas and universal harmony.

Musical Metaphors

Musical imagery in Shelley's poetry and prose ranges from common musical tropes such as the Aeolian harp to more unexpected themes, such as his presentation of music as the agent of revolutionary change, particularly through the image of a musical female empowered by love. While his view of poetic and musical representation may vary, he makes use of consistent types of musical imagery, which, though their formulation and application differ widely, can be easily organized into three main categories.[26] The first

---

[24] Shelley, *A Defence of Poetry*, Norton 2, 512.

[25] Shelley, *Prometheus Unbound*, IV. 415, Norton 2, 281; *A Defence of Poetry*, Norton 2, 535.

[26] These categories are partially borrowed from Sue Coffman, *Music of Finer Tone: Musical Imagery of the Major Romantic Poets* (Salzburg: Institut für Anglistik und Amerikanistik, Universität Salzburg, 1984).

category, *musica instrumentalis*, includes: human-produced music and musical instruments, such as harps, lyres, and people singing; Wordsworthian images of the positive, often overpowering music of nature and the natural sublime; and, concurrently, more Gothic, negative images of music as a supernatural force. The second and third categories, namely *musica humana*, the motions of the human body and soul, and *musica mundana*, celestial music or the music of the spheres, both emerge out of Shelley's emphasis on the primacy of harmony, defined as a union or synthesis of different elements, as well as his interest in the interrelationship between music and poetry as sound and words. In sum, these musical images show the development of Shelley's ideas on music and the ways in which it becomes a significant factor in his presentation of both the inward life of the poet as well as his external duty to communicate universal truths.

For a poet whose work Robert Browning called 'moved by and suffused with a music at once of the soul and sense',[27] Shelley's poetry contains relatively few descriptions of actual performances of concert or drawing room music. This is highly typical for the Romantic era, particularly for the male poets who had more limited training in the art of music. Shelley, like Wordsworth, Coleridge, and Byron, was more impressed with more individualistic images of a voice or voices captured in song, often accompanied by a lyre, harp, guitar, or other instrument. As John Minahan has shown,[28] Keats is the exception to this rule because his own considerable musical abilities gave him more fluency with actual performed music. Despite Shelley's acquired love of opera and other concert music after 1817, there are few mentions of organized musical ensembles and performances in his poetry; and drawing room instruments and the concert stage function to provide critical context or dramatic backdrop. In *Julian and Maddalo*, the madman is described as 'sitting mournfully | Near a piano', '[h]is head [...] leaning on a music book' and '[h]is lips [...] pressed against a folded leaf' (273–4, 278, 280), though we do not hear him play. Similarly, in *Epipsychidion*, the narrator tells Emily that he has 'sent books and music' (519) as an essential element of the utopic isle to which he beckons her.

In contrast to the infrequency of actual concert music, Shelley relies upon a range of musical instruments and images of a voice or voices singing to illustrate the inevitable processes of Nature, as well as the activities of a poet at work and his sources of inspiration. The preponderance of harps, lyres, lutes, guitars, flutes, reeds, and other instruments, in addition to references to musical winds, echoes, flows of water, and birdsong, in his poetry is symptomatic not only of the fundamental role of music in the Romantic perception of the natural world and its elemental forces; but also, for Shelley, it reveals the degree to which music eventually permeates his definition of poetry and the process of poetic creation. Shelley's later lyrics, particularly familiar examples like 'Ode to the West Wind', 'To a Sky-Lark', his Homeric hymns, and the Jane Williams lyrics, contain relatively optimistic depictions of musical instruments as the tools of divinely skilled or inspired artists who help the poet experience the beauty of music—moments that move

[27] Robert Browning, 'An Essay on Percy Bysshe Shelley', in *Peacock's Four Ages of Poetry; Shelley's Defence of Poetry; Browning's Essay on Shelley*, ed. H. F. B. Brett-Smith (Oxford: Basil Blackwell, 1937), 71.
[28] John Minahan, *Word Like a Bell: John Keats, Music and the Romantic Poet* (Kent, OH: Kent State UP, 1992).

from exasperation to catharsis as he embraces a seemingly more stable vision in which music and poetry somehow become intertwined.

However, the formulation of musical instruments in Shelley's poetry written before 1816 is generally less organized, borrowing heavily from the Gothic tradition and other sources. In *Alastor* and other poems, including 'Mont Blanc' and even 'Hymn to Intellectual Beauty', he presents two interpretations of the Aeolian metaphor: the first is the Wordsworthian notion of the 'gentle breeze', a beneficent natural force which brings inspiration to the poet; and the second notion, based on Coleridge's 'Eolian Harp', is a supernatural, synaesthetic force that can beguile and mislead the poet, causing him to confuse the line between silence and music, dream and reality. As discussed above, Shelley's agonized perspective on language and the limitations of his own poetic voice strongly drew him to the idea of music without words as well as the corollary relationship between music and silence. The pauses between sounds (and, in turn, words)—as well as the absence of them—signified for Shelley an awareness not only of how the revelatory effects of music connect its auditor to the ethereal world of thought and the imagination but also of the inescapable fleetingness of these experiences and, of course, of life itself. It is in this vein that Shelley utilizes musical imagery as a way of depicting moments of awe and dissatisfaction with the natural sublime. The music of nature becomes a way of mediating between his own sense of a poet's duty to uncover and communicate the secret truths of nature and his own sense of inadequacy over the capability of his words, as language, to capture these experiences. In 'Mont Blanc', he writes of the soothing yet uncanny sounds of the natural world as '[t]he chainless winds' that come to 'hear—an old and solemn harmony' (22, 24). In 'Hymn to Intellectual Beauty', which was written in the summer of 1816, an encounter with Intellectual Beauty, like the 'memory of music fled' (10), is ecstatic yet unsatisfying for the narrator, though he finds comfort in the recognition that its 'light alone' (32) like 'music by the night wind sent | Through strings of some still instrument' brings 'grace and truth to life's unquiet dream' (33–34, 36). Although the image of a 'speechless music' cripples the poet in these poems as well as in *Alastor* and *Queen Mab*, Shelley returns to this idea in Act III of *Prometheus Unbound* with the image of the 'mystic shell', the sound of which is 'both sweet and strange' (III. iii. 70, 71). However, the music of this shell, unlike his earlier uses of the idea of music without words, fills '[t]he abysses of the sky, and the wide earth', beginning 'a change' (III. iv. 99, 100) that literally brings an end to the Jovian age that enchained humanity and heralds the new Promethean age of peace and liberty.

While his scepticism never abates, Shelley's use of musical imagery in his later works reveals a renewed confidence towards the role of art in the potential amelioration of the 'moral and physical state of mankind' as well as a significantly improved understanding and appreciation of music, particularly vocal music.[29] The image of a voice or voices singing is dominant in his later works because it sets forth a refined model for the process of poetic inspiration and the activity of the imagination. In particular, he frequently

[29] Mary Shelley, 'Preface', *Posthumous Poems of Percy Bysshe Shelley* (London: John and Henry L. Hunt, Covent Garden, 1824), p. iv.

relies upon images of voice to describe the presence of a divine power in nature, whether as wind, echoes, or bird song. In 'Ode to the West Wind', for instance, the poet seeks to find strength in the wind, which is presented as the impetus of natural change as the 'Dirge | Of the dying year' (23–4) but also as an all-powerful 'voice' that the poet asks to '[m]ake me thy lyre, even as the forest is' and to '[b]e through my lips to unawakened Earth | The trumpet of a prophecy! O Wind, | If Winter comes, can Spring be far behind?' (57, 68–70). In 'To a Skylark', the skylark sings 'profuse strains of unpremeditated art' (5) and 'hymns unbidden' (38) that are '[b]etter than all measures | Of delightful sound' (96–7), which the poet suggests that if he were to learn:

> [...] half the gladness
>   That thy brain must know
> Such harmonious madness
>   From my lips would flow,
> The world should listen then—as I am listening now.
>
> (101–5)

In all of these examples, music becomes a radical vehicle for change, as the poet longs to harness his revelatory experience with the musical voice and its incumbent access to the fundamental beauty and harmony of the divine.

Images of vocal or choric performances, whether solo or accompanied by instruments, take on a deeper complexity as Shelley associates them with human singers. In 'Song of Pan', which, along with 'Song of Apollo', was written for Mary Shelley's drama *Midas*, the speaker observes how nature itself falls 'silent as even as Tmolus was, | Listening [Pan's] sweet pipings', which suggests the divine-like power of a singing voice to overpower even the natural world. In his post-1817 works, Shelley's fascination with music's affective capacity to bypass reason and impact the human imagination forms the basis of a strong conceptual link between music, love, and poetry, which is often figured through the vehicle of a woman singing. The negative association between music and women present in his earlier works evolves into a more nuanced duality between the positive powers of music when associated with love and its invidious nature when associated with the carnal world. Under the influence of a vocally gifted female who is empowered by love, music is transient, formless, and has a unique connection to the divine. However, without love as a harmonizing force, music represents the poisonous, unnatural forces of the earthly world that have the power to consume or destroy. For instance, unlike the 'veilèd maid' of *Alastor*,[30] the female figure in *Epipsychidion* 'whose voice was venomed melody' (256) is an earthly being who is the antithesis of the ethereal veiled maid the speaker sees in his sleep. Although music here is described as a formless art, its source is corrupted, mortal, and thus is noxious to the poet. Although this negative association between vocalized sound and the mortal world recurs throughout his later poetry, Shelley is nonetheless more concerned with the positive impact of vocal performance because of his personal associations between music and specific women of his acquaintance as well as of its potential use as a model for experience of

---

[30] See Shelley, *Alastor*, Norton 2, 149–91.

poetic inspiration. Over and over in his later poetry, musical women empowered by love not only function to carry the poet to a new realm of ecstasy but also to symbolize utopic renewal or a sense of universal change, whether literal or figurative, as a part of Shelley's desire to achieve social and political reform. His lyrics and smaller fragments to music, frequently denigrated by critics such as F. R. Leavis for their sentimentality, evoke the power of vocal music, even improvisatorial song, to affect the imagination more powerfully than poetry, despite the impossibility of sustaining these experiences due to the nature of sound. For example, the fragments Shelley wrote for Claire Clairmont in the summer of 1817, including the evocative 'To Constantia', celebrate the power and enchanting beauty of Claire's 'singing, where the musical and sexual gift are successfully united in evocation'.[31] In *Prometheus Unbound*, the character of Asia, who is Prometheus' lover and literal other half, represents freedom and revolution through the redemptive powers of love, which is imaged in terms of a synaesthetic fusion of music and light. At the end of Act II, after their encounter with Demogorgon, Panthea observes that Asia has changed, noting that she can 'scarce endure | The radiance of [Asia's] beauty' but, like the effects of music, can 'feel' that Asia has 'changed' (II. v. 16–18). This fusion of music, light, and love culminates in a lyrical exchange between Asia and Prometheus, figured as the 'Voice (*in the air, singing*)', first with the 'Life of Life!' lyric and then with Asia's 'My soul is an enchanted boat', in which she declares that 'by the instinct of sweet Music driven' (II. v. 90)

> The boat of my desire is guided—
> Realms where the air we breathe is Love
> Which in the winds and on the waves doth move,
> Harmonizing this Earth with what we feel above.
>
> (II. v. 94–7)

Although the female voice is strongly associated with music in Shelley's poetry, his overall conception of music is not exclusively feminine. While Paul Vatalaro suggests that Shelley's consistent connection between music and women stems from a fundamental perception of music as feminine vs. poetry as masculine, a dualism which ultimately stems from a 'fear of estrangement from his own poetic voice',[32] the music of the human voice and, indeed, music itself are not strictly feminine. When, in poems like 'Orpheus' and *Prometheus Unbound*, the male voice becomes alienated from the poetry of its own voice, it returns to this power not through a union with the musicalized feminine so much as through a restoration of its own fundamental musicality, which incorporates a balance of elements. In *Prometheus Unbound*, we learn that Prometheus was separated from the power of his own voice at the utterance of the curse against Jupiter. While Prometheus' reconciliation with his original vocal authority occurs via Asia, who represents the forces of music and love, it is important to recall Asia's capacity as the other half of Prometheus' soul: she is part of him. Her blinding music-like radiance not only symbolizes her reunion with Prometheus and the restoration of his power, but foretells the

---

[31] Richard Holmes, *Shelley: The Pursuit* (London: Weidenfeld and Nicolson, 1974), 242.
[32] Paul Vatalaro, *Shelley's Music: Fantasy, Authority, and the Object Voice* (Farnham: Ashgate, 2009), 2.

return of the natural order and harmony of the universe that is celebrated in Act IV. In this way, Shelley reveals his interest in harmony as a synergy or union of forces, in addition to the reconciliation of opposites. For Shelley, it is not simply a matter of reuniting the masculine and the feminine or the poetic with the musical. Rather, he is arguably concerned with the ideas of synthesis and interdependency. In terms of music, this becomes a question of how to make music a part of poetry or at least to link the two arts together in order to make the language of poetry more powerfully effective—ideas which both strongly connect to his perception of love and poetic inspiration. In *Epipsychidion*, he tells Emily:

> And we will talk, until thought's melody
> Become too sweet for utterance, and it die
> In words, to live again in looks, which dart
> With thrilling tone into the voiceless heart,
> Harmonizing silence without a sound.
> Our breath shall intermix, our bosoms bound,
> And our veins beat together; and our lips
> With other eloquence than words, eclipse
> The soul that burns between them [...]
>
> (560–74)

In these lines, the lovers talk until their words take on the formlessness of music, even without sound; and this transformation, in turn, causes their physical beings to unite with their spiritual. The wordless, soundless music of the lovers that '[h]armonize[s] silence without a sound' establishes love as a process of purified synaesthesia through the musicalization of language: words are ultimately inadequate to express thought, and it is only by becoming musical that they are able to become the fullest expression of love.

The idea of harmony dominates Shelley's descriptions of *musica humana*, which involves the motions of the human body and soul and the poetic process, as well as his depiction of *musica mundana*, which includes celestial or universal music. Harmony, defined as a consonance or unity of elements, signifies both the natural rhythm of the human body and mind as well as the fundamental order or organized music of the cosmos. Shelley's definition of harmony comes closer to melody in Rousseauian terms rather than harmony in the traditional eighteenth-century sense of an organized succession of sounds. Building upon the conventions of classical drama and modern dramatic forms like the Italian opera, Shelley's *Prometheus Unbound* presents music as harmony, consonance, and natural order, whereas sound and noise represent disharmony, dissonance, and disorder. Reading works like *Julie, ou la nouvelle Héloïse*, an epistolary novel in which Rousseau sets out many of his ideas on music, exposed Shelley to many of the basic precepts of late eighteenth-century musical aesthetics, including debates over the fundamental nature of music as either harmony, in this case defined as a mathematical organization of musical tones or intervals, or melody, defined as an organized succession of sounds designed to have a pleasant effect on the ear. The distinction between these conceptions of musical melody and harmony provided Shelley with a powerful model through which to describe his conception of the process of poetic inspiration as well as of the human mind. His conception of harmony as the underlying principle of the inner workings of the human body and mind evinces itself in his definitions of love as well as that of poetic inspiration. Shelley's readings of scientific works acquainted him with the wave theory of sound as well as medical theories on the processes of the human body and mind. These sources fed his interest in the idea of the fundamental harmony or vibrations of the human body and mind. In many of Shelley's works, the concept of harmony, when connected with poetry and love, signifies the impetus for and presence of socio-political change. In *The Mask of Anarchy*, music connects to patriotic ideals of liberty, freedom, and democracy as the 'voice' that inspires the poet and echoes the spirit of 'Liberty!' (335). Similarly, in 'Ode to Liberty', the poet describes the success of the Spanish revolutionaries as '[a] glorious people vibrated again' (1). As discussed earlier with reference to the 'mystic shell' of *Prometheus Unbound* as well as Asia's transfiguration, Shelley embraces the transformative powers of music and harmony to connect to larger concepts of universal order. Indeed, he combines inherited notions of celestial music or the music of the spheres with contemporary definitions of harmony and melody to form a utopic vision in which harmony and the music of vibrations reveals the triumph of liberty and democracy over tyranny and love and truth over the deceptive forces of evil. This concept of musical harmony provides him with a powerful model through which to describe his understanding of the process of artistic inspiration. Although Shelley, like his peers, is attracted to Wordsworth's musical notion of poetic inspiration as a 'gentle breeze' that sweeps over the passive poet-as-harp, he eventually abandons it in favour of a notion in which human beings play a more active role in creative inspiration. In his *Defence*, he writes:

> there is a principle within the human being, and perhaps within all sentient beings, which acts otherwise than in the lyre, and produces not melody alone, but harmony, by an internal adjustment of the sounds or motions thus excited to the impressions which excite them. It is as if the lyre could accommodate its chords to the motions of that which strikes them, in a determined proportion of sound; even as the musician can accommodate his voice to the sound of the lyre. (*Norton 2*, 511.)

Like the 'unseen musician' (*Norton 2*, 516) that he describes later in the *Defence*, Shelley here relies upon the evocative image of the formlessness of music to describe how artistic inspiration occurs through a harmonization of basic sensory perceptions with the deeper processes of the imagination.

SHELLEY'S 'MUSICAL' STYLE AND FORMS OF MUSIC

The depth of Shelley's attraction to the unifying concept of harmony and music in general is strongly evident in his versification, his poetic form, and his overall poetic style, particularly in work written in the last five years of his life. While early works like the

'Songs' in *St. Irvyne* and the potentially operatic 'antiphonal songs' of 'Fragment. Supposed to Be an Epithalamium of Francis Ravaillac and Charlotte Corde' reveal his early interest in musical forms, these works are mainly traceable to inherited models and do not exhibit the lyrical variety and metrical sophistication of his later works. Although it is perhaps critical folly to trace direct biographical influences in literary works, Shelley's exposure to music and ideas of music from 1817 onwards is strongly evident in the increased prosodic variability of his verse as well as an increase in his use of lyrical and dramatic forms closely related to music. As early as the summer of 1817, he began to experiment with writing poems based on his musical experiences, and by 1818, he was contemplating creation of a longer *dramma per musica* or 'lyrical drama' inspired by both classical drama as well as his recent exposure to the contemporary musical stage.

Indeed, Shelley's new understanding of the operatic and theatrical traditions can be felt in longer poems such as *The Cenci, Prometheus Unbound*, and *Hellas*, in which he builds upon his already extensive knowledge of classical drama and other inherited poetic models to expand and innovate upon traditional poetic style and form. For example, the complex alternation of lyrical and prose forms in *Prometheus Unbound* demonstrates the influence of his understanding of musical sources like the Italian *opera buffa*, classical hymnody, the French *ballet d'action* or choral ballet of Noverre, and the musical philosophy of German Romantics. Shelley's strong attachment to works like A. W. Schlegel's *A Course of Lectures on Dramatic Art and Literature*, which was his book of choice on the boat to Italy in 1818, as well as his immersion in the world of Mozartian opera between 1817 and 1818, not only establish his exposure to eighteenth-century music and musical aesthetics, but also the theoretical and formal role of music in Italian, French, English, and classical drama. These experiences confirm his burgeoning interest in the relationship between poetry and its sister arts of music and drama as a new path or model for his poetic endeavours.

The influence of music on Shelley's poetic style and prosody is perhaps most clearly evident in the fact the word 'musical' has been used without much qualification as a defining characteristic of his poetic works since the early Victorian era. Heeding John Hollander's warnings about discussions of 'musical poetry', it is sufficient to observe that these readers are responding to a range of factors within his poetry, including his word choice, his syntax, his expansion upon traditional poetic metre and versification, and his extensive use of lyrical and dramatic types, such as the lyric, ode, ballad, and the hybrid musico-poetic form that he labelled 'lyrical drama'.[33] Between 1818 and 1822, he authored a profusion of lyrical poems that have strong conceptual and formal links to music, including 'To a Skylark', 'Ode to the West Wind', the Homeric hymns, and the Jane Williams lyrics. These shorter lyrics as well as more epic poems like *Prometheus Unbound* demonstrate both a tighter prosodic control and a more complex metrical scheme than his earlier works. While this is evidence of an inevitable maturation and honing of his poetic craft, the strong presence of musical imagery in these poems as well as his use of

---

[33] John Hollander, 'The Music of Poetry', *Journal of Aesthetics and Art Criticism* 15 (1956), 232–44.

musical forms arguably reveal the demonstrable impact of his knowledge of music to the practice of poetry. Although Shelley obviously possessed a passing interest in musical forms throughout his life, his mature poetry demonstrates an in-depth knowledge of the structure and thematic organization of these music-related poetic forms. Longer dramatic works like *Prometheus Unbound* and *Hellas* represent more extended attempts to incorporate musical form into poetry through experiments with imbuing classical dramatic forms with lyrical or musical ideas. In particular, *Prometheus Unbound* reveals Shelley's adaptation of the traditional choral interludes from classical drama into a different poetic model that more closely resembles the alternation of recitative and aria found in the Italian *opera buffa*.[34]

In all, the presence of musical ideas and musical forms within Shelley's poetic repertoire signifies his continual desire to improve his skills as a poet and to find a way to connect the art of poetry to the higher order of the imagination. While his interest in an interdependency between music and poetry arguably may arise from a fundamental belief in the ultimate superiority of poetry over music because of its cognitive nature as language, Shelley nonetheless sees in music a potential model through which to widen the influence and powers of poetry by harnessing music's unique ability to affect human consciousness and the imagination. The world of music and musical aesthetics in parallel with his own experiences with music and his literary inheritance provided him with many different ways through which to envision a heightened kind of poetry closely allied with music that becomes the highest form of art because of its ability to affect the mind, emotions, and, in turn, the imagination. As the poet tells Emily, the object of his adoration, in *Epipsychidion*:

> We—are we not formed, as notes of music are,
> For one another, though dissimilar;
> Such difference without discord, as can make
> Those sweetest sounds, in which all spirits shake
> As trembling leaves in a continuous air?
>
> (142–6)

Taking a Rousseauian interest in the melodic power of the voice to affect the human soul, Shelley ultimately emphasizes music as the ideal pathway by which two souls can meet. From this basic configuration, Shelley argues in *A Defence of Poetry*, human society, its laws, and its culture arise (and thus, history, which he sees as a cyclical rather than a linear process of growth and decay, is best interpreted through art, specifically through poetry).[35] In this way, Shelley's musical conception of love as a process of harmonization—an almost electrically charged spiritual synergy—between a soul and its antitype becomes a symbolic configuration representative of the complex relationship between humanity and Nature, one that can be both political and private, demonstrating his fervent faith in the capacity of poetry to reveal the perfectibility of humanity.

---

[34] See Jessica Quillin, "'An assiduous frequenter of the Italian opera': Shelley's *Prometheus Unbound* and the *Opera Buffa*', *Romantic Circles* Praxis Series, *Opera and Romanticism*, <www.rc.umd.edu/praxis/opera/quillin/quillin.html>.

[35] Shelley, *A Defence of Poetry*, Norton 2, 516–19.

Select Bibliography

Coeuroy, Andre. 'The Musical Inspiration of Shelley'. Trans. Theodore Baker. *Musical Quarterly* 9.1 (1923), 82–95.

Coffman, Sue. *Music of Finer Tone: Musical Imagery of the Major Romantic Poets*. Salzburg: Institut für Anglistik und Amerikanistik, Universität Salzburg, 1984.

Conrad, Peter. *Romantic Opera and Literary Form*. London: University of California Press, Ltd, 1977.

De Palacio, Jean. 'Music and Musical Themes in Shelley's Poetry'. *Modern Language Review* 59 (1964), 345–59.

Hollander, John. *Images of Voice: Music and Sound in Romantic Poetry*. Churchill College Overseas Fellowship Lectures, no. 5. Cambridge: W. Heffer & Sons, 1970.

Minahan, John. *Word Like A Bell: John Keats, Music and the Romantic Poet*. Kent, OH: Kent State UP, 1992.

Pollin, Burton. *Music for Shelley's Poetry: An Annotated Bibliography of Musical Settings of Shelley's Poetry*. New York: Da Capo Press, 1974.

Rogers, Neville. 'Music at Marlow'. *Keats–Shelley Memorial Bulletin* 5 (1952), 20–5.

Quillin, Jessica. 'Shelleyan Lyricism and the Romantic Historicization of Musical Aesthetics'. *Keats–Shelley Journal* 54 (2005), 133–47.

—— '"An assiduous frequenter of the Italian opera": Shelley's *Prometheus Unbound* and the *Opera Buffa*'. *Romantic Circles* Praxis Series. *Opera and Romanticism*. <www.rc.umd.edu/praxis/opera/quillin/quillin.html>.

Temperley, Nicholas. Ed. *The Athlone History of Music in Britain*, V: *The Romantic Age, 1800–1914* (London: The Athlone Press, 1981).

Tetreault, Ronald. 'Shelley at the Opera'. *ELH* 48 (1981), 144–71.

Vatalaro, Paul. *Shelley's Music: Fantasy, Authority, and the Object Voice*. Farnham: Ashgate, 2009.

Winn, James. *Unsuspected Eloquence: A History of the Relations between Poetry and Music*. New Haven: Yale UP, 1981.

....

CHAPTER 34

SHELLEY, SHAKESPEARE,
AND THEATRE

....

BERNARD BEATTY

SHELLEY's four plays (*Prometheus Unbound*, *The Cenci*, *Oedipus Tyrannus; or, Swellfoot the Tyrant*, and *Hellas*), two substantial unfinished plays (*Charles the First* and the 'Unfinished Drama'), and his substantial translations of Goethe's *Faust* and Calderón's *El mágico prodigioso*, add up to a sizeable portion of his poetry. Many of his other poems and lyrics, explicitly or implicitly, presuppose a dramatic placing of their voice.[1]

Jeffrey Cox has argued that Shelley was 'a powerful dramatist who worked with the theatrical conventions of his day in order to remake the stage for the future'.[2] This has truth but elides 'drama' and 'theatre', whereas the gap between dramatic and theatrical tradition—evident already in the distance between Milton's *Samson Agonistes* (published 1671) and Wycherley's *The Country Wife* (first performed in 1675)—widened in Shelley's lifetime. Dramatic tradition is a contested idea at the behest of writers and thinkers; theatrical tradition is a complex fact answerable to theatre companies and audiences. *Prometheus Unbound* is a version of one; *The Cenci* and *Charles the First* of the other.

Something in Shelley consciously resisted the theatre. He was appalled when he first saw Kean playing *Hamlet* in October 1814 by 'the loathsome sight of men of [*sic*] personating characters which do not and cannot belong to them' (*Journals: MWS* I, 35). This is linked with his Puritan and rational dislike of religious rituals.[3] Yet, by temperament he is drawn both to rituals and to impersonation. He engages both with dramatic and theatrical tradition.[4]

---

[1] G. M. Matthews was perhaps the first to challenge the prevailing view that Shelley's lyrics are dramatically placed rather than self-expression. See 'Shelley's Lyrics', in D. W. Jefferson (ed.), *The Morality of Art: Essays Presented to G. Wilson Knight* (London: Routledge and Kegan Paul, 1969), 195–209.

[2] Jeffrey Cox, 'The Dramatist', in Timothy Morton (ed.), *The Cambridge Companion to Shelley* (Cambridge: Cambridge UP, 2006), 65.

[3] See his disparagement of Catholic rituals in the preface to *The Cenci* (Longman, 2, 732, ll. 102–10).

[4] Byron always loved the theatre from his Harrow days. Shelley did not. Medwin, Hogg, Peacock, and Mary Shelley all comment on his early dislike of the theatre but he attended operas (especially

Plays, until Chekhov, are usually structured through connected actions or one dominant action but, as Stuart Curran has reiterated, Romantic drama is remarkable for 'its focus not on action but on non-action'.[5] Shelley is not primarily interested in action yet he wants change, believes in it, and seeks to represent it. He does so by distinguishing between action and transformation.

A preference for transformation rather than active change will only work in a certain kind of drama. Both *Prometheus Unbound* and *Hellas* presuppose historical action: the failure of the French Revolution and the early progress of the Greek Revolution respectively. Nevertheless the main event in *Prometheus Unbound* is the letting go of a past action which enables a present transformation to take place. The powerlessness of Mahmud in *Hellas* is of a piece with the inconclusive early events of the Greek Revolution. Dramatic tension is only operative in the opposition between blank verse discourse and 'The music of breath-suspending song' (*Laon and Cythna*, XII. 4597).[6] Roughly speaking, Shelley's verse discourse is tethered to present and past 'reality', whereas song is the agency of a transformed future. Some blank verse, especially in Act IV of *Prometheus Unbound*, is, as it were, trying to turn into song, and the Furies in Act I use both blank verse and song, but in *Hellas* Shelley makes the division between discourse and song absolute. Power lies in the powerlessness of song which alone can make 'the world's great age' (1060) begin anew.

Shakespeare's theatre is the Romantic exemplum of power in powerlessness. Keats's and Hazlitt's insistence on Shakespeare's pre-eminence as dramatist—precisely because he knows how to relinquish authorial control in order to acquire negative capability—gives it a rationale. Shakespeare's characters retain their free will rather than express his preferences yet his imagination has placed them where they are. In the Preface to *The Cenci*, Shelley explains this by his own, tongue-in-cheek yet earnest, aesthetic theology: 'Imagination is as the immortal God which should assume flesh for the redemption of mortal passion' (*Longman*, 2, 733). The imagination redeems not by any further act but solely through its incarnation (i.e. taking form) and thus representing communicable transformation. Shelley's theology of the imagination prohibits positive action.

Swellfoot the Tyrant is an exception to this. It, too, is made up of blank verse and song but its drama does not consist in their opposition but in a sequence of events that parallel the trial of Queen Caroline which took place just before the play was written (July 1820). These events lead to a climactic action in Act II scene ii:

Mozart's) in 1817–18. In 1818, he saw Eliza O'Neill several times and overcame his initial dislike of Kean's acting. The fullest account of the extent of his actual theatregoing is in Stuart Curran's indispensable *Shelley's 'Cenci': Scorpions Ringed with Fire* (Princeton: Princeton UP, 1970), esp. 158n. See also Ernest Sutherland Bates's still useful *A Study of Shelley's Drama, The Cenci* (New York: Columbia UP, 1908), 47–8.

[5] Stuart Curran, 'Shelleyan Drama', in Richard Allen Cave (ed.), *The Romantic Theatre: An International Symposium* (Totawa, NJ: Barnes and Noble, 1986), 71.

[6] All quotations from Shelley's poetry and drama taken from *Longman* unless otherwise stated. All references to Shakespeare are to William Shakespeare, *The Complete Works*, ed. Stanley Wells and Gary Taylor (Oxford: Clarendon Press, 1988).

> PURGANAX, *after unsealing the* GREEN BAG, *is gravely about to pour the liquor upon her head, when suddenly the whole expression of her figure and countenance changes; she snatches it from his hand with a loud laugh of triumph, and empties it over* SWELLFOOT *and his whole Court, who are instantly changed into a number of filthy and ugly animals, and rush out of the Temple. The image of* FAMINE *then arises with a tremendous sound, the* PIGS *begin scrambling for the loaves, and are tripped up by the skulls; all those who* EAT *the loaves are turned into* BULLS, *and arrange themselves quietly behind the altar. The image of* FAMINE *sinks through a chasm in the earth, and a* MINOTAUR *rises.* (Longman, 3, 708)

The Queen rides off on the Minotaur, who is also John Bull, to hunt her husband and his court who are her enemy and the enemy of the people of England. There is more action in this single paragraph than in many pages of Shelley's verse.

Nevertheless this action is magical. It belongs in a ritual. Laon and Cythna end up in an unspecified 'Temple of the Spirit' (XII. 4815) but the Temple of Famine has an exterior (Act I) with a statue and altar, and an interior (Act II. ii) with priests, ceremonial trumpets, a table of food, and—in this like a Christian church rather than a classical temple—a high altar with steps leading up to it. Though satirized, the privileged figure of Liberty implicitly acknowledges the setting as sacred space when she kneels in front of the altar and prays to the statue of Famine who, apparently, grants her petition. Shelley calls Liberty 'it' three times in the stage direction which is at odds with Liberty's use of 'her' (II. ii. 101) to describe herself. Similarly, the green bag functions as comic object in a trial which delivers a verdict and as a ritual object which possesses the magical power to transform men into beasts just as the loaves dedicated to Famine can turn pigs into bulls.

Shelley's reason disliked religious rituals but his imagination constantly shaped sacred spaces and symbolic actions. Rousseau's translation, in *The Triumph of Life*, from life to living death, for instance, is accomplished by a rite of communion in a 'crystal glass' (358) or 'cup' (404) of which the unsealing and emptying of the green bag's liquor over Swellfoot is the comic precursor.[7] The two theatre texts that he chose to translate—*El mágico prodigioso* and *Faust*—depend upon the reality of magic and ritual transaction.

The Cenci is purportedly more realistic. It originated in Shelley's reading of a well-known Roman horror story, his visit to the building associated with it, and seeing what he thought was a picture of its principal character. Many poems by Byron have a similar genesis (*The Prisoner of Chillon*, for instance, was generated by visiting the castle and learning the story of Bonnivard), but it is unusual for Shelley. The origins of the play are bound up with its intention to be 'of a more popular kind' (*Letters: PBS* II, 108).

Shelley deliberately turned to the contemporary theatre in the very midst of his writing that drama—*Prometheus Unbound*—which is the antithesis of popular theatre in form and subject matter. *Prometheus Unbound* centres in forgiveness which transforms the cosmos; *The Cenci* centres in revenge which leaves an unreformable historical world as it is. Why should Shelley choose the theatre to represent an unreformable historical world?

---

[7] *Major Works*, 615, 617.

There are three ways of reading the play but only one answers this question. Michael Scrivener, for instance, argues that the audience 'realizes that only a radically different society, based on principles that transcend patriarchy, could permit the emergence of an innocence which does not contradict itself'.[8] In favour of this view is the timing of the play just after the 'Peterloo Massacre' and Beatrice's use of the phrase 'Aye, something must be done; | What yet I know not' (III. i. 86–7) which its author later used of that event (*Letters: PBS* II, 116). The appropriate reaction to Jonson's *Volpone*, similarly, is to supply a morality which none of the characters in the play actually exhibit. But *Volpone* is a satirical drama and this strategy is common in satire. *The Cenci*, unlike *Swellfoot the Tyrant*, is not a satire in any useful sense.

The second reading is apparently suggested by Shelley's Preface: 'It is in the restless and anatomizing casuistry with which men seek the justification of Beatrice, yet feel that she has done what needs justification [...] that the dramatic character of what she did and suffered, consists' (*Longman*, 2, 731). Cenci, Beatrice, Orsino, and Giacomo interpret themselves but their interpretation is not the same as our judgement.[9] Shelley is perfectly correct in thinking that his audience will notice the discrepancy and find it dramatic. But this interpretation won't work either, for it puts all the emphasis on 'what she did and suffered' whereas the play does no such thing. Shelley knows this, for the crystal clear 'what she did and suffered' is quite different in emphasis from his opaque later statement:

> The crimes and miseries in which she was an actor and a sufferer are as the mask and mantle in which circumstances clothed her for her impersonation on the scene of the world. (*Longman*, 2, 735)

Here, 'actor and sufferer' pick up 'what she did and suffered' but action and suffering are transferred from reality ('crimes and miseries') to theatre ('impersonation', 'scene'). Hence the word 'actor', which in the first part of the sentence suggests 'one who does something', turns out to mean 'one who performs on a stage'. The mediating simile ('as the mask and mantle in which circumstances clothed her for her impersonation') suggests that his earlier formulation is a misdirection. Hugh Roberts has argued that Shelley's Prefaces 'tell us too much' and this bears him out.[10] *The Cenci* invites us less to distinguish between judgement and sympathy than between acting an action, acting a part, and giving a performance. Orsino acts a part, the murderers act in the sense of carrying out an action, Beatrice performs, compels others to her performance, and tries to teach her mother how to act but she cannot (IV. iv. 34–46). These distinctions can only be made clear in the theatre, not in Prefaces. Shelley's ability to make them shows why, despite his reservations, he is attracted to theatrical impersonation and, like Shakespeare,

[8] Michael Scrivener, *Radical Shelley: The Philosophical Anarchism and Utopian Thought of Percy Bysshe Shelley* (Princeton: Princeton UP, 1982), 196.

[9] Michael O'Neill points out that although the vocabulary of self-awareness is everywhere in the play, 'it is more accurate to regard the play as deconstructing the idea of "self-awareness"'. *The Human Mind's Imaginings: Conflict and Achievement in Shelley's Poetry* (Oxford: Clarendon Press, 1989), 75.

[10] Hugh Roberts, 'The Communicative Strategies of Shelley's Prefaces', in Alan M. Weinberg and Timothy Webb (eds.), *The Unfamiliar Shelley* (Farnham: Ashgate, 2009), 198.

to actors whose performances he can imagine. Shakespeare's frequent use of the notion that the stage represents the world, because the world operates like a theatre ('the scene of the world'), will become the central focus of Shelley's two essays into the London theatre.

I concur, therefore, with Margot Harrison who argues that *The Cenci* stresses the centrality of models of theatrical performance.[11] Her approach accounts for all rather than some features of the play, makes it some sort of success rather than a failure, and it exposes the interesting connections between Shakespearian and Shelleyan theatre.

The Cenci has various sub-plots but it pivots round two actions: a rape and a murder. These actions—one altogether unrepresented, the other reported—are themselves related and together generate the trial scene which concludes the play. Nevertheless, the play does not really work through these actions, partly because they occur in a frame-work of self-anatomizing and accident supported by its twelve soliloquies (*Macbeth* has seven, *Lear* nine, *Hamlet* and *Othello* have ten) and speeches whose average length is longer than in any play of Shakespeare. It is performances rather than actions that count and speeches are a form of performance. So Shelley who, five years earlier, had disliked Kean and impersonation, now seeks him out to be Cenci because he can best perform violence in speech and gesture. Similarly he insisted that Beatrice should be played by Eliza O'Neill whom Shelley had seen play Bianca in Milman's *Fazio* (*Journals: MWS* 1, 92 and *Letters: PBS* II, 504). It is Bianca rather than Fazio who comes to dominate this play just as Beatrice comes to dominate the other Cenci of the title. And O'Neill's virtuoso performance matched the part. Kean was, notoriously, not an ensemble actor. He sought to dominate the huge space of the new Drury Lane Theatre. So Shelley chose two actors associated with a new style of playing Shakespeare (Kean came to fame through playing Shylock, and O'Neill through playing Juliet) who would vie for dominance in a play which is about the performance of dominance. The sequence of the play is to be set up by Kean's performance as Cenci, then O'Neill's as Beatrice, and finally the set-piece of the trial which critiques but sustains the idea of theatrical performance upon which the play has wholly depended.

Foregrounding performance is a mark of Shakespeare's own theatre. The displacement of Julius Caesar by Brutus and the use of a trial scene to end *Measure for Measure* provide clear precedents for the structure of *The Cenci*. Bryan Weller argues that it reverses *Lear*: 'In *The Cenci*, he creates a myth of paternal tyranny to counter Shakespeare's myth of filial ingratitude, and the inversion is mirrored at the centre of the drama.'[12] This would make the play, like *Prometheus Unbound*, a subversion of its precedent, but Shelley's originality here has nothing to do with ideology. It uses rather than subverts an idea of theatrical performance inherent in Shakespeare's art but emotively refashioned by Romantic acting styles. Shelley switched from detesting theatrical impersonation to seeing it as offering a new solution to problems that always haunted him.

[11] Margot Harrison, 'No Way for a Victim to Act? Beatrice Cenci and the Dilemma of Romantic Performance', *Studies in Romanticism* 39.2 (2000), 187–211.

[12] Bryan Weller, 'Shelley, Shakespeare and the Binding of the Lyric', *Modern Language Notes* 93.5 (1978), 913.

The implications of this change for his later poetry are considerable but its possibility is rooted in the tales which his sisters recall their brother telling them: 'we dressed ourselves in strange costumes to personate spirits or fiends, and Bysshe would take a fire-stove and fill it with some inflammable liquid and carry it flaming into the kitchen.'[13] Impersonation goes hand in hand with ritual.

Shelley puts two very different things together. The first is the idea that Shakespeare writes like Dante in his concern with 'the operations of the human mind'.[14] The second is the new style of acting associated especially with Shakespeare's tragedies which now foregrounds one or two celebrity performances that 'embody the deeply irrational fears and longings of an audience deeply committed to extreme emotional response'.[15] The peculiar character of *The Cenci* is explained by the privileging of the performing self over the introspective self. In this it inverts *Macbeth*.

Cenci performs all the time. The main scene in the first act reveals him stage-managing a banquet, broadly reminiscent of that in *Macbeth* (III. iv), to which guests have been invited only to have their expectations grotesquely overturned, as in the second banquet of Shakespeare's *Timon of Athens*, just as the Count has intended. We see him imagining and planning his performance as a rapist in Act II.

Beatrice is not like this. She always has the compelling presence of a great actress, it is true, and can stand up to Cenci's tyrannical performance at the end of the banquet by a commanding performance of her own (I. iii. 146–59), but she is here like a great orator who gives a performance which performs her own projected self. After the rape, we encounter a second kind of performance. Her self-consciousness in the midst of her extreme disturbance ('My God! I never knew what the mad felt | Before' (III. i. 24–5)) belongs to her, but the performance itself belongs to the actress performing the part of Beatrice; like the Maniac in *Julian and Maddalo* or Shakespeare's Ophelia, she is not in control of her melodramatic outpourings.

Then, in an extraordinary scene for which I can think of no parallel, Shelley shows the process by which Beatrice steps, permanently, into a third kind of performance where her skills and the skill of the actress who performs the part wholly coincide. In Shakespeare's theatre we would expect a soliloquy to explain this new direction or simply a change of time or scene (as with Timon who is absent from the stage for three scenes in the centre of the play), but Shelley chooses a stage direction, *She retires absorbed in thought* (III. i. 179), which is as powerful as the stage direction that tells us that Coriolanus holds his mother's hand in a silent pause of action (V. iii. 183). Unlike Macbeth, whose initial trance-like state (I. iv. 141) has sourced his will to kill Duncan but then finds that this destructively persists alongside his acting self (III. i. 10–13), Beatrice enters once only into a comparable enabling suspension which then leaves her after having transformed her. She is set aside, in full view of the audience but inaccessible in her mental processes, for twenty-seven lines (III. i. 179–206) whilst Orsino and Lucretia

[13] Thomas Jefferson Hogg, *The Life of Percy Bysshe Shelley* (London: Routledge, 1906), 22–3.

[14] Preface to *Prometheus Unbound* (Longman, 2, 473).

[15] Joseph W. Donohue, Jr., *Dramatic Character in the English Romantic Age* (Princeton: Princeton UP, 1970), 83.

both edge round the possibility of murdering the Count. In this space of time, she has arrived at the same conclusion but, unlike these who remain exactly as they are, or Macbeth who finds himself stuck with dual consciousness, there can now never be any gap between her self and her performance. Her new authority derives from this. Harrison suggests that for her 'acting is a mean of self-preservation, not self-transformation',[16] but I don't see why it should not be both. Beatrice does not get a new self exactly but the authority, which has been intermittently hers, becomes a permanent possession (ascribed to God in the first instance) which ensures her perfect performance thereafter. She talks of a 'holier plea' and 'atonement' immediately (III. i. 212, 215), and later describes the murder as an exorcism (IV. i. 6–8) in which ritual performance is not at odds with integrity.

Action is usually thought to bring about the being of the doer. It is hideously so in *Macbeth* though the play is as much interested in the separation of Macbeth's being from his act as it is in the act's consequences. I will return to this point later since the relation between the two is the main subject of Shelley's play too. But in the ritual world of holy acts, the ritual does not exist as efficacious unless it is enacted by an already accredited performer (e.g. a priest).[17] Theatre archaically originates out of ritual and often replicates it without actually being it. In *The Cenci*, we have a double sense of the murder as fact and ritual as we do in *Julius Caesar* which Shelley had read a few weeks before beginning his play (*Journals: MWS* II, 673). For Brutus it is a purifying sacrifice, so he can urge his fellow assassins to 'bathe our hands in Caesar's blood' (III. i. 107) in order to efface the crude fact stated in the earlier direction: *They stab Caesar* (III. i. 76). The audience sees both actions—ugly and aestheticized. In *The Cenci*, we only hear how the murder is carried out but it is clearly ugly ('And then we threw his heavy corpse i' the garden' (IV. iii. 46)). Macbeth's ugly acts are set in careful contrast with the ritual world of Edward the Confessor who cures by 'hanging a golden stamp' about the necks of the sick (IV. iii. 154). Beatrice urges an ugly act sharply distinguished from her encasing of it in an imagined sacred ritual over which she presides as a being set apart. Here, her habitual emphasis on anatomizing the self becomes irrelevant. Roger Blood puts it neatly: 'Beatrice, who understood herself perfectly well, loses what she knew by acting',[18] by which he means performing a stage role. He is wrong to see this as pure loss but he is right in connecting it with the absence of *anagorisis* in the play. A theatrical performer and a priest enacting a ritual are incapable of self-criticism since their habitual self does not exist apart from its performance. This is why the play is not interested in inner conflict. Giacomo's doubts about the ethics of parricide in scenes i and ii of Act III are made to seem beside the point simply because his is a lesser performance. The audience begins to recognize that such may be the familiar centre of many plays but not this one. The distinction, both evident and blurred, between ugly act and aestheticized performance, which does lie at the centre of *The Cenci*, parallels the distinction between act and being

[16]   Harrison, 'Beatrice Cenci and the Dilemma of Romantic Performance', 210.

[17]   See Laurence Hemming, *Worship as a Revelation* (London: Burns and Oates, 2008), 47.

[18]   Roger Blood, 'Allegory and Dramatic Representation in *The Cenci*', *Studies in Romanticism* 33.3 (1994), 382.

in *Macbeth* though of course, in the last two scenes of that play, the distinction disappears. It parallels, too, the distinction between song (which can transform) and discourse (which cannot) in *Prometheus Unbound* and *Hellas*. It corresponds, yet again, to the deliberately blurred change in *The Mask of Anarchy* (98–129) where Hope lies down before the advance of the cavalry (which represents the ugly actions of Peterloo) but is transformed into a giant invulnerable, all-powerful shape who nevertheless retains her soft steps (118). Power and powerlessness, ugliness and aesthetic performance, merge in the single image of the maid 'walking with a quiet mien' though 'ankle-deep in blood' (129, 127). The image sustains itself perfectly against the facts just as Beatrice does. In *The Mask of Anarchy*, a mist arises at the point of transition (102). Exactly the same thing happens in *The Cenci* at the point where Beatrice's being changes ('What is this undistinguishable mist of thoughts' (III. i. 170–1)). The word 'mist' is here more important than 'thoughts' for it is the shape-erasing 'undistinguishable' mist, not any psychological change that could be disclosed through a soliloquy, which enables Beatrice to emerge out of it transformed into a being who now exists only as an adept performer.

Beatrice's sudden horror of dying (V. iv. 48–75) could be seen as a betraying chink in this magic armour but since her speech is so openly modelled, in spirit if not letter, on Claudio's similar horror in *Measure for Measure* (III. i. 118–32), it does not contradict our sense of Beatrice as a supreme performer. Most of the evident parallels between words and actions in *The Cenci* and Shakespeare's plays function in the same way. They foreground performance as object of attention as well as means in the play. The most obvious ones are the parallels between Cenci's murder and that of Duncan in *Macbeth*. It does not matter that this makes Lucretia incongruously act like Lady Macbeth any more than Giacomo's bizarre lamp ritual and lines (III. ii. 51–2)—which make him, ludicrously, resemble Othello (V. ii. 7) for a moment whilst Cenci becomes Desdemona—is a flaw. What Shelley achieves through these obvious allusions is a sense that past theatre provides ready prompt-books for characters as well as authors. Shelley's defence in his Preface of his reuse of 'a sublime passage' in Calderón's *El Purgatorio de San Patricio* (*Longman*, 2, 733) works in the same way. Criticism, from the nineteenth century to the first half of the twentieth century, constantly explored the extent of Shelley's borrowings from Shakespeare in *The Cenci*.[19] The notion of intertextuality has made this seem less exceptional.

The setting for Beatrice's final performance is the judicial court—an extra-theatrical world which is itself a kind of theatre. Truth is not its concern. The court, proceeding by torture rather than by investigation, relies on confession and the display of personality under stress as the theatre does. If this is indeed 'the scene of the world' then Beatrice's impersonation of an innocent woman commends itself to our imagination in the theatre (which always depends upon good performances) as the best thing possible in the world

[19] See the notes to *Longman* for the major ones (except for the allusion to *King John*). Also see Bates, *A Study of Shelley's Drama*, 55 n. 2; D. L. Clark, 'Shelley and Shakespeare', *PMLA* 54 (1939), 277–86; Beach Langston, 'Shelley's Use of Shakespeare', *Huntington Library Quarterly* 12.2 (1949), 163–90; Sara R. Watson, 'Shelley and Shakespeare: An Addendum; a Comparison of *Othello* and *The Cenci*', *PMLA* 55 (1940), 611–14; Frederick L. Jones, 'Shelley and Shakespeare: A Supplement', *PMLA* 59 (1944), 591–6.

as the play presents it, if not to our suspended moral sense. This is why the play can sweep to its masterly conclusion where Shelley transforms a detail from III. iv of *King John*. There Constance enters '*distracted, with her hair about her ears*' (16–17), is asked by King Philip to bind it up, which she does, and then unbinds it to match the 'disorder in my wit' (102). Beatrice, by contrast, asks her mother to bind her hair for her and offers to do the same for her mother. This ritualized 'holy act' before execution is also presented as a normal and typical act of feminine life ('How often | Have we done this for one another!' (V. iv. 163–4)), much as Emilia's undressing of Desdemona the night before her murder (*Othello*, IV. iii) represents gentle, settled, feminine habits. The sequence which concludes *The Cenci* is always praised, and rightly so, for in combining a perfect ritualized action, immediately before heads are brutally severed, with a comely domestic feminine act, we are left with an implicit answer to the question that otherwise would bother us: if good performance is the only available value in the play why should that of Beatrice be superior to that of her father?

Performance in *The Cenci* is mainly a matter of words, apart from Cenci's invitation to a banquet, and Beatrice's use of her physical presence and compelling eyes. A particularly telling image here is Orsino's acknowledgement that Beatrice's image, 'as the hunter some struck deer | Follows me' (I. ii. 12–13). Orsino uses a similar figure at the end of the scene ('I were a fool, not less than if a panther | Were panic-stricken by the antelope's eye, | If she escape me' (I. ii. 89–91)). The image of the antelope, however ludicrous the possibility, is imagined as causing panic. It would be foolish to be subdued by Beatrice's 'awe-inspiring gaze', for she is only 'A friendless girl' (I. ii. 84, 87); nevertheless, the weak girl, like the weak antelope, may paralyse a wilful consciousness. Beatrice is in the position of the hunter in the first simile and the hunted animal in the second so she has both active and passive power over tyrant Pope, father, and would-be seducer even though she is struck (raped) and killed (executed) by them. Shelley uses the same image of himself in *Adonais* (33, 297) for pathos in the manner of Cowper, but associated with power in passivity, for he compares himself to Christ (34, 306). It underlies, too, Hope's transformation from stricken victim to conqueror in *The Mask of Anarchy*. The end of *The Cenci* sustains it in a yet bleaker world where Beatrice abandons and denounces Hope.

The play concludes with an ordinary act which no longer exists in its ordinary private context. It is now performed in public. The audience on stage know that it is the prelude to the end of all Beatrice's performances. The audience in the auditorium instantly recognize that it is the last scene of the play itself. Its positioning reifies, as the play's final word, the gentleness that Beatrice (and women) sustain over against the world of arbitrary authority, sexual violence, and torture masquerading as justice that the play has presented as 'the world'. Cenci's is an unmistakably extreme performance of the norms of that world. His actions and his performance are of a piece. But Beatrice is able to separate performance from action. Macbeth is exalted by his double sense of exaltation by an external Fate and his curious mixture of awe and desolation at the spectacle of his interior. The former exaltation can and will be taken from him and thus the gap between his act and his being will finally be closed off. Beatrice's initial separation occurs because of her rape and her refusal publicly to acknowledge it but her inner authority, unlike

Macbeth's, has no outside source. It is generated in the mysterious place of silence from which she emerges as consummate performer, innocent whatever she does. She is as much aware that her exaltation depends upon her performance as her audience on and off stage is. For this reason, whilst Macbeth can persuade no one of his innocence, Beatrice can persuade almost everyone. It is almost like Luther's idea of justification by faith where the old criminal Adam, whilst remaining a criminal, is rendered wholly innocent by another new Adam. Since, in Beatrice's case, she is both 'an actor and a suf-ferer' (*Longman*, 2, 735), this exalted other is also herself.

Shelley's dramas offer a possible scenario of a wholly transformed world. Shelley's theatre can offer no such vision but, instead, offers a salvific performance which only the theatre could make visible. I am using 'salvific' in the same strange way that Shelley talks about imagination's redemptive assumption of flesh in his Preface. Outside the theatre (and the imagination) this salvation 'saves' no one, but Shelley offers it as his equivalent to an incarnation that of itself redeems 'mortal passion'. In this way, Beatrice's assertion 'Ay, something must be done' (III. i. 86), which, in the first instance, foreshadows the ugly act of murder, is reclaimed at the end of the play for this perfectly performed inter-play that displaces power based on physical violence by a triumphing courtesy depend-ent on gentleness. It is both curious and instructive that Iona Taurina is also shown '*tucking up her hair*' (*Longman*, 3, 709) as she leaps onto the back of the minotaur and sallies out to defeat Swellfoot the Tyrant and his crew. Beatrice triumphs over tyranny and death by her gracefully sustained actions in the face of her inability to defeat them.

I have left one major emphasis out of this account. For whom are Beatrice and Cenci performing? For a theatre audience of course, yet they are not consciously in a theatre but standing in the scene of the world. Theatre audiences authorize and expect perform-ances but 'the world' as such cannot authorize them. Beatrice and Cenci are quite explicit as to who does so. The author of their performance and their ability to perform is God. Here I part company with Margot Harrison who says: 'Christianity provides an unim-peachable script for the drama of her vengeance' and, even more bafflingly, 'the articles of the Catholic faith are visible [*sic*] presented'.[20] Harrison is wrong, surely, to imagine that virtually any paid-up Christian of 1599 or any other time would imagine that God authorizes parricide, the wish that one's children be dead, or a delight in the exultant exercise as opposed to the patient abnegation of the will. Cenci thinks like atheist Marlowe's Tamburlaine ('I that am term'd the Scourge and Wrath of God'),[21] not the his-torical Pope Clement VIII. Harrison points to a real problem, however. Neither histori-cal context nor the presumptions of a later audience will render credible Cenci's and Beatrice's confidence that they act as God's agents. Beatrice describes her moment of change in these terms:

[20] Harrison, 'Beatrice Cenci and the Dilemma of Romantic Performance', 198, 197.
[21] *Tamburlaine*, Part One, III. iii. 44. Christopher Marlowe, *The Complete Plays*, ed. J. B. Steane (Harmondsworth: Penguin, 1969), 142. Beatrice uses the same word to justify her killing: 'The God who knew my wrong, and made | Our speedy act the angel of His wrath' (V. iii. 114–15), and Giacomo says that his father presented himself as 'God's scourge' (III. i. 316).

> I have prayed
> To God, and I have talked with my own heart,
> And have unravelled my entangled will,
> And have at length determined what is right.
>
> (III. i. 218–21)

We know that this means that she has resolved to have her father killed; no audience thinks that she has in fact talked to God (no actress would look upwards or momentarily fall to their knees during Beatrice's withdrawal *absorbed in thought*). It is the absolute and new authority in her ego ('I', 'I', 'my') which alone has 'determined what is right' that is apparent. Beatrice is closer to stanza 16 of 'Ode to Liberty' where the poet looks to a world without priesthood in which 'human thoughts might kneel alone | Each before the judgement-throne | Of its own aweless soul, or of the power unknown' (231–3) than she is to prayer. She has used an idea of God to authorize the course of action that she has herself decided upon in her obligingly complaisant 'mist of thoughts'. Her presumption is performed as assertion and so she believes it herself. What she says is not true, but that does not matter, for the play is neither concerned with historical exactitude nor truth. Instead an idea of God is a property within the play within the consciousness of Beatrice and Cenci. 'God' authorizes for them the privileged nature of their performances which, in turn, can infect others to make the same recognition. This is created theatrical fact rather than authorization by historical reference ('this is how people thought in 1599'). It enables Shelley to elevate Cenci from melodramatic villain into a force that only Beatrice and the audience can understand so long as the play lasts.

Cenci's God persists but Beatrice's does not. Like her father, she expects God to vindicate her immediately but is haunted by the idea that God will abandon her (II. i. 16) or does not exist (III. i. 100). When the execution is certain, her mother tells her to trust 'in God's sweet love' (V. iv. 75), but Beatrice replies that neither God nor anything else appears to undo injustice 'as regarded me' (V. iv. 84). There may be no one else to trust except God but 'my heart is cold' (V. iv. 89), and she makes a lengthy speech recommending hopelessness (V. iv. 96–120). This means that she now has to author her own performance and the play's conclusion. In her final two speeches she shows that her heart is not cold for she says farewell to 'my tender brother', maintains her exquisite courtesy to Camillo ('Give yourself no unnecessary pain, | My dear Lord Cardinal' (V. iv. 158–9)), which is witty since it precedes her own necessary pain, and then engages in the delicate by-play with her own and mother's hair. For the first time in the play, her performance in her own 'unblinking eye' as well as ours stands on its own in a blank and Godless universe which cannot be transformed.[22] Here, nevertheless, she continues to assert through religious vocabulary what that performance has always asserted:

> the faith that I
> Though wrapped in a strange cloud of crime and shame,
> Lived ever holy and unstained.
>
> (V. iv. 147–9)

---

[22] Stuart Curran's nice phrase in 'Shelleyan Drama', 75.

Beatrice paraphrases and clarifies, as it were, Shelley's own Preface ('the crimes and miseries in which she was an actor and sufferer are as the mask and mantle in which circumstances clothed her for her impersonation on the scene of the world'). She declares this to be a 'faith' by which she means a salvific truth asserted against the perceived facts. This still depends upon a 'strange cloud' which is heir to the 'undistinguishable mist' that enables her transformation.

It is hard to imagine anything more moving than the moment in the twenty-second Book of the *Iliad* when Hector discovers that what he thought to be the presence of a friend helping him to fight Achilles was a deception mounted by Athena so that, bereft of all human aid and divine presence, he is absolutely alone to face a ghastly and humiliating death. Unlike Macbeth, he gains stature and the scene gains pathos by his bearing in this last abandonment. Macbeth of course is exalted by his increasing desolation and isolation throughout the play but not by his discoveries that one by one all his miraculous gifts of preservation are mere tricks by 'juggling fiends' (V. x. 19). His death therefore is wholly unexalted. Shelley achieves a similar effect to the death of Hector through elevating domestic feminine acts into an equivalent heroism. Stuart Curran helpfully characterizes the play's 'self-reflexiveness' as 'watchful, cautionary' rather than 'playful',[23] but the final scene of the play has an austere playfulness as its final word.

What is present in but left out of the centre of *The Cenci*—sub-plots, contingency, minor characters, and the recalcitrance of history—is placed at the centre of *Charles the First*. Charles I, Marvell's 'royal actor' on the 'tragic scaffold',[24] is gentle in himself but implicated in violence. He will be called upon to give a performance which will be analogous to that given in the opening masque. The masque observed by a plebeian crowd exterior to it confirms the customary Shakespearian parallel between life and stage as the Second Citizen points out (I. 35–6; quoted from *H*). Its aesthetic is in contrast with the ugly anti-masque of recalcitrant 'reality' ('which serve as discords do | In sweetest music' (I. 175–6)).

But Shelley submits to his Holinshed in this play far more than he does in *The Cenci*. R. B. Woodings has shown how carefully Shelley had read a number of sources but was most influenced by David Hume's sympathetic account of Charles and his circle, except in the characterization of Laud.[25] As a result, he produces a text openly imitating chameleon Shakespeare in its reliance on divergences of opinion and character. Shelley's submission to historical facts is duplicated in his play by Charles's powerlessness in the face of events and confident surrounding opinions. Shelley's dramatization of himself as Julian, subjected to the more powerfully articulated opinions of Byron as Maddalo, is a parallel instance. Charles is, presumably, to be somewhere between Beatrice and Sultan Mahmud. He is both an innocent performer authorized by God and a helpless, but implicated and guilty, observer of unpalatable contingencies and forces more powerful

---

[23] Ibid. 77.

[24] 'An Horatian Ode upon Cromwell's Return from Ireland', 53, 54, in *Andrew Marvell*, ed. Frank Kermode and Keith Walker (Oxford: Oxford UP, 1990), 83.

[25] R. B. Woodings, 'Shelley's Sources for *Charles the First*', *Modern Language Review* 64 (1969), 267–75.

than he is. How this would have been worked out is unclear and it seems likely that Shelley could not sustain the energy to represent a world so wholly resistant to his preferred version of it. Nora Crook, who accepts the relation between *Charles the First* and *The Triumph of Life*, vigorously contests the view that the play was unfinished simply because in it 'Shelley was at war with his own convictions' and says that Vane would have been his exemplar.[26] Vane might well have been exemplary but surely Shelley would seek to avoid evidently privileged voices in a work designed for the theatre?

What succeeds in *The Cenci* cannot succeed here, for Charles's performance cannot be separated from his actions (he is a weak patriarchal king rather than a strong victim of patriarchal rape); nor can a comeliness in his actions prior to a bloody but ritualized execution be left as some kind of equivalent to Beatrice's final salvific authority of word and gesture in performance. This is to surmise, of course, that the play would have ended, as *The Cenci* does, with Charles's trial and death. This is probable, for the presence of Archy as court fool makes Charles into a Lear figure and Act II was to have ended 'with Parliament in the ascendant and the execution of Strafford for treason'.[27] What is so striking is the whole-heartedness with which Shelley approaches an actual political scene whose outcome would not appeal to him, and attempts to show in purely theatrical terms and on Shakespeare's scale (the first two acts represent seven years) the distinctions and crossovers between action and performance, power and powerlessness, that always intrigued him.

I have argued that Shelley's conscious move to the theatre makes him substitute the distinction between performance and action for that between action and transformation customary in his dramas and much of his poetry. Yet this discloses the extent to which all of Shelley's poems depend upon privileging performance to a greater or lesser extent. Obvious examples are the utilization of the performer's breath to enact the fitful energy of the West Wind, or to initiate the last stanza of *Adonais*, the theatrical transition from ecstatic power to powerlessness in the last five lines of *Epipsychidion*, and Shelley's self-dramatization as Julian and as 'one frail Form' (*Adonais*, 31, 271). 'Letter to Maria Gisborne' is an *improvvisatore*'s performance for its private recipient; the last three stanzas of *Adonais* are a carefully scripted one for the public. In 'With a Guitar. To Jane', Shelley offers a performance of himself as Shakespeare's Ariel to Jane Williams as Miranda who lives with him in a world of role-play based on the theatre. The implied dream-island setting of the lyric suggests that Shelley's *Epipsychidion* too, though sourced to Dante, is an extended performance for the reader which depends upon Teresa Viviani, like Jane Williams, already accepting the dramatic role that Shelley has assigned her.

Such a crossover works in miniature and on a large scale. Beatrice's 'mask and mantle' are transferred in *A Defence of Poetry* to great poets for 'The distorted notions of invisible things which Dante and his rival Milton have idealised, are merely the mask and mantle in which these great poets walk through eternity enveloped and disguised'

[26] Nora Crook, 'Shelley's Late Fragmentary Plays: "Charles the First" and the "Unfinished Drama"', in Weinberg and Webb (eds.), *The Unfamiliar Shelley*, 311, 299. Also see her 'Calumniated Republicans and the Hero of Shelley's "Charles the First"', *Keats–Shelley Journal* 56 (2007), 141–58.
[27] Crook, 'Shelley's Late Fragmentary Plays', 298.

(*Norton* 1, 526). The later text illuminates the early one. Beatrice's 'impersonation on the scene of the world' parallels Dante and Milton's 'walk through eternity enveloped and disguised'. They do so, for Shelley, because the immortal purity of their verse is wrapped up in Christian ideological dressing. They are real not in this but in the shaping of their works which, despite their tainted but accidental clothing, remain untainted. In exactly the same way, therefore, Beatrice, who is clothed in 'crimes and miseries', retains an untainted character not in some inner self which can be anatomized, but in her acting performance which upholds a realized ideal. In this she claims and acquires a 'holy and unstained' (V. iv. 149) character just as Dante and Milton 'walk through eternity'.

Shelley does not put Shakespeare with Dante and Milton here, because Shakespeare, as chameleon dramatist, does not idealize 'distorted notions of invisible things'. Yet Shakespearian and Shelleyan theatre does show performers who are analogous to these poets. His use of the word 'impersonate' in the dedication of *The Cenci* is a striking clue to his realization of this. His own poems have merely impersonated 'my own apprehensions of the beautiful and just' (*Longman*, 2, 725). He turns now to 'sad reality' where he, as author, will have to impersonate 'passions which I had never participated in' (*Letters: PBS* II, 189) but there, of course, places an actress as Beatrice who is impersonator of 'the beautiful and just' in the centre of a London theatre. The young Shelley, we recall, had 'dressed in strange costumes to personate spirits or fiends', later rejected Kean's theatrical personation, but then sought it out. His essay into Shakespearian theatre was designed to bring together what he had separated: poetical integrity and theatrical performance.

Select Bibliography

Bates, Ernest Sutherland. *A Study of Shelley's Drama, The Cenci*. New York: Columbia UP, 1908.

Blood, Roger. 'Allegory and Dramatic Representation in *The Cenci*'. *Studies in Romanticism* 33.3 (1994), 355–89.

Clark, D. L. 'Shelley and Shakespeare'. *PMLA* 54 (1939), 277–86.

Crook, Nora. 'Shelley's Late Fragmentary Plays: "Charles the First" and the "Unfinished Drama"'. *The Unfamiliar Shelley*. Ed. Alan M. Weinberg and Timothy Webb. Farnham: Ashgate, 2009. 297–312.

Cox, Jeffrey N. 'The Dramatist'. *The Cambridge Companion to Shelley*. Ed. Timothy Morton. Cambridge: Cambridge UP, 2006. 65–84.

Curran, Stuart. *Shelley's Cenci: Scorpions Ringed with Fire.* Princeton: Princeton UP, 1970.

Donohue, Joseph W., Jr. *Dramatic Character in the English Romantic Age*. Princeton: Princeton UP, 1970.

Erkelenz, Michael. 'The Genre and Politics of Shelley's *Swellfoot the Tyrant*'. *Review of English Studies* 47.188 (1996), 500–20.

Moody, Jane. 'Romantic Shakespeare'. *The Cambridge Companion to Shakespeare on Stage*. Ed. Stanley Wells and Sarah Stanton. Cambridge: Cambridge UP, 2002. 37–57.

Morton, Timothy. 'Porcine Poetics: Shelley's *Swellfoot the Tyrant*'. *The Unfamiliar Shelley*. Ed. Alan M. Weinberg and Timothy Webb. Farnham: Ashgate, 2009. 279–96.

Richardson, Alan. *A Mental Theater: Poetic Drama and Consciousness in the Romantic Age.* University Park, PA: Penn State UP, 1988.

Rossington, Michael. 'Shakespeare in *The Cenci*: Tragedy and "Familiar Imagery"'. *Shakespearean Continuities: Essays in Honour of E. A. J. Honigmann.* Ed. John Batchelor, Tom Cain, and Claire Lamont. Basingstoke: Macmillan, 1997. 305–18.

Tetreault, Ronald. 'Shelley at the Opera'. *English Literary History* 48 (1981), 144–71.

Thomson, Peter. 'Acting and Actors from Garrick to Kean'. *The Cambridge Companion to British Theatre, 1730–1830.* Ed. Jane Moody and Daniel O'Quinn. Cambridge: Cambridge UP, 2007. 3–19.

Woodings, R. B. 'A Devil of a Nut to Crack: Shelley's *Charles the First*'. *Studia Neophilologica* 11 (1968), 216–37.

Worton, Michael 'Speech and Silence in *The Cenci*'. *Essays on Shelley.* Ed. Miriam Allott. Liverpool: Liverpool UP, 1982. 105–24.

CHAPTER 35

....

SHELLEY, THE VISUAL ARTS, AND CINEMA

....

SARAH WOOTTON

SHELLEY is commonly regarded as a poet of *vision*, an aesthetic and/or political *visionary*. The importance of the *visual* in Shelley's poetry and prose, and the visual reception of his work, has, by contrast, received less attention. Two poems by Shelley that respond directly to works of art, the sonnet 'Ozymandias' and the fragment 'On the Medusa of Leonardo in the Florentine Gallery', provide the focus for much of the criticism that has emerged on this topic. For example, Neville Rogers's article 'Shelley and the Visual Arts' is concerned with establishing Shelley's 'vivid' sense of the visual through an analysis of 'On the Medusa'.[1] Shelley's ekphrastic poems have also been read alongside those of John Keats, most notably 'Ode on a Grecian Urn' and 'On Seeing the Elgin Marbles', which serves to highlight a discrepancy in the literature on these Romantic poets.[2] While Keats's visual legacy has been the subject of ongoing scholarship, illustrations to and paintings of Shelley's work have gone largely unnoticed.[3] Similarly, the interest in Byron's cultural heritage, particularly as it relates to film and adaptation, has yet to take hold in Shelley studies. This chapter examines the significance of the visual arts in Shelley's own

[1] Neville Rogers, 'Shelley and the Visual Arts', *Keats–Shelley Memorial Bulletin* 12 (1961), 8–17 (11). Following Rogers's lead, Shelley's poem has been the subject of various critical and theoretical approaches. See, among others, Grant F. Scott, 'Shelley, Medusa, and the Perils of Ekphrasis', in Frederick Burwick and Jürgen Klein (eds.), *The Romantic Imagination: Literature and Art in England and Germany* (Amsterdam: Rodopi, 1996), 315–32; William Hildebrand, 'Self, Beauty and Horror: Shelley's Medusa Moment', in G. Kim Blank (ed.), *The New Shelley: Later Twentieth-Century Views* (Basingstoke: Macmillan, 1991), 150–65; and Carol Jacobs, 'On Looking at Shelley's Medusa', *Yale French Studies* 69 (1985), 163–79.

[2] Grant F. Scott regards Shelley's 'On the Medusa' as the nightmarish culmination of the portrait poem and offers the following comparison with Keats's 'Ode on a Grecian Urn': 'The urn teases rather than accosts the speaker and prefers to engage him in a more civil form of rivalry.' See *The Sculpted Word: Keats, Ekphrasis and the Visual Arts* (Hanover, NH: University Press of New England, 1994), 132.

[3] See, among others, George H. Ford, *Keats and the Victorians: A Study of his Influence and Rise to Fame 1821–1895* (London: Archon Books, 1962); and Sarah Wootton, *Consuming Keats: Nineteenth-Century Representations in Art and Literature* (Basingstoke: Palgrave, 2006).

work and subsequently explores his continued creative presence in a wide range of artistic media. Section I is concerned with Shelley's descriptions of Italian sculpture and painting, and will concentrate on the often overlooked *Notes on Sculptures in Rome and Florence* and Shelley's letters to Thomas Love Peacock; section II will explore some, although by no means all, of the artwork that has been inspired by his poetry; section III will focus on Shelley's afterlife on screen.

I

Rogers declares, in the article mentioned above, that 'When Shelley went into a Florentine picture gallery the Renaissance came under the appraising eye of one of its most illustrious sons and heirs.'[4] Apart from the opening descriptions of the Arch of Titus and *Laocoön and his Sons* in Rome, the *Notes on Sculptures in Rome and Florence*, as they have come to be known, are the result of Shelley's frequent visits to the Uffizi gallery during the period between mid-October and mid-November 1819.[5] In a letter to Maria Gisborne, Shelley records:

> I have seen little of Florence. The gallery I have a design of studying piece-meal, one of my chief aims in Italy being the observing in statuary and painting the degree in which & the rules according to which that ideal beauty of which we have so intense yet so obscure an apprehension is realized in external forms.[6]

Shelley enthuses over the sculptures in the Uffizi, describing *Bacchus and Ampelus*, in note 53, as 'A lovely group', but he can be equally cutting; an urn is dismissed as 'over-sculptured' while 'Leda' is merely 'A dull thing'.[7] As Jennifer Wallace comments, Shelley is 'eager to avoid [...] passive admiration', and is not governed, commendably so, by popular tastes; he omits those celebrated sculptures, such as the *Venus de' Medici*, that ranked highly on the list of attractions for eighteenth- and nineteenth-century visitors, concentrating instead on lesser-known works.[8]

Whereas Shelley sets himself apart from travel writers of the period, deeming their 'show-knowledge' to be 'the common stuff of the earth', the poet's zeal for Greek sculpture accords well with Johann Joachim Winckelmann's influential theories on

⁴ Rogers, 'Shelley and the Visual Arts', 16.

⁵ Buxton Forman published sixty notes, under the title *Notes on Sculptures in Rome and Florence*, in a limited issue of 1879 and then again in 1880. No manuscript of the notebook survives, and E. B. Murray argues that what Forman published was based, 'in all likelihood', on 'a Claire Clairmont notebook' with relevant transcriptions by her. See E. B. Murray, 'Shelley's *Notes on Sculptures*: The Provenance and Authority of the Text', *Keats–Shelley Journal* 32 (1983), 150–71 (150).

⁶ *Letters: PBS* II, 126.

⁷ *Notes on Sculptures in Rome and Florence*, in *The Complete Works of Percy Bysshe Shelley*, ed. Roger Ingpen and Walter E. Peck, 10 vols. (London: Benn, 1965), VI, 328, 313, 320. Subsequent references to the *Notes on Sculptures* are given in the text.

⁸ Jennifer Wallace, *Shelley and Greece: Rethinking Romantic Hellenism* (Basingstoke: Macmillan, 1997), 161.

the subject.[9] A recurring emphasis on drapery and delicacy attests to Shelley's familiarity with Winckelmann's work, as does the priority accorded to a noble or 'ideal beauty'. Winckelmann's belief that 'perfect' beauty could exist in art is reflected in Shelley's motives for studying the sculptures in the Uffizi, as quoted in the paragraph above, and such comments as 'the Bacchus is immortal beauty' in the notes themselves (320). Daniel Hughes claims that Shelley's interest in the visual arts was restricted to 'archetypes [...] the suggestiveness and ideality of images themselves'.[10] However, in disregarding Shelley's *Notes on Sculptures* to concentrate on the Medusa poem, Hughes overlooks the poet's complex views on beauty. Shelley is as concerned with 'lifelike' representations as he is with ideals; of *Thetis*, for example, he states: 'the face far from idealism seems to be a real face of much energy and goodness' (326). Conversely, a statue of Venus, described in note 38, is deemed to be admirable, and has 'great perfection and beauty of form', but, crucially, lacks feeling (325). Shelley's reflections on beauty are a defining feature of the *Notes on Sculptures*, yet they are neither prescriptive nor limited to received notions of an ideal.

Shelley's responses to classical sculpture are remarkable for their lack of reverence. A parenthetical aside in his description of 'An Athlete', 'Curse these fig leaves; why is a round tin thing more decent than a cylindrical marble one?' (315), demonstrates the 'unstuffy attitude' that Timothy Webb sees as characteristic of the poet's interest in Greek art and literature, while the description of statue 54 is refreshingly down to earth: 'Leda with a very ugly face. I should be a long time before I should make love with her' (329).[11] Shelley can be coolly detached in one appraisal and passionately evocative in the next. Note 2, a description of *Laocoön and his Sons* in the Vatican, illustrates Frederick S. Colwell's praise for Shelley's 'candid and spontaneous reactions to works of art'.[12] For Shelley, initially recalling Lessing, the subject of the *Laocoön* is a 'disagreeable one', but it is a 'miracle of sculpture' (310–11). It is the human drama, the relationship between the father and his sons, that animates the sculpture for Shelley and that he, in turn, reanimates through his prose. The 'father's love' is similarly a feature of Byron's stanza on this statue in canto IV of *Childe Harold's Pilgrimage*, and his line on the 'Laocoön's torture dignifying pain' is echoed in Shelley's description of 'a majesty that dignifies torture'.[13] However,

[9] Letter to Thomas Love Peacock dated 23 March 1819. The edition of Peacock's letters referred to is *Peacock's Memoirs of Shelley with Shelley's Letters to Peacock*, ed. H. F. B. Brett-Smith (London: Henry Frowde, 1909). Subsequent references to these letters are dated in the text. For a more detailed discussion of Winckelmann's theories about Greek art and their influence on Shelley, see Timothy Webb, 'Romantic Hellenism', in Stuart Curran (ed.), *The Cambridge Companion to British Romanticism* (Cambridge: Cambridge UP, 1993), 148–76.

[10] Daniel Hughes, 'Shelley, Leonardo, and the Monsters of Thought', *Criticism* 12.3 (1970), 195. Hughes makes some interesting connections between Shelley and Leonardo da Vinci, most notably Leonardo's Deluge Drawings, Shelley's sketches and Act IV of *Prometheus Unbound*, despite the doubtful provenance of the painting in the Uffizi.

[11] Timothy Webb, *Shelley: A Voice Not Understood* (Manchester: Manchester UP, 1977), 192.

[12] Frederic S. Colwell, 'Shelley on Sculpture: The Uffizi Notes', *Keats–Shelley Journal* 28 (1979), 59.

[13] Lord George Gordon Byron, *Childe Harold's Pilgrimage*, IV. 160, 1433, *Lord Byron: The Major Works*, ed. Jerome J. McGann, Oxford World's Classics (Oxford: Oxford UP, 2000), 194.

Shelley takes issue with Byron's fusion of mortal and immortal traits in the principal figure, discerning, instead, the subtle emotions conveyed by the younger son, 'surprise, pain, and grief seem to contend for mastery', and the immediacy of the effect: 'We almost seem to hear his shrieks'. He is also attuned to the intricacies of the *Laocoön* and admires its 'anatomical fidelity and force', despite elsewhere castigating the study of anatomy: 'Every limb, every muscle, every vein of Laocoön expresses, with the fidelity of life, the working of the poison, and the strained girding round of the inextricable folds, whose tangling sinuosities are too numerous and complicated to be followed.'[14]

Shelley's appreciation of Greek literature as 'endlessly potential, a rich matrix of energizing possibilities rather than a rigid pantheon of unrivalled perfections' is equally apparent in his descriptions of Greek art.[15] The poet is most impressive when responding to works, like *Laocoön and his Sons* and *A Statue of Minerva*, where the fusion of intense feelings, the interconnectedness of sorrow, pain, and joy, can make 'grief beautiful' (322). What Shelley refers to as the 'poetic harmony of marble' (331) is palpable in note 29:

> The flowing fulness and roundness of the breast and belly, whose lines fading into each other, are continued with a gentle motion as it were to the utmost extremity of his limbs. Like some fine strain of harmony which flows round the soul and enfolds it, and leaves it in the soft astonishment of a satisfaction, like the pleasure of love with one whom we most love, which having taken away desire, leaves pleasure, sweet pleasure. (319–20)

In this instance, Shelley's focus on the fluid lines of the sculpture leads seamlessly into abstract meditations on love. The appreciation of a telling artistic detail is often the most rewarding, for Shelley, in terms of philosophical contemplation. The poet's sensitivity to movement, in particular, breathes life into the inanimate sculpture; the impression of their 'delicate and flowing forms', mentioned earlier in the same note, prompts a lively and imaginative vision of the figures conversing as they saunter along. In terms of form, Shelley duly notes the contrasting lines in 'Vasa Borghese A Parigi', for instance, and rejects attempts at restoration as 'villainous'.[16] Yet in his last note, a description of *The Niobe*, Shelley demonstrates both his command and reassessment of technical excellence. The figure's beauty is so affecting that it transcends the medium through which it is conveyed—it is 'beyond any effect of sculpture'—while the dimensions of the work, and the perspectives from which it can be viewed, intensify its 'potential' or 'energizing possibilities' which allow 'the spectator the choice of a greater number of points of view, in which to catch a greater number of the infinite modes of expression of which any form approaching ideal beauty is necessarily composed' (330).

Shelley's responses to other visual arts, including Italian painting, are recorded in letters written principally between April 1818 and April 1819 to his close friend the novelist

---

[14] Byron also fixes on the 'strain | And gripe' of the old man battling, in vain, with the snake.

[15] Webb, *Shelley: A Voice Not Understood*, 204. Shelley is unconstrained in the *Notes on Sculpture* by Lessing's ideological objections to *ut pictura poesis*.

[16] See *Julian*, III, 311. Shelley's contempt for restoration is evident in notes 19, 21, and 24.

Thomas Love Peacock. The letters 'comprise a unique collection within the Shelley canon that', according to Benjamin Colbert, 'has received very little attention'.[17] Such neglect is curious given the insights these letters offer into Shelley's imaginative sensibilities and the composition of such seminal works as *Prometheus Unbound*. This poem was informed by Shelley's response to the marble statues in the Uffizi and, as the poet tells us, was 'chiefly written upon the mountainous ruins of the Baths of Caracalla, among the flowery glades, and thickets of odoriferous blossoming trees, which are extended in ever widening labyrinths upon its immense platforms and dizzy arches suspended in the air', a scene also described in a letter to Peacock dated 23 March 1819.[18] Shelley is captivated by the Italian scenes and art he experiences long before his visits to the Uffizi in Florence. In a letter from Rome, dated 20 November 1818, Shelley enthuses about Spoleto, 'the most romantic city I ever saw', and the aqueduct that provides an unrivalled vista ('I never saw a more impressive picture'). The appreciative tone of his letters does not render his impressions undiscerning or predictable, however. Towards the end of the letter in which Shelley responds, in moving terms, to the solemn site of the Protestant Cemetery, he is struck by the treasures of Naples, Herculaneum, and Pompeii, yet he also records earlier misgivings: a tour around the Bay of Baiae leaves the poet feeling flat, even though it is mentioned in *The Sensitive Plant* and inspires the line on 'a pumice isle' in 'Ode to the West Wind' (32), and his introduction to Naples is marred by witnessing a fatal assault (22 December 1818).

While Shelley admits to a 'propensity to admire', he is equally anxious that his recollections should not appear trite (23 March 1819). In Rome, the poet seeks to distance himself from fellow travellers: 'The tourists tell you all about these things, and I am afraid of stumbling on their language when I enumerate what is so well known' (23 March 1819). Nevertheless, although he confesses to having forgotten the names of the places and works of art he has seen, paintings by Guido Reni and Raphael, among others, make an impression. Shelley is struck by images that evoke complex and, sometimes, conflicting feelings, such as Guido's depiction of Samson; here, the poet focuses on a defeated Philistine 'with the slight convulsion of pain just passing from his forehead, whilst on his lips and chin death lies heavy as sleep' (9 November 1818). As well as prizing Raphael's *The Ecstasy of St Cecilia* for a 'unity and perfection […] of an incommunicable kind', Shelley also deflects attention onto the figure of St John, 'languid with the depth of his emotion'. The 'ideal' beauty of the Raphael captivates the poet, yet he is also drawn to that which is strange and even grotesque in art. In response to Guercino's *Madonna Bambino san Bruno*, Shelley observes the contrast between the heavenly host of Virgin and Child with accompanying angels and the shrivelled figure of St Bruno in a robe of 'yellow, putrefied, ghastly hue'.

There are, for Shelley, some religious works where artistry is diminished by the subject matter. The poet's aversion to Michelangelo is evident in his description of 'A Bacchus by

[17] Benjamin Colbert, *Shelley's Eye: Travel Writing and Aesthetic Vision* (Aldershot: Ashgate, 2005), 118.

[18] *Major Works*, 230.

Michael Angelo' in the *Notes on Sculptures*, 'the most revolting mistake of the spirit and meaning of Bacchus' (329), and in his thoughts on *Moses*, a statue that is 'distorted from all that is natural and majestic' (25 February 1819). Of *The Last Judgement*, Shelley writes 'I cannot but think the genius of this artist highly overrated [...] he has no sense of beauty'. However, the perceived moral deficiency of the work does not prevent Shelley from warming to the fresco as he traces the various methods of torture depicted and responds to the energy of acute suffering. In his evocation of this hellish scene, the product of what he concedes is a 'great imagination', Shelley rises to some of the most vivid poetry in the letters—for instance, 'The blood-red light of the fiery abyss glows through their dark forms.' It is testament to the intensity of his feelings for this work that Shelley passes over some 'very sweet and lovely' paintings by Raphael, Titian, and Guido immediately afterwards.

In addition to his responses to Italian painting, Shelley's letters to Peacock are concerned with Italian landscapes and architecture. With regards to the former, Shelley often perceives the landscape as a work of art. The scene of a waterfall is wrought by a rock 'precisely resembling some colossal Egyptian statue of a female deity', which directs the flow and visual effect of the water (22 July 1816). As is evident in the sketches that adorn his notebooks, Shelley has an eye for shapes; the 'irregular spires' of some pine trees, 'pyramidal crags', and the fractured surface of a glacier, 'broken into a thousand unaccountable figures', are instances of what he later refers to as the 'inequality and irregularity of form [...] requisite to force on us the relative idea of greatness' (22 July 1816; 25 February 1819).[19] A preoccupation with form, space, light, and texture recurs throughout the letters and comes to the fore in the 'View from the Pitti Palace' in the *Notes on Sculptures*. A further parallel between the notes and the letters is the significance of movement and sound to an appreciation of the scene. Shelley is inspired, in equal measure, by gentle motions, 'the late leaves of autumn shiver and rustle in the stream of the inconstant wind, as it were, like the step of ghosts' (26 January 1819), and the constant yet changing noise of the Velino at the *Cascata delle Marmore*.

Shelley's reactions to Italian architecture, most notably what he sees in the capital, lead to the excited exclamations: 'Come to Rome'; 'Rome is yet the capital of the world' (23 March 1819). Among the many sites he visits, Shelley's response to the Arch of Titus, included in the *Notes on Sculptures*, employs a semantic field of reference inflected with the violent acts depicted on the reliefs ('the fury of conflagrations', for instance, 309). The conflict between admiring architecture and condemning the Roman Emperor commemorated similarly arises in a description of the Arch of Constantine, but does not

---

[19] Shelley's fixation with form emerges in the many dynamic, and often curious, sketches of trees, boats, profiles, architecture, and landscapes in his notebooks. Of the reiterative visual trope of trees—be they abstract or naturalistic, marginal or elaborate—it is the shape of the leaves and the contours of the canopy that seem to hold the poet's interest. This proliferation of tree images indicates an organic interplay between drawing and drafting that is discussed at greater length in Nancy Moore Goslee, 'Shelley at Play: A Study of Sketch and Text in His "Prometheus" Notebooks', *Huntington Library Quarterly* 48 (1985), 211–55, and Neville Rogers, *Shelley at Work: A Critical Inquiry* (Oxford: Clarendon Press, 1956).

feature in a description of the Colosseum immediately before. The emphasis in both this letter, dated 22 December 1818, and a prose fragment entitled *The Coliseum*, begun 25 November 1818, is on the amphitheatre as ruin.[20] Shelley's letter details, in terms almost identical to Helen's account of the Colosseum in the work of that name, a process of Nature reclaiming the shattered forms and chasms of this once man-made structure:

> It has been changed by time into the image of an amphitheatre of rocky hills over-grown by the wild olive, the myrtle, and the fig-tree, and threaded by little paths, which wind among its ruined stairs and immeasurable galleries: the copsewood overshadows you as you wander through its labyrinths, and the wild weeds of this climate of flowers bloom under your feet.

Here, as elsewhere in the letters, Shelley melds the organic with the abstract.[21] The flourishing flora reproduces an *impression* of the amphitheatre in which the 'labyrinths', now fashioned from colonizing vegetation, simultaneously erase and echo the underground tunnels of the *hypogeum* with their grisly past. In *The Coliseum*, the old blind man, who can be seen as representing an ideal reader or substitute author of the letters to Peacock, argues that when 'we enter into the meditations, designs and destinies of something beyond ourselves, [...] the contemplation of the ruins of human power excites an elevating sense of *awfulness* and beauty' (*Julian*, VI, 304; emphasis added). Shelley explores, through this weathered emblem of a bygone civilization, the involved relationships between art, time, and perceptions of the sublime; moreover, the poet is developing an aesthetic that accommodates contrasting yet sympathetic modes of vision and expression.

II

Shelley's preoccupation with the visual is reflected in the artists who were inspired by, or share an affinity with, his work. Michael O'Neill has recently traced the cross-currents between Shelley's poetry and Turner's paintings, stating, 'many Shelleyans think of their poet as Turneresque'.[22] O'Neill's focus on the intensity and evanescence

---

[20] See *Julian*, VI, 297–306. Sophie Thomas considers the importance of the Coliseum as ruin in *Romanticism and Visuality: Fragments, History, Spectacle* (Abingdon: Routledge, 2008), 68–73. See, also, Timothy Clark, 'Shelley's "The Coliseum" and the Sublime', *Durham University Journal* 85 (1993), 225–35; Colbert, *Shelley's Eye*, 177–84; and Sarah Peterson, 'Mediating Vision: Shelley's Prose Encounters with Visual Art (1818–1820)', *Keats-Shelley Review* 22 (2008) 112–31.

[21] When at the Baths of Caracalla, another ruin now open to the elements, Shelley is transported into a state of sublime reverie by the 'undecaying investiture of nature' that adorns the desolate scene (23 March 1819).

[22] Michael O'Neill, 'The Inmost Spirit of Light: Shelley and Turner', The 2008 Kurt Pantzer Memorial Lecture Part I, *Turner Society News* 109 (2008), 7. See, also, J. Drummond Bone, 'Turner and Shelley: The Sense of a Comparison', in Frederick Burwick and Jürgen Klein (eds.), *The Romantic Imagination: Literature and Art in England and Germany* (Amsterdam: Rodopi, 1996), 202–22.

of their Romantic vision also accords with the dynamic indeterminacy that Shelley prized in Italian art, as outlined in section I. Shelley's visual reception gains momentum in the Victorian period. The Pre-Raphaelites and their followers were animated in their admiration of the 'rebel' poet, and awarded him two stars in their 'List of Immortals'. Dante Gabriel Rossetti felt a particular empathy with Shelley; he duly wrote a sonnet to the poet, first published in *Ballads and Sonnets* (1881), and even included the ghost of Shelley in a skit written for Jane Morris, 'The Death of Topsy' (1878). Sylva Norman claims that 'These votaries eat, breathe, dream, and drink their Shelley, smoke him in their pipes, and fill their pens with him.'[23] Walter Crane was one such 'votary' whose painting *My Soul is an Enchanted Boat* refers to Asia's speech in Act II, scene v of *Prometheus Unbound*, and depicts an angel conducting the boat 'Upon the many-winding river' (II. v. 79).[24] The scene of a woman floating downstream, accompanied by swans, connects this image with the many Victorian depictions of Tennyson's 'The Lady of Shalott', most notably Crane's own version of 1862, Arthur Hughes's renditions of 1863 and 1872–3, and John William Waterhouse's popular painting of 1888. Among the late Victorian artists who engaged directly with Shelley's work was Arthur Hacker. His painting *The Cloud* was exhibited at the Royal Academy in 1902, accompanied by the following lines from Shelley's poem: 'And I all the while bask in Heaven's blue smile, | Whilst he is dissolving in rains' ('The Cloud', 29–30). The painting, which focuses on a reclining female nude, captures the erotic charge between the genii and the Spirit, as well as the shifting weather patterns, which Shelley's poem celebrates. A curved sunbeam leads our gaze from the woman's legs to the base of the canvas where a male figure emerges from the brilliant cloud to fall and dissolve into the shadowy darkness of rain.[25]

An artist for whom Shelley proved even more significant during the late nineteenth and early twentieth century was Waterhouse. Of the two volumes of poetry that are known to have been in the artist's library, one is by Shelley, dated 1880, and decorated with sketches.[26] Of these sketches, *Listening to my Sweet Pipings* became an oil painting of 1911 that takes its name from a line, 'Listening my sweet pipings', in 'Song of Pan' (5, 12).[27] Similar paintings of the 1890s, particularly *A Hamadryad* and

[23] Sylva Norman, *Flight of the Skylark: The Development of Shelley's Reputation* (London: Max Reinhardt, 1954), 227.

[24] Crane also produced a watercolour, 'Shelley's Tomb in the Protestant Cemetery in Rome', in 1873. Norman claims that Crane's tendency to 'free thought' had been induced, 'to a point', by reading Shelley. See *Flight of the Skylark*, 252.

[25] The following lines from Shelley's *Adonais* are inscribed on Hacker's gravestone: 'Peace, peace! he is not dead, he doth not sleep— | He hath awakened from the dream of life—' (39, 343–4).

[26] The edition of Shelley's poems owned by Waterhouse was *The Poetical Works of Percy Bysshe Shelley* (London: George Routledge and Sons, 1880). This copy, along with the artist's copy of Tennyson's poems, was recently on display at the Royal Academy of Arts. See Elizabeth Prettejohn, Peter Trippi, Robert Upstone, and Patty Wageman, *J. W. Waterhouse: The Modern Pre-Raphaelite* (London: Thames & Hudson, 2008), 232.

[27] Most modern editions of Shelley's poetry, including the one referred to here, give lines 5 and 12 of 'Song of Pan' as 'Listening my sweet pipings'. The title of Waterhouse's painting retains the wording as given in Mary Shelley's 1839 edition of her husband's work.

A Naiad (both 1893), indicate a 'paganist nostalgia' that, according to Peter Trippi, 'grew from his [Waterhouse's] love of Ovid, Shelley and Keats'.[28] In viewing Greek myth through the lens of these poets, Waterhouse's Pan is rendered unthreatening and his sirens sympathetic, as opposed to the monstrous lures characteristic of the *fin-de-siècle*.

It was, however, in the medium of book illustration that the visual potential of Shelley's work was realized. In his introduction to an edition of Shelley's poetry, Walter Raleigh passes a telling if pessimistic judgement:

> There is no great poet who offers a more hopeless task to the illustrator, if by illustration is understood a drawing that helps to the understanding of the poem. But Art begets Art, and there is surely nothing illicit about an embroidery of fair designs suggested by a reading of the poems.[29]

Raleigh's aesthetic imperative that 'Art begets Art' is equally evident in, and can be traced back to, Shelley's creative exchanges with the visual arts. Rather than cataloguing or explicating the sculptures in the Uffizi, for example, the poet's responses generate his own works of art in poetry and prose. Certainly, on the one hand, Shelley's poetry did not have the immediate pictorial appeal of Keats's or Tennyson's poetry for a Victorian audience, nor did it generate an equivalent demand for lavish illustrations; on the other hand, Shelley's poetry was considered suitable material for fine printing. One volume, published in 1860, contains only two poems, 'Ode to the West Wind' and 'The Question', and each page is illustrated with botanical watercolours that wrap around the gold text. The appropriately titled *Gems from Shelley* does not, perhaps, 'add' anything to a reading of these poems—unless we see the profusion of flora and fauna as emphasizing the organic—but the volume does demonstrate that Shelley's work, like Keats's, could be fashioned into an *objet d'art*.[30] Nature and landscapes emerge as staple subjects for illustrations to works by or on Shelley. *Shelley and his Friends in Italy*, written by Helen Rossetti Angeli and published in 1911, contains sixteen illustrations that were inspired by places, such as the Baths of Caracalla and the Protestant Cemetery in Rome, that Shelley visited and wrote about, while *Nature Poems*, published in the same year, contains a further sixteen watercolours by William Hyde that attempt to capture something of the atmospheric luminescence of Shelley's poetry.[31] Landscapes continued to appear alongside Shelley's poems in the latter part of the twentieth century with the publication of three thin volumes: Duine Campbell's black and white prints with an additional colour wash illustrate *Italian Idylls* of 1968; Anne Clements adopts a similar style in her rather abstract prints of 1977; and Patricia Machin's illustrations of 1985 consist of bright,

[28] Peter Trippi, *J. W. Waterhouse* (London: Phaidon, 2002), 127.
[29] *Poems by Percy Bysshe Shelley*, introd. Walter Raleigh, illustrated by Robert Anning Bell (London: George Bell and Sons, 1902).
[30] *Gems from Shelley* (London: Paul Jerrard & Son, 1860).
[31] Helen Rossetti Angeli, *Shelley and his Friends in Italy* (London: Methuen & Co, 1911); Percy Bysshe Shelley, *Nature Poems*, illustrated by William Hyde (London: Hutchinson & Co, 1911).

innocuous scenes, except for the inclusion of the dejected poet huddled amongst the pretty marginalia of flowers and birds.[32]

The poem with the most visual appeal for illustrators proved to be *The Sensitive Plant*, with its dense descriptions and impressionist hues. A woman in a long gown with wavy hair, illustrating the lines 'A Lady, the wonder of her kind, | [...] Tended the garden from morn to even' (II. 5, 9), adorns numerous editions of Shelley's poems; one such illustration situates the lady indoors, watering a pot plant, in what appears to be a Victorian parlour.[33] In the introduction to a slim volume of *The Sensitive Plant*, F. B. Money-Coutts praises the 'sweet-sounding [...] gossamer verses' of a poem that is equalled only by Keats's 'La Belle Dame sans Merci' for its ethereal qualities.[34] The black and white illustrations that follow are finely detailed, but remain little more than semantically flat decorations. A few illustrators did, however, rise to the aesthetic challenges presented by this poem. Charles Robinson, the illustrator of a sumptuous edition of the poem, combines diverse styles: black and white line drawings reminiscent of Aubrey Beardsley; full-page colour plates; and vignettes in grey tones with an additional colour. The plate illustrating the popular lines from the beginning of Part II is ornate and vibrant with a dense profusion of flowers carpeting the scene: yet the path that leads the viewer into the image is 'lost', as in the poem, or rather obstructed by pots out of which cascade blossoms that partially obscure stark stone carvings of cherubs (I. 52).[35] The illustration captures the following description of a resplendent yet forced beauty: 'And all rare blossoms from every clime | Grew in that garden in perfect prime' (I. 39–40). The vignettes are populated by playful fairies and cherubs who, in their state of Blakean innocence, are also vulnerable, isolated and sometimes fearful. The 'plumèd insects' (I. 82), for example, display brilliant flashes of orange light, but their disproportionate size in relation to the cherubs exposes a typically Shelleyan ambivalence about beauty. Likewise, on page 60, a cherub dangles beneath a fish, holding its barbel, to observe the 'sea-flower [that] unfolded beneath the ocean' (II. 8): this image links to both a dark yet pretty plate of fish swimming in a lily pond *and* the image of an infant who is oblivious to a predatory water snake that slithers onto the scene. Here, the dialogue both within and between Robinson's illustrations reflects the indeterminacy and near-tragic doubleness that characterize *The Sensitive Plant*. In Part III, the infants, now grown older, cover their nakedness and

[32] Percy Bysshe Shelley, *Italian Idylls*, illustrated by Duine Campbell (Leicester: Offcut Press, 1968); Percy Bysshe Shelley, *Lines and Fragments*, illustrated by Anne Clements (Belfast: Crannog Press, 1977); and *Shelley*, A Webb & Bower Pocket Poet, illustrated by Patricia Machin (Exeter: Webb & Bower, 1985). John Buckland-Wright's small wood engravings of landscapes, nature, and birds illustrate Percy Bysshe Shelley, *Poems*, introduction by Richard Church (London: Folio Society, 1949). This volume was reprinted in 1973. More recently, engravings by Simon Brett accompanied Percy Bysshe Shelley, *Collected Poems*, ed. Neville Rogers, introd. Richard Holmes (London: Folio Society, 2008).

[33] See Percy Bysshe Shelley, *Favorite Poems* (Boston: James R. Osgood and Company, 1877).

[34] Percy Bysshe Shelley, *The Sensitive Plant*, illustrated by F. L. Griggs (London: John Lane, 1902). More noteworthy illustrations include those by Jessie Marion King for *Poems of Shelley*, The Golden Poets Series (Edinburgh: T & E. C. Jack, 1907). King also produced an intricate border to decorate 'Hymn to Intellectual Beauty'.

[35] Percy Bysshe Shelley, *The Sensitive Plant*, introd. Edmund Gosse, illustrated by Charles Robinson (London: William Neinemann, 1911), 61.

appear alongside aged spectres that foretell winter and death. Furthermore, the threat that was concealed within the garden, 'the decaying dead | With a spirit of growth', is no longer a nightmarish vision, but an animated figure with looped tendrils of rotting vegetation that resemble 'rags of loose flesh' (III. 64–5, 68). Robinson intensifies the horror of Shelley's imaginings when, in one plate, he replaces the fauna that 'drowned | In an ocean of dreams' with a wave of children's contorted faces (I. 102–3). Another plate shows a cherub weeping, like the sensitive plant in stanza 21, as he kneels atop an urn of withered plants.

Even more gloomy and 'obscure' are the twelve full-page black and white designs by Laurence Housman for a volume of *The Sensitive Plant*, dated 1898.[36] Confirming Housman's own assessment, that they were 'the best drawings I ever did', a contemporary critic, Charles Kains-Jackson, declared that the illustrations were 'beyond what any of the great illustrators of the Victorian era from 1850–70 achieved. It has the precision and the decision, the design and the detail of the great pre-Raphaelites, but it is free from their invincible quaintness.' Rodney Engen also considers them to be 'among his most carefully considered, delicate and successful ink drawings'.[37] The frontispiece, entitled *Death in the Garden*, sets the mood for this series of sympathetic drawings; a circular procession of mourners leads the reader into the poem, despite this scene not appearing in the poem itself until the beginning of Part III. These unsettling figures intrude into a picture of the lady smelling roses in her garden. Both this image and *The Shadowed Doorway*, so called because a bower of ivy casts a shadow on the lady's skirt, hints at the dark undertones of a fairy tale (a technique employed to great effect in Housman's illustrations to Christina Rossetti's *Goblin Market* in 1893). It is out of the colonizing climbers that a gaunt, fragile man—representing the spirit of the sensitive plant/poet—is born; he is shortly after depicted in a corner of *Night in the Garden* wrestling with the undergrowth that threatens to engulf him. A far worse fate awaits our sensitive plant, however, as Housman introduces the pagan figure of Pan into the garden. This Pan is not the benign faun of Waterhouse's *Listening to my Sweet Pipings*, but a harbinger of death. Housman's Pan stalks and then vanquishes the sensitive plant. Pan is also visible through an archway in the last illustration, *The Garden Entombed*, where we see the anguished poet tethered to his frozen form. Housman is, in many ways, fabricating his own macabre vision of Shelley's poem, yet his illustrations echo the sorrowful tone in the final stanza of 'Song of Pan' and gesture towards the aesthetic complexity of *The Sensitive Plant*.[38] As the conclusion of Shelley's poem distances the reader from the plight of the sensitive plant and questions our sense of whether 'love, and beauty, and delight' are, indeed, subject to decay, so Housman's final illustration pictures the plant's inability or unwillingness to escape the bonds that tie him to a 'tragic' end of his own devising (Conclusion, 21). The plant's failure to transcend an earthly state, despite the wings that

---

[36] Percy Bysshe Shelley, *The Sensitive Plant*, illustrated by Laurence Housman (London: Aldine, 1898).
[37] Rodney Engen, *Laurence Housman*, The Artist and the Critic Series 1 (Stroud: Catalpa Press, 1983), 84. Housman cited ibid. 84; Charles Kains-Jackson cited on 121.
[38] Shelley's poem offered Housman 'certain symbolic challenges which appealed to his own love of visual imagery' (Engen, *Laurence Housman*, 84).

now appear at his feet, visualizes Shelley's commentary on the limits of human perception and comprehension. In the light of this image, all Housman's illustrations can be seen as 'the shadows of the dream' (Conclusion, 12).

III

Portrayals of Shelley on screen represent another aspect of the poet's visual afterlife that has been largely overlooked by scholars. His first appearance on film was in *The Bride of Frankenstein*, a cult horror movie directed by James Whale in 1935.[39] Shelley makes a brief appearance at the beginning of the film when Mary Shelley announces her new tale, the 'sequel' to Whale's earlier film of *Frankenstein* released in 1931. The four-minute prologue apparently became, for the director, the most important scene in the film.[40] The real interest of this opening scene, where domestic harmony reigns between the attentive husband and his cosseted wife, derives from Byron's fascination with Mary and the seeming incongruity between her angelic appearance and her Gothic imagination; when Byron refers to her as an 'astonishing creature', he makes a link between author and creation—here reinforced by the same actress, Elsa Lanchester, playing both Mary Shelley and the bride of the title—that will resurface in later films of the Romantics. Douglas Walton's limited performance as Shelley in this film signals a number of important trends. First, film portraits of Shelley are nearly always connected to the events that took place in the summer of 1816, 'the period', as Ramona M. Ralston and Sidney L. Sondergard argue, 'most interesting to popular imagination'.[41] Percy Shelley's significance as a Romantic poet is, thereby, overshadowed by the cultural legacy of Mary Shelley's frequently, and freely, adapted novel, *Frankenstein*. Second, a focus on the poet's relationship with his wife, as well as with Claire Clairmont, is nearly always supplanted by Byron's intrigues with these, and other, women.

Ivan Passer's *Haunted Summer* (1988), a film that explores the group dynamics at the Villa Diodati, concentrates on the relationship between Mary Shelley and Byron, with the pair sleeping together in the closing scenes—the film moves towards the physical consummation of their apparent mental connection—and hints at Byron's influence over and possible jealousy of Shelley.[42] Eric Stoltz portrays Shelley as a sensitive and

---

[39] The films discussed in this chapter are, in order, *The Bride of Frankenstein*, directed by James Whale (Universal, 1935); *Haunted Summer*, directed by Ivan Passer (Cannon, 1988); *Rowing with the Wind* (*Remando al viento*), directed by Gonzalo Suárez (Ditirambo, 1988); *Byron*, directed by Julian Farino (BBC, 2003); *Gothic*, directed by Ken Russell (Virgin Vision, 1986); *The Saint*, directed by Phillip Noyce (Paramount, 1997); and *Lewis*, Series 2, 'And the Moonbeams Kiss the Sea', directed by Dan Reed (ITV/WGBH, 2008).

[40] See Ramona M. Ralston and Sidney L. Sondergard, 'Screening Byron: The Idiosyncrasies of the Film Myth', in Frances Wilson (ed.), *Byromania: Portraits of the Artist in Nineteenth- and Twentieth-Century Culture* (Basingstoke: Macmillan, 1999), 138–9.

[41] Ibid. 141.

[42] The film of *Haunted Summer* is adapted from the novel of that name by Anne Edwards.

playful poet. The audience is reminded of the poet's 'subversive' activities and beliefs, but it is Claire Clairmont's description of Shelley as 'sweet' and 'adorable' that sum up his character in this film. Shelley's tenderness and affability, at least in the first part of *Haunted Summer*, forms a direct contrast to another portrayal of Shelley that appeared in the same year. In *Rowing with the Wind* (*Remando al viento*), Valentine Pelka's Shelley threatens to kill himself in front of William Godwin; later, after his son William's death, he contemplates suicide for a second time.[43] Pelka's Shelley is intense and passionate, introducing himself to Byron as 'atheist and democrat', and becomes increasingly daring when, for example, he arrives for lunch with Leigh Hunt and his wife completely naked.

Shelley is equally earnest in a BBC biopic of Byron's life screened in 2003.[44] For Oliver Dimsdale's Shelley, poetry is a vehicle for expressing revolutionary views; when discussing the conflict in Greece, for instance, he reprimands Byron: 'This is not lyric poetry. This is politics and battle.' The two-part biopic also recreates the events of late August 1818, when the two poets rode together on the Venice Lido and discussed the issues that were to inspire Shelley's *Julian and Maddalo*, a poem that Byron quotes from in these scenes when dismissing his friend's idealism: 'You talk Utopia' (179). Drawing heavily on the philosophical 'conversations' of *Julian and Maddalo*, Shelley is cast as the optimist to Byron's pessimism.

Shelley previously provided a foil for his friend and fellow poet in Ken Russell's infamous film *Gothic* (1986) where we witness Byron take centre stage as a satanic conjuror of hallucinatory nightmares. Russell's film does, however, feature an affectionate relationship between Byron and Shelley, if only to add a hint of homoeroticism, and stresses Shelley's enthusiasm for science (whereas Pelka's Shelley scoffs at its limitations). *Gothic*'s more unwelcome legacy for subsequent screen portrayals of Shelley include an increasing dependence on drugs and attempts to 'diagnose' the poet. Julian Sands's Shelley, in *Gothic*, explains that his fear of being buried alive is the result of narcolepsy while, in *Rowing with the Wind*, Mary Shelley reveals that her husband has suffered from 'persecution mania' since childhood. In addition, a consequence of the depraved games orchestrated by Byron in *Gothic* is the appearance of Mary's monster. This film, *Haunted Summer*, and *Rowing with the Wind* all suggest that the physical manifestation of their dark imaginings will be responsible for the impending deaths of Shelley, Byron, and the children they fathered who died in infancy. Taking this idea further, in *Rowing with the Wind*, the monster is connected to the intimacy between Percy and Mary. After experiencing a disturbing vision of his wife, Percy Shelley declares 'Nothing I see means anything unless I share it with you. You are in every page I read; every word I write, every

[43] Gonzalo Suárez won six major awards in Spain where the film was a commercial and critical success (see Ralston and Sondergard, 'Screening Byron', 145).

[44] By contrast, Shelley has made a number of appearances in well-known comedy series: *Monty Python's Flying Circus*, series 4, episode entitled 'Michael Ellis', and *Blackadder the Third*, episode entitled 'Ink and Incapability'. Shelley is also one of the Romantic writers to appear alongside Benjamin Zephaniah in the satire *Dread Poets' Society*. *Monty Python's Flying Circus*, directed by Ian MacNaughton (BBC/Python (Monty) Pictures, 1974); *Blackadder the Third*, directed by Mandie Fletcher (BBC, 1987); *Dread Poets' Society*, directed by Andy Wilson (BBC, 1992).

thought and every landscape', and he continues 'Your breath is my breath [...] but the look in your eyes is not like mine. [...] I was afraid because your thoughts were not my thoughts.' Later, after the creature visits Mary and repeats Percy's sentiments, this avowed attachment becomes overlaid with monstrous connotations; while Shelley's greatest fear is mental estrangement from his partner, Mary's is a loss of autonomy.

In the films discussed thus far, Shelley is portrayed as fragile and somewhat childlike. In *Rowing with the Wind*, Byron's line about his friend, 'He is an angel who beats his wings in the void', rephrases Matthew Arnold's famous verdict on the poet.[45] The influential image of an 'Ariel' Shelley assumes significance in a more recent film, which does not feature an appearance by Shelley as such, but includes references to the poet and his work. In *The Saint*, a film of 1997, the scientist who invents cold fusion is also an admirer of Shelley's poetry. Among Dr Emma Russell's diagrams and formulae are regular jottings about what could be described as an infatuation with Shelley and her daily visits to the Shelley Memorial. The sculpture, housed in University College, Oxford, conveys to Russell a sense of 'very personal loss', with 'so much pain and so much passion', and she describes 'the way it glows. And how the light enfolds him in silence, taking care of him.'[46] What Russell sees as the purity of Shelley's poetry, embodied by Edward Onslow Ford's sculpture, acts as a catalyst for her scientific breakthrough and ensures that she maintains her ideals over its non-commercial applications. This dialogue between the arts and the sciences, with Shelley as intermediary, is the main point of interest in an otherwise unmemorable film.

An episode of the popular detective series *Lewis* (a spin-off from *Inspector Morse*) ends with another loving close-up of the Shelley Memorial. The episode, entitled 'And the moonbeams kiss the sea', screened in 2008, begins with a young man reciting the last stanza of 'Love's Philosophy':

> And the sunlight clasps the earth
> And the moonbeams kiss the sea;—
> What are all these kissings worth,
> If thou kiss not me?
>
> (13–16)[47]

The version of the poem chosen, combined with the idyllic scene of a couple painting beside a river, initially suggests a sentimental reference to Shelley. However, the girl's bold response,

---

[45] In his essay on Byron, Arnold writes: 'Shelley, beautiful and ineffectual angel, beating in the void his luminous wings in vain.' See Matthew Arnold, 'Byron', *Essays in Criticism: Second Series* (London: Macmillan, 1892), 203–4.

[46] See frontispiece on page xxii. For a history of how the sculpture came to be in its current location, see R. H. Darwall-Smith, 'The Shelley Memorial; or, The Monument Nobody Wanted', *University College Record* 12.4 (2000), 74–84. I am grateful to Dr Robin Darwall-Smith for providing me with a copy of his article. For a discussion of the sculpture's aesthetic merit, or 'poetic realism', see David J. Getsey, '"Hard Realism": The Thanatic Corporeality of Edward Onslow Ford's *Shelley Memorial*', in *Body Doubles: Sculpture in Britain, 1877–1905* (New Haven: Yale UP, 2004), 119–41; and Francis Haskell, 'The Shelley Memorial', *Oxford Art Journal* 1 (1978), 3–6.

[47] See *Major Works*, 774 for the textual variants of the penultimate line.

'Do I get a kiss?', and his rebuff, 'I'm working', immediately deflates our romantic expectations. Later, when the same girl reads from a passage in *Frankenstein*, her college friends deem it to be 'terminally naff'. Allusions to the Romantics reading from and writing ghost stories at the Villa Diodati, the inspiration for previous films, are now the subject of satire: yet an image of the monster, from the 2004 Folio edition of the novel, leaves a more lasting impression. The girl, Nell, is composing a series of letters that suggest Percy Shelley wrote *Frankenstein*.[48] The letters, created by Nell as art, result in murder when two Oxford professors, one of whom is a Romantic poetry specialist, try to sell them along with some forged manuscripts. Nell is cast in the Mary Shelley role—as the author of a 'monstrous' sequence of events, taking the viewer back to the connection between author and creation in *The Bride of Frankenstein*—with her friend and artistic collaborator, Philip, quoting from *Adonais* and 'The Question' as well as 'Love's Philosophy'. Philip is thought to be autistic, another 'condition' that Shelley, by inference, suffered from; he obsessively paints the same spot on the river, gazing at cloud formations, as Nell tries to revolutionize art. While this oddly congenial couple invites us to rethink the intellectual dynamic between Percy and Mary Shelley, the murders are linked, significantly, through Percy Shelley, the 'main man', as Philip refers to him. Here, for once, the spotlight remains on the Percy Shelley figure.

This chapter has examined the importance of the visual arts to Shelley and his influence on them. Although it has not been possible to consider every visual representation of the poet, from portraits and busts to sculptures, as well as paintings of his funeral pyre and final resting place, I hope to have given an indication of his varied visual reception. Shelley's investment in the visual arts is nowhere more apparent than in his inspired and engaging evocations of Italian sculpture, painting, architecture, and the landscape. *Notes on Sculptures in Rome and Florence* and Shelley's letters to Thomas Love Peacock are concerned with exploring and challenging artistic media, and both works offer invaluable insights into the aesthetic vision that informs some of his most seminal poems. Artists, in turn, have engaged with the creative potential of Shelley's poetry. Most notably, Charles Robinson and Laurence Housman's respective illustrations to *The Sensitive Plant* constitute visual commentaries on the ephemeral beauty and aesthetic ambiguity of Shelley's poem. Film portraits of Shelley have, perhaps, not proved so fortunate: at best, the poet is portrayed as a subversive or an angel; at worst, he is a bit part in the events that inspire Mary Shelley's *Frankenstein* and a bystander in the relationship between his wife and her creation, or his wife and Byron. Shelley fares better in films that move away from the Villa Diodati to focus on more meaningful synergies between his poetry and popular culture.[49] In *Lewis*, Detective Sergeant Hathaway adopts a thoughtful Shelleyan persona after a crisis of faith leads him to reject his former vocation as a priest; he refers to Shelley as one of the 'guys in the band', while Lewis declares him to be 'every student's favourite role model', according him a cult status. If nothing else, recent attempts to 'sex up' Shelley—associating him with addiction, subversion, and teen angst—provide increasing evidence of the poet's lasting, and increasingly memorable, visual afterlife.

[48] For relevant evidence of Percy Shelley's role in the composition of *Frankenstein*, see *MYR* IX.
[49] A promising avenue for future research would be the aesthetic conversations with Shelley's poetry in films such as *The Painted Veil*, most recently adapted from Somerset Maugham's novel in 2006.

SELECT BIBLIOGRAPHY

Burwick, Frederick and Jürgen Klein. Eds. *The Romantic Imagination: Literature and Art in England and Germany*. Amsterdam: Rodopi, 1996.

Colbert, Benjamin. *Shelley's Eye: Travel Writing and Aesthetic Vision*. Aldershot: Ashgate, 2005.

Colwell, Frederic S. 'Shelley and Italian Painting'. *Keats–Shelley Journal* 29 (1980), 43–66.

—— 'Shelley on Sculpture: The Uffizi Notes'. *Keats–Shelley Journal* 28 (1979), 59–77.

Getsey, David J. '"Hard Realism": The Thanatic Corporeality of Edward Onslow Ford's *Shelley Memorial*'. *Body Doubles: Sculpture in Britain, 1877–1905*. New Haven: Yale UP, 2004.

Goslee, Nancy Moore. 'Shelley at Play: A Study of Sketch and Text in his "Prometheus" Notebooks'. *Huntington Library Quarterly* 48 (1985), 211–55.

—— *Shelley's Visual Imagination*. Cambridge: Cambridge UP, 2011.

Murray, E. B. 'Shelley's *Notes on Sculptures*: The Provenance and Authority of the Text'. *Keats–Shelley Journal* 32 (1983), 150–71.

O'Neill, Michael. 'The Inmost Spirit of Light: Shelley and Turner'. The 2008 Kurt Pantzer Memorial Lecture, Part I. *Turner Society News* 109 (2008), 7–12. Part II. *Turner Society News* 110 (2008), 6–8.

Peterson, Sarah. 'Mediating Vision: Shelley's Prose Encounters with Visual Art (1818–1820)'. *Keats–Shelley Review* 22 (2008), 112–31.

Rogers, Neville. 'Shelley and the Visual Arts'. *Keats–Shelley Memorial Bulletin* 12 (1961), 8–17.

....

CHAPTER 36

SHELLEY'S SCIENCES

....

MARILYN GAULL

BERTRAND Russell, mathematician, analytical philosopher, and fierce logician, described his accidental discovery at the age of 15 of Shelley's *Alastor or the Spirit of Solitude*: 'Entranced', he said: 'Here I felt was a kindred spirit, gifted as I never hoped to be with the power of finding words as beautiful as his thoughts.'[1] Later, he confessed, 'a passionate personal love of him—more than for any one I know'.[2] And in his *Autobiography*, 'I spent all my spare time reading him and learning him by heart [...] I used to reflect how wonderful it would have been to know Shelley and to wonder whether I should ever meet any live human being with whom I should feel so much in sympathy.'[3] Had he written about Shelley, he said, the poet would not have emerged as Arnold's 'ineffectual angel' but as 'a tough customer given to revolver shooting and to modern industrialism'.[4] Russell, like so many others, responded to Shelley's passion, atheism, liberal politics, rebellious nature, observational skill, and the assimilation of a scientific and mythic view of nature that anticipates later challenges to human survival. Together, these characteristics are more significant for Russell than the idealism, strongly associated with Shelley, on which Russell blamed all the social, political, and even scientific problems of the nineteenth century.

The best of Shelley's readers, like Russell, are often scientists as well as political and religious radicals. In *Science and the Modern World*, Russell's friend and collaborator Alfred North Whitehead elevated Shelley's science above his poetry, claiming that Shelley 'loved science' and 'never tired of expressing it in poetry'. What the hills were to the youth of Wordsworth, a chemical laboratory was to Shelley. How could the power and significance of science in Shelley's poetry have been so long overlooked, he wondered. 'It is unfortunate', he comments, 'that Shelley's literary critics have, in this respect,

---

[1] Bertrand Russell, *Fact and Fiction* (1961; New York: Routledge, 1994), 12.

[2] Quoted in Gladys Garner Leithauser, 'The Romantic Russell and the Legacy of Shelley', *Russell: The Journal of Bertrand Russell Studies* 4.1 (1984), 31–48.

[3] Bertrand Russell, *Autobiography* (1967; New York: Routledge, 1998), 35.

[4] Bertrand Russell, *The Collected Stories of Bertrand Russell*, ed. B. Feinberg (London: Allen and Unwin, 1972), 297–8.

so little of Shelley in their own mentality. They tend to treat as a casual oddity of Shelley's nature what was, in fact, part of the main structure of his mind, permeating his poetry through and through. If Shelley had been born a hundred years later, the twentieth century would have seen a Newton among chemists.'[5]

Being a Newton among anything during and after the Romantic period was a mixed blessing since so many artists and chemists, philosophers and writers, including Joseph Priestley, Blake, and Goethe, had questioned Newton's materialism, mechanism, objectivity, optics, mathematical notation, even his sanity and religious convictions. Appropriately, Wordsworth depicted him in *The Prelude* as 'Voyaging through strange seas of Thought, alone' (1850, III. 63).[6]

Following Whitehead, other scientists were drawn to Shelley: Carl Grabo in *A Newton among Poets* and his later *The Magic Plant*, and Desmond King-Hele, an award-winning astro-physicist and expert on Erasmus Darwin, in *Shelley: His Thought and Work*,[7] gave Shelley a voice in the scientific community. Kenneth Neil Cameron, a tough-minded analytical philosopher in the Bertrand Russell tradition, in both *The Young Shelley* and *Shelley: The Golden Years*[8] claimed that Shelley's science was integral to his poetry. Similarly, recent scholars with science backgrounds or interests have shown how Shelley anticipated modern physics, quantum theory, and chaos theory.[9]

Recognizing the compatibility of science and poetry, these scientists, philosophers, historians, and radical political theorists carried on the Romantic tradition of relating art and science: Wordsworth saw poetry as 'the history or science of feelings', as he said in the note to 'The Thorn', and believed, as he said in the Preface to *Lyrical Ballads*, that both science and poetry found 'pleasure' in their respective knowledge.[10] Shelley spoke of 'Science, and her sister Poesy' (*Revolt of Islam*, V. 51, 2255) and saw poets as 'men of science',[11] at one time considered the 'science of things' more important than 'the science of words' (*PBS: Letters* I, 318). Even the word 'scientist'—coined

---

[5] Alfred North Whitehead, *Science and the Modern World* (New York: Free Press, 1925), 84.

[6] Quoted from *William Wordsworth: The Prelude 1799, 1805, 1850: Authoritative Texts, Contexts and Reception: Recent Critical Essays*, ed. Jonathan Wordsworth, M. H. Abrams, and Stephen Gill (New York: W. W. Norton, 1979), 95. All quotations from *The Prelude* will be from this edition.

[7] Carl Grabo, *A Newton among Poets: Shelley's Use of Science in Prometheus Unbound* (1930; New York: Gordian Press, 1968); *The Magic Plant: The Growth of Shelley's Thought* (Chapel Hill, NC: University of North Carolina Press, 1936); Desmond King-Hele, *Shelley: His Thought and Work* (Teaneck, NJ: Farleigh Dickinson UP, 1960).

[8] Kenneth Neil Cameron, *The Young Shelley: Genesis of a Radical* (New York: Macmillan, 1950); *Shelley: The Golden Years* (Cambridge, MA: Harvard UP, 1970).

[9] Arkady Plotinsky, 'All Shapes of Light: The Quantum Mechanical Shelley', in Betty Bennet and Stuart Curran (eds.), *Shelley: Poet and Legislator of the World* (Baltimore: Johns Hopkins UP, 1996), 263–73; Hugh Roberts, *Shelley and the Chaos of History: A New Politics of Poetry* (University Park, PA: Penn State UP, 1997); Mark Lussier, *Romantic Dynamics: A Poetics of Physicality* (New York: Palgrave Macmillan, 2000); Richard Holmes, *Shelley: The Pursuit* (London: Weidenfeld & Nicolson, 1974); *The Age of Wonder: How the Romantic Generation Discovered the Beauty and Terror of Science* (London: Pantheon, 2009).

[10] William Wordsworth, *William Wordsworth: The Major Works*, ed. Stephen Gill (Oxford: Oxford UP, 1984), 594.

[11] Unless otherwise stated, quotations from Shelley's works are taken from *Norton 2*.

at Coleridge's request by William Whewell in 1833—was an analogy for artist, an alternative to 'natural philosopher', the phrase which Shelley and his contemporaries would have used.

Would one even discuss the relationship between art and science as if they were alternative modes of being were it not for C. P. Snow, who, within only two years of Russell's declaration, claimed that writers and humanists had usurped the title of intellectual from the scientists whom they did not sufficiently respect.[12] Ever since, historians of both science and literature have restated, refuted, or affirmed this fallacious proposition—although many claim it is a division they intend to overcome. Yet the evidence proves that in England, from about 1750 to 1830, arts, sciences, and literature all existed in a seamless pre-disciplinary culture. Some scholars imply that the poets were not very good at science and that the scientists were wary of poetry. Not so: their common conversation included William Blake, who engraved and illustrated the papers of the Royal Society and Erasmus Darwin's *Botanic Garden* and, correctly, objected to Newton's 'particles of light' (since by then suspicion was growing that light moved in waves) and concluded *The Four Zoas*: 'The dark Religions are departed & sweet Science reigns' (9, 855).[13] Erasmus Darwin was a legitimate scientist, doctor, and author of massive epics yoking ancient myth with contemporary science. Wordsworth began life as a mathematician and Keats as a pharmacist; William Herschel, a musician, who, as an astronomer, cultivated what he called 'the art of seeing';[14] Coleridge recommended chemistry to treat depression; Byron wrote about geology; and Adam Smith originated the idea of imagination (which Shelley thought science needed more of). Humphry Davy, who had he not been the first chemist 'probably would have been the first *poet* of his age',[15] according to Coleridge, revised the proofs for Wordsworth's Preface to *Lyrical Ballads*. In *Les Rêveries du promeneur solitaire* (1770), a source for *Alastor*,[16] Rousseau declared that 'I am crazy for botany—it just gets worse every day [...] I am going to become a plant myself one of these mornings.'[17]

Philosophers, artists, and writers shared the same interests as science: 'man, nature, and human life', as Wordsworth identified the theme of *The Excursion*. It was part of their shared thinking and being. For Shelley, 'Nature and culture' are the same and the human 'mind [...] inseparable from its world'.[18] As Ted Underwood puts it: 'To say that his theory of poetry was "modeled" on science would understate the connection. It developed out of natural philosophy (and philosophical poetry) in a way that makes it impossible

[12] C. P. Snow, *The Two Cultures and the Scientific Revolution* (Cambridge: Cambridge UP, 1959).

[13] *The Complete Poetry and Prose of William Blake*, rev. edn., ed. David V. Erdman (Garden City, NY: Anchor/Doubleday, 1982), 407.

[14] William Herschel, *The Herschel Chronicle: The Life Story of William Herschel and his Sister Caroline Herschel*, ed. Constance A Lubbock (Cambridge: Cambridge UP, 1933), 105.

[15] 'On the Poetry of Humphry Davy', *The Gentleman's Magazine* 8 (April 1837), 339.

[16] Edward Duffy, *Rousseau in England: The Context for Shelley's Critique of the Enlightenment* (Berkeley and Los Angeles: University of California Press, 1979), 94.

[17] Bernard Kuhn, *Autobiography and Natural Science in the Age of Romanticism: Rousseau, Goethe, Thoreau* (Aldershot: Ashgate, 2009), 43.

[18] Timothy Morton, 'Nature and Culture', in Timothy Morton (ed.), *The Cambridge Companion to Shelley* (Cambridge: Cambridge UP, 2006), 186.

to say where scientific reasoning ends and poetic reasoning begins.'[19] And Robert Mitchell writes that *Queen Mab* 'is founded on the premise of a reciprocal relationship between science and poetry, in which the visions of poetry are supported by science, but the progress and programs of the various sciences are themselves unified by a vision that only poetry can provide'.[20]

The unified vision of science and poetry originates in natural philosophy, for which science was not just another name: natural philosophy provided the common discourse of literature, art, theology, and philosophy until about 1840, when it was gradually replaced with the more specialized sciences that in turn were organized into professions and disciplines, with credentials, protocols, languages, institutes, clubs, and publications. Although the scientist was often represented during the period as a recluse, like Faust, Dr Frankenstein, or Manfred, deranged and testing the limits of the forbidden, the sciences in fact were transparent, public, accessible, often social, and narrative. Geology, astronomy, chemistry, even basic mathematics were common knowledge, popular, performed, shared, leisure activities for ladies and gentleman with the time and means. The occult and pseudo-sciences survived, alchemy next to chemistry, astrology in a new birth next to astronomy, bleeding and cupping next to transfusions, mesmerism, magnetism, phrenology, among conflicting theories of life. But even before there were such distinctions between science and pseudo-science, science itself, though often treated as a single collective practice, was divided into genres, like literature, like life itself; to adapt Keats's image, science was 'a Mansion of Many Apartments':[21] some dark and forbidding, others blinding with light, but all inviting exploration, awakening curiosity about the empirical world, the 'everlasting universe of things' as Shelley referred to nature in the first line of 'Mont Blanc'.

All the new sciences secularized nature and human life. Traumatic events such as storms, comets, plagues, volcanic eruptions, human diseases, or birth defects were no longer miracles or divine messages but challenges to existing theories of nature and of human life. Shelley's philosophical range, his materialism, idealism, and/or scepticism, depending on which time in his life and which scholar one reads, prepared him for all the conflicts between the old theological versions of nature and the demands of the new sciences, the rocks and vapours, the forces and substances.

Like Shelley, those who studied these sciences were self-taught, learning from books, experience, discipleship, and experiment. For example, for Priestley, chemistry and physics were nearly interchangeable. He followed his instincts, experimented with lightning and oxygen, invented carbonated water, wrote a book on electricity and another on English grammar. The different sciences, however, had distinct protocols, which Shelley encountered, practised, and incorporated in his verse. Some, like chemistry, are experimental; others like geology, medicine, meteorology, and astronomy are

[19]   Ted Underwood, 'The Science in Shelley's Theory of Poetry', *Modern Language Quarterly* 58 (1997), 302.

[20]   Robert Mitchell, '"Here is thy fitting Temple": Science, Technology and Fiction in Shelley's *Queen Mab*', *Romanticism on the Net* 21 (2001), <erudit.org/revue/ron/2001/v/n21/005964ar.html>.

[21]   John Keats, 'Letter to John Hamilton Reynolds, 3 May 1818'; *The Letters of John Keats 1814–1821*, ed. Hyder Edward Rollins, 2 vols. (Cambridge: Cambridge UP, 1958), I, 280.

observational, describing, collecting, and organizing specimens from fossils to human anatomy; others like physics are theoretical. British mathematics was peripheral to the new sciences: Euclid's geometry and the new arithmetization of experience in statistics and probability were irrelevant to the boundless spaces, the unpredictable trauma and fathomless time revealed in the new astronomy and geology. Whether for their own amusement or for practical application, scientists such as Thomas Beddoes who experimented with nitrous oxide, John Dalton who measured rainwater, or Davy who was charged with finding a solution to mine explosions, combined the empirical and the abstract as well as narrative and theory; they experimented on themselves as Shelley did, inhaling noxious gases and receiving electric shocks.

Shelley's generation was the first to be born into a world with electricity and nitrous oxide although no one knew how to use either of them. His generation understood theories of light, sound, colour, and oxygen, its origins and functions in human life. In medicine, they experienced vaccination, stethoscopes, blood transfusions, considered disease as invasive rather than a disorder, believed that defence is available, that diagnosis is possible, that pain is not inevitable, and that some physical disease is psychosomatic, a word the *OED* traces back to Coleridge (in 1834; see the word's first definition). From Thomas Malthus, they had proof that population was growing; from William Herschel that the universe is growing as well, with multiple, infinite, and fathomless galaxies; and from James Hutton that they inhabited an earth so old and mysterious that its origins and ends were unknown and unknowable; that humans were preceded on this earth by animals which were now extinct. Shelley's generation was the first to live with pocket watches, domestic clocks, personal time, diaries, schedules, and the whole social drama of the timely and belated that they bring into the world. His was also the first generation to live with tin cans to preserve food, bicycles, umbrellas, sewing machines, cotton underwear, carbon paper, telegraphy, gas lighting, batteries, light houses, photography, carbonated water, raincoats, matches, typewriters, domestic stoves, and the first prototype of a computer—Charles Babbage's 'difference machine', invented in 1821, a year before Shelley was drowned. All of this helped to anchor life in the terrestrial, to offset the dimensions of space and time that contemporary science was revealing, and to offer secular solutions for the lost promises of organized religion.

It was a contentious and exciting time to be interested in science, and in which everything was challenged and debated: creation theory, transmission and heredity, evolution, life itself, its origins and ends, growth, perception, the particles and imponderable fluids that comprised the universe, even the Euclidean certitudes. In science, however, revolutions are slow and the new does not merely displace the old.[22] Rather, those who cared about science lived in 'half truths', to adapt a phrase of Keats's, attempting to reconcile new ideas with old, still conflicted over whether they were practising science or natural philosophy. Shelley shared this divided state of mind. With all these possibilities, Shelley, like Erasmus Darwin, was a syncretist, yoking together all kinds of otherwise conflicting ideas: he concluded, as physicists eventually would, that light was both a

---

[22] See Thomas Kuhn, *The Structure of Scientific Revolutions* (Chicago: University of Chicago Press, 1962).

particle and wave, an abstract power and a function in photosynthesis, which in turn, to him, was also an aesthetic symbol and a mythic sign. But, however risky, impulsive, and advanced, Shelley's science derived from an earlier generation: his sources (like his radical politics) were late Enlightenment: Priestley, Erasmus Darwin, Herschel. Even the inventions he most enjoyed, the solar microscope, air pump, balloon, and steam boat, were expressions of the 1780s rather than the nineteenth century.

However philosophical his interests, Shelley, like Davy, required all sciences to have political and social applications. He bought the latest equipment, the solar telescope, the air pump, a 'galvanic trough', an electrical machine, and launched 'fire balloons' to disperse political messages before anyone even considered balloons suitable for communication and wrote a sonnet to them. While Benjamin Franklin, then American ambassador to France, feared after the first balloon flight in 1783 that France would use them to invade England, Shelley, according to Hogg, reputedly considered them liberating:

> It would seem a mere toy, a feather, in comparison with the splendid anticipations of the philosophical chemist; yet it [...] promises prodigious faculties for locomotion, and will enable us to traverse vast tracts with ease and rapidity, and to explore unknown countries without difficulty. Why are we so ignorant of the interior of Africa?—why do we not despatch intrepid aeronauts to cross it in every direction and to survey the whole peninsula in a few weeks? The shadow of the first balloon [...] as it glided over that unhappy country, would virtually emancipate every slave, and would annihilate slavery for ever.[23]

In fact, balloons, like electricity and nitrous oxide, had been an entertainment, decorated with mythic figures and a zodiac, launched in a carnival atmosphere, a mania that lasted over forty years without a real purpose. It was, however, the first great public science, a democratization of knowledge, aerial theatre, like comet watching, that aristocrats and the populace could enjoy.[24]

Similarly, Shelley's steamboat venture was a recreation, and the technology commonplace by 1819. In 1789, Erasmus Darwin, among others, described using steam for human transportation, even for flight: 'Unconquered Steam!' would 'Drag the slow barge, or drive the rapid car; | Or on wide-waving wings expanded bear | The flying-chariot through the fields of air'.[25] Steam boats had been used to cross the English Channel in 1803, and by the next year, 1804, the first steam locomotive did a nine-mile run in England. To Shelley, however—in 1819, in Italy, investing in Henry Reveley's experiment to build a steam boat—steam locomotion was magic, dramatic, and new. He enjoyed the process, the workshop, the forging, depicting himself 'Plotting dark spells, and devilish enginery' (Letter to Maria Gisborne, 107), finding drama and delight in the production. The project, however, was never completed.

[23] Thomas Jefferson Hogg, The Life of Percy Bysshe Shelley, ed. Edward Dowden (London: Routledge, 1906), 50.

[24] Jennifer Tucker, 'Voyages of Discovery on Oceans of Air: Scientific Observation and the Image of Science in an Age of "Balloonacy"', Osiris: Science in the Field 2nd series 11 (1996), 144–76.

[25] Erasmus Darwin, The Botanic Garden: A Poem, in Two Parts (London, 1791).

Grabo, King-Hele, Cameron, and others document Shelley's textual sources for his science. For form, ideas, and tactics, Erasmus Darwin was the most influential. *The Botanic Garden* (1789, 1791), *Zoonomia: or, the Laws of Organic Life* (1794), *Phytologia* (1800), and *The Temple of Nature* (1803) both in their texts and notes offered visually engaging, narrative, and mythic representations of contemporary science from evolution to atomic theory, geology, astronomy, botany, and chemistry. Initially Darwin's poetry inspired *Queen Mab* and later was subtly assimilated in *Prometheus Unbound*. His footnotes explained photosynthesis, electricity, magnetism, generation, metabolism, combustion, light, Herschel's expanding universe, Hutton's timeless one, and even climate, which Darwin, like so many of his contemporaries, believed was getting colder, that deadly glaciers were expanding, and that steam power could be used to haul the arctic glaciers to the tropics. For Shelley in *Queen Mab*, the cold would be overcome by everyone's becoming vegetarian, peaceful, rational, and the earth shifting on its axis. For both Darwin and Shelley, climate change was a human responsibility.

Erasmus Darwin also set a precedent by adapting old literary forms and even old theories to the new sciences. In footnotes and texts, Darwin revived the Greek myths and the Rosicrucian figures derived from them to explain the old sciences that he believed the myths represented. In the old and the new, he revealed the symbolic, philosophic, mathematical, and religious beliefs on which he believed all sciences were based.[26] In Darwin, Shelley saw illustrated the multiple levels on which knowledge exists and can be conveyed. Darwin's influence appears in Shelley's cyclical concepts of time, nature, and human life, in which the empirical, aesthetic, scientific, religious, mythic, allegorical, symbolic, personal, and political exist seamlessly.

From childhood on, Shelley, like Coleridge, was preoccupied with physical and mental disease. His diseases, discomforts, anxieties, diagnoses, and care illustrate the medical thought and practice of his time. As a young boy he tried to cure his sisters' chilblains with electricity and, reputedly, recovered his daughter from a wet-nurse whom he believed would corrupt her moral nature through breast milk.[27] In Darwin, a famous diagnostician who attributed disease to bad water, air, climate, diet, or the developing field of genetics, Shelley found explanations for his symptoms, and precedent for his complex vegetarianism, its implications for health, morality, and social improvement. Others, from Pythagoras, the most Promethean of ancient scientists, to Joseph Ritson, classicist, linguist, and collector of ancient ballads, lay behind Shelley's emphatic statement in *A Vindication of a Natural Diet* (1813) that there 'is no disease, bodily or mental, which adoption of vegetable diet and pure water has not infallibly mitigated' (*Murray: Prose*, 83). Of course, having made such a public statement about the advantages of vegetarianism, he could not reveal his own illnesses without discrediting it.

For his persistent kidney disease, he tried cures from mercury to magnetism, avoiding a brutal surgery without benefit of anaesthesia, the cure that would kill, as he called it

---

[26] See Noel Jackson, 'Rhyme and Reason: Erasmus Darwin's Romanticism', *Modern Language Quarterly* 70 (2009), 171–94 and Alan Richardson, 'Erasmus Darwin and the Fungus School', *Wordsworth Circle* 33 (2002), 113–16.

[27] Ann Wroe, *Being Shelley: The Poet's Search for Himself* (New York: Vintage, 2007), 26.

in his poem 'The Magnetic Lady to her Patient'. While his discomforts and some of his diseases were real, others were imaginary: nervousness, melancholy, cancer, typhus, 'inflammatory fever', consumption, 'elephantitus', heart disease, madness, according to those who knew him including his father. He had access to the best doctors: Dr Lind, his earliest tutor, had been physician at court and saved him from being sent to a madhouse as a boy; William Lawrence, the controversial surgeon caught up in the Vitalism debates, recommended his going to Italy; and the sociable and altruistic Dr Vacca in Pisa assured him that he was not dying, advising him to give up medication and doctors, to relax, get more exercise, and buy a horse.[28]

While the Vitalism debates seem remote from medicine, were it not for anatomy, the common subject among medical practitioners, the conflict over the sources of life itself would never have arisen. The question: which comes first, the form or the life principle? John Abernethy, a disciple of John Hunter, the legendary anatomist, lecturing at the Royal College of Surgeons between 1814 and 1819, believed that there was a life principle analogous to electricity, added to the body. William Lawrence, his disciple and Shelley's doctor, proposed that there is no soul, that life is the expression of form, and, in keeping with the other sciences of the day, especially geology, that any knowledge of life's origins is 'forever beyond our reach'.[29] While the debate was inconclusive, following Abernethy, many intellectual giants from Goethe to Emerson wanted to believe in an over-soul, a world spirit, that connects the mind, soul, and body, the plants, animals, and human beings, and accounts for evolution. Vitalism also prepared for other more valid scientific theories, and inspired Mary Shelley's *Frankenstein, or the Modern Prometheus* (1818) and the perennial ambition to create artificial life. Finally, the debates and demonstrations moved the concept of life itself, the origins, conduct, and end, from the churches to the theatres and lecture halls, secularized it, as the sky, the earth, nature itself was being secularized in the other sciences.

Chemistry, in which Whitehead thought Shelley would have excelled, was to the poet and his contemporaries 'entertaining knowledge',[30] a performance art, as common as astronomy, geology, even mathematics, practised by the wealthy in little home laboratories such as Shelley's, experimenting with predictable ends or just out of curiosity. Even leaving room for Hogg's exaggeration, as a chemist, Shelley was careless, unfocused, disorderly, and even ridiculous were he not dangerous: 'Books, boots, papers, shoes, philosophical instruments, clothes, pistols, linen, crockery, ammunition, and phials innumerable, with money, stockings, prints, crucibles, bags and boxes, were scattered [...] as if the young chemist, in order to analyse the mystery of creation, had endeavoured first to re-construct the primeval chaos.' The carpet was stained from aborted fires, bottles of 'noxious and nauseous fluids', with which he 'besmeared and disfigured himself and his goods'. Someday, Hogg feared, Shelley would set the whole college on

---

[28]   Bieri, 236.

[29]   See Alan Richardson, *British Romanticism and the Science of Mind* (Cambridge: Cambridge UP, 2001) and Sharon Ruston, *Shelley and Vitality* (Basingstoke: Palgrave, 2005).

[30]   See David Knight, 'Popularizing Chemistry: Hands-on Hands-off', *Hyle* 12.1 (2006), 131–40.

fire, or, more likely, 'blind, maim, or kill himself' because he used all his dishes to mix chemicals.[31]

On a professional level, chemistry and physics were hard to distinguish: chemistry, the more comprehensive, dealing with the nature of matter, elements, atoms, fire, gases, weather, agriculture, even the alchemy from which it evolved, and physics, the intangibles, imponderables, subtle airs and fluids, forces, movements, energies, light, sound, heat, electricity, magnetism. Chemistry was the most popular and accessible science, and chemists (who, like the physicists, preferred to be called natural philosophers) like Davy, Priestley, Dalton, Faraday, even Luke Howard who classified clouds, were the best performers and writers offering the most engaging public lectures, the most versatile and relevant.[32] According to Davy in his introduction to his lectures on chemistry at the Royal Institution (1802), 'Chemistry is that part of Natural Philosophy which relates to those intimate actions of bodies upon each other, by which their appearances are altered, and their individuality destroyed' and applies to 'all the substances found upon our globe', the small and large, and the 'phænomena of combustion, of the solution of different substances in water, of the agencies of fire; the production of rain, hail, and snow, and the conversion of dead matter into living matter by vegetable organs, all belong to chemistry'.[33]

This idea of converting the dead to the living ranged from using mulch to fertilize flowers and vegetables to using electrical currents to animate dead frogs and criminals (one of the sensational public galvanic experiments). Such resurrections extended the secularization of nature that had been taking place in astronomy and geology to the life sciences, biology, zoology, medicine, to human life itself: to be resurrected, one did not have to be a god such as Adonis, or the son of a god, or a fictional monster, such as Mary Shelley's in *Frankenstein*. Rather, like the ancient Persephone myth, death and rebirth were part of the natural cycle, one as well suited to history, economics, and politics as to biology. Even on a molecular level, the ancient cyclical narrative revived. Erasmus Darwin, following Lucretius, both poet-scientists, depicted all life, all matter, everything observable, experienced, and even invisible as comprised of indestructible atoms, constantly circulating from the dead to the living and back again, conferring a curious form of molecular immortality:

> So erst the Sage [Pythagoras], with scientific truth,
> In Grecian temples taught the attentive youth;
> With ceaseless change, how restless atoms pass,
> From life to life, a transmigrating mass;
> How the same organs, which to day compose
> The poisonous henbane, or the fragrant rose,
> May, with to morrow's sun, new forms compile,
> Frown in the Hero, in the Beauty smile.
> Whence drew the enlighten'd Sage, the moral plan,

---

[31] Hogg, *Life*, 54–6.

[32] See Knight, 'Popularizing Chemistry: Hands-on Hands-off', 131–40 and Jan Golinski, *Science as Public Culture: Chemistry and Enlightenment in Britain, 1760–1820* (Cambridge: Cambridge UP, 1999).

[33] *The Collected Works of Sir Humphry Davy* (London: Smith, Elder and Co, 1839), II, 307.

> That man should ever be the friend of man;
> Should eye with tenderness all living forms,
> His brother-emmets, and his sister-worms.[34]

In *A New System of Chemical Philosophy* (1808), Dalton explained that 'No new creation or destruction of matter is within the reach of chemical agency. We might as well attempt to introduce a new planet into the solar system, or to annihilate one already in existence, as to create or destroy a particle of hydrogen.'[35] And Shelley, in *Queen Mab*: 'not one atom of yon earth | But once was living man' (2, 211–12). The corollary, a devastating idea for those who need to believe that individuality matters, that identity exists, is that the 'ultimate particles of all homogenous bodies are perfectly alike'.[36] In his poetry, Shelley, like Darwin, tried to rescue the individual, the singular dimension, the 'minutest atom' that is constantly changing into something else.

Among the scientific concepts of the 1790s, based on this cyclical concept, photosynthesis is the most controversial and also the most comprehensive. Photosynthesis requires all the elements, rain, sun, and organic matter, to produce the oxygen on which all human and animal life depends while cleansing the air of poisonous gases. As the basic mechanism of life, photosynthesis began 3.5 billion years ago; however it was not until 1793 that Priestley explained it to the British public, and it took another fifty years for the public and for philosophers to accept that they participate in the same natural processes as their pets, farm animals, and decorative gardens. Everything that lives depends on the 'all-sustaining air', as Shelley referred to it in *Prometheus Unbound* (I. 754), a poem Michael O'Neill describes in his book of that title as 'an exercise in deep breathing, an eco-utopian search for and journey into a transformed [...] ideological atmosphere'.[37]

Before Priestley, and Erasmus Darwin who brought his theories into the literary and mythological world, Shelley's powerful, allusive, and coherent image of plants breathing and air as the gift of life would not have been possible. For Shelley, everything breathes, participates in the cycle: the river Arve, the 'breath and blood of distant lands', 'Breathes its swift vapours to the circling air' ('Mont Blanc', 124, 126). Vitalism, with its emphasis on electricity, souls, and origins, marginalized photosynthesis and its implicit challenge to a spiritual and political elitism. Shelley, celebrating the 'breath of Autumn's being' ('Ode to the West Wind', 1) and the 'all-sustaining air', wrote literally the 'poetry of life', something he found wanting in contemporary science.

Shelley's astronomy was also based on a combination of experience, texts, and scientific theory. In England, the 'golden age' of astronomy, the 'comet-crazed century',[38] as one art historian called it, began in 1780, with more comets, meteors, and representations

---

[34] Erasmus Darwin, *The Temple of Nature; or, The Origin of Society* (London, 1803; IV, 417–28).

[35] John Dalton, *A New System of Chemical Philosophy* (London: Bickerstaff, Strand, 1808), I, 212.

[36] Ibid. 143.

[37] Michael O'Neill, *The All-Sustaining Air: Romantic Legacies and Renewals in British, American, and Irish Poetry since 1900* (Oxford: Oxford UP, 2007), 16.

[38] Roberta J. M. Olson and J. M. Pasachoff, *Fire in the Sky: The Decisive Centuries in British Art and Science* (Cambridge: Cambridge UP, 1998), 109.

of them than any time before or since. Domestic and public telescopes, poetry, paintings, festivals, comet parties, even textiles, cartoons, and hat-ornaments registered the heightened astral activity. In 1799, meteor showers, the moist climate enhancing their visual effects, appeared to be flashes of lightning or rockets according to *The Gentleman's Magazine*; and, from 1801 to 1802, global asteroid storms convinced astronomers that their origins were outer space and not debris thrown off by the earth. Like so many other aspects of nature during the Romantic period, the heavens and sky were secularized but also expanded.[39]

Shelley's textual sources in astronomy included Milton, Herschel, Erasmus Darwin, and his first tutor, Herschel's friend Dr James Lind.[40] Across his poetry appear conflicting images of the heavens including the 'boundaries of the sky', repeated references to the 'dome of | Heaven' ('Mont Blanc', 108, 140–1), and the 'intense inane' of *Prometheus Unbound* (III. iv. 204). Shelley's is an evolving heaven, infinite, populated with stars, planets, asteroids, evolving nebulae, lunar volcanoes, and extra-terrestrials. In *Queen Mab*, Shelley describes the sky as a 'black concave' (1, 243) and explains in a footnote:

> Beyond our atmosphere the sun would appear a rayless orb of fire in the midst of a black concave. The equal diffusion of its light on earth is owing to the refraction of the rays by the atmosphere, and their reflection from other bodies. Light consists either of vibrations propagated through a subtle medium, or of numerous minute particles repelled in all directions from the luminous body. Its velocity greatly exceeds that of any substance with which we are acquainted: observations on the eclipses of Jupiter's satellites have demonstrated that light takes up no more than 8′ 7″ in passing from the sun to the earth, a distance of 95,000,000 miles.

Fascinating here is Shelley's recognition of light as both particle and wave and the precise numbers grounding this fantastical adventure.

Hogg claimed that Shelley knew little mathematics and 'treated the whole notion of their paramount importance with contempt'.[41] Both were probably more mathematical than they realized, as most people in England were. Everyone who had been in school, and many who weren't, knew Euclid, the axioms, the rhetoric, the syntax, the style of thought, abstract and logical; their lives were shaped by it. As a Platonist, Shelley was at least a metaphysical geometer if not a physical one, believing in ideal forms, prime numbers, and truths that exist whether anyone proves them or not. Euclidean rhetoric suffused the culture and, largely through the Freemasons, was political as much as numerical, the most famous example being Thomas Jefferson's axiomatic opening lines to the *Declaration of Independence*: 'We hold these truths to be self-evident, that all men are created equal.' And whether it was just a figure of speech or a figure for poetry, Shelley himself showed his familiarity with Euclidean rhetoric when he claimed in *A Defence of Poetry* that poetry 'is at once the centre and circumference of knowledge'; it 'comprehends

[39] Roberta J. M. Olson, *Fire and Ice: A History of Comets in Art* (New York: Random House, 1987); Olson and Pasachoff, *Fire in the Sky*.

[40] See Christopher Goulding, 'Shelley's Cosmological Sublime: William Herschel, James Lind, and "The Multitudinous Orb"', *Review of English Studies* 57 (2006), 783–92.

[41] Hogg, *Life*, 51.

all science, and that to which all science must be referred' (*Norton* 2, 531). Throughout his poetry he alludes to shapes, surfaces, forms, angles, and symmetries, his imagination clearly informed by geometry. He described Peter in *Peter Bell the Third*, his parody of Wordsworth, as 'polyhedric Peter, or a Peter with many sides' in the dedicatory letter to Thomas Brown (*Norton* 2, 415–16), and the destructive lightening in *Prometheus Unbound* as 'perpendicular now, and now transverse' (IV. 277). In an essay fragment, *A Discourse on the Manners of the Antient Greeks*, he describes the 'astonishing invention of geometry, that series of discoveries which have enabled man to command the elements and foresee future events, before the subjects of his ignorant wonder, and has opened as it were the doors of the mysteries of nature'.[42]

As with all the sciences he knew, Shelley assimilates different mathematical concepts—some contradictory, aesthetic, mystical, philosophical, religious, political, biological—that had accumulated around geometry. He may have refined his boyhood geometry with readings from Thomas Taylor, one of his vegetarian sources, who translated Pythagoras, another mathematical vegetarian, and from Proclus. Erasmus Darwin presented several strains of Euclidean thought, the classical, mystical Pythagoreans and the Rosicrucians, the subject of Shelley's early Gothic novel *St. Irvyne or the Rosicrucians* and the source of the excesses which led to Darwin being parodied in *The Loves of the Triangles*. The Pythagorean world transcended mathematics and the spatial abstractions of Euclidean geometry: number is beauty, but life depends on process, on transformation not form.

Geology, astronomy, chemistry, biology, the sciences that most interested Shelley, were non-mathematical, narrative even for the scientists themselves, personified and animate with plots, intersections, conflict, struggle. These sciences presented abstractions, immensities, indeterminacies, infinities for which existing British mathematics were not suited. Mathematicians including William Frend, Charles Bonnycastle, and John Playfair, the great geologist, rejected imaginary and negative numbers and anything that could not be empirically demonstrated: Herschel's boundless universe, Hutton's 'fathomless' one, Priestley's invisibles, and Dalton's particles (so many he was 'confounded with the thought').[43] Shelley reflects these contradictions in *Queen Mab*, which opens (as does *Laon and Cythna*) with a quotation from Archimedes, among the greatest geometers of antiquity, commenting on the lever: 'Give me somewhere to stand, and I will move the earth' (*Norton* 2, 16). Shelley thus invokes a geometrical basis for social action. And while he offers that precise footnote on how long it takes light to travel in *Queen Mab*, the poem itself reflects the challenges of number in this new universe of 'Countless and unending orbs' (2, 73), 'Innumerable systems' and 'countless spheres' (1, 253–4), 'infinity within, | Infinity without' (7, 21–2), 'interminable multitudes' (3, 227), and 'the indefinite immensity of the universe [...] a most awful subject of contemplation' (Shelley's note to 1, 252–3).

[42] Quoted in James A. Notopoulos, *The Platonism of Shelley: A Study of Platonism and the Poetic Mind* (Durham, NC: Duke UP, 1949), 405.
[43] Dalton, *New System*, 212.

Such mysteries of nature and of human life acquired definition, boundaries, dimensions from another mathematics, a 'quantifying spirit' as it has been called, that flourished among all classes and levels of literacy: counting, enumeration, number theory, accounting, statistics, and the revival of classical probability.[44] To mathematicians, natural philosophers, and social thinkers, everything, even the earth, could be and was measured and weighed, the stars and people counted and accounted for. Probability theory overcame the loss of belief in destiny, fate, certitude, or Godwin's and later Shelley's Necessity, and shaped an economy of gambling, insurance, and statistics. Numbers ruled what Shelley in *A Defence of Poetry* called the 'grosser sciences' (*Norton 2*, 530),: Malthus' brutal ratios of population and resources, Adam Smith's circulating wealth, Jeremy Bentham's 'pleasure calculus', the tyranny of majorities which troubled even a populist such as Shelley. In *A Defence*, Shelley invokes the great Euclidean mathematical tradition to empower poetry as the 'centre and circumference', as opposed to the enumerative one:

> We have more moral, political and historical wisdom, than we know how to reduce into practise; we have more scientific and œconomical knowledge than can be accommodated to the just distribution of the produce which it multiplies. The poetry in these systems of thought, is concealed by the accumulation of facts and calculating processes […] our calculations have outrun conception […] The cultivation of those sciences which have enlarged the limits of the empire of man over the external world, has, for want of the poetical faculty, proportionally circumscribed those of the internal world; and man, having enslaved the elements, remains himself a slave. (*Norton 2*, 531, 530)

Shelley's poetry captures boundless and vast spaces and the eons of time: his response was not enumeration, but form, poetic form.

Romanticism coincided with the Golden Age of Geology, a period of public drama and conflict between two schools: those who believed the earth had been divinely created and then destroyed as punishment for human sin, the Catastrophists, and those who believed that the origins and ends were unknowable and that the earth had been evolving independent of human or divine intervention, the Uniformitarians. Shelley, according to Hogg, dismissed a geology lecture he attended at Oxford as 'stupid', 'tiresome', and 'nothing but stones, stones, stones'. As with his other sciences, however, from observation, experience, historical and contemporary theories, Shelley developed an original, comprehensive, and imaginative image of earth history. His primary influence was James Hutton, whose Uniformitarian *Theory of the Earth* (1795) depicted an earth that was constantly changing, shaped by the wind and rain as well as volcanic eruptions and earthquakes; these latter phenomena, as with astral events, increased all over the world in frequency and severity during the period. From his observations on a

[44] Tore Frangsmyr, J. L. Heilbron, and Robin E. Rider (eds.), *The Quantifying Spirit of the 18th Century* (Berkeley and Los Angeles: University of California Press, 1990). See also my 'Romantic Numeracy: The Tuneless Numbers and Shadows Numberless', *Wordsworth Circle* 22 (1991), 124–31 and 'From *Tristram Shandy* to Bertrand Russell: Fiction and Mathematics', *British Society for the History of Mathematics Bulletin* 25 (2009), 81–91.

hillside in Scotland, he inferred a gradual, cyclical process, like photosynthesis, or nebulae that connect the 'mineral system of this earth with that by which the heavenly bodies are made to move'. Reconciled to the pitiless processes of nature, its indifference to human needs, Hutton saw 'no vestige of a beginning, no prospect of an end', instead a 'deep time', its challenges and deprecations: 'Time which measures everything in our idea, and is often deficient in our schemes, is to nature endless and as nothing.'[45] Hutton's image was Shelley's, from the molecular to the celestial, vast spans of time, the evolving landscapes, the creative and destructive powers of wind, rain, sun, inner fires, earthquakes, and ice, and the 'sublime science' as Wilson calls it, of living glaciers.[46] Such ideas shaped 'Mont Blanc': 'how hideously | Its shapes are heaped around! rude, bare, and high, | Ghastly, and scarred, and riven' where the 'old Earthquake-daemon taught her young | Ruin', 'a sea | Of fire, envelope once this silent snow' (69–74) and ultimately, the glacier, 'a flood of ruin' (107), overthrowing 'The limits of the dead and living world' (113). The events, powers, and forces in 'Mont Blanc' terrify because they have all the qualities of divinity without the responsibility, because they are secular and indifferent to human suffering: 'So much of life and joy is lost. The race | Of man, flies far in dread; his work and dwelling | Vanish, like smoke before the tempest's stream, | And their place is not known' (117–20). As with photosynthesis, Herschel's universe, and Dalton's atoms, in Hutton's geology and its dramatization in 'Mont Blanc', human history is overcome by natural history. As Noah Heringman points out, Shelley's was a romance with rocks, glaciers, volcanoes, earthquakes, forces and powers he sensed even when he did not understand them.[47]

As poet, Shelley also gave voice to Hutton's opposite, George Cuvier's catastrophic geology. First published in France in 1811 and translated into English in 1817 as *Theory of the Earth*, Cuvier's catastrophism restored the theological narrative to geology: the fossil bones and irregularities in the landscape memorialize an angry god who destroyed the earth and all living things, multiple times perhaps, by flood, earthquake, and meteors. The same forces Hutton had seen shaping the earth, in Cuvier became weapons, punishment for human sins. Like Byron, drawing on the apocryphal *Book of Enoch* in *Cain* and *Heaven and Earth*, Shelley overcame the theology to engage the visual, aesthetic, and dramatic impact of catastrophism. In *Prometheus Unbound* he depicts the originating flood, the 'melancholy ruins | Of cancelled cycles', 'ruin within ruin', the population, 'mortal but not human', 'lie, | Their monstrous works and uncouth skeletons, | Their statues, homes, and fanes' 'Huddled in grey annihilation' along with the 'anatomies of unknown wingèd things, | And fishes which were isles of living scale, | And serpents, bony chains, twisted around' (288–305). Here Shelley dramatizes the pointless cruelty in religious interpretations of nature which, in comparison with the vision of 'Mont Blanc', is far worse than the secular.

---

[45] James Hutton, *Theory of the Earth: With Proofs and Illustrations* (Edinburgh, 1795), I, 276, 304, 215.

[46] Eric G. Wilson, *The Spiritual History of Ice: Romanticism, Science and the Imagination* (New York: Palgrave, 2003), 74.

[47] Noah Heringman, *Romantic Rocks, Aesthetic Geology* (Ithaca, NY: Cornell UP, 2004).

Not yet subjected to scientific overview, weather played a definitive role in the new sciences, the art, music, and writing of the Romantic period, and Shelley is exquisitely sensitive to weather from every perspective. As late at the 1770s, weather depicted in literature and art was primarily textual, acquired from reading or paintings; poets, writers, artists, even natural philosophers worked indoors, from their studios, libraries, laboratories, secluded and domestic spaces such as the parlour sofa on which William Cowper wrote *The Task*, one of the longest loco-descriptive poems in the language. The poor, vagabonds, rustics, sailors, pedlars, owned the weather and with it weather-lore, all that could be known of weather, especially how to interpret and predict it in terms other than divine signs of pleasure and discontent.

However creatively writers and philosophers considered British weather, the climate itself was cold and inhospitable to human life. England was frozen in a little ice age from 1560 to 1860, with only brief periods of relative warming, and during the Romantic period, from 1790 to 1830, had endured a particularly frigid period of decreased solar energies, called the 'Dalton Minimum' after John Dalton. Atmospheric dust from volcanic eruptions, mostly in Iceland but also in the distant Philippines, fourteen of them between 1783 and 1817, also obscured the sun: Tambora in 1815, the largest and most famous, turned 1816 into a year without summer: failed crops, hunger, poverty, disease, the apocalypse Byron described in *Darkness*.[48]

To be a science, to be climate rather than a collection of weather events, weather required technology, balloons, and telegraphy to communicate distant and forthcoming phenomena. In London, Luke Howard, a Quaker chemist, advanced the idea of forecasting by identifying and naming the clouds by shape (another geometric skill), explaining how they functioned in weather systems, and how to interpret them as secular rather than sacred signs. Howard's *Essay on Clouds* (1803) was republished often, inspiring Goethe to write poems about him and Constable to spend a summer learning the vocabulary of clouds. Howard's essay may also lie behind the amazing description in Shelley's 'The Cloud', composed in Italy between 1818 and 1820, which some consider so accurate a description that it is still cited by meteorologists when considering the complicated and mysterious nature of storms. However, it is still, as Webb wrote, 'beyond the reach of versified meteorology', a characteristically layered account of the allegorical, symbolic, mythic, and functional meanings of a natural event which becomes in Shelley's hands a cultural one.[49]

'Ode to the West Wind', the poem Bertrand Russell most closely identified with, describes the wind as 'Uncontroulable' (47), 'tameless, and swift, and proud' (56); the poem best illustrates how Shelley assimilated art, politics, contemporary science, and the nuances of weather. It was 'conceived and chiefly written', Shelley says, 'in a wood that skirts the Arno, near Florence, and on a day when that tempestuous wind, whose temperature is at once mild and animating, was collecting the vapours which pour down

[48] Gillen D'Arcy Wood, 'Constable, Clouds, Climate Change', *Wordsworth Circle* 38.1–2 (2007), 25–38; Jonathan Bate, 'Living with the Weather', *Studies in Romanticism* 35 (1996), 431–7.
[49] Timothy Webb, *Shelley: A Voice Not Understood* (Manchester: Manchester UP, 1977), 246; also see F. H. Ludlam, *The Times Literary Supplement*, 1 September 1972.

the autumnal rains. They began, as I foresaw, at sunset with a violent tempest of hail and rain, attended by that magnificent thunder and lightning peculiar to the Cisalpine regions' (*Norton 2*, 297–8). A recurrent seasonal wind, with different names depending on where it is experienced, in the folk tradition causes illness, lassitude, melancholy, distemper, even criminal behaviour, but always arouses superstition, narratives, and song. Shelley's West Wind does it all: inspires, admonishes, punishes, blesses, buries, revives, disappoints, creates, and destroys; it has something of the mythic winds of the Old Testament, the geological winds of Hutton, and the actual autumnal winds. Although he is the source of the power he attributes to the wind, Shelley depicts himself as blasted, alienated, exiled, his own powers failing as one more victim in a history of suffering prophets: Orpheus, Job, Christ.

Shelley reflects the perennial wary and suspicious attitudes toward weather, not totally scientific or artistic, with lingering spiritual connotations, anthropomorphic, the floods, earthquakes, perfect storms, without meaning, without a divine origin or history. To his careful and informed observations of impending storm, of the interconnectedness of nature, of how weather events suffuse every aspect of nature, the sky, the sea, the foliage and human beings, to this knowledge of encounter, the record of a moment, he adds a rich and layered textual knowledge: Luke Howard's classification of clouds, Humphry Davy on vapours, Erasmus Darwin on everything, the biblical Job and God speaking in the whirlwind, the Greek Orphic tradition, the metaphoric winds of revolution, the aesthetic symbol of wind as literal inspiration, the 'correspondent breeze', as Wordsworth called it (*The Prelude*, 1850, I, 35). As Shelley wrote in the fragment *On Love*: 'In the motion of the very leaves of spring in the blue air there is found a secret correspondence with our heart. There is eloquence in the tongueless wind [...]' (*Norton 2*, 504).

As a poet, Shelley helped disseminate the scientific experiences of his day to his contemporaries and to his heirs even into the twentieth century, not only the concepts but also the human responses. In his representations of the major ideas of Romantic science—the cyclical and evolutionary concept of life, the secularization of nature, the indeterminacy of scientific speculation, the relatedness of all things, the displacement of human beings—Shelley helped change the narrative of natural history from a linear and hierarchical one to a recurrent and reciprocal one and helped change the human role from observer to participant in nature. For scientists such as Russell, Whitehead, King-Hele, and Cameron who sensed a kindred spirit in him, he connected them to their mythic and natural origins; for poets, he identified the beauty in the sciences, the shared mysteries, the common creative experiences, and the power of art.

SELECT BIBLIOGRAPHY

Burwick, Frederick. *The Damnation of Newton: Goethe's Color Theory and Romantic Perception.* Berlin: Walter de Gruyter, 1986.
Coleman, William. *Biology in the Nineteenth Century: Cambridge Studies in the History of Science.* Cambridge: Cambridge UP, 1978.

Crowe, Michael J. *Modern Theories of the Universe from Herschel to Hubble*. Chicago: University of Chicago Press, 1994.

Dawkins, Richard. *Unweaving the Rainbow: Science, Delusion, and the Appetite for Wonder*. New York: Penguin, 1998.

Eiseley, Loren. *Darwin's Century: Evolution and the Men who Discovered It*. New York: Anchor, 1961.

Gaull, Marilyn. *English Romanticism: The Human Context*. New York: W. W. Norton, 1988.

Hankins, Thomas. *Science and the Enlightenment: Cambridge Studies in the History of Science*. Cambridge: Cambridge UP, 1985.

Holmes, Richard. *The Age of Wonder: How the Romantic Generation Discovered the Beauty and Terror of Science*. London: Pantheon, 2009.

Lee, Debbie, Peter J. Kitson, and Tim Fulford. *Literature, Science, and Exploration in the Romantic Era: Bodies of Knowledge*. Cambridge: Cambridge UP, 2004.

Porter, Roy. *The Greatest Benefit to Mankind: A Medical History of Humanity*. New York: W. W. Norton, 1999.

Robson, Eleanor and Jacqueline Steadall. Eds. *The Oxford Handbook of the History of Mathematics*. Oxford: Oxford UP, 2009.

CHAPTER 37

SHELLEY, TRAVEL, AND TOURISM

BENJAMIN COLBERT

In her note on *The Revolt of Islam*, Mary Shelley remarked that Shelley 'was very fond of travelling, and ill-health increased this restlessness' (*H* 156) and elsewhere, 'But for our fears on account of our child [Percy Florence], I believe we should have wandered over the world, both being passionately fond of travelling' (*H* 636).[1] While scholars have been long attuned to Mary Shelley's travels, her extensive readings in travel writing, and her own contributions to the genre, the importance of travel and travel writing (his own and that of others) for understanding Shelley's poetic sources, methods, intentions, and contexts has been only gradually appreciated.[2] Nevertheless, Mary Shelley's notes to *The Poetical Works* (1839) consistently relate place of composition to the nature and texture of Shelley's works, and her earliest statement in this vein, from her preface to *Posthumous Poems* (1824), articulates this as a principle pervading his work:

> [...] every page of his poetry is associated in the minds of his friends with the loveliest scenes of the countries which he inhabited. In early life he visited the most beautiful parts of this country and Ireland. Afterwards the Alps of Switzerland became his inspirers. 'Prometheus Unbound' was written among the deserted and flower-grown ruins of Rome, and when he made his home under the Pisan hills, their roofless recesses harboured him as he composed 'The Witch of Atlas,' 'Adonais' and 'Hellas'. In the wild but beautiful Bay of Spezia, the winds and waves which he loved became his playmates.[3]

---

[1] Compare Shelley's letter of 20 July 1820 to Thomas Medwin, then touring the mountains around Geneva: 'how much I sympathise in the delights of your wandering. I have a passion for such expeditions' (*Letters: PBS* II, 218–19).

[2] See Select Bibliography below. For Mary Shelley, see Jeanne Moskal, 'Travel Writing', in Esther Schor (ed.), *The Cambridge Companion to Mary Shelley* (Cambridge: Cambridge UP, 2003), 242–58.

[3] Mary Shelley, 'Preface', in Percy Bysshe Shelley, *Posthumous Poems, 1824* (Oxford: Woodstock Books, 1991), p. v.

Her emphasis on homes, harbours, and sublime domestication makes of Shelley a cosmopolitan poet understood best by those ('his friends') who have travelled, who have seen what he has seen; readers' memories become adjuncts to poetry that itself aspires to the status of memorial or monument. While Shelley's preface to *The Revolt of Islam* describes the ideal education of the living poet in terms of solitary wandering, or travel to distant, extreme environments ('Danger [...] has been my *playmate*' (*H* 34, emphasis added)), Mary Shelley counters with an image less of defiance than incorporation, and, in so doing, grants to Shelley his most wished-for status, the poet of nature whose works live on *in* nature. Readers, like tourists, follow in the footsteps of writers, learning to read the places that have been hallowed by poetry and the poetry by place.

By contrast, it would seem, Shelley sets himself the task of seeing what others do not. 'I always seek in what I see the manifestation of something beyond the present & tangible object' (*Letters: PBS* II, 47), he writes to Thomas Love Peacock from Ferrara, and elsewhere he rails against travel writings that devote themselves to 'shew-knowledge [...] "the common stuff of the earth"' (*Letters: PBS* II, 89).[4] He takes what James Buzard refers to as an 'anti-tourist' stance characteristic of the period,[5] 'tourism' and its derivatives being words only then attaining currency, usually in the pejorative. But Shelley, for all his resistance to populist modes of travel and his avoidance of and disdain for the English abroad in Geneva, Rome, and Florence, nevertheless finds himself 'play[ing] the tourist deftly' (*Letters: PBS* I, 475), following beaten paths, hiring guides, visiting tourist sites, reading travel narratives and guidebooks, writing travel prose and poetry, sketching, and positioning his own reflections in contradistinction (or harmony, as the case may be) with touristic conventions.

What makes Shelley most interesting as a tourist/traveller is his self-analysis, his attempt to come to terms with tourism as an epistemological and cultural phenomenon. Many of his poems—including 'Ozymandias', 'Mont Blanc', 'Lines Written among the Euganean Hills', 'Ode to Naples', and *Adonais*, to which one might add Shelley's prose fragment *The Coliseum*—problematize the beholding eye of the traveller-observer;[6] and still others embed travel and travellers into their narrative frames: *Alastor*, *Prometheus Unbound*, *Epipsychidion*, and *Hellas*.[7] But the quality of self-reflection comes to the fore with Shelley's literary tourism, a phenomenon Nicola Watson has recently called a typically romantic practice involving 'habits of writing and memorialisation' growing alongside a new interest in the birthplaces, homes, haunts, and tombs of writers and their fictions.[8] Mary Shelley's own revision of Shelley's literary life in her notes and prefaces

---

[4] Shelley quotes from Godwin's *Mandeville*, immediately after Mandeville describes his own 'disposition to walk gloomily [...] and [...] shut myself up disdainfully in my own contemplations' (William Godwin, *Mandeville: A Tale of the Seventeenth Century in England*, 3 vols. (Edinburgh, 1817), III, 328). Shelley thus supplements his opposition to 'shew knowledge' with a rebuke against solipsism.

[5] James Buzard, *The Beaten Track: European Tourism, Literature, and the Ways to Culture, 1800–1918* (Oxford: Clarendon Press, 1993), 4–7.

[6] See Benjamin Colbert, *Shelley's Eye: Travel Writing and Aesthetic Vision* (Burlington, VT: Ashgate, 2005), 141–60.

[7] Unless otherwise indicated, citations from poetry in this essay will be to *Norton 2*.

[8] Nicola J. Watson, *The Literary Tourist: Readers and Places in Romantic and Victorian Britain* (London: Palgrave Macmillan, 2006), 10.

may be seen as an extension of this kind of touristic intertextuality, the layering of text, place, and affective identification between tourist-readers with absent authors. After outlining Shelley's travels, then, this chapter considers, first, the relation of his travels to 'literary' tourism, the making 'permanent' of poetry in and through place, and, second, Shelley's attraction to tombs, ruins, and places inscribed by the dead as a special kind of literary tourism: necro-tourism.

SHELLEY IN TRANSIT

Although he 'perused with more than ordinary eagerness the relations of travellers in the East', according to Thomas Jefferson Hogg,[9] and later entertained a voyage to Greece and the Levant, Shelley's travels were nevertheless circumscribed within Britain, Ireland, and continental Europe, and were marked by a tension between 'restlessness' and a desire to find a dwelling place, a place of belonging even in exile. Before going up to Oxford, he visited beauty spots in Wales near Cwm Elan, the estate belonging to the family of his cousin and first love, Harriet Grove, and after being sent down, Wales continued to fascinate as a potential spot for establishing a radical community. From 1811 to 1813, Shelley travelled hectically though England, Scotland, Wales, and Ireland: fleeing with Harriet Westbrook from London to Edinburgh and a Scottish marriage; residing temporarily in Keswick near Robert Southey; crossing twice to Ireland on political and literary missions; and wandering through North Wales and later Devon in search of an elusive homestead.

It was not until the second phase of his travels between 1814 and 1816 that Shelley began to construct his own poetic identity as a traveller/tourist-observer. This period began with Shelley's six-week (second) elopement tour, in which he, Mary Godwin, and Claire Clairmont joined the first wave of continental tourists after the cessation of hostilities with France in 1814. He began a travel journal with Mary and together they recorded their journey to Switzerland through sombre, half-ruined French villages in the wake of the Allied armies. They also followed idealized routes mapped out in the writings of William Godwin, Rousseau, and Tacitus, and read aloud from Mary Wollstonecraft's *Letters from Sweden, Denmark, and Norway* (1796) on the return voyage up the Rhine. Back in England, Shelley transmuted and relocalized these experiences in *Alastor* (1815), a poem featuring a traveller-poet who 'seeks strange truth in undiscovered lands', while in *The Revolt of Islam* (1817), Shelley describes the 'education peculiarly fitted for a Poet' in terms of his own continental travels: 'I have trodden the glaciers of the Alps, and lived under the eye of Mont Blanc [...] I have sailed down mighty rivers [...]' (*H* 34).

Here Shelley refers also to his second continental tour during summer 1816, when he, Mary Shelley, and Claire Clairmont established their residence near the shores of Lake

---

[9] Thomas Jefferson Hogg, *The Life of Percy Bysshe Shelley*, 4 vols. (London: Edward Moxon, 1858), I, 108.

Geneva, not far from Byron's Villa Diodati. Shelley and Byron launched their troubled friendship with a boating trip round the lake, taking in the 'classic ground' associated with Rousseau's *Julie, ou la Nouvelle Heloïse* (1761), already on the beaten track of tourists; the Shelley party also followed well-trodden paths to Mont Blanc and the glaciers of Montanvert, Shelley composing the first drafts of 'Mont Blanc' on this tour. Like other tourists, Shelley described his impressions in letters home, his first efforts in extended travel prose. Under Mary Shelley's editorial hand, these letters to Peacock, some of her own (perhaps originally addressed to her sister Fanny Imlay),[10] the journal of the 1814 tour, and 'Mont Blanc', were collected as *History of a Six Weeks' Tour through a Part of France, Switzerland, Germany, and Holland: with Letters Descriptive of a Sail round the Lake of Geneva, and of the Glaciers of Chamouni* (1817), one of eighteen British travelogues treating those regions published that year, but a rare example of collaborative work between male and female companions.[11]

As early as March 1812, Shelley entertained the idea of travelling to Italy, and his party considered crossing the Alps during both the 1814 and 1816 continental tours.[12] By autumn 1817, Shelley and Mary Shelley were forming plans once more to take up residence in Italy, prompted by Shelley's health worries, and they left England on 12 March 1818. Again Shelley began writing descriptive travel letters to Peacock—a total of eighteen between 6 April 1818 and 1 April 1819[13]—and Peacock, Mary Shelley, and probably Shelley himself recognized in them the basis for a travel publication.[14] Shelley takes his reader over the Alps to Milan, to the 'divine solitudes of Como' (*Letters: PBS* II, 16), to Pisa, the Bagni di Lucca, and, between June and August, on excursions in surrounding locales. Another sequence of travel followed, as the Shelleys shifted their residence to a villa in Este, the Casa I Capuccini, loaned to them by Byron. In late September, after the death of their infant daughter Clara, the Shelleys lost themselves in sightseeing around Venice, and Shelley began reflecting on his experience of Italy thus far in 'Lines Written among the Euganean Hills'. In early November, the party made their way to Rome and Naples, taking in Ferrara, Bologna, Spoleto, and the Falls of Terni, before entering Rome on 20 November. In a long journal letter to Peacock written from Naples nearly a month later, Shelley describes Rome as a revelation: 'The impression of it exceeds any thing I have ever experienced in my travels' (*Letters: PBS* II, 58). With his principal guidebook at hand, John Chetwode Eustace's *Classical Tour through Italy* (3rd edition, 1815), as well as the Italian Canto (fourth) of *Childe Harold*, Shelley surveyed critically the ruins of the

---

[10]   See *Letters: MWS* I, 19 n. 1.

[11]   For the Shelleys' 'collaborative spirit and non possessive attitude' and 'the experience they shared as tourists', see George G. Dekker, *The Fictions of Romantic Tourism: Radcliffe, Scott, and Mary Shelley* (Stanford, CA: Stanford UP, 2005), 202; 202–9.

[12]   For 1814, see *Letters: PBS* I, 276, 305; for 1816, see Shelley's remarks to Godwin of 21 February 1816 on 'our Italian scheme' (I, 453).

[13]   Fifteen survive. For a reconstruction of the Shelley–Peacock correspondence, see *The Letters of Thomas Love Peacock*, ed. Nicholas A. Joukovsky, 2 vols. (Oxford: Clarendon Press, 2001), I, p. lix.

[14]   Responding to Shelley's letters from Bologna and Rome, Peacock advised his friend: 'if you bring home a journal full of such descriptions [...] they will attract a very great share of public attention' (*Letters of Thomas Love Peacock*, I, 160).

ancient city—triumphal arches, the Forum, temples, and tombs—sensitive to aesthetic, historical, and political nuances at every step. The letter then conducts Peacock on the road to Naples, and, from there, two excursions to local points of interest, the first to Baiae Bay, and the second to Vesuvius ('after the glaciers the most impressive expression of the energies of nature I ever saw' (*Letters: PBS* II, 62)). Resident at Naples from around 28 November to 28 February 1819, Shelley visited Pompeii and Paestum, and studied painting and sculpture at the *Studii* (Royal Museum), composing gallery notes as well as the descriptions in the letters to Peacock. Throughout March and April, he revisited his haunts in Rome, adding detailed descriptions of the Baths of Caracalla, the Colosseum, St Peter's, the fountains, and statuary. With the death of his son William on 7 June, however, the travel letters cease. The Shelleys relocated first to Livorno and, after a residence in Florence from October to February 1820, Pisa, their final residence in exile. Nevertheless, the months of Shelley's most intense travels coincided with a period of intense creativity, with travel experiences and images informing the major poetry as well as the fine travel prose that Shelley was writing at this time.

Literary Tourism

Shelley's earliest sojourns of 1811–13 are memorialized by scattered letters in which he takes stock of his surroundings, especially sublime landscapes.[15] And yet, it is remarkable how little Shelley records. He kept no travel journal or dedicated sketchbook; his letters, replete with political, religious, legal, and financial schemes and anxieties, break off abruptly from touristic descriptions, as if these were indulgences; even sights that impressed him deeply remain cloaked: there is no record, for example, of his six-day visit in March 1813 to the lakes of Killarney, an increasingly popular tourist destination that affected Shelley enough to recall the beauties of its 'arbutus islands' when visiting, five years later, Lake Como in Italy.[16] Traces of travel may be found in the lyrics collected in his never-published companion volume to *Queen Mab*, 'Minor Poems' (1813), which, as David Duff remarks, might be read 'if not quite as a travelogue then as a diaristic poetic record of the literal and symbolic journeys of Shelley's early life'.[17] In poems like 'Written on a Beautiful Day in Spring', 'On Leaving London for Wales', and 'The Retrospect. Cwm Elan, 1812', Shelley explores affective transformations of landscape, the colourings superadded by solitude and companionship, despair and love. The notion of

[15] See Cian Duffy, '"One Draught from Snowdon's Sacred Spring": Shelley's Welsh Sublime', in Damian Walford Davies and Lynda Pratt (eds.), *Wales and the Romantic Imagination* (Cardiff: University of Wales Press, 2007), 180–98.

[16] See *Letters: PBS* II, 6. For an account of the 'arbutus islands' of Killarney as Shelley might have experienced them, see Anne Plumptre, *Narrative of a Residence in Ireland during the Summer of 1814, and that of 1815* (London: Henry Colburn, 1817), 267–306.

[17] David Duff, '"The Casket of my Unknown Mind": The 1813 Volume of Minor Poems', in Alan M. Weinberg and Timothy Webb (eds.), *The Unfamiliar Shelley* (Burlington, VT: Ashgate, 2009), 50.

'rapture' is repeatedly invoked, sometimes as a delusional or illusory emotion, some-times as supra-rational or supra-sensual vision.

In the early letters, one also glimpses Shelley's desire to form associations between lit-erature and landscape as well as his attractions to literary destinations. During his first visit to the Lake District late in 1811, this desire is focused upon Southey: 'The scenery here is awfully beautiful. [...] but the object most interesting to my feelings is Southey's habitation. He is now on a journey [...]' (*Letters: PBS* I, 183, 14 November 1811). The charm of viewing Southey's residence did not survive Shelley's meeting the man, nor did Shelley's picturesque raptures outlast a closer acquaintance with Cumberland social inequities.[18] But, transferring his hopes of intellectual communion from Southey to Godwin, Shelley continued to develop links between literature and landscape, increas-ingly investing Wales as a rural ideal beyond taint. Expressing his disappointment that Godwin could not visit him there, Shelley confesses his 'fancy that I s{hould} first meet you in a spot like that in which Fleetwood met Ruffigny; that then every lesson of your wisdom might become associated in my mind with the forms of Nature [...] and each become imperishable together' (*Letters: PBS* I, 260). The powerful attraction to Shelley of the idealized sage Ruffigny in Godwin's novel *Fleetwood* (1805), as Newman Ivey White and Gavin de Beer suggest, led Shelley, during the summer of 1814, to colour his first views of continental Europe in the hues of Godwinian romance, with Uri and the republican haunts of Wilhelm Tell the destination in which Shelley and Godwin's daugh-ters could animate their personal hardships with republican ideals in a post-Napoleonic landscape hallowed by fiction.[19] De Beer's claim that Shelley had by this time 'made a system of following in the tracks of the heroes of William Godwin's novels' identifies a pattern for which Shelley desired an explanation, and the ruminations on the relation-ship between fiction and reality which emanated from his two continental tours, if not a cohesive theory, comes closer than any other writer of the period to integrating literary tourism into a unified conception of poetry, the poet, and social change.

In 1826, Mary Shelley recalled the elopement tour of 1814 as a 'new chapter [...] of our travels': 'it was acting a novel, being an incarnate romance.'[20] Such recollections strike a truer tone in the light of the *Fleetwood* itinerary. Other texts, too, played a part in Shelley's sense of place on the tour, some historical, such as Tacitus, with Shelley's imagi-nation longitudinally layering a history of republicanism onto visible monuments.[21] Another presence to have received less attention than it merits is *As You Like It*. On the forested route to Besançon, Claire borrowed a volume of Shelley's Shakespeare and

---

[18] See *Letters: PBS* I, 223, where Shelley writes to Elizabeth Hitchener that 'tho the face of the country is lovely the *people* are detestable', blaming the social rot on manufacturers and tourism. Shelley would repeat these anti-touristic sentiments in Geneva (see *Letters: PBS* I, 500–1).

[19] See Newman Ivey White, *Shelley*, 2 vols. (London: Secker & Warburg, 1947), I, 320; and Gavin de Beer, Commentary to 'The Journal of Claire Clairmont, 14–22 August 1814', *SC* III, 364.

[20] Mary Shelley, 'The English in Italy', *Westminster Review* (October 1826), quoted in *CC*, 'Appendix A', 442.

[21] Michael Rossington, 'Rousseau and Tacitus: Republican Inflections in the Shelleys' *History of a Six Weeks' Tour*', *European Romantic Review* 19.4 (2008), 321–33.

opened it to this romance on 17 August 1814, perhaps at the instigation of Shelley, who at other times during the tour superintended her reading, as when he set her to translate one of Rousseau's *Rêveries* (*SC* III, 350). Claire 'found the wild & romantic touches of this Play very accordant with the scene before me' (*CC* 25) and later recalled Shelley's explanation that 'poetry read in a room never came so near the soul as if read in a beautiful spot, in the wide open air' (*SC* III, 346).[22] The choice of *As You Like It* can hardly have been random, given the parallels between the Shelley party and the rag-tag pedestrian travellers, Rosalind (posing as a young man), Celia (rechristened 'Aliena'), and Touchstone—exiles from patriarchal persecution who refashion their flight to the wildwood, Arden, as a journey 'To liberty, and not to banishment'.[23] The Arden romance enhances nature's healing and nurturing powers with textual metaphors—the 'Tongues in trees, books in the running brooks, | Sermons in stones, and good in every thing' (II. i. 16–17)—that counter the subterfuge of tyranny, but parodies too the overly literal grafting of feeling onto landscape, the love poems that Orlando pins to trees and scratches in bark ('these trees shall be my books' (III. ii. 5); 'tongues I'll hang on every tree' (III. ii. 127)).[24] Besides its sceptical foundation for reflections on literary tourism that increasingly preoccupy Shelley, the play also addresses Shelley's anti-tourism through the haunting proto-Byronic figure of the melancholy traveller, Jacques, whose restlessness purchases 'experience' (IV. i. 26) at the expense of belonging and fellow-feeling.

The *History of a Six Weeks' Tour*, as Jacqueline Labbe argues, uses 'romance to emphasize the lost romance of the war-ravaged' France, a textual manipulation that undercuts even as it deploys a generic frame popular with readers.[25] In its earlier manifestations on the spot (reading Shakespeare and following Fleetwood) the mode also appears to mark out the beginnings of touristic self-awareness in the travellers, their sense that tourism calls into relief the disjunctions between the *beau idéal* of intellectual freedom and the colder realities of war, tyranny, and human suffering.[26] Certain it is that the two tours to the Continent in 1814 and 1816 are accompanied by a maturation of Shelley's touristic self-consciousness. Though he claimed to Peacock in 1816 that 'it will be long before I shall play the tourist deftly' (*Letters: PBS* I, 475), he had already imbibed enough travel writing to know when he was in danger of sounding conventional: 'I too had read [...] the raptures of travellers. I will be warned by their example' (*Letters: PBS* I, 495). While

---

[22] *CC* 25.

[23] Shakespeare, *As You Like It*, I. iii. 138, in *The Riverside Shakespeare* (Boston: Houghton Mifflin, 1974), 376. Parenthetical citations are to this edition.

[24] Compare the lines in Orlando's poem—'Why should this [a] desert be? | For it is unpeopled? No! | Tongues I'll hang on every tree, | That shall civil sayings show' (III. ii. 125–8)—with Shelley's 'Mont Blanc', part 3. Shelley too juxtaposes the 'desart peopled by the storms alone' (67) with the 'mysterious tongue' of the 'wilderness' (76) and the 'voice' of the 'great Mountain' (80), both of which teach, in Orlando's sense of the word, 'civil' lessons.

[25] Jacqueline Labbe, 'A Family Romance: Mary Wollstonecraft, Mary Godwin, and Travel', *Genre* 25 (1992), 225.

[26] Similar ideas are present earlier; see for example Shelley's poem 'The Voyage', from the 1813 volume of 'Minor Poems': 'O! why is a rapt soul e'er recalled | From the palaces of visioned bliss | To the cells of real sorrow!' (*CPPBS* II, 74, ll. 15–17).

Shelley does not always evade the diction of rapturous response, he does become increasingly interested in the textual layering of physical place and self-presence, how travel description might capture the authenticity of perception without severing nature from history.

This touristic self-consciousness emerges most clearly from Shelley's travel letters to Peacock, later collected into *History of a Six Weeks' Tour* (1817), as well as the travel poem first published there, 'Mont Blanc', and his ideas coalesced in his meditation on the touristic value of Rousseau's *Julie*. By the early 1780s, literary tourists began their pilgrimages to haunts around Lake Geneva described in Rousseau's novel, Sir John Moore being among the first English travel writers to enthuse over the superadded feelings of viewing the scene above Mellerie described by the hero, Saint-Preux, in letter 17, part 4 of the novel. In this letter, which Shelley cites in his account to Peacock also published in *History of a Six Weeks' Tour* (SC VIII, 33), Saint-Preux describes the spot where he had formerly given vent to his passion, after the lovers' first separation, carving Julie's name and verses of Petrarch and Tasso into the rocks (a gesture not unlike Orlando's in *As You Like It*). To this spot, he conducts the now married Mme de Wolmar on an excursion, during which their suppressed feelings for each other are barely stifled. Moore, whose account appeared in 1779, writes: 'I felt myself on a kind of classic ground, and experienced that the eloquence of that inimitable writer had given me an interest in the landscape before my eyes, beyond that which its own natural beauties could have effected.'[27] Shelley, writing some thirty-seven years later, puts it even more forcefully: 'This journey has been on every account delightful, but most especially, because then I first knew the divine beauty of Rousseau's imagination, as it exhibits itself in Julie. It is inconceivable what an enchantment the scene itself lends to those delineations, from which its own most touching charm arises.'[28]

Jack Donovan notes that tourists wavered on the question of whether Rousseau embellished nature with its most striking powers or nature Rousseau (with William Coxe and Byron championing nature's primacy and Shelley Rousseau's), but Watson rightly points out that Shelley's formulation contains an equivocal causality: '[Shelley] meditates upon the ways on which the landscape is changed by reading *Julie*, and the experience of reading *Julie* is changed by seeing the landscape.'[29] As his original letter, much edited for *History of a Six Weeks' Tour*, makes clear, Shelley had in fact first visited Mellerie *before* reading the relevant passages from the novel, and he had written about it to Peacock *afterwards* (SC VII, 32). Nevertheless, Shelley enters into the spirit of

---

[27] Sir John Moore, *A View of Society and Manners in France, Switzerland, and Germany*, 2 vols. (London, 1779), I, 255–6. In December 1814, Shelley read Moore's account of 1790s France, *A Journal during a Residence in France from the beginning of August to the Middle of December 1792*, 2 vols. (London, 1793–4).

[28] Mary Shelley and Percy Bysshe Shelley, *History of a Six Weeks' Tour 1817* (Otley: Woodstock Books, 2002), 107–8. Cited hereafter as *History* in the text.

[29] Jack Donovan, 'Laon and the Hermit: Connection and Succession', *Unfamiliar Shelley*, 96; Watson, *Literary Tourist*, 143 and 133–50 *passim*. Other important discussions of Shelley's visits to sites associated with Rousseau include Colbert, *Shelley's Eye*, 107–14 and Rossington, 'Rousseau and Tacitus', 328–9.

literary tourism completely thenceforth, delighting in the 'semblance of truth' discernible in the novel's poetic fictions; at Clarens, he remarks on the locals' conviction that Rousseau's creations really existed and reports his own effusion, 'A thousand times I said have Julie & St Preux walked on this terrassed road looking on the scene which now I see' (*SC* VII, 33). Shelley's sentimental suspension of disbelief here has a philosophical lining, for both the letter and consequent travel book return repeatedly to the problem of perception as retrospection. His conviction that Rousseau's imagination 'cast[s] a shade of falshehood [*sic*] on the records that are called reality' (*SC* VII, 33) calls attention to reality as contingent, a written account in competition with another kind of inscription, the 'monuments' (Shelley's word) to Rousseau of 'Mellerie, Chillon Clarens the mountains of La Valais & Savoy' (*SC* VII, 33). Literary tourism, for Shelley, confirms the power of the imagination to transform the future, making permanent in landscape the emotional truths expressed by 'poetry' in the past.

History of a Six Weeks' Tour enhances the social and political applications of this record-keeping, repositioning and developing more fully, for example, a passage in the original letter in which Shelley mentions the Empress Maria Louisa visiting Mellerie 'in remembrance of St. Preux' (*History*, 118). The travelogue also underscores the transformative narrative leading up to, in the last of the *Letters from Geneva*, Shelley's unmediated experience of nature, his first confrontation with Mont Blanc in the fullness of its presence, an extraordinary passage culminating in an extraordinary claim: 'All was as much our own as if we had been the creators of such impressions in the minds of others, as now occupied our own.—Nature was the poet whose harmony held our spirits more breathless than that of the divinest' (*PBS: Letters* I, 497). Shelley's previous attribution of topographical ownership to Rousseau and his fictions ('[*Julie*] ought to be read amongst its *own* scenes which it has so wonderfully peopled' (*SC* VII, 33, emphasis added)), establishes these heights of unmediated experience as analogous to literary creation. The word 'poet', too, anticipates the *Defence* where Rousseau is classified amongst the poets, those who extend 'the circumference of' being (*Norton 2*, 515); Rousseau exceeds his own limited morality ('prejudices' (*SC* VII, 33)) and approaches the power of nature (even as nature is figured in terms of poetry).

'Mont Blanc: Lines Written in the Vale of Chamouni', with which *History of a Six Weeks' Tour* concludes, forms a coda to these concerns, and may be read as a tribute to literary tourism. The opening section analogizes the relationship between the individual and the surrounding universe: just as the sound of a 'feeble brook' (7) is amplified by the many sounds that surround it, so the mind's a priori construction of 'reality' cannot be distinguished from the background of sense perception, the 'everlasting universe of things' (1). Thought, originality, individuality not only cannot be separated from the world, but more profoundly merge with it, become inseparable from perceptions. The analogy hearkens back to Shelley's ideas about Rousseau, the way in which 'genius' becomes permanent by becoming inseparable from, or inscribed in place; indeed Shelley compares Rousseau's indelible effect on the regions to 'a mighty river—whose waters are indeed exhausted but which has made a chasm among the mountains that will endure forever' (*SC* VII, 33). The poem examines the problem of how the artist, or 'genius', peoples scenes with his or her fiction and endures as a force for future generations. While moving beyond the individual case of Rousseau, Shelley recycles the imagery with which he conceptualizes Rousseau's power, transforming the 'mighty river' to a 'vast river' (10) and then reimagining the river in full flow (the revivified Rousseau in absentia) as the river Arve, the 'chasm among mountains' as the 'Ravine of Arve' (12).

Shelley extends his analogy from Rousseau's power, or the power of genius, to 'Power in likeness of the Arve' (16), now befitting Shelley's metaphysical enquiries regarding the nature of Necessity, time, and change. Yet the shift back to 'My own, my human mind' that 'renders and receives fast 'influencings,|'Holding' an unremitting interchange' (37–9) with nature, again recalls the origins of these ideas in the example of Rousseau, whose novel, Shelley wrote to Hogg, 'acquires an interest I had not conceived [...] when giving & receiving influences from the scenes by which it was inspired' (*SC* IV, 719). Shelley substitutes himself for Rousseau, and invokes the 'still cave of the witch Poesy' (44) which recreates the Ravine and leaves its trace in poetry, as the poem self-reflexively demonstrates. Questions remain—and the poem can do little more in what follows than re-emphasize the ability of the poet to 'Interpret, or make felt, or deeply feel' (83) the lessons of nature: how might 'Lines Written in the Vale of Chamouni' become indelible, permanently associated with the places they describe? How might Shelley become like Rousseau to future like-minded travellers, who seek to revivify his writings in the landscapes that inspire them?

Necro-tourism

Shelley's proleptic meditations on Rousseau—on how poetic composition prepares itself for its posthumous future—accord too with Shelley's attraction as a tourist to places associated with the famous dead. During his Irish tour of 1812, he sought out the unmarked grave of Robert Emmet, the Irish republican executed for high treason in 1803 after a failed plan to attack Dublin Castle. Emmet's heroic and much-reported declaration at his trial, 'When my country takes her place amongst the nations of the earth [...] then only may my epitaph be written,'[30] gave Shelley an opening for depicting the grave as its own epitaph ('On Robert Emmet's Tomb'), the force of Emmet's immaterial presence inspiring patriots and chastening the powerful. Something of the necro-tourist is surely present, too, in the choice of Mary Wollstonecraft's tomb at St Pancras Church in London as a rendezvous with Mary Godwin, as their intimacy developed.[31] In Italy, resident among the Euganean Hills, Shelley mentions 'Arqua where Petrarch's house & tomb are religiously preserved & visited' (*Letters: PBS* II, 43), and if he did not himself join the pilgrims, he did so imaginatively in his 'Lines Written among the Euganean Hills', which invokes, in

---

[30] *The Trial, of Robert Emmet, Esq. For High Treason [...] on the 19th Day of September, 1803* (Dublin: Holmes Charles, 1803), 56, quoted in *CPPBS* II, 360.
[31] Bieri, 278–9.

addition to 'Petrarch's urn' (200), 'Many a sacred Poet's grave' (187) including (again proleptically) the posthumous Byron in Venice.[32] Among the 'sights at Ferrara' that Shelley sought out on 7 November 1818 was the tomb of Ariosto (relocated to the Public Library in 1801) displayed with an exhibit of the poet's armchair, inkstand, a corrected copy of *Orlando furioso*, and other manuscripts ('I could fancy Ariosto sitting in it, & the satires in his own hand writing [...] & the old bronze inkstand [...] which belonged also to him assists the willing delusion' (II, 46)). '[W]riting as from among sepulchres' (II, 70) in Rome, Naples, and, above all, Pompeii, Shelley indulged his fascination with funerary rites, painting, sculpture, and architecture ('[The tombs at Pompeii] seem not so much hiding places for that which must decay as voluptuous chamber[s] for immortal spirits' (II, 74)). At Naples, he visited the Elysian Fields and Virgil's tomb (II, 76). Shelley's last recorded necro-tour was at Ravenna in mid-August 1821, in the company of Byron. Together they visited the tomb of Theodosius and, later that day, tombs of 'Empress Galla Placidia daughter of Theodosius the great', her husband, brother, and son. These latter Shelley dismisses as 'massy cases of marble', a testimony to the 'first effects of the Christian religion to destroy the power of producing beauty in art' (II, 322). By contrast, a few days later, Shelley writes: 'I have seen Dante[']s tomb & worshipped the sacred spot' (II, 355).

Shelley's worship at the shrines of departed genius and the 'willing delusions' he indulged in on the trail of Rousseau in Switzerland or at the Ariosto exhibit in Ferrara owe more than has been acknowledged to Godwin's *Essay on Sepulchres: or, a Proposal for Erecting Some Memorial of the Illustrious Dead in All Ages on the Spot Where Their Remains Have Been Interred* (1809). Shelley first read the *Essay* in 1814 (Reading List 1814, *Journals: MWS*, 86) and by December 1817 cites it, in a review for the *Examiner* of Godwin's *Mandeville*, as among Godwin's principal works—*Political Justice, Caleb Williams, St Leon*, and *Fleetwood*—underpinning his credentials as the age's most acute moral philosopher: 'The *Essay on Sepulchres* has all the solemnity and depth of passion which belongs to a mind that sympathises, as one man with his friend, in the interests of future ages, and in the concerns of vanished generations of mankind' (*Murray: Prose*, 276). Godwin was interested in the foremost of these 'vanished generations', the 'illustrious dead' of his subtitle, and proposed that they be remembered by a nationally funded system for marking noted graves with a simple wooden cross. Visitors to these 'places of sepulture' would follow an 'Atlas of those who Have Lived, for the Use of Men Hereafter to be Born': 'a Traveller's Guide, of a very different measure of utility, from the "Catalogue of Gentlemen's Seats," which is now appended to the "Book of Post-Roads through Every Part of Great Britain"'.[33] Shelley was especially taken with the analogy of 'one man with

---

[32] The lines in question here sum up the full range of literary tourism: interest in sites associated with poets' birthplaces ('As divinest Shakespeare's might | Fills Avon' (196–7)), poets' works ('As the ghost of Homer clings | Round Scamander's wasting springs' (194–5)), and poets' graves ('Petrarch's urn' (200)). The figure of the posthumous Byron is used to demonstrate that places of exile, too, can be visited on the literary tourist trail ('so shall be | The City that did refuge thee' (204–5)). See Colbert, *Shelley's Eye*, 141–60.

[33] William Godwin, *Essay on Sepulchres, Political and Philosophical Writings of William Godwin*, ed. Mark Philp, VI: *Essays* (London: William Pickering, 1993), 29, 30.

his friend' that Godwin uses by way of rationale for his scheme, effectively grounding the human need for memorial in a psychology of affection. When Shelley, in his letter to Peacock on Rousseau's 'overflowing of sublimest genius' in *Julie*, declares that 'The feelings excited by this Romance have suited my creed, which strongly inclines to immaterialism' (*SC* VII, 33), he echoes Godwin's essay ('I am more inclined to the opinion of the immaterialists') at precisely this juncture in the argument.[34] Equally telling, Godwin's analogy underpins his explanation of survivors' attachment to physical possessions (Ariosto's inkstand, for example), places where the remains of the dead are interred, and, by extension, places endowed with 'beautiful association[s]' from fiction ('the bare selection of the spot made by the author [...] for the imaginary exercise of such feelings').[35] In accounting for the life after death of writers ('They are not dead. They are still with us in their stories, in their words, in their writings, in the consequences that do not cease to flow fresh from what they did: they still have their place, where we may visit them'[36]) Godwin anticipates the fundamental outlines not only of Shelley's theorizing on literary tourism but also Shelley's notion of poets as 'unacknowledged legislators of the World' in *A Defence of Poetry* (*Norton* 2, 535). Like Shelley, who considers the subtle reach of poetry as global, Godwin argues that writing travels by hidden byways: 'I cannot tell that the wisest mandarin now living in China, is not indebted for part of his energy and sagacity to Shakespear and Milton, even though [...] he never heard of their names.'[37]

Godwin anticipates too Shelley's regard of Rome as one of the Western world's undisputed sites of the 'illustrious dead'. Shelley's meditations on Rome in his two journal letters to Peacock of 17–18 December 1818 and 23 March 1819 recall Godwin's *Essay on Sepulchres* in their dwelling on the city in terms of its monumentality, its fashioning forth through ruins the signs of past intellectual greatness. In the December letter, Shelley sketches his subject deftly, recounting his impressions of the Colosseum, the nearby Arch of Constantine, and the Forum, then summing up: 'Rome is a city as it were of the dead, or rather of those who cannot die, & who survive the puny generations which inhabit & pass over the spot which they have made sacred to eternity' (*Letters: PBS* II, 59). His phrase, 'city [...] of the dead', also recalls, as Shelley remarked in a letter around the same time to Hogg, the 'eloquent desolation of what Corinna calls the "City of the Dead"' (*SC* VI, 764). Madame de Staël's *Corinne; ou l'italie* (1807), refers rather to Rome as 'la patrie des tombeaux' ('the land of tombs') (quoted in *SC* VI, 766 n. 4), but Shelley's obliquity concentres de Staël's transnationalism into an architectural imaginary, emphasizing the civic nature of the dead, their inhabiting a space of connection and interrelationship, extending, *pace* Godwin, into the future.

With the death of his son William in Rome, Shelley's attitude towards the 'city of the dead' naturally altered. As he wrote to Amelia Curran, charged with superintending the erection and inscription of a memorial tablet marking William's grave, '[Rome] is more like a sepulchre than a city; beautiful, but the abode of death' (*Letters: PBS* II, 159). Nevertheless, the death of Keats on 23 February 1821 and his interment not far from William's grave in the Protestant Cemetery of Rome returned Shelley to consider the

---

[34] Ibid. 8.   [35] Ibid. 20.   [36] Ibid. 23.   [37] Ibid. 29.

relationship between necro-tourism and futurity in *Adonais*. However tempting it is to ignore the situational poetics of this 'highly wrought' (*Letters: PBS* II, 294) poem—and critics have customarily focused on the idealist or sceptical underpinnings of Shelley's intimations of immortality—its setting in Rome and invocation to future tourists crucially ground the poem and its ideals in a touristic economy whereby the afterlife of Keats can be seen in material forms. Shelley establishes this touristic frame in his prefatory sketch of Keats's 'place of sepulture', the Protestant Cemetery near the 'pyramid [...] of Cestius' and the ruins of what were once 'the circuit of antient Rome', an 'open space' in which vitality and rebirth (the winter 'violets and daisies') render death and decay illusory (*Norton* 2, 409–10): exactly commensurate with the power of poetry which such scenes both mirror and metonymically recall. While the sections of the poem that lament Adonais are among the most ethereal, idealized, and metaphysical verses in his oeuvre, Shelley is nevertheless careful to locate the poet's bier as a destination, 'that high Capital' (55) where Adonais finds 'A grave among the eternal' (58). 'Come away!', cries the speaker to the mourners, a curious beckoning to the spot in which (already) the grave cannot be contained ('the vault of blue Italian day | Is yet his fitting charnel-roof!' (58–60)).

If the narrator's grief locks up the circulation between poetry and nature that is the promise of literary tourism, the poem's anti-touristic modes explore moods of emotional stasis and immobility that mock the changing seasons and natural cycles (stanzas 18–20), poignantly figured by 'Lost Echo [...] amid the voiceless mountains' (127), the anti-image of the 'great Mountain' ('Thou hast a voice [...]' (80)) in 'Mont Blanc'. The mourners of Adonais, however, foreshadow the thaw of this winter of grief. As when Byron's fame 'Over his living head' is figured as an already 'enduring monument' (265, 266), or Hunt's posture is 'In mockery of monumental stone' (310), the mourners take on the monumental qualities of Rousseau and his creations in *Julie*; they function both as proto-necro-tourists and future objects of necro-tourism, visitors to the places of the dead and those who, when dead, will be visited. But it is the Godwinian moment that signals the lift in the poem around stanzas 38–9. 'They are not dead', writes Godwin in the *Essay on Sepulchres* of those whose graves mark places of pilgrimage, and Shelley follows suit: 'Nor let us weep that our delight is fled | [...]| He wakes or sleeps with the enduring dead' (334–6); 'Peace, peace! he is not dead [...]' (343). Godwin's sidereal metaphor for the 'illustrious dead' as 'stars that gild our mortal sphere' is paralleled by Shelley's comparison of Adonais and his compeers to 'stars' who climb 'to their appointed height' (390). And Godwin's call for literary tourism to become the guarantor of moral improvement is invoked by Shelley's own call to tourism in the culminating stanzas. There the speaker enjoins one who would understand the transformation of poetry and poet, made possible by death, to imaginatively *become* a star—'dart thy spirit's light | Beyond all worlds' (418–19). Then he gives an alternative to this impossible voyage: travel. 'Or go to Rome, which is the sepulchre | O, not of him, but of our joy [...]' (424–5):

> Go thou to Rome,—at once the Paradise,
> The grave, the city, and the wilderness;
> And where its wrecks like shattered mountains rise,
> And flowering weeds, and fragrant copses dress

The bones of Desolation's nakedness
Pass, till the Spirit of the spot shall lead
Thy footsteps to a slope of green access
Where, like an infant's smile, over the dead,
A light of laughing flowers along the grass is spread.

(433–41)

The description returns to the scene-setting preface and, beyond the poem, to Shelley's own travel letters on Rome, his description of the Baths of Caracalla: 'Never was any desolation more sublime & lovely [...] steep ravines filled with flowery shrubs [...] aerial pinnacles of shattered stone [...]'. The poem's invitation to tourism is foreshadowed by Shelley's to Peacock: 'Come to Rome. It is a scene by which expression is overpowered' (*Letters: PBS* II, 84, 85), and the poem responds to the letter's 'perplexed windings' (II, 85) with an affirmation of something beyond the visible: 'Rome's azure sky, | Flowers, ruins, statues, music, words, are weak | The glory they transfuse with fitting truth to speak' (466–8).

In the letter, Shelley's anti-touristic taunt at literary competitors who sought the 'fitting truth' of Rome ('Hobhouse, Eustace, & Forsyth will tell you all the shew-knowledge about it—"the common stuff of the earth"' (II, 89)), and his fear of 'stumbling' upon the language of tourists 'when I enumerate what is so well known' (II, 85), suggest other textualized landscapes in which his work might be situated, for stumble Shelley most definitely did, the web of competing discourses, as Keith Crook and others have shown, being woven wide by travellers on the spot and journalists who reviewed and debated their claims.[38] If literary and necro-tourism provided Shelley with a way of looking at his own art, and its power to produce culture, Romanticism's increasingly pervasive travel culture in which Shelley took his passionate yet reluctant place remains an important but underexplored context with which to appreciate his achievement as tourist, travel writer, and poet.

Select Bibliography

Brinkley, Robert. 'Documenting Revision: Shelley's Lake Geneva Diary and the Dialogue with Byron in *History of a Six Weeks' Tour'. Keats–Shelley Journal* 39 (1990), 66–82.

Clark, Timothy. 'Shelley's "The Coliseum" and the Sublime'. *Durham University Journal* 85 (1993), 225–35.

Colbert, Benjamin. *Shelley's Eye: Travel Writing and Aesthetic Vision.* Burlington, VT: Ashgate, 2005.

—— 'Bibliography of British Travel Writing, 1780–1840: The European Tour, 1814–1818 (excluding Britain and Ireland)'. *Cardiff Corvey: Reading the Romantic Text* 13 (2004) <www.cf.ac.uk/encap/romtext/articles/cc13_n01.html>.

Dekker, George G. *The Fictions of Romantic Tourism: Radcliffe, Scott, and Mary Shelley.* Stanford, CA: Stanford UP, 2005.

---

[38] See *Remarks on Antiquities, Arts, and Letters during an Excursion in Italy [...] by Joseph Forsyth, Esq.,* ed. Keith Crook (Newark, DE: University of Delaware Press, 2001), 'Introduction', pp. xi–lxiii; Stephen Cheeke, '"What So Many Have Told, Who Would Tell Again?" Romanticism and the Commonplaces of Rome', *European Romantic Review* 17.5 (2006), 521–41; and Colbert, *Shelley's Eye,* 124–41.

Donovan, Jack. 'Laon and the Hermit: Connection and Succession'. *The Unfamiliar Shelley*. Ed. Alan M. Weinberg and Timothy Webb. Burlington, VT: Ashgate, 2009. 85–100.

Duffy, Cian. ' "One Draught from Snowdon's Sacred Spring": Shelley's Welsh Sublime'. *Wales and the Romantic Imagination*. Ed. Damian Walford Davies and Lynda Pratt. Cardiff: University of Wales Press, 2007. 180–98.

Janowitz, Anne. 'Shelley's Monument to Ozymandias'. *Philological Quarterly* 63.4 (1984), 477–91.

Lee, Debbie. 'Mapping the Interior: African Cartography and Shelley's *The Witch of Atlas*'. *European Romantic Review* 8.2 (1997), 169–84.

Makdisi, Saree Samir. 'Shelley's *Alastor*: Travel beyond the Limit'. *Romantic Geographies: Discourses of Travel 1775–1844*. Ed. Amanda Gilroy. Manchester: Manchester UP, 2000. 240–57.

Mazzeo, Tilar. 'Travel Writing and Empire in the Shelley/Byron Circle: Introduction to Edward Ellerker Williams's *Sporting Sketches*'. *Romantic Circles Electronic Edition*. <www.rc.umd.edu/editions/sketches/sketches_intro.html>.

Pite, Ralph. 'Shelley in Italy'. *Yearbook in English Studies* 34 (2004), 46–60.

Reiman, Donald. 'Roman Scenes in *Prometheus Unbound*'. *Philological Quarterly* 46 (1967), 69–78.

Rossington, Michael. 'Rousseau and Tacitus: Republican Inflections in the Shelleys' *History of a Six Weeks' Tour*'. *European Romantic Review* 19.4 (2008), 321–33.

Watson, Nicola J. *The Literary Tourist: Readers and Places in Romantic and Victorian Britain*. London: Palgrave Macmillan, 2006.

Wilson, Milton. 'Travellers' Venice: Some Images for Byron and Shelley'. *University of Toronto Quarterly* 43 (1973–4), 93–120.

PART V

AFTERLIVES

CHAPTER 38

SHELLEY AND THE
NINETEENTH CENTURY

RICHARD CRONIN

WHEN news of Shelley's death reached England in August 1822, it was widely reported. The obituary in *The Gentleman's Magazine* noted, 'Mr Shelley is unfortunately too well known for his infamous novels and poems,' but went on to list his principal works, first amongst them 'Prometheus Chained'.[1] It is a revealing slip. By the time that he died Shelley was well known, his poems were not. 'The sale, in every instance of Mr Shelley's works has been very confined,' his publisher, Charles Ollier, admitted the year after his death.[2] One consequence was that throughout the century the afterlives of Shelley and of his poetry followed markedly divergent courses, exemplifying in this the difficulty that nineteenth-century readers and critics so often had in fixing the relationship between writers and their writings. The century's biographers often set themselves to describe the 'Life and Works' of their subjects, but such titles draw attention to a problem rather than resolve it. It is revealing that the two most influential essays on Shelley should have focused on the relation between the man and the poet. Robert Browning, unwittingly introducing a collection of forged Shelley letters, was provoked into a sharp distinction between objective poets whose personality is irrelevant to their work and subjective poets whose work is explicable only in relation to their personalities.[3] Matthew Arnold, writing in response to Edward Dowden's biography, confronted still more directly the discontinuity between the man and the work. Shelley the man might talk 'nonsense about tyrants and priests', was capable of monstrous self-deception, and showed himself wholly untrustworthy in sexual matters. But then there is a quite different Shelley, the Shelley of the poems, for 'it is his poetry, above everything else, which for many people

---

[1] *The Gentleman's Magazine* 92 (September 1822), 283.

[2] Quoted by William St Clair, *The Reading Nation in the Romantic Period* (Cambridge: Cambridge UP, 2004), 650.

[3] *Letters of Percy Bysshe Shelley: With an introductory essay, by Robert Browning* (London: Moxon, 1852), 1–44.

establishes that he is an angel'. Dowden's biography revealed much in Shelley that was 'ridiculous and odious', and yet 'our former beautiful and lovable Shelley nevertheless survives'.[4]

Shelley's poems left their mark on the poems of his successors. Shelley the man, on the other hand, more often provided material for the century's novelists. Forbidden by her father-in-law from writing her husband's biography, Mary Shelley seems to have found it impossible thenceforward to write a novel that did not surreptitiously evade the embargo. Shelley is transported almost 300 years into the future as Adrian, Earl of Windsor, in *The Last Man* (1826), more than 300 years into the past in *The Fortunes of Perkin Warbeck* (1830), and the same figure is recognizable in a contemporary setting as the central male character in *Lodore* (1835). Two years later, in 1837, Benjamin Disraeli introduced Shelley into his *Venetia* as the quaintly named Marmion Herbert. Shelley continued to make appearances in novels throughout the century. Before G. H. Lewes wrote his life of Goethe he had projected a biography of Shelley, and he shared his enthusiasm with his partner, George Eliot. The title of her *Blackwood's* story 'The Lifted Veil'[5] echoes Shelley's sonnet, 'Lift not the painted veil' not just because the poem is appropriate to the story's theme (the narrator of the story has access to the thoughts of others and to his own future, and finds the experience produces horror rather than enlightenment), but because the narrator, though he writes no poems, is a type of the poet, and for Victorian novelists Shelley is the supreme instance of that type. The woman he loves knows him as her 'small Tasso', but his 'half-womanish, half-ghostly beauty' and his neurotically heightened sensitivity clearly establish his Shelleyan character.[6] Like Shelley's Julian he is 'as a nerve o'er which do creep | The else unfelt oppressions of the earth' (*Julian and Maddalo*, 449–50). In *Middlemarch* Mr Brooke, who gives no reason to suppose he is a poetry reader, when struck by Ladislaw's youthful idealism describes him as 'a kind of Shelley'.[7] The young Daniel Deronda is characterized more searchingly by a fellow-feeling with the unfortunate 'as precocious in him as another sort of genius in the poet who writes a Queen Mab at nineteen'.[8] The association still suggests youth, but it suggests too an unwillingness to be reconciled to the world and the world's expectations. The same might be said of Angel Clare in *Tess of the D'Urbervilles*, who is, Hardy tells us, 'less Byronic than Shelleyan'. Hardy's remark is not entirely complimentary. It implies that, like the hero of *Alastor*, Angel Clare finds it impossible to reconcile the ideal woman of his dreams with the woman of his waking hours. Angel can only wholly love Tess at dawn when she seems 'ghostly, as if she were merely a soul at large'.[9]

The difference between the novelistic interest in Shelley as a man and the poetic interest that focused on his work is indicative of a literary culture that was divided, as it had

[4] Matthew Arnold, 'Shelley', *Nineteenth Century: A Monthly Review* 23 (January 1888), 23–39, reprinted in *Essays in Criticism: Second Series* (London: Macmillan, 1888).

[5] *Blackwood's Edinburgh Magazine* 86 (July 1859), 24–48.

[6] George Eliot, *The Lifted Veil, Brother Jacob* (Oxford: Oxford UP, 1999), 26, 14.

[7] George Eliot, *Middlemarch*, ed. David Carroll (Oxford: Clarendon Press, 1986), 50.

[8] George Eliot, *Daniel Deronda*, ed. Graham Handley (Oxford: Clarendon Press, 1984), 163.

[9] Thomas Hardy, *Tess of the D'Urbervilles*, ed. Scott Elledge (New York: W. W. Norton, 1991), 151, 103.

never been before, between a literature, typically poetry, that addressed itself to the few, and a literature, typically the novel, that addressed itself to the many. One reason for the prominence of Shelley in the period was that he seemed to straddle the divide. Mary Shelley had insisted on the exclusiveness of her husband's appeal, which did not extend to the 'ordinary reader'. 'It requires a mind as subtle and penetrating as his own to understand the mystic meanings scattered throughout the poem' (H 272), she wrote of *Prometheus Unbound*. Arthur Hallam agreed. Shelley, like Keats and Tennyson, wrote a poetry of sensation, and poetry of this kind, because it appealed to subtleties of feeling that most people do not share, could never be widely popular. Yeats, who greatly admired Hallam's essay,[10] joined him in vigorously advertising the esoteric nature of Shelley's appeal. But Shelley himself had been more ambivalent on this matter, and even Yeats acknowledged that in order to safeguard Shelley's unpopularity he needed to reject the rival representation of the poet offered by those who, incapable of registering the subtlety of his thought, branded him 'a crude revolutionist'.[11] It is only when Shelley works against the grain of his own nature that he 'writes pamphlets and dreams of converting the world, or of turning man of affairs and upsetting governments'.[12] But that was precisely the aspect of Shelley that most appealed to Yeats's fellow countryman G. B. Shaw, for whom the decisive proof of Shelley's genius was the survival of *Queen Mab* in 'small, cheap copies, blackened with the finger-marks of many heavy-handed trades'.[13] As he grew older, Yeats began to doubt that poetry needed to be an esoteric art. He came to celebrate Byzantium as a city in which the poet might speak to 'the multitude and the few alike',[14] a possibility that seemed scarcely available to poets of his own time: 'we may never see again a Shelley and a Dickens in one body, but be broken to the end.'[15] The formulation is revealing precisely because it resists the possibility of a very different Shelley, the Shelley who seemed to some of Yeats's predecessors precisely the poet of the recent past who most urgently addressed the interests of the multitude.

   In the years that Shelley was being independently discovered by members of the Victorian avant-garde such as Hallam and Browning, *Queen Mab* was selling so widely in pirated editions that it became known as the 'Chartist's Bible'. One of the more striking Shelleyan poems of the nineteenth century, *The Purgatory of Suicides*, a dream-vision written in Stafford Jail by the Chartist shoemaker Thomas Cooper, who had been convicted for incitement to riot after addressing a meeting of striking miners, is as strident in its denunciations of monarchy and priestcraft as *Queen Mab* itself. Even the poem's awkwardness—Cooper's thoughts very often have to be manhandled into the poem's Spenserian stanzas—has its own aptness. It becomes the poem's most moving enactment of Cooper's belief that the world will only be reformed when the 'sinewy artisan,

---

[10]   Arthur Hallam, 'On Some of the Characteristics of Modern Poetry, and on the Lyrical Poems of Alfred Tennyson', *Englishman's Magazine* 1 (August 1831), 616–28.

[11]   W. B. Yeats, 'The Philosophy of Shelley's Poetry', in *Essays and Introductions* (London: Macmillan, 1961), 66.

[12]   W. B. Yeats, *A Vision* (London: Macmillan, 1937), 91.

[13]   G. B. Shaw, 'Shaming the Devil about Shelley', *Albemarle Review* 2 (September 1892), 91–8.

[14]   *A Vision*, 279.   [15]   Yeats, *Essays and Introductions*, 296.

the weaver lean, | The shrunken stockinger, the miner swarth, | Read, think, and feel' (10, 16, 1–3).[16] There are even passages in the poem to indicate that Cooper has not confined his reading of Shelley to *Queen Mab* and *The Revolt of Islam*. In Book III it is *The Triumph of Life* that comes to mind when Empedocles and Cleombrotus leave the dreamer and

> join the toiling crew
> Of motley shapes and guises, that for aye,
> Clomb up to gain some peak, winning no view
> They sought, but seeming, still, their struggle to renew.
>
> (2, 45, 2–4)

After his death Shelley survived, it seems, in two very different guises, as an esoteric poet available only to a privileged minority, and as the poet of the recent past who meant most to the 'sinewy artisan, the weaver lean'. It was a double character that not only troubled Yeats, anxious to reject the 'crude' notion that Shelley was a political revolutionary, but a Chartist poet such as Ebenezer Jones. His Lord Apswern, 'The Naked Thinker',[17] is a direct descendant of Shelley's Prince Athanase. He retires each day, after ritually divesting himself of all his clothes, to a room in a tower from which he gazes on his subjects, determined, in a markedly Shelleyan way, to 'rend life's seemings, and | Drag out the things that are' (167–8). But his ability to tear the veil that hides from the multitude the reality of their lives serves only to support a pride that separates him from the subjects that he wishes, as a benevolent prince, to serve. His best efforts only reinforce his solitude. The poem ends bleakly: 'Yea, even in the lovingest lady's arms, | Lord Apswern is alone' (227–8). But such differences only confirm Shelley's cultural centrality in a century in which it was fiercely debated whether poets ought properly to speak to the many or fastidiously confine their addresses to the few.

The novelists of the period often noted Shelley's special importance to young men such as Thomas Cooper and Ebenezer Jones. G. H. Lewes had once been a young man rather like them. He had joined a philosophical club that met in a Holborn tavern, an experience that makes its way into *Daniel Deronda* (1876) when Mordecai takes Daniel to a meeting of a club of working men called 'The Philosophers'. As they enter the room one of the shabbily dressed young men is 'just finishing a quotation from Shelley', some lines from *Prometheus Unbound*.[18] In Kingsley's *Alton Locke* (1850) the Dean regrets that 'Shelley has had so much influence on [Alton's] writing'. He is, according to the Dean, 'a guide as irregular in taste, as unorthodox in doctrine; though there are some pretty things in him now and then'.[19] He is the poet that Hardy's Jude recognizes as his own. 'The poetry of liberty used to walk here,' says Jude to an unimpressed Arabella as they

---

[16] Quotations from *The Purgatory of Suicides* are taken from *Poetical Works of Thomas Cooper* (London: Hodder and Stoughton, 1877). The poem was first published in 1845.

[17] The poem is quoted from Ebenezer Jones, *Studies of Sensation and Event* (London: Pickering, 1879). The volume was first published in 1843.

[18] Eliot, *Daniel Deronda*, 485.

[19] Charles Kingsley, *Alton Locke* (London: Macmillan, 1881), 164.

walk through Oxford (or Christminster), and he most easily speaks his love for Sue Bridehead by repeating to her lines from *Epipsychidion*.[20]

In distinguishing between Shelley's principles and his prettiness Charles Kingsley's Dean raises another concern central to Victorian aesthetics. According to Arthur Hallam it is a 'gross fallacy' to suppose that 'because certain opinions are acute or profound, the expression of them by the imagination must be eminently beautiful'. It follows that a poetry designed to express such opinions, what Hallam calls a poetry of reflection, is inferior to the kind of poetry written by Shelley, Keats, and Tennyson, the poetry of sensation.[21] T. S. Eliot a century later was in sympathy with Hallam's position, but disagreed with him as to the kind of poetry written by Shelley. Shelley, according to Eliot, 'made use of poetry for expressing views',[22] a turn of phrase that makes it quite clear that in Eliot's view it would have been better not to have done so. The disagreement nicely illustrates how Shelley's work figured in a dispute central to Victorian aesthetics about whether poetry should be valued for its content or for its form. Like Hallam, J. S. Mill contrasted Shelley's poetry with Wordsworth's—Wordsworth's was the poetry of culture, Shelley's an untutored expression of the poetic temperament—and for Mill, as for Hallam, Shelley's kind was 'poetry in a far higher sense, than any other'.[23] Hallam and Mill were writing at the beginning of a tradition that represented Shelley as the exemplary poet. As Yeats put it when that tradition was approaching its end, Shelley became 'so completely identified with romantic contemplation that young men in their late teens, when I was at that age, identified him with poetry itself'.[24] For Walter Bagehot his lyrics—his example is the late lyric, 'There was a little lawny islet'—represent the 'perfection of pure art'.[25] Shelley's reputation for lyric purity was strongly assisted by the most influential anthology of the century, Palgrave's *Golden Treasury* (1861). Shelley is only the third best represented poet, after Wordsworth and Shakespeare, but the poems of theirs that Palgrave chooses share, many of them, a reflective cast so that Palgrave's anthology works to confirm Shelley's status as the nation's supreme lyric poet. This was a poet very different from the one admired by poets such as Thomas Cooper and Ernest Jones and fictional characters such as Alton Locke. Again what strikes is the oddly bifurcated character of Shelley's nineteenth-century reputation, a quality nicely touched on by Trollope in *The Eustace Diamonds* (1873), when Lizzie Eustace, seeking a refuge from the world and her own worldliness, takes a copy of Shelley down to a beach on the Firth of Clyde. She reads and memorizes the opening lines of *Queen Mab*, and thinks, in happy ignorance of the rest of the poem, 'How perfectly that boy-poet had understood it all!'[26]

---

[20] Thomas Hardy, *Jude the Obscure*, ed. Cedric Watts (New York: W. W. Norton, 1999), 420 and 277.

[21] Hallam, 'On Some of the Characteristics of Modern Poetry', 616.

[22] T. S. Eliot, 'Keats and Shelley', in *The Use of Poetry and the Use of Criticism* (London: Faber, 1964), 88.

[23] J. S. Mill, 'The Two Kinds of Poetry', *Monthly Repository* 7 (October 1833), 714–24.

[24] W. B. Yeats, *Explorations* (London: Macmillan, 1962), 375.

[25] Walter Bagehot, 'Wordsworth, Tennyson, and Browning; or, Pure, Ornate, and Grotesque Art in English Poetry', *National Review* 19 (November 1864), 27–67, 45.

[26] Anthony Trollope, *The Eustace Diamonds*, ed. Stephen Gill and John Sutherland (London: Penguin, 1986), 232–3.

Long before then Charles Kingsley had been struck by the same oddity, and wondered exasperatedly how those who recognized Shelley's principles to be 'very wrong' could still insist that his poetry remained '"so refined," "so beautiful," "so tender"'.[27]

For many in the nineteenth century Shelley, like his skylark, seemed an 'unembodied joy', so brimful of the poetic spirit that he had become almost incorporeal. Yeats holds that every poet must choose between two places of resort, 'Shelley's Chapel of the Morning Star' and 'Burns's beerhouse'.[28] It may have been because of his reputation for spirituality that Shelley and his work were so often invoked by Victorians reflecting on the relative value that should be attached to the body and the soul. But it was also surely because Shelley's spirituality was covertly recognized as being in such disconcertingly close neighbourhood to fleshliness. Swinburne in *Poems and Ballads* and in *Songs before Sunrise* clearly shows the impress of Shelley's republicanism, Shelley's eroticism, and Shelley's metres, and yet Swinburne was himself a leading member of what Robert Buchanan nominated 'the Fleshly School of Poetry'.[29] In 'Shelley's Skylark' Hardy stages a whimsical quest for the 'dust of the lark' (5) that had inspired Shelley's poem, by then the most celebrated lyric in the English language.[30] He plans to enclose the bird's remains in a rich reliquary of silver, gold, and gemstones so that it might fitly memorialize a poem inspired by a bird that, after all, had only 'lived like any other bird' (7) until it fell out of the sky, a 'little ball of feather and bone' (10). The poem seems at once to celebrate and to mock the imagination that can find a value in the lark's song so incommensurate with the 'meek life' (9) of the bird that had inspired the poem. Hardy added a subtitle giving the circumstances of the poem's composition '(The neighbourhood of Livorno: March 1887)'. The poem was written, he claims, not far from the beach where Shelley's body was burned in circumstances described by Dowden in his biography of the poet, published just a year before. Dowden relates how Leigh Hunt was persuaded to restore Shelley's heart, presented to him by Trelawny, to the poet's widow and how, after her death, it was discovered in a copy of *Adonais*, 'at the page which tells how death is swallowed up in immortality', a little heap of 'embrowned ashes, now shrunk and withered' that Mary had enclosed in 'a silken covering' and 'secretly treasured'.[31] Trelawny had rescued the heart, as Hardy dreams of rescuing the remains of the bird, from 'earth's oblivious eyeless trust' (2), a phrase into which Hardy compacts his sense of the absurdity of all such endeavours. Do those 'embrowned ashes' that Mary treasured have anything more to do with Shelley than Shelley's poem with the 'pinch of unseen, unguarded dust' (4) which is all that remains of the bird? It is a poem that casts its own odd, mordant light on the vexed relationship between the body of the poet and the body of his works.

---

[27] Charles Kingsley, 'Thoughts on Byron and Shelley', *Fraser's Magazine* 48 (November 1853), 568–76.

[28] Yeats, *Essays and Introductions*, 267.

[29] Robert Buchanan, writing under the name Thomas Maitland, 'The Fleshly School of Poetry: D. G. Rossetti', *Contemporary Review* 18 (October 1871), 334–50.

[30] Hardy's poems are quoted from *The Complete Poems of Thomas Hardy*, ed. James Gibson (London: Macmillan, 1976).

[31] Edward Dowden, *The Life of Percy Bysshe Shelley* (London: Routledge and Kegan Paul, 1969), 579.

Hardy ascribed 'The Darkling Thrush' to 31 December 1900, a date that seems to offer the poem as an elegy on the Romantic century. The plant stems score the pale wintry sky '[l]ike strings of broken lyres' (6), as if to signal the final loss of any Romantic faith in the consonance between human consciousness and the natural world. The crucial difference between Hardy's thrush and more typically Romantic birds such as Wordsworth's cuckoo, Keats's nightingale, and Shelley's skylark is that Hardy's bird is plainly visible and so it cannot be imagined as disembodied, freed from the mortality that attends all bodily things. The physical being of the 'aged thrush, frail, gaunt, and small' (21) offers an ironic commentary on the bird's 'carolings' (25) that seems to extend from the thrush to Shelley's skylark and the 'rapture' ('To a Skylark', 65) of its song. Shelley's bird, because it is unseen, allows no visible discrepancy between the character of its song and its bedraggled plumage, but the discrepancy is re-positioned rather than eradicated. The gap between the bird's song and its body is closed only to re-emerge in the gap between the song and its human admirer, who is saddened by a consciousness of all those things such as time and mortality of which the bird can have no notion. It remains oddly unclear whether Hardy is echoing 'To a Skylark' or repudiating it. Shelley wrote his songs of hope, after all, at a time of reaction, when it must have seemed that 'every spirit upon earth' but him had become 'fervourless' (15–16).

Hardy's poem may offer a cryptic clue as to why it is that Shelley, who is often assumed to hold the sunny view that he ascribes to his own Julian—'we might be all | We dream of happy high, majestical' (173–4)—should have been the darling of the century's gloomiest poets; of Thomas Lovell Beddoes, James Thomson, and Thomas Hardy. All three shared principles with Shelley: Beddoes shared his revolutionary commitments, Thomson his republicanism and atheism, and Hardy his atheism and objection to marriage, though none of them seems to have adopted the perfectibilarian character of much of Shelley's thought. Shelley, it may be, continued to fascinate such poets because they found in him a Yeatsian anti-self, recognizing that their own repudiations of all transcendental value had a dark exuberance that found its proper counterpart in the desperation with which Shelley proclaims his optimism, his determination 'to hope till Hope creates | From its own wreck the thing it contemplates' (*Prometheus Unbound*, IV. 573–4; quoted from *H*).

Yeats remembered how, in his youth, his 'mind gave itself' to Shelley's dream of 'a young man, his hair blanched with sorrow, studying philosophy in some lonely tower'.[32] In Shelley's Prince Athanase, who sits 'Apart from men, as in a lonely tower, | Pitying the tumult of their dark estate' (33–4), he found the figure who, throughout his career, best figured for him the possibility that the poet might assume a vantage elevated above ordinary humanity. It was a possibility that Browning seems to mock when his Childe Roland arrives at the dark tower, and finds a 'round squat turret, blind as the fool's heart' (182), as does James Thomson in *The City of Dreadful Night* in the figure of the man doomed to visit again and again the tower that 'merged into the heavy sky', surrounded by graves, where he first lost his faith (133–8). Even for Yeats the Shelleyan tower was crumbling. In 'My Descendants' he imagines his 'stark' tower

---

[32] *The Autobiography of William Butler Yeats* (New York: Macmillan, 1938), 171.

Become a roofless ruin that the owl
May build in the cracked masonry and cry
Her desolation to the desolate sky.

(14–16)[33]

And yet even in their travesties of Athanase's tower Shelley continues to guide his successors, for he had himself offered as its dark counterpart the tower of a lunatic asylum, the 'windowless, deformed and dreary pile' surmounted by a bell-tower of *Julian and Maddalo* (102). Poets such as Thomson and Hardy kick against the shallow enthusiasm for a great world spinning for ever 'down the ringing grooves of change' ('Locksley Hall', 182)[34] that they believe endemic to their era, but even Tennyson swithers between that faith and a sad nostalgia for the days that are no more. Shelley, the English poet most wedded to the future tense, who wore a ring engraved with the motto *Il buon tempo verra*, became a landmark by reference to which they could fix their own position, and a landmark the more familiar because Shelley's statements of optimistic faith so rarely manage to repress his own misgivings.

It was not coincidental that the figure of Shelley focused so many key Victorian concerns; on the relationship between the poet and his works, on whether the artist should address the many or the few, on whether art was an affair of the body or the spirit, on whether poems should be valued for the justice or the intensity of the sentiments that they express. These were all of them concerns that Shelley had anticipated. Evidence, Shelley claimed, that 'Homer was a drunkard, that Virgil was a flatterer, that Horace was a coward, that Tasso was a madman, that Lord Bacon was a peculator, that Raphael was a libertine', and 'that Spenser was a poet laureate' (he resists the temptation to 'cite living poets') would not threaten his conviction that the poet 'inasmuch as he is a poet' is 'the wisest, the happiest, and the best' of men.[35] The plots of *Prometheus Unbound* and *The Mask of Anarchy* are rather similar, but the two poems scarcely seem to be addressed to the same readership. 'You might as well go to a ginshop for a leg of mutton, as expect any thing human or earthly from me,'[36] Shelley told John Gisborne, wittily choosing a metaphor that invalidates the confession. Shelley is a didactic poet who can nevertheless insist in his preface to *Prometheus Unbound* that 'Didactic poetry is [his] abhorrence' (*H* 207). The special place that Victorian cultural commentators allowed Shelley was founded perhaps on an unspoken acknowledgement that Shelley had anticipated most of the more powerful objections that might be brought against his own work. But it owed still more to the ease with which Shelley's life and his work could be assimilated into the narratives of personal development that underlie so many of the poems and the novels of the nineteenth century.

According to Yeats it was 'young men in their late teens' who identified Shelley with poetry itself. For Eliot, 'an enthusiasm for Shelley' was 'an affair of adolescence:

---

[33] Yeats's poems are quoted from *The Collected Poems of W. B. Yeats* (London: Macmillan, 1967).

[34] Tennyson's poems are quoted from *The Poems of Tennyson*, ed. Christopher Ricks, 3 vols. (Harlow: Longman, 1987).

[35] *Norton* 2, 533–4.   [36] *Letters: PBS* II, 363.

for most of us, Shelley has marked an intense period before maturity'.[37] The representation of a taste for Shelley as a badge of immaturity might be expected in Modernist poets anxious to register their break with Romanticism. In fact Eliot points to an experience that seems to have been characteristic of Shelley's admirers almost from the first. The notion was taken to its logical conclusion by those who imagined Shelley living on after July 1822, so that, even for Shelley, 'Shelley' might be represented simply as a phase that he had to pass through. In his *roman-à-clef Venetia*, Disraeli imagines Shelley surviving to become a stooping figure, his hair streaked with grey, who looks back on his youthful career, and feels serenely detached from its fierce struggles. His feelings, he finds, on politics, religion, and marriage are 'very much modified', which is after all only to be expected, because 'a man at fifty' cannot even claim to be 'the same material being that he is at five-and-twenty' (Book 6, chapter 3). Most commonly, Shelley was imagined as surviving long enough to reconcile himself with the Church. Browning's view that 'had Shelley lived he would have finally ranged himself with the Christians'[38] was surprisingly prevalent. It was a conversion, according to Maria Jewsbury, anticipated by most of Shelley's admirers: 'most readers will, in Prometheus himself, feel and see but a shadow of *One*, whose name, to be suggested, needs not to be mentioned.'[39] Elizabeth Barrett offers *The Seraphim* (1838) as an experiment to determine how Aeschylus might have modified his *Prometheus Bound* had he lived 'after the incarnation and crucifixion of our Lord Jesus Christ'. She had already translated Aeschylus' play, but when she represents *The Seraphim* as 'a poem of imperfect form—a dramatic lyric, rather than a lyrical drama',[40] she reveals that it is Shelley rather than Aeschylus who is on her mind. Her seraphim, Ador and Zerah, respond to the Crucifixion in a lyrical duet closely based on the dialogue between Panthea and Ione as they witness Prometheus' torture in the first act of *Prometheus Unbound*. The Furies force Shelley's Prometheus to witness the death of one whose words when they outlived him became 'swift poison | Withering up truth, peace, and pity' (I. 548–59). Prometheus will experience their presence, they tell him, like 'foul desire round [his] astonished heart' (I. 489), a horror dissipated in the 'strange astonished smiles' (I. 668) with which, according to Elizabeth Barrett's seraphim, humankind will greet Christ's loving self-sacrifice. In *The Seraphim* Elizabeth Barrett takes over the task that, in Maria Jewsbury's view, Shelley had not quite completed. She reclaims *Prometheus Unbound* for Christianity. So too, less solemnly, did Nathaniel Hawthorne in one of his most charming *jeux d'esprit*. Shelley, who is only rumoured to have drowned, returns to England, and in the course of time is ordained. He is at present seeing through the press 'a volume of discourses, treating of the poetico-philosophical proofs of Christianity, on the basis of the

---

[37] Eliot, 'Keats and Shelley', 89.

[38] Robert Browning, 'Essay on Shelley', in *The Poems of Browning: 1847–1861*, ed. John Woolford, Daniel Karlin, and Joseph Phelan (London: Longman, 2007), 725.

[39] 'Shelley's Wandering Jew', *Athenaeum* 194 (16 July 1831), 456–7.

[40] *The Poetical Works of Elizabeth Barrett Browning* (London: Smith, Elder, and Co., 1904), 76 and 77. Elizabeth Barrett Browning's poems are quoted from this edition.

Thirty-nine Articles', and is thinking of co-writing a poem with Bishop Heber.[41] Even the hostile Charles Kingsley agreed that Shelley would, had he lived, have converted, but strongly suspects that he would have contrived to get even that wrong: he 'would have probably ended in Rome'.[42]

Shelley was not the only poet of his generation to die young, but he was the only poet who repeatedly inspired his successors to imagine his afterlife. Even T. S. Eliot invites us to 'guess' whether, had he lived, 'his mind would have matured' (90). Throughout the nineteenth century Shelley was pre-eminently 'the boy-poet', as Trollope's Lizzie Eustace calls him, and in this too he remains central to Victorian preoccupations, for there was no narrative that the Victorians found so compelling as the story of how the child made its transition into adulthood. Shelley was so central to so many nineteenth-century poets because he became a principal means by which they could mark their own ascent into full poetic manhood.

The Cambridge Apostles championed Shelley's reputation in the late 1820s. They instigated debates at their own university and at Oxford, where they insisted on his superiority to Byron, and they financed an edition of *Adonais*. One of their number, Richard Chenevix Trench, wrote that Shelley's poems, like Wordsworth's, Byron's, and Keats's, remain 'unintelligible to us, till we have gone through that very state of feeling to which they appeal; as, for instance, none can entirely comprehend "Alastor" who has not been laid waste by the unslaked thirst for female sympathies, and so with the rest'.[43] Trench wrote from Southampton, just before embarking on an enterprise best understood as a bold statement of his willingness to enter into Shelleyan states of feeling. Trench, along with his fellow Apostle John Kemble, was about to set sail for Gibraltar to enlist with General Torrijos who was planning an invasion of the Spanish mainland designed to oust King Ferdinand and restore the Spanish constitution. Meanwhile Tennyson and Arthur Hallam were on their way to the Pyrenees with money and dispatches for another Constitutionalist leader, General Ojeda, who was to time his march from the north to coincide with Torrijos's attack from the south. In the event, Torrijos's attempt was delayed until late November 1831, by which time Trench and Kemble had tired of waiting and had returned to England, which meant that they escaped the firing squad that on 11 December executed General Torrijos and all of those who had landed with him, including Trench's and Kemble's English associate Robert Boyd. These young Cambridge undergraduates were revolutionaries for three months in the summer and autumn of 1830, and their opinions in these months have scarcely any relation with their opinions before or afterwards. Back in Cambridge they quickly reverted to type, busying themselves in collecting a petition opposing the Great Reform Bill. They were at one in associating those mad months in 1830, months in which as if in an act of collective hallucination they persuaded themselves that they were bold revolutionaries, with

[41] Nathaniel Hawthorne, 'P.'s Correspondence', *United States Magazine and Democratic Review* 16 (April 1845), 337–45, reprinted in 1846 in *Mosses from an Old Manse*, 571.

[42] Charles Kingsley, 'Thoughts on Byron and Shelley', 571.

[43] Richard Chenevix Trench, *Letters and Memorials*, ed. Mary Chenevix Trench, 2 vols. (London: Kegan Paul and Trench, 1888), I, 73.

Shelley. Trench wrote to Kemble, when they were both safely back in England, and announced his change of opinion: 'I have given over despairing and reading Shelley, and am beginning to acquiesce in things just as they are going on.'[44] The brief engagement of these young men in Spanish affairs was, one suspects, a literary rather than a political exercise, an exercise that seemed necessary because they believed that they needed to live through Shelley's states of feeling before they could properly comprehend his poems. Before, one is almost inclined to add, they could fully comprehend their error.

Shelley's eroticism seemed for a time as exciting as his politics. *The Lover's Tale* was to have been the final poem in Tennyson's 1833 *Poems*, until, despite Hallam's protests, he withdrew it from the volume. Tennyson claimed that he had written it before he had read any of Shelley's poems, but this seems implausible: the poem offers an encyclopedic set of variations on Shelleyan themes. It describes a day spent by the 'lover', who is named Julian in the version of the poem that Tennyson finally published, wandering with his beloved, who is also his first cousin, through a gorgeous landscape, luxuriously deferring the moment when he will speak his passion. Happy and inattentive, Julian listens to the sound of his cousin's voice. Only gradually does he register that she is confessing her love for his best friend Lionel. Julian faints, and wakes to find Lionel tenderly ministering to him, but Julian does not recover his senses. He enters a state that seems to echo the Maniac's in *Julian and Maddalo*, and prefigure the madness of the speaker of *Maud*, in which he can no longer distinguish between the real world and his ghastly imaginings.

Julian and his cousin are Shelleyan lovers, each the mirror image of the other. Tennyson follows Shelley in locating the origin of love in narcissism, but he confesses it more flagrantly than even Shelley dared. Julian looks into his mistress's eyes in order 'To worship mine own image, laved in light, | The centre of the splendours' (1, 63–4). He dreams, in a passage even more awash with Shelleyan echoes than the rest of the poem, of a consummation of his love, but the consummation he imagines is a penetration of the self by the self, the consummation enjoyed by 'the rose', when,

> drunk with its own wine, and overfull
> Of sweetness, and in smelling of itself,
> It falls on its own thorns.

> (1, 265–7)

Unlike Laon, Julian is only in love with his cousin: the consanguinity remains within respectable bounds. But this serves in Tennyson's poem only to make possible a specularity more perfect than even Shelley conceived. The two were born 'on the same morning, almost the same hour' (1, 192), the children of two sisters. The girl's mother dies in childbirth, and, immediately afterwards, Julian's father dies, so that the two babies share a single mother and a single father, and may be laid together in a single cradle, less cousins than a miracle of nature, identical twins of opposite sex.

The Lover's Tale is a wordy poem—even in its unfinished state it extends to more than a thousand lines—but its wordiness is produced by Tennyson's employment of

---

[44] Ibid. 96.

two tactics, both of them derived from Shelley. First, as in *Epipsychidion*, a recognition of the inadequacy of language generates a spate of words. Julian denies that his love can be 'cabined up in words and syllables' (1, 470), and that acknowledgement in itself produces a sustained burst of eloquence. It is because his love cannot be spoken that Julian can only defer the moment when he will declare himself, and it is that deferral that produces the poem's second tactic, for it generates the landscapes that occupy so much of the poem. Because it is denied any other expression, his love overflows, flooding the world, transforming each and every object in it into the sign of an unspoken thought. As in *Alastor* or *Epipsychidion*, the world becomes a system of metaphors, in all of which the tenor is the same, the one, unspeakable object of his passion. In the poem's second and third parts Julian is deprived of his love object, deprived of the one referent that made sense of all his words, and in consequence his language runs mad: the literal and the figurative, reality and dream, merge, blur, and intermingle. It is a poetic language lapsed into chaos, but chaos of the peculiar kind that Shelley represents in *Julian and Maddalo*, 'such as in measure is called poetry' (542).

In *A Lover's Tale* Tennyson rehearses the defining features of Shelley's erotic poetry flamboyantly, enthusiastically, but not quite seriously. Throughout its length the poem verges on parody. Tennyson plays at being a Shelleyan lover in much the same way that in his jaunt with Hallam to the Pyrenees he was playing at being a Shelleyan revolutionary. In both cases Tennyson does not so much assume a manner that he later refuses as assume a guise precisely in order to cast it off. Shelley remained important to Tennyson throughout his career, but he is most important as the poet that Tennyson defined himself against. 'He seems to go up into the air and burst', said Tennyson of one Shelley lyric ('Life of Life').[45] The same metaphor struck him when he thought about the short, swift life of Arthur Hallam, and how it had ended in Vienna. The city ever since had seemed to Tennyson a City of Death, though Hallam himself had thought no city statelier, none more gay. For him it was a city where

> wheels the circled dance, and breaks
> The rocket molten into flakes
> Of crimson or in emerald rain.
>
> (*In Memoriam*, 98, 30–2)

The rocket still bursts, but for Tennyson the lyric moment is not the moment of its explosion. The lyric for Tennyson measures a lapse of time, it memorializes a moment that is always about to vanish, a moment properly figured by the slow downward drift of the rocket's bright fragments.

Browning became a poet under Shelley's auspices: when he was 14 a cousin gave him Benbow's pirated edition of Shelley's *Posthumous Poems*. It was not long before he was converted to atheism and vegetarianism, and had written *Pauline* (1833), a confessional quest poem in the tradition of *Alastor* that pays famous tribute to Shelley:

---

[45] Hallam Tennyson, *Alfred, Lord Tennyson: A Memoir*, 2 vols. (London: Macmillan, 1897), II, 500.

Sun-treader, life and light be thine for ever!
Thou art gone from us; years go by and spring
Gladdens, and the young earth is beautiful,
Yet thy songs come not, other bards arise,
But none like thee.

(151–5)[46]

In *Paracelsus* (1835), his second major poem, Paracelsus recognizes his other self in Aprile, a Shelleyan figure as uncompromising in his quest for love as is Paracelsus in his quest for knowledge, and yet in *Sordello* (1840), the third of this sequence of poems, the narrator claims that the poem can proceed only if Shelley absents himself:

Stay—thou, spirit, come not near
Now—not this time desert thy cloudy place
To scare me, thus employed, with that pure face!

(1, 60–2)

Shelley is expelled in a gesture of humility—were he present Browning would have no heart to 'play [his] puppets' (1, 72)—but there is also an implication that Shelley's 'pure face' disqualifies him from the kind of investigation that Browning proposes to conduct, that Shelley's 'white ideal', as Elizabeth Barrett expressed it in a phrase that Browning admired (Elizabeth Barrett Browning, *A Vision of Poets*, 406), blinded him to much that Browning found most compelling in human experience. It is unsurprising that by 1840, when he published *Sordello*, Browning should have outgrown the infatuation with Shelley that he was so ready to express seven years earlier in *Pauline*. It is a good deal odder that even in *Pauline* Browning insists that his Shelleyanism was no more than an episode:

And suddenly without heart-wreck I awoke
As from a dream: I said ''Twas beautiful,
Yet but a dream, and so adieu to it!'

(448–50)

It is an awakening that recalls the awakening of the hero of *Alastor* from his dream of the 'veiled maid' only to point the difference. When Shelley's hero wakes he 'eagerly pursues | Beyond the realms of dream that fleeting shade; | He overleaps the bounds' (205–7). Browning's young poet by contrast briskly resigns himself to his loss, and at once finds compensation in the consciousness of 'new powers'; 'wit, mockery, | Light-heartedness' (462, 463–4). This is dangerously like a lapse into cynicism, and yet it seems a necessary stage in the young poet's still incomplete progress towards maturity.

Browning, it seems, traced his birth as a poet to the sense of guilt out of which *Pauline* is written. It is a complex guilt because it accommodates at once the guilt of rejecting a youthful idol and the guilt of ever having idolized him in the first place, but in both its aspects it is closely associated with Shelley. In all three of these early poems

---

[46] Browning's poems are quoted from *Robert Browning; The Poems*, ed. John Pettigrew, 2 vols. (Harmondsworth: Penguin, 1981).

he conducts exorcisms, but despite all that effort Shelley continued to haunt him. 'Numpholeptos' was published close to the end of Browning's career, in 1876, and yet, just as clearly as *Pauline*, it derives from *Alastor*. The poem, like 'Childe Roland', is the monologue of a man so wearied in his quest that he seems no longer capable of imagining a successful outcome. Like the hero of *Alastor* he seeks union with a visionary maid, but unlike Shelley's hero he is sardonically aware that his quest is futile. She remains after all his travail as cold, moon-like, unattainable as she has always been, meeting his ardent gaze with a 'sad petrific smile' (133). The speaker may complain that she rejects his attentions in obedience to some 'thrice superfine | Feminity of sense' (144–5), but even as he voices his protest he recognizes it as the 'true slave's querulous outbreak' (148), and bends himself once more to his task. His quest takes an odd form. The nymph shines with a white, moony light, but the 'magic hall' in which she lives acts as a prism from which the light '[r]ays forth' through the whole of the 'fantastic world', '[s]haft upon coloured shaft' (59–64). One by one, the speaker follows these shafts of coloured light. He gives himself 'soul and body' to the yellow shaft, allowing himself to 'swim and swathe | In yellow licence', until he 'reek[s] suffused | With crocus, saffron, orange'. But he finds, when he returns to the magic hall, that the nymph only stares in wonder at a man become '[m]onstrous in garb' (80–8). At the end of the poem the speaker is about to set out on 'the crimson-quest' (150), unable still to accept the lesson that his long experience ought long ago to have taught him. His quest can never be successful because its success would involve a self-contradiction. He inhabits a mortal world of colour, of refracted light, from which there is no egress to the pure, white light of the nymph in which all those earthly colours have their origin. The explanation that Browning offers of why it is that such men as the hero of *Alastor* can never achieve union with any 'veiled maid' except in dream has a quasi-scientific rigour that seems at once grim and gruffly comic.

The poem seems to place Browning at a sardonic distance from his Shelleyan model, and yet it is a distance that mimics as much as it mocks a poem that Shelley had himself presented as a study in 'self-centred seclusion' (Preface to *Alastor*, H 15). It is because he is shut out from the 'quintessential whiteness' of the nymph that Browning's speaker is urged forth to 'swim and swathe | In yellow licence', and 'obtain experience of each tinge | That bickers forth' from the magic hall (100–1). In all this there is an exuberance at odds with his querulous complaints, as if he is a thinly disguised Fra Lippo Lippi, confident underneath it all that when he tumbles himself in all the colours that make up the mortal world he gets 'about the best thing God invents' (*Fra Lippo Lippi*, 218). But even in this he does not stray too far from Shelley, who explains in his *On Love* that we are redeemed only by our failure to achieve union with our ideal likeness, because it is that failure that 'urges forth the powers of man to arrest the faintest shadow of that without the possession of which there is no rest or respite to the heart over which it rules' (*Norton 2*, 504). Browning, it has been suspected, offers his poem not simply as an analysis of the human condition, but as a retrospective survey of his own married life. He had, after all, written to Elizabeth Barrett in one of his courtship letters, 'You speak out, *you*,—I only make men and women speak—give you truth broken into prismatic hues, and fear the pure white light.'[47] But even if this is the case, Browning might claim Shelley's authority, because 'Numpholeptos' seems to echo not only *Alastor*, but *Epipsychidion*, a poem in which Shelley's wife is figured as a 'cold, chaste Moon' (281) that shines with a 'soft yet icy flame' (283). In the end, it seems better to understand 'Numpholeptos' not as the long-delayed expression of a husbandly grudge, but as another of Browning's acknowledgements that dramatic poetry of the kind that he writes, poems in which 'men and women speak', remains parasitical on lyric poetry of the kind that his wife wrote, and of which, for Browning, Shelley remained the supreme exponent.

For Yeats as for Browning the point that the poet had reached in his development was best marked by the distance he had travelled from Shelley. Shelley, Yeats came to feel, lacked a proper relish for the physical world. Still more damagingly he 'lacked the Vision of Evil, could not conceive of the world as a continual conflict, and so, though great poet he certainly was, he was not of the greatest kind'.[48] This seems decisive, and yet it is a judgement that Yeats arrives at when identifying Shelley as a poet of Phase 17, where he is grouped together with Dante, Walter Savage Landor, and with Yeats himself. The acknowledgement makes it less surprising than it would otherwise seem that Shelley exerts his most powerful influence on Yeats precisely in those poems in which Yeats entertains his darkest imaginings. In 'The Second Coming', Yeats's baleful vision of a world in which '[t]he best lack all conviction, while the worst | Are full of passionate intensity' comes to him rather directly from *Prometheus Unbound*:

> The good want power, but to weep barren tears.
> The powerful goodness want: worse need for them.
> The wise want love, and those who love want wisdom;
> And all best things are thus confused to ill.

> (I. 625–8)

In 'Nineteen Hundred and Nineteen', an Ireland torn by civil war inspires in Yeats a bitter sense that all those, like Shelley and himself, who have ever succumbed to a passion for reforming the world are victims of a grotesque self-delusion, unable to see humankind for what it is, a pack of 'weasels fighting in a hole'. It seems an entirely unShelley-like perception, and yet it is a poem in which echoes of Shelley cluster thickly. The great whom the poem invites us to 'mock' because they 'toiled so hard and late | To leave some monument behind, | Nor thought of the levelling wind' (93–7) are close kin to Shelley's Ozymandias. *Alastor* was all through his career the poem of Shelley's that meant most to Yeats, but he had never rehearsed its theme with a more graceful concision than he did here: 'Man is in love, and loves what vanishes, | What more is there to say?' (42–3) Asia's great lyric from *Prometheus Unbound*, 'My soul is an enchanted boat', is suavely recalled; 'Some moralist or mythological poet | Compares the solitary soul to a swan' (59–60), but Shelley's swan that sails back from Age to Infancy until it passes through the barrier of Death and Birth to 'a diviner day' is reflected in a 'troubled mirror'. When Yeats's swan

[47] Robert to Elizabeth, 13 January 1845, *The Brownings' Correspondence*, ed. Philip Kelley et al. (Winfield, KS: Wedgewood Press, 1984), 10, 22.
[48] Yeats, *A Vision*, 144.

takes flight, and leaps 'into the desolate heaven' (79) it confirms Yeats in his 'ghostly solitude' (40), as the visionary in *Alastor* feels his solitude complete when he watches a swan as it rises from the shore 'with strong wings | Scaling the upward sky'. The image of the ascending swan completes Yeats's disillusionment:

> O but we dreamed to mend
> Whatever mischief seemed
> To afflict mankind, but now
> That winds of winter blow
> Learn that we were crack-pated when we dreamed. (84–8)

That, Yeats suggests, is the lesson that Shelley never learned, and yet it is the lesson that is very closely anticipated in *Alastor* when the flight of the swan leaves the visionary conscious of 'wasting' his 'surpassing powers | in the deaf air, to the blind earth, and heaven | That echoes not [his] thoughts' (288–90). Shelley, Yeats complained, could 'never see anything that opposes him as it really is'.[49] Yeats, by not seeing Shelley as he really was, was able to make of him a poet of the kind that he most needed, a poet that he could define himself by opposing. It was the role that Shelley played for many of his more attentive nineteenth-century readers.

SELECT BIBLIOGRAPHY

Barcus, James E. Ed. *Shelley: The Critical Heritage*. London: Routledge and Kegan Paul, 1975.

Bornstein, George. *Yeats and Shelley*. Chicago: University of Chicago Press, 1970.

Browning, Robert. 'Essay on Shelley'. *Selected Poems*. Ed. John Woolford, Daniel Karlin, and Joseph Phelan. London: Longman, 2010. 851–77.

Eliot, T. S. 'Keats and Shelley'. *The Use of Poetry and the Use of Criticism: Studies in the Relation of Criticism to Poetry in England*. London: Faber, 1933. 87–102.

Hallam, Arthur. 'On Some of the Characteristics of Modern Poetry, and on the Lyrical Poems of Alfred Tennyson'. *Englishman's Magazine* 1 (August 1831), 616–28.

Kingsley, Charles. 'Thoughts on Byron and Shelley'. *Fraser's Magazine* 48 (November 1853), 568–76.

Mill, John Stuart. 'The Two Kinds of Poetry'. *Monthly Repository* 7 (October 1833), 714–24.

Norman, Sylva. *Flight of the Skylark: The Development of Shelley's Reputation*. Norman, OK: University of Oklahoma Press, 1954.

Radford, Andrew and Mark Sandy. Eds. *Romantic Echoes in the Victorian Era*. Aldershot: Ashgate, 2008.

Shaw, G. B. 'Shaming the Devil about Shelley'. *Albemarle Review* 2 (September 1892), 91–8.

---

[49] Ibid. 143.

CHAPTER 39

....

THE INFLUENCE OF SHELLEY ON TWENTIETH- AND TWENTY-FIRST-CENTURY POETRY

....

JEFFREY C. ROBINSON

[...] every great poet must inevitably innovate upon the example of his
predecessors in the exact structure of his peculiar versification [...].

(P. B. Shelley, from *A Defence of Poetry*)[1]

It is only form
that can flower

(Thomas A. Clark)[2]

THE reputation of Percy Bysshe Shelley and his influence upon later poets illuminates
dramatically the fact that poetry can produce irreconcilable differences in understanding among poets and readers. At the Shelleyan poles stand on the one hand Arnold's
ineffectual angel,[3] a singer far above the world of social life; on the other hand is the radical political poet inspiring Chartists, Frankfurt School theorists, and the revolutionaries
in Tiananmen Square. These two positions invite a third one that reconceives Shelley's
poetry in a way that takes account of both 'lyric' and political radicalism.

In this chapter I will show how some politically and poetically radical twentieth- and
early twenty-first-century poets found in Shelley a model for formal experimentation

I wish to thank Elizabeth Robertson for her help with the construction of this chapter.

[1] *Norton* 2, 514.
[2] Thomas A. Clark, [published as a postcard] Moschatel Press, 2007.
[3] Matthew Arnold, 'Shelley', *Nineteenth Century: A Monthly Review* 23 (January 1888), 23–39,
reprinted in *Essays in Criticism: Second Series* (London: Macmillan, 1888).

and playfulness in poetry that together with an understanding of him as a figure of an unpredictable personal and radical political life and who was sensational in his death helped to form their own radical poetry and poetics. I will begin with brief discussions of three major precursors to this radical understanding: Yeats and Eliot, who acknowledged some of what the radical poets called on but came to very different conclusions, and in a somewhat similar vein a poet of the next generation, W. H. Auden; then I will turn for the rest of the chapter to the work of a range of avant-garde poets.

By looking at how these poets engage with Shelley, I hope to indicate that there can be more than one line and model of influence. The paradigm of influence *à la* Harold Bloom as it affects twentieth-century poets' responses to the canonical Romantic poets has been beautifully articulated in the primarily British line of poets by Michael O'Neill. Shelley's presence figures in many of the poets discussed by O'Neill, particularly notable being Yeats, Eliot, Auden, Spender, Stevens, Heaney, Mahon, Muldoon, Hill, and Fisher. These poets, and O'Neill's reading of them, represent one major way of registering and understanding Shelley's (and the Romantics') influence. O'Neill argues that the later poets participate in a 'strenuous tussle' with their Romantic precursors and are consequently interested in a 'dialectic' within the Moderns themselves, courting and drawn to Shelley's (and more generally the Romantics') visionary and utopian excess but then correcting those tendencies as a function of modern social realities through a sense of a more imaginatively temperate function for poetry itself.[4]

Some twentieth-century poets, however, have seen Shelley's influence as that which invites a recasting of his poems and his poetics (the principles upon which his poems are made) not in the mode of scepticism but in the mode of greater or more current realization of their visionary utopian possibilities.[5] For these poets Shelley is a poet of transformations, and, as the poet Michael Palmer has said, of 'radical alterity'.[6] The poets represented here—George Oppen, Robert Duncan, Robert Kelly, Gregory Corso, Barbara Guest, Susan Howe, Andrew Mossin, and Alan Halsey—bring to light, realize, and at times 'liberate' the thematic and formally radical elements of Shelley underlying the poetry, the poetics, and the man in his life and in his death. Indeed, in all cases, visionary transformation seems to demand an accompanying formal experiment. All of these poets, moreover, would assent to Barbara Guest's confession about Shelley as poetic guide for imaginations narrowed and stymied by dark times but wishing to break out of them: 'I assume his stewardship through the cold and mist.'[7]

The first modern poet strongly influenced by Shelley, and strongly influenced by Victorian views of him, was William Butler Yeats (1865–1939). Yeats as a young poet

[4] Michael O'Neill, *The All-Sustaining Air* (Oxford: Oxford UP, 2007), 1.
[5] See Jerome McGann, *The Poetics of Sensibility: A Revolution in Literary Style* (Oxford: Oxford UP, 1996) for an articulation of such distinctions in the interpretation of Romantic and Modern poetry and poetics.
[6] Michael Palmer, 'Some Notes on Shelley, Poetics and the Present', in *Active Boundaries* (New York: New Directions Books, 2008), 204.
[7] From 'Shelley in the Navy-colored Chair', reproduced in 'The Barbara Guest Memory Bank' (<http://www.asu.edu/pipercwcenter/how2journal/bg_memorybank/bg_memory.html#berssen>).

worshipped the Shelley of visionary utopias (*Laon and Cythna, Prometheus Unbound*) and the romantic alienated adventurer (*Alastor*).[8] He went so far as to pronounce *Prometheus Unbound* one of the 'sacred books' of the world.[9] Further into his career, however, he saw Shelley as a poet weakened by his radical politics: 'Shelley the political revolutionary expected a miracle, the Kingdom of God in the twinkling of an eye, like some Christian of the first century.'[10]

Wanting not to deny the power of Shelley as a figure of visionary Romanticism, Yeats, in some of the poems of his middle and late periods, developed a more complex response to the Romantic poet, constructing a poetry of 'dialogue' (as in his poem 'A Dialogue of Self and Soul'), in which the positions within the poem itself, as Michael O'Neill argues, swing from a visionary idealism to a scepticism about the validity of such idealism. 'Ego Dominus Tuus' and 'A Dialogue of Self and Soul', moreover, may find their origins in a roughly similar poem of Shelley's: 'Julian and Maddalo'. Yeats, in other words, picks up on the Shelley that is sceptical of himself, not the utopian, feminist, transgressive, intensely lyrical, and formally experimental poet. Similarly, in the essay on *Prometheus Unbound*, Yeats accounts for a way to continue his admiration of that poem in terms of what he sees as Shelley's critique of his own radicalism; Yeats calls it a 'nightmare-ridden work', one that 'forced him to balance the object of desire conceived as miraculous and superhuman, with nightmare'.[11]

In reading Shelley this way, Yeats confirmed or perhaps helped to create his view of the strengths and weaknesses of the poetry of Romanticism as a whole. In this he both reinforces the late nineteenth-century view of Shelley, as Richard Cronin has admirably sketched in his essay for this volume,[12] and sets the stage for what might be called the establishment High Modernist reading of both Shelley and Romanticism.

Yeats's view of this reading acknowledges the falling off from the visionary past and imagines the loss of the guiding presence of reason ('the worst | Are full of passionate intensity').[13] In 'Coole and Ballylee, 1931' Yeats declares his youthful Romantic identifications and the subsequent changes to modern life that for any alert poet must put an end to Romanticism:

> We were the last romantics—chose for theme
> Traditional sanctity and loveliness;
> Whatever's written in what poets name
> The book of the people; whatever most can bless
> The mind of man or elevate a rhyme;
> But all is changed, that high horse riderless,
> Though mounted in that saddle Homer rode
> Where the swan drifts upon a darkening flood.[14]
>
> (41–8)

[8] W. B. Yeats, *Essays and Introductions* (New York: Palgrave Macmillan, 1961), 65–95.
[9] Ibid. 67.   [10] Ibid. 419.   [11] Ibid. 420.
[12] See also Richard Cronin, *Romantic Victorians: English Literature, 1824–1840* (Houndmills: Palgrave, 2002).
[13] W. B. Yeats, *Collected Poems*, Picador Classics (London: Macmillan, 1990), 211. All quotations from Yeats's poetry will be from this edition.
[14] Ibid. 276.

In Yeats's assertion that the modern horse of poetry is riderless, all energy and passion but no consciousness, 'Romanticism', as appealing as it may be, becomes the word for that failure to acknowledge in art the 'cold' reality of the present; it is a failure of mind and of ideas.

T. S. Eliot agreed with Yeats that Shelley's ideas were immature, but Eliot makes clear what is really at stake: he, and presumably Yeats, do not approve of the merging of poetry with ideas as part of a radical political programme, particularly when 'poetry' means, as is true of Shelley, intense lyricism. In an enormously influential pronouncement, Eliot criticized Shelley precisely because the 'adolescent' poet insisted upon his 'ideas' and, more importantly, upon their merging with his poetry: 'Shelley both had views about poetry and made use of poetry for expressing views [...] I find his ideas repellent; and the difficulty of separating Shelley from his ideas and beliefs is still greater than with Wordsworth.'[15]

But why should visionary and lyric art, except in the mode of scepticism and irony, have to exclude political consciousness? Or, as Michael Palmer asks, in a brilliant essay on Shelley that finds the position of Eliot a major roadblock to the former's proper estimation in the contemporary world: 'And why must a poet be separable from his ideas? [...] What is most striking [...] is [Eliot's] rage against Shelley's ideas. Which, one cannot but wonder, seemed to Eliot the worst: Shelley's feminism, his progressive egalitarianism, his ecotopic perspective, his idealism joined with an active interventionism?'[16] Eliot's demand that poetry remain separate from ideas only applies because of the radical, transformative nature of Shelley's ideas and the (correct) assumption that the intense emotional response elicited from Shelley's poetry would spill over into the enactment of the ideas in social life.

This perspective on Shelley and more generally the Romantics provided by Yeats and Eliot has appealed enormously to the subsequent 'mainstream' tradition of poetry, from Auden and Spender in the 1930s, to the so-called 'confessional' poets such as Lowell, Sexton, and Plath in the 1950s and 1960s, to more recent British poets such as Larkin and Hughes. Auden, for example, was one of the first and most articulate poets to pick up on this tradition and propel it forward towards the present. He once wrote that the Romantic poets and their nineteenth-century followers 'turned away from the life of their time to the contemplation of their own emotions and the creation of imaginary worlds, Wordsworth to Nature, Keats and Mallarmé to a world of pure poetry, Shelley to a future Golden Age'.[17] Shelley, often a stand-in for Romantic sins, is one who characteristically puts the visionary at the centre of the work, staking all on it, as if a poem were equivalent to its vision. To the High Moderns this often appeared as an act of naive exclusion of the 'real' world, with all of its materiality and, at times, its tragedy and needed 'correction'. Thus Auden can tout in 'Musée des Beaux Arts' (1940) Pieter Brueghel's paintings of the Nativity and of the Fall of Icarus as properly representing those moments of vast cultural

[15] T. S. Eliot, 'Keats and Shelley', in *The Use of Poetry and the Use of Criticism* (London: Faber and Faber, 1964), 89.

[16] Palmer, 'Some Notes on Shelley', 203.

[17] Quoted in O'Neill, *The All-Sustaining Air*, 93.

and social significance by placing them alongside quotidian moments (the daily work of the ploughman, for example).

Poets like Auden and his followers attend to form not so much with experiment as with the placing of a kind of pressure on, or resistance to, the (Romantic) 'flow' of the line itself, an increase in its 'density' (over a perceived vagueness and airiness in 'the' nineteenth-century line), a packing together of consonant and stressed syllables. At other times these poets 'correct' perceived Romantic escapism into excessive 'poetic' diction by means of a more quotidian, 'prosaic' one. The language of 'Musée des Beaux Arts' resists figuration and 'the poetic' yet, in straightforward declarative sentences, speaks with assured praise for Brueghel's vision:

> About suffering they were never wrong,
> The Old Masters: how well they understood
> Its human position;[18]

Continuing the prosaic account of the painting, Auden then lengthens the line from these pentameters (the Wordsworthian or 'Romantic' line of subjective meditation) to a longer, freer one that actually includes the expanded world of daily, repetitive life:

> [...] how it takes place
> While someone is eating or opening a window or just walking dully along.

There is a significant difference, however, between Auden's formal attentiveness and that of the avant-garde: in 'Musée des Beaux Arts' the transformation of vision does not really occur. By contrast to Brueghel's painting in which the viewer is forced to see a plough-man and a falling Icarus simultaneously, to feel the stunning juxtaposition and thus revisit the entire cataclysmic mythological event in the presence of the quotidian, Auden's poem simply diminishes the significance of one part of the juxtaposition. 'For [the ploughman] it was not an important failure.' The reader is not asked to take in both events at once, as an act of imagination that alters the reality.

It is precisely the merging of politically progressive ideas, experiments with form, and, as Robert Kaufman has called it, 'song',[19] that drives the poetry and the poetics of the poets whom I will consider in the rest of this essay. All the poets we are about to discuss would agree with Palmer about the necessary unity of Shelley's poetry with his politically progressive 'ideas'. But a poetry that is simply a conduit for ideas does not raise people's hackles; only when ideas are wedded to the *form* of the poem, when it is 'song' and thus pleasurable aesthetically and apparently innocent of thought, does a poem stimulate a critic like Eliot to find its ideas repellent. It follows that poets who practise in the wake of Shelley demonstrate again and again a commitment to the trans-formation, or deformation, of poetic form as the way to activate those ideas through the destabilization of the very medium in which they are presented.

---

[18] W. H. Auden, 'Musée des Beaux Arts', in *Collected Poems*, ed. Edward Mendelson (London: Faber, 1994), 179. All Auden quotations are from this poem.
[19] Robert Kaufman, 'Legislators of the Post-Everything World: Shelley's *Defence* of Adorno', *ELH* 63 (1996), 707–33.

Leaving Yeats, Eliot, and Auden behind, I can now ask: what, then, in Shelley's life, poetry, and poetics might have appealed to and guided the radical poets of the twentieth and twenty-first centuries whom I shall be discussing? They perceived that Shelley was a poet who, in his work and in his life, rejected the prevalent (and still prevalent) notion that an ideal poem existed in order to unfold the inner life, the drama, of the speaking subject. In Shelley's own time William Wordsworth was the leading exponent of this understanding of poetic purpose. But Shelley argues (in *A Defence of Poetry*) that love is, and poetry should be, a 'going out of our own nature' (*Norton 2*, 517). While Wordsworth might not have quarrelled with this statement as such, he would not have embraced it in the way that Shelley's later, radical interpreters in poetry have done.

They saw his existence on the periphery of society, his exile, and his early death by drowning as standing for a life, a self, sacrificed to poetry and the political ideas embedded in it. This view of the poet seems to have had the emotional correlate for Shelley himself in a figure constantly pursued, at times violently, like the Actaeon described in *Adonais*, a self devoured or dismembered yet occasioning beautiful myth, an exiled person become a breathless 'form'.

These twentieth- and twenty-first-century poets consequently might have noted at least two characteristics in Shelley's work that follow from the extremism of a life sacrificed to poetry. First, that Shelley's poems are replete with imagery and literary figures, the 'poetry', so to speak, of poetry. Examples include the lyric songs embedded in *Prometheus Unbound*, many of which take a utopian orientation; or the paratactic figuration, the metaphor and metonymy, in poems such as 'To a Skylark' and *Epipsychidion*. This language often overwhelms the (classical) sense of figure as ornament to the narrative line or (Romantic) sense of personal monologue as the centre of the work. Secondly, later poets see in Shelley not a poet as a figure of stability but rather one performing and participating in transgressions and transformations. He was fascinated with mythic or fabulous personages who take distinct pleasure in unsettling the known borders and the constitution of the familiar. In *The Witch of Atlas*, for instance, he created a figure that causes grotesque changes to occur in people, the effect of which is not to destroy but to realign in a positive way their thinking about themselves, their goals, and their world. In this she is like Mercury (Hermes) the god of transformations, of playfully wicked transgressions, the crosser of thresholds. Shelley translated the great Homeric 'Hymn to Mercury' at roughly the same time that he wrote *The Witch of Atlas*. Part of the drama of the Homeric Hymn involves a kind of conversion of the god Apollo to the ways of the thieving genius of Mercury: poetry, Shelley argues, insists upon such transgressions and indiscretions.

Indeed, what these twentieth- and twenty-first-century poets see in Shelley may be what I have argued elsewhere is essential to the most vital faculty of Romantic poetics, the 'Fancy'.[20] To have figures like the Witch of Atlas and the god Mercury as pre-

---

[20] Jeffrey C. Robinson, *Unfettering Poetry: The Fancy in British Romanticism* (New York: Palgrave Macmillan, 2006).

siding geniuses over one's poetry may indicate a preference in Shelley for that poetic habit of mind—playful, dispersive, image-making, destabilizing, and often improvisational. In contrast to the 'Imagination' where the focus is reflective and synthetic in Coleridge's famous phrase, concerned with the 'balance or reconciliation of discordant qualities',[21] the 'Fancy' is perfectly content with the accumulation or juxtaposition of images from different domains of experience. The playfulness of the 'Fancy' in Romantic poetry, and in particular in Shelley's, belongs to the radical side of the poetic spectrum, in part because it indicates a mind attuned to 'reality' but liberated from its strictures.

This in turn encouraged a poetry less committed to convention in form, syntax, and language itself—a more experimental poetry became possible, one in which the radicalizing of form, as well as a writing in the present, became essential for a poet trying to alter conventional modes and structures of thought. Interestingly, Shelley's own poetry doesn't immediately call attention to itself as formally radical (although a poem like the aforementioned *Epipsychidion* could be said to reverse the formal ratio of the account of the speaker and the density of figure). But later poets unquestionably associate Shelley's merging of 'song' (form) and radical politics, which may turn out to be his greatest contribution to modern experimental poetry.

In the American Objectivist poet George Oppen's (1908–84) reworking of Shelley's 'Ozymandias' (also called 'Ozymandias'), one can discern that, generated by Shelley's poem, experiment with form goes hand in hand with critical analysis of the modern person in a world blanketed by the market economy:

> The five
> Senses gone
>
> To the one sense,
> The sense of prominence
>
> Produce an art
> *De luxe.*
>
> And down town
> The absurd stone trimming of the building tops
>
> Rectangular in dawn, the shopper's
> Thin morning monument.[22]

Oppen sustains by updating Shelley's theme for the present: the fate of monomaniacal tyrannies is recast as the success of the world of high commercial capitalism, seen as the tyranny of 'the sense of prominence' over the other five senses. Formally, and in keeping with the critique of the market economy, he revises the sonnet and the idea of the sonnet: with his spare, short lines he visually projects the critique of tyranny as a critique of

---

[21] Samuel Taylor Coleridge, *Biographia Literaria*, ed. James Engell and W. Jackson Bate (Princeton: Princeton UP, 1983), ch. 14, 2. 16.

[22] George Oppen, *New Collected Poems*, ed. Michael Davidson (New York: New Directions Books, 2002), 59.

the 'monumental' form of the sonnet. He further capitalizes on Shelley's emphasis on the pastness of Ozymandias, and the failure of monuments and the tyranny associated with them to last. For the politically radical Shelley the spirit of Ozymandias comes forward into the life of the Regency moment. Oppen seems to begin right here in his own present—mid-twentieth-century New York City—where there has been no ruin, nothing 'shattered'. Thus both poets engage in an important improvisational feature available to the poetry of participation; the poet doesn't meditate on or reflect upon his subject as much as he observes it.

Where lies the tyranny of the King of Kings?—in today's 'down town' world of shops, in which the only identifiable person is one whose attention to the world through 'the five | Senses' has vanished, through Ozymandias as the spectre of capitalism, to be replaced by identity as acquisition. The new 'monument' (the sinister last 'remaining' word in the poem) is not an empire as such but a department store. The only line to equal Shelley's in length is a ten-syllable line mocking the stony monumental one.

One could read Shelley's sonnet as a critique of 'the monumental' associated with the misuse of power in poetry as well as in society. If the sonnet is a 'monumental' abstract form, even visually chunky, in the spirit of the poem it deserves to be 'shattered' by a later poet: the otherwise characteristically (for Oppen) shorter lines seem to indicate the vanishing of the monumental or the ephemeralizing of it. Conversely, these very short lines have, as they do in much of Oppen's work (and in the work of other poets in the 'objectivist' tradition such as Louis Zukofsky and Lorine Niedecker), the sense of new beginning, of being slight eruptions of the visionary imagination out of the oppressive Ozymandian silence. The vertical length of Oppen's poem, if you count spaces between lines, comes to fourteen lines, the length of a sonnet: the poem's social critique has a correlate in formal revision.

Oppen's poem, then, is an example of a poetic *deformation*, in which an 'essence' of the vision or life of a form is sought by a radical reworking of form: in this case, the sonnet's requisite number of lines is kept but its horizontal vector, the ten-syllable line, is deformed. Deformation at once recalls the originating poem while it acts as a critique that simultaneously releases the energies of the original. In this case Oppen *is realizing*, or translating, or deforming, Shelley's vision of tyranny and critique of monumentality into the twentieth century.

The principle of deformation also works in the case of the North American poet Robert Duncan (1919–88), although here the poet intends to liberate a Shelleyan lyric from what he perceives as an outworn metrics. Simultaneously he works to release the erotic energies of Shelley's elegiac version of Ovidian myth by recasting the poetry of Shelley as a comedy. Duncan took Shelley's Ovidian lyric 'Arethusa' and made it new: 'Shelley's ARETHUSA set to new measures'. Using much of Shelley's language, imagery, and narrative, Duncan, from his point of view, updates and revivifies the Romantic's poem. The motive for the revision has been recorded in Duncan's letter to Denise Levertov in which he describes his experience of reading 'Arethusa' out loud with his partner Jess:

Then we tried the Shelley aloud, but its onrushing regular stresses and rimes rang ludicrous in our ears, as if they did monkey imitations of themselves, having lost some secret of conformity—yet something in the poem haunted and asked to be renderd [*sic*]. It was a bet too, over coffee, and I set myself to keep the current, the stream-form of the original, and wherever I could to keep the original intact: the basic thing was to get a shifting pace and pattern to it—to have pools, eddies, and fast and slow onrushes etc.[23]

Duncan's 'Shelley's ARETHUSA' 'deforms' the original in the sense that the actual words of Shelley and the exact movement vertically in the poem are maintained, but they are loosened from their older syntax, from their quite strict anapaestic foot and predictable two dimeters closed by a trimeter, and from grammatical archaisms ('Alpheus bold' becoming 'bold Alpheus'). Shelley's words become 'winged', floating, sliding. Duncan's version of Arethusa before Alpheus' chase catches the mobility that Duncan wants to restore:

> As if still asleep, she goes, glides or
> Lingers in deep pools.
>
> (11–12)[24]

Duncan's initial seemingly sceptical response to the Romantic's 'Arethusa' leads him not to a scepticism about Shelley's project but to an effort to realize the intention of the original and what 'haunted' him about it. The letter goes on to recount beautifully the impulse to bring more life to the original than Shelley's is perceived to have, to refresh the rhythm and the images, to allow a 'labor in love of form'. As Levertov's reply indicates, Duncan's version is like an 'inspired translation [...] one that didn't try to copy the original slavishly but to give it new life by imitating the spirit of it'.[25]

Duncan realizes Shelley's work in part by recasting the earlier poet's account of Ovid's mythic version of Alpheus, the river god, and the nymph Arethusa: Alpheus attempts to rape Arethusa, but the god of the ocean saves her by transforming both into the river itself where they live eternally together. Here is the final section of Shelley's poem:

> And now from their fountains
> In Enna's mountains,
> Down one vale where the morning basks,
> > Like friends once parted
> > Grown single-hearted,
> They ply their watery tasks.
> > At sunrise they leap
> > From their cradles steep
> In the cave of the shelving hill;
> > At noontide they flow

---

[23] *Letters of Robert Duncan and Denise Levertov*, ed. Robert J. Bertholf and Albert Gelpi (Palo Alto, CA: Stanford UP, 2003), 288.

[24] Robert Duncan, *Roots and Branches* (New York: New Directions Books, 1964), 78–83.

[25] *Letters of Robert Duncan and Denise Levertov*, 291.

> Through the woods below
> And the meadows of asphodel;
> And at night they sleep
> In the rocking deep
> Beneath the Ortygian shore;—
> Like spirits that lie
> In the azure sky
> When they love but live no more.

$$(73-90)^{26}$$

And here is Duncan's rewriting:

> When now from Enna's mountains they spring,
>   Afresh in her innocence
> Arethusa to Alpheus gladly comes.
> Into one morning two hearts awake,
>   at sunrise leap from sleep's caves to return
>   to the vale where they meet,
>   drawn by yearning from night into day.
>
> Down into the noontide flow,
>   into the full of life winding again, they find
> their way thru the woods
>   and the meadows of asphodel below.
> Wedded, one deep current leading,
>   they follow to dream
> in the rocking deep at the Ortygian shore.
>
>   Spirits drawn upward,
>   they are divided
> into the azure from which the rain falls,
>   life from life,
> seeking their way to love once more.[27]

Even though Duncan describes his complaint with Shelley on the level of prosody and idiom, his reworking starts with the revision of Shelley's account of the Ovidian myth itself, which operates in an economy of scarcity: if the human is absorbed into the natural, its human attributes—difference and identity, 'life' itself—vanish. They lose their maturity and become 'cradled' in the nature that receives them. There is an elegiac side to Ovid and to Shelley's version of him. But Duncan presents their transformation in an economy of abundance. Not only love but 'life' comes 'from life', and renewal of love, not its pastness, becomes the principle upon which the poems ends. One feels this in Duncan's rewriting of individual lines, both in their content and in the greater expansiveness of the lines themselves (compared to

---

[26] P. B. Shelley, *Poetical Works* (London: Oxford UP, 1967), 611–12.
[27] Duncan, *Roots and Branches*, 78–83.

Shelley's shorter ones) including a new density of sound in alliteration and assonance: 'Down into the noontide flow, | into the full of life winding again' (75–6). By seeking to liberate the sounds of poetry to match the onrush of the violent energies of desire and escape along with the suddenness of transformation, Duncan catches something fundamental that is not only latent in Shelley but something that 'haunted' both Duncan in his reading of 'Arethusa' and Levertov in her return to the Romantic poem.

Strikingly, a number of twentieth-century poets writing with Shelley's ideological and formal revisionism in view seek to liberate in a contemporary idiom what I referred to above as the playful poetics of the 'Fancy'. His late poems to Jane Williams have somewhat surprisingly spurred interest where one might not expect it, among the Beat Poets, past and present, and also in Frank O'Hara (of the New York School of poets) who wrote a short group of lyrics to the artist and friend Jane Freilicher: 'A Terrestrial Cuckoo', 'Jane Awake', 'A Mexican Guitar', and 'Chez Jane'.[28] In his versions, O'Hara recasts Shelley's playfully imaginative but also utopian and deeply felt love poems into a post-surrealist playfulness; he picks up and extends the casualness of Shelley's exchange (unusual in Romantic poetry) with his interlocutor. Formally he carries Shelley's poetics of the 'Fancy' (e.g. short-lined rhymed couplets in long, unending streams, whimsical mythmaking) into a poetry of comic juxtapositions of language and image.

At times Shelley's poems to Jane seem like short-line riffs on his massive poem of passion-love *Epipsychidion*. Although Shelley referred to one of them as an 'ariette',[29] they contain much passion and intensity, much utopian idealizing and erotic longing; it is in this context that their playfulness must be considered: 'A spirit interfused around | A thrilling silent life' (45–6). O'Hara pushes the fancy-fulness further, in the way of a post-surrealist New York poet. In 'With a Guitar: To Jane' Shelley gives her a gift of the guitar with a poem that ventriloquizes Shakespeare's Ariel and then creates a 'myth' of the guitar's creation. O'Hara extends this kind of creativity to a playfully erotic juxtaposition of images, indeed an updating of that Shelleyan density of image, but also to dancing a fandango to the strains of a 'Mexican Guitar':

> Our shouting knocked over a couple of palm trees
> and the gaping sky seemed to reel at our mistakes,
> such purple flashing insteps and careers!
> which bit with lavish envy the northern soldiers.[30]

In each of the examples discussed to this point, a poet not simply responds to but intervenes formally and thematically in or with reference to a poem of Shelley. The North American poet Robert Kelly, in his recasting of Shelley's 'Mont Blanc' in a thirty-eight-page blank verse meditation with the same title, makes the formal part of the intervention

---

[28] Frank O'Hara, *Meditations in an Emergency* (New York: Grove Press, 1957), 24–9.

[29] See Michael O'Neill, referred to in 'Shelley's Lyric Art', *Norton 2*, 625.

[30] O'Hara, *Meditations in an Emergency*, 28.

apparent from his comment prefatory to the poem:[31] 'Inscribed in the spaces of Shelley's "Mont Blanc"'. Not only asked to realize that Kelly's lines are massive intercalations between Shelley's, the reader also learns to think of the poem (both poems) spatially and comparatively: Shelley's poem appears at the back of the book for easy reference. This allows one to see easily how Kelly is 'deforming' it, including what he might mean by 'spaces'. Moreover, both front and back end-pages have copies of a detailed early map of the Mont Blanc region of France, with the rivers Arve and Drance figuring centrally. Not on the map but right near the beginning of the poem reference is made to the Hudson river near where Kelly lives in the United States, where he has been teaching at Bard College and has become an extremely prolific and heavily anthologized poet over the past half-century. Kelly's poem encourages one to look at Shelley's spatially as well, as a geography of mind. The 'spaces' in Shelley belong to that geography; thus it is Kelly's intention to fill them with his own language and thinking by following out Shelley's implications or to take them along new pathways. The inscriptions are the formal equivalent of his thematic, in this case philosophical, recasting of Shelley's meditation, in his 'Mont Blanc', on the sublime.

The speaker in Shelley's poem worries about the connection between a power outside the self and the mind of persons, a version of the sublime in which access to that power may 'repeal | Large codes of fraud and woe' (80–1). How, the poem continually asks amidst the speaker's overwhelming solitude in the presence of Mont Blanc, can one write about forces the origins of which are far vaster than any human faculty can imagine and yet which could have enormous power for the human mind? The emphasis ultimately falls on a capacity of the 'awful power' not to tyrannize but to free up that mind in its imaginings, a liberation that involves full acknowledgement of the mystery of the other.

Kelly recasts this drama of mind in terms of the presence of the other as his beloved; indeed this is the biggest 'space' in Shelley's text that Kelly fills: he turns the solitary meditation into an address to the beloved who is at once present and to be discovered. The poem moves back and forth from the Hudson river of home to the river Drance; the journey celebrates her presence and their fulfilment while it journeys far to discover the same thing, a *via negativa*. Charlotte, wife of the poet, moves back and forth between a figure of the quotidian, a comfort in the social scale, and a lover on the scale of, say (at least in imagination), Emilia Viviani or perhaps Jane Williams. The world swings from present-day New York State to the world-in-exile of Shelley and Byron (the cover of the book pictures the castle of Chillon). Similarly, in 'Mont Blanc' Kelly says of language that it is the 'network of its pasts'. Kelly, in other words, works precisely among the different registers of being found in the great epics—social, historical, mythic—and, like Shelley, asks, how does one define 'the human' in relation to outsized and mysterious embodiments of reality? In terms of the address to the beloved the poem becomes an intense and extensive exploration of love.

But why Shelley in the first place? In an amusing comment in the poem, Kelly declares: 'there is nothing north of Boston', presumably a reference to the title of an early book of

---

[31] Robert Kelly, *Mont Blanc* (Ann Arbor: OtherWind Press, Inc., 1994). This edition contains no page or line numbers.

Robert Frost and thus a swipe at one whom Kelly would deem (in Michael Palmer's term) a 'poet of accommodation'.[32] The journey of discovery therefore must go further afield than a quick car trip from New York State along the Massachusetts Turnpike to Frost's northern New England countryside. Moreover, Frost's poetics of containment will not suffice for the exploration of essential mysteries of love and power ('Visit the hidden'). This exploration includes in its purview the failures of modern societies to care for the inner as well as public lives of its members: he therefore must journey back to the radical Romantic Shelley.

The life and in some cases the death of the radical Romantic Shelley also fascinated twentieth- and twenty-first-century poets, sometimes as a biographical fact but always as a precise locus for what gives his poetry its authenticity as a visionary poet pushing for utopian solutions. This Shelley tragically but heroically 'sails' from the life of the social person into poetry—a 'world' of rhythm, song, and image.[33] In the late nineteenth century the poet Algernon Charles Swinburne, a great promoter of Shelley, wrote: 'He alone was the perfect singing-god; his thoughts, words, deeds, all sang together [...] Shelley was born a son and soldier of light, an archangel winged and weapon'd for angel's work.'[34]

Presumably an account of a poet-as-person resonates with a way of thinking about his or her poetics. In the 1950s through the 1970s the so-called Beat Poets revered the figure of Shelley as a precursor of a politically and poetically radical enthusiasm, a boy-man of poetic energies, for whom, like themselves, at least in principle, that level of high-energy resistance was required to counter the perceived repressiveness of post-McCarthy North America. The Jack Kerouac School of Disembodied Poetics, founded by Allen Ginsberg and Anne Waldman in 1975, and continuing to this day, championed this understanding of Shelley particularly in its first twenty-five years. And no one (other than perhaps Ginsburg himself and Diane di Prima) was more vociferous on the subject of Shelley than Gregory Corso, whose letters are full of praise of and identification with Shelley. 'If I heed all my Catholic upbringing then surely Shelley is in Hell. I once asked a priest, "Do you really think beautiful Shelley is in hell?" And he said, "He left his wife didn't he? Married another didn't he? Was an Atheist, wasn't he? Then surely his soul rests in hell." But I said, "Look at his poems, he loved God!"'[35] Corso wrote a poem of sheer hero worship, 'I held a Shelley manuscript (written in the Houghton Library, Harvard)', that openly rejects the kind of self-conscious distancing and criticism seen in Yeats's later poems and in his accounts of Shelley in *Autobiographies* and the essay on *Prometheus Unbound*: 'I would have taken the page | breathing in the crime!'[36] Corso's (and more generally the Beats') Shelley is authentic precisely because he is the *senex puer* who thrives at the peripheries of the consciousness of 'middle age', or that of the social

---

[32] Palmer, 'Some Notes on Shelley', 203.

[33] See in particular below: *The Text of Shelley's Death*.

[34] Algernon Charles Swinburne, *Essays and Studies*, 5th edn. (London: Chatto and Windus, 1901), 215.

[35] Gregory Corso, *An Accidental Autobiography: The Selected Letters of Gregory Corso*, ed. Bill Morgan (New York: New Directions Books, 2003), 117.

[36] Gregory Corso, *The Happy Birthday of Death* (New York: New Directions, 1960), 22.

person. Corso describes himself, playfully, in 'Sunrise', as 'A poetman | become an olding messenger boy | O silver tongue of spiritus!'

Such poems are less self-deprecating than they are defining of a quality to be preserved or reconstituted in the present. 'On Gregory Being Double the Age of Shelley' acts as a challenge to a poet who has long lived past the age at which 'authentic' poets like Keats and Shelley himself died; as such we should contrast the idea of this poem with Wordsworth's 'Resolution and Independence' in which the middle age of the speaker requires, in relation to the *Wunderkinder* Chatterton and Burns, a new poetics: how do you write poetry and survive? The result has been the mainstream tradition of lyric which privileges the poem of the drama of the lyric subject. But for Corso it is different: 'If Shelley gave me anything, it was a kind of nobility, an effort at plagiarizing the Gods as it were [...] He's a pure angel-man.'[37] That is, how do I survive and still be 'angel-man', still plagiarize the gods and not worry too much about craft, the curse of the non-visionary but resolute and independent ego?

Very similar to Shelley here, Corso's poet as 'angel-man', with the anticipation of a destabilized identity, at times leads him to promote, as ideal poet, the god of transformations and thresholds, Hermes or Mercury, just as Shelley (and Keats) did. For example, a favourite epithet (to be found in Shelley's *Defence of Poetry*) is 'herald', which chimes with the title of Corso's *Herald of the Autochthonic Spirit*. The herald, or 'messenger', is Hermes, 'the orphan god',[38] alone in these late days but crucial, as he was for the poet of Homer's 'Hymn to Mercury' and *The Witch of Atlas*, for an artist wishing emphatically to awaken the consciousness of citizens.

If Shelley's life, that merges the person with the poet, commands Corso's attention, Shelley's haunting death by drowning helps other poets to characterize the essence of Shelley's contribution to poetry. In the accounts of his death begun by contemporaries including Mary Shelley, Leigh Hunt, and Edward Trelawny poetry is intimately entwined with death: Shelley, depending on the account, is washed ashore holding the latest book of Keats, the plays of Aeschylus, or the plays of Sophocles in hand or in his pocket, while remnants of water-soaked Shelley manuscripts also belong to the constellation. The poets with whom I will conclude this discussion associate the merging of life, death-by-drowning, and work with poetry that gains its hold over us as social beings because it locates itself beyond or outside the social. Such poetry goes deeper into origins than does typically poetry of the drama of the lyric subject. Moreover, their preoccupation with drafts from Shelley points to an interest in Shelley as a poet of process or event rather than of finished artefact (writing a monumental poetry of recollection and pastness). These poets also associate the 'draft' with an open-form poetry of their own.

A beautiful poem by Barbara Guest, alluded to previously, 'Shelley in the Navy-colored Chair', that begins 'I sit so close to him [Shelley]' directly brings the drowned person into conjunction with a transformed, living language. She observes: 'He breathes into the alphabet I found upon my chair' and continues

---

[37] Corso, *Autobiography*, 273–4.
[38] Gregory Corso, 'Ancestry', in *Herald of the Autochthonic Spirit* (New York: New Directions, 1981), 21.

he failed to ride the unswept sea, and like
a nautilus drowned in heavy seas, windswept
like the alphabet he enriched [...]
To add more stanzas to this alphabet
is the view Shelley takes.[39]

To be transformative with our language requires a poetry that comes from the sources of life, the sea of his drowning, implicitly a place where language has not distinguished itself from the person uttering or writing it. This is the implication of a moment in Susan Howe's Preface to her book of (often lyric) essays *The Birth Mark*; writing about the use of manuscripts (Dickinson's, Hölderlin's, and Shelley's) and poets' engagements with them, she discusses one which 'was pulled from the wreck of the *"Don Juan"*—which the poet had hoped to christen *Ariel*'.[40] She focuses on the text at the moment of Shelley's death, the text dredged from the sea itself and 'heavily damaged by water, mildew, and restoration', which is to say that the 'product' cannot be separated from its physical history and the body of its author. Since they are drafts, the text cannot be separated from the process of its making. Moreover, Howe picks as specimens passages which themselves blur the boundary between the artefact and the person producing it: for example (transcribing the manuscript with fragments of the *Defence of Poetry*), 'A Poet is as- nightin gale who sits < > dar kness & sings to cheer its own so li tude w ith s w eet sounds [...]' or, from a fragment from *Adonais*, 'He is a portion of the loveliness which once he made more lovely.'[41]

Thus when Andrew Mossin in his fascinating long, open-form poem *Drafts for Shelley* (2001) says that it represents his effort to 'find "Shelley"',[42] he alludes to the feverish activity that occurred in 1822 to find or recover the body of the drowned poet. But here it stands for an extreme way of writing that at once recovers a 'complete' and immediate version of the earlier poet through and for the sake of an expanded version of the later one: drafts from Shelley (reproduced occasionally in Mossin's text) become drafts *for* him. In both cases drafts signify process, which in turn revives the person in the text. The finding of the poet, his or her recovery, becomes itself the construction of a poetry very much Mossin's own but unabashedly 'derivative', in which he, in the spirit of Howe's editing, 'often ventriloquized the repetitions, cross-outs, and rewordings that score the pages of his notebook and contribute to their physical and graphemic beauty'. 'I sought to erase and fracture the language of Shelley's "original," thereby arriving at a poem whose language remained Shelley's yet whose form was my own.' It is not difficult to see this as a poetic reclamation of the Actaeon-like dismemberments with which Shelley himself identifies and of the drowned body ravaged by water and the creatures feeding on him. The 'Shelley' reclaimed by poetry is not by any means solely the biographical and social person, not simply the ego against which Shelley and his Cockney companions protested, but attracts to himself like seaweed to the drowned body the 'portion of that

---

[39] Taken from 'The Barbara Guest Memory Bank' (see n. 6 above).

[40] Susan Howe, *The Birth-Mark: Unsettling the Wilderness in American Literary History* (Middletown, NY: Wesleyan UP, 1993). From the introduction (no pagination).

[41] Ibid.

[42] Andrew Mossin, *Drafts for Shelley* (Cedar Ridge, CA: Facture Books, 2001). The quotations here and subsequently come from an unpublished draft of an introduction to the book.

loveliness' that is his own poetry as well as all of the elements of the mythic and historical collective in which he has participated.

Mossin moves this process forward into his own life in a manner that recalls Kelly's shifting of Shelleyan solitude into the context of unalloyed love. Much of *Drafts for Shelley* was written during the two years marked by the births of his two daughters; in an effort to record that intense experience, what he describes as a trance, he would sit 'with the blue Bodleian notebooks on my lap and transcribe myself into Shelley/Shelley into myself'.

Finding Shelley means finding and collecting fragments of Shelley's poetry and presenting them as such: a constellation of fragments (Mossin writes in open-form fragments) that create a strangely new, unpremeditated and unanticipated, yet strangely familiar, Shelleyan, whole. Looked at in terms of the politics of literary history, such a poetic project as Mossin's refuses a sentimentalized or idealized version of Shelley and his poetry. This, I believe, is the main point of the extraordinary book-length poem by the British poet Alan Halsey, *The Text of Shelley's Death* (2001). Halsey exploits the fact that there are many accounts of Shelley's death, some eyewitness and some retrospective and second-hand; but no one account fully agrees with other accounts, and often the facts from one telling contradict those of another: 'the text of Shelley's death is an embodiment of contradiction.'[43] Memoirists and literary historians have attempted to resolve the differences or insist upon one authentic account, but Halsey takes a different approach: he presents all the variants, often in the spirit of a variorum edition. In other words, he wants the text of Shelley's death to honour, even celebrate, the contradictions. In contrast to almost all of the accounts of Shelley's death, which dwell in the spirit of pastness and the tone of elegiac loss, this one radiates the feeling of recovery.

Halsey makes it clear, by accepting the impossibility of knowing irrefutably 'what happened', that his construction works against an idealization of the poet that began with his death and that led directly to the Arnoldian Shelley of ineffectuality and to a certain chasteness under the guise of 'maturity' that one still sometime encounters in versions of this poet. Thus in a brief, three-quarter-page opening re-telling ('Everybody knows the text of Shelley's death'), Halsey concludes inconclusively: 'The boat disappeared into thick haze.'[44] The book that follows lays out many details that produce a thick haze, not to be suffered but to be embraced as the way to finding Shelley. The book assumes the dis-figuring, the fragmentation, and the dismemberment of body and work as the starting point. Halsey's characterization of Shelley picked from the shards of his language and the surrounding narratives belongs to a quotidian, erotic, often self-absorbed world but also one drenched in sounds, rhythms, and figuration.

Halsey's closing 'Index' becomes a lake or bay (*the* Bay of Spezia in which Shelley drowned) of poetic language. The alphabetical presentation of image phrases, replete with the ambiguous or multivalent nature of images, leads to a metamorphic flowing

---

[43]   Alan Halsey, *The Text of Shelley's Death* (Sheffield: West House Books, 2001), 61.
[44]   Ibid. 9.

of one image into another: reading it like a poem, one becomes aware of sound, of intense alliterative transmutations. The *topicality* that one usually associates with an index becomes all signifier and movement. There are no page numbers, nothing to look up; thus the language here isn't referential. Each letter of the alphabet, separated by a vertical space from the preceding and succeeding ones, becomes a 'poem', the letter a rule for the poem to follow, giving it a shape, but also open for any number of specific entries. It reads like an open-form or aleatory version of a Shelley poem (like Duncan's 'Shelley's ARETHUSA' and Kelly's 'Mont Blanc'). Here, for example, is the beginning of 't':

> Tempering the cold and radiant air
> That band of sister-spirits
> That planet-crested Shape
> That strange boat like the moon's shade
> That thinnest boat
> The boat of my desire[45]

The text of Shelley's death absorbs and transforms the poet-as-ego into a much larger and more poetic version of self, linked to mythological figures of his own referencing (like Prometheus or Mercury) and to poetic language. In his last paragraph Halsey writes: 'At moments the text reads as a sailing into metaphor into the unavoidable image of Shelley's own sea of metonymy and symbol: if this is an illusion it is one borne out by the outsider-tellers' reliance on a Shelleyan vocabulary.'[46] Halsey has given us a twentieth- and twenty-first-century Shelley of radical transformations, a Shelley whose poetic calling sacrifices normal life for a total world of images.

'The romantic kind of poetry is still in the state of becoming; that, in fact, is its real essence; that it should forever be becoming and never be perfected.'[47] The poets considered in this essay seem to understand Friedrich Schlegel's aphorism instinctively, in a conclusively different response from that of Yeats described earlier, in which Modernism and its sequellae are a falling off from Romanticism and even its predecessors. That Shelley, as quintessential Romantic poet, became a lightning rod for their continued acts of becoming and renewing tells us precisely how he 'flowed in' to their own thinking and making. As we have seen, part of the becoming these poets have participated in assumes the truth of Ezra Pound's dictum: 'All ages are contemporaneous in the mind.'[48] That is, Shelley seems to have inspired an immediacy or presentness in their making of poems. To the degree that 'Shelley' belongs to the past, he must not remain in the recollection of a modern poet but must be brought forward into 'now': his perceptions, his prosody and form, his politics, and finally the collective dimensions of his person must be 'found' now. Clearly not many poets of the past have evoked such an urgency for renewal:

---

[45] Ibid. 78.   [46] Ibid. 81.

[47] Friedrich Schlegel, from 'Athenæum Fragment #116', *Friedrich Schlegel's Lucinde and the Fragments*, trans. Peter Firchow (Minneapolis: University of Minnesota Press, 1971), 175.

[48] Ezra Pound, *Guide to Kulchur* (New York: New Directions, 1968), 57–9.

> Scatter, as from an unextinguished hearth
> Ashes and sparks, my words among mankind!
> Be through my lips to unawakened Earth
>
> The trumpet of a prophecy!
>
> ('Ode to the West Wind', 66–9)

SELECT BIBLIOGRAPHY

Allen Ginsberg Library, Naropa University: <www.Naropa.edu/naropalibrary/index.com> (for lectures/readings on Shelley by Diane di Prima, Gregory Corso, Allen Ginsberg, and others).

Fishman, Lisa. 'Shelley's "Secret Alchemy": Mercury Unbound'. Unpublished dissertation, University of Utah.

Halsey, Alan. *The Text of Shelley's Death*. Sheffield: West House Books, 2001.

Hoffman, Eric. 'Legislator of the Unacknowledged World: George Oppen and Shelley'. *All This Strangeness: A Garland for George Oppen*. Ed. Eric Hoffman. <http://www.bigbridge.org/BB14/OP-HOF.HTM>.

Howe, Susan. *The Birthmark: Unsettling the Wilderness in American Literary History*. Middletown, NY: Wesleyan UP, 1993.

Kaufman, Robert. 'Legislators of the Post-Everything World: Shelley's *Defence* of Adorno'. *ELH* 63 (1996), 707–33.

O'Neill, Michael. *The All-Sustaining Air: Romantic Legacies and Renewals in British, American, and Irish Poetry since 1900*. Oxford: Oxford UP, 2007.

Palmer, Michael. 'Some Notes on Shelley, Poetics and the Present'. *Active Boundaries*. New York: New Directions Books, 2008. 195–206.

Robinson, Jeffrey C. *Unfettering Poetry: The Fancy in British Romanticism*. New York: Palgrave, 2006.

Rothenberg, Jerome and Jeffrey C. Robinson. Eds. *Poems for the Millennium*, III: *The University of California Book of Romantic and Postromantic Poetry*. Berkeley and Los Angeles: University of California Press, 2009.

Skau, Michael. '*A Clown in a Grave*': *Complexities and Tensions in the Work of Gregory Corso*. Carbondale, IL: Southern Illinois UP, 1999.

CHAPTER 40

EDITING SHELLEY

MICHAEL ROSSINGTON

I

ONE reason for the complexity of Shelley's afterlife is the manner in which his poetry and prose have been edited since he died in 1822. It will have taken nearly 200 years from his death for complete scholarly editions of his oeuvre to emerge.[1] The absence of such fundamental resources has been, and remains, to student and non-specialist alike, a cause of puzzlement, if not consternation, especially since complete works of other Romantic poets are available in more than one modern scholarly edition. While the results of the cumulative labours of generations of scholars indicate a settlement of sorts on the horizon, a Shelleyan sensibility will be alert to the danger of supposing that any edition can present itself as definitive. No doubt long after the publication of those in prospect, his writing will continue to be mediated in debatable forms. Moreover, given such recent advances as the discovery of a copy of the *Poetical Essay on the Existing State of Things* (1811) and the first publication, with full scholarly apparatus, of a diplomatic text of the prose fragment known as *On Zionism* (?1820–1), it seems likely that the Shelley canon and its textual foundations will continue to be further augmented and refined in the future.[2]

While it appears that about seventy of Shelley's poems were published in his lifetime, there are approximately 300 in *H*, and over 450 are projected in *Longman*. To understand why establishing a canon, let alone editing it, has been such a protracted exercise requires an awareness of the history of Shelley's text,[3] and of the contexts in which he

I am most grateful to Nora Crook for comments on a draft of this chapter.

[1] *CPPBS* and *Longman* are in progress as is, following *Murray: Prose*, the second and final volume of the Oxford UP edition of *The Prose Works of Percy Bysshe Shelley*, ed. Michael O'Neill and Timothy Webb.

[2] H. R. Woudhuysen, 'A Shelley Pamphlet Come to Light', *Times Literary Supplement* 5389 (14 July 2006), 12; Nora Crook and Tatsuo Tokoo, 'Shelley's Jewish "Orations"', *Keats-Shelley Journal* 59 (2010), 43–64. A reading text was first published in Tokyo in 1923.

[3] For the history of the text, see *Longman*, 1, pp. xiv–xxii, *CPPBS* I, pp. xxii–xxix and *Murray: Prose*, pp. xxvii–xxx.

wrote and published during his lifetime. In a career of just twelve years he produced an astonishing amount of verse and prose. What he wrote was often contentious, a factor that contributed to his difficulties in getting finished work into print. Moreover, when he was published, the printed texts were often unsatisfactory. These issues alone would make for a considerable editorial undertaking. But its scale and complexity are conditioned by a further circumstance. In B. C. Barker-Benfield's words, '[t]he factor that ensured both the chaotic state of his unpublished texts and the artificial preservation of every remaining draft was his sudden death'.[4] A consequence of Shelley's abruptly terminated life is that manuscript drafts, often incomplete, and fair copies are the sole authority for a very significant proportion of his works.

That Shelley had only limited success in securing the publication of his poetry and prose in his lifetime is especially true of much of the substantial achievement of his last four, richly productive years. *The Witch of Atlas*, *Julian and Maddalo*, and *A Defence of Poetry* all appeared posthumously, the first two in 1824, the last in 1839, respectively three, five, and eighteen years after they had been sent to Charles Ollier for publication. His lack of a successful and communicative publisher in Ollier struck Shelley forcibly in Italy and ultimately led him in January 1822 to seek to terminate their relationship in anger: 'I will have nothing more to do with Ollier on *whatever terms* or for *whatever apology*' (*Letters: PBS* II, 387–8). From a publisher's viewpoint, however, Shelley was not a profit-making concern, and, as Charles Robinson has shown, he was in many ways well served by Ollier who reported in October 1823 that 'The sale, in every instance, of Mr Shelley's works has been very confined'.[5] Byron's capacity to sustain his glittering success in exile can only have reinforced upon Shelley that it was his lack of a marketable profile, not distance from London, that excluded him from the kind of attention he felt his work deserved. A sense of disadvantage is palpable in the bitter tone with which he urged Ollier (in vain) to mail him proofs of *Hellas* in November 1821: 'The whole might be sent at once: Lord Byron has his poems sent to him in this manner, and I cannot see that the inferiority in the composition of a Poem can affect the powers of a printer in the matters of dispatch &c.—' (*Letters: PBS* II, 365) In 1821–2 Shelley realized that friends who were also editors and publishers could be of benefit to him at closer hand. Leigh Hunt, in whose *Examiner* 'Hymn to Intellectual Beauty' and 'Ozymandias' first appeared, and who also published other short poems in Ollier's *Literary Pocket-Book* series (1819–23), was his best hope. Easing Hunt to Italy and drawing Byron in to the periodical venture *The Liberal: Verse and Prose from the South* (1822–3) constituted Shelley's attempt, post his 'ex-Ollierization', to fashion a viable, published future for himself (*Letters: PBS* II, 344, 388).

That Shelley was not a commercially successful author was in part because the publishing business was officially regulated by the very laws underpinned by Church and state which his writings challenged. So it is no wonder that even those sympathetic to his views declined some of what they were sent for fear of prosecution on the grounds of

---

[4] B. C. Barker-Benfield, *Shelley's Guitar* (Oxford: Bodleian Library, 1992), p. xii.

[5] Quoted in Charles E. Robinson, 'Percy Bysshe Shelley, Charles Ollier, and William Blackwood', in Kelvin Everest (ed.), *Shelley Revalued* (Leicester: Leicester UP, 1983), 209.

blasphemy or sedition. In autumn 1819 Hunt refused *The Mask of Anarchy*, Ollier *Peter Bell the Third* (the former was eventually published by Hunt in 1832, the latter by Mary Shelley in 1839). His track record had from the start been enough to make any prospective publisher wary. *Original Poetry by Victor and Cazire* (1810) was withdrawn from sale following the discovery of a plagiarism, while a substantial number of copies of *The Necessity of Atheism* (1811) were ordered to be incinerated. *Queen Mab* was the first major test of the boundaries of what was possible to express publicly in print and, in the end, the concerns of Thomas Hookham led to the private circulation of a limited number of copies rather than publication. Its piracy by William Clark in 1821 and subsequently by William Benbow (1821), John Brooks (1829), John Ascham (1834), and others in the 1820s and 1830s, adds an intriguing twist to Shelley's editorial afterlife. He was most frequently published and read from the mid-1820s onwards in a parallel universe, one that was unofficial and illegal.[6] In spite, or rather because, of the multiple, unauthorized editions of his works in circulation in the central decades of the nineteenth century a very significant expansion of his readership was effected. This is in marked contrast to the repeated scenario of his works being refused by publishers or censored or suppressed in his lifetime. Further to complaints about its atheistical and incestuous content, *Laon and Cythna* (1817) was forcibly transmuted into *The Revolt of Islam* (1818) and *Oedipus Tyrannus; or, Swellfoot the Tyrant* (1820) immediately suppressed. *Epipsychidion* (1821) was withdrawn upon Shelley's instructions,[7] re-emerging first in Galignani's *Poetical Works of Coleridge, Shelley, and Keats* (1829), technically a piracy, and only officially in 1839. The suppression of Mary Shelley's *Posthumous Poems of Percy Bysshe Shelley* (1824) after an injunction by her father-in-law, Sir Timothy Shelley, is therefore consistent with the history of Shelley's publications in his lifetime.

By any measure, a very large proportion of Shelley's verse and prose was thus untimely, its dissemination interrupted or prevented altogether. The consequences were several. Personal disappointment for the author, especially in the Italian period when such works as *The Mask of Anarchy* and *Oedipus Tyrannus* depended on ready channels through which to alert readers to the urgency of his critique of contemporary Britain that had occasioned them. For posterity, because a significant body of finished compositions were suppressed or remained unpublished at his death, their impact was delayed and often mediated at a significant temporal remove. In some cases, such as *Letter to Maria Gisborne*, poems did not enter the public domain in textually complete forms until many years after they were first circulated.[8] Moreover, as public interest in Shelley's writings increased sharply in the last three decades of the nineteenth century so the short print runs, lack of further editions (only *The Cenci* went into a second edition in Shelley's

---

[6] See William St Clair, *The Reading Nation in the Romantic Period* (Cambridge: Cambridge UP, 2004), 317–22, 680–2.

[7] Ollier told Mary Shelley that 'it was the wish of Mr Shelley that the whole of the "Epipsychidion" should be suppressed' (quoted in Robinson, 'Percy Bysshe Shelley, Charles Ollier, and William Blackwood', 209).

[8] Sent to its addressee in 1820, it first appeared in *Posthumous Poems* but was only published in its textually fullest form by Forman in 1877.

lifetime), limited numbers of surviving copies of suppressed works, and rarity of crucial manuscript witnesses all contributed to a steep rise in their market value. Shelley therefore represented a business opportunity for book collectors such as Harry Buxton Forman whose editing of Shelley, however impressive, was in some respects mercenary.[9]

Part of the challenge of editing Shelley lies in the consequences of the often unsatisfactory way in which his works were published in his lifetime. Since the mid-twentieth century, most scholarly editors of English literary works have seen their task as to produce texts which represent as closely as possible their author's final intentions and have adopted W. W. Greg's 'rationale of copy-text' as a guide. Greg offers an editor latitude in respect of substantive variants from the chosen copy-text, normally that closest to an author's manuscript (thus frequently a first edition), but advises that it be followed in matters of accidentals.[10] However, this approach is frequently unworkable in Shelley's case particularly because the texts of many poems published in his lifetime manifestly do not represent his intentions, especially in matters of punctuation. Because Ollier refused to send proofs to him in Italy, he relied on his friend Thomas Love Peacock in London to oversee corrections to the *Rosalind and Helen* (1819) and *Prometheus Unbound* (1820) volumes (*Letters: PBS* II, 29, 244). The consequences in the form of error-strewn texts clearly aggrieved him (*Letters: PBS* II, 117). On receipt of the latter he told Ollier: 'the *Prometheus* [...] is certainly most beautifully printed. It is to be regretted that the errors of the press are so numerous, & in many respects so destructive of the sense of a species of poetry, which I fear even with[out?] this disadvantage very few will understand or like' (*Letters: PBS* II, 246). This salutary experience led to his careful supervision of the printing of *Adonais* (1821) locally with the desired results, duly emphasized to Ollier: 'The poem is beautifully printed, & what is of more consequence, correctly: indeed it was to obtain this last point that I sent it to the press at Pisa' (*Letters: PBS* II, 311). While for Byron's editors the archive of his publisher John Murray remains an invaluable resource, Ollier's peripheral status meant that some of the most potentially useful manuscript sources for Shelley's editors, the proofs of published works in his possession, were never likely to survive. They were probably destroyed by his son in the 1870s.[11]

The final factor to be taken into account by an editor of Shelley is that a considerable number of poems written in the two years or so before he died were unfinished and exist solely in the form of rough drafts. The words are frequently difficult to decipher, where poems survive in more than one draft the relationship between them is not always easy to determine, and Shelley's intentions for such uncompleted poems are hard to fathom. In some cases, for example *The Triumph of Life*, described by William Michael Rossetti

---

[9] See Nicolas Barker and John Collins, *A Sequel to An Enquiry into the Nature of Certain Nineteenth Century Pamphlets by John Carter and Graham Pollard* (London: Scolar Press, 1983), 23–42.

[10] For helpful evaluations of Greg's rationale, see G. Thomas Tanselle, 'The Varieties of Scholarly Editing', in D. C. Greetham (ed.), *Scholarly Editing: A Guide to Research* (New York: The Modern Language Association of America, 1995), 9–32, and Marcus Walsh, 'Theories of Text, Editorial Theory, and Textual Criticism', in Michael F. Suarez and H. R. Woudhuysen (eds.), *The Oxford Companion to the Book*, 2 vols. (Oxford: Oxford UP, 2010), I, 156–63.

[11] Robinson, 'Percy Bysshe Shelley, Charles Ollier, and William Blackwood', 185.

as 'a stately fragment amid many minor *debris*',[12] one can be reasonably confident that they would have been further revised, then sent for publication. But this is not always certain. In respect of this body of work, Timothy Webb has noted that the editorial legacy is particularly problematical: 'Although his widow and the later nineteenth-century editors deserve great credit for their dedication to an extremely difficult undertaking, they must also take the blame for distorting and sometimes misrepresenting Shelley's achievement.'[13]

Taken together, these factors—that editions of works published in his lifetime are often unsatisfactory, that surviving press-copies of works sent for publication but not published (and proofs of those that were) are extremely rare, that he did not always have the opportunity to oversee publication, and that much of his poetry and prose was unfinished at his sudden death—all point towards the central importance to an editor of Shelley of access to the surviving manuscript authorities. This state of affairs prompted Jerome McGann, following the abandonment of Neville Rogers's Oxford English Texts edition in the 1970s, to claim, somewhat rhetorically, that 'a powerful case could be made for producing an edition of Shelley's *Complete Poetical Works* in which the copy-text for the poems would be, in almost all cases, the manuscripts'.[14] The history of the transmission of Shelley's writings only reinforces a sense of the significance of the manuscripts as well as the authorized printed texts. As Donald Reiman has explained:

> In the narrowest sense, the primary textual authorities for Percy Bysshe Shelley's poetry and prose are the manuscripts of his works written in his own hand, transcriptions prepared by Mary W. Shelley or someone else—such as Claire Clairmont or Edward Williams—who was working under his direction; the other primary authorities are the editions of his works that derive directly from manuscripts in one of the above categories—especially those editions for which Shelley read proofs.[15]

However, the only gradual process of locating and making accessible some of these primary textual authorities has delayed the business of securing the canon, then editing it. Herein lies the main reason why it has taken so long for scholarly editions of Shelley's complete writings to emerge. Mary Shelley, Shelley's first editor, had access, albeit incomplete, to more manuscript sources than any of Shelley's subsequent editors. But, since her death in 1851, the closer an editor was positioned, chronologically, to her early printed editions, the less likely it was that he or she would have access to the fullest possible range of manuscript witnesses. The most eminent Victorian editors of Shelley's poetry and prose, Rossetti and Forman, were knowingly constrained by incomplete access to then available manuscript sources, as was C. D. Locock, whose still useful early twentieth-century editions, although benefiting from his greater

---

[12] *The Poetical Works of Percy Bysshe Shelley,* 2 vols. (London: E. Moxon, 1870), I, p. xii.

[13] *Webb*, p. xxxiii.

[14] Jerome J. McGann, *A Critique of Modern Textual Criticism* (Chicago: University of Chicago Press, 1983), 109.

[15] Donald H. Reiman, 'Textual Authorities for Shelley', *Keats–Shelley Journal* 42 (1993), 58.

access than theirs,[16] are nevertheless limited. That the study of manuscripts in 'the Boscombe collection' was restricted under the custodianship of Mary Shelley's daughter-in-law Jane, Lady Shelley, had scholarly consequences well into the late twentieth century, albeit to a gradually lessening extent.[17] With an awareness that more textually significant evidence is available to scholars now than ever before, we may now turn to the progenitor of all editions of Shelley, his widow.

II

Recently bereaved, Mary Shelley knew in the late summer of 1822 that the editing of her husband's unpublished writings would contribute to maintaining her independence and professional identity: 'if Sir T[imothy] behaves ill, I hope to be able to support myself by my writings & mine own Shelley's Mss.' (*Letters: MWS* I, 260). But she also felt that writing a memoir of Shelley and editing his oeuvre was incumbent upon her: 'Well I shall commence my task, commemorate the virtues of the only creature on earth worth loving or living for' (*Journals: MWS* II, 434). Such a view may be identified with a tradition of honouring radical writers notably practised by her father William Godwin. Godwin's tributes to his wife Mary Wollstonecraft in the form of *Memoirs* (1798) and *Posthumous Works* (1798), published soon after her premature death, were a precedent. Within months of her husband's death Mary Shelley was occupied in 'collecting His manuscripts', that is, recovering as much as possible of Shelley's unpublished corpus not in her possession (*Letters: MWS* I, 252). To this end, she importuned her friend Maria Gisborne and Peacock, who arranged for the papers he elicited from Ollier to be shipped to Italy where they eventually arrived in May 1823, shortly before her return to England (*Letters: MWS* I, 260–1, 266–7, 291–2, 339).[18] She also began to transcribe the typically entangled drafts of poetry and prose from his notebooks (even as she was employed in copying Byron's poems). Her 1822–4 copybooks remain invaluable to editors of Shelley,[19] not least because in cases such as 'The Boat on the Serchio' they contain the sole authority for part of the text.[20] That she accomplished most of the task of gathering and transcribing within a year

[16] C. D. Locock, *An Examination of the Shelley Manuscripts in the Bodleian Library* (Oxford: Clarendon Press, 1903), C. D. Locock *The Poems of Shelley*, 4 vols. (London: Methuen, 1906–9), *The Poems of Percy Bysshe Shelley*, 2 vols. (London: Methuen, 1911).
[17] See Barker-Benfield, *Shelley's Guitar*, pp. xvi–xviii.
[18] See Peacock's letters to Mary Shelley of 2 September 1822, 18 October 1822, and 15 April 1823, in *The Letters of Thomas Love Peacock*, ed. Nicholas A. Joukovsky, 2 vols. (Oxford: Clarendon Press, 2001), I, 191, 195.
[19] These copybooks are (poems) Bodleian MS. Shelley adds. d. 7 (*BSM* II) and adds. d. 9 (Irving Massey, *Posthumous Poems of Shelley: Mary Shelley's Fair Copy Book* (Montreal: McGill-Queen's UP, 1969)), and (prose) adds. d. 6 (*BSM* XXII, Part I) and adds. d. 8 (*BSM* XX). Another of her notebooks, d. 2 (*BSM* X), contains fair copies of four Shelley lyrics that it seems likely she made after his death (*BSM* XXIII, 56).
[20] See Nora Crook (ed.), 'The Boat on the Serchio', *Keats–Shelley Review* 7 (1992), 85–97.

or so of Shelley's death, and in trying conditions (she was living in straitened circumstances with the Hunts near Genoa at the time), testifies to her scholarly will (*Letters: MWS* I, 300).

However, *Posthumous Poems*, 'foremost among the first editions of Shelley's verse',[21] was not exactly the edition of his work that she envisaged even as late as November 1823. In a letter to Jane Williams of January that year she revealed a prescient awareness that Shelley's standing as a writer might benefit from a gradual rather than immediate realization of her editorial project:

> I intend to publish my Shelley's Mss. in the Liberal. First—being out of England & Ollier behaving so ill it is almost impossible to do it in any other way.—I think also that they will do good to the work & that would best please him—Then when I am rich enough I will make an edition of all he has written—& his works thus appearing at intervals will keep him alive in the minds of his admirers. (*Letters: MWS* I, 306–7)

Soon after the demise in August 1823 of *The Liberal*, where she had expected *A Defence of Poetry* to appear, three admirers of Shelley guaranteed the sale of 250 copies of the publication of 'such MSS as [Mary Shelley] had of our S—' by the Hunt brothers (*Letters: MWS* I, 292, 384). However, she wavered between a volume of unpublished works alone and a complete edition, favouring the former as the best means in the contemporary climate of achieving her long-term objective, to establish the audience for Shelley he so lacked in his lifetime: 'it w^d be a specimen of how he could write without shocking any one—and afterwards an edition of the whole might be got up inserting any thing too shocking for this Vol.' (*Letters: MWS* I, 397). That she was in a position to deliberate resulted from her having so rapidly set in place the conditions in which, when the time was right, everything of Shelley's writings accessible to her could be made publicly available.[22] In the end she confined the volume to (mostly) unpublished poems, commenting that 'the poetry alone will make a large Volume' (*Letters: MWS* I, 404). Hunt's failure to supply a biographical notice contributed to publication being delayed until June 1824. The other half of the print run of 500 was underwritten by John Hunt, and over 300 copies had been sold before Sir Timothy's intervention (*Letters: MWS* I, 444).[23]

Though suppressed, *Posthumous Poems* was a limited success in fulfilling Mary Shelley's aim of widening Shelley's readership. But its publication has had lasting consequences, notably in the shaping of his poetic canon. Her Preface variously acknowledges the challenge of presenting texts of the majority of its contents that survived solely in draft form. Of *The Triumph of Life* she comments that it 'was left in so unfinished a state, that I arranged it in its present form with great difficulty'. Many of the poems in the

---

[21] Charles H. Taylor, Jr., *The Early Collected Editions of Shelley's Poems: A Study in the History and Transmission of the Printed Text* (New Haven: Yale UP, 1958), 8.

[22] For excellent analysis of her editorial achievement, see Michael O'Neill, ' "Trying to make it as good as I can": Mary Shelley's Editing of P. B. Shelley's Poetry and Prose', in Betty T. Bennett and Stuart Curran (eds.), *Mary Shelley in her Times* (Baltimore: Johns Hopkins UP, 2000), 185–97.

[23] See Roger Ingpen, *Shelley in England* (London: Kegan Paul, Trench, Trubner, 1917), 584.

substantial 'Miscellaneous Poems' section she characterizes as having been 'written on the spur of the occasion, and never retouched'; these she 'found among his manuscript books' and 'carefully copied'. In such circumstances it is not surprising that she proffers the rationale of exhaustive salvaging that underlies much of her edition with diffidence:

> I do not know whether the critics will reprehend the insertion of some of the most imperfect among these [Miscellaneous Poems]; but I frankly own, that I have been more actuated by the fear lest any monument of his genius should escape me, than the wish of presenting nothing but what was complete to the fastidious reader.[24]

The legacy of Mary Shelley's comprehensive principle, evident in the twentieth century,[25] is impossible to escape nearly 200 years later. Once published, fragmentary drafts of verse can hardly be demoted from their status as 'poems' in the Shelley canon and returned to their 'never retouched' state, which arguably makes an appendix to a scholarly edition their most appropriate destination. The investment in Shelley and his writings that gathered pace through the nineteenth century, largely as a consequence of Mary Shelley's editorial endeavours, brought with it an expectation in the twentieth that the textual foundations on which his reputation was based could be made more solid. Today, with greater access than ever to Shelley's manuscripts through *SC*, *BSM*, and *MYR* and the prospect of a Shelley–Godwin digital archive,[26] that expectation remains, and is not only confined to the scholarly community. But nowhere do Rossetti, Forman, Locock, or their successors explicitly ask a fundamental question, one that hardly dare speak its name. Is it possible, let alone prudent, to manufacture reading texts out of rough holographs that are in many cases far from being finished, label them as 'poems', then present them as part of the Shelley canon? This is because *Posthumous Poems* has made the very asking of that question all but impossible for subsequent editors before the late twentieth century.

More immediately, other consequences of the publication, then suppression, of *Posthumous Poems* followed. First, Mary Shelley was legally bound to hand over to Peacock the manuscripts she had assembled for a volume of essays and translations.[27] The effective impounding of this material, though it did not prevent her from publishing *On Love* in *The Keepsake for 1829* (1828), led her to assert on its publication in 1839 that his prose had 'long been due to the public'.[28] (This work, however, excluded *A Philosophical View of Reform*, which did not appear in a complete text until 1920, and *On the Devil, and Devils*, first published in 1880). Secondly, in the early 1830s, Thomas Medwin, cousin of Shelley, began to capitalize on the interest in his life and works

---

[24] *Posthumous Poems*, pp. vii–viii.
[25] See, for example, Sir John C. E. Shelley-Rolls and Roger Ingpen (eds.), *Verse and Prose from the Manuscripts of Percy Bysshe Shelley* (London: privately printed, 1934), p. ix: '[A]ny scrap of his verse, bearing the stamp of his individual genius, will be of interest to lovers of his poetry.'
[26] <http://shelleygodwinarchive.org>.
[27] See William Whitton (Sir Timothy Shelley's solicitor) to Sir Timothy, 5 August 1824, in Ingpen, *Shelley in England*, 581–2, and Peacock to Whitton, 18 August 1824, in *Letters*, ed. Joukovsky, I, 199.
[28] *Essays, Letters from Abroad, Translations and Fragments, by Percy Bysshe Shelley*, 2 vols. (London: Edward Moxon, 1840), I, p. v.

prompted by *Posthumous Poems*. He published poems and prose that he had in his possession, in notably unsatisfactory texts. For example, 'To—("The serpent is shut out from Paradise")' and 'To Jane ("The keen stars were twinkling")' appeared in 1832 in *Fraser's Magazine* and *The Athenæum* respectively, and further poems in *The Shelley Papers* (1833). Thirdly, some of the unauthorized editions of Shelley's poems of the late 1820s assumed greater textual authority than *Posthumous Poems* and some of the first editions. Benbow's *Miscellaneous Poems* (1826) incorporated several corrections from the errata leaf tipped in to only the later copies of *Posthumous Poems*, while the alterations to *Adonais* and *Hellas* authorized by Shelley that Mary Shelley sent to Cyrus Redding were incorporated in the Galignani edition of 1829 (*Letters: MWS* II, 86). This gave some credibility to the large claim that the Paris edition 'is infinitely more perfect than any of those published in London'.[29] The authority of some readings in some of the piracies, however, did not make them textually authoritative overall. This is of consequence, as Charles Taylor has shown, because when, in 1838, Mary Shelley accepted Edward Moxon's offer to publish a collected poetical works (*Letters: MWS* II, 300), Ascham's unauthorized edition of 1834 and Galignani served as printer's copy.[30] She seems not to have been able to correct proofs systematically against the textual authorities in her possession. Nevertheless, Mary Shelley viewed the second, one-volume edition of Shelley's poems as the fulfilment of her task, which she described as 'my most sacred duty'.[31] She presented it as 'a complete collection of my husband's poetical works' that allowed her closure: 'I do not foresee that I can hereafter add to or take away a word or line'.[32] The organization of the still most widely available complete paperback edition of Shelley's poems, *H*, is indebted to the 1839 collected editions with longer poems first followed by shorter poems (by year), each section appended with Mary Shelley's Notes that constitute the biography she always determined to write.

A new, energetic phase in the editing of Shelley began in the 1860s and 1870s. Further to Lady Shelley allowing him access to the Boscombe collection, Richard Garnett published *Relics of Shelley* (1862) which contained important additions to the canon of poetry and prose, though in flawed texts. Through Garnett's offices Rossetti consulted the notebook now known as Bod. MS. Shelley adds. e. 17 (*BSM* XII) in 1869 enabling him to improve upon the *Posthumous Poems* texts of *Charles the First* and *The Boat on the Serchio* in his 1870 edition.[33] However, although Rossetti was in many ways a sensitive and talented editor, this edition was badly received because of an excess of conjectural emendation that even he regretted. In restoring some readings in the second (unannotated) edition of 1870, he noted that 'one cannot be too chary of conjectural emendations, which, even if unsatisfactory to no one else, are more than likely to pall upon

---

[29] *The Poetical Works of Coleridge, Shelley, and Keats* (Paris: A. and W. Galignani, 1829), 'Notice of the Publishers'. On Benbow and Galignani, see Taylor, *The Early Collected Editions*, 11–22.

[30] *The Early Collected Editions*, 34–46.

[31] *The Poetical Works of Percy Bysshe Shelley*, 4 vols. (London: Edward Moxon, 1839), I, p. xvi.

[32] *The Poetical Works of Percy Bysshe Shelley* (London: Edward Moxon, 1840), p. xi.

[33] See Rossetti to A. C. Swinburne, 14 March 1869, *Selected Letters of William Michael Rossetti*, ed. Roger W. Peattie (University Park, PA: Pennsylvania State UP, 1990), 208.

oneself in the long run'.[34] Mathilde Blind, who also accessed the manuscripts through Garnett, corrected Rossetti's text in many readings.[35] Rossetti's revised edition of 1878 responded to the reviews of his earlier edition by Blind and others, and to Forman's landmark edition of 1876–7, by showing greater restraint in its emendations.[36] Forman's editorial endeavours have influenced all major editions of Shelley since. He described his main object as 'to put within the reach of students and the public generally as near an approximation as may be to the text that the poet intended to issue'.[37] His organizational principle of 'reprinting Shelley's various volumes in chronological order, and with the contents arranged as issued in his life-time',[38] is adopted in *CPPBS*, with acknowledgement to him (*CPPBS* I, p. xxix). However his relegation of *Queen Mab* to a section of 'Juvenilia', copied in *H*, was a departure from Mary Shelley's collected editions, and is not favoured by any recent edition.

III

The last quarter of a century appears to mark a new era in editions of Shelley's poems and prose. The present is informed by renewed scrutiny of the manuscript corpus and is thus deeply indebted to *BSM*, *MYR*, and *SC*. One consequence is the standpoint, in respect of a 'definitively irresolute' fragment poem such as 'An eagle floating in the golden [glory]',[39] that it 'does not or should not exist as a legitimate poem that may be perused in a collection'.[40] Nevertheless, while a guiding principle for contemporary editors is fidelity to Shelley's final intentions as evidenced in the relevant textual authorities (or, in the many cases where firm evidence is wanting, his hypothesized intentions), most consider themselves also to have a responsibility to the reader to provide intelligible texts. This readerly imperative need not result in scholarly integrity being compromised so long as the primacy of editorial judgements, which often differ because of the challenges noted above, is acknowledged.

Readers today coming to Shelley for the first time are in a fortunate position. *Norton 2* and *Major Works*, the most widely available paperback scholarly editions from North American and British publishers, comprise generous, judicious selections of freshly edited poems (including unabridged texts of most of the long poems) and prose, chronologically arranged. Like *Webb*, an earlier paperback anthology on broadly similar principles, these constitute significant advances in the history of Shelley's text in their

---

[34] Odette Bornand (ed.), *The Diary of W. M. Rossetti 1870–1873* (Oxford: Clarendon Press, 1977), 38.

[35] Mathilde Blind, 'Shelley', *Westminster Review* 38.1 (July 1870), 75–97.

[36] *The Complete Poetical Works of Percy Bysshe Shelley*, 3 vols. (London: E. Moxon, 1878), I, p. xviii.

[37] *The Poetical Works of Percy Bysshe Shelley*, 4 vols. (London: Reeves and Turner, 1876–7), I, p. xi.

[38] Ibid., p. xix.

[39] *Longman*, 3, 545–6.

[40] Michael Bradshaw, 'Reading as Flight: Fragment Poems from Shelley's Notebooks', in Alan M. Weinberg and Timothy Webb (eds.), *The Unfamiliar Shelley* (Farnham: Ashgate, 2009), 34.

own right. *Norton 2* is distinctive in seeking to preserve Shelley's original or preferred spellings; *Major Works* and *Webb* modernize but retain old forms (e.g. *sate, wrapt*) where sound or sense are affected. All three confront a particularly problematical legacy of earlier editions, the tendency to punctuate Shelley's texts overly and to regularize his use of capitals. Their common principle in such matters is to be minimally interventionist in respect of copy-texts and to make judgements informed by the evidence of Shelley's practice while, at the same time, bearing in mind the needs of today's reader.[41] This tension informs, in very different ways, the two ongoing editions of the complete poems. The stated aim of *Longman*, which modernizes spelling in keeping with the 'Longman Annotated English Poets' series (though with the provisos noted above), and arranges the poems chronologically by date of composition, is 'to keep always in mind [...] the editor's responsibility to shape an image of a body of texts, and to attempt a coherent representation of the literary past which can live for the present' (2, p. x). *CPPBS* is organized chronologically but conducted on different principles, defined as 'historical', and is methodologically informed by the challenges to Greg mounted since the 1980s. *CPPBS* distinguishes between 'released "poems" and unreleased "poetry"', and seeks to preserve the integrity of 'the poems that [Shelley] intended to publish, according to the groupings he arranged and in the chronological order he hoped to issue them'. *CPPBS* does not seek to modernize spelling and punctuation, following instead Shelley's 'preferred standards of grammar, pointing, and orthography as established by his MSS and published editions' (I, pp. xxix, xxx).

The present may thus be characterized as perhaps the least editorially intrusive chapter so far in the story of how Shelley has been edited. However, a Whig interpretation of the history of editing Shelley won't quite do. Some of the insights of the main nineteenth- and early twentieth-century players since his death have continued to enlighten the current, more professionalized and technologically minded editors. Moreover the central challenge that confronted Mary Shelley remains: to maintain a simultaneous awareness of the relevant textual authorities and the needs of the readers that Shelley so earnestly sought. That there continue to be different approaches to addressing this challenge testifies to the potential for yet further kinds of editorial venture in the future.

SELECT BIBLIOGRAPHY

Barker-Benfield, B. C. *Shelley's Guitar*. Oxford: Bodleian Library, 1992.
Bradshaw, Michael. 'Reading as Flight: Fragment Poems from Shelley's Notebooks'. *The Unfamiliar Shelley*. Ed. Alan M. Weinberg and Timothy Webb. Farnham: Ashgate, 2009. 21–40.
Crook, Nora. '"Casualty", Mrs Shelley and Seditious Libel: Cleansing Britain's Most Corrupt Poet of Error'. *Readings on Audience and Textual Materiality*. Ed. Graham Allen, Carrie Griffin, and Mary O'Connell. London: Pickering & Chatto, 2011. 61–74.
Everest, Kelvin. 'Introduction'. *Longman*, 1, pp. xii–xxxii.

[41] See 'Note on the Text' in *Webb*, pp. xxxiii–xxxv and *Major Works*, p. xxviii, and 'Textual Introduction' in *Norton 2*, pp. xvii–xx.

Forman, Harry Buxton. 'Preface'. *The Poetical Works of Percy Bysshe Shelley*. 4 vols. London: Reeves and Turner, 1876–7. 1, pp. xi–xl.

Housman, A. E. *The Confines of Criticism*. Ed. John Carter. Cambridge: Cambridge UP, 1969.

Murray, E. B. 'Introduction'. *Murray: Prose*. Pp. xxiii–lii.

O'Neill, Michael. '"Trying to make it as good as I can": Mary Shelley's Editing of P. B. Shelley's Poetry and Prose'. *Mary Shelley in her Times*. Ed. Betty T. Bennett and Stuart Curran. Baltimore: Johns Hopkins UP, 2000. 185–97.

Reiman, Donald H. 'Editing Shelley'. *Editing Texts of the Romantic Period*. Ed. John D. Baird. Toronto: Hakkert, 1972. 27–45.

——and Neil Fraistat. 'Editorial Overview'. *CPPBS* I, pp. xix–xxxix.

Robinson, Charles E. 'Percy Bysshe Shelley, Charles Ollier, and William Blackwood'. *Shelley Revalued*. Ed. Kelvin Everest. Leicester: Leicester UP, 1983. 183–226.

Rossetti, William Michael. 'Preface to the Revised Edition'. *The Poetical Works of Percy Bysshe Shelley*. 2 vols. London: E. Moxon, 1870. I, pp. xi–xviii.

——'Editing Shelley, etc.; Trelawny'. *Some Reminiscences*. 2 vols. New York: Charles Scribner's Sons, 1906. II, 358–97.

Shelley, Mary. Ed. *Posthumous Poems of Percy Bysshe Shelley*. London: John and Henry L. Hunt, 1824.

Taylor, Charles H., Jr. *The Early Collected Editions of Shelley's Poems: A Study in the History and Transmission of the Printed Text*. New Haven: Yale UP, 1958.

CHAPTER 41

SHELLEY CRITICISM FROM ROMANTICISM TO MODERNISM

JANE STABLER

OFTEN eclipsed by the glare of biography, critical writing on Shelley in the nineteenth century was polarized between views of his work as otherworldly and all too earthly. Newman Ivey White's magisterial account of Shelley's contemporary reception and the magnificently full annotated bibliography of Shelley criticism by Karsten Klejs Engelberg both reveal how difficult it was for later critics to steer between the extreme terms of reference established by Shelley's early readers.[1] For Romantic-period reviewers motivated by political animosity, Shelley's work was seen as a 'common sewer' or a 'dish of carrion' and the poet himself, in the words of the *Quarterly* in 1819, someone doomed to sink '"like lead" to the bottom'.[2] This grossly material Shelley persisted in one strand of critical reviewing throughout the nineteenth century, and makes an unexpected appearance in T. S. Eliot's objection to the 'bulk' of Shelley's oeuvre.[3] On the other hand, there was the equally partisan view of Shelley as *Ariel*, above his public in all senses (the legacy of Mary Shelley's editorial work, as we shall see). William Sharp's 1887 biography offered a corrective to this tendency to idealize the idealist:

> It is a common mistake to suppose that the poet was an ethereal being from his infancy onward; at no period [...] was he too far removed from common humanity to be other than a genuine creature of flesh and blood.[4]

---

[1] Karsten Klejs Engelberg, *The Making of the Shelley Myth: An Annotated Bibliography of Criticism of Percy Bysshe Shelley, 1822–1860* (London: Mansell, 1988); Newman Ivey White, *The Unextinguished Hearth: Shelley and his Contemporary Critics* (New York: Octagon Books, 1966).

[2] White, *The Unextinguished Hearth*, 168, 169, 142.

[3] *Selected Prose of T. S. Eliot*, ed. Frank Kermode (London: Faber and Faber, 1975; repr. 1980), 81.

[4] William Sharp, *Life of Percy Bysshe Shelley* (London: Walter Scott, 1887), 21.

But that such a reminder was necessary is a mark of how entrenched the versions of Shelley as a poet of flesh or spirit had become by the turn of the nineteenth century. 'There are two kinds of imagination', Arthur Symons wrote in *The Romantic Movement in English Poetry* (1909), 'that which embodies and that which disembodies. Shelley's is that which disembodies, filling mortal things with unearthly essences or veiling them with unearthly raiment.'[5] Tracing criticism of Shelley from Romanticism to Modernism is like watching a tennis match between a succession of Julians and Maddalos; it is sometimes hard to remember that Shelley's poetry has already imagined the positions of both players.

The only works of Shelley's that received significant critical attention in his lifetime were *Queen Mab, Rosalind and Helen, The Revolt of Islam, The Cenci*, and *Prometheus Unbound*. The *Alastor* volume was welcomed in Hunt's 'Young Poets' article which linked Shelley with the Cockney school; Shelley was also associated with the Cockneys through *Adonais* and the *Liberal*.[6] This allegiance explains why Shelley was perceived as a polemical rather than a lyrical poet during his lifetime, while his use of poetry as a vehicle for philosophical and political speculations explains why even sympathetic critics like Leigh Hunt felt that 'a great deal of Mr Shelley's poetry ought to have been written in prose'.[7] To disarm the hostility that Shelley's political and religious footnotes had attracted, Mary Shelley's edition of *Posthumous Poems* (1824) contained 'a specimen of how he could write without shocking any one'.[8] She subdivided the 1839 *Poetical Works* into utterly harmless Wordsworthian categories: 'the purely imaginative, and those which sprung from the emotions of his heart'.[9] For the best possible reasons, Mary Shelley's editing was designed to lift Shelley out of the gutter into which the rabidly biased journals of his day had cast him.[10]

There were points, however, where the extreme supporters and detractors of Shelley met as they tangled with Shelley's own imagery. For the readers like Symons, Shelley's poetry was the projection of an evanescent being; it was 'a glittering cobweb' or 'a cloudy procession of phantoms'.[11] A century earlier, Hazlitt's review of *Posthumous Poems* also employed the image of a 'veil of shadowy or of glittering obscurity' to describe the perplexing quality of Shelley's writing. Hazlitt's objections replicated an anti-Jacobin line of attack that detached Shelley from reality:

> MR SHELLEY'S style is to poetry what astrology is to natural science—a passionate dream, a straining after impossibilities, a record of fond conjectures, a confused

---

[5] Arthur Symons, *The Romantic Movement in English Poetry* (London: Archibald Constable & Co., 1909), 275.

[6] For a summary of Shelley's critical reception 1818–22, see White, *The Unextinguished Hearth*, 1–28. For Shelley as a member of the Cockney school, see Jeffrey N. Cox, *Poetry and Politics in the Cockney School: Keats, Shelley, Hunt and their Circle* (Cambridge: Cambridge UP, 1998).

[7] Leigh Hunt, *Lord Byron and Some of his Contemporaries (1828)*, 2 vols. (Hildesheim: Georg Olms Verlag, 1976), I, 355.

[8] *Letters: MWS* I, 397.

[9] *The Poetical Works of Percy Bysshe Shelley*, ed. Mary Shelley (London: Edward Moxon, 1840), p. viii.

[10] For a discussion of Mary Shelley's editorial work, see Michael O'Neill, '"Trying to Make It as Good as I Can": Mary Shelley's Editing of Shelley's Poetry and Prose', *Romanticism* 3.2 (1997), 185–97.

[11] Symons, *The Romantic Movement*, 275.

embodying of vague abstractions [...] Whatever was new, untried, unheard of, unauthorized, exerted a kind of fascination over his mind. The examples of the world, the opinion of others, instead of acting as a check upon him, served but to impel him forward with double velocity in his wild and hazardous career. Spurning the world of realities, he rushed into the world of nonentities and contingencies, like air into a *vacuum*.[12]

As with so many reviews from this period, Hazlitt equated style with personality, creating a quasi-Burkean vision of a heedless Shelleyan revolution against the 'old and established [...] [t]he weight of authority, the sanction of ages'.[13] Hazlitt's image of escaping air mixed a stock satirical trope with a reminder of Shelley's own interest in science— a bio-critical device Hazlitt first used in 'On Paradox and Common-Place' (1821) when he suggested that Shelley was 'intent upon startling himself with his electrical experiments in morals and philosophy'.[14]

Throughout the nineteenth century, as Timothy Morton has recently outlined, there existed a tension between views of Shelley as a political animal and as a dreamy lyricist.[15] In addition to this, critical writing on Shelley was troubled by more existential questions about the nature of Shelley's poetry as a vessel of light or darkness. The *Monthly Review* and *The Literary Gazette* used the Miltonic oxymoron 'darkness visible' to describe Shelley's style; *Blackwood's* admitted that it had found 'the light of poetry even in the darkness of Mr Shelley's imagination'.[16] A. C. Bradley's 1907 lecture 'Shelley's View of Poetry' observed that in Shelley's 'eloquent exposition' of his ideas, 'there is a radiance which almost conceals them from many readers'.[17] Criticism of Shelley's poetry was preoccupied with its apprehension of the physical world, Shelley's passage between divergent images, and the question of how much 'meaning may be obscurely conjectured by the reader'.[18] Shelley was 'a profound metaphysician' to his friends, but his poetry was seen to revolve around 'metaphysics of the worst kind' by less well-disposed readers.[19] The long-running debate about the role of metaphysics in poetry that marks Shelley's critical reception might account for T. S. Eliot's reconsideration of the Metaphysical Poets in the light of the Romantics, a possibility we shall discuss in more detail below. Hazlitt criticized Shelley's metaphysical cast of mind in 'On Paradox and Common Place':

> His bending, flexible form appears to take no strong hold of things, does not grapple with the world about him, but slides from it like a river [...] he puts every thing into

---

[12] William Hazlitt, *The Complete Works of William Hazlitt*, ed. P. P. Howe, 21 vols. (Tokyo: Yushodo, 1967), XVI, 270, 265, 267–8.

[13] Ibid. 268.   [14] Ibid., VIII, 149.

[15] Timothy Morton, 'Receptions', in Timothy Morton (ed.), *The Cambridge Companion to Shelley* (Cambridge: Cambridge UP, 2006), 36.

[16] White, *The Unextinguished Hearth*, 105, 222, 111.

[17] A. C. Bradley, *Shelley's View of Poetry*, English Association Leaflet No. 4 (London: The English Association, 1908), 1.

[18] White, *The Unextinguished Hearth*, 242.

[19] Percy Bysshe Shelley, *Posthumous Poems*, ed. Mary Shelley (Oxford: Woodstock Books, 1991), p. iv; White, *The Unextinguished Hearth*, 56.

a metaphysical crucible to judge of it himself and exhibit it to others as a subject of interesting experiment.[20]

Shelley's rapid pursuit of imagistic sequences was seen more positively by Leigh Hunt, who took the failure to 'grapple' diagnosed by Hazlitt and re-imagined it as the effect of over-grappling:

> Mr. Shelley's poetry is invested with a dazzling and subtle radiance, which blinds the common observer with light [...] He ransacks every thing like a bee, grappling with it in the same spirit of penetration and enjoyment, till you lose sight of the field he entered upon, in following him into his subtle recesses.[21]

Hunt wanted Shelley to be a pastoral, not a metaphysical poet: Shelley was more successful, according to Hunt, when working with a small scale and when he has 'laid aside his wings' and 'the spiritual part of him is invested with ordinary flesh and blood':

> He is [...] too fond, in his larger works, of repeating the same images drawn from the material universe and the sea. When he is obliged to give up these peculiarities, and to identify his feelings and experience with those of other people, as in his dramatic poems, the fault no longer exists.

That said, Hunt wished that the subject of *The Cenci* 'had been of a nature to startle nobody', anticipating Mary Shelley's concern when she came to arrange *Posthumous Poems*.[22]

The divergence between Hazlitt and Hunt in the 1820s defined the poles of Shelley criticism for the rest of the century. After the spiritualized version of Shelley that appeared in *Lord Byron and Some of his Contemporaries* (1828), Moore's *Life of Byron* (1830) resuscitated a more critical comparison with Byron: Shelley's life, according to Moore, 'had been, like his poetry, a sort of bright erroneous dream,—false in the general principles on which it proceeded, though beautiful and attaching in most of the details'.[23] Trelawny's *Recollections of the Last Days of Shelley and Byron* (1858) re-envisaged Hunt's contrast between a corpulent, corrupt Byron and a sprite-like Shelley, the world's most unlikely *enfant terrible*:

> Swiftly gliding in, blushing like a girl, a tall thin stripling held out both his hands [...] although I could hardly believe as I looked at his flushed, feminine, and artless face that it could be the poet [...] was it possible this mild-looking, beardless boy, could be the veritable monster at war with all the world?—excommunicated by the Fathers of the Church, deprived of his civil rights by the fiat of a grim Lord Chancellor, discarded by every member of his family, and denounced by the rival sages of our literature as the founder of a Satanic school?[24]

---

[20] Hazlitt, *Works*, VIII, 148–9.

[21] Hunt, *Lord Byron and Some of his Contemporaries*, I, 353–5.

[22] Ibid. 355, 368.

[23] Thomas Moore (ed.), *The Works of Lord Byron: With his Letters and Journals, and his Life*, 17 vols. (London: John Murray, 1832–3), V, 365.

[24] Humbert Wolfe (ed.), *The Life of Percy Bysshe Shelley*, 2 vols. (London: Dent, 1933), II, 172.

Trelawny holds up the two Shelleys of popular mythology, but endorses the sense that Shelley was a daemon of one kind or another. In 1821 the *Literary Gazette* had expected 'a cloven foot, or horn, or flames from the mouth' to mark the 'external appearance of so bitter an enemy to mankind'; after his death Shelley became 'angelic' 'an angel among his fellow mortals', 'seraphical', 'like a spirit that had darted out of its orb', '*veramente un angelo*'.[25] Neil Fraistat points out that the 'etherealizing and dis-embodying of Shelley was, in fact, a project fostered by most of the Shelley circle and by John Stuart Mill, F. D. Maurice and the Cambridge apostles'.[26] This project was to assuage 'the general anxiety that the increasingly empowered middle classes felt about the potentially transgressive power of poetry' especially as it related to politi-cal, sexual, and religious issues.[27] The angelic Shelley was further disseminated by the portrait of Shelley which was used for Finden's engraving for *The Life and Works of Lord Byron* and as the frontispiece for the 1839 *Poetical Works*.[28] This was an improved version of the 1819 portrait by Amelia Curran and it creates a Shelley radiating epicene youthfulness with hair in fiery points. Angels had a significant presence in nineteenth-century culture evident, for example, in the Pre-Raphaelite Brotherhood's fascination with the rapt moment, and the being between states. In this aesthetic con-text, Shelley's poetry was easily assimilated in the realm of the suggestive, evocative, ecstatic and—inevitably—ineffectual.[29]

From the 1830s onwards, pragmatic social critics inspired by Carlyle, Wordsworth, and Southey questioned the elevation of poetry above matters of fact. Henry Taylor's Preface to *Philip Van Artevelde* (1834) issued a manifesto urging reconnection between art and life. He saw Shelley as one of 'the PHANTASTIC SCHOOL' who existed 'in a region of poetical sentiment which did not permit them to walk upon the common earth, or to breathe the common air'. He allowed Shelley to possess a powerful and expansive imagi-nation, but detected

> an attempt to unrealise every object in nature, presenting them under forms and com-binations in which they are never to be seen through the mere medium of our eye-sight. Mr. Shelley seems to have written under the notion that no phenomena can be perfectly poetical, until they shall have been so decomposed from their natural order

---

[25] White, *The Unextinguished Hearth*, 56; Stuart Curran, 'Horace Smith's Obituary Panegyric on Shelley', *Keats–Shelley Journal* 37 (1988), 31; *Letters: MWS* III, 284; Hunt, *Lord Byron and Some of his Contemporaries*, I, 295; 300; John Mullan (ed.), *Lives of the Great Romantics: Shelley* (London: William Pickering, 1996), 112.

[26] Neil Fraistat, 'Illegitimate Shelley: Radical Piracy and the Textual Edition as Cultural Performance', *PMLA* 109.3 (1994), 410. See also Richard Cronin, 'Shelley, Tennyson and the Apostles, 1828–1832', *Keats–Shelley Review* 5 (1990), 14–40 and Timothy Webb, 'Religion of the Heart: Leigh Hunt's Unpublished Tribute to Shelley', *Keats–Shelley Review* 7 (1992), 1–61.

[27] Fraistat, 'Illegitimate Shelley', 410.

[28] Mary Shelley objected to the thick lips of the engraving done by Wedgwood for Galignani's *Poetical Works of Coleridge, Shelley and Keats* (1829). See *Letters: MWS* II, 100, 159 n.

[29] Fraistat makes the point that the radical pirated editions of Shelley had a much more subversive reputation, though the commercial failure of this venture limited the impact on Shelley's reputation. See Fraistat, 'Illegitimate Shelley', 412–15.

and coherency, as to be brought before the reader in the likeness of a phantasma or a vision. A poet is, in his estimation [...] purely and pre-eminently a visionary.[30]

According to Taylor, readers would close one of Shelley's books of poetry 'no more enriched [...] than by having gazed on so many gorgeously coloured clouds in an evening sky'; under Shelley's influence, poetry becomes a realm of 'anarchy and abstraction, where imagination exercises the shadow of an authority, over a people of phantoms, in a land of dreams'.[31] A few years before Turner's painting of *Juliet and her Nurse* was attacked by the Revd John Eagles in *Blackwood's* for disorienting imaginative excess, Henry Taylor worried about Shelley's 'unbounded indulgence in the mere luxuries of poetry' at the expense of 'relevancy' and the poet's 'discipline of his reasoning powers'.[32] Both anxieties were, as Philip Davis has pointed out, symptomatic of a wider concern about the function of poetry in society and, later in the century, the rigour of English Literature as a subject for university study.[33]

Towards the end of his life, Taylor softened his views on Shelley, but Ruskin went in the opposite direction, celebrating Shelley with Turner at the start of his career and then, in *Modern Painters* (1846), turning aside from his quotation of *Alastor* (illustrating the 'faculty of the contemplative imagination') to scold readers who might misconstrue his enthusiasm: 'Let it not be supposed that I mean to compare the sickly dreaming of Shelley over clouds and waves, with the masculine and magnificent grasp of men and things which we find in Scott.'[34] Ruskin's *Elements of Drawing* (1857) condemned Shelley as 'shallow and verbose', but in *Fiction Fair and Foul* (1880–1), Ruskin gathered Shelley with Rousseau, Byron, Turner, and himself as one of the only five men of modern times who were responsive to beauty and glowing with the 'volcanic instinct of Astraean justice'.[35]

John Stuart Mill shared the reservations of many thinkers (and the Romantics themselves) about the power of poetic dreamers. His review of 'Tennyson's Poems' (1835) argued that

> Where the poetic temperament exists in its greatest degree, while the systematic culture of the intellect has been neglected, we may expect to find, what we do find in

---

[30] Henry Taylor, *Philip Van Artevelde; A Dramatic Romance in Two Parts*, 2 vols. (London: Edward Moxon, 1834), I, pp. xxv, xiii, xxii–xxiii. The 84-year-old Henry Taylor later wrote to Swinburne: 'It is true that I designate [Shelley] as "purely and pre-eminently a visionary"; and I dwell too much, I am afraid, and in too depreciating a spirit, upon what I conceived to be a want of relevancy in his poetry to the truths of life and nature' (Algernon Charles Swinburne, *Miscellanies* (London: Chatto & Windus, 1911), 371–2).

[31] Taylor, *Philip Van Artevelde*, I, pp. xxiii, xxvi. In 1820, the *London Magazine* had used the same image to praise *Rosalind and Helen*: 'The rich yet delicate imagery that is every where scattered over it, is like the glowing splendor of the setting sun.' James Barcus (ed.), *Shelley: The Critical Heritage* (London: Routledge and Kegan Paul, 1975), 170.

[32] Taylor, *Philip Van Artevelde*, I, pp. x–xi, xxiii, xv.

[33] Philip Davis, *The Victorians* (Oxford: Oxford UP, 2004), 457–8. This anxiety did not emerge for the first time in the 1830s; as early as 1816, we find the *Eclectic Review* worrying about 'the fatal tendency of that morbid ascendency of the imagination over the other faculties, which incapacitates the mind for bestowing an adequate attention on the real objects of the "work-day" life, and for discharging the relative and social duties' (White, *The Unextinguished Hearth*, 107).

[34] John Ruskin, *The Works of John Ruskin*, ed. E. T. Cook and Alexander Wedderburn, 39 vols. (London: Allen, 1903–12), IV, 297. Also see J. Drummond Bone, 'Turner and Shelley: The Sense of a Comparison', *Ruskin Gazette* 1.4 (1990), 30–6.

[35] Ruskin, *Works*, XV, 227; XXXIV, 343.

the best poems of Shelley—vivid representations of states of passive and dreamy emotion, fitted to give extreme pleasure to persons of similar organization to the poet, but not likely to be sympathized in, because not understood, by any other persons.[36]

In 1859 in *Dissertations and Discussions*, Mill returned to his earlier thoughts on Shelley in relation to Wordsworth. Like many, Mill followed Mary Shelley's preface in recognizing that Shelley 'had not, at the period of his deplorably early death, reached sufficiently far in that intellectual progression of which he was capable'; Mill went on to pathologize Shelley's poetic achievement:

> He seldom follows up an idea; it starts into life, summons from the fairy-land of his inexhaustible fancy some three or four bold images, then vanishes, and straight he is off on the wings of some casual association into quite another sphere. He had scarcely yet acquired the consecutiveness of thought necessary for a long poem; his more ambitious compositions too often resemble the scattered fragments of a mirror; colours brilliant as life, single images without end, but no picture. [...]
>   To the same original fineness of organization, Shelley was doubtless indebted for another of his rarest gifts, that exuberance of imagery, which when unrepressed, as in many of his poems it is, amounts to a fault. The susceptibility of his nervous system, which made his emotions intense, made also the impressions of his external senses deep and clear: and agreeably to the law of association [...] these vivid sensations were readily recalled to mind by all objects or thoughts which had coexisted with them, and by all feelings which in any degree resembled them.[37]

As Mary Shelley had done, Mill attributed Shelley's style to nervous susceptibility,[38] but he also detected self-indulgence. Mill's perception of associative leaps and a teeming sensuous imagination might have linked Shelley with Elizabethan poetics, but, like many nineteenth-century critics, he saw Shelley's instability as symptomatic of a wider adolescent malaise.[39] Shelley might be seen as someone who got younger as the century progressed. In 1819, *Blackwood's* had admonished the 27-year-old poet for finding an easy refuge in obscurity after reaching 'the maturity of manhood', but Mary Shelley's scholarly annotation of Shelley's poetry continually reminded readers of her husband's youthfulness.[40] Her preface to the 1839 edition had presented Shelley as a perpetual child:

> The luxury of imagination, which sought nothing beyond itself, as a child burthens itself with spring flowers, thinking of no use beyond the enjoyment of gathering them, often showed itself in his verses [...] It is seldom that the young know what youth is, till they have got beyond its period; and time was not given him to attain this knowledge. It must be remembered that there is the stamp of such inexperience on all he wrote; he had not completed his nine-and-twentieth year when he died.

---

[36] John Stuart Mill, *Autobiography and Literary Essays*, ed. John M. Robson and Jack Stillinger (Toronto: Toronto UP, 1981), 413–14.

[37] Ibid. 359–60.

[38] See *Poetical Works*, p. ix.

[39] For a broader survey of the construction of adolescence in the nineteenth century, see Patricia Meyer Spacks, *The Adolescent Idea: Myths of Youth and the Adult Imagination* (New York: Basic Books, 1981).

[40] White, *The Unextinguished Hearth*, 110.

The calm of middle life did not add the seal of the virtues which adorn maturity to those generated by the vehement spirit of youth.[41]

Fraistat sees Mary Shelley's preface as a 'class-coded language of sensibility', and her angelic Shelley as a corporate work, 'sponsored by a nascent set of middle-class Victorian ideological positions'.[42] In her 1841 edition of the prose, Mary made strenuous efforts to assert the maturity of Shelley's philosophical views: 'his views', she claims, 'were defined and complete', but her preface also closed with a lament for his early death and a reminder that Shelley remained caught in the 'turbulence of youthful impetuosity'.[43] Mary's youthful Shelley persisted into the twentieth century, Symons suggesting that Shelley's view of love was 'the love of an enthusiast youth, or of his own hermaphrodite [...] Shelley is not perverse, but he is fascinated by every problem of evil, which draws him to contemplate it with a child's enquiring wonder of horror'.[44] In 1909 Francis Thompson wrote that

> Shelley's life frequently exhibits in him the magnified child. It is seen in his fondness for apparently futile amusements, such as the sailing of paper boats. This was, in the truest sense of the word, child-like [...] That is to say, it was not a mindless triviality, but the genuine child's power of investing little things with imaginative interest.[45]

Thompson found in 'The Cloud' what he called 'the child's faculty of make-believe'; *Prometheus Unbound* was also childlike: 'This childlike quality assimilated to him the childlike peoples among whom mythologies have their rise.'[46]

The childlike or adolescent or feminine persona was a defensive strategy called into being by Shelley's biographers, but it usually inflected criticism in a negative way as in Charles Kingsley's portrait of Shelley as

> utterly womanish. Not merely his weak points, but his strong ones, are those of a woman. Tender and pitiful as a woman: and yet, when angry, shrieking, railing, hysterical as a woman. The physical distaste for meat and fermented liquors, coupled with the hankering after physical horrors, are especially feminine.[47]

For Kingsley, Byron 'might, if he had reformed, have made a gallant English gentleman'. Shelley, on the other hand, 'if once his intense self-opinion had deserted him, would have probably ended in Rome, as an Oratorian or a Passionist'—that is in retreat from the world, under a quasi-female vow of obedience.[48] Apart from the hostility that was directed at Shelley 'in petticoats', there were more subtle attempts to diagnose the unique 'in between' state created by his poems. Elizabeth Barrett depicted Shelley as a poet in limbo:

> high, and yet too low; [an] elemental poet who froze in cold glory between Heaven and earth, neither dealing with man's heart, beneath, nor [...] aspiring to communion with [...] the heart of the God-Man. Therefore his poetry glitters and is cold.[49]

---

[41] *Poetical Works*, p. ix.   [42] Fraistat, 'Illegitimate Shelley', 411, 410.

[43] *Essays, Letters from Abroad, Translations and Fragments by Percy Bysshe Shelley*, ed. Mary Shelley (London: Edward Moxon, 1845), pp. ix, xi.

[44] Symons, *The Romantic Movement*, 271.

[45] Francis Thompson, *Shelley* (London: Burns and Oates, 1909), 35.   [46] Ibid. 45, 46–7.

[47] Charles Kingsley, *Miscellanies*, 2 vols. (London: John Parker, 1859), I, 314–15.   [48] Ibid. 311.

[49] Philip Kelley, Ronald Hudson, Scott Lewis, and Edward Hagan (eds.), *The Brownings' Correspondence*, 16 vols. (Winfield, KS: Wedgestone Press, 1984–2007), V, 60.

Her husband, by contrast, celebrated Shelley for his 'simultaneous perception of Power and Love in the absolute, and of Beauty and Good in the concrete, while he throws, from his poet's station between both, swifter, subtler, and more numerous films for the connexion of each with each, than have been thrown by any modern artificer'.[50] Browning's remark represents a rare attempt to reconnect the material and immaterial aspects of Shelley and unusually suggested that Shelley's stylistic 'films' did not obfuscate or baffle vision, but served as a passage between the two domains. Sadly, his essay does not go into details, but Browning's poetry allows us to trace his sensitivity to Shelley's artifice.

Carlyle was much more impressed by Browning's essay than by Shelley's poetry: he saw Shelley as 'a poor, thin, spasmodic, hectic, shrill and pallid being' more worthy of pity than adulation, and he agreed with Elizabeth Barrett's sense of Shelley as frozen and static:

> Poor Shelley, there is something void, and Hades-like in the whole inner world of him; his universe is all vacant azure, hung with a few frosty, mournful if beautiful stars; the very voice of him (his style &c), shrill, shrieky, to my ear has too much of the *ghost*![51]

In this we detect the pervasive influence of biography: Shelley's squeaky voice was much discussed in early reminiscences and memoirs.[52] Slipping into another well-worn bio-critical path, Browning's Essay acknowledged that Shelley 'died before his youth ended', and forgave him for it:

> Nor will men persist in confounding, any more than God confounds, with genuine infidelity and an atheism of the heart, those passionate, impatient struggles of a boy towards distant truth and love, made in the dark, and ended by one sweep of the natural seas before the full moral sunrise could shine on him. Crude convictions of boyhood, conveyed in imperfect and inapt forms of speech,—for such things all boys have been pardoned. There are growing pains, accompanied by temporary distortion, of the soul also.[53]

Metaphors of darkness and sunrise, the invocation of the sea, and the struggle towards truth show how Shelleyan cadences pervade his own critical reputation. Browning gives no detail on the 'imperfect and inapt forms of speech'—it sounds like a tactful school report on 'There is no God!' When Arnold wrote to Clough in 1852 about the future direction of poetry and criticism, he was at Milford Boys School, where, as an inspector of schools, it was his job to think about how to train young minds:

> More and more I feel that the difference between a mature and a youthful age of the world compels the poetry of the former to use great plainness of speech as compared with that of the latter: and that Keats and Shelley were on a false track when they set themselves to reproduce the exuberance of expression, the charm, the

---

[50] Robert Browning, *Shelley: The Man and the Poet* (Hull: J. R. Tutin [1908]), 29. This 'Essay on Shelley' prefaced the volume of twenty-five forged Shelley letters published by Moxon in 1852.

[51] Thomas Carlyle, *The Collected Letters of Thomas and Jane Welsh Carlyle*, ed. Clyde de L. Ryals and Kenneth J. Fielding, 37 vols. (Durham, NC: Duke UP, 1970–present), XXVII, 65.

[52] See, for example, Hazlitt's 'On Paradox and Common-Place' (Hazlitt, *Works*, VIII, 148).

[53] Browning, *Shelley*, 19.

richness of images, and the felicity, of the Elizabethan poets. Yet critics cannot get to learn this […] They still think that the object of poetry is to produce exquisite bits and images—such as Shelley's *clouds shepherded by the slow unwilling wind*, and Keats passim.[54]

Adolescence was supposed to be a progression to maturity: the problem with Shelley's poetry was that there was movement without progression. He hangs 'on the devouring edge of mental darkness', according to Thomas Medwin, borrowing lines from *The Cenci*.[55] Hanging on this edge was condemned as morbid introspection by later nineteenth-century critics. A keen sense of duty and civic responsibility led Arnold to require that poetry should respect boundaries and encompass 'religious wants'.[56] He explained his own sense of vocation in opposition to Shelley in a letter to his mother (3 March 1865):

> No one has a stronger and more abiding sense than I have of the 'daemonic' element—as Goethe calls it—which underlies and encompasses our life: but I think, as Goethe thought, that the right thing is, while conscious of this element and of all that there is inexplicable round one, to keep pushing on one's posts into the darkness, and to establish no post that is not perfectly in light, and firm. One gains nothing on the darkness by being, like Shelley, as incoherent as the darkness itself.[57]

The image of pushing posts into darkness establishes the poet as boy scout or perhaps an imperial explorer. For many Victorians, Shelley's poetry, as William Michael Rossetti observed, was faulty 'through vague idealism and want of backbone'.[58] There was something unmanly and unmanning about poetic indeterminacy.

Until 1886, however, idealized versions of Shelley's vehement youthfulness easily outweighed the more critical ones: Mathilde Blind's 1872 edition of Shelley was the apotheosis of biographical idealism:

> If we would in an embodiment of flesh and blood seek for that haunting aspiration which lurks more or less dimly in the minds of all of us; if we would seek for a being in whom the spiritual tendencies completely triumphed over the more material parts of nature […] if we would seek the purely human stripped of all its grosser adjuncts and see as in a mirror how little less than angelic it is given to man to be, let us turn with glad eyes and adoring hearts to Percy Bysshe Shelley.[59]

As Matthew Arnold pointed out in 1888, the lovely image created by Mary Shelley's editions of her husband's work survived little changed by Medwin, Hogg, and Trelawny. But Edward Dowden's two-volume biography of 1886 challenged Arnold's belief in Shelley

---

[54] Matthew Arnold, *The Letters of Matthew Arnold*, ed. Cecil Y. Lang, 6 vols. (Charlottesville, VA: University Press of Virginia, 1996–2001), I, 245. Ruskin singles out the same line for 'that continuous expression of slow movement which Shelley has so beautifully touched' in *Modern Painters*. Ruskin, *Works*, III, 364.

[55] Mullan (ed.), *Shelley*, 180.

[56] Arnold, *Letters*, I, 246.

[57] Ibid. II, 390.

[58] P. B. Shelley, *Adonais*, ed. William Michael Rossetti (Oxford: Clarendon Press, 1903), 1.

[59] *A Selection from the Poems of Percy Bysshe Shelley*, ed. Mathilde Blind (Leipzig: Bernhard Tauchnitz, 1872), pp. xxxvii–xxxviii.

as a 'superior' man.[60] Despite the reluctance of the Shelley family, Dowden relayed the precise sequence of Shelley's second (English) marriage to Harriet in March 1814, awkwardly close to the start of his relationship with Mary Godwin in May 1814. In 1852, Browning had referred to 'certain charges against his private character and life, which, if substantiated [...] would materially disturb [...] our reception and enjoyment of his works, however wonderful the artistic qualities of these'.[61] Dowden's biography substantiated those charges and Arnold lamented the appearance of a Shelley 'who [...] disgusts'.[62] This was made even worse by Dowden's attempt to exculpate Shelley: 'his sentiment makes me sick', wrote Arnold, seeing in Dowden the Romantic infection he had diagnosed in his letter to Clough: 'I am inclined [...] to lament that Professor Dowden has not steadily kept his poetic quality of fervour and picturesqueness more under control'.[63] He was particularly incensed by Dowden's quotation of the letter in which Shelley invited Harriet to come and join him and Mary in Switzerland, assuring her that though 'all else are either unfeeling or selfish', Harriet could trust him to be 'firm and constant'; Shelley ended with the commission that she should bring with her a copy of the separation settlement.[64] Human relationships as well as images blurred one into the other. Arnold groped for a word to describe the letter, and settled for the contemptuous '*bête*'.[65]

In the context of the volatile emotionalism he associated with political debates about Irish home rule, the critical issue for Arnold was now the cause that could explain 'Shelley's abandonment of Harriet in the first place, and then his behaviour to her and his defence of himself afterwards'.[66] He concluded that 'when the passion of love was aroused in Shelley (and it was aroused easily) one could not be sure of him, his friends could not trust him'. Adjusting the Mary Shelley–Leigh Hunt view of a Platonic, Pythagorean, angelic Shelley, Arnold regretfully identified 'an entirely human inflammability, joined to an inhuman want of humour and a superhuman power of self-deception'; he then rounded on people who maintained that Shelley's poetry was somehow unstained by his life:

> It is his poetry, above everything else, which for many people establishes that he is an angel [...] But let no one suppose that a want of humour and a self-delusion have no effect upon a man's poetry. The man Shelley, in very truth, is not entirely sane, and Shelley's poetry is not entirely sane either. The Shelley of actual life is a vision of beauty and radiance, indeed, but availing nothing, effecting nothing. And in poetry, no less than in life, he is 'a beautiful *and ineffectual* angel, beating in the void his luminous wings in vain'.[67]

Arnold's summative judgement on Shelley has been immensely influential.[68] In *Miscellanies* (1911) Swinburne felt obliged to counsel the 'Wordsworthians, from

---

[60] Matthew Arnold, *Poetry of Byron* (London: Macmillan, 1881), p. viii.   [61] Browning, *Shelley*, 17–18.
[62] Matthew Arnold, 'Shelley', *The Nineteenth Century* (January 1888), 37.   [63] Arnold, 'Shelley', 24.
[64] Edward Dowden, *The Life of Percy Bysshe Shelley*, 2 vols. (London: Kegan Paul, Trench & Co., 1886), I, 449–50.
[65] Arnold, 'Shelley', 32.   [66] Ibid. 36.   [67] Ibid. 39.
[68] For a recent critique of Arnold's essays in the light of Stopford Brooke's appreciation of Shelley, see Alan Weinberg, '"The Ineffectual Angel": Arnold's Misrepresentation of Shelley', *Keats–Shelley Review* 33 (2009), 82–96.

Sir Henry Taylor to Mr Matthew Arnold [...] to break themselves of [...] the habit of girding and gibing at Shelley as a morbid and delirious visionary, notable mainly for fantastic feebleness of moral idea and uncertain hold on moral fact: a nervous, unmanly, unreal, unwholesome sort of poet.[69] But the famous '*ineffectual* angel' image was not solely a response to biographical exposure: for Arnold, the evidence of Shelley's pursuit of Godwinian truth in his personal life simply confirmed long-standing, if vague, worries about poetic 'substance'. The nature of substance is, of course, a concern of metaphysics, and Arnold circled around a problem that had preoccupied Shelley's readers throughout the nineteenth century. The '*ineffectual* angel' is a quotation from Arnold's first verdict on Shelley's poetry at the end of his essay on Byron.[70] In that essay, Arnold acknowledged Shelley's 'gift of musical diction and movement', and allowed poetic value in 'snatches and fragments', but found: 'the incurable want, in general, of a sound subject matter, and the incurable fault, in consequence, of unsubstantiality'.[71] In the later review, Arnold takes for granted that 'Shelley is not a classic, whose various readings are to be noted with earnest attention'.[72]

In 1888 this was not quite true: William Michael Rossetti had devoted careful attention to the texts in his editions of 1870 and 1878. In 1886 he presented a lecture on *Prometheus Unbound* to the Shelley Society. In 1890, he published a detailed edition of *Adonais*. It is to the notes to such anthologies and selections that we can turn for more sustained attention to Shelley's poetry in the nineteenth century. Palgrave's editorial notes in *The Golden Treasury* (1861) had presented Shelley as a poet of 'wayward intensity' and 'obscurity'.[73] Palgrave anticipated Symons's sense that Shelley 'never saw anything, in life or art, except through a mist'; for Symons, therefore, Shelley was quite precisely 'the only poet who is really vague'.[74] While Ruskin directed his students away from Shelley as an object of study, *fin-de-siècle* aesthetes praised his accuracy of idealist perception. Walter Pater defined the attentiveness he found in Coleridge, Shelley, and Turner as a

> singular watchfulness for the minute fact and expression of natural scenery pervading all he wrote—a closeness to the exact physiognomy of nature, having something to do with that idealistic philosophy which sees in the external world no mere concurrence of mechanical agencies, but an animated body, informed and made expressive, like the body of man, by an indwelling intelligence.[75]

In *Essays and Studies* (1875), Swinburne also leapt to defend the effect of Shelley's imagery. His comment on the invocation to the Sun-girt city in 'Lines Written among the Euganean Hills' (thus in Mary Shelley) was:

> Mr. Palgrave's proposal of 'sea-girt' for 'sun-girt city' [...] may look plausible, but the new epithet is feeble, inadequate, inaccurate. Venice is not a sea-girt city; it is

[69] Swinburne, *Miscellanies*, 120.   [70] Arnold, *Poetry of Byron*, p. xxxi.
[71] Ibid., pp. vii–viii.   [72] Arnold, 'Shelley', 23.
[73] Francis Turner Palgrave, *The Golden Treasury of the Best Songs and Lyrical Poems in the English Language* (London: Collins, 1954), 539–40.
[74] Symons, *The Romantic Movement*, 281.
[75] Walter Pater, *Appreciations with an Essay on Style* (London: Macmillan, 1920), 90.

interlaced and interwoven with sea, but not girdled; pierced through with water, but not ringed about. Seen by noon from the Euganean heights, clothed as with the very and visible glory of Italy, it might seem to Shelley a city girdled with the sunlight, as some Nereid in the arms of the sun-god.[76]

In Rossetti's editorial work, we see a similar effort to trace and comprehend Shelley's associative process. Grappling with the text of *Adonais* (1890), Rossetti followed Shelley's passage between images and the 'economy' that made one thing melt into the next. Stanza 11 exemplified the problems for any critic who tried to separate out the different strands of the poem: On the lines, 'One from a lucid urn of starry dew | Washed his light limbs, as if embalming them', Rossetti noted,

> The expression 'starry dew' is rather peculiar: the dew may originally have 'starred' the grass, but when collected into an urn, it must have lost this property: perhaps we should rather understand nocturnal dew upon which the stars had been shining. It is difficult to see how the act of washing the limbs could simulate the process of embalming.[77]

Rossetti soldiered on with, 'and threw | The wreath upon him, like an anadem | Which frozen tears instead of pearls begem':

> The wreath is the lock of hair—perhaps a plait or curl, for otherwise the term wreath is rather wide of the mark. The idea that the tears shed by this Dream herself (or perhaps other Dreams) upon the lock are 'frozen', and thus stand in lieu of pearls upon an anadem or circlet, seems strained, and indeed incongruous: one might wish it away.[78]

'I am free to acknowledge that I think the whole of this stanza bad', Rossetti admitted in the notes to stanza 11:

> Its *raison d'être* is a figurative but perfectly appropriate and straightforward passage in Bion: Shelley has attempted to turn that into a still more figurative passage suitable for *Adonais*, with a result anything but happy. He fails to make it either straightforward or appropriate, and declines into the super-subtle or wiredrawn.[79]

The use of the seventeenth-century adjective 'wiredrawn' is interesting. It means 'Drawn out to a great length; stretched thinly; over-refined. Also: designating or resulting from subtle argument; ingenious, contrived' (*OED*), and it is strongly reminiscent of pejorative criticism of metaphysical poetry. Rossetti recognized Shelley's profusion of images as 'Elizabethan', and frequently identifies confusion in *Adonais*: 'The passage of Shelley is rather complicated'; 'the transition [...] is artificial, and not free from confusion'; 'The image is rather confused'.[80] What we see in this criticism is a version of Dr Johnson struggling with Shakespeare's quibbles or Donne's conceits. Indeed, Rossetti suggested that the image of clouds outweeping rain in stanza 10 'verges upon a conceit'.[81]

[76] Algernon Charles Swinburne, *Essays and Studies* (London: Chatto and Windus, 1875), 199 n.
[77] *Adonais*, ed. Rossetti, 110.
[78] Ibid. 111.   [79] Ibid. 112.   [80] Ibid. 115; 116; 119.   [81] Ibid. 110.

When Mary Shelley described Shelley's 'metaphysical strain', she clearly did not mean to group him with Donne, Cowley, Crashaw, and Marvell, but I would like to suggest that T. S. Eliot's famous revaluation of seventeenth-century verse in the essay 'The Metaphysical Poets' (1921) was informed by the contested critical reception of Shelley's poetry in the nineteenth century.[82] Yeats recalled Shelley's galvanic effect on the 1880s: 'he seemed to sum up all that was metaphysical in English poetry.'[83] In general surveys of English Literature, T. S Eliot is usually seen to be depressing the reputation of Shelley as he elevated Donne's status.[84] The essay itself is more complex, however. If we look at what Eliot saw as 'characteristically metaphysical', we might detect echoes of the earlier nineteenth-century reviews of Shelley: 'the elaboration [...] of a figure of speech to the furthest stage to which ingenuity can carry it'; 'development by rapid association of thought which requires considerable agility on the part of the reader'; 'telescoping of images and multiplied associations.'[85] All these characteristics are identified in Hunt's and Hazlitt's critical view of Shelley and their nineteenth-century critics. Hunt had worried that 'some of Mr Shelley's poems [...] look rather like storehouses of imagery, than imagery put into proper action'; his sense of Shelley's poetry as 'too involved' with 'remote meanings' was shared by other contemporaries who felt that the connection between Shelley's images was sometimes so fine as to be invisible.[86] Derwent Coleridge, for example had approved of the way that '[t]he pleasure which he caters, demands an exertion on the part of the recipient corresponding to its intensity.'[87]

Eliot's main approbation for metaphysical poets comes from his sense that their erudition was incorporated into their sensibility, that they possessed a 'direct, sensuous apprehension of thought.'[88] After this definition, Eliot mentions 'one or two passages of Shelley's *The Triumph of Life* that achieve a metaphysical realization of life'. In the later essay 'The Use of Poetry and the Use of Criticism' (1933), Eliot specified the moment in the poem which provides 'precision of image', 'economy', and 'greater wisdom' than in any previous poem:

> Then what I thought was an old root that grew
> To a strange distortion out of the hillside,
> Was indeed one of those (*sic*) deluded crew
> And that the grass, which methought hung so wide
> And white, was but his thin discoloured hair
> And that the holes he vainly sought to hide
> Were or had been eyes[89]

Eliot slightly misquoted the poem and rendered the lines more as a *vers libre* monologue than as Petrarchan *Trionfi*. Shelley, he argued, did not have a 'metaphysical or philosophical mind', but he could exhibit 'passionate apprehension of abstract ideas'.[90] It is a

[82] *Poetical Works*, p. ix.   [83] W. B Yeats, *Essays and Introductions* (London: Macmillan, 1961), 424.
[84] See, for instance, Chris Baldick, *The Modern Movement* (Oxford: Oxford UP, 2004), 257.
[85] Eliot, *Selected Prose of T. S. Eliot*, 60.   [86] Hunt, *Lord Byron and Some Contemporaries*, 358–9.
[87] Quoted in Fraistat, 'Illegitimate Shelley', 417.   [88] Eliot, *Selected Prose*, 63.   [89] Ibid. 82.
[90] Eliot returned to this passage in 'What Dante Means to Me' (1950). He quoted it with the preceding two and the succeeding six tercets as an example of 'the greatest and most Dantesque lines in

rare moment that allows Eliot's Shelley to escape from nineteenth-century biographizing habits and the habitual critique of 'confusion' before Eliot reverts to his grumble that Shelley 'never quite escaped from the tutelage of Godwin', adding that 'the weight of Mrs Shelley must have been pretty heavy too' (he did not specify which Mrs Shelley).[91] Eliot's appreciation for *The Triumph of Life* followed Dowden's sense that it provided evidence of a more mature mind and promise of 'a reconcilement between [Shelley's] pursuit of the ideal and his dealings with actual events and living men and women'.[92] Eliot clearly saw ways in which Shelley might leap the nineteenth century to be a modern precursor, and it is ironic that this perception emerged from an essay that also allows us to hear what is most Victorian in Eliot's criticism.

The early years of literary Modernism coincided with an intensive period of Shelley scholarship: Roger Ingpen published *Shelley in England* in 1917 and in 1926 Ingpen and Walter E. Peck began to publish the ten-volume *Complete Works of Percy Bysshe Shelley*. Despite the new availability of texts, the New Critics avoided any serious engagement with Shelley's poetic forms or verbal texture as Shelley's life continued to distract critical attention. The ubiquity of Andre Maurois's *Ariel* biography (1924) in second-hand book-shops and public libraries presents the Shelley that the followers of Eliot could never quite exorcize. Yeats's 1900 essay 'On the Philosophy of Shelley's Poetry' celebrated 'the flowing forms of his mind' without going into any close reading of the poetic forms themselves.[93] And in 1932 when Yeats wrote about Shelley again, he identified something 'dark, destructive, indefinite' in the poetry, stirring to life the biographical disquiet that had haunted Shelley across two centuries of criticism:

> When in middle life I looked back I found that he and not Blake, whom I had studied more and with more approval, had shaped my life, and when I thought of the tumultuous and often tragic lives of friends or acquaintance, I attributed to his direct or indirect influence their Jacobin frenzies, their brown demons.[94]

Select Bibliography

Allott, Miriam. 'Attitudes to Shelley: The Vagaries of a Critical Reputation'. *Essays on Shelley*. Ed. Miriam Allott. Liverpool: Liverpool UP, 1982. 1–38.

Barcus, James. Ed. *Shelley: The Critical Heritage*. London: Routledge and Kegan Paul, 1975.

Cronin, Richard. 'Shelley, Tennyson and the Apostles, 1828–1832'. *Keats-Shelley Review* 5 (1990), 14–40.

Engelberg, Karsten Klejs. *The Making of the Shelley Myth: An Annotated Bibliography of Criticism of Percy Bysshe Shelley, 1822–1860*. London: Mansell, 1988.

English [...] which made an indelible impression on me over forty-five years ago' (T. S. Eliot, *To Criticize the Critic and Other Writings* (London: Faber, 1965; repr. 1978), 130–2). Also see George Franklin, 'Instances of Meeting: Shelley and Eliot: A Study in Affinity', *ELH* 61.4 (1994), 955–90.

[91] Eliot, *Selected Prose*, 82.

[92] Dowden, *Shelley*, II, 506.   [93] Yeats, *Essays and Introductions*, 75.   [94] Ibid. 421, 424–5.

Fraistat, Neil. 'Illegitimate Shelley: Radical Piracy and the Textual Edition as Cultural Performance'. *PMLA* 109.3 (1994), 409–23.

Morton, Timothy. 'Receptions'. *The Cambridge Companion to Shelley*. Ed. Timothy Morton. Cambridge: Cambridge UP, 2006. 35–41.

O'Neill, Michael. '"Trying to Make It as Good as I Can": Mary Shelley's Editing of Shelley's Poetry and Prose'. *Romanticism* 3.2 (1997), 185–97.

Webb, Timothy. 'Religion of the Heart: Leigh Hunt's Unpublished Tribute to Shelley'. *Keats-Shelley Review* 7 (1992), 1–61.

Weinberg, Alan. '"The Ineffectual Angel": Arnold's Misrepresentation of Shelley'. *Keats-Shelley Review* 33 (2009), 82–96.

White, Newman Ivey. *The Unextinguished Hearth: Shelley and his Contemporary Critics*. New York: Octagon Books, 1966.

CHAPTER 42

··

SHELLEY CRITICISM FROM DECONSTRUCTION TO THE PRESENT

··

ARTHUR BRADLEY

In many ways, the story of Shelley criticism over the last thirty years is the story of contemporary literary criticism itself.[1] It is not simply that the study of Shelley inevitably reflects the vast intellectual, political, and institutional transformations that the study of literature has undergone in the period between 1980 and the present. At a deeper level, the proper name 'Shelley' has played a pivotal role in many of the defining movements of the period: Deconstruction; New Historicism; textual studies. Yet, what I want to canvass for in this brief history of key texts and debates in modern Shelley criticism is a more particular symbiosis between the evolution of Shelley studies and literary critical studies. To be sure, contemporary Shelley criticism—like all criticism—takes place within a literary, philosophical, and institutional context, but my hypothesis will be that this context *itself* remains, in a certain sense, recognizably 'Shelleyan'. If such a claim may seem wildly anachronistic at face value, it is really only an extension of one of the most persistent and remarkable proclamations within Romantic criticism over the last thirty years: everyone from Paul de Man, through Jerome McGann, to Philippe Lacoue-Labarthe and Jean-Luc Nancy are agreed that late modernity is—consciously or unconsciously, for better or worse, tragically, culpably, or euphorically—still living and thinking within a legacy bequeathed to it by Romanticism.[2] Perhaps, in the same way, Shelley's poetics might enable us to pose a disconcertingly critical question to any self-professedly 'contemporary', anti- or post-Romantic, critical consensus. To what extent, and in what ways, might criticism *still* be Shelleyan?

---

[1] I am very grateful to Simon Bainbridge for his helpful feedback on this chapter.

[2] Paul de Man, *The Rhetoric of Romanticism* (New York: Columbia UP, 1984); Jerome McGann, *The Romantic Ideology: A Critical Investigation* (Chicago: University of Chicago Press, 1983); Philippe Lacoue-Labarthe and Jean-Luc Nancy, *The Literary Absolute: The Theory of Literature in German Romanticism*, trans. Philip Barnard and Cheryl Lester (Albany, NY: State University of New York Press, 1988).

I

It is possible to find one—albeit ambiguous—answer to this question at the very beginning of the period under review in this chapter in the seminal collection published by the so-called 'Yale School' of criticism: *Deconstruction and Criticism* (1979). As is well documented, this landmark event in the history of modern literary criticism—which gathered together Derrida, Bloom, de Man, Hillis Miller, and Hartman together in print for the first time—was originally envisaged as a set of essays on Shelley.[3] However, the fact that the collection did not turn out that way—only the essay by de Man could really be called a substantive reading of the poet—was just one sign of the many intriguing tensions at the heart of the Yale project. First of all, the very idea of a 'Yale School' itself was always something of a myth: its principal member—Jacques Derrida—was not actually based at the University and nor could he, Bloom, de Man, Miller, and Hartman be said to share any collective project or methodology to compare with that of, say, the Geneva or Prague Schools. Perhaps today it is easier to say what the Yale critics were against rather than what they supported, namely, the still-reigning post-war critical hegemony of American New Criticism, literary history, and humanism: recall, for instance, de Man's dead-pan claim in the opening line of *Allegories of Reading* (1979) that 'the spirit of the times is not blowing in the direction of formalist and intrinsic criticism.'[4] Despite all the differences between and within the work of this distinguished collection of writers and thinkers, however, *something* was clearly happening at Yale in the late 1970s, and the existence of a 'Yale School' had become established as fact in the collective academic and journalistic consciousness by the beginning of the 1980s. If the precise significance of this episode has been interpreted in countless different ways, it is generally agreed that it represented a critical moment in the history of American literary theory and criticism more generally: the 'Yale School', for all its animus towards what de Man waspishly called 'monstrously predictable' appropriations of texts in support of 'methodological claims made all the more pious by their denial of piety',[5] marked the beginning of the hyper-professionalization of literary theory and criticism into a school, method, or technique of reading.[6] In other words, this entirely virtual 'institution' was deemed responsible for setting in motion the *actual* institutionalization of criticism.

As a result, the Yale School's reputation as Shelley critics today remains somewhat mixed. It is tempting to read the abortive history of *Deconstruction and Criticism* as a metaphor for their work more generally: what begins as a set of essays on Shelley quickly turns into something else entirely. For William Keach, whose *Shelley's Style* (1984)

---

[3] Harold Bloom et al., *Deconstruction and Criticism* (London: Routledge & Kegan Paul, 1979), p. ix.

[4] Paul de Man, *Allegories of Reading: Figural Language in Rousseau, Nietzsche, Rilke and Proust* (New Haven: Yale UP, 1979), 3.

[5] Paul de Man, 'Shelley Disfigured', in *Deconstruction and Criticism*, 68.

[6] Jonathan Arac, Wlad Godzich, and Wallace Martin (eds.), *The Yale Critics: Deconstruction in America* (Minneapolis: University of Minnesota Press, 1983) offers the best contemporary genealogy of the 'Yale School' phenomenon.

appeared at the peak of the Yale School's influence, Shelley's poetics simply became a vehicle to work through a pre-existing set of philosophical concerns about rhetoric, reading, and the inescapability of the figural: 'post-structuralist Shelleyans—stimulating as much of their work is—have been too little concerned with distinguishing the elusive activity peculiar to Shelley's writing from the problematic condition of language more generally.'[7] Such criticisms are echoed by Michael O'Neill who complains of the 'allegorizing crudeness' which leads the deconstructionists only ever to see the poems as examples of abstract theories of language.[8] Yet, the Yale School's emphasis on the condition of language in general also came to be seen—particularly in the aftermath of the rise of New Historicism and the de Man 'affair' of 1987 which reread his work in the light of the posthumous discovery of anti-Semitic literary journalism he wrote during the Second World War—as not just poetically but politically suspect. If Yale was at least partly a critique of the New Criticism, the New Historicism charged it with simply reproducing the ahistorical, de-contextualized formalism of the latter: what Leavis notoriously dismissed as metaphor run riot in Shelley's poetry is, for instance, positively recuperated by de Man as the essentially figurative status of our perception of the real.[9] Just as Cleanth Brooks valorized poetry as a hermetically sealed well-wrought urn, so it could be argued that the Yale School's particular spin on Deconstruction risked transforming Shelley's poems into small, perfectly self-contained auto-deconstructive machines which have always already dismantled themselves before the critic arrives on the scene.[10] Perhaps more importantly, from this perspective, the readings of Shelley in *Deconstruction and Criticism* are as depoliticized as any formalism: Timothy Morton argues as recently as 2006 that Deconstruction was 'quite deaf' to Shelley's politics, and particularly, to his 'intense awareness of blood and gore' and his 'meat and potatoes poetics of poverty and class struggle'.[11] In its own rather self-serving version of Romantic literary history, as we will see later on, we might say that New Historicism casts itself in the role of the eternally youthful Shelley—radical, engaged, politicized—standing over and against the politically senescent and imaginatively solipsistic later Wordsworth of Deconstruction.

To be sure, Paul de Man's 'Shelley Disfigured' (1979)—which is perhaps the single most influential work of Shelley criticism of the last thirty years—does not fit quite so comfortably into this triumphalist version of literary history. It is, after all, an essay on

---

[7] William Keach, *Shelley's Style* (New York: Methuen, 1984), p. xii.

[8] Michael O'Neill, *The Human Mind's Imaginings: Conflict and Achievement in Shelley's Poetry* (Oxford: Clarendon Press, 1989), 4–5.

[9] F. R. Leavis, *Tradition and Development in English Poetry* (Harmondsworth: Peregrine, 1967), 172. In Leavis's words, Shelley's poetry displays 'a general tendency of the images to forget the status of the metaphor or simile that introduced them and to assume an autonomy or right to propagate'.

[10] Rodolphe Gasché, 'Deconstruction and Criticism', in *Inventions of Difference* (Cambridge, MA: Harvard UP, 1994), 22–57. In Gasché's account, de Man's concept of literature simply transfers a—highly deconstructible—metaphysics of subjectivity, where the subject is thought in terms of his consciousness or presence to himself, onto the work of literature, where the literary text is deemed to be conscious or aware of its own rhetorical status (53–6).

[11] Timothy Morton, 'Introduction' to *The Cambridge Companion to Shelley* (Cambridge: Cambridge UP, 2006), 9.

Shelley's most sombre depiction of historical evolution: the grotesque pageant that is *The Triumph of Life* in which poets (Wordsworth), philosophers (Plato, Rousseau, Voltaire, Kant), and dictators (Napoleon) alike are all obliged to participate. At the same time, the essay is also a critique of the archaeological or recuperative fallacy on which so much literary history depends: the presumption that, if only we could find the origin or beginning—the real or authentic Shelley text—then we would be able to understand everything that flows from it. For de Man, Shelley's poem thus poses a critical vital question for any critic—this one included—seeking to posit it as the beginning of a story that inevitably culminates with our own arrival onto the historical stage:

> Such questions allow one to conclude that *The Triumph of Life* is a fragment of something whole, or romanticism a fragment, or a moment, in a process that now includes us within its horizon. What relationship do we have to such a text that allows us to call it a fragment that we are then entitled to reconstruct, to identify, and implicitly to complete?[12]

Perhaps de Man's own answer to this precarious question of entitlement—which unfolds through an almost classically Derridan process of forensically close reading and *de haut en bas* declarations—lies within the aporetic, double-sided process that he calls (dis-)figuration. What exactly does this process involve? On the one hand, what de Man calls 'figuration' is the structural 'element in language that allows for the re-iteration of meaning by substitution':[13] we can see this in the way in which Shelley's poem, for example, famously progresses via a series of transferences from one new figure upon 'life's false and fragile glass' to another. Now, the question inevitably arises here of how this arbitrary positing power of language—which operates quite independently of any original and animating intention—comes to be mistaken for stable, intentional, and referential language, and this brings us to de Man's other point. On the other hand, 'disfiguration' is the name de Man gives to the necessary but erroneous process by which 'we impose, in our turn, on the senseless power of positional language [i.e. figuration] the authority of sense and of meaning':[14] we can see this in the way in which, for all its ambiguities, *The Triumph of Life* has been endlessly valorized by Shelley's critics as an allegory for just about every moral or philosophical position imaginable.[15] Such, it seems, are the antinomies between which every reading of *The Triumph of Life*, and (if de Man is to be believed) the process of reading in general, must shuttle: figuration and disfiguration, sense and senselessness, chaos and narrative order. If 'Shelley Disfigured' has been criticized for being insufficiently 'Shelleyan' by a subsequent generation of critics—which simultaneously deems it both too formalist (Morton) and not formalist enough (Keach, O'Neill)—de Man's essay arguably remains the guilty conscience of any critic seeking mastery or ownership over

---

[12] De Man, 'Shelley Disfigured', 40.   [13] Ibid. 61.   [14] Ibid. 64.

[15] On the one extreme, William Hazlitt originally described *The Triumph of Life* as a 'new and terrific *Dance of Death*'. On the other, Donald Reiman detects an ameliatory Wordsworthian piety in the poem where the 'child *is* father of the man'. See William Hazlitt, review of Shelley's *Posthumous Poems*, in James Barcus (ed.), *Shelley: The Critical Heritage* (London: Routledge & Kegan Paul, 1975), 335–46 (342) and Donald H. Reiman, *Shelley's 'The Triumph of Life': A Critical Study* (Chicago: University of Illinois Press, 1965), 119–28. Quoted in de Man, 'Shelley Disfigured', 42.

what is Shelleyan and what is not, what is specific to the poetry and what is universal, what is a faithful response to the text and what is an instrumental appropriation of it. What exactly gives us the right to posit any singular reading of our own as a response to a complete and self-contained aesthetic or historical object signed in the name 'Shelley'?

For de Man, there can be no sense of historical triumphalism in his own reading of *The Triumph of Life*: it is no more immune to the seductions of disfiguration—that readerly imposition of illusory sense upon the senseless positing power of language—than any other. 'Any reading', he writes, 'is a monumentalisation of sorts'. Not only is the act of aesthetic or historical recuperation 'by no means necessarily a naïve or evasive gesture' but 'it certainly is not a gesture that anyone can pretend to avoid making'. What *would* be naive is to believe that this strategy 'can be a source of value', he writes, 'and has to be celebrated or denounced accordingly'.[16] Such is the trap into which pretty much all contemporary literary criticism falls in the critic's view: all of us—whether historicist or formalist—are in the business of constructing historical and aesthetic objects—*The Triumph of Life*, Shelley, even Romanticism itself—to which we stand in relation and against which we measure our own relative progress or decline. Nevertheless, it is possible to argue that not only does de Man fall victim to the (inevitable) gesture of monumentalization—of imposing symbolic or narrative order upon the arbitrary—but he even succumbs to the (in his view entirely avoidable) desire to *valorize* this gesture, whether positively or negatively. To be sure, de Man's reading of Shelley possesses none of the barely concealed exhilaration of, say, J. Hillis Miller—whose own reading quite patently delights in the 'inexhaustible' and 'unending' hermeneutic possibilities posed by *The Triumph of Life*,[17] but, conversely, it is not difficult to detect a moment of almost tragic *anagnorisis*, that heroic 'recognition' or 'knowing-back' of the will of the gods, in the famous conclusion to the former's essay:

> *The Triumph of Life* warns us that nothing, whether deed, word, thought or text, ever happens in relation, positive or negative, to anything that precedes, follows, or exists elsewhere, but only as a random event whose power, like the power of death, is due to the randomness of its occurrence. It also warns us why and how these events then have to be reintegrated in a historical and aesthetic system of recuperation that repeats itself regardless of the exposure of its fallacy.[18]

What exactly makes it possible for de Man to wrest such a vast world-historical insight from a poetic fragment? Perhaps it is tempting to reply that de Man *himself* finally completes and valorizes Shelley's fragment as a moral allegory—and I would use this term in a more orthodox sense than he does in his *Allegories of Reading* (1979)—for the radical and more or less tragic contingency of history. Whilst I cannot help but admire the magnificent pathos of the end of 'Shelley Disfigured' every time I read it, it is hard to suppress the suspicion (which may, of course, be merely my own act of disfiguration) that it is

---

[16] De Man, 'Shelley Disfigured', 68–9.

[17] J. Hillis Miller, *The Linguistic Moment: From Wordsworth to Stevens* (Princeton: Princeton UP, 1985), 178.

[18] De Man, 'Shelley Disfigured', 69.

every bit as much an aesthetic and historical recuperation of what its author calls 'the madness of words' as any other.[19] If *The Triumph of Life* apparently possesses enough meaning to be able to *warn* us not only of our temporal contingency, but also why that contingency must be reintegrated into a system, it can only be because de Man has himself repeated the recuperative fallacy of foisting historico-aesthetic value on the random event of this particular poetic fragment. Just like the humanists, formalists, and historians he takes to task, then, de Man cannot help but reconstruct, identify, and implicitly complete Shelley's fragment—albeit only as an allegory for both the impossibility/inevitability of such reconstructive labours. In this sense, then, the critic both best proves and destroys his own point about the inescapability of disfiguring Shelley: what makes it possible for us to even *recognize* the process of reading as disfiguration is itself an *act* of readerly disfiguration.

To what extent, to return to my guiding question, is it possible to speak of Paul de Man and the Yale School as still somehow Romantic or even Shelleyan—or is Romanticism merely an instrument to pursue other ends? It is possible, of course, to find many different sources for de Man's own work (from his European philosophical background in Husserlian phenomenology, Heideggerian ontology, and Sartrean existentialism, through his famous encounter with Derrida and deconstruction in the 1960s, all the way to his somewhat ambivalent relation to post-war American literary criticism) but one possible, if strangely neglected, source lies in a Romantic theory of *poiesis* itself. After all, de Man himself is one of those great Romantic critics for whom 'Romanticism' was never merely a thing of the past but in some sense the philosophical origin of the modern, finite, linguistically determined, and temporally bound subject that we all are: 'We carry it [Romanticism] within ourselves as the experience of an *act* in which, up to a certain point, we ourselves have participated.'[20] Now, what is 'Romantic' about 'Shelley Disfigured', in my view, is not simply its diagnosis of modern subjectivity but the way in which it proposes to, if not heal, then at least suture together, the wounds of that alienated subject. To give one example, what is particularly striking about the famous conclusion to de Man's essay is the enormous philosophical burden it places on what is, after all, 'just' a poem: Shelley's fragment becomes the basis for an entire deconstructive ontology of radical contingency or eventhood. If it strikes us as naive to think that a poem could somehow prove a vast ontological claim about the nature of history, though, such naivety (as well as our own very modern sense of embarrassment at it) has an obvious Romantic pedigree. For Philippe Lacoue-Labarthe and Jean-Luc Nancy, recall, Romanticism is nothing other than our naive belief in the possibility of a self-conscious work of art that would be capable of transcending and unifying the epistemological crises of modernity:

> [W]e are all still, and always, aware of the *Crisis* [*krinein*, to discern or criticize], convinced that 'interventions' are necessary and that the least of texts is immediately 'effective' ['*opératoire*']; we all think, as if it went without saying, that politics passes through the literary (or the theoretical). Romanticism is our *naïveté*.[21]

---

[19] Ibid.   [20] De Man, *The Rhetoric of Romanticism*, 50.
[21] Lacoue-Labarthe and Nancy, *The Literary Absolute*, 16–17.

Just as Schlegel and Novalis's naivety was to think that poetry could reconcile the oppositions of the Kantian critical system—epistemology and ethics, necessity and freedom, the sensual and the intelligible—so the only naivety remaining in de Man is the belief that it is in Shelley's fragment (as an exemplum of the artwork more generally) that the crisis of modern subjectivity can best be represented, allegorized, and (however futilely) prophesied.[22] Perhaps de Man's naivety here (which cannot simply be dismissed as naivety given that there seems to be no alternative to it) was one to which Shelley himself might also have subscribed: *A Defence of Poetry* (1821), after all, famously establishes a generalized idea of the poetic that gathers together art, criticism, philosophy, and politics into a single idiom through which the becoming of modernity will express itself. In an incisive essay on 'Shelley Disfigured', Deborah Esch also demonstrates the ways in which Shelley's theory of poetry in the *Defence*—'vitally metaphorical', 'arbitrarily produced', yet famously replete with (unacknowledged) legislative force—even anticipates the critic's own account of the figural, arbitrary, and yet inexorable positing power of language: 'De Man's critical insights, which enable us to return to Shelley's prose as well as his poetry with a renewed sense of their theoretical rigour, are arguably the poet's own, forgotten in the wake of historicising and aestheticising interpretations of his work.'[23] Such is the extent to which de Man still, perhaps, remains 'Shelleyan': what the proper name 'Shelley' signifies in his work is not simply one more historical or aesthetic object in the seamless history of literature but an important historical and theoretical precursor for his entire theory of reading as (dis-)figuration.

II

In the 1980s, New Historicism changed Shelley criticism forever—or at least it would have done so if the historicists themselves had not trained us to be suspicious of exactly such grand ahistorical claims. To start with, of course, it is *de rigueur* to note that 'New Historicism' was just as much of a mythical beast as the Yale deconstructionist dragon it slew: Stephen Greenblatt, the Renaissance scholar who is generally credited with inventing the term, made clear from the outset that it was 'not a repeatable methodology or a literary critical program'.[24] It is well-nigh impossible to detect any meaningful collective

---

[22] See Tilottama Rajan's 'Displacing Post-Structuralism: Romantic Studies after Paul de Man', *Studies in Romanticism* 24.4 (1985), 451–74 for a discussion of the Romantic genealogy of de Man's critique of intentionality.

[23] Deborah Esch, 'A Defence of Rhetoric/The Triumph of Reading', in Lindsay Waters and Wlad Godzich (eds.), *Reading de Man Reading* (Minneapolis: University of Minnesota Press, 1989), 71–2. See also Jerrold Hogle, *Shelley's Process: Radical Transference and the Development of his Major Works* (New York: Oxford UP, 1988) and Tilottama Rajan, *The Supplement of Reading: Figures of Understanding in Romantic Theory and Practice* (Ithaca, NY: Cornell UP, 1990) for groundbreaking accounts of Shelley that are equally sensitized to both theoretical and formal concerns.

[24] Catherine Gallagher and Stephen Greenblatt, *Practicing New Historicism* (Chicago: University of Chicago Press, 2000), 19.

voice emerging from Romantic New Historicism—whether in its British or North American guises—let alone from the work of such singular Romantic critics as Jerome McGann, Marilyn Butler, James Chandler, Paul Hamilton, Marjorie Levinson, Alan Liu, and Clifford Siskin. On the contrary, it might again be easier to say what the New Historicism was definitely *not*—American New Criticism, 'old' or traditional literary history, Yale deconstruction—rather than what it was. For Marjorie Levinson, whose manifesto 'The New Historicism: Back to the Future' (1989) offers a useful insight into the psychology of the movement at its academic and historical apogee, what characterized the New Historicist moment was, amongst other things, 'a direct assault upon Yale's present-mindedness'.[25] Yet, with the benefit of hindsight it is possible to wonder whether this assault was not itself merely a new species of presentism, taking its revenge on the suddenly *démodé*. If the Yale critics were not quite as different from their New Critical predecessors as they liked to pretend, New Historicism's self-professed 'resistance' to Yale (a theoretically loaded choice of word, to be sure, carrying clear echoes of Freud and even de Man) could itself be seen as something of a counter-strike in an ongoing theoretical civil war:[26] the North American Historicists' animus towards Deconstruction, in particular, often took the form of an embrace—not of anything so vulgarly empirical as archival research—but of rival theoretical models like Bakhtinian dialogism; Machereyan and Althusserian ideology critique, and Foucauldian genealogy. Perhaps this may be one reason why New Historicism shared not only many of the Yale School's high-theoretical presuppositions but also its bathetic institutional fate: what started out as an utterly singular, anti-methodological set of virtuoso readings has, as Hugh Roberts notes, become the 'zero-degree' basis of all literary study in the modern university.[27]

It goes without saying, of course, that none of this stopped New Historicism's own rampant historical revisionism with respect to Deconstruction and its other allegedly ahistorical predecessors in the 1980s and 1990s—but it should at least give us reason to ask whether *post hoc ergo propter hoc*. After all, it would be a gross historical error to presume that the Yale School's insistence upon the irreducibly linguistic experience of history was somehow tantamount to a denial of history per se that clearly stood in need of materialist correction. For Paul de Man, as he makes clear in the Preface to his *Rhetoric of Romanticism*, what was at stake was rather the uncritical way in which that history was pursued. '[O]ne feels [...] envious of those who can continue to do literary history as if nothing had happened in the sphere of theory', says a not-very-envious-sounding de Man, 'but one cannot help but feel somewhat suspicious of their optimism.'[28] Such remarks (which were written shortly before the critic's death in 1983) were presumably aimed at the traditional exponents of literary history rather than the vanguard of the

---

[25] Marjorie Levinson, 'The New Historicism: Back to the Future', in *Rethinking Historicism: Critical Readings in Romantic History* (Oxford: Blackwell, 1989), 19. In many ways, Levinson's real target in this essay is not the Yale School's presentism but the naive empiricism of nineteenth-century historiography.

[26] Levinson, 'The New Historicism', 55n.

[27] Hugh Roberts, *Shelley and the Chaos of History* (Philadelphia: Pennsylvania State UP, 1997), 3.

[28] De Man, *The Rhetoric of Romanticism*, p. ix.

New Historicists, but one cannot imagine the author of *Aesthetic Ideology* responding much more generously to the unreconstructed Marxism of, say, McGann's *Romantic Ideology* (1983):

> Literature is fiction not because it somehow refuses to acknowledge 'reality', but because it is not *a priori* certain that language functions according to principles which are those, or which are *like* those, of the phenomenal world. It is therefore not *a priori* certain that literature is a reliable source of information about anything but its own language [...] What we call ideology is precisely the confusion of linguistic with natural reality, or reference with phenomenalism. It follows that, more than any other mode of enquiry, including economics, the linguistics of literariness is a powerful and indispensable tool in the unmasking of ideological aberrations, as well as a determining factor in accounting for their occurrence. Those who reproach literary theory for being oblivious to social and historical (that is to say, ideological) reality are merely stating their fear at having their own ideological mystifications exposed by the tool they are trying to discredit. They are, in short, very poor readers of Marx's *German Ideology*.[29]

Just as McGann's historico-materialist critique of Wordsworth's retreat from the 'real world' of political engagement into the false consciousness of the egotistical sublime remains ideological—insofar as it confuses a linguistic state with a natural or phenomenal one—so New Historicism's own critique of Deconstruction's political quietism does not escape the clutches of language as easily as it might think. If de Man's intense interest in rhetoric really did render him 'deaf' to what Morton calls Shelley's 'meat and potatoes' poetics of poverty and class struggle, for instance, it could only have been because the former would have instantly recognized that such appeals to the real world beyond rhetoric are themselves rhetorical all the way down: what exactly are 'meat and potatoes' poetics, anyway, if not well-worn rhetorical tropes for a no-nonsense, robustly proletarian, and apparently rhetoric-free reality? Perhaps Robert Eaglestone makes the same point when he argues that 'History' plays the same role in the work of Marxist critics like Terry Eagleton that 'Life' once notoriously did for Leavis: both are empty, vaguely self-justifying signifiers that—for all their claims to extra-linguistic integrity—do not notably point beyond themselves.[30] In his painstaking attempts to demystify the pseudo-historical ideology of literary history—and to expose any rhetorical return to an allegedly trope-free point of origin for the trope that it is—de Man could even be said to be trying to out-historicize the historicists: 'Reading as disfiguration, to the very extent that it resists historicism, turns out to be historically more reliable than the products of historical archaeology.'[31]

For Shelley scholars today, what is perhaps most striking about the early years of New Historicism is the poet's comparative marginalization, even exclusion, from the critical debate, especially given his ubiquity under the reign of Yale. It is revealing, for instance,

[29] Paul de Man, *The Resistance to Theory* (Minneapolis: University of Minnesota Press, 1986), 11.
[30] Robert Eaglestone, 'Review of Terry Eagleton, *Literary Theory: An Introduction* (New Edition)', *Times Literary Supplement*, 17 April 2009, 13.
[31] De Man, 'Shelley Disfigured', 69.

that McGann's seminal *Romantic Ideology* devotes just five sustained pages to a discussion of the poet—less than any other of the so-called 'big six' Romantic poets— and nor does he feature in groundbreaking collections like *Rethinking Historicism* (1989). Apart from Kelvin Everest's subtle historico-materialist reading of the ideological evasions at work in a poem like *Julian and Maddalo*, Shelley is largely exempted from the kind of relentless ideology critique to which, say, Wordsworth and Coleridge were subjected throughout the 1980s.[32] To be sure, Shelley's comparative absence from New Historicism may be something of a back-handed compliment: it would be deeply redundant, after all, to accuse the author of 'To Wordsworth' (1814–15) of succumbing to the Romantic Ideology of the Wordsworthian Sublime. Yet, on another level, Shelley's explicitly political poetry, historico-materialist philosophy, and career-long political activism clearly also represented a challenge to the very idea of a 'Romantic Ideology' in the first place, together with the psychoanalytic/materialist depth model of repression, sublimation, and the unconscious upon which (in its earliest formation at least) it relied. Not only was the real, historical Shelley a million miles from the Victorian caricature of a hopeless idealist or escapist, McGann reports, but he was actually at the 'ideological vanguard' of the Romantic poets.[33] Perhaps this is why New Historicist readings of Shelley—in stark contrast to the hermeneutics of suspicion that dominated equivalent studies of Wordsworth or Coleridge in the 1980s—consistently represent themselves as recuperating a political radicalism within his work that had become increasingly submerged under successive waves of Victorian criticism, American New Criticism, and Deconstruction:

> Historicism has made us freshly aware that Shelley was deeply involved in the social and political events of his day, while providing fresh readings of his work that make us aware of how history and politics interweave with literary language in deep ways.[34]

If Wordsworth criticism was routinely convicted of being too Wordsworthian—too complicit with a Romantic ideology of the individual poet absorbed in his own sensuous and imaginative universe—it seems that New Historicism's problem with Shelley criticism is rather that it has never been Shelleyan *enough*. The story of Shelley criticism from Arnold's beautiful and ineffectual angel, notoriously monumentalized in the camp effigy at University College Oxford, to the disfigured textual fragment of de Man is, in other words, the story of an enduring mythologization, idealization, and de-politicization. This story comes to an abrupt and overdue end with the arrival of New Historicism to remind us—if indeed we needed reminding—that Shelley was, all the while, a human being deeply immersed in the social and political life of his time. Such a narrative of the decline and fall into ahistorical idealism may well seem self-aggrandizingly neat—what about the Chartist Shelley? Or the inspiration he offered to generations of socialists?

---

[32] Kelvin Everest, 'Shelley's Doubles: An Approach to *Julian and Maddalo*', in Kelvin Everest (ed.), *Shelley Revalued: Essays from the Gregynog Conference* (Leicester: Leicester UP, 1983), 63–88.

[33] McGann, *The Romantic Ideology*, 124.

[34] Timothy Morton, 'Introduction', *The Cambridge Companion to Shelley*, 10.

Can we really still see Deconstruction as apolitical some twenty years after its own ethical and political turn?[35]—but it remains the foundational myth upon which Shelleyan New Historicism rests: no one, it seems, ever noticed that Shelley was a political poet until around twenty years ago.

In a larger sense, we might wonder whether the real reason Shelley's voice is nowhere to be heard in New Historicism is actually because it is (silently) everywhere. It is perhaps no accident that the epigraph to Marilyn Butler's *Romantics, Rebels and Reactionaries* (1982)—which is generally, if not quite accurately, taken to be the *Ur*-text of British Romantic New Historicism—is from the famous Preface to *Prometheus Unbound*: 'Poets, not otherwise than philosophers, painters, sculptors and musicians, are in one sense the creators, and in another the creations of their age' (*Norton 1*, 135).[36] Accordingly, the New Historicist's job is not critically to expose some ideological illusion or evasion in Shelley's life or work—à la Wordsworth—so much as better to affirm the poet's own political radicalism: Shelley has always already historicized and politicized himself before the critic has arrived on the scene. One can perhaps see this in the way that the later waves of New Historicist criticism commend the poet for his uncanny political prescience in the fields of radical politics (Hoagwood), postcolonialism (Leask), and finally even in the field of literary and cultural historiography itself. Not only is Shelley largely immune to the ideology critique carried out by McGann, James Chandler argues, but the turn to history advocated by *Romantic Ideology* is itself nothing but a largely unconscious *return* to a Romantic model of historicism.[37] Nevertheless, Shelleyan New Historicism's self-conscious fidelity to Shelley's own historico-materialism inevitably carries risks as well—chief amongst which is the danger of remaining too close to, or uncritically reproducing, the voice of its literary precursor. To this critic, at least, the New Historicism's distinctive rhetorical mode—self-consciously radical, occasionally self-righteous, even pious in its appeal to larger historical or materialist forces operating beyond the agency of any individual—verges at times on an act of Shelleyan ventriloquism. Rereading the many New Historicist accounts of its own emergence as a literary critical discipline, for instance, one can't help but be struck by the (in one sense at least) classically Shelleyan story they tell of a progressive historical amelioration, enlightenment, and liberation that all too inevitably culminates with the movement's own arrival upon the historical stage: Jerome McGann, for instance, sees New Historicism as 'an escape from certain illusions we inherit and cherish from the past';[38] Marjorie Levinson speaks of the 'sense of emancipation' and 'enthusiasm' New Historicism brought about

---

[35] See the essays collected in Betty T. Bennett and Stuart Curran (eds.), *Shelley: Poet and Legislator of the World* (Baltimore: Johns Hopkins UP, 1996).

[36] Marilyn Butler, *Romantics, Rebels and Reactionaries* (Oxford: Oxford UP, 1982). In many ways, Butler's book is an orthodox work of literary history, but its appearance at the beginning of the 1980s has generally led it to be classified as a New Historicist text.

[37] Terence A. Hoagwood, *Skepticism and Ideology: Shelley's Political Prose and its Context from Bacon to Marx* (Iowa City: University of Iowa Press, 1988); Nigel Leask, *British Romantic Writers and the East* (Cambridge: Cambridge UP, 1992); James Chandler, *England in 1819: The Politics of Literary Culture and the Case of Romantic Historicism* (Chicago: Chicago UP, 1998), 36.

[38] McGann, *The Romantic Ideology*, 13.

when it liberated us from our 'interpretative norms',[39] whilst Mary A. Favret and Nicola J. Watson describe their 'feeling of optimism about the possibilities available to romantic studies in the contemporary academic environment'.[40] Whilst no one would deny the very real critical excitement the historical turn afforded for a generation of scholars bored or alienated by the *ancien régime* of Yale—bliss was it in that dawn to be alive, it seems, but to be a historicist was very heaven—it is difficult not to wonder about the Enlightenment and Romantic genealogy of New Historicism's own politics of affect.[41] For Timothy Morton, writing in his recent introduction to the *Cambridge Companion*, the history of Shelley scholarship is just as clearly depicted as an almost dialectical progression from the formalist, ahistorical excesses of American New Criticism, Phenomenology, and Deconstruction to the moment of *Aufklärung* that is New Historicism: '[W]e now have a more complex picture of Shelley than ever' (p. 10).[42] If this state is partly the fruit of the labours of the New Historicists themselves, it is also the outworking of an—again almost classically Shelleyan—historical logic of social enlightenment that exceeds any individual: liberal modernity's own contemporary historical concerns—social and political activism, resisting capitalism, overthrowing colonialism, saving the environment—happily turn out to be Shelley's concerns too because we are both part of the same evolving historical drama. Perhaps all this is true—we manifestly do have a more complex picture of Shelley than ever and his poetry certainly does have useful things to say to us today—but it reminds us, once again, of the extent to which New Historicism, like Deconstruction before it, remains, for better and worse, a Shelleyan enterprise. What would it mean for Romantic New Historicism if Shelley were not simply the name of another Romantic poet to be historicized but a key precursor for the very theory of history upon which historicism itself depends?

III

In the aftermath of the 'Theory Wars' of the 1980s (which seem almost as remote and mysterious to students today as the Napoleonic Wars), Shelley has resumed his status as just one more canonical Romantic poet amongst others. It is, nonetheless, still possible to detect recognizably Shelleyan topoi even amidst the 'anything goes' post-ideological pluralism of contemporary English. To begin with, it is no coincidence that Shelley scholars have made significant contributions to several major trends within contemporary scholarship such as the explosion in textual criticism and scholarly editions over

---

[39] Levinson, 'The New Historicism', 18.

[40] Mary A. Favret and Nicola J. Watson, 'Introduction', *At The Limits of Romanticism: Essays in Cultural, Feminist and Materialist Criticism* (Bloomington, IN: Indiana UP, 1994), 1.

[41] See, for example, Jon Mee's *Romanticism, Enthusiasm and Regulation: Poetics and the Policing of Culture in Romantic Britain* (Oxford: Oxford UP, 2003) for an excellent discussion of the discourse of 'enthusiasm' in the Romantic period.

[42] Morton, 'Introduction', *The Cambridge Companion to Shelley*, 10.

the last decade or so (*Longman*; *Murray*; *CPPBS*). For Shelley, as Andrew Bennett has shown,[43] his own textual, political, and technological afterlife was a crucial poetic concern and texts like 'Ozymandias', 'Ode to the West Wind', *Adonais*, and *A Defence of Poetry* raise the very questions that editors like Matthews and Everest or Reiman and Fraistat are still trying to answer almost 200 years later. What exactly is a 'text'? Who or what decides its meaning? Can or should authorial intentionality survive the poet's own finitude? To what extent do new technologies extend poetic immortality or efface it forever?

If contemporary literary criticism still asks Shelleyan questions, however, it would be very unShelleyan indeed to pretend that the history of ideas I have been narrating here has taken place within some sort of political, material, or institutional vacuum. It is only necessary to recall Bill Readings's now-classic study *The University in Ruins* (1996) to understand the changing institutional backdrop against which the study of Shelley criticism now takes place. As Readings powerfully shows, the modern university is no longer the post-Romantic guarantor of national culture and identity, but just one more business, measured by the same performance indicators as any other, dedicated to the delivery of an empty and homogeneous product called 'Excellence'.[44] For Scott Wilson, the rise of New Historicism and sister disciplines like textual studies, biography, and cultural history in the 1980s and 1990s (together with the decline of 'Theory' in the same period) can even be seen as the University of Excellence's response to Anglo-American governmental pressure to produce utilitarian, vocational, or otherwise 'impact'-driven research in the arts and humanities: New Historicism is, as its name indicates, a product of an entirely capitalist marketing logic of the 'new'.[45] Such a fetishization of novelty has itself been recycled with increasingly diminishing returns in movements like the New Aestheticism or the New Formalism.

Perhaps though—and this is the rather risky speculation with which I would like to conclude—it might be here, more than anywhere else, that the contemporary state of literary criticism remains 'Shelleyan'. To be sure, it is difficult to think of any bigger cliché about Shelley than to claim that he is the 'poet of mutability'—of infinite material change or transformation—but, as Paul Hamilton has recently observed, this philosophy of becoming remains one of the most complex aspects of his thought.[46] On the one hand, Shelley's embrace of a materialist philosophy of never-ending change operating above and beyond all personal and collective authority enables the poet to ontologize or naturalize his own political radicalism: Mahmoud, the Turkish despot in *Hellas*, is compelled to recognize that his empire will disappear just as naturally as spring follows winter. On the other, though, an affirmation of such an

---

[43]   Andrew Bennett, *Romantic Poets and the Culture of Posterity* (Cambridge: Cambridge UP, 1999).

[44]   Bill Readings, *The University in Ruins* (Cambridge, MA: Harvard UP, 1996).

[45]   Scott Wilson, 'The Economimesis of New Historicism (Or How New Historicism Displaced Theory in English Literature Departments)', *Journal of Cultural Research* 11.2 (2007), 161–74.

[46]   In many ways, Shelley's multiple and competing philosophies of history—idealist or materialist? Linear or cyclical? Progressive or regressive?—remain one of the richest and most complex areas of Shelley studies. See Paul Hamilton, *Percy Bysshe Shelley* (Tavistock: Northcote House, 2000), 3–9.

impersonal non-anthropocentric and non-teleological process logically entails the annihilation of *all* individual agency, creativity, and responsibility, not least the poet's own: the new Greek golden age which begins at the end of *Hellas* is clearly just as doomed as any tyranny. In this sense, we can perhaps begin to grasp why so many of Shelley's poems (*Alastor, Rosalind and Helen, Laon and Cythna,* 'Ode to the West Wind', *Adonais*) conclude with the physical—if not imaginative—death of the poet-figure: the poetry performs—acts out—the philosophy of becoming it simultaneously promulgates.

For me, Shelley's place within this larger philosophy of becoming—which simultaneously stretches backwards to the materialisms of Lucretius and Spinoza and forwards to philosophers of immanence like Bergson and Deleuze—might be one last reason why he remains our uncanny contemporary. It is not simply that the neo-Spinozan philosophical tradition to which he belongs is still one of the most dominant and influential areas of contemporary thought: witness the work of such figures as Deleuze/Guattari or Antonio Negri and the Italian School of Marxist philosophy. At a more radical level, the philosophy of infinite, non-teleological change to which Shelley subscribes has ironically—even tragically—become the dominant political ontology of our epoch: what began life as a radically charged *Naturphilosophie*—the affirmation of infinite material transformation—now recurs everywhere in parodic form as the absolute value, *modus operandi*, and *raison d'être* of neo-liberal modernity. If Shelley himself mobilized the philosophy of permanent transformation against the temporal and political status quo—Mahmoud, Ozymandias, Napoleon—a modern species of this very philosophy of immanent becoming is now being pressed into the service of maintaining global liberal hegemony. Perhaps the single most visible index of this is the fact that global liberal government today predicates every aspect of social, cultural, and political life from the university seminar room to the high street on the inevitability of radical, even apocalyptic, change: globalization of labour and capital; falling profit margins; market crashes; rising crime; uncontrollable immigration, and imminent terrorist attacks. Just as governance presupposes a state of permanent becoming as the basic condition of life itself, so it responds by normalizing an equally perpetual revolution: hyperbolic legislation; infinite debt; the permanent audit and target culture in UK schools, hospitals, and universities; the ever-growing Surveillance State; and, of course, the endless War on Terror.[47] In the same way as the Romantic poet famously declared that 'Nought may endure but Mutability' ('Mutability', 16, *Norton 2*), the modern political leader ironically rejoins: 'So what is the challenge? It is that change is marching on again [...] That's what we have been in New Labour. The change-makers. That's how we must stay.'[48] What could be more—or less—Shelleyan than this?

[47] See Michael Dillon and Julian Reid, *The Liberal Way of War: Killing to Make Life Live* (London: Routledge, 2008) for an acute exposition of this (literally) fatal logic in the field of contemporary international relations.

[48] Tony Blair, keynote speech to Labour Party Conference, 27 September 2005 <http://news.bbc.co.uk/1/hi/uk_politics/4287370.stm> (accessed 12 August 2009).

SELECT BIBLIOGRAPHY

Bennett, Andrew. *Romantic Poets and the Culture of Posterity*. Cambridge: Cambridge UP, 1999.

Bennett, Betty T. and Stuart Curran. Ed. *Shelley: Poet and Legislator of the World* Baltimore: Johns Hopkins UP, 1996.

Bloom, Harold, et al. *Deconstruction and Criticism*. London: Routledge & Kegan Paul, 1979.

Everest, Kelvin. 'Shelley's Doubles: An Approach to *Julian and Maddalo*'. *Shelley Revalued: Essays from the Gregynog Conference*. Ed. Kelvin Everest. Leicester: Leicester UP, 1983. 63–88.

Chandler, James. *England in 1819: The Politics of Literary Culture and the Case of Romantic Historicism*. Chicago: Chicago UP, 1998.

Clark, Timothy and Jerrold Hogle. Eds. *Evaluating Shelley*. Edinburgh: Edinburgh UP, 1996.

De Man, Paul. *The Rhetoric of Romanticism*. New York: Columbia UP, 1984.

Hogle, Jerrold. *Shelley's Process: Radical Transference and the Development of his Major Works*. New York: Oxford UP, 1988.

Keach, William. *Shelley's Style*. New York: Methuen, 1984.

Lacoue-Labarthe, Philippe and Jean-Luc Nancy. *The Literary Absolute: The Theory of Literature in German Romanticism*. Trans. Philip Barnard and Cheryl Lester. Albany, NY: State University of New York Press, 1988.

Leask, Nigel. *British Romantic Writers and the East: Anxieties of Empire*. Cambridge: Cambridge UP, 1992.

Levinson, Marjorie. 'The New Historicism: Back to the Future'. *Rethinking Historicism: Critical Readings in Romantic History*. Ed. Marjorie Levinson et al. Oxford: Blackwell, 1989. 18–63.

McGann, Jerome *The Romantic Ideology: A Critical Investigation*. Chicago: University of Chicago Press, 1983.

Morton, Timothy. Ed. *The Cambridge Companion to Shelley*. Cambridge: Cambridge UP, 2006.

O'Neill, Michael. *The Human Mind's Imaginings: Conflict and Achievement in Shelley's Poetry*. Oxford: Clarendon Press, 1989.

Rajan, Tilottama. *The Supplement of Reading: Figures of Understanding in Romantic Theory and Practice*. Ithaca, NY: Cornell UP, 1990.

INDEX

....